# History of the County of Ayr : with a genealogical account of the families of Ayrshire Volume 2 – Primary Source Edition

## James Paterson

# HISTORY

### OF THE

# COUNTY OF AYR.

# HISTORY

OF THE

# COUNTY OF AYR:

WITH A

## GENEALOGICAL ACCOUNT

OF THE

## FAMILIES OF AYRSHIRE.

BY JAMES PATERSON,

PRINCIPAL AUTHOR OF THE LETTERPRESS TO "KAY'S EDINBURGH PORTRAITS;" AUTHOR OF "THE
CONTEMPORARIES OF BURNS;" EDITOR OF "THE SONGS AND BALLADS OF AYRSHIRE;"
"THE POEMS OF THE SEMPILLS OF BELTREES;" "THE OBIT-BOOK OF AYR;"
"THE POEMS OF HAMILTON OF BANGOUR;" "SCOTTISH JOURNAL," ETC.

VOL. II.

EDINBURGH:

THOMAS GEORGE STEVENSON,

Antiquarian and Historical Bookseller,

87 PRINCES STREET.

SOLD BY JOHN DICK, BOOKSELLER, AYR.

M.DCCC.LII.

# PREFACE.

It is precisely five years since we wrote the Preface to the first volume of this work,—the twelfth part of an average long life! We do not say that the whole of this protracted period has been devoted to the undertaking. On the contrary, lengthened intervals occurred, during which no progress whatever was made with it. This arose out of events which cannot well be explained. The want of a Publisher—engaging to run the risk of the second volume—occasioned an unavoidable and serious delay. Nearly two years elapsed before Mr. Stevenson, the publisher, came forward, and undertook the responsibility of completing the work. Since that time, we have been enabled to move on—slowly, or more expeditiously, according to circumstances. No doubt, the attention required in managing the business of a printing-office, however small, has been a material drawback; still, when the magnitude of the undertaking is considered, the time consumed in bringing it to a close may not appear so extraordinary after all.

To us it has been, in one sense, a labour of pleasure, but, in another, of much anxiety; and, we may add, of considerable pecuniary loss. The work is of such a nature that it could not be expected from the sale, local and limited as the demand for such books usually is,—to yield anything like a remuneration for the research involved in it; yet, having put our hand to the plough, we could not think of abandoning it, even in the face of apparently insurmountable difficulties, and the certainty of reaping a very inadequate reward. But for it, we might have been engaged in more profitable pursuits, and avoided many annoyances to which our devotion to the undertaking exposed us. It is now finished, however, and we may mention these things by way of apology to our Subscribers, many of whom have to look back over a period of at least eight long years since they first added their names to the subscription list, not only for the delay, but also on account of not a few deficiences inseparable from a task so often interrupted. No work of the kind ought ever to be undertaken, save by men of "lettered ease and independence," who can afford to give their hobby full rein,—a life-time being scarcely sufficient to do justice to such an extensive field of enquiry as we have gone over

Sensible we are of the numerous defects of the work—its sins of omission and commission,—we might have been more full here, more accurate there, still, when the difficulty of obtaining information—especially anything like correct information—in reference to family history and the descent of property, is considered, some indulgence will be vouchsafed to us In the preface to the first volume, we took occasion to thank the representatives of the various families, to whom we had applied, for the ready manner in which they responded to our inquiries; and we have our renewed thanks to tender in a similar manner on account of this the second volume At the same time, we may state that there were exceptions In some instances not even a reply could be elicited—while, in numerous cases, where the ancient race is extinct, we had no source of information save the public records It is therefore little to be wondered at if our genealogies sometimes dwindle down to mere skeleton sketches—notes thrown chronologically together, no doubt, but wanting the muscular adhesion of a full grown pedigree. It may be proper to explain, however, that the "History of the County of Ayr," was in reality designed to partake more of the character of a *historical* than a *genealogical* work. We were less caring for minute family detail, than to trace the progress and division of land, and the origin and descent of the principal branches of the proprietors. If we are therefore occasionally less full in the pedigrees than some genealogists could wish, our apology is thus at hand.

Faulty as the work may be in this respect, yet such notes as we have been able to give, may lead to fuller expansion by members of the families themselves—who have a taste for genealogical inquiry—or by parties into whose hands the requisite family documents have fallen. Whatever may be the opinion of the public as to the merits or demerits of the work, we are glad to know that the design of it is appreciated, and that, by and by, there may be done for other counties of Scotland what we have attempted for Ayrshire.

Amidst discouragements of no ordinary description, we have great pleasure in tendering our best thanks—in addition to the gentlemen mentioned in the preface to the first volume—to David Laing, Esq. of the Signet Library, for his unvaried kindness and assistance, and to William Ranken, Esq. Glenlogan, and William Cooper, Esq. of Failford, for their valuable information and otherwise.

PRINTING-OFFICE, 90, SOUTH BRIDGE,
*Edinburgh, September* 1852.

# CONTENTS OF VOLUME SECOND.

*a*

# APPENDIX

# ACCOUNT OF THE PARISHES AND FAMILIES.

## PARISH OF DUNDONALD.

THE name is evidently derived from the Gaelic *Dun*, a fortified hill; and *Donald*, the name of a person—some warrior in those early periods of which we have no authentic history. The parish is situated at the north-west extremity of the district of Kyle. It was at one time much more extensive than it is at present. It forms nearly " an equilateral triangle, the length of the side of which is about seven miles. On the south-west side it is bounded by the shore of the Frith of Clyde; which, passing over the point at Troon (extending nearly a mile into the sea), runs almost in a straight line from the point at Irvine harbour to where the Rumbling and Po burns meet, and separate it from the parish of Monkton. On the north it is bounded by the water of Irvine, separating it from the parishes of Irvine, Dreghorn and Kilmaurs. On the south-east it has no natural boundary, but runs in a straight line from a point on the Irvine, a little below Caprington, to the above-mentioned point on the coast westward, on which side it is bounded by the parishes of Riccarton, Symington, and Monkton.*

The topographical character of the parish is well described by the writer in the *Statistical Account:*—" Within these limits the surface is marked by a very pleasing variety of appearance. All along the sea-coast and the banks of Irvine for a considerable way inland, the soil is almost a dead

level, or very gently undulated. But with a view, as it were, to make amends for this tiresome monotony, it rapidly swells up, towards one concentrating point, into eminences betwixt three and four hundred feet above the level of the sea. These form the Clavin hills, so called probably from the Celtic *Clai bhein*, signifying broadswords, which, when laid in a particular form, give a good idea of their appearance. From the tops of these eminences there is a most delightful prospect, said to comprise parts of fourteen counties; and it is questionable if, from an equal elevation, so fine a natural panorama, both for richness and extent, is anywhere to be met with in the lowlands of Scotland.

" At the foot of one of these hills, forming a rocky precipice, and well skirted with wood, lies the village of Dundonald. This, with the adjoining grey ruins of the castle, crowning an eminence in front of the village, gives it a very picturesque appearance. There is only one thing wanting to complete the picture, and that is water; the village being shut in from the sea by the intervening hills, while there is scarcely a stream deserving the name of a rivulet in the parish. This defect, however, tells more upon the eye than upon the comfort of the inhabitants; for, the soil being generally retentive, excepting towards the shore, springs are everywhere abundant; and the water is in general good, though in some places strongly impregnated with carbonate of iron."

There is reason, however, to believe that this defect did not always exist. The low ground between the precipice and the Castle Hill, through

---

* Statistical Account of the parish, admirably drawn up by the Rev. Alexander Willison.

which a small streamlet runs, and which is still marshy, has every indication of having at one time formed a loch. Indeed, none of the old castles were built unless in the immediate vicinity of a plentiful supply of water. This supposition seems confirmed by the fact, that the ground on which part of the village is built, is styled in the title-deeds the *fisherman's field*, from the person, no doubt, whose business it was to supply the castle with fish from the loch. At the lower extremity apparently of this sheet of water there are certain remains extant of a mill for grinding corn, which was probably at work long after the castle became tenantless and the loch partially drained

The climate is considered mild, though rather moist, from the immediate vicinity of the hills. The greater part of the land is under cultivation, and the soil is exceedingly varied, so that no particular crop is peculiar to the parish It is not behind the rest of Ayrshire in dairy produce.

There are no extensive plantations in the parish, though the interior part of it is well wooded At Anchans there are a few acres of natural wood, and some fine specimens of old trees near the mansion-house

The means of communication are good Besides roads in various directions, two railways pass through the parish These are the old tramroad, constructed by the Duke of Portland in 1810, between Kilmarnock and Troon—now relaid with rails by the Glasgow and Ayr Railway Company, who have leased the line—and the Glasgow and Ayr line, which passes along the coast for nearly eight miles.

There are two harbours properly within the parish—Irvine and Troon The former, however, is usually classed along with Irvine. Troon is technically considered only a creek of Irvine, although it is now the most important of the two A charter was obtained, by William Fullarton of Fullarton, from Queen Anne in 1707, for the purpose of constructing a harbour at Troon About that period, says the *Old Statistical Account*, "an offer was made to the proprietor by the merchants of Glasgow for feuing the adjoining land, and proceeding with the work, but their offer was rejected for a reason which, however ridiculous it may now appear, would be considered very cogent in those days—lest a rise should take place on the price of butter and eggs" The charter thus remained in abeyance till 1808, "when the Duke of Portland, who had previously purchased the estate of Fullarton, entered on the undertaking, which has cost from first to last about £100,000." There are two dry docks, and a wet dock has been constructed, while other improve-

ments are still going on "The harbour has a good lighthouse, supported from its own revenue; and on the Lady Isle, lying towards the bay of Ayr, but belonging to this parish; the merchants of Glasgow, more than half-a-century ago, erected two pillars for the direction of vessels "*

### HISTORY, CIVIL AND ECCLESIASTICAL.

"The first historical notice we have of the place," says the *Statistical Account*, "is in the time of the fifth Walter Stewart, who was styled of Dundonald, and was made Justiciary of Scotland by Alexander II, at St Andrews, in 1230. It is said, however, by Chalmers, that the manor and parish belonged to Walter, the son of Allan, the first Stewart, who held the whole of the northern half of Kyle in the beginning of the reign of William the Lion, and that it might have been granted to him by David I, or his successor, Malcolm IV. Nothing more is known, or even conjectured, regarding it until the reign of Robert II, who appears, by several charters dated at Dundonald, to have made it the place of at least occasional residence, from 1371 till the time of his death in 1390. This latter event is particularly mentioned by the Prior of St Serf's Inch, Lochleven —

' The secownd Robert of Scotland Kyng.
As God purwaid maid endying
At Downdownald in his countre.
Of a schort sickness thare deyd he.'—WYNTON

That his gentle, but ill-starred son and successor, Robert III, died in the same place, is also asserted by the same author; and though his authority on this point is disputed by Pinkerton and Fordonn, there are others of no mean authority, such as Ruddiman and Macpherson, who stand up in defence of the testimony of the poet But, be this as it may, there cannot be a doubt of his continuing to reside here some time after his father's death and it is probable, that it was honoured by occasional visits from his royal successors till the time of James IV. From the predecessor of this monarch, James III, Allan, first Lord Cathcart, obtained the custody of the castle, with the dominical lands, in 1482, and with this family they may be supposed to have continued for some time. The next account we have of it is in 1527, the date of a charter from James V, confirmatory of one probably given in his minority, and granting it in right of possession to a person of the name of Wallace, a cadet, in all likelihood, of the family of Craigie. In this descent it continued till 1638, when the proprietor, who appears to have been deeply involved in the

* Statistical Account

troubles of the time, by taking an active lead in the covenanting interest, made it over by sale to Sir William Cochrane of Cowden, the ancestor of the present Earl of Dundonald.* In 1726, it passed again into the possession of the Eglinton family, with whom it still continues; and all that now remains to the Dundonald family is merely the mouldering walls of the castle, with the mount on which it stands, extending to about six or eight acres of land."

So far the Statistical Account. From the Boyd charter-chest it would appear that Thomas, fifth Lord Boyd, had a charter of Auchans (the superiority probably) from John Wallace of Auchans, in 1599; and he and his successors seem to have had no small trouble in enforcing their rights—the vassals of Wallace having resisted their claims. The case came before the sheriff and his deputies, who failed to put their decrees into execution, until letters were obtained from the Signet, commanding them to end the matter, and "do justice to Lord Boyd." By a *novodamus*, in a charter of the twenty pound lands of Dundonald, obtained by Mr William Cochran in 1638, the Kirktown of Dundonald was erected into a free burgh of barony. This clause in the charter, however, never seems to have been acted upon.

Before the harbour of Troon was constructed, the point upon which it is built was used as a fishing creek, and immense quantities of smuggled goods were landed at it, and carried through the Dundonald hills into the interior. All along the coast the inhabitants were extensively engaged in the contraband trade. Many curious stories are told of their encounters with the revenue officers, whom they frequently defeated or outwitted.

In reference to the ecclesiastical history of the parish, Chalmers, in his *Caledonia*, states that it was "anciently of much greater extent than it has been in more modern times. It comprehended, on the east, the chapelry of Ricardstoun, which was formed into a separate parish long before the Reformation; and it comprehended, on the south, the chapelry of Crossby, which is now included in the united parish of Monktoun and Prestwick.†

The church of Dundonald, with its two chapels of Richardstoun and Crossby, was granted by the second Walter the Stewart to the Gilbertine convent, which he founded at Dalmulin, in 1229. When this convent was given up, in 1238, Walter granted the church of Dundonald, with its two chapels of Richardstoun and Crossby, to the monks of Paisley. The chapel of Richardstoun was established as a separate parish church, which belonged to the monastery of Paisley till the Reformation; as did, also, the church of Dundonald, with its remaining chapel of Crossby. The church of Dundonald was served by a vicar, who had a fixed stipend from the monks, out of the tithes of the parish, and some other profits.* In Bagimont's roll the vicarage of Dundonald was taxed at £5, 6s. 8d., being a tenth of its estimated value. At the epoch of the Reformation, the vicarage of Dundonald was held by Mr Hew Montgomery, to whom it yielded £60 yearly, besides 40 merks more, which were paid to two curates who did the duty. The rectorial revenues of the church of Dundonald were reported, in 1562, as producing to the monastery of Paisley £140 and 2 chalders 8 bolls of bear yearly. In 1587, the patronage, and the tithes of the church of Dundonald, were vested heritably in Lord Cland Hamilton, the commendator of Paisley, who was created Lord Paisley; and they descended, in 1621, to his grandson, James Earl of Abercorn. In 1653, the patronage of this parish passed, with the lordship of Paisley, from the Earl of Abercorn to Sir William Cochran of Cowdon, who, some years before, acquired from Wallace of Dundonald the estate of Dundonald. . . . In the beginning of the eighteenth century the patronage of Dundonald church passed, with the estate of Dundonald, to the Earl of Eglinton. They still belong to that family, and are at present held by [the Earl of Eglinton and Winton.] . . Within the castle of Dundonald there was anciently founded a chapel, which was dedicated to Saint Ninian; and an endowment was made for the support of a chaplain to perform divine service in it. The patronage of this chaplainry probably belonged to the Prince and Steward of Scotland; but, dur-

---

* We take this to be the date of transfer, instead of that given in the former Statistical Account, which is two years later; because that date is given without authority, and we find Sir William's name entered in 1638, as a member of the kirk-session, which could scarcely have happened before the purchase of this estate, as it was his only bond of connection with the parish.

† This is a mistake. Monkton parish is sometimes erroneously mentioned as the united parish of Monkton, Prestwick, and Crosby. The latter never was a separate parish. The records of the Presbytery of Ayr bear that, in 1631, the estate of Crosby, at the request of its proprietor, was disjoined from the parish of Dundonald, and for the sake of being nearer to religious ordinances, was joined to Monkton. In 1638, however, it was again wholly remitted to

Dundonald. It would appear that, subsequent to this latter date, the laird of Crosby erected the place of worship, the ruins of which still remain, for the accommodation of the neighbouring population, and it continued for some time as a preaching station, and for a while had a minister of its own.

* There belonged to the vicarage of Dundonald glebe lands, in various places, to the extent of ten merks, seven shillings and fourpence, of the old valuation. All these were acquired, about the epoch of the Reformation, which was equally the epoch of dilapidation, by Cuninghame of Caprington. There belonged to the church of Dundonald other church lands, which also passed into lay hands after the Reformation.

ing the reigns of James IV. and James V., and till the Reformation, the patronage was exercised by the Crown; there being, in those periods, no prince who was of full age."

Besides these chapels there appears to have been another, possibly of greater antiquity, not mentioned by Chalmers, called St Mary's Chapel. A very small portion of the building is still traceable. It was situated in the pass through the Clavin hills. The site now forms the garden of Hallyards farm. An excellent well, still called St Mary's Well, exists about a hundred yards west of the remains of the chapel.

It is said that a chapel once existed at a place called the chapel-hill, near the mansion of Hillhouse. In the garden wall, built nearly a century ago, the font stone is still pointed out.

The present church of Dundonald was built in 1803. The finishing touch, however, may be said to have been only put to it within the last ten years. The following paragraph recording the circumstance we quote from a local print:—"DUNDONALD.—Our village steeple—so long without a hand or tongue to note the flight of Time—has at length been furnished with both in a style that may well excite the envy of surrounding communities. The clock—which is the workmanship of Messrs Breckenridge & Son, Kilmarnock, who deserve great credit for the very substantial and elegant job they have made of it—was set a-going about ten days ago, and it continues to perform its important functions in the most accurate and faithful manner. The history of this valuable ornament is worthy of being recorded, as alike honourable to the heritors and the inhabitants of the parish. A sum amounting to upwards of £50—the unappropriated residue of a fund collected some years ago for the relief of the unemployed during a protracted stagnation of trade—having been handsomely offered by the heritors as a contribution on their part towards procuring the long-contemplated desideratum of a clock, the villagers and farmers in the neighbourhood immediately commenced a subscription, which was speedily augmented to nearly £30. These two sums conjoined enabled the committee not only to meet the charges of the Messrs Breckenridge, but to purchase a new and very melodious bell, the maiden tones of which were first heard pealing on Tuesday the 9th instant [1841], in honour of the arrival of the Earl and Countess of Eglinton and Winton in Ayrshire. The spire—not unhandsome in itself—is greatly improved by the neatly-figured and richly-gilt horologes that now grace three sides of its square, and prominently indicate the hours and minutes of the day. The old bell—

which, of course, has been superseded—is an object of antiquarian curiosity. It bears the following inscription:—"SANCTE EGIDIE ORA PRO NOBIS ANNO DNI M.CCC.LXXXX.vto. X." The English of which is—"Saint Egidius pray for us. In the year of our Lord Jesus Christ, 1395." St Egidius, though we cannot ascertain the fact, was in all probability the patron saint of Dundonald. . . . When the old church was taken down, and during the erection of the present one—built about the beginning of this century—the bell was carefully secured. Suspended between two trees, it continued to warn the parishioners to sermon in the churchyard, where the minister preached from a tent constructed for the purpose. Thus, after five centuries of faithful service, it has found, we believe, a resting-place at Newfield, where it will be sure to meet that care and respect which it deserves as a relic of former times."*

Owing to the distance of Fullarton and Troon from the parish church, places of worship, on the church extension principle, were erected there in 1837 and 1838, with ordained clergymen, who have *quoad spiritualia* districts assigned to them.

In the churchyard at Dundonald there are no memorials older than the beginning of the last century. William first Earl of Dundonald, who died in 1686, was, by his own direction, interred within the church, but without any funeral monument. There are no monumental remains of the families of the district.

The parochial records go as far back as 1602, being thus two years earlier than those of Ayr.† "The oldest volume, containing the records of session, is tolerably entire; nay, strange to say, much more so than any of the succeeding ones. It extends over a period of forty years, comprising a silent interval of sixteen years, and contains a great deal of parochial information that is curious and interesting. Among other entries of this kind, are minutes of the trial of Patrick Lowrie, warlock, and Catharine M'Teir, demit of witchcraft. These seem to have been cases of peculiar interest, and considerable judicial difficulty, from the minute detail of evidence adduced, and the length of time they appear to have been under trial. The attention of the session was more or less occupied by them for nearly five years—a term which would now-a-days do no small honour to a Chancery law-suit. Notwithstanding all this trouble, however, matters seem

---

* Since the death of Col. Crawfurd the bell has come into possession of the Free Church of Dundonald.

† The first entry is dated 3d January. It concerns a case of discipline, at which were present four elders and four deacons.

to have been left just where they began; no decision being recorded, probably from the parties leaving the parish, as we see, from part of the evidence, they threatened to do."* Patrick was accused of visiting the byres of the neighbouring farmers, walking in at one door and out at the other, without speaking: the cows invariably, after such visitations, became "seik," and gave blood in place of milk. Catherine M'Tier is the only witch mentioned in the records of the session, and escaped being burned by leaving the "kintra," as Lowrie is supposed to have done. The following are extracts:—

"23d March, 1602.—The quhilk day, Symon Wallace in Creux requyrit to schaw the manner of that uproir and tumult maid in the kirkyard immediatelie eftir the sermon on Sonday the 8th of Apryle last was, be him and his adherentis, and John Dickie in Curraith and his adherentis. The said Symon declarit in manner following: That he persaiving the said John Dickie to come by his accustomed manner with convocation of his friendis that day to the kirk, and that the said John Dickie had offendit him, he tuik the sam as done in contempt of him, quharupon quhen he saw the said John Dickie he bad him ga out of the kirkyard, and that thairupon the said John Dickie and his adherentis drew swordes to the said Symon, quhairupon thai cutit his ganging staf, quhilk onlie he had in his han, and na ither armour. The Session continuit thes matters to farther tryel.

"13th January, 1605.—Quhilk day Johne Wyllie, in Clavins, accused for noth yoking his pleuch on Yule day last; declarit that he was at the smiddie himself laying and mending the pleuch yrnes (irons), and the rest of the folkis wrocht at hame that day.

George Brackenrig accusit in lyk manner, declarit that he led peitis that day.

"17th March, 1605.—John Fergushill, younger in Haly, deferrit ane slanderous taill spokin to him by Agness Lyoun, spous to Petir Renkin in Parkheid; she aledgand upon George Lachland her author, as the said George Lachland aledgit Symon Muir his author, ' That the late minister of Kilwinning now departit this life was eardit with his mouth doun, and that he confessit that the minister of Ayr and Irvine, and he, had the wyt of all the ill wedder the year.'

"25th January, 1608.—The whilk day the Session ordained that Catherine Neil and James Dickie, leppiris, wha, with danger of infection of otheris, hants frielie the companie of utheris in this parochin, thocht they were clein, be chargit

be the officer to gae to Hew Wallace in Bogside, and agree with him for places in Kingease,* and gif it stand on Bogsides's pairt, to adverteis the Session, that be their travellis be and they may be addressit; and gif it failzie on the said leppiris' pairts, that they neither will repair to him, to the effect foresaid, nor seek to the places appointit for sic foul persones, to certifie them that they sal be publicklie dischargit this parochin.

"10th July, 1608.—The quhilk day Issobell Turnbill, in Lones, compearand befor the Session, was accusit of the selander of ane superstitious doing by her. Declared that she was sent for anes or twys be Catherine Walker, spous to John Dook in Chamber in Lonis, and that when she cam to her she took ane auld left foot scho of the husband's, and therin thrust the said Catherine's sair pap, and cast the said scho over the balk; and that she thrust her pap in the scho, and cuist it over the balk twys or thryse, and thereafter she grew seik.

"June 2, 1611.—Quhilk day the Session ordeined that help be maid to John Young to get remeid to his deiseas, after it be knawin gif the mediciners will tak him in hand, and quhat they will tak thairfor.

"8th November, 1629.—The quhilk day the minister publicklie out of the pulpit, by the authority of the Presbytery, did inhibit and discharge all sorte of charming, and resorting to charmers, consulting with wizards, sorcerers, and uthers of that sorte, certifeing all and sundrie who did so in time cuming, they should be chalengit criminallie thairfore, and followit and persewit with death, as for the crimes of witchcraft.

"16th October, 1636.—The quhilk day it was ordainit that the deacons, gif they neglect to come to gather at the kirk door on the Sabbath at thair appointit days, and be absent without ane lawfull excuse, sall be lyable to the penalty of six shillings and aught pennies, money, of penalty, toties quoties, as they are fund absent.

"24th April, 1637.—The quhilk day compeared William Watsoun in Croshie, and because he was to be married without the bounds of this parish, desired libertie to tak from our parishioners who was to accompany him at his marriage feist six shilling for their bridal lawing,† quhilk the Session granted, providing that he paid out of his consignatioune the sowme of twenty-four shillings to the poure.

---

* Statistical Account.

---

* See united parishes of Monkton and Prestwick for an account of Kingease hospital.

† This is a curious minute, the first of the kind we have met with. The Session seem to have considered it proper to defray at least a portion of the bridegroom's expenses, because he was going to be married out of the parish.

"20th February, 1642.—It was ordained to summond to the next day, John French, John M'Spoddan, John Small, and Adam Forgiskill, fugitives from the armie, and so guiltie of the sinne of perjurie; to heir their injunes according to the Presbyteries ordinance, to give signs of repentance in the public place the next day for the foirsaid sinne. (They appeared and were rebuked accordingly.)

"16th May, 1642.—The Session ordained that no woman be suffered to sit in the kirk in the time of sommer with plyds upon their heids, because it is a cleuck to their sleiping in tyme of sermon, and desyred the minister to exhort them gravelie the next day to the observance of the same.

"12th September, 1642.—The whilk day these persons following war ordained to be summond to the next day, for absenting themselfs from the publict thanksgiving to the Lord for his great mercies showen unto this land, in returning our armie in saiftie, and bringing of our King amongst us, and settling of the Kirk and State, on Tuysday last, to wit, Hew Fultoun, &c."

The records are chiefly occupied with cases of bastardy and Sabbath-breaking, and working on fast-days. It would appear that actual *fasting*—abstaining from both meat and drink—was enforced at this period. One case occurs in which a married woman, who was "with bayrne," is accused of having taken food, as she could stand out no longer. She was dismissed with "ane admonitioun." There are repeated notices of the "pest," which paid more than one devastating visit to Scotland during the seventeenth century.

The first volume contains a record of a different kind from the foregoing extracts, "and to Scotchmen at large, of a more interesting nature, namely, the solemn League and Covenant, to which are attached no fewer than 222 signatures. But of these, which is a lamentable proof of the low state of education at the time, 179 are subscribed by proxy, because, as it is stated, they 'could not wryt themselfis.'* It appears, however, that the eyes of the people were beginning to open to this defect, as we find them making arrangements two years afterwards, in 1640, for forming what may be considered the first parish school. The articles agreed on at a public meeting held for the purpose, and to be subscribed by the teacher on admission to the office, are certainly curious enough. The luckless man of letters was to be anything but a free agent; for

there was scarcely a part of his duty, even the most trifling, which was not laid down to him by rule, and according to which he was not commanded to walk on pain of deposition. The hours of teaching and recreation, the tasks for the children, the deportment to be borne towards him, the kinds of punishment, even to the particular kind of birch to be used, with the exact parts of the body to which it was to be applied, are all made the subject of minute description and legal enactment. What would a teacher now-a-days think if he were gravely called upon to subscribe such an article as the following? "That he shall attend at all hours when the children are in school, and not suffer himself to be withdrawn by drinking, playing, or any other avocation.' And more especially, when he takes a glance at No. 4, and sees that these hours in the winter months are from sunrise to sunset, and in summer from seven o'clock morning till six evening, without even the benefit of a Saturday's recreation; and that on the very Sabbath itself, he was to be always present in church with his little flock around him, to see, as the record bears, that they conducted themselves with propriety, and gave due attention to the ordinances of religion, of which examination on the following day was strictly to be made.*

---

* The following is a copy of the Regulations:—

*Orders to be subscrybed be him who shall have charge of instructing the youth heirafter at the Kirk of Dundonald, whereunto he shall ty himself under paine of deposition from his office, in caice of failzie after deu tryall and admonitions.*

1. The Mr. shall attend at all tymes when the children ar in schoole, and not suffer himself to be withdrawn by drinking, playing, or any other avocation.

2. If ony other inevitable necessitie draw him away a whole day, or the great part of it, he shall not faill to have some other in his absence to teach the schollers, and keip them in ordour.

3. If it shall happen that the Mr. have necessarie bussiness to withhold him longer nor the space of one day, he shall acquaint the Session therewith, or at lest the minister, if the haist of the matter cannot admit delay till the Session moit, that he may obtein libertie thairto.

4. Let the children in the moneths of October, November, December, January, February, meit in the morning at the sunne ryseing, and be dismissed at the sunne setting at nicht, except some younger ones, or those who ar fardest from the schoole, of whom some consideratioun most be had. All the rest of the yeir let the hour of gathering in the morning be seavin of clock, and the hour of skailling six; and such as learns latein wold always prevent (precede) the rest a prettie space.

5. Let the schollers goe to breakfast at nyne hours, and convein againe at 10. To dinner lykways at 12 hours, and returne at one afternoone, so neir as may be.

6. Let the Mr. pray gravelie and religiouslie everie morning before the schollers at their first meeting, and so at even before he dismisse them.

7. Let a task be prescrybed everie evening to ilk scholler in the Lord's prayer, belief, commands, graces, or catechisme, according to their age and progresse, whilk let

---

* Amongst those whose signatures were holograph, M'Kerrell of Hillhouse is the only one whose descendants are in possession of the family property.

"The minutes of session, after the conclusion of this volume till within the last few years, have been very carelessly kept. The next entry after 1643 is in 1702, the commencement of another volume. And for more than half a century after this date there are scarcely ten consecutive years of their transactions recorded. The register of baptisms, extending to four volumes, begins in 1673; that of deaths, in one volume, in 1763; and that of marriages, also in one volume, in 1823. The first of these is, in comparison, tolerably correct. But the other two are very incorrect, and hopelessly so, until more stringent measures are taken to compel the people generally to attend to such matters." *

them say everie morning before they enter to their ordinar lesson.

8. It most be caerfullie attended that the schollers be present at the sermons on the Lord's day, that they sit round about the Mr. silent, hearkening modestlie, and reverentlie; and have in reddines what they have observed, to say on Mononday morning, at quhilk tyme, as also on ilk Saturday, before they goe home, the Mr. wold spend at least ane half hour, opening up to them the grounds of religioun.

9. They who learne lentein most have a peice of that quhilk they have learned before, to say everie morning; quhilk being accuratelie examened, let thair lesson in author and grammer, if they be that farre advanced, be taught; and what difficultie occurs in them let it be pointed out to them. Let the pairts of their lesson quhairof they are to be examened be told them, whether belonging to etymologie or syntax in the author; and whatever is to them obscuir in the grammer.

10. Let them expone their lesson, and conferre of the parts thairof among themselves till nyne hours. When they enter at 10 hours let the Mr. heir them expone thair author and grammer. So much of the author as he may overtake, let it be examined at the said tyme, and what he misses then, let him overtake at one, afternoon; that quhen they ar to give ane account of their lesson, thair be no more to examein bot the grammer. Let them get a theme to turne into latein everie day betwixt eleven and twelve hours before noone, quhilk also let be a common wryting hour to the whole schoole. Let the theim be accuratelie examened ather presentlie after the making of it, or when they say thair lessons. Let everie day's lesson be said before they skaill, both play-days and others, that it prejudge not the morning peice.

11. Because no certane number of lessons can be appointed for them who learns Scots to get, it being a thing that depends on the tyme of the yeir, the number of schollers and thair proficience, in respect quhairof some will have more to say at a lesson, and others less, quhilk will take up tyme accordinglie; therefore, in this let the Mr. doe all that possible may be. And that thair be no neglect thairin, let the minister, with the best skilled of the gentlemen, everie quarter of the yeir at leist, stand by the Mr. in the schoole, till in our presence he have hearkened throuch all the children learning Scots; that according to the tyme spent thairin quhilk they shall missour with a glasse, they may direct the Mr. how many lessons he shall give them in the morning, before and afternoone, quhilk thair directioun the Mr. shall be bund to fulfill as if heir it were particularlie expressed. At quhilk tyme also the said minister and gentlemen shall take inspectioun of the estate of the schoole, try the childreins' proficiencie and the Mr.'s diligence and fidelitie in fulfilling all the points of his charge, and shall make report to the Session, that the Mr. may be commended and encouraged; or rebuked and admonished, accordingly, as the matter shall require. And if it shall be fund that the Mr. usis ony fraud to elude the tryall, as that he cause the children say longer lessons that day nor they use ordinarlie, or ony such, that this shall be ane fault mereting removeal from his charge.

12. For the children's better profiting, let those who are farder advanced in reading Scottish, whether print or writ, each of them have the charge of a young scholar who shall sitt beyde them, quhom they shall mak perfyte of his lesson, against the tyme come he shall be called to say, on the negligent pairtels pour'd, quhilk of the two soever it

shall be fund to have bein. And let the eldest scholler themselfs spelr at the Mr. quhat words they are ignorant of in thair own lesson. It being alwayes provydit that the elder scholler his furdering of the younger hinder not himself in his learning.

13. Let a speciall care be had of the children's wryting who ar meit for it. Let the hour named betwixt 11 and 12 be alotted to that exercise everie day, and farder to those whois speciall ayme that is. Let the Mr. make or mend their pens, rule their paper, cast their coppels, take inspectioun particularlie of every one's wryting, point out the faults; and learne them be ocular demonstratioun in his own practise before them how to mend. The Mr. most lead the hands of young beginners, stand over thair heid for thair directioun; and be goeing throuch all for thair furderance.

14. As the Mr. would be cairfull and conscientious to teach his schollers good learning, so wold he also learne them good maners, how to carrie themselfs fashionablie towards all. And for that purpose wold learn them gestures of courtessie to be used towards himself in the schoole, thair parents at home, gentlemen, eldermen and others, of honest fashion abroad. He wold put in thair mouths styles of compellation sutable to each one's place, to whom they speik; and how to compose thair countenance, eyes, hands, feet, when ony speiks to them, or they to them; and that they be taucht to abandoun all uncivell gestures, as skarting of heid, arms, &c.

15. And because mony, far lesse the tender youth, ar unable to abyde continuall bensell of learning, let them have for preserveing and sharpning thair inggens some recreatioun on the ordinar dayes, Tuysday, Thursday, and Saturday, in the afternoone, for the space of ane hour in the winter, or from October to Februar, and two hours the rest of the yeir. Bot let the Mr. see that they play not at ony unlawfull or obscene pastime, or such as may ather reddilie defyle or rent thair cloaths, or hurt thair bodies; and let a convenient place be choisen neirby the schoole, bot not at all the church-yaird, nor ony part of it, quhilk is 'Dormitorium Sanctorum,' a place for no ordinarie cevill imployment, let be the ludicrous; it serving for mourning rather than for playing and sporting, quhilk wold be keipit honest and separat for the owne use.

16. And finallie, as without disciplen no comprude can be keipit in ordour, so leist of all unbridled youth, thairfor it shall be necessarie that thair be in the schoole a common censour, who shall remarke all faults, and delate them to the Mr., of quhom account wold be taken once a week. And for more perfyte understanding of the childreins' behaviour thair wold be a clandestein censor, of quhom none shall know bot the Mr., and he who is employed in that office, that may secretlie acquaint the Mr. with all things. And according to the qualitie of the faults the Master shall inflict punishment, streeking some on the loof with a birk wand, belt, or pair of tawes, others on the hips, as their faults deserve; bot none at ony tyme, or in ony case, on the heid or cheiks. And heirin especiallie is the Mr. to kyth his prudence in takeing up the severall inclinations of his schollers, and applying himself thairunto by lenitie, allurements, commendations, fair words, some little rewards, drawing from vyce, and provoking to vertue such as may be wune thairby; and others by moderat severitie, if that be fund most convenient for thair stubborness. And let the wyse Mr. rather by a grave, austere, and authoritative countenance and cariage, represse insolence, and gaine everie one to thair dewtie then by strockes; yet not neglecting the rod quhair it is needfull.

* Statistical Account.

## ANTIQUITIES

The Castle of Dundonald looks dark and gloomy in the distance, and is not much improved by a closer inspection. Built on the summit of a detached conical eminence of considerable height, it must have been a place of great strength prior to the introduction of artillery. The building is not extensive—the area on which it stands being circumscribed. It, however, bears unequivocal evidence of having been one of the most magnificent strongholds of the age. Besides the massive oblong tower—at least three spacious stories in height, the remains of the courtyard and some interior structures still exist. The arch over the ground-floor is in good preservation, as well as some of the outer walls, particularly the northwest, but the stair is almost entirely gone. True to history and tradition, the ruins bear ample proof of the royalty ascribed to the building—the Stewart arms, with the lion of Scotland, appearing on various portions of it.

Boswell in his "Journal of a Tour to the Hebrides," states that Dr Johnson, who had the curiosity to visit the castle was very "jocular on the homely accommodation of King *Bob*, and roared and laughed till the ruins echoed." The learned lexicographer, however, might have preserved his gravity had he reflected on the comparative rudeness of the age, and the fact that it was originally a baronial, and at best only a private residence of the monarch. The baronial castles of England were not, with few or no exceptions, superior in the thirteenth or fourteenth century. It is not known at what time the castle was built or when it became ruinous; but Chalmers, in his *Caledonia* supposes that it was erected by Walter, son of Allan the first Lord High Steward of Scotland who had a grant of the land from David I, or Malcolm IV. This family possessed an extensive portion of Ayrshire—part of Kyle being still known as Kyle-Stewart, and on succeeding to the throne in the person of Robert II, in 1370 the castle, of course, became an appendage to the crown.

Opposite the Castle of Dundonald is a high and precipitous bank, clothed with wood part of which forms the boundary of the Auchans deer park where, not many years ago the sportive fawns might be seen enjoying themselves in all the wantonness of conscious security. The whole herd, however, have lately been removed to the Eglinton policies. Sweeping round the base of this pleasant and thickly planted bank, the visiter is delighted to find, in a gently sloping curvature, the venerable House of Auchans, said to have been, "for a long period, the residence of the Wallaces of Dundonald." Of this there can be little doubt, it probably having been built on the accession of that family to the property, though the structure is somewhat modern in appearance. This, however, may be accounted for by subsequent additions and improvements. The building, in the form of a right angle, has all the features of that half-castle half-mansion-house style which obtained in the latter end of the sixteenth and during the seventeenth century. One of the sides of the angle bears the date 1644, but, judging from appearances, it seems to have been a later erection than the other. As the land passed from the Wallaces to the Cochranes in 1640, the inference is that this portion of the building was the addition of the latter possessors. The house has been long in a state of decay, and it is somewhat surprising that the more recent part of the structure has suffered most. The roof is still kept entire, and in good repair; but, internally, the hand of time is ruinously apparent. Some of the apartments in the older division are occupied by the family in charge of the place. The last inhabitant of Auchans of distinction was the celebrated Countess of Eglinton, to whom Allan Ramsay inscribed his "Gentle Shepherd." On the marriage of her son Archibald, the eleventh Earl, in 1772 it became the jointure-house of her ladyship, where she died in 1780, at the advanced age of 91. Here the Countess was visited by Dr Johnson and his biographer, after their return from the Hebrides, in 1773. Of this interesting meeting Boswell has recorded the following particulars:—"Lady Eglintoune, though she was now in her eighty-fifth year, and had lived in the retirement of the country for almost half a century, was still a very agreeable woman. She was of the noble house of Kennedy, and had all the elevation which the consciousness of such birth inspires. Her figure was majestic, her manners high bred, her reading extensive, and her conversation elegant. She had been the admiration of the gay circles of life, and the patroness of poets. Dr Johnson was delighted with his reception here. Her principles in Church and State were congenial with his. She knew all his merit, and had heard much of him from her son, Earl Alexander, who loved to cultivate the acquaintance of men of talent, in every department .

In the course of our conversation, this day, it came out that Lady Eglintoune was married the year before Dr Johnson was born; upon which she graciously said to him that she might have been his mother, and that she now adopted him; and when we were going away she embraced him, saying, ' My dear son, farewell !" My friend was much pleased with this day's entertainment, and owned that I had done well to force him out."

A vast number of old papers, chiefly connected with the Eglinton family, are secured in one of the rooms at Auchans. It is unfortunate that they were not sooner attended to—many of them having been destroyed by persons who had no idea of their importance. Dr Johnson could not here have found occasion to complain of the want of timber, as he had done in other parts of Scotland—the wood around Auchans being both extensive and old. In the orchard, a portion of which exists, the pear, known over the country as the Auchans pear, was first produced. "The tree," says the *Old Statistical Account of Scotland*, "came originally from France, grew to a great height, and was not long ago (1793) blown down by a storm." Auchans has long been famed as a preserve for game.

About the beginning of the fourteenth century, the family of Fullarton erected and endowed a convent of Carmelites on the site now occupied by the town of Fullarton. The convent, which was dedicated to the Virgin Mary, continued to flourish till the time of the Reformation. The last prior, Robert Burn, foreseeing the approaching storm, alienated the lands, which went under the name of Friar's Croft, to Fullarton of Dreghorn. No traces of the edifice, or of the ancient mansion-house of its founders, which stood close by, are now to be found. And the only circumstance which gives a decided locality to the building, which at one time was disputed, was, that when the grounds some years ago were feued out for building, the foundation of the convent walls was discovered on digging, about fifty yards west from the old place of Fullarton. Friar's Croft, in the more ancient title-deeds, is described as being bounded on the east side by the road leading to *St Mary's Well*, and a ford in the river Irvine, adjoining this place, appears frequently in the old writs of Fullarton by the name of the *Friars-Fuird*.

The ruins of Crosby Chapel, "three-fourths of the walls of which still maintain their original height, stand close by the south entrance to Fullarton Park, and a mile north-west of the village of Monkton. It has been a building of small extent, measuring only forty-five feet in length and twenty-one in width. The only chiseled work that when more entire it presented, were a few mouldings, with the usual emblems of mortality, rudely carved on a recess in the interior of the north side-wall, denoting the burial place of the ancient family of Fullarton of that Ilk. This wall has, within the last twenty years, fallen down, and several of the carved stones have been employed

in patching up the remaining ones. The chapel was not of old standing, having been built subsequent to 1681, as a preaching station for the accommodation of the district, after the final reunion of the estate of Fullarton with the parish of Dundonald. Of the Popish structure which the chapel succeeded, neither vestige nor tradition has been preserved." One of the few monumental remains which the churchyard contains bears the following inscription in characters of bold relief round the margin :—"Heir . lye Corpis of ane Honorrabel man Callit David Hameltovne of Bothelhavche spovs To Elesone Sinclar in his Tyme Quha desist the 14 of Merche 1619."[*] Some intelligent individuals have been of opinion that it was the party thus commemorated who shot the Regent Murray. But it is a well ascertained fact, that the name of the person was *James* not *David*.

A more ancient relic than either of these still exists at Kemplaw, on the Auchans estate. This is the remains of a vitrified fort, which occupy a considerable eminence in the centre of the ravine or pass through the Clavin hills. It seems to have been intended to command the pass, though so very small that it could not have accommodated many warriors. That it was a place of strength, however, there can be little doubt, for, on the west, where there is no natural declivity, as on all the other sides, the outline of a fosse is distinctly traceable. The wall of the fort itself, which is circular, has a hollow passage round, of a conical form, and covered over with flags of sandstone, through which, when entire, a man might have crept on all-fours. Some years ago, a piece of iron was discovered in a mass of vitrified stone. It was about four inches in length, and shaped like an ear-ring. The position in which it was found indicated that it had been accidentally deposited there. The iron, with a portion of the mass of stone to which it adhered, was presented to the Ayr Mechanics' Museum.

On the heights above the farm of Harpercroft are the remains of two circular encampments. They are popularly ascribed to the Romans—but they are more likely, from their shape, to have been of British or Danish origin, belonging to the Roman period, or constructed during the invasions of the latter. "The largest of these," says the *Old Statistical Account*, "contains, within a circular embankment of loose stones and earth, ten acres of ground; and there is an inner circle of the same kind, and from the same centre, which encloses one of these acres. The other encampment is about two hundred yards distant. No artificial work has been raised on its north-east

---

[*] The Churchyards of Ayrshire. By William Dobie, Esq.

quarter, the steepness of the declivity being a sufficient defence. But on the south and west, the circular embankment is strong, and within is a platform, not exceeding an acre in extent."

---

## FAMILIES IN THE PARISH OF DUNDONALD.

### FULLARTONS OF THAT ILK.

THE most ancient possessors of the soil in this parish, next to the ancestors of the royal family, who had a gift of Kyle and Strathgryfe (now Renfrewshire), are the Fullartons of Fullarton, who are supposed to have been of Anglo-Saxon or Norman origin, and vassals of the Stewards.

That part of the barony of Fullarton, whence the family designation is derived, as also doubtless their surname, is situated in the immediate vicinity of the town of Irvine, upon the south-west side of the water of that name, and in the bailliwick of Kyle-Stewart, which is here separated from the district of Cuninghame.

To ancient Fullarton have been added, at different periods, particularly in the reigns of David II. and Robert II., several extensive and valuable properties adjoining to the south and east. The family held also, from an early period, lands in the island of Arran; and which they retained until about the close of the sixteenth century—but appear then to have been alienated to the family of Hamilton.

In this island also, at a very early period, settled a cadet of the family, which is said to have sprung from a second son named *Lewis;* in allusion to whom the descendants from this branch have always been distinguished by the patronymic of *MacLewis,* i. e. son of Lewis. *

The particular period, however, when the family of Fullarton first obtained lands and became resident in Kyle-Stewart, is very uncertain. Indeed, but very little progress appears hitherto to have been made in bringing to light materials, if such really exist, relating to the early history of private families. It seems corroborative of the tradition, that they came to Scotland along with Walter, ancestor of the High Stewards, that, in Shropshire, whence Walter is said to have come, several families of the name of *Fowler** have been seated from a very early period.

Fullarton, or, as in ancient deeds always written, "Foulertoun," † is obviously of Saxon etymology, and has most likely been derived from *office* or occupation: in corroboration of which, a Galfredus *Foullertoun,* whom there is reason to suppose was descended of this family, obtained from Robert I. a charter of some lands in Angus, together with the *hereditary office of fowler to the king,* in that county; in which office, he and his successors were obliged to serve the king's household with *wild-fowl* when he came to Forfar Castle, where this Fowler was to be entertained with a servant and two horses. ‡

It may be remarked, that the *situation* of the original castle of Fullarton seems also greatly to strengthen this supposition, being set down near the influx of the Irvine Water into the sea, in the immediate neighbourhood of an extensive tract of low marshy lands, many hundred acres of which, at no distant period, were overflowed promiscuously with the waters of this river and the tides

---

* On the landing of Robert de Bruce in Arran, during his disconsolate wanderings through the Highlands and Isles, this ancient branch of the House of Fullarton attached themselves to his interest, and followed his fortunes; for which, on recovering the throne of his ancestors, he, by a charter dated at Arnele Castle (in Cuninghame), in the second year of his reign, granted to Fergus Fullarton the lands of Kilmichall, &c., with the hereditary office of Coroner of the bailliedom of Arran. [See Notes to the "Lord of the Isles."]

This family have ever since possessed these lands through the direct line of male descent. They have in their possession an ancient seal of their arms, being the same with the bearing of the original family, with a crescent betwixt the otter's heads for difference; which seems to corroborate the fact of their descent from a second son, as related.

Coeval with the family of Kilmichall, but from a third brother, were the Fullartons of the island of Bute, who had the patronymic of MacCamie, i. e. son of James, which seems to have been the name of their original ancestor. They are often called Jameson.

From Kilmichall, again, have branched several other families, amongst whom, we must not omit to mention John Fullarton of Overtown, West Kilbride, whose literary and antiquarian taste is well known, and to whom we are greatly indebted for the very liberal manner in which he has tendered us the use of his extensive gleanings for the illustration of the present work.

* The arms of the family of Fowler, Gloucestershire, are, quarterly, azure and or; in the first quarter, a hawk's lure and line, or. This speaks directly to the name. The armorial achievements of the family of Fullarton, we conjecture, have been assumed as indicative of their territory; the crest seems of eastern origin, and probably connected with the period of the Crusades.

† The town, or possession of the Fowler.

‡ Nisbet, who states the original charter to be in the Earl of Haddington's collection.

of the ocean. The occupation, therefore, in this state, of so large a portion of land, and that, too, lying upon the very verge of the *Firth*, whilst the adjacent country was still thickly covered with natural wood, must necessarily have been peculiarly adapted for the pursuits of the *fowler*.

In the early annals of Scottish history, the sports of the field were by far the most frequent of the royal amusements. The kings, in imitation of the Norman sovereigns of England, were always the chief hunters; and in every shire they had a castle to accommodate them in these their favourite sports. Connected, also, with these establishments were the offices of *forester*, *falconer*, *hunter*, and, as clearly appears from the above mentioned charter, the *fowler*—all which ultimately became hereditary in particular families; and from which unquestionably have been derived respectively their surnames.

So far Robertson: but in strengthening his hypothesis he assumes too much. If the Fullartons were Anglo-Saxon or Norman followers of the Stewarts, derived from the *Fowlers* of Shropshire, it does not follow that they should be *fowlers* at Irvine. It seems as probable that they had no connection with the Shropshire *Fowlers*, the patronymic originating simply in the similarity of office—hence there might be persons of the name of *Fowler*, *Forester*, *Falconer*, or *Hunter* in various districts of the country, perfectly distinct in descent.

But to come to documentary evidence of the family:—

I. ALANUS DE FOWLERTOUN lived before the middle of the thirteenth century, and died about the year 1280; as may clearly be inferred from his son's charter of the lands of Fullarton, &c., by whom he was succeeded, namely—

II. Adam de Fowlertoun, who received a charter from James High Steward of Scotland, "Ade de Fowlertoun militi filio quandam Alani de Fowlertoun, *de terra de Fowlertoun in Kyle-seneseall, infra vic. de Are; et de terra de Gaylis;* et de piscaria de Irwyne." This charter is undated, yet it must have been granted *inter* 1283 *et* 1309, the period in which James held the office of High Steward. It was afterwards renewed in 1371.* He was succeeded by—

III. Reginald de Fowlertoun of that Ilk. This is distinctly instructed from his (Reginald's) son's charter, who succeeded him, as shall appear afterwards. In the family *tree*, this Reginald is stated to have been son of the preceding Adam; and this is most probably the fact. He had, besides his successor, two daughters, Johanna et Elena, who

appear in a resignation in favour of their brother, Sir Adam Fullarton, in a full court of Kyle, held at *Foullertoun*, the Thursday before the feast of St Barnabas, in April 1340. He had probably another son called David. David II. grants "ane pension to David Foulertoun."* He was succeeded by his son—

IV. Sir Adam Foullertoun of that Ilk, who, as already alluded to, had a charter by Robert, High Steward of Scotland, dated at Irvine, April 13, 1344,† wherein he is expressly designed, "son to Reginald Fowlertoun of that Ilk," of the lands of Fowlertoun, and Gaylis in Kyle-Stewart, with the bail fishings from *the Trune* to the water mouth of Irvine, and thence up the water (of Irvine) as far as the lands of Fowlertoun go; and also an annual rent of four merks and an half out of the lands of Shewaltoun. This charter bears, that Jean, Elen, and Marion, *sisters* of the said Reginald, had freely resigned all right they had in said lands, fishings, and annual rent: and the *reddendo* is a pair of white gloves at Whitsunday, and three *suits* of *court* at the Steward's Court of Kyle, in place of all other services.

There are still remaining, in possession of the family, many other documents in which Sir Adam's name appears; and, as stated by *Nisbet*, "he is frequently to be met with, as a witness, in the charters of King Robert II., designed, 'Dominus Adamus de Foullertoun dominus de Corsbie,' upon account that he had a charter of these last mentioned lands from that king." The charter here alluded to was not discovered by Robertson; yet, as Crosbie does not appear in the writs of Fullarton *before* this time, it is very probable that the fact is as stated by Nisbet.‡

Sir Adam doubtless, along with the High Steward, accompanied the army under David II. into England in 1346. *Bowmaker* relates, that before the Scottish army passed the English border, King David created several knights. He says, "De tyronibus suis quinque numero ibi militari cinxit gladio, viz. Stuart, Eglintoun, Craigie, Boyde, and Foullertoun." And being present at the disastrous battle of Durham, which immediately ensued, viz. on the 17th of the same month, Sir Adam Fullarton, along with King David, was there taken prisoner.* On David's release, October 3,

* Records of the Great Seal.

* Robertson's Index.
† Fullarton Charter-Chest.
‡ The manor of Crosby was a part of the extensive property which was acquired by Walter, the first Stewart, in Kyle. This manor was held, under the Stewarts, by Fullerton of Crosby, in the fourteenth century, and perhaps during an earlier age.—'Caledonia,' vol. iii. p. 506.
There is a paper in a roll of Robert I., entitled, "The Laird of Crosbie, his form of holding of his lands of Crosbie.—' Robertson's Index.
* Abercromby's Martial Achievements.

1357, the eldest son and heir of Sir Adam Fullerton was one of twenty hostages left in England, until payment of the king's ransom. It is therefore probable that Sir Adam returned home at this time, if not sooner.

His wife was Marjorie, a lady of the Stewart family, as Robertson supposes, from a charter she obtained of an annual rent out of the lands of *Troon*, granted by King Robert II. whilst he was High Steward—"Marjorie Foullertoun dilectæ *consanguineæ nostræ.*"* This charter Robert afterwards, on his coming to the throne, confirmed at Irvine, December 7, 1371. Her name occurs in a charter of confirmation by Robert II., dated "Doundonald, 4 Decemb. a. v. i.," "donationis quam Matheus de Crake fecit Ade de Foulertoun, militi, et *Marjoriæ,* spouse ejus, de duabus Marcis Sterlingorum annui redditus debiti ex Malendino de Crosby," &c. She is also named in her grandson's indenture with the Carmelite Friars, 1399.

By this lady he had two sons, whom we find mentioned in the writs of the family: 1. John, who predeceased his father; 2. David, who obtained a charter, from Sir Hugh Eglintoun of that Ilk, of the lands of *Laithis,*† upon the resignation of Thomas Laithis of that Ilk, to be holden *blanch* for payment of a *penny silver* at Whitsunday, at the *Cray* of Robertoun.

In 1392, Sir Adam Fullarton made a mortification out of his lordship of Cosbie to the Abbot and Convent of Paisley, "for the health of his soul, and the souls of his ancestors;" and, on his death, about the year 1399,‡ was succeeded by his grandson, his son—

V. John Foullerten, younger of Foullerton, having predeceased his father. As already noticed, he was one of the twenty hostages agreed upon, by treaty, 1357, to be left in England until payment of the king's ransom. The particular time, however, of his release out of England seems uncertain. Many of those first left were afterwards exchanged for others who went in their stead; and not a few died in confinement.

He received a charter from John, High Steward of Scotland, "de terris de Laithis, orientali et occidentali: et de terris de Harperland, cum pertinan; in Baronia de Kyle-Seneseali, infra vic. de Are." Which charter was afterwards confirmed at Scoon, March 5, 1373, by King Robert II., father to the granter.

* This conjecture is highly probable, more especially as the charter was granted while he was High Steward; but it was used for the king, in his charter, to style persons in the rank of baron "cousin."

† Allan, first Lord 'atheart, had a transaction with Dalrymple of Laith, 1474.——Peer. vol. i. p. 340.

‡ Thomas Foullertoun had a charter of "Ane twentie pund land in the earldom of Carrik," from David II. This Thomas was possibly a brother of Sir Adam.

It does not appear who he married; but he left a son—

VI. Reginald Foullertoun of that Ilk, who succeeded to the family estates, about the year 1399, on the death of his grandfather, Sir Adam. This is shown by an indenture, dated at Irvine, August 24, that year, entered into betwixt Reginald Foullertoun of that Ilk, heir to Sir Adam Foullertoun of that ilk, his *guid sire,* on the one part, and the *Provincial* and the Brethren of the Convent of the Carmelite Friars, near Irvine, on the other. By which contract the said Reginald obliged himself to pay to the Prior and Brethren of said Convent 40 merks sterling, for *meliorating* and upholding the houses of said Convent, and for also repairing the principal Kirk and Cloyster, *with the knowledge and consent* of the said Reginald; whilst the said Prior and Brethren oblige themselves, on the other part, in all time coming, to pray weekly upon the Lord's-day, or any other *feast* day, in the beginning of a mass, at the Great Altar, with an audible voice, for the souls of the said Sir Adam and *Marjorie* his wife, and especially for the said *Reginald* and Elizabeth *his* wife, their heirs and successors; and for the souls of all the faithful deceased.

The next, after *Reginald,* in chronological order, mentioned in the writs of the family, is styled—

VII. Rankine of Foullertoun, Lord of that Ilk. He is found so designated in another indenture, or more properly a decreet, with said Convent, pronounced by the Provincial of the order of the Carmelite, or White Friars of Scotland, given at *Irvine,* June 28, 1412, in which the family of Fullarton are declared to have been *founders* and *patrones* of this monastery.*

* *Copy of an Indenture, or Decreet, betwixt "Rankin of Foullerton, Laird of that Ilk," and the Provincial and Convent of the White Friars near Irvine, June 28th* 1412.

"This Indenture made at Irvyne the xxviij day of the moneth of Junij, the zher of our Lord a thousand four hondyr and twelve, bet. frrer William Coker, than beande Provincial of the quite frrers of Scotland, beand at Irrwyn on the ta part, and a worshipful Lord Rankyn of flowlertoun, Lorde of that ilk on the tother part, In maner, forme, and in Effect as after followse; that is to say it is cum till our eris that thar has bene syndry tymes great debaitt and stryfe betwixt the sd. worshipful Lord and our frrers dwellande in the sd. house of Irrwyne, sume for willfullnesse, and sume for defaute of knawlage as to the right of patronage of the sd. house of Irwyn, ffor the forsaid Lorde clemys that he solde be patron, and the frrers has sayd nay, ffor the qwilke debate the house and the personis tharin dwellande have syndry tymis sufferit disese and skaithe, the said Lorde cumand till us and requirand to se qwither he aucht to be patrone of the said place or noucht, we the hale chapter sittand apon this cause we haf fondyn the forbears of the said Rankyne beand ffoundours and patronis till our house of Irwyn. Qwharfor we haf gefyn decrete, and grantis, and be this present Indentur confirmys the said Rankyne of flowlertoun the foundourship of the said place of Irwyn, and all his airs lauchfully succedande eftir him, we forbiddande till ony frer or freris that now is

He was twice married: first to Elizabeth, mentioned in the indenture 1399, by whom he had a son, George, his successor, (of whom immediately.) His second wife was Marion, daughter of Wallace of Craigie, by which lady he had two sons, William and Adam; all of which is established from a charter, dated at Perth, July 20, 1428, by King James I., of the lands of *Drigarn*, &c. in Kyle Stewart, to Rankin Foullertoun of Crosby, and Marion Wallace his spouse, and after their decease to William Foullertoun their son, and the heirs of his body; which failzieing, to Adam Foullertoun, brother-german to the said William, and his heirs in like manner. This charter proceeds on the resignation of said Rankin;—and in terms of which, and a subsequent ratification thereof, to be immediately further noticed, William, the elder of Marion Wallace's two son's, succeeded to the lands of Drigarn (Dreghorn), &c., and was the first of that ancient and very respectable branch of the family of Fullarton. *

This laird of Fullarton predeceased his lady soon after the above settlement, and was succeeded by his son, of the first marriage,—

VIII. George Foullertoun of that Ilk, who, however, was most frequently designed "Laird of Corsby." He granted the charter of ratification, &c. above alluded to—dated at Ayr, January 19, 1430, by which he ratifies and confirms "the resignation some time made by his dearest

fadir, Rankin of Foullertoun, Laird of Corsby," of the lands of Dregirn, Newyall and Laithis; and Gayn Gifin, made by the King to his said dearest father, and till Marion Wallace his spouse; and after their decease, to William and Adam, their sons; and obliges himself and his heirs that he sall never raise mote, pleade claim, nae question to the said Marion, William, and Adam, nae to nane of their heirs belongand to the said lands of Dregirn, &c. And gif it happens him to failzie, as God forbid, he binds himself, his heirs, &c. to pay to the King of Scots 100 pund Scots; to St Mungo's work in Glasgow 100 pund do, and 200 pund to the said Marion, William and Adam.*

In 1439 he granted, out of the lands of Foullertoun and Shewalton, ten marks sterling, and five marks out of the ground of the Temples of Wester Templetoun, &c. to the Carmelite Friars near Irvine:—expressed thus in the sasine: " Levand. Deo et beate Marie, Priori et Fratribus Conventus Fratrum ordinis Carmelitorum de Irwine:" the said Prior and Convent paying yearly out of the said Temples, to St John and his ministers, the annual rent vsit and wont due to them therefrom; and. by another instrument, of the same date, he relieved the Convent of said annual rent, which was 10 shillings 10 pennies.

He obtained a charter, under the Great Seal, by King James III. in favour of himself; failing heirs male of his body, to William Foullertoun his brother; of the lands of Fowlertoun, Marrass, Shewaltoun, Harperland, and Wester Laithis; also Crosbie, Trune, Craikisland, and Russelsland; all lying within the Bailliarie of Kyle, and Sheriffdom of Are; as also of the lands of Knightsland, lying in the Isle of Arran—all proceeding on his own resignation, dated at Edinburgh, October 24, 1464.

It does not appear who this Fullarton married; but he had two sons: the elder, Paul, was contracted to marry a daughter of the laird of Craigie, as appears from a back-bond, granted by Adam Wallace of Craigie, to "ane Nobleman, George of Foullertoun, Laird of Corsbie,' which proceeds upon a narrative that there was a marriage appointed betwixt "Paul of Foullertoun, son and appearand heir of the said George, and Janet, daughter of the said Adam, conform to indentures entered into by the said Adam and George."

In contemplation of which marriage the said Adam Wallace gave to Fullarton the sum of nine score marks of tocher; and in security therefor,

or sall be in ony tyme to cum, under all payne that than may fall into the religion, that nane presume to impugne our decrete gefyne upon this mater; and gif ony presumys to say ony thing in the contrary that is before sayd, as God forbede that they sall, the forsaid Lorde or his ayrs, quhatsa thai be, for the tyme, sal abide the Provincialis cunnying, and sal pleinzhe til him quhatsa he be for the tyme, and he sal punys that fror or freris with help of the patron, gyf myster be as the cause requyres. Item, the said Rankyn is obliat till us that he and his airs sal supporet the place, and the freris tharin dwellande, as patronys in thair richtwis cause efter thair power in all tyme to cume, na he na his ayrs sal nocht annoye nor disese the place through na tityl of patronage but as it is grantit til him and thaim in this indenture, that is to say that what time the said Rankyn or his ayrs askys lefe at the priour of the house to entre in the place that than the priour sall . . . . . na supprycion to the place or to the personis, and gif ony supprycion be done in deide be him or his ayrs, he or his ayrs sal amende it as sie dede asks, or Ellis he or thai qwhatsumever thai be for the tyme sal remove oute of the place within xiiij dayis qwil it be amendit. In witness of the qwilk thing to thir present Indenture to the pt. remaynande with the said Lorde, the comon sele of the haile province, and with the sele of the provincial office, ar to put, and to the pt. remaynande wt. the said Convent, the forsaid Lord his sele is to put, the day, the moneth, and zher beforesaide."

* There is some reason for suspecting that Reginald and Rankin, No. VI. and No. VII., may be one and the same person. It is so far certain, at least, that in some legal writs respecting both, the names are Latinized alike—Ranulphus de Foullertoun: but, as in the annals of the family, they are held to be two distinct persons; an adherence is here had to that arrangement.

* There is a similar agreement and obligation in " The Memorie of the Somervilles," vol. I. p. 259.

until performance of said indentures, Craigie received an heritable conveyance of the lands of "Harperland, Marrass, and Gaylis" This bond, which contains various other items agreed upon, is dated at Irwyne, May 13, 1464 It may be remarked here, that, from the tenure of the last-mentioned charter of settlement, and from its being dated in the month of October immediately following this contract, it appears not improbable that the young laird of Fullarton had been prematurely cut off in the interim, and before consummation of his marriage, as, not long after this, on the death of his father, the representation of the family devolved upon the second son,

IX John Foullarton of that Ilk, who is mentioned in a sasine, given by Sir William Wallace of Craigie, Bailie of Kyle-Stewart, proceeding on his retour as heir to his said father, of the lands of Foullartoun, Tronc, &c , dated May 26, 1471

There is also amongst the family writs a letter of reversion, dated at Fullarton, 28th April, 1493, granted by James Esdaill, burgess of Irvine whereby he obliges himself to "a right worshipful man, John of Foullarton, Laird of that Ilk, and Corsbie," to resign in his favour the half of the lands of Marrass, upon the payment of three score marks Scots There is also another letter of this nature betwixt Fullarton and Lambart Wallace of Shewalton, of same date And the last time he appears in said writs is in a remission of all debts and fynes which he could require from Ninian Bawnatyne of Kames, under the hand of Andrew Mackeormy, Nottar Publick —dated May 9, 1494

Who he married does not appear but he died in the latter end of the year 1494, and was succeeded by his son,

X John Foullartoun of that Ilk, who was served heir to his father, in the whole lands of Fullarton, Corsbie, &c , Nov 10, 1494, but which he enjoyed only four years, as appears by his son's retour He married a daughter of Cuninghame of Caprington,* and left a son, who succeeded him, viz

XI John Foullarton of that Ilk, whose service and retour, as heir to his father, in the estates of Fullarton, passed November 10, 1507—at which time the lands are stated to have been nine years in nonentry

He granted a charter of the lands of Wester Lathis to Gavin Foullarton (probably brother to his father)† and Elison Dalrymple his spouse,

August 4, 1514 In this charter he is designed "of that Ilk," and "Laird of Corsbie"

His wife was Katherine Maxwell, daughter to umqll John Maxwell of Nether Pollock; which is evidenced by a liferent charter granted in her favour at the time of their marriage, June 10, 1515 On his death, in 1528, he was succeeded by his son,

XII John Foullartoun of that Ilk, who, when his father died, was only about eleven years of age , as seems probable from a sasine, under the hands of George Abernethie, N.P , in his favour of the nine mark lands of Dunrudyer, in the Isle of Arran and shire of Bute,* proceeding upon a retour as heir to his father, and which bears that these lands had been in non-entry for the space of ten years from the date thereof, May 8, 1538.

He married, about the year 1543, Kathrine, daughter to David Blair of Adamtoun, (omitted in Robertson's account of that family,) as is shown by a liferent sasine, amongst the Fullarton writs, in favour of said Kathrine Blair, "spouse to John Foullarton of Crosbie," of the lands of Fullarton (proper) and Marrass, dated April 5, 1543. On 17th December 1545, he alienated the lands of Shewalton, which are described as lying in dominio de Fullartoun, to Edward Wallace †

He acquired, May 10, 1546, the non-entry duties of the estates of Fullarton, &c , in Kyle, from David Blair of Adanton, who acquired right thereto from William Hamilton of Sanquhar, which last had them by the gift of King James V. Moreover, he obtained a charter, under the Great Seal, by Mary, Queen of Scots, dated Edinburgh, May 2, 1548, in favour of himself in liferent, and David Fullarton, his son in fee, of the lands of Fullarton, Marrass, and Gaylis , and of the lands of Corsbie, Craiksland, Sandhill, and nine acres of land, with the patronage of the kirk of Corsbie, proceeding upon his own resignation

On December 10, 1562, he granted to his son and apparent heir a charter of the mark land of Troon , and, October 31, 1564 he granted a commission, with consent of Kathrine Blair, his spouse, to his said son, to redeem certain lands from the persons therein named He also, with consent of his eldest son, David (February 8, 1566), alienated, to John Wallace of Dundonald, and Edward Wallace of Shewalton, the lands of Marrass, to-

---

* Genealogical paper relating to the Fullartons of Dudwick

† He was of the family of Dreghorn

* The name Dunrudyer seems to be a corruption of the Gaelic 'Touroider,' signifying Knightsland, and by which latter denomination they are actually so expressed in a charter by James III , 1484 Three of the witnesses to this sasine are Robertus Jamison, Coronator de Bute, Robertus Jamison de Makynock, and Nigello M'Camie (See remarks on this patronymic, page 12 )

† Excerpts from the MS book in the Public Records, entitled, "Repertorium Omnis Terræ"

gether with the fishing in the water mouth of Irvine, up to the bridge on both sides of the river, within the sea flood.* He was succeeded by his son,

XIII. David Fullarton of that Ilk. He was twice married; first, to Christian, daughter of James Hamilton of Bothellhaugh, and sister to David Hamilton, afterwards of the same place, by which lady he had three sons. 1. James, who succeeded him. 2. David; and 3. Robert, from whom it is supposed descended the first series of the Fullartons of Bartonholm. His second lady was Jean Lockhart, sister to Alexander Lockhart of Boghall, and relict of George Hamilton of Bogwood; but whether of this marriage he had any issue does not appear.† He granted a charter in favour of this last lady, of the lands of St Meddens and Craikslands, which was afterwards confirmed by King James VI. apud Halyrudehouse, November 4, 1600. Further, he granted a procuratory of resignation, in implement of a contract of marriage past betwixt James Fullarton, his son, on the one part, and John Fullarton of Dreghorn, Jean Mure, Lady Dreghorn, his mother, and Agnes Fullarton, her daughter, on the other part, for resigning the whole lands of Fullarton, Corsbie, &c., together with the mills of Corsbie and Fullarton; as also, the advocation and patronage of the kirk of Corsbie; in his Majesty's hands, in favour and for new infeftment to the said James Fullarton, his son, dated September 22, 1593. He was succeeded by his eldest son,

XIV. James Fullarton of that Ilk, who was retoured heir to his father in the barony of Fullarton, &c., by a precept, granted by Henry, Prince of Great Britain, and Steward of Scotland, dated May 2, 1605, and followed by sasine accordingly.

As already mentioned, he married Agnes, daughter of John Fullarton of Dreghorn,‡ by Jean Mure, daughter of Mungo Mure of Rowallan, by whom he had three sons and one daughter: 1. James, who succeeded him; 2. John, who was bred to a military life, and served several years in Germany;* after which, in 1639, he went to France, as lieut.-colonel to the Hon.

Alex. Erskine, brother to the Earl of Mar. In 1640, Louis XIII. advanced him to the rank of colonel in the French army. He acquired the estate of Dudwick, in the county of Aberdeen; was married, and left a family, who succeeded him in the estate.* The third son, William, was the first of the Fullartons of Craighall, in the shire of Ayr, but latterly of Carstairs, in Lanarkshire.† The daughter, Helen, was married to James Blair of Ladykirk, in Ayrshire. He was succeeded by his son,

XV. James Fullarton of that Ilk, who married Barbara, eldest surviving daughter of John Cuninghame of Cuninghamehead; all which appears from a charter (amongst the Fullarton writs) granted by James Fullarton of that Ilk, and Agnes Fullarton his spouse, of the ten pound land of Corsbie-Danatyne, and the twenty shilling land of Troon, in favour of James Fullarton, their eldest son, and Barbara Cuninghame, sister of William Cuninghame of Cuninghamehead, and longest liver of them, &c., dated Nov. 2, 1624. There is also another charter, of the same date and tenor, of these lands, by the same granters, to their said son and his spouse, but to be holden of the Prince, whereas the former was to be held of the granters.

Moreover he obtained a charter, under the Great Seal, by King Charles I., as father, tutor, &c. to Charles, Prince and Steward of Scotland, in favour of himself and Barbara Cuninghame, his spouse, proceeding upon his father and mother's resignation, of the same lands mentioned in the two preceding charters. This is dated at Edinburgh, August 1, 1634, in the end of which year, or beginning of the following, his father died, as may be inferred from the two sasines, March 26, 1635.

On November 20, 1634, he received a commis-

---

* MS. book in the Public Records, entitled, "Repertorium Om. Ter."

† This lady afterwards married George Schaw of Glenmuir. In the list of debtors to "William Browne, merchant burges of Air," who died in 1613, she is styled "Jeane Lockhart, Lady Corsbie, spous to George Schaw of Glenmuir."—GLAS. COM. REC.

‡ "James Fullertoun of that Ilk, and Nans Fullertoun his spous," occur in the testament of Issobell Colvill in Craigie-Symountoun. Feb. 1622.—IBID.

* He appears to have accompanied the first Duke of Hamilton in aid of the King of Sweden, in 1631.

VOL. II.

---

* This family appears to have followed the profession of arms; were highly respectable, and existed until the beginning of the present century. The last was General John Fullarton of Dudwick, a brave and gallant officer, who greatly distinguished himself in the Prussian and Russian service, in the latter of which he was promoted to the above rank. A gentleman who was acquainted with this distinguished veteran writes—"He was spoken of as having been a very brave officer, but of somewhat peculiar character and habits, acquired in foreign service, and latterly from advancing age; went little from home, or had little intercourse with the neighbouring proprietors —unless at public meetings, which he attended pretty regularly, in an old fashioned carriage, and accompanied by one or two Russian servants. He was a most respectable, and much esteemed country gentleman—was never married, so far as I have heard, and left no family. He was succeeded in his property of Dudwick by the family of Uday of Udny, in the same county, supposed to have been relatives, or connected with him.

† There appears to have been a fourth son. Mr Robert Fullartoun, son lawfull to James Fullartoun of that Ilk, is witness to a testament, Jan. 31, 1632.—GLAS. COM. REC.

C

sion, under the Great Seal, from King Charles I , appointing him Bailie of the Baliery of Kyle-Stewart How long this office remained in the family does not appear It was successively held by the families of Glencairn, Craigie, and Loudoun

This Fullarton of Corsbie was one of the two commissioners for the shire of Ayr in the Scots Parliament, anno 1643 In 1615, Feb 20, an act was past, appointing the Laird of Crosbie head sheriff of Ayr, " in respect that shyre had wanted a sheriff the 4 years bypast "*

The Laird of Corsbie and others disclaimed the Remonstrance in June 1651 † The family, however, seem to have afterwards taken part with the Presbyterians, for, by the act of oblivion, September 9 1662, Fullarton of Corsbie was fined in £2 000 Scots

By his lady, Barbara Cuninghame, he had three sons and three daughters 1 William, of whom afterwards, 2 James, who predeceased his father unmarried, 3 George, who succeeded to the estate of Dreghorn by a special destination, and ultimately succeeded his elder brother in Fullarton The daughters were 1 Elizabeth, who was married, June 20, 1649, to Robert Wallace of Carnhill, 2 May, who was married March 30, 1654, to Robert Alexander of Corseclays and had two daughters (1 Barbara who on the 27th Jan 1682, was married to Andrew Brown of Knockmarloch, and 2 Beatrice, who, on March 21, 1686, was married to a Mr Robert Wallace), 3 Barbara who, on November 22, 1662, was married to Patrick Macdowal of Freugh, in the county of Wigton, to whom she had issue, Patrick next representative of the ancient family and whose son, or grandson, succeeded to the estates and honours of the family of Dumfries.

He died in 1667, and was succeeded by his eldest son,

XVI. William Fullarton of that Ilk, who, in the retour of his service, dated September 26 of said year, is styled " Magister Wilhelmus Fullartoune de eodem, hæres Jacobi Fullertonne de eodem, patris ' —and it is observable that in almost all writs wherein he appears he is uniformly so styled ; which circumstance very probably arises from his having studied the profession of the law A rigid adherence to distinctions of this nature was peculiar to those times

On July 30, 1683, he and his brother, George Fullarton of Dreghorn, were, on suspicion of being concerned in the affair of Bothwell-Bridge, committed to prison ; and on the 2d of April fol-

* Balfour's Annals
† Do

lowing were indicted for trial, but the diet, it seems, was afterwards deserted *simpliciter* On this occasion, amongst other offences, they were charged with " harbouring and countenancing" their brother-in-law, Macdowall of Freugh This gentleman, as is well known, was amongst the most forward and zealous supporters of the Reformed Church

He received a charter, under the Great Seal, by King William III , of the whole lands contained in his retour as heir to his father; and further, the five pound land of Aldtoun, containing the little isle, opposite to the lands of Corsbie, called the Lady-isle, and containing a new erection of the hail lands and others" into a barony, to be called, in all time coming, the " Barony of Fullarton " This charter is dated " Edinburgh, December 9, 1698, et anno Regni nostri undecimo "

And again he obtained another charter, under the Great Seal, dated at Windsor Castle, August 5, 1707, by Queen Anne, erecting anew the whole lands, &c contained in the former, called and to be called, the Barony of Fullarton ; and further, constituting the port of Troon a free sea-port and harbour, with power to lift anchorage and other customs This charter also contains an erection of the town of Fullarton into a burgh of barony, with two annual fairs, the one to be held on the third Wednesday of July O. S , and the other on the first Thursday of November, also old style, likewise a weekly market on the Wednesdays, and further, with all the powers and privileges of any free burgh of barony within the realm.

He was thrice married first, to Elizabeth, daughter of Mr William Wallace of Elintoun, advocate, with whom he received 9000 marks *tocher*, and at the time of his marriage, July 29, 1662, his father resigned to him the following parts of his estate, viz the lands of Fullarton (proper), Gaills, Harperland, St Meddens, Willockstoun, that portion of land called the Sealand, Ronhill, and Brownlie, all to be holden of tho granter By this lady he had a daughter, Eupham, who was, in 1682, married to Sir William Wallace of Craigie, to whom she brought a marriage portion of £20,000 Scots, but had no surviving issue.

In 1669, he was contracted matrimonially, as appears by a document amongst the family writs, with Lady Elizabeth Cuninghame, sister to the Earl of Glencairn, and widow of William Hamilton of Orbistoun; but before the marriage could be solemnized, Lady Elizabeth was suddenly taken ill, and died

He married secondly, July 9, 1670, Anne,

daughter of John Brisbane, younger, of Bishoptoun, by Dame Mary Mure, daughter of Sir William Mure of Rowallan, and relict of Walter, third Lord Blantyre, but by this marriage he had no surviving issue. He married lastly, April 17, 1707, Margaret, eldest daughter of Alexander Dunlop of Dunlop, but without issue. This lady survived him, and was afterwards married to Sir Robert Denholm of West Shiels, Bart.

He died in 1710, leaving no surviving descendant—the paternal inheritance and representation of the family of Fullarton devolved upon his next surviving brother-german,

XVII. George Fullarton of that Ilk. He was concerned in the Bothwell-brig insurrection. As will be remembered, this gentleman had succeeded to the estate of Dreghorn; which property, on his coming to the family estates, he alienated. His retour of Fullarton is dated May 9, 1710. About the year 1670, he married Elizabeth, daughter of James Gray of Warristoun, in the shire of Mid-Lothian, by whom he had three sons and a daughter, as follows:

XVIII. 1. Patrick Fullarton, younger, of Fullarton—born in 1677; he received a judicial education, and afterwards practised at the Scottish Bar. He married Elizabeth, daughter, of Cleland of that Ilk, in the county of Lanark, (who survived him, and married A. Craufurd of Fergushill) by whom he had two sons and two daughters: 1. William, who succeeded his grandfather in Fullarton; 2. Patrick, who, in 1738, purchased the lands of Goldring, now called Rosemount. He married Miss Harper, by whom he had two sons, William and John, and one daughter. William, the eldest, added considerably to his paternal property, by purchase; and, with good taste and liberal management, improved and left it one of the best cultivated and most beautiful places in Ayrshire. He married Annabella, third daughter of Ronald Craufurd of Restalrig, W. S. He died in 1805. John was an officer in the Hon. East India Company's service, and died in India in 1804. The daughters were: 1. Anne, married, April 4, 1723, to Robert Wallace of Sauchrie, to whom she had issue; 2. Margaret, died unmarried.

2. Robert, from whom is descended the present family of Fullarton, of whom hereafter.

3. George, died young.

The daughter, Marion, was married, in 1711, to James Cuninghame of Auchenharvie; from whom is descended the present family of Auchenharvie.

Patrick, the younger, predeceased his father in 1709, so that the latter, upon his death, was succeeded, as before stated, by his grandson,

XIX. William Fullarton of Fullarton. By a disposition and tailzie, dated May 17, 1710, his grandfather resigned to him the whole lands and barony of Fullarton; and failing him, to and in favour of his brother-german, Patrick [Rosemount]; whom also failing, to Robert Fullarton, W. S., second son of the said George Fullarton the granter. This deed was afterwards confirmed by a charter, dated at Edinburgh, July 25, 1711, under the Great Seal, by Queen Anne. This gentleman devoted much time to the study of agriculture and rural science, and greatly improved and embellished the paternal estate. In 1745 he built the present house of Fullarton, in which, and its accompaniments, he showed a just taste, by the simplicity and unity of the design. Gardening and botany he also cultivated with much assiduity and success—particularly the latter, of which he was a devoted admirer. In May, 1751, he married Barbara, fourth daughter of William Blair of Blair, by whom he had an only son, his successor,

XX. Colonel William Fullarton of Fullarton, who was born January 12, 1754; and in the year 1759 was served and retoured heir to his father in the barony of Fullarton. He thus succeeded to his property when a child of little more than five years of age. He received his academical education at Edinburgh, and in his sixteenth year was placed under the government of Patrick Brydone, Esq., a gentleman of eminent literary attainments. With Mr Brydone he travelled on the Continent, and also accompanied him while he made the celebrated Tour in Sicily and Malta, in 1770. Of the early indications of young Fullarton's mind, which afterwards so greatly distinguished him, Mr Brydone, as he was preparing to proceed to these unfrequented islands, thus observes :—" Fullarton has been urging me to it [to proceed on the tour] with all that ardour which a new prospect of acquiring knowledge ever inspires him." With the same feeling, and in allusion to his early connection with this gentleman, Burns, in one of his poems, thus alludes to him :

> " Brydone's brave WARD I well could spy,
> Beneath old Scotia's smiling eye;
> Who call'd on Fame, low standing by,
> To hand him on ;
> Where many a patriot name on high,
> And hero shone."

In 1775, when only twenty-one years of age, he was appointed principal secretary to the embassy of Lord Stormont, at the court of France. In 1780, he communicated to the administration the plan of an expedition to Mexico against the Spaniards. This project having been approved of, he instantly set about putting it into execution, and with this view raised the 98th regiment of infantry. Sir John Dalrymple, in his *Memoirs of Great Britain*, gives the following account of the expedition

"It was planned and proposed to the Cabinet Ministers, by Colonel Fullarton of Fullarton, who acted in conjunction with the late Colonel, then Major Mackenzie Humberstone, the first of whom had never been in the army, both representatives of families amongst the most ancient of their country—young, generous, spirited, gay, and scholars  They raised 2,000 men at their own expense, with unusual dispatch, and involved their estates to a very large amount, by preparations for the expedition, agreeable to the terms upon which government had adopted the proposal

"The object of it was an attack upon the coast of Mexico, the troops were to sail to Madras, and be joined there by a body of Lascars, who were to proceed with them to one of the Laconian islands in order to refresh the men, and then to make for the coast of Mexico, in the tract of the Acapulca ships  Lord George Germaine added to this the idea of another expedition to the Spanish Main, which was to go across the South Sea, and join that on the coast of Mexico, and there is no doubt that, if the junction had been made, Spain must have immediately sued for peace  But the unexpected breaking out of the Dutch war obliged the expedition intended for Mexico to be sent upon an attack on the Cape of Good-Hope, and when that was found improper, it was employed in the war of India, where Colonel Mackenzie bravely fell in his country's cause  His friend (Col Fullarton) returned on the peace, covered with laurels, to defend her liberties in the senate "

As thus related by Sir John, on the interruption of the expedition to South America, Col Fullarton, with the troops under his command, proceeded to India, and with them served on board Commodore Johnston's fleet.  In May 1783, he received the command of the Southern Army on the coast of Coromandel—a force consisting of upwards of 13,000 men  His campaigns and operations with this army, in that and the succeeding year, were attended with a rapidity and brilliancy of success altogether unknown in that distempered and enervating climate  On his return to Europe, he published a work entitled " A View of the English Interests in India," &c —together with an account of his campaigns there in the years 1782, 1783, and 1784, in which work he has given a very particular and interesting narrative of these transactions, as well as much curious and valuable information relative to the history of our eastern empire

Colonel Fullarton was frequently a member of the House of Commons—twice was he returned for his native county of Ayr, the last time of which his election was unanimous

He was served heir of line, and representative of the family of Cuninghame of Cuninghamehead, Bart, in the year 1791—which representation is still in the present family of Fullarton

At the breaking out of the French war in the year 1793, he raised the 23d Light Dragoons, then called " Fullarton's Light Horse," and also the 101st regiment of infantry, and, in 1801, was appointed first Commissioner, or Governor, of the Island of Trinidad.  In this situation, however, he remained but a short time—returning in the year 1803

The short intervals he enjoyed from public employment were assiduously devoted to the study of science and literature  In 1793, at the request of the President of the Board of Agriculture, he wrote " An Account of the Agriculture of the County of Ayr, with Observations on the means of its Improvement," which the same year was printed, and generally circulated in the county and elsewhere  This Report, as also an Essay which he wrote in 1801, addressed to the Board of Agriculture in England, on the best method of turning grass lands into tillage, have been highly esteemed both for the accuracy of the scientific observations and the classical elegance of the composition

In the year 1792, he married the Honourable Marianne Mackay, eldest daughter of George, fifth Lord Reay, by Elizabeth, daughter of John, second son of Fairlie of Fairlie (formerly Dreghorn), Ayrshire

Col Fullarton died at London, 13th February, 1808, at the age of 54 years, deeply regretted by a numerous circle of friends, to whom he was much endeared, not more from his highly cultivated mind, in almost every branch of literature and science, than from his amiable dispositions, and condescending affability, which latter quality entwined him round the hearts and affections of his vassals and tenantry  He was interred within the church of Isleworth, where has been placed to his memory a marble tablet, with an appropriate Latin inscription

He left no male issue, and the representation of this ancient family devolved on his second-cousin, Colonel Stewart Murray Fullarton of Bartonholm, grandson of

XXI. Robert Fullarton, second son of George Fullarton of that Ilk, No XVII in this account  He was bred a Writer to the Signet, which profession he for many years practised  He wrote the genealogical tree of the family of Fullarton, formerly alluded to. He obtained the lands of Bartonholm and others from Captain William Fullarton of Bartonholm, the last of this ancient cadet of the family. In the deed of entail executed by Sir William Cuninghame, the third Baronet of Cuninghamehead, he and his heirs whatsoever were called to the succession of his estate and title; so that the present representative of the Fullarton family has a clear right to the Baronetcy of Cuninghamehead.* On the 15th March, 1716, he married Grizel Stuart, daughter of John Stuart of Ascog, in the Island of Bute, a cadet of the family of Bute: by whom he had several children, none of whom survived him, except his successor,

XXII. George Fullarton of Bartonholm, who was an officer in the army, and was much upon foreign service, particularly in North America, where he was present during the whole of the period generally denominated " the Seven Years' War."

He married, February 7, 1763, Barbara, sister of James Innes of Warrix, Ayrshire, by whom he had one daughter, John, and two sons: 1. Robert, who died in the year 1784, unmarried; 2. his successor,

XXIII. Stewart Murray Fullarton of Fullarton. His service and retour as heir male to the family of Fullarton is dated August 5, 1809. He entered early into the military service, and was, in 1812, commissioned Colonel of the Kirkcudbright and Wigton, or Galloway Regiment of Militia;

which situation he resigned upon being appointed, in May 1819, Collector of his Majesty's Customs at the Port of Irvine.

In January 4, 1796, he married Rosetta, daughter of Colonel Fullarton, his predecessor, (who died October 19, 1814), by whom he had eight sons and four daughters:

1. George, his successor, born 12th December, 1796.
2. William, born 3d September, 1799, died in 1809.
3. James, born 11th April, 1801. He was Lieut.-Colonel of the 26th N. I. Madras Army, and died at the Cape, whither he had gone for his health, on the 7th November, 1845.
4. John Campbell, born 2d October, 1802; Lieutenant Royal Navy.
5. Robert, born 16th March, 1806; died at Cawnpore, August 1839. M.D.; Assistant-Surgeon, H.E.I.C.S. Madras Army.
6. Stewart Murray, born 8th October, 1807, Captain 39th Regiment N.I. Bengal Army.
7. William, born 3d September, 1810, died in 1817.
8. Cranford Rose, born 19th October, 1814, died in 1815.

1. Barbara, born 3d June, 1798; married, 15th May, 1820, to Alex. H. Manners, Esq., W.S., and has issue.
2. Marianne, born 28th April, 1804; married, 24th December, 1826, to the Rev. Charles Bannatine Steven, minister of Stewarton, and has issue.
4. Annabella Cranford, born 1st March, 1813; died in 1814.

He married secondly, September 11, 1820, Isabella-Buchanan, only daughter of the late James Muir, M.D., Glasgow, and had issue

1. Elizabeth Muir, born 17th September, 1822.
2. Cranford, born 13th January, 1824; Lieut. 1st Regiment N.I. Madras Army.
3. Agnes Marion, born 21st June, 1825; died 15th April, 1848.
4. Robina Alexander, born 26th September, 1826.
5. William Fullarton, born 31st August, 1828; Ensign Royal Ayrshire Militia.
6. Blair, born 8th January, 1831.

Col. Fullarton died 20th May, 1844, and was succeeded by his eldest son,

XXIV. George Fullarton of that Ilk, Captain in the Kirkcudbright Regiment of Militia.

*Residences.*—From about the year 1500, this family appears to have resided chiefly at their *Place* of Crosby, which, in after-times, came to be called Fullarton-house. Part of the old mansion is still standing. The present house, as already mentioned, was begun in the year 1745. In 1791, Colonel Fullarton made considerable additions, in the form of wings, to the principal building: the whole, though not very large, has certainly a very graceful, dignified appearance. The situation is also singularly inviting; placed upon a dry and gently elevated lawn, about a mile from the margin of the sea, over which, to the picturesque and lofty Island of Arran, the view is uncommonly varied and extensive.

Fullarton-house is further embellished by many noble trees, particularly ash, sycamore and elm—

---

* The deed of entail was executed in 1711. It runs as follows: " To myself, and the heirs-male, lawfully procreate, or to be procreate, of my own body; whilk failing, to the heirs-female, lawfully procreate, or to be procreate, of my own body; whilk failing, to Robert Fullarton, Writer to the Signet, lawful son to the late George Fullarton of that Ilk, and the heirs of his body whatsoever, lawfully procreate, or to be procreate; whilk failing, to Patrick Fullarton, second lawful son to the deceast Mr Patrick Fullarton, advocate, and eldest son to the said George Fullarton of that Ilk, and the heirs whatsoever of his body, lawfully procreate, whether male or female; whilk failing, to Mrs Marion Fullarton, lawful daughter to the said George Fullarton of that Ilk, if she shall happen to be herself in life at the time of her succeeding to this tailzie, and to the heirs whatsomever of her body lawfully procreate; whilk failing, to Ann and Margaret Fullarton, lawful daughters to the said deceast Mr Patrick Fullarton, advocate, successively, they being in life at the time of their succeeding to this tailzie, and to the heirs-male or female lawful of their bodies; whilk failing, to Barbara Fullarton, Lady Freugh; whilk failing, to Patrick McDowal of Freugh, and the heirs of his body lawfully procreate, or to be procreate, whether male or female; whilk failing, to the heirs of Dame Elizabeth Cuninghame, my grandaunt, youngest lawful daughter of John Cuninghame of Cuninghamehead, and Elizabeth Edmonston, his spouse; the heirs lawful, whether male or female, of the said Dame Elizabeth Cuninghame, being Protestants, and no otherways; whilk failing, to George Fullarton, youngest lawful son to the said George Fullarton of that Ilk; whilk all failing, to my own nearest heirs whomsoever, heritably and irrevocably."

many of which have obtained to great size and beauty

*Arms*—Argent, three Otters' heads erased, gules. Crest, a Camel's head and neck erazed, proper. Supporters, two naked Savages, wreathed about the head and middle with laurel, and holding clubs in their hands, all proper. Motto —*Lux in Tenebris.*

In 1805 this domain was alienated to the Duke of Portland, whose residence in Scotland it now is The lineage of the Duke is too well known, in connection with the illustrious of the British Peerage, to require any account of his family here He is universally esteemed by his Scottish tenantry as a liberal and considerate landlord, while his name will go down to posterity as one of the greatest agricultural improvers of his time

## FULLARTON OF DREGHORN

The first of this family was,

I WILLIAM FULLARTON of Dreghorn, eldest son of Rankine Fullarton of that Ilk, by a second marriage with Marion, daughter of Wallace of Craigie He obtained the lands of Dreghorn from his father, who had a charter of them from James I, dated 20th July, 1428, in favour of him and his spouse, whom failing, to the said William, his son, and the heirs of his body He received a charter from Elizabeth Stewart, with consent of Adam Mure, her husband, of the lands of Lagland now Craighall, dated at Ayr, 24th January, 1454, in favour of himself and his spouse, Agnes, and which charter was confirmed by James II at Edinburgh, 26th July of that year He received also a charter of confirmation from James III, dated at Edinburgh, 24th October, 1466, of the lands of Dreghorn, Newhall, and Laiths, which had been left him by his father. He was succeeded by his son,

II William Fullarton of Dreghorn, who married Giles Hamilton, by whom he had four sons. Charles, Adam, David, and William, who are all mentioned in a charter granted by himself, and confirmed by James III, at Edinburgh, 1st November, 1485, of the lands of Ladyland, Barclengh, Knockgulrane, Dreghorn, and Laiths. He received also a charter of confirmation, dated 29th May, 1492, from John Fullarton of Fullarton, of the lands of Wester Laiths He was succeeded by his eldest son,

III Charles Fullarton of Dreghorn, who, on the 2d December, 1484, married Elizabeth Ross, daughter of George Ross of Hainng, by whom he had two sons—John and James, the latter of whom married Elison Dalrymple, of the family of Stair, and a daughter, Janet, who, on the 15th February, 1505, married John Campbell of Skeldon He was succeeded by his eldest son,

IV. John Fullarton of Dreghorn, who was seized in the lands of Dreghorn and others on the 18th December, 1518. He married Helen, daughter of Sir John Chalmers of Gadgirth, by whom he had two sons—John, and William, who married, 1st May, 1545, Agnes, daughter of Thomas Corrie of Kelwood; and a daughter, who married William M'Kerrell of Hillhouse. On the 9th July, 1522, he received a charter of confirmation from John Fullarton of Fullarton, in favour of himself and the said Helen Chalmers, his spouse, of the lands of Wester Laiths He died in 1546, and was succeeded by his eldest son,

V. John Fullarton of Dreghorn, whose retour is dated in 1546 He seems to have studied with a view to some of the learned professions. In the list of assize at the trial of the Archbishop of St Andrews and others, for attempting to restore Popery at Maybole, Kirkoswald, &c., in 1563, he is styled "Mr Jo Fullertone of Dreghorne." He took an active part in the affairs of the Reformation, and involved his estate very much on that account With a view of suppressing the Convent of Carmelite Friars, which his chiefs, the Fullartons of that Ilk, built in the thirteenth century, and for ages afterwards liberally supported, he purchased, on the 10th May, 1558, from Robert Burne, prior of the Convent, the lands of Friars Croft, and Dyets Temple, on which it was situated, near Trone, and to which they belonged. On the 4th September, 1562, he subscribed the famed Band, at Ayr, along with the Earls of Glencairn, Lords Boyd and Ochiltree, and a number of the gentlemen of Ayrshire, binding themselves to support and defend the reformed religion at all hazards against all its enemies, and upon Queen Mary's marriage with Lord Darnley, he went, on the 31st August, 1565, to Edinburgh, along with the Earls of Murray, Glencairn, and Rothes, Lords Boyd and Ochiltree, at the head of 1300 horse, in defence of the reformed interests He married Janet, daughter of Mungo Mure of Rowallan, by whom he had three sons,

1  John, his successor
2  Adam, who, on 31st July, 1593, married Agnes, only child of William Fullarton of Ardovie, in the county of Forfar.
3  James, who married Elizabeth Gray He was first gentleman of the Bed-Chamber to Charles I, by whom he was created a knight He was buried in Westminster Abbey, where an elegant monument is erected to his memory.

1  Agnes, who was married in 1593, to James Fullarton, younger of Fullarton, from whom the present family is descended

2. Marion, who married James Chalmers of Gadgirth, and had issue.

3. Elizabeth, who married John Wallace, younger of Mainford, and was provided for by her brother, on 17th June, 1599, in the lands of Arrothill.

He was succeeded by his eldest son,

VI. John Fullarton of Dreghorn, whose retour is dated 10th March, 1587. He received a charter from James VII., dated at Edinburgh, 5th June, 1599, of the lands of Arrothill. He married Janet, daughter of Sir Patrick Houstoun of that Ilk. This lady survived him, and afterwards married Sir George Craufurd of Lifnorris. He had three sons—

1. John, his successor.
2. David, who, on the 16th May, 1600, married a daughter of Craufurd of Lifnorris, who was provided for in the lands of Easter Templeton*.
3. William. In the testament of William Fullarton, minister of Dreghorn, in 1622, he is mentioned as "Mr William Fullarton, brother-germane to John Fullarton of Dreghorn."

He was succeeded by his eldest son,

VII. John Fullarton of Dreghorn, whose retour is dated 15th May, 1605. He married Christian, daughter of Wallace of Auchans, and relict, first, of Mr James Ross of Whiteriggs; second, of John Craufurd of Cranfurdland, to both of whom she had issue; but having no children to him, the succession devolved by special destination on his cousin, and second living son of James Fullarton of Fullarton,† who became

VIII. George Fullarton of Dreghorn, and upon the death of his brother, William Fullarton of Fullarton, without issue, in 1710, succeeded to the estate and representation of that family. He then sold the estate of Dreghorn to William Fairlie of Bruntsfield, who changed its name to Fairlie, and it is now the property and seat of Sir John Cuninghame Fairlie of Robertland and Fairlie, Baronet.

The armorial bearings of Fullarton of Dreghorn were the same as Fullarton of Fullarton, with a crescent for difference.

### FAIRLIES OF DREGHORN, AFTERWARDS CALLED FAIRLIE.

NISBET states, in his *Heraldry*, that the ancient

* In a legal document in reference to the lands of Holmes of Dundonald, dated April 3, 1609, he is styled "David Fullertoun of Knokinlaw, sone lawfull to vmqle. John Fullertoun of Dreghorne."

† There is a letter in our possession dated "Dreghorne, 31 December, 1677," addressed by "George Fullartoune" to his "Honored Cusing" "The Laird of Enterkine," in reference to some case of arbitration in which he appears to have felt keenly, so that he must have succeeded to Dreghorn before that year.

family of Fairlie of Braid, in the vicinity of Edinburgh, was descended from a natural son of Robert II.; and it is probable that Fairlie of Bruntsfield, in the same neighbourhood, was a cadet of that family. This supposition is strongly countenanced by the similarity of the armorial bearings of both families. From an inventory of writs in the charter chest at Fairlie, it would appear that

I. JOHN FAIRLIE, burgess in Edinburgh, bought the lands of Bruntsfield from Alexander Lauder of Halton in 1603. He had previously acquired the four oxengait lands of Restalrig from Robert Logan, portioner thereof. The disposition of these lands is dated 29th May, 1601. This John Fairlie was married to Elizabeth Watson, and had issue. He died before the 24th February 1607, for of that date

II. William Fairlie is served heir to his father, John Fairlie of Brountisfield. This laird of Bruntsfield had the honour of knighthood conferred on him soon afterwards; and, it should seem, enjoyed some adequate property distinct from these lands on which he himself lived; as it appears that he disponed of them to his son,

III. William Fairlie, very soon after his own succession. The charter conveying his lands—dated 3d September, 1608—is granted by Sir William Fairlie to William Fairlie his son, to be holden of the Laird of Halton, for the yearly payment of seventeen marks. Again, there is a charter, dated 30th September, 1618, "granted be Sir William Fairlie of Bruntsfield, to his son William Fairlie, of the four oxengait lands of Restalrig." Sir William Fairlie died before the 31st of March, 1626, on which day William Fairlie, his son, is served heir in the lands of Bruntsfield. There is a precept of *clare constat*, granted by John Lord Balmerino, to William Fairlie, son of Sir William Fairlie, of the four oxengait lands of Restalrig, dated in 1632.

IV. William Fairlie of Bruntsfield, who had acquired the lands of Little Dreghorn, in the county of Ayr, was, in the year 1689, appointed one of the commissioners for ordering out the militia. He was no doubt the son of the previous William Fairlie. Who he married does not appear, but he had at least two sons. John, the second son, married Barbara Mure, the heiress of Caldwell, without issue. In Law's *Memorials* he is thus noticed:—"Rowallan, elder and younger, and *Bruntsfield*, does retire and darn for a time." That is, *hid* themselves—this gentleman having evidently been concerned with them in the Bothwell-Brig insurrection, in which were implicated a great many Ayrshire gentlemen. He was apprehended in London, in June the same year;

but it does not appear that, in these perilous times, he suffered to any greater extent on account of his attachment to civil and religious liberty. He died before the 22d of May 1696, on which day his son,

V. William Fairlie of Bruntsfield, was served heir to his father William Fairlie of Bruntsfield. This gentleman dropped the designation of Bruntsfield, and assumed that of Fairlie, applied to the lands of Little Dreghorn, purchased by his father from the Fullartons. He married Jean Mure, only daughter of William Mure the last of Rowallan, (who afterwards married David, first Earl of Glasgow, and settled her paternal property on the issue of the last marriage, in preference to that of the first.) By this lady he had two sons 1 William, of whom afterwards, 2 John, Collector of the Customs at Ayr, who married Miss Bowman, daughter of John Bowman of Ashgrove, by whom he had an only child, Elizabeth Fairlie, who was married, in 1760, to George Lord Reay, being his second lady, to whom she had a son who died young, and three daughters.

VI. William Fairlie, the eldest son, succeeded his father in Fairlie. He was twice married first, to Miss Catherine Brisbane, daughter of Thomas Brisbane of that Ilk, by whom he had issue, of whom afterwards, and secondly, to Elizabeth Craufurd, second daughter of John Craufurd of Craufurdland, by whom he had no issue. She survived him more than sixty years, during which time she enjoyed a jointure off the estate. She married John Howieson of Brachead, in the county of Edinburgh, to whom she had two sons who died in infancy, a daughter, who died unmarried, and a daughter, Elizabeth, who married the Rev. James Moody, minister in Perth, by whom she had a son, William Howieson Craufurd, now of Craufurdland and Brachead, and a daughter, Isabella. Mrs Moodie died in April, 1823. Her mother, the dowager of Fairlie, died in 1802, at the very advanced age of 97, before the cause was decided that adjudged her right to the estate of Craufurdland. By his first lady, Mr Fairlie had a son, Alexander, and a daughter, Margaret, of whom afterwards.

VII. Alexander Fairlie of Fairlie succeeded his father in 1744, in which year his father's widow, as stated above, was married to John Howieson of Brachead. He was a gentleman of much ability and public spirit, taking an active part in the affairs of the county. He took a prominent lead in promoting agricultural improvement. He died unmarried, at an advanced age, in 1803—when he was succeeded by his sister,

VIII. Margaret Fairlie of Fairlie, who was married to William Cuninghame, at first designed of Auchinskeith; but, in 1778, having been served heir to the late Sir David Cuninghame of Robertland, he assumed that title, and was accordingly designed Sir William Cuninghame of Robertland, Bart., which title was at first conferred on his ancestor, Sir David Cuninghame of Robertland, who, in 1630, was created a Baronet of Nova Scotia, being amongst the most early creations to that dignity. Sir William had two sons 1 William; 2 Alexander, who was Collector of Customs at Irvine, and died unmarried.

IX. Sir William Cuninghame Fairlie of Robertland and Fairlie, succeeded his father in his paternal property in 1781, and his mother, the heiress of Fairlie, in Fairlie, in 1811. He married Anne, daughter of Robert Colquhoun, Esq. of St Cristopher's, and sister to Wm. Colquhoun, Esq. M.P. for Bedford; by whom he had issue.

1 William
2 Robert—died unmarried.
3 John, of whom afterwards.
4 Charles, who married Frances daughter of Sir John Call, Bart. of Whiteford, in Cornwall, and banker in London

1 Frances died in 1815
2 Margaret, married to John Cuninghame of Craigends
3 Anne, married to Sir William Bruce of Stenhouse

IX. Sir William Cuninghame Fairlie, of Robertland and Fairlie, the eldest son, succeeded his father in 1811. In June 1818, he was returned member of Parliament for Leominster. In the same year he married Anne, only daughter of Robert Cooper, Esq. of Foxford, Suffolk, banker at Woodbridge. He died in 1837, when he was succeeded by

X. Sir John Cuninghame Fairlie of Robertland and Fairlie, the present Baronet, who married Jessie, daughter of the late John Wallace of Kelly.

Fairlie-House is pleasantly situated on the brow of a gentle eminence, on the south banks of the Irvine water, about three miles west from Kilmarnock. It is an elegant, commodious, and remarkably well-constructed modern mansion.

### WALLACES OF DUNDONALD AND AUCHANS

The lands and castle of Dundonald formed part of the royal demesnes after the accession of the Stewart family to the throne. They constituted a portion of the principality of Scotland, established by Robert III., in 1404. Alan, first Lord Cathcart, had a grant of the custody of Dundonald Castle, and the dominical lands of Dundonald, from James III., in 1482. These lands of Dundonald continued for some time in the possession of the Cathcarts. John, the second Lord, had a charter, in 1505, of Colynane, Hilhouse, and Holmyss, in Ayrshire, in the hands of the King, by reason of forfeiture, for the alienation of the greater part of the same by Alan, Lord Cathcart, his grandfather, without consent of the King,* &c. The next possessors of the lands were the Wallaces, a branch, no doubt, of the Wallaces of Riccarton. The first of the name who is found in possession was—

I. William Wallace, who had a charter from James V. of the lands and barony of Dundonald; the charter and infeftment of feu approved by act of Parliament in 1527.

II. William Wallace of Dundonald was, in 1566, conjoined with Edward Wallace of Shewalton, in the purchase of the lands of Marress from the laird of Fullarton.

III. John Wallace of Dundonald, who is supposed to have married Agnes, sister of Walter, first Lord Blantyre, whose father, Sir John Stewart of Minto, died in 1583. He had issue, as appears from the latter-will of James Wallace, afterwards quoted, who must have been his son,

1. John, who succeeded.
2. James, who died unmarried.
3. Thomas, who appears to have married and had issue.
4. Agnes, married to Patersoun, baker, Edinburgh.

IV. John Wallace of Dundonald, was retoured heir to his father, John Wallace of Dundonald, in 1572. He had a brother, whose name occurs in a testamentary document as "James Wallace, brother-german to Jon. Wallace of Dundonald," in 1597. Thomas, fifth Lord Boyd, had a charter of the lands or superiority of Auchans from John Wallace, in 1599. The Boyds appear to have experienced considerable difficulty with the property, the Wallace tenantry having resisted their demands. Robert, sixth Lord Boyd, at last, in 1617, procured letters from the Signet, commanding the Sheriff and his deputies to put their decrees in execution, and do justice to Lord Boyd. "Johne Wallace, elder of Dundonald," is mentioned in a testamentary document, in 1604, so that he had a son, named after himself, who succeeded him.† He died about 1609, in which year we have the latter-will of his brother, James Wallace, formerly mentioned, which is curious, and in substance as follows:—

Testament, &c. of vmqle. James Wallace, bro-

ther-germane to vmqle. Johnne Wallace of Dundonald, the tyme of his deceis, Quha deceist in the moneth of Januar, 1609. Gevin vp be himself the 19 day of Januar, the said year, in as far, &c., and pairtlie gevin vp be Johnne Wallace of Dundonald, in so far as concernis the Inventar, &c., Quhome he constitutis his onlie executor, &c.

Inventar.

Item, the said vmqle. James being vnmareit, had all, &c. viz. the abuilzement of his bodie, estimat to thriescoir fyiftein punds. . . .

Legacie.

. . . Item the said James Wallace levis to his brother, Thomas Wallace, the sowme of fourtie markis money: mair, levis to him ane stand of broune freis: mair, ane pair of gray worset schankis. . . : mair, levis to him ane sword, qlk. is in the handis of Andro Leitch, sone and appeirand air to the Laird of Craig. Item, levis to Bessie Wallace, hir brother dochter, ane new cloik of Inglis claith, with ane neck of veluot. Item, levis to Agnes Wallace, relict of vmqle.

Patersoun, baxter, burges of Edinburghe, the sowme of Twentie pundis. Item, levis to Agnes Wallace, dochter to Johnne Wallace of Dundonald, ane pair of blankettis, ane dowblet and breikis of Spainis taffatie, cuttit out vpone taffatie of the cord, with some musick buikis, quhilkis ar in the handis of Thomas Porter, in Kilfuird of Dundonald. Item, levis to Andro Paterson, baxter, sone to the said Agnes Wallace, ane cloick of Scotts greine, and ane coitt and breikis of broune claith, pasmentit with blak pasmentis. Done at Edinburghe, the 19 Januar, 1609. Mathow Wallace of Garscadden, cautioner and souertie for Johnne Wallace of Dundonald, executor, &c. to vmqle. James Wallace, his brother-germane. Feb. 7, 1610.

From this document, it would appear that John Wallace of Dundonald died in 1609, or 1610. He was alive when his brother James made his will; and, from the preamble, he must have been dead when it was recorded in 1610. We also learn from it, that besides his heir, he had a daughter named Agnes. In the testament of William Wallace, minister of Failfuird, who died in 1616, mention is made of "Margaret Cathcart, relict of vmqle. Jon. Wallace of Dundonald." This was in all likelihood his widow. The name of Lady Faile was Janet Cathcart, probably a sister.

V. John Wallace of Dundonald is frequently mentioned in testamentary documents between 1610 and 1625, in which latter year Mathew Wallace of Dundonald occurs. John possibly died unmarried, and was succeeded by—

VI. Mathew Wallace of Dundonald. From the latter-will of "Johnne Stewart, brother-ger-

---

* Wood's Peerage, i. 340.

† "Item, in and to the annuall and dewitie restand awand to the said cedent, or that may appertene to him during his liftyme, furth of the lands of Dundonald, pertening to Johne Wallace, elder and zounger of Auchans."—King's Proclamation in reference to certain dwes owing to Mr Andro Boyd, minister at Eglishame.

mane to Archibald Stewart of Ardgowane," who died unmarried at Paisley, August 1627, it would appear that Mathew Wallace had married the relict of        Stewart of Ardgowane. Amongst other legacies, he leaves " to Janet and Agnes Wallaces, dochters lawfull to Mathew Wallace of Dundonald, the sowme of Threttein hundrithe marks money, equallie betuixt thame, and the anuelrent of the said Threttein hundrithe markis To radoune and appertein to Margrat Stewart, *his and their mother*, during hir lyftyme." "Margaret Stewart, spous to Mathew Wallace of Dundonald," died in the month of June 1628.* Her latter-will was made in favour of *Annabell* and *Marie* Wallaces, her daughters. By these documents, it would thus appear that there were four daughters of this marriage—1. Janet : 2. Agnes : 3. Annabell : 4. Marie.† Mathew Wallace of Dundonald was alive in 1641, in which year he is mentioned in the latter-will of " Marcoune Craufurd, Lady Armillane." Whether he had a son and heir, does not appear ; but a

VII. " John Wallace of Auchanes" is mentioned in a testamentary document, as cautioner for Wallace of Garseaddane, in 1643. The lands of Dundonald seem to have been sold to Sir William Cochrane, ancestor of the Earls of Dundonald, before 1638 ; but those of Auchans were probably retained for some years longer in the family. Colonel James Wallace, who headed the rising at Pentland, is believed to have been the last of the Wallaces of Dundonald and Auchans.‡

### COCHRANES, EARLS OF DUNDONALD.

This family is a branch of the family of Blair of Blair, and adopted the name of Cochrane, in consequence of a marriage with the heiress of Cochrane, at the close of the sixteenth century. William Cochrane of that Ilk,§ county of Renfrew, married Margaret, daughter of Sir Robert Mont-

gomerie of Skelmorlie, Ayrshire. He was living in 1593. Elizabeth Cochrane, daughter and heir, married—

I. ALEXANDER, son of John Blair of Blair, who took the name and arms of Cochrane. They had seven sons, all of whom were officers in the royal army. His second son,

II. Sir William Cochrane of Coldoun, who was knighted by Charles I., acquired the estate of Dundonald in 1638. He was created Baron Cochrane of Dundonald in 1647. The part he had taken in the civil commotions of the time, is evidenced by the proceedings of the Presbytery of Ayr, who—Feb. 28, 1649—debarred "Lord Cochrane" from renewing the solemn league and covenant, he having " been a Colonel in the late unlawful rebellion, and having went to Ireland to bring over forces," &c.* In 1654, he was fined in £5000 by Cromwell's act of grace and pardon. On the Restoration, however, he was made a Commissioner of the Treasury and Exchequer, and created Baron Cochrane, of Paisley and Ochiltree (having previously acquired the latter barony), and Earl of Dundonald, with remainder to the heirs-male of his body, failing which, to the eldest heirs-female of his body without division, and the heirs-male of such heirs-female, bearing the name and arms of Cochrane. The earldom, however, has continued in the male-line. He married Eupheme, daughter of Sir William Scott of Ardross, county of Fife, and had issue :

1. William, Lord Cochrane, who died, during the life of his father, in 1679, leaving issue by Katherine, daughter of John, sixth Earl of Cassillis,
   1. JOHN, second Earl.
   2. William, of Kilmaronock,† died 1717, having married Grizel, daughter of James Grahame, second Marquis of Montrose, and had issue.
     THOMAS, sixth Earl.
2. Sir John, of Ochiltree, from whom THOMAS, the eighth Earl.
1. Margaret, married, in 1676, to Alexander, ninth Earl of Eglinton, and had issue.
2. Helen, married to John, fifteenth Earl of Sutherland, and had issue.
3. Jean, married, first, John, first Viscount Dundee ; secondly, to William, third Viscount of Kilsyth, and had issue.

The Earl, in his old age, was accused, 1684, of having kept a chaplain with his son, then dying, 1679, who prayed for the success of those rebels

---

* Her testament recorded in the Commis. Rec. of Glasgow, 1630.

† One of the daughters is said to have married Robert Montgomerie of Whitefoord.

‡ Since the foregoing sheets were put to press we have been informed by the minister of Dundonald, that near to the house of Auchans, occupied by C. D. Gairdner, Esq., Commissioner to the Earl of Eglinton, a workman, while digging lately in a small mound of gravel, came upon an urn, containing some fragments of human bones. The urn, which was of very rude workmanship, was much injured in the removal, and having been imperfectly fired, has suffered more since by exposure to the air. Mr Gairdner sent the fragments to the manse, where they still remain. The urn seems to have been of British rather than Roman workmanship. There is no tradition of a tumulus having existed where the relic was discovered.

§ For the Cochranes of Cowden, or Coldoun, see Appendix.

---

* In 1650, William, Lord Dundonald, and Dame Scott, his spous ; Lieutenant-Colonell Hew Cochrane, brother to my Lord Cochrane, occur as debtors in the testament of " Johne Blair, tailzeour, merchand burges of Air," a relation of the Blairs of Adamton.

† Erroneously printed " Kilmarnock" in some of the Peerages. " I, Mrs Anne Cochrane, daughter of the deceast Mr William Cochrane of Kilmaronock, grants me to have received from the right honourable the Earle of Dundonald, the sum of five hundred merks Scots, and that in full of a year's annualrent of the principall sum of ten thousand merks," &c.—May 29, 1732.

in the west—those covenanters who defeated Claverhouse at Drumclog. The Earl died in 1686, and was interred in the church of Dundonald.

III. John, second Earl of Dundonald, grandson and heir, married, in 1684, Susanna, daughter of William and Anne, Duke and Duchess of Hamilton; he died, 16th May, 1690.

IV. William, third Earl of Dundonald, son and heir, died unmarried, 19th November, 1705.

V. John, fourth Earl of Dundonald, brother and heir, married Anne, daughter of Charles Murray, second Earl of Dunmore, and by her—who married, secondly, Charles, third Marquis of Tweedale—had issue, a son and three daughters, celebrated for their beauty in the poems of Hamilton of Bangour.*

1. William, fifth Earl.

1. Anne, married, 1723, to James, fifth Duke of Hamilton and Brandon.
2. Susan, married, first, to Charles Lyon, sixth Earl of Strathmore; secondly, 1745, to George Forbes.
3. Katherine, married to Alexander Stewart, sixth Earl of Galloway.

The Earl married, secondly, in 1715, Mary, Dowager of Henry Somerset, second Duke of Beaufort, but had no issue. He died 5th June, 1720.

VI. William, fifth Earl of Dundonald, son and heir, dying unmarried, aged 16, was succeeded in his uncntailed property by his nephew, James, sixth Duke of Hamilton, and in the title and entailed estate by his cousin and heir-male,

VII. Thomas, sixth Earl of Dundonald, son of William, second grandson of William, first Earl. He was born in 1702, and married Katherine, daughter of Lord Basil Hamilton of Baldoon. He died on the 28th May, 1737.

VIII. William, seventh Earl of Dundonald, son and heir, accompanied General Forbes to America, 1757, and was killed at the siege of Louisburgh. Dying unmarried, 9th July, 1758, the title devolved upon his kinsman and heir-male,

IX. Thomas Cochrane, seventh son of William Cochrane of Ochiltree, great-grandson of William, first Earl of Dundonald. He thus became eighth Earl of Dundonald. He married, first, Elizabeth,

* " But who is she, the gen'ral gaze
   Of sighing crowds, the world's amaze,
   Who looks forth on the blushing morn
   On mountains of the east new born?
   Is it not COCHRANE fair? 'Tis she,
   The youngest grace of graces three.
   The eldest fell to death a prey,
   Ah! snatch'd in early flower away;
   The second, manifold of charms,
   Blesses a happy husband's arms;
   The third a blooming form remains;
   O'er all, the blameless victor reigns:
   Where'er she gracious deigns to move,
   The publick praise, the publick love."

daughter of James Ker of Morristoun, but by her had no surviving issue; secondly, 1744, Jean, daughter of Archibald Stuart of Torrence, county of Lanark, Esq., and by her, who died 1808, aged 86, had issue—

1. Elizabeth, born 1745, married 1775, Patrick Heron of Heron, Esq.

1. Archibald, ninth Earl.
2. Charles, a major in the army, born 1749, married Katherine, daughter of Major Piteairn of the Marines, but by her—who remarried Charles Owen Cambridge of Twickenham, Esq.—had no surviving issue. Major Cochrane being sent by Sir Henry Clinton with despatches to Earl Cornwallis, then besieged at York Town, 1781, passed undiscovered in a boat through the middle of the French fleet, and safely delivered them. The Earl, in approbation of his intrepid conduct, appointed him one of his aides-de-camp; but in a day or two his head was taken off by a cannon ball, previous to the surrender of that ill-fated army, aged 32.*

* The following spirited, and rather clever letter, written by this brave officer, while on service in the American war, to his brother Archibald, ninth Earl of Dundonald, will be read with interest:—

"New Jersey, Brunswick, 8th March, 1777.

"DEAR BROTHER,—I regret that I should have allowed you to be the first who has made an apology for the silence that has prevailed 'twixt you and me since leaving England. I assure you it has very frequently been in my mind the writing to my relations in Scotland, and making you my best wishes, ere now; and it has not only been thought of, but several times attempted. A kind, however, of shame for having so long delayed it, joined to my of late unsettled, inconvenient life, has occasioned my having undone many of those things which ought to have been done. I beg that you will accept the will for the deed; and if the utmost sincerity can atone for the delay, my conscious heart assures me of forgiveness.

"I, about two months ago, received your kind letter inclosed by K. It was of a very old date, as indeed are most of them that find their way here. We understand that at home many of our friends make the same complaint. I don't know any other reason for it except the uncertainty of the passage, which must be evident, when I assure you that General Howe, since the 16th of October, has not received any accounts from England, and that is now near five months. If he receives accounts so unpunctually, we have hardly a right to complain.

"It gives me much satisfaction to see by yours that there is almost a finishing stroke of the pick put to all your labours, and that there is a near prospect of some return. You have gambled tolerably deep, to use a sporting expression; but I now hope, as you have so long thrown out, that you will now hold in, a good hand.

"I thank you for your views or offers towards me. Notwithstanding that my desires are very strong of one time or other enjoying the sweets of a domestic retirement, yet I shall never take any steps, or accept of an offer that will encumber, or tend to make me a dead weight on any relation, especially on one who, I fear, for some years will have his own fortune to make.

"With respect to my profession, I still like it above any in the world. I think it, however, an improper one for a person in my circumstances and situation, who has neither friends or a tolerable prospect of preferment before him. To speak impartially, what would I now have been, had I not become a Benedict?—exactly a lieutenant in the 7th regiment, after fifteen years being in the army. That a knock on the head should be ten thousand times more acceptable to one capable of reflection, and any share of ambition, is beyond doubt. Like Orlando, in 'As you like it,' —not Orlando furioso,—it might be said then; if dead, but

3 John, born 1750, died 1801 having married, 1800, Miss Birch of Pinner, county of Middlesex

4 James Atholl, in holy orders, born 1751, died 1823, having married, Mary, daughter of —— Simpson, Esq

5 Basil, of Auchterarder, county of Perth, born 1753, died 1826

6 Sir Alexander Forrester Inglis Cochrane, G C B., Admiral of the White, born 1758, married, 1788, Maria, daughter of David Shaw, Esq , and widow of Sir Jacob Wheate, Bart., Captain R N , and had issue He took the rank of Lieutenant, 1773, was wounded in Lord Rodney's engagement, 1780, made Post Captain, 1782, and promoted to a flag in 1804 In 1806, when under Sir J T Duckworth, he attacked the French squadron of Admiral de Siegler off St Domingo, and took or destroyed the whole, one of 120 and two of 84 guns, having his hat blown off by the wind of a cannon ball He received the thanks of the House of Commons for the conquest of Martinique, 1809, and died 1832

7 George Augustus Frederick, Colonel in the army, retired, born 26th November, 1762

8 Andrew James Cochrane Johnstone, born 1767, married, first, 1793, Georgiana Amelia Constance Gertrude, daughter and heir of the late Baron Le Clugny, Governor of Guadaloupe, and widow of M Raymond Godet, and by the first marriage had Elizabeth, born 1795, married William John, first Lord Napier

X Archibald, ninth Earl of Dundonald, son and heir, born 1748, married first, 1774, Anne, daughter of Captain James Gilchrist, R N , and by her, who died 1784, had issue,

1 Thomas tenth Earl
2 William Erskine, a Major in the army, and late of the 15th Dragoons

---

one killed that should be willing to be so could do one's friends no wrong, for there was none to lament him , the world no injury, for in it he had nothing—only that a place in it was filled up that might be much better supplied when it was made empty Poor Orlando' I have a sympathetic feeling for him, and might perhaps had similar ideas, had I not thought fit at times to act for myself

" I don't immediately wish to leave the army, I am too poor to do that I am well satisfied to try a ten years farther spell of it , and wish I could see any chance of getting on in it, or that I had friends who would endeavour to procure me some snug civil military employment that would help to make the conjugal pot boil I know many such things that would suit me extremely well, and might either give rank or the pence, and are far from being inconsistent with an officer's holding For instance, Major Maitland here has been clerk of the pipes so many golden years, with a SALARY SAUCE of £200, that his small pipes are almost turned into a golden drone Col Skene has held fifty employments these ten years, a score of which were devised on purpose for him , I wish he would sell one of them to me for the value of my company

" I like no aid-de-campship employments , they are too precarious, and don't last long enough for an Old Foggy Rank in the army is a very pretty pleasing, musical thing, with a name and no substance, and does vastly well until you are tired of it, which seldom fails, sooner or later, happening A troop of dragoons is a mighty sensible, snug sinecure, for particular people But some of Skene's or Maitland's tunes on the pipes is the most insinuating music in the world, played in the duet way, with my present a-company-ment I dare say, among my friends and relations, there may be one or other that understands composition, and has a soul for music , they will, I hope, be able, from the above notes, to get the tune completed in time, and have it played for my benefit But if they are discordant, or no composers, in the Graciosa way, I don't expect that they will attempt the strain, or any part of my above affectuoso

" Nor shall I be a bit discomposed, but must beg leave

---

3 Archibald, Captain R N , distinguished himself under his brother, when Lord Cochrane, in the Mediterranean, 1801 , died 1829, having married, 1812, Jane, daughter of Arthur Mowbray, Esq , and had issue,

1 Anna Jane, born 28th January, 1813
2 Caroline Elizabeth, born 11th June, 1814
3 Robert Alexander, born 18th March, 1816.
4 Basil Edward Arthur, born 23d December, 1817
5 Archibald Hamilton, born 2d June, 1819
6 Elizabeth Stuart, born 26th April, 1823

He married, secondly, 1788, Isabella, daughter of Samuel Raymond of Belchamp, county of Essex, Esq , and widow of John Mayne of Jeffont-Ewins, county of Wilts, Esq , she died 1808 ; thirdly, 1819, Anna Maria, daughter of Francis Plowden, Esq , and by her, who died 1822, had issue,

1 Dorothy, born March, 1820

The Earl, whose life was devoted to scientific pursuits, rather to the injury than the improvement of his fortune, is known by various patents and publications, particularly *A Treatise on the Intimate Connexion between Agriculture and Chemistry*, 1795 , he died 1st July, 1831, and was succeeded by his son,

XI Thomas, tenth and present Earl, better known as "the Gallant Lord Cochrane" The following account of this nobleman we copy from an article in *Bentley's Miscellany*, entitled, *Memoir of the Earl of Dundonald*——

---

to humbug and amuse myself with these manuscripts, and feast my thoughts with springs to catch woodcocks with I have been very holy of late, and made a new beatitude—
Blessed are they who expect nothing, for they
Will not be disappointed
I believe I have tired you long ago with my REVERIES , if not, nous re-verron

" We have had rather a disagreeable winter of it The light infantry, with which corps I am, have been much harassed during the winter, and are miserably ill lodged, my whole company, which consists of 53 men, are obliged to live in one small room, and I am in a pigeon-hole, with 11 officers where we eat, drink, and sleep I don't believe a man of this army, ever since the affair of Trenton, where the fatal security of the Hessians brought us into that sad scrape have had their clothes off, for my part, except one fortnight, I have not been uneased these ten months I have a Galloway plaid, which Jack sent me , this, a blanket, and a skin of a bear, is my principal baggage and bed It is the healthiest and most agreeable life in the world, could one divest themselves of reflection, and have no eye towards futurity, or the main chance.

" It is with much anxiety that every body expects a vessel from Britain We hear a war with France much spoken of In that case, I hope some one will endeavour to get me made major to one of the new raised corps. All my cotemporaries are so long ago, and I have as much desire, ambition, and know my business full as well as any of them

" When you have a few spare moments, you will oblige me much by giving me a few lines, and telling me how all goes on If you ever see any of my friends, I beg that you will be so good as give my best respects to any that are pleased to remember me, not forgetting my commanding officer, Mrs K , and though I have not the honour of yet knowing Lady Cochrane, I hope best wishes, and respectful compliments of a brother, will not be disagreeable or unwelcome That she and you may enjoy every possible happiness is the sincerest wish of, dear brother, yours affectionately, CH COCHRANE "

"Thomas Cochrane, Earl of Dundonald, was born in Scotland, December 14, 1775. His father, the ninth Earl of Dundonald, had passed the earlier part of his life in the naval service, while his later years were devoted to the pursuit of practical science, in which he made many useful discoveries. At the early age of eleven, Lord Cochrane entered as a midshipman under his uncle Sir Alexander Cochrane, a gallant and enterprising admiral. A tutor was provided for the boy; and thus, while he rapidly acquired a practical knowledge of seamanship, the higher pursuits of science and literature were not neglected. The romantic enthusiasm of his character was manifest at a very early age, and was evinced in many adventures. His age for some time delayed his promotion; but his gallantry in attacking some French privateers and gun boats, in the bay of Algeziras, was so appreciated by Lord Keith, that he at once appointed him to the command of the Speedy, a sloop of eighteen guns.

In February, 1801, he captured the Caroline a French brig; and in April he took several Spanish xebeques; but in the May of that year he achieved his first great exploit, in the attack and capture of the Spanish frigate El Jamo, off Barcelona. The inequality of force was truly alarming; the frigate mounted thirty-two guns, twenty of which were long twelve-pounders, and she had a crew of three hundred and nineteen men. On the other hand, the Speedy had only fourteen four-pounders, and her crew amounted only to fifty-two men and two boys. But this small crew was worthy of being commanded by such a captain. No sooner did Cochrane announce his intention of boarding his enemy, than men and boys proclaimed themselves ready to follow him. The surgeon was obliged to take the management of the wheel. The very audacity of the attempt disconcerted the Spaniards; they made a brief, spiritless resistance, and then threw down their arms.

Many similar achievements followed. During the ten months that Cochrane commanded the Speedy, he captured thirty-three vessels, mounting in all 128 guns, and manned by 533 sailors and marines. Unfortunately he fell in with a large French squadron, commanded by Admiral Linois, and was obliged to strike to such a vastly superior force. But his captivity did not last long; he was liberated on an exchange of prisoners, and promoted to the rank of post-captain in La Raison frigate.

On the renewal of the war after the peace of Amiens, Lord Cochrane was appointed to the Arab, and afterwards to the Pallas, of thirty-two guns. In her he made several valuable captures, particularly that of the galleon Il Fortuna, laden with specie to the amount of 150,000 crowns. It is highly honourable to the generosity of the captors that they returned 10,000 crowns to the Spanish captain and crew, as some alleviation of their misfortune.

In 1806 Cochrane made a daring and successful attack on a French squadron in the Garonne, a river of most dangerous and difficult navigation. He sent a detachment in his boats to cut out the corvettes, which were twenty miles up the river, and they succeeded in carrying La Tapaguese, a corvette of fourteen long twelve-pounders and ninety-five men, though she lay under the protection of two powerful batteries. Day dawned as they were bringing her off. Another corvette of larger size gave chase to recover the Tapaguese; but after an hour's fighting she was so roughly handled that she too would have fallen into the hands of the English but for the rapidity of the tide. During the absence of his boats, three ships of the enemy, mounting in all sixty-four guns, advanced against Lord Cochrane; but, though so large a portion of his crew was absent, he met them half-way, and attacked them so vigorously that they were driven on shore, where they lay complete wrecks. His next exploit was the destruction of the Semaphores on the French coast; then followed the storming of a battery; then a battle with a French frigate of vastly superior force, which would have been taken, had not two others been sent to her assistance, and several daring cuttings out of vessels in the teeth of forts and batteries. From the Pallas Lord Cochrane was transferred to the Imperieuse; and in her, between the 13th of December, 1806, and the 7th of January, 1807, he took and destroyed fifteen ships of the enemy, chiefly laden with wine and provisions.

Unfortunately for his fame, Lord Cochrane wished to add senatorial dignity to his professional honours. After a vain attempt in 1805, he was returned for Honiton in 1806, and subsequently became member for the city of Westminster. But he did not abandon the naval service; he rendered essential service to the cause of Spanish independence by a long series of brilliant exploits on the coast of France and Spain. In 1809 he performed his last great achievement in the service of his country—the destruction of the French shipping in the Basque Roads. Ten ships of the line, and some frigates, lay in these roads, protected by formidable batteries, and a dangerous shoal, which extended between them and the English blockading squadron, commanded by Admiral Gambier. Lord Cochrane formed a bold plan for the destruction of this squadron, and communicated it to the Admiral. He was, in consequence, sent to join Lord Gambier, and under him to take command of the attack which he had projected. Fireships and explosion-vessels having been prepared, Lord Cochrane, with his gallant crew, led the way, and the boom by which the enemy was protected was broken by the Mediator. The fireships immediately rushed through the opening, and were piloted into the midst of the French anchorage, in spite of a furious cannonade and discharge of shells from the batteries. Though some of the ships mistook their course, and others exploded too soon, the greatest alarm was produced in the French fleet. Three ships of the line, and a frigate of fifty-six guns, were burned; another ship of the line was so injured that she sunk a few days after, and seven others were driven on shore. The whole loss occasioned to the conquerors was only ten men killed and thirty-five wounded. For this exploit Lord Cochrane justly received the dignity of a Knight of the Bath, an honour more rarely accorded then than it is now.

Lord Gambier had from the very first opposed this enterprise, and he was much annoyed that the conduct of it was entrusted to Lord Cochrane, a stranger to his squadron. He did not, therefore, second the attack as heartily as he should have done, and he lost the opportunity of capturing and destroying the seven ships that had run ashore. Lord Cochrane, therefore, expressed his determination to oppose the vote of thanks to Lord Gambier when it should be proposed in Parliament. As Cochrane was in opposition, and Gambier a great favourite with the administration, party spirit was mixed with the question, and Gambier demanded a court-martial. After a long investigation he was acquitted; but the verdict of the court was not ratified by the country. Lord Cochrane was regarded with manifest dislike by the ministry, and he reciprocated the unfriendly feeling with interest. Instead of entering into this controversy, we shall content ourselves with quoting the opinion of Napoleon Buonaparte, whom no one can suspect of partiality.—" Cochrane," he said, " might and would have taken the whole fleet, and carried it out with him, had his Admiral supported him as he ought to have done. For, in consequence of the signal made by L'Allemand to the ships to do the best in their power to save themselves, *sauve qui peut*, in fact, they became panic struck, and cut their cables. The terror of the *brulots* (fire-ships) was such that they actually threw their powder overboard, so that they could have offered very little resistance. The French Admiral was an *imbecille*, but yours was just as bad. I assure you that if Cochrane had been supported, he would have taken every one of the ships."

Ministerial vengeance found an opportunity to vent itself on Lord Cochrane. He was induced by Mr Cochrane Johnstone and others to speculate in the funds. He was unfortunate, and lost severely. Some of those with whom he had been associated entered into a conspiracy to raise the price of stocks by diffusing false intelligence; they were detected and brought to trial. Lord Cochrane was included in the indictment, for his intimate connection with the parties gave reasonable ground for suspicion. The case was tried, June 21st, 1814, before Lord Ellenborough, a man of violent passions and prejudices, who too often displayed on the bench the fiercest feeling of a political partisan. By straining the circumstances of suspicion, his charge established an apparent inferential case against Lord Cochrane, he was found guilty, sentenced to a fine of a thousand pounds, imprisonment for twelve months, and exposure in the pillory. To this the Ministers added expulsion from the House of Commons, deprivation of his rank in the navy, and erasure from the list of Knights of the Bath. The whole country was indignant at this spiteful harshness. Lord Castlereagh, with great reluctance, was forced to assure the House of Commons that the exposure in the pillory would be remitted; and the electors of Westminster marked their sense of the proceedings by again choosing Lord Cochrane as their representative. He paid the fine with a thousand pound note, on which he wrote a spirited and characteristic protest against the harshness with which he had been treated, and this note is preserved among the curiosities of the Bank of England. Disabled from serving his country, Lord Cochrane took a part in the war of South American independence as Admiral of the fleet equipped by the new republic of Chili. Among his many heroic exploits in this capacity, there is one so graphically described by Captain Basil Hall, that we must make room for the quotation :—

' While the liberating army under General San Martin was removing to Ancon, Lord Cochrane, with part of his squadron, anchored in the outer roads of Callao, the port of Lima. The inner harbour was guarded by an extensive system of batteries, admirably constructed, and bearing the general name of the Castle of Callao. The merchant ships, as well as the men of war, consisting at the time of the Esmeralda, a large forty-gun frigate, and two sloops of war, were moored under the guns of the castle, within a semicircle of fourteen gun-boats, and a boom made of spars chained together. Lord Cochrane, having previously reconnoitred these formidable defences in person, undertook, on the 5th of December, 1820, the desperate enterprise of cutting out the Spanish frigate, although she was known to be fully prepared for the attack. His lordship proceeded in fourteen boats, containing 240 men, all volunteers from the squadron, in two divisions, one under the immediate orders of Captain Crosbie, the other under Captain Guise, both officers commanding ships of the Chilian squadron.

' At midnight the boats having forced their way across the boom, Lord Cochrane, who was leading, rowed alongside the first gun-boat, and taking the officer by surprise, proposed to him with a pistol at his head the alternative of ' silence or death;' no reply was made, the boats pushed on unobserved, and Lord Cochrane, mounting the Esmeralda's side, was the first to give the alarm. The sentinel on the gangway levelled his piece and fired, but was instantly cut down by the coxswain, and his lordship, though wounded in the thigh, at the same moment stepped on the deck.

'The frigate being boarded with no less gallantry on the opposite side by Captain Guise, who met Lord Cochrane midway on the quarter-deck, also by Captain Crosbie, the after part of the ship was carried sword in hand. The Spaniards rallied on the forecastle, where they made a desperate resistance, till overpowered by a fresh body of seamen and marines, headed by Lord Cochrane. A gallant stand was made for some time on the main deck; but before one o'clock the ship was captured, her cables cut, and she was steered triumphantly out of the harbour, under the fire of the whole north face of the castle. The Hyperion, an English, and the Macedonian, an American frigate, which were at anchor close to the scene of action, got under weigh when the attack commenced; and, in order to prevent their being mistaken by the batteries for the Emeralda, showed distinguishing signals; but Lord Cochrane, who had foreseen and provided even for this minute circumstance, hoisted the same lights as the American and English frigates, and thus rendered it impossible for the batteries to discriminate between the three ships; the Emeralda, in consequence, was very little injured by the shot from the batteries. The Spaniards had upwards of one hundred and twenty men killed and wounded; the Chilians had only eleven killed and thirty wounded.'

This extraordinary achievement put an end to the naval warfare in this part of the world, for though the Spaniards had two frigates and several other ships in the Pacific, they never ventured to appear on a coast where they were likely to meet the dreaded Cochrane. His lordship may be said to have put an end to the war by the cap-

ture of Valdivia, the last post which the Spaniards retained in Chili, February 20, 1820. From the service of Chili, Lord Cochrane passed into that of Brazil, where the Emperor Pedro recognised his merits by creating him Marquis of Maranham. On the conclusion of peace between Brazil and Portugal, he tendered his services to aid in the liberation of Greece, which were accepted. Here his career was brief and not very glorious, for he could not obtain the co-operation and support necessary to success. He returned home to England about the close of 1828, and retiring into strict privacy, devoted himself to the pursuits of practical science and mechanical invention.

Soon after the accession of William IV., the good-hearted sailor-king, who valued the inestimable qualities of Lord Cochrane, and keenly felt the injustice with which he had been treated, restored him to his place in the navy; after which his lordship, in the course of promotion, became Rear-Admiral. By the death of his father he became Earl of Dundonald, but after having tasted the charms of privacy, he appears to have been unwilling again to take an active part in public life. His proud spirit never recovered the unworthy mortification to which he had been unjustly subjected, and he sought restoration to the order of the Bath, not for the sake of the title, but as the most solemn revocation of the ignominy that had been unfairly attached to his name. The case of the brave but ill-used veteran was brought under the personal notice of the Sovereign. Queen Victoria thoroughly investigated all the proceedings that had occurred before she was born, and being convinced that injustice had been done, she commanded reparation to be made as graciously as the injury had been inflicted wantonly and harshly."

The Earl married Katherine Francis Corbet, daughter of Thomas Barnes, county of Essex, Esq., and has issue,

1. Thomas Barnes, Lord Cochrane, in the army, born 14th April, 1814, married, December 1, 1847, Louisa, daughter of W. A. Mackinnon, Esq. M.P., and has issue.
2. Horatio Bernard William, in the army, born 8th March, 1818, married, 29th October, 1844, Frances Jacobina, only daughter of Alexander Nicholson, Esq., and widow of George James Carnegie, Esq., nephew of William, seventh Earl of Northesk.
3. Elizabeth Josephine, born 8th March, 1820, died in Peru, in 1821.
4. Katherine Elizabeth, born 8th December, 1821, married, 27th February, 1840, John Wallis Fleming, Esq., eldest son of John Fleming, Esq. of Stoneham Park, Hants.
5. Arthur Auckland Leopold Pedro, born 24th September, 1825.
6. A son, still-born, 15th April, 1829.
7. Ernest Grey Lambton, born 4th June, 1835.

*Residence*—The Earls of Dundonald resided chiefly at their mansion in Paisley till about the middle of the last century, when Culross Abbey in Fifeshire became their ordinary place of abode. Towards the close of the century, the increasing embarrassments of the family, occasioned by the unfortunate scientific speculations of the Earl, compelled them to part with that fine property, as well as most of the others. The present Earl resides in London.

*Arms*—Argent, a chevron, gules, between three boars' heads, erased, azure.

*Crest*—A horse, passant, argent.

*Supporters*—Two greyhounds, proper, collared, and leished, or.

*Motto*—Virtute et labore.

## M'KERRELL OF HILLHOUSE.

The M'Kerrells have flourished from a remote period in the shire of Ayr. The name Kiriell appears on the roll of Battle Abbey; hence the family is presumed to be of Norman descent.

Kiriell, Kirel, Kirrel, or Kerrell, (as at various times spelt), is a surname now very rarely to be met with. It is said to exist in Sweden, another proof of Normanic origin in Scotland,* where the family of Hillhouse alone bears it.

The first of the name, and the most remote now on Scottish record, Sir John M'Kirel,† distinguished himself at the celebrated battle of Otterburn, 19th August, 1388, by wounding and capturing Reuel de Percie, who held the second command in the English host, and whose brother, the renowned Hotspur, was made prisoner by Sir John Montgomerie,‡ (from whom spring the Earls of Eglinton), in the same sanguinary conflict. That this Sir John M'Kirel was an ancestor of the Hillhouse family, the circumstance of the latter bearing the arms§ which he acquired by his

* There is a family of the name of M'Kerlie in Dumfries-shire, and several of that name throughout the kingdom. In the north of Ireland, the name of M'Garrel is frequently to be met with; but it is not known whether either of these two names are of the same origin with the family of Hillhouse.

† Mac, or "Son of," was a prefixture more peculiar to Scotland.

‡ The death of Sir John Montgomerie's son, Hugh, in this bloody raid, has been commemorated in the old and popular ballad of Chevy Chace:

Against Sir Hugh Montgomerie
So straight his shaft he set,
The grey goose wing that was thereon,
In his heart's blood was wet.

§ If heraldry may be trusted, and for long after its institution its purity as a science, and its utility still in restoring the severed links of affinity when broken asunder, through loss of documentary evidence, are manifest, the arms of this family must have been those of Sir John M'Kerel, for they are founded on the Percie coat, which was azure, five fusils in fess, or. The arms of M'Kerrel being, azure, three fusils, gules, on a fess, or, within a bordure engrailed

prowess in that celebrated battle, appears conclusive, although a chasm of nearly two centuries occurs in the pedigree.

The following is Froissart's account of the battle of Otterbourn, and the mention of M'Kirel:

"De touts les besognes, batailles et rencontres qui sont cy dessous en ceste histoire (dont ie traitte et ay traittè) grandes, moyennes petites, ceste cy, dont ie parle pour le present, en fut l'une des plus dures, et des mieux combattues sans feintise, car il n'y auoit homme, chevalier n'escuyer qui ne s'acquittast et fit son devoir, et tout main a main. Cette battaille fut quasi pareille a la bataille de Becherel: car aussi elle fut moult bien combattue e longuement. Les enfants au Compte de Northomberllande, Messire Henry et Messire Raoul de Persy (qui là estoient soueraines capitaines) s'acquitterent loyaument par bien combattre: et quasi pareil party, que celui, par qui le Comte de Douglas fut arrestè, auint et cheut a Messire Raoul de Persy; car il se bouta si auant entre ses ennemis, qu'il fut enclos, et durement naurè, mis a la grosse haleine, pris et fiancè d'un *Chevalier*, lequel estoit de la charge et du meme hostel de Moray, et l'appeloit on *Jehan Makirel*. En le prenant et fiançant, le Cheualier Escoçois demanda a Messire Raoul de Persy, qui l'estoit, (car il estoit si muiet que point ne le cognoissoit) et Messire Raoul (qui estoit si outrè que plus ne pouuait, et luy couloit le sang tout aual, qui l'affoiblissoit) luy dit; je suis Messire Raoul de Persy. Adonc dit l'Escoçois, Messire Raoul receoux ou non rècoux, ie vous fiance mon prisonnier. Je suis *Makirel*. Bien dit Messire Raoul, je le veicil, mais entendez a mois, car ie suis trop durement naurè, et mes chausses et mes greues sont là toutes emplies de sang. A ces mots estoit le cheualiere Escoçois ententif, quand delez luy il ouyt crier Moray et au compte: et recit le compte et sa banniere droit deiez a luy. Si luy dit Messire Jehan Makirel, Monseigneur, tenez. Je vous baille Messire Raoul de Persy pour prisonnier; mais faites entendre a luy, car il est durement naurè. Le Comte de Moray de ceste parole fut rèiouy moult grandement: et dit, Makirel, tu as bien gagnè les esperons. Adonc fit il venir ses gens, et leua charger Messire Raoul de Persy: lesquels luy banderent et etancherent ces playes. Si se tenoit la bataille fort et dure et ne sauoit on

for distinction, leaving no question but that in consequence of the capture of Percie, this formed one of those cases described by heralds of arms by conquest: for as M'Kerrel was then a knight, (chevalier in Froissart), and no honour or reward being recorded of him, it follows that this augmentation to, or grant of arms, was his reward; and their inheritage, coupled with Froissart's record, is the best of all proofs of the descent of the present family of Hillhouse from Sir John, and also of the correctness of one part of the tradition above.—BURKE'S COMMONERS.

encores lesquels en auroient le meilleur ; car ie vous dy qu'il y eut là plusieurs prises et recousses faites, qui toutes ne vindrent pas a cognaissance."

The tradition from sire to son bears that they came out of Ireland,[*] and it carries back the possession of the estate of Hillhouse full five hundred years, to the glorious era of Robert the Bruce—a period when vast changes occurred in the proprietary of the soil, and when the chiefs of numerous houses, still in a high state of prosperity, were endowed by that illustrious prince. This tradition, however, must be taken with caution. The forty-shilling land of Hillhouse does not appear to have existed as an independent property in the days of Bruce. It, of course, formed part of the large tract of country belonging to the High Steward, and was amongst the lands granted by the Crown to the Cathcart family, of which a renewed charter was obtained in 1505.[†] If the M'Kerrells were in possession of Hillhouse at this period, it must have been as tenants or vassals of the Cathcarts.

The first of the name, so far as we have discovered, in connection with the property, was—

I. WILLIAM M'KERREL of Hillhouse, who married, about 1570, Margaret,[‡] daughter of John Fullerton of Dreghorn, by Helen, daughter of Sir John Chalmers of Gadgirth. This lady died in 1612. From her latter-will, it would appear that M'Kerrell of Hillhouse was Sheriff-clerk of Ayr. The substance of this document is as follows :—

"Testament, &c., and Inuentar of the guids, &c. qlk. perteinit to vmqle. Margaret Fullertoune, spous to Wm. M'Kerrell of Hillhouse, Sheriff-clerk of Air,[§] within the parochin of Air, the tyme of his deceis, Quha deceist vpone the saxt day of September, the zeir of God 1612 zeiris, flatfullie maid and gevin vp be the said Wm. in name and behalf of Jeane and Margaret M'Kerrells, lautfull bairnes to the defunct, executouris datives, dewlie decernit, to her guids and geir, be decreit of the Commissour of Glasgow, the nynt day of August, 1617.

Inuentar.

Item, the said vmqle. Margaret and her said

spous, had the tyme foirsaid perteining to thame . . . the guids and geir vnderwrittin . . . viz. ane dussane of sylwir spoynes, pryce thereof xlviii lib. ; ane sylwir peice of aucht vnce wecht, or thereby, pryce thereof xxvi lib. xiiis. iiiid. ; ane sylwir goblat of sevin vnce wecht, or thereby, pryce thereof xxiii lib. vis. viiid. . . . . Item, in gold and sylwir lyand attoure that quhilk furneissit the hous to the nixt terme, xxx lib. Item, the Insicht of the said Wm. his hous, with the abuilzement of hir bodie, with ane gold cheinzie and taiblet, and thrie litle wowp ringis, estimat to ii° iiii$^{xx}$ x lib."

William M'Kerrell of Hillhouse survived till 1629. His name occurs in various documents previous to that year. He died at Hillhouse in the month of October. His testament was "flaytfullie maid and gevin vp be Mr Williame M'Kerrell, eldest lautfull sone to the defunct, and executour dative," &c. From these documents it would appear that he had more sons than his heir, and two daughters, *Jean* and *Margaret*. He was succeeded by his son,

II. Magister William M'Kerrel of Hillhouse, who appears in the retour, dated 1630, as proprietor of several lands in the parish of Dundonald, and of Knock Gall, in the parish of Ochiltree. Robertson puts this Mr William as grandson of the previous proprietor of Hillhouse, and Burke follows him ; but they are both certainly in error.[*] From the title "Magister," he appears to have been brought up to one of the learned professions. "Mr Wm. M'Kerrell of Hillhous" occurs as a debtor in the testament of "Adame Coninghame, elder, merchand, burges of Irwein,'" who died November, 1635. In 1636 he is retoured heir to his father in the fifty shilling land of Goldring (now Rosemount), and "a little piece of land called the Kemnock land." He was succeeded by his son,

III. William M'Kerrell of Hillhouse, whose retour is dated in 1643, and who, in 1659, was succeeded by his brother,

IV. John M'Kerrell of Hillhouse, who married about the year 1670, Elizabeth Wallace, daughter of the Bishop of the Isles. Their initials are engraved on the lintel of the garden-door at Hillhouse, having been removed from the old house, when taken down about fifty years ago. Amongst the Boyd papers, there is a bond, dated 1666, to John M'Kerrell of Hillhouse, in name and in behalf of his lawful children, *Robert* and *Anna* M'Kerrell, for certain moneys advanced in their name by Lord Kilmarnock. John M'Kerrell had thus, in all likelihood, been twice married,

---

* The advent of the family from Ireland does not millitate against their supposed Norman origin, if the swarm of Anglo-Norman adventurers who joined the banner of Earl Strongbow, and invaded that country in 1170, be taken into consideration.

† John, second Lord Cathcart, 1505, had a charter of Colynane, Hilhouse, and Holmyss, in Ayrshire, in the hands of the King, by reason of forfeiture, for the alienation of the greater part of the same by Alan, Lord Cathcart, his grandfather, without consent of the King, &c.—WOOD's PEERAGE, i. 340.

‡ In Robertson's 'Ayrshire Families,' and Burke's 'Commoners,' the name is erroneously stated to have been Elizabeth.

§ He is mentioned in various legal documents as Sheriff-clerk of Ayr, from 1603 till the date of this testament.

---

* In the retour, he is styled heir of William M'Kerrell of Hillhouse.

Robert and Anna being children of the first union. Among the Cochrane papers there is a discharge, dated 1675, by Elizabeth Wallace, relict of umqle. John M'Kerrell of Hillhous, tutrix testamentar to *Jeane* and *Elizabeth* M'Kerrell" her daughters, to the Earl of Dundonald for a year's interest on three thousand merks lent upon a bond belonging to her children. William Fullartoun of that Ilk, and Robert M'Kerrell, merchant in Irvine, were the guardians appointed in the testament. John M'Kerrell had thus died before 1675. He was succeeded by his son,

V. John M'Kerrell of Hillhouse, who wedded Elizabeth, daughter of William Fairlie of Fairlie, by his wife, Jane, only daughter of the *last* Sir William Mure of Rowallan,* and had issue,

1. William.
2. John.
1. Jean.
2. Elizabeth.

He was succeeded by his eldest son,

VI. William M'Kerrell of Hillhouse. This laird married Mary Vaux, of French extraction, whose family sought refuge in this country from the persecution which followed the revocation of the edict of Nantes. Her father was in holy orders, and one of the canons of St Paul's cathedral. By this lady he had William and John, with a daughter, Elizabeth. In 1713, William M'Kerrell of Hillhouse petitioned the Sheriff of Ayr, to order the Earl of Kilmarnock to deliver up certain bonds for five thousand merks lent upon heritable bond by his grandfather to M'Kerrell's grandfather, most of which had been paid up during the Earl's minority.† William M'Kerrell died before 1728, in which year he is mentioned in the Ayr Presbytery records as "the deceased William M'Kerrell of Hillhouse." He was succeeded by his elder son,

VII. William M'Kerrel of Hillhouse, at whose decease, unmarried, the estates devolved on his brother,

VIII. John M'Kerrel of Hillhouse, who married Margaret, sister of the late William Fulton, Esq. of Park, in the county of Renfrew, and had issue,

1. William, his heir.
2. John, married, first, Miss Hervey, of Edinburgh, and had
    1. John, married Anna, daughter of Herbert Buchanan, Esq. of Arden. John died in 1831, and left one daughter.
    2. Alexander, died in 1827.
    3. William, married his cousin, daughter of John Edward Wright, Esq. of Bolton on Swale.

* The Mures of Rowallan were of great antiquity and consideration in the shire of Ayr, and were distinguished by their alliance with the royal family of Scotland, through the marriage of King Robert II. (the first of the Stuart dynasty), with Elizabeth, daughter of Sir Adam Mure of Rowallan, when residing at his castle of Dundonald, in Kyle-Stewart.
† Boyd Papers.

He wedded, secondly, Helen Stuart, niece of Robert Morris, Esq. of Craig, and had a fourth son, Archibald.
3. Robert, who married Miss Shultz of Frankfort, and had one son and two daughters, viz.
    1. Robert, married Emily, daughter of Major-Gen. Stavely, C.B., and has issue.
    1. Margaret.
    2. Augusta Jane, married to Count Segure, the French charge d'affaires at Palermo.
4. Fulton, married, first, to his cousin-german, Elizabeth, daughter of Fulton of Hartfield, but had no issue. He wedded, secondly, Mary, daughter of James M'Call, Esq. of Braehead, and had three daughters, Sarah, Margaret, and Mary.
1. Margaret, married to the late Moses Crawfurd, Esq of Newfield, and had issue.
2. Mary, died in 1849.
3. Elizabeth, married to Colonel John Reid, of the Hon. East India service, and died, leaving a daughter, Elizabeth M'Kerrell Reid, who wedded James Campbell, Esq. of Treesbanks.
4. Jane, married to her cousin, Robert Fulton of Hartfield, late Lieut.-Colonel of the 79th Foot, with which regiment he served in Egypt and the Peninsula; she has issue,
    1. Robert Fulton, Captain in the 79th regiment, died in 1835.
    2. John Fulton, Lieutenant in the East India Company's service.
    3. William Fulton, a captain in 15th foot.
    1. Jane Fulton, married to her cousin, John Buchanan, Esq.
5. Marion, married to the late James Kibble, Esq. of Whittford and Greenlaw House, in the county of Renfrew, and had one son, Robert Kibble, who died in 1843.
6. Agnes, married to John-Edward Wright, Esq. of Bolton-on-Swale.

Mr M'Kerrell died in 1811, aged seventy-nine, and was succeeded by his eldest son,

IX. William M'Kerrell of Hillhouse, who married, first, Miss Reid, sister of the late Robert Reid, Esq. of Adamton, but had no issue. He wedded, secondly, Miss Govane, daughter of Robert Govane of Anderstone, by whom he had five sons and four daughters, viz.

1. John, his heir.
2. Robert, died in India.
3. William, died young.
4. Henry, of whom hereafter.
5. James, died in 1833.
1. Janet, died 1841.
2. Margaret, married Major John Crawford, late of the 44th regiment.
3. Anne, married to James Brown, Esq., and had issue: died in 1833.
4. Mary, died 1837.

This gentleman, who had the honour of raising, at Paisley, the first volunteer corps embodied in Scotland during the French revolutionary war, died in 1820, and was succeeded by his eldest son,

X. John M'Kerrell, who went in early life to India, in the Civil Service of the East India Company. He filled several important offices in India, and for nine years previous to his return, that of Master of the Mint at Madras. He died unmarried, in 1835, and was succeeded by his brother,

XI. Henry M'Kerrell of Hillhouse, formerly a merchant in Liverpool. He married Margaret Cochrane, daughter of John Paterson, Esq. Edinburgh.

*Arms*—Azure, three fusils, gules, on a fess, or, within a bordure engrailed.

*Crest*—An ancient warrior in armour, with a shield and spear, a star over the point of the latter.

*Motto*—Dulcis pro patriâ labor.

*Seat*—Hillhouse, four miles south of Irvine.

## THE WALLACES OF SHEWALTON.

Shewalton House, a modern erection, is situated on the left banks of the water of Irvine, about two miles eastward of the town of Irvine. The old manor place, which latterly became ruinous and uninhabitable, was one of those square towers of former times, adapted more for security than convenience. The situation is pleasant, and has been much improved by plantation.

The Fullartons of Fullarton were the overlords of this property. At what time it became possessed by a branch of the Wallaces is uncertain. The first of them known is,

I. LAMBERT WALLACE of Sewalton, who, in a letter of reversion, 20th May, 1473, binds himself to resign a rent of £3 out of the lands of Sewalton to his Lord, John de Fullarton of that Ilk, on getting payment of £60. Between him and the next known possessor, a period of fifty years elapses. *

II. Edward Wallace of Sewalton, who appears to have had some transaction with John Fullarton of that Ilk, in reference to the lands of Shewalton, on the 17th December, 1543. There was an Edward Wallace concerned in the purchase of the lands of Marress from the same party, on the 8th February, 1566; but whether he was the same Edward, it is impossible to determine. There is a John Wallace, "fear of Sewalton," mentioned in a legal document in 1583, and—

III. Edward Wallace of Shewalton is thus mentioned in 1586: June 20.—"This day Eduart Wallace of Sewaltoun comperit personall within the said paroche kirk" (of Ayr), &c. In another similar document, of date September 6, 1595, the following occurs: "The rycht honorabell William Wallace, tutour of Sewaltoun,"† and "Helene Dunbar, his spous," obtain renunciation and discharge of certain debts over a tenement in Air. Edward Wallace had thus died, leaving his heir in nonage. He was succeeded, at all events, by—

IV. Edward Wallace, who, in 1605, is styled "Edwart Wallace of Sewaltoun," in a testamentary deed of that date. The same name occurs in several other similar documents at a later period. He appears to have married Marjorie Dunbar, who died in July, 1614. In her latter-will she is styled "Marjorie Dunbar, spous to Edward Wallace of Sewaltoun." The inventory was made and given up "be said Edward, in namo and behalf of Robt., Edward, John, Agnes, Jeane, and Helein Wallaces, bairnes lawtfull to the deid." Amongst the debts owing by the deceased, were £226 to "Marcoun Wallace, sister to the said Edward." Edward Wallace seems to have died very soon after the demise of his spouse.

V. David Wallace of Sewaltoune is mentioned in the testament of William Lyn in Sewaltoun, in 1615. "Jonet Peiblis, Ladie Sewaltoun," occurs in the latter-will of James Porter in Sewaltoun, the same year. She was perhaps a daughter of John Peblis, Provost of Irvine. David Wallace was probably succeeded by a younger brother, of nonage at the time. At least there is a "Margrat Wallace, dochter to Wm. Wallace, *tutor* of Sewaltonne," * mentioned in a testamentary document, in 1619. The next found in possession is,

VI. "Edward Wallace of Sewaltoune, heir to Edward Wallace of Sewaltoun, *Proavi*," (his grandfather), served heir 25th March, 1624: Also, at the same time, to "Edward Wallace of Sewaltoun, *Patris*," (his father). Robertson states that this Edward Wallace "was, on his own resignation, succeeded by his son," *William*. This would appear to be correct from the inventory of writs in the possession of the present family of Shewalton, in which there is a charter, dated in 1627, "Edward Wallace of Sewaltoun, &c., who resigns these lands to his son, William." Notwithstanding, we find, in 1628, "Edward Wallace of Sewaltoun," and "Wm. Wallace, zounger *in* Sewalton," mentioned in a testamentary document of that date; and again, in 1630, 1633, and 1634. This may be explained, however, by the fact, that in cases of resignation, the father was generally styled by the property, though virtually in the possession of the son. He appears to have died in 1649, at least there is the testament recorded of "Edward Wallace, elder of Sewaltoun," who died in that year, "maid and gevin up be Mr Danid Conynghame, lait minister of Perstone, burges of Irvine, lautfull creditor to the defunct." We shall therefore assume that—

VII. William Wallace was in possession. He was, according to Robertson, married to Margaret Scott, daughter of Lawrence Scott, whom he conjectures to have been of the ancient family of

---

* Fullarton Writs.
† The tutor, as appears from a testamentary document, had a son called Edward.

* A Margaret Wallace, of the house of Shewalton, was the second wife of George Montgomery, second of Broomlands.

Scott of Scotts-Loch, by Irvine. He " soon after-wards," he adds, " resigns these lands to his son,"

VIII. Edward Wallace of Sewaltoun. The deed of resignation is dated 1633, and registered in 1654. In 1634, he is mentioned as tenant of Knadger-hill, Irvine, in a testamentary document. He married Janet Porter, only child of William Porter, merchant in Edinburgh. The marriage contract is dated 16th May, 1646. He had at least four sons: 1. *William*; 2. *John*,* who, in 1672, is served heir of provision to his father, Edward Wallace of Sewaltoun, in the £2 land of Whitehill; 3. *Lawrence*; 4. *Robert*, both design-ed, in the inventory of writs, merchants in Irvine, and brothers of William Wallace of Sewaltoun; also a daughter. He was probably twice married. In an obligation on the part of John Hamilton of Inchgothric, in 1670, to shut up a back gate leading to the Old Church of Ayr, Edward Wallace of Shewalton is mentioned as the first husband of Elizabeth More, then married to Major John Ful-larton. † Edward Wallace of Shewalton was ap-pointed, by Parliament, in 1649, one of the Com-mittee of Defence in the shire of Ayr. He was succeeded by his eldest son,

IX. William Wallace of Sewaltoun. He was served heir to his father, Edward, in these lands in 1670; and in the same year, married Mary, or Maria Boyle, only daughter of David Boyle of Halkshill and Dame Grizel Boyle of Kelburn, as appears from the marriage contract, dated 15th April, 1670. He and his father appear to have been involved in considerable pecuniary difficul-ties, as may be inferred from the several heavy sums that were from time to time borrowed from the lairds of Kelburn, Hunterstoun, and Smith-stoun, and others, all recorded in the inventory already mentioned. The last of these that ap-pear is dated 10th September, 1694, and he could not have lived long after that time, for his son,

X. Edward Wallace, who succeeded, is de-signed laird of Shewalton in a bond, dated the 8th of January, 1698, to David Boyle, laird of Kelburne, for the sum of £1136, 3s. 6d. Scots, in all probability, from the fractional parts of the sum, the bygone interest on his father's bonds. The laird of Shewalton is mentioned in the records of Parliament, as being on the Committee of De-fence in 1696. The different estates of Shewal-ton, Waxford, and Marress, appear to have all remained in the family till they were sold by this Edward, the last of the Wallaces, ‡ to William

Boyle, Esq., brother of David, first Earl of Glas-gow, and one of the Commissioners of Customs in Scotland. The contract of sale is dated 15th February, 1715,* and all these properties remain in a branch of the Glasgow family to the present day. The Waxford property had been acquired by Edward Wallace of Shewalton in 1565.

### BOYLE OF SHEWALTON.

I. THE HON. PATRICK BOYLE, third son of John, second Earl of Glasgow, by Helen, his wife, daughter of William Morrison, Esq. of Preston Grange, county of Haddington, married, first, Agnes, daughter of William Mure of Caldwell, Esq., by whom (who died in 1758) he had no issue; and, secondly, Elizabeth, daughter of Alex-ander Dunlop, Professor of Greek in the Univer-sity of Glasgow, by whom he had (with other children who died unmarried)

1. John, his heir.
2. David, now of Shewalton.
1. Helen, married, in 1795, to Thomas Mure, Esq. of Warriston, and died in 1805.
2. Elizabeth, married, in 1800, to Rear-Admiral John Rouctt Smollett of Bonhill and Auchindonan, county of Dumbarton, who died 6th May, 1842.

Mr Boyle died in 1798, and was succeeded by his son,

II. John Boyle of Shewalton, Colonel of the Ayrshire Local Militia, who died unmarried, 30th January, 1837, and was succeeded by his brother,

III. The Right Hon. David Boyle of Shewal-ton, Lord Justice-General, and President of the Court of Session, born 26th July, 1772; married, first, 24th December, 1804, Elizabeth, eldest daughter of the late Alexander Montgomerie, Esq. of Anniek Lodge, brother of Hugh, twelfth Earl of Eglinton, and had by her,

1. Patrick, a member of the Faculty of Advocates, Prin-cipal Clerk of the High Court of Justiciary, M.A., a Justice of the Peace, and Commissioner of Supply for Ayrshire, born 29th March, 1806, married, 17th Au-gust, 1830, Mary Frances, second daughter of Sir Ro-bert Dalrymple Horn Elphinstone, Bart. of Horn and Logic Elphinstone, and has issue.
  1. David, born in 1833.
  2. Robert Elphinstone, born in 1837.
  3. Alexander James, born in 1842.
  1. Elizabeth Magdalene Græme.
  2. Louisa Laura.
  3. Mary Helen.
2. Alexander, Commander R.N., born 9th March, 1810.
3. John, born 9th September, 1819.

---

* In 1675, John Wallace, son of Edward Wallace of Shewalton, resigns the tenements within the yards com-monly called Craigie House, and lands of Whitehill, in favour of Sir Thomas Wallace of Craigie.

† Town Records of Ayr.

‡ Edward Wallace of Shewalton, notwithstanding, con-

tinued to fill his place among the Commissioners of Supply for the county of Ayr. He was one of the most regular attenders, and his name occurs in the sederunts so late as 1720.

* William Wallace, "a brother of Shewalton's," appears in the Ayr Presbytery records, 19th December, 1722. His wife, Margaret Kennedy, had twins before marriage. He was then in Kirkcudbright.

4. William, Lieutenant 15th Foot, born 25th January, 1821.
5. Archibald Thomas, born 14th April, 1822.
1. Elizabeth, married, in 1828, to James Hope, Esq. third son of the Right Hon. Charles Hope.
2. Helen, married, in 1829, to the late Sir Charles Dalrymple Fergusson of Kilkerran, Bart.
3. Hamilla Augusta.
4. Eleanora Charlotte.

Mr Boyle married, secondly, 17th July, 1827, Camilla Catherine, eldest daughter of the late Hon. David Smythe of Methven Castle, Perthshire, a judge of the Court of Session, and has by her,

1. George David, born 17th May, 1828.
2. Robert, born 2d December, 1830.
3. Henry Dundas, born 1st February, 1833.
1. Amelia Laura.

*Arms*—Quarterly: 1st and 4th, or, an eagle, displayed, with two heads, gules; 2d and 3d, per bend, embattled, argent and gules; over all, an escutcheon, or, charged with three stags' horns, erect, gules, two and one.
*Crest*—An eagle, displayed, with two heads, per pale, embattled, argent and gules.
*Motto*—Dominus providebit.
*Seat*—Shewalton.

### CUNINGHAMES OF COLLELLAN.

In the appendix to *Nisbet*, vol. ii., this family is stated "to be come off that of Caprington," and Robertson supposes the statement to be likely, "from the circumstance of the first of them, for three generations in succession, being of the name of *Adam*." A manuscript genealogy, written about 1704, says, however, that Alexander, Earl of Glencairn, the Great Reformer, had a natural son by a daughter of Lord Sempill, and that this natural son was the ancestor of the House of Collellan. Be this as it may, the family seems to have been related to the Cuninghames of Caddell, who were a branch of the Cuninghames of Glengarnock. The first of them on record was,

I. ADAME CUNINGHAME of Clolynane, who lived during the latter half of the sixteenth century. He married a daughter of John Mure of Rowallan. His successor is mentioned as—

II. Adame Cuninghame, son of the late Adame Cuninghame of Clolynane and Jeane Mure, in 1589–90. He was retoured heir to his father, 21st October, 1600. Adame Cwynghame of Clolynnan occurs in the testament of "Agnes Cwynghame, spous to Wm. Cwynghame of Clonbeith," who died in 1612. The property had probably been acquired by his father from the Cathcart family, in whose possession it was in 1548. He was succeeded by his son,

III. Adam Cuninghame of Collellan, whose retour, as heir to his father, is dated in 1623. The next in succession appears to have been,

IV. Alexander Cuninghame of Collellan, who has a charter in favour of himself and Margaret Cuninghame, his spouse, dated 15th December, 1631. "Alexander Cvynghame of Cullellane" is mentioned as one of the "kinsmen and freindis" in the latter-will of "Adame Cvninghame, elder, merchand, burgess of Irwein," in 1635. "Margaret Conynghame, Lady Clolynane, elder, and Conynghame, hir buirne," appear as creditors in the testament of James Thomesone, merchant, Irvine," in 1646, from which it may be inferred that her husband, Alexander Cuninghame, had been previously deceased. This is confirmed by the following extract from the Commissary Records of Glasgow:—

"Omissa Conynghame. We (the Commissaries), Be the tenour heirof, of new againe ratifie, approve, and confirme the saidis Margaret Conynghame, relict of umqle. Alex. Conynghame of Cullellane, Johne Conynghame of Caddell, Johne Conynghame of Baidlen, principall executoris, &c., nominat, &c., to the said umqle. Alex. Conynghame, in and to the sowme of ffour hundreth merks, &c., adebtit and awand be umqle. Rot. Conynghame of Cassiltone, baillie of Kilmairis," &c., 1653.

Robertson supposes that this laird of Collellan had been twice married, because he finds amongst the Fullarton writs a charter from the Earl of Dundonald, in favour of Alexander Cuninghame of Collellan and his spouse, Catherine Brown, dated 18th December, 1635. But this must have been his successor, the Alexander Cuninghame of Collellan, *younger*, whom he also finds mentioned.

V. Alexander Conynghame of Collellane is mentioned in a testamentary document in 1652. He married Katherine Broune, daughter of Broune of Mott. He died in August, 1660. In the "Inventar," in his testament, occurs the following: "Item, nyne beeskeps (attour the airschip on), the most part of them being of the third cast, pryce of them all xxlib."

"Latter-will and Legacie.—I, Alex. Coninghame of Collellane, being for the present seik and disseasit in body, &c., have thought good to mak and sett doun this my testament and latter-will as follows: Haveing heirtofor maid bondis and provisions in favouris of my childrein, who ar as zit vnforisfamiliat, To wit, and the first, I mak and constitute Katherine Broune, my lawfull spous, to be my only executrix of all my haill guids and geir, &c.; and I do heirby mak and constitute Johne Coninghame of Caddell, John Coninghame of Baidland, Mr Johne Coninghame, minister at

Cumnock, Robert Broune of Mott, Hew Coninghame, last baillie of Irving, Mr Wilham Coninghame, minister of Kilbryd, to be tutors testamenters to *Robert, Alexander, William, Eupham, Beatrix,* and *Jonet* Coninghams, my lawfull childrein And I doe nominat John Coninghame of Caddell, John Coninghame of Bedland, elder and zounger, Rot Broune of Mott, Wm Monfod of that Ilk, Mr Jon. Coninghame, minister at Cumnock, Hew Coninghame, last baillie of Irving, and Mr Wm Coninghame, minister at Kilbryd, to be oversiers to my children, to be helpfull to them and remanent of my childrein who ar zit unfornsfumhate," &c

VI Robert Cuninghame of Collellan was retoured heir to Alexander Cuninghame of Collellan, his father, in 1669 In 1674, he sold the lands of Collellan, under reversion, to Alexander Cuninghame, son to the deceased William Cuninghame of Clonbeith He appears to have died before 1684, in which year there is a decreet against the heirs of Alexander Cuninghame of Collellan, *decesit*, Alexander, younger of Collellan, and Robert Cuninghame, the son of the younger Alexander, to enter heirs in special to them, at the instence of Adam Fullarton of Bartonholme Robert thus died without leaving any male issue In 1691, Adam Fullarton had a disposition and assignation of the said lands, granted by the heirs portioners of the saids Alexanders Cuninghame, father and son, and Robert, the grandson, all of Collellan, to the said Adam Fullarton

The line of descent of the Cuninghames of Collellan now underwent a complete change

VII John Cuninghame of Collellan, heir to Alexander Cuninghame, his father, and probably grandson of William of Clonbeith,* to which Alexander the lands of Collellan were sold under reversion by Robert Cuninghame of Collellan, in 1674, had a precept of *clare constat*, dated 1st December, 1699 for infefting him in half of the lands of Collellan, by Adam Fullarton He was succeeded by—

VIII Alexander Cuninghame of Collellan, who, along with John Mure, represented the burgh of Ayr in 1698 and 1700. He was most likely a brother of his predecessor. In 1701, Alexander Cuninghame of Collellan was appointed a Commissioner of Supply for the county of Ayr He married, 17th April, 1686, at Paisley, Margaret Walkinshaw, as appears from a private record on the blank leaf of the family Bible They had a numerous family, of whom only two

* The Clonbeith Cuninghames were descended from the Aiket family

reached mature years, James, his successor, and Elizabeth, married, first to Robert Montgomerie of Broomlands, and, secondly, to Provost Glasgow of Irvine, by neither of whom had she issue

According to a note in the family Bible, this Alexander Cuninghame "died at Shens, near Edinburgh, upon Fryday the threttin day of July, 1705, and was buried on the Saturday after, at fyve of the clock at night, at Enterckin's tomb, in the Grey-Friers churchyard, Edinburgh"

IX James Cuninghame of Collellan succeeded his father He was quite an infant at the time, having been born on the 7th April, 1704 His name frequently occurs in the sederunts of the Commissioners of Supply for the county from 1732 till 1748 He married, at Hamilton, on the 5th May, 1727, Margaret, daughter of Sir Mark Carse of Cockpen, in Mid-Lothian By this lady (who died of a declme on the 8th of March, 1733, in the 28th year of her age) he had two sons, Alexander and William, and a daughter, Elizabeth, all of whom died in infancy. Also a daughter, Rachel, married, in 1754, to Alexander Hamilton of Grange, third son of Robert Hamilton of Grange, and had issue. He married, secondly, before the year 1737, Susana, daughter of Thomas Cuninghame, the last of Mountgreenan By this lady he had a son, Loudoun Cuninghame, who went to America, where he was killed accidentally by a shot from his companion's fowling-piece He had also two daughters, Margaret, who died unmarried in 1813, in the 76th year of her age, and Elizabeth, who died in infancy

Besides Collellan, the Cuninghames possessed the lands of Friars-Croft and Dyets-Temple, in the vicinity of Irvine In April, 1749, there was a disposition of them, *inter alia*, by James Cuninghame and his spouse, Susana, to the trustees for his creditors The estate having been broken up about this period, the property was acquired by George Fullarton of Bartonholme.

Collellan is situated about four miles south of Irvine, near to the high road to Ayr. The old mansion is now occupied as a farm-house.

## WALLACES OF GALRIGS, OR GARRIX, NOW CALLED NEWFIELD

The first of this family with whom we meet was

I. WILLIAM WALLACE of Gariggs October 16, 1578, John Hamilton of Barnweill grants " sasing " of all and haill the xx s. land in Tounheid of Barnweill, occupiet be William Wallace of Gariggs, &c, and of the four lib land of Barnweill-Hereis, &c., in warrandice of the said xx s. land to Wm. Wallace, sone and air apperand to Wm. Wallace in Gariggis, &c., conforme to the said precept, &c., maid thereupoun," &c. The Wallaces *in* Galriggis thus appear to have been different parties from the Wallaces *of* Galriggis, though probably nearly related. That they were of some consideration is apparent from the following rather curious extract* from the testament of "Jeane Houstoun, spous to Williame Craufurd, elder of Lefnoreis," who died in 1608. "Debtis awand to the deid . . Item, be Jeane Fullertoun, spous to Robert Wallace in Galrigis, ane taiblet of gould, price thriscoir sax pund xii s. iiii d.; mair, be the said Robert Wallace, ane Arabic duket, price fiftie pund. Item, ane havie nobill, price ten lib. Item, ane dowbill soucrane, pryce sax pund. Item, ane Spaneis peice, pryce sax pund. Item, mair be the said Jeane, twentie ells of small borclaithes, pryce of the elne saxtein schillingis . . mair be hir, saxtein elnes servitour lynning, pryce of the elne viii s."

II. Robert Wallace " of Galrix " is mentioned alongst with " Mr William Wallace, minister at Symontoun " and others, as one of the overseers appointed in the testament of Robert Wallace of Ronhill. He and his wife were infeft in the " thrie pund land of Holmis " by David Fullarton, son of John Fullarton of Dreghorn, on the 18th May, 1609. Robert Wallace of Garricks is also mentioned in the testament of " Jonet Campbell, relict of vmqle. Mr David Mylne, minister of Dundonald," who died in 1618. His wife, Jeane Fullertoun,† died in the month of May, 1619. Her testament contains the following : " Legacie.—At Galrigis the 20 day of May. the zeir of God 1619. The quhilk day the said Jeane Fullartoune maks, nominats, &c., the said Robert Wallace of Galrigis, hir spous, hir onlie executor, &c. Item, the said Jeane Fullarton levis to Mr Wm. Fullertoune, hir brother germane, the sowme of ane thousand merks money, at his returning fra the kingdome of France, quhere he now is," &c. In 1625 the name of Robert Wallace of Galrigis again occurs as cautioner in the testament of Mr Alexr. Sibbald, minister of Dundonald, He had a daughter married to John Blair of Hilhouse, a son of David Blair of Adamton, and a son called

*William.* This appears from the testament of John Blair of Hilhouse, who died in 1626 :— " Debts awand In, . . Be Robert Wallace of Galrigis, his father-in-law, the sowme of ane hundrith punds money of annuell of his tocher guid," &c. His spous, Nans Wallace, is appointed Tutrix to her son, and failing her and others mentioned in the testament, " Mr Williame Wallace, younger of Galrigis, tutor," &c. " Robert Wallace of Garrikis " occurs in the testament of William M'Kerrell of Hilhous in 1629, and in that of Robert Barclay of Pierstoune in 1631. In 1636 both he and his son, " Mr Williame Wallace, fear of Galrigis," appear in the list of debtors to " James Norwall, merchant in Kilmarnock." Robert Wallace died in the month of September, 1642. The inventory of his effects was " faithfullie maid and gevin vp be Hew Wallace of Vnderwood, lawfull creditor to the defunct," &c.; " Mr Williame Wallace, sone to vmqle. Robert Wallace of Galrigis, cautioner."

III. Mr Williame Wallace of Garrikis is mentioned as a debtor in the testament of Margaret Boyd, Kilmarnock, December, 1645. His name occurs in another testamentary document in 1648, and again in 1652.

IV. William Wallace of Galrigis, son, or probably grandson of the foregoing, sat as one of the Commissioners of Supply for Ayrshire at the sederunt, August 5, 1714; and again, for the last time, in 1720.

The property of Galrigs, situated about a mile from the village of Dundonald, was acquired soon afterwards by Captain LAWRENCE NUGENT, whose name appears in the sederunts of the Commissioners from 1725 to 1758. He appears to have changed the name to *Newfield*, by which designation he is mentioned in the Presbytery records in 1723, as well as in the burgh records of Ayr in 1725, and subsequently. He held some situation in connection with the Customs.

## CRAUFURD OF NEWFIELD.

The late Col. Craufurd of Newfield claimed to be chief of the name of Craufurd. He traced the descent of the family from Robert Craufurd of Nethermains, third son of Patrick Craufurd of Auchinames.*

I. MOSES CRAUFURD, third son of Captain Robert Craufurd of Nethermains, married Marion Francis, of the family of Francis of Stane, and

---

* May 26, 1582, John Schaw of Haly " Gaif heretabill stalt and sasing to Wm. Wallace, as sone and air to vmqle. Wm. Wallace in Garrigis, of the fyve lib. land of Heleis, of auld extent, liand within the baillerie of Kylestewart, &c.—MASON'S NOTES.

† This is no doubt the same party referred to in the testament of Lady Lifnoris. If so, her husband, formerly " in" Galrigs, had become, either by succession or otherwise, " of" Galrigs.

---

* In the testament of Patrick Crawfurde of Auchinames, dated " at Corsbie the xii day of Decr. 1648 zeiris," " Robert Crawfurd of Nayr. Maynes, also my lawfull sone," is mentioned as one of the witnesses.

had a son, Archibald, named after his cousin-german, the last of Auchinames, then resident at Corsby, who died in infancy, and a daughter, Christian. He wedded, secondly, Janet Allason, grand-daughter of Allason of Curreath, and had by her, who died in 1738,

1. Robert, his heir.
2. Archibald, whose son, Moses, emigrated to America, and had a son, Moses, a lieut. R. N., lately deceased.
3. David; 4. Jane; 5. Elizabeth.

Mr Craufurd died in 1723, and was succeeded by his eldest son,

II. Robert Craufurd, born in 1707, who married Marion Brison, co-heiress of the lands of Groateholme, in the parish of Kilwinning, and dying in 1772, was succeeded by his eldest surviving son,

III. Moses Craufurd, who went to India about the year 1765, and there attained the rank of Major in the Company's service. He was second in command at the capture of Becchigar, a strong hill-fort on the Ganges, and was left in command of that place with a garrison of two thousand men. Returning home in 1783, he purchased the estate of Newfield, and married in two years after, Margaret, eldest daughter of John M'Kerrell of Hillhouse, by whom he had issue—

1. Robert, his heir.
2. John, Major 44th foot, who, serving during the Peninsular war, was present at the battles of Salamanca and Orthes, and wounded and taken prisoner in the latter engagement.
3. Archibald, Major of Artillery in the E.I.C.S., who married Octavia, daughter of the late Colonel James Phelp, of Caston House, county Leicester.
4. Patrick, M.D., who died in India.
1. Margaret, married to the Rev. Dr Alexander Hill, Professor in the University of Glasgow.

Major Craufurd died in 1794, and was succeeded by his eldest son,

IV. Robert Craufurd of Newfield, representative of the Craufurds of Craufurd, Crosby, &c.; Colonel-commandant of the Ayrshire Yeomanry, and one of the deputy-lieutenants. He married, in 1813, Frances, daughter of the late Henry O'Brien of Blatherwick Park, county Northampton, and dying in 1843, left issue,

1. Robert, his heir.
2. Patrick-Reginald.
1. Frances.
2. Emma, married, 15th June, 1841, to George Walker, Esq. of Eastwood, Notts.
3. Julia.
4. Letitia.

V. Robert Craufurd succeeded his father in 1843. He is an officer in the Rifle Brigade.

The estate of Newfield was sold, soon after his father's demise, to Mr Finnie, a London merchant, but originally from Kilmarnock, now also deceased. The property, however, remains in possession of this gentleman's family.

*Arms.*—Quarterly: 1st and 4th, gules, a fesse, ermine, for Craufurd of Craufurd; 2d and 3d, argent, three escutcheons, sable, for Loudoun of Loudoun; and a central coat, gules, thereon a fesse, ermine, surmounted by two spears, salterwise, for Crosby.

*Supporters.*—Two stags, gules.

*Crest.*—A phœnix rising from the flames, gules.

*Mottoes.*—" God shaw the right;" and " I bide my time."

## WALLACES OF RONHILL.

JOHNE WALLACE of Ronhill died in the month of November, 1609 He left a son, Adame Wallace, who, by his testament, was constituted his only executor. Robert Wallace of Galrigs, Mr William Wallace, minister of Symontoun, &c., were appointed overseers.

The Wallaces in Dundonald parish seem to have been all pretty nearly related. Adam, originating with the Riccarton family, was a prevailing name amongst them. Ronhill is now a farm on the Newfield estate.

## M'CLUNE, OR M'CLEANE, OF HOLMES OF DUNDONALD.

This family seems at one time to have possessed considerable property. The first of them connected with the parish of Dundonald was, in all probability,

I. ROBERT M'CLUNE of Holmes, who died at Largs in April, 1647. He was succeeded by his son,

II. Robert M'Clune, whose retour, "in 3 libratis terrarum de Holmes de Doundounell," is dated 10th August, 1647. He was succeeded by,

III. David M'Clean de Holmes, hæres of Robertii M'Cleane de Holmes of Dundonnell, whose service to the lands is dated July 31, 1673.

The property was soon afterwards acquired by the Earl of Dundonald. It first appears in the retours of that family in 1690. Previous to the M'Clunes coming into possession, Holmes had belonged to the Fairlies of that Ilk. By a legal document, dated 13th April, 1609, it appears that the late John Fullarton of Dreghorn, father of David Fullarton of Knokinlaw, had granted letters of reversion to Sir Robert Fairlie of that Ilk, which letters of reversion had been assigned over by Sir Robert to William M'Kerrell of Hillhouse.*

* Mason's Notes.

# PARISH OF DUNLOP.

## ETYMOLOGY, EXTENT, &c.

Chalmers is no doubt correct in ascribing the etymology of the parish to the Celtic, *Dunluib*—not *lub*, as he has it, however,—which signifies the hill, at the bend or winding. There is a hill, or *dun*, in the vicinity of the village, near which a small stream, called the Glazert, describes such a bend as to render the place still characteristic of its Celtic etymology.[*]

Dunlop is quite a rural parish. It lies south-east of Beith, from which it is divided by the Lugton water. It is bounded on the north-east by the county of Renfrew, and south and south-west by the parish of Stewarton. Its extreme length, from south-west to north-east, is about four miles; and it is a little more than four miles in breadth. The greater part of the parish lies in Ayrshire, and the lesser in the county of Renfrew. There are 4462 acres in Ayrshire, and 700 in Renfrewshire.

Topographically speaking, the parish is composed of a number of small hills and ridges, rising from 50 to 130 feet above their corresponding hollows, though the highest point is calculated to be above 560 feet above the level of the sea. Many of the little hills present steep fronts of naked rock, very picturesque and romantic. The principal elevations are Braikenheuch, where, tradition says, one of the Cuninghames of Aiket was killed by the Montgomeries, during the memorable feud which existed between the families of Montgomerie and Cuninghame. Braikenheuch is about a mile and a half from Dunlop village. From its summit one of the most interesting prospects is obtained which can be found in the west of Scotland, embracing, as it does, an extensive view of the parishes of Lochwinnoch, West Kilbride, Dalry, Kilbirnie, Kilwinning, Stevenston, Irvine, &c.; the Firth of Clyde, with the Islands of Arran, Holy Isle, Plada, Ailsa, and the beautiful point of Troon. Far in the north towers the western ridge of the Grampians—Benlomond, Benledi, &c.; and towards the south, the eye rests on the bold, rocky coast of Carrick. Dunlop, or more properly, Boarland Hill, is a delightful round eminence, a little to the west of the village of Dunlop. Barr Hill is a pleasant eminence in the barony of Aiket. Knockmade Hill is the most elevated ground in the parish. It is on the estate of Col. Mure of Caldwell. There are several other notable eminences, such as Craignaught Hill and the Chapel Craigs—the whole presenting a series of delightful green hills, with fertile vales lying between, the haunt, no doubt, of numerous fairies, in the days of superstition.

Dunlop parish, as might be expected from its undulating surface, is well watered—having numerous springs and rivulets. The principal stream is that of the Lugton, which rises out of Lochliho,[*] in Renfrewshire, and joins the Garnock near Kilwinning, after coursing through the parish about fifteen miles. Corsehill Burn divides the parish from Stewartoun, while the Glazert intersects the centre of it, falling at length into the Annick, a tributary of the Irvine. Formerly there was a lake in the parish, called Halket Loch, covering about ten acres of land. It was drained, however, some time since, at the joint expense of the surrounding proprietors, and now forms an excellent meadow. Previous to this, the crops in the vicinity were much subject to mildew. Except on the larger estates, where plantations have been cultivated with considerable care, the parish is deficient in shelter, and has a bare aspect. It is also behind in agricultural improvement—the attention of the inhabitants having for a long time been chiefly directed to the dairy, which is carried

---

[*] Dunloppe Kirk, prettily seated at ye confluence of three small brookes.—PONT.

[*] Anciently 'Loch le Bog Syde,' so called in a charter by Robert II. to Hew de Eglintoun (from 1371 to 1390). It signified the Bogside Loch. In process of time it came to be changed to Lochleboch, or Lochlevoch—so termed in the conveyance of the Duke of Hamilton to Mure of Caldwell, in 1754. It is now generally termed Lochlibo.

on to great perfection, especially in the making of cheese. *Dunlop cheese* is universally celebrated. This description of cheese—made with sweet milk, in place of skimmed, as was generally the practice —is said to have originated with Barbara Gilmour, who had, with many others, been driven into exile in Ireland, during the troubles in the reign of Charles II. It has been affirmed that she derived the idea of employing the whole milk from the Irish; but this seems extremely doubtful, seeing that the Irish do not understand cheesemaking at the present day.* Of late, considerable progress has been made in draining on the larger estates, particularly that of Dunlop; and altogether the climate is more salubrious now than it used to be, although the district has all along been considered one of the most healthy in the west of Scotland, if the longevity of the inhabitants is to be regarded as a test of purity. There is a limestone quarry on the farm of Laigh Gameshill, and the parish is well intersected with roads, by which the lime, burnt or unburnt, can be easily conveyed to wherever it may be required. The turnpike from Paisley to Kilmarnock runs through it, but none of the railways intersect it.

## HISTORY, CIVIL AND ECCLESIASTICAL.

The lands of Dunlop appear to have been held under the De Morvilles, who possessed all Cuninghame, by a powerful family of the name of Ross. Timothy Pont says,—" Boirland over and nether ar ye possesions of the Earl of Cassilles. Heir of old duelt Gothred de Ross, a famous and potent nobleman, of grate reputatione, quho, having his residence heir, enjoyed ample possessions abroade in ye countrey, and ves for ye tyme shriffe of Aire, his jurisdictione then extending over Carrick, Cuninghame and Kyill, of quhom, in the minority of David ye II., our annals remembreth thus; *Ae juvante conatus eorum Gotofride Rossio præfecto juridico Aerensi, breui totam Carrictam, Coilam et Cuninghamiam, in suas partes traxerunt.*" As a proof that there had been a castle on Boarland, or Dunlop Hill, the residence, we may presume, of Gothred de Ross, the foundation of a ruin was removed some years ago by a late pro-

prietor. A diligent observer may yet perceive the traces of the ruin. On the east side of the hill there are the remains of a deep trench, cut from the top, in a straight line, half way down its side. In the charter chest of the burgh of Irvine there is a notarial copy of an inquiry made in 1260, respecting some lands in litigation between Dom. Godfrey de Ross and that burgh. The Rosses seem to have taken part with the Baliol faction in the struggle for the Scottish crown, and their possessions of course became forfeited. There is a charter, for example, by Robert I. to Robert Boyd, of the lands of Kilmarnock, Bondingtoun, Hertschaw, &c., " que fuerunt Johannis de Balliolo, Godfridi de Ross, filii quondam Reginaldi de Ross, Willielmi de Mora, et Roberti de Ross." In the subsequent reign of David II. the Rosses were still farther reduced by forfeitures. William Murray, son to Maurice Murray, had a charter from that monarch, of lands within the barony of Stonehouse, by " the forfaultrie of Godfred Ross." The parish is now divided into a great many small proprietorships. So early as 1640, according to a manuscript valuation among the Dunlop papers, there were no fewer than thirty-three heritors.

There are no very notable historical events connected with the parish of Dunlop. Craignaught Hill was the scene of the sanguinary feudal conflict between the Stewarts and Boyds, as related in the introductory sketch (vol. i.) to this work. The ground where the battle took place is a romantic spot, near Neilstoun (parish of Dunlop) in Renfrewshire.

Chalmers says,—" The church of Dunlop belonged, in former ages, to the monastery of Kilwinning. The monks enjoyed the rectorial revenues, and a vicarage was established for serving the cure. In Bagimont's Roll, as it stood in the reign of James V., the vicarage of Dunlop, in the deanry of Cuninghame, was taxed £5, 6s. 8d., being a tenth of the estimated value. At the Reformation, this vicarage was held by Mr John Houston; and the whole profits of his benefice was leased to William Cuninghame of Aiket, for payment of £78 yearly. At the same epoch, the rectorial tithes of the church of Dunlop produced to the monks of Kilwinning only £40 a-year, having been leased by them for that sum. Of the lands which belonged to the church of Dunlop, a part, consisting of two merk lands of the ancient extent, was appropriated to the vicarage, and the remainder was enjoyed by the monks of Kilwinning. The whole passed into lay hands after the Reformation. In 1566, the church lands of the vicar of Dunlop were granted, in fee-firm, to William Cuninghame of Aiket, by Mr John Houston,

* The Rev. Thomas Brisbane, who wrote the Statistical Account of the parish, in 1795, is believed to have been the originator of this statement. Ayrshire has been celebrated from an early period for its dairy produce. Bishop Leslie, in his "De Origine Moribus et Rebus Gestis Scotorum Libri Decem," &c., written before 1578, speaks of Ayrshire as producing the 'best cheese,' and plenty of butter; also bees and bee-skeps, not a few—aits, barley, &c. In the same work he tells us that that portion of Stirlingshire lying towards the west, was renowned for the best cheese.

the then vicar of Dunlop, with consent of Gavin Hamilton, the commendator of Kilwinning; the patron of the said vicarage. The vicar reserved, however, to himself and his successors, the manse, garden, and an acre of land, adjacent to the manse. The lands thus granted, being two merk lands of the ancient extent, continued with the family of Cuninghame of Aiket. At the end of the seventeenth century, the rectorial church lands of Dunlop appear to have been acquired by the Earl of Eglintoun. In 1603, the patronage and tithes of the church of Dunlop were granted to Hugh Earl of Eglintoun, with many other churches that belonged to the monks of Kilwinning. After that date, the family of Dunlop of Dunlop appears to have claimed a right to the patronage of the church of Dunlop. The patronage was, however, held by the Earl of Eglintoun at the Restoration, and it has since continued with that family. The parish church of Dunlop was rebuilt about the year 1765. It stands at the village of Dunlop." This building having become too small for the population, a new church was built by the heritors in 1835. The manse was built in 1781; but a considerable addition was made to it in 1814.

It is not known at what time Dunlop was erected into a parochial charge. The earliest notice of it occurs in the chartulary of Paisley, from which it appears, that in 1265, " John de Reston" was perpetual vicar of the parish church of Dunlop. In 1505, Sir Andrew Marshall, the vicar of Dunlop, was chamberlain to the archbishop, and one of the vicars-general of the archbishoprick. John Major, or Mair, the instructor of Knox, appears from the old register, entitled, " Annales Universitatis Glasguensis," to have been vicar of Dunlop from 1518 till 1523.

In 1540, Alexander, the abbot of Kilwinning, granted to the Court of Session a pension of £28 yearly from the vicarage of Dunlop. This pension was formerly granted from the vicarage of Kilbirnie, but was now given from the vicarage of Dunlop, because it was of greater value.

Hans Hamilton, son of Hamilton of Raploch, appears to have been the first Protestant minister of this parish, having entered on the charge in 1563. In the " Register of ministers, exhorters, and readers, and of their stipends after the period of the Reformation," published by the Maitland Club, there is the following entry with regard to Dunlop : " John Hamilton, vicar and exhorter, the thryd of the vicarage, extending to xxvi li., providing he wait on his charge betym, 1567." As there can be no doubt that this was the same person, it is presumed that Hans, or Hanis Hamilton, the name by which he is usually designated, was a corruption of the Latin, Jo-

hannis.* Hans Hamilton was succeeded in the charge by Hew Eglintoun, who died in 1647. As the records of Presbytery, during the time of his incumbency, are lost, little is known about him. From an incidental notice in the record of the Presbytery's proceedings at a subsequent period, it appears that he was under process at the time of his death, but the cause of the process is not specified.† In 1648, one year after the death of

* James Hamilton, Viscount Clandeboyes, was the eldest son of Hans Hamilton, vicar of Dunlop. He was sent to Ireland by James VI. in the year 1587, along with James Fullerton, to keep up a correspondence with the Protestants of that kingdom, and communicate intelligence from time to time as to the designs of the Irish in the event of Queen Elizabeth's death. The better to conceal their design, they opened a school in Dublin for the education of Protestant youths. After teaching privately for several years, they were appointed to fellowships in Trinity College, then newly founded, and by their talents contributed much to establish the high character which it soon acquired. After the accession of James to the throne of England, James Hamilton, who had discharged his mission to the satisfaction of the king, was rewarded by extensive grants of forfeited lands in the county of Down and elsewhere ; and after being employed in several important services, was at length, in 1622, elevated to the peerage, by the title of Viscount Clandeboyes and Baron Hamilton. This title became extinct on the death of his grandson, Henry Earl of Clanbrassil. Lord Clandeboyes' five brothers having followed him to Ireland, shared his good fortune. Their numerous descendants, the Hamiltons of Down, Armagh, Dublin, and Carlow, with their various collateral branches, are still possessed of great wealth and influence. From them are descended the noble families of Clanbrassil, Roden, Massareene, and Dufferin. The first of these having become extinct through the failure of heirs in the eldest branch of Hans Hamilton's family, was granted to one of the descendants of a younger son, but has again become extinct. Archibald Hamilton Rowan, so well known from his connection with the Irish rebellion, was the lineal descendant of Hans Hamilton's second son, Archibald.— STATISTICAL ACCOUNT.

In the east corner of the churchyard of Dunlop, there is a tomb erected by the Viscount Clandeboyes in memory of his father. On a flagstone on the floor is the following inscription : " Heir lyis Hans Hamilton, vicar of Dunlop, quha deceist ye 30 of Maii 1608, ye aige of 72 zeirs, and Janet Denham, his spous." Under a marble arch, with two marble pillars of the composite order, in front, are two statues kneeling on a marble monument, in the attitude of devotion, and habited according to the fashion of the times. In the wall is a marble slab, having an inscription, stating that Hans Hamiltoune was the son of Archibald Hamiltoune of Raploch; his wife a daughter of James Denham of West Shields; that they lived together forty-five years, during which period he served the cure at this (Dunlop) church—offspring, six sons and one daughter. His daughter, Jean Hamiltoune, married to Wm. Muir of Glanderstone. Erected by their son, James, the first Viscount Clandebois, of the kingdom of Ireland.

† The following is an extract from his testament : " At the parosche kirk of Dunlope, the second day of December 1646 zeirs. The quhilk day Mr Hew Eglintoune, minister at Dunlope, nominats and constitutes Marione Hamiltone, his spous, his onlie executrix and universall intromitrix with his haill guidis, &c. Item, first of all, he lieves, assignes, &c., to the said Marione, his spous, the sowme of ane thousand merks money, &c. Quhilk sowme of ane thousand merks he ordaines to be in compensatione, &c., to hir of the said thousand merks money quhilk I and my airs ar oblessit to pay to hir at my deceis, &c., conforme to his band grantit to hir thairupone, of the dait the xxvi.

Hew Eglintoun, Gabriel Cuninghame was settled. He was ejected in 1663, and restored again by the indulgence of 1672, when Mr William Mein was associated with him in the charge of the parish. After this he seems to have fallen under the suspicion and displeasure of the government; for on the 2d of April, 1683, he was indicted, along with some others, " for aiding, assisting, and corresponding with Mr John Cuninghame, late of Bedlane, a notorious traitor." Failing to appear, " he was denounced and put to the horn, and his moveable goods ordered to be escheat and brought into his majesty's use, as an outlaw and a fugitive." He is mentioned by Wodrow as having lived till after the Revolution; but whether he was restored to his charge before that period does not appear.* He seems to have been a person of considerable eminence, and to have taken a prominent part in the deliberations of the Presbyterian ministers in those distracted times.

The following is a list of the ministers since the Revolution:

John Jameson, ordained 21st September 1692, died 1706.†

James Rowat, ordained May, 1707: translated to Jedburgh September, 1732.‡

Robert Baird, ordained 28th March, 1734, died 27th March, 1756.

James Wodrow, D.D., ordained 1st September, 1757; translated to Stevenston, October, 1759.

John Fullarton, ordained 25th September, 1760; translated to Dalry, 16th March, 1762.

John Graham, ordained 12th May, 1763; translated to Kirkinner, 30th June, 1779.§

Thomas Brisbane, ordained 27th April, 1780, died May, 1837.*

Matthew Dickie, admitted from Limerick, 8th May, 1834, assistant and successor. He left the church at the late disruption.

William Gebbie is the present incumbent.

The parochial registers do not go farther back than 1700, and were very irregularly kept until about 1780.

The school-house at Dunlop was built in 1641, as appears from the following inscription over the door:

" 1641.

" This school is erected and endowed by James, Viscount Clandeboyes, in love to his parish, in which his father, Hans Hamilton, was pastor 45 years, in King James the Sixt his raigne.

" JcLV."

" It is still in pretty good repair; but though it affords to the schoolmaster what may be called legal accommodation, it does not afford such accommodation as a well-qualified teacher ought to have. If, as the inscription intimates, the school was ever endowed by Lord Claneboyes, all knowledge of the source whence the endowment was derived is now lost." †

### ANTIQUITIES.

At a place called the Chapel Craigs, about half a mile from the village of Dunlop, there existed until lately the ruins of a chapel, which was dedicated to the Virgin Mary, and had an appropriate endowment for the support of a chaplain. It is not known whether this was the parish church before the Reformation, or a chapel distinct from it. It stood upon a rock, on the side of a rivulet, which was crossed by steps, called the *lady's steps* —which steps, however, have been superseded by a bridge. A beautiful stream of water gushes

---

day of Januaril 1626 zeiris: and the haill rest of my free guids I lieve, &c., equallie betwixt John, Jeane, and Elspet Eglintones, my bairns," &c. [Magister Hugo Eglintoun, minister at Dunlop, had a retour, 26th July, 1634, as heir to Archibald Eglintoun, his father, in the lands of the vicar of Mernis, in the parish of Mernis. He had a son, Hew, a merchant in Glasgow, who died while a young man, in 1649.]

* He seems to have been restored to his charge. " Mr Gabriel Cuninghame, minister of Dunlop," gives a discharge to the laird of Craigends for £120 Scots, January 21, 1690. He died in 1692, as appears from a document signed by William Cunynghame of Ashinyards, executor dative of vmqle. Mr Gabriel Cunynghame, minister at Dunlop, dated 22d July, 1692.

† This John Jameson was a poet of no small pretensions. Some fragments of his poems exist in MS.

‡ Mr James Rowat, minister at Dunlop, married Agnes, daughter of James Muir of Roddans, or Rhoddens, son of William Muir of Glanderstoun. A son of Mr Rowat was Professor of Church History in Glasgow College from 1752 to 1762.

§ His great hobby was farming, and he had some ground leased on which he built a small round tower in which he might study his sermons, while overlooking the farming operations! The small tower is still standing, and is called by the people " The Folly." He became very unpopular with his flock.

* Mr Brisbane had natural wit, and possessed much shrewdness and common sense, but was very miserly. The late celebrated Dr Fleming of Neilston used often to assist Mr Brisbane on sacramental occasions. The Doctor, as is well known in the west of Scotland, was a great advocate of church accommodation. In the pulpit it was frequently the Alpha and Omega of his discourses. Taking a walk one Sabbath evening with Mr Brisbane, after having indulged in his favourite theme in the church, he still complained bitterly that he had not sufficient " accommodation" in his parish. Mr Brisbane, turning away from him, rejoined him in a little, saying: " Saunders, I ha'e been making an epitaph for you." " And what is it?" said the Doctor. " I will let you hear it,"—repeating, with due emphasis, the following lines:

" Here, underneath this stone,
Is Dr Fleming's station;
Ance sairly scrimpt for room, but now
He's got accommodation."

† Statistical Account.

from the rock. The existence of this chapel has given name to a number of localities around. A few hundred yards south-west of the site of the chapel, on the gentle swell of the hill, is a Druidical stone, called the *Thugart stane*, supposed to be a corruption of *the grit stane*. It appears at one time or other to have been a rocking-stone. The base is so covered with rubbish, that it has now lost its vibratory motion. It lies on the farm of Brandleside, and the tenant is bound in his tack to protect it, by neither removing it, nor cultivating the ground for a considerable number of square yards around it. Above the site of the chapel, a pathway was cut out of the solid rock, leading to the top of the hill, where tradition says there was a burying-place belonging to the chapel. The pathway is nearly obliterated, a quarry having been opened in the place a number of years ago.

Until within these few years, two beautiful small monuments stood on the top of Barr Hill, in the barony of Aiket. They were well built, the stones being firmly cemented with lime; and about twelve feet high. They were taken down, in a spirit truly worthy of a vandal age, and the stones applied to agricultural purposes. At the foot of Barr Hill, on the right bank of the Glazert, stands now, with only one exception, the most ancient building in the parish—Aiket Castle. It is a strong square tower, with a side of thirty feet: it was originally four stories in height, but, in modern times, has been reduced to three. An addition has likewise been built to the east side. The walls, at the base, are upwards of seven feet thick. There was an inscription above the principal entrance, but it has long ago been obliterated. A tradition exists that the stones of the building were quarried from the hill in its neighbourhood, and conveyed thither by being handed from one man to another. The castle stands on a small rock overhanging the water of Glazert. In ancient times it was surrounded with a moat.

### TRADITIONS.

Like every inland rural parish in Ayrshire, Dunlop has many traditions attached to certain localities. Of course, the great enemy of mankind has been seen in various shapes. Tam Giffen, the reputed warlock, wandered much in this parish, and many anecdotes are related of him of a mar-

vellous kind, which appear to have been believed by the peasantry until within a late period. It was believed that he frequented the midnight meetings of ghosts, fairies, &c. On one occasion he entered the farm-house of Gills, a little to the west of the village. On being asked where he had been the night previous, he replied, "I was just at a meeting o' witches, an' we settled it yestreen, that the wee wean at the Grange is to dee the nicht." Which happened according to his prediction.

Long ago, a noted cadger, who went under the cognomen of " Young Robin," although his " haffets were lyart and gray," saw several amazing " sights." One night, returning home from Kilmarnock on horseback, rather late, when the moon was clear and bright, he was a little surprised to find that he was riding in company with a headless horseman, whose steed was likewise minus the head. He spurred his weary steed to its utmost speed, thinking, like Ichabod Crane, to outrun his " eerie" company; but, strange to say, he did not gain one inch on his rival. He again reined in his steed, thinking the spectre horseman would fly past him, but the strange horseman likewise did the same. Wearied in his efforts to get away from the unearthly equestrian, he hurried on towards the village, still in company with the fiend, whose mysterious steed galloped along without making the least noise with his hoofs on the stony road. When crossing the bridge, the " headless horseman," with his steed, sprung high in the air and vanished in a " flaucht o' fire." At another time he was returning from Glasgow with a horse and cart. On the road near the Camore, a lonely spot, there was in a field a number of bushes close by the roadside, where the fairies were reported to hold " merry meetings." It was far advanced in the night ere he reached this " haunted spot," and when he arrived, his ears were greeted with sweet melody of a very enchanting kind. Looking round he perceived a vast concourse of little people dressed in green, his horse became frightened and ran off, breaking the cart, which contained a barrel of ale, which was stove, and all the ale lost; so terrified was Young Robin that, for several weeks afterwards, he durst not go to the door when it was dark.[*]

* Young Robin's apparitions were probably an invention to monopolise the trade of cadging or merchandise in the district.

# FAMILIES IN THE PARISH OF DUNLOP.

## DUNLOP OF DUNLOP.

This family is of ancient origin, as are almost all those whose patronymics are derived from locality, for there can be little doubt that the district of Dunlop gave the name to the family. It is impossible, however, to trace the line of succession accurately in the more early part of its history. Several breaks occur, and in some instances the links have to be supplied more by induction than direct evidence. As we have seen, the district of old belonged to the Rosses, whose seat is supposed to have been the ancient stronghold of Boarland. It is a tradition, that the Dunlops were "servitours," or vassals of this family. Pout says—"Dunlop, ane ancient strong house, fortified with a deipe foussie of watter, and planted with goodly orchards. It is named Hunthall, because, say they, the ancient possessor thereof wes huntsman to Godefred Ross. The quhole bounds and grounds heir about, and all Macharnock Moore, wes of old a mightie forrest." The castle, or strong house of Dunlop, stood on the banks of a little rivulet called Clerkland burn, which divides the parish from Stewartoun. It is unknown at what time the original square tower was erected. One of the more modern additions bore the date 1599. The site is now occupied by the handsome modern mansion, built by the late Sir John Dunlop, Bart., in 1831. The first to be met with is,

I. DOM. GULIELMUS DE DUNLOP, who appears in a notarial copy of an inquest, in the charter-chest of the burgh of Irvine, in 1260, in a cause betwixt the burgh and Dom. Godfredus de Ross. The next is,

II. Neil Fitz-Robert de *Dulap*,* who, in 1296, appears in the Ragman Roll, and whom Nisbet conjectures to have been of Dunlop. The property, shortly after this period, seems to have been alienated from the Dunlops, probably, as has been conjectured, on account of their having taken part, along with their superiors, the Rosses, on the side of Baliol, in the contest for the Scottish crown. The link in the family chain is therefore irremediably broken.

III. James Dunlop was in possession of Dunlop, as appears from a valuation of the county of Ayr of the fourteenth century. He was succeeded by,

IV. John de Dunlop, who, in 1407, has a charter from Hugh de Blare. The next in succession probably was,

V. Alexander Dunlop of Hunthall,* whose identity is ascertained by a transaction of his grandson, as after stated. He is mentioned by Rymer as of that Ilk in the reign of James I. He was possibly the son of the preceding, and father of—

VI. John Dunlop of that Ilk.

VII. Constantine Dunlop† of that Ilk is presumed to have been the son of the preceding. In 1483, he has a transaction respecting the *entry* of the lands of Hunthall, that had been in arrear since the time of his grandfather, Alexander Dunlop.

VIII. Alexander Dunlop of Dunlop, brother of Constantine Dunlop, whose retour, as Dunlop of that Ilk, is dated 1476, was succeeded by his son. In 1489, he was appointed by Parliament—among other Lords, or Barons, as they are termed—to collect the bygone rents and casualties of the Crown, in Stewarton and Kilmarnock, along with Alexander Boyd, doubtless of the Kilmarnock family, as we find him, soon after, permanently established chamberlain of that family. He is also mentioned as a member of an inquest on the retour of Mathew, Earl of Lennox. Constantine Dunlop died in 1505, leaving (with a daughter, Janet, married to James Stuart, Sheriff of Bute, great-grandson of King Robert II.) a son and successor.

IX. John Dunlop of that Ilk, whose infeftment is not dated till 1507. This gentleman married in 1492, Marion Douglas, and had one son, Alexander, and a daughter, who married Hugh Maxwell of Auldhouse. He died in 1509, and was succeeded by his son,

X. Alexander Dunlop, who, in 1537, is in possession of the lands of Hunthall, or Dunlop, and of the presentation of the parish and patronage of Dunlop Church. He married Ellen Cuninghame of Glencairn. By a charter under the Great Seal, in the reign of Queen Mary, and protectorship of Arran, he settled his estate on his five sons in succession—James, William, Constantine, Robert,

---

* Dulap, or Dulap, is the vernacular pronunciation in the district at this day.

* John, Earl of Buchan, had a charter of the lands of Dunlop in 1413. This Alexander Dunlop was, therefore, probably the first of the Dunlops who re-acquired the property.

† Constantine Dunlop of Hunthall, or Dunlop, is a witness to the infeftment of the Queen of James IV. in the lordship of Kilmarnock, in 1504.

and Andrew. He died about the year 1549. Margaret Dunlop, "of the family thereof," who was married to Archibald Lyon, a son of the family of Glammis, in 1540, was probably a daughter of this laird of Dunlop.

XI. James Dunlop, the eldest son, succeeded. His retour is dated in the year 1549. He married Isabel, daughter of Gavin Hamilton of Orbieston, and is said to have had two sons, James and Allan. He was succeeded, however, by

XII. Alexander Dunlop of Dunlop, of whom there appears to be no account in the family record. His existence, however, in 1558, is proved beyond doubt by the Criminal Records.* He was succeeded by his son or brother,

XIII. James Dunlop of Dunlop, in 1596. He married Jean, daughter of Sommerville of Cambusnethan, by whom he left four sons:

1. James.
2. John, who purchased the lands of Garnkirk.
3. Thomas, who married Grizell, daughter of Cochrane of that Ilk, and from this alliance are descended the Dunlops of Househill.
4. Robert, to whom his father left the lands of Bloak.

He died in April, 1617, and was succeeded by his eldest son,

XIV. James Dunlop of that Ilk, who married, in 1614, Dame Margaret Hamilton, widow of the Bishop of Lismore, or Argyle, and daughter of Gavin Hamilton, Bishop of Galloway. He and his lady are mentioned in testamentary documents, in 1615, 1616, and 1617, as *younger* of Dunlop. His mother survived his father, as we find "Margaret Hamilton, Lady Dunlop, zounger," mentioned in another testamentary document in 1618.† He died in the month of May, 1634; the inventory of his effects was made and given up "be Mr Johane Dunlope, brother-germane to the defunct, lautfall creditor."‡ Resisting the attempt of Charles I. to introduce Episcopacy, the estate of Dunlop had been made over to John of Garnkirk, for the purpose of security. This deed was acted upon in 1633, when his brother took possession, and in five years after made resignation to his nephew,

XV. James Dunlop, who obtained a charter, under the Great Seal, of the lands of Dunlop. He married Elizabeth Cuninghame, daughter of Alexander Cuninghame of Corsehill, by whom he had two sons and two daughters:

1. Alexander, his successor.
2. John.

* See vol. i. p. 66.

† Jeane Somervell, Ladie Dunlope, died in 1645, in which year her testament is dated. Her son, Thomas Dunlop of Househill, was her only executor.

‡ John Dunlop, brother-german to the laird of Dunlop, lent 1200 merks to Sir William Cochrane of Cowdoun, in 1639.

1. Jean, married, in 1674, to William Ralston of that Ilk.
2. Marion, married to David Montgomerie of Lainshaw.

James Dunlop of Dunlop was a warm supporter of the Presbyterian cause, and suffered both by imprisonment and fines accordingly. About 1667, when the Pentland Hill rising took place, he made over a considerable part of his lands to the Earl of Dundonald, probably as a measure of safety against forfeiture. He was amongst the number of Ayrshire lairds, who, according to Wodrow, were imprisoned in 1665, and not liberated till 1667, and then only in consequence of granting a bond to keep the peace, under a heavy penalty; his penalty, in particular, being rated at 12,000 merks. He was succeeded by his son,

XVI. Alexander Dunlop. He does not appear ever to have obtained possession of the property made over to the Earl of Dundonald. He suffered severely in the public cause. Wodrow mentions that he was imprisoned on the 30th July, 1683, on suspicion of being concerned with the Bothwell Brig Covenanters, and was compelled to give up a part of his estate, besides a bond for £12,000 Scots to appear in November following. He was indicted anew in April, 1684, when he made over to his son, John, the lands which had been settled upon him on his marriage. He emigrated soon after to America, and was appointed, 1685, Sheriff of South Carolina. He married, in 1667, Antonia Brown, daughter of Sir John Brown of Fordel,* by whom he obtained the lands of Rossie, which he sold in 1669. On his marriage, his father made over to him the valuable possessions of Muirshields, Over and Nether Oldhalls, Galloberries, and the barony of Peacockbank.

XVII. John Dunlop, his son, succeeded to Dunlop. In 1684, he got a disposition to the lands that had been settled on his father, Alexander; and, in 1685, the Earl of Dundonald resigned to him those lands of which he got a conveyance from his grandfather, James: and, in 1687, he had an adjudication against his said grandfather, by which he got possession of all his estates. In 1688, he had part of them erected into a free barony, by the name of the barony of Dunlop. He does not appear ever to have been married, and dying in 1706, was succeeded by his brother,

XVIII. Francis Dunlop of Dunlop. He was among the gentlemen called upon, at the Union in 1707, to witness the deposition of the Scottish

* Sir John Brown died of a fever at Leith, being a prisoner, September, 1652.—BALF. ANNALS. In the year 1825, his portrait remained in the dining-room of Rowallan House, his widow, Dame Mary Scott, having married the laird of Rowallan.

regalia in the Castle of Edinburgh * In 1715, he took an active part against the Chevalier, and was Lieutenant-Colonel, under the Earl of Kilmarnock, of a regiment of fencible cavalry then raised He married, first, Susan, daughter and sole heiress of John Leckie of Newlands, by whom he had,

1 John · of whom afterwards
2 Hugh, who died a student at Glasgow College, in his 17th year
3 Alexander, Major of the Enniskillens, which he commanded in the unfortunate expedition to Carthagena, in 1741, and died on his return to Britain, unmarried
1 Antonia, married to Sir Thomas Wallace, Bart of Craigie, but died without issue

Secondly, he married a daughter of Sir —— Kinloch of Gilmerton, and widow of Charles Campbell, by whom he had two daughters

1 Frances, died unmarried
2 Magdalene, married to Robert Dunlop, R N, and had two children

He died in 1748, and was succeeded by his son,

XIX. John Dunlop of Dunlop,† who on the resignation of his father, Francis, in 1748, was infeft in the estate In 1745 he was deputed by the gentlemen of Ayrshire, together with Sir Thomas Wallace of Craigie, to offer the assistance of the county to the Duke of Cumberland He married Frances Ann, last surviving daughter of Sir Thomas Wallace of Craigie, Bart (by his first wife, a daughter of Colonel Agnew of Lochryan), by whom he had seven sons and six daughters

1 Francis, died young
2 Sir Thomas, who succeeded to the estate of his maternal grandfather, and took the name of Wallace of Craigie
3 Alexander, died young
4 Andrew, who died unmarried, in 1804 This gentleman served in the first American war, and attained the rank of Major He afterwards raised a regiment of horse, called the Ayrshire Fencible Cavalry, which he commanded until its reduction in 1800
5 James, of whom presently
6 John was in the army, but early retired on half-pay, married his cousin, Frances Magdalene, as above, by whom he had seven sons and four daughters, and died in 1831 leaving issue—
    1 John Andrew Wallace, a member of Council at Bombay, who married Elizabeth, daughter of Dr Sandwith, E I C S, by his wife, Jane Bamien Boye of Gaften in Sweden, who died in 1843, leaving issue, Robert Henry of the Bengal Civil Service, born in 1823, Madeline Anne, Elizabeth Joanna Emily, and Rosalind Harriet Maria.

7 Anthony entered the navy early in life. He married Ann, daughter of Alexander Cuninghame, Esq., brother of Sir William Cuninghame of Robertland, by whom he had four sons and three daughters

Frances, the third daughter, was married to Robert Vans Agnew, Esq of Barnbarrow, and had five sons and four daughters

Rachel, the fourth, married to Robert Glasgow of Mountgreenan

XX. James Dunlop, the fifth son, succeeded, in 1784, on his father's resignation, to the estate of Dunlop, his only remaining elder brother, Sir Thomas, the second son, having succeeded to the estate of Craigie He served in the American war, during which he attained the rank of Major In 1787 he proceeded to India as Captain in the 79th regiment, where he remained thirteen years, and commanded one of the assaulting columns at the storming of Seringapatam, where he was severely wounded He returned soon afterwards to England, and served at home In 1810, having attained the rank of Major-General, he was appointed to the command of a brigade in the fifth division of Lord Wellington's army, and he remained at the head of that division during the campaign of 1811 In 1812, General Dunlop was elected Member for the Stewartry of Kirkcudbright, as he also was in the two ensuing Parliaments He married, in 1802, Julia, daughter of Hugh Bailhe, Esq, a younger son of Bailhe of Monckton, and had issue—

1 John, his heir
2 Hugh, Lieutenant R N, married, in 1831, Ellen Clementina, only daughter of Robert Cockburn, Esq
3 Andrew Robert, died in 1831
1 Anna, married in 1824, to Francis John Davies, Esq, Captain in the Grenadier Guards, and died in 1825
2 Frances, married in 1838, to Alexander E Monteith, Esq, Sheriff of Fifeshire

General Dunlop died in 1832, and was succeeded by his son,

XXI. John Dunlop of Dunlop, born in 1806—an officer in the Grenadier Guards, who married, first, in 1829, Charlotte Constance, daughter of General Sir Richard Downs Jackson, K C B, and by that lady had issue—

1 James, his heir
2 Charlotte Constance

He married, secondly, 29th December 1835, Harriet Primrose, eldest daughter of the Earl of Roseberry Sir John, who represented the county in Parliament, was created a Baronet in 1838 He died 3d April, 1839, and was succeeded by his son,

XXII James Dunlop of Dunlop, the present Baronet

Arms—Quarterly 1st and 4th, argent; 2d and 3d, quarterly; 1st and 4th, gules, a lion, rampant, argent, 2d and 3d, gules, a fesse, chequy, argent and azure an eagle with two heads displayed, gules

* He was the youngest of five brothers There were also two sisters Of the other four brothers nothing is known, but that one of them went out in the unfortunate expedition to Darien, and was never more heard of The eldest sister, Margaret, was married to William Fullarton of Fullarton, being his third wife, without issue, and whom she survived She was married, secondly, to Sir Robert Denham, Bart, and left two sons The youngest was married to an English gentleman of the name of Brewster, who was forfeited in the "ill times" She likewise left two sons These four boys, losing their parents in infancy, were educated at Dunlop with Francis Dunlop's own sons

† John Dunlop, younger of that Ilk, was admitted a burgess of Ayr in 1733

*Crest.*—A dagger in a dexter hand, and all proper.

*Motto.*—Merito.

### CUNINGHAMES OF AIKET.

The Cuninghames of the "two merk, six shilling and eight pennie land of auld extent of Aiket-over, exclusive of Auldhall," were descended of Bedland, who were cadets of Glencairn.

I. ALEXANDER CUNYNGHAME got a grant of " Owr-Aitkead" from James III. or IV., which lands had fallen to the Crown by recognition, in consequence of the heiress, Elizabeth Cunynghame of Bedland, having disposed of them to John, Lord Hay of Yester, without the superior's consent. Alexander Cunynghame married Jean Kennedie, sister of the first Earl of Cassillis. His name occurs in the Acts of the Lord's Auditors, date 16th October, 1479.*

II. Robert Cuninghame of Aiket married Helen, daughter of Caldwell of that Ilk. He is witness to a charter of Hunter of Hunterstoun, in 1535.†

III. William Cuninghame married Helen, daughter of Colquhoun of Luss. He and his family were guilty of the slaughter of Sir John Muir of Caldwell, in 1570. His wife, Helen Colquhoun, was accused before the Justice-Depute, of administering poison to him in October, 1577, but she did not appear. ‡

IV. John Cuninghame of Aiket married Helen Barclay, a daughter of the laird of Carfin. Issue :

1. Alexander, his successor.
2. William, concerned in the murder of Lord Eglintoun, in 1586.
3. Margaret, wife of the Laird of Langshaw. She betrayed Lord Eglintoun in 1586.
4. Matilda, married to Cuthbert Cuninghame of Corshill.

V. Alexander Cuninghame of Aiket was one of the accomplices in the murder of Hugh, Earl of Eglintoun, on the 19th April, 1586. He was shot by the Montgomeries § near his own house.

He married Dorothea Ross, and had issue :—

1. James Conynghame.
2. Malster Alexander, who died about 1644, without issue.

VI. James Cunynghame of Aiket occurs in the Commissary Records of Glasgow, 1607, 13, 15, 20, 28. " Jacobus Cunninghame, laird of Aiket," was admitted a burgess of Ayr in 1625. William Cunynghame, *Tutor of Aiket,* is mentioned in the testament of John Lockhart of Bar, 1614. On the 6th September, 1601, he is served as heir to Alexander, his father, in the 33s. 4d. land of Bustoun, in Kilmaurs, but he does not appear to have made up any title to Aiket.

VII. William Cunynghame of Aiket, who is retoured heir to his great-grandfather's father, William Cuninghame of Aiket, 21st March, 1644. He had another retour of the same date, as heir of his father. He married Anna, only daughter of Thomas Inglis of Corsflat, town-clerk of the burgh of Paisley, by whom he obtained a considerable fortune. Her father, by his testament, 27th April, 1625, appointed Mr Fullarton, minister of Beith, as one of her trustees. He had expressed a wish that his daughter should be married to Montgomerie of Hesilhead, her kinsman, but her fate was otherwise. Aiket was of dissipated habits, and used his lady in a brutal manner. The following notice of her circumstances occurs in Baillie's letters, 20th August, 1641 :—

" Friday, 6th.—A world of Bills came to be referred to the Parliament: Among the rest, Anna Inglis complaining that her husband, young Aiket Cunynghame, having received 40,000 merks tocher with her, had deserted her after frequent tormenting of her with strokes and hunger, he debauching all with harlots in Paisley. We sent two with this bill to the Parliament to get present order. The justice of God was in this matter. The damsel's father had left her to be married to Mr Hugh Montgomerie of Hesilheid, her wife's near cousin. After, his (widow) falls in conceit with Allan Lockhart, and gives herself to him, and by

<hr/>

* Millar's Genealogical Notes.
† The Abbot of Kilwinning set in tack to Aiket, his heirs, &c., the parsonage and vicarage teinds of Dunlop for four lifetimes and five nineteen years. See a case as to the validity of a sub-tack granted in 1655, by Hugh Lord Montgomerie to Muir of Caldwell, in prejudice of this long tack.—MORRISON'S DECISIONS.
‡ Pitcairn's Criminal Trials.
§ Robert, Master of Eglintoun, obtained a commission by the " Secret Counsaill," ratified by act of Parliament, to expel the denounced rebels from the Places of Robertland and Aiket, to put in six men in the former, and four in the latter house, at the rate of £6 per man per month, to be recovered from the readiest sums that could be raised on these respective estates. Thus it continued till another decreet of the Secret Counsail was obtained by the Cuninghames, 25th March, 1591, and ratified by Parliament,

5th June, 1592, whereby the laird of Robertland was received into the number of his Majesty's subjects, and restored to his Place and lands ; but ordering him to give a full discharge to the Master of Eglintoun for his intromissions. The same favour was, at the same time, extended to the wife of Alexander Cuninghame, styled Dorothea Ross, Lady Aiket, who complained bitterly of "the destruction of the policie of the place of Aiket, housis, yairdis, orcheardis, and growand tries, sua that the samyn has been rwinous and laid waist, but door, windo, lok, ruf, or hut ony repair, and the dewties prescrivit, rigourouslie exacted, to the grit wrack of the puir tenantis, quha ar not addetit in sa mickle mail as is extortionat be thame." Her ladyship, however, had also to grant a discharge to the Master of Eglintoun for his intromissions, and to become bound, under a penalty of 5000 marks, to reset neither her husband nor any other person concerned in the above murder while they lay under a process for it.

his persuasion, makes her daughter, when scarce twelve years of age, without proclamation, to be married to his cousin, Aiket. For her reward, her husband, Allan, leaves her to pay 10,000 merks of his debt, which made her a poor vexed widow."

This was followed by an action of reduction, which Anna Inglis brought with the view of setting aside her contract of marriage with her husband, on the plea of minority and lesion.* He refused his concurrence; but the court found it competent for her to carry on the action in her own name, as the husband was the party to defend—8th July, 1642.† He had a retour, 30th May, 1640, in 2 merk 6s. 8d. land of Over-Aiket, as heir of William Cuninghame of Aiket, his grandfather.

VIII. James Cunynghame of Aiket married Euphan, daughter of William Russel, minister of Kilbirnie. He feued the 18s. 4d. land of "Nedder Auldhall," called Collennan Auldhall, to John Neilson, eldest son of Archibald Neilson of Auldhall, Collennan, 11th September, 1660.

IX. James Cunynghame of Aiket, who, in his service as heir to his father, James, 29th July, 1695, is designed *Captain*. He commanded a company in the Earl of Glencairn's regiment at the Revolution, which he exerted himself in raising. He was an active promoter of the Scots Darien Expedition, in the records of which he is designed Major James Cuninghame of Aiket. He went along with the expedition, having been appointed to the chief command; but he is understood to have proven somewhat restive, and speedily returned to Scotland, leaving the colony to its fate. He petitioned the Scots Parliament, 23d August, 1704, for compensation for alleged losses sustained in consequence; stating that he had been employed by the Company trading to Africa; that he went as a counseller, along with the first ships to Caledonia; and that, besides neglecting his own private fortune, there were due him of arrears £145, 12s. sterling, and £270 sterling for the support of his company in the Earl of Glencairn's regiment, which he had defrayed from his own estate. In 1705 he was allowed so much of his claim out of the Poll Tax, imposed for the support of the army, the remainder to be paid when the whole tax was collected. Major Cuninghame distinguished himself by his opposition to the Union, in 1707. He married Dorothea M'Adam, daughter to the laird of Waterhead, and had issue. His affairs becoming embarrassed, he was obliged to part with the estate.

* Les-age, or non-age, or lesion, a term in Scots law.
† Morrison's Decisions.

What became of his family is unknown. Robertson mentions that two ladies who had lived in Ayr some years before he wrote, were said to be the last of the family of Aiket. There was a process before the Presbytery of Ayr, 22d April, 1730, against Alexander Cuninghame of *Aikhead*, and his wife, Anna Crawfurd, daughter of the laird of Kerse, for irregular marriage. This was, in all likelihood, the son of the preceding James Cuninghame of Aiket.

## DUNLOPS OF HAPLAND, SUBSEQUENTLY OF BOARLAND.

Alexander Dunlop of that Ilk, who died about 1549, settled his estate of Dunlop, or Hunthall, on his five sons in succession, viz.:

1. James Dunlop, who succeeded to the lands of Hunthall, or Dunlop.
2. William Dunlop.
3. Constantine Dunlop.
4. Robert Dunlop; of whom afterwards.
5. Andrew Dunlop.

I. ROBERT DUNLOP, fourth son of Alexander Dunlop of that Ilk. He was designed of Hapland,* and is mentioned by that designation as a debtor in the testament of Thome Lauchlan, whose settlement was written out by Alexander Lumsdane, curatour, in 1551. He must have had a large offspring:

1. Adam Dunlop; of whom afterwards.
2. A son; of whom afterwards.
1. A daughter, who was married to John Maxwell of Auldhouse, whose progeny by this marriage succeeded to the lands of Nether Pollok or Pollick.†

II. Adam Dunlop of Hapland. He died in or before 1573, without male issue; for his nephew succeeded to the estate.

III. John Dunlop was retoured, January 26, 1573, as heir-male or of entail—hæres masculus sive talliæ—of Adam Dunlop, his uncle, in the 6 merk land of Hapland in property and tenendry, of auld extent, in the parish of Dunlop. Johnne Dunlop

* There is a Gilbert Dunlop mentioned in a remission to Cuthbert Lord Kilmarnock, in 1498.
† This John Maxwell of Auldhouse acquired "Meikle Glanderstoun," &c., in 1553. He had confirmations, in 1572, of two charters from the Abbot of Paisley, dated in 1562. He was alive in 1578. Succeeded, John, his father, in 1548. Issue—
1. George Maxwell of Auldhouse, minister at "Mernes," (Mearns) was a witness to the will of Gabriel Maxwell, minister at Inchinan, April 1621. He died in November, 1648. He married Janet, daughter of John Millar of Newton (by Gells, daughter of Pollick of that Ilk); by whom he had, 1. John, his successor. Married, secondly, Jean, daughter of William Muir of Glanderstoun; by whom he had, 2. William, ancestor of the Maxwells of Springkell, Baronets. He married, thirdly, Janet Douglas, daughter of the laird of Watersyde; by whom he had, 3. Hugh Maxwell, who married Marion, heiress of Maxwell of Dalswinton.

of Hapland was one of the assize between the families of Hessilheid (Beith parish) and Scotstoun, 1st December, 1576. *

IV. David Dunlop "niffered" or excambied with Patrick Cunningham † the lands of Hapland for the lands of Boarland, before 1597, in which year Patrick Cuninghame is mentioned in a testamentary document as now "laird of Hapland."

V. Dunlop of Boarland.

VI. John Dunlop of Over Boarland married Elizabeth Walkinshaw. Their land, in 1650, was valued at £100 Scots, supposed to have been valued by Cromwell's agents.

VII. John Dunlop of Boarland, married to one Montgomerie from the "Heigh Corce," in Stewarton parish. Issue—

    1. John Dunlop of Boarland.
    2. James Dunlop of Loanhead.
    1. Margaret, who died young.

VIII. John Dunlop of Boarland, married to Mary, daughter of William Clerk, portioner of Shitterflat, by Margaret Simpson, about 1740. Issue—

    1. John.
    2. William.
    3. James.
    4. Robert.
    1. Mary.
    2. Margaret.

IX. John Dunlop of Boarland married Jean Gilmour. She was one of three daughters, heiresses, portioners of the Tailend (Dunlop parish.) They had a large family, who all died without issue, except two daughters,‡ viz.—

    1. Mary, who had the half of Boarland, married to Andrew Brown of Craighead. She died in 1839, at the Hill, the property of her mother's brother-in-law. Issue now alive—
        1. John Brown, married to —— Duncan, and has issue—
            1. Jean Brown.
    2. Jean Dunlop, portioner of Boarland, married Thomas Reid of Balgray, and has issue—
        1. Robert.
        2. John.
        1. Jean.

## PORTERFIELD OF HAPLAND.

I. GABRIEL, son of Master John Porterfield of that Ilk, by his second marriage with Jean Knox,

daughter of the laird of Ranfurlie. His father gave him the lands of Blairlin, in 1568. He is supposed to have been the father of,

II. Gabriel Porterfield, of the four pund land of Porterfield, who infeft, 21st January, 1618, Mariot Crawfurd, his future spouse, in Gills, Lothrihill, the Templeland and Maynes of Hapland, with the mansion-house, lyand within the parish of Dunlop, together also with a lyferent of £100 Scots. This Mariot was sister-german of George Crawfurd, younger of Liffnorris. Witnesses, Alexander Cunynghame, elder, of Corsehill, Hugh Cunynghame, servitor to Sir William Cunynghame of Capringtoun, &c. Subscryvit at the Place of Corsehill. "Gabriell Porterfeild of Hapland" is mentioned in a testamentary document in 1620.

*Jeane Porterfeild*, married to Robert Hamiltoune of Torrence, who died within the burgh of Glasgow, December 1658, was probably a daughter of this laird of Hapland. She left, "in legacy to Elizabeth and Mary Porterfeilds, dochters lawfull to vmqll. Gabriel Porterfield of Haipland, the sowme of sex hundreth merks money, equally betwixt them," &c.

III. Gabriel Porterfield of Hapland, son no doubt of the foregoing, married Jean Maxwell. They made a contract of alienation with Mr David Dickson, minister at Irvine, 24th December, 1633, of their 44s. land of Crawfield, in the parish of Beyth, in liferent, and his son, in fee. He and his spouse had a conjunct liferent sasine in the two merk and half land of Dunlophill, Wattirland, and Halketh, with the loch thereof, on a charter of Robert Montgomerie of Hesilheid, dated 24th May, 1634. Both had also a precept of sasine, 29th July, 1637, in the fyve merk land of Aikhead-Wallace, on a sale charter from William Wallace of Johnstoun (in Renfrewshire) and Agnes Porterfield, his spouse. Gabriel Porterfield of Haipland had another sasine of the four pund land of Brockilmuir, from William Cunynghame of Lagland. The Baillie in that part was John Porterfield of Greenend.

Sir Johne, son of Sir James Cunynghame of Glengarnock, by a disposition, dated at Castle-Cunynghame, in the county of —— in Ireland, 28th June, 1632, disposed to Gabriel Porterfield of Hapland and Jean Maxwell, his spouse, the lands of Crawfield, in the parish of Beith. He was a witness to a certain paper, dated 3d November, 1641, but died before 1648. He had issue,

    1. John, his successor.
    2. Alexander, who succeeded his brother.
    3. Elizabeth,(?) wife of Mr Hugh Peebles, minister at Lochwinnoch about 1659. Two of their children died, and were buried in the churchyard, in 1656. They had surviving,

---

    † Cunningham of Boarland was concerned in a foray against Drumlanrig in 1650. The Cuninghames of Boarland were probably of the Aiket family, into whose hands the property possibly fell through the marriage of Alexander, the first of Aiket, with the sister of the Earl of Cassillis.

    ‡ The late Mrs Steven of Port-Glasgow mentioned, as a family tradition, that there were nine lairds of the name of Dunlop successively inherited Hapland and Boarland—the tenth generation being two heiresses.

1. Marion Peeblis, married to James Cochrane—cousin and chamberlain to the Earl of Dundonald—of Mainshill, before 1687.
2. Jean Peeblis, married to John Wallace of Neilstounsyde, ancestor of the laird of Kelly.
3. Catharine Peeblis, married to Matthew Hammill of Roughwood, in 1681.
4. Daughter, married to Alexander Cunynghame of Cairneurran, in Kilmalcolm parish.

4. Mariot (or Mary?) Porterfield, married to Robert Fergushill of that Ilk, 8th February, 1685, who infeft Mariot Porterfield, his future spouse, in his mansion-house, and the lands of Auchintiber.

IV. John Porterfield of Hapland, 19th October 1648, had a retour, as heir-male of Gabriel Porterfield, his father, in the four pund land of Brockwelmure, part of Caprington; five merk land of Aiket-Wallace, &c.; two merk and half land of Dunlop Hill, &c.; part of Wattirlandis, with the corn-mill, &c.; part of Halkhead, with the loch, &c. He was also retoured, 4th January 1619, as heir to his father, in the four merk land of Leffnoreis, the pendicle called the Ward, the ten shilling land of Blackwodhill, in Kingiskyle, and in the twa merk land of Snaidis (vel Snaidis) in the barony of Auchinleck. The laird of Hapland was ruling elder in the parish of Dunlop in 1649. He died without issue, and was succeeded by

V. Alexander Porterfield of Hapland, who had a retour, 5th October, 1653, as heir to his brother, John, in the four pund land of Brockwellmuir, &c. He had a retour, 5th October, 1653, as heir of his father, Gabriel, of Leifnorris, and pendicle called Ward, ten shilling land of Blackwoodhill, in Kingskyle, twa merk land of Snaidis, &c. He also had a retour, 3d November, 1654, as heir of John, his brother, in the four merk land of Leifnoreis, and the ten shilling land of Blackwoodhill, within Kingskyle.

VI. Gabriel Porterfield of Hapland sold the Crawfield, 15th December, 1676, to John Peebles, to be holden of the disponer. This disposition was signed at Hapland; witnesses, Alexander Cunynghame, younger of Robertland, Magister James Cunynghame of Tour of Kilmaurs, &c. James Steill of Muirstoun, writer in Beith, was factor of this estate in 1708. He left an account of his intromissions; and mentions the lady as in her widowhood. He was succeeded, probably, by his son,

VII. Gabriel Porterfield of Hapland who married Elizabeth Cuningham, daughter of the laird of Craigends, about 1720. Issue—

1. Alexander Porterfield of Hapland. He fell from his horse in returning from Stewartoun, about 1765 or 1770, and was killed, unmarried.
1. Johanna Porterfield, married to Thomas Trotter of Mortonhall, and other extensive possessions in Mid-Lothian and Berwickshire. Their share of Hapland consisted of the manor-place of Hapland, and about 200 acres of land. General Trotter was a son of this union, and the property is still possessed by their descendant, Sheriff Trotter.

2. Margaret Porterfield, married to John Hamilton of Barr, in the parish of Lochwinnoch, in 1751. They had a numerous family.
3. Lillias Porterfield, married to William Sommerville of Kennox. Their daughter married to Colonel Macallister of Loup, in Kintyre, and also proprietor of the remainder of Hapland.
4. The third daughter married a common tradesman, and was disinherited.

## GEMMELLS OF TEMPLEHOUSE.

There are several small proprietors in the parish of Dunlop, whose families can boast of considerable antiquity. Amongst these may be mentioned the Gemmells of Templehouse, whose ancestors were in possession of the property before 1570, in which year

1. PATRICK GEMMIL of Tempilhouse was one of the jury on the trial of "William Cuninghame of Aiket, William Fergushill, Florence Craufurd, and John Raeburn of that Ilk, delatit of the slaughter of vmqle. Johnne Mure of Cauldwell."

From an "Inventory of the writs of all and haill the Templeland of Dunlop Hill, commonly called Templehouse," it would appear that, in June 1596, the foresaid Patrick resigned the Templelands into the hands of the superior, Lord Torphichen, in favour of his eldest son,

II. John Gemmill, and Isobel Ross, his spouse, in liferent, and to John Gemmill, their son, his heirs and assignees, in fee. John Gemmill died before his father, and apparently without surviving issue,[*] for there is a precept of clare constat, dated 24th October, 1617, granted by Robert Montgomerie of Hesilheid and Tempill Connynghame, in favour of

III. Patrick Gemmill, brother to the late John Gemmill, who died last vest and seised in the said lands, reserving to Patrick Gemmill, father to the said John Gemmill, his liferent over the said lands. He was succeeded by his son,

IV. John Gemmill of Templehouse, who had a charter from his father, dated 15th December, 1656, of the lands of Templehouse, in implement of a matrimonial contract with "Agnes Smith, his future spouse, and langest livend of them twa."

V. John Gemmill of Templehouse succeeded his grandfather. He had a precept of clare constat, dated 13th November, 1754, granted by Mr William Wallace of Cairnhill, "in favour of John Gemmill, as nearest and lawfull heir to the deceast John Gemmill of Templehouse, his grandfather."

* John, the grandson of Patrick, though he must have died young, appears to have been married, for "Elizabeth Howie, spous to Johnne Gemmill, zounger of Tempilhous, in the parochin of Dunlop," died in the month of August, 1616.

The instrument of sasine following thereon is dated 5th December, 1759. He was succeeded by

VI. John Gemmell of Templehouse, who had a precept of *clare constat*, by Thomas Wallace, Esq. of Cairnhill, dated 8th April, 1789, " in favour of John Gemmell of Templehouse, only son of Patrick Gemmell, who was eldest lawful son of John Gemmell of Templehouse, as the nearest and lawful heir of his said grandfather." He was infeft in the lands 20th September, 1790. He was succeeded by his son,

VII. John Gemmell of Templehouse, father of

VIII. John Gemmell of Templehouse, the present proprietor.

### DUNLOPS OF LOANHEAD OR AIKET.

I. JAMES, second son of John Dunlop of Boar-land, the seventh laird. He was styled of Loanhead, or of the Mains of Aiket. He married Agnes, daughter of John Service of the Holms of Cauf, in the parish of Dalry. His son,

II. James Dunlop of Loanhead, or the Mains of Aiket, married Agnes, daughter of James Black, Pennel, now of Locherbank, Kilbarchan parish. He died at Beith, 1st June, 1829. Issue—

1. James Dunlop, merchant in Glasgow, and others. He married Marianne, only daughter and heiress of the late Andrew M'Millan, Esq., merchant in Port-Glasgow, on the 26th August, 1817. He died in the beginning of July, 1843. Issue—
   1. James W. Dunlop.
   2. Robert Dunlop.

The collateral branches of the Dunlops were numerous.

# PARISH OF FENWICK.

There can be little doubt that Chalmers is correct in deriving the name of this parish from the Anglo-Saxon, *Fen-uic*, signifying the village at the fen, or marsh. The marshy nature of the surrounding country, though now greatly drained and improved, amply supports the accuracy of the derivation. There is a hill in the vicinity of the village or villages of *Finnick*, called Fenwick Hill.* It is, however, scarcely prominent enough to have given the name to the district.

The parish is about nine miles long, and upwards of six broad—resembling, in form, an oblong square. It is bounded on the east by the parishes of Loudoun and Kilmarnock, on the south by Kilmarnock, on the west by Stewartoun, and on the north, by Mearns and Eaglesham.† The highest part of the parish is about 700 feet above the level of the sea, to which height it attains by a gradual ascent. The higher and lower portions of the parish present very different features. The land in the former is almost wholly pastural, while in the lower it is capable of the highest cultivation, and produces excellent crops. The lower portion is, consequently, thickly dotted with farm-steadings, while the upper is thinly peopled. Rowallan and Craigendunten Moors occupy the greater portion of the upper range. The pasture, however, is good, and excellent stock is reared upon it. No small portion of the soil has been of late reclaimed by draining, and large patches of cultivation intersect the moorlands. The mosses are extensive, and dangerous to life, some farms having not less than a hundred acres of it within their boundaries. The climate is consequently moist, yet it seems to be healthy, if we may judge from the longevity of the inhabitants.

* There were two "Finnicks,"—"Finnick-hill" and "Little Finnick."—possessions of the Mures of Rowallan.
† Statistical Account.

## HISTORY, CIVIL AND ECCLESIASTICAL.

Fenwick was originally a portion of Kilmarnock parish. The disjunction took place by Act of Parliament, in 1641. It is thus of comparatively modern erection. The act directed that the parish should be called the *New Kirk of Kilmarnock*. The populace, however, in matters of this kind, pay little attention to Acts of Parliament. It was popularly called Fenwick, from a small village at a short distance from the church—which name has long been universally recognised. The new church was built in 1643, and a minister planted in 1644, provision having been made for his maintenance from the tithes of the old parish of Kilmarnock. Around the new church a village gradually arose, called New Fenwick, or the Kirktown, which is now of more importance than the original village. By the Act of 1641, the patronage of the church was settled on the Earl of Kilmarnock, but in the reign of Charles II. it passed to the Boyles of Kelburne, and now belongs to the Earl of Glasgow.

The first minister of the parish was the celebrated Mr Guthrie, whose memory is still greatly revered in the district. At his settlement among them, it is understood that the people were sunk in deep ignorance and barbarism, and Mr Guthrie had the merit of producing, in the course of the twenty years he continued in the parish, a decided change for the better. Great multitudes flocked from Glasgow, Hamilton, Lanark, and the adjacent districts, to hear Mr Guthrie's sermons, so popular did he become. Wodrow, in his *History of the Sufferings of the Church of Scotland*, has preserved the following commission to *Rowallan* "to bear down vice," as illustrative of the mode by which this change was effected. "At Fenwick, December 2d, 1674.—The whilk day the heritors and kirk-session of Fenwick convened, by virtue of the 22d Act of the 3d Session of the 2d Parl. of King Charles II., entituled, ' Act against Profaneness,' of the date September 1672, did, according to the appointment of the foresaid Act, nominate, likeas by these presents we do nominate William Muir of Rowallan, younger, residenter within the said parish, as most fit to execute the penal statutes of several Acts of Parliament against cursing, swearing, and other profanenesses exprest in the foresaid Act, and other Acts therein specified : And did, likeas, by those presents do appoint and earnestly desire Sir William Muir of Rowallan, elder, to present this unanimous nomination of the said William Muir, younger of Rowallan, to the effect foresaid, to the right honourable and noble lord the Earl of Eglintoun, Baillie of Cuningham, and to entreat his lordship to grant commission, in terms of foresaid Act, and a deputation to the said William Muir of Rowallan, younger, for convening the persons, transgressors of the foresaid statutes against profaneness, and to judge them according to law. In witness of these premises we have subscribed these presents," &c. He had made himself too conspicuous, by his zeal in the cause of the Covenant, to be overlooked by the government after the Restoration; so that he was among the " outed" in 1664—which event he survived little more than a year. His remains were interred at the Cathedral of Brechin, in the vault of Pitforthy, to which family he belonged.

Under such a ministry, it is to be presumed that the inhabitants of the parish would be emulous of the religious zeal of their gifted pastor. We accordingly find that a stern resistance was maintained against the government. One of the most distinguished officers " among the Covenanters (Captain John Paton) was a native of the parish. He was born at Meadowhead, of which his father was farmer, and was himself employed in agriculture till the age of manhood, when he went abroad, and engaged as a volunteer in the German wars. For his heroic conduct at a siege, he was raised *per saltum* to the rank of captain. On his return to Scotland, his courage and military experience gave him a prominent place in the transactions of his persecuted country. Of his prowess in battle many instances are recorded. He fought at the battle of Worcester, where he distinguished himself by his services, and so deeply impressed General Dalzell with admiration of his courage, that long afterwards, when Paton had been condemned, he applied to the king for his pardon. At Bothwell it is said he acted as colonel, though he did not retain the title. After the defeat of Bothwell he was declared a rebel, and a price offered for his head. His escapes were numerous and romantic. He afforded shelter in his house at Meadowhead to several of the persecuted ministers ; and it is said that Mr Cargill baptized at one time twenty-two children in his house. He was at last taken at Floak, in the parish of Mearns. On his way to Kilmarnock, he was accidentally met by General Dalzell, who affectionately embraced him, and assured him that he would apply to the king for his pardon. The General kept his word, and solicited and obtained the pardon; but Bishop Paterson inhumanely detained the order till after the execution. His Bible, which he handed to his wife on the scaffold, along with his sword, are still preserved as heir-looms by his descendants. The people of Fenwick, in gratitude for his services, have erected a tombstone to his memory." *

There are still the descendants of another family in the parish who sternly resisted the oppression of the times—we mean the Howies in Lochgoin, a remote farm in the south-eastern extremity of the parish. " The house," says the writer in the *Statistical Account,* " is altogether inaccessible on the east to horsemen, and an active man could not, even though acquainted with the locality, at night cross the moss, by which it is defended, but at the risk of his life ; and no stranger could venture across it with safety, even in daylight, without a guide. On the west, the only direction from which it can be approached, a sentinel was always stationed in time of danger, whence he could command an extensive view of the whole country as far as Ailsa Craig and the hills of Arran, and thus no body of troopers could reach the house before the inmates had time to escape into the morasses. A situation like this was invaluable to the Covenanters, and it was the point at which the utmost vigilance and attention of the dragoons were naturally directed. Twelve times was the house plundered, and as often did the people escape. On such occasions, the money was removed, and buried in the neighbouring mosses. It happened once that they were nearly taken by surprise, and had only time to conceal the coins, without being able to reach the spot. In spite of all subsequent search, it remained in the moss for more than a century, when the place was accidentally discovered. After an extensive search, some scores of British and foreign coins were discovered. These are preserved by the family as very interesting relics. The Fenwick flag, which waved at Bothwell, Kilsyth, and Drumclog, is also preserved" at Lochgoin.†

* Statistical Account.
† The Rev. Edward Irving paid a visit to Lochgoin, and is said to have looked upon this relic "with an interest almost amounting to devotion."

The churchyard of Fenwick attests the nature of the struggle to which the inhabitants were subjected during what is called the Second Reformation in Scotland. It contains two tombstones, upon which are inscribed the following memorials —

1. " Here lies the dust of John Fergushill and George Woodburn, who were shot at Midland by Nisbet and his party, 1685 "

> " When bloody prelates, once these nations' pest,
> Contrived that cursed self-contradicting test,
> These men for Christ did suffer martyrdom,
> And here their dust lies waiting till he come ''

2 " Here lies the body of James White, who was shot to death at Little Blackwood, by Peter Inglis and his party, 1685 "

> " This martyr was by Peter Inglis shot,
> By birth a tiger rather than a Scot
> Who that his monstrous extract might be seen,
> Cut off his head, and kick'd it o'er the green,
> Thus was that head which was to wear a crown,
> A football made by a profane dragoon "

## ANTIQUITIES.

The ruins of the strong house of Polkelly, now the property of the Earl of Glasgow, still remain They occupy a portion of the rising ground north of Muiryet, on the main line of road between Glasgow and Kilmarnock This tower, with the lands of Polkelly, was one of the earliest possessions of the Mures of Rowallan It has long been in ruins

The church, built in 1643, still exists, and the oaken pulpit, occupied by Mr Guthrie, is regarded with no common interest Within these few years, and probably still, the old practice of preaching by the sand-glass was kept up " When the preacher has announced the text from which he is to preach, the precentor brings forth from a small box a half-hour sand-glass, which he places on an iron stand When the glass has run out, he removes it, and the preacher after that only adds what he finds necessary " *

## TRADITION

The writer in the *Statistical Account* appends the following as a note to his account of the parish We cannot vouch for its accuracy, but think it worthy of copying. It has, no doubt, some foundation in fact. *Pathelly* Hall is probably a popular mistake for *Polkelly*, which was of old

----

* Statistical Account.

called *Pothkelly* " There is a tradition connected with a house in this parish which is worth recording King's Well has long been known as a principal inn between Glasgow and Kilmarnock. It stands on one of the most elevated spots in the parish, and is flanked on the west by a deep flowmoss, over which a road has been formed within the last few years with extraordinary difficulty, the moss being in many parts so soft that a dog could not have walked across without sinking. At some distance from King's Well stood Pathelly Hall, a baronial residence of the Cochranes, at that time a place of some importance, but of which there is now hardly a vestige. Hither one of the Jameses was proceeding to administer justice on occasion of some feud or foray, of which the details have not been preserved The affair was sufficiently serious to occasion no slight apprehensions on the part of those who had the misfortune to be implicated, and the approach of the monarch awakened many conflicting emotions of hope and fear. After a long ride over very difficult ground, and in one of the highest and most exposed districts in Scotland, his Majesty had at last acquired an appetite too sharp to be compatible with comfort He was obliged therefore to alight at the nearest house, which happened to be a peasant's cottage The gudewife supplied him with very homely cheer; but luxury was then in a great measure unknown, and a king would have been contemptible who could not *rough it* with the hardest of his subjects. After a hearty meal, he was proceeding to depart, when the good woman told him that her husband was one of the prisoners whose trial had been the main object of his journey, and that he surely never would have the heart to hang a man after having eat his breakfast sitting in his arm-chair This appeal the rules of hospitality rendered irresistible. When he reached Pathelly Hall, he singled out the husband of his hostess, lectured him on the impropriety of his conduct, and dismissed him with an admonition to be a better bairn He next commenced his investigation, and finding eighteen of the prisoners guilty, hung them up forthwith on a hawthorn, which is still pointed out, and displays obvious marks of great antiquity On his way to Pathelly Hall, his horse drank at the spot where the King's Well now stands, and shortly afterwards sunk in a quagmire, which is still called the King's Stable. His Majesty long remembered the ride, of which he used often to detail the particulars, and the Ayrshire roads were represented as impassable."

# FAMILIES IN THE PARISH OF FENWICK.

No family of note appears to have resided in the parish of Fenwick, except the Mures of Polkelly. This is sufficiently accounted for by the originally bleak nature of the greater portion of the district, and the fact of its having belonged in large tracts to adjacent proprietors, such as Rowallan, now possessed by the Marquis of Hastings, Crawfurdland, Cuninghamehead, &c. A few small proprietorships have recently sprung up.

## MURES OF POLKELLY.

The first of the Mures of Polkelly, according to the historian of the Mures,[*] was Ranald More, a kinsman of Sir Gilchrist More of Rowallan, who had come from Ireland, and aided him in his feuds with the Cumins, as well as fighting under his banner at the Largs, where Sir Gilchrist obtained great credit for his prowess. To this Ranald More he gave the house and lands of Polkelly, together with a portion of the Muir of Rowallan, which property continued in the possession of Ranald's family till the marriage of the heiress, Janet Mure, grandchild of Ranald, with Sir Adam Mure of Rowallan, once more united the estate with Rowallan. It was, however, branched off a second time by the son of this Sir Adam, also Sir Adam Mure of Rowallan, who gave his second son, Alexander, "the barronie of Pokellie, together with the lands of Limflare and Lowdowne hill, qherein his lady was infeft." This occurred, we should suppose, before the middle of the fourteenth century. The property thus settled upon Alexander, was further enhanced by the acquisition of the lands of Hareshaw and Drumboy, all within the district of Cuninghame, although described in the precept by Lord Galloway and Annandale, for giving infeftment, as lying in the "Barronie of Strachanan and Scherefdome of Lanrick," which precept is dated in 1417.

The house of Polkelly, of the surname of Mure, continued a distinct branch from Rowallan, "verie neer ane hundereth and fyftie yearis," till towards the end of the fourteenth century, when, by the death of William Mure of Polkelly and all his male children, the whole inheritance became the property of Robert Cuninghame of Cuninghamehead, who had sometime previously married Mar-

garet, his daughter and heir. Polkelly continued in possession of the Cuninghamehead family till the death of the last of them, in 1724, when it was soon afterwards acquired by the Earl of Glasgow.

*Finnickhill* and *Little Finnick* also latterly belonged to minor branches of the Mures of Rowallan. They were long possessed, however, by the Arnots of Lochridge, in the parish of Stewartoun. Sir Gilchrist More, already alluded to, gifted to "Edward Arnot the two finnicks, for yearlie payment of ane paire of gloves at S. Lawrence Chapell, and of ane paire of spures at S. Michaell's Chapell, embleames of reddie service." One of these Fenwicks, called Wat, or Wattis, Fenwick, now the Kirktoun, was acquired by Robert Mure, apparently a son of Rowallan, from "Andrens Arnot de Watt fenik, fillius et heres apparen. ednardi Arnot de lochrig," in 1497.[*] Notwithstanding this alienation of "vatt fanike," the Arnots seem to have resided at Fenwick until a comparatively recent date. The testament of Alexander Arnot of Lochrig, who died in November, 1623, is dated "at Fynnick, the xxi day of November," in that year; and the conclusion of the document states, that "thir presents ar writtin be me, Alexr. Conynghame of Corshill, at the directioun of the said Alexander Arnot, *in his awn hous of Fynnick*," &c.

## GARDRUM.

The lands of Gardrum, with those of Skerneyland, Ladeside, and Laighmoor, in the neighbourhood, belonged, prior to the Reformation, to the Abbey of Kilwinning. After that period, they fell into the hands of Alexander and John Hamilton (father and son) of Grange. This appears from a decree of the Court of Teinds, dated 8th July 1635, charging them with minister's stipend for these lands, Fenwick being then in the parish of Kilmarnock.

Not long afterwards, Gardrum fell into the hands of James Kelso (of the Kelsoland family probably), whom we find making a disposition of Gardrum—18th December, 1697—in favour of his son, James Kelso, younger.

Again, James Kelso, younger, gives a disposi-

---

[*] "The Historic and Descent of the House of Rowallane."

[*] Historie of Rowallan.

tion of the lands of Gardrum in favour of Mathew
Hopkin, merchant, Kilmarnock, dated 19th June,
1703; who makes them over to Ninian Bannatyne,
chamberlain to Lord Boyle, his wife, Barbara
Wilson, and David Bannatyne, their eldest son,
on the 10th September of the same year; and in
1710, they receive a feudal right from Alexander
Hamilton of Grange.

David Bannatyne of Gardrum* died in 1784
or 5.† He was succeeded by his brother, a drug-
gist in London, whose retour in the lands of Gardrum, Skerneyland, Laighmuir, and Ladeside, is
dated 10th January, 1785.

Ninian Bannatyne was succeeded, 6th August,
1790, by Dugald Bannatyne, merchant, Glasgow;
and, on the 2d February, 1791, Dugald is succeeded by John Carse of Meiklewood, Alexander
Hamilton of Grange being still feudal superior.

In March, 1793, John Carse was succeeded in
the proprietorship of Gardrum by James Dunlop
of Polkelly, who, in turn, in 1819, gave place to
Robert Lindsay of Horselybrae, whose grandson,
Robert, is the present proprietor. His ancestors
long resided either at Bruntland or Dalmerster-
nock, in the parish of Fenwick.

It may be mentioned that, in 1793, March 7,
James Dunlop granted to William Sheddan sixteen acres of the lands of Gardrum, commonly
called Gardrum-miln. This portion, therefore,
does not belong to the present proprietor. A
small property, part of Gardrum, called Tristrimhill, afterwards Blackfauld, consisting of two acres
or thereby, was also disposed of about the beginning of the last century, by the younger Kelso, to
James Gilkison, smith, Tristrimhill, of which

three enclosures were made. This latter portion, however, has again been attached to the
Gardrum property, which is regarded as a goodly-
sized and well-conditioned farm.

### LOCHGOIN.

The Howies in Lochgoin are a family of old
standing. They are said to have sprung from a
family of Waldenses, who took refuge in Scotland.
The earliest notes we have of them is from the
testament of " Johnne Howie in Lochgoyne, within the parochin of                , the tyme of his
deceis. Quha deceist in the moneth of Februar,
1614, ffaythfullie maid and gevin vp be his awin
mouth, &c. . . . . . Legacie—At Lochgoyne, the
xviii day of Februar, 1614—The quhilk day, &c.
Quharin he nominatis, constituts, &c., Dorathie
Gemmill, his wyfe, and Arthore Howie, his sone,
his onlie executouris, &c. To equallie distribute
the deids' pairt amangis the said Arthor, William,
Stein, Andro, Alexander, and Agnes Howie, his
bairnes," &c.*

The pretensions of the Howies to a considerable
antiquity are thus well-founded. Lochgoin forms
part of Rowallan Moor, so that they had been
originally tenants of that ancient barony. John
Howie, who died in 1793, was the author of the
*Scots Worthies*—a work of universal fame. His
son also, John Howie, was the author of a work
called the *Fenwick Visions*, in which there is a
singular record of visions of armies, in battle array, &c., seen in the parish of Fenwick, immediately before the rebellion of 1745, and the breaking out of the long war with France.

---

* David Ballantine of Gardrum was elder for Ayr to the
General Assembly, in 1744.—AYR RECORDS.
† Captain John Ballantine, late of Gardrum, gave £10 to
the poor of Ayr, in 1780. He was probably a son or brother of David.

---

* Johnne Howie of Lochgoyne, and James Howie, his
brother, occur in the testament of Johnne Landellis, pas-
singer, in Kilmarnock, April, 1615.

# PARISH OF GALSTON.

The name of the parish is one of the few in Ayrshire derived apparently from the Anglo-Saxon. Chalmers supposed it to have originated with some person of the name of *Gall*, to which was added *tun*, or *town*, signifying Gall's possession. Chalmers makes a near guess at what may be considered the truth. In early records the name is spelled *Gallystoun*, or *Gaulistoun*, the name of a place also in Galloway. In the reign of David II. James Boyd had a charter of " the lands of Gauylistoun, in Galloway, quhilk *John Gauilstoun* forisfecit." Thus we see that Galston in Galloway was so called from a person of the name of *Gauil; and* though we cannot show that Galston in Ayrshire belonged to the same party, yet it was similarly written, and was no doubt similarly derived.

Galston is situated in that division of Kyle called Kyle-Stewart, from its belonging to the High Steward of Scotland, the great overlord of the district. "Its greatest length is about 13 miles, and its greatest breadth about 4½; but its figure is very irregular, and accordingly its superficial extent is found to be scarcely 28 square miles. It is bounded on the east by the river Aven, which divides it from the parish of Avendale; on the north by the Irvine, which separates it from London and Kilmarnock; and on the west by the Cesnock, which divides it from Riccarton and Craigie." * On the south it is bounded by Mauchline and Sorn.

The topographical appearance of the parish presents considerable variety—hill and dale mingling in admirable confusion. Burns says, in his "Holy Fair,"—

> " The rising sun oure Galston muirs
> Wi' glorious light was glintin';"

* Statistical Account.

so that we have here a picture of wildness associated with the running streams and rich valleys of the Irvine, the Burnawn, and the Cesnock—the banks of which latter stream are the scene of one of Burns' early and most exquisite lyrics:

> " Her voice is like the ev'ning thrush
> That sings on Cesnock banks unseen,
> While his mate sits nestling in the bush,
> And she's twa sparkling, roguish een."

The highest of the eminences is called, appropriately enough, Distinct-horn. It is situated near the south-eastern extremity of the parish, and is about 1100 feet above the level of the sea. To the north-west of this is Molmont-hill, nearly 1000 feet high. "The general character of the soil," says the Statistical Account, "in the higher and eastern parts of the parish, is loamy and sandy, with a considerable tendency in many places to peat; in the lower and western parts, the most prevalent soil consists of different varieties of clay. In the eastern parts, which are generally covered with heath, there are found many trunks of trees of considerable magnitude. One of these was lately dug up from a piece of mossy ground, which appears formerly to have been a small lake, about 500 feet above the level of the sea. It proved to be a magnificent oak, with a straight trunk, which had once been 48 feet long, and is still 3½ feet in diameter at the upper extremity. Two large pieces, in good preservation, are now kept at Lanfine garden. Whether this tree and its fellows, already mentioned, are to be regarded as the remains of the Caledonian Forest mentioned in the Classics, or to be referred to a still more ancient epoch in the history of our globe, must be left for the decision of more competent authorities than the writer of this account. Along the south bank of the Irvine there are from 400 to 500 imperial acres of rich holm land, which appear evidently to have been formed by successive deposits from the river. It is certain, at least, that the river has at some period traversed almost every part of this rich tract, and it may be remarked, to the same purpose, that the uniformity of the soil and subsoil throughout its whole extent, as well as the considerable difference of level at the two extremities, preclude the supposition of its having been deposited at the bottom of an ancient lake." The only streams in the parish of Galston are those already alluded to—the Irvine, which bounds the parish and divides Kyle from Cuninghame the Aven, the Burnawn—a small rivulet which joins the Irvine at the village of Galston, and the Cesnock, which also joins the Irvine at the western boundary of the parish The only lake now in the parish is that of Loch Gait, an insignificant marsh Bruntwood Loch, which was much frequented by water-fowl, has wholly disappeared, having been drained a number of years ago. As in most of the other parishes of Ayrshire, rapid strides have been made in agricultural improvements

### HISTORY, CIVIL AND ECCLESIASTICAL.

The scene of the successful rencontre between the patriot Wallace, and the English convoy under Fenwick, in 1297, took place near to Loudoun Hill but within the boundaries of the parish of Galston * Bruce lay with his army at Galston, previous to overthrowing the English army under Sir Aymer de Valence, not far from the same spot, in 1307 The cairn, which is said to mark the vicinity of these battles, says the Statistical Account, "is still in existence, in the vicinity of Loudoun Hill, though considerably diminished by the repair of the neighbouring stone fences The ' rude fortification,' however, which is said in the former Statistical Account to have sheltered Wallace and his handful of followers, performed the same office to a much more numerous body of warriors, probably not less than a thousand years before It is evidently a Roman camp, chosen and fortified with all the military science for which that celebrated people were distinguished Its ramparts, though much reduced by time and the depredations of the husbandman, may be distinctly traced throughout its whole extent, and the Prætorian and Decuman gates are in a state of tolerable preservation The original camp, to which these remarks apply, is 180 yards long, and 114 broad, but there is another enclosure upon a lower level towards the south which seems to have been added upon a subsequent occasion, to accommodate a larger force, or perhaps originally de-

signed for the quarters of the allies This addition lengthens out the parallelogram to 258 yards. It does not appear that there have been any gates at the extremities of the Principia ; and indeed it is not to be expected from the nature of the ground, which, on the right and left sides, slopes downwards for twenty or thirty yards, with the declivity of a rampart. Upon one of these slopes there was found, in 1831, a silver coin in good preservation, having this inscription—CÆSAR AVGVSTVS DIVI F PATER PATRIÆ. This coin is now in the possession of Thomas Brown, Esq , the proprietor of the estate on which the camp is situated, who is also in possession of another Roman coin, found along with many more, a little to the eastward, in the parish of Avendale, and inscribed, DIVVS ANTONIVS * These facts and observations, taken in connection with the existence of a Roman military way, which may still be traced on the opposite bank of the Irvine, furnish incontestible evidence that the parish of Galston has received at least one visit from the masters of the world, and it furnishes a striking proof of the stupendous scale upon which that wonderful people conducted their affairs, that marches and encampments, too trivial to be recorded in their military histories, have thus certified their own existence during a period of not less than 1600 years In connection with these Roman remains, may be mentioned another military station on the Galston bank of the Aven, about two miles farther to the south It is nearly surrounded by the river, and fortified, where it is not so, by a rampart and ditch Its traditionary name in the neighbourhood is Main Castle, which, as there is not the slightest vestige of a castle in the modern sense of the word, involuntarily suggests to the classical scholar the Latin designation of Minora Castra In the absence of evidence, therefore, to establish any other hypothesis, it may not improbably be conjectured to have contained a detachment of the army stationed on Allanton Beg."

With all due deference to the respected writer in the Statistical Account, it seems fully more probable that the small encampment, thus described, was a British fortlet and not a Roman station. In the vicinity of the Roman encampments there are invariably to be found one or more native strengths, for we must recollect that almost every inch of ground was contended for against the advancing enemy Its being on the Galston, or opposite side of the Aven from the Roman encampment, is in itself evidence of its having been

---

* See vol i p 26

* Numerous coins have been discovered from time to time in the parish of Galston Mr Brown is in possession of a variety of silver pieces bearing the names of Alexander, David, and Edward

a British encampment, constructed to observe the movements of the foe. The banks of the Doon, which, like the Irvine, was also traversed by a Roman way, are studded, in a similar manner, with British entrenchments, at points commanding a view of the Roman line of road.

The traditional name of Main Castle renders it probable that a castle actually occupied the spot in later times than the era of the Romans. There is good reason for believing that castles existed in this country at a much earlier period than is generally supposed; and, as other instances prove, the fact of the existence of any particular building soon becomes lost after all vestiges of it have been removed. There is, no doubt, some foundation for the tradition, otherwise, why is the term castle not traditionally applied to all similar Roman or British remains?

In more recent times, during the momentous struggle connected with the Reformation, Galston parish sustained a part fully equal to the rest of the country. Her chiefs, Cesnock, Bar, and Galston, took decided parts in the struggle, and were well sustained by their dependents. In the list of fugitives proclaimed by Government in 1684, twenty belonged to Galston parish.

Galston village, which no doubt had its origin in the ancient tower belonging to the early proprietors of the lands of Galston, is now a thriving village, with a population of upwards of 4000. It is delightfully situated on the south banks of the Irvine, nearly opposite the policies of Loudoun Castle. It has the best means of communication, the roads in the vicinity being both excellent and numerous.

As to the ecclesiastical history of the parish, Chalmers says, " the church of Galston was dedicated to St Peter, and a fair was annually held at Galston on St Peter's day, the 29th of June.* The fair has declined in business and importance, but the custom of lighting fires on the neighbouring hills, on the evening before the fair, is still continued.† The church of Galston was granted to the Convent of Red Friars, which was founded at Faile, in 1252; and it continued to belong to that establishment till the Reformation. The church was served by a vicar, who had a stipend of five chalders of victual, yearly, with a manse and glebe; and the brothers of Faile enjoyed the remainder of the revenues. In Bagimont's Roll, as it stood in the reign of James V., the vicarage of Galston was taxed at £4, being a tenth of the

estimated value. At the epoch of the Reformation, the vicar's income of five chalders of victual was let for the payment of 50 marks, or £33, 6s. 8d. yearly, which was greatly under its real worth. Besides the five chalders of victual, which was payable to the vicar, the minister, or chief of the Convent of Faile, drew from the parsonage tithes of Galston nine chalders two bolls of victual, yearly, at the period of the Reformation. Out of this, he was obliged to pay £40 annually to the exhorter, whom the Reformers placed in the church. Before the year 1471, a chapel was founded in the tower of Galston, which was dedicated to the Virgin Mary; and a chaplain was endowed for performing divine service in it. On the 3d of November, 1489, Mr John Charteris, as chaplain of Galston,* obtained a letter of confirmation of the lands of Lenfene, in Kyle-Stewart, which were settled on him for life. In 1578, the patronage of the chapel of Galston belonged to Campbell of Cesnock. The chapel was not then used; but the right of patronage seemed to give a right to the property of the chapel. After the Reformation, the patronage of the parish passed through the hands of several proprietors, and was at length acquired, in 1787, with a large estate in the parish, by Miss Scot of Scotstarvit, [late] Duchess of Portland." The old church, which was superseded by a new one in 1808, was built before the Reformation. The new church—of " a neat quadrangular building,"—occupies the site of the old, and is surrounded by the ancient burying-ground. In the interior of the church, below the north gallery, a tablet of black and white marble, bears as under : " The burial place of the Campbells of Cesnock and their descendants, the Campbells of Mayfield, extends in front of this wall 12 feet by 8 feet. To perpetuate their remembrance, this plate is put up by Bruce Campbell of Mayfield, Anno 1809."

On the east wall of the galleries, to the right on entering from the staircase, is a handsome mural monument to the memory of an illustrious native of Galston, Lieut.-Col. Hutchinson ; and to the left is another design of the same school, bearing a long record of the births, marriages, and deaths of the ancient, but now extinguished family of Nisbet of Greenholm. Both of the monuments are of marble. That of Colonel Hutchinson has the following inscription :—" In memory of George Hutchinson, Esq. of Galston, late Lieut.-Col. of his Majesty's Ninety-eight Regiment of Foot. During the American war, he was first aid-de-camp to the Right Honourable Earl Percy, and Deputy Adjutant-General of the Grand Army.

---

* In 1797, Sir Alexander Campbell of Cesnock obtained an act of Parliament for holding "yearly fairs and mercates at the towns of Galstoun and Riccartoun."

† These fires are no doubt the remains of the Druidical festival at the summer solstice.

* Alexander Arbukill was curate of Galston in 1551.

His martial abilities, undaunted bravery, and heroic feats, had long attracted the notice of his sovereign, who was graciously pleased to honour him with seven different commissions. He fell a sacrifice for his country in an Engagement in India, the 5th of September 1782, aged 46 years.

"Be thou faithful unto death,
And I will give thee a Crown of Life."

The monument of the Nisbets bears this record.

"Sacred to the memories of Archd Nisbet of Greenholm, Esq , descended of Nisbet of that Ilk, eminent in King David the First's reign, 1126, eldest son of Robert and Barbara Nisbet, who left issue six sons and four daughters  Born 6th Oct 1689 , married Elizabeth Hogg, 6th August, 1727 , died 25th Sept 1764, aged 75 years.  Had issue five sons and seven daughters by his wife Elizabeth, daughter of Hogg of Harcarse, who died 23d Aug 1756, aged 46 years  Also Ann, then daughter, born 1 Nov 1732, died 20 Aug 1749, aged 16 years "

" Sacred also to the memories of David Nisbet, M D , youngest son of Robert and Barbara Nisbet , born 10 July, 1703, married 2 Sept 1736, the eldest daughter of Sir Thomas Rinton, died 29 March, 1773, aged 70 years, leaving no issue  Also David, fourth son of Archd and Elizabeth Nisbet, born 18 Jany 1742, married Sophia Williams 8 May, 1773  This monument is erected by their fourth son, David

*Data sunt ipsis quoque fata sepulchris " *

The churchyard furnishes more than one memorial of the part which the parishioners took in the civil and religious struggle of the seventeenth century —

" This stone is erected by public contribution in the parish of Galston, in honour of those belonging to it who suffered at the glorious era of Scotland's Covenanted Reformation  May it stand for ages as a Monument of Abhorrence at Tyranny in Church and State, as a grateful and well-merited tribute to those illustrious men who successfully struggled to resist it  May it excite in the breasts of posterity an attachment to the Noble Cause of Religious and Civil Liberty, and if ever circumstances should require it, an ardour to emulate the noble deeds of their ancestors "

The west face of the stone, bearing the following inscriptions, has cut across the upper part of it a representation of " Galston's Covenanters' Flag "  On the centre of the banner is engraved a thistle, and above it an open book, bearing " God is ever the same."  Around the ends and top of the flag runs the motto, " For God and State, Kirk and

* Greenholm is in the parish of Loudoun

Covenants, and the work of Reformation," with " Galston," along its lower unfurled extremity. Above this representation is cut " Renewed in 1823," and below all is the following inscription :

" In Memory of John Richmond, younger of Know, who was executed at the Cross of Glasgow, March 19th 1684, and interred in the High Churchyard there, and James Smith, East Threepwood, who was shot near Bank on Burn, Ann 1684, by Capt Inglis and his dragoons, and buried there

" Also James Young and George Campbell, who were banished in 1679, and the Rev Alexander Blair, who suffered imprisonment, 1673 "

East Face —At the top is a miserably executed bas-relief, meant to represent one man shooting another, and between whom is a sand-glass two-thirds of their stature.  Above this scene is an open book, marked Rev. xii. & 11, and below is cut as under :

' Here lies Andrew Richmond, who was killed by bloody Graham of Claverhouse, June 1679, for his adherence to the Word of God and Scotland's Covenanted work of Reformation

" Where bloody tyrants here did rage
Over the Lord's own heritage,
To persecute his noble cause
By mischief framed into laws "
*     *     *     *     *

The remaining lines are covered by the soil *

In reference to education, it is gratifying to be able to state that it is ample.  Besides the parish school, there is now a free school, erected and endowed from £4000 left for that purpose by Charles Blair of Longhouse, one of the heritors of the parish  Another legacy of £1000 were left by John Brown of Waterhaughs, to be expended in clothing and educating an equal number of children from the parishes of Loudoun and Galston

The parish records extend as far back as 1568, although they have not been regularly kept till 1692.  The oldest of the registers is devoted to baptisms  The session minutes exhibit the usual routine of business, and the constant labours of the session to reform the habits of the people  In reference to morality, Galston does not seem to have been at all in advance of the other parishes of Ayrshire—Sabbath breaking,† and promiscuous sexual intercourse prevailing to no inconsiderable extent ‡

In 1592, when the records began to be regu-

* The Churchyards of Ayrshire  By William Dobie
† 23d March, 1628 —George Lockhart of Tempill, and John Adame of Brewlands, having been summoned before the session, "confest the break of the Sabbath be striking ilk ither "
‡ 24th September, 1628.—A scale of penalties resolved to be exacted from fornicators

larly kept, the "purse of the puir" is put down —2d April—as amounting to xlij s. 7d.

Some idea may be formed of the interior of the old church from the following minute:—"27th August, 1626. The qlk. day the sessioun condescendit that George Lockhart of Tempill his dasse sould stand and remaine still in the south-eist nuik of the kirk, with the forme qrof. it is presently set vp, ay and quhile the sessioun think expedient to build ane laft, at quhat tyme the height of the said dasse sall not exceed the cor-balls," &c.

14th January, 1629.—No caution to be exacted in proclamations of marriage. As in most other places, it had been the practice to demand pledges from the parties "buikit."

19th August, 1638.—"Qlk day the Laird of Barr delyvered to the sessioune xiii s. 4d. qlk. rested of the xiiij libs. that was send to Edinburgh to buy the Kirk Byble."

This was probably the first "Kirk Bible" possessed by the parish, although there had been an act of the Privy Council passed in 1575, ordaining "fyve pundis" to be collected in "every perochin" for the purchase of a Bible. The act is in itself curious—"That In euerith paroche kirke thair be a Byble remaining In sic forme as salbe thocht expedient be the kirke, and allowit and sett furth be our auctoritie, and that thair is gude characters and printing Irnis already within oure Realme, proper and sufficient for Wirking and Imprenting of the said Bible, and that zit the charge and hasard of the wark wilbe great and sumptuous, and may not well be performit without enery parochin, as weill to Burgh as Landwart, advance aforehande the sowme of fyve pundis, viz. for the price of the said Bible, weill and sufficientlie bunde In paist or tymmer, foure pundis xiij s. iiij pennies, and for the Collectioun the vther sax shillingis and aucht pennies : Thairfore our saide Regent, Nobilitie, Estaittis, and Counsall allowing of the saide overture, and willing to extende our auctoritie to the furtherance thereof, hes ordanit that the said sowme salbe collectit of euery parochin be the Bischoppis, &c., and brought to Alexander Arbuthnot, burgess of Edinburgh, the furnissar of the said warke."

This act had a double purpose, to extend the use of the Bible, and promote the printing of it in Scotland. Five pounds was the sum condescended upon by the Lords of Council as the price of the Bible and Collection; but we see that Galston had forwarded to Edinburgh no less a sum than fourteen pounds "to buy the kirke Bible."

Galston kirk, like those of most of the other parishes, had its Reader after the Reformation. On the 19th March, 1639, the session ordained

that the Reader, Hector Campbell, should have no wages, remuneration for his services arising from certain gratuities. By another minute, 27th December, 1639, it was statute that the session-clerk, for the performance of certain duties as reader, "and for the gude attending on ane schoole," should have "three schillings Scots from ilk fyre house within the paroche," &c.

From the proximity of Galston to Loudoun Hill, the rendezvous of Montrose after the victory of Kilsyth, the parish seems to have been in a very excited state at the time. Various parties were subsequently brought before the session to answer for their misdeeds.

"June 16, 1646.—Present, minister, Galstoune, Sornbeg," &c., certain parties were summoned for buying plundered goods from the enemy, i.e. the soldiers of Montrose. "Lykwyse compeirit James Finlay and Johne Browne, for going to Bodellbrig quhen the enemie ware ther, but denyed they stepit ther at all, and confessed that they bought a horse; lykwyse that James Findlay restored his to the owner of it, and Johne Browne hes oblished himself to restoure his lykwyse if it be challenged. However, censure ut supra.

"June 23, 1646.—Qlk day compeirit Wm. Mortoune, for buying plundered goods from Kilmarnock, quho confessed he bought some wool, but nothing else, and lykwyse that he restored it to the owner, whose censure is ut supra. Lykwyse compeired Geo. Stinstoune for the same business, quho confesses he bought a pair of old plyds, but hes not yet restored them, but hes promised to restore them if they be awned, quhose censure is ut supra."

A number of others were at the same time before the session for similar offences.

July 25, 1646.—William Law, to answer the slander of slaying another man's bull in time of confusion.

## OLD BUILDINGS.

The most ancient buildings extant in the parish are those of Bar Castle and Cesnock House, the former possessed in early times by the Lockharts of Bar, and the latter by the Campbells of Cesnock. There is no remains of a strong-house which can be assigned as the residence of the Keiths or Stewarts of Galstoun. The "tower of Galstoun" frequently occurs in old writs, and Chalmers mentions the fact of a chapel having been erected in it, so that such a building must have existed at some period or other. The castle of "Gastoune" is, in short, mentioned as in existence at the same time with that of Bar, by

Sir James Balfour, in his manuscript "Collection for the Shires of Scotland." No vestige of it, however, now remains, and "the oldest inhabitant" has no recollection of ever hearing of it. Bar Castle is now almost surrounded by the village, though originally the situation must have been at once secluded and pleasant. The tower is planted on a gentle knoll on the banks of the Burnawn. It is a massive oblong square, of moderate height, and still in good preservation—a modern slate roof having been substituted in place of the ancient stone flags. The principal entrance was by a short outside stair, reaching to the first floor above the keep. There is scarcely any vestige of additional buildings having at any time existed in connection with the tower, which seems to have retained its pristine character of a "tower," long after these buildings, by additions and alterations, had generally begun to assume the name of *places*, or mansion-houses. Bar Castle was a favourite haunt of a well-known, but unfortunate local poet of no small merit, John Wright, whose "Retrospect," and other poems, are highly creditable to the unlettered muse of Scotland. He repeatedly alludes to the tower, but more especially in one of his small pieces addressed to "Bar Castle"—

> "Bar Castle' tenantless and wild'
> Dome of delight' dear haunt of mine'
> The shock of ages thou hast failed
> Since fell the last of Lockhart's line,
> Thou, left a hermit, to grow gray
> O'er swallow, crane and bird of prey"

The walls of the old garden, though somewhat dilapidated, still enclose a space of ground devoted to gardening purposes, and in a field adjacent stands a majestic elm, among the branches of which, according to tradition, Sir William Wallace, upon one occasion, concealed himself from his foes. Whether this may be the case or not, the tree is of undoubted antiquity, as its huge sapless, hollow trunk, and bare extended withered arms, clearly evince. It is celebrated as "The Warrior's Tree," in a pleasant little volume of prose and poetry, entitled, "Recreations of Leisure Hours,"* by Archibald M'Kay, author of the "History of Kilmarnock," &c.

> "The vision has passed, but the warrior's tree.
> Though fading 'neath Time's chilling blight,
> Still waves its broad branches alone on the lea,
> The haunt of brave Wallace the Wight"

"In the trunk of the tree," says Mr M'Kay, "is a cavity ample enough to contain several persons; and apart from the story of Wallace, to the lover of nature it cannot fail to be highly interesting."

Cesnock House, which is still inhabited, is situated about a mile and a-half from Galston, farther up the Burnawn. It occupies a steep bank at one of the numerous bends of the stream, forming a natural defence on two sides of the building, and probably it was at one time defended on the other by a trench, cut from bank to bank of the picturesque Burnawn, whose beauties are depicted in language of intense local attachment by the poet already mentioned—

> "Clear, wild, romantic rill! at sound of thee
> How thrilled affection throbs through every vein!
> A lovelier fountain search were vain to see;
> From hills so rich, ne'er leaped into the main
> Thy likeness yet, nor rolled through wealthier plain
> The genius of thy waters is the maid
> That moistened Eden—and, unhurt, here reign
> Peace, love, primeval purity, arrayed
> In garb that pececancy to stain yet never strayed"

Cesnock House is a large building—several additions having, from time to time, been made to the original square tower—the whole forming rather more than three sides of a square. It yet retains, even in its deserted state, an air of mellowed grandeur, if not magnificence, amply attesting the wealth and importance of the family who once resided within its walls. It is surrounded with some fine old trees, and commands a pleasant view of Loudoun Castle, on the opposite side of the Irvine, and of a great portion of the valley

---

## FAMILIES IN THE PARISH OF GALSTON

### KEITHS, STEWARTS, AND ROSSES OF GALSTON.

Wood, in his *Peerage of Scotland*, supposes that Sir John Keith, Great Marischal of Scotland, who died before 1270, had a third son, ancestor of the

KEITHS OF GALSTOUN, in Ayrshire,† and father of the gallant Sir William Keith of Galstoun, who

---

* Kilmarnock H Crawford and Son, 1844
† Sir Edward de Keith, Great Marischal of Scotland, who succeeded in 1324, married Isabel de Keith, said to be of the family of Galstoun

repulsed the English with extraordinary valour at Berwick, in 1318. He accompanied Sir James Douglas on his expedition to Palestine with the heart of King Robert I. in 1330. He commanded in Berwick in 1333; was ambassador to England in 1335, when he obtained a safe-conduct for himself and sixty horsemen in his retinue, and was killed at the siege of Stirling with his own lance, 1336. He "left a daughter, Johanna Keith, heiress of Galstoun; married, first, to a gentleman of the name of Hamilton;* secondly, to Sir Alexander Stewart of Derneley, and had issue by both." This explains a charter, confirmed during the regency of the Duke of Albany, by Johanna de Keth, *Domina de* Gallystoun, to her son, Andrew de Hamyltoun, of her lands of Gallystoun, in the barony of Kyle, and shire of Are, viz., Tholock, Uvermomunde, Langsyde, Bryntwod, Sorne, Kirktoun, and Dundivane. The original charter is dated at Dalserff, the 10th December 1406. Among the witnesses to the charter are William de Hamyltoun, and John Stewart, sons of the said Johanna, the latter son being designated *Domina de* Crukystoun. *John Cambell of Gallystoun* is also a witness to the charter, so that the Keiths had only possessed part of the lands of Galston.

The next possessors we find of Galston were the STEWARTS—no doubt a branch of the Stewarts of Darnley.

I. William Stewart, *feodatarii de Galstoun,* whose son,

II. Thomas Stewart of Galstoun, was retoured as heir of his father, March 24, 1603, viz., " in terris de Galstoun, molendino et straith, et brasina, apud ecclesiam parochialem de Galstoun, cum 3 acris terræ eisdem spectantibus, in baronia de Tarboltoun,† et balliatu de Kyle-stewart." Old extent, £16, 13s. 4d.; new extent, £83, 6s. 8d. Thomas Stewart of Galstoun is mentioned in a variety of documents, from 1601 till 1643. In 1632 occurs the testament of Jeane Ros, spous to Thomas Stewart of Galstoun, who died in December, made and given up by the said Thomas Stewart, in name and behalf of *Margaret* and *Barbara*‡ Stewarts, their lawful bairns. He married, again, Anna Ross, a sister of his former wife. This appears from the testament of Dame Mareoune Boill, relict of vmqle. James Archbishope of Glasgow, who died in November 1636, " maid and gevin vp be

Thomas Stewart of Galstoune, hir sone-in-law," &c. " Legacie—At Glasgow, the 24th day of September, 1636 zeiris.—The quhilk day Dame Mareoun Boill, &c. Item, I heirby nominat Thomas Stewart of Galstoun, my sone-in-law, and Anna Ros, my dochter, conjunctlie, &c., my onlie executours, &c. Item, my saidis debtis being payit, I leive the rest that sall be free to be devydit betuixt the said Thomas Stewart his bairnes procreat betuixt him and vmqle. Jeane Ros, my dochter, and the said Anna Ros, my other executrix, sche being in lyf," &c. Thomas Stewart of Galstoun frequently occurs in the session records, and his name is mentioned in a testamentary document so late as 1643. He appears to have been succeeded by

III. Lodowick Stewart of Galston, who married Agnes Hamiltone.* He died at Glasgow, in May 1650, leaving apparently no issue. By his latterwill he made over his whole substance to his uncle, George Rosse of Brownhill, Renfrewshire, brother of his mother, who was afterwards styled

I. GEORGE ROSSE of Galstone.† He married, first, Grissell Maxwell, who died at Paisley on the 4th of April, 1647, leaving at least a daughter, Anna Rosse. From her testament, it appears that William Maxwell of Kowglen was the tutor of the deceased. The daughter only survived till the 4th of October of the same year. He married, secondly, Jeane Stirling, of the house of Glorat, and died in July, 1655, leaving two sons, *George* and *Munga*, but whether by his first or second wife does not appear. The following is the substance of his testament: " Lattre-will and legacies.—At Glasgow, the xix day of July, 1655. The quhilk day George Rosse of Galstone, &c., constituted William Andersone, yr., portioner of Newtone, his sole executour, &c., lykas he nominats, makes, and constitutes William Barkelay of Peirstone, James Rosse of Thornetone, and the said William Andersone, or any two of them, tutouris testamentouris to George and Mungo Ross, his lawfull children, during the zeiris of thair pupilaritie, &c. Item, he lieves in legacie to Alexander Rosse, his naturall sone, &c., the soume of ane thowsand markis, &c. Item, in caice it sall pleis God to remove the said George and Mungo Ross, his childrein, befoir they sall attaine to the aige of sevintein zeiris compleit, then, and in that

---

* The gentleman, as Wood elsewhere shows, was Sir David de Hamilton, an ancestor of the ducal house of Hamilton, who died in 1392.

† John Stewart, Lord of Kyle, eldest son of Robert, the Steward of Scotland, granted the lands of Tarbolton and Drumley to his cousin, Sir John Stewart of Darneley.

‡ 30th July, 1626.—Baptized to the laird of Galstoun ane lawfull daughter, callit Barbara.—Witnesses, Bar and Sornbeg.—PARISH RECORDS.

* Agnes Hamiltone, Ladie Galstone, occurs in the testament of Michaill Maire of Dalley, 1648. She could hardly be the wife of Thomas Stewart of Galston, although he may have married a third time.

† There were Rosses, proprietors to a considerable extent, in Galston parish before this time. Mathew Ross of Hayning was served heir of his father, " Magistri Mathei Ros de Hayning," April 15, 1619, " in terris de Hayning paroche (Hayning-Ross), Overton, Netherton, Rance, Roddingis," &c.

caice, he lieves in legacie to the persones eftir specifit, &c., to witt, to Jeane Stirling of Glorat, his
spous, the equall half of that sonne of aught thowsand markis that is dew to him be Sir Mungow
Stirling of Glorat, be vertew of his contract of
marriage; as also, to the said Katherine Rosse
of Dreghorne, the soume of ane thowsand markis,
quha is dochter lawfull to the said vnqle. John
Rosse of Dreghorne; ffarder, the said George
Rosse does heirby lieve to the said Alexander
Rosse, his sone, in caice it sall pleis God that the
said George and Mungo Ross, his childrein, sall
depairt this lyfe, &c., all and haill, the sowme of
ane thowsand markis," &c.

II. George Ross of Galstoun, one of the Commissioners of Supply in 1715.  He married, first,
Lady Christian, third daughter of James, second
Earl of Loudoun; secondly, the widow of Alexander Cranfurd of Kerse.

Previous to this, the greater portion of the lands
of Galstoun, Bar, Hayning, and other properties,
had been acquired by the growing family of Cesnock.  In 1580, we find Charles II. as heir of
Charles, Duke of Lennox, retoured, amongst
others, in the lands of Galstoune.

## LOCKHARTS OF BAR.

In the Ragman Roll (about 1297) there is a
" Malcolm Lockhart del Conte de Air," possibly
the progenitor of the Lockharts of Bar.  That
the family was of ancient standing, and had considerable ramifications in Ayrshire, there is no
doubt.  The Lockharts, during the sixteenth and
seventeenth centuries, were amongst the leading
citizens of the burgh of Ayr, some of them being
merchants of no small enterprise.  The first with
whom we meet in charters is,—

I. ANDREW LOCKHART, who had a charter of
the lands of Bar, Gallartlands, Makiswodeis, and
Newtoun, in the barony of Walter's Kyll, from
Robert III.  No date is given, but it must have
been between 1390 and 1400, the limits of that
monarch's reign.  John Lockhart, probably a
brother, or his son, had a charter of the lands of
Dalry, Auchinbert, in the barony of Walter's
Kyll, from the same monarch.  The next that
appears is,—

II. John Locarde de le Bar, one of the jury in
a dispute between the burgh of Irvine and Francis
of Stane, respecting the right to a piece of muir
ground.  The paper containing the decision, in
the archives of Irvine, is dated 1417.

III. Johne Lockhart of Bar, whose name first
occurs in connection with a feud with the Stewarts
of Ochiltree, in 1550.*   John and Hugh, his brothers-german, are also mentioned in the Criminal
Records.†  Lockhart was a zealous supporter of
Knox, and in the same year was warmly engaged
in the spoliation of various churches.  His name
occurs in a "remission to Robert, Lord Boyd, by
Henry and Marie, for assisting the Duke of Chasselherault in taking the Castles of Haddington
and Draffin," dated 23d April, 1560.‡  "In the
beginning of the year 1556, Knox was conducted
by Lockhart of Bar, and Campbell of Kinean-
cleugh, to Kyle, the ancient receptacle of the Scottish *Lollards*, where there were a number of adherents to the Reformed doctrine.  He preached in
the houses of Bar, Kineaneleugh, Carnell, Ochiltree, and Gadgirth."§  He signed the band, along
with a number of other Ayrshire gentlemen, for
the protection of Knox, when the Reformer proceeded to that county on his famous expedition
to meet Abbot Kennedy, of Corssraguel, at Maybole, in 1562.  He married a daughter of Mure
of Rowallan, relict of the laird of Newark.  He
had issue,

> 1.  James, who predeceased him.  On the 10th July, 1568,
>     was baptized William Lockhart, son to James Lock-
>     hart, younger of Bar.‖
> 2.  John, who succeeded.

He died in or before 1575, in which year his son,

IV. Johne Lockhart of Bar was served heir.
He seems, like his father, to have taken an active
interest in public affairs.  Knox mentions that
" the young laird of Bar" was " a traveller" in
the affair of a projected marriage between Queen
Mary and the King of Sweden, in 1562.  This,
however, must have referred to his elder brother,
James.  He married a daughter of Mure of Rowallan, he and his father having thus married two
sisters.

V. George Lockhart of Bar is mentioned in
the testament of John Campbell in Boirdland, in
1601.  George Lockhart of Bar again occurs in
the testament of "Williame Brown, merchand
burges of Air," in 1613; while "Johne Lockhart of Bar and his wife," are also mentioned in
the same document.

[It would appear from what follows (No. VIII.),
that the lands of Bar passed about this time from
the Lockharts of Bar into the hands of their relatives, the Lockharts of Boghall, near Ayr.]

VI. Johnne Lockhart of Bar, who died in
1614, and from whose latter-will the following is
an extract:—"Testament, &c. and Inuentor, &c.

---

* Vol. i. p. 952.
† He had another brother, Alexander, killed, according
to Knox, at the siege of Leith.
‡ Boyd Charter Chest.
§ M'Crie's Knox.
‖ Parish Records.

qlks. perteinit to vmqle. Johnne Lockhart of Bar, . . . Quha deceist in the moneth of Aprile, 1614, ffaytfullie maid and gevin vp be his awin mouth, &c.

. . . . . . . . . . To Johnne Lockhart, sone to *George Lockhart, sumtyme of Bar,*[*] to be payit to him eftir the deceis of his fether and mother, the sowme of fyve thowsand and thrie hundrith markis. To William Cvnynghame, tutor of Aiket, Twa thowsand and sevin hundrith markis. To Jeane Cvnynghame, dochter to the Laird of Robertland, Twa thowsand twa hundrith markis. . . . To James Campbell of Steinstoun, his bairnes, aucht hundrith markis.

Legacie. At Air, the saxtein day of Aprile, 1614, The quhilk day the said vmqle. Johnne committis his saull to God, his creatour and maker, to be with him in glorie as redeimit with the pretious bluid of his saviour and redeemer, Jesus Chryst; and ordanes his bodie to be bureyt in the kirkzaird of Air, in the burial place of his vmqle. father. Item, he nominats, &c. Marcoun Cvnynghame, his spous, Johnne, Margret, and Jonet Lockharts, his bairnes, his onlie executouris, &c. Item, he willis and ordanes the said Marcoun Cvnynghame, his spous, to intromit, &c., quhill the said Johnne Lockhart, his sone, be twentie ane zeir of age compleit, quherby scho may keip and hald him at the scholls credutioune and vertew, quhill they may defray and pay to the said Johnne Lockhart of Bar, his Lawfull debtis awand be him. Item, the said Johnne Lockhart of Bar loveinglie intreitis, requeistis his honorabill and loving Maisters, Alexander Erle of Dumfermling, Chanceler of Scotland, my Lord Abircorne, my Lord of Lowdoun, and Sir Claud Hamiltoun of knyt, to tak the patronomie of his puir wyf and bairnes, and to sie thame nocht opprest nor wrangit. Item, he wills and requeistis his guid freindis, Wm. M'Kerrell of Hillhouse and Johnne Power, merchand, burges of Edinburgh, to concur with his wyf and bairnes in all the lautfull adois, as he wold evir bein reddy to do the lyk for thame. Item, he levis to the puir ane hundrith markis, [he concludes by several small bequests to his servants,] and this testament, maid at day, zeir, and place foirsaid, befoir thir witness, *Hew Lockhart*, his brother-germane, George Masoun, notar," &c. Marconn Cvnynghame, Lady Bar, died in January, 1623.

VII. John Lockhart of Bar, son of the preceding, succeeded. He died in April, 1624. He seems to have died suddenly, as he is one of the

<hr>

[*] In the testament of the master of Loudoun, 1612, John Lockhart is mentioned as "son to George Lockhart, sumtyme of Bar."

executors appointed in the testament of George Campbell of Cesnock, who died in February of the same year. It was probably a daughter of this laird of Bar, Margaret, who was married to Neil Montgomerie of Lainshaw, about 1630.

VIII. Johnne Lockhart of Bar was served heir to Alexander Lockhart of Boghall, his grandfather, in the lands of Boghall, &c., 24th June, 1630. His name, which is attached to the "solemn league and covenant," in 1640, repeatedly occurs in the session records from 1626. He is mentioned as one of the overseers in the testament of Mr Alexander Blair, minister at Galston, in 1643, and "Jon. Lockhart of Bar" again occurs in a similar document, in 1651.

IX. John Lockhart of Bar and his lady, Barbara Jamieson, are mentioned in the town records of Ayr, in 1672. Sometime before, the estate of Bar, and others in the vicinity, were acquired by the Campbells of Cesnock. In 1686, the lands of Cesnock, Galstoun, *Barr*, &c., belonging to Sir Hugh and George Campbells, were disjoined from the Crown in favour of John Viscount Melfort.

### SCHAWS OF SORNBEG.

The Schaws of Sornbeg were a branch of the ancient family of Hayley. They appear to have acquired Sornbeg, and other lands, from the noble house of Cathcart by wadset. The first of them was,

I. ANDREW SCHAW of Sornbeg, son to Hayley. He was infeft in the lands of Sornbeg, Polkemmet, Whitburn, and other lands in the shire of Ayr and Linlithgow, &c., 21st May, 1447.

II. Alexander Schaw of Sornbeg and Polkemmet, his son, resigned the lands of Polkemmet in favour of Sir Robert Hamilton of Preston, in 1486. He was succeeded by his son,

III. William Schaw of Sornbeg. He was infeft in the lands of Polkemmet and Sornbeg on the 14th March, 1486, and in the lands of Flockside, in the shire of Renfrew, 20th April, 1487. He was succeeded by his son,

IV. John Schaw of Sornbeg, who was infeft in the lands of Flockside, &c., 28th May, 1529.

V. Andrew Schaw of Sornbeg, his son, was served heir in special to William Schaw of Sornbeg and Polkemmet, his grandfather, in the five pound land of old extent of Helington; five pound land of old extent of Knockindale; fifty shilling land of old extent of Goldring; the lands, barony, and fortalice of Sornbeg, and others, in the shire of Ayr, 18th December, 1547. The lands of Polkemmet, Sornbeg, Foulshiels, &c., having fallen into the hands of Queen Mary, by reason of non-entry, in 1549, they were gifted to David Hamilton of Preston, in trust, it would appear, for Andrew Schaw, the nearest heir, upon which he obtained a charter, under the Great Seal, in favour of himself and John Schaw, his son, dated 4th March, 1550. In 1555, he purchased the lands of Hayley from his relative, John Schaw. The sasine, proceeding upon a charter of feu-right, was in favour of " Andre Schaw and *Robert Schaw*, his son, of Sornbeg." In 1589, Andrew Schaw was infeft in the lands of Flockside, upon a precept forth of the Chancellary, as heir to his father, John; and, on the 2d March, 1590, he obtained a charter from Queen Mary in favour of himself and his son, John,* of the lands of Sornbeg and others. He married Helene Ross, who died in 1551. Her testament is dated at Galston, the last day of February in that year. It was written in Latin by Alexander Arbukill, curate of Galston. She directed that her body should be buried in the church of St Peter of Galston, and that 4s. should be given toward the repair of the church of Glasgow. Her executors were, Andrew Schaw, her spouse, and John, Robert, and William, her sons. Amongst the debts owing was a sum of £253, 6s. 8d. Scots, due by Hugh Wallace of Carnell, restand of a contract of marriage between John Schaw, son and heir of Andrew, and Helen Wallace, daughter of the said Hugh. Amongst the witnesses was William Schaw, brother of Andrew. He was succeeded by his eldest son,

VI. John Schaw of Sornbeg, who married, 28th April, 1550,† as already indicated, Helen Wallace, daughter of Wallace of Carnel, or Cairnhill. He was succeeded by his son,

VII. John Schaw of Sornbeg, in 1592. He was infeft upon a precept forth of the Chancellary, as heir to Andrew Schaw, his grandfather, in the foresaid lands of Sornbeg, Hedington, Knockindale, Goldring, &c.; and, on the 28th October, 1608, he was infeft in the lands of Polkemmet, &c., as heir to John Schaw of Polkemmet, his father. In 1615, upon his own resignation, he obtained a charter from James VI. erecting the haill lands into the barony of Sornbeg; and, in 1620, he granted a charter to his son, Patrick, at his marriage, of the lands of Polkemmet.

Agnes Dunbar, Ladie Sornbeg, who died in 1603, must have been the wife of this laird of Sornbeg. In her testament, she constituted " Mr Ard. Drummuire, scholemaster at Air, hir guidsone, and Janet Schaw, hir dochter, his spous,

executouris and intromittouris with hir guids and geir." She left " ane zoung kow" to her " oye, John Drummuire."

The laird survived till 1623; at least there was a John Schaw of Sorubeg died in that year, who had a daughter, *Agnes*, married to Johne Masoune in Barnaiche. He was succeeded by his son,

VIII. Patrick Schaw of Sornbeg. He is mentioned as of Sornbeg in the testament of Robert Broune, merchand in Kilmarnock, in 1628, although his service as heir to his father did not take place till 25th August, 1631. He signed the " Solemn League and Covenant" in 1640, and his name occurs in testamentary documents, and in the parish records, down till 1646. He resigned in favour of John, his son, and John, his grandson, who were infeft under the Great Seal in 1699. He married a daughter of Durham of Duntervie, by whom he had his heir, and, as appears from the parish register, another son called *Thomas*. " 24th of July 1626.—Baptized to Patrick Schaw of Sornbeg ane lawfull soune, caillit Thomas; witnesses, John Lockhart of Bar, Johne Neilsoune of Maxwood."

IX. John Schaw of Sornbeg, his son and successor, married, in 1651, Isabel Boswell, second daughter of David Boswell of Auchinleck, by whom he had,

X. John Schaw of Sornbeg, who married Marion Kennedy, daughter of Kennedy of Kilhenzie. He had a mortification of his property in 1672. He had issue :

1. John, his successor.
2. Alexander, writer in Edinburgh.
1. Anne, married to Graham of Drynie.
2. Catharine, married to Mackenzie of Suddie.

XI. Captain John Schaw of Sornbeg held a commission in the First Royals, with which regiment he served in America. He was served heir to his father and grandfather in 1720.

## CAMPBELL OF CESNOCK.

It seems to be pretty satisfactorily shown by Robertson, from the entail executed by Hugh Lord Loudoun in 1613, that the ancestor of the Cesnock family must have been a second son of George Campbell, No. VII. of Londonn. The name, however, has not been ascertained.

I. —— CAMPBELL of Cesnock. He married Lady Janet Montgomerie, seventh daughter of Hugh, first Earl of Eglintoun. This appears from the Records of Parliament, 7th November, 1513, —the Earl having become surety for his daughter, Janet, Lady Cesnock.

II. John Campbell of Cesnock, no doubt the son of the foregoing. He married Janet, third

---

daughter of Sir Hugh Campbell of Loudoun, his cousin-german,—which marriage, according to Craufurd, took place in 1553. He was succeeded apparently by his son,

III. George Campbell of Cesnock, mentioned in Knox's History of the Reformation before 1550.

IV. George Campbell of Cesnock was served heir to his father on the 16th of October, 1578, in the £42 lands of Cesnock and Galston,* of old extent, which, in the reckoning of those times, makes a very considerable property. There is also a Crown charter, dated 6th February, 1597, in favour of George Campbell of Cesnock, and Agnes Cuninghame, his spouse, a lady of the Caprington family.

Robertson supposes that this is the George Campbell of Cesnock mentioned in the Loudoun entail of 1613, and who, after the death of his first wife, married secondly a daughter of Ker of Kersland. There is good reason to believe, however, that they were two different persons. Besides the long interval between the succession and the death of the party, according to Robertson, and the fact of two marriages, the *second* George, according to our view of the matter, is styled " *Mr* George Campbell of Cesnock," in a testamentary document in 1600,—showing that he had been brought up to some of the learned professions, and must have been a different person from George No. IV., probably his son.

V. Mr George Campbell of Cesnock married Anna, daughter of Daniel Ker of Kersland. In Kersland's will, 1613, " George Campbell of Cesnock" appears as a creditor for " thrie thowsand markis" " restand of his tocher guid, conforme to his contract of mariage."† His name also occurs as one of the legatees in the will of the Master of Loudoun, who died in 1612, and as a creditor for eleven hundred and fifty marks in that of Lady Loudoun, in 1617. He was one of the commissioners appointed by Parliament, in 1608, to regulate the price of hides, " buits and shoone," in consequence of " the grite and extraordinair derth and pryces rasit vponne the buitis and shone through all pairtis of this countrey." He died in 1624. The following is an extract of his will :— " Legacie.—At the towre of Galstoune,‡ the tent day of Februar 1624.—The quhilk day George

Campbell of Cesnok nominats, &c., Anna* Ker, my spous, my only executrix, &c. Item, I nominat, &c., the said Anna Ker, my spous, tutrix testamenter to Hew, George, † and Margaret Campbells, my bairnes, procreat betwixt me and hir; and ordanes in speciall Alexr. Erle of Eglintoune, John Lord of Loudoun, Sir William Cvnynghame of Caprington, knyt, and David Dunbar of Enterkin, to be oversearis, &c. . . . . with the assistance of Kersland, my guid-brother, and the laird of Blackbie (?) That my leving be tane vp for the weile of my hous, and releif of my burdingis, as they sall answer to God. Item, I ordane my said spous to content and pay thir legacies vnderwrittin to the persones eftir specifit, viz. Imprimis, to the distressit minesterie, and to be distributit be sicht of Mr James Cvnynghame, minister at Cesnock, Mr James Greg, minister at New Mylnes, Mr James Inglis, minister at Daylie, and Mr James Bonar, minister at Mayboill, the sowme of fyve hundrith markis." How long his lady, Anna Ker, survived him, does not appear, but she was alive in 1630. He was succeeded by his son,

VI. Hew Campbell of Cesnock, who, on the 27th May, 1630, was retonred heir to his father in the £20 land, old extent, of Cesnock, the eighth part of the muir of Galstoun, and the fourth part of the muir of Cesnock,—from which it appears that the property, though still extensive, had been considerably reduced. He married Lady Elizabeth, second daughter and co-heiress of George, Master of Loudoun, and with her obtained considerable estates, part of the family lands of Loudoun; so that, besides being the male representative of that noble family, the descendants of this marriage are also nearest in blood to the Loudoun Campbells, failing the descendants of Lady Margaret, the eldest sister. By this marriage, according to Robertson, there were four sons:

1. George, born in 1639,‡ who was knighted in his fathers time.
2. James, ancestor of Treesbanks.
3. Captain Hugh Campbell of Barquharrie.§
4. John, ancestor of Fairfield.‖

Hew Campbell of Cesnock was a member for the county of Ayr in the Parliament which met in 1639 and 1641, and in which Charles I. attended in person. He was of the Presbyterian party

---

* Part of the lands of Galston only—a portion being then in the possession of the Stewarts of Galston.

† George Campbell of Cesnock obtained the lands of Tulloch, which formerly belonged to William Wallace of Dulland, and Andrew Faulds, from Alexander Nisbet of Greenholm, 12th June, 1613.—BOYD PAPERS.

‡ The Cesnock portion of the lands of Galston had thus contained the old tower.

* In the testament of Margaret Schaw, Riccartoun, she is styled " Nans Ker, Lady Cesnock."

† " George Campbell, brother-german to the laird of Cesnock," is witness to a baptism in 1637.

‡ George, son to Hew Campbell of Cesnock, was baptized 17th March, 1639. Witnesses, Johne Lord Loudoun, John Lockhart of Bar.—PAROCHIAL REGISTER.

§ It is somewhat doubtful whether Captain Hugh was a son or grandson of Sir Hew. If a son, he must have been nearly 60 years of age when he married, in 1702.

‖ This is also questionable.

during the troubles which led to the death of
Charles I  In 1643 the laird of Cesnock was one
of the committee of war, and, along with the lairds
of Rowallan and Houstoun, had the command of
all the cavalry of the county, save those of Carrick, which were to be commanded by such as the
Earl of Cassillis "sall appoynt"  He had the
same appointment in 1648.  He opposed the establishment of the Commonwealth in Scotland,* and
was one of the representatives of Ayrshire in the
Parliament held in 1649 and 1650 by Charles II
in person  He appears to have been knighted
about this time, for in 1649, we find Sir Hew
Campbell of Cesnock supplicating Parliament to
have his purchase confirmed of the hundreth and
nine merkland of Riccarton, which he had acquired
from the laird of Craigie, elder, Sheriff-depute of
Edinburgh  He was appointed Lord Justice-
Clerk by the Parliament of 1649, and is so styled
in the records, but it appears he declined to act

Sir Hew took no part in public affairs at the
Restoration in 1660, and it seems rather unaccountable, in the absence of any specific charge
against him, that he should have been one of those
exempted from the act of indemnity passed in
1662  On the contrary, he was subjected to
heavy fines, first of £800 Scots, and again of
£1500  In 1665, Sir Hew was confined in the
Castle of Edinburgh for two years, and not liberated till he granted a bond to keep the peace
No reason was ever assigned for such tyrannical
procedure  In 1683, both Sir Hew and his son,
Sir George, were thrown into prison, on a charge
of having been concerned in the rising at Bothwell  In 1684, Sir Hew was brought to trial  He
was defended by his friend, Sir Patrick Hume of
Polwarth, advocate, but, as related by Wodrow,
he would have been convicted but for the breaking down of a witness apparently suborned and
paid to give evidence  The witness was so conscience struck with the manly appearance of Sir
Hew at the bar, that he would not confirm, on
oath, what he had previously declared  Sir Hew
was in consequence acquitted †

Notwithstanding of their acquittal, both father
and son were still detained in prison; and in the
following year were again put upon trial as acces-
sories to the Ryehouse Plot  At the trial, the
Cesnocks, elder and younger, admitted that "they
were at the meeting mentioned in Monro's deposition, and threw themselves upon the king's mercy."  The Parliament accordingly found the dit-
tay proven, and sentence of forfaulture was pronounced against them—their lives being spared,
in consequence of their having thrown themselves
upon the mercy of the court  Their estates were
accordingly annexed to the Crown, and Sir Hew
and his son ordered into confinement in the Bass,
until his majesty's pleasure should be known.  The
following year, 1686, the estate was disjoined from
the Crown, and conferred upon John Drummond,
Viscount of Melfort, one of the cabinet, by whom,
it is supposed, the accusation against the Campbells had been chiefly urged  The property is
thus described in the Act —"The lands and barony of Riccarton, the lands and barony of Cesnock and Galstoun, with the tower of Cesnock,
and pertinents, the lands and barony of Castle-
mains and Cumnock, and the lands and barony of
Haining-Ross—all lying within the sheriffdom of
Ayr, formerly possessed by Sir Hugh and Sir
George Campbell, some time of Cesnock."

Sir Hugh Campbell did not long survive his
unjust forfeiture and harsh treatment  It should
seem that, on account of his infirmities, he had
been relieved from his imprisonment in the Bass,
and had come to Edinburgh, where he died, on
the 20th September, 1686, which appears from
an old memorandum-book, in the possession of a
descendant —"Monday, September 20th, 1686
Sir Hugh Campbell died this day, in his son
Hugh's chambers, in Edinburgh, of seven days
sickness, which he contracted on the Monday
night previous.  He was buried by torch light, at
6 o'clock on the Thursday following, in the Grey-

* It is, however, somewhat questionable whether he was
hearty in this opposition  In 1650, Lord Mauchline and
Colonel Robert Montgomerie complain to Parliament, that
of the 500 horse appointed to be raised in Ayrshire, only
116 had been brought in by the Earl of Eglintoun, and
139 by Cesnock, while Colonel Kennedy of Kirkhill had
not brought in his number

† His own defence was,—" That though several field-
conventicles had been kept in the country where he lived,
yet he had permitted none to be upon his ground, that
neither himself, children, or servants, had been present at
any of them, that as he kept his own parish church regularly, so, missing two of his servants there one Lord's-day,
he caused them to be kept out of his gates till the Sabbath
was over, and next morning called for them, paid them
their wages and dismissed them, that during the time of

the libelled rebellion, he was so far from encouraging it,
that he retired to Gilchrist (perhaps writ for Gilcherscroft,)
a strong house, and abode there till it was over, that he
had put off his ground all his tenants who were said to be
at Bothwell, as soon as they were convict, that if he was
found guilty in that matter, he was most willing to underly
the law, but he knew he was innocent, that one of the witnesses adduced against him he never saw before, as far as
he knew, but could prove he had declared in several places
that he would do Cesnock an ill turn, because he had informed about a murder he (the witness) had committed "
The proof against him simply amounted to this—" That
the pannel having met with the persons mentioned coming
from the rebels in arms, June 1679, and having asked them
where they had been, and when they had told him they
had come from the westland army, he said, he had seen
more going to them than coming from them, and he having asked them if they were to return, and they answered
they knew not, said to them, he liked not runaways, and
that they should get help if they bide by it "—Wodrow

friars' churchyard, aged 71 years in March, 1686. Note.—I understand that Sir Hugh Campbell's death was occasioned by being at that time, in consequence of some false information, taken to the Canongate jail, which brought on bad health, and killed him."

Soon after the Revolution, there was an act passed in Parliament, rescinding all the forfeitures and fines that had occurred since the year 1665. The lands of Cesnock were consequently restored to the family.

VII. Sir George Campbell of Cesnock was served heir to his father on the 5th March, 1691. In the previous year he had been appointed Lord Justice-Clerk, and one of the Lords of Session. Sir George married, in 1665, Mrs Anna M'Mouran, heiress of an estate in Fife, as appears from a charter in his favour, dated the 24th of November of that year. By this lady he had three daughters: Mary, the eldest, was married to William Gordon of Earlstoun, without issue. Christian, the youngest, was married to Dr Francis Pringle. The second daughter, Margaret, was married in 1697, to Sir Alexander Hume, advocate, afterwards Earl of Marchmont. He was the second son of Sir Patrick Hume of Polwarth, the great friend of the late Sir Hugh Campbell, and of the family; and who had himself suffered great hardships during the persecutions that preceded the Revolution; but in reward for his signal services, had been, in 1696, constituted Lord High Chancellor of Scotland, and, in 1697, was created Earl of Marchmont.

VIII. Sir Alexander Hume, on the death of Sir George, assumed the name of Campbell, and, in right of his wife, succeeded to the property of Cesnock. He was a man of great abilities, and filled, at different times, several high and confidential offices in the State. He became second Earl of Marchmont, on the death of his father, in 1724, his elder brother, Patrick, Lord Polwarth, having died in 1710. He himself died in 1740. By his lady, Margaret of Cesnock, he had four sons:—

1. George, Lord Polwarth, who died in 1724, in the twenty-first year of his age.
2. Patrick, who died the same year.
3. Hugh, of whom afterwards.
4. Alexander Hume Campbell, a twin-brother with Hugh. He married Miss Pettis; but died without issue in 1760, in the fifty-third year of his age.

There were four daughters, of whom two were married, but only one had issue, namely,—

Lady Anne Hume Campbell, married to Sir William Purves of Purveshall, Berwickshire.

IX. Hugh, third Earl of Marchmont, third son of Sir Alexander Hume Campbell, the second Earl, succeeded his father in 1740. He died in 1794, in the eighty-sixth year of his age. He was a man of distinguished abilities, and of great political and literary talents. He was one of the representative Peers of Scotland from 1750 till 1784, "during which he punctually attended the House of Lords, taking an active part in business, being exceeded by none in Parliamentary information and experience." He was twice married: first, to Miss Anne Western, by whom he had Patrick, Lord Polwarth, who died young, and three daughters. He married, secondly, Elizabeth Crompton, by whom he had a son, Alexander, Lord Polwarth, afterwards a British Peer, by the title of Lord Hume of Berwick. The Earl alienated the ancient estate of the Campbells, concentrating his whole property in Berwickshire, the more ancient seat of his own family.

*Arms of Cesnock*—Girony of eight pieces, or and sable, for Argyle; within a bordure, gules, charged with eight escalops of the first; and a canton, also girony of eight pieces, ermine and gules, for Loudoun.

*Crest*—A Phœnix head erased, or.

*Motto*—Constanter et prudenter.

The arms of *Hume Campbell* are to be seen on a brass plate, still on the door of Cesnock house.

The property of Cesnock has passed through various hands since it was alienated by the Marchmont family. The Dicks of Cesnock seem to have been the next proprietors. John Dick of Cesnock had a daughter, baptized October 17, 1719, called Marjory;[*] and, again, a son, whose name is not mentioned, on the 11th February, 1721. Cesnock was subsequently acquired by John Wallace, second son of John Wallace of Cairnhill, who possessed it before 1778, in which year, 23d September, "John Wallace of Cesnock" had a son, *William*, baptized.[†] He had another son, *James Maxwell*, baptized, born 21st February, 1783. Soon after this, in 1787, Cesnock was acquired by the trustees of Miss Scott, late Duchess of Portland, and it now remains in the hands of the Duke.

CAMPBELL OF BARQUHARRIE AND MAYFIELD.

There were several branches of the Cesnock family, the principal amongst whom, connected with the parish of Galston, was the Campbells of Barquharrie and Mayfield. According to Robertson,

* Session Records.
† Ibid.

I CAPTAIN HUGH CAMPBELL of Barquharrie
was the third son, or grandson, of Sir Hugh Campbell of Cesnock and Elizabeth, second daughter
of George, master of Loudoun   He married, 5th
June, 1702, Margaret Boswell, second daughter
of David Boswell of Auchinleck, by Anne, daughter of James Hamilton of Dalziel, and had issue

II  Hugh Campbell of Barquharrie, afterwards
of Mayfield,* Comptroller of the Customs at Ayr.
He married, 10th January, 1727, Margaret,
daughter of David Henderson of Tinochside, by
whom he had, says Robertson, three sons, Hugh,
Claud, and Bruce.  He had, however, at least
another son, whose name occurs as follows in the
parochial registers   "Hume Campbell, son of
Hew Campbell of Barquharrie, was born and baptized at the Tower of Cesnock, the 15th of January, 1712," but this son may have died young

III  Bruce Campbell, the youngest, was designed of Mayfield and Milrig, or of Hillhouse, as
he is sometimes styled in the parochial registers,
from which it seems probable that his elder brothers had died early, or unmarried   He married
Annabella, daughter of James Wilson, Esq , Kilmarnock, by whom he had issue —

1　Hugh of Barquharrie, Captain in the 85th regiment,
　　who married, 18th December, 1797, Sophia, youngest
　　daughter of Thomas Barber Esq of Greasley in Not-
　　tinghamshire and dying at Bath, 5th January, 1824,
　　left issue
　　　1　Hugh Bruce of Barquharrie, now residing at Not-
　　　　tingham, born 8th April 1808, who married, first,
　　　　Anne daughter of —— Hurd, Esq of Kentish
　　　　Town, by whom he had no issue, and, secondly,
　　　　in October, 1832, Elizabeth daughter of E Werge,
　　　　Esq of Hexgrave Park, Nottinghamshire
　　　2　Thomas Alexander
　　　3　William
　　　4　John
　　　1　Anne, married to the late George Douglas, Esq
　　　　of Roddinghead, Ayrshire
　　　2　Annabella, married to William Comyn, Esq of
　　　　the county Clare
　　　3　Sophia Elizabeth married to Denis Browne, Esq
　　　　of Brownestown, Ireland
2　Bruce born 4th May, 1773, Captain E I C's Naval
　　Service, died unmarried
3　Alexander born September, 1778,† a Captain in the
　　74th regiment, and of distinguished bravery  Of his
　　services particularly at the memorable battle of Assaye,
　　honourable mention is frequently made in Col Welch's
　　"Reminiscences of India"  He died of his wounds,
　　in October, 1 05   The Duke of Wellington, on hear-
　　ing of his death, wrote a very complimentary letter to
　　his brother dated Berkley Square, March, 1806  "He
　　was an officer," says the Duke, " with whom I had the
　　advantage of serving frequently, and I never knew
　　one of his rank and situation in whom I could place
　　more confidence, with a more certain belief that my
　　expectations from him would not be disappointed "
4　John, late in Sornbeg
5　William, born 4th May, 1788, died in January, 1830

* Mayfield was part of the lands of Galston, formerly
belonging to the Stewarts
† "Alexander, son to Bruce Campbell of Hillhouse, born
23d September, 1778 "—PAROCHIAL REGISTER

1  Euphemia, married to her cousin, Hugh Wilson, Esq,
　　Kilmarnock, and died in 1817, leaving a son, Hugh
　　Campbell Wilson
2  Marianne, died in April, 1825, unmarried

Besides these, there are the baptisms of a son and
two daughters recorded in the parish registers
Bruce Campbell of Mayfield had a son, whose
name is not given, born on Thursday, 20th January, 1774, "about half an hour after 11 at
night ." "Susanna, daughter to Bruce Campbell
of Hillhouse, Esq., born on Sabbath, 23d of September, 1777," and "Margaret Boyd, daughter
to Bruce Campbell of Hillhouse, born 11th February, 1782 "

Mr Campbell died in February, 1813, aged 79
He sold the estate of Milrig, which formed part
of the paternal property acquired from Cesnock,
to Colonel Hughs, who, in turn, disposed of it
to the late —— Gordon, Esq of Milrig   It is
now possessed by Captain A. D. Tait.

*Arms*—Girony of eight pieces, or and sable,
within a bordure, gules, charged with eight escallops, of the first, and a canton, also girony of
eight pieces, ermine and gules
*Crest*—A Phœnix head, erased.
*Motto*—Constanter et prudenter

There were several other families of the name
of Campbell, all connected with Cesnock or Lou-
doun, in the parish of Galston, such as Campbell
of Windyhill, Campbell of Waterhaughs, &c.
Amongst other small proprietors, there were the
Lockharts of Templil, Adams of Brewland, Neil-
souns of Maxwood, Rosses of Hayning, Meikles
of Clokisland, Patouns of Straith, Richmonds of
Pennsland, Mitchells of Escherzairdis, Mitchels of
Littlemont, &c *
Of the modern proprietorships of Lanfine and
Holmes we have little information
The lands of Lanfine belonged to the Church.
In 1489, as Chalmers states, Mr John Charteris,
as chaplain of Galston, obtained a letter of con-
firmation of them for life  After the Reformation,
they were acquired by Lockhart of Bar, who took
an active part in the overthrow of the Popish
ecclesiastical structure   The properties of Green-

* The following list of the heritors of Galston parish
occurs in the presbytery records, 26th April, 1727 :—" The
heritors of Galston being called, there compeired John,
Duke of Glasnock, for the Earl of Marchmont , the lairds
of Greenholm, Waterhaughs, Bruntwood, Bankhead, Mr
Fawsyde, by his letter, Alexander Morison of Cowrsbrae-
head, John Aitain, for David Crawford, John Browning
of Bankhouse, John Adam of Brewlands, John Gebbie of
Middlethird, William Findlay of Crofthead, Alexander
Meikle of Strath, John Woodburn of Ashyards, James
Young of Whitehorn, Alexander Meikle of Priestland,
Hugh Brown, for John Smith of Ashyards, John Aiton of
Tilloch and Growcraig; James Brown of Ronaldcamp "

holme* and Lanfine were acquired by JOHN BROWN, of the well-known Glasgow banking firm of Carrick, Brown, & Co., who was succeeded by the late NICOL BROWN of Lanfine. The present proprietor, THOMAS BROWN, second cousin of Nicol, is liferented in the lands of Lanfine. He is heir to his brother of Langside, near Glasgow.

The Holmes appears to have been the lands styled of old "Stewart-Gallesholme," or the holm lands of Galston. They were purchased from the Earl of Marchmont in 1770, by Mr Patrick Clark, merchant. "Janet Clark, daughter of Patrick Clark of Holmes and Margaret Fairley, being their fourth daughter, born 21st June, 1785."† They had also a daughter, born at Holmes, 5th June, 1789. On the death of Mr Clark, in 1796, the Holmes was purchased by the late MUNGO FAIRLIE, one of three brothers who made fortunes in the East and West Indies. Mungo died a bachelor in 1819, and was succeeded by his nephew, the present proprietor, JAMES FAIRLIE of Holmes.

### FAIRLIE OF HOLMES.

The Fairlies, of whom Holmes is a branch, are understood to be descended from the Fairlies of that Ilk, near Largs. About 1650, the principal part of the property was alienated to Boyle of Kelburn. A cadet of the family,

I. THOMAS FAIRLIE settled in Irvine about the middle of the seventeenth century, and married Jane Francis, of the ancient family of Francis of Stane, and had one son,

---

* The estate of the ancient family of Nisbet, in Loudoun parish.

† Parish Register.

II. James, who was twice married, and had a family by both wives. By his first, Jane Davidson, there were three sons, the eldest,

III. John, married Agnes, eldest daughter of Mungo Mure of Bruntwood, and had issue, four sons and three daughters, the eldest son,

IV. James, of Bellfield, shire of Ayr, and formerly of Jamaica, married Sarah Bell, relict of John Mitchell, Esq., and had issue, three daughters and one son,

V. James, the present proprietor of Holmes, Lieut.-Colonel Commandant of the Ayrshire Yeomanry, a deputy-lieutenant and justice of the peace of the county of Ayr. He succeeded his father in 1819, and his uncle, Mungo Fairlie of Holmes, in the same year. He married, in 1821, Agnes Maria, eldest daughter of the late William Fairlie of London, and formerly of Calcutta, and has issue,—

1. James, Bengal Light Cavalry.
2. William, merchant in Calcutta.
3. Mungo.
4. John Robert, Madras Light Cavalry.
5. Edward.
6. Patrick.
7. Charles Hay.
8. Henry Alexander.
1. Margaret Ogilvy, married R. H. H. Knightley, Esq. of H.M. 7th regiment.
2. Sarah Adelaide.
3. Agnes Maria.
4. Mary Jane Sophia.
Louisa Emmeline Ann, and Thomas Francis, died in infancy.

Arms—Argent, on a cheveron sable, between three water budgets of the second, as many mollets, or, all within a bordure ermine.

Crest—A lion's head couped proper.
Motto—Meditare.

# PARISH OF GIRVAN.

The name of this parish is of Celtic derivation
The town of Girvan, where the church stands, was
of old called *Inver-Garvan* from its being erected
at the mouth of the river Garvan, which here enters the sea  *Gari-Ivan* or *Garvan* signifies
the rough or rapid river—a name peculiarly descriptive of the Girvan  The river thus gave the
name to the town, and the town to the parish.*

"This parish,' says the Statistical Account,
"lies on the sea-coast of Carrick, about midway
between the well-known points of Bennan and
Turnberry.  Its length, from south-south-west to
north-north-east, is nine imperial miles, and its
breadth from two to seven miles  The mean
breadth, as nearly as can be computed, is four
miles, which gives a surface of 36 square miles, or
19,000 acres  It is bounded on the east by the
parishes of Dailly and Bar  on the south by the
parish of Colmonell, on the west, for nearly its
whole length, by the sea, and on the north by
the parish of Kirkoswald "

The parish is somewhat mountainous, a ridge of
hills, of considerable height, stretching diagonally
across the district  The highest point of this rather commanding range is not less than 12,000
feet above the level of the sea.  "On the south
side of it the ground is high and coarse and where
not cultivated, covered with heath  On the north
side, though not uniformly level, it is low, and of
fine quality "  The climate, in consequence of the
inequality of the surface, is of course variable—
being much colder in the high than the lower portions of the parish, still, from the light, dry quality of the soil, it is on the whole most salubrious
Springs of water are both excellent and numerous,

and there are at least three running streams connected with the parish—the Girvan, the Lendal,
which falls into the sea at Carleton Bay, and the
Assel, a tributary of the Stinchar  There are,
however, only two small lochs in the parish, Loch-
ton and Laggan

Whatever may have been in ancient times, there
is now no natural wood in the parish, and but a
few patches of modern plantation.*  The late Sir
Hew Dalrymple Hamilton of Bargany was the
first to plant on a small scale, and since his time
several of the proprietors have followed the example  As in most other parishes, great improvements have been made in agriculture.  The statement of the writer in the Statistical Account furnishes the best evidence of this  Forty years ago,
he says, "there were about 1700 head of black
cattle, and 214 scores of sheep, in the parish ;
whereas now there is only about the one-half of
either  The cattle were then almost all of the
Galloway breed, and the sheep of the small black-
faced kind  These have been succeeded, the former by the Ayrshire breed, chiefly for the dairy,
and the latter, by a much larger boned stock of
the black-faced, and in some instances, by Che-
viots  The reason of the decrease in the numbers
of live stock, therefore, are obvious  In the first
place, the animals are both heavier and better fed
than formerly, and, in the second place, there is
now a much greater proportion of the land bearing grain than there was at the period above al-

---

* Burns thought the name of the river so "horridly pro-
saic," that, in his inimitable song,

"Behind yon hills where Girvan flows,"

he changed it to "Lugar," which he deemed more poetical

---

* This is somewhat curious  Abercrummie, in his "Description of Carrick," written shortly before the Revolution
in 1688, says  "No countrey is better provyded of wood,
for alongst the banks of Dun, Girvan, and Stinchar, there
be great woods, but especially in Girvan, whereby they
serve the neighbourhood, both in Kyle and Cuninghame,
for timber to build countrey-houses, and for all the uses of
husbandrie, as cart, harrow, plough, and barrows, at verie
easie rates, and the sorts are birch, elder, sauch, poplar,
ash, oak, and hazel, and it is ordinary throughout all that
countrey, and every gentleman has by his house both wood
and water, orchards, and parkes "

luded to." Since the Statistical Account was written, however, a still greater advance has been made in the science of farming; and tile-draining, then scarcely begun in the parish, has been extensively carried into operation.

The Bay of Girvan is well frequented by the best kinds of white-fish; and salmon-fishing has long been carried on at the mouth of the Girvan, formerly by net and coble, but latterly with the more destructive stake-net.

## HISTORY, CIVIL AND ECCLESIASTICAL.

Girvan is a burgh of barony. The charter was originally granted by Charles II., in 1668, to Mr Thomas Boyd of Ballochtoul, and renewed by King William to Sir Archibald Muir of Thornton, in the year 1696. Abercrummie, in his "Description of Carrick," gives rather an amusing account of the *new burgh of Girvan:*—" And near to the influxe of the sea, upon a levell ground, high above the water, stands the kirk of Girvan, and the parson's house, on the north syde of the churchyard. Opposite to which, on the other syde of the river, lyes a pleasant links, with conyware;* and at the foot of it is a salmond-fishing, at the mouth of the river, and a station for boats that come from Ireland or the Highlands. Southward from the kirk of Girvan stands the tower of Ballachtowll, a monument of the builder's folly, being raised five story high, without a staircase, and no more but one room in each story. It has neither garden or orchard, nor planting, but stands in the midst of rich corn-fields. The builder of this house, Boyd of Penkill, procured a patent for building a new burgh at Girvan, whose situation and streets he designed and marked out in these barren sands, on the south syde of the water mouth of Girvan, and erected a pole for the crosse thereof; but this design never took effeet, not an house having been built there, save (one?) and that scarcely within the compass of the bounds assigned his towne; yet it hath four faires, one for every quarter of the year, that give the names of the new burgh of Girvan to these sandy knowes. Amongst which, there is one spot that is not to be passed without observation, which is called Knockoshin; upon which the head courts of this jurisdiction are kept and held, and all the vassalls compear there, and seems to retaine something of the ancient custome of our nation, that the king's vassals were convened in the field, lyke a rendezvous of souldiers, rather than any house for ceremony and attendance." The charter remained in abeyance till 1785, when, in consequence

of the great increase of the town, it assumed the liberties and privileges of a burgh, which it has since continued to enjoy. " It is beautifully situated on a fine bay, and commands a magnificent view of the sea; of the north coast of Ireland; of the rock of Ailsa; of the mull and promontory of Cantyre; of the islands of Sanda, Arran, Plada, Little Cumbrae; part of Bute, and the hills of Cowal."* The number of inhabitants in the parish is upwards of 7,000, the greater portion of whom reside in the town, and are employed in the cotton trade. There is a harbour at the mouth of the Girvan, which has been much improved of late, and affords great facilities to the shipping of grain, coals, and other commodities, rendering Girvan one of the most important outlets on the coast of Carrick. The want of a convenient harbour was long felt by the inhabitants of Carrick, "Though this country," says Abercrummie, writing some two hundred and fifty years ago, " be (washed) with the sea, for the space of 24 myles and upwards, yet there be no convenient harbours or bays, for receiving of ships; so that none resort (to) it but small boats and barks from Ireland or the Highlands, and their best receptacle is the broad lands of Turnberry, and the mouths of *Dun, Girvan,* and *Stincher:* and of all these three, Girvan is the best; and for the fishing-boats, they have no other shelter but to draw them up the length of the water-mark, when they come ashore, and then to (launch) them when the tyde puts them afloat againe." Such continued to be the state of the harbour of Girvan until within these few years.

Though Girvan remained an insignificant place[†] —as witness the abortive efforts of Ballochtoul to raise it in the scale of burghs—until very recent times, it seems to have possessed a bridge over the Girvan as early as the close of the sixteenth century—a convenience which many places of greater importance did not enjoy. This fact is known from " The Historie of the Kennedyis,"[‡] where a certain rencontre is said to have occurred at "the brig of Girwand." Towards the close of the seventeenth century, however, the bridge seems to have wholly gone to decay, or been swept down, for we find the Presbytery of Ayr, March 4, 1696, ordering a letter to be written to Lord Bargany respecting the building of a bridge over the water of Girvan at the *new church*—if there was any vacant stipend, of which he was patron, the same to be applied to the erection of the bridge. Bargany replied that he would devote a year's vacant sti-

---

* Cuningar, or rabbit-warren.

* Statistical Account.
† In 1791, it contained only 1012 inhabitants.
‡ Original Manuscript, with Notes and Illustrations, by Robert Pitcairn. Edinburgh: John Stevenson. 1830.

pend of Maybole, and also of Daillie, towards the building of the bridge.* Several years elapsed, however, before any progress was made with the bridge; for in July 1701, the Presbytery require the Lord Bargany to build a boat for the Girvan until the proposed bridge should be constructed. The Presbytery assigned as a reason for urging Lord Bargany on the subject, that many lives were lost by persons going to church attempting to ford the river when flooded.

Chalmers, as usual, supplies us with the ecclesiastical history of the parish of Girvan. The church, dedicated to St Cuthbert, was " granted to the monks of Crossragwell, which was founded by Duncan Earl of Carrick. It was confirmed to that monastery by Robert I. and Robert III., under a charter, wherein the church was called ' Ecclesia Sancti Cuthberti de Invergarvane.' This church continued in possession of the monastery of Crossragwell till the Reformation. The monks enjoyed much of the revenues; the remainder belonged to the vicar, who served the cure, as settled by the Bishop of Glasgow. John, the vicar of the church of Garvan, swore fealty to Edward I. in 1296. In Bagimont's Roll, as it stood in the reign of James V., the vicarage of ' Geraven,' in the deanery of Carrick, was taxed £2, 13s. 4d., being a tenth of its estimated value. In a rental of Crossragwell Abbey, which was given in officially after the Reformation, it was stated that the church of Girvane produced to that monastery 260 bolls of bear and meal yearly. In the old parish of Girvan, which was much larger than the present, there were several chapels. In the south of the parish, there was the chapel of Kildomine, which was dedicated to the Holy Trinity.†  . . . In the northern part of the parish, there was, in former times, a chapel dedicated to St Donan, a Scottish saint of the ninth century, whose festival was celebrated on the 17th of April. This chapel, which was named from him Chapel-Donan, stood on the lands of Cragach, near the sea-coast, more than a mile and a-half north-north-east of Girvan. In the charter of Robert III., before mentioned, to the monks of Crossragwell, he confirmed to them, among other estates, the twenty-shilling lands of the chapel of St Donan of Cragach. In 1617, the patronage of the parish church of Girvan, with the other property of Crossragwell Abbey, was annexed by act of Parliament to the Bishoprick of Dunblane; reserving, however, the rights of Peter Hewet, as commendator. On the final abolition of Episcopacy, in 1689, the patronage of the church of Girvan was vested in the King, to whom it now belongs. In 1653, the south-east part of the old parish, lying on the river Stincher, was detached from this parish, and made part of the new parish of Bar, which was then established. When this large detachment was made from the parish of Girvan, it received some additions, both on the north and on the south."

So far Chalmers. He does not tell us when the old or new churches of Girvan were built. From the letter of the Presbytery to the laird of Bargany, in 1696, in reference to building a bridge over the Girvan at the *new church* previously alluded to, we should suppose that the church of Girvan had then been recently built; but this does not appear to have been exactly the case, for, in 1701, mention is made of the church having undergone repairs, and of the building of the manse*. It may have been denominated the new church, in contradistinction to the old, though built some considerable time previously. The present church, according to the Statistical Account, was built about 1780.

The parochial registers do not go farther back than 1733, and being chiefly a register of births, they present no feature of interest. There is no doubt that older records were at one time in existence, but they probably experienced the fate of not a few other similar documents, by being handed over to the huckster or tobacconist.

## ANTIQUITIES.

The only antiquities of which the parish can boast are five circular encampments, generally regarded as ancient British strengths. They occupy the ridge of hills already described, and all of them command a view of the sea. One of them is somewhat remarkable as having two parallel ditches. These encampments, in all likelihood, belong to the period of the Danish, Irish, and Scottish* invasions. Formerly there were a number of cairns in the higher part of the parish; but we regret to say that they have nearly all been removed for the purpose of building fences. " On removing one of them," says the Statistical Account, " there was found, in a kind of coffin, formed of broad thin stones, an earthen urn, unglazed, and rudely ornamented. It held about the quantity of two English pints, and contained a small portion of something like ashes."

---

* An Act of Parliament was passed in 1696, warranting Lord Bargany to employ the vacant stipends of Maybole and Colmonell, of which churches he was patron, in building the proposed bridge.
† See Parish of Bar, vol. I.

* The Scots from Argyle under Alpin.

# FAMILIES IN THE PARISH OF GIRVAN.

## KENNEDIES OF ARDMILLAN.

We have not been fortunate enough to trace the origin of the Kennedies of Ardmillan upon documentary evidence; but there is reason to believe that they were of the house of Bargany. The author of "The Historie of the Kennedyis," says, there "hes of it cumin the Houssis of Ardmillane, Dunneane, Bennane, Kirkhill, Bardrohatt." This is supported by the fact, that the first of them with whom we meet was,

I. THOMAS KENNEDY, usually styled "the gudeman of Ardmillan,"[*] who bore the honours of the house of Bargany at the funeral of Gilbert, the seventh laird of Bargany, who fell in the feud fight with the Earl of Cassillis at Pennyglen, in 1601. According to the historian already alluded to, he attempted, by reason of his relationship, to procure the tutory of Bargany, but was defeated by the greater interest of Josias Stewart, brother to the Lady Bargany. His name repeatedly occurs in testamentary documents from 1604 till 1637, in which latter year he died: "Test. &c. of Thomas Kennedy of Ardmillane, . . . Quha deceist in February, 1637 zeiris: ffaytfullie maid and gevin vp be Hew Kennedy, now of Ardmillane, sone lautfull to the defunct and executour dative," &c. He married Marion Wanfred, Lady Dronghame.[†] He was succeeded by his son,

II. Hugh Kennedy of Ardmillan, who was served heir to his father on the 18th September, 1640, in the 23 merk lands of old extent of Ardmillan, with numerous other properties, in all forming a large estate. It comprehended the lands of Kilsanetniniane, Boyndgrange, Drumfairne, Barjarge, Over and Nether Aldeans, Knokcormill, Templelands of the church of Girvan, Drumbayne, Archanroche, Ellerkinnoch, Letterpyne, Ballochdowane, Balmanache, &c. On the 20th of July, 1642, the "goodman of Ardmillan" supplicated the Presbytery of Ayr, that his "twentie pund land of Ardmillan" might be annexed to the parish of Colmonell, to which the Presbytery agreed, under protest that the junction should not be prejudicial to the College of Glasgow. He married Jean, daughter of Thomas Kennedy of

Baltersan, tutor of Culzean.[*] Robertson states that he married Margaret, daughter of John Blair, younger of Blair, so he must have been twice married. He had a son, who, in 1645, seems to have favoured Montrose. "Ardmillan, younger," occurs in the list of disaffected. And farther, "Thomas Kennedy of Ardmillan, younger," confessed before the Presbytery that he had supped with Alaster M'Donald in Kilmarnock accidentally—that he carried a letter to the laird of Culzean—and that he went to Peebles on the way to Philiphaugh. This Thomas Kennedy, younger of Ardmillan, must have been married; for in the Presbytery records, in the course of the year 1646, there are various minutes in reference to a "scandale of adulterie between the Laird of Culzean, elder, and the Lady Armillan, *elder*."[†] In 1647, Ardmillan, younger, confessed on his knees before the Presbytery his compliance with the enemy, and was forgiven; and, two years afterwards, he was received into communion with the Church. Thomas Kennedy, younger of Ardmillan, died apparently without issue before his father, who was alive in 1652.[‡]

Hugh Kennedy, elder of Ardmillan, left two daughters, one of whom married James Craufuird of Baidland before 1658, in which year he is styled of Ardmillan, and the other Sir Alexander Kennedy of Culzean. Craufuird, in consequence of this marriage, succeeded to the property of Ardmillan.

## CRAUFUIRDS OF ARDMILLAN.[§]

X. William Craufuird, younger of Ardmillan. In June, 1691, he threw himself and some succours into the fortress of the Bass, in the Firth of

---

[*] In old documents, the proprietors of Ardmillan invariably bore this title. The distinction between LAIRD and GUDEMAN had reference to the titles of the property, whether held from the Crown, or merely from a feudal superior.

[†] Thomas Kennedy of Ardmillan and Marion Wanfred, Lady Dronghame, his spouse, are mentioned in the town records of Ayr, 7th June, 1608.

[*] "Historical Account of the Noble Family of Kennedy," &c. Privately printed, 1849.

[†] These records afford an instructive illustration of the power of the Church courts at the time: "2d June, 1647.—Compeired Sir Alex. Kennedy of Colzean." He denied that he had converse with the Lady Ardmillan—especially that he was with her alone in a chamber compting money, or that he bedded in the same chamber, where she and her husband were. At a subsequent diet, the report was not found clearly proven against the parties; but the case was continued. On the 14th July, however, they were ordered to be censured as adulterers, and the act formerly passed against them, [prohibiting their keeping company], to remain in full force.

[‡] His name occurs in a testamentary document of that year.

[§] For the Craufuirds of Baidland, of whom the Craufuirds of Ardmillan are a continuation, see vol. i. p. 418.

Forth. which was so long held out by the adherents of King James, and was the last place in the kingdom that surrendered to King William. He married Margaret, daughter of Kennedy of Baltersan, and had issue —

1 Archibald, his successor
2 James, who settled in England  His descendants are a considerable family in Sussex
1 A daughter, married to David Craufurd of Drumsoy, whose son, David, was Historiographer to Queen Anne for Scotland, from which marriage also descended John Craufurd of Auchnames

XI  Archibald Craufurd, his eldest son, succeeded in 1712 *  He was a keen Jacobite, and after the rebellion of 1745, had to remain for several years under hiding in Edinburgh  He married Marion Hay, a descendant of one of the branches of the Tweeddale family, by whom he had two sons —

1 Archibald
2 Thomas, of whom afterwards

He died in 1748, when he was succeeded by his eldest son,

XII  Archibald Craufurd of Ardmillan  He married Anne, daughter of Robert Kennedy, Esq of Liverpool, and on his death, in 1784, was succeeded by the eldest son of that marriage,

XIII  Archibald Craufurd of Ardmillan, W S  His father having been deeply involved in the unfortunate copartnery of Douglas, Heron & Co the estate was brought to a judicial sale during his minority, when it was acquired by his uncle, Thomas Craufurd  Archibald married Margaretta, youngest daughter of his uncle, and had issue —

1 John Macmiken
2 Thomas
3 Archibald—all of whom died young
4 Robert heir presumptive of Kilsancunnian, died s p aged 27
5 Hugh, died in Jamaica, aged 18
6 Thomas who succeeded to the estates of Grange and Kilsancunnian in 1840  He is male representative of the Craufurds of Baidland and Kennedies of Ardmillan  He married 13th June 1843, Elizabeth Fraser, second daughter of David Stewart Galbraith, Esq of Mackrihanish and Dromore, in Argyleshire
7 Hamilton Cathcart
8 John Graham of Gartur, in Stirlingshire, and Threemile-river, in Jamaica  Died May 1840
1 Margaret eldest daughter, married July 8, 1831, to William Handley Sterndale, and has issue
2 Marion, married obscurely
3 Ann, and five other daughters who died young

He died 16th May, 1824

XIV  Thomas Craufurd, second son of Archibald, No XI, acquired Ardmillan by purchase, as above stated  He had served in the army, and held a lucrative office, under government, at Bristol, by which means he was enabled to preserve the estate in the family  He married, first, Anne,

daughter of John Taylor, Esq of East Sheen, in the county of Surry, by whom he had issue, and, secondly, Jane, daughter of the Rev. Hugh Hamilton of Girvan  He died in 1793, leaving —

1 Archibald, his successor
1 Anne, married Macmiken of Grange
2 Margaretta, married her cousin, Archibald Craufurd

Mrs Jane Craufurd, relict of Thomas Craufurd of Ardmillan, died May 25, 1825, aged 80 *

XV  Archibald Clifford Blackwell Craufurd, now of Ardmillan, a Major in the army, and late a Captain in the 78th Highlanders  He served in India, and at the taking of the Cape of Good Hope in 1795.  He married Jane, daughter of Dr Leslie, and has issue

*Arms of Craufurd of Baidland*—Gules, on a fesse ermine, between three mullets, argent, two crescents interlaced of the field

*Motto*—Durum patientia frango

*Arms of Kennedy of Ardmillan*—Argent, a cheveron, gules, between three cross crosslets fitched sable, within a double tressure.

*Crest*—A game hawk, hooded and belled

The representative of both families quarters these respectively  first and fourth, Baidland; second and third, Ardmillan  The present proprietor of Ardmillan, and the junior branches of the family, bear gules, a fesse ermine, with the interlaced crescents, the hawk, and the above motto

*Seat*—Ardmillan House, about two miles south from the town of Girvan  In Balfour's Collections, Ardmillan is called a castle, and a glowing description is given of it by Abercummine  "Next to this (Turnberry) is the castle of Ardmillane, so much improven, of late, that it looks like a Palace, built round, court-wayes, surrounded with a deep broad ditch, and strengthened with a moveable bridge at the entry; able to secure the owner from the suddain commotions and assaults of the wild people of this corner, which on these occasions are sett upon robbery and depredation, and to enable him the better to endure a seige, he is provided of well in his court, and a hand-mill in the house, for grinding meall or malt, with which two lusty fellows sett a-work will grind a firlott in the space of ane hour  It is well surrounded with orchards that yeild plenty of apples and pears, and one more particularly, that for its precocity is called *the early pear of Ardmillan*, of a very pleasant tast.  In the year    . happened a strange conjunction 'twixt a Jackdaw and a Magpie that paired together, built their nest, and brought forth ther young, resembling more the jackdaw than the magpie "

---

* About this time, or shortly afterwards, Baidland was sold to Hugh Macbride, merchant in Glasgow

* Headstone in old churchyard, Ayr

## TROCHRIG.

Trochrig, mentioned by Abercrummie as one of the old houses of the gentry in the parish of Girvan, was in his time, and long afterwards, in the possession of the Boyds, a branch of the Kilmarnock family. He says, "on the north syde of the River (Girvan) downward, and up toward the hill, about a myle from the River, stands the House of Trochreg, which belongs to the Boyds; which family hath produced two great men, famous in their generation, and great lights in the church of God. One was James Boyd, Archbishop of Glasgow, who maintained the honour of his character by a vertuous and exemplary lyfe, and strenuously defended the lawfullness of his office against the insults of our first zealots, Mr Andrew Melvin and his accomplices.* The other was his son and heir,† who, following the study of Divinity, merited the Chair in the College of Saumure, in France; and thence, was brought to be Principall of the Colledge of Glasgow; whose learned Commentaries on the Ephesians are well known, and justly had in great estimation."

I. JAMES BOYD, the first of Trochrig, was the Archbishop of Glasgow, above referred to by Abercrummie. He was the second son of Adam Boyd of Pinkill, brother to Robert, Master of Boyd, who was father of Robert sixth Lord Boyd. Keith, in his Catalogue of Scottish Bishops, gives the following account of him : " During the Earl of Marr's regency, a new kind of episcopacy having been set up, Mr James Boyd of Trochrig, (in 1572), a very worthy person, received the title of the See of Glasgow, and he exercised the office of particular pastor at the Cathedral Church, the barony of Glasgow being then the parish that pertained to that church. This Bishop Boyd was the second son of Adam Boyd of Pinkill, brother to the Lord Boyd. When the legality of the episcopal functions came to be first called in question by the assembly, in the year 1578, he learnedly and solidly, both from Scripture and antiquity, defended the lawfulness of his office; yet, the animosities, which he then perceived to be in the hearts of a great many, so far impaired his health, that he died in the month of June, 1581." This eminent churchman was the second Archbishop of the Protestant faith in Glasgow. He was preceded by John Porterfield, and succeeded by Robert Montgomery. ‡ He was buried in the choir of the Cathedral, and laid in the same sepulchre

with Bishop Gavin Dunbar. He married Margaret, daughter of James Chalmers of Gadgirth,* who long survived him. " Margaret Chalmeris, Lady Trochrig," occurs as a creditor "for hir fermes of the said lands of Grange, the said crop 1611," in the testament of George Hutchesoune in Grange, Mayboill, March, 1612.

II. Mr Robert Boyd of Trochrig was served heir to his father, the Archbishop, 16th February, 1608, in the ten pund land of Trochrig, with the mill, the five merk land of Barneile, M'Cryndle, and Snaid, A. E. £13, 6s. 8d. He was one of the most learned men of his time—having been Professor of Divinity, first at Saumur, in France, and subsequently in Glasgow and Edinburgh. He was the author of the well-known Commentary on the Ephesians. The following brief summary of the career of this eminent theologian is from a manuscript in the College of Glasgow: " Born at Glasgow in 1578—taken from Glasgow to Trochrig on the death of his father, in 1581—sent to the school at Ayr—studied afterwards at Edinburgh, where he got the degree of A.M., in 1594, or thereby—left Scotland in 1597—arrived in France, May 7th, same year—taught at Thouars —was made Professor of Philosophy at Montauban, 1599—went to Saumur in 1600—in 1607 Mr Boyd travelled through Germany, Holland, England, and Scotland. In 1608 he returned to Saumur, and was chosen Professor of Divinity there. He came over to Scotland in 1610—returned same year to Saumur—married at Saumur, in May 1611, Anne Malverin—returned to Britain in 1611—settled in Glasgow in December same year—was made Principal of the College in January 1615."

In 1621 he resigned the Principality, and removed his family and furniture to Trochrig, where he resided, except when called occasionally to Edinburgh for a few weeks, till 1622, when he was called to be Principal there. He resigned, however, next year, and, in 1626, was called and admitted minister of Paisley. In April of the same year, a riot was committed on his house, and he demitted his charge in September following.

Having fallen into bad health, he went to Edinburgh for medical advice, and died there 5th January, 1627. The following is an extract of his latter-will :—

" The Testament, testamentar, and Inventar of the guidis, geir, debts, and sowmes of money quhilks perteint to vmqle. Mr Robert Boyd of Trochrig, within the parochin of Kirkoswall,† the tyme of his deceis, Qha deceist in the monethe

---

*  Abercrummie was a keen supporter of Episcopacy.
†  Mr Robert Boyd of Trochrig.
‡  The latter, having been compelled to demit the See, became minister of Symington in 1587.

---

*  From Wodrow's MS. Life of Trochrig he appears to have had a sister married to James Chalmers of Sauchrie.
†  This is a mistake, Trochrig is in Girvan parish.

of Januar Jai vi^c and Twentie sevin zeirs: fayt-
fullie maid and gevin vp be his awin mouth, In
sa far as concernes the nomination of his executrix, nominat be him in his Latterwill and Testament, and legacies eftir-mentioned, and pairtlie
maid and gevin vp be Anna Demaliverin, onlie
executrix nominat be the defunct; In sa far as
concernes the vpgeving of ye Inventar of the defunct's guids, geir, debts awand In and Out, as the
samyne testament of the date vnderwrittin mair
fullie proports.

### Inuentar.

Item, the defunct had, the tyme foirsaid, the
guids and geir vnderwritten of the availls, qualities,
and pryces eftirspecifit, viz. Certane buiks, all
estimat to Jai v^c lib. Item, the Insicht of the
hous in utincills and domicills, with the abuilzement of the defunct's bodie (by the airschip), estimat to j^c lib. Item, twa ky and ane stoitt, pryce
of the peice xii lib. Inde xxxvi lib.

　　Summa of the Inventar, Jai vi^c xxxvi lib.

Debts awand In. [Under this head occur a variety of money transactions with the tenantry of
Trochrig, Barneill, &c., and other persons. In
all, these credits amount to Jai Lviii lib. iiii s.].
Next we have

### Debts awand Out.

Item, there was awand be the defunct, the
tyme foirsaid, the sowmes of money following
To the persones efterspecifit, viz. To Mr Hew
M'Kaill, for ane zeirs fie, Lxvi lib. xiii s. iiii d.
To Jonet Ramsay, nurcis, for ane zeirs fey xl lib.
To Johnne Tod, gairdner, for ane zeirs fey
xxiiii lib. To Alex. Ramsay, for ane zeirs fey
viii lib. To Marcoun Gairner, for ane zeirs fey
vii lib.

　　Summa of the Debts out j^c lvii lib. xiii s. iiii d.

Restis of Frie Geir, debts deducit

　　　　　　　　　jjaiv^c xxxvi lib. ix s. 8 d.

. . . . . . . . . . . . . .

### Legacie.

At Edinburght, the Twentie fyift day of December, the zeir of God, Jai vi^c and Twentie sex
zeirs, The quhilk day I, Mr Robert Boyd of
Trochrig, calling to mynd the certantie of daith,
and the incertantie of the tyme and place, and
being willing to declair my latterwill and testament, Haiff thairfoir nominat my loveing spous
Tutrix to my eldest sone, and to our haill remanent childrein, during the zeiris of thair pupulla-
ritie; and failzeing of hir be deceis or marriage,
I nominat my honorable and loveing kinsman,
Thomas Boyd of Pinkill, conjunctlie,* Tutours to

　　* There seems to be some omission here. Some other
person was evidently intended to have been named along
with Pinkill.

the saids bairnes; and failzeing of the ane he deceis, as God forbid, the vther being on lyf, being
assured that they, or other of thame, will not only
assist my said loveing spous in the richt administration of the said office of Tutourie, swa lang as
scho sal happin to be Tutrix, bot likwayis quhen
the said office sall accres to thame, will mayst cairfullie dischuirge the samyne for the guide of the
saids pupillis. I leif in legacie to Mr Alexander
Boyd, sone to vmqle. Mr Williame Boyd, The
sowme of ane hundrithe marks, and to Robert
M'Call, my servand, Ten punds, and to Alex.
Ramsay, my servand, Ten punds, without prejudice to the feyis that sall be dew to thame the
tyme of my deceis. Item, I leive to Mr Johnne
Ker, minister at Prestoune, and Johnne Hamiltoune, hypothecar, burgess of Edinburght, the
sowme of ane hundrith merks, to be vplifted of
the first and reddiest of my stipend restand awand
to me of the Kirk of Paisley, to be imployed
be thame, and failzeing the ane, the vther onlyf,
to sich vses as I have maid knawn to thame.
Item, I leif to my guid freind, Doctor George
Sibbald, 'Scaligeri Commentarie in Arristotelein
de Historia Animalum,' as ane small taiken of
my love to him. Item, I leive Twenty punds to
help to by ane bell to the Kirk of Daylie, and
Twentie merks, including thairin the ten merks
alreaddy promeist be me to the bigging of the
brig of Girvane. And last, I leive fourtie merkis
to be distribute amongest the puir of the parochin quher I sall happin to depart this lyf. And
I leif the haill rest of the thrid of the guids and
geir qnhilk cumes vnder my testament to my
childrein, Johnne, Margrat, and Jonet Boydes,
to be equallie devydit amangst thame, and to be
imployed to thair behuif. In witnes quherof I
haue subscryvit thir presents, at Edinburght, the
xxv day of December, the zeir of God, Jai vi^c and
Twentie sex zeirs, Befoir thir witness, Mr Robert
Boyd of Kippis, Mr James Robertoune, advocatts,
and Michaell Melvill, servitour to the said Mr
Robert Boyd, and writer of the premiss. Sic
subr. Mr Robert Boyd of Trochrig, Mr Robert
Boyd, witnes, Mr James Robertoune, witness,
Michaell M'Gill, witnes.

Confirmed at Glasgow, June 8, 1627. Mr
Johnne Chalmeris of Sauchrie, cautioner."

III. Mr John Boyd of Trochrig was served
heir to his father, April 21, 1640. He had a
daughter married to Sir William Bruce of Stenhouse, Bart., and a son.

IV. Robert Boyd of Trochrig, who succeeded
him. He refused the Test in 1683, and was
thrown, in consequence, into prison. He obtained his liberty, August 7, 1685, on payment of a
fine of one thousand merks for church irregulari-

ties, and giving a bond and caution, for two thousand pounds sterling, to live regularly and orderly. He was alive in 1724, in which year his name occurs in the Ayr Presbytery records. He married a daughter of William Craufurd of Auchnames, and was succeeded by his son,

V. John Boyd of Trochrig, who, in 1752, was served heir-male to Alexander Boyd of Pinkill, the last of that branch, who died in 1750. He died himself without male issue.

VI. Ann Boyd of Trochrig, his daughter, married William Boyd Robertson, to whom she had a daughter, and who alienated the property.

Trochrig, or Trochraigue, was acquired upwards of forty years ago by the late James Fergusson of Monkwood, advocate, and by him sold to his brother, the late Mr John Hutcheson Fergusson. It is now possessed by his son, John H. Fergusson of Trochraigue, at present residing in Calcutta.

### BALLACHTOULE.

Ballachtoule, another of the old houses of the gentry mentioned by Abercrummie, was in the possession of the Grahams of Knokdoliane in the sixteenth century. Robert Graham of Grougar, as heir-male of entail of John Graham of Knokdolian, was retoured in the lands of Ballachtoule, April 16, 1606. From Abercrummie's Account of Carrick, it would appear that, about the middle of the seventeenth century, Ballachtoule belonged to Thomas Boyd of Pinkill, who obtained the charter constituting Girvan a burgh, in 1668, and who built the tower of Ballachtoule on the lands laid off for the new burgh. Ballachtoule was acquired by Sir Archibald Muir of Thornton, in 1696, and shortly afterwards by Gilbert Stewart, designed of Ballachtoule, in various documents. He was alive in 1726. In 1746, it was purchased by William Wilson, writer in Edinburgh, in virtue of a decreet of adjudication obtained by him against William Stewart, chirurgeon in Edinburgh, only surviving son of the late John Stewart of Ballachtoule, merchant in Kilmarnock, heir general to Gilbert Stewart of Ballachtoule, his father. Ballachtoule is now the property of the Bargany family, who are the superiors of the burgh of Girvan.

### TROWAIR.

Troweir, or Trowair, also noticed by Abercrummie. It was in his time, and still continues to be, in the possession of the Cathearts of Carleton. William Cathcart, heir of Allan Cathcart of Wattirheid, his father, was retoured in the twelve merk lands of Trowair and Killonh, 9th April, 1631; and in 1662, Hugh Cathcart of Carleton is served heir in the lands, amongst others, of Trowair.

# PARISH OF IRVINE.

There can be little doubt that the parish of Irvine, like those of Ayr and Girvan, derived its name from the town, and the town from the river Irvine. In old charters, the name is generally spelled *Irwyn*, sometimes *Errin*, or *Yrewin*; and Chalmers presumes that it may be a corruption of the British or Celtic *Ir-Avon*, signifying the clear river, which is certainly characteristic of the Irvine throughout the greater part of its course.

The parish of Irvine is bounded on the east by that of Dreghorn; on the west, by Stevenston; on the north, by Kilwinning and Stewarton; and on the south, by the water of Irvine. The parish comprehends an area of about five square miles, or 2644 acres. The surface is throughout level. In the lower part of the parish, the soil, originally pure sand, has been pretty generally converted into a fertile loam in the course of cultivation. Towards the interior, however, it is naturally of a strong, adhesive clay; but it has also been greatly improved by cultivation. Good crops of all kinds of grain, and green cropping, are grown in the parish, particularly of potatoes and turnips.

There are no lochs of water in the parish, but it is well supplied with springs and running streams.

## HISTORY, CIVIL AND ECCLESIASTICAL.

The history of the town of Irvine may be said to constitute that of the parish. The origin of the burgh is assuredly lost in the " mists of antiquity." It may possibly date its rise so far back as the days of the Romans, for there is no doubt that that wonderful people traced the Irvine, as well as the Doon, westwards to its junction with the sea. We are not aware that any remains of Roman masonry have been dug up at Irvine, as

there was at Ayr; but it seems extremely likely that one of their stations was fixed on the high ground, on the banks of the Irvine, where now stands the town. Roman implements of war, and other vestiges of their presence, have been found in the vicinity—thus corroborating the fact of their having continued the causeway, still traceable at particular parts of the banks of the Irvine, all the way till the confluence of the water with the sea. These, however, are, to some extent, merely conjectural notions as to the rise of the burgh of Irvine. Of its great antiquity, at the sametime, there can be little doubt. Chalmers considers it the most ancient town in Ayrshire. He says:—" It is certain that the town of Irvine, and the castle, under the protection of which it arose, were in existence before the castle and the shiretown of Ayr were founded. Hoveden refers to *the castle* of 'Irewin,' in Cuninghame, as a place of note in 1184." We have great respect for the research of Chalmers, but he sometimes forgets his own statements, and his deductions are not always to be depended upon. No doubt, the period referred to by Hoveden is a few years earlier than the erection of Ayr into a royal burgh by William the Lion, who at the same time built a *new* castle at Ayr ; but that both a town and a castle existed previously at Ayr, seems plain from the words of the charter itself. There is evidence to show that the *new* town, or Newton of Ayr, with its castle, existed early in the thirteenth century; so we can have no difficulty in believing that there must have been an *old* town long previously.

We put forward these remarks, not from any desire to claim a greater antiquity for the one burgh than the other, but because they bear us out in an opinion, founded upon similar facts, that towns and castles are of more remote antiquity in Scotland than most people imagine. It is usual to assign their origin to the infusion of

Norman blood after the conquest of England; but though it might be difficult, or rather impossible, to *prove*, by *documentary evidence*, that castles existed prior to that period, yet the more we study history—and particularly local history—the more are we convinced that such towns and castles as those of Ayr and Irvine originated earlier even than the Danish invasion. There are various remains of castles built by the Romans in England, and are we to suppose that they did not introduce the art into Scotland?

None of our local historians have ever attempted to point out the remains, or the site, of the Castle of Irvine, mentioned by Hoveden. . There are the remains of only one castle in connection with the burgh, called the Seagate Castle, supposed by Robertson to have been built as a jointure-house by the Eglintoun family, sometime after 1361—a central stone in a vaulted chamber in the lower story having engraved upon it the united arms of Montgomerie and Eglintoun. It is not improbable, however, that this was the site of the castle referred to, the present ruin having been a re-building, after the union of the houses of Eagleshame and Eglintoun.* What makes this supposition the more likely is the fact, that anciently the sea flowed much nearer the town than it does at present—so much so as to form a complete defence, on the south and westward, to the castle. No situation could be more appropriately chosen. Indeed, had there not been a castle existing previously upon the spot, and if it had merely been meant as a jointure-house, as Robertson supposes, it is hard to conceive why a site in such proximity with the town of Irvine should have been chosen, when so many other and more appropriate might have been selected. Supposing the Seagate Castle to have been the original stronghold of Irvine, it would have been as nearly as possible about the same distance from the Cross of Irvine as the Castle of Ayr was from the Cross of Ayr, and in every respect similarly protected by the river and the sea.

Be this as it may, we proceed to trace the rise of Irvine upon more certain data. The earliest of the Crown documents preserved in the charter chest of the burgh is a precept by Robert I. under the Great Seal, dated 14th February, 1308, commanding his Justiciare, &c., to protect the burgh, burgesses, and community of Irvine. The next is a charter by Robert I., 12th May, 1323, declaring that the burgesses of Irvine, and their successors, shall be free from toil, &c., " as is more

fully contained in a charter granted thereupon to the same burgesses, by Alexander the Second, King of Scots, of venerable memory, our predecessor."* This charter by Alexander II., whose reign extended from 1214 to 1249, and which has been lost or destroyed, may be considered as the first possessed by the burgh. The boundaries and privileges of the incorporation of Irvine are shown by another charter by King Robert II., dated 8th April, 1372, proceeding on an inquest made at the king's command, concerning a dispute between Ayr and Irvine in reference to the boundaries and liberties of the respective burghs. By this inquest it was clearly found, that Irvine had been sixty years and upwards, and from time past memory, in possession of the liberties of the whole barony of Cuninghame, and of the baronies of Largs, " pro suis tam mercandisis et mercimoniis in eisdem libere exercendis."†

These were the mercantile boundaries of the burgh of Irvine, including the whole of Cuninghame and Largs,‡ as those of Ayr extended over the whole of Kyle and Carrick. The heritable boundaries of the burgh, however, are not so easily ascertained, though they were no doubt clearly enough stated in the charter of Alexander II. now lost. That they were pretty extensive may be inferred from a charter by the Duke of Albany, dated 24th July, 1417, proceeding upon an inquest ordered by the governor, regarding the right to a piece of muir claimed by William Fraunees of Stane, situated about midway up the parish, when the jury unanimously found that the right lay with the burgh of Irvine. Also from a notarial copy, 12th May, 1444, of an indenture, dated June, 1260, entered into between the Lord Godfrey Ross and the burgesses of Irvine, regarding their respective rights in the tenement of Hormissoch (Ormsheugh) and the wood of Longhurst. It was arranged that Godfrey should have right to all the ploughed and ploughable part of the said tenement, and an exclusive right to the said wood—the burgesses to have a right of common pasture over the whole of the said tenement, except the arable ground and the wood, neither party to have power to cut the wood. The property of Ormsheugh is still farther up the parish than the lands of Stane. In 1689, the lands then belonging to the town were lotted in twenty-six lots of three acres each. These were,—Kidneuk and Redburn; Murray's Land;

---

* The old square tower is of great antiquity, and much older than the other parts of the building. The portion in which the chamber with the arms occurs, is much more modern, and built of quite a different stone.

* This charter superadds an immunity to the burgesses of Irwyne, and their successors, from a toll which, previous to this new grant, they were in the habit of paying in the burgh of Ayr.

† These and other charters were subsequently confirmed by James I., James IV., and James VI.

‡ Largs is now a portion of Cuninghame, though then a distinct barony or baronies.

Macfade's Rig; Bogside Land and Loan; Groat-holm; Rottenboag; Spittalmeadow; Divet Park; the value of the whole amounting to £606, 13s. 4d. Scots.

The jurisdiction of the Magistrates of Irvine* extended over the entire heritable boundary of the burgh. Early in the sixteenth century, a dispute occurred between the Earl of Eglintoun, Bailie of Cuninghame, and the Magistrates, as to their respective powers of administering justice. At length a contract of agreement was entered into, 10th February, 1522, settling their respective jurisdictions. The Magistrates' right was admitted to extend over the freedom of the burgh, burgh woods, burgh lands, and community; while the Earl was to "keep the heid fair" of the burgh of Irvine, holden on the 15th of August yearly. The feuds and slaughters usually prevailing at this annual gathering, are referred to in the contract as a principal reason why the Earl, as Bailie of Cuninghame, should keep the fair.

By a charter under the Great Seal, 20th March, 1572, James VI. conferred on the authorities the power of holding Justiciary Courts within the Court-house of Irvine, for trying residenters within the burgh for the crimes of pickery, theft, and receipt of theft, by a jury of honest men, inhabitants of the burgh. Crimes, however, of a deeper die were frequently tried before this court. In 1586—18th December—"Master William Montgomerie, Arthur Montgomerie, his sone and appeirand air," were summoned before the Justiciary Court of Irvine, to answer at the instance of ——— Patersoun, "sone and air of vinquhill Archibald Patersoun, burgess of Irwin," for "violent and masterfull spoliatioun." And on the 20th October, 1625, was tried "per Allanum Dunlop nobis praefectum dicti burgi," "Alexander Banks, sone of Robert Banks, flesher, for the slaughter of Gilbert M'Alister, heilland man, slain in Stevenston yesterday, and brought in by the Earl of Eglinton, as baillie of Cunningham, and repledgit from his court to the jurisdiction of this burgh, as ane of yair inhabitants."

The town was repeatedly involved in disputes, particularly with the burgh of Ayr, as to their jurisdiction. So late as 1694, they had to defend themselves against the encroachments of the Commissary Court of Ayr, who had "proceeded to judge some of the inhabitants of this burgh (Irvine) for alleged calumnies and other crimes, although the burgh had appeared and produced their charters of resignation, which were altogether disregarded and contemned."

* The burgh was governed by a Provost, Baillies, and Councillors—in all, 17.—Sederunt, Sept. 1628, Allan Dunlop, Lord Provost.

Irvine does not appear to have ever been a walled town, but it was enclosed with gates, or ports, one at the west end of Glasgow Vennel, and the other at Eglintoun Street. The town then, as now, consisted chiefly of one main street, running parallel with the river. It is impossible to trace the extension of the burgh with any degree of satisfaction. It must, however, have been rather an inconsiderable town before the end of the fourteenth century. Up till that period, it had no public place for the authorities to meet in. In 1386, a charter was obtained from Robert II., dated 22d October, granting ground in the market-place for building a *Council-house,* &c. on payment of a blench duty of a penny of silver if demanded allenarly. This charter was confirmed by Robert III.

One of the most ancient evidences of the privileges of the burgh of Irvine—we mean the Cross—was removed in 1694. The minute, ordering the removal of this interesting relic, is dated 7th September, and to this effect: The Cross to be taken away, and the stones to be applied towards erecting the meal market-house, now a-building, in respect there is great want of freestone for that new work, and that the Cross, being of an old fashion, and inconvenient, doth mar the decorum of the street and meal market-house. We are not aware that a drawing of this relic anywhere exists.

It does not appear that the town possessed any town clock before 1686, in which year, 31st March, the Council give orders to David Buchanane, smith, "to make ane clock for the vse of the said burgh." The same year, 9th July, Adam Gray, wright, is appointed "for coopring of the toune clock and ringing of the Tolbuith bell, for the space of ane zeir." Salary 40 merks.

We are not aware that Irvine ever was the seat of any particular species of manufacture; but much of its importance, no doubt, arose from the harbour, which was at one time the principal one on the Clyde. Its advantages seem to have been purely natural; but as the sea began to recede its capabilities gradually diminished. The first document which occurs in the Irvine archives in reference to the harbour, is a contract, dated 3d August, 1572, between the magistrates and "John Wallace of Dundonald, Edward Wallace of Shewalton, and Robert Wallace, his son and heir apparent," by which the Wallaces, in consideration of 200 merks, sold to the burgh "ane sufficient quantity and roume of ground of their landis of Murrass, extending to the quantity of twelf fallis broad, for louseing and landing of their Schippis, Barkis, and Bottis, with their merchandice, and the merchandice of whatsumever utheris that sal happen to resort towards the said Burch upon the foresaidis landis of Murrass on ayther syd of the watter of Irwyng, with ane sufficient gaite and passage through the foresaidis lands for free Ische and Intres to and frae the said water, togedder with ankerage and ankerfauld upon the saidis landis," &c. This would seem to have been the first attempt at the construction of a regular harbour for shipping. A few years afterwards—15th August, 1579—James VI. granted the customs of the burgh to the magistrates, amounting to twenty-nine merks yearly, for the space of five years, to enable them to repair their haven and port. In "Timothy Pont's Cunningham Topographized," printed in 1620, the harbour of Irvine is called "the chieff porte of the country of Cunningham. The porte and harbry being now much decayed from quhat it was anciently, being stopt with shelves of Sand which hinder the neir approach of shipping."

" As appears from the map which accompanies Pont's work," says the Statistical Account, "the confluence of the rivers Irvine and Garnock had not taken place at the time to which it refers, for he describes the Garnock as emptying itself into the sea, about two miles from the mouth of the river Irvine. Indeed, long subsequent to Pont's time, the sea came up close to the town, and vessels were loaded and discharged at what was then and is now termed the Seagate. Within the memory of persons now alive, the sea has receded considerably on this coast; and very considerably since 1620, for the lower part of the Seagate is now nearly half a mile from the sea. Some time subsequent to the period at which Pont wrote, Thomas Tucker published a report (in 1656) upon the settlement of the revenues and customs in Scotland. He had been sent by the Government of England, for the purpose of introducing order into the collection of the revenues of the excise and customs, and was appointed one of the commissioners of the Scottish board. The district concerning which he was to report, consisted of 'Glasgow, Newarke, Greenocke, Fairly, Colburgh, Saltcoates, Bute, and, lastly, Irwyn.' 'Irwyn,' says he, ' a small burgh towne, lying at the mouth of a river of the same name, which hath some time been a pretty small port, but at present clogged and almost choaked up with sand, which the western sea beats into it, soe as it wrestles for life to maintaine a small trade to France, Norway, and Ireland, with herring and other goods, brought on horseback from Glasgow, for the purchasing timber, wine, and other commodities to supply theyr occasions with. The vessels belonging to this district are, viz. to Glasgowe, 12, viz. 3 of 150 tons, 1 of 140, 2 of 100,

1 of 50, 3 of 30, 1 of 15, 1 of 12. Renfrew, 3 or 4 boates of five or six tonnes a-piece. Irwin, 3 or 4, the biggest not exceeding sixteen tonnes."

The shipping of Irvine had thus been in a very low state in 1656. The Civil War had no doubt somewhat to do with such a state of affairs. Shortly after the Restoration, however, matters began to assume a better aspect. By a minute of the Council, 29th June, 1677, it was ordered that "the haill stanes lying at the ends of the bridge be taken to the shore for the laying of a kasey (causeway) for the good of the harbour, and ease and advantage of the vessels;" and by another minute of the 3d August, of the same year, all the able-inhabitants were ordered " to go out, at tuck of drum, and take stones out of the water for the laying of ane key at the Bar of Irvine." There is also, amongst the town's papers, a precept, of the same date, by Corsbie [Fullartoun of that Ilk] in " favour of the burgh, for six bolls beir for helping to build ane key at the Bar of Irvine." A considerable traffic seems to have been maintained with Ireland about this time and subsequently, chiefly in the importation of grain, no doubt in return for the products of this country. On the 22d January, 1676, it was enacted by the Council, that meal and malt, &c., imported within the precincts of Irvine by strangers, should be first offered to the community of the burgh. A curious illustration of this rule, as well as of the miscellaneous nature of the traffic with Ireland, occurs in a minute of the town council, October 4, 1687, to the effect that there had been offered to the town, by a merchant from Carrickfergus, a large importation of goods, and that he was to be allowed to sell the same in the market, if the magistrates did not by next day accept the offer.

Various acts were passed by the legislature, in the reign of Charles II. and subsequently, imposing a duty on the importation of Irish grain, with the view of checking the trade, which was alleged to drain the western districts of money, and depreciate the value of home grown corn; but the merchants of Irvine continued their importations in defiance of law, partly in the belief that their privileges as a burgh entitled them to do so. The Statistical Account, quoting Fountainhall, gives the following example of this in 1712: "Thomas Gray, merchant in Irvine, and others, were dilated before the justices as criminals for this offence, and for their contumacy in not appearing, were fined in £100 sterling each, under the penal statutes against the importing of Irish meal. Gray suspended, and stated various important pleas,— 1st, That the burgesses of Irvine were not subject to the jurisdiction of the county justices, and that the magistrates had the power of repledging them. This plea was repelled, and the right of repledging found to be in desuetude. 2d, That it was not competent to refer the fact on which the charge rested to the oath of party. This was also repelled, and the court found it provable by oath, as well as usury and the like. 3d, That the fine was most exorbitant. The court found that the offenders should not be all classed alike, for one who had only brought in a boll or two was not to be so deeply fined as he who had brought in a hundred, and had reiterated his transgression," &c.

Towards the close of the sixteenth century the trade of the harbour of Irvine had greatly increased, and, in 1760, it was ranked as the third port in Scotland—Port-Glasgow ranking first, and Leith second. Irvine was the chief seat of the customs on the Ayrshire coast.* The principal imports are timber and grain from America, and butter and grain from Ireland; and the exports consist almost wholly of coals.

The parochial church of "Yrewin," which we find first mentioned in the chartulary of Paisley so far back as 1233,† belonged to the Abbey of Kilwinning, by the monks of which, who levied the revenues, a vicarage was established for the service of the church. The earliest document in the archives in reference to the Church is a deed of mortification, dated September, 1323, by Thomas, surnamed Baxter, burgess of Irvine, of an annual rent of 37s. 10d. to the chaplain of the parish church of Irvine, &c., for the welfare of his own soul and that of his wife, Eda. This deed was sealed with the seal of the abbot of Kilwinning and the common seal of the burgh. None of the impressions, however, are preserved. The next is another deed of mortification, dated 1st March, 1418, by Mr William de Cunynghame, perpetual vicar of the church of Dundonald, son of the Lord William de Cunynghame, Lord of Kilmaurs, of various tenements in the burgh of Irvine, &c., to maintain two chaplains in the church of Irvine for prayers for the souls of himself, of his father, of Agnes, his mother, &c., at the altars of St Catharine and St Ninian, in the parish church of Irvine, &c., of which two chaplains, the bailies and community of Irvine, after the death of the mortifier, were to have the presentation. In a subsequent deed by the same party, dated 26th July, 1426, assigning certain tenements in

Irvine to the Church, for the health of "James I., King of Scots, and his Queen, Johanna," he is designed canon of Glasgow as well as vicar of the church of Dundonald. This last deed is confirmed by a charter of James I., dated 28th July, 1426.

"Before the Reformation," says Chalmers, "there was at Irvine a chapel dedicated to the Virgin Mary, which stood on the bank of the river, near to the parish church;" and he quotes a grant in favour of this chapel by Lady Loudoun, in 1451. Amongst the Irvine charters, however, there is a notarial instrument, dated 16th November, 1446, being a species of sasine, setting forth a deed of mortification by Lady Alicia Campbell, Lady Lowdonhill, of an annual rent of five merks out of two tenements within the burgh of Irwyne to the chaplain who should officiate at the altar of St Michael in the *new aisle* of the Virgin Mary, within the parish of Irwyn. This was followed by a charter of confirmation by the same lady, dated 3d January, 1451, in which the previous mortification is repeated, and the annual rent of four additional tenements devoted to the support of St Mary's Chapel. The *new aisle* may therefore be regarded as having been only recently erected at the time of Lady Alicia's first grant, and to have been merely an extension of the parish church.

On the 6th September, 1502, James Chalmyr of Gadgireth resigned an annual rent of 40 pence, payable out of a tenement in Irvine, for the support of the chaplains officiating at the altars of St Ninian and Catharine, within the parish church. There is also a similar mortification by Rankin Brown, burgess of Irvine, dated 16th November, 1506. In 1540, Alexander Scot, the provost of the collegiate church of Corstorphin, granted five roods of land, in the burgh of Irvine, a tenement in the same, and a piece of land beside the bridge of Irvine, two acres of land at the said burgh, and annual rents to the amount of £6, 2s. 4d., from a number of tenements within the said burgh, for the purpose of building a chapel within the parish church, and maintaining a chaplain. The charter under the Great Seal, confirming this grant, is dated 10th February, 1541. The original is in the Irvine charter chest. Chalmers mentions, that "at Bourtrehill, in the country part of the parish of Irvine, a mile distant from the town, there was formerly a chapel, with a burying-ground."

"From the rental of Kilwinning, which was given in officially to government in 1562, it appears that the monks received from the church of Irvine yearly, 39 bolls of meal, 9 bolls and 2 firlots of bear, £17, 6s. 8d. for part of the tithes

---

* Ayr is now the chief—Irvine is the custom-house for Irvine, Troon, and Ardrossan.

† In a dispute between the Abbot and Monks of Paisley and Gilbert, the son of Samuel of Renfrew, in 1233, the first examination of witnesses took place in the parochial church of "Yrewin," before the Deacons of Carrick and Cunninghame and the Schoolmaster of Ayr.

leased, and 'four hugguttis of wine.' At the same epoch of the Reformation, the vicarage of Irvine was held by Thomas Andrew, who made a return on the 3d of March, 1561-2, stating that the fruits and revenues of that vicarage had been let for forty years past, at 40 marks yearly."*

In 1572, this same Thomas Andrew, vicar of Irvine, feued the church lands belonging to his vicarage, to Patrick Brown of Boroughland, for a feu-duty of five shillings Scots, being one shilling in augmentation of the old rental.†

In 1562, immediately after the Reformation, the burgh of Irvine received a perpetual grant of all the revenues and property which had belonged to the Church for the purpose of establishing a public school at Irvine. The instrument of sasine conveying the gift, is dated 5th October, 1564, and proceeds upon a royal precept, dated 8th June, 1562, bearing that a perpetual grant had been made to the provost, bailies, councillors, and community of the burgh of Irwyne, and their successors, "of all and singular the lands, houses, buildings, churches, chaplinaries, orchyards, gardens, crofts, annualrents, trusts, rents, profits, emoluments, farms, alms (lie Daill silver), anniversaries, alterages, and prebendaries within any church, chaplainary, or colledge, founded by any patrons of the same within the liberties of the burgh of Irvine: as also, six bolls of multure belonging to the Carmelite's Order, all united into one tenement, to be called in time coming the King's foundation of the school of Irvyne." This seems to have been the first step towards the institution of a public school in Irvine; but it appears not to have been immediately acted upon; for there is a charter from James VI., ten years afterwards, dated 8th June, 1572, including all the subjects enumerated in the previous grant, and proceeding upon the narrative of his Majesty's desire to enable the people to establish schools in all the burghs. It does not appear that the "King's foundation of the School of Irvyne" was ever matured by the authorities. No doubt a schoolmaster was maintained by the burgh, although we do not find any notice of the fact in the Council records, till a minute of the 16th Apryle, 1686, states that the authorities had "aggreid with William Clerk, scholemaster at Beith, ffor serving as scholemaster of this burgh for the space of ane yeir,"—salary, "twa hundreth merks for the said yeir." There can be no doubt, however, that a parish school had existed long previously at Irvine. The present academy, towards the erection of which the town contributed largely, was built in 1814.

* Chalmers' Caledonia.
† Original feu-charter in the archives of Irvine.

In Pont's Cuninghame Topographised (1620) Irvine is thus described:—"The toune is a free Royal Burghe, and is governed with a Provost and his Baillies. In it is a fair church, and the Baillie Courts of Cuninghame ar ther keipt by the Earl of Eglintoune and his deputts. Neir to the toune the river Irwyne is overpassed by a faire stone bridge; neir to vich was formerly a frierrey of the order of the Carmelitts,* founded of old by the Laird of Fulartoune de eodem. Ther is plenty of salmond taken in this river, and the toune bears for ther armes, argent, a Lyone chained, gules." A new bridge was built at the expense of the burgh in 1746, and widened and improved in 1827. The present church was erected on the site of the old in 1774. "The revenue of the burgh," says the Statistical Account, "is derived chiefly from landed property. In the year 1697, it amounted to £1557, 2s. 7d. Scots, and the expenditure to £1431, 6s. 7d. Scots. In the year 1840, the revenue amounted to £1675, 6s. 11d. sterling, and the expenditure to £1567, 15s. 4d. sterling." As in most other burghs, no small sociality seems to have prevailed under the old regime. Amongst the loose papers in the archives of Irvine, there is a goodly roll of tavern-keepers' accounts against the burgh. For example, the "Account due be the Toune of Irvin to Janet Garven, Beginning 23 January, 1686," till Nov. 10, amounted to the round sum of £84, 14s. 4d. Scots. One of the items runs thus:

"Jan. 30.—It. The Magistrats and Councill when they were subscryving the tacks betwixt my Lord Montgomerie and the toune, flour pynts of wyne, and for Aill, Brandy, tobacco, and pypps, 20s, . . . . . £05 00 00."
Only think of the Magistrates and Councillors of the present day enjoying their tobacco and pipes at the public expense!

*Memorabilia connected with the Burgh:*

The following notes from the papers and records of the burgh may be amusing, while they serve to illustrate particular passages both of local and general history:—

1529.—Discharge by the Earl of Rothes, the Abbots of Whithorn, Arbroath, &c., as Lords Compositors, to the Bailies of Irving, for composition of £33, 6s. 8d. for the Raid of Solway.—Dated at Air 12th February.

1540.—Letter of protection by James V. under his Privy Seal, dated 7th August, in favour of the Provost, &c., showing the disturbed state of the times.

* This friary was on the Fullarton side of the river, in the parish of Dundonald.

1546.—Commission by Queen Mary, with consent of the Earl of Arran, 15th August, proceeding on a narrative of the burgh of Irvine being infected with a plague, and therefore granting to the Magistrates, while the plague continued, the same powers of justiciary which the Justice-General possessed, to enable them to enforce the necessary regulations, &c.

1549.—Licence and warrant by Queen Mary, under the hand of the Regent, Earl of Arran, as her tutor, narrating, that "for the composition of sax scoir pundis money of our realm, hes grantit and given licence to our louitts the prouist, bailzies, and haill communitie of our burgh of Irvine, to remane and byid at hame fra our oist and army devisit to conuene on Roskene muire the xx day of October instant, for resisting of our auld inemies of England, and recovering of the forts of our realme presentlie in their handis," It further narrates that the Provost and Bailzies had paid the composition, and that the inhabitants delayed to repay the same; the Regent therefore grants warrant to " command and charge all and sindrie the burgesses inhabitantes, wedeis, alsweill women as men," " to relief and mak thankfull payment to the saidis Provost and Bailzies of the foirsaid compositione . . within the dayis next after they be chargit, under the pane of rebellione, and putting of thame to our horne." Dated at Hamilton, 9th October, the seventh year of the Queen's reign.

1569.—Discharge by Alexander Earl of Glencairn, commonly called the " Good Earl," to the burgh of Irvine, for £52, 6s. 8d., for furnishing men for recovering the Castle of Dumbarton, &c. Dated at Finlayston, 27th December.

1572.—Letters of protection by Archibald Earl of Argyle.

1583.—Letter from James VI. " To our traist freindis the Prouost, Bailzies, and Counsel of our Burth of Irving:—Traist freindis, we greit you hairtlie weill. It hes plesit God, to our contentment, and we ar assurit na less to the commoun lyking of all our affectionate subjectis, to blis with appeirance of successioun, our darest bedfallow the quene being with child, and neir the tyme of hir delyuerie.—Quhilk and vther wechtie effairs geving occasioun of a mair necessar deliberatioun and adwyse of our nobilitie and estaittis nor at any tyme heirtofoir, we have thocht meit to desyre you maist ernistlie, that ye faill not, all excuses set apairt, to addres your commissioners towards us heir at Halyruidhous the xi day of Januar next to cum," &c. From Halirnidhouse the xviij day of December.

1584.—Letter from the Earle of Mar and Goury, the Abbots of Dryburgh, Cambuskenneth, &c.

to the Provost and Bailies of Irvine, stating that they have declared their mind to the Lord Boyd, to be shewn unto them in some matters of consequence, tending to the " suirtie of God's true religion and professors thairof, the welfair of the Kingis majestie and commonwealth of the haill realme, whereanent we desire you effectuously to give him ferme credit." From Stirling, xxi September.

1593.—Letter from Lords Blantyre, Newbottle, and others, respecting imposts on wyne.—3d January.

1644.—Letter from the Marquis of Argyll, dated 9th August, for 2000 weight of powder for the service of the Committee of Estates; with receipt by John Campbell, servant of the Marquis, for the same in 20 barrels.

1656.—Paper signed by Lord Cochrane, Cessnock, Rowallane, &c., bearing that Mr Robert Barclay, Provost of Irving, had craved payment of a bed, &c. Dated at Kilmarnock, 30th May.

1670.—George Erskine, procurator-fiscal, represented to the Counsell ane ryot and misdemeanour committed be Sir Alexander Cunynghame of Robertland and others, his assotiats, vpon the 12th instant, within the said burghe, within the hous of Arthour Hamiltone, toune-clerk of this burghe, &c.

1671.—Discharge from Alexander Earl of Eglintoun to the Magistrates for 200 merks, their fourth year's answering for militia horses.—13th December.

——." A true Accompt of the Disbursements and Losses by John Dunlop, qll. he was Magistrat of Irvin, in tyme of Alaster Macdonald, In the tyme of the sectaries prevailing after the defeat at Hamiltoun,"—amounting in all to £811, 13s. 4d. Scots. He desired the burgh to refund him. He had been summoned to Kilmarnock and Glasgow, and among other items occurs the following:—" Imprimis, ane fedder bed and its furnitour, to the garrisone in Eglintoune, which I never gat back, £30."

1675.—The Council order three pounds to be paid Thomas Thomson, to mend a wound in his child's head, he being in poverty.—May 12.

1676.—Price of ale fixed by the Council at 28d. the pint; beer, 32d.; cake of oat bread, 30d.; candle, 4s. 4d. per lb.—20th Feb.

1677.—Provost Blair complains to the Council against Dean of Guild M'Goun for calling him a fool, &c. Admitted to proof.—Sept. 27.

1678.—Intimation to the Council that a millstone in Kameshill, also a blue bonnet, had been bought for the Holme miller, if Magistrates would accept them.—Aug. 23.

——.—Archibald Dickson of Towerland to pay

£40 Scots for his entry in lands of High Myre.—Memorandum, that Mathew Gray and Robert Dickie, tenants of the burgh, have not got allowance of their disbursements anent the Hielandmen and sojours, but ordained to be allowed them as other noblemen and gentlemen allow to their tenants, &c.—Sept. 27.

1678.—Large meeting of the inhabitants held in the church to elect a committee to act in the town's affairs. Seventy persons are mentioned in the sederunt. Twenty merchants and five traders were appointed.—Oct. 31.

——. Nov. 1.—Another large meeting held in the quere of the church to name a committee for electing the Magistrates.*

1680.—Provost Boyle ordered by Council to ryde over to Ayr with the first convenience, and do his utmost to remove the quartering (of the military) that is presently on the burgh.

1686.—William Hendersone, weaver, obtains ten pounds from the burgh as a gratuity to repair his house, which had accidentally fallen down. He was fourscore years of age, and poor.—30th Jan.

——.—Ane hundreth punds Scotts money voted by the Council to defray the expense of the Provost in attending Parliament (John Montgomerie, Provost.)—23d April.

——.—Persons appointed by the Council to oversee the sett of the Doura coal-heughs,† &c.—28th May.

——.—The Magistrates and Council sign a bond to support William and Mary.—July 9.

1687.—Shewalton and Bailie Wallace appointed commissioners, with Sir William Wallace of Craigie, to repair to Castle Drummond, and commune with the Earl of Perth, Lord High Chancellor, anent the affairs of the burgh.—Oct. 15.

1688.—The Council agree to build pews in the meeting-house for their convenience.‡—Jan. 3.

——.—Magistrates apply to Government for the gift of " a plack to the pynt, or 20s. the boll of malt," to defray the amount of cess, and pay off other debts.—March 15.

——.—Thomas Wallace of Alderslie, advocate, appointed to manage the town's affairs in Edinburgh.—April 17.

——.—" Considering that there is a party of Major-General Graham of Claverhouse his troops hath been quartered upon this burgh for some time back, for the additional supply due by this burgh to Sir Hugh Wallace of Inglestane, and which supply had been uplifted, and was still resting by the late Magistrates; therefore, order the said party to quarter upon the late Magistrates for the same, and to pound for the quartering money, if necessary."

1688.—The burgh to put forth men, horse, and furniture, in obedience to his Highness'* proclamation.—Oct. 12.

——.—£160 Scots to be instantly advanced to the Provost and John Crawfurd of Banneik, to ryde for the town,† and more to be sent them, if they have occasion to tarry long in his Majesty's service.

In respect of the great burdens under which the burgh at present laboured, the Magistrates were not able to outreik men, horse, and furnitour for the foregoing use. Resolved, that one month's cess be laid upon the inhabitants for the said outreik, &c.—Oct. 12.

——.—The 5000 merks contributed to procure the gift of 20s. on the boll of malt, to be brought back from Edinburgh, and applied to the most pressing debts.‡—Oct. 23.

1689.—Letter from the Prince of Orange, dated at St James's, 5th February 1689, addressed to the Town-Clerk, requiring the whole burgesses to meet and choose their commissioners for the meeting of the Estates, to be held at Edinburgh on the 14th March, &c.—Feb. 25.

Alexander Cuninghame of Cherrylands was appointed.—March 6.

——.—Order for payment of £9, 14s. 4d. to the Provost for expenses incurred by him with Lord Eglintoun and Lieutenant-Colonel Grahame and others, along with the inhabitants, at Kilwinning, at the burial of one of Lord Montgomerie's men; also for attending a county meeting at Ayr.—May 14.

——.—Town to be guarded by " twenty fenceable men each night, in case the officers transiently on the spot refuse to do so."—May 7.

——.—Fencible men called out, and ammunition brought from Ayr. They are formed into two companies, with two pair of colours—" one pair being the town's arms, the other the king or kingdom's arms," &c.—May 7.

——.—Innkeeper's to give nightly a list of all persons lodging with them.—June 21.

——.—" Fencible men within Cuninghame to rendezvous to-morrow within the town's Ebertie, under the command of the Laird of Kilbirnie, their Colonel." Town's companies " to go forth

---

* These meetings, as the reader will perceive from the dates, occurred during the struggle for civil and religious liberty under Charles II.

† Coal was early wrought in the parish of Irvine.

‡ Taking advantage of the Act of Toleration, a meeting-house, apart from the parish church, had been built in Irvine. The resolution of the Council to build " pews," was obviated by the Revolution.

VOL II.

* The Prince of Orange.

† To appear in arms.

‡ The proposed plack a pynt of dues was obtained in November following.

to Townend in their best armes and joyn them."
—July 3.

Such was the display of arms deemed necessary to aid in guaranteeing the infant Revolution of 1688, which, a few years afterwards, was felt to be so firmly established, that we find the burgesses of Irvine with ample leisure and inclination to attend to the amusements of the people.

1694.—Appoint a silver tumbler to be made at the town's expense, as the prize to be run for at the race which is to be at this place on the last Tuesday of October current.—Oct. 12.

Irvine, or Bogside Races, have been long famous.

### The Presbytery Records.*

Irvine was somewhat famous as a place of execution in the era of witchcraft. No fewer than twelve witches were there executed at one time, in the month of March, 1650, and four more in the course of a few weeks afterwards.

15th June, 1647.—The plague surmised to be in Kilwinning, and that the sickness at Largs still continues.

15th Sept. 1647.—The Presbytery, in terms of the Assembly's ordinance, ordains that a thanksgiving be solemnly keeped the last Lord's-day of this instant, for thir causes: 1st, That the Lord hath been pleased to grant so glorious a victory to our army employed against the rebels in the Hielands. 2dly, That in the time of England's confusions, and our fears from them, it has pleased the Lord to give us the benefits of a General Assembly, which, with great unanimity, has issued forth a public declaration against the *errors in England*. 3dly, That the Lord hath been graciously pleased to keep the pestilence from spreading over the face of the land, &c., &c. Mr John Nevoy is returned from the army, and gave the brethren hearty thanks for their care in supplying his kirk in the time of his absence.

26th Oct. 1647.—Collections ordered for Largs, where the people were very destitute. Some individuals in the bounds of the Presbytery having gone into England, and got married, contrary to the order of the kirk, the General Assembly to be applied to for instructions how the Presbytery are to proceed in censuring the said persons. Sums collected for Largs: From New Mills, 152 pounds 8s. 4d. From Irvine, 200 merks; Kilmaurs, 102 merks; Kilbirnie, 50 pounds. From Stewarton, 111 pounds; Kilwinning, 100 pounds; Dreghorn, 43 pound 8s.; Dalry, 48 pound 20 merks; Ar-

drossan, 50 merks. From Perston, 40 pound viii merks. Three clergymen appointed to speak to the Erle of Eglinton anent the plantation of Perston.

16th May, 1648.—The Presbytery having read and examined a letter from the Commission of the Kirk, dated at Edinburgh, 28th April 1648, to the end that there may be some testimony and evidence extant of the zeal and faithfulness of the commissioners of the kirk in the cause of God, does ordain that the special heads and clauses of the said letter should be inserted and registered as follows: The first head bears a narrative of the commissioners' proceeding towards the present Parliament, which had gone on and concluded ane engagement in war against England before satisfactory answer was given to the desire of the kirk, relating withal, that they did conceive the liberty of the kirk much prejudiced by the Parliament proceeding to determine in these things, which so nearly and highly concerned religion, without the advice and consent of the kirk, whereupon the commissioners of the kirk does find themselves pressed for the preservation of the liberties of the kirk, according to the word of God. Second clause: Because there was just fear of overturning the whole word of God in three dominions. They require that a solemn fast may be kept the last Sabbath of May, for entreating the Lord for the means of help in the day of this our great need. A third clause bears ane exhortation to the brethren of the Presbytery, that they not only withdraw themselves from giving any assistance and concurrence to the Parliament in the matter of the engagement between the two nations, but also be ready to give a testimony of their affection to the cause as they shall see need, and to give timeous warning unto all against the snares and temptations of the times; exhorting likewise that the brethren may labour to be of one mind in the Lord, that by his means the boasting of the adversary may be put to silence. The fourth clause is anent the reading of a short information relating to the Parliament declaration, which is to be made known to the people, and they are exhorted to get copies of the same, to the end that they may not be ensnared by specious pretences. The several heads of the letter aforesaid being read over again in the Presbytery's audience, were unanimously approven, the information to the people appointed to be read the first Lord's-day, the fast agreed unto to be kept upon the day above mentioned, and that Mr Hew M'Kaile, Mr John Bell, and Mr John Nevoy, shall draw up the causes of the fast out of the commissioners' letter, to be given to every brother, that they might be publicly read upon the day of the intimation.

---

* We are indebted for the following notices to a correspondent of 'The Irvine Monthly News-Letter.'

The Presbytery also agree to a supplication to be made to Parliament, embracing the foresaid matters.

25th July, 1648.—Some of the brethren cited before the Committee of Estates for being at Mauchline Moor, although they had persuaded the people who were there present to disband and go home to their houses.

15th Dec. 1648.—The Presbytery gave various directions regarding those who had been out in the late unlawful engagement, directed, *inter alia.* 11th, Those who were active in quartering of sojures in the unlawful engagement, or being employed to quarter those who rose up for the good cause, did either declare themselves unwilling or absented themselves. They are to make a personal acknowledgment, and to be sadly and gravely rebukit. Further, it is agreed upon and concluded, that all who are to make a personal acknowlegment, if they be elders, are to be suspended from the exercise of the eldership for a day or two.

2d Jan. 1649.—On a report that some persons in the family of Lady Semple, then residing at Southanan, did absent themselves from church, inquiry directed, that in case Lady Semple remain there, some course be taken with that family.

13th Feb. 1649.—It is appointed that Elizabeth Bruntfield and Bessie Duel, two of my Lady Semple, her servants, for the present at Southanan, for their absenting themselves from the public ordinances, shall be cited before the session of Largs.

19th Feb. 1649.—The Presbytery, taking into consideration the diverse combats that have been fought, and the challenges to duels within the bounds of the Presbytery, &c., do appoint the Assembly's Act, 12th Aug. 1648, to be publicly intimated by every brother in the congregation, that none may pretend ignorance.

8th May, 1649.—Elizabeth Bruntfield and Bessie Duel, my Lady Semple, her two servants, are gone out of the country.

22d May, 1649.—At trials of Mr Wm. Rodger, in relation to a call to the ministry of Kilbirnie, "The Presbytery having considered what common head was most fit and useful to be handled in reference to the times, does condescend upon that *De jure magistratus circa sacra,* quhilk is prescribed to the said William to be handled when the Presbytery should appoint a diet."

At a visitation at Kilmarnock, 19th June, 1649, anent ane seperstitious image that was upon my Lord Boyd his tomb, it was the Presbytery's mind that his Lordship should be written to that he would be pleased to demolish and ding it down, and that if he did not, then the Presbytery was to take a farther course.

14th August 1649.—Compeared the two bailies of Irvine, and did represent to the Presbytery the great skaith and damage that the town had sustained through fire, and did desire a contribution from the several parishes for re-edifying of the houses that were burnt. The Presbytery having heard their desires, do unanimously condescend thereunto, and that the contributions should be gathered with the first conveniency, and brought in.

20th Nov. 1649.—Thomas Cumming having been required to sign the Covenant, "he gave in a paper, declaring that, notwithstanding all the pains the brethren had taken upon him, he could not do so without sin." The Presbytery finding him obstinate, and unwilling to receive information, does appoint that, without further delay, he renew the Solemn League and Covenant upon Sabbath come-fortnight, publicly, in the kirk of Kilmaurs; and that before renewing the same, he acknowledge that he has given scandal and offence to the people of God, and that Mr William Guthrey preach that day, and tender the Covenant to him; and in case he do refuse, that Mr William Crooks make report, that the Presbytery may go on in process against him.

15th Dec. 1649.—Compeared Thomas Cumming, who offered to take the Covenant privately before the Presbytery; that rather than take it publicly, would venture upon excommunication, imprisonment, and a scaffold; because to do it publicly, was to make him suffer as an evil-doer, &c., &c. The Presbytery think it altogether unjust and ridiculous, and therefore directed that he receive the Covenant on the first Lord's-day. Poor Thomas' courage evaporated; and on 1st Jan. it was reported that he had taken the Covenant as enjoined.

24th Sept. 1649.—The moderator of the Presbytery (Mr Thomas Bell), upon the grounds and presumption of witchcraft that are holden forth against Elizabeth Graham in Kilwinning, having written for a commission to try the said Elizabeth; the commission is returned, whereupon it is appointed that some of the brethren go to the Erle of Eglinton, and speak his Lordship that that commission may be put in execution, and that his Lordship may be pleased actively to concur.

24th Oct. 1649.—Upon the presumption of witchcraft that was holden forth against Elizabeth Graham in Kilwinning,[*] the Presbytery did

* In a work entitled "Satan's Invisible World Discovered, by Mr George Sinclair, Professor of Philosophy in the College of Glasgow," there is an account of the proceedings against Elizabeth, or Jessie Graham, one of the parties mentioned in the minutes of Presbytery. It is stated to

conclude that the Committee of Estates should be written to for ane commission to put the said Elizabeth to an assize, if their Lordships should think the presumption relevant, and the draught of the letter that was drawn up by Mr James Ferguson is approven as fit to be sent.

19th March, 1650.—The bailie of Cuninghame having signified to the Presbytery, that upon Thursday next an assize was to be holden upon twelve persons who had confessed the sin of witchcraft, and that the execution was to be upon Friday the morn thereafter, and that it was fitting a minister should be appointed to wait upon every one of them that they might be brought to a farther acknowledgment of their guilt, the Presbytery having considered the foirsaid, does, in order thereto, appoint these brethren following to wait upon the execution the said day, viz., Mr Ralph Rodger, Mr James Ferguson, Mr Wm. Russel, Mr R. Urie, Mr Alex. Nisbet, Mr James Roman, Mr Wm. Rodger, Mr And. Hutchison, Mr Wm. Castellan, Mr James Clandening, Mr Rob. Aird, Mr Wm. Crookes, and Mr Gabriel Cuninghame.

22d April, 1650.—The Presbytery finding that the sin of witchcraft was growing daily, and that in the several parishes meikle of the hidden works of darkness was discovered and brought to light in the mercy of God, and that several were apprehended, and in firmance for that sin, did meet

occasionally this day to hear and receive the confessions of some, of the said sin of witchcraft, that they might recommend the same to the Lords of Privy Council, for the issuing forth of a commission of assize to sit upon the said persons; and after hearing the Presbytery, do judge the confessions of the persons following relevant to be recommended: Inprimis, of Margaret Couper in Saltcoats, who was apprehended by the Bailie of Cuninghame, upon presumption of witchcraft and common *bruit*, who confessed the renunciation of her baptism, carnal copulation with the devil, and the taking of a new name from him. Item, the confession of Janet Robison in Monkcastle, of Sarah Erskine in Largs, of John Shedden there, of Margaret Montgomerie in Irvine, of Jean Hamilton, Marion Cuninghame, and Euphame Dickie, there, of Janet M'Kie in Dalry, Catherine Robison, Agnes Glen, and Bessie Ewing there, likewise of Violet Mudie in Kilbride, all which did confess before famous witnesses the renouncing of their baptism, copulation with the devil, taking of a new name from him, and several apparitions of the devil to them, and some of them by and attour, did confess. Further, the Presbytery being informed that there were several persons in Dalry, who, partly upon presumption, partly upon delation, and partly upon *mala fama*, were apprehended by the Judge Ordinary for witchcraft, who continued still impenitent, therefore it is appointed that Mr Patrick Colville, and Mr W. S. Russel, shall go to Dalry, and deal with the said persons for bringing of them to ane confession. Likewise the confession of Catherine Montgomerie in Saltcoats, who did confess, beside the renunciation of her baptism ; the appearing of the devil ; the taking of a new name from the devil ; copulation with him, and sundry malafices, and the alluring and drawing on of others to the devil's service, is found relevant and clear, and recommend it amongst the rest.

The Bailie Depute of Cuninghame, (north district of Ayrshire,) having represented to the Presbytery that sundry persons, who were suspected of witchcraft within the bounds of the Presbytery, were apprehended (contrary to the privilege of the bailiary) without a warrant from him, the foresaid representation being heard and examined by the Presbytery, they do judge it expedient that no person or persons suspect of witchcraft as said is, be apprehended and put in firmance by any person, without a warrant from the Bailie of Cuninghame or Depute; and in case any person be apprehended before a warrant can be obtained and had, that word be presently sent to the bailie thereof.

The confessions of several persons in Largs, of

have been given by the minister of the parish. It appears, that in a fit of drunkenness Jessie had threatened another woman, who ten days afterwards was taken ill and died. Jessie was apprehended and imprisoned in the steeple on a charge of witchcraft. She lay there for thirteen weeks, the minister constantly visiting her. But she remained obdurate, denying her guilt. He was under great doubts on the subject, when fortunately a celebrated witch-finder, named Hogs, made his appearance, and having examined Bessie, found the mark in the middle of her back. Into this mark Hogs inserted a large brass pin; and as Bessie did not appear to feel it, and no blood flowed, this was considered strong evidence. The minister was a good deal nonplused, however, because the chief man in the parish, (we presume Lord Eglinton,) and other judges, had declared it to be "mere clatters." Another circumstance appears to have given the minister some anxiety, which was, his fear that the assize would not condemn Bessie, unless he advised them to do so, which he was not very clear about doing. In this dilemma he prayed for directions how he was to proceed, and as he appears to have considered it by a special interposition, he was induced to listen at the door of the prison, accompanied by the bellman, where they overheard Bessie conversing with the foul fiend: although the minister could not understand their conversation, the bellman did; at the same time the bellman appears to have got such a fright, that he nearly tumbled down the stair of the steeple in his haste to get away from so dangerous a personage. Of course this was conclusive of Bessie's guilt, and her fate was soon settled. Finding she must die, poor Bessie prayed earnestly for forgiveness of her sins, but denied most obdurately the witchcraft, and the minister very sagely discovered that this was a device between Bessie and the devil to deceive him, but he was too knowing to be thus taken in, and Bessie suffered according to her sentence, impenitent to the last.

the sin of witchcraft, being read and examined, are recommended to the Committee of Estates for issuing furth of a commission to put the said persons to ane assize, that so the land may be purged of that abominable sin.

30th April, 1650.—Some of the brethren, viz. Mr James Ferguson, moderator, Mr Alex. Nisbet, Mr Thom. Bell, Mr J. Rowat, Mr A. Hutchison, Mr Ralph Rodger, Mr Wm. Rodger, Mr Jas. Clandening, Mr Robt. Urie, and Thos. Guthrie, ruling elder, did convene to receive and examine the confession of Maal Montgomerie in Largs, Mall Small and Isobel Maillshead there. Siklike of Margaret Isset in Kilwinning, who had confessed ilk ane of them their guiltiness of the sin of witchcraft; and after examination of the foresaid confessions, they are found relevant to be recommended for issuing furth of a commission to put them to ane assize.

7th May, 1650.—Because there is to be ane execution of four persons upon Saturday next, at Irvine, for the sin of witchcraft, the Presbytery does appoint three ministers, viz. Mr James Ferguson, Mr Matthew Mowat, and Mr Andw. Hutchison, together with the minister of the place, to attend the execution the said day.

Three ministers to go to Dalry, and deal with those persons apprehended for the sin of witchcraft, and continuing impenitent, to bring them to a confession of their guilt, if it be possible.

Isobel Allan in Kilwinning, being trilapse in fornication, compeared, and because she was under the suspicion of witchcraft, and withal great with child, &c., delay proceeding in the meantime.

The confession of Geiles Buchanan in Ardrossan, and Janet Hill there, wherein was contained their acknowledgment of the abominable sin of witchcraft in renouncing their baptism, taking a new name from the devil, having carnal copulation with him, and being at diverse meetings with him, being read and examined, are judged clear to be presented to the Lords of Privy Counsel or Committee of Estates, for granting and giving a commission to put the said persons to ane assize.

28th May, 1650.—The confession of Wm. Semple in Kilburnie, and Agnes Houston there, being apprehended by the Bailie Depute of Cuninghame, for the sin of witchcraft, and acknowledging the same before witnesses, being read and examined, are to be recommended to the Committee of Estates for the issuing furth of a commission to put the said persons to ane assize.

Mr Wm. Guthrey, and the two ministers of Stewarton, are appointed to deal with some persons within the parish of Dreghorn, apprehended for the sin of witchcraft, both upon presumptions and delations, for bringing them to ane confession.

16th June, 1650.—Having heard the confession of Jean Hamiltown, Isobel Hutchison, Marion Boyd, of Agnes Dunlop and Jean Swan, in Irvine, of witchcraft, how that they had renounced their baptism, taken a new name from the devil, &c., being read, are found to be clear, to be recommended to the Committee of Estates for a commission.

James Robertson and his wife, indwellers in Irvine, apprehended to be cited before the Presbytery for writing a letter to Barbara Montgomerie, now apprehended for the sin of witchcraft, wherein they dissuade her from confession of that sin, and desiring her by any means to keep her tongue, and all the world will not get her life.

2d July, 1650.—The confession of two persons in Irvine, having acknowledged their guiltiness of witchcraft, viz., Thomas Brown and Isobel Carse, likewise of ane Samuel Elves, an Englishman, who had been a common beggar this many years in the country, being read, are judged clear to be holden furth to the Committee of Estates for a commission to put them to ane assize.

In 1697, a fast to be observed for various sins, among others the sin of witchcraft. Three people in Ardrossan, charged with using a charm to preserve their cattle from disease, who declared they did it ignorantly, and professed their grief, are sharply rebuked, and ordered back to their session to be rebuked.

19th July, 1698.—The Presbytery appoint Mr Pat. Warner, their commissioner, to attend with other ministers, the meeting of Parliament, for prosecuting of the recommendations of the General Assembly against popery and witchcraft.

This is the last instance in which witchcraft is mentioned. There are several cases where parties were brought before the Presbytery for consulting spaewives for the purpose of recovering stolen goods, the last instance occurs in the year 1735.

A number of individuals were brought before the Presbytery at different times charged with malignancy, and being concerned in the unlawful engagement. Among others the Earl of Glencairn, Lords Montgomerie and Boyd, the lairds of Roberland, Knock, Baidland, Cambskeith, &c., and the sons of Lainshaw and Magbiehill; all these parties appear either to have given satisfaction to the kirk, or evaded it by keeping out of their jurisdiction, in which cases the Presbytery applied to their brethren, in the part of the country to which the culprits had gone, to follow up the proceedings against them. The following are a few of the cases mentioned: Janet Cunninghame in Kilmaurs, for cursing of all those who went out in the public cause, (i. e., those who went out to oppose parties employed in the unlawful engagement,) ordered to be cited. Adam Simpson cited for malignancy, viz. drinking to the confusion of all that were contrary to the engagement, calling the ministers deceivers of the people. That he did curse the people of God—that he called Mr Robert Aird ane ass and fool, because he said the Parliament ought only to be obeyed in the Lord. Simpson asked who were his accusers. The Presbytery answered, "That *fama clamosa* was enough for the Presbytery to own it, albeit there was none to accuse him."

Aug. and Sept. 1649.—Lord Montgomerie, and others, applied to be allowed to confess their sin in joining the unlawful engagement, which appears to have been granted after having sufficiently humbled themselves and submitted to the kirk. The ladies did not escape. "Concerning the Lady Robertland, Mr Andrew Hutchison is appointed to try what was her carriage in the time of the unlawful engagement."

April, 1650.—Process against the laird of Knock continued notwithstanding of his removal to Ireland. They had, since 1647, hunted this unfortunate laird all over Scotland, and he appears at last to have taken refuge in Ireland.

7th May, 1650.—The laird of Robertland appeared, but said he was not yet convinced of the unlawful engagement. The Presbytery being "desirous to go about all lawful means for the gaining of the gentlemen," appointed Mr Pat. Colville and Mr Wm. Guthrie, to go and labour with him to convince him.

### Custom-House Records.

Much has been said by our local romancers on the subject of smuggling on the coast of Ayrshire during the last century. Many marvellous stories have been told of the feats of those engaged in the contraband trade, and of the great extent to which it was carried. The following extracts from the Custom-house records show that there is at least good foundation for some of the traditional averments still current amongst the peasantry in the smuggling districts:—

1728, Sept. 27.—A letter from the collector and comptroller, mentions a vessel, the *Prosperity* of Kilbride, having arrived at Saltcoats, on 6th September, with a cargo of brandy, woollens, &c., accompanied by a king's sloop, to prevent the cargo being run. The avowed object for coming to Saltcoats being to take in salt, in addition to her cargo. The master delayed sailing on pretence of having met with damage, and being unable to proceed on her voyage.

28th Oct.—Another letter states that a mob had attacked and robbed the vessel, after having severely beaten the officers in charge, and on 7th November, they reported that one of the officers "was dangerously ill, and his life much doubted of from the bruises he had received on that occasion."

1728, Nov. 7.—The Custom-house attempted to be robbed. At this period it appears to have been the practice when tobacco was shipped, to send troops from Glasgow to guard the vessels till they sailed.

1730, Nov. 10.—A letter from the Commissioners mentions that a troop of dragoons was quartered at Kilmarnock, another at Kilbride, and 50 men at Irvine, Saltcoats, Beith, &c., "for the assistance of the officers of the customs in the execution of their duty."

1730, Dec. 3.—The collector and comptroller directed, "not to receive any Old Bank notes in time coming, as the Old Bank" (we suppose the Bank of Scotland) " have come to a resolution to alter the form of their notes, above twenty shillings value, whereby they have reserved to themselves an option, whether they will pay their current cash notes on demand, or within six months thereafter, which being a proceeding of a very extraordinary and uncommon nature, and attended with great inconveniency, &c. &c." In 1775, we find the collector and comptroller ordered not to take Glasgow bank notes.

1731, Sept. 23.—From Commissioners, mentioning their having dismissed James Crawfurd, surveyor, Alexander Kennedy, landwaiter, and the collector's clerk, for being concerned in a fraud on the revenue, by shipping lately at Saltcoats, on board the *Moses*, a considerable quantity of peats and stones as tobacco.

[This James Crawfurd was a son of Viscount Garnock, and if he had had a family and descendants, his heir would have now been Earl of Crawfurd. James Crawfurd was the *alleged* ancestor of Crawfurd, the Irish schoolmaster, who, about forty years ago, laid claim to the title and estates of the Earldom of Crawfurd.]

1732, April 12.—Commissioners mention that they had received information from the Isle of Man, that thirty sail of vessels were loading brandy and other goods for Ireland and this country.

1733, July 6.—Francis Porter, cooper and tidewaiter, understanding from Kilwinning, that on Friday last, there were 16 or 18 carts there, which came empty from Glasgow, in order to assist at the re-landing tobacco along the coast, (our tidesmen observing always when any of our own carters stir,) went with some others of our own tidesmen that night to Saltcoats, where they mostly suspected it to be, and with the assistance of Mr

Charles Hamilton, landwaiter, and other officers there, carefully watched that night, and nothing occurred; only they observed several of Mr B.'s sons, going to and fro, about his storehouse there. In the morning, Mr Hamilton went along the coast to learn what had become of the carters that were at Kilwinning, and on his way understood they had gone a bye-way to Peucorse, for fear of being discovered; but by the tracks in the sand, was led to that old castle where the carts lay, and their horses grazing hard by. Likewise in a creek hard by that castle was a lighter, loaded with tobacco, from Port-Glasgow; he being suspicious they had put part ashore the night before, went on board of her and saw their cocket, which was for Fort-William and Inverary, and saw her full. He kept spies on her several nights, which they understanding, thought it most proper to bring her about to Saltcoats, and they have now got a warrant to land it. Mr Hamilton since informs us, that that night 20 of the hhds. had been put on shore, and some of them came the length of Arneal, (where Mr B. has been at Goat-Whey this summer,) on their way to the storehouse at Saltcoats, but the spies informing him that the officers were out, drove it all back again to the lighter. We are of opinion that the trick intended, was to have landed the 43 hhds. on board the lighter, without any despatch, and to have sent the lighter with the coast cocket to the Isle of Man, or some part of the Highlands, where they may have re-landed tobacco, and by the cloak of the coast cocket, to have brought home the same quantity of tobacco, which they judge not safe to risque without one, and to land it regularly in order to get their coast bond cancelled.

1733, July 19.—Last night there came 40 or 50 armed men from Beith (as we suppose), and broke open the Custom-house, and took away a considerable quantity of the brandy, rum, teas, &c., that was condemned in exchequer, and fallen into the officers' hands at sale; also most of the parcels claimed by the Admiral, and calico and other goods which lay for payment of the duties. They set guards round the house, so that neither the officers who were on watch in the house, nor the collector's servants, could get out to alarm the other officers, till a forward maid-servant of the collector's went out at a back window, three stories high, on the roof of the adjoining house, and so got down and alarmed the surveyor. Had it not been for her getting out, and making this alarm, together with the shortness of the night, also the strength of the door, which took them a good deal of time to undo, they had left nothing, &c., &c. Troops are requested by the comptroller.

1733, August 10.—It is flagrant up and down the country who were concerned in it (the robbery of the Custom-house), and there has been strange debates among themselves about the division. Last week, two of our officers went round the country, and to Beith, incognito, and learned the whole people concerned, and particularly got one of the carriers, who was present, to meet Ladyland and me yesterday here, and made a full confession. He happened to be unmercifully beat, which made him make the clearer confession. There are others abused also, from whom we expect a like discovery. But the whole affair must lie dormant till the soldiers come to the country, for without them there is no attempting to secure any of them.

1733, August 13.—Upon Saturday last, one James Ker, in Crunock, in Beith parish, came and told me that a sub-tenant of his had acquainted him of his being willing to discover the whole, so being he would be pardoned. He also told me that the ringleaders of that base crime were entering into an association and solemn oath not to discover any part of that fact; and that whoever refused to do so were in danger of being murdered by the rest; and that if I would give this Ker what would maintain this person, either at home or elsewhere he might be obliged to go to, which I undertook. He brought him, and he made the confession enclosed, which I think is more full than the one made here the beginning of the week.

Note.—The confession is not copied in the letter-book.

1733, September 12.—Yesterday morning, one of the officers of excise here brought 12 casks of brandy, which they seized in one of the *present magistrates'* houses, and this morning, betwixt two and three, a mob to the number of 50, armed with guns and other offensive weapons, attacked the Custom-house, who, after an hour's hard work, broke open the door leading to the warehouse. I made all the resistance I could, having none but myself and a servant in the house, and alarmed the neighbourhood sufficiently, though without success, they being all in the mob's interest, and such of the officers as lived near the Custom-house were sent out by a sham information, so that I had no access of getting them any notice; however, by the methods used, they were diverted from their main design, not having got the warehouse broke. I have too great reason to believe that such mobs are connived at by *those whose business it is to suppress them.*

1733-4, January 31.—We were yesterday informed by Mr Charles Hamilton, land-waiter at Saltcoats, that the *Eagle* of this place, John Boggs, master, wherein Mr B. had shipped tobacco for London, lay still there, as also the empty lighter that brought it about from Clyde, notwithstanding they might often have sailed with a fair wind; that for eight days past, there were lodged in about Saltcoats and Kilwinning (where Mr B. is for the present), several carts and two horses in each, that came from Glasgow empty; that he and the officers, who are all on their guard, do observe them all convened at Mr B.'s storehouse, ready to put some base object in execution, and as soon as they learn the officers are out, the carts are locked up in the warehouse, and the horses dispersed. Mr B. has, since the carts have been here, given some of the tidesmen sham information where brandy lay at some distance, in order to carry them off, but in vain. He also informs us that their design is to land this here, and to carry tobacco along with our coast cocket, which he might have re-landed in the Highlands. The officers have been so fatigued, that we were obliged to send others to relieve them. He begs us to entreat your honours would use your influence to get the half of the command that lie here removed to Saltcoats; for though he should see them in the execution of any unlawful thing of the kind, he could not propose to make a seizure good among such robust fellows as these carters are. We are hopeful, through the officers' vigilance, to break Mr B.'s plan in this attempt of re-landing tobacco, without warrant, as was done last year, with respect to that parcel shipped for England on board the *Thistle*, of which John Boggs was also master.

173½, February 28.—We received yours of the 25th. In answer, please know that the *Eagle* of Saltcoats sailed on Monday last, and has on board 25 hhds. leaf, and 7 hhds. roll tobacco, containing 25,688 pounds. John Boggs is gone master. The lighter which took this tobacco from Clyde, took in a few coals, and sailed some days before the *Eagle*, pretending to be bound for Belfast, though we have cause to suspect she is to be employed in assisting them to execute some base scheme. We learn the *Thistle* is now at Dublin, on her way from Hamburgh to Belfast. Enclosed is a return of a seizure of snake root, made by the officers here. The party at Saltcoats shall be ordered to return to Glasgow in a day or two, when she may be fairly off the coast.

1764, March 26.—From collector and comptroller to Commissioners. Be pleased to know that we have been lately informed, that for a considerable time past both the officers of the Customs and those of the Excise in this collection, and in the collection of Ayr, who have been in use to make seizures of brandy and rum at the Troon point, about four miles from this port, have compounded with the smugglers, and still continue to do so, generally at the rate of four casks to each officer—at the same time allowing several hundred casks of spirits to be conveyed away into the country in their presence; and further, that their composition is such with the smugglers, that the few casks received by them by way of composition, are sometimes first laid on the shore and set apart by themselves, there to remain untouched by the officers till the residue of the cargo be landed, and all the residue conveyed into the country as aforesaid. As this collusive practice must greatly encourage the smugglers, and also augment the illicit and very pernicious trade of running of spirits into this precinct, and as we are very apprehensive that certain of the officers of the Customs here under our immediate inspection are too much concerned in those compositions, (with a greater body of exeisemen who pretend to have authority from their board to compound, and who have made our officers in some degree believe so,) we thought it our duty to acquaint your honours of the same, that such methods may be taken in order to the suppression of every collusive practice tending to the encouragement of smuggling, as to you shall deem fit.

This method of compounding has intimidated some of the officers, so far as they dare not attempt to make a seizure unless they unlawfully join with those that compounded, and therefore find it impracticable to do any service to the revenue in making search for run goods, and we cannot help acquainting your honours, that upon the 8th or 9th day of February last, John Harper, tidesman here, and James M'Nillie, landwaiter at Ayr, made a seizure at the Troon point of several packages of teas, &c., landed out of a wherry in the forenoon of that day, and were deforced, cut, beat, and abused by the smugglers and their abettors, and the goods which they were in possession of, resened.

Your honours will also be pleased to know that the wherry put off again, and in the night of the said day, she returned and landed several hundred casks of spirits at the Troon point, after a composition had been made by a great many other officers both of the Customs and Excise, and other aiders and abettors.

Your honours will be pleased to know, that after inquiry made here as to the nature of frauds carried on between the Isle of Man and Scotland, we find that as the Isle of Man is so situated, and that as it is not above six or seven hours' sail from the nearest port of Scotland, and but about twelve hours' sail from this port, it is now more than ever become the greatest storehouse or magazine for the French and other nations to deposit prodigeous quantities of wines, brandies, rums, &c., coffee, teas, &c., and other Indian goods, and all manner of goods and merchandizes that pay high duties in Great Britain or Ireland, or are prohibited to be imported into these kingdoms, which are afterwards carried off in small boats and wherries built for that purpose, and smuggled upon the coast of Scotland to an enormous degree, as well as upon the coast of England and Ireland, which no method has yet been found out to prevent in any degree, (not one in a hundred of the boats, wherries, or vessels concerned in the smuggling trade being taken at sea, or seized afterwards); it cannot therefore be supposed that it can much longer be suffered to be carried on to such an exorbitant height.

Your honours will further be pleased to know, that this is all the information we can obtain here with respect to the nature and manner of the frauds carried on between the Isle of Man and Scotland in general; but we beg leave to acquaint you, that smuggling into this part of Scotland has so far increased, that it is believed that goods thence have been smuggled into the precinct of Irvine to the value of 20,000 pounds in the last twelve months, notwithstanding of the king's cruizers, and the endeavours of certain of the officers of the Customs and Excise upon land to suppress it.

We cannot pretend to make out a list of all the goods imported into the Isle of Man, and afterwards smuggled upon the coast of Scotland; but enclosed we send your honours a list of the several kinds of goods that have been given into us from our inquiry, together with the trivial duties said to be paid thereon to the proprietor of the island.

A list of goods imported into the Isle of Man, said to pay duties to the proprietor of the island as under, and afterwards smuggled into Scotland, viz.——

Brandies, rum, and geneva, one penny per gallon; arrack, twopence per gallon; wines, one halfpenny per gallon; tobacco, one halfpenny per pound.

The following goods 2½ per cent. *ad valorem*, viz.——

Teas, silks, and other India goods, Barcelona hankerchiefs, French lawns, silks, gloves, and laces, chocolate, coffee, china ware, spiceries, India drugs, and groceries.

*Report by R. M'Clure and A. Crawfurd, Oct. 1764.*

Between seven and eight in the morning, we descried a boat coming into the Troon, which proved to be a small Isle of Man one, and which we believed contained foreign spirits. She no sooner arrived, than about 100 men, mounted on horses, having large sticks in their hands, accompanied with some women, instantaneously came

down from the country, and took possession of the Troon; and though we immediately made an attempt to seize the said boat and spirits, we could by no means get access to her for the mob, who threatened to put us to death if we offered to touch her or what was in her. However, the spirits having been immediately landed, we stood by in order if possible to seize any part of the same, when conveying into the country, and accordingly we then laid hold on three carts, with six casks of the spirits in each, but had no sooner made a seizure thereof, than we were attacked by one ——— ———, servant to ——— ———, in Loans of Dundonald, and by three other men unknown to us, and disguised in sailors' habits, all well provided with great sticks, who deforced us of the seizure, while others, also unknown to us, drove off the carts and spirits, swearing every moment to knock us down, and sometimes lifted up their sticks ready to lay on blows, upon which we made off with an intention to go for Irvine, (seeing we were so unequal in force, and that all the spirits were conveyed up into the country,) and in our way, about a quarter of a mile from the Troon, we met with John Cousar.

1764, Oct. 20.—From collector and comptroller. We have received your letter of the 15th ult., acquainting us that your honours had received undoubted information that large quantities of rum and tea were to be smuggled from the Isle of Man, at Troon, Heads of Ayr, or Turnberry, when the nights were dark and favourable for the purpose, and therefore directing us, and all the officers under our direction, to exert ourselves upon that occasion, and to inform you of our proceedings.

We beg leave to acquaint your honours that, in obedience to your said order, we and all the other officers have used our utmost endeavours to disconcert the smugglers in the execution of their intended fraud, and that notwithstanding thereof, no seizure has been made by any of us since the receipt of that order, excepting four kegs of rum, by John Harper, tidesman; that the said four casks of spirits are part of a wherry, and of a boat's cargo, directly from the Isle of Man, and landed at the Troon yesterday, and the whole of the spirits and a parcel of tea, &c., conveyed into the country before the said John Harper, and Robert M'Clure, and Andrew Crawfurd, tidesmen, could make up to the smugglers. That John Harper was cut and much abused by sundry cadgers and carriers, supposed to have come from Glasgow and the country adjoining, whose names are unknown to him and the other tidesmen. That the said officers were so much obstructed in the execution of their duty, and threatened by persons well known to them, that they could not make themselves masters of one keg more, out of about 150 cart and horse loads of spirits, &c., conveying further into the country by a huge number of country folks, a great part of whom were resolute and desperate fellows, being present at their threatening and obstructing the said officers, and who were aiding and assisting in conveying away the run goods. That the said tidesmen went out to the Troon upon a venture, and afterwards finding a necessity for a party of the military, they immediately called out the same, but before the party could make up, the whole of the run goods were conveyed away into different parts of the country and concealed.

We further beg leave to acquaint you, that it is our humble opinion, that the most effectual means of suppressing smuggling at the Troon, (which has arisen to a very enormous degree), would be for your honours to order a cutter, well manned, a constant station at the Troon, and never to leave that station but in the case of them seeing smuggling wherries and boats going past. We are also humbly of opinion, that were one other cutter stationed at the Heads of Ayr, where we are informed smuggling is carried on very considerably, and a third to cruize between the Heads of Ayr and Mull of Cantyre, this would be of much more service to the revenue than any method that has hitherto been fallen upon.

29th August, 1766.—The collector and comptroller report, that the vesting the ports in the Isle of Man in his Majesty, has had the effect of suppressing in a great measure the smuggling from that quarter; but that they are informed that great quantities of rum from Belfast has been run at Troon and other places, as well as on the coast of Galloway.

1768, August 17.—From Commissioners, mentioning that they had received information that the smuggling trade from Holland had increased to an enormous height upon the coast of Scotland.

1768, December 8.—From collector and comptroller, stating that a party of smugglers, eight in number, or upwards, on horseback, with casks under them, had, between seven and eight o'clock in the evening of the previous day, crossed the bridge at Irvine, the river being flooded; that they had been intercepted by the revenue officers —some shots having passed on the side of the officers, and many blows on both sides; and that two of the smugglers had been seized and committed to prison.

1769, February 21.—From collector and comptroller, mention that a vessel, the *Diamond*, having arrived from Dublin, and officers placed on board, that between twelve and one o'clock the previous night, a party of about twenty men had boarded her, and tied the officers, and carried off a quantity of goods concealed on board.

Of the ecclesiastical history of the parish of Irvine since the Reformation, the Statistical Account affords a succinct outline. "The first Presbyterian minister of Irvine, Mr Thomas Yonng, was inducted in 1570. He was succeeded by Mr Alexander Scrimseour in 1598; and in 1610, he and several of his brethren were charged by the Lords of Secret Council with the crime of harbouring 'John Campell *alias* Fadder Christostome, ane known traffiequing priest.' Mr Scrimseour, in 1618, was succeeded by Mr Dickson, who was deprived of his office by the Court of High Commission; but was afterwards restored through the influence of Alexander the Sixth Earl of Eglintoun. Mr Dickson was translated, and became Professor of Divinity, first at Glasgow, and subsequently at Edinburgh, where he died in 1662. His place as minister of Irvine was filled by Mr Alexander Nisbet, whose character is well stated in his epitaph, as written by one of his brethren in these words: 'Grande aliquid vultu nituit, gressuque decoro; grandius in magni dotibus ingenii.' After Mr Nisbet, Mr George Hutchison became minister of Irvine. Not giving obedience to his bishop, he was first silenced by the Parliament in 1662, and subsequently, in the same year, he was banished from Edinburgh; but, upon their passing the act of indulgence, he was authorised by the Privy Council, in 1669, to exercise the ministry at Irvine, where he died. Contemporaneously with Messrs Dickson, Nisbet, and Hutchison, Mr James Ferguson was minister of the adjoining parish of Kilwinning, and in conjunction with these eminent individuals, he formed the design of publishing brief expositions of the Scriptures. In part, this plan was carried into effect. Mr Dickson, *inter alia*, published his 'Expositio Analytica omnium Apostolicarum Epistolarum.' Mr Nisbet published an Exposition of the two epistles of Peter, and also an Exposition of Ecclesiastes. From the pen of Mr Hutchison, the public received an Exposition of the Book of Job, of the Minor Prophets, and of the Gospel according to the Evangelist John. Mr Patrick Warner succeeded Mr Hutchison in 1688. Mr Warner met with great discouragements from his people in the prosecution of his ministry. Greatly oppressed by these discouragements, he submitted the reasons of demission to the Presbytery of Irvine in 1702. Upon the retirement of Mr Warner in that year, Mr William M'Knight became minister of Irvine, and remained in this situation till 1750, when he died. His successor, Mr Charles Bannatyne, was translated from Kilmorie, in Arran, and died soon after he laid the foundation of the New Church, in 1774.

During the preceding year a church was formed in Irvine, in connection with the Synod of Relief. The first stated pastor of this new church, viz. Mr James Jack, was not ordained till 1777. The vacancy occasioned in the Established Church by the death of Mr Bannatyne was filled up by the appointment of Dr James Richmond, who closed his ministry in 1801. During his incumbency, and in the year 1782, Mr White, the second minister of the Relief Church, was ordained to that office, and, in 1783, he was deposed for error in doctrine, and for contumacy. His errors were adopted under the influence of a Mrs Buchan. It appears from the autograph letters of this woman, and from the correspondence of some of her followers which we have seen, that, by herself and by them, she was considered as being the spirit of God dwelling in flesh,—as being, in short, the incarnation of the Holy Spirit. From the terms of the libel against Mr White, we learn that by him, and as we infer by her, it was held, first, that sin does not adhere to the believer; secondly, that Christ tasted death for all men; and, thirdly, that, whilst the bodies of Saints under the New Testament are the temples of the Holy Ghost, the Saints under the Old Testament were not favoured with this distinction. To the honour of the inhabitants generally, and more especially of the Relief congregation, her doctrines and pretensions excited feelings of abhorrence. Petitions were presented to the magistrates, in which, by Dissenters as well as Churchmen, the magistrates were called upon to apprehend her, and proceed against her as a blasphemer. They did not do this; but they proceeded to dismiss her from Irvine. 'To protect the woman from insult,' as we learn from the Statistical Account, by Dr Richmond, 'the magistrates accompanied her about a mile out of town; but, notwithstanding all their efforts, she was grossly insulted by the mob, thrown into ditches, and otherwise ill-used by the way. She took up her residence, that night, with some of her followers, in the neighbourhood of Kilmaurs; and, being joined by Mr White and others in the morning, the whole company, about forty in number, proceeded on their way to Mauchline, and from thence to Cumnock, and to Closeburn, in Dumfries-shire, singing as they went, and saying that they were going to the New Jerusalem.' This occurred in May, 1784; but the woman soon died, and the establishment being broken up, the imbecile fanatics, who had followed her, returned to their former places of abode. Mr White was deposed in 1783, and Mr Peter Robertson was

ordained as pastor of the Relief Church, in 1784. During his ministry the building was enlarged; and Mr Robertson died on the 30th January, 1819. He was succeeded by Mr Archibald Maclaren, who was ordained on the 23d March, 1820, and died on Saturday, 11th September, 1841.

Dr James Richmond died in 1804, and was succeeded by Mr James Henderson, who died in 1820." The Rev. John Wilson was admitted to the charge on the 22d June of that year. The Rev. Mr Brown is the present incumbent. Up to 1785, the stipend of this parish was seven chalders of victual, chiefly meal, and near £100 Scots. The augmentation granted at that time was £400 Scots. The last augmentation was granted on the 19th June, 1816, and commenced with crop 1816. As then granted, the stipend consists of eighteen chalders of victual, with £10 sterling for communion elements. Originally, the glebe was about one and a-half acres, but subsequently an addition was made to it of six and a-half acres. The manse, which is commodious and handsome, was built in 1820.

The parish, as well as the Presbytery records, are in a very imperfect state.

## ANTIQUITIES.

The only existing antiquities in the town and parish of Irvine are the remains of the Seagate and Stane Castles. Of the former, Robertson says, "It belongs to the Earl of Eglintoun, and is supposed to have been intended as the jointure-house of the dowager ladies of that family. There is no date upon it; but from the circumstance of the united arms of Montgomerie and Eglintoun being engraved upon a central stone in a vaulted chamber in the lower story, it must have been built since the union of these two families by marriage, in 1361; and that it could not be much later than that period, may be inferred from its structure as a house of defence, in which are many arrow-slits for bows, but no gun-ports for cannon or other fire-arms, which were seldom omitted in fortified places erected after that time. In this old castle there remains still, quite entire, one of the most perfect specimens of the Saxon or Norman round arch that is perhaps now to be met with in Britain. It is erected over the principal gateway into the house. A square tower in one of the corners is evidently much more ancient than the rest of the building,* as may be con-

* This is corroborative of our suggestion, that the Seagate Castle is the ancient castle of Irvine alluded to by Hoveden.

cluded not only from the rest of the building, but from the stone being greatly more decayed from the action of the weather."

All that remains of the ancient residence of Stane is a square tower of small dimensions. It is kept in repair by the Eglintoun family, whose property it is.

The churchyard of Irvine has some pretensions to antiquity, the present church having been built on the site of the old. One of the oldest tombstones is that erected to the memory of John Peebles of Broomlands, Provost of Irvine, who died in 1596.

Another monumental stone contains the following to the memory of the Montgomeries of Broomlands: "Here lyes Hugh Montgomery of Broomlands, who died in November, 1658, aged 92 years. Also, Margaret Calderwood, his spouse. Also, George Montgomery of Broomlands, their son, who died May 6, 1700, aged 86. Also, Anna, Barclay and Margaret Wallace, his spouses. Also, Hugh Montgomery of Broomlands, their son of

the first marriage, who died December 3, 1728, aged 83 years, in the 55th year of his marriage with Jean Brown, his spouse; and the said Jean Brown, who died December 8, 1728, aged 83 years. Also, Robert Montgomery of Broomlands, their son, who died January 11, 1740, aged 63 years. Also, Hugh Montgomery of Broomlands, their son, who died February 24, 1766, in the 80th year of his age."

There are also headstones to the memory of James Blackwood and John M'Coull, who were executed for being concerned in the rising of Pentland.

### EMINENT PERSONS CONNECTED WITH IRVINE.

Galt, the novelist, and Montgomerie, the poet, are both claimed as natives of Irvine.

The celebrated Robert Barclay was Provost of Irvine, and a Commissioner to the English Parliament in the reign of Charles I.

---

## FAMILIES IN THE PARISH OF IRVINE.

There are several extensive and valuable properties within the parish of Irvine, but few families of any note seem to have permanently resided within its bounds. The most ancient of these were the family of

### STANE, OR STONANRIG,

A lordship extending to upwards of 300 acres of good land. The first of the family we find mentioned is "William Frawncies of le Stane," who occurs in the charter of the Duke of Albany, already alluded to as in the archives of the burgh of Irvine, dated 24th July, 1417. The family of Frances was connected by intermarriages with the best in the district. It, however, failed in the male line in the beginning of the sixteenth century,* when the heiress was married to a younger son of the Earl of Eglintoun.

### MONTGOMERIES OF STANE.

I. WILLIAM MONTGOMERIE of Greenfield, third son of Hugh, first Earl of Eglintoun, married, in 1508, Elizabeth, only daughter and sole heiress of Robert Frances of Stane, with whom he got the barony of Stane, St Bride's Kirk, and Bourtreehill. He built a castle on the lands—the ruins of which still exist—with his coat of arms thereon, being the same as those of Eglintoun, with a proper distinction.

Mr William Montgomerie had a licence from the King, dated 2d January, 1532, to remain from the army on the Borders, in consequence of sickness; but his son and heir, and household, according to his estate, were to pass to the army.*

"The laird of Blair askit instruments that Mais-

---

* Robertson, writing in 1825, says, "Cadets of the family remained in respectable circumstances, in the town of Irvine and vicinity, to the present times; of whom Mrs Cowan, and her sister, Miss Frances, are the only survivors now of the name — though diverged among many

other families through intermarriage. It is a name otherwise little known in Scotland, and apparently of English origin." Henricus Franceys was one of the "Burgenses et cives de Berawyk" who subscribed the Ragman Roll.—RYMER. The arms of the Stane family, according to the seal of Robert Frances, appended to the contract of marriage between Montgomerie of Greenfield and his daughter, were a mascle between three stars.
* Pitcairn's Criminal Trials.

ter William Montgumry declarit in presence of the lords, that quhen he past to red the maling callit ⸻, pertening to Jonet Coluile, that the said laird of Blair deforcit him not, nor he saw him nocht on that ground." *

William Montgomerie of Stane and Greenfield died previous to the 3d September, 1546. He had issue :

1. Arthur, who succeeded.
2. Hugh Montgomerie of Stane, of whom afterwards.

II. Arthur Montgomerie of Stane succeeded his father. He married Elizabeth, daughter of John Fairlie of that Ilk, who died without issue. Arthur Montgomerie of Stane is mentioned in the latter-will of Hugh, second Earl of Eglintoun, who died on the 3d September, 1546. He is there appointed, along with many other friends of the family, respectively and successively, tutor to the young Earl. He appears to have been succeeded by his brother Hugh, who is also designed of Auchinhood.

III. Hugh Montgomerie of Stane and Auchinhood, sold the barony of Stane, in 1570, to Hugh, third Earl of Eglintoun. He married Elizabeth, daughter of Blair of Adamtoune,† by whom he had a son, Hugh, who succeeded.

IV. Hugh Montgomerie of Stane, who, according to the Broomland's Manuscript, took first the designation of Stane, then of Auchinhood, then of Bowhouse.‡ He married Margaret, daughter of Calderwood of Peacockbank, and died in 1658, aged 96. It appears that he married, secondly, a lady named Peebles, probably of the Broomlands family. He left issue three sons and two daughters :

1. Hugh, who succeeded him in Bowhouse.
2. George Montgomerie of Broomlands, born in 1614, of whom afterwards.
3. Robert, from whom Northcove.
1. Janet, married to John Thomson of Gawcadden, but had no issue.
2. Helen, married Ninian Barclay of Warrix, and had issue.

V. Hugh Montgomerie of Bowhouse succeeded his father. He married Margaret, daughter of ⸻ Swinton, merchant in Glasgow, by whom he had a son,

VI. Hugh Montgomerie of Bowhouse, who succeeded his father. He married Margaret, daughter of ⸻ Durry, merchant in Glasgow, by whom he had a son,

VII. Hugh Montgomerie of Bowhouse, who succeeded his father. He married Margaret, daughter of George Montgomerie of Broomlands, his cousin, but died in 1718 without issue.

## MONTGOMERIE OF BROOMLANDS.

The Broomlands consisted of the upper and nether Broomlands, lying partly in the parish of Irvine, and partly in the parish of Dreghorn. They belonged for many years to a family of the name of PEIBLES, merchant burgesses of Irvine. "Johnne Peblis of Brumlandis" is mentioned in the latter-will of "Robert Peblis, burges of Irveiu, and ane of the baillies thairof," who died September 16, 1605. He was, along with "Johnne Peblis, Knodgerhill," and others, appointed one of the tutors to the young family of the defunct, to whom they were evidently nearly related. John Peibles appears to have been succeeded by "Patrik Peibles of Brumelands," whose name occurs in the testament of John Stewart, Beith, in 1616. In 1625, 4th November, Mariote Peibles was served heiress of John Peibles of Broomlands, her father, while James Peibles of Knogerhill* was retoured in certain lands as heir-male. The Broomlands were subsequently acquired by,

I. GEORGE MONTGOMERIE of Broomlands, second son of Hugh Montgomerie (3d) of Stane and Auchinhood. He was twice married ; first, to Ann Barclay, daughter of the laird of Perceton, by whom he had two sons and a daughter :

1. Hugh, who succeeded his father.
2. William Montgomerie, a merchant, and one of the magistrates of Edinburgh. He married, and had three sons ; 1. William. 2. George. 3. Hugh; who all died unmarried. This line failed in the year 1745.†
Jean, married John Montgomerie of Bridgend, and had issue.

George Montgomerie of Broomlands married, secondly, Margaret Wallace, of the family of Shewalton, by whom he had issue, six sons and one daughter :

1. George Montgomerie, married Janet, daughter of George Garven, clerk of the bailiery of Cuninghame, by whom he had a daughter, Margaret, married to Alexander Simpson, surgeon in Edinburgh, and had issue.
2. Alexander Montgomerie of Assloace, (living 1704, when he was Commissioner of Supply in Ayrshire,) married Margaret, daughter of Alexanger Montgomerie of Kirktonholme, by whom he had issue—four daughters:—

---

* Acts of Parliament, vol. ii. p. 313.
† Hamilton of Wishaw's Historical Notes of Lanarkshire and Renfrewshire.
‡ The sale of the property, in 1570, must have been by his father, as he would only be about four years of age at the time. He may, however, have had a lease or wadset of Stane, hence his first designation. Auchinhood was part of the barony of Eagleshame, so that the family would seem to have had only a leasehold interest in that property also.

---

* Knogerhill is now the property of the burgh of Irvine, acquired by purchase. It fell to an heiress, Jean Peebles, heir of her uncle, John Peebles, who sold it to Hugh Kilpatrick, burgess of Irvine, in 1670, and who, the same year, disposed of it to the burgh. As the magistrates were superiors of the lands, they had no doubt originally belonged to the corporation.
† Broomlands MS., Geneal. Fragmenti.

1  Janet, married to James Somerville of Kennox, and had issue
2  Penelope, married to Sir David Cuninghame of Corsehill, and had issue
3  Margaret, married to Mr Forbes of Waterton, and had issue
4  Anne, married George Moore of Leckie, but had no issue
3  Robert, died without issue.
4  Ninian, died unmarried
5  John Montgomerie of Wrae, left succession
6  James Montgomerie, merchant in Edinburgh, married Mary, daughter of Mathew Stewart of Newton, but died without issue

A daughter, married to Hugh Montgomerie of Bowhouse, but had no issue

George Montgomerie of Broomlands died 7th May, 1700, aged 86 years, and was succeeded by,

II  Hugh Montgomerie of Broomlands, his eldest son, who married Jean, daughter and heiress of Robert Brown of Moile, by whom he had five sons and three daughters

1  Robert, who succeeded his father
2  George Montgomerie  He was Captain of a merchant ship, and died at Jamaica, in 1739, unmarried
3  Hugh Montgomerie, who succeeded his brother, of whom afterwards
4  William Montgomerie, was a Cornet of Dragoons  He married Jean, daughter of John Brisbane of Bishoptoune, by whom he had a son and a daughter —
    1  John Montgomerie of Arthurstone, born 1723  He married and settled in Fife, but died without leaving issue
    2  Jean his daughter, married Robert Ramsay, merchant in Dundee, and had issue, their daughter married Mackenzie of Coul and left descendants  William Montgomerie died before 19th October, 1753, as appears by his son's "receipt of a legacy of that date"
5  Alexander Montgomerie, was Captain of a Letter of Marque ship, and died in the East Indies unmarried
1  Margaret, married to Charles Binning of Pilmore, advocate, and had issue
2  Jean, probably married to William Kelso of Hullerhurst, who is said to have married a daughter of Hugh Montgomerie of Broomlands, by whom he had a son, William Kelso of Hullerhurst
3  Ann, married to Edward Ker, merchant, and one of the magistrates of Irvine, and had issue

Hugh Montgomerie died in December, 1728, aged 80 years, and was succeeded by his eldest son,

III  Robert Montgomerie of Broomlands, who married Elizabeth, daughter of Mr Alexander Cuninghame of Collelland  He died 11th January, 1740, without issue, and in the 63d year of his age,* and was succeeded by his brother,

IV  Hugh Montgomerie of Broomlands,† who had been Provost of Campbelton, in Argyleshire, and married Mary, daughter of the Rev Mr James Boes, minister of the gospel at Campbelton, by whom he had one son and three daughters :

1  Charles, who succeeded him
1  Jean Montgomerie, of whom afterwards
2  Elizabeth, married the Rev Mr David Campbell, minister of Southend, in Kintyre, and had issue, a son,

* Broomlands MS
† Author of the 'Broomlands MS' elsewhere referred to in this work.

Charles Montgomerie Campbell, who married and had issue
3  Mary, married to Adam Dickson, merchant in Glasgow, and had issue

Hugh Montgomerie of Broomlands married, 2dly, Margaret, daughter of Mr Learman of Moneymore, in the county of Derry, by whom he had no issue  He died about 1767, and was succeeded by his only son,

V. Charles Montgomerie of Broomlands, who sold that estate, and died in 178-, unmarried.  He entered merchant burgess of Glasgow, 24th January, 1754  It was in his time that the large tree of the family of Eglintoun was completed.  Mr Dickie, writer in Kilmarnock, an excellent penman, was employed to write the tree, which was elegantly done, and of such large dimensions as to require stretchers of wood to keep it open when consulted  He was undoubtedly heir-male of the Eglintoun family  The family of Broomlands claimed precedency over that of Lainshaw, from an expression in a deed relating to the Hon William Montgomerie of Stane and Greenfield, the ancestor of the Broomlands family, in which that gentleman is styled second son of Hugh, first Earl of Eglintoun  This however, was subsequent to the death of John Lord Montgomerie, the eldest son, who was killed in the streets of Edinburgh, in 1520, in the fray popularly called "Cleanse the Causeway," so that at the time the deed alluded to was drawn out, the Hon. Sir Neil Montgomerie of Lainshaw was eldest, and William of Stane and Greenfield, second (surviving) son of Hugh, first Earl of Eglintoun  After the death of Charles Montgomerie of Broomlands, the representation of that family devolved on his eldest sister,

VI. Jean Montgomerie, eldest daughter of Hugh Montgomerie of Broomlands, who married Mr Henry Eccles of the Excise, by whom she had a daughter, Margaret  Mrs Eccles survived her husband many years, and chiefly resided in Greenock, but occasionally visited her friends in Irvine.

She died at Glasgow in 178-, and was interred in the burial-place of Dr George Montgomerie, physician in that city, who was a relation of the family of Bourtreehill  It was to Mrs Eccles that the family tree came on the death of her brother, Charles.  She sent it to England to her nephew, Mr Charles Montgomerie Campbell, but it appears that it has been lost since.  After her death, the representation of the Broomlands devolved upon,

VII  Margaret Eccles, her daughter, who died about 1828.  She married a Mr Henderson, and had issue.

1.  Archibald Montgomerie Henderson, Ensign 71st regiment, or Highland Light Infantry  He was with his

regiment at the battle of Waterloo, and retired on half-pay sometime afterwards. He died without issue. A daughter, married to Mr Seton, who, with her husband, died in 1841, leaving issue.

### BOURTREEHILL.

The greater portion of this valuable barony—about 800 acres—lies in the parish of Irvine, the remainder in that of Dreghorn. It formed of old part of the large possessions of the Morville family, and in the " time of the Brucean contest, it was possessed, through marriage of two ladies of that house, by William de Ferrars and Alan la Suche." The lands were afterwards confiscated by Robert the Bruce for their adherence to the party of the Balliols, their kinsmen, and conferred on Roger de Blair of that Ilk, " or rather an annuity of four chalders of meal out of their lands; for one should suppose that the rent would have been much more, even though the territory should not have been so extensive as at present."* In 1685, and 1696, Bourtreehill belonged to the Skelmorlie family, from whom it was purchased by Peter Montgomerie, merchant in Glasgow, whose son (probably) James Montgomerie, sold the property to Robert Hamilton, prior to 1748.

Robert Hamilton of Bourtreehill, born 5th January, 1698, was the eldest son of Hugh Hamilton of Clongall, merchant in Ayr. He and his younger brother, John, ancestor of the Hamiltons of Sundrum, were long resident in Jamaica, where they possessed the estate of Pemberton Valley, and acquired very considerable wealth. He married, and had several daughters:

1. Jane, married to the Earl of Craufurd and Lindsay.
2. Frances, died unmarried, in 1798.
3. Elinora, married to Hugh, 12th Earl of Eglintoun.
4. Margaret, married to Sir John Cathcart of Carleton, without issue.

Robert Hamilton of Bourtreehill died 4th June, 1773, aged 75. He was succeeded in Bourtreehill by his eldest daughter, the Countess of Craufurd, who died October 6, 1809. The Countess was succeeded, as heir of entail, by her sister, Dame Margaret Hamilton Cathcart, widow of Sir John Cathcart of Carleton, who died in 1785. She died April 25, 1817, aged 73, when the property devolved upon her nephew, the present Earl of Eglintoun.

### ARMSHEUGH,

A property of about 300 acres of excellent land, belonged, in 1260, as appears from a contest with the burgh of Irvine, previously mentioned, to Sir Godfrey de Ross of Stewarton. It afterwards came into the possession of John Balliol, King of Scotland, and on the triumph of Bruce, was conferred by that monarch on " Sir Reginald de Craufurd, of the Loudoun family; or at least two chalders of oatmeal, that John Balliol was wont to receive yearly from these lands, was given to Sir Reginald. In 1482, it appears along with Doura and Patterton in a charter to Lord Boyd, making part of the jointure lands to his mother, the Princess Mary, sister of James III. In 1654, and from that time, down to 1697, it appears in various retours among the lands belonging to the Montgomerie family of Skelmorlie, in which it was latterly conjoined with the lands of Bourtreehill, also belonging to the same family. It belongs at present, and has for a long time past, to the Earls of Eglintoun.* Part of the lands is in the parish of Kilwinning.

### BALGRAY.

This property " extends to 300 acres of arable land, of a heavy and not unfertile soil, and is at present divided into four distinct possessions. On them all there are suitable mansions, each amid its own plantations, making a good appearance in the country. over which they all command an extensive prospect. This ancient barony, in 1361, is contained in a charter, along with the conterminous lands of Armsheugh, Dowra and Patterton, to Sir Hugh de Eglintoun of Eglintoun, and would pass of course, with the rest of the property of that potent baron, to Montgomerie of Eagleshame, who married his only daughter and heiress in the same year. The succession of proprietors in these lands appears from the progress of writs, to the present time, to be as under:—

1. In 1542, they are contained in a charter to Gilbert, first Lord Kennedy.
2. In 1540, ditto to Gilbert, third Earl of Cassillis.
3. In November, 1600, they were conveyed by John, fifth Earl of Cassillis, to Neil Montgomerie, younger of Lainshaw, who,
4. In 1602, conveyed them to William Mure of Rowallan.
5. In 1630, disponed by Sir William Mure to David Cuninghame, afterwards Sir David of Auchenharvie.
6. In 1684, sold by Sir Robert Cuninghame of Auchenharvie to Hamilton of Grange, who,
7. In 1710, sold them to James Montgomerie of Pereeton Hall (now Annick Lodge), and who,

* Robertson's Cuninghame.

* Robertson's Cuninghame.

8. In 1748, sold them to Robert Hamilton of Bourtreehill.

9. In 1760, sold by the Bourtreehill family to the family of Montgomerie of Kirktonholme, or Corsehill.

10. In 1786, sold, by a judicial sale, to Richard Campbell, William and Robert Reid, and John Niven.

11. In 1795, the above Richard Campbell sold his part of them to

12. William Reid of Stacklaw Hill; and about the same time, the above John Niven sold his portion to Thomas Dunlop, which is now possessed by his son, Robert Dunlop; whilst the descendants of the above William and Robert Reid, and William Reid of Stacklaw Hill, enjoy the other portions, each in severalty." *

### BARTONHOLM.

Part of this property is nearly encircled in a link of the Garnock, and is among the richest holm-land in the county. There is also upon it one of the best going collieries in the neighbourhood. The property belongs to George Fullarton of that Ilk, an account of whose family is given under the head of " Families in the Parish of Dundonald."

" There are," says Robertson, " many other properties, of considerable value, in the parish— as Towerlands, consisting of 70 or 80 acres of fine land, situated near to Bourtreehill House, and surrounded by its land on all sides; Chalmers' Houses, nearer Irvine, very rich land; as also is Lochwards, in the same quarter; Holm Mill, on the Irvine water; Scotsloch, on the north side of the town. There is also Bogside and Snodgrass, along the Garnock, extensive lands, belonging to Lord Eglintoun, partly very valuable, partly sandy soil—all incumbent on coal. The burgh itself is a great heritor in its own parish, having 500 acres or more in full property."

---

* Robertson's Cuninghame.

# PARISH OF KILBIRNIE.

Chalmers derives the name of this parish from the church, which he reasonably supposes to have been dedicated to *St Birnie* or *Birinus*, a bishop and confessor, who converted the West Saxons, and died in 650.* It is curious, however, if this was the fact, that all tradition of his festival, which occurs on the 3d December, should have been forgotten, "whilst that of St Brandane, the Apostle of the Orkneys, is still commemorated on the 28th of May, under the modernised appellation of Brinnan's Day, the great annual fair of Kilbirnie."†

The parish is bounded, on the north and east, by Lochwinnoch and Beith; on the north-west, by Largs; and on the south and west, by Dalry. It is from seven to eight miles in length, and about two and a-half in breadth, and has been calculated to contain nearly 9,000 Scots acres.

The topographical features of the parish are well described in the Statistical Account. It consists of "two naturally well-defined sections, viz., a lower and altogether an arable division, and a more elevated and extensive one, combining with a considerable portion of arable land a great extent of green hill-pasture, bog, and moorland. The lower section, lying in the position of north-east and south-west, along the boundaries of the parishes of Beith and Dalry, is partly flat, especially towards the south-west, but more generally its surface is varied with gently-marked swells and depressions. This division, which is nearly four miles in length, and about the medium breadth of a mile and a-half, does not, therefore, possess any striking features, unless it be the bright expanse of Kilbirnie Loch, extending along two miles of its eastern confines, and the winding course of the water of Garnock, which flows through its upper

* Several other places in Scotland are called Kilbirnie.
† Statistical Account, drawn up by William Dobie, Esq., Grangevale, Beith.

part from north to south, but which, after passing within a quarter of a mile of the south-west extremity of the loch, forms the eastern boundary of the lower part. West and north-west of this fertile and highly-cultivated division, the ground assumes a much greater variety of position and form; in addition to which, it rises somewhat rapidly, until it swells into airy upland pastures considerably beyond the reach of cultivation. These verdant uplands are succeeded by dreary tracts of moss and heath, and irregular ranges of dusky hills, of an extent equal to fully one-third of the superficies of the parish; and, taken altogether, compose a region, doomed alike by climate, inaccessibility, and soil, to hopeless sterility. The lowest land in the parish is about 93 feet above the level of the sea, and the highest, which is the Hill of Staik, situated on its north-west boundary, has an altitude above the same level of 1691 feet. From the summit of this hill, the most elevated in the district of Cuninghame, as well as from several of the adjacent heights, panoramic prospects of an extent, variety, and magnificence, may be enjoyed, unsurpassed by anything in the west of Scotland.

"There are numerous perennial springs of excellent water in this parish, but none have yet been discovered possessing medicinal virtues; that especially of Birnie's Well, situated about a quarter of a mile north of the ruins of Kilbirnie Place, to which it had been conducted by pipes, is alike remarkable for its strength, and the superior quality of the water. The Garnock and the Maich, the latter forming the northern boundary of the parish, are the only streams of any note. The Garnock rises at the base of the hill of Staik, and traverses the district in the direction of south-east. About a mile and a-half from its source, it forms a wild and romantic waterfall, called the Spout of Garnock, which, after heavy rains, presents an animated spectacle, strongly in contrast with the immobility and stillness of the surrounding scenery. Nearly three miles farther down, it winds in melancholy murmurings round two sides of the precipitous knoll, on which are perched the tottering ruins of Glengarnock Castle. Descending thence for a short distance through a wooded ravine, it hastens over a rocky channel, and after skirting the village of Kilbirnie, quietly pours its accumulated waters through a strath of much beauty, in the lower part of the parish. It then pursues its devious course through the parishes of Dalry and Kilwinning, and, after being considerably augmented by many tributary streams, falls into the sea at Irvine. Like other mountain rivers, a heavy fall of rain renders, in a short time, the Garnock an impassable torrent, a little way from its source; while during the summer months, it is frequently fordable at nearly all points within the parish. Its banks are tame, presenting, in their whole extent, no charms to the admirer of picturesque scenery: the immediate environs of Glengarnock Castle, and of the waterfall, alone excepted.

"The source of the Maich is close by the south side of the Misty-Law, in Renfrewshire. It runs in a direction nearly parallel to the Garnock, from which it is nowhere more than a mile and a-half distant. After a sinuous course of about five miles in a deep channel, occasionally fringed with natural wood, this 'lonely moorland river' enters Kilbirnie Loch from the north, to which it is by much the most steady and abundant contributor. Kilbirnie Loch lies in the south-east quarter of the parish, and constitutes part of its boundaries in that direction. It is a beautiful sheet of pellucid water, and forms a noble feature in the widespread landscape. Its banks, though tame, are remarkably clean, and, where not adorned with trees, arable fields slope gently to its margin. It extends a mile and a-half in length, is scarcely half a mile in breadth, and its greatest depth is about five fathoms and a-half. Besides the Maich, the loch receives supplies from the Mains and the Bath burns, streamlets which have their sources close by the town of Beith; and its only outlet is by the Dubs Water, which discharges itself into Lochwinnoch Loch. It is well stored with pike, perch, trout, and eel, and is betimes the resort of the wild duck and heron. The loch forms part of the estate of Kilbirnie, although that property does not extend around one-half of its circumference.*

"The soil in the lower or south end of the parish is a deep alluvial loam of great fertility. Ascending the river it gradually changes into a rich clayey loam, while to the east, along Kilbirnie Loch and part of the course of the Maich, it is a light red clay, resting on a stiff clay subsoil. West of the Garnock, clayey loam likewise prevails, and occasionally adhesive clay mixed with sand, varied with numerous stripes of meadow ground, almost every farm in this quarter having two or more acres of this valuable ground. The soil of the higher grounds being incumbent on trap and limestone, is light and dry, and its fertility is sufficiently evinced by the excellency of the pastures. The moorish uplands are generally moss of various depths, resting on a light-coloured clay, and the more level parts are much broken by hags and pools of stagnant water."

There is much want of plantation in the parish. Early in the present century, about thirty acres were planted on the estates of Ladyland and Kilbirnie, which are thriving well; and a few fine old trees still surround the ancient house of Ladyland, but very little "now remains of the noble sylvan embellishments of the parks and pleasure-grounds" which once distinguished the Castle of Kilbirnie.

"Great and striking improvements, by draining, liming, and enclosing, have been effected in this parish, within the present century, by various individuals, and in particular, by the late William Cochran, Esq. of Ladyland. This gentleman, besides adding considerably to the extent of his arable grounds, by an extensive and skilful style of draining, beautified much his estate by clumps and belts of plantations, and was, by the consequent increased productiveness of the soil, in the course of a few seasons, amply indemnified for all his outlays. He was, moreover, the first agriculturist in this quarter who introduced the enclosing and irrigation of waste lands, by which, according to Aiton, in his 'Agricultural View of the County of Ayr,' 'land not worth more than 3s. or 4s. an acre, produced to Mr Cochran upon 11 acres, 3000 stones, county weight, or 4500 stones English, of good hay.' Another portion of his estate, consisting of 129 acres, he raised, by his mode of improving it, from 1s. 6d. per acre, to about £1 of yearly value. In all his undertakings he was eminently successful, and most strikingly illustrat-

---

* Kilbirnie Loch is thus noticed by Bellenden, the translator of Boece: "In Cunninghame is ane loch namit Garnoth, nocht unlike to Loch Donae, full of fische." It was subsequently called Loch Thankart. In 1628, David Cunynghame of Robertland is served heir of David Cunynghame, his father, in the lands and barony of Glengarnock, "et loch de Loch Thankart." It belonged to the Cuninghames of Glengarnock, but the Craufurds of Kilbirnie dis-

puted their right, and, in the spirit of the times, these families called out their tenants and retainers, and broke one another's boats. A case between them is reported, 16th July, 1626, (Mor. Dict. p. 10,631), from which it appears that both parties had the loch included in their titles. The Craufurds of Kilbirnie subsequently acquired right to the barony of Glengarnock, and there was no longer room for dispute on the subject. Sir John Craufurd's right was ratified by Parliament in 1641.

ed how much might be accomplished within the compass of half an ordinary life, by art and industry,

'When science plans the progress of their toil.'

Since their introduction by Mr Cochran, agricultural improvements have been widely extended here, all of which received a fresh impulse, a few years ago, by the succession of the Earl of Glasgow to the estate of Kilbirnie, comprising three-fourths of the parish. Several of the largest arable farms on that extensive property are in every species of improvement rapidly advancing to the limits of perfection; while the hope may apparently be safely indulged, that the period is not distant when all the land in the parish, susceptible of profitable cultivation, will be in an equally improved condition."

### HISTORY, CIVIL AND ECCLESIASTICAL.

Apart from the history of the families connected with the locality, there are few details of a historical character at all pertaining peculiarly to the parish. There are no traditions, even, worthy of record, though, from the number of tumulii at one time existing, there can be no doubt that events, important to our ancestors, occurred within its boundaries at some period or other.

The parish, though now divided among a number of proprietors, was formerly possessed by three only, and was accordingly divided into three baronies, which division is still nominally adhered to. These are—Kilbirnie, Glengarnock, and Ladyland. The barony of Kilbirnie was the most extensive, consisting of upwards of 5000 acres, of the most fertile quarter of the parish. The barony of Glengarnock extends over about 1400 acres, of which more than 1000 are arable. Nearly 700 acres of the best of it, with the superiority of all the rest, now belong to the barony of Kilbirnie. The barony of Ladyland contains upwards of 1800 acres, nearly the one-half of which is arable—the remainder, consisting of excellent upland pastures, and a considerable extent of moorland. About 400 acres of the arable land are held by twelve different proprietors.

St Brinnan's, or Brandane's Day (third Wednesday of May), is the principal fair in Kilbirnie. It has long been famed as a horse-market. The value of the horses brought together for sale on this occasion, have been calculated to amount to not less than £8000 or £9000 annually. A good deal of cooper-work, in the shape of milk and culinary utensils, used to be disposed of; and much general business is still transacted. Two other fairs, or holidays, were formerly observed. The first of these, the Trades' Race, was held on the first Tuesday of July; the second, Craufurd's Day —a cow fair, instituted, it is said, by the Craufurds of Kilbirnie—on the last Tuesday of October. Both have been discontinued.

Though a church had long existed at Kilbirnie, and the privileges of a burgh of barony had been obtained by John Craufurd of Kilbirnie in 1641, the existence of the village of Kilbirnie is of very recent date. In 1740, there were only three houses in it. What with manufactures, and the recent impulse given to the locality by the Ayr and Glasgow Railway, and the vicinity of numerous iron-works, it is now a thriving and spirited community, containing not less than 2000 inhabitants.

"The church of Kilbirnie," says Chalmers, "belonged anciently to the Monastery of Kilwinning. The monks enjoyed the rectorial tithes and revenues, and a vicarage was established for serving the cure. At the Reformation, the parsonage tithes of the church of Kilbirnie were held on a lease, from the abbot and monks of Kilwinning, for the inconsiderable sum of £8 yearly. The lands which belonged to the church of Kilbirnie passed into lay hands after the Reformation. In 1603, the patronage and tithes of the church were granted to Hugh Earl of Eglintoun, with many other churches, that had belonged to the monks of Kilwinning. The patronage of the church continued with the family of Eglintoun at the Restoration, and it still remains with that family."[*]

"In the Books of Adjournal, commencing in 1507, mention is made of Robert Peblis, in Brockly, being convicted of a felony done in the house of John Skeoch, capelano in Kilbirny. This is the first notice we have met with of a resident chaplain. In 1543, James Scott was vicar of Kilbirnie. Prior to that year, the Abbot of Kilwinning had granted to the College of Justice a yearly pension of £28 Scots from the vicarage of Kilbirnie; but on the 15th of December, a mandate by the abbot, ordering said sum to be taken from the vicarage of Dunlop, is ratified by Parliament. In 1567, Mr Archibald Hamilton was vicar and exhorter, with the thryd of the vicarage, amounting to £31, 2s. 2d. He was forfeited in 1571, for joining with his clansmen, the Hamiltons, in defence of Queen Mary, and was succeeded by Robert Crawfurd, vicar and reader, who had the haill vicarage. His successor was Mr John Harriot, who died prior to 1619, as in that year Mr William Russell, minister of Kilbirnie, appears as a debtor in the testament of Alexander Boyd, one of the regents of Glasgow College.[†] In 1670,

---

* Chalmers' Caledonia.

† On the 15th June, 1647, Mr Russell complained to the

Mr William Tullidaff was admitted under the first indulgence, and in 1672, Mr Patrick Anderson was conjoined with him. Mr Tullidaff did not conform to the wishes of the court, and was in consequence subjected to many hardships. On 8th July, 1673, he was fined in the half of his stipend for not observing the 29th of May, the anniversary of Charles's restoration, and in 1684, he and others of the indulged ministers were imprisoned. At the Revolution in 1688, Mr John Glasgow was admitted, and remained in the charge until his death in 1721, when he was succeeded by Mr James Smith, who died 11th February 1733."*

The church of Kilbirnie, an object of great interest to the antiquary and genealogist, "is situated about half a mile south of the village, at the base of a gentle rise forming the westward boundary of the fertile valley watered by the Garnock. The fabric is a simple oblong in form, measuring sixty-five feet in length, by twenty-nine and a half in breadth, with wings or aisles extending north and south from its eastern extremity, and a plain square tower of moderate elevation attached to the opposite gable. Both the church and tower are covered with deep roofs, and the west gable of the latter is crowned with a small belfry. The aisles, which are of unequal dimensions, have been

Presbytery, that John Braidine, one of his parishioners, had called his doctrine "dust and grey meal." The said John Braidine being summoned before the Presbytery for the offence, "compeared 29th June, and ingenuously confessed his fault. The Presbytery, considering how prejudicial such speeches were to the whole ministrie, after mature deliberation, does ordain, that first upon his knees he make ane confession of his fault before the Presbyterie, and yrafter to goe to his owne congregation, and there in the public place of repentance make ane acknowledgement of his fault likewise; and Mr Hugh M'Kaile to go to Kilbirnie to receive him."—He submitted, and was absolved.

* On his tombstone in Kilbirnie churchyard is the following epitaph, said to have been composed by Patrick, second Viscount Garnock:—

"Bethia Barclay erected this monument in memory of her dear husband, Mr James Smith, minister of the gospel in Kilbirny, who died 11th of February, 1733.

"And though after my skin worms destroy this body, yet in my flesh shall I see God.'

    Buried here lys a worthy man,
    Whose life, alas! was but a span;
    He pleasure took by God's command,
    To lead us to Emanuel's land.
    He was a blessing to our place,
    Where he did preach by power of Grace,
    Bidding us Jesus' footsteps trace,
    And from all sinning strive to cease.
    To us, alas! he is no more;
    His soul triumphs in endless gloir;
    Why should we then his death deplore,
    Who joined has the Heavenly choir?
    To make his character compleat,
    Nature blest him with temper sweet,
    Kind to his own, to all discreet.
    All who do love his memory,
    Must like him live, and like him dy,
    Then ye'l enjoy eternity,
    In ever praising the Most High."†
† Statistical Account.

added at different periods to the original structure, the oldest being the one projecting southwards. It is built of jointed ashlar, and ornamented with a few indifferently formed mouldings: the body of the church and tower being of common masonry, with the quoins and facings of the apertures of roughly chiseled freestone. Over a window of this aisle, in a panel, are cut the armorial bearings of the name of Cuninghame, with the date 1597, and the letters I. C. and K. C., being the initials of Sir James Cuninghame of Glengarnock and his lady, Katherine, second daughter of William, seventh Earl of Glencairn. The north wing, which is considerably the largest, contains, besides the Crawfurd gallery, a private apartment and entrance lobby, and under these, in impressive contiguity, is the family burial vault. This is the most modern and best built part of the church, having been erected by Sir John Cranfurd in 1642, as is testified by his initials, and the date being cut in raised characters on the gable of the aisle. That the main part of the edifice is of much older standing than the earliest of these additions, seems obvious from the greater strength and simplicity of the masonry in that part of the building, and though not prepared to assign a date for its construction, yet, as the south or Glengarnock aisle was built only thirty-seven years subsequently to the Reformation, it can scarcely be doubted that the body of the structure was a place of public worship prior to that great era in the history of the country. The church is, however, chiefly remarkable on account of the carvings in oak with which the Cranfurd gallery and the pulpit are profusely decorated, and the numerous heraldic proofs on the former of the ancestral gentility of John, first Viscount Garnock, by whose commands all these adornments were executed early in the last century."*

Along the front of this stately family-seat, there are no fewer than sixteen armorial escutcheons genealogically arranged, besides two elaborate representations of the Viscount's honours. "There are, besides, two paintings on the paneling of the walls at each end of the gallery, which, though but of slender artistical merits, are worth mentioning. The right hand panel contains a representation of the Jewish legislator holding the Tables of the Law, and the other the High Priest, arrayed in his pontificals. Both of these paintings are so wasted, that in a short time the decayed canvas will be unable to maintain its situation."

"Besides these illustrations of the ancestral dignity of the house of Garnock on the gallery,

* This and the subsequent quotations, in reference to the church of Kilbirnie, are from an excellent account of it by William Dobie, Esq., Grangevale, Beith.

there are on other parts of the church three repetitions of the conjoined bearings of Craufurd and Lindsay. One of these, which is a painting in oil, and an exact transcript of the armorials in the central arcade, is on the front of a loft running across the western portion of the church, erected some seventy years ago. The second is on the pulpit, and bears simply the impaled coats of Craufurd and Lindsay. The other is suspended over the Glengarnock aisle, and the shield, which is of an oval form, is tastefully inwreathed with palms, and ensigned with a Viscount's coronet, the bearings in every respect being the same as those first referred to. An empty picture frame, affixed against the moulding, above the armorials last noticed, contained, until lately, a beautiful specimen of the ornamental cipher. It was a painting, or in other words, the letters J. C. M. S., composing it, were in gold, artistically shadowed on canvas of a bright blue colour. On its falling down, the cloth, when handled, crumbled into dust; and thus, as in countless similar cases, was lost that which, by a little timely attention, might have still withstood the wasting influence of many years. . . . In a state of decay, fast verging to the like condition, though their disappearance will not excite so much regret, are two funeral escutcheons placed against the opposite side walls of the church. That to the right of the Craufurd gallery retains only one of its ghastly mementos, while the other, which was probably put up on the demise of the first Viscount, one-half of its blighted quarterings still retain their places, the number, form, and arrangement of which appear to have been, of course, precisely the same as those on the gallery.

"There remains yet one coat armorial to be noticed. Besides the peculiarity of being the only one within the church unconnected with the house of Garnock, its date shows it to be of considerably older standing than the more elaborately insculped and artfully emblazoned armorials of that family. It is cut on the back of the Ladyland family pew, and occupies only the dexter side of the shield, the other half having been left plain. The bearing is a mullet between three cinque foils, but the bordure, waved, the special mark of difference of Hamilton of Ladyland, has been omitted. Over the shield is the date July, 1671, in raised characters, but the initials W.— C.— I.— G., planted against its sides, are those of the father and mother of the late Mr Cochran of Ladyland, and must have been put there since 1756, the year of their marriage.

On the pulpit, an object which attracts the attention of every visitant, "the most prominent of the carvings is a winged female figure, the emblem of religion, standing on coiled serpents, and holding in her right hand an olive wand. Beneath the serpent is a richly carved ornament, in outline, resembling somewhat an ancient lyre. The lower part of the compartment is occupied by a kind of divided pediment, composed of two fillets, and finished with circular flowers, from which, across the last mentioned ornament, extends a festoon of bay leaves. The fillets, which are five inches apart, enclose three cherubs' heads on each side of the pediment, the field of which is decorated on the right hand with a thistle, and on the other with a rose. The space between the figure representing religion and the pediment, is ornamented with wreaths of fruit and foliage, terminating in grinning masks, and doves with sprigs of foliage in their beaks; the interstices being semé of stars, while at each extremity of the canopy stands a half-draped juvenile figure blowing a trumpet.

"Besides the gallery and pulpit there are several lines of carved cornices, scroll and other ornamental work, on different parts of the church, but the common-place form of these, and their indifferent execution, demand nothing beyond a passing notice. Little indeed, if any, of the sculptured work, which we have attempted to describe, is calculated, on account of spirited handling, or delicate finish, to elicit commendation from the finical connoisseur; by much the greater part of it, though effective enough at some distance, bearing too many marks of the gouge and the chisel to stand a close inspection. To the rough and unfinished condition of the carvings, generally, may not improbably be ascribed the origin of the tradition, that the artist brought them all into their respective forms unaided by other implement than his knife.

"The interior of the church was formerly used by the Kilbirnie, Glengarnock, and Ladyland families, as their place of sepulture. Of this once common, though baneful practice, excepting a flag-stone forming part of the pavement of the passage between the gallery and the pulpit, there are now no visible indications. The stone bears only the engraved figure of a two-handed sword, with a slightly sunk fillet or groove cut around the margin. The memory of him who lies beneath it has long since sunk into oblivion; for, though we have heard it stated, that this memorial denoted the last resting place of Sir John Cranfurd of Kilbirnie, who died in 1661, it does not seem at all likely that this distinguished person should have been buried elsewhere than in the vault erected by himself in 1642.

"The apartment over the vault, which is entered by the same outside stair as the gallery, is in keeping with the desolate condition of every thing in this parish once belonging to the extinguished house of Craufurd and Garnock.

'Now to the dust gone down, their houses, lands,
    And once fair spreading family dissolved.'

Shortly after the death of the last Earl in 1808, the apartment was denuded of its garniture by the order of his sister, the late Lady Mary Lindsay Craufurd. Long previously, however, to this, it had ceased to be the resort, occasionally, on Sundays of noble lords and high-born dames, and was only used at the period adverted to as the rendezvous where the tenants of the Kilbirnie estates met on rent days to pay their devoirs to the factor. For several years past it has not even been thus employed, though it is not improbable it may yet serve some purpose still more at variance with its original destination. The pictures that once adorned its walls, and which are still remembered with garrulous regret by a few of the older parishioners, consisted of drawings in water colours of Kilbirnie House, Glengarnock Castle, and engravings of scriptural and allegorical subjects. That several of these possessed considerable merit we are induced to believe, by their having been deemed worthy of a place in so splendid a mansion as Craufurd Priory; nor would the view of Kilbirnie House, unless it had exhibited a master's hand, been especially noticed in a description of that august residence, drawn up by the celebrated Delta of Blackwood's Magazine. The only other matter regarding these specimens of the graphic skill of a former age that we can state with certainty is, that they were all dispersed by auction shortly after the demise, in 1833, of the noble person by whose orders they had been withdrawn from the apartment."

" By much the most interesting monument in the burying-ground is the 'stately tomb,' erected in 1594, by Captain Craufurd of Jordanhill, for himself and his lady. It stands a few yards south of the church, and is of a quadrangular form, measuring nine feet and a half in length, six feet in width, and six feet six inches in height. It is built of chiseled freestone, and covered horizontally with the same material; and, though still entire, has been long in a state ripe for repairs. The walls are finished at the angles with columns composed of three bottels, separated by hollow curves, which are enriched with the Gothic astragted ornament, and over each of the bottels is carved a mask, by way of capital. The only other decorated external feature of this 'pretty stone monument,' as it was designated by Timothy Pont, already quoted, is a cornice composed of alternating cima-reversas and quarter-rounds, surmounting the walls. Through an aperture in the east end of the monument, aided by a faint light admitted through slits in the south and west walls, are seen the recumbent statues of the gallant captain in military garb, and of his spouse in the costume of the time. The figures have the hands joined on the breast as in prayer, and, though at first look but indifferently seen, the light soon becomes strong enough to repress all regret that these rude efforts of the untutored stone-cutter are not more distinctly visible. On the exterior of the north wall, the following inscription, which has been cut in large raised characters, may still be traced :—

GOD . SCHAW .
THE . RICHT .

| Heir . Lyis . Thomas . | And . Ionet . Ker . His . |
| Cravfvrd . of . Ior . | Spovs . Eldest , Doc . |
| danhil . Sext : Sou . | Iter . To . Robert . Ker . |
| To . Lavrence . Crav . | Of . Kerrisland . |
| fvrd . of . Kilbirny . | 1 . 5 . 9 . 4 . |

" In the centre of the inscription is engraved a shield bearing, quarterly, Craufurd and Barclay, and for crest, a figure, by its irregular outline meant probably to represent a rock, in allusion to Dumbarton Castle. The motto, 'God . Schaw . The . Richt.' was conferred on Captain Craufurd by the Earl of Morton, in memory of the conflict at the Gallow-Lee, in 1571, betwixt the factions of the King and Queen. Captain Craufurd died 5d January, 1603, and was buried alongside of the inscribed wall of the monument, as is still indicated by a flat stone bearing his name.*

" There is no other memorial in the churchyard of so old a date as the one just described, by nearly half a century; but there are three or four flat stones, bearing the figure of a sword, to which we would not hesitate to assign an antiquity considerably more remote. These stones are each seven feet in length, and one foot nine inches broad at the top, and three inches less at the lower end. Between the handle of the sword and the upper verge of the stones, is cut, within a circle sixteen inches in diameter, a figure seemingly intended to represent a cross, with an annulet in each of its quarters. On account of these figures, but especially of that of the sword, it has been alleged that these unlettered memorials commemorate at least the fact of so many Knight Templars having been buried here, though there is no other evidence, nor even a whisper from tradition, adduced in support of the notion.

* The name of Captain Cranfurd has been rendered famous by his adventurous exploit of storming the almost impregnable fortress of Dumbarton, in 1571. In consideration of this extraordinary feat of courage and dexterity, which Sir Walter Scott held to be unparalleled in ancient or modern history, Captain Craufurd received a grant of several lands in the neighbourhood of Glasgow, whence his title of Jordanhill, besides an annuity of £200 Scots during his life, payable out of the Priory of St Andrews.

" The remains of Tam Giffen, the reputed warlock of the district, lie beneath the hearthstone of the Watch-house, erected about twenty-five years ago in the south-east corner of the churchyard. A few of his ridiculous sayings, by means of which he 'kept the country-side in fear,' and procured a ready amous, are still preserved in the parish, and certainly convey but a low idea of the intelligence of the peasantry in this quarter a hundred and fifty years ago, when a sturdy beggar's idle tales could

" Touzle a' their tap, and gar them shake wi' fear.' "

The parish records commence in 1688; but numerous and long gaps occur, especially in the minutes of session. What remains presents little worthy of quoting, being chiefly a record of the immorality of the district.

## ANTIQUITIES.

Under this head, we cannot do better than continue our quotations from the carefully drawn up article in the Statistical Account :—

" Various tumuli have, at different times, been accidentally explored in this parish, and in some of which urns filled with calcined bones have been found, and in others stone coffins containing human remains. Early in the century, three stone coffins, but without the addition of any mound over them, were discovered on the right bank of the Garnock, about a quarter of a mile below Kilbirnie Bridge; one of them contained a large urn filled with burnt bones; but in neither of the other two, nor in one opened about the same time on the opposite bank of the river, near to Nether-Mill, and close to the base of a large barrow or mound, were found any relics whatsoever. About thirty years ago, the late Mr Cochran, in the course of his agricultural improvements, had occasion to remove a slightly elevated tumulus, situated on the lands of Ladyland, in the centre of which a small urn was found containing ashes. The urn, until lately, was to be seen in the Museum of Glasgow College, to which it was presented by Mr Cochran, but it appears now to be either lost or withdrawn from that collection. In 1836, a stone coffin, containing remains of human bones, was discovered on the farm of Langlands, about three quarters of a mile north of Kilbirnie. The tumulus over it was by much the most remarkable object of the kind in this quarter. It stood on the level part of a field, skirted by the Garnock on the west, from which it was fifty yards distant. It was of a circular form, 100 feet in diameter, and six feet in height. Originally, it had been much higher, but, about the beginning

of the century, a great quantity of stones were taken from its summit to form a road in the neighbourhood. What remained of it in 1830, was composed of stones of various dimensions intermixed with earth. Few of these were heavier than a man could carry, excepting a row placed seven feet within the line of the base, and some three or four feet apart, each of which might weigh half a ton. The coffin or chest, which was formed of six flat stones neatly fitted together, measured 2 feet 7 inches in length; 1 foot 9 inches in breadth; and 1 foot 7 inches in depth. It was situated in the centre of the tumulus, and its longitudinal position was north and south. It contained nothing but bones very much decayed, and the greater part of which lay in its south end. Many of these, on being handled and exposed to the air, crumbled into dust, but several of the fragments which have been preserved can be distinctly recognised as belonging to the human species. In the spring of 1837, every vestige of this primeval monument was removed. The mound situated at Nether-Mill, incidentally mentioned above, is of an irregular pyramidal form, about 18 yards in length, 9 in breadth, and between 5 and 6 in height. It is, we doubt not, artificial, and has apparently been formed by excavating the adjoining bank, which overlooks it. This opinion, though not supported by popular belief or local tradition, is strengthened by the unstratified appearance of the composition of the mound, and by the circumstance of the stone coffin already noticed being discovered in its immediate vicinity.

" Coin.—In tilling a field last year, near the ruins of Glengarnock Castle, there was turned up a silver coin about the size of a modern shilling. It is in excellent preservation, having apparently been little worn, and weighs about one drachm thirty-five grains. The obverse bears the Scottish shield and crown, supported by the letters M. and R. Legend, Maria . Dei . G . Scotor . Regina. 1556. On the reverse, a large cross, with four less in its quarters. Legend, In . Virtute . Tua . Libera . Me. It is of pure silver, or appears to be so; it feels like malleable iron; the modern silver coinage like cast-metal.

" Kilbirnie House.—The stately ruins of the ancient house or Place of Kilbirnie, are situated a mile west of the village, and overlook a considerable extent of country beyond the valley, beautified with Kilbirnie Loch, and fertilized by the Garnock. The surrounding grounds fall gently towards this valley, and are varied but slightly by a shallow dingle, on the margin of which stands the ruined mansion. The building, which has been erected at two widely different periods, consists of an ancient quadrilateral tower, and a modern addition, extending rectangularly from its east side. The tower is 41 feet in length by 32 feet in breadth, and its walls are 7 feet thick. Its height has been divided into four stories, the lowest of which is vaulted and without a fire-place. The second, which consisted of a hall, 26 feet long, and 18 feet wide, has likewise been vaulted, and lighted tolerably by a window in its south wall, and another facing the west. Above the hall have been two tiers of chambers; but of their subdivisions there are no traces left. Access to the different floors and to the roof, has been gained by a narrow spiral stair in the north-east angle of the building. A way fenced with a parapet has gone round the top, all of which has fallen down, as well as every vestige of the roof, which was probably of the high triangular form, common to such castellated mansions. It is impossible, from any peculiarities in the masonry of this feudal tower, to ascertain the period of its construction. The absence of gun-ports in its walls—a provision of defence with which every stronghold erected subsequently to the use of fire-arms was furnished —seems to imply that it was built, at the latest, in the early part of the fourteenth century, and consequently in the days of the Barclays, the most anciently recorded lords of the barony. The modern part of the edifice was built about 1627, and must have proved a satisfactory increase of light and airy accommodation to that afforded by the sombre tower. It extends 74 feet, is 25 in width, and has been three stories in height, besides the attics, the pedimented windows of which have risen above the lower line of the roof, as have likewise the hanging turrets at the extremities of the principal façade. Much of the exterior walls of both parts of the building is still entire; and, as is frequently the case in similar ruinous structures, the most ancient part is the least dilapidated. Most of the interior divisions have, within these few years, fallen down, a few of the vaulted apartments excepted, and in these the "lazy steer and sheep" have been long permitted to find a shelter. The building was entirely destroyed by fire accidentally kindled on the 1st May, 1757, and from which, as it occurred at an early hour of the morning, the Earl of Crawfurd with his infant daughter and the domestics, had little more than time to escape.* Eighty years of exposure to the weather have much lessened, and greatly enfeebled what the fire had spared; while, during this long period, all the contiguous pleasure-grounds have been torn up by the plough, or permitted to run waste. The noble straight-lined avenue, full twenty yards in breadth, has returned to a state of nature:—the gardens situated to the west, instead of flowers and shrubs, are allotted to the rearing of potatoes and turnips; and of the orchard grounds no traces are now to be found. The high walls with which they were enclosed are everywhere breaking down, and all the fine old timber, which had beautified and sheltered "the Place" for ages, and afterwards added much to the grandeur and interest of its ruins, has disappeared within the last thirty years.

"*Glengarnock Castle*.—The ruins of Glengarnock Castle stand on a precipitous ridge or knoll, overhanging the Garnock, about two miles north of Kilbirnie. This brawling stream skirts two sides of the knoll; and as the ravine through which it flows is fully eighty feet in depth, the position, under the ancient system of warfare, must have combined security with the means of easy defence. The only access to the castle is from the northeast, in which direction the ridge, upon which it is situated, is connected with the adjoining field. At the distance of thirty yards from its entrance, a depression in the ground indicates what has been the course of a dry moat, by which, and a drawbridge, the approach is said to have been protected. The ground-plan of this ancient stronghold could, until lately, be easily traced; and as a portion of the exterior walls still remains nearly the original height, its appearance when entire may, with little difficulty, be yet shadowed out. From notes and measurements taken a few years ago, it may be described in general terms, as having consisted of a quadrilateral tower, with a court of less elevated buildings extending from its east side. The entrance has been from the eastern extremity of the latter. This façade is 46 feet long, and has been about 24 feet in height. A court or passage, 59 feet in length, lay between the entrance and the tower, on each side of which has been a range of two-storied apartments. The

---

* The cause remained long unaccountable. The carpenters had nearly finished their operations. They were working in the garret story. They had no fire there, and by way of precaution, they locked the doors of the apartments in the evenings when they left off work, and carried the keys with them. They had left, however, the garret or sky-light windows open. It was through these that the fire found access from a foul chimney that was set on fire by one of the ladies of the family, having inadvertently thrown the melted grease in the socket of a candlestick into a grate in the lower story, about the time she retired to bed. Even the firing of the chimney was not at the instant discovered, as the flame did not issue from below, but altogether at the top of the vent. This circumstance, which was known to one only of the female servants, or rather to a nurse, employed at that time in nursing Lady Jean, who was afterwards Countess of Eglintoun, was carefully concealed at the time; and the burning was always accounted supernatural, till about twenty-four years after, when, on the death of the Earl, it was divulged.—ROBERTSON'S CUNINGHAME.

tower is 45 feet long, 33 feet wide, and its height has been above 40 feet. Its upper and now only accessible story has consisted of a hall occupying the whole extent within the walls, and the imbowed ceiling of which has been 20 feet in height. It has been lighted both from the court and from the exterior walls. One of the windows overlooks the rugged chasm through which murmurs the Garnock, and from two narrow apertures facing the east, the eye may yet revel over a beautiful extent of the district bearing the same name as the old lords of the castle. From the hall, a narrow circular stair led to the upper part of the building, which has been surrounded by a parapet wall. The ruins show neither the arrow-slit nor gun-port of defence, so common in similar old houses. Perhaps the situation was of itself so secure as to render unnecessary the ordinary means of repelling an attack. The uniformity of style in all castellated mansions, erected prior to the discovery of gunpowder, renders it hazardous to be precise regarding the date of their construction. Few, however, conversant with such remnants of feudal architecture, would hesitate to assign to the ruins of this stronghold, an antiquity as remote as that of any remains of masonry in the west of Scotland. It is not, therefore, improbable that Glengarnock Castle may have existed in the time of the De Morvilles, though the conjecture of its having been the residence of these ancient lords of Cuninghame, appears entitled to nearly the same consideration as that of its having been the castle of Hardyknute. It may be added, in justification of so minute an account, that the ruins of this castle will soon cease to be an object of interest to the local antiquary, or to form a picturesque feature in the landscape. The storms of January 1839 overthrew the north wall of the tower, containing between 4000 and 5000 solid feet of masonry; and unequivocal symptoms portend, that, at no distant date, the bed of the Garnock will receive the greater part of the time-worn remains.

"*Ladyland House.*—The old house of Ladyland, briefly characterised by Pont, circa 1609, as a 'strong tower,' was demolished in 1815, with the exception of about 20 feet in length and 25 feet in height of its north elevation. This fragment is six feet in thickness, and as compact as the solid rock. A pedimented stone, which belonged to a door or window of the building, but which is now placed over an entrance to the adjoining garden, bears the initials W. H. I. B., and the date, Anno 1669. The date records, doubtless, the period of some repairs, or perhaps the year the estate was acquired by Hamilton of Ardoch, as there cannot be a question of the existing fragment of masonry having formed part of the 'strong tower' noticed by Pont, and in which, a few years previously to his visiting the district, had resided Barclay, the unfortunate friend of Montgomerie, the poet, as had likewise, probably, all his ancestral possessors of the barony of Ladyland. In taking down this ancient strong-house, there were found, in a cavity in one of the walls, a little above the foundation, four small urns, a painted drinking glass, and a large jaw bone, supposed to have been that of an ox. The urns were neatly formed of common clay, three of which were filled with an unctuous kind of earth, and one of them, besides the earth, contained the breast and side bones of a chicken. Two of the urns had handles, and all of them were tightly closed with shreds of trimming or woven cloth, the most of which, on being taken out, crumbled into powder. Part of these relics are preserved by Mrs Cochran of Ladyland, as is a small coin found in the grounds adjoining the tower. The coin is of some compound metal, and bears the legend FESTINA LENTE; but the date and the impress on both sides appear to have been effaced by long circulation."

## FAMILIES IN THE PARISH OF KILBIRNIE.

### THE BARCLAYS AND CRAUFURDS OF KILBIRNIE.

The oldest possessors of the barony of Kilbirnie, so far as there is any record, were the Barclays, supposed to have been a branch of the very ancient family, the Barclays of Ardrossan.

I. SIR WALTER BARCLAY, derived, as *Craufurd* supposes, from Sir Walter Barclay, Lord High Chamberlain of Scotland in 1174, married Margaret, daughter of Sir John Craufurd of *Craufurd-John*, by whom he obtained one-half of the lands of Craufurd-John.

II. Hugh Barclay, who was in possession of half the lands of Craufurd-John in 1357.[*] He was succeeded by—

III. Sir Hugh Barclay, designed of Kilbirnie, as well as of half the lands of Craufurd-John, in 1397. Sir Hugh had two sons—*Adam*, who succeeded; and *Archibald*, the first of the Barclays of Ladyland, soon after 1400.

IV. Sir Adam Barclay, styled in a charter, in 1429, " Adam filius domini Hugonis de Kilbirny." He left issue, a son,

V. Sir John Barclay of Kilbirnie and Craufurd-John, who died without male issue in 1470, and whose only daughter, Marjory, was married to,

I. MALCOLM CRAUFURD of Greenock, the fifth in descent from Sir John Craufurd of Craufurd-John,[†] by which the heirs-male and heirs-line of this family became united. He had a charter from James IV., in 1499, " Malcolm Crawford de Greenock, terrarum de Kilbirnie, dimidietat baroniæ de Crawford-John." There were four sons and a daughter of this marriage :—

1. Malcolm, who succeeded.
2. James, first of the Craufurds of Monock.
3. Thomas.
4. John.

Isabel, the daughter, was married to Sir Adam Cuninghame of Caprington.

II. Malcolm Craufurd of Kilbirnie and Craufurd-John, who, on the 24th April, 1499, had a resignation from his mother of the barony of Kilbirnie and others. He married Marion Crichton, daughter of Robert, Lord Sanquhar, by whom he had two sons, *Robert* and *John*.

III. Robert Craufurd of Kilbirnie and Craufurd-John, son of the preceding, had a charter of the whole lordship of Kilbirnie, on the 8th May, 1499, on his father's resignation, who reserved a competency to himself. He married Margaret, daughter of Semple of Eliotson. He died in 1513, and was succeeded by the only son of the marriage,

IV. Laurence Craufurd of Kilbirnie. He exchanged the lands of Craufurd-John, with Sir James Hamilton of Fynart, for the lands of Drunry, in 1528. He married Helen, daughter of Sir Hugh Campbell of Loudoun, by whom he had six sons and two daughters ; of the sons, Thomas, the sixth, was ancestor of the Craufurds of Jordanhill. He died in 1541, and was succeeded by his eldest son,[‡]

V. Hugh Craufurd of Kilbirnie,[*] who fought in the battle of Langside, May 13, 1568, on the part of Queen Mary. He married, first, Margaret, daughter of Colquhoun of Luss, by whom he had a son, who succeeded him ; secondly, Elizabeth, daughter of Barclay of Ladyland, by whom he had a son, William, of Knightswood, who married Jean, daughter of Andrew Craufurd of Baidland ; also, a daughter, Marion, married to John Boyle of Kelburne. He died in 1576, and was succeeded by his son of the first marriage,

VI. Malcolm Craufurd of Kilbirnie, who married Margaret, daughter of Cuninghame of Glengarnock, by whom he had two sons and a daughter. He died in 1592, and was succeeded by his eldest son,

VII. John Craufurd of Kilbirnie, who married Margaret, daughter of John Blair of that Ilk, by whom he had three sons and two daughters.[†] It was in this laird's time (1602) that the place of Kilbirnie was broken into, and a number of valuable articles abstracted. " Johnne Crawfurd, sumtyme in Auchinloch, now (1606) in Auchinbothe," was put upon his trial for the robbery, 26th February, 1606. The indictment, which is curious, is as follows :—

" Forsamekill as he, accompaneit with Thomas Wilsoun in Wallase, with divers vtheris thair complices, cowmoun thewis, in the moneth of Nouember, the yeir of God 1m. VIc. and twa yeiris, come to the place of Kilbirnie, the Laird being than furth of this realme, and his Lady being than in Grenok, ten myle distant fra the said place of Kilbirny : and thair, vnder sylence and cloud of nycht, brak the said Place, at the North syde thairof, enterit within the samin, and thiftiouslie stall, concelit, ressett and away-tuik, furth thairof, and furth of the cofferis than standing within the said Place, ane figuret velvet goune, ane blew bend of taffetie, ane ryding cloik and skirt of broun cullerit claith, wrought with siluer pasment ; ane blak velvet dowblet, cuttit out and wrocht with silk cordounis ; ane pair of broun veluet breikis, wrocht with cordounis of gold, ane lowse goun of grograne, ane skirt of broune satene, ane broun saittene dowblet, twa hwidis with craipis ; togidder with ane pair of blankettis, quhairin he band all the saidis claithis and abulzements : Quhilkis guidis and geir pertenit to the

and are apperand to Laurence Craufurd of Kilbirny, of all gudis, movabill and vnmovabill, &c. quhilkis pertenit to the said Laurence, Eschete for falseing and flenzeing of ane proces of apprizing, led at his instance agains Johne Cunynghame (‘1c. merkis’ of composition.)

[*] He was one of the assize at the trial of the Laird of Bishoptoune, Oct. 8, 1541.

[†] Margaret Blair, Lady Kilbirny, and John Crawford, her spous, occur in the testament of vmqle. Marcoun Barclay, who deceist April 1603.—GLASGOW COM. REC.

---

[*] Craufurd's Peerage.

[†] Sir John Craufurd is said to have been the second son of Sir Reginald Craufurd, who married the heiress of Loudoun ; but there is some confusion in the family tree, which it would be difficult, if not impossible, to clear up in a satisfactory manner.

[‡] 1540, June 11.—Lettre of gift to Hew Craufurd, sone

said Johnne Crawfurd of Kilbirnie and his spous. Lyke as, att the same tyme, he with his complices, brak vp the said Johnne Crawfurdis Charter-kist, standing within the said Place, and thiftiouslie stall, conceilit, ressett and away-tuik, furth thairof, ane grit number of the said Laird of Kilbirneis speciall euidentis and writtis, togidder with the saidis guidis and geir and abulzements, he and his complices had and convoyit away with thame, and disponit thairvpoun att thair pleasour; and he wes airt and pairt of the thifteous steilling, conceiling, resetting and away-taking of the saidis guidis, geir, writtis, euidents and vtheris aboue writtin, and of the breking of the said Place, in maner, and att the tyme forsaid; quhilk wes notourlie knawin. To the takin, (token) he, with his wyffe and seruand-wemene, delyuerit bak agane to the Lady Kilbirny, within the duelling house of Cuthbert Crawfurd in Parkfut, in presens of the said Cuthbert Crawfurd, Hew Gavin in Boig, William Allane in Manis, Thomas Harvie in Brocklirhill, Mungo Allane in Sarslie, Hew Starrie in Banksyde, and George Kelso in Brighill, the perticuler abulzements following, viz. the saidis cuttit out velvet dowblet, the broun velvet brekis, the lowse grograne goune, the broun satene skirt, ane broune satene dowblet, the said figurit velvet goune, the said broun ryding cloik and skirt, with the saidis twa huidis, quhilkis wer thifteouslie stollin and away-brocht be him and his complices, furth of the said place, att the tyme foirsaid: To the takin also, he being examinate him selff, in presens of the Minister, eldaris and deakinnis of the Kirk of Kilbirnie, he grantit and confessit the haifing of the said blew taffatie bend, with certane of the said Laird and Ladies writtis and euidentis, bot wald nocht declair how he came be thame; as the Extract of his Confessioun, heirwith produceit to schaw, beris: To the takin lykwayis, the said Johnne, being charget of befoir to find cautioune to haif comperit before the Justice, at ane certane day bygane, to vnderly the law for the foirsaidis crymes, he than, for disobedience of the said charge, past to the horne; as the Hoirning lykwayis schawin beiris."

Notwithstanding the strong evidence here adduced, "the assise, be the mouth of Williame Orr in Lochrig, chancellor, for the maist pairt, ffand, pronuncet and declairit the said Johnne Crawfurd to be clene, innocent and acquit of airt and pairt of the breking," &c.

John Craufurd died, as the following extract from the Commissary Record of Glasgow shows, in 1622. "Testament dative and Inventar of the guidis, &c. qlk. pertenit to vmqle. Johnne Crawfurd of Kilburnie the tyme of his deceis, Quha deceist in the monethe of Januar, the zeir of God

1622 zeirs. ffaytfullie maid and gevin vp be Johnne Crawford now of Kilburnie, lawfull sone to the defunct, and executour dative decernit to his guids and geir be decreit of the Commissary of Glasgow, 27th Merche, 1622, &c. *Inventar—* . . . Item, ane boitt wt. hir furnitor, Rowing and sailling graithe, estimat to je li. Item, in the bornes and bornezairdis of Kilburnie, Grenok, and Fairlie Crevoche, rextive. Sax scoir bolls aitts, price of the bole v li. 6s. 8d. Cond. the penult day of May, 1622. Hew Crawford of Jordanehill, Cautr."

VIII. John Craufurd of Kilbirnie, son of the testator, rebuilt, or rather made additions to, the house of Kilbirnie in 1627. He married Lady Mary Cuninghame, daughter of the Earl of Glencairn, by whom he had two sons and two daughters, one of whom, *Anne*, married Sir Alexander Cuninghame of Corsehill. He died in 1629, and was succeeded by his eldest son,

IX. Sir John Craufurd of Kilbirnie, who was knighted by Charles I., and took part in the Civil Wars. He married, first, a daughter of Lord Burleigh, by whom he had no issue; secondly, Magdalene, daughter of David, Lord Carnegie, by whom he had two daughters:—

1. Anne, married to Sir Archibald Stewart of Blackhall, from which marriage descended the family of Blackhall and Ardgowan.
2. Margaret, who married Patrick, second son of John, the fifteenth Earl of Craufurd and first of Lindsay.

Sir John died in 1661. The representation of the family now fell on Cornelius Craufurd of Jordanhill, as heir-male; but in the estate of Kilbirnie, Sir John was succeeded by his youngest daughter,

X. Margaret Craufurd, and her husband, Patrick Lindsay, who now, in consequence of the entail, assumed the name of Craufurd of Kilbirnie. Of this marriage there were seven children. Both husband and spouse died suddenly in 1680, having been carried off by a malignant fever. Their deaths are thus detailed in Law's Memorials:— "October 1680. In one week's tyme, dyed, first, the Lady Kilburnie, daughter to the late laird of it, on the 12th of that instant, and her husband, the laird, second son of the Earl of Lindsay, who gott that estate by marrying this laird's daughter, dies also upon the 15th of that instant, both of a feaver. The Sabbath before, they were at the celebration of the Lord's Supper at the kirk of Beith. On the day they sickened, the laird's dogs went into the closs, and an unco dog coming in amongst them, they all set up a barking, with their faces up to heaven howling, yelling, and youphing; and when the laird called upon them, they would not come to him, as in former times, when he called upon them. The death of thir spouses was much lamented by all sorts of people. They left seven children behind them; within a few days after, the Lady Blackhall, her sister, being infected with the same disease, (for it was a pestilentious fever,) and coming to Kilbirnie to wait on the funeralls, she also dyes there." It would appear that a considerable party of the citizens of Glasgow had attended the funeral of these distinguished individuals, for on the 21st December following, the town-council ordained "John Robesoune to have ane warrand for the soume of thrie hundreth sextie punds, nyne shilling Scots, payed be him for the expenses and hors hyres of these that went to the buriall of Kilbirnie, his Ladie, and to the buriall of the Ladie Blackhall."

XI. John Craufurd of Kilbirnie, the eldest son, was served heir, 4th December, 1690. He took an active part in those measures which led to the Revolution, and, as stated in our account of the parish of Irvine, commanded the Fencible men of Cuninghame in 1689. In 1693, he was chosen member of the Scots Parliament for the shire of Ayr, and again in the first Parliament of Queen Anne. In 1705, he was raised to the peerage by the title of Viscount Mount Craufurd, which he afterwards got altered to that of Garnock. He married Lady Margaret Stewart, daughter of the Earl of Bute, by whom he had five sons:—

1. Patrick, his successor.
2. John.
3. James, sometime connected with the Customs at Irvine, and the reputed ancestor of John Lindsay Craufurd, the Irish claimant of the honours and estates of Craufurd.
4. David.
5. Charles; and three daughters.

He died 25th December, (o. s.) 1708, and was succeeded by his eldest son,

XII. Patrick, Viscount Garnock. He married Miss Home, daughter of George Home, Esq. of Kelly, by whom he had two sons and three daughters. His eldest daughter, Margaret, was married to David first Earl of Glasgow, of whom the present Earl is descended. He died 24th May, (o. s.) 1735, and was succeeded by his only surviving son,

XIII. George, third Viscount Garnock, who succeeded to the honours of Cranfurd, &c. on the death of John, the eighteenth Earl. He married Jean, daughter of Robert Hamilton, Esq. of Bourtreehill, by whom he had three sons and two daughters:—

1. George, who succeeded.
2. Robert. 3. Bute; both of whom died unmarried.
1. Lady Jean, married, in 1772, to Archibald, Earl of Eglintoun, but died in 1778, in her twenty-first year, without issue.
2. Lady Mary, of whom afterwards.

Lord Garnock died in 1781, and was succeeded by his eldest son,

XIV. George Lindsay Craufurd, fourth Viscount Garnock, twentieth Earl of Craufurd, and sixth Earl of Lindsay, Lord-Lieutenant of Fife, and a Major-General in the army. His Lordship died unmarried in 1808, and was succeeded in his estates in Fife, Dumbartonshire, and Ayrshire, by his only remaining sister,

XV. Lady Mary Lindsay Craufurd, of Craufurd, Lindsay, and Garnock. Her Ladyship remained unmarried, and enjoyed the property till her death, in 1833, when the estates fell to George, fourth Earl of Glasgow, in right of his descent from Margaret, the eldest sister of the first Viscount Garnock.

*Arms*—The arms of the Viscount Garnock, as represented in the Craufurd gallery of Kilbirnie Church, are as follow: Two coats impaled, Baron and Femme; the first bears quarterly, first and fourth, azure, three cross patees, or, for Barclay; second and third, gules, a fess, cheque, argent and azure, for Lindsay; and by way of surtout, gules, a fess, ermine, the maternal coat of Craufurd; the second bears, or, a fess, cheque, azure and argent, for Stewart, his Lordship having married Lady Margaret Stewart, only daughter of James, first Earl of Bute. The shield is timbered with helmet, coronet and mantling, befitting the quality of Viscount, and on a wreath of the principal tinctures of the coats, for crest, a stag's head erased proper, collared, ermine, and between his attires, or, a cross crosslet, fitche, of the last. On an escroll is the motto, "Hinc . Honor . Et . Salus." Supporters, on the dexter a man robed in green, striped with gold, and carrying on his right arm a shield charged with the fess, ermine, of the Craufurds, and on the sinister, a horse, sable, the whole standing on a compartment on which are the words, "Sine . Laba . Nota."*

* Lest the accuracy of any part of the above blazon should be called in question, we shall briefly notice what appears to be three errors committed in the 'getting up' of this handsome achievement. The first is the omission in the sinister coat of the double tressure flowered and counter-flowered with fleur-de-lis, gules, assumed by the first Earl of Bute in addition to the simple coat of Stewart. The second is in the tincturing of the supporter of this coat, viz., a horse, sable, whereas in the Bute achievement, from which it is taken, and of which it is the dexter supporter, the horse is argent, bridled gules: and thirdly, the mantlings, which are or, doubled sable, appear to be faulty, inasmuch as they are not of the tinctures of the arms within the shield, as was the rule of old with us, nor are they agreeable to the English practice, which of late, says Nisbet, "our heralds have followed, who have all the mantlings of gentlemen and knights red without, and lined or doubled with white within, and those of dignified nobility also red, but doubled ermine."—(Account of the Church and Churchyard of Kilbirnie, by W. Dobie, Esq., Grangevale, Beith.)

## CUNINGHAMES OF GLENGARNOCK.

As already stated, this barony was anciently in the possession of a family of the name of Riddell, supposed to have been descended from the Riddels of Teviotdale. The Cuninghames acquired the property by marriage.

I. REGINALD, second son of Sir Edward Conyngham of Kilmaurs, by his wife, Mary, daughter of the High Steward of Scotland, living about 1292, married Jonet Riddell, the heiress of Glengarnock.* His son,

II. Sir Gilbert Conyngham of Glengarnock married Ann Lyle, daughter of Sir Allan Lyle, Sheriff of Bute, who turned to the English interest, and became keeper of the castle of Rothesay. The vassals of the Stewarts there rose and put Sir Allan Lyle to death. Gilbert de Conyngham del Comte de Aire, swore fealty to Edward about 1296.

III. Donald Conyngham of Glengarnock, living about 1310, married Elizabeth, daughter of Linn of that Ilk.†

IV. John Conyngham of Glengarnock (about 1330) married Jean, daughter of Sir Ronald Crawfurd of Loudoun.

V. Robert Conyngham of Glengarnock (about 1360) married Magdalene, daughter of Blair of that Ilk.

VI. John Conyngham of Glengarnock (about 1380) married Elizabeth, daughter of Conyngham of Kilmaurs.

VII. William Cuninghame of Glengarnock, who, about the commencement of the fifteenth century, married Christian, daughter of Sir Humphry Colquhoun of Luss. His son,

VIII. Sir Humphry Cuninghame of Glengarnock, married Jean, daughter of Buchanan of that Ilk. About the year 1459, he had a daughter, Agnes, married to Sir Andrew Moray of Abercairney.

IX. William Cuninghame of Glengarnock, his son and successor, married, about 1470, Ann, daughter of Montgomerie of Ardrossan.

X. Sir William Cuninghame of Glengarnock, married, about 1480, Mary, daughter of Sir William Edmonston of Duntreath. He was witness to a charter granted by Alexander, Lord Montgomerie and Laird of Giffyne, signed at Ardrossan, 20th July, 1452.

The Lords Auditors, 5th August, 1473, decreits that Thomas, Lord Erskine, Johne, Lord Dernele, and *William of Conyggam of Glengarno*, sall pay to Walter Stewart of Morfie and Patric Steruiling, fyftie ky and oxin, twa horss, ane meir, ane chartour, twa ringis of gold, &c.

In the actioun, 17th May, 1474, persewit be a venerable Fadir, George, Abbot of Inchechaff, and his Convent, against *William of Conyggam of Glengarnok*, *Thomas* and *William*, his sonnes, anent the destructioun and doun castin of the mylne lade and dam of Dunfallie, perteining to the said Abbot, the Lords decreits that the Conynggams sall big up again the dam, &c. on their awn expenses.

Another accioun, 12th October, 1494, be the said Abbot agane said William and Thomas, for the wrangwis withhalding thair Place of Inchaneray, &c. Senteus againes the said Conynggams.*

Issue :—

1. Patrick.
2. Thomas.
3. William.

XI. Patrick Conyngham of Glengarnock died before 1478.

XII. Umphra Conyngham of Glengarnock attended a Parliament at Edinburgh (as one of the barons) 2d April, 1481. He married Marjorie Scott, daughter of the laird of Balweirie.

In ane actioun, 12th October, 1478, before the Lords of Conncill, be Umphra Conynggam of Glengarnok, as air to umquhill Patric of Conynggame, aganis Alexr. Conynggam of Lekkie and James Norie of Bochopil, for the wrangwis withholdin of the gudes of airschip of said Patric, the Lords decreits that said Umfra nocht to have airschip of said Patric becaus he had nane heritage.

The Lords of Conncill, 14th October, 1478, assignis to William of Conynggam, the 11th Januar, to prufe that umquhill Patric of Conynggam, his brothir, sauld him 22 young schepe, &c.

Umphra Conyngham of Glengarnock, on 12th October, 1478, as air of Patric, pursues for airschip of moveables; but is non-suited, because Patrick had no heritage.

The Lords assigns, 14th October, 1478, to Alexr. Conynggam and James Norie, executouris to Patric of Conynggam, 11th Jan., to prufe that the twentie four yowis and twentie thre lammis taken be William of Conynggam was the said umquhill Patrikis gudis, and byrnt with his Birn.

The Lords, 20th October, 1478, ordains that Patric Erskine deliver agane to James and Alexander Conynggam, executouris to umqule. Patric Conynggam, the mails of the lands of Clotherok,† and the cornes that was prysit for said umqle.

* Acts of the Lords Auditors, pages 29, 33, and 36.
† Clockodrick, in the parish of Kilbarchan, about two miles from Johnshill, Lochwinnoch.

♥ Millar's MS.          † Ibid.

Patrikis herezeld gife he hes takin the said corn or maills.

Compeirit before the Lords Auditors, 12th March, 1478, Umphra Conynggam of Glengarnock, Patrick of Galbraith, and Donald Fischer, summond at the instans of David Barcla, parishe clerk of Kilbirnie, and protestit, &c.

Before the Lords Auditors, 26th Feb. 1483, it was appunctit and accordit betwixt Johne Inglis of Culquhalye, on the tae pairt, and Umfra Conynggam of Glengarnok, on the tithir pairt, anent, &c. The Lordis decreitis that Umfra sall pay to said Johne, nyne tidie kye, nyne thre yeir auld, and tuelf merkis for three chalders of aittis.*

Umphra Conyngham of Glengarnock had a crown charter, including the Baldalloch, Paleyaris, and Kifassettis properties in 1505.

XIII. William Conyngham of Glengarnock, who married Isabella Cuninghame. It was probably in this laird's time that a grant of the forest of Buchan, in the lordship of Galloway, dated July 8. 1526, was obtained by the family. In 1527, William Cuninghame of Glengarnock was fined for intercommuning with Hugh Campbell, the Sheriff of Ayr, then at the horn for the slaughter of the Earl of Cassillis.

XIV. William Cuninghame of Glengarnock, who was slain at Pinkie, was probably the son of the foregoing. His mother, at all events, " Lady Isabella† Cunyngham,' was alive at the time. Before taking his departure for the army, he made his will, of which the following is a literal translation :—" Death is certain—the hour most uncertain. Hence it is that I, William Cuninghame of Glengarnock, taking my way to rencounter our old enemies, and, in the event of sudden death, make and ordain my testament and last will. In the first place, I give and leave my soul to Almighty God, the most blessed Virgin Mary, and all saints, and my bones to be buried where it shall please the Most High. And I leave iiij pence to the fabrick of St. Kentigern, and xx pound to be given to a chaplain duly ordained to pray for my soul in the parochial church of Kilbirny. Also, I leave to Sir Robert Cunyngham, chaplain, x merkis of money; likewise I leave to the Friars Minor of Air and Glasgow, xx merkis. Also, I appoint and ordain that my tenants have the liberty of compounding their debts. Further, I appoint my executors, viz., Elizabeth Synclair, my wife, and Lady Isabella Cunyngham, my mother, only; and I leave my four best horses to my four sons, in such a way that the eldest shall have the first choice of the same, viz., ay the eldest to

cheis first, and that the heirship horse shall stand to my heir for his choice. I leave to Alexander Cunyngham, my younger son, the younger horse called the ' scur staig,' and to John Blair, my son-in-law, the younger horse, called the ' brown staig.' I grant and assign to Elizabeth Cunynghame, my daughter, relict of the late Alexander Schaw of Sauchguy, that sum of 400 merkis, resting upon the lands and buildings of Sir John Makghe, vicar of Arbruthven, lying within the city of Glasgow; as also, that sum of 200 merkis, owing by the said Sir John, I assign to the foresaid Elizabeth, towards relieving my executrices of the forementioned sum of 700 merkis due to the said Elizabeth. Moreover, all my goods, moveable and immoveable, my debts being taken out and paid, I give and leave to my three daughters, to be distributed and apportioned at the will of my executrices aforesaid, as they shall answer to the Supreme Judge." This testament was made by the mouth of the departing, " the xxix day of the month of August, in the year of our Lord 1547, my manuel subscription bearing testimony, at Glengarnock." Follows the form of subscription, " William Cunyngham of Glengarnock, with my hand." This testament was confirmed, &c., 4th November, 1547.*

It was probably this William Cuninghame of Glengarnock who was engaged in so many of the local feuds of his time. The Books of Adjournal† show, that in 1530, May 23, " William Cunynghame of Glengarnock, David C. of Robertland, and thirty-seven of their followers, found caution to appear at the Justice-aire of Air, to underly the law for art and part of the forethought, felony, and oppression done to Gabriel Sympill, lying in the highway, in feir of weir, near Ormysheuche, awaiting his arrival, for his slaughter, of forethought, felony, and old feud."

In 1503, November 20, he was engaged in the feud between his chief, the Earl of Glencairn, and Lord Sempill, and had to underly the law for assisting the Master of Glencairn in attempting the slaughter of Lord Sempill. " William Cunynghame of Glengarnock, David C. of Robertland, and Robert C. of Auchinhervey, with sixteen others, found caution to underly the law at the same Justice-aire, for art and part of the forethought felony and oppression done to Robert Snodgerse, Mark Sympill, and Patrick Young, coming with convocation of the lieges to the number of 100 persons, in warlike manner, on the (3d) day of September last, within the lands of the said Robert, and forcibly seizing and imprisoning

---

* Acts of Lords Auditors.
† The name Isabella, seems favourable to the belief that she was the spouse of William.

* Statistical Account.
† Pitcairn's Criminal Trials.

him, &c. The parties, both Cunynghames and Sempills, were bound over to keep the peace, under the pains of 5000, 2000, and 1000 marks each, according to their respective ranks."

William Cuninghame married Elizabeth, daughter of Lord Saint-Clair. Issue:—

1. John, who succeeded.
2. William, who died intestate before his father. The inventory of his effects was confirmed before the Commissary Court of Glasgow, on the 5th of January 1547. He is styled in that document "Will. Conynghame, filii quond. nobilis viri Willmi. Conynghame de Glengarnok." His executors dative were Isabella, Johanna, and Agnes Cuningbame, "sorrores legittime."
3. Cuthbert.
4. Alexander.
1. Elizabeth, married to Alexander Schaw of Sauchie, who died before 1547.
2. Isobel, married to William Porterfield, younger of that Ilk, in 1506.
3. Margaret, married to John Blair of that Ilk.
4. Johanna.
5. Agnes.

XV. John Cuninghame of Glengarnock succeeded his father. Robertson supposes him to have been twice married, as he had a daughter, Jean, married in 1565 to John Shaw of Greenock, who could not have been the daughter of Margaret, daughter of Malcolm, third Lord Fleming, whom he married in 1548. He had also a daughter, Margaret, married to Malcolm Craufurd of Kilbirnie. He had, according to Millar's MS., twelve sons:—

1. William, who predeceased him.
2. John, the first of Caddell, &c.

And five daughters, viz. Lady Blair, Lady Kilbirnie, Lady Greenock, Lady Fullwood, and Lady Duchall. Like his predecessors, this Laird of Glengarnock entered pretty deeply into the feuds of his time. In 1555, January 8, "John Cunnynghame of Glengarnok, Cuthbert C. of Cochrane, and Alex. C., his brothers,[*] John C. of Croy, and thirty-two others, found caution to underly the law at the next Justice-aire of Air, for convocation of the lieges to the number of thirty persons, armed in warlike manner, and coming under silence of night, in July 1554, by way of hamesucken, to the house of Humphrey Galbrayth in Eister Glenne, breaking up the doors thereof, entering the same, and searching for him for his slaughter, committed on forethought felony." He lived to a great age. In 1591, June 19, Sir Patrick Houston of that Ilk, &c., was "dilatit of airt and pairt of the slauchteris of vmqle William Cuninghame, oy (grandson) of the auld Laird of Glengarnok, and vmqle. Johnne Cwningham, his sone naturall, committed with convocationne, of the causing of the said Sir Patrick, the ferd day of Apryle last-

was, vpoun sett purpose and provisionne." The pursuers for this slaughter were, "Johnne Cwninghame of Glengarnok," and "William Cuninghame, zounger of Glengarnok." As already stated, the "Auld Laird" survived the younger.[*] He died, however, before 1596.

XVI. William, who died before his father, married Mary Sinclair, daughter of Lord Sinclair, and had issue:—

1. Sir James, who succeeded his grandfather.
2. William of Quarreltoun, who obtained from his father the lands of Quarreltoun, Paisley parish, in 1583. He married[†] and had issue.
    1. Robert of Quarreltoun, married Margaret Wood. He died in 1632, and left, in their minority:
        1. Robert.
        2. William.
        3. John.
        4. Margaret.
        5. Isobel.[‡]
    2. James, executor of his father's will, died in 1614.
    3. Margaret, married to Robert Blair of Lochwood, died in 1614.
3. James, died May 18, 1544.
4. Jean, married to her cousin, John Schaw of Greenock, in 1565.
5. Andro went to Ireland. Durie, in his Decisions, mentions him as living in 1626.

XVII. Sir James Cuninghame of Glengarnock. "Jan. 29, 1595-6, James Cunynghame of Glengarnok ordained to be denounced, for not 'compeiring personalie' before the King and Council, 'tuicheing the removing of the fleid standing betuix him and Schir Patrik Houstoun of that Ilk, knt. and his freindis," &c. He succeeded in 1599, and was served heir to his father in 1601. In 1602, January 15, James Cwninghame of Glengarnok was "dilatit of art and part of the slauchter of vmqle. Williame Cuninghame in Walzaird." In 1609, "Sir James Cuninghame of Glengarnock" was one of the assize on the trial of Sir James Makconeill of Knokrynsay, knt., &c. He appears to have been knighted about this time. His name occurs in several testamentary documents, a few years previously, as James Cuninghame simply. In the testament of "Hew Garven, notar, toune-clerk of Irwein," in 1610, however, it occurs thus: "Item, be Sir James Cunynghame of Glengarnok the sowme of Thrie hundrith thretty-thrie pund vi s. viii d."

He married, about the beginning of the seventeenth century, Lady Catherine, daughter of James, seventh Earl of Glencairn, by whom he had three sons and a daughter:—

---

* This shows that John Cuninghame of Glengarnock was the son of William who died at Pinkie, Alexander, who was left the 'seur staig,' having been the younger son. Robertson was doubtful on the point.

* William the young laird died before 1592, as Robertson quotes a sasine subscribed at Glengarnock, 7th September, 1592, by John of Glengarnock, and James his grandson and heir apparent.

† "The Kirkland Rosses, in Renfrew parish, made intermarriages with the Sempills of Fulwood, Whytefuirds of that Ilk, and Cunynghams of Quarreltoun."—ROBERTSON'S CRAUFURD.

‡ Wishaw.

1. John, the representative of the family.
2. William, of Balluchaw, in Ireland, whose daughter, Pannel, married Sir James Colquhoun of Luss, about 1670.

The daughter married James Boswell of Auchinleck.

Having got into pecuniary difficulties, Sir James "assigned, in 1609,[*] the lands of Glengarnock in behoof of his creditors, and went to Ireland, where he had got a grant of 12,000 acres of land from King James VI.[†]

XVIII. John Cuninghame, representative of the family of Glengarnock. With the view of recovering the wadset lands of Boquhan, he sold the lands of Crawfield, Beith parish, to Gabriel Porterfield of Hapland, and Jean Maxwell, his spouse. The deed of sale was dated at Castle-Cuninghame, Ireland, the penult day of January, 1643.[‡]

*Arms*—Argent, a shake-fork, sable, charged with a cinque foil of the first.

### THE OTHER CUNINGHAMES OF GLENGARNOCK.

DAVID CUNINGHAME of Robertland bought the barony of Glengarnock, and was infeft in it, 15th October, 1628. His second son, Alexander, who married Elizabeth, daughter of John Cuninghame of Cambuskeith, resided at Ladyland in 1647.[§] He joined the Marquis of Montrose, and was rebuked for doing so in the kirk of Kilbirnie. He appears to have garrisoned the old castle of Glengarnock in the royal cause. The following notice occurs in reference to this:—"Debursit be the lieut, Bigert, and Ramsheid, to Alexander Cunyngham his garrison of Glengarnock, £51, 15s. 9d. July, 1651, the half, £25, 17s. 6d."

The Robertland family sold the barony of Glengarnock in 1651 or 1652, to

I. Richard Cuninghame, son of William Cuninghame, clerk of the Signet, and depute-keeper of the Privy Seal, who died before 1646. William was the second son of James Cuninghame of Aishinyairds, in Kilwinning parish—a branch of the Craigends family. Richard married, in 1654, Elizabeth, daughter of James Heriot of Trabroun, and niece of the celebrated George Heriot, founder of Heriot's Hospital in Edinburgh. This lady

had possibly some relations in the vicinity of Glengarnock, for Maister John Heriot was "minister of the word" at Kilbirnie in 1615. Maister John married Jean Barclay, and had a daughter, Jean Heriot, married to Hugh Montgomerie, Irvine, in 1615. Richard is said to have received £12,000 Scots by his wife.[*] He died in or before 1671, and his wife in March 1672. They were both interred in Glengarnock aisle in Kilbirnie kirk. They had twelve children, of whom six as follows:

1. Richard, his successor.
2. John went to Ireland. He occurs in 1676.
3. William, born at Glengarnock. He received from Alexander Cuninghame of Craigends, 17th August, 1687, part of 1250 merks addebted to "Robert, my brother, now in America, conforme to a letter from said Robert, directed to Janet Cunynghame, Lady Craigens, his father-sister."
4. David Cunyngham, son of unquhile Richard of Glengarnock, witness to the seisin of his brother Richard of Glengarnock's creditors in 1671.
5. Alexander, fifth son, born at Glengarnock in 1665. He was ordained minister of Dreghorn in 1695, and died in 1712. He married Janet, daughter of Aikenhead of Jaw, in Stirlingshire. Issue, among others—
   1. William Cunyngham, who married his cousin, Elizabeth, daughter of Robert Cuninghame of Cayen, in St Christopher's, in the West Indies. He had several children, but all without issue.
   2. Richard Cunyngham, minister at Symington, who died in 1760. He married Ann, daughter of Mr Murray, merchant in Edinburgh, who died in 1775. Issue, three children:—
      1. Elizabeth Cuningham,[†] married to George Bannatyne, minister at Craigie, and thereafter one of the ministers of Glasgow. He was son of Mr James Bannatyne, who was minister of the College Church of Edinburgh. Issue, five sons and a daughter, all of whom died without issue except Richard Bannatyne, who married Jean, daughter of Robert Allison of Fowtown. He died in 1815, leaving five sons.
      2. Alexander Cuningham, minister at Symingtoun, succeeded his father. Died in 1782, in his 46th year, unmarried.
      3. Robert Cuningham went to Blandford in Virginia. Died in 1796. He married Martha Baird, an American lady. Issue, two daughters, who died unmarried; and two sons, viz. 1. Alexander Cuningham, married. 2. Richard Cuningham, unmarried (when the Bannatyne Manuscript was written). Both are, or were, settled at Petersburgh in Virginia.[‡]
6. Robert Cunyngham, born at Glengarnock in 1669, son of Richard and Elizabeth Heriot. He went to America, or to the West Indies, before 1687, when he wrote to Lady Craigends, his aunt, craving Craigends for 1250 merks due to him. He gained a considerable fortune, and purchased an estate called Cayen, in St Christopher's. He married, first, in 1693, Judith Elisabeth de Bonnisson, daughter of Daniel de Bonnisson of Morlaix, in France, by his wife, Mary de Barat, sister of Charles de Barat, Seigneur de la Bodie,

---

[*] The name of Sir James Cuninghame of Glengarnock occurs in several testamentary documents connected with the locality as late as 1615, at which period he appears to have still remained in Scotland.

[†] Durie mentions, that being engaged in a law plea in 1626, Sir James Cuninghame of Glengarnock borrowed 1000 merks from Walter Forrester upon his lands of Boquhan.

[‡] Beith Papers.

[§] Notwithstanding, he was elected ruling elder for the parish in 1649.

[*] He appears, however, to have been in pecuniary difficulties, for John Watt, in Edinburgh, had the half of Glengarnock in wadset, 24th January, 1667.

[†] She survived Mr G. Bannatyne, her husband, and died in 1802.

[‡] Bannatyne MS. used by Mr Robertson in his Ayrshire Families.

Lieutenant-General to the King of France, and Governor of the Citadel of Lyle in France.* He married, secondly, in his old age, Mary Garnier, his housekeeper. He had by his French lady fifteen children, most of whom died young. Among others:—

1. Daniel, sixth son, who married Elizabeth, daughter of Anthony Hodges, Governor of Montserrat. He died in 1772, aged 72. He had four children:
    1. Elizabeth Philadelphia, married to Charles Pearce of London.
    2. Robert, died at Montserrat.
    3. Henrietta, married to John Knight of Seacastle, Worcestershire.
    4. Anthony, married Harriet Rook.
4. Susanna, (by Mary Garnier) to whom he left his Scots estates of Baidland of Dalry, and Craig of Kilmaurs. This lady married Major Hay of Nunraw, in East-Lothian.†

II. Richard Cunynghame of Glengarnock, born at Glengarnock in 1656. He was served heir to the property 5th June, 1671. His father's debts were greatly beyond what had been calculated upon; and the young heir was so distressed by his creditors, that his education was neglected.‡ The estate of Glengarnock was bought by Patrick Lindsay of Kilbirnie, in 1672 and 1677.§ Richard Cunynghame attained his majority in 1677. Having been dispossessed, and "roupit" out of his inheritance, he married the heiress of Baidland, Elizabeth Cuningham, about 1686. He was alive in 1710,|| about which period he made up the following memorandum of his family:—

1. Richard, born 2d February, 1687. He was in the army in Flanders in 1710.
2. John, born 1st October, 1690. An apprentice to a surgeon in 1710.
3. Ann, born 16th June, 1692.
4. Alexander, born 13th July, 1694.
5. Euphame, born in March, 1696.
6. Robert, born 2d January, 1699.
7. Margaret, born in May, 1701. Married to John Wilson, in Irvine, in 1743. She married, secondly, John M'Dowall, factor to Castlesemple, in 1749.
8. —— born 12th July, 1702.
9. William, born 21st November, 1703.
10. Mary, born 14th March, 1705.

* Nisbet's Heraldry.
† Craig was sold, in 1780, to the brother of the present Robert Morris of Craig; and Baidland-Cuninghame, about 1783 or 1784, to the Earl of Glasgow.
‡ This is noticed among the family papers in 1673.
§ The rental of the whole barony of Glengarnock, comprehending 23 farms, was, in 1672, as follows:—"Sum total of money rent, £2480; of meale, 52 bolls; of malt, 14 bolls, inde 66 bolls; of fouls, § hens, ½ capons, 24 dozen and a-half of caponis. By the mylne ane dozen; with 25 aikers of land, plowed, harrowed, wedd, shorne, inned, and stackt, and the mains for myselfe, which I value at ——."
[From the account of the Chamberlain, John Cuninghame of Wattiestoun, second son of Sir David Cuningham of Robertland. In his papers occurs the following notices in reference to the property of Glengarnock:—
"The 27 Apryle, 1672, for the outrick of Blew Coats, £27, 10s. 0d.
"28 May, 1672, for three weekis mayntenance of the militia, the fourt pairt is £90, 0s. 0d.
"For collecting fyve punds inde £90, 2s. 2d. allowit to Johne Cunynghame as the maister's pairt, with fyve pund for the tennents of waist land, inde £95, 2s. 2d.]
‖ Craufurd's Renfrewshire.

VOL. II.

(Besides, says Richard, I have a son and four daughters, dead.)

III. A son who went to the West Indies, where he married and had three sons. They were living in 1777, according to the Bannatyne manuscript, which ended in that year. "It should seem that this Richard did not retain this property; for we find it the possession of his brother Robert.

"Note.—This account is collected chiefly from the Bannatyne MS., with the perusal of which I have been favoured by Mrs Bannatyne, widow of Richard Bannatyne, son of the late minister of Craigie."*

LADYLAND—BARCLAYS.

The earliest possessors of this barony, so far as seems known, were a branch of the Barclays of Kilbirnie. The first of them, according to Crawfurd's Peerage, was

I. ARCHIBALD, second son of Sir Hugh Barclay of Kilbirnie, who had the dimidieatum terrarum de Ladyland bestowed upon him by his father. It is out of our power, however, to trace the descent of the family in a connected manner. Some generations passed over, the next we find on record is,

II. David Barclay of Ladyland, who was one of the jury, in 1564, on the trial of Patrick Houstoun of that Ilk, for assaulting Archibald Hamilton of Cochno on the street of Dumbarton.† His wife was Margaret Craufurd, probably of the Kilbirnie family. Issue:

1. Hew Barclay, his heir, of whom afterwards.
2. David.
1. Elizabeth, married to Hugh Craufurd of Kilbirnie.

This was the "Laird of Ladyland" who, in May 1568, was with Queen Mary's party at Hamilton, and who, no doubt, fought at the subsequent battle of Langside.

III. Hew Barclay of Ladyland was a poet, and the friend and companion of Montgomerie, the author of "The Cherry and the Slae." Two of his sonnets, the one addressed to Captain Montgomerie, and the other to Ezekiel Montgomerie of Hesilhead,‡ are preserved in Laing's edition of the poems of Montgomerie. These were written in the author's happier days, about 1580, and display no small talent. The first of the sonnets is full of quaint humour. He represents himself as in the country, "hotching on a sped," "draiglit

* Robertson's Ayrshire Families, vol. 1 p. 313—318.
† Criminal Trials.
‡ Ezekiel, younger son of the laird of Hesilheid, was styled of Weitland, Kilbarchan parish. He was chamberlain to his kinsman, Lord Sempill.

Q

in dirt, vhylis wat evin to the skin;" and regretting his absence from his correspondent, who, with his friends, was " birling at the wyne," and " puing Bacchus' luggis."

The poet, unfortunately, got himself embroiled in the civil commotions of the times; and with characteristic enthusiasm took part with the losing side. In 1592, he was seized and imprisoned in the Tolbooth of Edinburgh, for being concerned in the Popish plot. He was, however, set at liberty, by the king's directions, in 1593, on finding four sureties for his re-entering in ward in Glasgow at his majesty's pleasure. In this somewhat critical position, and sensible of the danger of his political predilections, he disponed, in 1593, all his lands of Ladyland to his brother David, under a liferent to Margaret Craufurd, his mother, and that of Isobel Stewart, his spouse. Soon after this he fled to Spain; from whence he returned in 1597, and contrived to get possession of the Craig of Ailsa, with the view of holding it in aid of the designs of the party with which he was connected. His enemies, however, were too active for him. He was discovered while laying in a store of provisions, and being pursued, he either fell by accident, or threw himself intentionally into the sea, and was drowned.

He left no issue. His lady long survived him. " Isobel Stewart, Lady Ladyland," occurs in the testament of John Barclay, Kilbirnie, July 1618.[*]

IV. Sir David Barclay of Ladyland succeeded his brother in 1599, and died in 1606, leaving issue :

1. David, who succeeded.
2. William, burgess of Irvine. He married Margaret Cunynghame. They were infeft in a certain tenement in that burgh in 1819.
3. Hugh, witness to a sasine in 1616. His name occurs in a similar document in 1619.

V. David Barclay of Ladyland was served heir to his father, 27th March 1606. His name occurs in various documents, testamentary and otherwise, from the year 1616 till 1621, inclusive. In 1621, he is mentioned in the testament of " David Stewart of Fairlie Crevoche, within the parochin of Stewarton;" from which it may be inferred that his aunt, Isobel Stewart, Lady Ladyland, was of that family. He seems to have been in easy circumstances; for, in 1617, he gave some money in loan to Lord Sempill, over the lands of Lochhead. He is supposed to have married a daughter of Alexander Cuninghame of Corschill,[†] and left issue.

VI. David Barclay of Ladyland was retoured heir to his father, " Sir David Barclay, knight, of Ladyland and Auchinniff," united in one dominum, in 1629. He was very unfortunate. His father had happened to become cautioner for a debt in 1621, which debt had never been liquidated. In 1631, he was pursued for this debt, as heir of his father, by the Laird of Cloberhill, parish of Stewartoun. The Lords of Session ordained Ladyland to pay the claim, with expenses. This seems to have ruined him; for, in the same year, John Blair of Cloberhill was infeft in the lands of Ladyland, which, from that time, ceased to be held by the Barclays.

Sir David Cuninghame became Laird of Ladyland about 1654. The property was then valued about £546, 17s. 8d.

## LADYLAND—HAMILTONS.

Ladyland was acquired by,

I. CAPTAIN WILLIAM HAMILTON of Airdoch,[*] parish of Kilwinning, between 1662 and 1667. He was the first of the Hamiltons styled of Ladyland. He was one of the witnesses to an infeftment of Montgomerie of Bogstoun in 1682, in which document he is styled " Williame Hamiltone de Ladyland." He was a keen Presbyterian, standing boldly up against Prelacy. He refused the test, notwithstanding his commission as a captain in the service of the king, and was disarmed, by order of the secretary at war, in 1684. He appears, however, to have been restored to his rank soon afterwards, as he fell in battle, fighting against the French, before 1690. The name of Captain William Hamilton of Ladyland is to be found among the Commissioners of Supply for the county in 1667, and in 1686.

Captain Hamilton married, in 1662, Janet, daughter of John Brisbane of that Ilk,[†] and had issue :

1. John, who succeeded.
2. Lieutenant William Hamilton, styled " of Gilbertfield," though he was only tenant, not laird of that property. He served in " my Lord Hyndford's regiment." Gilbertfield is situated within the parish of Cambuslang, Lanarkshire. He was the author of several poetical pieces, one of which, " The Last Dying Words of Bonny Heck, a famous Greyhound in the Shire of Fife," appeared in Watson's " Collection of Comic and Serious Scots Poems, both Ancient and Modern," printed at Edinburgh in 1709. He is, however, better known as the friend and correspondent of Allan Ram-

---

* Glas. Com. Rec.
† Kennedie of Kirkmichael's Peerage and Baronage, MS.

* Captain William was the fifth in descent from Andro Hamilton of Airdoch. See Parish of Kilwinning.
† The stone, with the initials W. H.—I. B. 1669, which formerly belonged to the old tower of Ladyland, had evidently been placed there by the Captain and his lady as a memento of their accession to the property. It had probably been put up on the occasion of some repairs in 1669, but they were in possession of Ladyland two years previously.

say, several of his familiar epistles having been printed along with the poetical works of Ramsay. He also rendered into English Blind Harrie's Life of Sir William Wallace, which was published in 1722. Burns says: "The two first books I ever read in private, and which gave me more pleasure than any two I have read since, were the Life of Hannibal and the History of the Acts and Deeds of Sir William Wallace. . . . . The story of Wallace poured a Scots prejudice into my veins, which will boil along there, till the flood-gates of life shut in eternal rest." Gilbertfield spent the evening of his days at Letterick, where he died at a great age, 24th May 1751. It appears from the following entry in the parish records of Kilbirnie that he was married: "Baptized, at Kilbirnie, 15th June 1693, Anna, lawfull daughter of William Hamilton, brother-german to the Laird of Ladyland, and —— Hamilton, his spouse." Gilbertfield had probably been on a visit to Ladyland with his family at the time.

II. John Hamilton of Ladyland and Airdoch. He had a retour, 3d September, 1690, as heir to Captain Hamilton of Ladyland, his father, in the five merk land of Ardoch, &c., "with the house called the Woodsyde, within the paroch of Kilwinning." He married Margaret, daughter of Sir John Schaw of Greenock, before the year 1690.*

Robert Caldwell, merchant, at the Kirk of Lochunioch, in 1703, "sauld ane dyeed belt to the Laird of Ladyland, at 6s. 10d.; and to the chaplain, ane cased inkhorn, at 11s. Scots." †

Ladyland was sold by Hamilton, about 1710, to Ensign Henry Moncrieff, Collector of Cess for Renfrewshire, who must have sold it soon afterwards to the Earl of Eglintoun; for his lordship granted a disposition and assignation of the lands of the Mains of Ladyland, comprehending Byres, Cockstoun, the Ford, Dykebank, Ladyward, Milnsyde, &c., with the Manor Place of Ladyland, to William Cochran of Edge; and gave a precept of *Clare Constat* of the same, dated 18th January, 1718.

After parting with the estate, Ladyland went to the north of Ireland, many of his kinsmen, especially the relations of his lady, having settled there in former times.

By his lady Hamilton had a numerous family. The offspring of these, in the female line, still remain in Ireland, and are in flourishing and affluent circumstances. Part of the following births are extracted from the Kilbirnie Record, which began in 1688, subsequently to the birth of the first of the family:—

1. William Hamilton, of whom afterwards.
2. Elizabeth Hamilton, dochter of the Laird of Ladyland and Margaret Schaw, his lady, christened 31 Jan. 1690.
3. Gavin Hamilton, son to the Laird of Ladyland and Margaret Schaw, his spouse, 27 October, 1691. Died young.
4. Margaret Hamilton, married, in Ireland, to the Rev.

Patrick Bruce, minister of Killeleah, County-Down. In 1718.

This Mr Bruce was descended from the Bruces of Airth, Stirlingshire. Their son, James Bruce, married a daughter of the Hon. and Rev. Henry-Hervey Aston, D.D., fourth son of John, Earl of Bristol, in 1762. Their son, Bruce of Downhill, County-Londonderry, was created a Baronet, 29th June, 1804.

5. Rabina Hamilton, daughter of the Laird of Ladyland, christened 20 October, 1702.
6. Charles Hamilton, son of the Laird of Ladyland and Margaret Schaw, christened 20 November, 1704. He succeeded to the estate of Craiglaw, after his brother's death, in 1747.

Hamilton bought a large estate in Ireland, which he named Ladyland, after his Scots lands. It is still called Ladyland.

III. William Hamilton of Ladyland in Ireland. He sold the Irish property and returned to Scotland, having purchased the estate of Craighlaw, in Wigtonshire, of which lands he had a charter 26th July, 1744.

He married his cousin, Isobell M'Dowall, daughter of the Laird of Logan. No issue. He died before 1747. He was succeeded by his brother,

IV. Charles Hamilton of Craighlaw, who was Collector of the Customs of Irvine. He was Provost of that burgh for twelve years, two in and two out of office alternately, from 1758 to 1782. He was born at Ladyland, in Scotland, in 1704, but was partly educated in Ireland, where he continued about thirty years. He married Sarah M'Dowall, another of the ladies of Logan, by whom he had issue:—

1. John, who died unmarried after 1760.
2. Ann, married to Major John Peebles in Irvine. They had an only daughter, Sarah Peebles, who was married to Col. John Cuninghame of Caddell.
3. Isobel.
4. William, of whom afterwards.
5. Catharine.
6. Charles.

Provost Hamilton made a provisional deed to his younger children in 1760. His eldest son was John. His landed estates were Craighlaw, in Wigtonshire; and Garvoch, in Renfrewshire. He appointed tutors for his children, viz. Andrew M'Dowall of Banktoun, Senator of the College of Justice, their grand-uncle; John M'Dowall of Logan; Mr Patrick M'Dowall, merchant, his brother; Mr Andrew Adam, minister of Whithorn, their uncles; Mr Robert Hunter, minister of Kirkowan, and James and Michael Bruce, their cousins. He died, in 1783, at Irvine.

V. William Hamilton of Craighlaw, M.D., in Kilmarnock. He resided at Kilmarnock House, and was one of the early patrons of the Poet Burns, having become security, along with others, to John Wilson for the printing of the first edition of his Poems. He married the only child of

* Kilbirnie Record.
† Caldwell's Count Book.

Edward Cairns of Girstounwood, in the Stewartry of Kirkcudbright. He died in 1798. Mrs Hamilton lived at her house of Parkhill, in the parish of Dalry. She died there, 9th March, 1844, aged 85. They had issue, two sons and ten daughters, all of whom died unmarried, except the following :—

1. William Charles of Craighlaw, of whom afterwards.
2. Catharine, married to Major William Cochran of Ladyland, 5th Sept. 1815.
3. Harriet, married to the Rev. Thomas Thomson, minister of Dalry.
4. Isabella, a posthumous daughter. She is of Parkhill.

VI. William Charles Hamilton of Craighlaw. He is or was an officer in the Tenth Hussars. He married Ann, eldest daughter of the Rev. Dr Stewart, minister of Kirkowan, and has issue :

1. Christiana Grace Agnes.
2. Annelia.
3. William Charles Stewart.

*Arms*—Gules, a mullet betwixt three cinque foils, all within a border waved, argent.

*Motto*—Honestus pro patria.

## LADYLAND—COCHRANS.

I. William Cochran of Edge, who purchased the property of Ladyland from the Earl of Eglinton before the 8th January, 1718, was the son of Cochran of Ferguslee, and grand-nephew of the Earl of Dundonald.* He married Margaret

---

* Robertson. The statement, however, is somewhat doubtful. According to other information, William Cochran of Edge, parish of Lochwinnoch, was the grandson of Robert Cochran of Muirscheill.

Orr, of Easter Gavin and other lands, by whom he had a son and five daughters. He died on the 21st December, 1765, and was succeeded by his son,

II. William Cochran of Ladyland, who, in 1756, married Janet, daughter of Robert Glasgow of Pudevenholme, part of the estate of Glengarnock, by Jean, daughter of John Cuninghame of Wattieston, (representative of Robertland,) by whom he had six sons and four daughters. He died on the 13th of February, 1803, and was succeeded by his eldest son,

III. William Cochran of Ladyland, who married, on the 5th September, 1815, Catherine Hamilton, great-grand-daughter of John Hamilton, the last of Ladyland, and had two daughters, *Agnes* and *Janet Glasgow*. He died 1st July, 1832, leaving his eldest daughter the lands and mansion-house of Ladyland, and his second daughter the estate of Beltrees, in the parish of Lochwinnoch and county of Renfrew.

IV. Agnes Cochran of Ladyland, married, in April, 1841, William Charles Richard Patrick of Waterside, advocate, second son of the late Dr Robert Patrick of Trearne and Hessilhead, (*vide* Patrick of Trearne) who, in terms of the entail, took the name and quartered the arms of Cochran of Ladyland. Issue :—

1. Robert William.
2. Catherine Hamilton.
3. Harriet.

The arms of Cochran of Ferguslee were the same with those of Dundonald, with a suitable brotherly difference, viz. argent, a chevron, gules, betwixt three boars' heads erased, azure.

# PARISH OF WEST KILBRIDE.

---

THIS parish is called *West* Kilbride, to distinguish it from Kilbride parish, in Lanarkshire, which is called *East* Kilbride. The name is derived from St Brigid, or *Bride*, to whom the church was no doubt dedicated. A fair, called *Brides'-day*, has been held immemorially at the Kirkton or village. Anciently it was observed on the 1st of February, but latterly on the second Tuesday of that month. The parish is bounded on the north by the parish of Largs; on the east and south-east by those of Dalry and Ardrossan, and on the west by the sea, or the Firth of Clyde. The figure is triangular, extending in length about 6 miles, while its medium breadth is not above 2½ miles, and contains in all about 8650 Scots acres.

The topographical appearance of the parish is irregular. Its inland boundary is marked by a chain of hills, a continuation of those of the western part of Renfrewshire and Largs, which here gradually decline until they altogether terminate at the southern limit of the parish. Besides these, there are several other eminences, such as Law, Ardmill, Tarbert, and Kame hill, the latter of which rises nearly 1000 feet above the level of the sea. From numerous points of the parish a splendid view may thus at all times be commanded of the Firth of Clyde, which here begins to expand itself as it opens towards the sea below the Cumbray Islands. There are, of course, many picturesque openings along the coast, particularly that of Portincross promontory, which overhangs the sea. The promontory is terminated by Ardneil Bank, or "Goldberrie Head," which Pont describes as "grate heigh rocks, making a headland, and running in the maine oceane." "This majestic wall of rock," says the New Statistical Account,* "rising, where highest, to perhaps

little less than 300 feet perpendicularly, ranges in a straight line along the water's edge, from which it is merely separated by a narrow slip of green land, and extends to about a mile in length. Along the bottom, the precipice is richly fringed with natural coppice, in which the oak, ash, hazel, and hawthorn, are thickly interwoven; upwards, the glossy ivy is widely spread, whilst gray lichens, intermixed with large patches of a bright golden-colour succeed, lining the bold front to its utmost verge. Viewed from the plain below, the effect is highly impressive and sublime; whilst to approach its terrific summit, the vivid description by Shakspeare of the cliff of Dover is fully realised. The general mass of these stupendous rocks consists of dark red sandstone, lying horizontally; but for a considerable space where highest, the sandstone, about midway up, is surmounted by a beautiful brown porphyry. This portion, dividing itself into three distinct and deeply separated cliffs of equal height and uniform appearance, has immemorially obtained the poetical cognomen of the *Three Sisters*, otherwise three Jeans, perhaps *Nuns?* And truly it were not difficult, in their stately and solemn austerity, to conceive a fanciful resemblance to the veiled sisterhood. According to tradition, diamonds were contained in this part of the precipice." With the exception of Ardneil Bank, "the shore is low and shelving, consisting of alternate sandy bays and reefs of sandstone." The sands of Southanan, lying in a deep and sheltered curvature, "extend fully two miles in length." They are "frequented by immense flocks of wildfowl, chiefly of the duck tribe, and contain, likewise, large beds of cockles and mussels, besides other varieties of shell-fish, as the clam," &c. About one-half of the parish consists of pasture, the hills being clothed with beautiful green verdure, interspersed with heath. The cultivated lands stretch, in greater or lesser breadth, out along the coast,

---

* Drawn up by John Fullarton, Esq. of Overton.

or are interspersed among the hills, giving a varied and lively aspect to the appearance of the locality. There is a considerable portion of wood lands, most of which is planted, as on the estate of Hunterstoun, where the plantations are in a very thriving condition. On the estates of Southanan and Corsbie, the wood is natural. There are no lakes nor rivers in the parish, although it is well watered by springs and streamlets, the four most considerable of which are Gourock, Millburn, Southanan, and Fairly burns. Southanan rivulet is "distinguished by its picturesque cascade and beautiful sylvan banks."

### HISTORY, CIVIL AND ECCLESIASTICAL.

From the existence of numerous hill fortlets facing the sea, called "castlehills," it has been inferred that the inhabitants of Kilbride, in common with other portions of the coast of Scotland, were frequently called upon to resist the bold inroads of the Danish invaders; and tradition avers that this was particularly the case upon the well-known descent of Haco in 1263. It is said, that at the Hill of Goldberry, a detachment of the Norwegians was attacked and defeated by a detachment of Scotsmen under Sir Robert Boyd, ancestor of the noble family of Kilmarnock, for which services he received a grant of land in Cuninghame. The Kilmarnock family continued, from their large possessions in Kilbride, bestowed upon them by Robert the Bruce for their aid in the national cause, to have great influence in the parish; and from the well-known leaning of that family to what was called the national party, in contradistinction to the reforming or English interest, the inhabitants were led to take part in not a few of those conflicts to which the civil disturbances of the sixteenth and seventeenth centuries gave rise. The Lairds of Hunterstoun and Monfode fell at Pinkie in 1547, and Robert Boyd of Portincross, with his son Archibald, and many others, supported their chief in the cause of Queen Mary at the disastrous battle of Langside. The parish of Kilbride, consequently, makes no great figure during the persecutions — the moderate views of the leaders of the district preventing those zealous outbursts by which other portions of the west of Scotland were distinguished. The only other incident worthy of notice, peculiar to the parish of Kilbride, in connection with the general history of the country, is the sinking of one of the large ships of the Spanish Armada, in 1588, near the Castle of Portincross. This unfortunate vessel, after the dispersion of the fleet, had found her way into the Clyde, and perished

in "about ten fathom water, at no great distance from the shore," on a clear sandy bottom. The sinking of the ship was superstitiously ascribed to the incantations of Geils Buchanan, a noted witch in the vicinity, who, it is said, sat on the promontory of Portincross, twirling her spindle, and as the thread lengthened, the voyagers went down. Tradition affirms, what seems highly probable, that part of the crew were saved. In 1740, an attempt was made to recover property from the vessel by means of a diving-bell.* A number of brass and iron cannon were obtained from the wreck, all of which were carried off, save one, which still lies on the beach beside the old castle. Subsequent to the union, the same spirit of opposition to Whig dominion led them extensively into the practice of smuggling, which assumed a most formidable character over the greater part of Scotland. The session records of Kilbride bear ample evidence of this—as, for example:

"May 25, 1720.—This day the session was informed that some person was seen lately carrying off brandy upon Sabbath morning, &c.

"Oct. 22, 1721.—This day compeared William King, and was examined about baking bread in his house upon the Lord's-day. He did not deny but that it might be done, but neither he nor his wife knew anything of it. He told that there was a great confusion about his house that day, with soldiers and custom-house officers, who came up to take brandy on that day, &c.

"Jan. 17, 1722.—This day the session was informed of Robert M'Caltyre, in Broomcraig of Hunterstoun, his having abused with reproachful names Jean Kell, and particularly for calling her a damned hypocrite in a public company, and on

* De Foe's Tour, vol. iv. 1779.
More than one vessel of the formidable Armada perished on the west coast of Scotland. Dr Smollet, in his novel of 'Humphrey Clinker,' (Lond. 12mo, 1771,) says, "Mull affords several bays where there is safe anchorage; in one of which, the Florida, a ship of the Spanish Armada, was blown up by one of Mr Smollett's ancestors. About 40 years ago, John Duke of Argyle is said to have consulted the Spanish registers, by which it appeared that this ship had the military chest on board. He employed experienced divers to examine the wreck, and they found the hull of the vessel still entire, but so covered with sand, that they could not make their way between decks; however they picked up several pieces of plate that were scattered about in the bay, and a couple of fine brass cannon."
The following is extracted from Martin's Description of the Western Isles, p. 253, published in 1716:—"One of the ships of the Spanish Armada, called the Florida, perished in this bay, (Tobermory, Isle of Mull,) having been blown up by one Smallet of Dunbarton, in the year 1588. There was a great sum of gold and money on board the ship, which disposed the Earl of Argyle and some Englishmen to attempt the recovery of it; but how far the latter succeeded in this enterprise is not generally well known, only, that some pieces of gold and money, and a golden chain, was taken out of her. I have seen some fine brass cannon, some pieces of eight, teeth, beads, and pins, that had been taken out of that ship."

a Sabbath morning, in his own barn, where Archibald M'Kellip was brought in dead, having killed himself with drinking of brandy the night before.

"Jan. 31, 1722.—Robert M'Caltyre being called, compeared; and being asked, how he came to fall on his neighbour with such foul language and reproachful names, and particularly for calling her a damned hypocrite? he answered, he said nothing but what she deserved, and was provoked too, because she charged him with Archibald M'Kellip's death. The said Jean told, that as she was coming to the church on the Sabbath morning, she saw a gathering of people about the said Robert's barn; she drew near to see what it was, and understanding the occasion of the gathering, all she said was, "Fy upon you, Robert, and your brandy!" He was rebuked.

"Aug. 29, 1724.—The session being informed, that it is become a practice for young women to carry loads of brandy, some twelve, some sixteen miles out of the parish, &c.

"Sept. 1, 1725.—This day there was a report of the Sabbath's being lately profaned by persons concerned in the brandy trade. Ordered, that inquiry be made into it by the elders against their next meeting.

"Oct. 3, 1725.—This day reported, that the rise of the last session day's information concerning the profanation of the Sabbath, was, that some herds falling on some casks of brandy that was hidden in the moss, and abusing themselves with it.

"Jan. 21, 1757.—It was reported that Mr Kennedy, schoolmaster, deals in the *running* business," &c.

The village of Kilbride, or the Kirktoun, originated, as in most other instances, with the plantation of the church in the locality. At what time this occurred is unknown. It was probably, however, subsequent to the foundation of the monastery of Kilwinning, in 1140, of which it was a dependency. The monks of Kilwinning "enjoyed the rectorial tithes, and other revenues; and a vicarage was established for serving the cure. In Bagimont's Roll, as it stood in the reign of James V., the vicarage of Kilbride, in the deanery of Cuninghame, was taxed at £2, 13s. 4d., being a tenth of the estimated value. At the Reformation, the vicarage of Kilbride produced, on an average, £40 yearly. At the same epoch, the rectorial tithes of the church of Kilbride produced yearly to the monks of Kilwinning 79 bolls 2 firlots of meal, 53 bolls of bear, and £8 in money, for a part of the tithes, which were leased for that sum. In 1503, the patronage, the tithes, and lands of the church of Kilbride, were granted to Hugh, Earl of Eglintoun, with many other churches that belonged to the monastery of Kilwinning. The patronage and the tithes continued in this family, and the Earl of Eglintoun is now patron of the church of Kilbride and titular of the tithes."*

There were several chapels in the parish of Kilbride before the Reformation. One of these stood on the sea-coast, about a mile and a quarter south from the church of Kilbride, which, from it, was named *Chapel-toun.* At Southanan, a seat of the Sempill family, in the northern part of the parish, John, Lord Sempill, in the reign of James IV., built a chapel, which was dedicated to Saint Annan, or Saint Innan; and Lord Sempill granted, for the support of a chaplain in it, an annual rent of 10 marks from the lands of Meikle and Little Kilruskan, with two sowmes of pasture grass in the Mains of Southanan, and an acre of land, on the north side of the cemetery, belonging to the said chapel, for the chaplain's manse. This grant was confirmed by the king in June 1509. The ruins of the chapel are still extant, in the front of the fine mansion of Southanan, which is also in ruins, and stood on the sea-coast, nearly three miles north from the church of Kilbride. In the island of Little Cumbray, which is in the shire of Bute, but belongs to the parish of Kilbride, there was, in former times, a chapel dedicated to Saint *Beyd,* a Scottish virgin and saint, who is said to have died in 896 A. D., and was commemorated on the first of November. The ruins of this chapel are still to be seen." †

The parish church underwent considerable enlargement in 1732, and has been repeatedly improved since. It is, however, a very incommodious and mean-looking edifice. It is at the same time pleasantly situated on a rising ground in the centre of the village, and with its burying-ground encircled with spreading ash and plane trees, has rather a pleasant and picturesque appearance. The village contains upwards of a thousand inhabitants.

The earliest of the parochial records, the register of births, commences November 6, 1691; the register of baptisms is continued from 1693; and the minutes of kirk-session commence February 15, 1716. These latter exhibit the usual zeal of the kirk-session in enforcing the observance of the Sabbath, and in hunting out and punishing the backslidings of the people. The details, as in most other instances, are often gross and indelicate, yet not a few of the minutes are worthy of quotation, as illustrative of the times:

"Aprile 19, 1716.—It being represented to the session that one Colin Black, quho has for some time resided in this paroch, had, sometime after harvest last, driven cattle belonging to Mr Crawford, on Sabbath-day, from Caldwall Law

---

* Caledonia.　　　† Ibid.

to Corsbie Park; and that the said Colin being to leave the place, desired a testificate from the session, he having brought one with him to the paroch, and produced it to the elder of the quarter, the session appointed their officer to cite him the next session: and withal recommended it to the minister to advise with the presbytery anent the censure due for such a trangression, in regard the session, on some considerations, was not unanimous thairanent.

"May 13, 1716.—Black was rebuked in session, and obtained his testificate.

"Same day.—It being represented to the session that the Sabbath was much profaned in several places of the paroch, especially Arneil, by children meeting and playing together, and by persons come to age flocking together and feeding their cattle, the session unanimously agreed that the several elders, upon the Sabbath, after last sermon, should go through their respective quarters and take notice of persons guilty of such abuses, in order to their being informed against; and that intimation of this act be made to the congregation Sabbath next, by the minister from the pulpit.

"May 1, 1717.—The said day, the gentlemen, heritors residing in the paroch, viz. Hunterstoun, Carlung, and Kirkland, waited on the session, and chose Mr Alexander Glas to be their schoolmaster.

"May 22, 1717.—The said day the session unanimously chose Mr Glas foresaid to be their session-clerk, and ordered the registers to be committed to his care. Item, they appointed William King, wright, to repair the school; to put up a bed, a clay brace, and a partition.

"This day, the session was informed by one of the elders, of a bark coming to the Little Isle on Sabbath se'enight, wherein there were two belonging to the paroch, viz. James Or and Heugh Thomson; and that they, with the rest of the crew, came on shore about nine of the clock at night; and that they, with the help of some people in the isle, viz. William Harper, Patrick Montgomery, Jane Moor, and Elspa Syre, did draw down a boat in order to transport one of their crew to the Fairly. The session taking this to their consideration as a gross prophanation of the Lord's-day, appointed the minister to enquire into the truth and circumstances of the business, and to cause summon the foresaid persons against next meeting of the session.

"March 9, 1718.—This day there was an intimation made from the pulpit of an act of the synod, for a voluntary collection in favour of ministers in Pensilvania. And the said collection amounted to £28 Scots.

"June 18, 1718.—The said day, the minister acquainted the session that he designed to dispense the sacrament of the Lord's Supper to the congregation, and desired them to think on the most proper time. The session having deliberate on this matter, told that it behoov'd to be before the middle of July, because of the herring fishers.

"July 15, 1718.—This day, appointed that none of the Cummunion Tables be lent out at fairs, or such times.

"August 20, 1718.—This day, it was represented to the session that William King, coupar, and Anne Cuninghame, his wife, had been guilty of horrid cursing and imprecations against James Bole and his family.

"Oct. 29, 1719.—A thanksgiving day appointed by the synod for deliverance from the Spanish invasion; and for the late good harvest.

"Jan. 3, 1722.—This day, the session taking to consideration that the school-house, which was build upon the glyb, and att the expence of the session, had been much abused of late at bookings and penny weddings; and that the kirk furms, which was borrowed on these occasions, were also abused; they do hereby discharge the same in time coming.

"July 21, 1723.—This day, the minister inquired at the elders how the fast-day was kept through their several quarters. John Orr told it was very ill observed in the low part of the Tarbert; that immediately after their going home from sermon, they went and pilched their horses, and went down to the Sandilands to get them loaded.

"Informed also, that James Robison, with his boat's crew, went off, late on Tuesday night before the fast, in the expectation of a loadening of prohibite goods, and did not stay to observe the fast. Ordered to be summoned before the session.

"May 17, 1726.—This day, the session taking to their serious consideration the abuse that's like to creep in att bankets on the Lord's-day, by inviting excessive number of people to their feast—sometimes two dozen and upwards—the intertainment of whom cannot be without a great deal of unnecessary work on the Sabbath, the session unanimously agree that these excessive numbers be discharged; and that when baptisms happens upon the Sabbath, there be not above six persons present, besides the family; and that intimation of this be made from the pulpit the next Sabbath.

"May 31, 1727.—This day, information was given in against William Cochran, in Brakenlie, weaver, by his gross forgettfullness of the Sabbath, in working at his imployment.

"May 28, 1729.—This day, Hugh Hill, in Glend-head, having represented to the session his bodly affliction by reason of the king's evil in his thighs, and that he was advised to go for Moffat wells for cure, but had nothing to bear his charges, ordered that there be a publick collection made for him, and that the minister make intimation of it from the pulpit, &c.

"July 9, 1729.—This day, reported that the minister, att the desire of Mountain elder, had called for Alexander Cunningham, wright in Kilwinning, to take a look of the kirk, who accordingly came, and to the best of his judgement, told that it was in the most ruinous condition of any kirk he had seen of this long time. For which reason, thought the sacrament could not be conveniently given till the rest of the gentlemen concerned be acquainted, in order to a speedy reparation of it. Ordered further, that the minister speak to them about this affair."

Under the head of "eminent men" connected with the parish of Kilbride, two individuals deserve to be mentioned—Dr Robert Simson, Professor of Mathematics in the University of Glasgow, the well-known translator of Euclid, and General Robert Boyd, Lieutenant-Governor of Gibraltar during the memorable siege of that fortress in 1782. Both of these gentlemen derived their origin from the parish of Kilbride. The former was the son of John Simson of Kirktonhall, and the latter belonged to the class of small farmers, having, by extraordinary perseverance and talent, raised himself to the rank of a General in the army.

### ANTIQUITIES.

Under this head, the writer in the New Statistical Account says, in reference to the fortlets or "castle hills" already alluded to: "They stand at unequal distances, apparently as suitableness of situation offered—some scarcely half a mile, others a mile and a-half apart. In particular, they occur at Boydston, Glenhead, Seamill, and Ardneill. They are all constructed in the same manner, and are of very limited dimensions. A portion of the bank is detached on all sides, and rounded conically; the enclosure on the summit, of about 30 or 40 feet in diameter, is surrounded by a rampart from 6 to 8 feet in thickness, faced on both sides with large undressed stones neatly laid, the interstice being filled up with small stones, intermixed with earth. That at Ardneill stands on a finely isolated eminence called Auldhill,* and in front of the enclosure or prætorium, there is an esplanade of 40 or 50 paces in length,

* Auldhill is a vitrified fort

very exactly formed and levelled. Something similar exists at Seamill, but the rest are confined to the circular rampart alone. Conjecture assigns these structures to the era of the Danish incursions, which seems not improbable; but they may belong to a still higher antiquity.* Tumuli have likewise been accidentally explored here, in which were found urns containing calcined human bones and ashes. Near the Castlehill at Seamill, about four years ago, whilst the new line of the coast road was being executed, two entire urns of this sort were dug out in a stratum of gravel, about three feet below the surface, but without any mound being raised over them. One of these, it is believed, has since been deposited in Anderson's Institution in Glasgow. These urns were formed of coarse red clay, of very rude manufacture, yet well proportioned, and modelled in the vase form. In hardening, the fire appears to have been applied solely to the inside of the urn, that part being changed to a dark colour, whilst the outside remains of the natural red."

Some years ago, a very splendid silver brooch, of beautiful workmanship, having a Runic inscription, was found near Hunterston. This is supposed to have been a relic of the invasion of Haco—a large tumulus of stones having formerly existed at the spot where the skirmish with a party of Danes, already alluded to, is said to have taken place.† Several ancient graves were discovered near the place.

There are the ruins of five houses or castles in the parish, viz., Portincross, Law, Crosbie, Hunterstoun, and Southanan.

The first of these, *Portincross*, or *Ardneill*, is perhaps the most ancient. It is in the style of a fortalice, built on a "ledge of rock projecting into the sea, under the bold promontory to which it gives name, a singularly wild and romantic situation." Whether it ever was a royal resi-

* A few years ago, an opening being made in the ground outside of the rampart at Seamill, a considerable quantity of charcoal of wood, bones of cattle, and deer's horns, some of which appearing to have been sawn asunder, were found a few feet below the surface, the materials of the wall having fallen down over the place.

† 4th April, 1831.—Andersonian Soiree, of Glasgow. Mr Hunter of Hunterstoun, exhibited an ancient brooch lately found on his estate. This splendid and beautifully wrought antique is of silver, ornamented with rich and elegant filigree work in gold, and is in perfect preservation. On the back of it there are two inscriptions in the Runic character, viz. Maloritha a dalk this: in English—Maloritha possesses this brooch: Dolk Osfrida—the brooch of Osfrida. The names are both females, and apparently Scandinavian. Mr Repp, F.S.A., who has written an elaborate memoir on this remarkable antique, is of opinion, that it cannot be referred to a later period than the twelfth century. It was found near an ancient cairn, which tradition points out as the scene of a skirmish in which Mr Hunter's ancestor routed a party of Norwegians, at the battle of the Lein—, in 1263.—GLASGOW HERALD, 8th April, 1831.

R

dence is unknown; but it is certain that several charters of the Stewart kings were signed at "Arnele," or Portincross. One of these deeds, granted by Robert II., is in the possession of the ancient family of Hunter of Hunterstoun. It is said that Robert I. occasionally resided at Portincross. "The probability is," says Mr Fullarton, in the Statistical Account, "that these sovereigns, in passing to and from Dundonald in Kyle, and Rothesay in Bute, had been in use to cross the channel at this point, and may occasionally, as circumstances or inclination suggested, have prolonged their stay at this convenient station. Contemplating the narrow walls of this sea-beat tower, it is certainly difficult to conceive it should ever have afforded accommodation to the prestige of a royal court; yet, when we reflect on the circumscribed nature of even Dundonald itself, the favourite residence of these same sovereigns, the contrast by no means appears so extraordinary." Mr Fullarton adds, in a foot-note, that in an inventory of the effects within the fortalice of Portincross, taken in 1621, it appears, *inter alia*, to have contained "ten fedder beddis, with their furnishings, which is so far illustrative of the manners of these times; for it is clear two or three of these must have belonged to each chamber."

*Croshie Castle* stands amidst some fine old wood, about a mile east of the village of Kilbride. It was inhabited at the beginning of the seventeenth century, when Timothy Pont made his survey. He says: "Crosby toure is the habitatione of William Craufurd of Auchnaims, by divers thought to be chieffe of the Craufurds. He holds the same of the Earls of Glencairne. This surname is very ancient, and did memorable service under King Alexander the 3d, at the batell of Largis, by quhome their good service wes recompensed with divers great lands and possessiones. According to the old common rithme:

' They had Draffen, Methweine, and rich erth Stevinstone,
Cameltoune, Knockawart, and fair Lowdoune.'

Fra this king, lykewayes, they have amongst them a traditione that they had their armes." Croshie is peculiarly interesting to the admirers of Scottish patriotism, as there can be no doubt that it is the original "Tower of Crosbie" where Wallace found shelter with his uncle, Reginald Craufurd, during his outlawry by the English authorities. Blind Harry represents Wallace and his uncle as coming from Corsby on the morning of the "Blac Parliament," when so many of the leading men of the county were put to death in the Barns of Ayr. On arriving at Kingcase, in the vicinity of Ayr—

" With heidfull hast then sperit wicht Wallace
At Schyr Ranald for the charter of pece,
It is lewyt at Corsbe, in the kyst."

Wallace and his uncle discover that the bond of peace entered into with the English had been left at Crosbie in the charter chest. There is a Crosbie in Kyle, but that property belonged to the Fullartons of Fullarton, and never was in the possession of the Craufurds. It is, therefore, the walls of Crosbie Castle, in the parish of West Kilbride, that gave shelter to the hero of Scotland; and great is the pity that they should ever be allowed to go to ruin. Tradition has assigned numerous hiding-places to Wallace; but the fact of his having been repeatedly at Crosbie with his uncle, during his younger years, as well as after he had unsheathed the sword in defence of his native land, cannot be reasonably doubted.

*Law Castle*, or the Tower of Kilbride, is situated on an eminence adjacent to the village of Kilbride. The walls are entire, and have a stately appearance. The situation commands a delightful view of the Clyde westward.

*Hunterstoun.*—The old fortlet, consisting of a tower and other buildings, of the Hunters of Hunterstoun, is still entire, being occupied as a farm-house. It originally occupied a narrow tongue of land, jutting into a deep morass, a site well chosen for security. It is surrounded with trees, and has altogether a picturesque and interesting appearance, although recent agricultural improvements, by draining the morass, have deprived the ancient strong-house of one of its chief characteristics.

*Southanan* was one of the mansion-houses of the Sempill family, to whom the property belonged from the time of Bruce. It is situated close upon the sea; and though it has long been in a state of decay, it still bears evidence of its former splendour. The site is beautifully wooded, and is altogether one of the most delightful on the coast.

### Island of Little Cumbray.

This island, though in the shire of Bute, is attached *quoad sacra* to the parish of Kilbride. It is about 1¼ miles in superficial extent, and at the highest nearly 600 feet above the level of the sea. It has long been in the possession of the Eglintoun family: "October 28, 1515.—Lettre to Hew Erle of Eglintoune, making him and his assignais, keeparis, overscaris, correkaris, and suplearis of the *Isle of Litill Comeray*, the dere, cunyngis, and wild bestis being thairin, quhill the kingis perfite age of xv yere; becaus Robert Huntare of Huntarestoune, forrestar of heritage of the said isle, is nocht of power to resist the personis that waistis the samyn, without suplie and help," &c.

The ancestors of Hunter of Hunterston were thus the heritable keepers of the Island of Little Cumbray, which was no doubt included in the principality of Scotland, when that appendage to the crown was erected by Robert III. in favour of his son in 1404. Notwithstanding the above letter to the Earl of Eglintoun the island remained in possession of the family for two hundred years afterwards. They also, it appears, claimed a right to the falcons bred on the Red Farland Rocks, in the Great Cumbray, situated on the property of South Kames. It is related that a serious dispute took place betwixt the Governor of Dumbarton Castle, as representing the king, and the Laird of Hunterstoun, regarding the right to the said falcons, which were claimed by the king as royal birds. The Laird having refused either to give up his right, or to appear before the king at Edinburgh, when summoned, the Governor was ordered to go with a force to seize him, when, it is said, the refractory Laird, having been joined by his neighbours, succeeded in repulsing the Governor with loss. It is not known how the matter ended.

George Ker, brother of Mark Ker, Lord Newbattle, was pursued by Mr Andro Knox, minister at Paisley, accompanied by some scholars from Glasgow, and apprehended in the Isle of Cumbray, on the 27th December, 1592. Ker was a Roman Catholic, and bore letters to Spain, whether he meant to pass by sea, taking shipping at the Fairlie Roads, for the purpose of promoting the threatened invasion from Spain.

Near the middle of the Island of Little Cumbray there exist the remains of a square tower, the first story of which is vaulted. During Cromwell's stay in Scotland, the Eglintoun family retired to the Little Cumbray—residing, no doubt, in this small building, the dimensions of which are only 28 by 15. It is said that the tower was destroyed by the soldiers of the Commonwealth, the Earl of Eglintoun having made himself highly obnoxious to the Protector.

Mr Fullarton, in the Statistical Account, quotes a curious contract, dated in 1568, from the burgh records of Glasgow, showing that the tower of Cumbray was among the other residences of the Eglinton family:—"Hew Erle of Eglintoun," contracted with "George Elphinstoun, glassinwricht, burges of Glasgow, that the said George suld uphald and mantene the places of Ardrossan, Eglintoun, Polnone, Glasgow, and Cumray in glassin wark, as also the place of Irvin;" and for all which, Elphinstoun was to receive yearly, "twa bollis meill, and ane stane cheis," " and gif it happinis the said Erle to hald hous in ony of thir foir-saidis places when it sal happin, the said George to wirk, the said George shall have his meit the time that he wirks, and als when the said George tursis creillis of glas and leid to Irvyn, Ardrossan, Eglintoun, and Cumray, the said Erle sal caus ane carrage hors to turs the samyn out of Glasgow."

The ruins of the tomb and chapel of St Vey, still in existence, occupy the top of the hill, a short distance northward of the castle. In the tomb there are two flat stones, one of which has long been broken in two, bearing " some ornamental tracery, such as is usually to be seen on those ancient monuments called Danish stones, but no vestige of any inscription is to be observed in any of them. This enclosure, which is of a square form, and of very limited dimensions, was originally surrounded by a stone wall, but of which only the foundation now exists. There is a tradition that this chapel, another at Ardrossan, and a third at the Garrock-head, in Bute, were all served by one and the same priest, who, of course, journeyed *per vices* among them."

At Shanniwilly point, some urns and fragments of ancient instruments of war were found in tumuli, which the Earl of Eglintoun caused to be opened about thirty years ago. They were all carried to Eglintoun Castle.

# FAMILIES IN THE PARISH OF WEST KILBRIDE.

Before the contest for the Scottish crown in the thirteenth century, the lands of West Kilbride seem to have been chiefly in possession of the Baliols and Rosses. After the succession of Robert the Bruce, however, a change took place—the lands of the Baliols, and most of those of the Rosses, having been forfeited to the Crown, and conferred by the King upon the most faithful of those chiefs who had supported him throughout his arduous struggle. As then divided, the parish consisted of seven baronies, which division, with little modification, still exists.

## SOUTHANAN BARONY,

situated on the northern extremity of the parish, is the largest. It extends to upwards of 2400 acres. It belonged to the noble family of Sempil, upon whom it was conferred by the Crown after the forfeiture of Baliol. Although this family occasionally resided at their beautiful mansion of Southanan, built in the Italian style, yet Castle Sempil, in Renfrewshire, was their principal seat, and they are justly held to be a Renfrewshire family. Therefore it does not fall within our scope to give an account of them here. When the first breaking up of the family occurred, more than a hundred years ago, the property was purchased by Alexander, ninth Earl of Eglintoun, and it has since remained with his descendants.

## HUNTERSTOUN,

situated to the west of Southanan, along the coast, extends to about 700 acres. The *Hunters of Hunter, or of that Ilk*, are one of the most ancient families in the district. No trace can be had of their origin, but there is scarcely a doubt that the estate of Hunterstoun has been in the family since, at least, the beginning of the twelfth century, or a period of about 750 years, and how much longer cannot now be ascertained. That the family is of Norman origin seems, however, extremely probable, from the circumstance of the oldest of the family on record, being a "Norman Huntar." The name, till a comparatively modern period, was always spelled "Huntar," and the proprietors styled themselves "Huntar

of that Ilk." At a remote period, a singular manner of subscription was adopted, as can be seen in many old papers, viz. "Robert Huntar of Huntarston" signed himself always "RoHuntarston," and "Patrick Huntar of Huntarston," "PaHuntarston," and the like.

In the Ragman Roll the name "Ailmer de la Huntar" occurs, and that he was an ancestor of the present family is placed beyond doubt, inasmuch as the subscriptions come regularly down the coast. Among others we find Hugo de Montgomerie (Skelmorley), then Fraser of Knock, Hugo de Boyle (ancestor of the Earl of Glasgow). Ailmer de la Huntar, Barclay of Ardrossan, &c. Another ancestor, a Quintigern Huntar, was killed at the battle of Flodden, where the slaughter of the Scottish nobility was so great, and so disproportionate to that of their followers, but which can be easily accounted for by adverting to the speech of Lord Lindsay to the Scottish lords before the battle, in which he says "for none, my Lords, have remained but gentlemen, the commons have all departed from us for lack of victual." In these days, when there was no commissariat, an army could only be kept together for a short period; and it would appear that the wealthier portion of the army alone, and their immediate retainers, had remained with the king, the others having departed in search of food or plunder, and in this state the battle, so fatal to Scotland, took place.

The possessions of the family were originally much more considerable than at present, a great deal of land having been sold by the great-grandfather of the present proprietor. Besides the properties of Hunterstoun and Campbeltoun, which still remain in the family, they possessed at one period Annan-Hill, near Kilmarnock, called formerly Annan-Hill-Huntar-Longmuir, in the parish of Kilmaurs; Highlees, in Dalry; South Kames, in the Great Cumbra; the Island of Little Cumbra; the Holy Island, or Lamlash, with a part of the opposite shore; and several families of the name of Hunter still remain in Arran and the Great Cumbra.

The proprietors of Hunterstoun were foresters in heritage of the Island of Little Cumbra, it being a royal deer park.

The cadets and descendants of the family are numerous. Among these may be mentioned the following:—

1. Hunters of Barjarg, in Dumfries-shire, descended from Quintigern Huntar, killed in 1540.

2. Hunter of Restenet.

3. Drs William and John Hunter, physicians in London, descended from Francis, third son of Patrick Hunter of that Ilk, who died in 1674.

4. Hunter of Kirkland, descended from Robert, second son of Robert Hunter, who died in 1680.

5. Orby Hunter of Croydon Abbey, descended from James, third son of Robert Hunter, who died about 1680.

6. Hunter of Thurston, in Haddingtonshire.

7. Hunter of Doonholm, in this county.

8. Mr David Hunter of London, descended from David, third son of Patrick Hunter, who died in 1739.

9. Hunter Blair of Blairquhan.

As already stated, the oldest of the family of whom any distinct record is preserved, is Norman Huntar, who lived between 1214 and 1249. As the lands, however, are never known to have been in the possession of any other family, and as there can exist no reasonable doubt that they were acquired at a period not very long subsequent to the Norman Conquest, in the year 1066, they must have been in the family at least 150 years before the time of the said Norman Huntar, so that he may safely be assumed as the sixth in the genealogical enumeration of the family. Nisbet, in his remarks on the Ragman Roll, states that, in an ancient charter, certain lands were bounded " terris

VI. Normani Venatoris." The next on record is

VII. Ailmer de la Huntar, who was one of the Magnates Scotiæ, who, in 1296, subscribed the noted submission to Edward I. of England, in the question between Baliol and Bruce, relative to the Scottish crown, (see Ragman Roll and Nisbet's remarks). As this Ailmer was alive in 1296, and the next on record, William, seems to have succeeded in 1375, at least one generation must have intervened, so that the ninth will be

IX. William Huntar, who obtained a charter from Robert II.—" Willmi. Hunt— totam ter-'am de Arnele, cum fit. quæ fuit Andre Cambell militis......Apud St'velyne sedo. die Maij Anno regni nri. Q'rto (1375)*. These lands are now called Campbelton, from their original owner, the said Sir Andrew Campbell, and are still in the possession of the family. So long an interval again occurs between this William and the next on record, who was also a

XI. William, that at least another generation must have intervened. He was infeft in High-lees, in the parish of Dalry, by a sasine from Andrew Linn of that Ilk, dated 4th March, 1452, though these lands appear to have been in possession of the family from a much earlier period. His son,

XII. Archibald Huntar of that Ilk, married Jean Craufurd, of the family of Corseby, in the vicinity, by whom he had a son,

XIII. John Huntar of that Ilk, who married Margaret, fourth daughter of John, second Lord Cathcart, by Margaret, daughter of Sir William Douglas of Drumlanrig, by whom he had a son,

XIV. Robert Huntar of that Ilk, who, on the 5th September, 1517, was infeft in the Island of Lamlash. He married Margaret Craufurd, another of the ladies of Corseby, and by her he had a son,

XV. Robert Huntar of that Ilk, who married Janet Montgomerie, daughter of Montgomerie of Giffen, and widow of John Craufurd of Craufurdland. His son,

XVI. Mungo, or Quintigern Huntar of that Ilk, was served heir to his father in 1540. He was killed at the battle of Pinkie, on the 10th September, 1547. By his wife, daughter of James Hamilton of Torrance, he had two sons:

1. Robert.
2. ———, ancestor of the Hunters of Barjarg.

He was succeeded by his eldest son,

XVII. Robert Huntar of that Ilk. He was served heir to his father in the five merk land of Campbeltoun, 2d October, 1548. He was one of those Ayrshire gentlemen who subscribed the Band in defence of the Reformed religion, on the 4th of September, 1562. He married Margaret Craufurd, a daughter of Thomas Craufurd of Auchnames, by Marion, daughter of Montgomerie of Hesilheid, by whom he had issue:

1. Robert.
2. Francis.
3. Jean, married to the Rev. Robert Cuninghame, minister of Barnweil, brother of Hugh Cuninghame of Carlung, to whom she had two daughters:
   1. Jean, of whom afterwards.
   2. Catharine, married to Robert Cuninghame of Auchinharvie, 4th May, 1616.

He was succeeded by his eldest son,

XVIII. Robert Huntar of that Ilk, who was served heir to his father on the 23d May, 1598, in the lands of Campbeltoun, Annan-hill and Highlees. He married Margaret,* daughter of

---

* " Margaret Peblis, Lady Hunterstone, for wairs," appears in the list of debts " awand to the deid," in the testament of " Allexr. Cunynghame, elder, merchant burgess" of Irvine, 1611.—GLAS. COM. REC.

Provost Peeblis of Irvine,* a family of considerable respectability, and possessed of several properties in the neighbourhood; but he died without issue in 1616, as the following extract from the Commissary Records of Glasgow show:—

"The Testament dative and Inventar of the guidis, geir, &c. quhilks pertenit to vmqle. Robert Huntar of Huntarstoune, within the parochin of Kilbryd, the time of his deceis, quha deceist in the monethe of Maij, the zeir of God 1616 zeiris, ffaithfullie maid and gevin vp be Patrik Huntar, now of Hunterstoune, executor dative, &c.

"Inventar.

"Item, the defunct had the time foirsaid perteining to him, as his awin proper guids and geir, and in his possessioune, the guids and geir vnderwrittin, of the availls, qualities and pryces eftirspecifit, viz. Twa ky, pryce of the piece x lib. inde xx lib. Item, in the borne, four bolls beir, pryce of the boll vi lib., inde xxiiii lib. Item, the insicht of the hous in vtincills and domicills, with the abuilzement of the defunct's bodie, estimat to xxxvii lib vi s. viii d.

"Summa of the Inventar lxxvii lib. vi s. viii d." His lady survived him. She is mentioned in the testament of "John Tempiltoun in Hilhous, parochin of Kilbryde," May 1617, as a creditor of "ferme the said zeir 1617, vii firlots beir," &c. "Mair to hir, ane mas of herring, pryce lib. vis. viii d."

Having no issue, the Laird of Hunterstoun settled his estate on the husband of his niece, Jean Cuninghame, as above (No. XVII.), who married

XIX. Patrick Huntar, (son of William Huntar of Binberry-yards, parish of Ayr) great-grandson of Mungo Huntar of that Ilk (No. XVI.), as appears from a charter in the possession of the present Hunterstoun. He had a retour of the lands of Ardneil-Hunterstoun and Campbeltoun, as heir of entail and provision, of Robert Hunter of Hunterstoun, 11th July, 1618. His name occurs, among those of other gentlemen, in the Committee of War for Ayrshire, in the troublesome times of 1647.† The issue of this marriage was,

1. Robert.
2. The Rev. Henry Huntar, minister of Dromore, who died without issue.
3. Francis, from whom, it is supposed, the family of Hunter of Long Calderwood was descended, and of which family were the celebrated Drs William and

* She seems to have been his cousin. Provost Peeblis, who died in 1603, left his spouse, "Mareoun Hunter," his only executrix, and appointed Robert Hunter of Hunterstoun one of the guardians of the family.
† Parl. Rec.

John Hunter, physicians in London, who were born at Easter Kilbride, in Lanarkshire, in the years 1718 and 1728, whose grandfather is stated to have been a younger son of Huntar of Huntarston.

1. —— married to Alexander Cuninghame of Carlung.
2. Jean, married to David Kennedy of Balmaelanachan, and of Craig, in Carrick, about the year 1683.*

In 1662, we find the laird of Hunterston fined in £600 by one of Middleton's arbitrary acts. He was succeeded by his eldest son,

XX. Robert Huntar of that Ilk. In 1674, he was served heir of conquest to his immediate younger brother, the Rev. Henry Huntar. He married Elizabeth, daughter of Patrick Craufurd of Auchnames, by whom he had issue:

1. Patrick.
2. Robert, ancestor of Kirkland.
3. James, who was bred to the bar. He married Margaret Spalding, by whom he had General Robert Huntar, who died Governor of Jamaica in 1734, who was married to Lady Mary Dalziel, only child of James, fourth Earl of Carnwath. His descendants are the Orby Hunters of Croyland Abbey, Lincolnshire.
4. Hugh, who was a physician in Kilmarnock.

He married, secondly, a daughter of Cuninghame of Aiket, by whom he had no issue, and was succeeded by his eldest son,

XXI. Patrick Huntar of that Ilk, whose retour is dated on the 19th January, 1680. He married Marion, daughter of John Cuninghame of Langmuir, by whom he acquired that property, and had issue:

1. Patrick.
2. Henry was ordained minister of Mearns in 1713, and died in 1738.
3. John.
1. Dorothea, married to Henry Cuninghame of Carlung, and had a numerous issue.
2. Marion, married, in 1694, to John Peeblis of Crawfield, without issue.
3. Margaret.

He died in 1699, and was succeeded by his eldest son,

XXII. Patrick Huntar of that Ilk, who married Marion, eldest daughter of Thomas Craufurd of Cartsburn, by whom he had issue:

1. Patrick, who died in his father's lifetime, in 1732.
2. Robert.
3. David, who married Miss Milliken of Port-Glasgow, by whom he had Patrick Hunter, merchant in London.
4. Henry.
5. Thomas.
1. Rebecca, died unmarried.
2. Elizabeth, married to Mr John Hyndman of Lunderston.
3. Marion, married to Hugh Muir.
4. Dorothea, married, first, to Mr Kelso of Hullerhirst, and, secondly, to Mr Hugh Weir of Kirkhall.
5. Margaret, married to Mr Caldwell, merchant and shipmaster in Greenock.

He died 9th November, 1789, and was succeeded by his eldest surviving son,

* See Nisbet, vol. ii. App. 41.

XXIII. Robert Hunter of that Ilk, who married Miss Aitchison of Glasgow, by whom he had issue:

1. Thomas Orby, } died young.
2. Patrick John. }
1. Eleonora, who succeeded.
2. Marion.
3. Elizabeth.

He died in 1796, and was succeeded by his eldest surviving daughter,

XXIV. Eleonora, who married her cousin, Robert Caldwell Hunter, by whom she had issue:

1. Robert.
2. Patrick, died in 1828.
3. Norman, died in 1836.
1. Eleonora, died in 1833.
2. Marion Crawfurd, died in 1830.
3. Margaret.
4. Janet.

Robert Caldwell Hunter died 22d August, 1826, and was succeeded by his eldest son,

XXV. Robert Hunter of that Ilk, the present proprietor. He married, in 1836, Christian, eldest daughter of Crawfurd of Cartsburn, and has issue:

1. Jane.
2. Eleonora.

*Arms*—Vert, three dogs of the chase courant, argent, collared or, on a chief of the second, three hunting horns of the first stringed, gules.

*Crest*—A greyhound sejant, argent, collared or.

*Motto*—Cursum perficio.

The old castle of Hunterston, as already mentioned, still exists. It was originally merely a square tower, the walls of which are of great thickness.

A new mansion-house, at a short distance, was built by the late proprietor, Robert Caldwell Hunter. Situated near to the sea, and looking up the Firth of Clyde, directly in front are seen the villages of Fairlie, Largs, Dunoon, and Millport, with their numerous and scattered villas; as also, the picturesque old castle of Fairlie, with the beautiful grounds and plantations of Kelburne, whilst farther off, are seen towering above the nearer and lower hills, the rugged mountains of Argyll and Dumbarton shires, called "Argyll's Bowling Green," with Ben-Cruachan in the distance. More to the left, are the islands of Bute, the Great and Little Cumbras, and Arran, with its magnificent mountain range, beyond which is seen the coast of Kintyre, whilst the remarkably shaped Paps of Jura are seen in the far west, terminating a view of singular beauty, scarcely surpassed in this or any other country. Ardneill Banks, extending two miles along the shore, are partly in this property, and partly in that of Mr Craufurd of Auchnames.

In the possession of the family are many curious and very old charters, papers, and letters, several of the former so injured by time as to be quite illegible.

## ARDNEILL, OR PORTINCROSS.

The ancient name of this property, which lies south of Hunterstoun, was Ardneill, usually spelled *Arnele*, from the Celtic, signifying a hill. "Ard-neill, or Nell's Knope," says Pont, "ye possession of Archibald Boyd, Laird of Portincrosse, and Ard-neill." Latterly, it became better known by the designation of Portincross,* the name given to the promontory or bay where the ruins of the castle stand. Ardneill anciently comprehended part of the lands of Hunterstoun as well as of Portincross. The property, however, has long been limited to about 700 acres, extending upon both sides of the promontory eastwards to within three quarters of a mile of the village of Kilbride.

Ardneill, in early times, belonged to the family of Ross, who held extensive possessions in Renfrewshire and Ayrshire, under Baliol, of whose pretensions to the throne of Scotland they were zealous abettors; but on the triumph of the Bruce, their estates became forfeited, and were bestowed by that monarch upon those adherents who had most firmly stood by him in the long and arduous struggle so gloriously consummated on the field of Bannockburn. Ardneill, or Portincross, formerly belonging to Godfrey de Ross, son of the deceased Reginald de Ross, was gifted to Sir Robert Boyd of Kilmarnock, in the first year of his reign (1306.)

The first of the Boyds designated of Portincross was,

I. ROBERT, third son of Sir Thomas Boyd of Kilmarnock, and grandson of Sir Robert, the friend and supporter of the Bruce. Crawfurd, in his Peerage, says: "I have seen a charter on the 10th June 1444, *Per Thomam Boyd de Kilmarnock dilecto avunculo† Roberto Boyd terrarum de Arneil.*" The next representative of this family is at the distance of more than a century from the last-mentioned date—namely,

II. Robert Boyd of Portincross, who, about the year 1550, married Elizabeth, third daughter and one of the co-heiresses of David Fairlie of that Ilk, by his wife Catharine, daughter of Lau-

---

* Supposed to be derived from "Portus-crucis," the port of the cross.

† "Avunculus," according to Ducange, in the middle ages, was often used for "patruus."

renee Craufurd of Kilbirnie. His name occurs as one of the assize in a criminal case in 1562. His son,

III. Archibald Boyd of Portincross, succeeded him. In Robertson's *Ayrshire Families, Archibald* is altogether omitted, and the writer supposes Robert No. II. to have been succeeded by his "son or grandson," also called Robert. Amongst the Boyd papers in the Kilmarnock charter chest, however, there is a contract between Robert Lord Boyd and *Archibald* Boyd of Portincross, by which the latter obliges himself to "obtene himself heritablie and sufficientlie infeft and seasit in all and haill the ten merk land of Portincross and Ardneil" before the decease of his father, Robert Boyd; contract dated 19th April 1572. The father had no doubt assigned the property to his son before his death—hence the occasion of the contract. Archibald is also mentioned in other documents—as, for instance, the following: "The testament-testamentar, latter-will, and inventar of the guidis and geir perteining to vmquhile hew boyde, sone lawfull to vmquhile *Archibald boyde* of *portincross,* burges of Irwen, quha deceist in ye moneth of October, the zeir of God Jai vi and ten zeiris, maid and gevin vp be his awin mouth in his awin dwellinghous in Irwen, ye xxvj day of October ye said zeir," &c. "Robert boyd of Portincross, Ard. boyde vnder ye hill," his brother, were witnesses to this document, so that Archibald Boyd of Portincross must have died before 1610, the date of the testament. This accords precisely with the date of Pont's survey of Scotland, who states that Archibald Boyd was the laird of Portincross. Archibald Boyd had thus several sons :

1. Robert, his successor.
2. Hew, burgess of Irvine. He married Marcoun Ros. of the Bordland family, and had issue several daughters, but apparently no sons. Niniane Barclay, Robert Barclay, and Hew Barclay, are all mentioned as his sons-in-law in his testament. He left, of "free geir," at his death, £386, 10s. Scots, to be divided in three parts.[*]
3. Archibald, "under the hill."

IV. Robert Boyd of Portincross succeeded, as we have seen, before 1610. His name repeatedly occurs in testamentary documents. He married Jean Montgomerie, sister of Sir Robert Montgomerie of Skelmorlie, who died in December 1621, and from whose testament and latterwill it appears that besides *Robert* his heir, he had several sons and daughters :

"The testament, testamentar, and inventar of the guidis, geir, debts, and sowmes of money, quhilks perteint to vmquhile Jeane Montgomerie, spous to Robert Boyd of Portincross, within the parochin of Kilbryd, the time of hir deceis, quha deceist in the moneth of December, the zeir of God Jai vi c. twentie ane zeiris, ffaithfullie maid and gevin vp be hir awin mouth, as hir latterwill and testament, of the date vnderwrittin, mair fullie proports.

"Inventar.

Item, the defunct and hir said spous had, the tyme foirsaid, perteining to thame, and in their possessioun, the guids and geir vnderwrittin, of the availls, qualities and pryces efterspecifit, viz. ane quhyt hors, pryce xl lib. Item, ane dvne hors, pryce xl lib. Item, four auld pleughe naigis, pryce of the peice x lib., inde xl lib. Item, aucht tydie ky, pryce of thame all lxxxxvi lib. Item, auchtein zoung quoyis, pryce of thame all lxxxx lib. Item, sax stirks, pryce of them all xlii lib. Item, of aittis in the borne and bornezaird, thriescoir bolls aitts, pryce of the boll iiii lib., inde ii c. xl lib. Item, of beir in the borne and bornezaird, togidder with the ferme beir restand awand be the tennents, extends to ane hundrit and xii bolls, pryce of the boll vi lib., inde of beir and ferme inde v c. lxxii lib. Item, ane boitt, with her graith, pryce lxvi lib. xiii s. iiii d. Item, ane skout, (?) pryce x lib. Item, pleughe and pleughe irnes, with carris and harrowis, pryce viii lib. Item, ten feddir beddis and vii bowsters, estimat to i c. lib. Item, twelf pair of blankettis, pryce of the pair thrie lib., inde xxxvi lib. Item, thrie caddayis, pryce of thame xxiiii lib. Item, four sewit coveringis, pryce of thame xxvi lib. xiii s.

* The inventory may be curious, as showing the intercourse between the coasts of Ireland and Scotland at the time. It is as follows :—"Ane gray naig, by the airschipe hors, pryce xxvj lib. Item, tway ky, with the stirks, pryce xxvj lib. xiii s. iiii d. Item, thrie zoung ky in Ireland, estimat to xxx lib. Item, in the borne and bornezaird, Ten bolls beir, pryce of the boll v lib., inde l lib. Item, the threttie bolls aittis, pryce of the boll, with the foddir, iiij lib, inde je. xx lib. Item, sex bolls salt, pryce of the boll xl s., inde xij lib. Item, twa kists of bogheids, with als mony rungis to set thame vp, pryce of all xvj lib. Item, auchtein fir dailis, pryce of thame all nyne lib. Item, auch dussane of Ireland buirdis, at fourtie shillings ilk dussane, inde xvi lib. Item, twa stanes of woll, pryce of the stane v lib. xiii s. iiii d., inde lvi lib. xiii s. iiii d. Item, sax feddir beddis, by the airschipe, pryce of the piece, with their furnitour, xiiij lib., inde fourscoir four lib. Item, Tuentie twa pair of scheittis, by the airschip, pryce of the pair onrheid,

xx s., inde xxii lib. Item, buird claithes, and fyve dussane of serveitts, by the airschip, pryce of all xiii lib. vi s. viii d. Item, thrie dussane and ane half of pewdir plaittis, with twa dussane and thrie trunscheouris, all estimat to xxxvi lib. Item, an brasin basen, by the airschip, estimat to l s. Item, thrie pynt stopis and thrie choppein stopis, by the airschip, all estimat to aucht pund. Item, twa brasyne chandleris, by the airschip, estimat to xx s. Item, thrie litle kists and ane chyre, by the airschip, estimat to xx s. Item, sax aylwir spwnis, by the airschip spwne, with twa brokin spwnis, pryce of thame all xx lib. Item, thrie auld gunis, by the airschip, estimat to iiij lib. Item, the abuilzement of the defunct's bodie, by the airschip, estimat to ane hundrith punds.———Summa of tha foirsaid inventar vi c. lxxxxvii lib. iii s. iiij d."—Such were the "guida and geir" belonging to a respectable burgess of Irvine during the sixteenth, and at the beginning of the seventeenth century.

iiiid. Item, four auld caddais, pryce of thame x lib. Item, sax auld coveringis, pryce of thame vi lib. Item, thrie pair of courtingis, pryce x lib. Item, ten pair of lyning scheitts, pryce xl lib. Item, of round scheittis and hardin claith, estimat to xx lib. Item, thrie pair of heid scheittis, estimat to sax pundis money. Item, twelf codwaris, pryce v lib. Item, fyve buirdclaithis, pryce x lib. Item, four dussane of serveittis, pryce x lib. Item, aucht breid claithis, pryce vi lib. Item, four lang towallis, pryce iii lib. Item, ane compter claith, pryce xii lib. Item, nyne [cntihornis] pryce iii [or viii] lib. Item, thrie chancleris, twa bassingis, ane lawer, ane pewldir stoip pryce of thame all xiii lib. vi s. viii d. Item, twa dussane twa plaittis, twentie ane truncheours, twa salsours, and ane saltfalt, twa wattir potts, pryce of thame all xv lib. Item, four pottis, thrie speitts, with ane pair of rakis, pryce of thame xvi lib. Item, ane litle caldroune, ane kettill, thrie pannis, ane girdill, thrie cruiks, ane chymnay, pryce of all xxxvi lib. Item, of kistis, beddis, and vther inspret within the defunct's hous, with the abuilzement of his bodie, estimat to lxvi lib. xiii s. iiii d.
——Summa of the inventar, jaj vi c.lxxv lib.

\* 　 \* 　 \* 　 \* 　 \*

## " Legacie.

" At Portincors, the xix day of December, the zeir of God jai vi c. and twentie ane zeiris, the quhilk day Jeane Montgomerie nominat Robert Boyd of Portincors, hir husband, executour. Item, my will, and I ordane my husband, to help our bairnes, *Nans, Elspeth,* and *Barbara* Boyds, eftir this maner, viz. to Nans viii c. merks, to Elspeth vii c. merkis, and to Barbara fyve hundrith merks. And to our eldest sone *Robert*, ane hundrith merks, and ane broune naig, to *George*, thrie hundrith merkis, to *Archibald* thrie hundrith merkis, to *Gavin* thrie hundrith merks, and to *James* thrie hundrith merks. And farder, I requiest my husband, for the love that has been betwixt my husband and me, and for the favour he beiris to our bairnes abonewritin, to give the thrid part of the movabill gudis and geir that apperteins to ws, to be equallie devydit amangis our four zoungest sones, George, Archibald, Williame and James, and our thrie dochters, Nans, Elspeth, and Barbara Boydis. And I leif my brother, Sir Robert Montgomerie of Skelmorlie, and George Montgomerie, our brother, to be overseers to my bairnes; and ordanes thame, with my husband, to gif the portioun that is left to ony of my dochteris to the rest of our bairnes, incais, as God forbid, ony of thame abuis their bodeys in harlotrie," &c.

V. Robert Boyd, *fear*[*] of Portincross, eldest son of the preceding, appears to have predeceased his father. According to his " testament dative," he died in March 1634. The " inventar of the guids, geir, debts and sowmes of money" perteining to him were given up by " Jeane Bronne, dochter lawfull to vmquhile Robert Bronne of Burrowland, lawfull creditor to the defunct." He married Elizabeth Cuninghame, daughter of Alexander Cuninghame of Waterstoune, by whom he probably had a son, who succeeded his grandfather. He had, at all events, a daughter, *Elizabeth*, who is mentioned in his testament, *ad omissa*, " geiven vp be Allexr. Cvnynghame of Watterstoune, guidsire to Elizabeth Boyd, dochter lawfull to the said vmquhile Robert Boyd of Portincross." In this testament, *ad omissa*, he is styled *fear* of Portincross; and in another document, where " Elizabeth Cvnynghame, Lady Portincors " occurs, in 1636, he is called " hir vmquhile husband, Rot. Boyd, zounger of Portincors."

VI. Robert Boyd of Portincross, on the 19th July 1658, was served heir to his " guidsire," (grandfather) Robert Boyd of Portincross, in the five merk land of Ardneill, &c. He died before the year 1668, leaving a son,

VII. Robert Boyd of Portincross, who had a charter from William, Earl of Kilmarnock, of the ten merk lands of Portincross and Ardneill, dated October 2, 1668. He had also a charter under the Great Seal, of the five merk lands of Arneill, dated December 14, 1671.[†] Whom he married is not mentioned; but he had a son, Robert, and a daughter, Grizel, of whom afterwards. The son married, before the year 1693, Antonia, daughter of Sir Robert Montgomerie of Skelmorley, Bart.,[‡] by Antonia, daughter of Sir James Scot of Rossie, and a son named Hugh, and a daughter, Lilias, both of whom died young.

VIII. Robert Boyd, younger of Portincross, predeceased his father, leaving no surviving issue, upon which his father disponed the barony of Portincross and Ardneill, 13th April 1712, to his grandson, William Fullarton Boyd, eldest son of the above named Grizel Boyd, his only daughter, by Alexander Fullarton, Esq. of Kilmichail, in the Island of Arran,[§] whom she married, perhaps, before the year 1680, and to whom she had, be-

---

[*] " Fear." In this instance, seems to have signified joint proprietor.

[†] Both in an inventory of writs of Craufurd of Auchinames.

[‡] Parish Register.

[§] The Fullartons of Arran are believed to be derived from the same stock as the Fullartons of that Ilk.

sides the said William, another son named Robert, of whom afterwards, and five daughters, *Margaret, Janet, Geils, Antonia,* and *Grizel.* Janet married James Fullarton of Corse, and left issue. Mrs Grizel died at Kilmichail, March 14, 1722.*

IX. William Fullarton Boyd of Portincross, who thus succeeded his grandfather, took the name of Boyd; and, in the year 1714, married Grizel Campbell, only daughter of Angus Campbell, Esq., Captain of Skipness, by Jean, third daughter of Sir James Stuart of Bute, Bart., ancestor of the noble family of Bute, by whom he had an only son, *John,* and four daughters, the eldest of whom, *Elizabeth,* married to Donald Macdonald, Esq., Collector of Excise at Campbelton, and left issue.

The above William Fullarton Boyd alienated the ancient family estate of Portincross to Patrick Craufurd of Auchinames, on the 19th of November 1737, together with the corn-mill of Drummilling, which last he had acquired from Alexander Cuninghame of Carlung, in the year 1725. He afterwards possessed the lands of Balnakil, in Cantyre, where he died some time subsequent to the year 1765. He was succeeded by his only son,

X. John Boyd, younger of Portincross, who, after his father's death, resided at Skipness with his maternal relations, where he died unmarried, about the year 1785.

The heirs-male of the elder son of the marriage betwixt Mrs Grizel Boyd of Portincross and Alexander Fullarton of Kilmichail, having failed in the person of the last-mentioned Mr Boyd, we now return to the second son of the marriage,

XI. Robert Fullarton, afterwards of Overton, who was born at Kilmichail, June 8, 1693, but does not seem ever to have used the name of Boyd in addition to Fullarton. He married first, in 1723, Anna Cuninghame of Carlung, by whom he had a son, *Henry,* and a daughter, *Grizel,* who both died in infancy. Mrs Anna Cuninghame died January 15, 1728. He married, secondly, Mrs Anne King, about the year 1732, by which marriage there were three sons, and as many daughters. About the period of his first marriage, he acquired the lands of Overton, part of the estate of Carlung; and dying in June 1750, was succeeded by his eldest son of the second marriage, namely,

XII. William Fullarton of Overton, who, in consequence of the death of his cousin-german, No. X., became the nearest heir-male of the marriage betwixt Mrs Grizel Boyd of Portincross

and Alexander Fullarton of Kilmichail. This William had a disposition from his father of the lands of Overton, May 6, 1749. He married, in the year 1783, Mary Tarbet, West Kilbride, and left issue three sons and a daughter:

1. John, his successor.
2. Francis, who went young to sea, and was some time a midshipman on board H. M. brig 'Tigress.'
3. William, writer in Glasgow.
4. Robina.

He died in the end of the year 1793, and was succeeded by his eldest son,

XIII. John Fullarton of Overton, formerly a lieutenant in the 71st regiment. Mr Fullarton is well known as one of our most devoted and talented local antiquaries; and not a few publications, illustrative of the family and other antiquities of the county, are indebted to his industry and pen.

The ancient tower or castle of Portincross continued to be the residence of the proprietors until after the restoration of Charles II., when it was relinquished for a mansion-house of a very different style of building, where they resided until the alienation of the property. The old castle, however, still continued to be occupied by fishermen, and other inferior tenants, until about the year 1739, when, having been unroofed by what was termed "the windy January," it was forever after consigned to ruin and decay.

*Arms of the Boyds of Portincross*—A star in chief was all the distinction from the arms of the Kilmarnock family. Crest and mottoes the same.

### BUNTINE OF KILBRIDE.

The property of Kilbride, along with Ardneill or Portincross, was conferred upon Sir Robert Boyd, by Robert the Bruce, in 1306, and it continued in the possession of the Kilmarnock family until the latter part of the eighteenth century. Lawcastle, a stately tower, whose ruins still exist in a pretty entire state, was one of the residences of the noble and respected house of Boyd. In 1670, William, third Earl of Kilmarnock, alienated this property, along with the lands of Drummilling and Boydston to

· Major Hugh Buntine, who, it is said, acquired both reputation and money in the Parliamentary Wars. From his armorial bearings, which were, argent, three Bunten birds proper, and on a chief, azure, a sword fessways of the first, hilted and pommelled or—crest, an arm, grasping a sword—motto, *Fortiter et Fide,* it has been supposed that he was descended of the

---

* Inscription on her tombstone in the churchyard of the parish of Kilbryd, Arran.

Buntines of Ardoch. Be this as it may, it is evident that his ancestors were connected with the immediate locality in which he in after life chiefly resided. For example, a " *Wm. Buntein, servitour to the Earl of Eglintoun,*" occurs as a creditor in the testament of Janet Rodger in Kilwynning, who died in December 1620; and the death apparently of the same William Buntein took place six years afterwards. His testament is called " the Testament of William Buntein in Kilwynning, who deceast October 1626." That Major Hugh Buntine was the son or a near relative of this William Buntein is more than probable from what is known of his history. It seems likely, presuming that his father, or other near relative, was servitour to the Earl of Eglintoun, that he first joined the army, in the great civil war, under the banner of the Earl of Eglintoun, or of his son, Lord Montgomerie.

Robertson, who wrote from family information, states that " Major Buntine was a man of great respectability, and enjoyed a high reputation in the Parliamentary armies during the civil wars. He distinguished himself, in particular, in the battle of Philiphaugh, where, on the 13th of September 1645, General David Lesly annihilated the army of Montrose, till then deemed to be invincible. Cromwell had a high opinion of Major Buntine's talents, and appointed him to be Muster-Master of Horse in Scotland: a situation in which it is believed he acquired a considerable part of his fortune. He built a large house in Kilwinning in 1681, and spent the latter part of his life in it.

" During his residence in Kilwinning, he was appointed one of the trustees on the Eglintoun estate, which, from the troubles of the preceding times, had become very much embarrassed. At one time it was in contemplation to sell part of the lands in order to pay off the debt; but this resolution was successfully opposed by Major Buntine, who suggested such judicious arrangements, founded on the basis of strict economy, that the incumbrances were gradually extinguished, leaving the estate entire. This good service was gratefully acknowledged by the Eglintoun family, who ever afterwards kept up an intercourse, on the most friendly footing, with Major Buntine and his relatives the Baillies.

" Previous to this he had acquired the lands of Kilbride, from William the first Earl of Kilmarnock, in the year 1670, and took out a crown charter in the following year—disjoining these lands from the lordship of Boyd, and erecting them into a free barony, to be called, in all time coming, the Barony of Kilbride, and which he assumed as his own designation, and under which

title he appears several times as a Commissioner of Supply for the County of Ayr, towards the latter end of the seventeenth and beginning of the eighteenth centuries. He had also a share in the troubles of the times, during the reign of Charles II. This, indeed, from the party he adhered to in the civil wars, was what might have been expected; but he managed his matters so cautiously as to come off with little loss. Of what family he was, I have no information; but from his armorial bearings, so similar to those of Buntine of Ardoch, there appears reason to conclude that he was of that house."

Robertson may be right in his conjecture; but there can be little doubt that he was immediately descended from " Wm. Buntein, servitour to the Earl of Eglintoun," who died in Kilwinning in 1626. Major Buntine disponed the Barony of Kilbride to his nephew, William Baillie of Monktoun, in 1714, shortly after which period it is supposed he died. In politics the Major was highly patriotic, and at the Union in 1707 he is said to have declaimed against that measure in no ordinary terms.

### CRAUFURDS OF CORSEBIE AND AUCHINAMES.

The old and extensive estate of Corsebie, comprising about 1500 acres, lies towards the east of the parish. It consists of arable, meadow, moss, hill pasture, and heath land, with a considerable portion of natural wood. The earliest proprietors of this property on record were a branch of the great family of Craufurd. It would seem, from the adage quoted by Pont, in reference to the possessions of the Craufurds—

" They had Draffen, Methweine, and rich erth Stevinstone, Cameltoune, Knockawart, and fair Lowdoune "—

that the last mentioned estate was amongst the latest acquirements of the family. Notwithstanding, it would appear that the Craufurds of Corsebie were immediately descended from the Loudoun branch. It seems to be generally understood, though the earliest records of the Craufurds of Corsebie and Auchinames were accidentally destroyed by fire in Edinburgh, that the first of Corsebie was,

I. SIR REGINALD DE CRAUFURD, but whether "brother carnalis" to Hugh Craufurd of Loudoun, father of " Sir Reginald Craufurd of Loudoun, Sheriff of Ayr, who was murdered by the English at Ayr, in 1297," seems somewhat questionable. There can be little doubt that Sir Reginald of Loudoun, and Sir Reginald of Corsebie, the latter uncle to Sir William Wallace, existed contemporaneously; hence the inference that they were not full brothers, although there are various instances in great families of two brothers being called by the same name. Be this as it may, the mother of Sir William Wallace is pretty satisfactorily shown to have been a daughter of Sir Reginald Craufurd of Loudoun, while it is equally clear that Sir Reginald Craufurd of Corsebie was the *uncle* of Sir William Wallace. This could not have been the case, however, if Robertson is correct in stating that Sir Reginald of Corsebie was the "brother carnalis" of *Hugh*, grandson of the first Sir Reginald of Loudoun, who, from the period in which he lived (1220), could not have been the grandfather of Sir William Wallace. In the reign of Robert I., there is a charter to "Reginald Craufurd of ane annuale out of Ormischue," in the parish of Irvine; but whether this was Sir Reginald of Corsebie, or Sir Reginald of Loudoun, son of Sir Reginald who was killed at the Barns of Ayr, does not appear. There is no reason for supposing, as Robertson does, in another edition of the *Ayrshire Families*, that Hugh, brother of Sir Reginald of Loudoun, who died in 1303, was the first of Auchinames.

A hiatus takes place in the family line between Reginald Craufurd of Corsebie, who became the first Baron of Auchinames, the ancient property of the family in Renfrewshire, and his next successor on record; but there is no reason to doubt the accuracy of Craufurd, the historian of Renfrewshire, who, writing in 1710, says that the Craufurds had been in possession of Auchinames well-nigh 400 years before that time.

The next on record condescended upon by Robertson, who follows Craufurd, is *Thomas* Craufurd of Auchinames, whose father, he presumes, may have been named *Hugh*. There is, no doubt, much guess work in attempting to lay down the order of descent at this stage of the history of the family; but to us it appears probable that the first Sir Reginald was succeeded by another,

II. Reginald Craufurd of Auchinames, whom we presume to have been the son of the former. At all events, a Reginald Craufurd of Renfrewshire appears as a witness to a charter by Robert, the High Steward, in 1358. This could hardly have been the *first* Sir Reginald, uncle of Sir William Wallace, who could not have been less than 121 years of age in 1358, although he might well have been his son.

III. Thomas Craufurd of Auchinames appears in a charter of confirmation by Robert III., dated at Arncill, on the 24th October 1401. In the same year, according to Craufurd, this Thomas of Auchinames made a mortification "for the health of his soul, and of his wife, and for the soul of *Sir Reginald Craufurd, his grandfather*,"

the founder, probably, of the house of Auchinames.

IV. Archibald Craufurd received grants of the lands of Thirdpart, Predvick, and Drumver, from his father, Thomas Craufurd of Auchinames, in 1427. On the death of his father, he succeeded to Auchinames. He married Margaret Douglas, daughter of Sir William Douglas of Pierston, and left two sons:

1. Robert, who succeeded him.
2. Thomas, ancestor of the Craufurds of Thirdpart.

V. Robert Craufurd of Auchinames, son of Archibald, was, according to Nisbet and Douglas, twice married—first to Margaret Douglas, daughter of George, Master of Angus, and sister to Archibald, the great Earl, who married the widow of James IV., daughter of Henry VII. of England, by whom, says Robertson, he had a daughter married to Semple of Noblestoun. He next married Marion Houston, daughter to Houstoun of that Ilk, by whom he had three sons—*James, Henry*, and *Robert*—in whose favour he granted a charter in 1483, and in 1484 gave sasine of his whole lands to his eldest son, James, reserving his own liferent. He was slain at the battle of Flodden, in 1513, and was succeeded by his eldest son.

It is evident, from these dates, that a great mistake has been committed. George, Master of Angus, himself fell at Flodden, and could not have been so aged a man as that his youngest daughter of six (so says Douglas), could have been married at such an early period to this Baron of Auchinames, that the sons of his second wife could have been of age—three of them—by 1483. In place, therefore, of Robert, the *father*, having been the son-in-law of George, Master of Angus, it must have been Robert, the *son*, that married the Lady Margaret, or, as others say, the Lady Isobel Douglas, and who died at Flodden. It is farther corroborative of this, that in 1513, Noblestoun was given by Sempill of Fulwood to his son Robert, and Margaret Craufurd, his wife, apparently on their marriage. Craufurd, in his account of the family of Noblestoun, calls the lady "a daughter of the house of Auchinames,"—a mode of expression which would not have been used had she been the daughter of the chief of that house.

VI. James Craufurd of Auchinames, who had a charter of the lands of Corsebie and Munnock in 1498, and appears in other charters dated in 1526 and 1533. He was succeeded by his son,

VII. Thomas Craufurd of Auchinames, whose name occurs in the Books of Adjournal, Nov. 13, 1537, so that he must have succeeded before that period. In 1539, he obtained a gift of the non-entries of the lands of Auldmuir, said to have been a hundred years in arrear. He married Marion, daughter of Montgomerie of Hazelhead, by whom he had three sons, all in succession lairds of Auchinames. He died in 1541, and was succeeded by the eldest son,

VIII. John Craufurd of Auchinames, who was killed at the battle of Pinkie, 1st September 1574, and was succeeded by his brother,

IX. William Craufurd of Auchinames. He married Annabella, daughter of Chalmers of Gadgirth, by whom he had a son, James, who died before himself, but who had previously married Elizabeth, daughter of William, sixth Earl of Glencairn. The marriage contract is dated 2d September, 1579. As part of the tocher, the said noble Earl bound himself " to pay to James Craufurd of Auchinames the sowme of £1000 Scots, within the paroch kirk of Irvine, &c. And also the said Erle binds himself to hald and honorabillie sustein the said Elisabeth in familie with thame togidder with the said James Crawfurd of Auchinames, with his gentilman and vnder serwane to ilk ane of thame, ffor all the tyme and space of thrie yeiris nixt eftir the compleiting of the said marriage at Finlaystoun." James Craufurd of Auchinames died soon after the marriage.* He left an only daughter, Jean Crawfurd, born in 1582, upon whom were settled the lands of Corsbie, and of whom afterwards. On the death of William Craufurd, he was succeeded in the barony of Auchinames by his brother,

X. Patrick Craufurd, who also succeeded his nephew, James, in the lands of Auldmuir and Whiteside, both in 1585. He married a daughter of Frazer of Knock, by whom he had his successor,

XI. William Craufurd of Auchinames, who married Margaret, daughter of Sir Patrick Honstoun of that Ilk. He appears to have died before 1611, as "Dame Margaret Houstone, Ladie Auchnenis," occurs in the testament of Hew Boyd in Kirktoun, who died in April of that year, as a creditor for the "byrun dewties of the ballis thriescoir sax punds." In the same document appears " —— Craufurd of Auchnemis, zounger, for 1611 zeiris dewtie of the ballis xl lib." Lady Auchinames survived her husband till 1642, as witness her latter-will :

"Legacie.—At Auchinames, the xiiii day of May Jai vi c. fourtie twa zeiris. The quhilk day I, Dame Margaret Honstoun, relict of vmquhile William Craufuird of Auchinames, &c. ordaining my bodie and corps to be bureid amange the faithfull with my said husband at Kilbarchane, vpone the charges eftirspecifit. Throgh guid to mak and set doune this my latterwill and testament as followis, To wit, in the first, I have maid and constitute, &c., Patrik Craufuird of Auchinames, Elizabethe Craufuird, my loveing bairne, and Elizabethe Naper, my oy, all thrie conjunct equall and vniversall executouris, &c. And leist ony questioune sould aryse, I have declared and devydit, and left in legacie as followis, viz. In the first I ordane the sowme of thrie hundrithe merks money, loying besyd me, to be taiken and bestowit vpone my said honest buriall. Item, I have gevin and left in frie gift presentlie, and left in legacie, to Williame Craufurd, appeirand of Auchinames, my oy, ane sylwir tas, or cowpe, ane sylwir futtit cope, an xi silwir spones, to be keipit be him with the hous of Auchinames as ane memoriall. Item, I leive and presentlie give to the said Elizabeth Craufurd, my dochter, and Elizabeth Naper, my oy, equallie betuixt thame, all the inspreche, &c. of my hous, being within the dooris, except my best furneisched fedder bed, dornik buird claithe, capbuird, and the mekill kist above, quhilk I left and presentlie gevin and delyverit to the said Patrik Craufuird of Auchinames, my eldest sone, &c. Be thir presents, wryttin be James Craufuird, sone lawfull to the said Patrik Craufuird of Auchinames, my oy, and subscryvit with my hand at Auchinames, &c.* Befoir thir witnesses, Johne and Patrik Craufuirdis, my oyes, and Johnne How of Damptoune. Sic subscribitur, I, Dame Margaret Houstoun, &c. with my hand at the pen, &c., becaus I can nocht wryt myself, &c."

From this document it appears, that William Craufurd of Auchinames and his spouse had issue :

1. Patrick, who succeeded.
2. Elizabeth, married to Sir Alexander Napier of Lawrestone, Knight, and had issue a daughter, Elizabeth.[†]

XII. Patrick Craufurd of Auchinames, as appears from the foregoing documents, succeeded his father before 1611. He married his cousin, Jane Craufurd, heiress of Corsbie, by which union the ancient estates of Auchinames and Corsbie were again united. "They had a numerous issue," says Robertson, "of whom one of the daughters was married to Frazer of Knock." This

---

* The said Elizabeth Cuninghame was married secondly to Alexander Cuninghame of Craigends. The marriage took place in 1586 or 1587.

---

* He was a notary-public.

† This daughter died "ane zoung woman unmarried," within the burgh of Glasgow, in 1650. Her whole "guidis and geir" consisted of "ane pair of virginallis estimat to xl lib." In her testament she is called Margaret, so much for the accuracy of the Commissary Court. "James Craufurd, sone lawfull to umquhill Patrike Craufurd of Auchinames, and Elizabeth Craufurd, sister-germane to the said umquhill Patrike," were appointed her only executors.

does not appear, however, from the latter-will of Patrick, who died in the month of January 1649.

"Legacies.—At Corsbie, the xii day of December 1648 zeiris. The quhilk day I, Patrik Crawfurde of Auchinames, being seik in bodie, &c. Item, I make, nominat, and constitute Jeane Craufurd, my loveing spous, executrix, vniversale intromitterix with all and sundrie guidis, geir, &c. perteining to me, &c. Quhilks debtis and sowmes of money I ordane to be payit, in ordour as they are abovewrittin. And being so done, I, for the faythfull and loveing dewtie keipit and done to me be my said spous thir manie zeiris bygane, and for the love I have and aw to hir, I have friclie disponet and left in legacie to hir, hir aires, executrixis and assignis, all and sindrie my foirsaidis guidis, &c. And leist seditious persones sould contradict thir presents directlie or indirectlie I ordane the same to stand firme and stable as ane law to all over quhome I have fayrlie power, according to the trew meaning therof, wnder all hiest paine that I may imposie. Be thir presents, wrettin be James Crawfurd, my sone, and subscryvit with my hand, at day, zeir and place foirsaid, befoir thir witnesses, Wm. Crawfurd, younger of Auchinames, my sone, Rot. Huntare, younger of Hunterstone, my sone in law, and Robert Crawfurd of Nayther Maynes, also my lawfull sone," &c.

Amongst the "Debts awand Out" mentioned in the testament, occur the names of "Margaret Crawfurd, my second lawfull dochter," "Johne Crawfurd, my sone," "Mr Hugh and Jeane Crawfurdis, my bairnes," "Patrik Crawfurd, also my sone," and "Katherine Crawfurd, my youngest dochter."

There were in all six sons and three daughters of this marriage, viz. :—

1. William, who was infeft in the 12 pund land of Auchinames, 12th May 1649.
2. James, W.S., and father to Patrick Craufurd, Counsellor-of-Law, London.
3. Captain Robert of Nethermains, in Kilwinning Parish.
4. John.
5. Patrick.
6. Mr Hugh, minister at Cumnock, and grandfather of Hugh Craufurd of Garrive.

1. Jeane.
2. Margaret, married to Robert Hunter of Hunterstoun.
3. Katharine.

XIII. William Craufurd of Auchinames was infeft in the twelve pound land of Auchinames in 1649. He married Anna, daughter of Sir Coll Lamont of Ineryne, in Argyleshire, by whom he had a son and three daughters—the latter were respectively married to Houston of Houstoun, Kennedy of Kilhenzie, and Boyd of Trochrig. He was succeeded by,

XIV. Archibald Craufurd of Auchinames, his only son. His retour is dated 20th April 1676. He was imprisoned on the 30th July 1683, on suspicion of being concerned in the affair of Bothwell-Brig; and again indicted 1st April 1684, but the charge was deserted simpliciter. He married, first, Margaret, second daughter of Porterfield of Duchal, or of that Ilk. The marriage contract is dated 16th October 1672. Her tocher was £8000 Scots. Issue of this marriage:

1. William, who succeeded.
2. Anna, married to James Bruce of Powfowls, to whom she had issue.
3. Jean, married to Patrick Craufuird, merchant, Edinburgh, afterwards of Drumsoy,* and had issue.
4. Margaret, married to "a worthy man, about, 1720 —— Young of Killicantie."

He married, secondly, in 1696, Annabella Stewart, daughter of John Stewart, younger, of Blackhall, who died in his father's lifetime. Of this marriage there was no issue. She had previously been married to William Porterfield of that Ilk, to whom she was living. She was living in 1701, when a marriage contract between her daughter, Jean Porterfield, and James Farquhar of Gilmilnscroft, was drawn out. In that document the bride's mother is styled "Annable Stewart, now Dowager of Auchinames." The bride's tocher was 8000 merks Scots.

His only son, William, married Helen, daughter of Sir Thomas Burnet of Crimond, Physician to King William, and brother to Bishop Burnet, by whom he had only one daughter, Helen, who married Patrick Edmonston of Newton, and had issue. He died, in 1695, before his father; when an arrangement was made, by which the estates of Auchinames and Corsbie were retained to Jane, the second daughter of his father, Archibald, and to her husband, Patrick, the male representative of the Craufuirds of Drumsoy. Patrick Craufuird of Drumsoy and Auchinames died in 1733, and was succeeded by his eldest surviving son,

XV. Patrick Craufuird of Drumsoy and Auchinames, member for the county of Ayr in 1741 and 1747, and for Renfrewshire in 1761. He married, first, Elizabeth, daughter and co-heir of George Middleton, Esq., a banker in London, and had two sons,

1. John, his heir.
2. James, Col. in the Guards, and Governor of Bermuda. He died s. p. in 1811.

He married, secondly, Sarah, daughter of Lord Sempill, by whom he had a daughter, Sarah, who died unmarried in 1796. He died in 1778, and was succeeded by his eldest son,]

XVI. John Craufuird of Drumsoy and Auch-

---

* See the account of Craufuird of Drumsoy, parish of Coyiton, vol. i, p. 327.

inames, M.P. for Old Sarum in the Parliament of 1768, and afterwards for the county of Renfrew, in the Parliament which assembled in October 1774. This gentleman, who was the associate and friend of Charles James Fox, died unmarried in 1814, and was succeeded by his cousin,

XVII. John Craufurd of Auchinames and Crosbie, who, in 1814, was served heir to his great-grandfather, John Craufuird of Drumsoy and Auchinames. He married Sophia-Marianna, daughter of Major-General Horace Churchill, and great-granddaughter of Sir Robert Walpole, and has issue:—

1. Edward-Henry-John, born in 1816.
2. Frederick-Angustus-Buchanan, born in 1822.
3. Robert-Emilius-Fazakerley, born in 1824.
4. George Ponsonby, born in 1826.
1. Katherine-Horatia.
2. Georgiana-Janet.

*Arms*—Quarterly; 1st and 4th, gules, a fesse, ermine; 2d, a stag's head, erased, gules; 3d, argent, two spears in saltier, between four spots of ermine.

*Crests*—A stag's head, erased, gules, between the attires a cross-crosslet fitchée; 2d, a phœnix, proper, rising from the flames.

*Mottoes*—Tutum te robore reddam; and, God show the right.

*Seat*—The proper seat of the family is Crosbie Castle, now in ruins; but they possess a neat cottage residence in the immediate vicinity of the Old Castle of Portincross, which is also their property.

### CUNINGHAMES AND BOYDS OF CARLUNG.

The lands of Carlung, lying conterminous with the village of Kilbride, formed part of the church lands of the collegiate church of Kilmaurs. At the Reformation, they fell into the hands of the Earl of Glencairn. Drummilling, the other portion of the church lands, were gifted to the Lord Boyd. Carlung, long afterwards, continued in the possession of a cadet of the Glencairn family. The first of the branch was,

I. HUGH CUNINGHAME, third son of William, fourth Earl of Glencairn. He had previously possessed the lands of Watterstoun, near Kilbarchan, in Renfrewshire, which, in 1538, he had obtained from his father, then Lord Kilmaurs. The next* we find mentioned was,

II. Archibald Cuninghame of Watterstoune

who was killed by the followers of Lord Eglintoun, during the feud which so long prevailed between the Cuninghames and Montgomeries. As this occurred towards the close of the sixteenth century, the next no doubt was,

III. Robert Cunynghame, elder of Watterstone, whose name occurs in the list of "Debtis awand to the deid," in the testament of Alexander Cunynghame, elder, merchant in Irvine, who died in 1611. His son, "Allexr. Conynghame, zounger of Watterstoun, Jeane and Sara Conynghames, his sisteris," are mentioned in the list of "Debtis awand be the deid," in the testament of "Jeane Porterfield, spous to Williame Muire, zounger of Rowallane," who died in 1612. Robert Cuninghame of Watterstoun was alive in 1618, in which year his name occurs in another testamentary document. He appears to have died, however, before December 1622. He had thus, at least, three children:

1. Alexander, his successor.
2. Jean.
3. Sarah.

IV. Alexander Cuninghame of Watterstoune occurs in the testament of "James Conynghame of Aischinzairdis," who died in December 1622; also in that of Robert Boyd of Portincross, who died in March 1634, where he is mentioned as the father-in-law of the deceased. He had thus a daughter, *Elizabeth*, besides his heir,

V. Alexander Cuninghame of Carlung, who, on the 18th February 1658, was served heir to his father, Alexander Cuninghame of Carlung and Watterstoun, in the corn-mill of Drummilling. It must have been this Alexander, and not his "father," as stated by Robertson, who married, about the year 1640, a daughter of Patrick Hunter of Hunterstoun. He was succeeded by his next brother,

VI. Joseph Cuninghame of Carlung, whose retour is dated 18th March 1664. He was succeeded by his only remaining brother,

VII. Henry Cuninghame of Carlung, who was served heir to his brother, last mentioned, in the corn-mill of Drummilling, June 11, 1674. He married Dorothea, daughter of Patrick Hunter of Hunterstoun, by which marriage he had nine sons and six daughters. Of the daughters, two were married:

1. Marion, married to John Boyd, of the family of Pitcon.
2. Anna, married to Robert Fullarton of Overton.

He was succeeded, before the year 1704, by his eldest son,

* Robertson supposes that there was another, Hugh, in succession, from his finding the name recorded in a charter of John Cuninghame of Caddell, in 1572; but this was probably the first Hugh of Watterstoun.

VIII. James Cuninghame of Carlung, who appears in the list of Commissioners of Supply, 5th August 1704. It is uncertain whether he ever was married, but he was succeeded by his immediate younger brother,

IX. Alexander Cuninghame of Carlung, who, by a precept of Chancery, dated November 14, 1724, was infeft heir in *special* to his father, Henry Cuninghame of Carlung, in the corn-mill of Drummilling. He married, about the year 1728, Margaret Wallace, but left no surviving issue, for he was succeeded by his next and only brother,

X. Henry Cuninghame of Carlung, who is a subscribing witness to a deed dated January 6, 1739. He died unmarried, when the estate devolved upon his sister,

XI. Marion Cuninghame of Carlung, the last remaining child of her father, Henry Cuninghame of Carlung, and Dorothea his wife. She married, as already stated, John Boyd, of the Pitcon family, by whom she had a son,

XII. John Boyd of Carlung, who succeeded his mother in that property. He was brought up to a mercantile life, and passed a number of his younger years in America. On his return, he settled at Carlung, which he greatly improved, and built the present house. He acquired the adjoining lands of Corse from James Fullarton of Corse, which had been alienated by his maternal uncle, Alexander Cuninghame of Carlung. He married Elizabeth Hunter, daughter of Robert Hunter of Kirkland, by whom he had two sons, *John* and *William*, who died young; and two daughters, *Jean* and *Marion*, of whom afterwards. He died in 1786, and was succeeded by his only remaining son,

XIII. John Boyd of Carlung, who did not long survive his father, as he died in 1792. He was succeeded by his two sisters,

XIV. Jean and Marion Boyd, heirs-portioners of Carlung. Jean, the eldest, previous to her brother's death, was married to her cousin, Robert Hunter of Kirkland. Marion married the Rev. Robert Steele, minister of the West Parish of Greenock, and had issue one son and eight daughters.

In 1799, the lands of Carlung and Corse were alienated by the two heiresses to Archibald Alexander of Boydston, whose family still possess them.

The modern house of Carlung is planted in a commanding situation, within a mile north-west of the village of Kilbride. The old mansion, supposed to have been built in 1560, was situated about a hundred yards northward of it.

## SIMSONS OF KIRKTOUNHALL.

Kirktounhall is a small property adjoining the village of West Kilbride. The name is obviously derived from the situation of the dwelling-house—which is comparatively of recent construction—near to the street of the *Kirktoun*. The house, as well as the property, derive interest from the fact of their having at one time belonged to Professor Simson of Glasgow, the celebrated restorer of Euclid. The progenitors of this eminent individual are said to have resided from time immemorial at the *toun*, or farm, of North Thirdpart, on the estate of Ardneill. The first of the Simsons of Kirktounhall mentioned in the writs of the property, however, was

I. Robert Simson of Kirktounhall. Upon a tombstone in the churchyard of Kilbride, dated 1695, he is designed "writer in Kilbryde." In the year 1660, he built the house called Kirktounhall. Who he married does not appear, but her initials, "M. W.," are recorded on the tombstone, as well as on a sun-dial, designed by Dr Simson, the remains of which still exist in the garden of Kirktounhall. From an entry in the Parish Register of Kilbride, it would appear that his son had succeeded to the property, in, or prior to, the year 1724.

II. John Simson of Kirktounhall, there is reason to suppose, was a younger son of the family,[*] and that, about the above date, he succeeded an *elder* brother, who had then died without issue. He was regularly bred a merchant in Glasgow, and became a member of the Merchant House in 1683, the date of his burgess ticket. About the year 1685, he married Agnes, daughter of the Rev. Patrick Simpson, minister of Renfew, by Agnes Hay, daughter of John Hay of Renfield. By this lady he had the extraordinary family of seventeen sons, without any daughters. Only six of them, however, came to manhood:

1. Robert, the celebrated professor, and successor to his property.
2. Patrick, who was educated for the church, and afterwards settled minister at Coventry, in England.
3. Thomas Simson, M.D., Professor of Medicine in the College of St Andrews, known by several professional works. He married, about 1724, a daughter of Sir John Preston of Prestonhall, in the county of Fife,[†] by whom he had four sons and two daughters:

---

[*] In Robertson's 'Ayrshire Families,' the writer says: "A letter, which I have seen, addressed to him by Professor Simson, his son, dated 'Glasgow, December 27, 1722,' is thus superscribed, ' To Mr John Simson, merchant in Glasgow, at West Kilbryde;' and in which letter the writer makes particular inquiry for the health of his uncle, with whom his father appears to have been upon a visit. In this letter, Dr Simson also mentions his mother as being then living."

[†] Sir John was forfeited in 1715.

1. John, died unmarried.
2. Robert, who was educated for the medical profession, and ultimately settled as a physician in Coventry, where he married his cousin-german, Anne, daughter of his uncle, the Rev. Patrick Simson, by whom he had three sons and two daughters.
3. Patrick, a clergyman of the Church of Scotland, who died unmarried.
4. James, M.D., who succeeded his father as Professor of Medicine in the College of St Andrews. He died unmarried.
1. Agnes, married to Professor Wilson of St Andrews, to whom she had a family. One of the daughters was the first wife of the late Lord Jeffrey, of distinguished memory.
2. Preston, married to Professor Craigie of St Andrews, and had issue.
4. John Simson, bred a writer in Edinburgh, who afterwards became chamberlain to the Lord Elphinston. He married Agnes, second daughter of John Prentice, merchant in Glasgow, by Annabel, daughter of Porterfield of Duchal, and obtained with her the lands of Wester Balloch, Dunbartonshire, by whom he had a large family, none of whom married, save two sons and a daughter.
5. Matthew Simson, a merchant in Glasgow, where he resided, and died 20th November 1769. He married, in 1724, Marion, eldest daughter of John Prentice and Annabella his wife, by whom he had nine sons and one daughter, none of whom married, save one daughter, Marion, married to Michael Erskine, merchant in Glasgow.
6. William Simson, the youngest of the six sons, went to sea, and obtained the command of a merchant vessel. He died unmarried.

John Simson of Kirktounhall acquired the lands of Knockeward, in the parish of Ardrossan, from William Mure of Caldwell, in 1713. He died, as appears from the Session Records of Kilbride, in the spring of 1731, and was succeeded in the property of Kirktounhall by his eldest son,

III. Robert Simson, M.D., Professor of Mathematics in the University of Glasgow, who, March 14, 1732, obtained a precept of *Clare Constat* of the " fifty shilling land of the five pound land of Overtoun, formerly called the south and east quarters, with the mansion-house, &c. of the same, now passing by the name of Kirktounhall."* Dr Simson was born on the 14th of October, O.S. 1687. His career as a scholar, and the ability with which he filled the Mathematical Chair of the College of Glasgow for a period of fifty-eight years, are too well known to require repetition here.† Dr Simson died at Glasgow in his 81st year, in the month of October 1768, and was interred in the Blackfriars' burying-ground, where a marble tablet is placed in the wall to his memory. He was never married, and his valuable collection of mathematical works were left as a legacy to the College of Glasgow. He was succeeded in the property of Kirktounhall by

* Title-deeds of the property.
† See an "Account of the Life and Writings of Dr Simson, by the Rev. Wm. Trail, LL.D.," &c. 4to. London. 1812.

IV. " Robert Simson, eldest, or only son of his nephew, Dr Robert Simson, physician in Coventry." Mr Simson, the direct representative of the family, was educated at Oxford, and entered from thence into the army. He was an officer in the 9th light dragoons, and subsequently in the 2d regiment of foot; but he ultimately returned to Oxford, where he obtained the degree of LL.B., and entering into holy orders, became vicar of St Michael's in Coventry, to which living he was presented by the late distinguished statesman William Pitt. He married Miss Tandy, an English lady.

*Arms*, in the possession of a descendant of the family—Argent, on a chief vert, three crescents of the first.

*Crest*—A Fraze, argent, allusive to the descent of the name Simson from the Frasers, as is generally held.

*Motto*—Semper virens.

The property of Kirktounhall was purchased by Captain Ritchie from the representative of Professor Robert Simson in 1789, and now belongs to Francis Caldwell Ritchie, Esq., his nephew.

## HUNTER OF KIRKLAND.

This family is derived, by immediate descent, from that of Hunterstoun.

I. Robert Hunter, second son of Robert Hunter of Hunterstoun, by Elizabeth, daughter of William Craufurd of Auchinames. He studied for the ministry, and was placed at Kilbryde before 1688. He bought the lands of Kirkland from Craufurd of Craufurdland, his wife's uncle, in 1686. He married, in 1675, Margaret, daughter of John Hamilton of Grange, near Kilmarnock, and had issue :—

1. Robert Hunter of Kirkland.
2. Margaret, married to Mr William Castlelaw (son probably of Mr William Castlelaw, minister at Stewarton about 1650) in 1713.
3. Rebecca, married to Mr Robert Cameron, minister of Beith. He died in 1735. His relict collected his stipends, as received from George Kerr of Dockray, for payment of his teinds for 1735. Receipt dated at Mainshill, 6th February, 1736.
4. Elizabeth, married to John Montgomerie of Barradger, in Beith parish, in 1720, second son of Robert Montgomerie of Craighouse, and grandson of Montgomerie of Bogstoun. Issue :—
   1. John, who went to sea and died unmarried.
   2. Gavin, surgeon, who died at Antigua in 1760.
   3. Captain Robert, born in 1728, died unmarried.
   4. Margaret, died unmarried.
   5. Rebecca, born, in 1726, at Barradger, and married to William Wilson, merchant in Kilmarnock. She died in 1814, aged 86. She had previously con-

T

veyed Barradger to Lieut. Colonel Cameron, Ayr, her kinsman.[*]

Mr Hunter demitted his charge 3d May 1698, and died before 1713.

II. Robert Hunter of Kirkland, who purchased part of the lands of Drummilling, adjacent to his own, which still remains in the family. He married Margaret, daughter of Bailie Munro of Irvine, by whom he had:

  1. George, who succeeded him.

  1. Margaret, married to William Cuninghame, son of Cuninghame of Monktonhill.
  2. Elizabeth, married to John Boyd of Carlung.

II. George Hunter of Kirkland. He married, first, his cousin, Dorothea, daughter of John Boyd, of the Pitcon family, by whom he had several children, who all died young, except his son, who succeeded him. He married, secondly, Mary, daughter of Cuninghame of Monktonhall (another near relative), by whom he had also several children, most of whom, save a daughter, Dorothea, died in early life. His son,

IV. Robert Hunter of Kirkland, succeeded him. In 1791, he married his cousin, Jean Boyd Cuninghame, eldest daughter of John Boyd of Carlung. This lady died on the 24th of March 1825. Issue:

  1. George.
  2. Robert.

  1. Jean.
  2. Marion, who married, 1st February 1825, John Woodrop of Dalmarnock,[†] maternally descended of the family of Hamilton of Holmhead.

*Residence*—Kirkland House, in the village of Kilbride.

*Arms*—Same as Hunterstoun, with a mark of cadetcy.

*Tarbet.*—The Rosses of the barony of Tarbet were a branch of the once powerful family of that name, who held large possessions in Cuninghame, under the Baliols, and in whose reverses the most of them participated. The Rosses of Tarbet, a property extending to about 500 acres, however,

continued in possession of it until the year 1450,[*] when they alienated it to their namesake, Ross of Hawkhead. It belongs now to the Earl of Eglintoun.

*Orchard*, on which stands Law Tower, one of the seats of the Kilmarnock family, derived its name, no doubt, from its actually having been the orchard belonging to that great mansion. It is supposed by Robertson that the tower was erected "about the year 1648, when Thomas, the Master of Boyd, married the Princess Mary, sister to James III., and was then created Earl of Arran. It is so far certain, that there is a charter on record, dated the 14th October 1482, of the lands of Kilbride, Dalry, Nodesdale, Kilmarnock, &c., to that Princess, in liferent, and to her son, James Lord Boyd, in fee; on none of which places was there a house equal in magnificence to this, or so suitable for a lady of her rank." It is a stately fabric, well lighted, one of the sides containing eight windows; and in evidence of its comparatively modern construction, it is furnished with gun-ports in its lower story. This pleasant little property was acquired by Robert Boyd of Dykehead, in 1759, from the Misses Baillie, whose predecessor, William Baillie, acquired the whole barony of Kilbride from Major Buntine, in 1714. Robert Boyd, the purchaser, was succeeded in Orchard by his son, Thomas Boyd of Orchard, who, dying without male heirs, it fell to his two daughters.

*Springside.*—This rather extensive property, consisting of about 200 acres, formed part of the barony of Kilbride. It was purchased, in 1790, from Mr James Fairie, in Irvine, by Mr Robert Hyndman, of the Hyndmans of Lunderston in Renfrewshire—a family of long standing and respectability. He married Jean, daughter of Thomas Boyd of Orchard, and was succeeded by his son, John Blair Hyndman, Esq., W.S., of Springside and Burrowland. He never practised the law, but lived at Springside as a country gentleman, and died unmarried in 1844. He left a natural daughter, Margaret Blair Hyndman, married to John Ritchie, Esq. of Seamill, second son of Francis Caldwell Ritchie, Esq. of Kirktounhall.

*Boydston.*—This estate, the property of Archibald Boyd, Esq., who resides at Carlung, extends to about 200 acres, and is the most southerly in the parish. It is attached, *quoad sacra*, to the parish of Ardrossan.

---

[*] The monumental stone in Ayr Kirkyard no doubt refers to this family:—"Erected, 1819, in memory of Captain Cameron and his spouse, Mary Adair, daughter of William Adair of Prestwickshaws, and granddaughter of the Rev. William Adair, minister of Ayr. Also, in memory of Capt. Thomas Humble, who died 11th Nov. 1819, husband of their daughter, Rebecca; and of their son, Lieut.-Colonel Robert Cameron, of the Hon. East India Company's Service, who died 11th Aug. 1826."

[†] "Alexander Wardrop of Dalmarnock," in 1676, was fined in 50 merks for attending conventicles.—LAW'S MEMORIALS.

[*] History of Renfrewshire.

# PARISH OF KILMARNOCK.

ETYMOLOGY, EXTENT, &c.

THE name of the town and parish of Kilmarnock is evidently derived from the church, which " was dedicated to Saint Marnock, a Scottish saint of very early times, who was commemorated on the 25th of October, on which day there was formerly held at Kilmarnock an annual fair, now held on the third Wednesday of October." The parish is about nine miles in length, and four in breadth, —the number of superficial acres, 8340. It is bounded on the east by Loudoun; on the north and west by Fenwick and Kilmaurs; and on the south by the river Irvine, which separates the Presbyteries of Ayr and Irvine, and divides the district of Cuninghame from that of Kyle. The parish was originally of much greater extent, comprehending the whole of the parish of Fenwick, which was detached from it in 1641.

The appearance of the parish is that of a rich and highly cultivated country, presenting few rugged or barren spots. It may be considered as a plain, somewhat undulated, the valley of the water of Kilmarnock, running from east to west, alone presenting anything of the picturesque in scenery. There are no lochs or streams of any extent, save that of the Kilmarnock water, in the parish. The soil, as described by a former writer, is strong and rich, " consisting of clay, with a mixture of sand; and near the moors, some moss. There are some fine holms along the banks of the Irvine, consisting of sand and fine loam, brought down by the river, and left on its banks by the floods." On the south and west, the soil is lighter than towards the north. The introduction of tile-draining, in 1820, by the Duke of Portland, one of the most extensive proprietors in the parish, has vastly improved the capabilities of the soil; and it may well be said that nowhere has agriculture been carried on with more success than in the parish of Kilmarnock, where a society for promoting the science was established so early as 1792. In the northern part of the parish there are considerable plantations, but few of any consequence towards the south and west.

## HISTORY, CIVIL AND ECCLESIASTICAL.

Kilmarnock, whether of the parish or the town, dates back, no doubt, to an early period; but it does so chiefly in reference to its ecclesiastical history. The site of the church of St Marnock may have been that of a Druidical temple—for it is well known that the early promoters of Christianity everywhere, as well as in this country, judiciously endeavoured to plant the cross in the locality, if not upon the very spot, where the fires of Baal had previously burned. The history of the church of Kilmarnock cannot, however, be traced, with any degree of certainty, before the erection of the monastery of Kilwinning, in the twelfth century, to which it became an appendage. Pont, in his description of Cuninghame, states, that " it was built by the Locartes, lords of it [the barony] and dedicat to a holy man, Mernock, as vitnesses the records of Kilvinin Abbey."[*]

" The church of Kilmarnock," says Chalmers, " belonged of old to the Monastery of Kilwinning. The monks enjoyed the tithes and the other revenues, and found a curate to serve the cure. As the parish was formerly large, and a great part of it fertile, the produce of the tithes was considerable. At the Reformation, the monks enjoyed, as an income from the tithes of Kilmarnock, 347 bolls 2 firlots and 1 peck of meal; 21 bolls 2 firlots and 1 peck of bear; and £33, 6s. 8d. in money—being the rent of a part of the tithes, which were leased for payment of that sum yearly.

[*] It is much to be regretted that the charters of Kilwinning Abbey have either been destroyed or lost.

The lands which belonged to the church of Kilmarnock passed into lay hands after the Reformation. In 1619, Archbishop Spottiswoode, who was the commendator of Kilwinning, transferred the patronage of the church, with the tithes of Kilmarnock, to Robert Lord Boyd,* who was proprietor of the lordship of Kilmarnock; and he obtained a charter from the king of this property in August 1619. The patronage continued, at the end of the seventeenth century, in this family. In the eighteenth century, the patronage passed from the Earl of Kilmarnock to the Earl of Glencairn, from whom it was purchased, about the year 1790, by Miss Scott, late Duchess of Portland, to which family the patronage still belongs." M'Kay, in his "History of Kilmarnock," quotes a very interesting document illustrative of the privileges enjoyed by the parishioners of Kilmarnock in Popish times. It was translated from the original Latin some years ago, for one of the local prints, and is as follows:—

"In the name of God, amen. Be it evidently known to all men by this present public instrument, that in the year of the incarnation of the Lord 1547, on the 17th, 18th, 19th and 20th days of the month of November, the sixth of the Indiction and of the Pontificate of the Most Holy Apostolic Father and our Lord Paul III., by Divine providence Pope, the thirteenth year.— In presence of us notaries public and witnesses subscribed, compeared personally the parishioners of the parish Kirk of Kilmarnock, to whom the election of the parish priest thereof is known of full right to belong (quibus electio clerici parochialis ejusdem pleno jure dignoscitur pertinere), namely, Allan Cunynghame, James Cunynghame, senior, John Kirkland, George Tailzeour —[Here follow the names of the other parishioners, amounting to about three hundred in number]—neither actuated by force or fear, fallen into error, or circumvented by guile, but at their own simple, pure, free, and spontaneous good will, from their own certain knowledge gave and preferred and every one of said parishioners for himself separately and successively gave and conferred, as by the tenor of the present public instrument they give and confer, and every one for himself gives and proffers their voices of election, and their votes for the office of Clerk (or

Priest) of the said parish Kirk of Kilmarnock (now vacant by the death and departure of umquhile Thomas Boyd of Lyne, last Parish Clerk and possessor of the said Kirk), to a worthy and distinguished young man, Alexander Boyd, son of a renowned man, Robert Boyd, master of Boyd, of Kilmarnock, and they elected and nominated, as by the tenor of the present public instrument they elect and choose the said Alexander Boyd as a proper person in and to the office of Parish Clerk of Kilmarnock; and they publicly inducted and admitted, as by the tenor of the present public instrument they induct and admit the said Alexander, personally present, to the real, actual and corporal possession of the said office of Clerk of Kilmarnock, by delivery to him of the Bell, Cup, and Sprinklers of Holy Water, and the keys of the doors of the said Kirk of Kilmarnock, with the accustomed solemnities and ceremonies as use is: on the said Alexander, or his doer, procurator, or substitute, undertaking and performing the duties and services belonging to said office during the whole time of his life, with all and sundry its rights, revenues, feus, teinds, endowments, and profits whatsoever to be enjoyed, used, and possessed, without any impediment, obstacle, or contradiction whatever. Upon all and sundry of which, as in the premises, the said Master of Boyd, in the name and on the part of his foresaid son, asked of us notaries public subscribing an instrument, or instruments to be constructed.—These things were done within the foresaid parish of Kilmarnock, and parish Kirk thereof on the days, in the year, month, Indiction and Pontificate, as above, in presence of Robert Boyd, son of Patrick Boyd of Hungryhill; John Boyd of Nairstoun; James Cunynghame of Clonbeith; James Wyllie; and Robert Colvile; with several other witnesses called and required to the premises.

"Subscribed by George Boyd and John Parker, notaries, with the usual docquets."

Such is a brief outline of the ecclesiastical history of Kilmarnock. It would be interesting to trace the town from the first plantation of the church of Marnock, on the winding banks of a rivulet, then unpolluted by anything more impure than the floods of winter, but now thick and muddy with the debris of a large population and numerous manufactories. In the absence of all documentary proof, in the earlier stages of its existence, imagination may be allowed to exercise some sway. Besides the church, round which most of our towns, villages, and hamlets have sprung up, there was a mill in early times at Kilmarnock, so that it possessed a combined source of attraction to the surrounding neighbourhood.

---

* This transfer was originally in the form of a lease, to the effect that Robert, sixth Lord Boyd, had tack and sett of the parsonage teinds and sheaves of the parish of Kilmarnock, for nineteen years, from John, Archbishop of Sanct Andrews and Abbot of Kilwinning, for nine score fifteen lbs. 8s. 2d. usuall money of this realme. The lease, which is preserved in the Kilmarnock charter chest, is dated 27th June 1612. It has the seal of the Abbot of Kilwinning attached to it in excellent preservation.

M‘Kay, the historian of Kilmarnock,* establishes the fact of the mill very clearly: "The Cross of Kilmarnock [one of the most spacious of any town in the west of Scotland] was, in early times, the site of a corn-mill, which was driven by a lade or stream that flowed through the same spot.† *Sheelinghill*, or *Sheilinghill*, near the railway station, is so called from being the place where the corn was *sheild* or prepared for grinding. Regarding the exact time of the erection of the mill we have no information. It appears, however, by the following extract from the town treasurer's book, to have been removed about the beginning of the eighteenth century: '1703, June 26.—Paid to Ballyie Hunter for the street wher the *miln* stood, £21, 9s. 4d. Scots.'‡ We may likewise state, that the name of the last occupant of the mill was Rankin, from whom are descended the Rankins of Wardneuk, in this parish, and also William Rankin, Esq., postmaster of Kilmarnock. The new mill, at a short distance from the town, on the banks of the Irvine, was also occupied at one time by the same Rankins, and was built, we believe, as a substitute for the one at the cross; hence it obtained the name of the *new mill*."

The mill and the church of Kilmarnock stood thus in close proximity, and the town seems gradually to have grown up, clustering round them, or lengthening itself along the various roads or avenues by which they were approached. Kilmarnock had also the advantage of being situated on the great line of road leading from Glasgow to Ayr, and formed a convenient halting-place or stage on the way. The consequence was, that the town, as it began to increase, gradually became elongated out of proportion in the direction of the leading thoroughfare, north and south. Speaking of Kilmarnock, about the middle of the eighteenth century, M‘Kay says it had "a mean and inelegant appearance. The streets were crooked and narrow; the houses were low and poorly lighted; and to many of them that were two stories high were attached outside stairs, that not only confined the already limited thoroughfares, but gave to the houses themselves a rude and clumsy aspect. The principal streets at that time were those now called High Street, Soulis Street, Fore Street, Back Street, Strand Street, and Sandbed Street, which, with some buildings at the Cross, which was nearly square, Nethertonholm, and a few back tenements and lanes, formed the whole of the town."

The first recorded attempts at improvement occur in 1702, shortly after the town had obtained a charter of the common good of the burgh from the Earl of Kilmarnock, when it was enacted, evidently with the view of encouraging building, that all feuars were to have liberty to raise stones in any part of the Craigs, they being always first obliged to acquaint the magistrates. In the same year, it appears an act had been passed ordering the streets to be causewayed, one of the minutes running thus: The Strand, in conformity with the act for causewaying, to be causewayed. The Earl of Kilmarnock, Lairds of Fergushill, Pitcon, and Langlands, together with the *Provost** of Kilmarnock, order the bailies to proceed with the causewaying.

In 1726 a penn or drain was completed in Strand Street, for the sanitary improvment, of course, of the locality.

In 1733 pumps were first erected at the Cross. The minute ordering this to be done is dated 23d July, where it is also stated, that "Bailie Gilchrist and widow Black having carried a penn, or the syver, near to the well a good length, the same to be carried on to Kockmarleoche house," &c. But where this house stood we have no knowledge.

In 1735, 11th August, the Tolbooth, then much out of repair, was ordered to be renewed. This building stood at the corner of Cheapside, and was bounded by the water of Kilmarnock. Its situation and appearance is well described by M‘Kay. It "was situated west from the Cross, nearly opposite the present Crown Hotel. It was a gloomy looking structure, two stories high, with shops on the ground floor facing the street. Immediately behind these, down a lane at the west end of the building, was the Thieves' Hole; and above were two dungeon-like apartments, called the Tolbooth, at the stair-head of which hung the *juggs*, or iron collar, in which petty delinquents were doomed to stand for a given time. The part of the upper flat nearest the Cross formed the Hall, or Court-house, the entrance to which was by a broad outside stair faced with a parapet. From the head of this stair the whole of the market-place was seen; and here, on public occasions, such as kings' birth-days, the Bailies and Councillors, accompanied by the Lord of the Manor, would assemble to drink his Ma-

---

* A History of Kilmarnock, from an early period to the present time, &c. By Archibald M‘Kay, author of "Recreations of Leisure Hours," &c. Kilmarnock. 1848.

† Which lade, having been covered over, now serves as a drain for carrying away the waste water of the upper part of the town.

‡ The "mills of Kilmarnock" are mentioned in the Town Books in 1686.

* We do not find the name of Provost anywhere else mentioned.

jesty's health, and give other loyal and patriotic toasts."

There is at least one notable record in the Town Books of the accuracy of this statement, and that refers to the Hanoverian succession. The inhabitants of Kilmarnock have long been famed for their constitutional principles, and on this occasion they shone conspicuous :—10th Aug. 1714.—The said day King George was proclaimed in a most solemn manner. The Earl of Kilmarnock, his bailies and the gentlemen above named* being present, and the haill inhabitants standing in array at the Cross, the Council-house stair-head covered with carpet, a large bonfire at the Cross, and ringing of the bells, all the royal healths were drank, and several other loyal healths; and the night concluded with the greatest demonstration of joy; and advertisement put in the Gazette thereof. Bailie James Thomson read the proclamation to Robert Paterson, who proclaimed it.

On the death of George I., in 1727, the Earl of Kilmarnock sent an express with the intelligence, ordering the train-bands to be in readiness to proclaim the Prince of Wales as George II.

The Tolbooth had been in a very indifferent state at the time we refer to—more gloomy and incommodious than described by Mr M'Kay. It had only one apartment, the "Black Hole," for the reception of prisoners, male and female, an evil which at length engaged the attention of the Town Council. 27th August 1737—As "frequently men and women are put in the prison promiscuously, and sundry inconveniences occasioned by there being only one prison, do agree now, in separation of the Tolbooth, that one partition be made therein, so as there may be two distinct prisons."

There had been a clock and bell attached to the Tolbooth at an earlier period than is shown by the town records. The first notice we find of it occurs 2d Feb. 1730, when Thomas Wallace, gunsmith, is appointed keeper of the clock, and to ring the bell, with a salary of 20 merks, and ten merks more, to be paid by the Kirk session. In 1735, when repairs were ordered to be made on the Tolbooth, Robert Craig, clockmaker, was commissioned to make a new clock, which he undertook to do for £25 sterling. 17th Dec. 1744, the bell was ordered to be rung at six o'clock morning, and eight evening.

A considerable impetus was given to the improvement of the town on the acquisition of the lands and superiority of Kilmarnock by the Earl of Glencairn in 1749. For example the following

minute: "22d June 1749.—The Earl of Glencairn, now superior of the burgh, is inclined to purchase the whole grounds within the town's enclosure, at the end of the town, next to his wards, with Barbadoes Green, that he may the better be enabled to extend his policy and improvements there, which being considered by the Council, and the situation of their right to the same grounds, and burden of the ministers' stipend affecting the same, and the advantage that may accrue to the place by his Lordship being encouraged to resyde in it, they are unanimously of opinion and resolve to do all that lyes in their power to serve his Lordship in the matter, on reasonable terms, and with safety to the town." A committee was appointed to treat with the Earl, then in town, and the following was the result: 22d June 1749.—The committee met his Lordship.—The present rent of the lands being £292 Scots, and the stipends payable to the second minister furth thereof and the town's other lands, being £320 Scots yearly, the said Earl has condescended to relieve the Town Council of the whole stipend in lieu and satisfaction of the price of the lands; which being considered by the Council, and that they reap £28 Scots yearly of benefit by the sale, they unanimously resolve to agree to the terms, giving Barbadoes to the Earl, reserving, however, a feu-right to bleach on the green between the houses and the water, and of access to the wells. Also to uplift and dispose of the annual rent of three thousand five hundred merks Scots as a part of the said stipend stipulate by the writs thereof to fall into the Town Council's hands when a vacancy happens, &c.

Those acquainted with the locality will have no difficulty in understanding the extent of the ground thus disposed of. Kilmarnock House, the policies of which the Earl wished to improve and extend, had been built, or partly built, by the forfeited Earl of Kilmarnock, as a family residence after the destruction of Dean Castle, the ancient stronghold of the barony.

In 1752 two improvements were suggested, the building of the town bridge—the one, we presume, which still stands, connecting Sandbed with the Strand—and the Green Bridge—lately superseded by a new one. The use of the town quarries were to be given for the erection of both; and in the case of the town bridge the Commissioners of Supply were to be applied to for aid, the old bridge "being inconvenient." To these schemes the Earl of Glencairn was a liberal subscriber.

The building of the town bridge, however, does not appear to have been carried into effect at that time; for in 1762 we find a minute—March 31

---

* We have omitted the names.

—to the effect that the new bridge shall be built on the site of the old—the old having become much injured by the floods; and again, so late as March 1, 1766, the Council resolve to "apply for one hundred pounds from the shire, voted some time ago towards building the bridge, on condition that a parapet should be built upon the Sandbed dyke, and the flesh-market removed therefrom.—Resolve to build a flesh-market, also a bridge and parapet at flesh-market, &c.

Thus we see that the flesh-market was originally held in the Sandbed, and that the present flesh-market, with the bridge, was built subsequent to 1766.

One of the greatest improvements carried into effect by the Earl of Glencairn, was the opening up of the new street between Kilmarnock and Riccarton, together with the square called Glencairn Square, which was done in 1765.

In March 1770 contributions were entered into to build a bridge at David M'Kean's steps. Stones were to be allowed from the town's quarries and winter course, but the bridge was not to be considered a town's bridge. We know not whether this bridge was ever built. In the same year it was projected that a weigh-house should be built, and the subscribers for a bridge at Townhead were allowed at the same time to quarry stones from the town quarries. The weigh-house, however, was not contracted for before the 17th April 1781, so that the authorities of Kilmarnock in former times could not be accused of doing any thing without due deliberation.

Kilmarnock, as it stands, may be considered quite a modern town; and many of its inhabitants can recollect the formation of what are now the principal streets, as well as the building of most of those shops and other tenements which constitute its acknowledged superiority. The great era of the improvement of Kilmarnock, in point of architecture and the widening of the streets, may be set down as commencing with the beginning of the present century. The old Council-house was taken down, and the new and new Council Rooms built, about the year 1805. The new bridge opened up a new and comparatively spacious passage through the town, which, in the course of some years afterwards, was followed by the opening of Portland and King Streets, taking away from the old and crooked thoroughfares that superabundance of traffic they were so ill capable of sustaining, but of which they had so long possessed the entire monopoly.

The rapid extension of Kilmarnock, so remarkable within the memory of its existing inhabitants, is no doubt to be attributed, partly to its central position as the heart of a rich agricultural and mineral district, but still more, perhaps, to the manufacturing and trading enterprise of its inhabitants. To trace the origin of this mercantile spirit cannot fail to be interesting, and we shall endeavour to do so as far as the records of the burgh, and other sources of information, enable us. These records, it is to be regretted, do not extend to a remote period. The first charter erecting Kilmarnock into a burgh of barony was granted in favour of Thomas fifth Lord Boyd;[*] a second was obtained in 1672, in favour of William the first Earl of Kilmarnock, whose grandson, the third Earl, in 1700, gave a charter to the town of the whole common good, consisting of "the common greens of the said town, shops under the tolbooth thereof, the weights, pocks, and measures, the troan,[†] and weights thereof, and the customs of the faires and weekly mercats, and all other customes belonging to the said burgh and barony." It is thus apparent that there can be no burgh records of an ancient date. The first of the "Kilmarnock Books" preserved commences 15th June 1686, when "the haill tenants of the burrow of Kilmarnock and Grougar [were] directed to mak payment to the Earll of Kilmarnock, and his chalmerlane, in his name, of all maills formerly due, or now due to them, for the Whitsunday ending the year 1686," &c. The sederunt is styled, "The Court of the Town and Burrow of Kilmarnock and Grougar, holden in the Tolbuith of Kilmarnock," &c. Although a burgh of barony at this time, Kilmarnock did not enjoy the privilege of a magistracy, the lord of the manor, or his chamberlain, who, in 1686, was Charles Dalrymple, [‡] presiding in the court as bailie.

The first magistrates of the burgh of Kilmarnock were appointed in 1695, as the following extract from the records show:

"16th Aug. 1695.—Master Robert Stewart, and Mr John Boyd, one of the regents of the College of Glasgow, tutors-testamentars to ane noble Earl, William Earl of Kilmarnock, &c., for the better administration of justice, seeing "that the office of baillie cannot be dewlie exercised in the persone of ane man," appoint the following magistrates and councillors for one year: Charles Dalrymple, writer (factor to the Earl); Alexander Muir, elder; Robert Wright; Mathew Habkin; Robert Milligane; William Morris and Jasper Tough, apothecaries; James Adam and James

---

* Boyd charter chest.

† Before the erection of the weigh-house, the "troan" stood at the Cross. It was a wooden erection, consisting merely of a roof supported by three or four pillars.

‡ He lived in Langlands House.

Wilsone, bonnet-makers; William Sloss, and James Smith, in Backsyde, skinners; James Cathcart, and James Gilkieson, hammermen; John Miller, taillzeor; William Bracunrig, shoemaker, and James Thomsone, weiver, to commune with the saids bailies in the management of the common goods and public affairs of the said burgh, for the space foresaid." [John M'Leslie, present bailie, and Robert Paterson, merchant, were the baron bailies alluded to.]

The first act of the Council was to the effect, that an extract should be got of the town weights of Irvine, that the town weights might be adjusted thereby; and that Friday should be the market-day in all time coming.

From this period, the Earls of Kilmarnock and their successors, as lords of the manor, continued to appoint the magistrates of the burgh annually. This was done from a leet, or list of persons, selected by the Council, a deputation of whom waited upon the Earl at the Castle of Dean. In 1723, the Council had an opportunity of electing their own bailies. The minutes bear, that "as the Earl of Kilmarnock was out of the country this year, and the time expiring for presenting the leet of five persons, out of whom two to be chosen for bailies, therefore, conform to the town's right, granted by the late Earl of Kilmarnock,* appoynt Mungo Moor, &c. to go to the place of Dean this day (11th October 1723) or to-morrow, and thereat, under form of instrument, to present and make offer of the list chosen by the Town Council, upon the 3d of September last, in terms of the town's right, &c. This having been done, and no commission arrived from the Earl, the Council, on the 15th of October, declared the right of election to lie with themselves. The same thing occurred in 1732:—"14th Oct. 1732.—Instrument produced of having been at the Dean, and offered thereat the leet of five for the bailies, and there being no commission from the Earl of Kilmarnock, the Council declare the privilege of choosing the bailies to have devolved upon the Council."

The Earl appears at last to have become alive to the danger of his repeated omissions in this respect, and still detained abroad, he next year took care to furnish his Countess with the neces-

sary authority to act in his absence. This led to an assertion of independence upon the part of the Council, commensurate probably with the growing importance of the burgh, but hardly to be expected from a small body of burgesses towards their feudal superior. The substance of the minute is as follows:—29th September 1733. Produce extract of commission from the Earl of Kilmarnock in favour of Anna Countess of Kilmarnock, authorising her to constitute bailies, &c. And the question being put as to the right of the Earl to delegate his power, the Council "judge it expedient to avoid disputing on that head for the present year, out of regard for the family, and agrees to sustain the Countess's commission as sufficient to authorise her, but prejudice allways to the Town Council to quarrell the validity of any such commission for the future, and declare that their present acquiescence shall noways homolgate the same."

The last time the Earl of Kilmarnock appointed the magistrates of the burgh was on the 30th September 1745, by which time his lordship had engaged in the unfortunate rising under Prince Charles-Edward. The mandate was dated the 26th of that month.

In 1746, Oct. 13, the Council produced "ane instrument," &c. "taken against James Boyd of Kilmarnock, Esq. commonly called Lord Boyd,* on the 29th of September last, offering to him the leett, and containing his reasoun of refusal to nominate, and no commission having been received of any one empowered to nominate the Council, declare the choosing to fall upon the Council."

In 1747-8 the leet was presented at the "manor place of Dean, James Boyd, Esq. being furth of the kingdom," when the nomination as formerly devolved upon the Council themselves.

In 1764, the lands and superiority of Kilmarnock having previously passed into the hands of the Earl of Glencairn, the Earl refused to nominate bailies from the leet—probably in consequence of the riot which had taken place a short time before at the induction of the Rev. Mr Lindsay to the Low Church, when both patron and presentee were treated with no small disrespect. With their usual independence, the Council forthwith proceeded to appoint the magistrates themselves. The dispute, however, was not easily laid. In 1766, the Earl having still declined, the Treasurer repaired with the leet to Dean Castle, as of old, and having performed this ceremony, the nomination was held to devolve upon the Council.

---

* In the charter of 1700, such contingencies were thus provided against: "And in caice it shall happen us, our airs or successors forsaid, not to be living within the forsaid bounds the time of the offering the forsaid leittis, then and in that caice, the saids bayllies and counsell for the time, making up and offering the forsaid leitts to us and our forsaids at our manor-place of Dean, in presence of ane nottar and witnesses as efficirs, shall be also valide, effectuall, and sufficient to them to elect and choose haylies in manner forsaid, as if we, our airs or successors, were personally present."

* Son of the unhappy Earl, and who succeeded to the title and estates of Errol.

The Earl, however, seems to have brought the matter before the Court of Session, and in 1769 obtained a decreet declarator in his favour.

In 1786, the bailies were nominated by Miss Scott, afterwards Duchess of Portland, who had in that year purchased the estate of Kilmarnock from the Glencairn family. Next year, however, we find the magistrates protesting against the nomination of "Miss Henrietta Scott and her curators;" and the matter seems to have been adjusted by a quorum of the commissioners of the Earl of Glencairn and Miss Scott appointing the bailies.

Thus we have the origin of the civic government of Kilmarnock. By the charter of William third Earl of Kilmarnock, the burgh was empowered to elect seventeen councillors, and of these two bailies were appointed out of a leet of five by the superior. As barons of Kilmarnock, the family of Boyd had also the right of "pit and gallows," and in the "Head Courts of the lands and barony of Kilmarnock and Grougar," continued to exercise their rights down to the abolition of feudal jurisdictions in 1746. In 1551, before the first charter was obtained, erecting Kilmarnock into a burgh of barony, Lord Boyd had a commission of justiciary for trying certain persons in Kilmarnock.* There can therefore be little doubt that the Lords Boyd actually judged in criminal causes, and the rising ground, now the site of a dissenting church, still called the Gallows-knowe, was, it may be presumed, the spot upon which the culprits suffered capital punishment. There are, however, no records of the "Head Court" of Kilmarnock at so early a period—the first we find, as previously stated, dating no farther back than 1686.

One or two extracts from these books may not be inappropriate here. No small portion of the minutes relate to cases of debt. The first entry of general interest refers to the troublous times immediately prior to the Revolution:—

31st July 1686.—The quhilk day, we, the tenants within the toun of Kilmarnock under-subscribed, bind and oblige us that we, our families, cotters and servants respectively sall serve personallie and regularlie, under the pain of the tenant, cotters and servants contravening, their leving of the half of their movables, respectively each for their ownselves, conform to the 24th act of the first Parliament of King James the seventh.

[To this minute 63 signatures are attached. A number of the tenants, however, did not subscribe the minute, in consequence of which their tacks were declared null.]

* Original document in Kilmarnock charter chest, dated May 1551.

VOL. II.

13th July 1686.—The quhilk day James Thomson, ane of the dragoons of horse, Adam Black's companie, was decerned to pay to John Tod, cutler in Kilmarnock, the sum of 3s. 4d. Scots; and the said John Tod to give up to James Thomson his wyflis body cott, quhilk was pandit for threepence, and paid to the said James.

1687.—An act passed, that in consequence of the hazard to which the inhabitants were exposed by disorderly persons becoming tenants of houses, no house should be let in future to any one who could not bring a certificate of character satisfactory to the bailie, the tenants at the same time obliging themselves to free the town of all begging by their cottars. [The peasantry must have been in a very low state at this period.]

1695.—[The Council having then been appointed]. Several acts were passed for regulating the social condition of the town, such as no ale to be sold by vintners after ten o'clock on Saturday nights, and that their jugs and stoups should be properly adjusted; and certain parties were appointed to keep a proper account of the common goods of the burgh against Michaelmas.

1698.—Enacted, that in case any refuse the appointment of bailie, they should pay a fine of £50 Scots.

1702.—Act against swearing and banning, drunkenness, &c.

1711.—That all persons sell or retail their meal in the mealmarket, and not elsewhere.*

1723.—Enacted, that no party before the bailie court shall employ a procurator, unless by mutual consent, or both parties having procurators.

1724.—Burgess entry-money first exacted.

—— The October mercat of horse and kyne, on the last day of the fair, to be held in the town's common green in future, in place of the Holm, which is enclosed.

26th July 1726.—In presence of the Earl of Kilmarnock, agree to alter the days of the fair, in consequence of their frequently falling on a Saturday. To be held as follows:—The fair formerly held on the 15th and 16th July shall be keepit on the 3d Wednesday and Thursday of the said month; and the fair formerly held on the 25th and 26th days of October to be keepit up the 3d Wednesday and Thursday of the said month.

1727.—Burgess-tickets formerly £18, 18s. Scots; but none to be admitted in future under £24.

18th Nov. 1729.—Iron weights to be substituted for lead ones in the meal mercat.

* According to M'Kay's History, the mealmarket was built in 1705, and rebuilt in 1840. It is situated in the High Street.

1st Dec. 1730.—£300 Scots to be cast among the inhabitants for the support of the poor.

1785.—No country butcher to be allowed to sell butcher meat in the burgh unless on the market day.

No account of the common good of the burgh was kept earlier than 1692. From 1690 to 1692 the income amounted to £1484, 13s. 4d. Scots; the expenditure to £1215, 11s. 6d. From 1726 to 1727—one year—the income was £2765, 17s. 7d. Scots; the expenditure £2929, 15s. 5d.

With reference to the trade of the burgh, it seems to be admitted on all hands that a trade in leather, shoes and bonnets, had sprung up at a very early period. Significant of these branches or incorporations, a bonnet, a pair of leather breeches, and a pair of shoes used to be paraded annually at Fastern's E'en races, as the nominal reward of the victors, and that from time immemorial. Of the six incorporated trades of Kilmarnock, speaking of modern times, that of the bonnet-makers is held to be the oldest, their charter dating back to 1646; but there must have been an incorporated body as early as 1603, for in an act passed by the Town Council in 1713, commencing, "We, William Earl of Kilmarnock," &c. special reference is made to a law passed by his predecessor and his bailie in 1603, prohibiting all persons from "dressing hose or stockings made by any persons that are not *incorporate in the trade.*" It is evident, therefore, that there was an incorporate body, either of stocking or bonnet-makers, in or before 1603, although it seems probable from the minute that the incorporation of bonnet-makers also exercised the craft of hose or stocking making. It is apparent that the town of Kilmarnock had attained to considerable importance as a place of trade and manufacture towards the close of the sixteenth century. Pont, who made his survey of Scotland about the beginning of the seventeenth century—1609—speaks in a lively strain of the appearance of Kilmarnock: "Kilmernock-toune and Kirk is a large village, and of grate repair. It hath in it a weekly market; it hath a fair stone bridge over the river Mernock, vich glydes hard by the said toune till it fallis in the river Irving. It hath a pretty church, from vich the village, castle, and lordschip takes its name," &c. At this period, as we have seen, it carried on the making of hose, stockings and bonnets, and no doubt shoemaking and leather-tanning.* M'Kay, in his history, states that about the year 1646 the bonnet trade "was in a flou-

rishing condition, and fears seem to have been entertained by the followers of the craft that it was then passing too rapidly into other hands. In glancing over the charter of this venerable corporation, we find that a court was 'holden at Kirkdyke the twenty ane day of December sixteen hundred and fourty seven years, by a noble Lord, James Lord Boyd, John Cunninghame of Redlaw and John Mowat, his Lordship's bailies,' and that about thirty bonnet-manufacturers 'compeared,' and complained of various abuses having crept into the craft, such as feeing each other's servants, and servants leaving their masters' work to do their own. At this court it was ordained that "no servant or other person presume to take up work at their own hand until first he be thought worthy by the craft, and have given in his *sey* [trial-piece] to them."

That the trade in "milned stockins" was one of very considerable importance during the seventeenth century is evident from the various attempts made to promote its efficiency, when symptoms of decay had begun to manifest themselves at the beginning of the eighteenth century. In 1711, for example, the Town Council enacted, that owing to the great abuse and decay of the trade in milned stockings, all stockings wrought for milning to be brought to the inspector appointed to see that the manufacture was properly carried on. An act was passed, at the same time, rescinding several previous enactments in reference to "milned stockings."—"We, William, Earl of Kilmarnock," &c. The act then goes on to refer to a law passed by his predecessor, with consent of the Bailie of Kilmarnock, in 1603, by which no master nor servant dress hose or stockings made by any persons that are not incorporate in the trade, under the pain of five pounds Scots; and farther, that no master or servant dress any stockings but to such as are to wear them themselves, the person or persons to be employed in dressing to acquaint some of the trade or others [the parties appointed for this purpose] and to have their allowance to do so. None of the trade to buy from any person but hose or stockings milned or raw: and also, considering an act passed by himself in 1706, which confirmed the original rights granted by his predecessors, no person to make hose, stockings or bonnets save for their own use, unless sighted and allowed by the visitors, &c.

Another minute of the Town Council, 11th Aug. 1713, is to the following effect: The bonnet-makers having monopolised and enhanced the dressing of all milned stockings to one person, a member of the corporation, to whom the privilege was rouped yearly for the payment of an inconsider-

---

* The first notice we find in reference to the latter trade in the Council Records occurs in 1687, when an act was passed against washing skins in the miln-dam.

able sum to the trade, and this practice having been petitioned against, as well as the whole corporation of bonnet-makers convened and examined thereanent, the Council find, that at the time of their approving and confirming the former privileges of the trade, "the trade of milned stockings in Kilmarnock was come to little or no perfection; the bonnet-makers and others incorporate with them might then be able to furnish all such stockings that occasion offered to sell; but since that time the said incorporation being very sensible and convinced they were not able themselves to furnish and supply the country and kingdom, and also countries abroad, with these stockings, have hitherto, notwithstanding of their privileges above written, allowed and permitted all persons that had a mind to use their employment that way, and having dressed to these persons their stockings, without obliging them to enter," &c. and the said trade in stockings is so far improved and advanced that it is become beneficial and advantageous to the community of our said burgh, and intending the farther promotion and advancement of so good a project of trade, have lately, with our Bailies and Town Council of Kilmarnock, passed ane act for the better regulation thereof, appointing visitors to inspect all such stockings, and stamp all that are sufficient thereof with the town's seal, provided for that effect; and conceiving it inconvenient that the dressing of stockings should be monopolised, all who deal in spinning, carding, working or vending said stockings, should be obliged to incorporate. All former acts on the subject were consequently repealed; and all monopoly prohibited in dressing stockings, every person being free to make their own stockings, provided they employ members of the incorporation to dress them, who must do it at a reasonable rate, otherwise they are free to get them dressed where they please.

The manufacture of milned stockings must at this period have formed one of the staple products of Kilmarnock. That the trade of Kilmarnock, however, was not limited to a single branch or two is apparent from a minute of Council, dated 30th Nov. 1725, when certain parties were appointed for stamping, according to the act of Parliament regulating the goodness, length and breadth of serges, fingrums, (?) playding and linen clothes. In 1726 [15th May] the "Town agree to give £30 Scots for the encouragement of the linen trade in the town and parish of Kilmarnock to the owner, and £6 Scots to the weaver, of the best white linen web of 84 ells or above, divided as the law directs, and spun and wrought within the town or parish of Kilmarnock." Such was

the public spirit of the worthy burghers of Kilmarnock at the commencement of last century.

The trade in milned stockings seems to have occasioned great anxiety in the community. In spite of every effort it continued to decay, no doubt from causes which could not be controlled. Still renewed attempts were repeatedly made to remove the supposed cause of the decline; as for example the following minute, which we give at length:—

"14th June 1729.—The milned stocking trade having fallen off, in consequence of abuses in the making, the former act of 1712 is revived in full force, with the additional clauses—That all the said stockins be made of the finest wool, plucked or clipped, and that they be made of one colour and fineness from end to end; and the whole stockins made for common sale to men to be of such fineness as that one pair shall not take under five cutts of yearn, and not under sixty two loops on each wire.* Item, that the maker shall be obliged upon oath to report to the visitors what faults he shall find in the stockins, either before or after walking; so also that the dressers dress none that are faulty; nor shall they fraudulently conceal or patch up the faults, but report the same likewise to the visitors upon oath. Item, that none of the said stockins shall be accounted sufficient that are woven upon the bonnet-makers' pricks, and that the yearn be spun and twinned as slack as possible. Item, that any stockins found insufficient by the visitors shall be clipped an inch or two in the head, and burnt bare in the upper part of the foot with an iron, and shall also suffer a fine at the sight of the visitors, not exceeding six shilling Scots upon ilk pair; and that all insufficient stockins shall be sent by the visitors, after the first inspection thairof, straight to the miln for wacking, and be returned by the wacker to the visitors, to be dressed at the owner's charges. Item, that all stockins sold or exposed to sale within the toun or precincts thereof, without being inspected by the visitors, shall be confiscate till payment of twelve shilling Scots on ilk pair. And that none of the inhabitants shall dress or expose to sale any of the said stockins either within the town or anywhere else till first they be inspected, under the said penalty of twelve shillings Scots for ilk pair, the dresser's wages being always under the regulation of the Baillies and Town Council. And lastly, none of the said stockins to be contracted for raw, till once they be milned and scoured,

---

* The stockings had thus been wrought or knitted with wires, and afterwards subjected to the fulling mill—hence the name of "milned stockings."

under the penalty of six shillings Scots for ilk pair sua sold or contracted for, both to the buyer and seller. Declaring there is nothing in this act to hinder the making of unlaid stockins for women, providing such stockins be made conform to the regulations, except as to wideness and length."

The incorporation of glovers—18th Sept. 1729 —lay a petition before the Magistrates and Council, complaining that certain masters, journeymen and apprentices, had "sold leather breeches without being stamped." The Earl of Kilmarnock, who seems to have taken a great interest in promoting the trade of the burgh, together with the Bailies and Council, pass a stringent law against all who either sell or buy leather breeches unstamped.

2d Oct. 1729.—Similar complaints having been made of abuses in "the manufacture of wisecaps, commonly named striped capes, a stringent act, similar to that in reference to milned stockings, was passed regarding the manufacture of these caps.

Another minute, 25th May 1730, states that the act respecting the "manufacture of wisecaps" is to be put in full force, owing to the decay of the trade.

Serges, a description of woollen cloth for women's petticoats, is frequently mentioned in the records, and seems to have been a branch of manufacture of some consideration about this period. 4th June 1734, the trade of serges so much decayed, in consequence of using coarse wool, the Council enact that no coarse wool is to be purchased for that manufacture.

17th Feb. 1737.—A committee appointed to take into consideration the state of the "course and paceloom coverletts made or sold in the burgh," in order that they may be inspected and stamped.

23d June 1737.—The Earl of Kilmarnock present in Council. New regulations made for the serge manufacture, which, in spite of all previous exertions, was not conform to act of Parliament.

1742.—Former acts to be enforced in reference to the serge and stocking manufacture.

Notwithstanding these various enactments, occasioned by the alleged decay of particular branches of trade, the town of Kilmarnock seems to have been steadily increasing in commercial importance, insomuch that, on the 11th April 1745, the Earl of Kilmarnock present, the Council agree to petition Parliament next session for the privilege of imposing two pennies Scots on the pint of ale, publicly brewed and vended in the town, as funds were wanted to make various improvements commensurate with the *increased importance of manufactures.*

" The manufacture of woollen cloths," says M'Kay, " was introduced about the year 1728 by Miss Maria Gardiner, (half-aunt to the late Lord Kilmarnock,) who, through a praiseworthy spirit of patriotism, and for the encouragement of useful arts, brought spinners and weavers of carpet from the town of Dalkeith, then distinguished for its woollen products. Under the encouraging auspices of this lady, the carpet trade, which is now one of our chief sources of wealth, increased, comparatively speaking, to a considerable extent; and we feel somewhat surprised that her memory has not been preserved in the town by some public memorial . . . . We regret that it is not in our power to give a more extended notice of Miss Gardiner. Even the place of her nativity and the time of her death are unknown to us. It appears, however, from Loch's "Essays on the Trades and Fisheries of Scotland," that she lived to an advanced age; for she was alive in 1777 or 1778, about fifty years after she introduced the woollen manufactures."

It is strange that no notice of Miss Gardiner, and the introduction of so important a branch of manufacture, is to be found, in so far as we have discovered, among the records of the burgh; but we think the origin of what is still called, par excellence, " the factory" may be traced from the Town Books. The first notice we find in reference to wool is to this effect:—26th Dec. 1728.—Robert Boyd having been appointed *wool sorter* by the Trustees for Improving the Fisheries, &c., he is to have ground and be allowed to build a work-place, with store-house and grass field, at the Old Dam.

Farther, another minute of the Town Council, in the same year, states that the Council " in consideration of the Board of Trustees having appointed Robert Boyd, sorter of wool for this burgh, gave him ground upon the most convenient spot of the Old Dam, to build a *woollen factory* at his own charges, the town reserving the right to take it from him at the end of three years, on paying his outlay."

No more occurs in reference to the woollen manufacture until 1743, when we find the Council giving a piece of ground " to the Society erecting a house at the Greenhead for manufacturing coarse wool, to straight their side-wall to join the washing-house at the Greenhead."

We know not whether the woollen factory projected by Robert Boyd was ever erected, or whether the scheme had merged into the hands of the Society here alluded to; but it is evident that the latter was the origin of the extensive work still known as the Greenside Factory. What inclines us to believe that they were one and the same, is the fact, that in virtue of the reservation in the grant to Robert Boyd in 1728, to take the work from him at the end of three years, we find the Town Council, in 1773, disposing of the whole premises to "Richard Oswald, Esq. of Auchincruive; John Campbell and William Coats, merchants in Glasgow; John Hunter, jun., merchant, Kilmarnock; James Wilson, senior, merchant, Kilmarnock; James Wilson, junior, merchant, there; William Cuninghame, merchant, Glasgow; Elizabeth and Barbara Cuninghame, only children and nearest lawful heirs of the deceased Alexander Cuninghame, merchant in Glasgow; John and Hugh Parkers, merchants in Kilmarnock, and William Boyd, carpet weaver there —all partners in the company of the said woollen manufactory in Kilmarnock, known by the firm of James Wilson and Company, according to their respective shares." This was, no doubt, the woollen factory at the Greenhead.

Loch, in his "Essays," states, that about the year 1777 there were two hundred and forty looms employed in the weaving of silk, which had been introduced seven years previously; sixty-six looms in the weaving of carpets; forty in the weaving of linen; thirty in the weaving of blankets; thirty in the weaving of serges and shalloons; twenty in the weaving of duffles, together with six frames for the making of stockings. There were also two tanyards, and a good trade in shoes. The blanket manufacture was carried on by Robert Thomson and Company. The other principal merchants and manufacturers were James Wilson and Son, and Messrs Parker, Hunter and Smith. From this period the trade of Kilmarnock went on flourishingly for many years. In addition to the old staple manufactures of the place, the weaving of muslin and the printing of calicoes was introduced. Before the close of the eighteenth century, the annual value of the manufactures was estimated as follows:—Carpets, £21,400; shoes and boots, £21,216; skins tanned, £9,000; sheep and lamb skins dressed, £6,500; printed calicoes, £6,500, &c. During the early part of the present century, while the war continued, the increase and prosperity of Kilmarnock was not less extraordinary. The first serious check experienced was during the general stagnation in 1816, and since it has been subjected to all the various depressions which almost periodically overtake the country; still the commercial spirit of the people is of the most elastic description, adapting itself with decided tact and talent to whatever promises the greatest amount of remuneration for the time. The introduction, in 1824, of worsted shawl printing, fabrics which had long previously been produced of superior quality by

the looms of Kilmarnock, gave a fresh impetus to the trade; and at one period no fewer than 3000 looms were employed in producing them. The printing business, as it is termed, grew to an amazing extent, employing, as it did, in 1847, no fewer than about 2000 hands, including boys and girls.

The gradual increase of Kilmarnock, previous to the current century, may be gathered from various circumstances. In 1547, at the election of Alexander Boyd as parish clerk, there were about three hundred parishioners, or, as we shall presume, heads of families, which, multiplied by five, the usual average of a family, give about 1500 inhabitants of all ages. In 1731, the inhabitants had become so numerous, that the parish kirk was incapable of affording the necessary accommodation. On the 11th January of that year, the Town Council resolved to build "a new and additional church, in consequence of the populousness of the parish."[*] The Earl of Kilmarnock, Mr Orr of Grougar, and other principal proprietors, to be memorialised on the subject. The Earl and Mr Orr entered warmly into the design, contributing 1000 merks between them towards the fund. The latter also procured some subscriptions in Glasgow. The Town Council of Kilmarnock advanced £30 sterling towards the building. By the 6th May 1731, the subscriptions for the new kirk were in such a forward state, that the Council appointed Charles Dalrymple of Langlands, and James Rae of Walston, one of the bailies, and others, to choose and purchase ground for the kirk. 7th Nov. 1734.—Four shillings Scots imposed upon the boll of malt brewed within the burgh, over and above the usual custom, until the expense of the new kirk be defrayed, and "ane thousand merks" to be borrowed in the meantime for that purpose.[†] 2d March 1737.—Committee appointed to arrange about the letting of seats in the new kirk, and "ane yearly allowance to Mr Hill, present incumbent, for his encouragement," &c. 18th April 1737.—Twelve hundred merks to be borrowed to pay off the debts owing for the new kirk. 31st Oct. 1737.—The Earl and Council consent to an act of the head court of the burgh, agreeing to give £30 sterling yearly for an assistant to Mr Hill out of the vacant stipend and customs on malt, and also to a fund of not less than five hundred merks yearly for "ane assistant to Mr Hill, to be levied from the duties and customs on malt, and seat

* The inhabitants were unwilling to aid in the building, unless sittings were secured to them in proportion to their contributions.

† The thousand merks were borrowed from the Society of Merchants.

mails of the new kirk," so soon as there shall be constant service in it. 31st Oct. 1737.—Mr Robert Dow agreed upon as a fit assistant to Mr Hill. 21st Oct. 1738.—Commission to wait upon Mr Robert Hall, preacher of the gospel, to signify the heritors and Town Council's resolution to apply to the next Presbytery to moderate in a call for his supplying the present vacancy, and to acquaint him, that as the new church is now built, he must lay his account to preach both forenoon and afternoon on the Sabbath-day during his incumbency. 22d Nov. 1738.—Town give the heritors of the parish security that the fabric of the new church will be upheld. 4th April 1739.—Committee appointed for drawing up a scheme of division of the new church seats, according to the amount of subscription. 8th April 1739.—Mr Dow demits his charge as assistant, having been called to Ardrossan. 9th May 1739.—The Earl of Kilmarnock leaves the appointment of an assistant to the Council, who appoint Mr William Boyd in place of Mr Dow. 6th Sept. 1739.—Committee finds the whole value of the seats in the new kirk to be £41, 6s. 8d. sterling. The expense of the fabric and building of the kirk, &c. amounted to £850 sterling, or thereby. The contributors to have their rooms in the kirk at twenty years' purchase of the yearly value, with the burden of the assistant's salary after mentioned, and upholding the kirk as formerly settled. The non-resident contributors to be advertised of this, in case any of them should claim a share. That as one-half, or more, of the kirk will be in the Council's hands and disposal, so that they might claim an equality with the contributors in setting of the seats, yet, for their ease and benefit, allows the contributors their choice of the whole kirk, excepting the Earl of Kilmarnock and Magistrates' seats, a pew or two for the ministers, and a division or two in the lofts. The highest contributor to have the first choice, and so on in rotation. Those entitled to half seats to have the privilege of purchasing the other half. The town either to let or sell their share of the seats, the proceeds, after bearing their proper share of the ministers' stipends, &c., to go to the building of a steeple. Not above £13 sterling of the ministers' salary to fall upon the kirk seats, wherein the proprietor to be rated yearly in a sum not exceeding sixpence on the pound advanced. Upon what was waste, the whole sixpence to be paid the first year. 31st Oct. 1763.—The Council denude themselves of the chapel to the managers, which was done by a bond.

Such is an outline of the origin and completion of the chapel of ease, now a parish church, designed the High Church of Kilmarnock.

The number of the inhabitants, in 1763, according to Dr Webster, was nearly 5000; in 1792, 6776; in 1801, 8079; in 1811, 10,148; in 1821, 12,769; in 1831, 18,093; and in 1841, 19,398. The increase, it will thus be observed, has been most marked since 1821.

Having thus traced the rise and progress of Kilmarnock, we may, before proceeding to recall the more prominent of those historical events with which the district is connected, string together a few miscellaneous gleanings, that may not be uninteresting to the local reader:—

1710.—The town contributed £50 Scots towards the fund of the Society instituted by her Majesty (Queen Anne), for the promotion of Christian knowledge.

1723.—Adam Dickie appointed to apply to the Town Council and inhabitants of Glasgow for a contribution towards defraying the expense of building a bridge over the Irvine.

27th April 1724.—This day, the two bailies, or any of them, appointed to attend the meeting of the Commissioners of Supply at Ayr, on Thursday the 7th of May, to solicit their consent to levy tenpence upon the hundred pound for one year, and what further they shall think of towards the erection of a bridge at Riccarton; and also to impress upon the neighbouring parishes the propriety of driving sand and stones for the building, the Council of Kilmarnock being willing to undertake the building of the bridge.

23d May 1724.—The Commissioners agree, on condition of the Council advancing one hundred pounds sterling, which the Council consent to, there being at the time subscriptions for seven or eight hundred pounds Scots in the town, and five hundred merks allowed by the Earl of Kilmarnock and his curators, and that there is three hundred and fifty merks in the town's hands of vacant stipends, and therefore ordain bond to be granted to the Commissioners for the same.

1735.—The streets first cleaned by public subscription, the magistrates heading the list.

Aug. 16, 1729.—It is agreed, on a petition from Hugh Fairlie, merchant, late here, now in Kilmaurs, that the treasurer only exact presently twelve pounds Scots from him of his bill of twenty-four pounds granted for his burgess fyne; and that the other twelve pounds shall not be demanded till he shall either return to reside in the place, or desyre his freedom therein. Declaring, that he has no privilege of burgesship in tyme coming, till the whole bill is paid.

5th Jan. 1736.—In consequence of the Council's application to the Earl of Kilmarnock about a schoolmaster, Mr James Smith, teacher, Dalkeith, is recommended, and the Council appoint him. As Mr Robert Montgomery, formerly teacher, still retained the session-clerkship, the town agree to give Mr Smith £5 sterling yearly till he is installed in the clerkship. [Mr Montgomery having refused to vacate the school without a consideration, he is guaranteed in £20 yearly, provided he gives up both school and session-clerk.]

17th April 1736.—Montgomery having still refused to give up his charge, the Council agree to support Mr Smith, in case he should contest a process, and be restored to his charge; and for his encouragement, promise him one hundred merks yearly, beside the sixty pounds formerly promised, and to provide him with a convenient house in which to teach the scholars, during the time Montgomery may continue to hold his situation. The Earl of Kilmarnock coincided in this resolution.

11th May 1736.—John Boswell of Balmuto interposes with Mr Montgomery, who agrees to resign on the terms formerly proposed.

In reference to the origin of the burgh school, M'Kay says: "We learn from authentic records, that on Thursday, 23d March 1727, the session of Kilmarnock being met and constituted—the Rev. Mr Paisley, moderator:

'Inter alia—The session agree to give forty pounds Scots per annum for encouragement of an English school, but only during pleasure, the Town Council granting twenty pounds Scots for the said end.'

On the 17th November 1728, the session being met and constituted—

Sederunt—The Rev. Mr Paisley, moderator, with Mr Hill and the elders:

'Inter alia—The session, finding that the Presbytery will not sustain their grant of forty pounds yearly for encouraging an English school, unanimously agree to stop further payment of the said grant.'

This was the origin of the burgh school of Kilmarnock, which was merged into the Academy in 1807. From 1736 till 1748 the salary was forty pounds Scots, or £3, 6s 8d sterling yearly; and from the latter date it varied till 1803, when Mr Andrew Henderson, the incumbent at that time, got it increased to L15, in consideration that the parochial schoolmasters had got an augmentation of their salary."

There was, however, a school in Kilmarnock at a much earlier period. Amongst the Boyd papers in the Kilmarnock charter chest, there is a scroll of a grant by James Lord Boyd—"ffor the pious zeale and love we have for the educatioune and learning off zoung ones, and for keiping ane schoole within the parocheine of the Old Kirk of Kilmarnock, and for provisioune of ane constant rent and stipend for holding ane schoolemaister in the said parocheine of the Old Kirk of Kilmarnock, quho may also serve as musician in the said Old Kirk in all tyme coming." The Earl being patron of the said kirk, assigns and allocates certain teinds and vicarage dues for the above purpose. There is no date to this scroll, but there can be no doubt that the granter was James eighth Lord Boyd, who died in March 1654; and from the words of the document itself, making special reference to "the Old Kirk of Kilmarnock," it is apparent that it must have been written after 1641, the year in which the parish of Fenwick was disjoined from that of Kilmarnock, the church of which was called "the New Kirk of Kilmarnock." It therefore follows, that the grant for the erection of the school must have been made between the years 1641 and 1654.

15th June 1736.—The town gives L.30 sterling to aid the coal work at Dean, on the same terms as the other subscribers, in consideration that it will be of great benefit to the town.

This was, we should think, the first coal dug in the parish of Kilmarnock, so long had that mineral wealth upon the Kilmarnock estates, which in our own times has added so much to the prosperity of the community, been allowed to lie dormant. The coal, it seems, was wrought without sinking, and the field in the neighbourhood of Dean Castle still wears the appearance of having been the scene of extensive operations.

22d May 1741.—In consequence of the dearth and scarcity, one hundred bolls of meal to be purchased of a cargo arrived at Irvine from the north of Scotland—not above L.10 Scots per boll.

"19th May 1744.—We, the Earl of Kilmarnock, the Baillies, Thesaurer, and members of the Town Council of Kilmarnock above named and subscribing, all convened in Council, being deeply sensible of the pernicious consequences of the immoderate use of French wines and spirits, in public houses, drinking of tea thro' the kingdom, especially amongst the people of lower ranks, which is carried to so extravagant an excess, to the great injury of this nation, by the exportation of their specie, discouragement of the national produce, and detriment to the constitution of the people, by all which the nation is reduced to the last ebb, and is upon the brink of destruction, do therefore resolve and promise that from and after the first day of July next to come, we and each of us will moderate and discourage the drinking of tea in our severall familys; that we will not drink in any publick house, or drink or use any way in our private houses any

French brandy or other French spirits; and, as much as lyes in our power, discourage the drinking and importation of French wines; that we will encourage and assist the officers of the revenue in preventing the clandestine importing of French wines and spirits, and of tea, and suppressing the smuggling and vending of them in the country by wholesale or retail, and bringing to punishment all persons guilty thereof, by publicly informing and putting the laws in execution against them; and that we will exhort the communty, as well as our tennants, cotters, and servants, to do their duty on the same accounts; that we will encourage all public houses who do retail strong ale, twopenny ale, and spirits made from malt and other grain, and will discourage all those who sell and retale French brandy and other spirits." *

The contraband trade was carried on to a great extent at this period, hence the attempt of the Earl and other influential parties to check the consumption of foreign spirits, which was no doubt highly injurious to the nation in every sense.

Aug. 26, 1745.—The Earl and Council present. Heard petition read praying for the priviledge of imposing two pennies on the ale, &c.

The Earl of Kilmarnock had thus taken a deep interest in the welfare of the burgh by presiding at the Council meetings up almost to the very hour in which he engaged in the unhappy affair of 1745-6.

May 6, 1751.—A shank (coal-pit) agreed to be sunk in the holm of the town's ground adjoining the Dean Park, where coal had previously been wrought without sinking. The coal at the Dean works had become scarce by this time.

—— Seeing the inconvenience of keeping the timber mercat (the fuel market?) at the Cross, some other place to be found for it.

1751.—The old school-house burnt, and new one to be built on the same site.

Nov. 17, 1753.—The Council order a water machine, or fire-engine, to be purchased; the first article of the kind, no doubt, in the burgh.

21st Nov. 1764.—Resolve to prosecute Mr Dalrymple of Orangefield for L.6 sterling, due for the gin and other machinery of the town's coal-work, which he got four years ago.

Dec. 19, 1767.—The state of the public roads seems to have engaged the attention of the community at this period, for we find the Town Council acting with the committee of gentlemen appointed to inquire into the state of the respective trusts.

May 3, 1768.—The Whipmen's Society sanctioned by the Council.

Sept. 12, 1771.—General Paoli, and Count Barzinski, ambassador from the King and States of Poland at the Court of Great Britain, visited Kilmarnock on the Sabbath-day, during divine service, to stay a few minutes only. The eldest magistrate, following the instructions of the Council of the previous day, presented them with the freedom of the burgh. This occurred on the 8th September. The General and Ambassador replied in French.

Nov. 17, 1772.—James, Lord Kilmaurs, one of the Councillors.

March 8, 1787.—The Council, understanding that it is proposed that the present mail coach which runs to Carlisle, shall proceed as far as Glasgow, by the way of Lockerby, Douglas Mill, &c., through a mountainous and almost uninhabited country, are desirous that the said coach should go by Aunan, Dumfries, Sanquhar, Kilmarnock, &c., to Glasgow, which would be a more commodious and speedy conveyance; they therefore appoint the magistrates, &c., to draw up a memorial to the Postmaster General of Scotland on the subject.*

M'Kay has an amusing chapter on the pastimes and amusements of the inhabitants of Kilmarnock, and quotes the following extracts from the treasurer's accounts, as illustrative of the hearty manner in which the king's birth-days were held:

1718, Feb. 6.—Payt. for six load of coals for a bonfire, L.1, 16s. Scots.

Feb. 12.—For ale for the Queen's birth night, L.1 Scots. Ribbon for cockade to drummer's bonnet, 4s. Scots.

March 4.—Paid at the Bailie's order to James Boyd for ale drank at the cross on Queen's birth night, L.1, 4s. Scots.

1719.—Paid to Bailie Moris for wine on King George's birth day, L.9, 18s. Scots.

1737.—Paid for raisings and Almonds at King's birth day, L.1, 7s. Scots. For ringing the bell, nuts, gunpowder, &c., L.3, 19s. Scots. For 2 blew bonnets to John Lawry and Stenson at the King's birth day, 12s. Scots.

1740.—Given Robert Cumming for necessarys to repairing his drum, being broke at King's birth day, L.3, 12s. Scots.

1770.—By Wm. Wilson 15 bottles Port at King's birth day, at 18s. sterling per dozen,

---

* To this minute is attached the holograph signature of the Earl of Kilmarnock. It is written in a round, legible hand.

* The memorial proved ultimately effectual. The coach, the first that ever passed through the narrow streets of Kilmarnock, was called the Camperdown.

L.1, 2s. 6d.   By Alexander Mitchel 6 pints Rum made into punch King's birth day, L.1, 16s. Sterling.

"1789.—To Nathan Hodge for attending King's birth day, 5s. Ster." This individual was a barber, and attended, we believe, to make and serve out the punch to the bailies and councillors.

"But one of the most important days of amusement," continues the author, "was Eastern's E'en, which was given up some time ago, after having been held annually for five centuries."* "We have never heard any of our aged townsmen talk of the Maypole, or rural festival of the first of May, being observed in the district. The following entry, however, in the Town Treasurer's book, for 1780, would imply that such was the case about that period:—"Paid Robert Fraser, for *dressing a Maypole*, 2s. 6d. sterling." This is certainly the latest notice of the Maypole in Scotland with which we are acquainted—that pastime having been strictly put down by act of Parliament immediately after the Reformation.

Curling in winter was a favourite amusement of the Kilmarnock burghers in ancient times as well as the present. "The Cross, too," says M'Kay, "strange as it may appear, was sometimes converted into a curling pond. The late Robert Montgomery, Esq. of Bogston, who was the eldest son of Bailie John Wilson, merchant, Kilmarnock, and who adopted the name of Montgomery on inheriting the above mentioned estate, told our informant, James Dobie, Esq. of Crummock, Beith, that his father (Bailie Wilson) curled, in 1740, at the Cross of Kilmarnock, for twenty-three successive days, excepting Sundays. The water was raised from a well, probably the present Cross well, and was dammed up for the purpose. The winter of 1740 was very severe, and long talked of as the hard winter."

The author of the "History of Kilmarnock" has apparently overlooked the Bowling Club. This healthful and pleasant pastime used to be, and still is, we believe, a favourite with the wealthier classes of Kilmarnock. The following minute of Council throws some light on the origin of the Club:—5th March, 1764.—Relieve Wm. Paterson of any claim upon his father's representatives for a shooting prize of L.5, which was, in or about the year 1740, put into the defunct's hands towards erecting a Bowling Green and purchasing bowls, as being then thought a more agreeable diversion than shooting, on his obligation for repeating the same, if ever a

majority of the contributors demand it for any other use. Thus we see that bowling had not been practised in Kilmarnock before 1764; but how soon afterwards we cannot say, although there can be little doubt that the L.5 for a shooting prize lodged in the hands of the father of William Paterson was the origin of the Bowling Club.

There is no historical event of much importance connected with Kilmarnock, and yet there are not a few incidents having reference to the locality which ought not be overlooked by the topographical historian. In vol. i., p. 37, of this work, we were led to make some remarks on "Makyrnokis way," at a pass of which, according to Barbour, Sir James Douglas and about forty adherents defeated a thousand of the English troops under Sir Philip de Mowbray. We were led into these by the statement of David M'Pherson, who, in explanation, says "Makyrnockis way is a narrow pass on the bank of Makyrnock Wattyr," near Kilmarnock. We have since found that "Makyrnockis way" was a path through the forest which at one time overspread the greater part of the north part of Cuninghame, including the parishes of Dunlop, Beith and Stewarton,* so that Kilmarnock cannot, as M'Pherson would have it, lay any peculiar claim to the pass where De Mowbray was so signally overthrown.

Pont ascribes another somewhat obscure incident to the locality: "Item, not far from Kilmarnock, in ye midell of ye river Irwin, wes the Read Steuart slaine, after he had receaved a Responce from a vitch yat he should not perrish nather in Kyle nor zet in Cuninghame, the said river being the merch betwixt the two, and being in nather of them."

Were tradition, or Chambers' "Picture of Scotland," to be credited, Dean Castle, in the vicinity of Kilmarnock, must have had the honour of a visit from the troops of Edward I.—"The ancient family of Crafurdland," says this authority, "was always in strict league with their neighbours, the Boyds of Dean Castle; and there was a subterraneous communication between the two houses for the mutual use of both, in case of either being besieged. An authentic and most valuable anecdote, illustrative of the ancient modes of life, is preserved in connexion with this conveniency, the orifice of which was only closed up at Craufurdland on the late modification of the house. It was the fortune of Dean Castle to be beleaguered by the troops of Edward I., who, being unable to reduce it by force, lay for three months around it, in the hope that a famine in the garrison would

---

* The author does not give his authority for this statement, although we believe the amusement to have been of ancient origin.

* Chartulary of Paisley.

ultimately make it surrender. To their infinite surprise, the garrison of the Castle one morning hung a great display of new-killed beef over the battlements, and tauntingly inquired if the besiegers were in need of provisions, as the garrison had a considerable quantity which they did not expect to use. At this the English commander, unable to solve the mystery, thought proper to raise the siege, and try his arms upon some fortress of less inexhaustible resources." Unfortunately for the authenticity of this "authentic and most valuable anecdote," the Boyds were not in possession of Dean Castle during the reign of Edward I. It was not until after the final triumph of Bruce at Bannockburn that he conferred these lands, forfeited by John de Baliol, upon his faithful adherent, Sir Robert Boyd.[*]

After the accession of the Boyds, the tenantry both of the burgh and barony of Kilmarnock, no doubt, frequently followed the lord of the manor to the field in the various conflicts, civil as well as foreign, in which they were engaged: but the page which is freshest and most distinctly marked in the annals of Kilmarnock, refers to the long struggle for civil and religious liberty during the seventeenth century. As already shown in the first volume of this work, pp. 116, 117, &c. Alaster M'Donald or M'Cole, nephew of the Lord of the Isles, who commanded the Irish division in the army of Montrose, established his headquarters in Kilmarnock immediately after the victory of Kilsyth in 1645, as well to inspire confidence in those friendly to the cause as to levy contributions from those opposed to it. There is no tradition or record, however, of any material loss sustained by the inhabitants at this particular crisis.

Another General of still greater notoriety honoured Kilmarnock by making it his head quarters. This was General Dalziel, with his soldiers, after the battle of Pentland in 1667. He is said to have exacted fifty thousand merks—an enormous sum in these days—from the inhabitants of the burgh, and to have enacted many cruelties in suppressing the attenders of conventicles—all of which have been duly chronicled in Wodrow and the "Scots Worthies," and are too well known to be repeated here.

Kilmarnock also suffered severely during the "Highlandman's Year," as it is called, when the Highland Host was brought down by the executive to live at free quarters among the Western Whigs in 1678. The loss sustained upon this occasion by "the town of Kilmarnock, and lands belonging to my lord within the parish, quarters, dry quarters, and plunder, [was] £5918 Scots." According to some authorities—we forget whether Robert Chambers is amongst the number—it was not all loss to the burghers, for they gained the art of manufacturing blue bonnets from the Highlanders! We need not remind our readers of the authenticity of this statement, if they have paid attention to the various extracts produced from the town records in reference to the trade of Kilmarnock.

In 1683, according to Wodrow, Lieut.-Colonel Buchan held a court at Kilmarnock, when several parties were tried for their alleged concern in the rising at Bothwell. Amongst others, John Nisbet of Hardhill was condemned for his share in that affair. He was executed at the Cross of Kilmarnock on the 14th April 1683. "The spot where the gallows stood," says M'Kay, "is still marked by the initials of his name, formed with white stones, at the south corner of the Cross."

The Revolution of 1688 brought a happy release to the persecuted; and by none was it hailed with greater enthusiasm than the people of Kilmarnock. In 1715, when the Earl of Mar unfurled the standard of the Pretender, they gathered strongly, and with great spirit, under the Earl of Kilmarnock, in defence of the House of Hanover. At the general muster of the Fencibles at Irvine, in August 1715, the Earl, according to Rae's "History of the Rebellion," appeared "at the head of above five hundred of his own men, well appointed, and expert in the exercise of their arms." Rae goes on to state, in compliment to the gallantry of the men of Kilmarnock, that "on Sabbath the 18th of September, two gentlemen from Glasgow came here [Kilmarnock] representing the danger the city was in by the number and nearness of the enemy, who were reported to be marching straight thither in order to surprise it, while it wanted sufficient defence through the absence of their own men, who, at the desire of the Duke of Argyle, were marching to Stirling. This sudden and surprising alarm so animated the people, that on Monday, September 19, they universally assembled in arms by the sunrising, and in presence of the Earl of Kilmarnock, offered cheerfully to march forthwith to Glasgow; and accordingly, 220 men, who were best prepared, marched with the greatest alacrity (even those who contributed for the subsistence of others not exempting themselves), and having come to Glasgow that day, to the great satisfaction of the inhabitants, were received and entertained with all the marks of friendship and gratitude. Next day

---

[*] It is said that Sir Robert had two charters of these lands from Robert I., one in 1308, and the other in 1316. The latter we have seen. It is preserved in good order in the Boyd Charter chest at Kilmarnock. It is dated 3d May in the tenth year of King Robert's reign.

the Earl came in himself with 120 men, whose presence very much added to the general satisfaction and courage of the city; and so they were the first of all the western parts that came to the assistance of Glasgow, excepting Paisley, who, lying only about six miles off, were in about two hours before them. Next day they entered upon duty, keeping watch and ward night and day, till Saturday the 1st of October."

The Kilmarnock men, headed by the Earl, next proceeded to Perthshire, and were stationed at Gartatan House from the 3d to the 13th of October, to overawe the celebrated Rob Roy and his band of Macgregors. They were relieved by the Stirlingshire Militia, and returning to Glasgow, were "honourably dismissed" on the 21st of November.

True to their constitutional principles, the men of Kilmarnock took no part with their unhappy chief, the last of the Earls of Kilmarnock, in the gallant but hopeless attempt to restore the House of Stuart in 1745. A tradition is current that his lordship endeavoured to shake their loyalty, by inducing them to join the standard of the Prince. This is not supported by any evidence; and the Earl himself, in his petition to the Prince of Wales, states, "that he influenced neither tenant nor follower of his to assist or abet the rebellion; but on the contrary, that between the time of the battle of *Preston* and his unhappy junction with the rebels, he went to the town of Kilmarnock, influenced the inhabitants as far as he could, and by their means likewise influenced the neighbouring boroughs to rise in arms for his Majesty's service, which had so good an effect that two hundred men of Kilmarnock appeared very soon in arms, and remained all the winter at Glasgow, or other places as they were ordered."

The only allusion to this period we have found in the Town Records is as follows: "13th September 1745.—The Council agree [the Earl not present] that, in the present critical conjuncture, when threatened with ane invasion into the neighbourhood of this conntrey, and because of the many stragling people and strangers in the place from the Highlands and other parts of the countrey, the town-guard be raised, and kept each night by a sufficient number of men."

M'Kay tells an amusing anecdote illustrative of the loyalty of the burghers of Kilmarnock: "A party of marauders," he says, "had come so far west as the town of Stewarton; and, in consequence of their arrival there, a report was instantly circulated that a considerable body of the insurgents were on their march from Glasgow to the west, for the purpose of ransacking Kilmarnock. This rumour created an unusual sensation

in Auld Killie. The town-drummer speedily patrolled the streets, and gave warning of the approaching danger; at the sametime he announced that a public meeting would be held at the Netherton, for the purpose of devising measures for the protection of life and property. A large number of weavers, shoemakers, and bonnetmakers, were soon on the ground, armed with old swords, muskets, and other weapons. After two or three thrilling speeches had been delivered, respecting the cruelty and thievish propensities of the Highlanders, it was agreed that the meeting should march in a body to meet the invaders, and give them battle before they reached the outskirts of the town. It was resolved that the women, during the absence of their husbands, should contrive means for securing everything that the mountaineers were likely to covet, such as pewter-plate, wearing apparel, &c., which they immediately did, by sinking the former in the open wells at the back of their houses, and by concealing the latter about the hedges in the vicinity. In the meantime the Kilmarnock heroes, with flying colours, passed through the centre of the town, up Soulis Street and Townhead, thence to the highway leading to Glasgow; but, on coming to *Craigspout*, they learned from some travellers that the report which had caused so much alarm was all a hoax! —that no soldiers were on the road—that the Pretender and his army had left Glasgow, and were supposed to be on their way to Stirling. Our worthy volunteers then returned to the town; and, on arriving at the Cross, discharged their muskets into the air, gave three hearty cheers for King George, and, *unscathed* by *dirk* or *broadsword*, repaired to their respective dwellings.

"The majority of the inhabitants, therefore, were opposed to the House of Stuart, and we have heard of only one man whose principles inclined to the side of the Jacobites; but he evidently wanted the chivalrous spirit with which the true followers of 'bonnie Prince Charlie' were actuated. This individual was commonly called *Auld Soulis*, from the circumstance of his residing in the house next to Lord Soulis' monument. A day or two previous to the battle of Falkirk he left Kilmarnock, and went to that town to gratify his curiosity, as he said, by seeing Prince Charles and his army. When he arrived in Falkirk, he was immediately accosted by some of the Highlanders, who asked, with an air of authority, whence he had come? He answered that he had come from Ayrshire, was friendly to the Prince, and was an acquaintance of the Earl of Kilmarnock, to whom he had a letter. "Join our party then, an' pe tam to you," said one of the Highlanders, "an' no pe stanin' there like some stupid deevil, or hy

Got her nainsel's dirk shall mak you do your duty." Auld Soulis, on hearing such vehement language, began to wish he was again in Kilmarnock; but, anxious to see the battle, which was expected every hour to commence, he contrived to linger about the place until it was over; and besides seeing the hostile encounter, he had the satisfaction of beholding the young Pretender conducted by torch-light to his lodgings in Falkirk. Next day Auld Soulis was seized by the insurgents, and commanded to follow them in their march towards Stirling, and lead a horse on which were placed two wounded men. Afraid to act contrary to orders, he took the horse and men under his charge, and proceeded slowly behind the army; but, on coming to a turn in the road, where an eminence concealed him from their view, he left the two invalids to their fate, and hurried homeward, carrying along with him a loaf he had got for their use. He had not gone far, however, when he was met by several hungry Highlanders, who plundered him not only of the loaf, but of the very shoes that were on his feet. We may add, that Auld Soulis, in the course of two or three days, was again in Kilmarnock, amusing his friends with an account of his wonderful adventures at Falkirk."

The news of the decisive battle of Culloden was received with so much delight by the inhabitants of Kilmarnock, that they held a public rejoicing on the subject—a fact sufficiently attested by the following entry in the treasurer's accounts:—" Acct. of Entertainment at Rejoicing on the victory of Colodin fight, to Will. Walker, May 1746, £17 Scots." "About the sametime," says M'Kay, "the Duke of Cumberland's birthday was celebrated here, and £7, 10s. Scots expended by the bailies and councillors on the occasion."

Notwithstanding the decided opposition of the inhabitants to the cause espoused by the Earl of Kilmarnock, the Town Council, on the 20th July 1746, unanimously petitioned the Government in behalf of their unfortunate chief. No appeal, however, as is well known, could save him.

In 1764, the peace of Kilmarnock was greatly disturbed by the violent settlement of the Rev. William Lindsay in the second charge of the Low Church. The presentee was inimical to the majority of the parishioners, but the patron, the Earl of Glencairn, was inexorable, and a riot was the consequence. Burns, in his "Ordination," thus alludes to the affair:

"Curst common sense, that imp o' hell,
  Cam in wi' Maggie Lauder."

Mr Lindsay was a preacher of liberal sentiments —too liberal for the "true blue" professors of " Auld Killie"—hence the bard's allusion to "common sense." Margaret Lauder was the name of the clergyman's wife; and as she had been formerly in the service of the Glencairn family as housekeeper or governess, it was presumed that the appointment had been obtained through her influence. On the day of induction an immense crowd collected, and a serious riot ensued. The Earl of Glencairn was himself struck on the cheek with a dead cat, and several others of the gentlemen and clergymen were more or less abused and injured. The following account of the riot is from the " Caledonian Mercury" of July 21, 1764:—" By a letter from Kilmarnock we learn, that on Thursday se'ennight, the day appointed by the General Assembly for the transportation of the Rev. Mr Lindsay from the Cumbraes to Kilmarnock, the patron, with a number of gentlemen and ministers, went to the church, in order to proceed in the settlement; but divine service was not well begun, when a mob of disorderly persons broke into the church, throwing dirt and stones, and making such noise, that Mr Brown, the minister who officiated, could not proceed, on which the patron with the gentlemen and ministers, retired to a house in the neighbourhood; 'tis said Mr Lindsay is to be ordained in the Presbytery house of Irvine."

The authorities of Kilmarnock waited upon the Earl of Glencairn, and affected to be very wroth against the abettors of the riot; and, on the 20th July 1764, the Council offered a reward for their apprehension. A number of persons were accordingly apprehended. Referring again to the " Caledonian Mercury" of 1764, we find that " Alexander Thomson, William Wyllie, James Crawford, John Hill, Adam White, David Dunlop, William Nemmo, William Davies or Davidson, Hugh Thomson, alias Bulloch, with Robert Credman, tradesmen and journeymen in Kilmarnock, were indicted for raising a tumult at and in the church of Kilmarnock at the settlement of Mr Lindsay as minister of that parish in July last. The last seven were acquitted by the jury, and the first three found guilty, and sentenced to be imprisoned for a month, and whipt through the streets of Air, and to find caution for keeping the peace, and a good behaviour for a twelvemonth."

The "Scoffing Ballad" alluded to by Burns, has been preserved in "The Ballads and Songs of Ayrshire,"* and in "The History of Kilmarnock."

* T. G. Stevenson, bookseller, 87 Princes Street, Edinburgh.

Various serious fires have occurred in Kilmarnock. One in 1670, according to the author of "Caledonia," "when a public collection was made for the sufferers by the direction of the Diocesan Synod; and again in 1800, when upwards of thirty houses, as well as the Holm School, were destroyed. The houses were roofed with thatch, and the weather being dry, the fire spread with great rapidity.

Another serious accident occurred the following year, on Sabbath the 18th of October 1801, in the old Low Church. The building, which was at best limited and incommodious, had long been considered in an unsafe state. On that day it was particularly crowded, and a small piece of plaster having fallen from the roof, or as some said a seat cracked in one of the galleries, a panic ensued, and in the wild and tumultuous rush to escape from what they conceived to be a falling fabric, a scene of indescribable confusion and suffering followed. Twenty-nine persons were killed on the spot, and upwards of eighty more injured. A liberal subscription was immediately entered into by the magistrates of the burgh, and the wealthier classes in the vicinity, as well as by the nobility and gentry of the county, which in so far tended to the relief of those who had been deprived of their "bread-winner." The church, after inspection, was immediately taken down, and the present new, large and commodious building erected nearly on the same site, so anxious were the heritors to remove all risk of a similar catastrophe.

We have thus glanced over all that may be considered notable in the history of Kilmarnock. It remains only to be stated, to the credit of the people, that during the French war they were not behind their forefathers in the manifestation of their loyalty when danger was apprehended. Two regiments were formed in the parish, the Sharpshooters or Rifles, commanded by Captain James Thomson, and the Volunteers, commanded by Major Parker of Assloss; and the military enthusiasm of the period was kept alive by a continued series of military exercises, mock battles, sieges, &c., so that both regiments attained considerable perfection in the art of war. Even during what is called the "Radical period"—1819–20—a body of volunteers was formed, and continued in arms so long as it was deemed necessary. The mass of the inhabitants of Kilmarnock at this time, however, were decidedly opposed to the policy of the Government, and some of them had made themselves rather conspicuous at public meetings, and as members of private clubs; so much so that they became marked men in the eyes of the Government officials. Many

of the inhabitants must still recollect of the town being surrounded, on the morning of the 14th April 1820, by the regiment of Edinburgh Yeomanry Cavalry, accompanied by a piece of ordnance, or flying artillery, which, placed in position at the Cross, remained there ready for execution in any direction. The inhabitants were greatly surprised at this sudden invasion, the object of which was to command all the roads and avenues leading to or from the town, so as to prevent any one from escaping, while a vigorous search was being made for the ringleaders of the disaffection in the town. The officers of the law, however, missed their mark it is understood; the more guilty having been made aware, through some channel or other, of what was intended, made their escape some time previously. On turning over some of the Edinburgh periodicals lately we were amused to find the event celebrated in a humorous song, which we deem worthy of being transferred to our pages, as illustrative of an event which may perhaps engage the attention of some future local historian. It is as follows:—

### THE WESTERN CAMPAIGN.[*]

#### Air—"Black Joke."

Let us sing of the heroes that marched from yon town,
To keep liberty up, to put Radicals down,
   With their long spurs and sabres so bright;
Their majestic manœuvres in cross-road and lane—
Their walk on the hill, and their trot on the plain—
The butts that were shed, and the beeves that were slain,
Stamp'd immortal renown on the Western Campaign,
   And the long spurs and sabres so bright.

Through Auld Reekie thy note, Preparation! was heard,
The hallooing of Honne, and the bellow of Baird,
   For their long spurs and sabres so bright.
At their magical call, what a muster began!
What a figging of horse! what a rigging of men!
Lawyers flung by the fee-book to furbish their pops,
And mettlesome merchants strode fierce from their shops,
   With their long spurs and sabres so bright.

'Twas at Bathgate this war might be said to commence,
To the tune, as was fitting, of "D—n the expense!"
   By our long swords and sabres so bright.
As the Waterloo cheesemongers batter'd the French,
So these nurslings of luxury, stretched on a bench,
In a pitiful pot-house durst patiently snore,
Or boldly bivouack'd round a bowl on the floor,
   All in long spurs and sabres so bright.

Yet ere long they were destined still higher to soar,
In endurance heroic, on Slammanan Moor,
   In their long spurs and sabres so bright.
On that scene of devotion there twinkled no star:—
The occasional flash of a lighted cigar
Scarce sufficed to distinguish a friend from a foe,
Or the wet Mandarin from a turnip scare-crow,
   Spite of long spurs and sabres so bright.

[*] This song is, we believe, one of the many standard ditties of the Edinburgh Yeomanry Cavalry's Mess. It was written by one of themselves, in jocular commemoration of a march to Lanarkshire and Ayrshire, when these districts were in a disturbed condition in the spring of 1820.—[Note by the author we presume.]

Neither pot-house, nor pent-house, nor pea-shed was here,
Nor the heart-stirring clunk of one cork of small-beer,
    To greet long spurs and sabres so bright ;
Yet, all sleepless and fagged, when to Airdrie they came,
Colonel Smith canters in with a visage of flame ;
" There's a thousand hot colliers," quoth he, " I've just
    seen
Reviewed by old Soult on a farmer's back green ;
    Go it, long spurs and sabres so bright !"

There was mounting in haste beside Airdrie's canal :
Every pistol was cock'd—some were loaded with ball—
    Besides long spurs and sabres so bright.
Over ditches and dikes, and through marshes and mire,
They gallop—you need not be told they perspire ;
Sure the fault was not theirs, if they nothing espied
But a gay penny-wedding upon the hill-side,
    With their crack'd fiddles and favours so white.

" Hey for Glasgow, that hot-bed of wealth and of war,
There at least you'll not baulk us," quoth every hussar,
    With his long spurs and sabres so bright.
Call inactive, an please you, these traitor poltroons,
But accord the just meed to unwearied dragoons ;
Mars approved of their vigour at dinner and lunch,
And Broomielaw Naiads pour'd oceans of punch
    O'er the long spurs and sabres so bright.

In the dead of the night, with twelve pounders behind,
To surprise strong Kilmarnock, more fleet than the wind
    Rode the long spurs and sabres so bright.
Their investing that city of ill-disposed men,
Might have honoured a Condé, a Saxe, a Turenne ;
But their march had been bent by the Kilwinning Fly,
And the cursed cowl-knitters escaped, being shy
    Of their long spurs and sabres so bright.

When one greasy disciple of Carlisle and Hone
Had surrendered his shuttle, ' Te Deum' was blown
By young Napier, who flourish'd his bugle so bright.
Next they Straven blockaded :—if weavers were fled,
At least whisky and gingerbread staid in their stead ;
So the holsters were cramm'd, and the leaguer was raised,
And the old women, lighting their cutty pipes, gazed
    After long spurs and sabres so bright.

Bellona thus bearded, Minerva struck dumb—
To Auld Reekie once more the Invincibles come,
    With their long spurs and sabres so bright :
O, what grateful caresses, from matron and maid,
Must reward their exertions in storm and blockade ;
Trophies bloody and bloodless are equally sweet,
And ladies must yield them, like Rads, when they meet
    With the long spur and the sabre so bright.

The Session books date back to 1644, but they
were not kept with any degree of regularity until
a much later period. They present little of interest even to the local reader ; and we have already
quoted so largely from more important records
that we deem it unnecessary farther to advert to
them.

### ANTIQUITIES.

That the Romans, who traversed the banks of
the Irvine from its source to its junction with
the sea, had a station at Kilmarnock is very possible. The site of the encampment is supposed
to have been the Knockinlaw, where the Powder
House now stands, an eminence, as the name
implies, commanding an extensive view of the
surrounding country. In the vicinity, until within
these few years, there was a well, long known as
the " Roman Well," and not far from it various
urns and other remains of antiquity have from
time to time been dug up.

In the town of Kilmarnock itself there are few
vestiges of antiquity. The most remarkable is
that of Soulis Cross, which gives its name to one
of the streets. It formerly consisted of " a rude
stone pillar, about eight or nine feet high, on the
top of which was fixed a small gilded cross." In
1825 the inhabitants of that quarter of the town
raised a subscription with the view of renewing
the monument, which had become greatly dilapidated. A handsome fluted pillar has accordingly
been erected in the same spot, in a niche of the
wall which surrounds the High Church, fronting
the street, bearing this inscription :—

> " To the memory of Lord Soulis, A.D. 1444.
> Erected by subscription, A.D. 1825.
> ' The days of old to mind I call.' "

Tradition states that Lord Soulis was an English
nobleman, and that he was killed by an arrow
from the cross-bow of one of the Boyd family.
M'Kay, in his " History of Kilmarnock," gives
the tradition at length, and mentions, in evidence
of the skirmish which is said to have taken place
between the contending parties, that in " 1825,
Mr Clark, farmer of Knockinlaw, when cutting a
drain near the spot where this encounter is said
to have happened, found at a considerable depth
beneath the surface, a sword of rather ancient
appearance ; but whether it was one of those used
in the skirmish we have described is matter for
conjecture,"[*] It seems to be now impossible to
trace the true history of the monument.

The present steeple of Kilmarnock formed part
of the old church, taken down in 1801 after the
melancholy catastrophe already mentioned. It
bears the date 1711. The church itself, from its
construction, with galleries and inside stairs, could
not have been of ancient standing, however inadequate to the wants of the parish or deficient
in construction. It could not have been the
" pretty church " spoken of by Pont, in which,
he says, " are divers of ye Lord Boydes progenitors buried, amonges quhome ther is one tombe
or stone bearing this inscription and coate :[†]

---

[*] If there is any truth in this tradition, the party by
whom Soulis was slain must have been either Robert Boyd,
created a peer of parliament in 1459, or his brother Sir
Alexander Boyd of Duncow, who was considered " a mirror of chivalry." Chalmers, author of " Caledonia," is
inclined to consider the whole as a fable, there being no
Lord Soulis in Scotland, " either as a friend or an enemy
at this period." There is usually, however, some foundation for tradition.

[†] A shield with the fesse cheque so well known as the
family arms.

Hic jacet Thomas Boyde, Dominus de Kilmarnock, qui obit septimo die mensis Julii 1432, and Johanna de Montgomery, eius spousa. Orate pro iis. Ther is also ane vther tombe, not so ancient of Robert Lord Boyds, quheron is this epitaph:

Heir layes yat godly noble, wyse Lord Boyde,
Who Kirk and King and Commonveill decord,
Vich ver, whill they this jevell all inloyed,
Manteined, governed, and councelled by yat Lord.
His ancient housse (oft perilled) he restored;
Twisse sex and sexty yeirs he lived, and syne,
By death, ye third of Januar deuold,
In anno thrysse fyve hundereth aughty nyne.

Neir also unto this Robert Lord Boyd, layes interred Robert last Master of Boyde, who deceased in anno 1597."

In the kirkyard there is a stone commemorative of two martyrs, who were beheaded in Edinburgh in 1666, and whose heads were set up in Kilmarnock. The inscription is as follows:—
"Here lie the Heads of John Ross and John Shields, who suffered at Edinburgh, Dec. 27th, 1666, and had their Heads set up in Kilmarnock.

Our persecutors mad with wrath and ire,
In Edinburgh members some do lye, some here;
Yet instantly united they shall be,
And witness 'gainst this nation's perjury."

Another memorial of " the Persecution " is to be found in the following inscription upon " a plain but neatly executed stone," also in the burying ground:—" Sacred to the memory of Thomas Finlay, John Cuthbertson, William Brown, Robert and James Anderson, (natives of this parish), who were taken prisoners at Bothwell, June 22nd, 1679, sentenced to transportation for life, and drowned on their passage near the Orkney Isles. Also, John Finlay, who suffered martyrdom, 15th December 1682, in the Grassmarket, Edinburgh.

Peace to the Church! her peace no friends invade,
Peace to each noble martyr's honoured shade:
They, with undaunted courage, truth, and zeal,
Contended for the Church and country's weal,
We share the fruits, we drop the grateful tear,
And peaceful altars o'er their ashes rear."

The fate of John Nisbet of Hardhill, executed at the Cross of Kilmarnock, is also recorded on a stone in the kirkyard:—" Here lies John Nisbet, who was taken by Major Balfour's Party, and suffered at Kilmarnock, 14th April, 1683, for adhering to the word of God and our Covenants. Rev. xii. & 11.

Come, reader, see, here pleasant Nisbet lies,
His blood doth pierce the high and lofty skies;
Kilmarnock did his latter hour perceive,
And Christ his soul to heaven did receive.
Yet bloody Torrence did his body raise,
And buried it into another place;
Saying, ' Shall rebels lye in graves with me?
We'll bury him where evil doers be!' "

*Dean Castle.*—The ruins of Dean Castle, once the seat of the noble, but unfortunate family of Boyd, are situated within a mile and a half of Kilmarnock. They stand on a gentle rising ground on the banks of the Kilmarnock, formerly called, according to tradition, the *Carth* Water:

" The Water of Carth rins by the Dean,
That anee was Lord Boyd's lodgin':
The lord wi' the loupen han',
He lost his title and his lan'."[*]

This rhyme refers, of course, to the last Earl of Kilmarnock, who forfeited his title and estates by taking part in the rebellion of 1745. The " loupen hand " is in allusion to the crest of the family, which is a dexter hand, couped at the wrist, erect, pointing with the thumb and two next fingers, the others turning down, with the motto, *Confido.* The castle originally consisted of a single, but strong, massive, oblong tower; built, as Grose conjectures, about the beginning of the fifteenth century. According to Pont, who thus describes it, it must have had a much earlier origin:—" It is a staitly, faire, ancient building, arrysing in two grate heigh towers, and built around courteways vith fyve low buildings; it is veill planted, and almost environed vith gardens, orchards, and a parke. It belonged first to ye Locartts, Lordes therof, then to the Lord Soulis, and now the chieffe duelling almost for 300 zeirs of ye Lords Boyde. Neir to it is ther a stone crosse, called to this day Soulis Crosse, quher they affirme ye Lord Soulis wes killed." The authority of Pont for this statement seems doubtful, in so far that in the charter granted by Robert the Bruce to Sir Robert Boyd, dated 3d May 1316, the lands are stated to have previously belonged to John Baliol. The probability is, therefore, that the castle was built about this period. Besides the two towers, as described by Pont, one of the sides of the square is formed by the ruins of a more modern and commodious suite of apartments. This addition was no doubt built by James eighth Lord Boyd, who succeeded to the title and estates on the death of his nephew in 1640. The arms of the family, with his initials, and an inscription below, are still, though much defaced, distinguishable on the wall facing the court. The inscription, which cannot now be clearly made out, seems to have been readable in 1789, when Grose took his drawing of the ruins. He gives it as follows:—

" James Lord of
Kilmarnock
Dame Katherine Creyk
Lady Boyd."

This lady was daughter of John Craik, Esq., of

* Taken from the recitation of an old inhabitant of Kilmarnock, between 80 and 90 years of age.

the city of York. It is thus pretty evident that the modern part of the castle was built some time after 1640. But the fact is still rendered more certain by an enumeration of the *plenishing* of the castle at the death of Thomas, fifth Lord Boyd, in June 1611, which shows, from the extent and nature of the articles, that the square tower only was then in existence. This list occurs in a charge upon a decreet obtained before the Lords of Council, at the instance of James Elphinstone of Wodsyde, "donatour of [a] *gift of eschiet of* vmquhile Thomas Lord Boyd" against Dame Elizabeth Wallace, relict of the late Lord. This document, which bears to have been served on the 25th July, 1612, is amongst the Boyd papers. The list may be interesting to our readers, as illustrative of the furnishing of a nobleman's house in Ayrshire, 239 years ago. We shall therefore make no apology for copying it *verbatim* from the original—

"Twa cowpis of siluer, every ane of thaim vechtain ten unce of siluer; ane lang carpet, half worset half selk; ane schort carpet for the chalmer buird; ane lang green buird claithe, the lengthe of the haill buird; twa schort greine buird clathis for the chalmer buird; four enschownis of tripe veluet;* four cushownis of carpet ruche vark; thrie schewit cushownis of the forme of cowering vark; four cushownis of ruishe vark; twa lang buird claiths of flandiris damais; saxteine seruietis † of damais; ane lang dornick ‡ buird claithe; ane lang damais towell; ane cower buirde claithe of small lynyng; ane dusoun of dornick seruiettis; ane braid dornick towell; twelt lang lyning buird claithis; four dosun and ane half of lyning seruietis; fywe buird claithis of grit lynyng; fywe dosoun of round lynyng seruicitis: aucht towellis of roun hardine; four drinking clathis, twa thairof sewit with selk, and the vther twa plaine; twa lynyng drinking claiths; ane copbuird claith; ane down bed; aucht feddir beddis, with aucht bowsteris effering thairto; auchteine codis, pairtlie filed with downis and pairt with fedderis; auchteine pair of dowbill blankettis; fywe cowerings of ruishe vark; ane fair rallow caddow;§ sevin houshaild coweringis; saxteine pair of lynyng scheittis; twa pair of heid schettis of small lynyng, schewit with quhyet vork and perling; twa pair of heid scheittis, schewit with black selk; ane pair of plaine heid scheittis; sax pair of heid scheittis; ten cod-

waris* of small lyning, schewit with black selk; sax codwairis of small lynyne unschewit; ane stand of stampit crambassie† vorset courteinis, with ane schewit pand effering yrto; ane stand of greine champit curteinis with ane pand effering yrto; ane vther stand of gray champit‡ vorset courteinis, vith the pand effering yrto; ane stand of greine pladine courtainis, with the pand effering yrto; ane stand of quhyet schewit courteinis; ane pair quhyet vowen courteinis, with the pand effering yrto; seventie pewdir plaitis; ane dusoun pewdir trunchoris; ten coweris of pewdir; sevinteine saisceris; two new Inglis quart stowpis; twa new quart flacownis; thrie ale tyne quart stouppis; twa ale tyne quart flacownis; ane tyne pynt stoup; twa new chalmer pottis; four new tyne chandilieris; fywe grat brassin chandilieris; ane grit morter of brass, and ane iron pester; twa tyne bassings, with ane lawer of tyne; five grit brass panis; thrie meikle brassin pottis, and ane lytill brassin pot; twa iron pottis; ane grispan of brass, and ane pair of grat standard raxis; fywe lang speittis; ane grit iron tank; ane meikill frying pan, and ane grit masking fatt; thrie gyill fattis; twa meikill barrals; four lytill barralls; ane burnest, and twa grit iron chimnays; twa pair of taingis; ane chalmer chimnay; twa lang hall buirds; thrie furmis; ane schort hall buird; twa chalmer buirdis; twa chyiris of aick; ane copbuird of aick; sax buffet stuillis; ane meikill bybill; twa meikill meill gurnells of aick; thrie cofferis; twa grit kistis of aick for keiping of naipperie; four less kistis, and ane candill kist; twa stand bedis of aick."

From this inventory may be traced the furniture peculiar to the various apartments in the tower, which consisted of four stories or flats. The first, vaulted, was no doubt used partly as the keep and partly as the kitchen, to which the " twa grit iron chimnayis," the " standard raxis," the " fywe lang speittis," and other culinary implements, belonged. The second, which is also vaulted, formed the large or grand hall. Judging of it even in its now ruinous state, it must have been a capacious and splendid apartment. It extended the whole length and width of the building. The roof is of great height. The large " burnest" (burnished) chimney would grace the fire-place. The two chairs of oak would also belong to it. It may seem rather curious that there should be only two chairs in a nobleman's castle; but the fact is easily accounted for, when it is known that seats of another de-

---

\* Tripe veluet—an inferior kind of velvet.
† Seruietes (servettis)—table napkins.
‡ Dornick—a species of linen table-cloth.
§ Rallow caddow—a kind of streaked or rayed woollen cloth.

---

\* Codwairis—pillow-slips.
† Crambasie (crammasay)—crimson.
‡ Champit—having raised figures.

scription were used. The chairs, in all likelihood, were placed at the head of the "buirds" or tables, which, from the number of them—two long and one short—seem to have formed a double row: one of the long upon each side, and the short running across at the head of the hall. Stone seats, projecting from the walls on both sides, still remain; so that, with the three forms—mentioned in the list—placed parallel with the "buird" in the centre of the floor, there would be a double row of seats to each set of tables. These covered with Flander's damask; the stone seats, as well as the forms, laid over with cushions of velvet or carpet rush work; the walls, no doubt, covered with tapestry;* and the hall lighted up with five great brazen chandeliers, some idea may be formed of the splendour of the apartment on occasions of festivity, when the oaken chairs were filled by the noble host and hostess of the castle, and the cushioned seats with the fair and gallant of the land. On the third floor there seems to have been two principal chambers, besides smaller apartments, one only having a fire-place, as there is no more than one "chalmer chimnay" mentioned in the list. This apartment would contain one of the "twa stand bedis of aich," with the down bed, the head sheets of fine linen "schewit with black selk and perling," the pillow slips of fine linen sewn with black silk, and the curtains of *crammasy* worsted. Add to this the carpet-covered "chalmer buird," three or four of the "sax buffet stuills," with the walls hung with tapestry, and we have, in all likelihood, a fair picture of the state bed-room of the Lords Boyd in the sixteenth and beginning of the seventeenth centuries. The other chamber would be furnished after a similar and not much inferior fashion. The fourth and highest story would be occupied with the other beds—there having been nine in all, " ane down bed" and "aucht feddir beddis." For these there were "auchteine pair of dowbill blankettis"—two pair of double blankets for each, besides coverings.

Such was the plenishing of Dean Castle in 1611. Save "ane meikle bybill" (Bible) it does not appear that there was a book within its walls. According to tradition, the castle was destroyed by fire, through the carelessness of a laundry maid, in 1735, while the Earl of Kilmarnock was absent in France. We know, from the town books of Kilmarnock, that the Earl was in France

in 1732-3—the Countess having been then empowered to manage his estates in his absence; so that the tradition is probably correct. It is said the first notice his lordship had of the event was in a London newspaper, on his arrival from France.

*Craufurdland Castle.*—This ancient residence has been greatly augmented by recent additions, all in excellent keeping with the character of the building. The centre, erected by the present proprietor, is a fine Gothic structure. The most ancient part of it, the tower, is said, although upon what authority we know not, to have been " built prior to the days of William the Conqueror." The walls are of great thickness, and no doubt claim a remote antiquity. The situation of the castle is truly a delightful one. It stands on the summit of a steep bank, overlooking Craufurdland water, which bounds the estate upon one side, while Fenwick water limits it on the other, both of which streams take their rise in the neighbouring moors, and uniting at Dean Castle, form the Kilmarnock water. " In the vernal season of the year," says the historian of Kilmarnock, " the romantic bank on which Craufurdland castle is situated is covered with a beautiful sheet of yellow daffodils, indigenous to the soil. On this delightful spot Mrs Craufurd assembles yearly, in April, about 700 or 800 children, who are all supplied with a large bouquet. Some years the floral display is so luxuriant, that half as many more children might carry off its golden honours." The castle is surrounded with wood, and there are numerous shady avenues in the vicinity, as well as a beautiful lake, upon which, in the winter season, the animating game of curling is keenly contested by the curlers of Fenwick, Kilmarnock, &c., all of whom are made welcome by the proprietor.

*Rowallan Castle.*—This mansion, deserted and in decay, save one or two apartments occupied by the baron bailie, is delightfully situated on the banks of the Carmel water. There are different dates upon the building, which is of singular construction, with various initials, and the three mullets and a moor's head, the arms of the family. The principal and more ornamental part of the mansion appears to have been erected in 1562. There is, however, the fragment of a tower of much higher antiquity, situated on a projecting rock immediately in the rear of the more modern building. This is supposed to have been the birth-place of Elizabeth More, first wife of Robert II. of Scotland; and was anciently called, no doubt from its situation, the Craig of Rowallan. The Rowallan family were zealous sup-

---

* No mention is made of tapestry in the inventory, but it was then common in the houses of the nobility, and probably it might be regarded as a fixture. It was only to the moveables and a certain sum of money that the gift of escheat to Elphinstone extended.

porters of the Reformation, and the covenanted cause of Scotland. Conventicles were not unfrequently held within the mansion, and one of the apartments, in which are preserved two "Kirk stools" of the period, still bears the name of the "Auld Kirk."

## EMINENT PERSONS CONNECTED WITH THE PARISH.

*Sir William Mure of Rowallan,* author of the "True Crucifixe for True Catholikes," a metrical version of the Psalms of David, &c., deserves to be noticed under this head, although an outline of his history and character will fall to be given when we come to the genealogical account of his family. We may observe, in passing, that he was a poet of no small reputation in his time, though few of his pieces are now known.

The name of another and more popular poet, the Ayrshire Bard, can never be mentioned without calling forth the recollection that it was in Kilmarnock where the first edition of the Poet's works was printed, and where he met with some of his earliest and kindest patrons.* It is intimately associated, too, with several of his most spirited productions, "The Ordination," "The Twa Herds," "Tam Samson's Elegy," &c. Referring to the Poet's frequent visits to Kilmarnock, and his intimacy with some of its most intelligent inhabitants, the historian of Kilmarnock remarks that "nothing has been said, so far as we are aware, respecting the house of Sandy Patrick, in which the Poet was wont to spend many merry evenings in 'Auld Killie,' with the hero of one of his finest poems, namely, Tam Samson, and other boon companions. Sandy, who was married to a daughter of Mr Samson's, brewed within his own premises the *cap ale*, which the old sportsman used to drink with Burns and other social cronies after a day's shooting. Sandy's Public, which consisted of two stories, and which was famed

'Thro' a' the streets and neuks o' Killie'

for its superior drink, was situated at the foot of Back Street, (at that time one of the principal thoroughfares of the town,) and was called 'The Bowling Green House,' from being near to the old Bowling Green, which lay immediately behind it, in the direction of the present George Inn. But, like Sandy himself, and the other jolly mortals who were accustomed to assemble within

its walls, the house which the presence of genius had hallowed, and which would have been an object of interest to many at the present day, is now no more, having been taken down about the time that East George Street was formed. In our humble opinion, however, the name of Sandy Patrick is worthy of a place in the biographies of the Poet, along with those of Nanse Tannock, Lucky Pringle, and Johnnie Dowie.

"Burns tells us, in a note to the 'Elegy on Tam Samson,' that this worthy sportsman, on one occasion, when going on a shooting excursion, 'expressed a wish to die and be buried in the muirs,' and that ' on that hint he composed his elegy and epitaph.' From a respectable source, we have learned the following additional particulars regarding the origin of the piece. On the occasion referred to, Mr Samson was longer than usual in returning from his 'fields.' Burns was then in Kilmarnock, and being in company with Mr Charles Samson [nephew of the sportsman], the conversation turned upon the shooting season. ' By the bye, Burns,' said Charles, ' have you heard anything of my uncle to-day?' ' Not a syllable,' replied the Bard; ' but why that question?' ' He has been longer than his wont in returning from his sports,' answered Charles, ' and his wish about dying among the muirs has, perhaps, been realised.' ' I recollect the words of the game old cock, but I trust it will turn out otherwise.' The Poet, however, became a little thoughtful; and, taking a piece of paper from his pocket, wrote the first draught of the elegy and epitaph. In the course of the evening Mr Samson returned, safe and sound. A meeting of his friends took place, and Burns, of course, was one of the party. To amuse them he read the elegy. ' Na, na, Robin,' cried the subject of the poem, ' I'm no fond o' that mournfu' story; I wad rather ye wad tell the world that I'm hale an hearty.' Burns, to gratify his friend, retired for a short time to another apartment, and wrote the *Per Contra*, with which he immediately returned, and read to the company:—

' Go Fame, and canter like a fillie,
Thro' a' the streets and neuks o' Killic;
Tell every honest, social billie
    To cease his grievin';
For, yet unscathed by death's sleg gullic,
    Tam Samson's livin.'

The rehearsal of the verse, we need scarcely say, restored the old sportsman to his wonted good humour."

The late *Sir James Shaw, Bart.,* some time Lord Mayor and City Chamberlain of London, though a native of the neighbouring parish of Riccarton, spent his early years, and received his education in Kilmarnock. During the whole

---

* See memoir of John Goldie, "terror o' the Whigs," in "The Contemporaries of Burns."

course of his successful career in London, he continued a warm friend to the land of his nativity; and many an adventurous son of "Auld Killie" owed his success in life to the generosity and untiring solicitude of the honourable Baronet. The charities of Kilmarnock, and whatever might tend, in a public way, to the advancement of the burgh, found in him a warm supporter. In the Town-Hall there is an excellent full-length portrait of Sir James. He is attired "in a full court suit, with the robes and insignia of Lord Mayor of London. He appears as if in the act of speaking in Guildhall, and holds the King's warrant of precedence (which regulated his place in the procession at Lord Nelson's funeral,) in his right hand, which rests upon the top of the table supporting the city mace and the sword of state. There is properly speaking, no back ground, although a fine fluted column upon the right hand of the baronet, and the drapery of a curtain on his left, fill up the painting." This portrait was painted by J. Tannock, Esq., another eminent native of Kilmarnock, who, in his profession as an artist in London had experienced, like many others, the kind patronage of the Lord Mayor, and presented by him to the Magistrates and Town Council of

Kilmarnock in 1817. After the death of Sir James, which occurred in 1843, the authorities of Kilmarnock, sensible of the debt of gratitude they owed to the deceased, subscribed £50 towards erecting a statue in honour of the Baronet. The subscription list was speedily augmented to nearly £1000, contributed chiefly by those who had benefited, in India and elsewhere, by his influence. The statue, executed by Mr James Fillans, from a block of Carrara marble, was erected at the Cross of Kilmarnock on the 4th of August 1848.

Amongst the flatteringly numerous crop of mechanists, artists, prose writers and poets, which Kilmarnock has in the present age produced, the name of *Thomas Morton* cannot be omitted. His Observatory, constructed by himself, has long been the pride of his townsmen; and he has gained undying reputation by the invention of the barrel or carpet machine, which conferred a great boon on the carpet establishments. This machine has been in some measure superseded by the Jacquard loom, which Mr Morton has also much improved.

*Templeton*, the vocalist, and *Macmillan*, the ventriloquist, are both natives of Kilmarnock.

---

# FAMILIES IN THE PARISH OF KILMARNOCK.

The parish of Kilmarnock, in its original extent, comprehending that of Fenwick, seems to have been divided into five baronies, viz.—Kilmarnock, Grougar, Rowallan, Craufurdland, and Polkelly. Grougar never had any castle or mansion-house, and all the rest, save Polkelly, are situated within the modern bounds of the parish of Kilmarnock, though the greater part of the baronies of Rowallan and Craufurdland are in the parish of Fenwick.

### THE BOYDS OF KILMARNOCK.

In the Boyd charter chest we found a fragment, in a hand apparently of the beginning of last century, entitled "A Genealogical Deduction of the Noble Family of Boyd." The writer says, "as for the origin of this antient family, I can say nothing, only I have seen a very antient genea-

logie of the Stewarts in manuscript, whereby in the Reign of K. Alex. ye 1st, Robert, a younger son of that noble family was ancestor of The Boyd, the sirname Stewart then not being fixed as the sirname of that illustrious house, the bearing of ye family of Boyd seeming to favour this account, which is a fess checke, the same with the bearing of Stewart, differing only in tincture; but of the antiquity of this family I have not seen any memorable mention untill that Robert De Boyd is one of the witnesses in a contract of aggrement betwixt the viladge of Irvine and Ralph of Eglintoun, anno 1205, as is evident from the originalls yet extant in the town of Irvine's charter chest, of whom descended Sir Robert De Boyd, who was by King Robert ye 1st rewarded of the merit of his good services to that Prince with the Lordship and barony of Kilmarnock upon the forfaultour of the Lord Soulls, anno 1320, from which"———. So ends the fragment.

The writer was probably Charles Dalrymple of Langlands, chamberlain to the Earl of Kilmarnock, and from a jotting on the margin, subtracting 1205 from 1709—making the Boyds of 504 years standing at that time—it seems to have been written in the latter year. Upon what authority he states that Sir Robert de Boyd obtained the "Lordship and barony of Kilmarnock upon the forfaultour of the Lord Souls, anno 1320," we know not. The statement is quite opposed to the charter granted by Robert the Bruce. According to the best of our genealogists, Cranfurd and Wood, the first of the family was,

I. SIMON, brother of Walter, the first High Steward of Scotland, and youngest son of Alan, the son of Flathald. He was a witness to the foundation charter of the Monastery of Paisley, 1160, in which he is designed *frater Walteri, filii Alani, dapiferi.*

II. Robert, his son, is said to have received the surname of *Boyt*, or *Boidh*, from his fair complexion, so expressed in Celtic, which must have been then the prevailing language of the Lowlands as well as of the Highlands. He is designed nephew of Walter the High Stewart, in the chartulary of Paisley. Robert Boyd, no doubt the same individual, is witness to a contract between Ralph de Eglintoun and the town of Irvine in 1205, which charter was in existence when Cranfurd wrote his History of Renfrewshire in 1710, but is now lost. The author of the fragment, written in 1709, which we have already quoted, seems to have also seen this charter.

III. Robert, called Boyt, or Boyd, is to be found in a charter of the lands of Halkhill, 1262; the same party, it is believed, who distinguished himself at the battle of Largs, in 1263, and obtained a grant of land in Cuninghame. It is not known, however, where the lands were situated.

IV. Robert Boyt swore fealty to Edward I. in 1296; but joined Sir William Wallace in 1297. He was in all likelihood the same person, designated Sir Robert Boyd, who was one of the first associates of Robert the Bruce, in his arduous attempt to restore the liberties of Scotland in 1306, although Wood places Sir Robert as No V. in the genealogy. What makes this the more probable is the fact, that Boyd was regarded as a warrior of considerable standing. Harvey, in his "Life of Bruce," thus alludes to him, in describing the various positions of the leaders at Bannockburn:

"Ranged on the right the Southron legions stood,
And on their front the fiery Edward[*] rode;

[*] Edward Bruce, brother to the King.

With him the EXPERIENCED BOYD divides the sway,
Sent by the King to guide him thro' the day."

For his faithful adherence to the cause of Bruce, says Wood, he had a grant from that monarch, *Roberto Boyde, militi, dilecto et fideli nostro,* of the lands of Kilmarnock, Bondington, and Hertschaw, which were John de Baliol's; the lands of Kilbryd and Ardnel, which were Godfrey de Ross's, son of the deceased Reginald de Ross; all the land which was William de Mora's, in the tenement of Dalry; with seven acres of land, which were Robert de Ross's, in the tenement of Ardnel: all erected into an entire and free barony, to be held of the King. He had also a charter of the lands of Nodellesdale; and a third, granting Hertschaw in freeforest.[*]

He was one of the guarantees of a treaty of peace with the English, 1323. He was taken prisoner at the battle of Halidonhill, 19th July 1333; and died not long afterwards.[†] He had three sons:

1. Sir Thomas.
2. Alan, who commanded the Scottish archers at the siege of Perth, under the Steward of Scotland, 1339, and was killed there.
3. James, witness in a charter 1342.

V. Sir Thomas Boyd of Kilmarnock, the eldest son, had, from King David II., a grant of the forfeiture of William Carpenter, and accompanied that monarch to the battle of Durham, in 1346, where he was taken prisoner with his royal master. He had three sons:

1. Sir Thomas.
2. William, ancestor of the Boyds of Badinheath, in Strathearn.
3. Robert, first of the house of Portincross.

VI. Sir Thomas Boyd of Kilmarnock had a remission from Robert Duke of Albany, governor of Scotland, in 1409, for the slaughter of Neilson of Dalrymple. He married Alice, second daughter and co-heir of Sir John Gifford of Yester, by whom he had a son,

VII. Sir Thomas Boyd of Kilmarnock, who was one of the hostages for the ransom of King James I., 1424. His annual revenue was then estimated at 500 merks. He married Joanna Montgomery, daughter of Sir John Montgomery of Ardrossan, and died 7th July 1432.[†] He had issue:—

[*] In Robertson's Index, among the missing charters of King Robert I. are five to Robert Boyd, of Duncoll and Clark's lands, in Dalswinton; to Robert Boyd, son of William Boyd, the lands of Duncoll, and the barony of Dalswinton and lands of Dulgarthe; to Robert Boyd, of the lands of Glenkin; of the five penny land of Trabeache, in Kyle regis: and of the five penny land of Trabeache, in Kyle. Also a charter of David II. to John Boyd, of the lands of Gnayllstoun, in Galloway, forfeited by John Gnailstoun.

[†] As we have already seen from Pont, a monument was erected to him and his wife in the church of Kilmarnock.

1. Sir Thomas.
2. William, Abbot of Kilwinning.

VIII. Sir Thomas Boyd of Kilmarnock having, from old feud, slain Sir Alan Stewart of Dernelly in 1439, Alexander Stewart, brother of Sir Alan, went in pursuit of him, and the two parties, for each were accompanied by their followers, having met at Craignaught Hill, in Renfrewshire, 9th July 1439, a severe conflict ensued, and Sir Thomas was killed. He had issue:

1. Robert, who succeeded.
2. Sir Alexander Boyd of Duncrow, a mirror of chivalry, appointed to superintend the military exercises of King James III. 1466; executed 22d Nov. 1469.
1. Janet, married to John Maxwell of Calderwood.
2. Margaret, married to Alexander Lord Montgomerie.

IX. Robert Boyd of Kilmarnock was created Lord Boyd in 1459. He rose to great distinction, and had many high offices intrusted to him. On the death of Bishop Kennedy, in 1466, Lord Boyd and his sons, together with his brother, Sir Alexander Boyd of Duncrow, may be said to have had for sometime the supreme command in Scotland. His Lordship was in fact appointed, 25th October 1466, governor of the kingdom till the sovereign came of age. His son, Thomas, who was created Earl of Arran, was married to Mary, eldest sister of the King; upon which event it is supposed that the splendid castle, called Law Castle, at Kilbryde, one of the seats of the Boyd family, was built. In the *Introduction* to the present work, we have already given an outline of the rise and fall of the house of Boyd at this time, with several original documents, showing how careful they had been to extend their influence, by bonds of alliance and mutual support, with the heads of families and parties in power. All their efforts, however, were unavailing; and at length, driven to rebellion, Lord Boyd fled to Alnwick, where he died in 1470. His brother, Sir Alexander of Duncrow, was taken prisoner, and beheaded on the Castlehill of Edinburgh, 22d Nov. 1469.

Lord Boyd married Mariota, daughter of Robert Maxwell of Calderwood, by whom he had issue:

1. Thomas, Earl of Arran.
2. Alexander.
3. Archibald, first of the Boyds of Bonshaw.
1. Elizabeth, married to Archibald, fifth Earl of Angus.
2. Annabella, married to Sir John Gordon of Lochinvar.

X. Thomas Earl of Arran, married the eldest daughter of James II. The island of Arran was granted to him as her dower, and erected into an earldom, in order to elevate the station of her husband, by a charter dated 26th April 1467.* The Earl and his royal consort had also a grant of the lands of Stewarton, Tarrinzean, Turnberry, and many other properties in various districts of Scotland. In short, so elevated was his position, that the nobility became jealous; and while he was absent on the Continent, in 1468, on the well known matrimonial commission for a wife to James III., he and his whole family fell into disfavour with the weak-minded monarch, and flying abroad with his wife, who met him on his arrival at Leith, he died at Antwerp, where, according to Buchanan, a magnificent monument was erected to his memory by Charles the Bold.* His wife had previously been brought back to Scotland, through the influence of the King; but, according to Drummond, " instead of having access to her brother (the king) she was kept at Kilmarnock, the chief house of the Boyds, as in a free prison." She was, in 1474, after the death of the Earl, married to James Lord Hamilton, and had two charters, dated 14th October 1483, of the liferent of all the lands which had belonged to Robert Lord Boyd, and Thomas Boyd his son. By her first husband she had:

1. James.
2. Margaret, married first to Alexander, fourth Lord Forbes; secondly, to David, first Earl of Cassillis, without issue. She is called 'Grizel' by Wood; but, according to the Boyd charter chest, Margarett had the lands of Thorntoun, in the lordship of Kilbryde and sheriffdom of Lanark, conferred upon her while Lady Forbes; and also the lands of Balgray, by David Lord Kennedy, the last of which deeds is dated in 1532.

XI. James, only son of Thomas Earl of Arran, was restored to the property of the family—which had been forfeited—by two charters, dated 14th October 1482, to his mother in liferent, and to him in fee.‡ He was slain, either by treachery or open assault, in 1484. His death does not seem to have been ever inquired into. In Boethius' " Chronicles of Scotland," he is said to have been slain by Lord Montgomerie; and in the history of the Craufurds of Craufurdland, one of that family is stated to have died of wounds he received at the Wylielie, when attending James Earl of Arran, who was there killed by the Earl of Eglintoun. He died, according to Boyd of Trochrig, " in ipso adolescentis flore periit inimicorum insidiis circumventus." His sister, Margaret, was served heir to him in 1495.‖ The representation of the Kilmarnock family now devolved upon

XII. Alexander Boyd, second son of Robert Lord Boyd, who had charters of the lands of

---

* This charter we have seen in the Boyd charter chest at Kilmarnock.

* The Earl was esteemed one of the most accomplished and best men of the age.
† This accords with Craufurd, who calls her Margaret.
‡ Charter in the Boyd charter chest at Kilmarnock.
‖ Retour in Boyd charter chest.

Railston, in the barony of Kilmarnock, 30th of Nov. 1492, of Bordland, 1494 ; and he was made Bailie and Chamberlain of Kilmarnock for the Crown in 1505. By an indenture, dated Edinburgh, 27th June 1508, Margaret, Queen of Scots, with the consent of her right excellent and illustrious spouse, James IV., "maikis" and "lattis" to Alexander Boyd in Kilmarnock, and to his heirs, "ane or mae," the lordship and lands of Kilmarnock, Dalry, Nodisdail and Kilbryde.* He married a daughter of Sir Robert Colvill of Ochiltree, by whom he had issue :

1. Robert.
2. Thomas, ancestor of the Boyds of Pitcon.
3. Adam, ancestor of the Boyds of Pinkill and Trochrig.

XIII. Robert Boyd, the eldest son, had charters, according to *Wood*, of the King's lands of Chapelton, and land and castle of Dundonald. 1st June 1537. According to *Craufurd*, he was restored to the title of Lord Boyd in 1536, and had a grant from King James V., whom he faithfully served at home and abroad, of the lordship of Kilmarnock, 20th May 1536.(?) This date, queried by *Wood*, appears to be wrong ; at least there is in the charter chest at Kilmarnock, the original "Instrument of Instalment" of Robert Boyd "in the toun and Castle of Kilmarnock," dated 5th May 1534. On the accession of this Robert Boyd, who was styled Gudeman of Kilmarnock, he seems to have revived the feuds existing between his house and that of Eglintoun. He and his friends had slain Patrick Montgomerie of Irvine, from old feud, no doubt, in December 1528,† and the matter having been taken up by the Earl of Eglintoun, a commission, consisting of Robert, Archbishop of Argyle, and a number of the heads of families connected with the west of Scotland, met "at Glasgow, the seventh day of May, ye zeir of God ane thousand five hundreth and thretty zeirs" (1530), for the purpose of bringing the quarrel to an amicable issue. The opposing parties were "Hew Earl of Eglintoun, his barnis, brethryn, freynds, lands and housands for ye ta part, and Robert Boyd de Kilmarnock, Mungow Muir, Master of Rowallane, thair barnis, brethryn, freynds, servands and housands for the other part." By the settlement entered into at this time, which was to make up for all bygone slaughters and injuries on both sides, it was agreed that Robert Boyd of Kilmarnock should accept, "for the slauchter of his chief"—no doubt James Earl of Arran—the "sowne of twa thousand merks," to be paid by instalments, &c.*

Robert Boyd of Kilmarnock seems to have been a person of judgment and resolution, and bent on the restoration of his house. For this purpose he entered into bonds of mutual support with various powerful parties in the state, such as the Earl of Argyle and Robert Lord Fleming; while maintaining a close friendship with the Muirs of Rowallan and others of his more immediate neighbours, he was able to maintain his place against the more powerful barons of the district. At the battle of "Glasgow Field," as it is called, fought in 1543, between the Earl of Lennox and the Regent Hamilton, and their adherents, during the minority of Mary, Robert Boyd of Kilmarnock and his friend Mungo Mure of Rowallan, at the head of a small party of horse, valiantly thrust themselves "into the midst of the combat," and decided the fate of the day favourably for the Regent Hamilton. For this piece of timely service the Gudeman of Kilmarnock was rewarded with the family lands, which he held in tack, as well as the family honours. It would appear that the Glencairn family had laid some claim to the barony of Kilmarnock, during the forfeiture of the Boyds, for upon the back of this restoration, it seems to have been necessary for Queen Mary to grant a letter discharging the execution of any letters at the instance of the Master of Glencairn, charging "Robert Boyd, or any otheris withhaldaris of the Castell of Kylmarnock, to deliver the same to hym or his servandis"—29th October 1593.† On the 11th March 1544 he was served heir of James Boyd, his father's brother's son, in the lands and baronies of Kilmarnock, Dalry, Kilbride, &c.‡ He had a confirmation from Queen Mary of all the estates, honours, and dignities that belonged to the deceased Robert Lord Boyd, his grandfather, with a novodamus 1549. It is supposed he died in 1550. Previous to his death he had resigned the lands and lordship of Kilmarnock to his son. He married Helen, daughter of Sir John Somerville of Cambusnethan, by whom he had.

1. Robert.
2. Margaret, married to John Montgomerie of Lainshaw.

XIV. Robert, fourth Lord Boyd, had a charter of the lands and lordship of Kilmarnock, on

---

* Boyd charter chest.

† A remission was afterwards obtained for this offence. The remission is in the charter chest.

* The original of this agreement is in the Kilmarnock charter chest; also of several discharges for all offences from Queen Margaret from 1510 to 1536.

† Boyd charter chest.

‡ The retour, and other legal papers following thereupon are in the Charter chest at Kilmarnock.

his father's resignation, 6th September, 1545. He married, in 1535, Margaret, daughter and heiress of Sir John Colquhoun of Glins, and had a charter—" to Robert Boyd of Glin, and Margaret Colquhoun his wife "—of the lands of Balindoran, in Stirlingshire, 18th Feb. 1546-7. As mentioned in the introductory essay to this work, Lord Boyd was a warm supporter of the cause of Queen Mary, and introsted by her with the management of the most important affairs. In the Boyd charter chest there are several commissions and letters to Lord Boyd, signed by the unfortunate Queen. Like his father, he endeavoured to support his house by alliances with influential parties, and by bonds of man-rent with the smaller barons of the west country.[*]

Notwithstanding the settlement entered into by the houses of Kilmarnock and Eglintoun in 1530, the feud between them still continued, Sir Neil Montgomerie of Lainshaw[†] having been killed by Lord Boyd and his adherents[‡] in a skirmish in the streets of Irvine in 1547. This slaughter was warmly resented by the Montgomeries, and the Master of Boyd scarcely dared appear openly in the county for some time. He had, in fact, along with Mowat of Busbie and others, to give bond to Neil Montgomerie of Lainshaw, to go to France, and remain there during his pleasure. At length, in 1561, the affair was made up between the parties, Lord Boyd appearing at the Cross of Irvine, and paying a fine to the son of the deceased Sir Neil Montgomerie.[||] The feud thus staunched, a close friendship seems to have ensued between the two houses; at least among the Boyd papers there is " ane mutuall band between Hew Erl of Eglintoun and Robert Lord Boyd," dated 25th August 1563. There was also a bond of mutual support between Robert Lord Boyd and Hew Craufurd of Kilbirnie, dated Ryesholme, 18th July 1567, wherein it is stipulated that, in return for the services of " Hew Craufurd, his friends, servands," Lord Boyd shall, in case of his death, protect his spouse, Isobella Barclay and her bairns.[§]

Lord Boyd had a respite for nineteen years given by Queen Mary, with the " consent of our deirest cousing and tutor, James Duke of Chattellarailt, Earl of Arran, Lord Hamilton, Protector and Governor of our realme," for " his tressonable art and part and assistance gevin be him to John, vmquhile Johne Erle of Levinax, aidand aganis our maist noble fader of gude mynde, quham God assolze, and his authoritie, in arrayit battell, besyde our burgh of Linlithgow, our said vmquhile derrest fader being thair present, and his banner being displayit for the tyme," &c. Dated the last day of March 1552. He and his friends were also engaged with the Duke of Chasselherault in taking the castles of Haddington and Draffin, for which offence he had a remission from Henry and Mary, including all those engaged with him, dated 23d April 1560.[*] In these eventful times, we next find his lordship engaged in the association formed in favour of Queen Mary at Hamilton, 8th May 1568, and fighting at the battle of Langside, in consequence of which he and his two sons, Thomas, Master of Boyd, and Robert of Badinheath, were compelled to leave the country by order of the Regent. During their absence, the Laird of Knockdolian attempted to dispossess Lord Boyd of the bailiary of the barony of Grougar; but his friends, under " Sanderis Boyd, chamberland to the said Lord Boyd," mustered in great force, and prevented Knockdolian from holding his intended court. At length, when the cause of the Queen became desperate, he had the address to gain favour with the Regent Lennox, and on the 8th September 1571, had a remission under the Great Seal for appearing against the king at Langside.

On the 12th of August previous to this, an agreement was made at Stirling (12th August, 1571) between the Earl of Morton, Chancellor of Scotland, and the Earl of Mar, on the one part, and the Earl of Argyle, Cassillis, Eglintoun, and Lord Boyd, on the other, that " from the troubled state of the realm, his Majesty being inanymat, and his mider (mother) being in the realm of England, and with a view to the settlement of the same to his hienes's obedience, subscrive a bond to that effect.

" They sal have a remitt to thame, thair friends and servandis, for not obeying and serving the King in tyme bygane, and for all other causes except the murther of the King's fadder, to our soneraine Lord and the Earl of Murray, his hie-

---

* Amongst others he had a bond of man-rent from John Cochrane, zoung laird of Bischoptoun, dated 30th Sept, 1546.

† Sir Neil was the father-in-law of Margaret, sister of Lord Boyd, then Master of Boyd.

‡ Nisbet, repeated by Robertson. The date may be questionable, though the fact is certain. It is evident, however, that the deed was committed by Robert the fourth Lord Boyd, and not by his father, the third Lord, better known as ' Gudeman of Kilmarnock,' as inferred by the historian of Kilmarnock, for in the account of the affair in the Rowallan memorandum he is styled " the Maister of Boyd."

|| See vol. 1. p. 64.

§ Witnesses to this document, Thomas Master of Boyd,

James Boyd of Trochrig, Hew Montgomery of Hessilheid, James Boyd.

* Boyd charter chest.

nes lait regent, for murther, slaughter, revissing of women, theft, and witchcraft, exceptand furth of the said exceptioun slauchter and other crymes comittit in the commoun cause, or depending vpoun, qlk sall alwyis be comprehendit vnder the said remitt.

"Also, as my saidis lordis of Argyle, Cassillis, Eglintoun and Boyd, may procure to the king's obedience and service, sal have the like appointment as they justly gett, being in the like state as they now are in.

"And seeing the intention of the noblemen on baith parts is to preserve the quietness and commoun weill of the realme, and that the same can not be, rather hindred mor, be vptaking of the eschaits and guidis of the persons now aiding to the kingis obedience for crymes attributed to thame, . . . . in the commoun caus, and depending thairon. Thairfor all escheattis of the noblemen above written, thair freinds or servandis, disponit upon the accessoris of the commoun caus, or depending thairon, sall tak na effect aftir the dait heirof, bot be simplie dischargit," &c.

The Boyd papers show, in conformity with this agreement, that Lord Boyd had been careful to strengthen his position by cultivating the support of others. He had a bond of man-rent, dated "Irwin, tent day the moneth of November 1571," from "William Fairlie, bruder german to James Fairlie of that Ilk," in return for which my Lord Boyd gave him the "threttie shylling land of auld extent of Byrehill, in the perochin and regalitie of Kilwinning;" another from John Fergushill of that Ilk, dated at Aslos, 26th October 1572; and a third from the Laird of Lochrigis, "Andro Arnet, zoungare;" binding himself and heirs at all times to "ryde and gang" with the said Robert Lord Boyd, dated 1st Feb. 1573. The peace of the realm was still farther secured by a bond of friendship, dated 13th June 1578, between Hew Earl of Eglintoun, Lord Montgomerie, William Erle of Glencairn, Robert Lord Boid, Mathew Campbell of Loudoun, Knt., Sheriff of Air, John Wallace of Craigie, for himself, Hew Master of Eglintoun, James Master of Glencairn, Thomas Master of Boid, Hew Campbell of Tarringan, &c. There was also a bond of mutual assistance between Lord Boyd and the Laird of Blair, dated 2d March 1575; and a bond of man-rent from Robert Colquhoun, Laird of Cambustrodain, January 1575.

From the epitaph preserved in the church of Kilmarnock in memory of Lord Boyd, previously quoted—

"Heir lies yt godlie, noble, wyis lord Boyd," &c.—

it might have been supposed that he was a person slow to the shedding of blood. Such was not the case, however, as the various feuds in which he was engaged sufficiently attest. In revenge of the slaughter of Sir Robert Colville of Ochiltree, his maternal grandfather, Lord Boyd, Thomas Master of Boyd, and others, waylaid and slew John Mure, in the Well, on his way home from Ayr, in August 1571, the month immediately prior to his obtaining the remission already mentioned. Of course these slaughters may be attributed more to the spirit of the times than to any peculiar blood-thirstiness on the part of the individual.[*] In 1589, Robert Lord Boyd paid 350 merks to John Muir of Rowallan, "in full of all claims for the slauchter of his father," in presence of Mr Robert Wilkie, minister of Kilmarnock, one of the witnesses, Muir at the same time obliging himself to enter into friendship with Lord Boyd.[†]

James VI. is known to have acted on the principle that those who were faithful to his mother could hardly prove false to her son—hence many who espoused most heartily the cause of Queen Mary enjoyed the greatest share of his confidence. One of these was Robert Lord Boyd. Amongst the Boyd papers there is a letter from James VI., dated 14th March 1577, requiring Lord Boyd to attend at Stirling, to consult with others of his nobility as to the demission of his last regent, the Earl of Morton, and as to his assuming the government in his own person. Lord Boyd must have at this period held the office of General Collector, as there is an order from the Regent, dated 13th May 1577, desiring him as "General Collector" to pay £200 to the College of Glasgow. There are also letters from the King, in 1577, requesting his attendance at Stirling, on the 8th of December, with the view of settling the disturbances in the west. About the same time the Lords of "Counsell, with consent of James Earl of Morton, discharge Robert Lord Boyd and his tenantis, inhabitantis and ocuperis of his ten pund land of Gliu, and ten pund land of Dinnerbok, Auchinburlie and Spittale, liand within our sheriffdome of Dunbartane, to Robert Boyd of Badinheith, and his tenantis, inhabitantis and occuparis of his fyve pund land of Badinheith, within the sheriffdom of Striviling and seven pund land of Galbers (or Gawers) and Resk, within the sheriffdom of Renfrew, to Humphra Colquhoun of Luss and his tenantis, inhabitantis and occuperis of his fyftie three pund 8s 4d.

---

* It is stated by Bannatyne that Lord Boyd visited Knox, when the latter was on his death-bed, to beg his forgiveness, probably for the part he had taken in favour of Queen Mary and the Catholic party.

† Boyd charter chest. Document dated 14th Sept. 1589.

land of the baronie of Luss, "to remane and byde at hame fra our raid and army appointit to convene and meit our said cousing and regent at Dumfries, upon the tent day of October restant, ffor persute and invasioun of the thevis and outlawis, disturbaris of the peace and quietness of our realm"—dated 6th Oct. 1577.

These documents show in what estimation the services and character of Lord Boyd, notwithstanding the slaughters and feuds in which he had been engaged, were held by the sovereign and his regent. He was twice appointed an extraordinary Lord of Session, which office he filled till his retirement in 1588, and was one of the commissioners sent to negotiate a treaty with England in 1578, and again in 1586. In 1583 he had a pass (4th Sept.) from James VI. to go abroad for five years, for "doing of his lefull affairs," with six persons in company.* By this pass it appears he intended to visit France and Flanders. He was not allowed, however, to remain long abroad; for there is a letter from James VI., dated 11th Feb. 1585, recalling him from abroad, to take his place in Council, in which letter he is highly complimented for the commendable fidelity always reported of Lord Boyd.

Lord Boyd died on the 3d of January 1589, aged 72; his lady, Margaret, or Mariot Colquhoun, in Feb. 1601. They had issue:

1. Robert Master of Boyd, who had a charter of the lands of Auchintuerlie, in Dumbartonshire, 14th Oct. 1540, and died without issue soon afterwards.
2. Thomas fifth Lord Boyd.
3. Robert Boyd of Badenheath, in Stirlingshire. He acquired various properties in Lanarkshire. He was tutor to his nephew, Hew fifth Earl of Eglintoun. He had the keeping of the fortalice of Lochwood, with the pertinents and lands, in the barony of Glasgow, disponed to him by James VI., with consent of the Regent Morton, 4th March 1572. He had a pass to France, from James VI., for three years, "having certain lefull effaires to do within the realme of France, and specialie for visiting of our traist cousing, Robert Lord Boyd, his fader," dated 23d April 1585. He had another, in 1587, for the same purpose.†
4. Egidia, married to Hew fourth Earl of Eglintoun.
5. Agnes, married to Sir John Colquhoun of Luss.
6. Christian, married to Sir James Hamilton of Avondale, and had issue.
7. Elizabeth, married to John Cuninghame of Drumquhassell.

XV. Thomas fifth Lord Boyd, the eldest surviving son, succeeded. He was served heir in special to his father Robert Lord Boyd, 20th March 1589.‡ He had been engaged, as we have seen, in most of the feuds and public transactions which had occupied the attention of his able and politic

* Pass in charter chest.
† Kilmarnock papers.
‡ Retour in charter chest.
VOL. II.

father. He seems to have suffered much from ill health. In 1579—July 14th—"Thomas Master of Boyd" had a pass from James VI. to go abroad for three years, for the benefit of his health. The pass runs thus:—"We, understanding that our cousing, Thomas Master of Boyd, is vext with ane vehement dolour in his heid, and other discises in his body, as he cannot find sufficient ease and remeid within our realme, bot is in mynd to seik the same in forein cuntries, quhair the samyn maist convenientlie may be had, thairfor be the tenor heirof gevis and grantis licence to the said Thomas Maister of Boyd to depart and pas furth of our realme, to the partis of France, Flanderis, Wall of the Spa, and otheris partis, quhair he pleises, thair to remain for seiking of cure and remedy of his saidis discasis, for the space of thrie zeiris after the dait heirof; and will and grantis that he sall not be callit nor accusit thairfor criminalie nor civilie be ony maner of way in tyme coming, nor sall not incur ony skaith nor danger thairthrow, in his person, landis, nor guidis, notwithstanding quhatsomever our actis, letters, statutes, proclamationis or charges, maid or to be maid, in the contrair, or ony pains conteint thairin. Anent the quhilks we dispens be thir presentis. Attour we haif takin, and be thir presentis takis oure said cousing, his kin, freinds, tenentis and servandis, duelland vpon his proper landis, his and thair landis, heretages, benefices, actionis, causs, possessionis, guidis and geir, in speciall protection, supplie, maintenance, defence and savegaird, to be unhurt, vnharmit, unmolestit, troublit, or in onywais pursewit, for the caus foirsaid, during the said space of thrie zeires. Discharging heirfoir our justice, justice clerkis, the sairvand advocattis, judgeis, ministeris of our lawis, and thair deputtis and vtheris our officiaris, liegis and siclike, off all calling, accusing, vnlawing, or in onywais proceeding criminalie nor civilie agains our said cousing, Thomas Master of Boyd, and his saidis kin, freinds, servandis and tenentis, duelland within his proper landis, for his departing and remaning furth of our realme, as said is, pounding, troubling, or in onywais intrometting with thame, thair landis or guidis thairfoir, and of thair offices in that part for evir. Providing always that our said cousing do not attempt nathing in prejudice of us, our realme and religioun, publielie preachit and professit within our realme, or otherwais this our licence to be null and of none availl, force, nor effect. Gevin vnder our signet, and subscrivit, with our hand, at our castell of Striviling, the xiiii day of Julij, and of our reigne the twelfth zeir—1.5.7.9.

(Signet attached) JAMES R."

z

In 1583 Thomas Master of Boyd had licence to " repair to foreign pairts for doing of his lefull erandis." The following year he seems to have been concerned in the insurrectionary movement at St Johnston, or perhaps previously in the "Raid of Ruthven"—for, by a warrant of the King and Council Thomas Master of Boyd was ordered into ward at Aberdeen, within a circle of six miles of the city, 10th May 1584. He accordingly surrendered himself prisoner at Glasgow on the 11th of the same month, and entered himself at Aberdeen on the last day of it. He was not, however, long detained a prisoner, having had a licence from the King " to go furth of his present ward," 16th July 1585.* In 1580, while yet Master of Boyd, he gave his bond of service to his father, Robert Lord Boyd.

In 1591, 17th December, Lord Boyd resigned the lands and barony of Kilmarnock, &c. in favour of his son, Robert Master of Boyd,† and had a charter, 12th January 1592, erecting the same into a free lordship and barony to himself in life-rent, and Robert Master of Boyd, his son, in fee, and the heirs-male of his body, with a long restriction of heirs-male to the exclusion of heirs-general. He had also a charter of the lands of Bedlay, 8th March 1596. He had sasine of the lands of Knockindon and Hairschaw in 1590; a charter from Robert Cuninghame of Netherton, of the lands of Overtoun ;‡ and a charter of Auchinas in 1599.|| The lands of Bogside were wadsett to Thomas Lord Kilmarnock by James Mowat of Busbie, redeemable on payment of 800 lbs.; contract dated Edinburgh, 12th July 1603. He disponed the five pund land of Corsbie to William Wallace, minister of Failfuird, upon a back-bond, for 1720 merks, 18th August 1597.§

That Thomas Lord Boyd continued to be subjected to ill health is amply evinced by the Boyd papers. In 1595 he had a pass to go abroad for " remedie of his diseises" for five years; another dated at " Halirudhouse, the first day of March 1600;" and a third, to repair to England or any other place for his health, dated " Whitehall, 28th March." He had a licence, dated 18th December 1600, to stay at home from the wars, and board himself where he pleased, in consequence of his infirmities, the son of Robert late Master of Boyd to act in the same manner that

his father would have done under the circumstances.*

Notwithstanding his many ailments, Lord Boyd lived till June 1611. According to Wood, he married Margaret, second daughter of Sir Mathew Campbell of Loudoun. He must, however, have been twice married, as Elizabeth Wallace is mentioned as relict of Thomas Lord Boyd in a legal document in 1611. If Wood is correct, his issue were by the first marriage :

1. Robert Master of Boyd, who died in May 1597. He married Lady Jean Kerr, eldest daughter of Mark second Earl of Lothian, by whom he had
 1. Robert sixth Lord Boyd, born in November 1595.
 2. James eighth Lord Boyd.
 " Jeane Kerr, maistres of Boyde," is mentioned in several testamentary documents in 1609 and 1610.† She afterwards married David tenth Lord Craufurd.
2. Sir Thomas Boyd of Bedlay. He married Grissell Conynghame, daughter of Jeane Blair, Lady Montgrenan. Contract of marriage dated 22d October 1603.‡
3. Adam, who married Marion, (not Margaret) Galbraith, sister of Robert Galbraith of Kilcroich. He had the forty shilling land of the Nethermains of Kilbirnie given him by his father.
4. John. He had the five merk land of Whiteside, in the parish of Largs and Bailiary of Cuninghame, from his father. " Johnne Boyd, sone to my Lord Boyd," is mentioned in the testament of " Marcoun Seller, spous to Robert Broune, merchand, within the parochin of Kilmarnock, who deceist in 1614.||
 1. Marion, married to James first Earl of Abercorn.
 2. Isabel, married to John Blair of that ilk.
 3. Agnes, married to Sir George Elphinstone of Blythswood.

James Elphinstoun of Woodside, probably some relation of Sir George of Blythswood, had a " gift of escheate and liferent of all gudis, geir, movabills and unmovabills, debtis, takis as weill of landis as of teyndis, steidings, rowmes, possessions, cornis, cattle, insicht plenishing, &c. quhilk perteint of before to our traist cousing Thomas Lord Boyd, the times of his denuntiation." What " times" these were does not appear. Thomas Lord Boyd was put to the horn, 13th May 1611, shortly before his death, at the instance of John Bell, minister of Calder, for non-payment of teinds; and in 1622 Elphinstoun obtained a decreet against *Elizabeth Wallace, relict of the late Thomas Lord Boyd,* to restore certain moveables appropriated by her.§ El-

---

* Charter chest.
† The instrument of resignation following thereon is dated 10th January 1592.
‡ The sasine upon this charter is dated 3d April 1617.
|| Sasine upon this charter also in 1617.
§ Charter chest.

* We know not whether it was in consequence of any derangement occasioned by the Master of Boyd, which must have taken place before 1600, but there is a document in the family charter chest which bears that Lord Boyd, on the 10th September 1595, gave notice to his tenants to resume their lands; and this was done in presence of John Caldwell of Annanhill, James Mowat of Busbie, James Edmistoun of Airds, Patrick Craufurd of Auchinames, &c.
† Glasgow Commissary Records.
‡ Charter chest.
§ Glas. Com. Rec.
§ The inventory of the effects in Dean Castle, in connection with this case, we have given elsewhere.

phinstoun appears to have paid 3000 merks to Thomas Lord Boyd, and the action was brought against Dame Elizabeth Wallace for alleged intromitting with his lordship's estate.

XVI. Robert sixth Lord Boyd, eldest son of Robert Master of Boyd, succeeded his grandfather. He was served heir to his father in the lands and barony of Kilmarnock, &c. 12th October 1614. He had previously a gift of the ward and nonentry of the said lands, dated 19th August 1612.[*] He had a disposition of the lands of Menfurd, which comprehends a great part of the town of Kilmarnock, from John Wallace of Menfurd, dated 27th July 1619; and a tack of the parsonage teinds and sheaves of the parish of Kilmarnock from the Abbot of Kilwinning, dated 27th June of the same year. In 1621 he resigned the lands, lordship and barony of Kilmarnock, for new infeftment, to himself in liferent, and Robert Master of Boyd, his son, in fee. The precept of sasine, proceeding upon a charter under the Great Seal of the said Procuratory of Resignation, is dated 29th March 1621.[†] Lord Boyd died in August 1628, aged 33. The following is the substance of his latter-will:—

" The Testament, Testamentar, and Inventar of the guidis, geir, &c. quhilk perteint to vmqle. Robert Lerd Boyd, within the parochin of Kilmarnock, the tyme of his deceis, quha deceist vpone the xxviii day of August, the zeir of God jaj vi c. twentie aucht zeirs, &c.

" Inventar.—Item, the said vmqle. nobill Lord, Robert Lord Boyd, had perteining to him the tyme of his deceis . . . . Item, the sawing of ane boll quheit,[‡] estimat to the ferd corne pryce of the boll with the fodder viii lib., inde xxxii lib. . . . Item, on the Litle Maynes of Badinhaithe, occupiet be Johne Wod, sevin bolls corne, &c.

Summa of the Inventar, ii aj ix c lxxxxi lib.

" Debts awand In.—Item, thair was awand, &c. be Mr Johnne Hutchesoun of Scottistoun, vi c lxvi lib. . . . . Item, be the tennents of Badinhaithe of the teynd victuall of the crop 1628, &c. Item, be the tennents of Myvettis, Wardheid, Blairtin, Garvin, Gavok and Lochwod, the teynd meill the said zeir [1628] xxiiii bolls meill, pryce of the boll viii lib. Item, be the tennents of Gawan and Risk, the teynd victuall, &c. Item, be the tennents of Badinhaithe the ferme meill the said zeir, 1628, nyne bolls meill, &c. Item, be parochineris of Kilbryde, restand of the teyndis of the crep 1628 zeiris, xxii bolls meill, &c.

Item, be the tennentis of my ladie's lyfrent land in Fyff, restand be thame for the fermes in the zeir of God 1628 zeiris, viiixx bollis meill, &c.

Summa of the debtis In, vii aj iii c and lxxxxv libs. iiis. iiiid.

" Debtis awand Out.— . . . . Item, to the Kingis Majestie of blenche dewtie of the landis of Medrois,[*] xiiii lib. vi s. viii d. Item, to my Lord of Glasgow, the few dewtie of Lochwod, x lib. Item, to my Lord of Blantyre, the tak dewtie of the personage teyndis of Medrois vii lib. xvi s. . . . . Item, to Allexr. Erle of Eglintoune for the tak dewtie of the lands of Kilbryde, xix lib. Item, to my Lord of Glasgow of bygane dewties of the hous in Glasgow callit the persone's mans, xvi lib. x s. . . . Item, to James Boyd, the defunctis brother, for his dewtie, thrie hundrith xxxiii lib. vi s. viii d. . . . . Item, to the Reidair at the Kirk of Kilmarnock his pensioun, xx lib., &c.

Summa of the debtis Ont, vi aj i c and lxxii lib. xvi s. ix d.

\*　　　\*　　　\*　　　\*　　　\*

" Followis the Deidis Latterwill and Legacie of ane nobill Lord, Robert Lord Boyd.

" At Edinburgh, the sevintein day of October, the zeir of God jai vi c and twentie thrie zeirs, The quhilk day I, Robert Lord Boyd, knawing the certantie of deathe, the vncertantie of the tyme and place, and being willing, for the guid of my childreing, to mak my latterwill and testament, in sa far as concernes the nominatioun of executouris and tntouris to my childreing, Thairfoir I, be thir presents, maks and constituts my lnifing spous, Dame Christiane Hamiltoune, my only executourix with my guids and geir, geving to hir full power to give vp inventar thairof, and to conferme the samyne. And likwayis I nominat my said loveing spous Tutrix to my eldest sone, Robert Boyd, and to our haill remanent bairnes, desyring her alwayis to tak the advys and counsall, in all her effairis, of the Erle of Melros, hir father, Thomas Lord of Binnie, hir brother, Andro Bischope of Argyll, George Elphinstoun of Blythiswood, knyt., Sir Thomas Boyd of Bollinschaw, knyt., and Mr Robert Boyd of Kippis, or the maist pairt thairof, as convenientlie scho may have thame. [These parties are nominated to succeed Lady Boyd, in case of her decease or marriage, as tutors to his son and younger children. He thus concludes:—

" Assuring myself that they will loveinglie and cairfullie dischairge the dewties thairin for the guid of my bairnes, as my full trust and confidence in thame," &c.]

---

* Charter chest. " The Wardatours of the Lordschip of Boyd" occur in a testamentary document, dated Feb. 1816.

† Charter chest.

‡ Wheat was a scarce article in Ayrshire at this period.

* Probably a mistake for Melrois.

Lord Boyd married, first, Margaret, daughter of Robert Montgomerie of Giffen, relict of Hugh fifth Earl of Eglintoun, without issue (she died in 1615);[*] secondly, as we have seen, Lady Christian Hamilton, eldest daughter of Thomas first Earl of Haddington, relict of Robert tenth Lord Lindsay of Byres, by whom he had issue :

1. Robert seventh Lord Boyd.
1. Helen, who died unmarried.
2. Agnes, married to Sir George Morrison, Dairsie, in Fife.
3. Jean, married to Sir Alexander Morrison of Preston Grange, in the county of Haddington, and had issue.
4. Marion, married to Sir James Dundas of Arniston.
5. Isabel, married first to John Sinclair of Stevenston; secondly, to John Grierson, fiar of Larg, whose wife she was in 1647, when she was served heir of her sister Helen.
6. Christian, married to Sir William Scott of Harden.

XVI. Robert seventh Lord Boyd, the only son, was served heir of his father 9th May 1629. He had a tack of the teinds of Melros in 1638. About the same period the family had the teinds of Govan, as well as those of the vicarage of Glasgow. Lord Boyd married Lady Anne Fleming, second daughter of John second Earl of Wigton; but he died of a fever, without issue, on the 17th November 1640. He was succeeded by his uncle.

XVII. James eighth Lord Boyd, second son of Robert Master of Boyd. He was served heir to his nephew 10th April 1641. During the great civil war he was a steady supporter of royalty, and was fined by Cromwell in the sum of £15,000. His support of the royal cause seems to have embarrassed him considerably, as we find his lordship wadsetting the lands of Dalry, with the manor house, Rysdalhmuir, Flott, Noddisdaill, Baillicland, Harplaw, Ryelies, Ryeburne, Tourhill, Howrat, &c., " extending to ane fourtie merk land, lying within the bailiary of Cuninghame," to Sir William Cochrane of Cowdoun, knt. Calculating victual at ten merks per boll, these lands yielded the sum of 1248 libs. 13s. 4d. Scots. He also wadsett several portions of land in the barony of Kilmarnock, having previously borrowed 6000 merks from Sir William. He disposed of the teinds of the lands and barony of Powkellic to Sir William Cuninghame of Cuninghamehead, 3d November 1646.[†]

Notwithstanding the disturbed times in which he lived, Lord Boyd seems to have paid great attention to the trade of Kilmarnock, as well as to the improvement of its social condition generally, having instituted " ane schoole within the parocheine of the old Kirk of Kilmarnock," for " the educatioune and learning off zoung ones." He built, it is presumed, the more modern part of Dean Castle. His lordship married Catherine, daughter of John Craik, Esq. of the city of York, by whom he had issue :—

1. William, who succeeded.
1. Eva, married to Sir Robert Cuninghame of Robertland.

XVIII. William ninth Lord Boyd was served heir of his father in the barony of Kilmarnock, &c. 28th February 1655. He was created Earl of Kilmarnock, by patent to him and his heirs male, 7th August 1661 ; and had a charter of the barony of Kilmarnock 30th July 1672; also of Kilmarnock and Grougar in 1679.[*] He had a disposition of the " forty shilling land of old extent of the Kirkland of Kilmarnock, with the glebe lands thereof," from John Hamilton of Grange, dated 22d June 1677. He disposed of the lands of Hairschawmuir to John Boyd, merchant, Edinburgh, 6th July 1670, in payment of money borrowed from the said John.[†] His lordship died in March 1692. By his lady, Jean Cuninghame, eldest daughter of William ninth Earl of Glencairn, High Chancellor of Scotland, he had issue :

1. William second Earl of Kilmarnock.
2. Hon. Captain James Boyd.
3. Hon. Captain Charles Boyd, who died at Namur in September 1737.
4. Hon. Robert Boyd.
1. Lady Mary, married to Alexander Porterfield of Porterfield.

XIX. William second Earl of Kilmarnock succeeded his father in March 1699, but died in May the same year. He married Lettice, daughter of Thomas Boyd of the city of Dublin, and had two sons—

1. William, who succeeded.
2. Hon. Thomas Boyd, who became a member of the Faculty of Advocates in 1710. He married Eleanora, daughter of Sir Thomas Nicholson of Carnock, in the county of Stirling, Baronet, who, in her widowhood, married John Craufurd of Craufurdland.

XX. William third Earl of Kilmarnock was served heir to his father 20th July 1699, and took the oaths and his seat in Parliament 6th July 1705. He had a new patent of his title

---

* Lady Loudoun, who died in January 1617, left to her " saidie dochters, Jeane and Margaret Campbells, equallie betuix thame, the haill goldsmyth work, joells, abuilzements and vthers, left and disponit to me, be vmquhile deame Margaret Montgomerie, Ladie Boyd, content in ane particular inventar, subscrivit be ye said vmquhile deame Margaret, of the date at Sorne, the    day of    the zeir of God 1615 zeiris."

† Charter chest.

---

* Charter chest.
† Amongst the family papers there is a ' Clare Constat ' in favour of Lady Margaret Boyd, spouse of Sir Thomas Foulis of Reidfoord. This lady was a daughter of John Boyd, Dean of Guild of Edinburgh, and had sasine of the lands of Hairschaw, 27th December 1680. She and her husband disposed of the annual rent of Hairschaw to John Boill of Kelburn in 1681. Sir Thomas Foulis was a Lord of Session

and dignities from Queen Anne in 1707. As we have had occasion to narrate elsewhere, his lordship was a steady supporter of the Revolution Settlement, and displayed great military zeal in opposing the rebellion of 1714. He acquired the lands of Beinsburne and Pape's Brae, in the vicinity of Kilmarnock, from John M'Leslie, 26th February 1703. He died in September 1717, leaving by his lady Euphane, eldest daughter of William eleventh Lord Ross, an only son,

XXI. William fourth Earl of Kilmarnock. The records of the burgh of Kilmarnock, as we have previously shown, bear ample proof of the interest taken by his lordship in the affairs of the community. Unfortunately for himself he became attached to the cause of the Pretender, and joined his standard at Edinburgh immediately after the battle of Preston. Prince Charles had been entertained at Callendar House on his progress towards the capital, when, it is understood, the Earl had pledged himself to the cause. The Earl was appointed Colonel of the Horse, was with the army of the Prince in England, and acted a prominent part at the battle of Falkirk, after its return to Scotland. At the decisive field of Culloden, his lordship was taken prisoner, and conveyed to the Tower in London, where, having been convicted of high treason, he suffered decapitation, 18th August 1746. Various reasons have been assigned for his lordship's desertion of the constitutional principles in which he had been so religiously brought up; but the chief cause, as he himself has stated, seems to have been the embarrassed position of his affairs. That he deeply regretted his conduct, apart from any hope of pardon it might bring him, there appears to be no good reason to doubt; for, although his lordship confesses to an indulgence in some of the fashionable vices of the times, his innate sense of truth and justice can hardly be questioned. "While in prison," says the historian of Kilmarnock, "his lordship wrote a letter to his lady, one to his eldest son, and another to his factor, the late Boyd Paterson, Esq. The latter of these is in the possession of Mr Paterson's great-grandson, M. T. Paterson, Esq., Deanside, who has kindly permitted us to copy it. In a striking manner it exhibits the sterling honesty of the writer; and, on that account, we insert it in our pages, convinced that it will be perused wish considerable interest. It is as follows:—

'Sir,—I have commended to your care the enclosed packet to be delivered to my wife, in the manner your good sense shall dictate to you will be least shocking to her. Let her be prepared for it as much by degrees and with great tenderness as the nature of the thing will admit of. The intire dependence I have all my life had the most just reason to have on your integrity and friendship to my wife and family as well as to myself makes me desire that the enclosed papers may come to my wife through your hands, in confidence that you will take all pains, to comfort her and relieve the grief I know she will be in that you and her friends can. She is what I leave dearest, behind me in the world, and the greatest service you can do to your dead friend is to contribute as much as possible, to her happiness in mind and in her affairs.

' You will peruse the state before you deliver it to her, and you will observe that there is a fund of hers I dont mention, that of 500 Scots a year as the interest of my mother-in-law's portion, in the Countess of Errol's hands, with I believe a considerable arrear upon it; which as I have ordered a copy of all these papers to that Countess, I did not care to put in. There is another thing, of a good deal of moment, which I mention only to you, because, if it could be taken away without noise it would be better; but if it is pushed, it will be necessary to defend it:—that is a bond which you know Mr Kerr, Director to the Chancery, has of me for a considerable sum of money, with many years interest on it, which was almost all play debt. I dont think I ever had fifty pounds, or the half of it, of Mr Kerr's money, and I'm sure I never had a hundred, which however I have put it to in the enclosed Declaration that my mind may be intirely at ease. My intention, with respect to that sum, was to wait till I had some money and then buy it off by a composition of three hundred pounds, and if that was not accepted of, to defend it; in which I neither saw, nor now see anything unjust, and I leave it on my successors to do what they find most prudent in it.

' Beside my personal debts mentioned in general and particular in the State, there is one for which I am liable in justice, if it is not paid, owing to poor people who gave their work for it by my orders. It was at Elgin in Murray, the regiment I commanded wanted shoes. I commissioned something about seventy pairs of shoes and brogues, which might come to about 3s. or three and sixpence each, one with another. The magistrates divided them among the shoemakers of the town and country, and each shoemaker furnished his proportion. I drew on the town for the price, out of the composition laid on them, but I was told afterwards at Inverness that, it was believed, the composition was otherwise applied, and the poor shoemakers not paid. As these poor people wrought by my orders, it will be a great ease to my heart to think they are not to lose by me, as too many have done in the course of that year, but had I lived I might have made some inquiry after: but now it is impossible, as their hardships in loss of horses and such things, which happened through my soldiers, are so interwoven with what was done by other people, that it would be very hard, if not impossible, to separate them. If you'll write to Mr Innes of Dalkinty at Elgin (with whom I was quartered when I lay there) he will send you an account of the shoes, and if they were paid to the shoemakers or no: and if they are not, I beg you'll get my wife, or my successors, to pay them when they can.

' Receive a letter to me from Mrs Boyd, my Cousin Malcomb's widow; I shall desire her to write to you for an answer,

' Accept of my sincere thanks for your friendship and good services to me. Continue them to my wife and children. My best wishes are to you and yours and for the happiness and prosperity of the good Town of Kilmarnock, and I am Sir your humble Servant,

KILMARNOCK.

' Tower of London, Augt. 16, 1746.'

" The letter to his son was written on the day previous to his execution. We cannot resist presenting it to our readers; for, besides giving us a glimpse of the *heart* and *mind* of the unfortunate nobleman, it inculcates instruction of the highest importance :—

' Tower, 17th August, 1746.

' DEAR BOYD,—I must take this way to bid you farewell, and I pray God may for ever bless you and guide you in this world, and bring you to a happy immortality in the world to come. I must likewise give you my last advice. Seek God in your youth, and when you are old he will not depart from you. Be at pains to acquire good habits now, that they may grow up and become strong in you. Love mankind, and do justice to all men. Do good to as many as you can, and neither shut your ears nor your purse to those in distress whom it is in your power to relieve. Believe me, you will find more joy in one beneficent action, and in your cool mornings you will be more happy with the reflection of having made any one person so, who, without your assistance, would have been miserable, than in the enjoyment of all the pleasures of sense—which pall in the using—and of all the pomps and gaudy shows of the world. Live within your circumstances, by which means you will have it in your power to do good to others. * * * Prefer the public interests to your own, wherever they interfere. Love your family and your children, when you have any, but never let your regard for them drive you on the rock I split upon, when on that account I departed from my principles, and brought the guilt of rebellion on my head, for which I am now under the sentence justly due to my crime.* Use all your interest to get your brother pardoned, and brought home as soon as possible, that his circumstances and bad influence of those he is among may not induce him to accept of foreign service, and lose him both to his country and his family. If money can be found to support him, I wish you would advise him to go to Geneva, where his principles of religion and liberty will be confirmed, and where he may stay till you see if a pardon can be procured him. As soon as Commodore Barnet comes home, inquire for your brother Billie, and take care of him on my account. I must again recommend your unhappy mother to you. Comfort her, and take all the care you can of your brothers; and may God, of his infinite mercy, preserve, guide, and conduct you and them through all the vicissitudes of this life, and, after it, bring you to the habitations of the just, and make you happy in the enjoyment of Himself to all eternity."

The Earl of Kilmarnock married Lady Anne Livingstone, only surviving child and sole heiress of James fifth Earl of Linlithgow and Callendar, by Lady Margaret Hay, second daughter of John twelfth Earl of Errol, and by her, who died, it may truly be said, of a broken heart, at Kilmarnock House, on the 18th September 1747, had three sons :—

1 James Lord Boyd. He served in the Scots Fusileers at the battle of Culloden, and was, of course, opposed to his father. By a trust-deed, dated 1732, and confirmed by the House of Peers in 1752, he recovered the lands of Kilmarnock, which had been forfeited, and which he afterwards sold to the Earl of Glencairn. On the death of his grand-aunt, the Countess of Errol in her own right, he succeeded to the title of Earl of Errol in 1758. He died at Callendar House in 1778.

2. Hon. Charles, was engaged at Culloden in the ranks of the Pretender. He fled to the island of Arran, and there concealed himself for a year. He at length found his way to the Continent, where he married a French lady, and after a residence there of twenty years, a pardon to all the rebels having been then granted, he returned to Scotland. In 1778, Dr

Johnson and his friend Boswell, when on their tour to the Hebrides, spent some time with him and his brother, the Earl of Errol, at his seat of Slain's Castle, in Aberdeenshire.

3. Hon. William. He served in the royal navy, and was promoted, in 1761, to a company of the fourteenth foot.

The present Earl of Errol is the direct descendant of the Kilmarnock family in the male line. In the Peerage of the United Kingdom he is Baron Kilmarnock of Kilmarnock.

### MURES OF ROWALLAN.

Much light was thrown upon the genealogy of this ancient family by the publication, in 1825, of "The Historie and Descent of the House of Rowallane, by Sir William Mure, Knight of Rowallan, written in or prior to 1657 ;" but the writer seems to have fallen materially into error, in reference to the early history of the family. He holds that the Mures, or Mores of Rowallan, originally came from Ireland; and the editor of the "Historie" is the more inclined to believe in the Celtic origin of the name, that in "most early writings" the "preposition de is omitted, which so invariably accompanies all early Saxon designations." Now, this is not the fact—Wilielmi de Mora, and Laurentii de Mora, occur in two charters granted by Robert I., so that no argument can be drawn from this as to the Celtic derivation of the Mures, or Mores. Nevertheless there may have been a tradition in the Rowallan family that their ancestors came from Ireland—a tradition perhaps similar to that which exists in Carrick in reference to the family of Kennedy; but we are inclined to think that it rests on no better ground than that those who spoke the Erse, or Celtic language, were called Erse, or Irish, in contradistinction to the Normans and Saxons introduced into the country by the Crown. Like the Kennedies, the Mures may have been of the ancient race of Scotland, for it is well known that Ayrshire was decidedly a Celtic district until comparatively modern times.

If the Mures of Rowallan really were a direct offshoot of the O'Mores of Ireland, it is plain that the writer of the "Historie" could not claim for them the distinction of being at the head of the name in Scotland, because the Crown charters show that there were Moores, or Mores, contemporaneously in various parts of Scotland. The author, in tracing his ancestry, ventures no farther back than Sir Gilchrist, who is said to have distinguished himself at the battle of Largs in 1263, and he brings to his assistance a Ranald More, "who had come purposlie from Ireland,"

* This looks like an admission on the part of the Earl that he had joined the standard of the Prince through the counsel of his lady, although he elsewhere repudiates the fact. The passage, however, may be understood to mean that his love for his family had unduly urged him to attempt the bettering of his fortune by the desperate measure of rebellion.

to whom Sir Gilchrist gave " the lands of Polkellie," one of the oldest inheritances, if not the *only* one, belonging to the family at the time. There is something questionable here; for it appears by the charters of Robert I. that the Mures had been pretty extensive proprietors in the county on his accession to the Crown, which could hardly have been the case if their settlement in the district had been so recent; neither does the fact accord with the author's statement as to the antiquity of the family inheritance.

With these preliminary remarks, which will be better understood as we proceed, we shall endeavour to trace the descent of the family.

According to the author of the " Historie," Rowallan had been in possession of the Mures previous to the reign of Alexander III., from which they were dispossessed by the powerful house of Cuming, and the owner, Sir Gichristl More, was " redacted for his safty to keep close in his castle of Pokellie." After the battle of Largs, however, upon which occasion Sir Gilchrist received the honour of Knighthood in reward of his bravery, he " was reponed to his whole inheritance." " Sir Gilchrist," continues the author, " for preventing of more occation of trouble, and for settling of his owne securitie and firmer peace made allyance with this partie of power, and maried Isabell, his onlie daughter and heire, by accession of whose inheritance, to witt of the lands of Cumiuside, Draden, and Harwoods, his estate being enlarged." The editor, however, remarks, that it is " fully as probable, even from his own showing, that Polkelly was the more ancient inheritance of his family, and that Rowallan was acquired solely by the marriage of the heiress, Isabell, as is generally held."* But to follow our author—" After the death of Sir Walter Cumine, Sir Gilchrist now secured not onlie in the title and full possession of his old inheritance, but also in his *border lands quherin he succeided to Sir Walter forsaid within the Sherefdome of Roxburgh*, being sensible and mindfull of the deserving of his freinds and followers in time of his troubles, deals with all of them as became a man of honour, bestowing vpon each some parcell of land according to his respect, intrest or (happly) promise to the persone. He disponed to his kinsman Ranald More, who had come purposlie from Ireland for his assistance in time of his troubles, and tooke share with him of the hazard of the battell, the lands of Pokellie," &c. Now there is evidently a complete jumbling of times and circumstances here. In the reign of David II. Maurice Mur-

ray had a charter " of the *waird of Walter Cuming of Rowallan, in vic. de Roxburgh, with the lands thereof*." It is thus apparent that the Rowallan lands in Roxburghshire were not in possession of Sir Gilchrist at this period; and it is next to impossible that the same Sir Gilchrist Mure, who fought at the battle of Largs, could have been alive in the reign of David II. Indeed he is stated by the author to have died in 1280. No reliance, therefore, is to be placed on the " Historie " by Sir William farther back than can be corroborated by concurrent testimony. The immediate ancestor of Sir Gilchrist appears to have been

I. " DAVID DE MOORE," mentioned in a charter by Alexander II. between 1214 and 1249,* who is stated to have been " the head of the house of Rowallane." This is extremely probable, at least, he is the first on record. That he possessed Rowallan, however, is doubtful, though the lands of Polkelly, chiefly in Renfrewshire, may have belonged to him. He was probably succeeded by

II. Sir Gilchrist, who fought at the battle of Largs. He is said, as already mentioned, to have disponed the lands of Polkelly to his kinsman, Ranald More, but of this there is no evidence.† The author of the " Historie" refers to a charter " extant, granted by him to his daughter Anicia, of the lands of Cuthsach, Gulmeth, Blaracharsan, with the woods thairof purchast from Molid, together with Garnegep and Calder, rowmes now not knowne by these names. The pasturage thairin specifyed being bounded vpon the north side from Drwmbwy dieth by Swinstie burne, maks evident that the lands of Pokellie have been at that time in the hands of the disponer, and a proper part of the mure of Rowallane," &c. With his daughter Anicia, married to Richard Boyle of Kelburne, he is said to have given the lands of Polruskane, " for payment of ane pound of Comine seed in name of blensch ferme yearlie from these times, till by God's good providence they are now brought in againe, to the house by lawfull purchase. He gifted likwise the lands of Ardoch (now Crawfurdland,) to Johne Crawfurd and aires, for service of waird and reliefe, and to Edward Arnot the two finnicks for yearlie payment of ane pair of gloves at St Lawrence Chapell,

* Nisbet's Heraldry.

* History of Renfrewshire.
† Reginald More had a charter from Robert I., of " the lands of Templestown and Scheills, (Edinburghshire), given to him by Rodulphus Lindsay, dudum magister hospitalis St John Jerosolomitani." Ronald More, Chalmerlan, had a charter of the " lands of Formerteine, Akintor, Aboyn, Meikle Morfey, Douny, and Caverays, whilk was Isabel Balliol's, heir to Thomas Balliol [Lanerk] from David II."

and of ane pair of spurs at St Michaell's Chapell, embleames of reddie service.* Last it is recorded that he builded the Mures Ile at Kilmarnock, and decored the same with funerall monuments, and mortified for mantainance of the Preist who did officiat at the altar thairin, to the Abacie of Killwining, the lands of Skirnalland, for which reasone the nomination of the priest forsaid (a custome which constantlie continued till the restoring of religion) was proper to him and his successors."† Sir Gilchrist, who had evidently been the means of vastly increasing the family estates, although there is no evidence of his being in the possession of Rowallan, is said to have died "about the year 1280, neer the 80 year of his age." He was buried, says the historian, "with his forfathers in his owne buriell place in the Mures Isle at Kilmarnock," a statement certainly involving an anachronism. If he was the builder of the Isle, he could not well have been buried with his forefathers, unless they had been disinhumed for the purpose. He had, by his lady, Isabell Cumine :—

t. Archibald, his heir.

1. Elizabeth, married to Sir Godfrey Ross.
2. Aniela, married to Richard Boyle of Kelburne.

He was succeeded by his son,

III. Archibald, who was slain at Berwick, where the army of Baliol was wholly routed, in

1298. He married a daughter of Sir John Montgomerie of Eastwood, and by her had,

1. William, his successor.*

1. Margaret, married to George Dunbar of Cumnock.
2. Jonet, married to ——.

IV. William, heir and successor, is honourably mentioned in an indenture† of truce with England, in the nonage of King David, wherein he is designed Sir William. He is probably the same individual mentioned in the charter of Robert I. to "Robert Boyd, of the lands of Kilmarnock, Bendingtoun, Hertschaw, &c.—que fuerunt Johannis de Balliolo, Godfridi de Ros, filii quondam Reginaldi de Ros, Willielmi de Mora, et Roberti de Ros." The Mures, from theri connection with the Cumins, had probably been in some measure opposed to the claims of the Bruce, hence the acquisition of their lands by the followers of King Robert. Part of the lands granted by the King to Fergus Ardrossan of Ardrossan, belonged to Laurentii de Mora. According to the author of the "Historie," Sir William died about the time David II. was taken prisoner at the battle of Durham, fought on the 17th October 1346. If he was the same Sir William mentioned in the indenture, however, he must have been alive at a much later period, as there is a Willielmus More mentioned in the M'Farlane MSS. as living in 1363. Reynold, son and heir of Sir William More, was one of the hostages left in England on David's redemption in 1357; and the editor of the "Historie" presumes that if Sir William was of Rowallan, that Reynold, his heir, may have died while in England, and the succession devolved upon his younger brother, Adam. This is extremely probable; but, at the same time, it is impossible to say whether these William Mores belonged to the Rowallan or Abercorn Mures. William More, for example, had a charter of "the barony of Abercorn, by the resignation of John Graham," from David II. Sir William married "a daughter of the house of Cragie, then Lindsey," and by her had, at all events, his successor,

V. Sir Adam, "who having been bred a long time in his father's auld age with the management and weight of all his affaires both private and more publick, in these rougher times, found the less difficultie to apply himself by a more easie method to mantaine the lott and fortoune left by his predecessours, now in his own hand."

---

* These chapels are stated by the author to have been situated at Bankend and Well, near Rowallan, places still known, but no vestige of the chapels remain.

† The following notices concerning Mure's Isle have been collected from the Session records of Kilmarnock :—

"Sess. 2 August 1649.—The whilk day, the minister and elders being conveinet in Session, and having concluded with advyce of the presbytery at the last visitation of the Kirk, for the better accommodation and furtherance of the people, both in seeing the minister and hearing the word, that the pillar and pen, divyding the yle called the Mures' yle, as being held and acknowledged from ancient tymes the proper buriall place of the house of Rowallan and Cranfurdland," &c.

"At Kilmarnock, the fyft day of Jully, one thousand six hundred and seventie six yeares, it is agreit and endit betwixt the parties following. To wit, Sir Wm. Mure of Rowalland, knyght, with consent of Wm. Muir, younger thereof, his son, and John Cranfurd of Cranfurdland, with consent of John Cranfurd younger thereof, his son, on the other part, in this manner following: That the said John Cranfurd of Cranfurdland, shall alter his seat that is situat within the north yle of the old church of Kilmarnock, commonlie called the Muires' yle," &c.

In 1695, the aisle was ordered by the Session to be repaired and seated; but the seats were to be raised when the family had occasion to bury there.

The school-house at Kilmarnock having been burnt, the children were, for a short time, taught in the aisle; its bad air and dampness caused fever to prevail amongst them, and it was soon abandoned as a school-house.

Some of the sepulchral monuments, with which this aisle was "decored," might be seen some years ago, and may perhaps still be seen in the garden of the house, once occupied by Captain Thomson, in the foregate, Kilmarnock.

---

* The ancestors of the Mures of Caldwell and Auchindraine are supposed to have been brothers of William.

† This indenture, according to a note on the margin of the "Historie," was in the possession of Mr Thomas Crawfurd, Professor of Philosophy and Mathematics in the University of Edinburgh, and author of the Notes on Buchanan's History, &c.

It appears from the " Historie," that the family had suffered considerably during the war of independence, maintained first by Wallace, and afterwards by Bruce; and Sir Adam is eulogised for his prudence in having improved and enlarged their dilapidated inheritance. Sir Adam[*] is said to have married Janet Mure, grand-daughter of Ronald More, heiress of Polkellic, by which the latter estate was rejoined to Rowallan. By this marriage, he had :

1. Sir Adam, his successor.
2. Andrew, " uncle to the king," (Robert III.)
1. Elizabeth, married to Robert, the High Steward, afterwards King of Scotland. There existed at one time much dubiety as to the reality of this marriage. All our early historians, down even to Buchanan, were of opinion that the union had never been legalized by marriage. The author of the " Historie," however, quoting from a " deduction of the descent of the house of Rowallane," collected by Mr John Lermonth, chaplain to Alexander Archbishop of St Andrews, says " That Robert, Great Steward of Scotland, having taken away the said Elizabeth, drew to Sir Adame her father ane instrument that he should take her to his lawfull wyfe, which myself hath seen, saith the collector, as also ane testimonie, written in Latine by Roger M'Adame, preist of our Ladie Marie's Chapell."[‡] " Mr Lewis Innes, Principal of the Scots College at Paris, first completely proved the fallacy of Buchanan's account of King Robert's marriages, by publishing in 1694, a charter granted by him in 1364, which charter showed that Elizabeth More was the first wife of Robert, and made reference to a dispensation granted by the Pope for the marriage. That dispensation was long sought for in vain, but was at length discovered in 1789, at which time a dispensation for the marriage of Robert II. with Euphame Ross was found."[‡] Ample proof of the union exists in the Crown charters. For example, there is a charter by David II. " to Robert, Great Stuart of Scotland, of the lands of Kyntire, with the advocation of the kirks thereof in fee; and to John Stewart, his son, gotten betwixt him and Elizabeth More, daughter to Adam More, Knight, and failzeing of him, to Walter, his second brother."[§] Also, a charter by Robert III. " to Andrew Mur, uncle to the King, of ane pension of £20 sterling furth of the great customs on both sides of the Forth, until said Andrew or his heirs should be heritably seised in a £20 land in some convenient place."[‖] Elizabeth More, the first wife of Robert II., is said to have been a woman of great beauty, and to have attracted the attention of the High Steward during the troublous times of Edward Baliol, when he was frequently compelled to seek safety in concealment. Dundonald Castle, then the chief residence of the Stewarts, was no doubt the " scene of King Robert's early attachment and nuptials with the fair Elizabeth." From this union are descended the existing race of British sovereigns, as well as most of the crowned heads of Europe.

VI. Sir Adam, the eldest son, succeeded his father. He is the first of the Mures whom we find styled " of Rowallan" in any of the public charters, although there can be no doubt that his father had been in possession of that property, for Sir Adam had a charter of the barony, on the resignation of his father, from Robert III., dated at Irvine, in the second year of his reign (1891.) He married " Dame Joanne of Dannestone (Danielstoun),[*] daughter to the lord of that family." There is a charter from Robert III. to " Adam More of Rowallan, and . . . . Danielstonn, his spouse, of the lands of Polnekill, Grey, Dumblay, Clunche, Clony, Herber, Darlache, Balgrum, in the barony of Cuninghame, vic. Air ; the lands of Ayntslare ; by resignation of Jonet Danielstonn."[†] Sir Adam " carried away," says the author of the ' Historie,' " as appears with emptie surmises and hopes founded on court favours (not well enoughe acquent with the rocks in the way'), made unawares a new rent in his estate, and provyded his second sone, Allexander, to the barony of Polkellie, together with the lands of Limflare and Lowdowne hill, qherin his lady was infeft in liferent, and wer given out by him, now the second time, to the great damnage and prejudice of his house and posteritie, and not without a deserved note of improvidence and winadvertance to the good thairof. However, at that time the Court seemed to smile vpon him, his proper estate considerable, his friendship strong, and of the greatest of these times. He gave a quartered coat of the armes of Mure and Cumine. The hoarsenes and aspperitie of the Irish pronunciation of his tittle and lands is forgoten, and Rigallane is now Rowallane, Pothkellath is now Pokellie, &c., and More is Mure by the Court dialect." Sir Adam seems to have predeceased his lady, as she had letters purchased from Robert Duke of Albany, " dispensing with the recognition of the barronie of Polkellie and others her lands pertaining to her be terce or otherwise, dated at Downe, in Munteith, anno 1415, the tent year of his governale." In these letters she is designed Dame Joanne of Danielstoune, " wife to whilome our Cussine Adame Mure of Rowallane." Sir Adam died in 1399.[‡] He had issue by his lady:

1. Archibald, who succeeded.
2. Alexander of Polkellie[§] He had, from David II.,

---

[*] Ade More had a charter of lands from Robert I. In the reign of David I., there is a charter of " excambion betwixt Alexander Livingstoun of that Ilk and Ade More, knight."

[†] Supposed to be " Our Lady's Kirk of Kyle," in Monkton parish.

[‡] Remarks by the editor of the ' Historie.'

[§] Robertson's Index.          ' Ibid.

---

[*] Danielstoun of that Ilk. The possessions of this ancient and opulent family, whose chief messuage was the castle of Finlaystoun, Renfrewshire, devolved to Margaret and Elizabeth, daughters and co-heiresses of Sir Robert Danielstoun of that Ilk, about the beginning of the fifteenth century.—' Crawf. Hist. of Renf.'

[†] Robertson's Index.

[‡] Adam More de Rowallan is a witness to a charter by Robert II. " Fergusio de Foulertone de Arane terras nostras de Orqwbonyne," &c. " apud Arnele, 26to die Novembris, anno regni secundo (1372)."

[§] " Alexandri More," had a charter " de terris de Kynchumbr," from David II.

"Carta confirm. carte concesse per Alexandrum de Elfynstoun, Dominum ejusdem, Alexandro More, filio quondam Ade More, militis, terre de Kychumbr, in baronia de Stanhous, (quam Dominus Godfridus de Roos dedit Alexandro de Elfynstoun, patri dicti Alexandri, in excambio pro quadam petia terre in Ertibeg): testes in originali carta non inseruntur in recordo; carta confirm. data fuit apud Edynburgh, 4 Junii, a. r. 33 (1363)."[*] From the Earl of Douglas, who married Margaret, daughter of Robert III., he had the lands of Hareschaw and Drumbowy by a precept of infeftment dated in 1417. He is said to have "adventured himself" for the Earl of Douglas "in all his noble undertakings." So also is it said of

3. Rankine, or Reginald, "commonlie called of Abercorne," says our author," not that he had these lands in heretage, for that doth never appear by historic nor evident that hath ever come to my hands, notwithstanding of the common tradition thairanent, being established thair as Bailliffe and a chief officer wnder his lord, the Earle of Duglass, having charge of his men thair in all his noble atcheifements."[†] The deceadants of Rankine, to the third generation, are said to have been steady supporters of the house of Douglas. The last of them died in defending the castle of Abercorn against King James, when the house of Douglas was wholly overthrown. "The Mures of Skemore and Kittiemore (?) both houses now perished and quyte out of memorie, wer said to have been the oulie remnants of that race "—(i. e. the race of Reginald.)

---

VII. Archibald Mure of Rowallan succeeded. He married Euphame Kennedy, daughter of the Knight of Dunnuir,[‡] by whom he had a son, Robert. He is said by the author of the 'Historie' to have "died in battell against Ingland, 1426 ;" but here the editor remarks, that this part of the account is "obviously erroneous, as nothing in history, of this nature, corresponds to the date 1426, or with James II.," and supposes the battle in question to have been that of Sark in 1448. By a charter of "George Fullertoun, lord of Corsbie," in 1430, it appears that

VIII. Robert More of Rowallan was in that year Sheriff-Depute of Ayrshire. He may have been the son of Archibald, who died in 1426. Robert was probably succeeded by a son or a brother, named

IX. Archibald Mure of Rowallan, who may have been slain at the battle of Sark in 1448. The author has thus probably omitted two successors in the descent of the family, from his confounding the time of the two Archibalds, for he seems to be positive that a "Robert succeeded to his father Archibald." Archibald Mure of Rowallan married Isabel, third daughter of Sir John Montgomerie of Eglintoun, who appears from 1405 to 1425.

[*] Robertson's Index.
[†] This seems to be the correct view of his position, and he is probably the "Ranaid More, Chalmerlan," whom we have previously noticed as having obtained a charter of certain lands from David II. Sir William More of Abercorn occurs frequently in the charters of David II.
[‡] Ancestor of the present Marquis of Allsa.

---

X. Robert Mure of Rowallan. He is described as a frequenter of the " court in the minoritie of King James the Third. He was ane man black hared, and of ane hudge large stature, therefore commonlie called the Rud[*] of Rowallane. The king in his bearne head proponed to round with him, and as he offered swa to doe, dang out his eye with the spaug of ane cocle-shell. He was a man regarded not the well of his house, but in following court, and being unfit for it, waisted, sold, and wadset all his proper lands of Rowallane, quhilk may be an example to all his posteritie. He married Margerie Newtoune, daughter to the laird of Michaell-hill, in the Merse. Ane druncken woman, and ane waistor man, quhat made then this house to stand but the grace of God." The following document, printed in the Appendix to the "Historie," seems to refer to this "waistor man" and his son :—

"K. Letters in favoures of Robert Mure of Rowallane, and his sonne Johne.
Ctra.
Archibald Cranfurd of Cranfurland.
"JAMES, be the grace of God King of Scottis till our Shereff of Are and his deputis greting, ffor sa mekle as it is humlie menit and complent to ws he our louit schouitour Robert Mure of Rowallane, apoun Archibald Craufurd of Craufurlland, That quhar be has be fenist [feigned] informacioun of ane byle [bill] of complaint, purchest our lettres direct to zow, our said Sheref, and zour deputis, to distrenze him for a sowme of money optenit be the said Archibald apone the said Robert and ymquhil Johnne Mure his sone, of the quhilk sowm the said Robert has payt his parte thairof efiir the tennour of the Decrett optenit apone him be the said Archibald before the Lordis of our Counsale. Nevertheles, that ze intend to distrenze the said Robert for the haile sowme, to his grete dampnage and scaitht, and in contrar justice gif it sa be. Our Will is herefore, and we charge zow straithe, and commandis that ze gif our last lettres direct to zow, purchest be the said Archibald, wer to put our vtheris lettres direct to zow apone ane act in the said mater of before to execucioun, that ze exe̅ct the samyn deulie as efferis. And gif oure saidis last lettres wer purchest vtherwaise apone ane byle of complaint, that ze lauchfully summond warne and charge the said Archibald, purchessar of our saidis lettres, to compere before ws and our Counsale at Edinburghe, or quhar it sall happine ws to be for the tyme, the xii day of October nixt to cum in the houre of caus, with continuacioun of days, bringing with him our saidis vtheris lettres last purchest be him in the said mater, to be sene and considerit gif thai be procedit of justice or noucht. And gif thai refer noe̅t to our saidis vtheris lettres direct to zow apone the said act in the said mater of befor. And forthair to answere to ws and at the instance of the said Robert in the said mater in sa fer as law will, with intimacione to the said Archibald as efferis, Deliuering thir oure lettres be zow deulie execut and indorsit as efferis again to the berare. Gevin vndere our Signet at Falkland the vii day of September, and of our regnne the aucht zere [1495]."

The "Rud of Rowallane" died in 1504. He had issue :

1. John, who succeeded.
2. Robert, in the Well, whose descendant, John, was slain by the Boyds at Prestick Kirk, near Ayr, in 1571.

[*] 'Rud' means a person of great strength, and not disinclined to a fray.

3. James, in Craig,
4. William, of Cocktries.
1. —— married to —— Boyde of Hietrie.

XI. John Mure of Rowallan succeeded, apparently on the resignation of his father, Robert. He married " Elizabeth Stewart, daughter to the first Lord Evandale, whose mother was daughter to the Earle of Crawfurd, called Earl Beardie." He had issue :

1. John, his successor.
2. Archibald, called " mickle Archibald,"
3. Patrick Boyd.  "Nov. 3. 1508.—" Patrick Boyde, brother to the Laird of Rowalloun," and twenty-seven others. " was convicted of art and part of convocation of the lieges against the act of Parliament, coming to the Kirk of Stewarton, in company with John Mure of Rowallan, for the office of Parish Clerk of the same Kirk, against Robert Cunynghame of Cunynghamehede and his servants, in the year 1508."*
4. James.  "James Muir, brother to the Laird of Rowalloun, was, in 1508, convicted of art and part of the forethought felony and oppression done to John Mowat, junior, Laird of Busbie, and Andrew Stevinstone, in the town of Stewarton, in company with the Laird of Rowalloun."†
1. Lady Macfarlane.
2. Lady Balquider.
3. The gudewife of Clarkland, Peacock-Bank, &c.

He is said to have died in 1501, before his father; but, according to the foregoing document, his death must have occurred prior to 1495.  A long feud had existed between the Lairds of Rowallan and Craufurdland, the former being the superiors of the lands of Ardoch (afterwards called Craufurdland), which was carried to considerable excess during the lives of Robert and John.  The evidents of both houses are said to have been destroyed in the course of the struggle.  In a Justice Eyre, holden about 1476,‡ by John Lord Carlisle (Chief-Justice of Scotland on the south side of the Forth), at the burgh of Ayr, Robert Muir of Rowallan, and John Muir his son, and divers others their accomplices, were indicted for breaking the king's peace against Archibald Craufurd of Craufurdland.

XII. John Mure of Rowallan succeeded his grandfather.  He married Margaret Boyd, third daughter of Archibald Boyd of Bonshaw, brother to the Earl of Arran.  This lady, in her youth, was mistress to James IV.  She afterwards " procured to herself the ward of the Laird of Rowallan, John Muir, and married him."  They had sasine of the lands of Warnockland, the gift of James IV., dated January 1498.§  They had issue :

1. Mungo, who succeeded.
2. Alexander, of Ormsheugh.
3. Patrick.
4. Adam.

1. Lady Newark; contract of marriage dated 1568: secondly, married to the Laird of Bar, thirdly to the Gudeman of Baldoon.
2. Lady Sorbie, in Galloway.
3. Lady Bar, younger.
4. Lady Portincross. *

John Mure of Rowallan, " ane very worthie man," died at Flodden in 1513.  He was succeeded by his eldest son,

XIII. Mungo Mure of Rowallan.  He appears to have greatly improved the old fortalice of Rowallan, having " raisit the hall vpone four vouttis [vaults], and laiche trance, and compleitit the samen in his awin tyme."  He is described as " a man of singular valour, and very worthie of his hands, quherof he gave good proofe in divers conflicts."  It was this laird of Rowallan who, with Robert Boyd, Gudeman of Kilmarnock, gave the Duke of Hamilton such signal assistance at the skirmish called the " Field of Glasgow."  In a memorandum of " the behaviour of the house of Kilmarnock towards the house of Rowallane, and of their house towardis them,"† published in the appendix to the " Historie," his services are thus recorded:—"It is wnderstandit that Mungow Muir of Rowallane, quhois mother was Boyd, joynit with Robert Boyd, Guidmane of Kilmarnock, in seeking revengement of the slauchter off James Boyd, the Kingis sisteris sone,‡ quho sould have bene Lord Boyd, bot befoir he was fullie restoirit was slaine be the Earle of Eglintoune. Nixt, my Lord of Glencairne proposing ane richt to the barronie of Kilmarnock, procleamit ane court to be holdin at the Knockanlaw, quhair the said Robert Boyd, Guidmane of Kilmarnock, and Mungow Muir of Rowallane, with the assistance of thair freindis, keipit the said day and place of court, offirit battel to the said Earle of Glencairne, and stayit him from his pretendit court hoilding. Thirdlie, the foirsaid Robert Boyd, Guidmane of Kilmarnock, and the said Mungow Muir of Rowallane, enterit in the field of Glasgow, the said Mungow being lairglie bettir accompanied then the foirsaid Robert. They behavit themselfe so valiantlie in that facht, that the Duik Hammiltone, quho reckonit both his lyfe and honour to be preservit be thair handis, maid the said Robert Boyd, Guidmane of Kilmarnock, Lord Boyd, lyk also as he revardit the said Mongow Muir with dyvers fair gifts.  The said Robert Boyd hichlie esteimit of the said Mungow Muir of Rowallane, and gave him the first place of honour, al his dayis, acknowleging the alteratione of his estait to the worthines of the said Mungowis handis:

---

* Criminal Trials.          † Ibid.
‡ This date must be wrong, although it is said to be from the Craufurdland papers.
§ Rowallan writs.

* This lady seems more likely to have been a sister of John Mure of Rowallan.  "Roberto Boyd . . . . et Isabell Mwr ejus sponse," appear in a charter dated 1520.
† Rowallan writs.
‡ Son of Thomas Boyd Earl of Arran.

this is knawin zit to ould living men." Like a brave warrior, as he appears to have been, Mungow "died in battell at the Black Satterday" [Pinkie-cleuch] in 1547.* He married Isabel Campbell, daughter of Sir Hugh Campbell of Loudoun, Sheriff of Ayr,† and had issue:—

1. John, who succeeded.
2. Archibald, of Areulane and Cotland.
3. Mr Patrick, parson of Ferne.
4. Hugh, of Blacklaw and Skirualland.
5. Robert.

1. Isobel, married to Hugh Wallace of Carnel.
2. Agnes, married to John Dunbar of Blantyre.
3. Elizabeth, married to John Dunbar of Mochrum.
4. Margaret, married to Patrick Fleming, younger of Barrochan.
5. Jonet, married to Mr John Fullarton of Dreghorn.
6. Marion.‡

XIV. John Mure of Rowallan. He is said to have taken "great delyte in policie and planting. He builded the fore wark, back wark and woman house,§ frome tho ground." Another account states, that "he plantit the orchrarde and gairdein, sett the vppir banck and nethir bank, the birk zaird befoir the zett." He is said to have "lived gratiouslie;" yet the following "Letter of Sleance, by Alexr. Cowper," shows that he was not altogether free from the prevailing spirit of the times:—"Be it kend till all men be thir present lettres, me Alexander Cowpair, masone in Killwyning, nocht compellit, coacted, nor seducit be ony maner of waye, but of my awin frie motive and voluntarie will, wyth consent and assent of honorable men, Johnn Fergushill of that Ilk, Johnn Cowpair of Brigend, Killwyning, Thomas Adameson, Blais Tarbet in Corshill, my cheife and capitall branchis, bayth on my father syde and mother syde, to haife remittit, pardonit and frelie forgevin; and be the tennour heirof remittis, pardonis, and frelie forgevis, Johnn Mwre of Rowallane, Williame Mwre his sone and air appeirand, Johnn Mwre and Mongow Mwre his sonnes, also Archibald Boyd of Portincors zoungar, and Patrik Glasfurde, thair complices, kin, freindis, allys, assistaris and parttakaris, the crewall wonding, hurting and bluding of me, the said Alexander, to the great effusioue of my bluyde, done and committit be the saidis persones, thair seruandis and complicis, vpone the day of Februar, the zeir of God Jaj v° thre-

seoir and ten zeris [1570]." Subscribed, "At Irwin and Killwyning," 16th and 17th March, 1571. According to the memorandum already quoted in reference to the good offices interchanged between the houses of Kilmarnock and Rowallan, it would appear that this Laird of Rowallan had shown great friendship to Robert Master of Boyd, after the slaughter of Sir Neil Montgomerie of Lainshaw. He, with his vassals, was the means of saving the Master's life when pursued by the Montgomeries at Bogside. "The said Robert Maister of Boyde seimit nevir to forzett that kyndlie turne. Efter the field of Laugsyd the said Robert being Lord Boyd, fell in the disfavour of the Regent Murray; how kyndly he was ressavit in the place of Rowallane be the said Johne Muir laird thairoff, it is weil knavin to dyvers within the perishenne zit living, both men and wemen. The said Robert Lord Boyd being commandit be the authority to passe affe the country, . . . . the Laird of Knockdoliane proponit to have dispossessit him off the bailiarie of Grugar, bot be the diligens of Sauderis Boyd, chamberland to the said Lord Boyd, the freindis of the Lord Boyd war adverteisit of the said Laird of Knokdolianes intentione, and com to Grugar at the appointit day of the Laird of Knockdolianes court halding, quhair Jhon Muir of Rowallane not only conveinit his awin forcis, bot also purchest his nichtbouris of Kilmauris and Cunninghamcheid . . . . and past to the zoudmest [furthest] boundis of Grugar to resist the said Laird of Knockdoliane, that he and his freindis suld nocht get leiff to sett their foot wpone no grund of Grugar to hauld thair court unfochtin with. It is also weil knawin be liveing men that Hew Earle of Eglintoune, quho died in Edinbruch, cem accompanied with his freindis to the Blackbyre, and tuik Andro Puickane, Guidman of Blackbyre, my Lord Boydis tennant, upon allegance that he was a theiffe, the foirsaid Jhone Muir of Rowallane, with his awin folk, the rest of the perishenne, met the foirsaid Earle of Eglintoune at Bines burne, quho wes constrainit to delyvir the said Andro Puikane, lyk as he did to Jhone Crawford of Crawfurdland, quho for eschewing of bloodshed delyvirit his bond to the said Earle of Eglintoune for redelyvery of the said Andro Puikane wpon the said Earlis lawfull requisition. For all thir gnid deidis done be the house of Rowallane to the house of Boyd, thair is gret liklines of wnkyndly and wngraitfull meiting, quhilk nather God nor man will allow off. Gif it be that ony freind of the house of Boyd doutis of this informatione, quhat wes done by Mungow Muir neidis no prof, for it is certaine, and quhat wes done be Jhone

---

* He is mentioned in the testament of Bernard Mure of Park, 2d. October 1547.

† Mungo Mure was amerciated, in 1527, for resetting and supplying Hugh Campbell, Sheriff of Ayr, then at the horn for the slaughter of the Earl of Cassillis.

‡ All mentioned in a deed by Dame Margaret Boyd in favour of John Mure of Rowallan, eldest son of Mungo Mure of Rowallan, dated October 1550.

§ The editor remarks that "the part of the budding called the 'woman house,' was perhaps that which contained the old kitchen, and the rooms of the domestic servants; which part, with the old tower on the Crag of Rowallan, forms the east side of the castle.

Muir may be verified by living men. The process of this present actione sall be extractt and laid up with this informatione, to teiche and instruck our posterityis of the true kyndnes that was amongst our forbearis: and gif thair be ony alteratione, thairfra, to consider in quhois wyt it is."

This memorandum must have been drawn up by William Mure of Rowallan, the son and successor of John; for it appears that the family tree must be right, and the author of the " Historie " wrong, in reference to the death of John. According to the former, he died in 1581, and to the latter, in 1591, at the age of 66. He was alive in 1589, when Thomas Master of Boyd was " dilatit of the slauchter of vmquhile Johne Muir in the Wall, committit in the moneth of August 1571."* " Williame Mure, apperand of Rowallane," was one of the sureties. This slaughter appears to have been committed in revenge of " Robert Colwyngis (Colvin or Colvil) slauchter " by the Mures, Alexander Boyd, father of the fourth Lord Boyd, having married a daughter of Sir Robert Colvill of Ochiltree. In 1571, Lord Boyd and John Mure of Rowallan were charged by the Regent Mar to appear before the Secret Council, with a view to adjust the feud which prevailed between the houses of Kilmarnock and Rowallan, so that the cause of " wnkydly and wngraitfull meiting " between the parties had originated in the time of John Mure of Rowallan, before the memorandum was drawn up by his son, evidently in reference to the action begun in 1588 or 1589. There can, in short, be no doubt that 1591 is the proper date of the death of John Mure of Rowallan. He had a " Precept of Clare Constat," of " all and haill" the " lands and toune of Ingerstoune," &c.; also the half of the " toune and lands of Spitlehaugh," &c. " all lyand within the baronie of Lintoune, Regality of Dalkeith and Sherefdome of Peebles." These lands were originally granted " be Sir Thomas Aitoune, called Preband of Ingerstoune of the Colledge of St Nicolas, the Bishop in Dalkeith within the diocie of St Andrews, with consent of me, Archibald Boyd, Provest of the said Colledge Kirk, and Preband Chapterly conveened, and of ane noble Eurle, James Earle of Mortoune, Lord Dalkeith, patron of the said Colledge Kirk, to Mungo Muire of Rowallan [father of the above John]," &c. " to be holden of the Prebands of Ingerstoune and their successors, in few ferme,'—for

certain feu duties, specified, ' and [for] building and vpholding vpon the saids lands, housses and policie necessar and agreeable to the said ground. Dated the twenty day of December, Jaj vᶜ fourtie and fyve years, [1545] under the scall of the Preband and Chapter of the said patron."* He had, in 1588, as the following letter shows, the present of a horse from the Earl of Morton:—

" Traist Cousing, after hertlie commendationis I mind, God willing, to pass furth of this realme for sum occasionis. I have thocht gud to remember zou by my gray coursour in an taiken of my favour. I think ze sall find him als meit an haikney for zour self or zour wife to ryd vpoun as ony uthyr, for I chosit him to have been presentit to the King quhen the Scots horse suld have been send to the Duke of Gwies. Swa wishing the welfare of zourself, zour wife and barnis, I commit zou to God. Off Dumfrese, the 21 day of Februaro 1582.
                                        Zour very friend
                                            J. MORTONE."

The following letter was addressed to the Laird of Rowallan by Queen Mary, on her escape from prison in 1568; but as he had subscribed the " Band" in support of the Reformation in 1562, in which year he also sat in Parliament, it is not probable that he attended the summons:—

" Traist Friend, We greit zou weil. We believe it is not unknawin to zou the greit mercie and kyndnes that Almythie God of his infinit gudnes hes furthschevin towart us at this tyme in the deliverance of us fra the maist straithes pressoun in quhilk we ware captive, of quhilk mercy and kyndnes, we cannot enough thank, and therefore we will desire zou, as ze will do us acceptable service, to be at us with all possible [speed] on Settirday the aught of this month, be aught hours afternene or sooner gif ze may, weil accompanyt with zour honeurable friendis and servantis, bodin in feir of weir, to do us service, as ze sall be appointit, because we knaw zour constance at all tynnes. We neid not mak longeir letters for the present, bot will bid zou feir-well.—Off Hamilton, the 6 of May 1568, and that ze with the folks bait on fute and horse be heir on this next Sunday at the fordest.
                                            MARIE R."

John Mure of Rowallan married Marion Cuninghame, daughter of the Laird of Cuninghamehead, whose mother was a daughter of the Earl of Glencairn, and had issue:—

1. William, who succeeded.
2. John of Cassincarrie.
3. Mungo, concerned in the slaughter of Hew fourth Earl of Eglintoun, for which he had a remission. He died in London in November 1632, and was "honourablie buried in Westminster Church." He greatly lamented the " crying sinne of innocent blood."
1. Lady Adamton, who died in January 1632.
2. Lady Newark : married, secondly, to the Laird of Lochnaw, Sheriff of Galloway.
3. Lady Collellan ; married secondly, to the Gudeman of Dundonald.

XV. William Mure of Rowallan succeeded his father. He is described as " of a meik and gentle spirit, and delyted much in the studie of phisick, which he practised especiallie among the poore people with very good success. He was ane religious man, and died gratiouslie in the

_____
* In the Letters against Thomas Lord Boyd, published in the appendix to the " Historie," the date, apparently by mistake, is printed 1569.

_____
* Rowallan writs,

yeare of his age 69, the yeare of our lord 1616."
The following is an extract of his latter-will:—

" The Testament, testamentar, and Inventar
of the guidis, geir, debts, and sowmes of money
quhilk perteint to vmquhill William Muir, elder
of Rowallane, within the parochin of Kilmarnok
the tyme of his deceis, quha deceist in the moneth
of November 1616, then ffaythfullie maid and
gevin vp be his awin mouth, in swa far as concernis the nominacioun of his executour and
debtis awand out be him; and pairtlie maid and
gevin vp be Williame Muir of Rowallane, his
sone and executour nominat be him in his latter-
will and testament vnderwritten, in swa far as
concernes the geving vp of the Inventar of his
guidis and geir and debts awand in to him, as the
samyne of the date vnderwrittin mair fullelie
proports.

" Inuentar.
" Item, the said Wm. had perteining to him the
tyme of his deceis, &c., viz. ffourscoir and thrie
tydie ky, at xiii li. vi s. viii d.; forrow ky, with
the stirks, fourtie ane, at do.; thrie bulls, at viii
li.; nyntein stotts and quoyis of 3 zeir auld, at
viii li.; twentie fyve stottis and quoyis of 2 zeir
auld, at vi li.; threttie nyne stottis and quoyis of
12 months auld, at iii li. 6s. 8d.; ffiftie auld
scheip, at x li.; twentie four lambis, at xx s.;
thrie cursour staigis of thrie zeir auld, at 13 li.
6s. 8d.; twa gray filleis, of baith, xxxiii li. 6s. 8d.;
twa twelfmoneth auld foills, price of baith, 6 li.
13s. 8d.; ane auld broune meir in Lochgoyne,
p. 24 li.; ane meir in Fynnikhill, 26 li. 13s. 8d.;
twa work hors in Gamhill, bayth 33 li. 6s.; twa
work hors in Well, 66 li. 13s. 4d.; in the Maynes
of Rowallan, four work hors, at 26 li. 13s. 4d.;
in Righill, ane broune hors, 33 li. 6s. 8d. In the
bornezaird of Darfallache, Well, Gamhill and
Fynnikhill, conforme to the pruifis of the haill
staks cassin, of aitts fyve hundrith threttie sevin
bolls, at, with the fodder, iiii li. Item, of beir
in the saidis bornezairdis, thriescoir ten bolls, at
vi li. 13s. 4d., &c.

" Debts awand In.— . . Be Johnne Howie in
Lochgoyne, &c. for the crop 1616, 60 stains cheis,
at 20s. Be the tennentis of Lochrig, for the
personage teyndis of the landis of Lochrig, &c.
the crop 1615 and 1616, 12 bolls meill, price of
all 80 li. Mair, be the said tenents, of alterage
teyndis for the said land, thir saxtein zeiris bygane, be zeir 3 li. . . Be Agnes Miller for hir
husband's herizeld [hirsel] xx li. (Neill Montgomerie of Langschaw occurs as indebted 33 li.
And Johne Boill of Kelburne, conforme to his
band, 33 li. Mair be him, for relief and nonentres
of the fyve pund land of Polruskane, lx li., togidder with the sowme of fiftie pund for the price

of fiftie pund wecht of Cvmyng,* awin of by-
rune blanche to the said sowmes of dewtie, conforme to his band. Be Andro Arnot, fear of
Lochrig, conforme to his band, lxxx li.)

        *           *           *

" I, Williame Muir of Rowallane, knawing
thair is nothing mair certane nor death, &c. As
for the thingis of this worlde, I nominat Wm.
Muir, my sone and appeirand air, my onlie executour, &c. Item, I ordane the said Wm. Muir
my servand, to be relevit at the hands of Robert
Dunlope of the haill lyme bocht this instant zeir,
laid vpone the lands of Balgray; because the
said Wm. is onlie condicioune maker for me, and
the said lyme cum to my awin vse. And for
samekle as be verteu of ane contract of mariag
maid betuix me and Wm. Muir, my sone, Wm.
Muir, my oy, on the ane part, and Johnne Dundas of Newlistoune, Margaret Creichtoune, his
spous, and Anna Dundas, thair dochter, on the
other part, ffor mariage than to be solemnized,
and now perfytit, betuix the said Wm., my oy,
and the said Anna Dundas, I, be verteu of the
said contract, bes disponit to my said sone, and
to the said Wm. Muir, my oy, certane my guids,
&c." [Subscryvit at Rowallane the thrid day of
September 1616 zeirs.]
Sir William married Jonet Maxwell, daughter
of the Laird of Newark, whose mother was a
daughter of the Laird of Craigends, and had
issue:—

1. Sir William, who succeeded.
2. John, of Blacklaw, slain at a combat at Beith.  He
married Helen Wallace, daughter of Sibilla Stewart—
her father's name not mentioned.  Contract dated
Kilmarnock, August 21, 1604.  Prior to Dec. 6, 1631,
this lady again married William Wallace of Prestwickshaws, which so far ascertains the time of Blacklaw's death; for, at that date, she, with her husband,
is a party in a contract of marriage betwixt Elisabeth
Mure, evidently her daughter, and Edward Wallace
of "Sevealltoune."  Another daughter, Jean Mure,
married George Campbell, then younger of Auchman-
och: "Contract of mariag betwix Arthor Campbell
of Auchmanocht and George Campbell his sonne,
Wm. Wallace of Prestickshaws and Helene Wallace
his spous takand burdine for Jeane Mure," &c.  Dated
at Kilmarnock, June 9, 1632.
1. Lady Langschaw.
2. Lady Skeldone Campbell.

XVI. Sir William Mure of Rowallan was
served heir of his father in the " 5 mercatis terrarum de Grange," 10th March 1620. " This
Sir Williame was ane stronge man of bodie, and
delyted much in hounting and halking. He died
in the yeare of his age 63, and of our Lord
1639." He married, first, Elizabeth Montgomerie, daughter of the Laird of Hessilheid,
" whose mother was one of eleven daughters

---
        * " Comine seed," see page 183.

(all married to considerable persones) to the Lord Sempill." She had issue:—

1. Sir William, who succeeded.
2. Mr Hugh, preacher at Burstone in Norfolk in England. He entered a student in the University of Glasgow in 1618.
1. Marion, Lady Pinkill.

Secondly, Jeane Porterfield, daughter of the Laird of Duchall, by whom he had—

3. Alexander, of Little Sessnock. He died in the month of September 1635.

She died in 1612. Her latter-will runs thus:— "The Testament, &c. of vmquhile Jeane Porterfield, spous to Williame Mwire, zounger of Rowallane, the tyme of hir deceis, quha deceist in the moneth of Junii 1612 zeiris, flaythfullie maid and gevin vp be the said Williame, in name and behalf of Allexr. Mwir, lawfull sone to the deid, executour dative, dewlie decernit to hir guids and geir," &c. The inventory of her "guidis and geir" is curious, as illustrative of the household furnishings and personal attire belonging to ladies of her rank in the seventeenth century:—

"Inuentar.

"Item, the said vmquhile Jeane and her said spous had, the tyme foirsaid, &c., viz.: In the first, twa silk gownes, ane thairof of plain silk, callit *telar miltum*, and the other figorit taiffatie, baith estimat to jc lb. Item, ane veluot cloik, furoit with plusche, and the four lapis lynit with satein, estimat to xxx lb. Item, ane veluot dowblat, with ane skirt, estimat to xl lb. Item, ane auld dowblat and skirt, estimat to iiij lb. Item, ane cloik of burret, estimat to viii lb. Item, ane ryding cloik of violat hewit claith, estimat to ten lb. Item, ane dowblat and skirt of blak Spanes taiffatie, all estimat to thrie lb. Item, ane auld broun freis skirt gowne, and twa auld gownes of sie bombasie, all estimat to x lb. Item, twa Scottis scarlot wylicoits, estimat to xiiii lb. Item, fyve quarters of            taiffatie, estimat to vi lb. Item, twa hnids, with the trappis, estimat to viii lb. Item, twa auld taiffaties, estimat to viii lb. Item, twa pair of auld playds, estimat to x lb. Item, ane ryding skirt of violat hewit claith, estimat to thrie lb. Item, twa auld furneissit wemen saidills, baith estimat to x lb. Item, fyve ells of Scottis scarlot claith, estimat to x lb. Item, sax ells of mixit hewit claith, estimat to ix lb. Item, four ells and ane half of gray claith, estimat to iiij lb. Item, aucht ells of raw litting claith, estimat to iii lb. Item, four feddir beddis and four bowsteris, estimat to xxxiii lb vi s viii d. Item, nyne coddis, thrie lb. Item, fyve pair small lyning sebeittis, xiii lb. Item, threttein pair of round sebeitts, xx lb. Item, twa peir of walkit blankattis, v lb. Item, thrie

pair of playding blankattis, iiii lb. Item, fourtieane ellis playding to be blankattis, xiii lb vi s viii d. Item, ane auld Ireland mat, xxx s. Item, four sewit coveringis vnlynit, xiii lb vi s viii d. Item, fyve coveringis of woll, and fyve coveringis of hair, all nyne lb. Item, nyne small and aucht round codwaris, iii lb. Item, thrie pair of auld courtingis, iiii lb. Item, tuelff ells of Scottis reid scarlot to be courtingis, viii lb. Item, fyve pendicles, l s. Item, twa lynning buirdclaithis, vi lb. Item, fyve round buirdclaithis, v lb. Item, ellevin small lynning servitouris, and ellevin round, v lb. Item, ten harden servitouris, xx s. Item, twa dussane of round servitouris, xl viii s. Item, twa breidclaiths, xx s. Item, four round hardin towells, xx s. Item, aucht ellis of round hardin, xxvii s viii d. Item, nyne sewit euschanes, iiii lb. Item, fyve silwir spones, pryce thairof, xv lb. Item, ane lang speit, vi s viii d; ane hingand cruik, xx s; ane fut [or suit] buird, xx s. Item, thrie chyris, xxx s. Item, ane gould ring set with ane dyamont, estimat to xxx lb. Item, ane ring set with ane rubie, estimat to ten lb. Item, ane neck chinze of gould, with ane taiblet of gould, estimat to thriescoir lb: ane chaddow of orien pairll, estimat to x lb. Item, mair in Warnokland, four stand bedis, estimat to iiii lb. Item, the thrie kistis, vi li."

Sir William married, thirdly, Sarah Brisbane, of the house of Bishoptoun. She had many children, but only three daughters lived to be married:—

2. Margaret, Lady Barrochan.
3. Marie, married to Lord Blantyre; secondly, to the Laird of Bishoptoun; thirdly to the Laird of Melgum, in Angus.
4. Jeane, married to Sir John Schaw of Greenock, the first Baronet of that name.
5. Lillias. "Lillias Muir, dochter to the Laird of Rowallane," occurs in the testament of Jonet Kelso, spouse to "Johne Birshane of Rosland" in 1627.
6. "Margaret Muir, relict of vmquhill Mr Zacharias Boyd," confirmed as one of the executors of her husband in the Commissary Court in 1654, was probably of this family. She afterwards married Mr James Durham, one of the ministers of Glasgow, who died in June 1658. In his latter-will "Sir Williame Mure of Rowallane, knyt," occurs as a debtor in the "annell rent of ellevin thousand merks."

Lady Rowallan survived her husband a number of years. "Dame Sara Birsbane, relict of vmquhill Sir Williame Muire of Rowallane," died in Irvine in September 1648.

XVII. Sir William Mure succeeded his father. As we have seen from the testament of his grandfather, he married, first, Anna Dundas, daughter of the Laird of Newlistoun, which event took place in 1615. She had issue:—

1. Sir William, who succeeded.
2. Captain Alexander, slain in the war against the rebels in Ireland.
3. Major Robert, married Anne, second daughter of Sir

James Maxwell of Calderwood, widow of the Laird of Newhall.

There were several daughters of this marriage, one of whom was married to the Laird of Ranfurly. Sir William married, secondly, Dame Jane Hamilton, Lady Duntreth, and by her had two sons and two daughters:—

4. James.
5. Hugh.
1. Jeane.
2. Marion.

"This Sir William," says the "Historie," of which he was the author, was pious and learned, and had ane excellent vaine in poyesie; he delyted much in building and planting; he builded the new wark in the north syde of the close, and the battlement of the back wall, and reformed the whole house exceedingly. He lived religiouslie and died Christianlie in the yeare of [his] age 63, and the yeare of [our] Lord 1657."

Some farther notice, however, of Sir William, the author of "The True Crucifixe," seems only a just tribute to his memory. He appears to have early cultivated a taste for the muses, and some verses in Latin, on the death of his grandfather, occur among his juvenile pieces. His manuscript poetry is considerable. Among the larger pieces is a translation of some books of Virgil; a religious poem which he calls "The Joy of Tears," and another, "The Challenge and Reply." Several of his pieces have been published. In the "Muse's Welcome," a collection of poems and addresses made to King James, on his visiting Scotland in 1617, there is a poetical address to the King at Hamilton, written by Sir William Mure of Rowallan. In 1628, he published a poetical translation of the celebrated "Hecatombe Christiana" of Boyd of Trochrig, together with a small original piece called "Doomesday." In 1629, he published "The True Crucifixe for True Catholikes." For some years after 1629, he seems to have been employed on a version of the Psalms, which was much wanted in Scotland at that time. The old English version was not popular; and the one executed by King James, and Sir W. Alexander of Menstrie, was so disliked, that the Bishops would not press it upon the Church. King James' version was not sanctioned by the Assembly, and some expressions in it gave offence to the people, e. g. the sun was called 'The lord of light,' and the moon, 'The pale lady of the night.' Though this version was rejected, still, many wished that the old one should be improved, or a better one substituted in its place. Several gentlemen attempted particular psalms; but a version of the whole was undertaken by Sir William Mure of Rowallan, which he seems

to have finished in 1639. Principal Baillie, who attended the Westminster Assembly, as Commissioner from the Church of Scotland, in a letter, dated at London, January 1st, 1644, says, 'I wish I had Rowallan's Psalter here, for I like it better than any I have yet seen.' It does not, however, appear that Sir William's version was transmitted to the Assembly; Mr Rous's, which was recommended by the English Parliament, was finally adopted, and has ever since been used in Scotland; but the committee appointed to revise Mr Rous's version, were instructed to avail themselees of the help of Rowallan's. The following is a specimen of Sir William's version:

### PSALM 15.

Who in thy Tabernacle stay,
Lord, who sall dwell with thee
2. upon thy holie mount? the man,
that walketh uprightlie;
Who just is in his works and wayes;
whose mouth and mynd aggree
3. in uttring of the trenth; whose tonge
is from backbyting free.

Hee who no evill to his freend
intends; hee, who taks head
his neighboure, nor defam'd to heare,
nor his reproache to sprend.
4. Vyle personnes in whose pureer eyes,
contemptible appeare,
but faithful men, that fear the Lord,
are honord and held deare.

Hee, to his hurt, thogh having sworne,
whose faith no change doth staine.
5. by biteing usury, who makes
not by his money gain.
hee, 'gainst the innocent, for brybs
who hath not partiall prov'd,
The man who these things shall attayne
shall in no time be mov'd.

The attention of Sir William was not entirely devoted to literary pursuits. He took his share in the burden of the duties of civil life, being a member of the parliament held at Edinburgh, June 1643, and of the 'committee of Warre,' for the sheriffdom of Air in 1644. He was also with the Scottish army in England, in 1644, and was present in some engagements between the royal and parliamentary forces, as the following letter to his son interestingly attests:—

"Loveing Sone,—We are now lying before Newcastle, engaged anew to rancounter with new dangers, for we are to adventure the storming of the toun if it be not quickly rendered by trenty, wherof ther is very smal appearance, for they look very quickly for ayde to releave them. They are very proud as yet, for oght we can perceave, and those that come out to us resolute . . . . for the most part they are Reformer officers, under the commandment of the Earle of Craufard and Mackay. We have had diverse bowts with them, and on Satterday last their day, a sound one, wherein we had good sport from the sunryseing till twelve a'clock, both parties retreeting and chairgeing by touers, without great losse to eyther, for our General Major shew himselfe that day both a brave and a wise commander; and if it had not been so, we could not but have had great losse, for we were put back over the water at the last; for their forces grew, and we had no armes but pistoles, and they played upon us still at a very far distance with muskets and long fowling peeces. I am keept heir now beyond my purpose wpone necessity, haveing the only chairge of the regiment till Col. Hobert, the Lieut. Colonel, and Major come heir, who have bein all in very great danger, but are now pretty well recovered, so that I expect them heir very shortly. I am engadged in credit, and cannot leave such a chairge, of such consequence, in ane abrupt maner, quhilk might hazard the breaking of the regiment, notwithstanding of the wrgent necessity that I know calls for my presence and attendance wpon my owne affaires at this time, which in so far as yee can be able ye must have ane ey to.

I have written to Adame Mure, to whom yee shall also speak and requeist, that he must take the whole care and chairge of my harvest, and stay constantly at my house for that effect, and I will sufficiently recompense his paynes. Yee may be now and then visiting my workers, and hasting them to their dwty, as your owne affaires may permitt. It is very long since I heard from you, and am vncertane whither yee received my letters written since the battle at Longmarston Moore. I know I will hear from you by this bearar, again whose retourne to me I hope to be ready, to take a voyage home. Praying heartily the Lord to blesse you, your bedfellow and children, till our happy meeting, and ever I rest

Youre loveing father,<br>S. W. M. Rowallane.

From Tyne-side before Newcastle
  the 12 of August 1644.

I blesse the Lord I am in good health and sound every way. I gote a sore blow at the battle upon my back with the butt of a musket, which hath vexed me very much, but specially in the night, being deprived therby of sleep, but I hope it shall peece and peece weare away, for I am already nearby sound. I thank God for it."

Sir William was one of the Remonstrators, who " brunt the Gaite of Drumlanrig, and plundered and waisted the lands," in 1650.* He was succeeded by his eldest son.

XVIII. Sir William Mure of Rowallan, in the end of the year 1657. April 13, 1658, he was served " heir of Sir William Mure of Rowallan, Knight barronet, his father—in the lands and barronie of Rowallane, extending to ane 100 mark land of old extent, within the bailliarie of Cunynghame, unite in the barronie of Rowallane : * * * 5 merke land of Grang :—40 shilling land callit the Townend of Kilmarnock." This Sir William was firmly attached to the Reformed doctrines, and was the intimate friend of the celebrated Mr Guthrie, first minister of Fenwick. It is said that conventicles were held in the house of Rowallan during his time. Whether on this account or not, it is certain that he suffered much during the troubles of the Church of Scotland. He was imprisoned in 1665, in the Castle of Stirling, together with the lairds of Cuninghamehead and Nether-Pollock. When other gentlemen were liberated upon the bond of peace, in 1668, these three were still retained in confinement; but, in the year following, upon the re-

moval of Bishop Burnet, from Glasgow, they presented a petition for release to Lauderdale, the Commissioner, which was granted. In 1683, he again fell under the suspicion of the Court, and was apprehended, together with his eldest son, in London. They were sent from London to Edinburgh, and committed prisoners to the Tolbooth. In the same year his second son, John, was taken prisoner, and carried to Edinburgh. In a short time, the health of the young laird of Rowallan required indulgence, and he was allowed to be removed from the prison to a private house. In April, 1684, they were both discharged, upon giving a bond of £2000, to appear when called. Sir William died in or about 1686. He married, about 1640, Dame Elizabeth Hamilton, daughter of James Hamilton of Aikenhead, Provost of the city of Glasgow. He had issue :—

1. William, who succeeded.
2. John, witness to the marriage contract of his sister.
1. Jean, married to James Campbell of Treesbank.

XIX. William Mure of Rowallan, the last lineal representative of the family, succeeded his father in 1686, as appears from the following retour of his service—" March 2, 1686, Willielmus Muir de Rowallan, haeres Domini Willielmi Muir de Rowallan, patris." He was entered a student at the University of Glasgow in 1660. His share in the afflictions of his father has been already noticed. This did not shake his attachment to the church for which he suffered. His name frequently occurs in the records of the parish of Kilmarnock. He is mentioned there, for the last time, in 1695, in a commission to defend a process of translation before the Synod. He married about 1670, Dame Mary Scott, apparently heiress of Collarny, in Fife, by whom he had three children :—

1. Anna, born July 1671.
2. Margaret, born July 1672.
3. Jean, born April 1778.*

He died in 1700, as appears from the following warrant :—

" His Majesty's High Commissioner, and the Estates of Parliament, in respect of the decease of William Mure of Rowallan * * Do grant order and warrand to the Sheriff principal, &c. to the effect they may choice an Commissioner to the said Parliament in place of the said William Mure of Rowallan," &c. †

XX. Dame Jean Mure of Rowallan, his only surviving daughter, and sole heiress, succeeded. This lady married, first, William Fairlie, of Bruntsfield, afterwards designed of Fairlie, to whom she had

---

* His name appears in the roll of persons to be proceeded against by the Earl of Queensberry for the damage sustained.

* Register of Kilmarnock.
† Acta Parl. Gulicl. Nov. 5, 1700.

issue.* She married, secondly, David first Earl of Glasgow, by which marriage she had three daughters:—

1. Lady Bettie, died in infancy.
2. Lady Jean, who, by special destination, succeeded to the family estates of Rowallan, &c.
3. Lady Anne, died unmarried.

Jean Mure, Countess of Glasgow, &c. &c. &c. died, Sept. 3, 1724, and was succeeded by her eldest daughter of the second marriage.

XXI. Lady Jean Boyle Mure of Rowallan. She married the Hon. Sir James Campbell of Lawers, K. B., third and youngest son of James second Earl of Loudoun. He entered the army at an early age, and served on the Continent, under the Duke of Marlborough.† He commanded the British horse at the battle of Fontenoy, 30th April, 1745, when he was mortally wounded, one of his legs being carried off by a cannon ball. He expired soon afterwards, and was buried at Brussels. He had a daughter, Margaret; and a son who succeeded.

XXII. James Mure Campbell, born 11th Feb. 1726. He assumed the name of Mure on succeeding to the estate of Rowallan; he was elected Member of Parliament for the county of Ayr, in 1754 ‡—succeeded his cousin John, fourth Earl of Loudoun, on the 27th April, 1782, and died on the 28th April, 1786, being then a Major-General in the army. He married, in 1777, Flora, eldest daughter of John Macleod, of Rasay, and by her, who died in 1780, had an only child,

XXIII. Flora Mure Campbell, born in August,

---

* "Fairly of Brunsfield, near Edinburgh, who were burgesses of Edinburgh, give out that they are come of the Fairlys of Braid, and wear a coat of arms as a cadet of that ancient family. William Fairly, of Brunsfield, having married a daughter of Sir William Mure's, of Rowallan, this induced him to sell his estate in the east, and purchase the lands of Dregorne, in Kyle, within the Sheriffdom of Air, which he got by a new charter cald fairly, and styled himself of that ilk, though he had no relation to the family of Fairly of that ilk," [in Largs, Cuninghame.]—' CRAUF. MS. BAR. Tradition still points out the spot where Fairlie was married to the heiress of Rowallan. The ceremony was performed by a curate, in the fields, about a quarter of a mile from the house of Rowallan, at a tree, still called the marriage tree, which stands on the top of a steep bank, above that part of the stream called " Janet's kirn."

† At the battle of Malplaquet, while the victory was yet doubtful, Lieutenant Colonel Campbell, with a party of his men, rushed with great fury against the French, and cutting all before him, returned the same way back. This sally contributed not a little to turn the fortune of the day. It was, however, made a subject of censure; but Prince Eugene, the commander-in-chief, allowing that emergencies might exist which justified a transgression of rules, on the day after the battle, in the face of the whole army, thanked Colonel Campbell for having exceeded his orders.

‡ " Lieut.-Col. James Muir Campbell of Rowallan, Esq. of Lord Geo. Sackville's Dragoons," admitted an honorary burgess of Kilmarnock in October 1756.—KILK. REC.

1780, Countess of Loudoun, Baroness Mauchline, &c. &c., who succeeded to the ancient patrimonial inheritance of her ancestors, the Mures of Rowallan. Her Ladyship married, 12th July 1804, Francis, Earl of Moira, Marquis of Hastings, by whom she had issue; particulars of whom will fall to be given in the account of the Loudoun family.

*Arms of Mure of Rowallan.*—Three mullets, for Mure; and three Cumin, or wheat sheaves for *Cumin*, parted per pale; with a Moor's head for a crest.

The following description of the castle of Rowallan, published in the Appendix to the "Historic," is more minute than the brief notice we have given elsewhere:—" Closely environed by aged trees, many of which have attained to great size and beauty, in the hollow tract of the stream, this venerable mansion affords a very perfect specimen of an early feudal residence, progressively enlarged, and fashioned to the advancing course of civilization and manners. The original fortlet, of which only the vaulted under apartment remains, occupied the summit of a small isolated crag, in the course of the rivulet, which, here dilating, obviously has formed a kind of lake around its base, of which many indubitable proofs still remain; thus giving to the castle-crag all the appearance of an islet-rock—from which circumstance, it may still be suggested, may have been derived its Gaelic appellation, ' Rowallan.'

In the mutations of the Carmel, the bed of the stream around the rock has long been consolidated into a firm and verdant small link, circumfluently washed by the now restrained brook; thus giving space for the intermediate and more modern buildings which constitute the present fabric. These are united to, and partly embrace the rocky base of the fortalice, which they, on three sides, obscure from the view; together, they form a small quadrangle, enclosing an open area in the centre, from the pavement of which springs a sombre yew, an appropriate accompaniment of the deserted and mouldering walls around; and combine, or rather contrast, almost all the modifications of architecture which obtained from about the end of the fifteenth to the beginning of the eighteenth century.

The southern front, the principal and more ornamental part of the building, however, was erected about the year 1562, by John Mure, of Rowallan, and his lady, Marion Cuninghame, of the family of Cuninghamehead. This appears from the following inscription on a small tablet at the top of the wall:—JON. MVR. M. CVGM. SPVSIS. 1562. On the right of which is placed the family arms, having the three garbs for *Cumin* depicted on the field, two in chief, and one in base ; whilst on the left side of the tablet is sculptured the paternal bearing of his lady—a shake fork betwixt three garbs, also for Cumin, one in chief, and two in the flank points ; the tinctures, it will readily occur, must have been varied in both instances to suit this arrangement. As stated in the account, the more usual manner of marshalling the achievements of the family of Rowallan, was by *quartering*. The Crest, a *Moor's head*, which also appears sculptured near the same place, is probably allusive of some feat performed during the Crusades against the Saracens — in the old *Fam. Tree*, it is alluded to as the ' bludy heid.'

Various other fragments of emblematic sculpture, initials and dates, appear in different parts ; in an ornamental compartment over the principal door, at the top of a long flight of steps, is cut in stone the Royal Arms of Scotland, with the supporters and regal accompaniments, surmounting the family shield, emblazoned as above.

### CRAUFURDS OF CRAUFURDLAND.

According to an old MS. history, in the possession of the family, the Craufurds of Craufurdland—who have retained their original lands for a much longer period than any other branch of the great Craufurd family—trace themselves from Sir Reginald de Craufurd, Sheriff of Ayr, who, about the commencement of the thirteenth century, married the heiress of Loudoun. By this marriage, it is said, there were four sons, the third of whom,

I. JOHN CRAUFURD, was the first of the family. By his father's donation, he had many lands in Clydesdale, and in right of his wife, Alicia de Dalsalloch, possessed, if not all, at least a good part of that barony, all which, (sometime possessed by his eldest son,) by marriage of his daughter, came to the Cumins, who gave to his second son, called John Craufurd, the lands of Ardach or Craufurdland, in contentation of his right to the whole, as heir male to John Craufurd, his father, or to his elder brother.*

II. John Craufurd, first Laird of Craufurdland, second son of the above John Craufurd, and grandson of Sir Reginald Craufurd, Sheriff of Ayr, lived in the days of King Alexander II. (inter

1214 et 1249,) and was succeeded in the said lands by his eldest son,

III. John Craufurd of Cranfurdland, who lived in the days of Alexander III. (inter 1249 et 1285,) and was succeeded by his eldest son,

IV. James Craufurd, who was a follower of Sir William Wallace, his cousin, and is one of those who are marked to have been present in 1297, at Wallace's election to be Warden of Scotland, at the Forest-Kirk in Selkirkshire. He was succeeded by his eldest son,

V. —— Craufurd of Craufurdland, who died about the year 1350, and was succeeded by his eldest son,

VI. John Craufurd of Craufurdland, who acquired a new confirmation of the lands of Ardach, alias Craufurdland, from King Robert III., which charter is dated at Dundonald in the year 1391, in the second year of his reign, he having succeeded in anno 1390.* Of this John Craufurd are descended the families of Giffordland and Birkhead in the shire of Ayr. He was succeeded by

VII. —— Craufurd of Craufurdland, his eldest son, who died without issue, and was succeeded by his brother,

VIII. Sir William Craufurd of Craufurdland, son of the above John Craufurd, a man of great bravery and fortitude, who had the honour of knighthood conferred on him by King James I. This Sir William was at the siege of Crevelt in France in the year 1423, where he was severely wounded and taken prisoner, and was one of the captives released with King James I. of Scotland, 1424. He was succeeded by his eldest son,

IX. Rankine Craufurd of Craufurdland, married about the year 1430. He had three sons :—

1. William, his successor.
2. Robert, who was educated as a churchman.
3. Andrew.

He was succeeded by his eldest son,

X. William Craufurd of Craufurdland. He lived in the days of King James II., and married Janet Hamilton, daughter of the Laird of Bardewic, by whom he had three sons—

1. Archibald, his successor.
2. William, who married —— Nisbet, the heiress of Cultness. He was the first of the Craufurds of Dean.
3. Thomas Craufurd of Amlaird.

He was succeeded by his eldest son,

XI. Archibald Craufurd of Craufurdland. He lived in the reign of King James III. ; was twice married:—first to Jean Kennedy, daughter of

---

* This is contrary to the " Historie " of the Mures of Rowallan, wherein it is stated that the lands of Ardach were gifted to " Johne Crawford and his aires for service of waird and releife."

* " Carta to John de Crawfurd of Ardacht, of the lands of Ardacht, within the dominium of Rowalane, the barony of Cuninghame, and shire of Ayr, to be holden blench of the Lairds of Rowallane."—Rob. Index. This seems favourable to the statement of the author of the " Historie."

Gilbert Kennedy, second Laird of Bargany, by whom he had a son, *Robert*, of whom afterwards. He married, secondly, —— Boyd, widow of Hugh Muir of Polkellie, eldest daughter of Archibald Boyd of Narston and Bonshaw, by whom he had two sons and a daughter:—

1. Thomas, from whom are descended the Craufurds of Classlochie and Powmill in Kinross-shire.
2. William Craufurd, Secretary to the Earl of Morton, who settled in Tweeddale, and of whom the Craufurds in that country are descended.
3. Jean, married to —— Cathcart of Waterhead.

His father-in-law, Archibald Boyd of Bonshaw, had three daughters—the Lady Polkellie, above-mentioned, was the eldest; the second was Elizabeth, Lady Lochleven, of whom the Earl of Morton is descended; the third was Margaret Boyd, who in her youth was mistress to King James IV., and bore to him Alexander Stewart, Archbishop of St Andrews, and Jean, Countess of Morton. She being a great favourite in the Court, and cousin to Dame Elizabeth Boyd, daughter to Robert Lord Boyd, and Countess of Angus, whose husband, Archibald Earl of Angus, then Chamberlain, had the greatest power in the state. By his means and her own, Margaret Boyd brought her cousins the Boyds into the factorship of the barony of Kilmarnock, their ancient patrimony—lately fallen to the Crown by forfeiture; in the possession of which they continued upholden by the Earl of Angus, till such time as they were restored again by the Duke of Hamilton, Governor, after the battle of the field of Glasgow in 1545. She brought about the marriages of her other sisters to the Lairds of Lochleven and Cranfurdland. In consideration of which last marriage, she, donator in presence of the said Archibald Earl of Angus, Chamberlain, " apud Boghall prope Biggar, 17mo. Decembris 1493," disponeth to Archibald Cranfurd of Craufurdland her kinsman (as she calls him,) the ward of the lands of Craufurdland. The words are "Honorabili viro Archibaldo Craufurd de Craufurdland, consanguineo meo wardam terrarum de Ardach, et omnium terrarum infra dominium de Craufurdland, tam proprietatis quam tenendriæ, per donationem S. D. N. Regis."—She got Elizabeth Muir, daughter of her sister the Lady Polkellie, to be married to Robert Craufurd, young Laird of Cranfurdland, for which cause she procured to him the *kindness* and tack of the lands of Walston, from the said Archibald Earl of Angus, anno 1494, which Walston lands are part of the Barony of Kilmarnock, and then belonged to the crown, and were afterwards possessed by the said Robert's successor. The feud which had so long prevailed between the Mures and Craufurds, was, by means of this Dame Mar-

garet Boyd, at length extinguished, and a new charter, upon resignation, granted to the Laird of Craufurdland of the lands of Ardoch—at the first the whole holding ward—thereafter, a five merk land of the Mains, holding blanch; the rest ward.

XII. Robert Craufurd, the eldest son, was styled of Auchencairn in Nithsdale, during his father's lifetime. He stood also infeft in the lands of Redhall in Annandale, holding ward of the King. He married Elizabeth Muir, daughter of the Laird of Polkellie, by whom he had three sons:—

1. John, his successor.
2. William, Laird of Walston, married —— Mowat, daughter to the Laird of Busbie, by whom he had John Craufurd of Walston, who married Isabell Craufurd, heiress of Giffordland, and also of William Craufurd of Beanscroft.
3. James Craufurd, vicar of Kilbryde.

Robert Craufurd of Auchencairn died, before his father, of the wounds he received at the Wyllie-lee, in company with his father, attending James Boyd, son of Thomas Earl of Arran, who was killed there by the Earl of Eglintoun. This happened in 1484.

XIII. John Craufurd of Craufurdland, eldest son of the said Robert Craufurd, succeeded his grandfather, Archibald Craufurd. By his prudent conduct, he composed the feud betwixt the Boyds and Montgomeries, and received in marriage Janet Montgomerie, daughter to the Laird of Giffin, by whom he had two sons:—

1. John, his successor.
2. Archibald, born after his father's death, was parson of Eaglesham, and as such had a manse in the Drygate of Glasgow, which he conveyed in free property to his chief, the Laird of Craufurdland. He was also a Lord of Session, Secretary and Almoner to Queen Mary of Guise, Regent, with whose corpse he was sent to France, in 1560, to see it deposited in the Benedictine Monastery of St Peter at Rheims, where her own sister, Renee, was then Abbess. When in France, he got a commission from her daughter, the unfortunate Mary Queen of Scots, renewing to him his office of Secretary and Almoner, and expressive of her obligations for his great services rendered to her late mother; which commission, supposed to be the first granted to a Scotsman, is dated at Joinville in France, the 17th April 1561:[*]

[Queen Mary, after her arrival in Scotland, August 1561, was permitted to have Popish worship in the chapel at Holyroodhouse. Some French noblemen, who had accompanied her in her voyage, were then with her, and many of her servants were natives of France. The Sacristan, or keeper of the sacred utensils, was Sir James Paterson, who probably was one of her officiating chaplains, and one of the Popish Knights. Riotous attacks were sometimes made upon the

---

[*] The original commission is preserved among the family papers at Craufurdland.

chapel, and there was danger of its being rifled at any time when she might be absent from Edinbugh. It was probably, therefore, upon this account that the Queen, January 11, 1561-2, directed Sir James Paterson to deliver to her valet de chambre, Servais de Conde, the furniture of her chapel, to be kept by her respectable Almoner, Mr Archibald Craufurd, in the wardrobe of her palace at Edinburgh, from whence it could be easily conveyed as often as was necessary. The following is the inventory of these curious ornaments:—

"Item imprimis, tua blew damaiss capis stripit with gold. Item, tua reid welnouss [velvet] champit with gold. Item, ane fyne caipe of claith of gold on blew welnouss feild. Item, three black welnouss earpis [perhaps carpets] for the mort, ane of them studit with gold. Item, tua tunikillis [small coats or vests] with ane chesabill of blak welnouss for the mort stand, with three albis annits stolis [long vests or robes] and sarnonis and purse. Item, twa auld alter towalls. Item, ane frontole, and ane pendikill of black welnouss studit with gold. Item, four tunikillis, twa chesabillis of fyne clayth of gold, with three albis stolis, sarnanis, annitts, and purse. Item, ane mess buik of parchment, with ane nobt artiphenate of parchment. Item, ane coffer, with lok and key, within the quhilk thair is part of this foresaid garniture. Item, ane pendakill of silk, ane frontoll of clayth of gold and purpour velvat. All this geyr receivit be me, Sernais, varlot of Chalmer to our Soverane, at hyr command, the 11me daye of Janver anno 1561, before me, David Lamerol."

There follows in the French language the acceptance of the above ornament by " Sernais de Conde, vallet de chambre de la Royne." His subscription is dated à Lilleboun, 11me de Janvier 1561. It is remarkable that in the above inventory no mention is made of crucifixes, or images of any kind: if such had been in the chapel the zeal against Popery was then so great, that the chapel would have been immediately destroyed. No mention is made of the sacred vessels, some of which were perhaps contained in the coffer.—Keith, says, that in June 1567, after the Queen had been committed as a prisoner to the Castle of Lochleven, " Alexander Earl of Glencairn went to the palace of Holyroodhouse, accompanied by his own servants only, and demolished the chapel, with all its ornaments and furniture."

In June 1567, the Queen was conducted in the night time and in disguise, as a prisoner, to the Castle of Lochleven. She was spoiled of all her princely ornaments, and clothed with a warm brown cassock. " The Lords took an Inventory of all the plate, jewels, and other moveables, within the palace of Holyrood-house; and yet this was not all, for we are likewise informed that they spared not to put violent hands on her Majesty's cupboard, melted the specie thereof, and converted it into coin, thereby to forge a staff to break her own head. The Queen's cupboard amounted to sixteen stone weight."

It appears, however, from the Craufurdland papers, that she found means to put into the hands of Mr Archibald Craufurd her Almoner, certain pieces of plate for the service of her table, which he faithfully kept in his possession till November 1567; at which time they were demanded from him, by the Treasurer, Mr Robert Richardson; and on the 13th of that month were delivered by the said Treasurer to James Stewart, Earl of Murray, Regent of the kingdom, who granted the following acquittance to Mr Archibald Craufurd :—

" We, James Erl of Murray, Lord Abernethy, and Regent of Scotland, grantis me to haif ressavit be the handis of Maistr Robert Richartson, Tresurer, fra the handes of Maistr Archibald Craufurd, Parson of Eaglesham, this sylver work, under quhilk he had in keeping of the Quenis Maijeste.

" Item imprimis, ane sylver chaless, with the patery [border] gylt. Item, twa sylver chandelaris gylt. Item, ane watter fat [vase] with ane watter stik [spout] gylt. Item, ane sylver bell gylt. Item, ane purse with ane boist gylt. Item, ane cowip [cup] with ane cower [cover] and ane sayer [salver] gylt. Item, ane erowat with ane lyd gylt. Item, ane flakkon with ane charger gylt. Item, twa ball crowatts, and discharges the said Maistr Archibald hereof be this our acquitance, subscribit with our hand at Edinbroch the thirteenth daye of November, in the zier of God 1567 zeirs.

" JAMES REGENT."

The above Archibald Craufurd, among the many acts that distinguished his life, and proved him so worthy of Royal confidence, built the West Church of Glasgow, and the Bridge of Eaglesham. He died unmarried.

The before-mentioned John Craufurd of Craufurdland was a youth of a noble spirit and great resolution. He accompanied James IV. to the fatal field of Floudoun, where he lost his life in the flower of his age, with his royal leader, anno 1513. His widow, Janet Montgomerie, married Robert Hunter of Hunterston, of whom the present family of Hunterston are descended. He was succeeded by his infant son,

XIV. John Craufurd of Craufurdland, who married Margaret Blair, daughter to John Blair of that Ilk, (by Lady Elizabeth Montgomerie, daughter of Hugh, first Earl of Eglintoun), by whom he had three sons and five daughters :—

1. John, his heir.
2. Thomas, who married Margaret Craufurd, heir-portioner of Giffordland, sister to Isabel Craufurd, spouse to John Craufurd of Walstoun.
3. Robert, died unmarried.
1. Janet, married to James Aucheneross of that Ilk.
2. Agnes, married to Hugh Montgomerie of Smithson, Bailie of Kilwinning.
3. Elizabeth, married to Alexander Arnot of Lochrig.
4. ———, married to Archibald Dunlop of Auchenskeith.
5. Marion, married to John Currie in Gardrum.

He had also a natural son, Robert, for whom he purchased the lands of Nethertown of Kilmarnock, then belonging to the crown. This Robert was at the battle of Pinkie, and died of the wounds he received there.—He got a charter under the Great Seal from King James VI., *Johanni Craufurd de Craufurdland, terrarum de Giffordland*, &c., in Ayrshire, dated 27th March 1576. He died anno 1583, in the 71st year of his age, and was succeeded by his eldest son,

XV. John Craufurd of Craufurdland, who upon his father's resignation got a charter under the Great Seal, *Johanni Cranfurd juniori de Craufurdland, terrarum ecclesiasticarum de Kilbryde,* &c. in Ayrshire, dated 12th Feb. 1581. He also, during his father's lifetime, got from Mary Queen of Scots a gift of the ward of the lands of Reidhall, lying within the Stewartry of Annandale ; the deed of gift, having the Queen's signature attached to it, is dated at Edinburgh, the 26th December 1561, and is in possession of the Craufurdland family. He married Margaret, daughter of Hugh Wallace of Cairnhill, by whom he had four sons and three daughters :—

1. John, his heir.
2. Hugh, portioner of Rutherglen, was married, and had several sons, who all went to Germany and settled there.
3. Robert of Howrat, died unmarried.
4. Archibald, Constable of Dunbarton Castle, and one of the Bailies of that Burgh.
1. Janet, first married to George Campbell of Stevenston and Dreat-hall ; secondly, to Mungo Campbell of Cowfauldshaw; thirdly, to John Darleith of that Ilk; of all which marriages she had issue, who heired all their families.
2. Elizabeth, married Robert Fergushill of that Ilk.
3. Marion, married to William Shaw of Malnholm, died without issue.

This Laird of Craufurdland was a man of eminent abilities, and great spirit ; and though he lived in a splendid manner, yet he did not encumber his paternal estate. He died anno 1603, aged 70, and was succeeded by his eldest son,

XVI. John Craufurd of Craufurdland, who married first, in 1590, Helen, daughter to James Chalmers of Gadgirth, by whom he had a son, *John*, his successor, and three daughters :—

1. Janet, married to Alexander Cuninghame of Waterston and Carlung.
2. Agnes, married to Thomas Craufurd of Walstoun, portioner of Giffordland.
3. Helen, married to William Rankine of Sheil.

He married, secondly, Christian Wallace, daughter to the Laird of Auchans, then widow of Mr James Ross of Whiteriggs, and thereafter Lady Dreghorn, by whom he had a son and daughter:—

Robert, who got from his father the lands of Monkland, and married Catherine Davidson, daughter of Patrick Davidson of Sheil, burgess of Ayr. Their only son, John, dying soon after his father, without issue, the lands of Monkland returned to the family of Craufurdland.

Catherine married Robert Stewart of Barskimming.

In conjunction with John Craufurd, his father, he gave contentation to the Laird of Rowallan, in 1602, for the wardholding of the fourteen merk land of Ardach, alias Craufurdland, which originally held blanch of Rowallan as superior, (but of late had been taken to hold ward), at the reconciliation betwixt the families in 1511. He died in 1612, aged 42. His son,

XVII. John Craufurd, in 1610, married Elizabeth Cuninghame, daughter to Alexander Cuninghame of Corsehill, who bore him two sons :—

1. John, who succeeded.
2. Alexander, who died an infant.*

He was a young man of great life and spirit. He died, of a hurt received at foot-ball, a little before his father, anno 1612, aged 21. His widow married Sir David Barclay of Ladyland, and his infant son,

XVIII. John Craufurd of Craufurdland, born in 1611, succeeded his grandfather in 1612 ; and, June 15, 1613, was served heir both to his grandfather and great-grandfather.† In 1630 he married Janet Cuninghame, daughter of the Laird of Craigends ; by her he had seven sons and five daughters :—

1. John, his heir.
2. Alexander Craufurd of Fergushill, who married, first, Elizabeth Maxwell, daughter of John Maxwell of Southbar, by whom he had two sons and three daughters; secondly, he married Isabel Henderson, daughter of Henderson of Baikie, and relict of Bryce Boyd of Pitcon, by whom he had a son and daughter.
3. William, was a merchant and burgess of Glasgow. He married Martha Miller, daughter of John Miller, of the Barskimming family, by whom he had four sons and a daughter:—
    1. Anthony.
    2. Matthew, who married, first, Agnes Stewart, daughter of Alexander Stewart of Torrence; secondly, Esther Fletcher, co-heiress of Cranstoun, by whom he had seven sons and one daughter, of whom afterwards.
    3. John.
    4. James, and a daughter.
4. James, was a surgeon.
5. Archibald, died in Africa aged 20.
6. Robert.
7. Thomas.
1. Elizabeth, married John Hamilton of Grange, by whom she had two sons and six daughters.
2. Agnes, married John Campbell of Kingincleugh, to whom she bare two sons and a daughter.
3. and 4. Isabella and Anne, died in infancy.
5. Janet, married to William Craufurd of Dalleagles, to whom she bare five sons and two daughters.

He married, secondly, Margaret Skeene, daughter of —— Skeene of Hallyards, and relict of William Fairlie of Bruntsfield ; and again, for his third wife, Elizabeth Inglis, daughter of —— Inglis of Ingliston, and relict of Dundas of Breastmiln, but had no issue by the last two marriages. He died 1686, aged 75, and was succeeded by his eldest son,

XIX. John Craufurd of Craufurdland, who,

---

* "Archibald Craufurd, brother to the Laird of Craufurdland," occurs in a testamentary document in 1620.
† Thomas Craufurd of Walstoun was tutor of Craufurdland.

in 1667 married Anna Stuart, daughter of Sir Archibald Stuart of Castlemilk, by whom he had three sons and four daughters :—

1. John, his heir.
2. Archibald.
3. James.
The daughters all died young.

This gentleman met with much trouble in 1684, on suspicion of being concerned in the Bothwel-Brig insurrection ;* and, in particular, was confined in prison. He died in 1693, and was succeeded by his eldest son,

XX. John Cranfurd of Craufurdland. He married Elizabeth Kerr, daughter of Mark Kerr of Morriston, by whom he had five sons and three daughters :—

1. John, his heir.
2. and 3. died without issue.
4. William, was a writer in Edinburgh, who also died without issue.
5. Andrew, was a surgeon in Lord Mark Kerr's Dragoons; afterwards settled at Preston in England, but died at Edinburgh, in December 1762, without issue.
1. and 3. daughters died unmarried.
2. Elizabeth, of whom afterwards.

He died in 1744, and was succeeded by his son,

XXI. John Cranfurd of Craufurdland, who married, in 1719, Robina Walkinshaw, daughter and heiress of John Walkinshaw of that Ilk, Laird of Bishoptoun; upon which marriage he added the name and arms of Walkinshaw to his own, and by her he had several children, who all died young, excepting John Walkinshaw Craufurd, his eldest son and successor. He afterwards married Elenora Nicolson, daughter of Sir Thomas Nicolson of Carnock, and relict of the Hon. Thomas Boyd, advocate, brother-german to the late Earl of Kilmarnock, by whom he had no issue. He died at Newcastle, Jan. 10, 1763, and was succeeded by his son, the said

XXII. John Walkinshaw Craufurd of Craufurdland, who early entered the army. In August 1761, he was appointed Falconer to the King, for Scotland. He was an intimate friend of the unfortunate Earl of Kilmarnock, who suffered with others for the attempt to restore the house of Stuart. He attended him to the scaffold, and, it is said, held a corner of the cloth to receive his head; he afterwards performed the last sad office of friendship, by getting him interred. For the public exhibition he then made, he was put to the bottom of the army list. He rose to be Major-Commandant of the 115th Regiment of Foot, and latterly to the rank of Lieut.-Colonel in the army. He was present at the battles of Dettingen and Fontenoy, where he distinguished himself. He died at Edinburgh, unmarried, aged 72, Feb. 1793, settling his estate, by a deed made on his death-

* Law's Memorials.

bed, upon Thomas Coutts, banker in London. His aunt and nearest heir, however, Mrs Elizabeth Craufurd, instituted an action of reduction of this settlement, and after a long litigation, carried on by her and her successor, the deed was reduced by a decree of the House of Lords in 1806, by which the succession to this ancient estate returned into its natural channel.

XXIII. Elizabeth Cranfurd of Craufurdland, daughter to the before-mentioned John Craufurd of Cranfurdland and Elizabeth Kerr of Morrieston, and aunt to the last John Cranfurd, married, first, William Fairlie of that Ilk, by whom she had a daughter, who died in infancy. She afterwards married, 3d June 1744, John Howieson of Braehead in Mid-Lothian, head of one of the oldest families in that county, by whom she had two sons, *William* and *John*, who died in infancy, and two daughters :—

1. Elizabeth.
2. Margaret, who died, unmarried, in 1801.

Elizabeth Craufurd died at the advanced age of 97, at Braehead in Mid-Lothian, in 1802, and was succeeded by her only remaining daughter,

XXIV. Elizabeth Howieson Craufurd of Craufurdland and Braehead, who united in her own person the representation of these two ancient families, which had always been in the male line, till the former came to her mother, and the latter to herself. She married the Rev. James Moody, one of the ministers of the gospel at Perth, who assumed the name of James Howieson Moody Craufurd, to whom she had seven children :—

1. John Craufurd Howieson, died in infancy.
2. Alexander, born 1780, died 1796.
3. William Howieson Craufurd.
1. Elizabeth Beatrix, died in infancy.
2. Margaret.
3. Elizabeth, died in infancy.
4. Isabella.

Elizabeth Howieson Craufurd died on the 1st of April 1823, and was succeeded by her only remaining son,

XXV. William Howieson Craufurd of Craufurdland and Braehead. In 1808, he married Janet Esther Whyte, only daughter of James Whyte of Newmains (nephew and sole heir of Veitch of Dawick, and ought to have assumed his name, being his representative) and his wife, Esther Craufurd. The father of the said Esther Craufurd was the lineal male descendant of William, third son of John Craufurd of Craufurdland and Janet Cuninghame of Craigends his wife, before mentioned.

It is a remarkable coincidence, and worthy of record, that a female descendant of this collateral male branch of the family, is now united to the only male descendant of a female on whom the representation devolved, upon the failure of the direct male line of this ancient family.*

Issue of this marriage :—

1. John Reginald Craufurd, born 30th August 1811. He married, in 1847, Mary Dundas Hamilton, fifth daughter of John Hamilton, Esq. of Sundrum, by whom he has a daughter, born Feb. 1848.

1. Elizabeth Constantia, born 18th Oct. 1813, married in 1845 to James Ogilvie Fairlie, Esq. of Coodham, by whom she has a son, born in 1847.

As proprietor of Braehead, Mr Craufurd had the honour, in terms of the reddendo in the charters of that estate, *Servitium lavacri in nomine albæ firmæ,* of performing that service to his Majesty George IV., at the banquet given by the city of Edinburgh, on the 24th August 1822, as thus described by authority :—" As soon as the King had dined, a silver basin, containing rose water, was brought to his Majesty, by William Howieson Craufurd, younger of Braehead, who, in right of his mother, as proprietrix of Braehead, who, in the county of Mid-Lothian, claims this privilege: the service performed being the ancient tenour by which the estate of Braehead is held. He was attended by Masters Charles and Walter Scott, the one a son, the other a nephew of Sir Walter Scott, Bart., as pages, attired in splendid dresses of scarlet and white satin. The former holding a silver ewer, and the other a salver, with a damask napkin of Scottish manufacture, and of the finest texture. In offering the basin, Mr Howieson Craufurd knelt down to his Majesty, who, after he had dipped his fingers

---

* The descent of this lady is as follows:—William, third son of the before-mentioned John Craufurd and Janet Cuninghame, who lived in the days of the unfortunate Charles I., married, as has already been stated, Martha Miller, daughter of John Miller, by whom he had four sons and one daughter. Mathew, the second of these sons, with whom only we are at present interested, married, first, Agnes Stuart, daughter of Alexander Stuart of Torrence, by whom he had one child, a daughter, married to Sir William Dalrymple of Cousland; secondly, Esther Fletcher, co-heiress of Cranston, whose mother was Esther Cuninghame, a daughter of the Laird of Enterkine, and she herself grand-daughter of the Bishop of the Isles. By her he had seven sons and one daughter: Mathew, the eldest son, was a man of singular worth and merit. John, his second son, possessed of similar endowments, was a physician, and got his diploma at Leyden. He married Janet Orr, daughter of John Orr of Barrowfield and Grugar, then a family of great wealth and consequence in Glasgow, by whom he had five sons and two daughters. Martha, only daughter of the above Mathew Craufurd and Esther Fletcher, married John Orr of Barrowfield and Grugar, (brother of the above Janet Orr,) to whom she had several children. Mathew, the eldest son of John Craufurd and Janet Orr, died, unmarried, at Edinburgh 1815. John, second son of John Craufurd and Janet Orr, married Mary Johnston of New-York, by whom he had one son, John, and two daughters. Esther Craufurd, the only one of the before mentioned five daughters of John Craufurd and Janet Orr, who was married, had, by her husband, James Whyte of Newmains, as already stated, three sons and one daughter; which daughter, Janet Esther, is the wife of the present William Howieson Craufurd, as above.

---

in the water, and wiped them with the napkin, acknowledged the service with an affability and grace peculiarly his own.*

*Arms of Craufurd of Craufurdland.*—Gules, a fesse ermine. *Crest.*—A marble pillar, supporting a man's heart proper. *Motto.*—*Stant Innixa Deo.*

---

### Howieson of Braehead.

" The *Howisons of Braehead,*" says *Wood,* in his account of the Parish of Cramond, published in 1794, " are by far the most ancient family of the parish, having subsisted there upwards of 350 years, a longer period than any of the numerous families that have had interest in this district have done." The following is the pedigree adduced by this genealogist:—

I. John Howison, was a burgess in Edinburgh in 1450. His son,

II. James Howison, had a charter of Cramond-Regis in 1465. His son,

III. George Howison, was witness to a sasine of Sir John Moubray of Barnbougle, 9th October 1511, of the lands of Coleairny, to his uncle William Moubray, ancestor of the present family. His son,

IV. Andrew Howison, of Cramond-Regis, had a charter dated Feb. 10, 1555. He married Elizabeth, daughter of —— Bathgate. His son,

V. John Howison of Braehead, in Cramond-Regis, who had a charter dated Dec. 13, 1575—died in 1618. He married Janet, daughter of Alexander Moubray in Dalmeny, (descended of the ancient family of the Moubrays, Dukes of Norfolk,) by whom he had, besides his successor, a daughter, Elizabeth, who was married to William Murray of Romanno, ancestor of the Murrays of Stanhope, to whom she had a son, Adam, who was ancestor of the Murrays of Cardon; and a daughter, Margaret, from whom are descended the Murrays of Cringaltie.

VI. Alexander Howison of Braehead, who died in 1637. He married a daughter of —— Haldane in Saughton, by whom he had a son,

VII. James Howison of Braehead, who was buried at Cramond 20th March 1680. He married Alison, daughter of Ramsay of Blackcraig, by whom he had a daughter, Agnes, married to

---

* The silver ewer, basin and towel, together with the rose water, used by his Majesty at this banquet, are in the possession of the proprietor at Braehead. The foregoing service had its origin, according to tradition, in an adventure of one of the Stuarts, Kings of Scotland, in which he was overmatched by a band of gipsies, and rescued by the farmer in Braehead.

James Dundas in Southfield, four children who died young, and a son who succeeded him,

VIII. Alexander Howison of Brachead, who died 18th April 1703, aged 67. He married Martha, daughter and heiress of William Young in Craigleith, by whom he had several children, who died young, or without issue, and a son who succeeded him,

IX. William Howison of Brachead, who died of a fit of apoplexy, on his way home from Cramond church, 28th Feb. 1729, aged 63. He married Margaret, daughter of John Mitchel of Alderstone, by whom he had a daughter, married in 1735 to Mr William Dauling; a son Charles (the sixth of the family), who died in 1780); and five more children, who died young—besides his eldest son, who succeeded him,

X. John Howison of Brachead, who died 12th May 1787, aged 74. He married Elizabeth Craufurd, daughter of John Craufurd of Craufurdland (No. XXII. in that family), and relict of William Fairlie of that Ilk, by whom he had, as before stated, a daughter,

XI. Elizabeth Howison of Brachead, who was married in 1777 to the Rev. John Moodie, one of the ministers of Perth, (who *jure uxoris* became Laird of Brachead), to whom she had several children, as already noticed. Dying in April 1823,

XII. William Howieson Cranfurd, now of Craufurdland, her only surviving son, succeeded her in Craufurdland, and Brachead.

*Arms of Howieson of Brachead.*—Argent, a heart proper, on a chief, Azure, three fleur de lis, or. Supporters, two husbandmen, in the dress of the fourteenth century: one holding a flail, and the other a basin and napkin.—*Crest*, a dexter hand erect and couped at the wrist. *Motto*, " *Sursum Corda.*"

*Seat.*—Brachead is a modern small mansion, snugly masked under the shade of its own old timber, near to Cramond Bridge, in the county of Mid-Lothian, about five miles north west of Edinburgh.

### HAMILTONS OF CAMBUSKEITH AND GRANGE.

The progenitors of the Hamiltons of Cambuskeith, now called the *Mount*, is derived by *Craufurd* and *Wood* from Walter, second son of Sir David, *filius Walteri de Hamilton*, the third in the line of succession from Gilbert de Hamildun, the founder of the Ducal house of Hamilton. Craufurd further states that *Hamilton* of *Grange*, in Ayr-

*shire*, was the representative of the Cambuskeith Hamiltons. This is very probable, although neither Crawfurd nor the writer of the family genealogy in Robertson's *Ayrshire Families*, prove it to be the fact. We shall, however, follow the latter account, said to be drawn from family writs, so far as it appears to be correct. The first recorded in these documents is

I. David Hamilton of Cambuskeith, who had a charter of the lands of Blairmead from his uncle (*patruus*) Alan Hamilton of Lethberd, which was confirmed by the over lord, Archibald Earl of Douglas, Lord of Galloway and Annandale, at Peebles, on the 29th January 1411.

II. James Hamilton of Cambuskeith, who was served heir to his father David in 1436. He married Marjory, daughter of Sir James Hamilton of Preston, by Margaret, daughter of Sir James, afterwards Lord Hamilton, by whom he had his successor,

III. John Hamilton of Cambuskeith, who married Marion, daughter of Sir John Maxwell of Calderwood, by whom he had a son,

IV. Alexander Hamilton of Cambuskeith, who was served heir to his father John in 1489. His name occurs as one of the assize in a criminal case in 1512; and he was amerciated for intercommuning with the Sheriff of Ayr in 1527.[*] He married Marion, daughter of Sir Adam Cuninghame of Caprington, by Isabel, daughter of Sir Malcolm Craufurd of Kilbirnie, by whom he had a son,

V. John Hamilton of Cambuskeith, who in 1542 appears in the Scots Acts of Parliament as one of the curators of John Hamilton of Fynart. He was killed on the Muir of Glasgow, May 1544.[†] He married Margaret, daughter of Cuninghame of Leglane, by whom he had a son,

VI. John Hamilton of Cambuskeith, who was served heir to his father, John, in 1546. He did not, however, long enjoy the property, as he died intestate in September 1547. His relict, *Joneta Muntgumery* was confirmed *executores datui* the following January. He left issue:

1. John. " his son and heir apparent."
2. Elizabeth, " his daughter."[‡]

" William Hammiltone, Tutour of Cammiskeyth," was charged with celebrating mass, and attempting to restore Popery at Kirkoswald in 1563.[||]

VII. John Hamilton of Cambuskeith. It was this John, probably, who married Catherine Far-

* Criminal Trials.
† Pollock Diurn. p. 32.
‡ Glas. Com. Records. John No. VI. and John No. VII. seem to have been regarded as one and the same person by the writer in Robertson.
§ Crim. Trials.

quhar, daughter of the Laird of Gilmilnscroft, by whom he had two sons :—

1. John, his successor.
2. William, afterwards Sir William Hamilton of Sorn.*

He was succeeded by,

VIII. John Hamilton of Cambuskeith, who was served heir to his father, John, in the lands of Cambuskeith in 1561, and to his grandfather, John, in the lands of Pophill, Burnhill and others, near to Craufurdland and Kilmarnock Castles, on 1st May 1572. He married, first, Jane Montgomerie, daughter of the Laird of Haiselheid, by whom he had his successor, and probably a daughter, *Elizabeth* ;† secondly, he married Janet Stewart, daughter of Mr Mathew Stewart of Minto, by whom he had a son, according to the writer in Robertson, *David* of Ladyton, which lands he obtained from his father, in 1571, and who married Marion Campbell daughter of the Laird of Ducathall.

The following extract from the *Notarial Book* of John Masoun, notary in Ayr, possibly refers to this period :—" June 28, 1582.—The quhilk day, Katherine Hamiltoun, dochter to vmquhile Johne Hamiltoun of Colmiskeyth, knyt., past to the personal presens of Johne Wallace of Dundonald, and there, for the sowme of ane hundreth merkis, money of this realme, instanlie payit to hir be the said John, &c. resignit, and simplie renuncit in his handis, as in the handis of hir superiour, as heretabill possessour of the landis vnderwrittin. All and haill ane annuelrent of ten merkis money zeirlie, to be vpliftit furth of all and haill the landis of Litill Monktoun manis, or ony part therof, annalyit to hir be Dauid Hammiltoun of Bothuelhauch, sumtyme heretabill possessour of the saidis landis, to remane with the said John and his airis for ever. And attour the said Katherine oblist hir and hir airis, gif ned be, to infeft the said Johne and his airis, he chartour and sasing tharintill, haldand of himself," &c.

IX. John Hamilton of Cambuskeith or Grange. He was retoured heir to his great-grandfather, John, in the lands of Overmure and Carlingcraigs, 3d Nov. 1603. He married Janet, daughter of William Cuninghame of Caprington, by whom he had no issue. His brother-in-law, William of Caprington, is said to have obtained unfairly a

charter under the Great Seal of the ten pound land of Cambuskeith in 1598. " Johnne Hammiltoun of the Grange of Kilmarnok " is mentioned as one of the assize in a criminal case in 1608. He died before 1615, in which year " vmquill Jonn. Hamiltoun of Grange " occurs as a debtor in the testament of " Mr Johnne Luif," Kilmarnock. He was alive in 1612, so that his death must have occurred between the years 1612 and 1615.

The writer in Robertson states that the representation of the family now devolved on his brother *David* of Ladyton. No proof is adduced of this, but it seems probable from the fact that Ladyton was the property of the family. It does not appear, however, that David succeeded his brother, or that he was ever styled of Grange, as we find

X. " Alexander Hamiltoun of Greng " mentioned in the testament of John Hutchesoun in Bog, Galston parish, in June 1616. He was retoured heir to his father, David, in the lands of Grange, 10th January 1617. He married Agnes (not Elizabeth) Craufurd, neice of the Laird of Lochnorris, by whom he had two sons :—

1. John, who is erroneously said to have died young.
2. Robert, said to have been the successor of his father.

XI. John Hamilton of Grange. His name occurs in various documents. In 1618 John Hamilton of Grange disposed of his annual rent on the lands and barony of Kilmarnock to the Boyd family, which he seems to have again acquired, for, in 1634, John Hamilton of Grange has infeftment of the annual rent furth of the lands and baronies of Kilmarnock and Grougar.* " Johnne Hamiltoun of Grange occurs in the testament of Margaret Speir, &c. Dreghorne, July 1623, as a creditor " for the maillis and dewties of thair mailling," &c. " Johne Hamiltoun, *fear*† of Grange " occurs as a debtor in the testament of " Johne Andersoune, schoolmaster at Kilmarnock " in 1629. In 1630 " Johanes Hamilton of Grange " was admitted a burgess of the town of Ayr.‡ He appears to have married Margaret Knox, for we find " Margaret Knox, Ladie Cambuskeith " mentioned in the testament of Elizabeth Arnot, in Kilmarnock, in 1632. John Hamilton of Grange appears in a testamentary document so late as 1658. He probably left no issue, and may have been succeeded by his brother,

XII. Robert Hamilton of Grange, who was retoured heir to his father, Alexander, 19th December 1661. He married Margaret Hamilton,

* William Hamilton of Cambuskeith was imprisoned for attending Mass, May 19, 1563.

† " The testament, &c. of vmquill Elizabeth Hamiltone, sister Germane to Johne Hamilton of Grainge besyde Kilmarnok, quha deeelst vpon the day of Junii the zeir of God 1611 zciris. This Elizabeth was unmarried, and must have been the sister of John who was retoured heir to his father in 1603. Grange had thus been adopted as the designation of the family at an earlier period than the writer in Robertson supposes.

daughter of the Laird of Neilsland, by whom he a son,

XIII. John Hamilton of Grange, who, married Elizabeth Craufurd, daughter of the Laird of Craufurdland, by whom he had two sons and six daughters, of the latter of whom, Margaret, was married, in 1675, to Robert Hunter of Kirkland. He was succeeded by his eldest son,

XIV. John Hamilton of Grange, who, in 1677, was retoured heir of his father, John. By a deed, dated 22d June 1677, he disposed of the " forty shilling land of old extent of the Kirkland of Kilmarnock, with the glebe lands thereof," to the Earl of Kilmarnock.* In 1685, he acquired part of the lands of Stevenston-Campbell from Robert Cuninghame of Auchenharvie; and about this time also he acquired the barony of Stevenston-Cuninghame from the Glencairn family ; the mansion-house of which, Kerila, under the name of *Grange*, became, the residence as well as the title of the family.† He married Rebecca Cuninghame, daughter of Alexander Cuninghame of Craigends, by whom he had issue a daughter, Janet, married to William Warner of Ardeer, and an only son,

XV. Alexander Hamilton of Grange, who succeeded him, and married, about the year 1730,‡ Elizabeth Pollock, eldest daughter of Sir Robert Pollock of that Ilk, by Annabella, daughter of Walter Stewart of Pardovan, by whom he had issue :—

1. John, | successively Lairds of Grange
2. Robert, | successively Lairds of Grange
3. Alexander. He married Rachel Cuninghame, daughter of James Cuninghame of Collellan, by whom he had a son, Alexander, and four daughters:
  1. Elizabeth, married Robert Cuninghame of Auchenharvie, and had issue.
  2. Margaret, married the Rev. Thomas Pollock, minister of Kilwinning, and had issue.
  3. Joana, married Edward M'Cormick, Esq. advocate, late Sheriff Depute of Ayrshire, and had issue.
  4. Jane, died unmarried.
4. James a proprietor in the West Indies, and father of General Hamilton, the celebrated statesman and patriot in the United States, who fell, greatly regretted, in a duel with a Mr Burr
5. Walter, | both died unmarried.
6. George, | both died unmarried.
7. William, married Jean, daughter of Robert Donald, Esq. and had issue.
8. Joseph.
9. William, who died in infancy.

Of his two daughters, one died in infancy, and the other, *Elizabeth*, was married to Alexander Blair,

---

* Boyd papers.
† Kerila Castle continued to be the mansion-house of this family till about fifty years ago, when the present house of Grange was built on a fine situation, at a little distance from the old Castle of Kerila.—STAT. AC. OF SCOT.
‡ He was in the same year admitted a burgess of Ayr.—AYR RECORDS.

Esq.. surveyor of the customs at Port-Glasgow, son of William Blair of Blair, and had issue.

XVI. John Hamilton of Grange, the eldest son, succeeded. He died unmarried, and was succeeded by his brother,

XVII. Robert Hamilton of Grange, who, dying also unmarried in 1774, was succeeded by his nephew, son of Alexander Hamilton, the third brother.

XVIII. Alexander Hamilton of Grange, advocate, and Lieut-Col. of the late 2d Regiment of Ayrshire Local Militia. He disposed of the Grange, in 1792, to Miss Scott, afterwards Duchess of Portland, who had previously, 1787, purchased Cambuskeith, the more ancient property of the family. He built the new house of Kerila, previous to 1790, and died in 1837.

Dying without issue, the representation of this ancient family descended to Captain John Brown, of the 23d Fusileers, his grand-nephew, only son of the marriage between Major George Vanbrugh Brown of Knockmarloch and Elizabeth Cuninghame, eldest daughter of the marriage between Robert Cuninghame of Auchenharvie and Elizabeth Hamilton, eldest sister of the second Alexander Hamilton.

Alexander Hamilton having left large debts, Captain Brown disponed the estate to trustees for the creditors, by whom it has been sold. The lot with the mansion-house of Kerila was purchased by Gavin Fullarton, Esq., now of Kerila. Mr Fullarton is descended of an ancient and respectable family in Ayr and Renfrewshire. He went early to the West Indies, and is proprietor of a large estate in Demerara, but has now retired, and settled on his estate of Kerila, which he has greatly improved by drainage and otherwise, and become one of the most active, spirited, and intelligent farmers in the neighbourhood.

*Arms.*—Gules, a lion rampant, argent (for the Earldom of Ross); betwixt three cinque foils, ermine (for Hamilton). *Crest*, an oak tree proper. *Motto*, in an escroll above, *Viridis et Fructifera*.

Cambuskeith and Grange, from which the family took the title, are in the neighbourhood of Kilmarnock.

## WALLACE OF MENFUIRD.

The property of Menfuird comprehended a considerable portion of the town of Kilmarnock. At the Townhead of that burgh there is a place still called the "Menfuird Lane." The earliest possessor of the lands of Menfuird, as a separate property, was

I. John Wallace of Menfuird, who had a charter of confirmation, under the Great Seal, of the lands of " Menfuird of Kilmarnock " from John Ross of Drumgrange (parish of Dalmellington, we presume), dated 17th March 1523. The superiority of these lands seems to have been disponed to the Kilmarnock family, for we find Robert Lord Boyd granting a charter of the said lands to

II. Hugh Wallace of Menfuird, dated 27th June 1567; and again, another charter of the same lands to John Wallace, son to the said Hugh Wallace, dated 15th June 1570.* In March 1575, " Hugo Wallace de Monyfurde " was served heir of his father's brother, Bartholomew Wallace, in the lands of Corshall in Kyle Stewart. " Hew Wallace of Menfurde " occurs in the testament of Agnes Speir, relict of Robt. Paton, in Caithburne, parish of Kilmarnock, in 1577. The " Gudman of Menfurde " is mentioned in a similar document in 1602. He seems to have been succeeded by his son,†

III. " Johne Wallace of Menfuird," who, in 1611, is mentioned in a testamentary document as the landlord of the house of Margaret Finlay, spouse to John Boyd, merchant in Kilmarnock. This John Wallace was unfortunate enough to be involved in a law process with the Boyd family, amongst whose papers there is a "decreet of certification in an improbation, Robert Lord Boyd against John Wallace of Menfuird, before the Lords of Council," dated 29th July 1618. Also a " disposition by the said John Wallace and his spouse to Robert Lord Boyd of the lands of Menfurd, wauchmill, teinds, and pertinents, dated 27th July 1619." The small but valuable property of Menfurd was thus swallowed up by the superior.

## ASSLOSS OF ASSLOSS.

There can be little doubt that this was a family of considerable antiquity, though apparently of no great influence. The first of them we have met with is,

I. " JACOBO AUCHINLOSS, apparenti de eodem," who had a charter of confirmation, " terrarum

de Auchinloss," from Queen Mary, dated March 10, in the first year of her reign (1543). His father appears to have been then alive, and had assigned the lands to him. " James Assinloss of that Ilk " is one of the assize in a criminal case in 1562.* He seems to have been succeeded by

II. James Assloss of that Ilk,† who, together with his son, *Adam Assloss*, resigned the five merk land of Assloss, with " the toure, fortalice, manor house, milnes, fyschings," &c. in favour of Robert Lord Boyd, on the 10th Nov. 1592.‡ Thus we see that Assloss had all the conveniences of a regular feudal residence.

In 1601 (9th Feb.), Thomas Lord Boyd appears before the Commissary Court of Glasgow, complaining of the delay of Adam Asslos, younger of that Ilk, in infefting him in the aucht shilling land and pertinents of Judas-hill, according to contract of the 9th and 11th days of December 1595, with the consent of his wife, Jean Blair, his lordship having given him 400lb money of this realme.‖

III. " Adame Aslos of that Ilk," son of the foregoing, succeeded. His name occurs, as " cautioner for the bairnes," in the testament of " Patrick Tran, Provost of Irwein " in 1611. He is mentioned as a debtor in the testament of Kathrein Broune, in Cranfuirdland, to the amount of " vi lb for fetchit aill ;" so also is " James Aslos, his sone, for hay and certane fetchit aill, viii lb."

IV. James Aslois of that Ilk occurs in the testament of James Gemmill in Raith in 1616. He was served heir of his father " Adami Aslois de eodem, in 5 mercatis terrarum de Aslois," &c. Nov. 1, 1617.§ " James Aslos of that Ilk and his wyf" appear as debtors in the testament of " Wm. Cvmyng, chapman in Kilmarnok" in 1621; and he is mentioned in a similar document so late as 1637.

Such are the few notices we have gleaned of the family of Assloss, now extinct. The name appears to have been originally *Auchinloss*, and to have varied, by different modes of spelling, until it settled into the present orthography. Towards the close of the seventeenth century, the

---

* " Martene Wallace, brother germane to Hew Wallace of Mynfurd," is a witness to a resignation of property, 31st July 1576.

† The " Trinitie land of Symontoun " is mentioned in a proclamation of assignation, of certain debts, by Thomas Lord Boyd, to Mr Andro Boyd, minister at Eglishame, made at the cross of Ayr, 29th June 1602, as belonging to " Johnne Wallace, younger, of Mainfurd."

* Criminal Trials.

† It was probably this James, "laird of Assloss," who married a daughter of John Mure of Rowallan, which John succeeded to the estate in 1547.

‡ Boyd Papers.

‖ " James and Adame Asloss, elder and zounger of that Ilk," are mentioned as debtors to Thomas Lord Boyd in the proclamation of assignation, in 1602, formerly referred to.

§ These lands resigned, in 1592, as we have seen, to Robert Lord Boyd, appear in the services of that family from that period downwards. They must only have held the superiority, however.

property passed into the hands of a branch of the Montgomeries of Broomland, whose names appear frequently, in 1702, and again in 1704, in the list of the Commissioners of Supply for the county of Ayr. The last of the family was Janet Montgomerie, who was married to James Somerville, the first of the Kennox family in Ayrshire. This lady, with the concurrence of her husband, sold the lands of Assloss, Nov. 19, 1725, to John Glen, merchant in Kilmarnock. Mr Glen married Juliana, daughter of Provost M'Taggart of Irvine, by whom he had two sons John and William; also a daughter, Margaret, married to John Parker of Barleith. Mr Glen disponed the lands of Assloss to his son, John Glen, who, dying without issue in 1795, was succeeded by his brother, William Glen of Assloss, who dying also without issue, in 1801, was succeeded by his nephew, William Parker, son of John Parker of Barleith. William Parker of Assloss married, in 1788, Agnes, daughter of William Paterson of Braehead, and had issue *John Parker*, now of Assloss, and two daughters.

The old "toure, fortalice," and "manor house" of Assloss have long ago disappeared. The present modern mansion is situated about a mile north of Kilmarnock. The lands lie between the two branches of the Kilmarnock water, and the house is delightfully placed amidst its own plantations on the summit of the shelving banks of the main branch.

### ANNANHILL.

The lands of Annanhill appear to have been for some considerable time in the hands of a family of the name of Caldwell.

*John Caldwell of Annanhill*, we find mentioned in the Boyd papers as a witness in 1605. In 1606, Robert sixth Lord Boyd had a charter of certain lands from apparently the same John Caldwell. He seems to have been succeeded by

*William Caldwell of Annanhill.* He is mentioned in the testament of John Montgomerie of Bridgend, as cautioner upon a bond for Thomas Neving of Monkridding, in 1612. He married *Jeane Dunlope*, sister to William Dunlop of Craig.* He seems to have been succeeded by

"*Mr William Cauldwell*" of Annanhill, whose spouse, Beatrix Broune, died at Irvine in November 1641. By her latter-will, their daughter, Elizabeth, was appointed sole executrix.

Shortly after this Annanhill became the property of a family of the name of M'Taggart, pro-

bably of Irvin. A William M'Taggart, taylor, burgess of Irvine, appears amongst the Boyd papers in 1681; and William M'Taggart, younger of Annanhill, obtained some property from Adam Fullarton of Bartonholme, 3d March 1693.*

### DUNLOP OF ANNANHILL AND BONNINGTON.

Annanhill was purchased, in 1796, from William Anderson, Esq., by the late William Dunlop, Esq., who built a commodius mansion-house on the property, in the style of the period. It has been greatly added to, and the property very much improved by plantation, since 1815, by the present proprietor, who bought the adjoining lands of Bonnington in 1817, from Captain Armstrong, son-in-law of the late General Dalrymple, so that altogether the estate is now a most valuable one, more especially on account of the rich seam of coal which extends throughout it.

The late William Dunlop, Esq. married Harriet, daughter of William Paterson of Brachead, by whom he had: *James*, his successor; Captain *William* Dunlop, deceased in 1839; and Margaret, also deceased, who married Robert Buchanan, Esq. of Ardoch, merchant in Glasgow.

*James Dunlop, Esq. of Annanhill and Bonnington*, married Mary Anne, eldest daughter of the late James Haldane, Esq. and has issue, *William Henry*, and other four sons and one daughter.

The mansion-house of Annanhill is pleasantly situated on a rising ground a short distance west of Kilmarnock, and commands a good view of the surrounding country.

GROUGAR.—This valuable property is situated towards the eastern boundary of the parish, and marches with that of Loudoun. It extends to considerably more than two thousand acres, nearly all arable land, of the best quality. About the time of the Brucean contest, it belonged to William de Ferrars and Alan de la Suche, in consequence of their marriage with two co-heiresses. Being partizans of Baliol, they were of course forfeited, and their possessions were conferred by Robert I. on his steady adherent, Sir Robert Cuninghame of Kilmaurs, by a charter dated 1319. In 1515, it belonged to Logan of Restalrig, whose other large possessions in the Lothians and Berwickshire were soon after forfeited, and probably this place also. The next who appears as Laird of Grougar, was Graham of Knockdolian, in 1606;

---

* Com. Rec.

* Boyd papers.

then Campbell af Loudoun, in 1613 ;—Boyd of Kilmarnock, in 1616, down to 1699. It has been in various hands since. The Orrs of Barrowfield had it a considerable time ; then the representatives of Sir George Colebrook ; and next the late William Blane, Esq., who died in 1837, and was succeeded by his eldest son, David Anderson Blair Blane, in the civil service of the H.E.I.C. It does not appear that there was ever a mansion-house upon it.

# PARISH OF KILMAURS.

ETYMOLOGY, EXTENT, &c.

THE writer in the *New Statistical Account* surmises, from the spelling of the name *Kilmures*, in some of the older records of session, that it has some reference to *Marie*, "and if so, it is probable that the *Kil* was dedicated to the mother of our Lord"—a very slender hypothesis certainly. "The ancient church of Kilmaurs," says the author of *Caledonia*, "was dedicated to saint Maure, a Scottish saint, who is said to have died in 899; and she was commemorated on the 2d of November. The name of the church was, as usual, formed by prefixing the Gaelic *Cil*, which is always pronounced *Kil*, to the name of the saint; and *Kil-maure* was changed to *Kil-maures*," or Kilmaur's, in the possessive case. The parish is "situated betwixt that of Kilmarnock on the east, and Dreghorn on the west, terminating in a point betwixt them on the north-east; and on the south it is bounded by the water of Irvine, which separates it from Kyle. The length of it, from SW. to NE. is about six miles, and the greatest breadth across to that direction, is about two miles and a quarter. It extends to nearly nine square miles of surface."*

The soil is deep and fertile throughout, well calculated for wheat and bean crops. Tillage, however, as in other parts of Cuninghame, prevails to a considerable extent. The surface is undulating, but without any very picturesque variety—although as a whole, it presents a panorama upon which the eye can rest with innate satisfaction. Extensive cereal fields, interspersed with rich pasture, and clumps of plantation occupying the summits of the gentle eminences, the parish appears in reality "as one well cultivated garden." There is only one stream or rivulet, of any consequence in the parish. It has its

source in the muirs of Fenwick, and runs the whole length of the parish from east to west. It is called Kilmaurs water, although farther down it takes the name of the Carmel, by which it is known until it loses itself in the sea.

## HISTORY CIVIL AND ECCLESIASTICAL.

Kilmaurs town is a burgh of barony, erected by a charter of James V., between 1513 and 1542, in favour of Cuthbert Earl of Glencairn, and his son William Lord Kilmaurs. By a charter from the Earl of Glencairn, and his son Lord Kilmaurs, dated at Glasgow 15th November 1577, "the five-pound land of Kilmaurs, consisting of 240 acres (280 in fact) was disposed to forty different persons in feu-farm, on payment of eighty merks yearly, or two merks for each lot, with an exclusive privilege to these fenars, 'of buying or selling, of brewing or making malt, and of all other art or trade, as that of shoemakers, skinners, carpenters, woolsters, &c." This was no doubt meant for the encouragement of handicraftsmen to settle and form a community at Kilmaurs. These possessions are called "the tenements of Kilmaurs."

Kilmaurs had at one time a reputation for the manufacture of cutlery.* The *steel mills*, erected at the Nether Mill of Ayr about 1740, were made by Robert Craig of Kilmaurs. Clock-making formed also a thriving branch of business in the burgh. These arts, however, have long ago ceased to flourish there; and none but the common crafts indispensable to all rural districts, are to be found within its boundaries.

The town is pleasantly situated on the Kilmaurs water, the gentle eminence on which it is

---

* Robertson's Cuninghame.

* "Though the cutlers have passed away," says the writer in the STATISTICAL ACCOUNT, "their fame survives in the Ayrshire proverb, 'as gleg as a Kilmaurs whittle,' which cut, it was said, an inch before the point."

planted looking towards the south. It consists principally of one street, having a town-house, with a steeple and clock in the centre. Its appearance, at the beginning of the seventeenth century, is thus described by Pont :—" Kilmaerstoune, Castell and Kirk. The toune is a large village, seated in a good soyle, and very populous. The castell is ane ancient, strong building, belonging to the Earl of Glencairne, environed with a faire parke, called Carmell wod, from the vatter of Carmell that runs by it. The church is veill bult, and is the comone sepulture of the Earlls of Glencairn, Lords Kilmauers.—Kilmauers, that is the church, or cell of Mauers, alleged by the vulgar a holy man."

The origin of the town of Kilmaurs is, like most other places, to be traced to the Church, which is of considerable antiquity. So early as 1170, " Robertus filii Wernebaldi,"* granted the church of Kilmaurs (ecclesiam de Kilmauro), in the township of Cuninghame (villa mea de Cunygham), with half a caracute of land, to the monks of Kelso.† This charter was confirmed by Richard Morville, Great Constable of Scotland, and Lord of Cuninghame, the superior ; also by Engleram, Bishop of Glasgow, who died in 1174. It was farther confirmed by Robert, the son of Robert (the granter) son of Wernebald, in 1189 ; and by Walter the Bishop of Glasgow in 1232. In 1245, William, the Bishop of Glasgow, confirmed to the prior of Lesmahago the church of Kilmaurs, in Cuningham, reserving to William de Cuninghame the tenure thereof for his lifetime. The Prior of Lesmahago‡ obtained a confirmation of the same church, from the Dean and Chapter of Glasgow, in 1246.‖ " An account of the property of the Monks of Kelso, which was made up by them, in the reign of Robert I., states that they had the church of Kilmaurs, in rectory, which used to be worth £40 yearly. The church of Kilmaurs continued to belong to the monks of Kelso till the Reformation. The monks enjoyed the rectorial revenues, and a vicarage was established for serving the cure. In Bagiment's Roll, as it stood in the reign of James V., the vicarage of Kilmaurs, in the Deanry of Cuninghame, was taxed at £2, 13s. 4d.; being a tenth of the estimated value. At the Reformation, the vicarage of Kilmaurs was held by Mr Andrew Layng,§ who stated that it produced, from the tithes of wool and lambs, and from Easter fines,

and other articles, about £30 yearly ; but that corspresents, umest clathes, and pasch fines, amounting to about 10 merks, not having been paid of late, this sum ought to be deducted. We may recollect that corspresents, umest claithes, and such objects, were severely satirized by Sir David Lindsay, in his poetry, at a somewhat earlier period. The vicar's church lands had been let, for twenty years past, to Cuninghame of Robertland, for the small rent, yearly, of eight merks. Out of the whole the vicar paid twenty merks annually to the curate who served the cure. There belonged to the church of Kilmaurs a considerable extent of church lands, a part of which were appropriated to the vicarage, and the remainder were held, by the monks of Kelso, with the rectory of the church.

" The glebe and church lands, which belonged to the vicar, were usually leased. William Cuninghame, who had a lease of these lands, that expired in May 1476, attempted to continue violent possession, after the expiry of his lease ; for which he was prosecuted before the officials of Glasgow, who excommunicated him. Cuninghame was also prosecuted by Mr William Twedy, the vicar, before the Lords Auditors of Parliament, who pronounced a decree in favour of the vicar, against Cuninghame, on the 10th of July 1476.

" The whole passed into lay hands after the Reformation. A small portion of the church land, called the Girnal Croft, was granted, in fee, during 1505, by Robert, the Abbot of Kelso, to William Cuninghame of Craigends, for payment of 6s. 8d. yearly. In 1633, when Charles I. established the Bishoprick of Edinburgh, he granted to the Dean of Saint Giles's the church of Kilmaurs, with all its tithes and revenues. After the final abolition of Episcopacy, the patronage of the church of Kilmaurs was acquired by the Earl of Eglintoun, whose family has since retained it."*

*Keith* states that " Kilmaures was founded the 13th of May 1403, for a Provost and eight Prebendaries, with two singing boys, by Sir William Cuningham of Kilmaures." This is a mistake. Sir William, 13th May 1413, made a bequest of certain lands for the celebration of divine service in the church of Kilmaurs, for the safety of his own soul, his parents, and *Henry de Cuninghame, the founder* of the church.† Henry, who lived in the reign of Alexander III., is thus affirmed to have been the founder of the church, although, as we have seen, the church of Kilmaurs was

---

* Progenitor of the Glencairn family. † Chart. of Kelso.
‡ Lesmahago was a cell of the Monastery of Kelso.
‖ Chart. of Kelso.
§ Samuel Hendersoun, sone to Alex. Hendersoun, Redar at Kilmauris" is witness to a document dated Jan. 23, 1585.

* Chalmers's Caledonia.
† Original charter.

dedicated to the monks of Kelso during the previous century.

The church of Kilmaurs is an old building, and various additions have apparently been made to the original erection. It appears to have undergone certain improvements about 1670, in which year Sir John Cuninghame of Lambrughton, patron of the churches of Dreghorn and Kilmaurs, petitioned and obtained the sanction of Parliament, to have the vacant stipends applied in repairing the churches and manses of these parishes. The church of Kilmaurs was always used as the cemetry of the family of Glencairn.

The parochial records, (a register of births and marriages), commence in 1688, but were not regularly kept till 1783.

There was a chapel at Busbie, in the southern division of the parish, "which had an appropriate endowment for its chaplain. After the Reformation, the chapel was allowed to fall into ruins; and the endowment was appropriated by the patron. The patronage appears to have belonged to the Eglintoun family in 1661; but how long that family had held it, or when they acquired it, is uncertain."[*]

### ANTIQUITIES.

*Kilmaurs Castle.*—Of the Castle of Kilmaurs, described by Pont, there seems to be now no certain remains. From Pont's map, however, where the castle is dotted, and Carmel wood (still so called), the "fair parke" by which it was environed, some idea of its situation may be formed. It appears to have stood some distance east of the church, probably, as conjectured by Robertson, on the farm called *Jock's Thorn*, where some ruins can still be pointed out. It is curious that its position should be a matter of dubiety. When Pont surveyed the district, about 1608, the Castle of Kilmaurs existed in all the pomp of family distinction—and, now, about two hundred and forty years since, so is its grandeur worn out even of the traditional mind, that its site cannot be identified with certainty.

*Tower*, or *Tour*.—On the lands so called, in an orchard adjacent to the parish kirk, there are the remains of a tower, "forming part," says a correspondent, "of an old monastic building, which at one time was joined to the church, and must be of very ancient date,[†] as it is mentioned in an old work,[†] that Sir Hugh de Morville resided there, in the twelfth century, while engaged in building a part of Kilwinning Abbey . . .

The Cuninghames of Tour dwelt in it as late as 1630; and the door of an adjoining pigeon-house bears that date."

*Busbie Castle.* — This is the only other remain of a feudal residence extant in the parish. "The style of building," says Robertson, "seems to belong to the middle of the fourteenth century—having both gun-ports and arrow slits in the walls as means of defence. The antique decoration of the *twisted cable* in the architraves, indicates the same era." The castle, which consists of a single but high and massive tower, has long been roofless, and is falling to decay.

*The Glencairn Aisle*—The burial aisle of the Glencairn family stands close by the church. It has within it a curious and elaborately carved monument to the memory, it is said, of the Lord Chancellor Glencairn (William ninth Earl) erected in 1600.[*] It is a beautiful specimen of ancient sculpture. It is composed of six columns—three at each of its extremities, the innermost being about eight feet apart—and over all of which extends an entablature, returned above each of the columns, and sustaining in the centre a compartment formed by small pilasters, flanked with scroll-work, and crowned with a divided pediment. All the three columns are of different forms, and recede literally the one behind the other, just as much as permits the free return of their respective basis and capitals. The two inner and most advanced columns have cylindrical shafts, with Corinthian capitals; the second are of an octagonal form, with a row of leaves on the capitals; and those forming the extremities of the monument are square and plain. The space between the innermost columns is formed into a deep recess, where are placed full sized half-length figures of the Earl and Countess, and an ornamented inscriptive panel. The spaces below the recesses are ornamented with bas-reliefs, and the capitals and shafts of the principal columns are elaborately covered with flowering buds and other designs. The "glorieous towme" erected in the Bargany aisle at Ballantrae, to the memory of Gilbert Kennedy, killed in a feud with the Earl of Cassillis near to Mayhole in 1601, seems to be almost a literal copy of the Glencairn monument at Kilmaurs. The aisle was repaired in 1844 by the late Sir Alexander Montgomerie Cuninghame, Bart. of Corsehill, and the monument is in tolerable preservation.

---

* Chalmers's Caledonia.
† We know not the work to which our informant refers.
VOL. II.

* There must be a mistake in all the accounts we have seen of this monument. It could not be to the memory of the ninth Earl, if erected in 1600, for that nobleman died in 1644.

D 2

*Tumuli.*—There are several barrows, or places of ancient sepulture, in the parish. One of these was accidentally thrown open a few years ago. "As two men," says the *Kilmarnock Journal*, were engaged digging in a field on Mr Fulton's farm of Waterpark, parish of Kilmaurs, they came upon two stone coffins a considerable way beneath the surface. On removing the lids with their spades, observing that they contained nothing but a quantity of earth, of a deeper colour than the surrounding soil, and that there were no valuables of the olden time to reward their discovery, they very coolly broke them up, and proceeded with their work. They subsequently, however, met in with other sepulchres, of the same rude construction, to the number of six in all, and the examination of these unknown remains has caused considerable speculation. It was found, on examination, that each of the coffins contained a small quantity of calcined bones, collected into a heap in the centre of the coffin. And it was remarked by a workman, that the stone jambs of the stronger and more recently uncovered grave themselves bore traces of having been exposed to the action of fire; so that it is probable the reduction of the bodies to ashes not being completed (probably from haste) at the interment, the stones of the sepulchre were themselves heated, like the ovens used by the Indians in cooking their meat, to render the pulverization as perfect as possible. The lid of the most substantial of the graves laid bare, appeared to have been sunk about two feet beneath the surface. On admeasurement, we found its width to be twenty-one inches, and its length thirty-six inches. It is rectangular. Its depth we could not well ascertain, from its being filled up with stiff, wet clay, of which, we understand, when opened, it was perfectly clear, containing only about two inches of water, and its depth at that time appeared to be from twelve to eighteen inches. These graves have been found within the circuit of one of three large barrows or tumuli, situated on either bank of the Carmel water; the tumulus to which they pertain being, as already stated, upon Waterpark farm, and the others being situated upon Greenhill farm—the most remarkable of the three, indeed, being close to Greenhill farm-house. The surface being now pared from the Waterpark cairn, it presents the usual aggregation of stones piled over the forgotten dead of ancient times. We understand that the Rev. Mr Robertson, and Dr Sloan of Kilmaurs, and others, have visited the spot, and that no doubt exists of the bones being human remains; Dr Sloan having identified the cap of a shoulder and the socket bone of the eye. The only conjecture that can be formed respecting these interesting discoveries is, that here lie the accumulated dead of some great conflict; a surmise somewhat confirmed by our observation respecting the marks of haste evinced in reducing the bodies to ashes."

*Antedeluvian Remains.*—Nearly forty years ago, two large pieces of bone, or ivory, supposed to have been the tusks of some huge animal, were found, in the course of excavation, at an immense depth, in the Woodhill Quarry.

# FAMILIES IN THE PARISH OF KILMAURS.

## CUNINGHAMES OF KILMAURS, EARLS OF GLENCAIRN.

There seems to be considerable diversity of opinion in reference to the origin and name of the widely-spread and once powerful family of Cuninghame. In the historical sketch introductory to this work,* we coincided in the opinion of Robertson, in his *Description of Cuninghame*, that the name was derived from the Celtic *Cuinneag*, a butter churn, or *Cuinneag'am*, the churn district, and we are still inclined to adhere to this derivation. The names of places were almost invariably given, in the ancient language of the country, from some peculiar feature of the district, and not from individuals, unless, as in the case of *Kyle*, from the chief actor in some great historical event.

* Vol. i. pp. 3-4.

The leading branches of the family, however, are understood to repudiate this derivation, and to adhere to that of Buchanan, who states that Cuninghame, in the Danish language, signifies the *King's House;* but neither history nor tradition attempts to show that any Danish king ever had a *hame,* or home, in the district. Buchanan was a classical scholar, but totally ignorant of the Gaelic; hence his overlooking the only genuine source of all topographical etymology—the original language of the inhabitants.

It seems unquestionable that the district was known by the name of *Cunigham,* or *Cuninghame,* long before the adoption of patronymics in this country—consequently the family derived their name from the district, and not the district from the family. The De Morvilles were Lords of Cuninghame long before the Kilmaurs family had risen to importance. It is also evident that the early possession of the family was called *Cunigham,* probably from its being situated in the centre of the original bounds of the district—before the addition of Largs—as well as from its antiquity as a stronghold.\*

It is farther urged, however, against the Celtic etymology of the name, that in all old writings it is invariably spelled *Cunyngham, Conynghame,* or otherwise, but never without the *n,* as in *Cuinneag'am,* or *Cunigham.* Now, this is not the fact. In the earliest record known to be extant in reference to the family—the grant of the Church of Kilmaurs to the Monastery of Kelso, in 1170, by " Robertus filii Wernebaldi"—the name is distinctly *Cunygham,* without any mark of elision—" Ecclesiam de Kilmauro . uilla mea de Cunygham cum dimidia carucata terre ad ipsiam ecclesiam pertinente." So is it spelled in all the confirmations of this charter, by the family and others, down till 1269, when " Domino Willielmo de Cunyngham " appears as a witness in a contract between the Abbots of Kelso and Melros. Even the granter of the church of Stapilgortum to the Abbey of Kelso, in 1153, who is believed to have been an offshoot of the Kilmaurs family, " Willielmus de *Cuniggeburch,*" follows the same pronunciation; so did the families of *Cunigham* of Caprington, and *Cunigham* of Cuninghamhead, until within two hundred years ago.† The same orthography occurs in the *Obit Book of the Church of St John of Ayr.* In short it is the common mode of pronouncing the name amongst the peasantry at the present day.

The argument, we think, is thus conclusive as to the Celtic derivation of the name of the district. It, however, by no means follows that the family who assumed the name were of Celtic origin also. It has been supposed that they are of Danish descent—probably in coincidence with Buchanan's etymology of the "King's House"—or at all events of Saxon. But this is mere conjecture. All who held tenures under the De Morvilles are believed to have been foreigners; which we consider a false idea, although many of them were Normans or Saxons. An old writer, Van Batsea, in his history of the Kings of Scotland, states that this family are descended from one Friskin, who, when Malcolm fled from Macbeth towards England, after the murder of King Duncan, concealed the Prince from his pursuers, by forking hay or straw over him, and for this service King Malcolm, after his restoration, conferred the Thanedom of Cuninghame upon his preserver.

We need scarcely say that this is fabulous, seeing that the overlords of Cuninghame were the De Morvilles; although there is a tradition to the same effect, omitting the name, so generally known among all ranks and classes of the Cuninghames, that it is difficult to avoid believing that it has some foundation in fact. The arms of the family, argent, a shake-fork, sable, with the motto, " over fork over," have evident allusion to some such occurrence.

But perhaps the most surprising account of the origin of the family—at least to modern inquirers—is that put forward by a writer in the beginning of the seventeenth century. We copy from MS., and are not aware that his work \* was ever printed :—

" And morrover, I am able to prove at this present tyme, 1622, ther is not see maney noble men as zit of on surname in all Europe as professeth the name of Cuming, sua that they wer all with ther lands and livings in one realme, and to qualifie and make my alleageance good I have insert heir as after followeth :—

" The names of ther hous's, stylls and surnames, quho professeth themselves to be laufullie descended of the said surname of Cumings, quhilk certainlie I have in part be some of ther oune confessiones; for being at super in the Earl of Glenkairnes hous in Kilmarnok [Kilmaurs] quher my Lord wes present with his sone the Maister ; as also the old Laird of Watterstoun, Cuninghame to his surname, and my Lord goodsire's brother, quho did all thric confess and confer that Cuming wes ther right surname, quilk wes

\* If there is any truth in the tradition that Sir Hugh de Morville resided in the old Tour of Kilmaurs, while part of the Abbey of Kilwinning was built, it countenances the supposition.
† Robertson's Cuninghame.

\* An account of the Cuming family.

to be seen in my lord's ancient evidents, as my old Lord did confess at this tyme in presence of the wholl companie, quher ther wer divers noblemen. And as for the surname of Cunnynghame, they took it of that province quhilk wes called of auld Cunynghame, as Cumirnauld wes called Cumingshald. Lykas our armes, the thrie beare schaves, in gravin stone in the said house of Cumirnauld is ther to this day, as ane evident left be the Cuming's predecessor, quho wes Lord thereof (to witt) ffirst the Earle of Menteith, quho wes most ancient of that surname, and nixt the Earle of Buchan, quho succeidit to him. Sicklyk Cunnynghame, quhich is seavin myles above Dunkell, wes callit Cumingstoun befoir our banishment, quhen as the Cumings wes Earles of Atholl. This with many mor accidents hes chainced to that surname since the fall, quhilk is ane lamentable greif to ther posteritie."

Unfortunately for this vexatious historian of the Cumings, the "ancient evidents" of the family do not bear out his statement. The Cuninghames are as old as the Cumings themselves; and no evident has ever been produced to shew that their patronymic was at any time Cuming. Of the antiquity of the family there can be no doubt. They were in possession of the township of *Cunigham*, as we have seen, before 1170; but there is every probability that they had been settled there at even an earlier period. *Willielmus de Cuniggeburch*, who granted the church of Stapilgortun to the monks of Kelso in 1153—seventeen years before Robert the son of Wernebald gave the church of Kilmaurs to that Monastery—did so for the soul of his uncle, Godfred—*per anima Gaufredi avunculi mei*—thus showing that they at least were not newly settled in the country when these bequests were made. That the *Cuniggeburchs* and the *Cunighams* were branches of the same family is countenanced by the fact of their both making grants to the same Monastery. If the Monastery of Kilwinning was in existence in 1170, as is generally allowed, we can scarcely account for Robert of Cunygham's presenting a gift to the monks of Kelso in place of those of Kilwinning, who were introduced by his own overlord, unless from some strong family motive; and if so, the inference is that the Cuniggeburch branch was the eldest. But enough of speculative deduction. The first of the Ayrshire Cuninghames on record unquestionably is,

I. WERNEBALD, who may be supposed to have been in possession of the manor-place of Cuninghame about 1130 or 1140. *Crawfurd* in his MS. History, states that Robert, the grandson of Wernebald, was the first to assume the surname of Cunynghame. This is questionable, however.

There is a Galfrides de Cunynghame who appears as a witness in a charter from King Malcolm IV. to the Abbey of Scone, who is presumed to have been a younger son of Wernebald. But this is no proof of the surname having been then adopted. At this early period parties were often designated by the district to which they belonged, as, for example, *Nigellus de Carrick*, long before the patronymic became settled. Certain it is that none of the family are designated by their surname in the Kelso chartulary until a later period.

II. Robert "filii Wernebaldi," who granted the church of Kilmaurs and half a caracute of land "in meum villam de Cunygham" to the Abbey of Kelso in 1170. He had previously—inter 1153 et 1156—made a donation, with consent of his wife, Richenda de Barclay, heiress of "Sir Humphrey de Barclay of Glenfarqbarlin," to the Abbey of Aberbrothic.*

III. Robert, "filius Roberti filii Wernebaldi" confirmed the grant made by his father to the Abbey of Kelso, which was also confirmed by Richard de Morville, Constable of Scotland, before 1189.

The next who is met with, according to Crawfurd, is *Richard*, who was witness in a grant by Allan, son of Rolland the Constable, in the reign of Alexander II. This Richard, it may be conjectured, was son of the preceding, and brother, though Crawfurd appears to have thought he was father of

IV. Robert, who had a son designed

V. Robert, son and heir "Domini Roberti de Cunyngham," witness in a charter from Alexander Senescallus Scotiæ, to the monks of Paisley, in the reign of Alexander II., about the year 1240. *Wood*, in his Peerage, introduces this Robert as the son of the Robert who had a transaction with Richard de Morville, fully fifty years previously, which is double the time usually calculated for a generation; and as Crawfurd says there was a *Robert* after Richard, we think it presumable that there were four Roberts in succession.

VI. Henry,† probably son of Robert, had a charter of the barony of Kilmaurs, thenceforward the designation of the family, from Alexander III. A very old copy of the original document exists.‡ He married it is said the heiress of Glengarnock.

VII. Sir William Cunnyngham of Kilmaurs, the eldest son, according to *Wood*, is mentioned in records dated 1269 and 1275.‖

---

* Chart. of Arbroath.
† Hervey, in Wood's Peerage.
‡ Family papers.  ‖ Chart. of Caldingham.

VIII. Edward Cunynghame of Kilmaurs. Mention is made of him in a record dated 1290.[*]

IX. Gilbert Cunynghame of Kilmaurs.[†] It is said he was one of Robert Bruce's nominees in the competition with Baliol. His second son, Sir *James*,[‡] was ancestor of the Cuninghames of Hassendean and Barns. His third son, *Donald*, was, according to *Douglas*, ancestor of the Cuninghames of Shalloch, &c. In the *Ballentyne MS.* Gilbert is called *Gilmore*, and is said to be the ancestor of Belton, Barns and Aiket. *Hugh* Cunynghame does not appear in any pedigree of the family we have seen. He had charters from Robert I. of the lands of Lambrachton and Polquharne, " dilecto consanguineo nostro " Hugoni de Cunynghame.[||] As both these properties afterwards belonged to the Kilmaurs family, it is not unlikely that Hugh died without issue.

X. Sir Robert Cuninghame of Kilmaurs. He swore fealty to Edward I., in 1296, but nevertheless joined Bruce. Roberto de Cunyngham had a charter of the lands of " Lambrachtoun et de Grugere " from Robert I.[§] His second son, *Andrew*, is said to have been ancestor of the Cuninghames of Ballindalloch, Drumquhassel, Balbougie, Banton, &c. " Dilecto consanguineo nostro *Andrew de Cunynghame* and Margaret his spouse, had a charter of the lands of Kyndeny, in Perthshire, from David II. dated Jan. 16, 1331, which was confirmed in 1333.

XI. Sir William Cunynghame, apparently son of the preceding, succeeded him in Kilmaurs. He married Eleanor Bruce, and during her life was styled Earl of Carrick. He had a charter of the Earldom of Carrick from David II. It has been generally supposed that the Lady Eleanor brought him no family,[¶] and that his successor and other sons were by a former marriage. The reverse seems to be the fact. Sir William must have married Eleanor Bruce previous to 1361, the supposed date of the patent of Earldom.[*] In 1368, however, there is another charter of the lands of Kincleven, in Perthshire, from David II.

" dilecto consanguineo nostro Willielmo de Cunynghame, militi, et Margareta, sponse sua," &c.[*] As these lands did not descend in the Kilmaurs family, or to any of the name of Cunynghame, so far as known, it may be supposed that Sir William had at least no male issue by Margaret. Eleanor Bruce, his first wife, must have been alive in 1366, in which year Sir William is styled " Domini de Carrik " in a charter of confirmation to him of the lands of Polquhairn, &c. So that his second marriage must have taken place between that period and 1368.

Margaret, according to some authorities, was the name of the son's wife also ; but the charter above noticed could not be in the son's favour, for, of date 1384, there is a letter extant from John Earl of Carrick, Prince of Scotland, confirming an obligation " dilecto consanguineo nostro Willielmo de Cunynghame,[†] *filio*, militi "—the word filio clearly proving that the father was then alive. Robert, the eldest son, was one of the hostages for David II. in 1359. He predeceased his father. *Thomas*, the third son, was ancestor of the Cuninghames of Caprington, Enterkine, and the first Cuninghames of Bedland,[‡] the second son,

XII. Sir William Cuninghame of Kilmaurs, succeeded before 1400, for of that date he resigned his property in the hands of the Sovereign, and obtained a new charter[||] in favour of himself and his heirs male ; whom failing, to each of his brothers, *Thomas*, *Alexander*, and *John*, in succession, and their heirs male ; whom failing, to certain other near relatives of the name of Cuninghame and their heirs male also, &c. of the lands and baronies of Kilmaurs, Lambrachton, Kilbride, Skelmorlie and Polquharne, in the county of Ayr ; the lands and barony of Redhall, in the county of Edinburgh ; the lands of Nevy in Forfar ; the barony of Hassendean in Roxburghe ; and lands of Ranfurly in the barony of Renfrew, proceeding on the resignation of the said Sir William.

---

* Chart. of Levenax.
† Paisley Chart.
‡ Jacobi Cuningham had a charter of the lands of Hassingden, from Robert I.
§ Original Charters, dated 1321-1322.
§ Great Seal Record.
¶ Because the title did not descend in the family of Kilmaurs, genealogists have been misled on this point. The patent is on record, but incomplete, being without a date. Those immediately preceding and following it are dated 1361. As it contains a simple grant of the Earldom to Sir William himself, without any mention of heirs, it was evidently intended that the title should revert to the elder branch of the Bruce's family, to whom it rightfully belonged.
* Original extract, dated 1633.

* There were several confirmations of this charter by David II.—amongst others as follows :—" David, Dei gratia, Rex Scottorum, omnibus, &c. Sciatis nes dedisse, concessisse, et hac presenti carta nostra confirmasse, dilecto consanguineo nostro Willielmo de Cunynghame, militi, totum comitatum nostrum de Carrik," &c.
† The title of Earl is here omitted, which seems conclusive that it was only conceded to Sir William during Eleanor Bruce's life. It is worthy of remark, also, that amongst the witnesses to this charter is Robertus Senescallus Scotiæ Comiti de Stratherne, as if the title of Carrick was still in abeyance.
‡ Original charter extant from Robert III. 8th July 1460.
|| In 1364 there is a dispensation " Fergusie Mackdanial, Dom. Candidæ Casæ et Margaretæ filiæ Willielmi de Cuningham, Domicellœ Glasguen."—STUART'S HIST. OF THE STUARTS.

Sir William married Agnes, not Margaret, Danyelstoun, eldest co-heiress of Sir Robert Danyelstoun, by which marriage he acquired a great addition to the family property.

There is a charter on paper (seemingly a copy of the principal document) still extant, from Willielmus de Conynghame, Dominus de Kilmaurs, granting the lands of Southwick, the two pound land near the west port of Kilmaurs, twenty-one acres adjacent to the chapel of St Maurice(?), the mill of Kilmaurs, and lands of Kilbryde-Cuninghame, in pure and perpetual alms for the sustentation of three presbyters, to celebrate divine service in the church of Kilmaurs, for the safety of his own soul, his parents, and Henry de Cuninghame, the founder of the said church, dated 13th May 1413.[*]

Sir William died in 1418. His second son, William,[†] was ancestor of the Cuninghamehead family; his third son, Henry, distinguished himself at the battle of Bauge in France, in 1421.

XIII. Sir Robert, the eldest son, succeeded. He was knighted by James I., and formed one of the jury of twenty-one members of Parliament for the trial of Murdoch Duke of Albany in 1425, at which the King presided in person. Sir Robert married Anne, only daughter of Sir Hugh de Montgomery of Ardrossan, and apparently left an only son, his successor. Sir Robert had a joint commission with Alexander Montgomery of Ardrossan " de custodia terrarum de Kyntyre et de Knapdale," 10th August 1430.[‡] He had a charter from the Duke of Albany, of the lands of Kilmaurs, Lambrachton, &c.

XIV. Sir Alexander Cunynghame of Kilmaurs, who married Margaret Hepburn, daughter of Adam Lord Hailes. His family were four sons :—Robert; William, first of the Craigends branch ; Alexander and Edward. According to Crawfurd he disponed his office of heritable Bailie of Cuninghame to his uncle, the second Lord Montgomerie, in the year 1454,[||] This is confirmed in Cuninghame of Aiket's history of the Glencairn family. He was created Lord Kilmaurs by James III., about the year 1450,[§] and appears to have been a strenuous

supporter of that monarch. At a later period, he took an active part against the disaffected nobles, who, having seized upon the person of the Prince, set up a government in his name, in opposition to that of the King his father. The hostile parties met, and fought at Blackness. Alexander Lord Kilmaurs was on the King's side, and for the service rendered by him and his friends on that occasion, as narrated in the patent, he was raised to the dignity of Earl of Glencairn, 28th May 1488. He was also present at the battle which took place near Stirling on the 11th June following, where James III. and the newly created Earl of Glencairn were both slain. The young King immediately issued a proclamation, afterwards drawn up into an act of Parliament, annulling all grants whatever made by the late King from the 2d Feb. preceding. The eldest son,

XV. Robert Cuninghame, could therefore only lay claim to the title of Kilmaurs, and was served heir to his father, Alexander Lord Kilmaurs, 24th Nov. 1488. He married Christian, daughter of Lord Lindsay of Byres, by whom he had two sons, Cuthbert and Archibald, and died about 1492, as appears from the date of an instrument of sasine in favour of his son and successor,

XVI. Cuthbert, who must have been very young at the time of his father's death. About this period took place the original quarrel with the Montgomeries, which led to the bitter and bloody feuds between the families for a century thereafter. Cuthbert, with the rashness of a youth, seems to have been the first implicated on the side of the Cuninghames. He and Archibald, his brother, Andrew and Guido Cuninghame, and others, were summoned before George Earl of Huntley, Justice-General south of the Forth, in a court holden at Ayr, 9th March 1498, and were found guilty of forethought felony, committed by them on Hugh Lord Montgomerie, when holding a court of the Bailliary of Cuninghame, and also for breaking the King's protection. For all which they were fined.

Cuthbert married Lady Mary Douglas, whose dowry was the lands and lordship of Kilmarnock, daughter of Archibald Earl of Angus, fifth of the name of Douglas,[*] and appears to have made use of his father-in-law's powerful influence at Court to obtain a renewal of the title of Glencairn.

In honour of the nuptials between James IV. and Margaret, daughter of Henry VII. of Eng-

---

* Mr William de Cunynghame, perpetual vicar of the church of Dundonald, son of the Lord William de Cunynghame, Lord of Kilmaurs, by a deed of mortification, dated 1st March 1418, granted certain tenements in Irvine, to maintain two chaplains in the church of that burgh, for prayers for the soul of himself, of his father, of Agnes his mother, &c.—IRVINE REC.

† It would thus appear that there had been a chapel dedicated to St Maure or Maurice(?), besides the parish church of Kilmaurs.

‡ Great Seal Record.

‖ Craw. Hist. of Renfrew.

§ Carta terrarum de Polquharne.

---

* Instrument of Resignation by the Earl of Angus in favour of Cuthbert Lord Kilmaurs, of the lands and lordship of Kilmarnock, dated 25th Jan. 1496. The Kilmarnock family were under forfeiture at this period.

land, in August 1502, a tournament was held, at which Cuthbert Lord Kilmaurs was one of the challengers, and was opposed by James Lord Hamilton. The festival lasted several days. Twenty-six gentlemen were knighted by the King, and on Sunday 13th August 1502, the Queen and Court being present, the King conferred the dignity of Earl on three Lords, by the ceremony of lincture or girding with the sword : —Immediately Marchmont, Herald, and his companions, cried—

"Largesse, James D'Arene Lord of Hamilton ;

Largesse, William Conte de Montrose, Lord of Graham ;

Largesse, Cuthbert Conte de Glencairn, Lord de Kilmaurs."

XVII. William, apparently only son of Cuthbert, by Lady Mary Douglas, was in possession of a great part of the family property before his father's death. He married, first, Catherine, daughter of Lord Borthwick, by whom he had no issue. It was under William Master of Glencairn that the Cuninghames, in revenge of the murder of Cuninghame of Watterstoun, by the Montgomeries, made a furious inroad upon the possessions of the latter, and succeeded in burning Eglintonn Castle, about the year 1523. Upon the death of his father, William became second Earl of Glencairn, though commonly called the fourth. The latter enumeration is most usual, and ought to be adhered to. Charles II. granted, in 1637, a confirmation of the original patent in 1488.* William, when Lord Kilmaurs, was appointed Treasurer of Scotland, 25th June, 1526, but held that office only a few months. As Earl of Glencairn, he was present at the battle and rout of Solway, in 1542, where he was taken prisoner by the English, and given into the custody of the Duke of Norfolk. His ransom was fixed at £1000. He was one of the ambassadors sent to England in 1543. By a second marriage, with Elizabeth Campbell, heiress of wester Loudoun, he had five sons :—

1. Alexander his successor.
2. Andrew, first of Corsehill.
3. Hugh, of Watterstoun.
4. Robert, minister of Failford.
4. William, said to have been Bishop of Argyle.

The last three are, we believe, set down according to seniority, but of this there is no proof. That

*Andrew* was second is known, because his descendants are named in the great settlement of the family property in 1614, immediately after those of *Alexander*, and before those of *Hugh*. No descendants of either *Robert** or *William* are mentioned in this entail. William the second, or rather the fourth Earl, died in 1547. He was succeeded by his eldest son,

XVIII. Alexander, fifth Earl of Glencairn, popularly styled *the Good Earl*, from his taking so very active a part in promoting the Reformation. He was the author of the famous "Ryme," entitled *Ane Epistle direct fra the halie Hermeit of Alareit, to his Brother the Grey Freirs*, preserved by John Knox in his "Historie of the Reformation "—

"I, Thomas, Hermit in Larcit,
Sanct Franeis Ordour de hairtilie greit," &c.

This "Ryme," as it is styled by Knox, exhibits so much of the true poetical vein as to lead to the belief that the author had not limited his muse to a single effort, and to a consequent regret that no more of his writings have been preserved. The Earl married, first Lady Johanna Hamilton, daughter of James first Earl of Arran, by whom he had two sons and a daughter ; the second son, *Andrew*, was prior of Lesmahago; the daughter, Lady *Margaret*, was married to John Wallace of Craigie. He married, secondly, Janet, daughter of Sir John Cuninghame of Caprington, by whom he had a son, *Alexander*, commendator of Kilwinning, who married Jean Blair, and was ancestor of the Cuninghames of Mountgreenan ; and a daughter, Lady *Janet*, married, first, to Archibald, fifth Earl of Argyle, and afterwards to Sir Humphrey Colquhoun of Luss. He died in 1574, and was succeeded by his eldest son of the first marriage,

XIX. William sixth Earl of Glencairn. He married Janet Gordon, daughter of Gordon of Lochinvar, by whom he had two sons and four daughters :—

1. James, his successor.
2. John, had the lands of Ross in Dumbartonshire conferred upon him. He had an only son, JAMES, and two daughters, ANNE and MARION. The son died unmarried previous to 1631. The daughters were married into the families of Somerville of Cambusnethan, and Bailie of Carsphin, both in Lanarkshire.

1. Lady Jean, married, first, to Haldane of Gleneagles ; secondly to Kirkpatrick of Closeburn, and thirdly to Ferguson of Craigdarroch.
2. Lady Margaret, married to Sir Hector Maclean of Dowart.
3. Lady Elizabeth, married, first, to James Craufurd,

---

* The Earls of Glencairn made numerous protests in the sittings of the Scottish Parliament in reference to precedency, apparently arising out of this hiatus between the two patents. In 1606, Eglintoun and Cassillis obtained a decree of the Privy Council, preferring them in the order of Parliament: but the Earl of Glencairn obtained a decree of the Court of Session, annulling that preference, in 1609.

* In 1540, Robert Cuninghame, at the age of 22, a BASTARD son of William Earl of Glencairn, was appointed minister of Failford.—EPIS. REG. SCOT. ii. 86-7. The minister of Failford, Robert Cuninghame, sat in Parliament, among the clergy, in 1546, and in 1550.

younger of Auchinames, and afterwards to Cuninghame of Craigends.

4. Lady Susanna, married to Napier of Kilmahew.

The Earl died in 1581, and was succeeded by his eldest son,

XX. James seventh Earl of Glencairn. He married, first, Margaret, daughter of Sir Colin Campbell of Glenorchy, by whom he had two sons, and six daughters,

1. William his successor.
2. " Johnne Cvnynghame of Cambuskeithe, within the parochin of Kilmaris." He is not mentioned in any of the genealogies. He died at Kilmaurs, 9th Feb. 1628. In his testament he ordains his body to be buried in the " buriall place of James Erle of Glencairn [his] father, within the paroch kirk of Kilmaris." He married Margaret Knox, of the Ranfurly family.* He left a son JOHN, to whom William Cuninghame of Craigends was appointed tutor. Cambuskeith thus appears to have fallen into the hands of the Glencairn family after its alleged unfair acquisition by the Cuninghames of Caprington.

1. Lady Jean, contracted to the Earl of Cassillis, but he marrying another, Lady Jean died the same day.
2. Lady Catherine, married to Sir James Cuninghame of Glengarnock.
3. Lady Margaret, married first to Sir James Hamilton of Evandale, secondly, to Sir James Maxwell of Calderwood.
4. Lady Anne, married to James second Marquis of Hamilton, and was understood to have an uncommon sway over the minds of her two sons, the Dukes of Hamilton, in the reign of Charles I., attended with important political consequences.
5. Lady Mary, married to John Craufurd of Kilbirnie.
6. Lady Susanna, married to Sir Alexander Lauder of Hatton.

The Earl married, secondly, a sister of the Earl of Carlisle, without issue. He died between 1614 and 1628. His successor,

XXI. William eighth Earl of Glencairn, died in 1631. He married Lady Janet Ker, daughter of Mark first Earl of Lothian, by whom he had three sons and five daughters. The second son, Colonel *Robert*, married Anne, daughter of Sir John Scot of Scotstarvit, by whom he had a daughter. Of the daughters,

1. Lady Elizabeth was married to Sir Ludovick Stewart of Minto.
2. Lady Jane, to Blair of Blair.
3. Lady Margaret, first to Beaton, of Creich; and, secondly, to Chisholm of Cromlix.
4. Lady Marion, first, to James first Earl of Findlater; and secondly, to Alexander Master of Saltoun.

He was succeeded by his eldest son,

XXII. William ninth Earl of Glencairn, a nobleman of a very energetic character. He was Colonel of the forces raised in 1644, during the civil war, in Ayr and Renfrewshire. He afterwards conducted the campaign of the royalists in the Highlands in 1653-4 with great ability, until the arrival of General Middleton; but the cause was hopeless, and no effort could avail. In 1661, after the Restoration, he was appointed Principal Sheriff of Ayrshire, and Bailie of Kyle-Stewart, for life, and died Lord Chancellor of Scotland, in 1644. He married, first, Lady Anne Ogilvie, daughter of James first Earl of Findlater, by whom he had four sons, two of whom, as Lords of Kilmaurs, predeceased himself, and two more were, in succession, Earls of Glencairn. He had also three daughters that were married:—

1. Lady Jean, to the Earl of Kilmarnock.
2. Lady Margaret, to Lord Bargany.
3. Lady Elizabeth, to William Hamilton of Orbiston.

He married, secondly, Lady Margaret Montgomerie, daughter of the Earl of Eglintoun, by whom he had no issue. He was succeeded by his eldest son,

XXIII. Alexander, tenth Earl of Glencairn. He married Nicholas, eldest sister and co-heiress of Sir William Stewart of Kirkhill, by whom he had an only daughter, Lady Margaret, who was married to John fifth Earl of Lauderdale, whose son, James Lord Maitland, had an only child, Jean, who was married to Sir James Ferguson of Kilkerran, and was mother of Sir Adam Ferguson, who became a claimant for the honours of Glencairn. Dying without male issue, in 1670, he was succeeded by his brother,

XXIV. John eleventh Earl of Glencairn. In 1690, " John Earle of Glencairne " presented a petition to Parliament, setting forth that his father had served Charles I. and II., until taken prisoner by Cromwell, for which he was allowed a precept of £8000 sterling, in consideration of his sufferings and services, which precept was never paid. He had purchased the forfeited estate of Gilbert M'Ilwraith of Dinmurchie, and some others, after the battle of Bothwell Bridge, thinking the price would be allowed out of the precept for £8000. He had, however, to pay the price of the properties; and now he claimed restitution. The petition was remitted to the Commissioners on forfeitures and fines, to report to next session. Parliament at length recommended the claim to the favourable notice of their Majesties. At the Revolution, the Earl of Glencairn, amongst others, offered to raise a regiment of soldiers in support of the new Government. He married Lady Jean Erskine, daughter of John ninth Earl of Mar, by whom he had an only son,

XXV. William twelfth Earl of Glencairn, who succeeded his father in 1703. He married Lady Henrietta Stewart, daughter of Alexander third Earl of Galloway, by whom he had eight sons, all of whom but the second died either in infancy or unmarried, and two daughters that were married:—

* This, we presume, is the "Margaret Knox, Ladie Cambuskeyth," supposed to have married John Hamilton of Grange, (see page 202).

4. Lady Margaret, who was married to Nichol Graham of Gartmore.

2. Lady Harriet, married to John Campbell of Seafield.

Also two daughters, who died unmarried. His lordship died in 1734, and was succeeded by his eldest surviving son,

XXVI. William thirteenth Earl of Glencairn. He married the eldest daughter and heiress of Hugh Macguire of Drumdow,* by whom he had four sons and two daughters. His eldest son, William Lord Kilmaurs, predeceased him unmarried in 1768; the second and third were in succession Earls of Glencairn; his fourth son died young. The eldest daughter, Lady Henriet, married Sir Alexander Don of Newton, and had issue; Lady Elizabeth died unmarried. His lordship died in 1775, when he was succeeded by his eldest son,

XXVII. James fourteenth Earl of Glencairn, who, dying unmarried in 1791, was succeeded by his only remaining brother. He was one of the earliest and kindest patrons of Burns, who celebrated his death in the well-known "Lament for James Earl of Glencairn."

XXVIII. John fifteenth Earl of Glencairn, dying in 1796 unmarried, the male line of this main stem became extinct.

Nichol Graham, Esq. of Gartmore, who married Lady Margaret, eldest daughter of William twelfth Earl of Glencairn, upon proving the failure of all the collateral heirs male, descended from him, was put in possession of the family property. As the failure of all other collateral heirs-male of the body of Alexander fifth Earl, has also been shown, the succession, with the family honours, is therefore open to the descendants of *Andrew*, second son of William fourth Earl, of whom Sir Thomas Cuninghame, Bart. of Corsehill, is the lineal male representative.

*Arms.*—Argent, a shake-fork, sable. *Crest*, a unicorn's head couped. *Supporters*, two conies proper. *Motto*, "*Over fork over.*"

*Seats.*—The chief residences were Kilmaurs House; Kerila, near the town of Stevenstoun, both in Cuninghame; and Finlaystoun, on the Frith of Clyde, in Renfrewshire, opposite Dumbarton Castle. It does not appear that the family ever resided at Glencairn in Nithsdale, from whence they took their title.

MOWATS OF BUSBIE, OR KOCKINTIBER.

The barony of Busbie consists of from 700 to 800 acres of excellent arable land. At what time it came into the hands of the Mowats is uncertain. Robertson surmises, from the architecture of Busbie Castle, that it was erected during the fourteenth century, and probably by the first of the Mowat family. This conjecture is supported by the existence of a charter, under the Great Seal, of which Robertson was ignorant, of the lands of Robertoun, in the Bailliary of Cuninghame, granted to David Mowat by Robert III. inter 1390 et 1406, which David was probably the first of the Mowats of Ayrshire. The surname, according to Nisbet, was anciently *Monte-Alto*, "of which the principal family is reputed to have been Mowat of Balquholie in Aberdeenshire. There were also," he continues, "two families in the west, Mowat of Stanehouse in Clydesdale, and Mowat of Busbie in Cuninghame, both families of good respect and well allied; but they are now decayed, the last about a century ago." It would appear that the foresaid David Mowat, who had a charter of Robertoun from Robert III., had also a charter of the "barony of Stanehouse, vic. Lanerk; the barony of Brochton, Winkistoun, Burlefield, vic. de Peebles." So that he was in all likelihood the progenitor of both the western branches of the name.

The Mowats were an ancient family. *Willielmus de Monte Alto* appears in the Ragman Roll, and the name frequently occurs in the record of the Crown Charters. A Sir Bernard Mowat accompanied Margaret of Scotland to Norway, in 1281, and with thirty-one others was drowned in returning.*

In the absence of all proof to the contrary, we shall assume that,

I. DAVID, who had a grant of Robertoun from Robert III., was the first of the Mowats of Busbie. The next on record, though one or two successors may have intervened, is,

II. Johanni Mowat, who had a charter of confirmation "de terris de le Moite, Knockintiber, Bogside," &c. from James III. inter 1460 et 1489. The charter is not complete, and wants the date. It was probably his daughter who was married to William Cranfurd of Walstoun, about the close of the fifteenth century.

III. Charles Mowat of Busbie had a charter of the same lands from James V., in 1541. He was, in 1546, appointed one of the curators of the young Earl of Eglintoun. He was, notwithstanding, next year concerned in the slaughter, along with Lord Boyd, of Sir Neil Montgomerie of Lainshaw, and had in consequence to remain

---

* An account of the Macguires of Drumdow will be given in the PARISH of STAIR.

* Balfour's Annals.

abroad for some time along with his lordship. He was slain by two sons of Lord Ochiltree, about 1577,* and was succeeded probably by his son.

IV. Charles Mowat of Busbie, whose name Robertson recollects having seen in some document dated in 1590.

V. "Jacobo, nepoti et hacredi Caroli Mowat de Knockintiber, Bogside, Corshouse," &c. had a charter from James VI., in 1571. "Jacobo Mowat de Busbie, et Jenncæ Wallace, ejus conjugi," had a charter "terrarum ecclesiasticarum de Dreghorne et Halbarnis de Oversyde" from James VI., 5th Jan. 1607; and another of the lands of Busbie, dated 2d June 1614. James Mowat of Busbie occurs in 1600, as a witness to a discharge given by the Laird of Blair to the burgh of Irvine. His name appears in the testament of Mathew Galt, in Bogsyde, as creditor for the rent of his fermes, crop 1600, "twa firlattis meill." In a similar document, in 1603, he is mentioned as proprietor of Knockintyber, otherwise Busbie. In 1608, he was appointed by Parliament, along with the magistrates of Irvine, to see that "Buitis and Shone are made and sold in conformity to the price of leather."† He married and had issue, for he and his eldest son, "James Mowat, zounger, of Busbie," are frequently to be met with in testamentary documents down to 1619. James seems to have predeceased his father, who was alive in 1621. A daughter, *Jean*, was married to Robert Pollock of that Ilk.

VI. John Mowat of Busbie, probably the brother of James, was served heir to his father, Charles Mowat of Busbie, in 1626.

It must have been this Laird of Busbie who was the subject of the following memorial of *Welsh*, preserved by Wodrow:—" His [Welsh's] influence upon and interest in the gentlemen and persons of all rank, through the shire of Air, was not small; they all, save the openly wicked and profane, had a veneration for him; though he spared not to reprove their sins, as far as he knew them. Mr Craufurd gives an instance of his holy freedom this way, as well as his propheticall spirit, which he had from the gentleman's own son, a worthy and pious minister, who was present, quhen his father told the passage with tears. There was much profanation of the Sabbath at a gentleman's house, about eight miles distance from Air, by great gatherings of people, upon that holy day, to the football, and other games and pastimes. Mr Welsh took the

liberty to write severall prudent and civil letters to the gentleman, desiring him to suppress the profanation of the Lord's day at his house. The gentleman, not loving to be received a Puritan, slighted all, and would not amend. In a little time after, Mr Welsh, riding that way, came to his gate, and called for the gentleman, who, coming out invited Mr Welsh in, which he declined, and told him he was come to him with a heavy message from God, quhich was, that because he had slighted the advice given him from the Lord, and would not restrain the profanation of the Sabbath, in his lands, and beside his house, therefor the Lord would cast him out of his house and lands, and none of his posterity should ever enjoy them. This was visibly fulfilled: and though the gentleman was in very good circumstances at the time, yet from that day forth all things went cross, and he fell into one difficulty after another, till he was compelled to sell his estate; and when he was giving the purchaser possession of it, he said with tears before his wife and children, 'Now Mr Welsh is a true prophet.' (This gentleman was, as I am told, Mouat of Busby, Mr Math. M.'s father.)"*

The last notice we find of the Mowats of Busbie in any local document is in the testament of "Archibald Cvnynghame of Kilmaurs," in 1634 . "Item, thair was awand . . in the first be *vmqle James Mowat sumtyme of Busbie*, as principall, and Robert Muir, sone lawfull to Robert Muir of Thornetoun, as cautioner, their bond, xxx lb vis. viiid."

The Mowats of Busbie had alienated part of their lands long before the final breaking up of the estate, the greater portion of which was ultimately acquired by the Eglintoun family. In 1661, Hugh Earl of Eglintoun was served heir to his predecessor, in the lands of Busbie, Knockintiber, and Robertoun. It had been in their possession, however, for some years previously. Among the Eglintoun papers there is a receipt for the rents of Robertoun and Busbie for crop 1638, amounting to " ane thousand four scoir sevinteine pundis, thretteine shillingis, four pennies." The Mowats of Busbie are now wholly extinct, and the name in Ayshire is rare.†

*The Arms* of Mowat, according to Nisbet, are: A lion rampant, sable, armed, gules, within a border of the second. *Crest*, an oak tree growing out of a rock, proper. *Motto*, " *Monte Alto.*"

---

* Crim. Trials.
† Parl. Records.

* The Rev. Mathew Mowat was minister of Kilmarnock in 1643, and until 1660.
† In 1641, Mr Hew Mowat was a servant to the Queen of Sweden.—BALF. ANNALS.

## RITCHIE OF CRAIGTON AND BUSBIE.

I. JOHN RITCHIE, "merchand burgess" of Glasgow, married Bessie Wallace, whom he survived. Her testament is recorded in the Glasgow Commissary Register, 6th April 1674. He is designed "elder" in the Glasgow Register of births, where he witnesses the baptisms of the children of his successor.

II. John Ritchie, who married Jean Somervell, and died 1710. His issue were:—

1. John, baptized 14th October 1687, died young.
2. Anna, baptized 6th February 1679.
3. Jean, baptized 5th February 1681.
4. John, of whom below.
5. Bethia, born 28th July, and baptized 6th August 1684.
6. William, baptized 30th January 1687.

III. John Ritchie, of Craigton, the eldest surviving son, was born 1st, and baptized 5th June 1682. He married Helen, daughter of John Adam, merchant in Glasgow, and by her, who died April 1765, had a numerous family. In 1746, he acquired the estate of Craigton, county of Lanark. He died in 1755. His will is dated 22d September of that year, and is recorded in the Glasgow Commissary Register. His issue were:—

1. John, born 2d, baptized 19th July 1720. He predeceased his father.
2. James, of whom below.
3. Thomas, born 22d, baptized 24th July 1723. He predeceased his father.
4. Mary, baptized 11th March 1725. She married, on 29th March 1753, James Dunlop, younger, of Garnkirk, and had issue.
5. Samuel, born 15th, baptized 27th November 1726. He died in infancy.
6. Jean, baptized 21st January 1728.
7. Samuel, baptized 2d March 1729. He died unmarried.
8. Helen, born 5th, baptized 19th July 1730.
9. Margaret, born 9th, baptized 14th October 1731.
10. Henry, baptized 26th November 1734. He married in 1767, Esther, daughter of William Craufurd of Balshagrie and Scotstoun, and had issue. He died 14th June 1792.
11. Robert, born 8th, baptized 16th May 1736.

IV. James Ritchie, the eldest surviving son, succeeded to Craigton, and was retoured heir to his father, before the Bailies of Glasgow, 30th January 1756. He acquired the estate of Busbie, of which he had a charter under the Great Seal, 23d February 1763. (Great Seal Record, lib. 106. No. 129.) He married, firstly, in 1758, Frances, daughter of Alexander Montgomerie of Coilsfield, and sister of Hugh 12th Earl of Eglintoun, and by her had issue two sons and two daughters:—

1. John, (a Colonel in the army), born 1st, baptized 3d November 1760. He married Elizabeth, daughter of George Bogle, Esq. but died without issue, having predeceased his father.

2. Alexander, born 15th, and baptized 16th June 1763.
1. Lillias, born 19th, baptized 22d July 1759. She married Hugh Hamilton of Pinmore, but died without issue, in 1817.
2. Helen, born 7th, baptized 12th March 1762.

James Ritchie married, secondly, on 20th May 1765, Catherine, daughter of Robert Kerr of Newfield, (son of Lord Charles Kerr, and grandson of Robert first Marquis of Lothian), and by her, who died at Craigton 24th September 1783, had issue five sons and seven daughters:—

1. Robert, born 5th, baptized 15th April 1767.
2. James, born 22d September, and baptized 6th October 1771.
3. Charles, born 1st, baptized 2d September 1772.
4. Henry, born 7th, baptized 28th February 1776.
5. Henry, who succeeded his father.
1. Elenora, died unmarried, March 1846.
2. Frances, married Hugh Wallace of Biscany, and died at Madeira in 1842, leaving issue.
3. Catherine.
4. Jean Douglas, married        Donaldson, M.D., and died without issue.
5. Mary, married Alexander West Hamilton, Esq. and died without issue.
6. Margaret Hamilton, married William Stirling of Cordale, Esq. and has issue.
7. Charlotte.

James Ritchie died 1799, and was succeeded by his only surviving son,

V. Henry Ritchie of Busbie and Craigton, born 15th August, and baptized 7th September 1777. He was served heir to his father before the Sheriff of Lanarkshire 18th December 1799. He acquired the estate of Cloncaird in the county of Ayr, and made it his principal residence during the latter part of his life. He married, firstly, Elizabeth, daughter of John Cathcart, Esq. and by her, who died in 1836, had issue:—

1. Elizabeth Cathcart, born 26th January 1807, died unmarried 1831.
2. Catherine, born 12th February 1808, died in infancy.
3. Mary, born 22d March 1810, died in infancy.

Henry Ritchie married, secondly, on 17th January 1838, Catherine, daughter of Sir James Fergusson of Kilkerran, Bart., but by her (who survives him) he had no issue. Henry Ritchie died 6th November 1843, and was succeeded in his estates of Busbie and Cloncaird by his nephew, William Wallace, Esq. son of his sister Frances.

*Arms* of Ritchie of Craigton and Busbie, matriculated in the Lyon Register.—Quarterly, first and fourth, argent, on a chief, gules, three lions' heads, erased, of the first; second and third, azure, a crescent, or, between three cross crosslets, argent.—*Crest*, an unicorn's head, couped, ermine, horned, or.—*Motto*, "Virtute acquiritur honos."

There is no mansion-house on the estate of Busbie, although Mr Ritchie, the purchaser of the property, at one time contemplated building a residence, and with this view laid out and planted a portion of it.

### DESCENT OF WALLACE OF BUSBIE.

I. JOHN WALLACE, third son of John Wallace of Riccarton, by the heiress of Lindsay of Craigie, married the heiress of Ellerslie, county of Renfrew, and by her acquired that property about the beginning of the reign of Robert III. (1390), which for more than a century had been held by a younger branch of the Riccarton family. He was succeeded by,

II. John Wallace of Ellerslie, mentioned in the Chartulary of Paisley 1432.

III. George Wallace of Ellerslie, was living in 1468.

IV. Patrick Wallace of Ellerslie, living between 1488 and 1513, was succeeded by his son,

V. William Wallace of Ellerslie, father of

VI. John Wallace of Ellerslie, who married a daughter of Cuninghame of Craigends, and had a charter of the lands of Ellenton 1530. He was succeeded by his son,

VII. William Wallace of Ellerslie, who had a charter of his lands in 1554. He married Catherine, daughter of Hugh Cranfurd of Kilbirnie, and was succeeded by his son,

VIII. William Wallace of Ellerslie, who, in 1556, obtained a precept of *Clare Constat*, as heir to his father, from his superior, William Wallace of Craigie. He married Jean, daughter of James Chalmers of Gadgirth. He was succeeded by his eldest son, *William*, whose grandson, *Hugh*, having no issue, alienated the estate of Ellerslie to Sir Thomas Wallace of Craigie in 1678.

IX. John Wallace, the second son, married Margaret, daughter and heiress of John Hamilton of Ferguslee, Renfrewshire, and thereby acquired that property previous to 1624. His eldest son, *James* of Lorabank, died unmarried.

X. William Wallace, the second son, married Margaret, daughter and heiress of Hugh Stewart of Neilstounside, and by her acquired that property. His eldest son, *John* Wallace of Neilstounside, left three daughters, who, in 1713, sold that estate, but the representation of the family fell to the second son,

XI. William Wallace, merchant in Glasgow, who acquired the lands of Overkirktoun, in the parish of Neilstoun. He had two sons, *John* and *Thomas*. John purchased Ellerslie from the Craigie family, and left an only daughter, married to Archibald Campbell of Succoth; but the male representation of the family went to

XII. Thomas Wallace, second son of William, who acquired the lands of Cairnhill. He married, in 1710, Lillias, daughter of William Cuninghame of Craigends, by whom he had four sons :—

1. William, of Cairnhill, whose male line is now extinct.
2. John, of Cessnock and Kelly, who is now represented by his son, Robert Wallace late of Kelly.* He was M.P. for Greenock in the Reform Parliament.
3. Hugh.
4. James.  Besides three daughters.

XIII. Hugh Wallace, the third son, acquired the estate of Biscany, in the island of Jamaica. He married Margaret, daughter of —— Whyte, Esq., of that island ; and by her had issue four sons and one daughter :—

1. Thomas, who died young.
2. Hugh, of whom afterwards.
3. John, who held a commission in the British Army, and died in India, unmarried.
4. William, Lieutenant-Colonel of the 20th Regiment of Infantry, fell at the battle of Vittoria. He died unmarried.
1. Margaret, the only daughter, married Andrew Houston of Jordanhill, county of Renfrew, and left issue.

XIV. Hugh Wallace, of Biscany, the second but eldest surviving son, was a Captain in the army. He married, in 1789, Frances, daughter of James Ritchie of Busbie and Craigton. He died in 1800, leaving issue :—

1. Hugh Ritchie of Biscany, Lieutenant H.P. 7th Fusiliers.
2. James Ritchie, lieutenant in the navy. He was lost at sea ; unmarried.
3. William, of whom afterwards.
4. John Ritchie, Doctor of Medicine, died in 1825, unmarried.
5. Thomas, died in the West Indies 1843, unmarried.
6. Robert.
1. Frances, died 1845.

XV. William Wallace, the third son, purchased the lands of Rhynd, in the county of Fife. In 1843, by the settlement of his maternal uncle, Henry Ritchie of Busbie, he succeeded to the estates of Busbie and Cloncaird. He married, in 1821, Janet Craufurd, daughter of Samuel Cooper, of Failford and Ballindalloch, by whom he has issue four sons and two daughters :—

1. Hugh James, died in infancy.
2. William.
3. A son, died in infancy.
4. Henry Ritchie Cooper.
1. Jeanette Ritchie.
2. Ellinor Harriet, died in infancy.

*Arms.*—Quarterly ; 1st and 4th, gules, a lion rampant, argent, within a border goboné of the last, and azure ; 2d and 3d, gules, a fess chequé, argent and azure ; the whole within a border, or.—*Crest*, an arm in armour holding a broadsword. *Motto*, " Pro libertate."

---

* Mr Wallace is now the acknowledged head of the ancient and renowned family of Wallace, all the collateral branches having failed in the male line. Failing him the representation will devolve upon the descendants of Hugh Wallace of Biscany.

## THORNTOUN.

This property, situated to the west of Busbie, is about 300 acres in extent. It belonged, of old, according to *Wood*, to one of the branches of the Montgomeric family. *Murchaw de Montgomery*, whose name appears in the Ragman Roll in 1296, is supposed by *Nisbet* to have been of Thorntoun—"one of the ancientest families of the name. John Montgomery of Thorntoun was forfeited in King James V.'s time, and his estate given to Lord Home; his only daughter was married to Sir Alexander Hamilton of Innerwick."[*]

Sometime thereafter the property passed into the hands of a branch of the *Mures*, probably of Rowallan. The first we find of them is

*James Muir of Thorntoun*, who is mentioned in a testamentary document in 1607. Hew Muir, younger, of Thorntoun, as well as his father, James, occur in the testament of Adame Galt, merchant, Irvine, in 1611. Hew seems to have predeceased his father. James Muir of Thorntoun married *Jonet Naper*, but of what family does not appear. She died in 1626, and in her testament James Muir elder and younger of Thorntoun are mentioned.

*James Muir of Thorntoun* succeeded his father. In 1634 "*Robert Muir*, sone lawfull to James Muir of Thorntoun," was cautioner on a bond with James Mowat of Busbie. The next we find was

*Sir Archibald Muir of Thorntoun*, Lord Provost of Edinburgh, who was knighted by King William in 1689. His daughter, *Margaret*, was married to John Cuninghame of Caddell, whose descendants still possess the property.[†]

## TOUR AND KIRKLANDS.

This small but prettily situated property formed part of the church lands of Kilmaurs, and was granted by the Abbot and Convent of Kelso, in 1532, to David Cuninghame of Robertland, in whose family and their descendants it remained until its purchase a few years ago by the present proprietor. Of the *Cuninghames of Kirkland*, we have gleaned only a few notices:—

*William Cuninghame of "Tour-lands"* was the "Laird thereof" when Pont made his survey of Cuninghme, towards the close of the sixteenth or beginning of the seventeenth century.

*Archibald Cuninghame of Kirkland* died in

1614. By his latter-will it appears he left his spouse—whose name is not mentioned—and six children:—*Patrik, David, Archibald, Adame, Bessie,* and *Margaret.*

"*Archibald Cunynghame of Kirkland*" occurs in the testament of Alexander Cvnynghame of Corshill, who died in 1615. "Mr David Cvnynghame, sone to Archibald Cvnynghame of Kirkland" occurs in the testament of John Harper, merchant in Kilmarnock, in 1630. In 1633, Patrik Cuninghame, *fear* of Kirkland, is mentioned in a similar document in 1633. Patrick seems thus to have been joint proprietor with his brother. Archibald of Kirkland died in April 1634, and was succeeded by his eldest son,

*Patrik Cvnynghame of Kirkland*, who died in July 1645, leaving "Elizabeth Hendersone, relict of the defunct."

Prior to this period the Tourlands seem to have been in the hands of a family of the name of Hay. *James Hay* was served heir of his father, *John Hay*, in Tourlands, 12th Dec. 1640.

In 1694 the property went to *William Watson*, through marriage, we presume, and continued with his descendants till 1814, when it passed by the female line to *William Cathcart*, of the Carlton family, formerly of Jamaica, who, on his death, in 1828, devised it to his nephew, George James Cathcart, brother of Sir John of Carlton, from whom it was purchased in 1841, by

*Robert Parker Adam*, formerly of Brazil, a merchant in Glasgow. The property was greatly improved by plantation while in the possession of the late Mr Cathcart; and Mr Adam, by rebuilding the mansion-house in the old English style, has made it a handsome and comfortable residence.

The family of the present proprietor has been for many years connected with the district. His great-grandfather, the Rev. John Adam, (who married a daughter of the Rev. James Campbell of Craigie), was minister of the parish of West Kilbride from 1716 to 1763, when he was succeeded by his son, the Rev. Dr Adam, afterwards of Greenock, who was proprietor of the lands of Lawhill, in Kilbride parish.

He married (1752) Elizabeth, daughter of William Parker of Barleith (Riccarton), by Mary Stuart, daughter of Hugh Stuart,[*] merchant in Glasgow. Their eldest son, *Robert*, who in-

---

[*] It is probable that this refers to Thorntoun near Dunbar, one of the early possessions of the Montgomeries.
[†] See Cuninghames of Caddell. vol. i. p. 231.

[*] John Adam, merchant in Glasgow, had three daughters, one married M'Call, ancestor of Daldowie, &c.; another married John Ritchie of Craigton, and was mother of James Ritchie of Busbie; another married Hugh Stuart of Castlesalt, two of whose daughters married respectively William Cooper of Smithstone, and William Parker of Barleith, county of Ayr.

herited Lawhill, died in north Carolina; their second son, *John William*, was a merchant in Greenock, and married his cousin Margaret, only surviving daughter of John Parker of Barleith, banker in Kilmarnock, and had a family, viz. *John*, *William*, *Robert Parker*, and *Elizabeth*.

Robert Parker Adam married, 1832, Margaret, second daughter of James Haldane, formerly of Auchans, (deceased 1840), by whom he has issue, a son, *William Parker*, and two daughters—*Mary Henry*, and *Margaret Parker*.

*Arms.*—Per pale, argent, a crescent, azure, between three crosses crosslet, fitchy, gules. Gules, a chevron, azure, between three Leopards' heads, or. *Crest*, a cross crosslet, surmounted by a sword proper, hilted and pommelled, or, placed in a saltire. *Motto*, " *Cruz mihi grata quies.*"

### CRAIG.

This property formed part of the barony of Robertoun, which, as we have seen, belonged at one time to the Mowats of Busbie. It seems, however, to have been acquired from them at an early period, by a branch of the Dunlop family, the first of whom we find mentioned is

I. Adam Dunlop of Craig, whose nephew,

II. William Dunlop of Craig, was served heir to his grandfather in 1576. He is mentioned in various documents, from 1618 downwards. He married " Grissall Mowat"—most likely a daughter of Mowat of Busbie—who died in 1618. Her effects were given up by her husband, in behoof of *Robert Dunlope*, " bairn lawfull to the defunct." He must have died in 1620,[*] for " William Dunlope, zounger, of Craig," is mentioned in a testamentary document in that year, and not in the next.

III. William Dunlop of Craig. His wife, Jeane Campbell, died in January 1621. Besides *William*, his heir, he had *Allane*, *Grisall*, *Jonet*, *Archibald*, and *Elizabeth*. He was alive in 1636, in which year " William Dunlope, zounger, of Craig," occurs in another testamentary document.

V. William Dunlope, elder, of Craig, and *Allane Dunlope*, zounger, of Craig, occur in a testamentary document in 1652. William, the elder, was alive in 1659.

The property of Craig, or a portion of it,

seems to have been temporarily in the possession of Mr David Mylne, minister of Dundonald, and his brother, also named David, goldsmith in Edinburgh. The latter was served heir to the former in 1618. " In 1780," says Robertson, " it was acquired from Dalrymple of Nunraw, in East Lothian, by Captain John Morrice. The house was soon afterwards burnt, when the present mansion was erected at a little distance west from the site of the old one, and is pleasantly set down on the top of a pretty steep bank on the north side of Irvine water, and commanding a fine prospect over the country to the west and south." Craig, however, seems to have belonged previously to *John Glasgow, Esq.* of *Craig*, Provost of Irvine, whose daughter, *Elizabeth*, married Robert Morrice, shipmaster in Irvine, who died 22d May 1796. John Morrice, Esq. of Craig, died 23d March 1788, aged 45. *Robert Morrice of Craig*, who succeeded, died 8th March 1827, aged 77.[*] He left the property to his sister, and, after her death, to William Pollok, M.D., a surgeon in the army, who assumed the name of Morrice—now William Pollock Morrice. He married Janet, only daughter of James Buchanan of Davanhill, merchant in Glasgow, and has two sons,—*Allan* and *Robert*—and three daughters.

### CARMEL BANK.

This small but pleasant property was anciently called the *Mott*, or *Moat*, and formed part of the estate of Busbie. The mansion is snugly situated on the banks of the Carmel. It belonged to *John Cuninghame of Carmel*, who died about twenty years ago. Having no family, he left the property to his brother, *Gilbert Cuninghame*, who died, without issue, in 1842, leaving it to his widow, *Elizabeth Pollock*, daughter of the late Rev. Mr Pollock, minister of Irvine.

*Robertoun.*—This rather extensive barony, consisting of about 1300 acres, was conjectured by *Robertson*, to have been at one time a wing of the Kilmaurs estate. Be this as it may, we have seen that David Mowat had a charter of the lands of Robertoun so early as the reign of Robert III. It was latterly acquired by the Eglintoun family, but is now parcelled out among a number of small proprietors.

---

* He had a sister, Jeane Dunlope, married to William Cauldwell of Annanhill.

* Tombstone in Irvine Churchyard.

# PARISH OF KILWINNING.

ETYMOLOGY, EXTENT, &c.

The name is evidently derived from St Winnin, a Scottish saint of the eighth century, whose memory was celebrated on the 21st January, and on which day a fair has long been held in Kilwinning. The parish is bounded on the west by Stevenston and Ardrossan; on the east, by Dunlop, Stewarton, and Irvine; on the south, by Irvine and Stevenston; and on the north, by Dalry and Beith. It contains upwards of 11,000 acres.

The parish, both in figure and appearance, is irregular. "Its surface," says the *New Statistical Account*, "gradually slopes upwards from the south-west to the north-east, and is varied by gentle undulations, but nowhere rises to any considerable elevation. It is intersected by the valleys of Garnock and Lugton; the former, open and cultivated; the latter, more narrow and woody. The view from the upland district is extensive and beautiful.

"The soil in the higher and central parts of the parish, is generally a thin clay, not fertile or productive, especially where the surface water has not been removed by tile drainage, though nearly the whole is under the plough, except what is occupied by plantations of forest trees. A better description of clay land is found on the slopes towards the river Garnock; and along its margin are some good loamy fields. From the town of Kilwinning towards the sea, there is a portion of light sandy soil, well cultivated and fertile. To the eastward, near Auchintiber, there remains probably sixty or seventy acres of a peat bog, which was formerly much more extensive, a considerable part of it having been reclaimed and improved in the course of the present century.

"The most considerable stream in this parish is the Garnock. It rises in the hills above Kilbirnie, about twelve miles from the town of Kilwinning, which it intersects, and after a remarkably circuitous and serpentine course through the low lands to the west, falls into the sea at the same point with the river Irvine. The Lugton, a small stream, flows out of Loch Libo, in Renfrewshire, enters this parish near its eastern extremity, and, after passing through the woods of Mountgreenan and Eglinton, falls into the Garnock, about two miles from the sea. The Caaf water, also a tributary of the Garnock, forms part of the boundary line, for a short distance, betwixt this parish and Dalry. At Craighead mill, it falls over a rock of considerable heighth, and forms a pretty little linn or cascade in a narrow wooded dell. There is a sheet of water, about a mile and a-half to the north-west of Kilwinning town, called Ashenyard, or Ashgrove Loch. It is not of great extent, and part of it is included in Stevenston. In the town and neighbourhood, an ample supply of the finest spring-water is obtained, as is almost invariably the case, throughout Scotland, around the sites of ancient monasteries, or other religious houses."

## HISTORY, CIVIL AND ECCLESIASTICAL.

"The history of the parish begins with that of the patron saint, from whom it derives its name.*

---

* This account of the Monastery of Kilwinning is from the pen of James Dobie, Esq., Beith, furnished by him to the NEW STATISTICAL ACCOUNT.

In the calendar of Scottish Saints, the date assigned to St Winnin or Winning, is 715. In Pont's MS. it is said, that 'Vinnin was a holy man wich came from Irland, with certane of his discipells and followers, and heir taught the Gospell; the place of his residence retaining still ye name Killvinnin, ye church or cell of Vinnin, unto quhome, as to a notable sante, ye superstitious posterity dedicated.' In the Proprium Sanctorum, a different parentage is given to St Winnin, as he is there said to have sprung of a noble family in Scotland. He was famous for his power in curing diseases, and for his control over the elements. In the parish of Holywood, a fountain of precious virtue sprung up on his intercession, and remained in repute until the beginning of the sixteenth century. A spring of fine water, a little to the south of Kilwinning manse, which still bears the name of St Winning's Well, was also celebrated for its virtues. But St Winnin could curse the waters as well as bless them, for on one occasion, when the river Garnock would not yield up any of its fish to one of his angling friends, the saint pronounced a malediction, on which the river ' left its bed, and followed another course adverse to nature.'*

" The fame and sancity of St Winnin led to the building of the splendid monastery, near the site of the more ancient church of this place. According to the commonly received account, it was founded in the reign of David I., A. D. 1140, by Hugh de Moreville, Constable of Scotland, the chief benefactor, if not also the founder, of Dryburgh Abbey. In the Pont manuscript, before quoted, however, a different origin is assigned to it, and the date of the foundation, or perhaps the completion of the buildings, is placed in the year 1591: ' It was foundit by a nobel Englichman, named Sir Richard Morwell, fugitive from his owne country for ye slaughter of Thomas Beccket, Archbichope of Canterburrey, (being one of them), in the raine of King Henry II. of England, quho, flying to Scotland, was, by the then Scots King (Malcolm IV. he elsewhere affirms), velcomed and honoured with ye office of grate Constable of Scotland, as also inriched with ye Lordships of Cuninghame, Largis, and Lauderdaill, quhosse posterity for divers generations possessed ye said office and lands. Now ye forsaid Richard being, as vald scime, touched with compunctione for ye safty of hes soule, (according to the custome of these tymes), did found this Abbey of Kilvinnen, in testimony of hes repentance; and first of all did bulde ye queir or cancell of ye said Abbey Church, endowing it with divers lands, as namely,

the 80 lb. land of Kilvinen, after this tennor, Damus forrestam nostram de Kilvinnen, ibidem deo servientibus ad pascendum porcos eorum et ac excindenda ligna ad constructionem Monasterii, una cum decimis tergorum tam cervorum quam damarum euisdem forrestae. Also, Alicia Loncaster, viffe to ye said Sir Richard, with consent of her said husband, dottes, in puram et perpetuam elimosinam the landof Bytth, Batth, and Threppewood to ye said Monastrey. Item, Dorathea de Morvil, daughter to ye said Sir Richard, and vyffe to Philippus de Horssey, accomplished ye fabrick of ye said monastrey, and hes sone, Dominus Valterus de Horssey, confirms to them ye same, and ye said foundatione, with ye donations and mortifications thereto belonging, is confirmed by Pope Honorius the 2d. Ano. 2do. pontificatus sui. These donations and foundations ar also confirmed by King Alexander III.; as also by Jocelinus Dei Gratia humilis Glasguensis Ecclesiae Minister Auctoritate Episcopali, &c. The revenues of this abbey ver grate, and maney by (over and above) their proper lands. The founder thereof, Sir Richard Morvil, layes interrid in the new cemetery of this church, under a tome of lymestone, framed coffin-vayes, of old polished vorke, without any superscriptioune or epitaphe. The structure of this monastery wes solid and grate, all of freestone cutte; the church faire and staitly, after ye modell of yat of Glasgow, vith a fair steeple of 7 score foote of hight, zet standing where I my selve did see it.'

" It is difficult to suppose that Pont, who refers in another part of his work to ' old records of ye monastery of Kilvinnen,' and here quotes the original charter of De Morville to the monks, should yet be mistaken as to the individual member of that family who founded the abbey. If the common accounts, however, of the reign of Malcolm IV. are to be relied on, it closed in 1165, and consequently he could not receive the murderer of Thomas a Beeckct, for that prelate was not slain till 1170. His murderers, we are told,* retired at first to Knaresborough in Yorkshire, which belonged to De Morville; from whence they repaired to Rome for absolution, and, being admitted to penance by Alexander III., were sent by the orders of that Pontiff to Jerusalem, and passed the remainder of their lives upon the Black Mountain, in the several acts of austerity and mortification. Pont says that the grants of the De Morville family to Kilwinning were ' confirmed by Pope Honorius II. Ao. 2do. pontificatus sui;' but the death of that Pontiff, according to

---

* Proprium Sanctorum, fol. 38.

* Mosheim, Eccles. History, vol. ii. p. 401. M'Lean's note.

Mosheim, (vol. ii. p. 393), happened in 1130. In Morton's Monastic Annals of Teviotdale (p. 290), the murderer of Thomas a Becket is said to have been the uncle of Hugh de Morville, Constable of Scotland, whose family became extinct 1196 (do. p. 59). It is highly improbable, indeed, that a sacrilegious assassin should have been welcomed by the Scottish monarch, and invested with lands and authority, at a period when the power of the Church of Rome had reached so great a height. It is possible, however, that Richard de Morville, son of Hugh, Constable of Scotland, may have founded the Abbey of Kilwinning in the latter part of the twelfth century, and that Pont, misled by that name, attributed the work to the murderer of Becket, and represented it as the atonement made to the Church for his crime. The date 1140 is adopted by the learned author of 'Caledonia;' but he does not give his authority, and the matter is involved in some obscurity, in consequence of the loss of the chartulary.

"Though the founder and the date of the foundation be thus uncertain, it is known that the abbey was richly endowed by different members of the De Morville family. Successive monarchs and noblemen, also, 'for the health of their souls,' and sometimes for relief to the souls of their ancestors, contributed by their pious benefactions to increase its revenues. The estates belonging to it included nearly the whole land in the parish of Kilwinning, and various properties in the parishes of Dalry, Beith, and Kilmarnock. At the Reformation, the revenue of the Monastery, exclusive of these property lands, amounted to £880, 3s. 4d. Scots; 67 chalders, 9 bolls, 3 firlots of meal; 14 chalders, 1 boll, 3 firlots, 3 pecks of bear; 8 bolls 1 firlot of wheat; 4 hogsheads of wine; 13 stirks; 140 capons; 100 hens; 268 cheeses; and 9 fathoms of a peat stack.* To the Abbey belonged the patronages and teinds of the following parishes, subject to the burden of stipends for the regular clergy, viz. Kilwinning, Irvine, Kilmarnock, Loudoun, Dalry, Ardrossan, Kilbirnie, West Kilbride, Beith, Dunlop, Dreghorn, Stevenston, and Stewarton, all in Cuninghame; Dumbarton and Kilmaronock, in Dumbartonshire; south and north Knapdale, in Argyll; Kilmory and Kilbride, in the island of Arran.

"The monks of Kilwinning were originally brought from Kelso, and were called Tyronenses, from Tyron, in the diocese of Chartres, where their order was first settled under St Bernard. It would appear that the usual artifices by which superstition was encouraged and confirmed in the Roman Catholic church, were not neglected by the occupants of this monastery. The fountains which had been blessed by St Winning continued in high repute, and one of them was believed to give warning of the approach of war, by flowing with blood on such occasions. R. Hoveden and Benedictus Abbas relate a portent of this kind as having occurred in the year 1184. ' In eadem vero ebdomada qua rex in Anglia applicuit, quidam fons aquæ vivæ, juxta ecclesiam sancti vinini, in occidentalibus partibus terræ regis Scotiæ, infra Cuninham, non longe a Castello de Irevin, mutatus in sanguinem, manavit puro sanguine per octo dies et totidem noctes sine intermissione. Et dicebant indiginæ quod simile portentum ibidem contingere solebat contra effusionem sanguinis. Sed numquam antea tam diu manavit ibi sanguinis manatio.'* This fact was mentioned by Lord Hailes, among the miscellaneous occurrences in the first volume of his Annals of Scotland. He was, in consequence, accused of credulity by the critics; and, in a subsequent edition of his work, he declares, that ' the author must still remain under that imputation, for he cannot submit to acknowledge that he does not believe that a fountain, near Kilwinning, ran blood for eight days and eight nights, without intermission. ' A recent occurrence tends to prove the truth of the story, and to vindicate the stubborn faith of the learned Lord. In 1826, when the square or green, in the town of Kilwinning, to the west of the monastery, was being levelled, the workmen came upon an old leaden pipe, about an inch in diameter, which ran from the walls of the building, in the direction of a fine spring, now called Kyles Well. This pipe had a considerable descent, and could not have been used for the purpose of drawing water from the well to the abbey. Through it, therefore, in all probability, blood, or some liquid resembling it, had been caused to flow into the fountain, and thus the credulity of the people was imposed upon, by the appearance of a miracle, which served to enhance the fame of the monastery, and the power of its priesthood.

"Few of the abbots of Kilwinning attained to much celebrity, or are noticed in history. One of them swore fealty to King Edward in the year 1296, and another, more patriotic, fell, with his sovereign, on the fatal field of Flodden. The last of the order, Gavin Hamilton, was the most distinguished. He was frequently employed, by Queen Mary and her party, in offices of great trust and responsibility. In 1566, he was admitted an extraordinary Lord of Session, on the Queen's letter. He appeared in her cause at the battle of Langside, and was among the commissioners

---

* Former Statistical Account and Beith papers. MS. collection by James Dobie, Esq.

* Ben. Abbas, p. 116.

- 2

at York, in 1568, for settling disputes between Mary and Elizabeth. In 1571, he was declared a rebel, in a Parliament held by the Regent Lennox, and in the same year, lost his life in a conflict, at Restalrig, near Edinburgh, between the Earl of Morton and the Queen's party.

"Gavin Hamilton, and his immediate predecessors in office, foreseeing the fall of the Roman Catholic Church, considerably dilapidated the revenues of the abbey, by conferring grants of its lands on their friends and relations. What remained at the Reformation was annexed, with all other church lands in the country, to the Crown. The King gave the office of Commendator to Alexander Cuninghame, third son of Alexander, commonly called the good Earl of Glencairn. He was bound to pay the salaries of the reformed teachers, in the parishes that held of the abbey, but appears to have been unwilling to recognize this obligation; for, in 1581, he was denounced and put to the horn, by John Boyd, "reider at Kilmarnock," for non-payment of his stipend. Imitating the example of the last Popish abbots, he conferred the estate of Mountgreenan, a valuable part of the abbey lands, on his son Alexander, in whose family it remained for several generations. In 1592, the whole remaining abbacy, or halydome, was erected into a temporal lordship, in favour of William Melville of Raith, then commendator, who soon after transferred his rights to Hugh fifth Earl of Eglintoun. By charter from the Crown, in 1603, these possessions were confirmed to the Eglintoun family, in whose hands they still remain.

"In 1560, the Estates of Scotland passed an 'act for demolishing such cloisters and abbey churches as were not yet pulled down.' The work of havoc was entrusted, in the western Lowlands, to the Earl of Glencairn, who, mindful of the dictum of Knox, ' pull down the nests, and the rooks will fly away,' destroyed that stately and splendid fabric, whose elegant remains still silently point to the sky. A part of the abbey church was afterwards repaired and fitted up as a place of Presbyterian worship. It continued in use till 1775, when it was removed, and the present parish church was built on its site. The ' fair steiple,' which Timothy Pont did see, remained till 1814, when it fell from natural decay. It was a huge square tower, 32 feet on each side, and 103 feet high. The following year, a beautiful tower, about the same height, and 28 feet square, was erected on the same situation, and separate from the church. The south gable of the transept, and one of its finely proportioned arches, a Saxon gateway, and some mouldering walls, are the only indications and memorials now extant of the once splenddid results of superstitious piety and Italian art."

*Masonry.*—" The art of executing very large and magnificent buildings in timber frame-work was carried to high perfection in the northern countries of Europe during the tenth, eleventh, and twelfth centuries. Owing, however, to the perishable nature of the materials, and to accidents by fire, these buildings were frequently either destroyed, or reduced to a state of extreme decay; so that the ruinous state of the ecclesiastical edifices in the northern parts of Europe became a serious subject of inquiry at Rome, and measures were taken to obviate the grievance. The Pope created several corporations of Roman and Italian architects and artisans, with high and exlusive privileges, especially with a power of settling the rates and prices of their labour by their own authority, and without being controlled by the municipal laws of the country where they worked. To the various northern countries, where the churches had fallen into a state of decay, were these artists deputed. In consequence of the exclusive privileges conferred upon them, they assumed to themselves the name of Free Masons, and under this title became famous throughout Europe. These corporations, from their first origin, possessed the power of taking apprentices, and admitting into their body such masons as they approved of in the countries where their works were carried on.* A party of these foreign artisans, aided by such workmen as they found in Scotland qualified to join them, are said to have constructed the monastery of Kilwinning. The architect or master mason, who superintended and carried on the work, was chosen master mason of the meetings of the brethren all over Scotland. He gave rules for their conduct at these meetings, and decided finally in appeals from all the other lodges in the kingdom. From this period, down to the fifteenth century, little is known of the history of masonry. It is acknowledged that Kilwinning continued to be the head-quarters of the order. In the notes to a French poem, *La Maconnerie,* published at Paris in 1820, p. 151, it is said, that " Jacques Lord Stewart recus dans sa loge a Kilwin en Ecosse, en 1286, les Comtes de Gloeester et Ulster, l'un Anglois, l'autre Irlandois." King James I. of Scotland, eminently distinguished for his knowledge and taste in polite literature and in the fine arts, not long after his return from England, patronized the mother lodge of Kilwinning, and presided as grand master, till he settled an annual salary, to be paid by every master mason in Scotland to a grand master, chosen by the brethren,

* P. F. Tytler's Hist. of Scotland, vol. ii. pp. 395, 396.

and approved by the Crown. It was required that this grand master should be nobly born, or a clergyman of high rank and character. He had his deputies in the different counties and towns of Scotland. Every new brother paid him a fee at entrance. He was empowered to regulate and determine such matters in dispute, between the founders and builders of churches and monasteries, as it would have been improper to bring before a court of law. James II. conferred the office of grand master on William Sinclair, Earl of Orkney, and Baron of Roslin. By another deed of the same King, this office was made hereditary in this very ancient and illustrious family. Earl William and his successors, Barons of Roslin, held their head courts, or, in the style of masonry, assembled their grand lodges at Kilwinning.* The mother lodge continued in possession of the highest authority, and granted charters of erection to other lodges, till the year 1736, when the Lord of Roslin, hereditary grand master, assembled thirty-two lodges in Edinburgh, and resigned all right or title which he possessed, or his successors might claim, to preside over the masonic order throughout Scotland. His resignation being accepted, the Grand Lodge of Scotland was constituted, consisting of representatives from other lodges throughout the kingdom, in whom was vested the right of legislating and of granting new charters, or confirming old ones, for the whole order, for which purposes a general meeting is held, and office bearers are elected annually. This usurpation was resisted for a time by the Kilwinning brethren, who continued to hold independent meetings, and to grant charters as formerly, till the year 1807, when the dispute was amicably settled, and the mother lodge relinquished her ancient privileges, joining the general association, along with the lodges that held of her."†

*Archery.*—Kilwinning has been long famed for its practice of Archery. It is well known that the use of the bow was enforced in every parish, by act of Parliament, until the introduction of fire-arms rendered it less essential, as a weapon of warfare. The periodical assembling of the people at the respective parish " butts," consequently fell into disuetude throughout the country generally. It seems, however, to have been regularly kept up at Kilwinning, with the exception of a few years prior to the Revolution, from about the year 1488. This is known by the following extract from the Register of the Company of Archers :—" Sept. 1688.—Shooting with bow and arrow at Butts and Papingo has been used and practised at Kilwinning by the inhabitants there-

of, for the space of two hundred years and upwards. The prize shot for at the game of the Papingo, in former times, was a piece of fine Persian taffettie, three ells long and three quarters broad, of several colours, red, blue, green, scarlet, &c. to the value of twenty pounds (Scots) at least, which they termed a Benn. The person who gained the same, by shooting down the Papingo upon the day appointed for that effect, had the said Benn tied about his waste as a badge of honour, and was thereupon denominated Captain, and making a parade through the town attended by the former Captains, each wearing about their wastes the Benns they had gained, and accompanied by the rest of the Archers. Each changekeeper brought forth to them ale and other liquors to drink the Captain's health, &c. The said ancient game turning into disuetude for some few years, was restored and again renewed at Kilwinning on the fourth day of September Javi (1600) and eighty eight, by

William Blair of that Ilk,
Hugh Montgomerie of Coilsfield,
Wm. Baillie, merchant, Edinburgh,
H. Stevenson of Mountgreenan,
J. Ferguson, writer, Edinburgh,
Mr James Stevenson, advocate,
James M'Bryde, writer, Edinburgh,
Francis Baillie,
John Ewing, writer, in Edinburgh,
William Hamiltoun,
James Maxwell,
Mr William Rodger,
Matthew Frew, merchant, Kilwinning,
And John Logan,

as appears by the original Constitution, who turned the prize, formerly used as above mentioned, into a piece of silverplate, and erected themselves into a society, and kept a register of their acts and customs, their several meetings, proceedings, &c. Since that erection several gentlemen of note and distinction, through many places of the kingdom, have been admitted members of the said society, of which the index in the following pages gives a particular account."

It appears from the Records that Hugh Montgomerie of Coilsfield presented the Society with the first prize at *the butts* in the year 1694. At the present time the annual prize is given by the senior member of the Society, who has not done so previously. Various regulations have since been made with regard to the Papingo prize. Since 1724 it has consisted of a silver arrow. The tournament at Eglintoun Castle, in 1839, gave a stimulus to chivalrous pastimes, and greatly added to the popularity of archery, so that the annual competition at Kilwinning has since been attended with a marked degree of interest, and greatly added to the number and respectability of the Company.

* Old Statistical Account.
† Robertson's Cuninghame, Appendix.

The Parochial Records date back to 1656, and have been kept with tolerable regularity until comparatively recent times.

A considerable town has, in progress of time, sprung up around the ancient fabric of St Winnin. In 1841, the population within its boundaries amounted to 5251, a considerable increase having been occasioned in later years by mining and railway operations. The town, or regality, was governed by a Baron Bailie, appointed by the Eglintoun family.

### Eminent Persons connected with the Parish.

Under this head may be mentioned *Robert Bailie*, afterwards the celebrated Principal of the University of Glasgow, and author, besides other works, of those letters and journals which throw so much light on the history of his own times. In 1622, he received Episcopal orders from Archbishop Low of Glasgow, and became tutor to the son of the Earl of Eglintoun, by whom he was presented to the living of Kilwinning. The exact period of his incumbency here is not ascertained. In 1626, he was admitted a regent in the college of Glasgow, and, having opposed the new ecclesiastical arrangements of Archbishop Laud, he was chosen to represent the Presbytery of Irvine in the famous General Assembly of 1638.

*James Fergusson*, of the Kilkerran family. He was esteemed by his contemporaries as a man of great piety and learning. He was invited to be Professor of Divinity in the University of Glasgow, but modestly refused. His works are, an " Exposition of the Epistle to the Galations, Ephesians," &c. and a volume of sermons, delivered at Kilwinning in 1652, entitled " a Brief Refutation of the Errors of Toleration, Erastianism, Independency, and Separation." This work was publised after his death. He died about the year 1666.

The late *Dr Ritchie*, Professor of Divinity in the University of Edinburgh, was minister of Kilwinning for a few years, between 1798 and 1802.

## FAMILIES IN THE PARISH OF KILWINNING.

### EGLINTOUN OF EGLINTOUN.

The large and valuable estate of Eglintoun, extending to upwards of 1700 acres in the parish of Kilwinning, belonged of old to the *Eglintouns of Eglintoun*, a distinguished and very ancient family. The first of them recorded appears to have been

*Eglin*, Lord of Eglintoun, in the reign of Malcolm King of Scots.[*] He was the father of

*Bryce*, who was the father of

*Hugh*, whose son and heir

*Rodolphus de Eglintoun*, occurs in a contract with the town of Irvine in 1205.[†]

The next who appears is

*Radulphus de Eglintoun*, probably grandson of the previous Rodolphus. His name is in the roll of the *Magnates Scotiæ*, who submitted to Edward I., 1296.

*Hew Lord Eglintoun* had various charters of lands from David II. Amongst others a charter of the lands of Bondington and half lands of Nortoun, in the barony of Rathow, in Lothian, and ane annual furth of Westhall. " Hugone Domino de Eglyntoun " occurs as a witness in a charter of confirmation by David II. to the monks of Kilwinning. He was Justiciary of Lothian in 1631, and one of the convention held, 1st September 1367, at Muirhouslaw, and from thence adjourned to Roxburgh, relative to the affairs of the Marches. " Hugo de Eglintoun, miles " had a confirmation of the lands of Nortoun, &c. from Robert II. in 1371; also of the lands of Allertoun, in the barony of Kilbryde, in Lanarkshire, the eight shilling land of Westhall, in the county of Edinburgh, and of the lands of Gyffeyn, in Kyle-Stewart, in the same year. Sir Hew de Eglintoun seems to have been twice married,[*] first to the heiress of Ardrossan, through whom that property came into the family, and by whom he had a daughter, *Elizabeth*, married to Sir John

---

[*] Malcolm Canmore reigned between 1057 and 1093.
[†] In this document Rodolphus is described as son and heir of Hugh, the son of Bryce, the son of Eglin, Lord of Eglintoun, in the reign of Malcolm King of Scots.

[*] Robertson corrects Douglas in reference to this. There is no other way of reconciling the facts, unless indeed there had been two Sir Hew de Eglintouns, the former married to the heiress of Ardrossan, and the latter to the King's sister, without issue.

Montgomerie in 1361; secondly to *Egidia*, half-sister to Robert II. and widow of Sir James Lindsay of Crawford, by whom it is supposed he had no issue. In 1372, he had a charter from Robert II., "Dilecto fratri nostro Hugoni de Eglyntoun, militi, et carrissime sorori nostre Egidie de Lyndesay sponse ejus, terre de Bonyngtoun, medietatis terre de Nortoun, cum dominio terrarum de Westhallis et del Cotraw, et quatuor marcarium et octo solidorum annui redditus ex dictis terris de Westhallis et Cotraw, in vic. de Edynburgh; apud Perth, 28 Junii, an. reg. 2d."

Also a charter of the forfaultrie of Michael de Lardener; of certain annuals within the sheriffdom of Air, whilk Robert de Bruys resigned, viz. 50s. out of Drumdow, 8s and 4d out of Stayre, 33s 4d out of Cars, 40s out of Monyhagane; and to Hew de Eglyntoun, knight, and Egidia, his wife, sister of the King, of the lands of Lochlebogside, in Renfrewshire. Robert II. gives charter confirming a contract dated 21st March 1374, betwixt Hew de Eglintoun, brother to the King, on the one part, and Hew de Aldestoun, on the other part," in reference to certain lands in Stirlingshire. The last of the Crown charters in which Sir Hew's name appears is a new grant to him "et Egidie de Lyndisav sorori Regis sponse suc," of the lands of Westhall and Cotraw," &c.

Sir Hugh is said to have died about 1374, but it is probable he lived some years beyond this. Robert II., from whom he obtained the last charter quoted, without date, lived till 1790. He is supposed to have been "the gude Schir Hew of Eglyntoun," mentioned in Dunbar's "Lament for the Death of the Makars;" and to his muse are attributed the romances of "Arthur" and "Gawan," and the "Epistle of Susanna," pieces not known—their names only being preserved in Wintoun's Chronicle.

On the death of Sir Hew de Eglintoun, the estates of Eglintoun and Ardrossan passed to the Montgomeries of Eagleshame, who quartered the arms of Eglintoun with their own, and made Eglintoun their chief residence afterwards.

### MONTGOMERIES OF EGLINTOUN.

"The first we find of that name," says the Broomlands MS. "is Roger, Earl of Montgomery, who lived in the Province of Normandy in France, in the year 906, who had a son called Earl Roger of Montgomery, who had a son called William Earl of Montgomery, who married Elizabeth Tripon, daughter of Janet, Dutchess of Normandy, and also daughter to the Earl of Botinet, who bore to him a son called *Roger* Earl of Montgomery, who came to England with William the Conqueror, to whom he was allied. He made him Constable of his army, which he commanded in that memorable battle of Hastings, in Sussex, which was fought in the year 1066, where Harold, King of England, was slain, and the victory and crown of England accrued to King William the Conqueror, for which singular service the said King William bestowed upon him very great gifts, and gave him the territories and honours of Earl of Arundel, Salisbury, and Chester."[*]

*Arnulph de Montgomerie*, Lord or Earl of Pembroke, fourth son of Roger, was the ancestor of the house of Eglintoun. When Henry usurped the crown of England, the house of Montgomerie remained faithful to the elder son of the Conqueror, Robert Duke of Normandy. Earl Arnulph crossed over to Ireland to obtain supplies for the war from Murtagh O'Brien, King of Munster, and was so kindly received that not only was his request granted, but he obtained the hand of his daughter in marriage.[†] The name of this Princess was Lafracoth, which name, in the *Historie de la Noblesse*, we find curiously applied, under a French form to her father, who is called "Lafracotte, Roi d'Irland." The name of this Princess would be thus pronounced by her husband's family, and some genealogical record may have existed in Eglintoun Castle before its destruction in 1528, in which it had been stated that Arnulph, the ancestor of the Scottish house of Montgomerie, had married "the daughter, Lafracotte, of the King of Ireland;" and when their cadet, Robert, went to France (about 1480) he has been careful to get proofs of his descent from the ancient French house transcribed, but a mistake has been made in the transcription,[*] and had suffered in the above mentioned

---

[*] The Broomlands manuscript, from which the above extract is taken, was composed by Hugh Montgomerie of Broomlands, about 1760. The earlier portion of it is presumed to have been gleaned from some ancient record of the family, a fragment of which may have escaped the general destruction of the evidents of Eglintoun in 1528, when the castle was consumed by fire in a foray led on by the Master of Glencairn. In a "Genealogy of the Family of Montgomerie, compiled from various authorities by the late Captain J. H. Montgomerie, 76th Regiment, formerly of Barnshill, in the County of Ayr," the MS. of which was kindly placed in our hands for some time by the author, the origin of the Montgomeries is traced back to the Counts of Hiemes, a territory in Lower Normandy forming part of the ancient Armorica, "who were hereditary before the reign of Pepin, who ascended the throne of France, in the year 749." Much of the writer's data is inferential, consequently it may be doubted, still his deductions are extremely probable.

[†] Welsh Chronicles.

[‡] This is a sample of Captain Montgomerie's style of hypothetical, though probable deduction.

manner; yet the passage shows indubitably that the marriage had been recorded in the family, in which record the French idiom had been retained in writing the lady's name. Indeed the genealogy of the Eglintoun family in *Lodge's Peerage*, of which Hugh fourth Earl of Mount-Alexander (in Ireland) was the author, bears the same testimony. The year 1100 is presumed to have been the date of Arnulph's marriage. In 1102 he, together with his brother, was expelled from England, and after Henry's reduction of Normandy in 1106, it is presumed that he took refuge with his mother's relations, the Countess of Perche, and her son, who was sovereign of most of the Province.

*Philip de Montgomerie*, the son of Arnulph, born about 1101, appears to have been named after his gallant uncle, who died at Jerusalem, about 1099, during the first crusade. Boethius, whose History of Scotland was published in 1526, before Eglintoun castle was destroyed, states that the ancestor of the Montgomeries came out of France; and at that time there is reason to believe that evidence existed that such was the fact, and that Philip de Montgomerie, the son of Arnulph, accompanied David Earl of Huntingdon from France to Scotland. That Prince, afterwards David I., it is well known, undertook a journey to France, for the purpose of visiting Bertrand d'Abbeville, the founder of the Tyronensian order of monks. Before he reached Tyrone, however, the monk was dead; but he brought over with him an abbot and twelve monks of this order, and placed them at Selkirk, where some of them had been settled about three years earlier. During this visit it is naturally presumed that David could not fail to make the acquaintance of the houses of Perche and Montgomerie, sovereigns of Tyrone, which accounts for the introduction of Philip, son of Arnulph, to the Scottish Prince, who accepted of an offer to accompany him to Scotland. Philip would no doubt do so the more readily that none of his father's territory in Wales remained to him, and from the enmity of Henry, who had expelled his family from their seats in Normandy.

I. PHILIP DE MONTGOMERIE, on settling in Scotland, appears to have been called the Welshman, or Cymbricus, synonymical with Cambricus. As his son and heir, *Robert* was called MacCymbric in Gaelic, a name inapplicable, if, as some would make out, Robert had been an emigrant from the English county of Salop, but proper if he was the son of a native of Pembroke. Philip married Lady Margaret, daughter of Cospatrick second Earl of March, which Earl died 17th September 1139; and from the circumstance of

his grandson, Sir John, having had children grown up before the end of the century, we should conclude that this marriage had taken place about 1118. It farther appears that the manor and castle of Thorntoun had come into the possession of the family at this period,* and in all likelihood as the Lady Margaret's dowry. It is about three miles and a half from Dunbar, and immediately opposite Innerwick Castle, divided from it only by a ravine, through which a stream flows, where the Montgomeries had early possessions, the latter holding from the Stewarts. The issue of this marriage was:—

1. Robert, who succeeded.
2. Hugh, who married Elizabeth, daughter of Adam de Gordon. He was a faithful attendant of Malcolm IV. on his northern expedition against the rebellious province of Moray, the inhabitants of which he reduced to subjection.† He was a resident at the court of that monarch, hence called "Aulicus," and designated of Boudjedworth, which, having been part of the royal domain of Jedburgh possessed by Malcolm IV., appears to have been the official residence of Hugh de Montgomerie. This designation proves that the Hugh de Montgomerie, son of Philip, of the Broomlands Manuscript, was the same with the Hugh de Montgomerie, "Aulicus," of the Macfarlane MS. By his said wife, Lady Margaret Dunbar, as she is called in the Broomlands MS., a name, as is well known, taken by the Earls of March, he had issue a son and daughter, viz.—
    1. Adam, who would appear to have been nephew of Richarde de Gordon, Lord of Gordon, who died about 1200. He probably married an heiress of the family of Constantine of Shropshire, some of whom had settled and obtained lands in Scotland, as appears from the chartularies. Adam de Montgomery, who died 18th Edward I., may have been his lineal descendant, and inheritor of his lands. From the arms of the next mentioned, there is reason to believe that they were descended from this branch.
    2. Egidia, or Giles de Montgomerie, who is mentioned in the Macfarlane MS.

There is every reason to believe that Philip de Montgomerie died soon after the birth of his sons.

II. Robert de Montgomerie, or Mundegrumbi, as we find it written, succeeded him in his lands of Thorntoun ‡ of Innerwick, which appear to have paid tithes to the Monks of Kelso. He was called MacCambric, or son of the Welshman.‖ He is designed Vice Comes of Lanerk in the mortification of Innerwick, and in another of a ploughgate of land of Innerwick, which last was granted to Nigellus de Constantine. He is also witness to the endowment charter of Paisley, by Walter, son of Alan, the Lord High Steward, between the years 1164 and 1174, on the 2d February of which last year, the Bishop of Glas-

---

* Broomlands MS. † Ibid. ‡ Ibid.
‖ That the Scots called Robert de Montgomerie MacCambric, clearly infers that his father was known to them as a Welshman, a fact they could not ascertain from his French name, though his family had added Welsh conquests to their English Earldoms.

gow, another witness of the same charter, died. He was also witness to another charter of the said Walter, inter 1173 et 1177, between which last date and 1180, he is said to have died. He was succeeded in his estate of Eaglesham, granted to him by the Lord High Steward, and Thorntoun, by his eldest son and heir,[*]

III. John de Montgomerie, miles. He married Helen, one of the daughters and co-heiresses of Robert de Kent of Innerwick, with whom he obtained a part of the estate of her father, which was held under the Steward of Scotland. This appears by a charter on the division of his lands, to which, amongst others, Alan de Mundegumorie, son of Sir John, is a witness, about 1190. It appears from the endowment charter of Paisley, that the church and tithes of Innerwick were granted to Paisley Abbey, and that the Kent's lands were held in such a way, that the lands of the Montgomeries that paid tithes to Kelso Abbey, must have been other lands at Innerwick, viz. Thorntoun. Sir John left issue by his wife, Helen de Kent, three sons:—

1. Alan, who succeeded.
2. Robert, who is witness to several donations to the Monastery of Paisley, between 1200 and 1230.
3. William, who witnessed a donation of the church of Dunsyre to the Abbot and Convent of Kelso, between 1180 and 1199.

IV. Sir Alan Montgomerie, or Mundegumbri, the eldest son, succeeded his father. He is designated *miles* in the chartulary of Kelso; and in his father's lifetime got a charter of divers lands in " tenemento de Innerwick," and is witness to many charters of donations to the Monastery of Paisley, between 1204 and 1231. He possessed lands at Innerwick, in East Lothian, and in Lanarkshire, of which Renfrewshire then formed a part, as appears from the chartularies of Kelso and Paisley. He witnessed the charter granted by Walter, grandson of the founder of the Abbey of Paisley, of the lands between Old Patrick and Espedie, in the time of Alexander II., and two charters by Alan, the said Walter's father, in the previous reign. He was also a witness to the charter of Robert Avenel, of his wood of Polwarth, to Richard, Abbot of Kelso, in 1221, at which time he, Sir Alan, settled with the said Abbot about his tithes of the lands of Innerwick, which had been in dispute between him and the Convent.[†] He died before 1234, and left issue three sons:—

1. Robert, designed ' miles.'
2. John.
3. Henry, who, with his brother, Robert, witnessed a charter of Walter the High Steward, in the period between 1204 and 1248, as appears from the Chartulary of Balmerino, in which they are called brothers.

V. Sir Robert de Montgomerie succeeded his father, and likewise is designated *miles*. Robert de Montgomerie, knight, and John his brother, are witnesses to a charter of Walter, Lord High Steward of Scotland, upon an excambion of the lands of Ingleston with the lands of Inverurie, inter 1240 et 1248. He was alive in 1258, in which year he was witness to a charter by Patrick Earl of Dunbar to the Monks of Coldingham. Dying without issue, before 1260, he was succeeded by his brother.

VI. Sir John de Montgomerie, who was witness to a donation by Walter the High Steward, inter 1240 et 1250. He was designed of Eastwood,[*] probably before he succeeded his brother. He died about 1285, leaving issue four sons and a daughter:—

1. John, his heir.
2. Murthaw de Montgomerie, " of the county of Ayr," according to Wood, and whom Nisbet supposes to have been of Thorntoun. He swore fealty to Edward I. in 1296.
3. Alan de Montgomerie of Stair and Cassillis. In the Haddington Collection there is a charter to " Alani de Montgomery, filii quondam Johannis de Montgomery, de terris de Stahare, &c. anno regis 22. There is reason to believe that he had three sons.
4. Thomas de Montgomery, of the county of Stirling, who swore fealty to Edward I. in 1296.
5. ———— de Montgomery, married to Archibald Mure of Rowallan.[†]

VI. Sir John de Montgomerie, designated " del Conte de Lanark " in Prynne's Collections —the lordship of Eaglesham and Eastwood, as well as the whole of Renfrewshire, being then in Lanarkshire. He was one of the Great Barons of Scotland summoned to appear at Berwick in 1291, and was afterwards, with many of his countrymen, obliged to swear fealty to Edward I. Notwithstanding, it is understood that he afterwards joined with the Bruce as soon as he began to assert his title to the Crown. He married Janet, daughter of the Lord of Erskine;[‡] and dying before 1357,[‖] left issue two sons and one daughter:—

1. Alexander, his heir.
2. ————, William de Montgomery, who, in 1390, was witness to a decreet of the Baron Court of Cammethan,

---

[*] Another son may have been Alan de Montgomerie, witness to a donation to the Monastery of Paisley, " tempore regis Malcome," who died in 1165.

[†] Broomlands MS. The manuscript is silent regarding the name of the Abbot, which, from the date, should be Richard. Robert Avenel married the sister of Helen de Kent, Lady de Montgomerie.—CHART. OF KELSO.

[*] Historic and Descent of the House of Rowallane.
[†] Ibid.
[‡] Broomlands MS.
[‖] If Sir John lived till 1357, he was probably 99 years of age when he died. We find that in 1252 Sir John de Montgomerie and Sir John Erskine were witnesses to a donation to the Monastery of Paisley. These were the parents of this Sir John and his lady, unless she was the grand-daughter of Sir John.

in favour of Sir Alexander Stewart of Darnley; and William Montgomery, who, in 1450, had a papal dispensation to Mary Helen Sempyll, may have been a son or grandson of this second son.

3. Marjory de Montgomery, senior, who was cousin to John de Montgomery, father of Marjory, junior, joined with her in the vendition of Cassillis to John Kennedy of Dunure, which was ratified by David II. in 1361-2.

VII. Alexander de Montgomerie, the eldest son, succeeded his father. He seems to have been a man of ability and trust, having been employed on diplomatic missions to England, connected with the affairs of the state. In a charter by David II., he is designed " Alexander de Montgomery de Eglisham, filius Johannis de Montgomery," &c. dated 1357. The following year, 1358, he was one of the Barons despatched to England to treat for the release of their captive sovereign ; and on the 24th October of the same year he had letters of permission to pass through England on his way abroad accompanied by a retinue of sixty horse and foot. Hume of Godscroft says that the Lord of Montgomerie married a daughter of William first Earl of Douglas, by his first wife, Margaret, daughter of the Earl of Dunbar and March, and had issue by her :—

Sir John, who was at the battle of Otterburne. A manuscript in the British Museum says, " Iste John Montgomery fuit nepos Magni Comiti de Douglas interfecti apud Otterburne;" and Camden gives the same testimony in his genealogy of the Scottish Peers. These agree with the ancient tradition :—

" Sir Hugh was slain, Sir John maintained
    The honour of the day ;
And with him brought the victory,
    And Percy's son away."†

As the legitimacy of Archibald third Earl of Douglas has been disputed, and the objections raised against it never having been satisfactorily refuted, it is therefore possible he had a daughter, of whose existence no documentary evidence has hitherto been discovered, which could establish the fact in a legal point of view. Such being the case, the authority above quoted may be considered sufficient to warrant the belief that a daughter of William Earl of Douglas, and half-sister of Earl James, really did marry Alexander de Montgomerie, or Lord Montgomerie, as his descendants continued to be very generally called, even before the peerage was granted, by whom he had issue a son, who succeeded him before 1388, namely,

VIII. Sir John de Montgomerie of Eaglesham and Eastwood. Nisbet says, on the authority of the original writs of the lands and estate of Bonnington :—" Alexander de Montgomery, chevalier, was his (John de Montgomerie No. VI.) son and heir, in the 1357, and is Dominus de Eglishame, as Sir John de Montgomerie de Egleshame, his son, in

† Ancient ballad.

the 1388, who obtained the great baronies of Ardrossan and Eglinton by the marriage of Elizabeth, the daughter and sole heiress of Sir Hugh Eglinton of that Ilk, one of the two great Justiciaries of Scotland in the reign of King David the second, anno 1361, by Giles, or Egidia, his wife, daughter of Walter the Great Steward of Scotland, and sister to King Robert II. The facts are well vouched from the original writs of the lands and estate of Bonnington, in Edinburghshire, which this lady gives to Alexander Montgomery, her second son, with consent of John Montgomery of Ardrossan, her eldest son."* It appears from this statement, that Sir John de Montgomerie, of whom we are now treating, is described in the writs of Bonnington, as son of Alexander, and grandson of John de Montgomerie. There is, however, a difficulty here, as already noticed under the head " Eglintoun of Eglintoun." The daughter of Sir Hugh de Eglintoun, by Egidia, sister of Robert II., could not be marriageable in 1361, seeing that her first husband was alive in 1357. The difficulty is attempted to be got over by supposing that, although contracted in 1361, the union may not have taken place till 1372, when Elizabeth de Eglintoun would be in her fifteenth year ;† still, though this were possible, it does not greatly mend the matter, as the eldest son of that marriage, who fought and fell at Otterburne, in 1388, would only be in his fifteenth year. *Probability* is therefore opposed to the alleged facts of Nisbet, in obviating the difficulty, by supposing that the heiress of Sir Hugh de Eglintoun was by his first marriage—the heiress of Ardrossan—and not by Egidia, the King's sister.

Upon the death of his father-in-law, between the 26th June 1376, and 5th Oct. 1378, when his widow received a dispensation to marry " Robert de Bevachtyn, a nobleman," Sir John de Montgomerie succeeded to the lordships of Eglintoun and Ardrossan. In 1388, he and his eldest son, *Hugh*, fought and distinguished themselves at the battle of Otterburne, where the latter was

* Nisbet must be wrong in the date assigned to this transaction, 1387, which ought to be 1397: for Sir John de Montgomerie was dead when his lady granted Bonnington to her second son, and he was living in 1396, when he granted to William de Blakeford, on the 8th October of that year, the lands of Ardbennane.

† That is presuming that Sir Hugh de Eglintoun and Egidia were married in 1358, the assumed date of the charter to Hew de Eglintoun of the lands of Bonnington. The lands of Bonnington and Nortoun were part of the dowry given to the Princess Marjory Bruce, by her father, Robert I., on her marriage with the High Steward. Amongst the charters of Robert I. there is one—" Charter to Walter Stewart in marriage with Marjory, the King's daughter, of the barony of Rathow . . . . the lands of Bonnington," &c.

slain. The spear and pennon of Percy were carried along with the body of the gallant youth to Edinburgh Castle, (from thence no doubt conveyed to the family burial place at Eaglesham or Kilwinning), and the trophies still remain in the possession of the noble house of Eglintoun. It is said that when the late Duke of Northumberland requested their restoration, the late Earl of Eglintoun replied—"There is as good lea land here as any at Chevy Chase, let Percy come and take them."[*] Sir John Montgomerie died before 1398,[†] and by his wife, Elizabeth de Eglintoun, who survived him, had four sons :—

1. Hugh, who died at Otterburne.
2. Sir John, who succeeded his father.
3. ———— to whom his mother gave a charter of the lands of Bonnington, in the barony of Ratho. He does not appear to have had any succession, as these lands returned to the chief of the family, and were included in the charter from James V. to Hugh first Earl of Eglintoun, dated 16th Nov. 1528.
4. Hugh, who may be presumed to have been born after the death of his elder brother, being of the same name. He was tutor to Hugh third Lord Montgomerie, who succeeded his father about 1480-1. He survived four generations of the chiefs of his family, and was probably 98 years of age at the time of his death, which occurred before 11th October 1484.

IX. Sir John de Montgomerie, Dominus Ejusdem, or of that Ilk, (by which title it appears that he was the male heir and chief of the French house of Montgomerie), succeeded his father before 1398. In 1402, he formed one of the chiefs of the Scottish army which invaded England, and was taken prisoner at the disastrous battle of Halidon Hill. He was in Scotland, however, in 1404, in which year he had occasion to introduce the reputed Richard II. to the court of Robert III. Tytler, in his History of Scotland, relates the circumstance as follows :—"King Richard II., it was affirmed, had actually escaped from Pontefract, and had found means to convey himself, in the disguise of a poor traveller, to the Western or Outer Isles of Scotland, where he was accidentally discovered by a lady who had known him in Ireland. He was treated, however, with great kindness, and given in charge to Lord Montgomerie, who carried him to the court of Robert III., where he was received with honour. It is certain that he lived and died in the Palace, within the Castle of Stirling, about nineteen years afterwards, and that he was buried with the name, state, and honours of that unfortunate monarch, Richard II." It is certain that a person, supposed to be Richard II., lived some years at Stirling, in the Palace, and died there. This is proved by the Treasurer's Accounts. Tytler obscurely hints at a secret negotiation carried on

by Henry IV. with the Lord Montgomerie, which he seems to suppose had reference to the dethroned King; but, as his lordship had taken him to court, and introduced him to the Scottish King, in the most prompt and honourable manner, there can be no room for suspecting him of any intention of betraying the unfortunate monarch.

Sir John Montgomerie was employed in various public duties, particularly in 1425, in reducing the fortress upon Loch Lomond, which was held out against James I. by Lord James Stewart, youngest son of Murdoch Duke of Albany. He died previous to 22d November 1429. He married Margaret, daughter of Sir Robert Maxwell of Caerlavrock, (ancestor of the Earls of Nithsdale), by whom he had issue three sons and three daughters :—

1. Alexander, who succeeded.
2. Robert, of Giffen, who is called the first of Giffen ; but as other branches of the house of Eglintoun were soon afterwards also designed of Giffen, it is evident that this and the other families of that designation could only have possessed portions of that extensive barony, of which the chief of the house of Montgomerie continued to be the superior. From the above mentioned Robert descended the Montgomeries of Machihill.
3. Hugh, mentioned in a charter, by Alexander Lord Montgomerie, dated at Polnoon, 29th July 1452.
1. Anne, married, 16th June 1425, to Robert Cuninghame of Kilmaurs.
2. Janet, married to Sir Thomas Boyd of Kilmarnock.
3. Isabel, married to Archibald Mure of Rowallan.

X. Alexander de Montgomerie, Lord Montgomerie, succeeded his father before 22d November 1429, as on that date "Alex. de Montgomery, Lord of that Ilk, is one of the assize in an action between the burghs of Renfrew and Dumbarton." He had, together with his brother-in-law, Sir Robert Cuninghame of Kilmaurs, a commission for the government of Kintyre, Knapdale, &c. dated 16th August 1430. He had charters, under the Great Seal, of a vast number of lands and baronies between the years 1430 and 1450. He was distinguished for his loyalty to James I. and his successor, and was a member, under both, of the Privy Council. He was employed in the negotiation of various important matters with England.

With regard to the creation of the Peerage of Montgomerie, it is difficult to assign anything like the precise date. Sir John Montgomerie, Lord of that Ilk, is stated to have been the first Lord Montgomerie, but his predecessors were styled Lord Montgomerie in history and genealogy many years previously. On the 3d July 1445, Alexander de Montgomerie, along with Duncan de Campbell, Patrick de Graham, William de Somerville, and Herbert de Maxwell, is styled "Parliamenti nostro Dominus," in the charter erecting the lordship of Hamilton, by James III., to which instrument these noblemen were witness. As the other parties mentioned were raised to the peerage, according to Douglas and other authorities, about that period, there is reason to believe that Alexander de Montgomerie, who was of equal rank, must have also been raised at the same time.

His lordship married Margaret, daughter of Sir Robert Boyd of Kilmarnock, by whom he had issue four sons and four daughters :—

1. Alexander Master of Montgomerie.

2. George of Skelmorlie, who got a charter from his father of the lands of Lochlibogside, Hartfield, and Coply.

3. John, who appears to have had lands in the barony of Giffen, and to have been designed of that property. He was witness to a proclamation at Irvine, 13th August 1488, by Carrick, pursuivant, and is there styled John de Montgomery of Giffen. He was ancestor of the distinguished house in France, of the Comtes and Marquis de Montgomery, into which family, in 1510, the feudal county of Montgomery re-entered in the person of Jacques de Montgomery, seignior de Lorges, who thus became Comte. His descendants in the male line are extinct, but in the female line the Marquis de Thiboutat became his representative.

4. Thomas, parson of Eaglesham. He must have been distinguished by his literary attainments, having been elected Rector of the University of Glasgow upon three several occasions, which office he held from 1476 till 1478; again from 1495 until 1497; and latterly from 1504 till 1510. He is called "nobilis vir" in the College Record; and is designed Thomas Montgomerie, parson of Eaglesham, dearest "eyne" to Hugh Lord Montgomerie, in a deed granted by that nobleman to Adam Alexander Montgomerie of Braidstone, son of his dearest eyne Robert Montgomerie of the Braidstane, given at the request of the said Thomas, and dated 3d January 1485. It appears that in his time, Alexander Lord Montgomerie had a property, and perhaps a mansion, at Glasgow, situated at the Dowhill, near the south boundary of the University grounds.* He died unmarried.

1. Margaret, the eldest daughter, married John Earl of Lennox, Lord Darnley. There is an indenture dated at Houston, 15th May 1458, between Alexander Montgomerie, knight, Lord of Ardrossan, on the one part, and Alan Stewart, Lord Darnely, on the other part, by which it was agreed that John Stewart, son of Alan, should marry Margaret, eldest daughter of the said Lord Ardrossan. By that indenture, Alan Stewart, Lord of Dernely, became bound to infeft the lady, his daughter-in-law, in 40 merks worth of land, viz. the lands of Drogalm and Drumley; and in case Alan aforesaid should happen to recover the estate of Lennox, then he was to infeft her in as much more as would make 100 merks of old extent. The issue of this marriage, from which Kings of Scotland and of Great Britain were to descend, was four sons and four daughters.

2. Janet, married a gentleman of the Kilmaurs family.

3. Elizabeth, married to John second Lord Kennedy of Cassillis.

4. Agnes, married William Cuninghame of Glengarnock.

Alexander Lord Montgomerie died after 6th June 1461, and before 14th October 1465, when his grandson and successor, Alexander second Lord Montgomerie, had a charter of the lands of Piltoun. His eldest son,

XI. Alexander Master of Montgomerie, carried on the line of the family. It is said erroneously that he acquired, in 1454, the heritable Bailliary of Cuninghame from Sir Alexander Cuninghame. This could not be the case, as he died in 1452, but it appears that he was actually in possession of that office several years earlier, by a grant from James III., dated 31st January 1448-9 :—"To Alexander de Montgomerie, eldest son of our dear cousin, Alexander Lord Montgomerie." There can be no doubt, however, that the family of Gleneairn, relations, and hitherto friends of the house of Eglintoun, were discontented, and considered themselves aggrieved by this high jurisdiction and regality having been conferred on the latter, and that a feud was the consequence, which raged between the families upwards of a century. The pretensions of the Gleneairn family seem not to have been well founded, as the commission appointed to inquire into the circumstances, composed of five persons of high rank, decided by a decreet arbitral, dated 12th January 1509-10, that Hugh Earl of Eglintoun had full and heritable right to the office of Baillie of Cuninghame; which would imply that the office, independently of a grant the Earl had received, 4th July 1498, had descended heritably to him from his grandfather, Alexander Master of Montgomerie. The Master of Montgomerie married Elizabeth, daughter of Sir Adam Hepburn of Hailes, who was next in command, under the Earl of Angus, of a Scottish army 4000 strong, which, in September 1435, defeated the English led by the Earl of Northumberland, at Piperdean, in the Merse, and by her had three sons and one daughter :—

1. Alexander, who succeeded his grandfather.

2. Robert. A charter was granted by Alexander Lord Montgomerie, in 1452, of the lands of Braidstone, "dilecto sue nepoti Roberto Montgomery." From him descended Sir Hugh Montgomerie, son and heir of Adam Montgomerie of Braidstone, who was created Viscount of Ardes, in Ireland; and his descendant, Hugh Viscount Ardes, was created Earl of Mount-Alexander, which title became extinct in 1757. From the younger branches of the house of Braidstone descended several families both in Ireland and Scotland, amongst others the Montgomeries of Barnahill, now Broomfield, in Lanarkshire, of which the late Captain John Hawthorn Montgomerie, of the 76th regiment, was representative.*

3. Hugh of Hesilhead, whose descendant, Robert Montgomerie of Hesilhead, left an only daughter, Mary, married to Macaulay of Ardincaple.

XII. Alexander second Lord Montgomerie, the eldest son, succeeded his grandfather before 14th Oct. 1465, and, according to Wood, soon after 1461, in which case he was the Alexander Lord Montgomerie, who, on the 10th Feb. 1465,

---

* College Records.

* Already noticed as the compiler of a "Genealogical Account of the Family of Montgomerie," in manuscript.

during the minority of James III., is mentioned in an indenture entered into at Stirling, between Lord Fleming and Gilbert Lord Kennedy, by which the former agrees that he shall not take away the King's person from the said Lord Kennedy, &c. Alexander Lord Montgomerie married Catherine, daughter of Gilbert Lord Kennedy, by whom he had two sons and a daughter :—

1. Hugh, who succeeded.
2. James of Smiston, from whom, we presume, descended Thomas Montgomerie of Smiston, Provost of Irvine in 1693.
3. John of Bowhouse, married a daughter of Ramsay of Montfode, but had no issue.
4. Helen, married to Sir James Bruce of Airth, and had issue.

He was succeeded by his eldest son,

XIII. Hugh first Earl of Eglintoun and Lord Montgomerie. He was under age at his father's death, and in consequence executed a revocation of all grants made during his minority, 11th October 1484. This nobleman was in great favour with James IV., who nominated him one of his Privy Council in 1489. He obtained a grant of the Constabulary of Rothesay, and was created Earl of Eglintoun in 1508.. His office of Bailie of Cuninghame provoked the hostility of the Cuninghames, whose chief was then Cuthbert Earl of Glencairn, and produced a succession of feuds. In 1526, the Cuninghames set fire to Eglintoun Castle, and in the conflagration the evidents of the family were wholly destroyed—a misfortune which induced James V. to grant to the Earl of Eglintoun a charter, de novo, of all his lands in Ayr, Renfrew, &c. In 1488, (17th Oct.) he was appointed to search for and punish trespassers in the jurisdiction of Cuninghame.* His lordship and the Earl of Huntley were constituted joint governors of Scotland by James V., in 1536, when he went to France for his bride, the Princess Magdalene. The Earl of Eglintoun was one of the Lords to whom the tuition of James V., when in his minority, was entrusted by James Duke of Albany, the Governor. His lordship married Lady Helen, daughter of Colin first Earl of Argyle, by whom he had six sons and eight daughters :—

1. Alexander Master of Montgomerie, who died young.
2. John, Lord Montgomerie, who predeceased his father.
3. Sir Neil Montgomerie of Lainshaw, whose male line is extinct—the heir of line being the representative of Robert Montgomerie, Esq., Lord Provost of Edinburgh, whose eldest daughter, Janet, married Mr David Spense, merchant in Edinburgh.
4. William Montgomerie of Greenfield, whose heir of line is the descendant of Jean Montgomerie, eldest daughter of Hugh Montgomerie of Broomlands, who married Mr Henry Eccles of the Excise.

---

* Pitcairn's Criminal Trials.

5. Hugh, who was killed at the battle of Pinkie in 1547. He married the daughter of John Lord Lyle.
6. Robert, Bishop of Argyle. He died unmarried, leaving three sons, who were legitimised by Act of Parliament, viz. Michael, Robert, and Hugh.
1. Lady Margaret, married to William second Lord Semple, and had issue.
2. Lady Marjory, to William second Lord Somerville, and had issue.
3. Lady Maude, to Colin Campbell of Ardkinglass.
4. Lady Isobel, to John Mure of Caldwell, and had issue.
5. Lady Elizabeth, to John Blair of that Ilk, and had issue.
6. Lady Agnes, to John Ker of Kersland, and had issue.
7. Lady Jonet, to the Laird of Cessnock.
8. Lady Catherine, to George Montgomerie of Skelmorlie, and had issue.

The Earl of Eglintoun died at an advanced age in November 1545. He was succeeded by his grandson, whose father was

XIV. John Lord Montgomerie, the Earl's eldest surviving son. He married Janet, daughter of Sir Archibald Edmonstone of Duntreath, by whom he had two sons :—

1. Lord Archibald, who died before his grandfather, unmarried.
2. Hugh, who succeeded his grandfather.

He was accused, 20th January 1556, of wounding William Cuninghame of Craigens. This had occurred on some public occasion, no doubt in consequence of the feud existing between the families. Craigens was Coroner of Renfrew. Lord Montgomerie was wounded in a battle fought with Sir William Cuninghame, Master of Glencairn, previous to 20th January 1507-8, in which several of the combatants lost their lives. He was unfortunately killed in the skirmish, on the High Street of Edinburgh, commonly called "Cleanse the Causeway," fought on the 2d May 1520, in which the families of Douglas and Hamilton were the principal actors. Christina, daughter of the Master of Eglintoun, married Sir James Douglas of Drumlanrig.

XV. Hugh second Earl of Eglintoun succeeded his grandfather. He married Marion, daughter of George Lord Seton, by whom he had issue :—

1. Hugh Lord Montgomerie.
2. Lady Agnes, married to Thomas Kennedy of Bargany.
3. Lady Margaret, died unmarried.

That the Earl, prior to his accession to the estates and honours of Eglintoun, had been one of the Justiciaries of Scotland, appears from the following entry in the Lord Treasurer's accounts in 1529 :—" To Lord Montgomery, Justice, remanand continualie at the Airis of Forfar, Perth, and Cowper, fra the first day of Januar to the xxiii day of Februar, to his expences ic xx li." His lordship died at Monkredding, near Kilwinning, 3d Sept 1546. By his last will and testament he directed his body to be buried in the choir of the Monastery at Kilwinning; and nominated Marion Seytoun, his wife, Hugh, his eldest son and heir, and James Houstoun, sub-dean of Glasgow, his executors. Hugh Montgomerie, his good-sire (Hugh Montgomerie of Smiston, we presume) was appointed tutor of his heir till he came of perfect age. His daughters, *Agnes* and *Margaret*, are mentioned in the codicil. He was succeeded by his son,

XVI. Hugh third Earl of Eglintoun. He married, first, Lady Jean Hamilton, daughter of James Duke of Chatelherault, and Earl of Arran, Governor of Scotland during the minority of Mary Queen of Scots; which marriage was dissolved in 1562, in consequence of the Pope's dispensation not having been obtained, the parties standing in the fourth degree of consanguinity. By this union there was no issue. By permission of the Bishop of Rome, he was allowed to marry Agnes (Margaret is stated to have been her name) daughter of Drummond of Innerpeffar, and widow of Sir Hugh Campbell of Loudoun, by whom he had two sons:—

1. Hugh Lord Montgomerie.
2. Master Robert Montgomerie of Giffen, whose only daughter, Margaret, by Jean, his wife, daughter of Sir Mathew Campbell of Loudoun, married her cousin-german, Hugh fifth Earl of Eglintoun, and secondly Lord Boyd, without issue.

1. Lady Margaret, married Robert first Earl of Morton, and had issue, of whom Sir Alexander Seton took the name and arms of Montgomerie, and succeeded his cousin, Hugh fifth Earl of Eglintoun. Lady Margaret was a celebrated beauty, and an amiable woman, as we learn from the poems of her admirer, Captain Alexander Montgomerie, author of "The Cherrie and the Slae," her cousin, and a gentleman of the Court of James VI.
2. Lady Agnes, married Robert Lord Semple, and had issue.

The Earl of Eglintoun was a steady supporter of the unhappy Mary Queen of Scots.[*] He was in arms in her behalf at Langside, in 1568, and with many other Barons of account, taken prisoner. The Earl was one of the leading nobles invited by the Earl of Bothwell to an entertainment in Edinburgh, with the view of obtaining their signature to a document approving of his marriage with the Scottish Queen; but it is said that, on learning what was expected of him, the Earl, in place of complying, left the house. As was the fashion at the time, the entertainment was given in a tavern, and called "Ainslie's supper," probably from the name of the landlord. It took place, according to some, on the 13th, and

to others, on the 10th April 1567. The Earl of Eglintoun was present at the Parliament in August 1570, called the Parliament with the hole in it, holden by the Regent Earl of Lennox, when Stirling Castle was taken by a *coup de main*, by Huntley, Lord Claude Hamilton, and others, on which occasion the Earl of Eglintoun was taken prisoner, with several other Lords, and carried off to Edinburgh, but subsequently liberated.[*] He died in the month of June 1585, and was succeeded by his eldest son,

XVII. Hugh fourth Earl of Eglintoun, who was barbarously murdered while crossing the Annock water at Stewarton on the 12th April 1586. This was done from old feud by a party of the Cuninghames and their friends, under the leadership of John Cuninghame of Ross, brother to James Earl of Glencairn, David Cuninghame of Robertland, Alexander Cuninghame of Aiket, and other gentlemen of the Glencairn family. The *Broomlands Manuscript*, after describing the tragical death of the Earl, says, in the true feudal spirit, "this unhappy fact cost much blood, and was afterwards honourably revenged by Master Robert Montgomery of Giffen, the nobleman's brother." The Earl, it seems, was twice married, first, to Lady Giles, daughter of Robert Boyd, by whom he had *Hugh*, his successor; secondly, to Helen, daughter of Thomas Kennedy of Bargany, by whom he had no issue, and who appears as his relict in the prosecution of the murderers of her husband.

XVIII. Hugh fifth Earl of Eglintoun, is styled in the letters of James VI., regarding the slaughter of his father, "our right traist cousing," and appears to have been a favourite of that monarch, who granted to him, his heirs and assignees, the dissolved Abbey of Kilwinning, with all its lands and titles, either in property or superiority, and erecting the same into a temporal lordship, together with the patronage of the parish churches—Kilwinning, Irvine, Dunbarton, Kilmarnock, Loudoun, Ardrossan, Kilbirnie, Stewarton, Dalry, Dunlop, Beith, Stevenston, Dreghorn, Pierceton, Kilbride and Kilmaconnel. This grant is dated in 1603. The Earl was twice married, first to Lady Jean Hamilton, daughter of James Duke of Chatelherault, who died without issue; secondly, to Margaret, daughter and sole heiress of Robert Montgomerie of Giffen. Dying without issue in 1613, he was succeeded, according to a contract between the Earls of Eglintoun and Wintoun, by Sir Alexander Seton of Foulstruther, who took the name and arms of Montgomerie, as well as the title of Earl of Eglintoun.[†] James

---

* Nimmo's Stirlingshire.　　　† Broomlands MS.

VI., then occupying the British throne, upon learning the circumstance, ordered his Privy Council of Scotland to convene Sir Alexander before them and discharge him from using the title of Earl of Eglintoun, as he was not the heir male of that family.* The Council accordingly wrote, addressing him "Mr Alexander Seton," but he refused to compear by that title, at the same time giving his reason, through the medium of Sir William Seton, his uncle, for adopting the title of Earl of Eglintoun, which was that he had been served heir to his cousin the late Earl. His Majesty, however, would not allow him to use the title, which was kept in abeyance for two years. He then assumed it again, having married Lady Anne Livingstone, daughter of the Earl of Linlithgow, and one of the maids of honour to the Queen. It is understood that Court influence was used to induce the King to accede to the title going to the son of the Countess of Wintoun, Lady Margaret Montgomerie, eldest daughter of Hugh third Earl of Eglintoun.

XX. Alexander sixth Earl of Eglintoun was her second surviving son. The *Broomlands MS.* says: "This Earl was among the number of those peers who engaged themselves against the King in the year 1638, upon the first commencing of our bloody civil war. He had the command of a regiment of the army that was sent to Ireland in the year 1642, towards the suppressing of the rebellion there. He was likewise personally engaged in the battle of Long-Marston-Moor, which was in the year 1643, in the service of the Parliament of England against the King, where he behaved with abundance of courage, yet his lordship still retained a respect and affection for his Majesty's person, and no man more abominated the murder of the King than he. He heartily concurred in, and was extremely satisfied with, the restoration of King Charles the Second, by whom he was constituted Captain of his Guards of Horse, in the year 1650; and next year, while he was raising forces in the western parts for the King's service, he was surprised at Dumbarton by a party of English horse, and sent prisoner to the town of Hull; and afterwards removed to Berwick-upon-Tweed, suffering likewise the sequestration of his estate, till the Restoration reponed in the year 1660." His lordship was one of the Privy Council of Charles I., and took a considerable share in the parliamentary business of the troublous times in which he lived. At the battle of Long-Marston-Moor, while the Earl was fighting for the liberty of the subject, his son, the Lord Montgomerie, was present on the side

of the King. In 1646, it appears that both he and his eldest son were present at the Camp at Dunse Law, in command of their respective regiments, forming part of the army of Covenanters, when King Charles, though at the head of a large army, "stooped to a treaty with his Scottish subjects. This treaty was soon broken, and the following year Dunse Law again presented the same edifying spectacle of a Presbyterian army; but the Scots were not contented with remaining there. They passed the Tweed, and in a skirmish at Newburn the English troops showed either more dissatisfaction or greater cowardice than at any former period." There is a tradition that during the usurpation of Cromwell, the Earl retired to the Castle of Little Cumbrae, which island belonged to the estate of Eglintoun.* The Earl was sarcastically called "the pious Eglintoun," by his opponents. He was also designated *Greysteel*, from the colour of his armour. He was a zealous Covenanter, and greatly encouraged the Rev. Mr Guthrie and Mr Dickson, well known ministers of his time. He died in the month of January 1661. He was twice married, first, to Lady Ann Livingston, by whom he had five sons:—

1. Hugh Lord Montgomerie.
2. Sir Henry, of Giffen, who died without issue.
3. Sir Alexander, a Colonel in Ireland, where he died without issue.
4. Col. James, of Coilsfield, ancestor of the present Earl of Eglintoun.
5. Major-General Robert Montgomerie was severely wounded at Marston-Moor, where he fought in his father's regiment. He defeated the English army, under Cromwell, previous to the battle of Dunbar, to which place the English retreated, in an action fought near Musselburgh, on the 31st July 1650. The following is the account of this affair in Balfour's Annals:—"One Wedinsday, 31 of July, Gen. Major Rob. Montgomery, and Colonell Straquhane, led out a pairty against the enemy, of 2000 horse, and 500 foote, and beatt him soundlie; and if he had had 1000 more, they had routed his whole army. They killed to him 5 Colonells and L. Colonells; mortally wounded L. Gen. Lambert,† and above 500 souldiers, and returned with no great losse." When Charles II. suddenly fled from Perth, Colonel Robert Montgomerie, amongst others, proceeded in pursuit, and persuaded his Majesty to return. Towards the end of the year 1650, General Montgomerie had an affair with the English, and forced his way, by Kilsyth, killing seven of the enemy, and taking four prisoners. Immediately after orders were given to the forces in the west that they join with Montgomerie, and receive his orders. At Stirling, on the 7th of May 1651, the army of horse being divided into seven brigades, Major-Gen. Montgomerie had the second brigade assigned to him, consisting of the regiments of the Earls of Linlithgow and Dunfermline, and Lord

---

* The heir-male was Neil Montgomerie of Lainshaw.

* Amongst the Eglintoun papers, in a note apparently of the expense incurred during the civil war, this entry occurs—"for a Jewel to David Leslie, six hundreth pound sterling."

† This is an error. He was taken prisoner and severely, but not mortally wounded.

Cranstoun. The following account of the gallant conduct of General Montgomerie at the battle of Worcester, is taken from the Boscobel Tracts:—"Major-General Robert Montgomerie commanded the brigade stationed at Powick Bridge, on the left bank of the Severn, and was opposed by Fleetwood and Ingoldsby, who advanced under a brisk fire to attack him. Montgomerie, after maintaining his post till his ammunition was expended, was forced to abandon Powick Bridge in disorder; and the Protector having at the same time overpowered the equally gallant defence offered by Pitscottie and his handful of men, only 300 Highlanders (by which the Republicans were enabled to cross the Severn, and outflank General Montgomerie) passed the Severn on pontoons, leaving Montgomerie in full retreat towards the city of Worcester." In this hard-fought though unsuccessful action at Powick Bridge, General Montgomerie was dangerously wounded. The Broomlands MS. states that the General "commanded the horse at Worcester, in the King's army, where he received divers wounds, and had the misfortune to be taken prisoner, whence making his escape out of the Castle of Edinburgh in disguise, in 1659, he got beyond the sea to the King, and returned with his master in 1660, being one of the gentlemen of his Majesty's Bedchamber. He married Margaret Livingstone, daughter of James Viscount of Kilsyth, by whom he had James, his son, and a daughter who died without issue." It is not stated when or where the gallant General died.

1. Lady Margaret, married, first, to John first Earl of Tweeddale; secondly, to William Earl of Glencairn.
2. Lady ———

Lady Ann Livingstone, Countess of Eglintoun, died in Nov. 1652.* The Earl married, secondly, Margaret, daughter of Walter Lord Buccleugh, by whom he had no issue. This lady died at Hull, in England, were the Earl of Eglintoun was confined a prisoner, on the 5th October 1651. Her body was embalmed, and brought home by sea to Dalkeith.†

A contract was entered into between the Earl of Eglintoun and Hugh Montgomerie first Lord Viscount Montgomerie of Ardes, in Ireland, by which the latter acknowledged the former as his chief, and agreed to hold his lands in Ireland of him, a white horse, presented to the Earl when he came to Ireland, being the symbol of his superiority, and relatively of each other's successors. The late C. K. Sharpe, Esq., maternally descended from the redoubted *Greysteel*, had in his possession a copy of the agreement, the original of which had been preserved in the archives of the house of Eglintoun as late as the time of Archibald the eleventh Earl, Mr Sharpe's grand-uncle. This curious document, which Mr Sharpe saw and copied, was ornamented round the margin with some miniature likenesses of the Earls of Eglintoun of the olden time, amongst the rest of *Greysteel* himself, and probably also Lord Hugh of Ardes, and some of his ancestors. This curious relic of the days of chivalry is probably still in existence.

XXI. Hugh seventh Earl of Eglintoun. "He was a very perfect loyalist in the time of the civil troubles, and raised a troop of horse in the year 1643, with which he marched in person, and fought valiantly at Long-Marston-Moor, and several other battles and skirmishes; and continuing to adhere faithfully to the royal cause, he was therefore excepted out of Cromwell's indemnity."* Antecedent to this he and his regiment were in the Scottish army which invaded England in 1640. Lord Montgomerie's signature is one of those appended to the dispatch from the army after the victory obtained at Newburn. It appears that Lord Montgomerie, in consequence of his attachment to his Majesty, had been declared incapable of public employment—having been concerned in the "engagement against England"—and petitioned to be relieved from this grievance, which was at length granted. His lordship appears to have afterwards risen very high in the confidence of the Committee of Estates. On the 17th January 1651, it is "ordered that the Lord Montgomerie have 6 barrells of that powder wich belongs to the publicke, wich was carried to the Isle of Bute, for the defence of his house, for wich the said Lord is to be comptabell to the publicke for."† As the family of Eglintoun had no castle or honse in Bute, the house alluded to must have been the castle of the Little Cumbrae, which castle was surprised and burnt by Cromwell's soldiers in 1653. His lordship married the Lady Ann Hamilton, daughter of James Marquis of Hamilton, by whom he had, in 1653, one daughter, Lady *Ann*, married to James Earl of Findlater, and had issue. He married, secondly, Lady Mary Leslie, daughter of James Earl of Rothes, by whom he had issue:—

1. Alexander Lord Montgomerie, who succeeded him.
2. Mr Francis, of Giffen.
1. Lady Mary, married to George Earl of Wintoun, and died without issue. ‡
2. Lady Margaret, married to James second Earl of Loudoun, and had issue.
3. Lady Christian, married to John fourth Lord Balmerino, and had issue.
4. Lady Eleanor, married to Sir David Dunbar of Baldoon, and had issue.
5. Lady Anne, married to Sir Andrew Ramsay of Abbotshall, and had issue.

Earl Hugh died in February 1669,§ and was succeeded by his eldest son.

---

* Broomlands MS.
† Balfour's Annals.
‡ The Earl of Wintoune being but a youth married Lady Mary Montgomery, the Earl of Eglintoun's eldest daughter, (who stayed in the wel . . . . and was contracted there in the year 1662. The marriage feast stood at her father's house in the west country, 4th Sept. 1662.—Lamont's Diary.
§ Ibid.

---

* Balfour's Annals.
† Ibid.

XXII. Alexander eighth Earl of Eglintoun, who came early into the Revolution, and was named one of the Privy Council in the year 1689. He died in the year 1701, at London, and was buried at Kilwinning. He left issue by his Countess, Lady Elizabeth, daughter of William Earl of Dumfries :—

1. Alexander Lord Montgomerie, who succeeded him. "In 1658, Jan., the Lord Montgomery's sone being at London about his father's business in Parliament, in reference to his fyne, without consent of his parents, married privately the Lord Dunipice his daughter, a gentlewoman bred in England, but having no title or no portion."
2. Major Hugh, who died without issue.
3. Major John, who likewise died without issue.
4. Lady Mary, who married Sir Andrew Agnew of Lochaw, Bart.

XXIII. Alexander ninth Earl of Eglintoun, was of the Privy Council, and one of the Commissioners of the Treasury to King William the Third, in 1700, in which year he sat and voted in Parliament, in place of the High Treasurer of Scotland, on the King's Letter. He succeeded to the title of Eglintoun in 1701; was a Privy Councillor to Queen Anne, and one of the Commissioners of the Chamberlain's Court 1711. He was chosen one of the sixteen representatives of the Scottish Peerage at the general election in 1710, rechosen in 1713. During the Rebellion of 1715, his lordship actively promoted the training and discipline of the fencible men of Ayrshire, and met the Earls of Kilmarnock and Glasgow, and Lord Sempill, at Irvine, where a general rendezvous of the fencibles of Cuninghame was appointed to be held, on the 22d of August 1715. "At which time, upon a short advertisement, there appeared on the common of Irvine, 6000 effective men, well armed and in good order, with their proper officers, who all made a handsome appearance, and expressed a great deal of zeal and loyalty for his Majesty King George, and a firm resolution to defend his Majesty's person and government against the Pretender and all other enemies whatsoever. The town of Irvine had a company of artillery, besides their trained bands, with three pieces of cannon, mounted on an eminence, wherewith they saluted the respective nobility, gentry, and battalions, as they came up; for there were the Earls of Eglintoun, Kilmarnock and Glasgow, the Lords Sempill and Boyd, with the haill of the gentry in that jurisdiction, and most of the clergy. After they had performed their exercise they were dismissed for the time." The Earl of Eglintoun was a nobleman of good parts and solid judgment, very prudent and attentive; he cleared the estate of a load of debt, and made several purchases of land. His lordship was thrice mar-

ried—first, to Lady Margaret Cochrane, daughter of William first Earl of Dundonald, by whom he had two sons and four daughters :—

1. Hugh Master of Eglintoun, died at the University of Glasgow, in 1696.
2. Master William.[*]
1. Lady Katherine, married James Earl of Galloway, and had issue. She died in December 1757.
2. Lady Eupham, married to George Lockhart of Carnwath, Esq., and had issue. She died at Carneway, 1st December 1732.
3. Lady Grace, married to Robert Earl of Carnwath, and had issue two daughters.
4. Lady Jean, married to Sir Alexander Maxwell of Monreith, and had issue.

His lordship's second countess was Lady Anne, daughter of George Earl of Aberdeen, Lord High Chancellor of Scotland, by whom he had one daughter, Lady Mary, married to Sir David Cuninghame of Milncraig, Bart., and had issue. Her superior beauty is the theme of Hamilton of Bangour's warmest praise. His third Lady was Susanna, daughter of Sir Archibald Kennedy of Colzean, Bart. by whom he had three sons and seven daughters :—

1. James Lord Montgomerie, who died young.
2. Alexander Lord Montgomerie, who succeeded.
3. Hon. Archibald, who adopted the military profession; rose to rank in the army; and succeeded his brother Alexander in his titles and estates.
1. Lady Elizabeth, married to Sir David Cuninghame of Capringtone, Bart., and had issue. In her widowhood she retired to the village of Troon, where she lived in remarkable retirement for some years. She died at Edinburgh, 19th Feb. 1800, aged 95.
2. Lady Helen, married to Lieut.-Col. John Stewart, brother-german to the Earl of Murray, and had issue.
3. Lady Margaret, married to Sir Alexander Macdonald of Slate, Bart., and had issue. This lady was exceedingly popular in the Highlands, and whether her zeal in the preservation of the Young Chevalier arose from attachment to his cause, which is the opinion generally entertained, or sprung from sympathy for the adventurous and gallant wanderer, every one must admire the dexterity of her ladyship, and applaud her for at once doing a good action, and saving the government of George II. from the obloquy of shedding the blood of the male heir of the royal house of Stuart. Lady Margaret was mother of the amiable Sir James Macdonald, whom she had the grief to survive. Her ladyship died on the 30th March 1799. She had three sons, of whom Alexander, created Lord Macdonald, and Archibald, survived her.
4. Lady Susanna, married to John Renton of Lamerston, and had issue. She died at Blackadder, 27th July 1754. Her daughter married Charles Sharpe, Esq. of Hoddam, whose son was the late C. K. Sharpe, Esq. of Hoddam.
5. Lady Christian, married to James Moray of Abercairney, and had issue. She died at Abercairney, 19th July 1748.
6. Lady Francis.
7. Lady Grace. She married against the wishes of the family, and lived for the remainder of her life in estrangement from them. Her husband was a Cornet Boyne of Bland's Dragoons. The Broomlands MS. does not mention her marriage, but says she died without issue. She died at Edinburgh, 15th June 1731.

* The Peerage calls him Alexander; the Broomlands MS. William.

Susanna Countess of Eglintoun was amiable, accomplished and beautiful. A portrait of her ladyship when young was in the possession of the late Mr Sharpe. He had also a miniature of her in her 81st year, when she was a fine looking, stout old lady. Her blue eyes grew lighter in colour as she advanced in years. Allan Ramsay's well known pastoral of the *Gentle Shepherd*, published in 1726, was dedicated to her ladyship by Hamilton of Bangour.

Alexander the ninth Earl died in 1729, and was succeeded by his eldest surviving son,

XXIV. Alexander tenth Earl of Eglintoun. He and his brother Archibald were first sent to Irvine school, and afterwards to Eton. He was appointed Governor of Dumbarton in 1749; and one of the Lords of the Bedchamber to the King, on the accession of his Majesty in 1760, which he resigned in 1767. His lordship was chosen one of the sixteen representatives of the Scottish Peerage, at the general election, in 1761, and re-elected in 1768. Under the act for abolishing heritable jurisdictions, in 1748, his lordship got for the redeemable sheriffdom of Renfrew, £5000; for the Bailliary of the Regality of Kilwinning, £800; and for the Regality of Cuninghame, £2000. In all £7800 in full of his claim of £12,000. Possessing considerable talents for parliamentary business, it was to his patriotic exertions that this country chiefly owes the act which abolished the optional clause of the Scottish banks, by which they had it in their power to refuse payment of their notes for no less than six months after demand. The valuable agricultural improvements throughout the county of Ayr are chiefly attributable to his lordship's uncommonly spirited exertions, and very refined and correct taste. His lordship instituted an agricultural society, over which he presided for many years. His own farm of Eglintoun, with the plantations, contained about 2000 Scottish acres, the whole planned and executed with such taste as to render the ancient seat of the family one of the noblest and most beautiful places in Scotland. His enthusiasm for agricultural improvement is shown in a characteristic manner in a letter dated London about the middle of last century, which we have seen. It was addressed to his brother, and written on the eve of a duel—his lordship having been "called out" in consequence of some remarks to which he had given utterance in his place in Parliament. It was one of the coolest productions under such circumstances that could have been imagined. After various instructions, in case he should fall, the epistle concluded with the laconic injunction—"mind the turnip drilling!" Sowing turnips in drills was then a novel process in agriculture. His lordship escaped unhurt from the hostile meeting, but he experienced a rencontre of a more disastrous nature. On Tuesday the 24th Oct. 1769, his lordship left Eglintoun Castle on horseback, his carriage and four servants attending him. He stopped at Ardrossan parks, and observing two men on the sea-shore, one of them with a gun in his hand, a person of the name of Campbell, an excise officer at Saltcoats, whom he had detected killing game on his estates about twelve months before, but passed from prosecution on his promising not to repeat the offence, he rode up to and him insisted on his delivering up his gun, which the latter refused to part with. The Earl, alighting from his horse, went towards Campbell, who cocked his gun, and retired, keeping it forward on his side and thigh, pointed towards his lordship. The servants then rode up, and a conversation ensued, Lord Eglintoun reminding Campbell of his former offence, and insisting to have his gun—Campbell, on the other hand, acknowledged it; but added, that, if he had trespassed either formerly or at present, the law was open; that he was resolved not to part with his gun; that he would sooner part with his life; desiring Lord Eglintoun to keep off if he regarded his own. The Earl replied that he could use a gun as well as he, and ordered one of his servants to fetch his fowling piece from the carriage. In the meantime he kept still advancing, and gaining on Campbell, circling and winding to avoid the muzzle of the gun. Campbell retired backwards till he stumbled on a stone and fell. In rising he fired at Lord Eglintoun, then within three or four yards of him, and lodged the whole charge in his left side. His lordship, laying his hand on the wound, walked some paces from the place, which was wet, and within tide-mark, and sat down on a green hillock, telling his servants that he was mortally wounded—adding that he intended no harm to Campbell, as his gun, which had been brought from his carriage a moment before, was not loaded. He was put into his coach, and carried to Eglintoun Castle, where he arrived a little before two o'clock. A physician and several surgeons were there before he reached it. All assistance was unavailing. He employed himself in giving orders, and writing directions about his affairs, making provision for his servants, and comforting his nearest relations, in which he discovered a tenderness, composure, and magnanimity that affected every person present. He died next morning. Sincere and steady in his friendships, and possessed of all the more amiable virtues, his lordship's death was long and painfully regretted. The Earl was unmarried, consequently the succession devolved upon his brother, who had been brought up to the profession of arms, and served a number of years in the army,

XXV. Archibald eleventh Earl of Eglintoun. He was a general in the army, Colonel of the Scots Greys, Governor of Edinburgh Castle, and one of the Sixteen Representative Peers, at the time of his death. He was born about the year 1733, and brought up to the profession of arms. He served with his regiment in America, where he commanded a successful expedition against the Cherokees, a powerful Indian nation, who had been at war with the British, and committed terrible ravages upon the colonists. His lordship married first, in 1772, Lady Jean Lindsay, daughter of George eighteenth Earl of Cranford, who died without issue in 1778, aged 21; secondly, Frances, daughter of Sir William Twysden, Bart. of Raydon Hall, in Kent, and had issue, two daughters :—

1. Lady Mary, born 5th March 1787, who succeeded to the large property purchased by the ninth Earl, and entailed upon her and her issue; married, 28th March 1803, Archibald Lord Montgomerie, eldest son of Hugh twelfth Earl, and had issue two sons.
2. Lady Susan, who died in 1805, aged 18.

Archibald eleventh Earl of Eglintoun died at Eglintoun on the 30th of October 1796, and was succeeded by his cousin, Col. Hugh Montgomerie of Coilsfield. We therefore go back to

XXI. Col. James Montgomerie of Coilsfield, fourth son of Archibald sixth Earl of Eglintoun. Like his brother, Hugh Lord Montgomerie, he fell under the displeasure of the Church and Parliament, in consequence of his adherence to the party of the King, and was declared incapable of holding any public employment. On the 17th of December, 1650, however, "the Lord Montgomery's bill, and his brother James his bill, on the Committee of the General Assemblie's recommendation, declared capable of publicke employment, and all acts of restraint against them repealed." Colonel Montgomerie married a daughter of Eneas Lord Macdonald of Ares, and had issue two sons and three daughters :—

1. Alexander, who succeeded his father.
2. Hugh, succeeded his brother.
1. Margaret, married to John Chalmers of Gadgirth.
2. Mary, married to Dunbar of Machrimore.
3. Elizabeth, married to Kennedy of Kirkmichael.

Col. James Montgomerie died before 18th October 1675, on which day Major-General Robert Montgomerie was served tutor-at-law to Alexander, Hugh, Mary, and Elizabeth, his children. He was succeeded by his eldest son,

XXII. Alexander Montgomerie of Coilsfied, who died not long afterwards, and was succeeded by his brother,

XXII. Hugh Montgomerie of Coilsfield, who

VOL. II.

married, first, Jean, daughter of Primrose of Carrington, by whom he had three daughters :—

1. —— married to William Hamilton of Letham.
2. —— married to Thomas Girvan or Garven, Esq. Provost of Ayr.*
3. ——, married to —— Burnet, Esq. and had Hugh, who died abroad without issue.

He married, secondly, Catherine Arbuckle, relict of Hamilton of Letham, a lady, it is said, of great beauty, by whom he had :—

1. Alexander, who succeeded.
2. Margaret, married to John Hamilton of Jamaica, and had issue.
3. Catherine, died unmarried.

XXIV. Alexander Montgomerie of Coilsfield, who married Lilias Montgomerie, daughter and heiress of Sir Robert Montgomerie of Skelmorlie, Bart., and had issue :—

1. Hugh, who succeeded him and his mother, and became twelfth Earl of Eglintoun.
2. Alexander Montgomerie of Annick, who married and had issue, and died 8th July 1802.
3. Thomas, died at Dumfries, in Virginia, 13th August 1793.
4. Archibald Montgomerie of Stair and Belmont.
5. Lieut.-General James Montgomerie of Wrighthill, Col. of the 74th regiment, and afterwards of the 90th. He was some time Governor of Dominica, and latterly appointed to the command of the Western District of Scotland. He was M.P. for Ayrshire in several Parliaments. He married, but had no issue. He died at Skelmorlie Castle, his usual residence. The Peerage says he served with distinction in the west.

1. Frances, married, in 1798, to James Ritchie of Busbie.
2. Lilias, married to John Hamilton of Sundrum, and had issue.
3. Margaret, married, in 1772, to John Hamilton of Bargany, without issue.

XXVI. Hugh twelfth Earl of Eglintoun succeeded his parents in the estates of Coilsfield and Skelmorlie; and on the death of his third cousin, Archibald the eleventh Earl, he became, in 1796, Earl of Eglintoun, &c. He entered the army about 1756, and saw considerable service in America, during the seven years war, as a Captain in the 78th, and subsequently in the First Royals. On the breaking out of hostilities with France in 1778 he was constituted Major, and afterwards Lieut.-Col. of the West Lowland Fencibles. At the General Election, in 1780, he was chosen M.P. for the county of Ayr, and rechosen in 1784. He vacated his seat in 1789, by accepting the office of Inspector of Military Roads, the duties of which he performed for some years with much advantage to the public. At the breaking out of the war in 1793, he had the commission of Lieut.-Col. of the West Lowland Fencible Regiment. Soon thereafter he raised a regiment of the line, called the Glasgow Regiment, which was reduced in 1795. He had also the appointment of Lieut.-Governor of Edinburgh Castle.

* See vol. ii. page 323.

2

At the general election, in 1796, he was a third time chosen M.P. for the county of Ayr; but his seat immediately afterwards became vacant by his succession to the Eglintoun titles and estates. At the first subsequent vacancy in the representation of the Scottish Peerage in 1798, his lordship was chosen to supply the place; was rechosen at the general election in 1802, and created a Baron of the United Kingdom, 15th February 1806, by the title of Baron Ardrossan, with limitation to the heirs male of his body. He was Lord Lieutenant of the County of Ayr, which he retained till his death.

His lordship was magnificent in all his undertakings. He rebuilt the Castle of Eglintoun, which was completed in 1802, and enlarged and improved the pleasure grounds on an extensive scale. He also rebuilt the mansion on his paternal estate of Coilsfield. The greatest of his undertakings, however, was the construction of a harbour at Ardrossan, which he calculated upon becoming, in connection with the canal from Glasgow to Johnston, the great shipping entrepot of the Clyde. This gigantic speculation involved his lordship in debt, to clear which the estate of Eastwood, and various smaller properties were disposed of.

As an illustration of the princely state maintained by the Earl, we quote the following account of a masquerade, given by his lordship at Eglintoun Castle in 1809, from the columns of the Edinburgh *Courant* of that year:—

" Among the social festivities which enliven Eglintoun Castle in Christmas times, on Tuesday last, [27th Dec. 1809], a grand masquerade was given by the Lord Lieutenant of Ayrshire, which was attended by a very great portion of the fashion and gaiety of the country.

" About nine o'clock at night the company in masks began to arrive. When the Castle gate was thrown open, the transition from the natural winter night gloom, which pervaded the serpentine paths through the shadowy policy, to the dazzling effulgence of the brightness and splendour of the radiant halls, was superlatively striking. Fronting the door, in the entrance hall, a beautiful transparent painting of the Eglintoun arms was fixed; in the niche of the saloon, opposite the grand organ, there was another transparency, representing Britannia, and above the door of the breakfast parlour, one representing an Italian dance. These, we understand, were by Mr Smith of Irvine. The taste and execution displayed, prove him to be an artist whose talents may be an acquisition to the country. Besides the ordinary lights which illuminate the entrance hall and saloon, hundreds of variegated lamps, in various fantastic forms, from the walls, from the fronts of the galleries of the saloon, and from the lustres, united in shedding rays like the meridian splendour of the sun-beams. On the railing of the staircase, a variety of evergreen shrubbery served to display variegated lamps, and to give equal light. At the entry to the large drawing-room, a gipsy den was situated; and in the middle of the room, on the right hand side, an inviting arbour, chequered with flowers, near to which a luxuriant display of evergreen shrubbery, all tastefully set off with variegated lamps, served, with the splendid mirrors, the rich furniture, and the noble grandeur of the apartments, to impress the spectator with the idea of an enchanted palace.

" Here, about ten o'clock, the characters in the masquerade had nearly assembled. Mr Sylvester Daggerwood, in capital style, was among the first who attracted notice. He was busily employed paying his respects to the company, soliciting their patronage to his benefit next Tuesday, and furnishing them with a bill of fare of the performances. Two farmers and a few sprightly country lasses seemed quite in character. A considerable group of old gentlemen, who seemed to have held commissions of the peace in the days of George the II., possessed of great garrulity, and very courteous address, afforded gallants to some ladies of similar standing, dressed in hoops, toupees, rich brocades, and apparently in a plurality of petticoats. One old gentleman in scarlet and gold appeared to possess a peculiar knack of making himself agreeable to all; he also seemed to enjoy a waggish pleasure in quizzing a lawyer, who appeared to have little employment. A French hair-dresser industriously proffered his services; but he was in two loyal a society; instead of being encouraged by the gay and the fashionable, who seemed to dislike him for his country airs, and regard his bowing and scraping and fawning, as symptomatic of a spy, and as dangerous to be trusted as a domestic, he could only prevail on a clownish watchman to submit to his dressing. A german peasant, and a woman in the grotesque costume of the country, excited particular notice; many a sprightly waltz they danced together, for they seemed from Hungary, where the blasting influence of the Corsican satellites have not destroyed mirth and jollity. A joyous old fiddler seemed much pleased to be employed by them, and shook his elbows with as much spirit as they cut their whirling capers. A portly Dutch skipper and a few British sailors were well supported. A Jew appeared in very natural style, purchasing old clothes. A lawyer, a Turk with two ladies, and one with none, two Chinese, a doctor, an Indian Prince and Princess decked out with a profusion of gewgaws, a Hindoo Brahmin, a Pilgrim, and a Quaker, were all interesting characters. An interesting country maid, spinning with a distaff, a number of flower and fruit girls, especially one who trundled a wheel-barrow with apples, attracted considerable notice. A fine and appropriate figure of Diana, and also of the Goddess of Peace, drew general attention. Portraits of two of the noble family graced the walls of the apartment, dressed in the Highland garb; and the appearance of Master Montgomerie, a nephew of the Earl's, in that attire, served to excite lively emotion and complacent anticipation. The Earl and the Countess were not masked, and mixed in the social throng with their characteristic affability and condescension. Our limits prevent us from noticing further this numerous and happy society. About one o'clock they withdrew; and, after taking off their masks, and enjoying in the saloon a hearty laugh at the frolic they had been parties in, they adjourned to the dining-room, where a supper, in the most superb style of elegance and plenty, was served up, presenting part of all the delicacies of the season, a dessert of the most choice and rare fruit, and a profusion of the richest wines, &c.

"In the midst of this rich repast the gong sounded, and the ghost of the governor, in Don Juan, stalked through the saloon into the dining-room. Four fiddlers were seated on a form in the saloon. Astonishment struck three of them, and they started up; the fourth being seated at the end of the form, and blind, and not participating in the impression, as if to produce a kind of sympathetic contrast to his brethren, upset it, and fell on the floor.

"Among those who excited most attention in the characters they had assumed, were Lord and Lady Montgomerie, and Lady Jane Montgomerie, Sir David and Colonel James Hunter Blair, Colonel and Mrs John Hamilton, Mr Solicitor-General Boyle, Colonel Brisbane, Colonel Burnet, Colonel A. W. Hamilton, the Miss Hamiltons of Sundrum, Mr Montgomerie, and the Mr Montgomeries of Annick, Colonel and Captain White, Major Logan,* &c. &c.

"On such occasions poets are generally inspired, and we have of course been favoured with the following song:—

---

* Major Logan was a poet and a musician of no mean rank. His execution on the violin was altogether peculiar, and truly exquisite. As a wit his reputation was scarcely inferior to his namesake, the Laird of Logan.

"A BALLAD,

TO THE TUNE OF HOOLY AND FAIRLY.

In Eglintoun Castle I take great delight,
Where I'm feasted all day, and amused every night;
But to sing all its charms it would puzzle me fairly;
When I try at a rhyme it comes hooly and fairly.
    Hooly and fairly, hooly and fairly,
    When I try at a rhyme, &c.

My Lord is benevolent, friendly, and true
To his king and his country, he's rivall'd by few;
This place shows his taste, that he's showed up so rarely;
Would you see all its beauties, gang hooly and fairly.
    Hooly, &c.

With cheerful good humour my Lady behold,
Who is always the same, and ne'er frigid and cold;
She's kind to the poor, when she sees them clad barely,
And in giving relief ne'er gangs hooly and fairly.
    Hooly, &c.

Montgomerie sae noble, and his lady sae sweet,
In Coilsfield's gay mansion have all things complete;
Love and wealth in their cup, fortune does not deal sparely,
Or, in filling it up, e'er cries hooly and fairly.
    Hooly, &c.

Lady Jean in her cottage,* sae neatly set out,
I suspect is some goddess that's come here about,
To instruct a' our wives to gae trig late and early,
Or in cleansing their house ne'er gang hooly and fairly.
    Hooly, &c.

Now in this happy circle may pleasure abound,
And wit, mirth, and frolic, go cheerfully round,
Till Aurora peeps in for to hint that 'tis early;
But I'm sure when we part 'twill be hooly and fairly.
    Hooly and fairly, hooly and fairly,
    I'm sure when we part 'twill be hooly and fairly."

The Earl of Eglintoun had a considerable taste for music, and is understood to have been the author of several popular Scottish airs. He himself played on the violincello, and occasionally took part in the many private concerts given at the Castle. His collection of violins —most of which fell into the hands of those who could not appreciate them, when the Castle was refurnished some years ago—were understood to be valuable. His lordship was much esteemed in the county—over which he so long held sway as Lord Lieutenant. In the County Hall there is an excellent full-length portrait of the Earl, in the Highland uniform, painted by public subscription, as a memorial of his worth and services.

The Earl married his cousin, Eleanor, daughter of Robert Hamilton of Bourtreehill, by whom he had issue:—

1. Archibald Lord Montgomerie, who was a Major-General in the army in Sicily, from whence returning in bad health, he died at Alicant, 4th January 1814, and was interred at Gibraltar. He married

---

* Lady Jane had a model cottage built near Eglintoun Castle, in the arranging of which she took great pleasure. Her ladyship has been distinguished throughout by her condescension and kindness to the poor. The Infant School at Ayr was chiefly instituted by her ladyship's liberality, and it bears her name.

Lady Mary Montgomerie, eldest daughter of Archibald eleventh Earl of Eglinton, and heiress of large entailed estates. Lady Mary married, secondly, Sir Charles Lamb, Bart., by whom she had issue, and died 12th June 1848. To Lord Montgomerie she had

1. A son, born and died 18th December 1803.'
2. Hugh Lord Montgomerie, a very promising youth, who, on his father's death, succeeded to that title. He died young, at Eglintoun Castle, 18th July 1817, to the great grief of his aged grandfather, who raised to his memory a handsome monument in the Park of Eglintoun, with an inscription commemorative of his sorrow, and of his interesting grandchild.
3. Archibald-William, who became Lord Montgomerie on his brother's death, and succeeded his grandfather as Earl of Eglintoun.

1. Lady Jane, married to the late Archibald Hamilton, Esq. of Carcluie.
2. Lady Lilias, married, first, to Robert Dundas Macqueen of Braxfield; secondly, to the late Richard Alexander Oswald of Anchincruive. Lady Lilias died 16th Sept. 1845.

The Earl of Eglintoun died on the 15th December 1819, aged 80 years, and was succeeded by his grandson,

XXVIII. Archibald-William thirteenth and present Earl of Eglintoun. In addition to the title of Eglintoun, his lordship has assumed that of Wintoun, having been served heir-male general of George fourth Earl of Wintoun, in December 1840, George fifth Earl, who was attainted in 1716, having left no issue. The Earl of Eglintoun and Wintoun is Lord-Lieutenant of Ayrshire, and Colonel of the Prince Regent's Royal Regiment of Ayrshire Militia. His lordship married, 17th Feb. 1841, Theresa, widow of Richard-Howe Cockerell, Esq., Com. R. N., and has issue :—

1. Archibald-William Lord Montgomerie, born 3d December 1841.
2. Lady Egidia, born 17th December 1843.
3. Hon. Seton-Montoliou, born 15th May 1846.

The celebrated Tournament at Eglintoun Castle, in 1839, brought the Earl prominently into public favour, and he has since well sustained his part in the influential position which he occupies.

*Arms.*—Quarterly, first and fourth, azure, three fleurs de lis, or, for Montgomerie: second and third, gules, three annulets, or, stoned azure, for Eglintoun; all within a bordure, or, charged with a double tressure, counter flowered, gules. *Crest*—a lady, representing Hope, richly attired, azure, holding in her dexter hand an anchor, and in her sinister the head of a savage by the hair—in some emblazonments, on an escrol above, the word *Towless* or *Ropeless*, i.e. without a cable.* *Supporters*—two dragons, vert, vomiting fire;

* In allusion, it is said, to one of the ladies of the family having slain a ruffian, in self-defence, while on a sea voyage, and unprotected.

the crest of Seton, Earl of Wintoun. *Motto*—" Garde Bien."

*Seats.*—Eglintoun Castle, Skelmorlie Castle, and Rozelle House, Ayrshire; Polnoon Lodge, Renfrewshire.

Eglintoun Castle, the chief seat of the family, is a modern building—not older than the beginning of the present century. The old castle, a strong but rude and incommodious edifice, was taken down soon after the accession of the late Earl, who built the present mansion on the site of the former one. It is an extensive, solid, and regular building, in the castellated form, and was finished, we believe, in 1802. The former Earls had done much to improve the property, and beautify the grounds in the vicinity of the Castle; but the late Earl spared no cost in rendering it altogether one of the most delightful in the west of Scotland. The ground for several miles in the neighbourhood being almost a perfect level, the Castle is not observed until within the range of the immediate policies. Surrounded by old oak and elm trees, it stands completely secluded from public gaze; but it is on that account not the less delightful. If nature there wears none of those grand and majestic features, arising from the stupendous rock and falling cascade, she puts on her sweetest and most winning smiles, and,

" With bowers of birch and groves of pine,
And hedges flowered with eglantine,"

enchants the visitor with the richness and placidity of her dominion. The Castle stands on a gentle eminence, past which, on the east and north, a small stream—the Lugton—flows smoothly and gently; and where, in a summer eve,

" The springing trout in speckled pride,"

may be seen clearing the " crystal flood " in myriads. The policies—which are very extensive—have been laid off with great care, and a taste studious of effect.

## MONTGOMERIE OF SMISTOUN.

The property of Smistoun or Smithston, as it is now called, extends to upwards of 400 acres, and is situated within a mile of Kilwinning. It belonged, in former times, to a branch of the Eglintoun family.

I. JAMES MONTGOMERIE of Smistoun, second son of Alexander second Lord Montgomerie, by his lady, Catherine, daughter of Gilbert Lord Kennedy, was the first of this family.* He mar-

* Broomlands MS.

ried Katherine, daughter of Lindsay of Dunrod, by whom he had a son who succeeded. James Montgomerie of Smistoun was living in 1526, in which year (August 1), his name occurs in Pitcairn's Criminal Trials. He probably died previous to 3d September 1546.

II. Hugh Montgomerie of Smistoun succeeded his father. The Broomlands MS. states that he held the office of Bailie of Cuninghame, which must be erroneous, as that office belonged hereditarily to the Earl of Eglintoun. It is possible, however, that he was Bailie of the Regality of Kilwinning. Hugh Montgomerie, guidsire brother's son of Hugh second Earl of Eglintoun, who died at Monkredding, 3d Sept. 1546, was appointed by that nobleman tutor to his heir, Hugh third Earl of Eglintoun; and failing him others were substituted in his room. He was probably father of

III. Hugh Montgomerie of Smistoun, Bailie of Kilwinning, who married Agnes, daughter of John Cranfurd of Craufurdland. On the 19th November 1572, Hugh Montgomerie of Smistoun is witness to the discharge of letters of sleance granted by Alexander Cowpar to John Muir of Rowallane. Hugh Montgomerie was one of the assize who, on the 15th of May, 1602, at Irvine, retoured Patrick Montgomerie of Blackhouse, heir to his father John. He was alive in 1623, in which year "Hew Montgomerie, zounger," is mentioned in the testament of William Conynghame of Dankeith. His son,

IV. Hugh Montgomerie of Smistoune had succeeded, however, before 1621, in which year "Hew Montgomerie of Smeystoun, thair master," is a creditor in the testament of "Jonet Montfold, spous to Johne Muir in Darnehog, (Kilwinning), for the landis of Quhythirst possest be thaime, the crop, &c. 1630." He died in 1635. "Legacie.—At his dwelling hous in Kilwynning, the xviii day of October 1634 zeiris. The quhilk day the said Hew Montgomerie maid, constitute and nominat Margaret Peblis, his spous, his only executrix, &c. In the first the said Hew Montgomerie of Smeystoune levis to James Bannantyne his oy aucht bolls meill. Item, he levis to the said James Bannantyne his kindnes and ryt of the hous he presentlie dwellis in, lyand in the green of Kilwynning, callit the Cornehouse," &c.

This Hugh Montgomerie was probably the last of Smistoun. Hugh Montgomerie of Nether Smistoun, who obtained a decreet in the Bailie Court of Cuninghame against the Laird of Auchinharvie,[*] 25th February 1690, was probably a

descendant of that family. The property seems to have passed immediately afterwards into the hands of a family of the name of Miller, from whom it was purchased by the ancestor of the present possessor.

## MACGOWN OF SMITHSTON.

This family is descended from a Presbyterian minister in Galloway—Alexander Macgown, minister of Mouswald—who lived in the reign of Charles II., and was possessed of considerable property in borough acres and houses in the town of Dumfries. From him are descended, maternally, the families of Corsan, Meikle Knox and Copland of Collieston. His son,

I. THOMAS MACGOWN, was sometime Provost of Irvine, and in 1690 puchased the estate of Smithston from John Miller, the former proprietor. In 1673, he married Margaret, daughter of the Rev. Mr Shaw, minister of Irvine, by whom he had a son and two daughters. The youngest daughter, Anne, was married to John Cumming, M.D. Irvine; the other died unmarried. He died in 1711, and was succeeded by his son,

II. Alexander Macgown of Smithston. He married, in 1710, Miss Maxwell, daughter of James Maxwell, Esq. of Barncleugh in Dumfries-shire, by whom he had issue four sons —Thomas, William, John and James—and three daughters. He was succeeded by his eldest son,

III. Thomas Macgown of Smithston, who was born in 1718, and died on the 21st Dec. 1791. He was thrice married, but had issue only—a son and daughter—by his second wife, Helen, daughter of the Rev. Robert Baird, minister of Dunlop. He was succeeded by his only son,

IV. Alexander Macgown of Smithston, who was a Captain in the 2d or Irvine Regiment of Ayrshire Local Militia. He resided generally on his estate, which he improved, and beautified considerably with plantations, and built the present house. He died on the 9th of Nov. 1815. He married, on the 7th May 1804, Janet Tod, fourth daughter of Robert Tod, Esq. of Knockendale,[*] banker in Irvine, by whom he had issue

* Robert Tod of Knockendale and Doura died in 1804. He was twice married, first, to Marion Mure, by whom he had three sons and five daughters, all dead; secondly, in 1784, to Jane Montgomerie, a descendant of the Braidstane and Blackhouse family, by whom he had issue, four sons and one daughter, of whom the only survivor is John Tod, a Major in the Madras army, who was much employed on service during a long residence in India and Ava. He married, in 1845, Janet Glasgow Brown, daughter of Hugh Brown of Broadstone.

three sons and two daughters, of whom two sons only survived. He was succeeded by his eldest son,

V. Thomas Macgown now of Smithston, a Major in the E.I.C. Madras Army, with which he has seen much service both in India and China. He married, in 1834, Mary M'Lean, Midlothianshire, by whom he has issue:—

1. Alexander.　　2. John Tod.　　3. Thomas.

1. Rose Elizabeth. 2. Mary.　　3. Margaret Miller.

The situation of Smithston House, on the banks of the Garnock, is romantic and beautiful, having high and finely wooded banks.

## MONTGOMERIE OF SEVENAIKERS.

This family is supposed to have been a branch of the Montgomeries of Smistoun.

I. WILLIAM MONTGOMERIE of Sevenaikers was one of the jury who served Patrick Montgomerie of Blackhouse heir to his father John, on the 5th May 1562.[*] He died before 1612. His wife, Jonet Montgomerie, died in February 1629. "Legacie.—At Sevenaikers, the 27th day of Januar, the zeir of God 1629 zeiris. The quhilk day the said Jonet Montgomerie maks, nominats, &c. with hir guids and geir," &c.

II. John Montgomerie, the eldest son, is styled "of Sevenaikers" in the testament of Agnes Cunynghame, spous of Wm. Cunynghame of Clonbeith, in 1612. His name occurs in several testamentary documents down to 1635, when it appears as one of the witnesses to the testament of Hew Montgomerie of Smistoun. He died before 3d May 1643,[†] when

III. John Montgomerie of Sevenaikers was served heir to his father John Montgomerie. He was succeeded by his son,

IV. Thomas Montgomerie of Sevenaikers, who was served heir to his father 26th June 1673.

The property, soon after this period, seems to have passed from the family either by marriage or sale.

* Records of Bailie Court of Cuninghame.

† "Wm. Montgomerie, brother to vmquhile John Montgomerie of Sevin Aikers," died at Irvine in August 1661. "Inventar.—Item, the defunct being ane man vnmaried had nae other gudis, &c. except, &c. viz. in the first, be Johne Montgomerie now of Sevin Aikers, je vi lib. &c. quhilk was awand to the defunct be vmquhile John Montgomerie of Seven Aikers, be his latter-will and testament, quhairof the said John his sone ingadgit to mak payment, &c. Legacie.—Lykeas I leive in legacie to Wm. Montgomery, my sone, the soume of fyve pund sex s. viii d. money of Scotland, and to Robert Montgomery, my brother german, and the said George Girvane, the haill remanent of my said soumes of money, &c., equally betwixt them, &c. At Irving the 1st Dec. 1657."

## MILLER OF MONKCASTLE.

This fine property—upwards of 360 acres—belonged to the Monastery of Kilwinning. The first lay proprietor recorded was James Duke of Chattelherault, who, on the 20th July 1552, had a charter of the Over and Nether Monkcastles. The property afterwards passed to a family of the name of Hay. In 1666, John Hay of Monkcastle conveyed these lands, and the adjacent lands of Craigmill (that had also belonged to the Monastery), to John Wallace, minister of the Largs. In 1703, George Wallace conveyed them to Adam Cuninghame, advocate, whose sister, Jean, with consent of her husband, David Forrester of Denovan, alienated them in 1723 to the present family.

I. WILLIAM MILLER, the founder of this family, had two sons, *William* and *Alexander*, both merchants in Glasgow. Alexander, who purchased the lands of Monkcastle in 1723, died soon after, when the property devolved upon his brother,

II. William Miller of Monkcastle, who was served heir of conquest to his brother, Alexander, 26th August 1725. He married, 24th October 1727, Jean, second daughter of William Nimmo of Bridgehouse, Linlithgowshire, and had two sons:—

1. William, his heir.
2. Alexander, merchant in London, who died unmarried in 1760.

He died at the advanced age of 97, in 1757, and was succeeded by his eldest son,

III. William Miller of Monkcastle, who married, 5th April 1773, Agnes, eldest daughter and eventual co-heir of George Cuninghame of Monkredding, and dying in December 1802, was succeeded by his only child,

IV. Alexander-William Miller of Monkcastle. This gentleman married, in 1800, Miss W. Warner, second daughter of Patrick Warner of Ardeer, and had issue:—

1. William, his heir.
2. Alexander-Cuninghame, now in Australia.
3. Patrick, died unmarried.

1. Agnes, married to Col. J. S. Wyllie, of the 29th Madras Native Infantry, and has issue.
2. Ellen, married to Captain Lancaster, E.I C. service, and left a son.
3. Jane-Nimmo, unmarried.
4. Janette-Hamilton, died unmarried.
5. Catherine-Anne, married to William-Cuninghame Haldane, Esq., Edinburgh.
6. Rebecca-Henrietta.

Mr Miller died 5th March 1828. He took great pleasure in agriculture, and retained a considerable portion of the estate in his own cultivation. He encouraged spade husbandry, and frequently reaped from sixty to seventy bushels of grain from the acre, where little more than thirty could have been expected by the plough. He built the modern house of Monkcastle. He was succeeded by his eldest son,

V. William Miller of Monkcastle, advocate. He married, 5th Nov. 1830, Anna-Maria, second daughter of the late Admiral Campbell, Portuguese Royal Navy. He died in 1846, leaving two daughters and his only son,

VI. William-Campbell Miller, now of Monkcastle, a pupil.

*Arms.*—Argent, a cross, moline, sable, between four hearts, gules. *Crest*—a lion, erect, holding in his paws a cross, moline, of the second. *Motto* —Forward.

*Seat.*—Monkcastle is an elegant building, occupying a commanding situation. The old manorplace or castle still remains, almost hid amidst its coeval woods. It was the country residence of the Abbots of Kilwinning Monastery, hence its name—*Monk Castle.*

## HAMILTON OF ARDOCH.

The first of the Hamiltons of Ardoch was

I. Andro Hamiltoun, third son of Robert Hamilton, fourth laird of Torrance, whose ancestor was David Hamilton, second son of Sir James de Hamilton of Cadyow, who lived about 1420. Andro Hamiltoun had a charter of the lands of Airdoch from the Abbot of Kilwinning. There is a precept in the Register of the Great Seal to Andro Hamiltoun of Airdoch, 16th July 1543, making him principal "Janitor and Master of Entrie of the Places, Castles and Pallaces of our Souerane Ladie, during life." He married, first, Catherine Park. They had a charter of part of Boydtoun, Thorntoun and Kilbryde, in Lanarkshire, 3d June 1546; secondly, Margaret Stewart. They had a charter of Cathkin and Netherurd, 20th January 1546. The next of the name, most likely his son, was

II. Gavin Hamiltoun of Ardoch, who was a witness to a document of Walker of Dalgarvan, in 1556. He was probably the father of

III. James Hamiltoun of Ardoch, who had a charter from Alexander, Commendator of Kilwinning, of the lands of Ruchbank, Crummock, Airdoch, &c. lyand within the Bailliarie of Cuninghame, 10th January 1583. He and Johnne Boill of Kelburn were cautioners for "Johnne Boill of that Ilk, quha infeftit the Laird of Craig-

ends in the 34s. 4d. land of Groitholm," &c.[*] James Hamiltoun is thus noticed in the latter-will of Robert Boyd of Badenheath, in 1611—"Item, I leif to James Hamiltoun of Ardoch, my cousing, my auld servand, my best hors, my ganging sword, and fyve hundrith merkis money, to be distribut be him amang his bairnes, at his awin discretioun." Airdoch was a witness to a Disposition in favour of Johne Lynn of that Ilk, in the 20s. land of Haleis, in the paroch of Dalry, 14th December 1614.[†] He is supposed to have died about 1633. In 1619 he is mentioned as a creditor " of alterage teynds " in the testament of Margaret Paterson in Barcraigs. A "Robert Hamiltoun of Airdoch" is mentioned in a testamentary document in 1618, and again in 1633. He was no doubt one of the Ardoch family, though not the laird.

IV. Maister Gavin Hamiltoun of Airdoch, so styled from his academical education, seems to have been in joint possession with his father, as he is styled "fear of Ardoche" in the testament of William Buntein, in 1626. He was served heir of his father, James, 13th Nov. 1633, in the 18s. land of Rouchbank; the 16s. land of Crummock;[‡] the 5 merk land, of auld extent, of Ardoch; the 12s land of Cassill-land, with the messuage lying adjacent to Ardoch; the lands of Stokward, Woodmeadows and Woodland; ten ruids of land callit Newparksyde; ane merkland of new extent of Eistwray; the 6s. 8d. land of new extent of Carlinmyrebrig; and ane aiker in Byreflat, with the malt-kiln, house, the une, with the bake-house, in Kilwinning; ane aiker in Wttir-Byirflat; ane rig of land, house and yaird in the lands callit Stabilcroft in Kilwinning. He sold the Southbrae, with the superiority of that house, (built by Hugh Crawfurd), to Robert Peebles of Mainshill.[§] He died in 1637 :—

" Test, &c. Mr Gavin Hamiltone of Ardoch, Kilwining, quha deceist in the monthe of Aprile 1636.

" Debts awand Out.—Item, thair was awand be the defunct, &c. To his sister, Katherin Hamiltone, aucht hundrithe marks, &c. Item, to his sister Isabelle Hamiltone fyve hundrithe marks, &c. To Wm. Hamiltone his brotheir lxvi lib. xiiis. iiiid.

" Legacie.—At Wodsyd, the auchtein day of Aprile 1636, &c. The said Mr Gavin Hamiltone ordanes and appoynts his brother germane, Mr Claud Hamiltoun of Ulterwood,‖ in Kilwynning,

---

[*] MS. Contract.
[†] Brown's Protocol Book.
[‡] Ruchbank and Crummock are in the parish of Beith.
[§] Summons by the Earl of Eglintoun in 1734.
[‖] Mr Claud Hamiltoun of Uttirwood was thus the brother, not the son, of Mr Gavin Hamiltoun of Ardoch. He

his onlie executour, &c., during the tyme of his sone's minoritie, &c. Item, the said Mr Gavin ordanes his eldest sone and air to pay twa thousand merks of his debts. Item, he ordanes his eldest sone and appeirand air to give to Andro, his brother, the sowme of flyve hundrithe punds at the tyme the foirsaids oversearis sall think expedient. Item, to his brother, William, (the same). Item, to his sister, Jeane, (400 merks). He ordanes that his sones, Andro and William, (have in part of their portions certain lands)," &c.

Mr Hamilton had thus three sons—*James, Andro* and *William*—and one daughter, *Jean.*

V. James Hamiltoun of Ardoch was retoured heir of Magister Gavin Hamiltoun of Ardoche, his father, 4th August 1637. He sold Ruchbank and Crummock, in 1643, to William Ralstoun of that Ilk. His lands of Ardoch, &c. were valued at £240, 3s. 4d. Scots, about 1650. "James Hamiltoun of Woodsyde * was served heir, 10th January 1667, of Maister Claud Hamiltoun in Kilwinning, in three quarters of the wood of Kilwinning, &c. and the house and garden in Kilwinning. He married by contract, Barbara, daughter of James Mure of Caldwell, in 1637.† He had issue :—

1. John Hamiltoun, his heir.
2. Captain William Hamiltoun.

VI. John Hamiltoun of Ardoch died unmarried. He was succeeded by his brother. [See Hamilton of Ladyland, Parish of Kilbirnie.]

### CUNINGHAME OF ASHINYARDS, NOW BOWMAN OF ASHGROVE.

Ashinyards, including the Wood, extends to between 300 and 400 acres of good land, the latter especially. Both properties are in the vicinity of Kilwinning. The lands are well sheltered and ornamented with a considerable extent of plantation. The house, though originally intended for a suit of offices, has, by some judicious alterations, been converted into a commodious residence. This was the ancient Ashinyards, long the residence of a branch of the Craigends family, from whom is descended the present proprietrix. The first of the Cuninghames of Ashinyards was

I. JAMES CUNINGHAME, second son of Gabriel Cuninghame of Craigends, third in descent from Alexander first Earl of Glencairn. He was styled *Camerarius de Kilwinning*, and acquired Eisenyards, as the property was then called, from the proprietor, John Russel, in 1567. He married Margaret Fleming, daughter of Alexander Fleming of Barrochan, by whom he had two sons :—

1. Alexander, his heir.
2. William, who became a Writer to the Signet in Edinburgh, and married Rebecca Muirhead, daughter of the Laird of Lenhouse, by whom he had :
 1. Richard, afterwards of Glengarnock.
 2. William.
 3. Janet, married to Alexander, seventh Laird of Craigends,* to whom, among other children, she had a daughter, Rebecca, married to John Hamilton of Grange.

He was succeeded by his eldest son,

II. Alexander, to whom, in his lifetime, according to *Robertson*, he executed an instrument of resignation, in favour also of Mariotta Fleming, spouse of the said Alexander, dated in 1594. This, however, must be a mistake, as, from the following excerpt of his latterwill, he does not appear to have been married. It was, besides, his brother, James, who married Marcoun Fleming :—

"Testament, &c. and Inventar of the guidis, &c. quhilk perteinit to vmquhile Allexr. Cwnynghame of Elschinzairdis, within the parochin of Kilwynning, the tyme of his deceis, quha deceist in the moneth of Junii, the zeir of God Jai vi c. threttein zeiris, ffaythfullie maid and gevin vp with his awin mouth, &c.

"Legacie.—At Eschinzairdis, the xvii day of Jvnii 1613 zeiris. The quhilk day the said Allexr. maks and constituts James Cwnynghame, his lawfull brother, executour and intromittour with his guidis and geir, and ordanes him to fulfill his will and command heireftir, &c. And levis to Hew Campbell, his brother in law, and Jeane Cwnynghame, his spous vi c. merks, and desyris thame to imploy the samyn to the vse and proffeit of the bairnes ; and levis to Johnn Cwnynghame,† his thrid lawfull brother, thrie hundrith merks ; and to Gawin [previously named Gabriell] Cwnynghame,‡ his fourth lawfull brother, iii c. merks ; and to Rot. Cwnynghame, his fyift lawfull brother, iii c. merks ; and to Wm. Cwnynghame, his zoungest lawfull brother, iii c. merks.

---

is mentioned in an Irvine document in 1619, and sat on the inquest of Robert Boyd of Pitcon, 5th December 1633. His lands in Kilwinning parish, about 1569, were valued at £66, 12s. 10d. Scots. He died about 1667, without issue.
* The house, in the parish of Kilwinning, was called Woodsyde.
† In Anderson's History of the House of Hamilton, he is said to have married Janet, daughter of William Hamiltoun of Dalserf, but no date is given. Probably he was twice married.

* Ballentyne Mannscript.
† "Johne Cvnynghame in Eschinzairdis," died unmarried in 1623.
‡ "Gabriell Cvnynghame, sone lawfull to vmquhile James Cvnynghame of Eschinzairdis," died at Ashinyards, 29th December 1623. He left three sons—Alexander, John, Gabriell—and one daughter, Marcoun.

And levis to Wm. Cwnynghame, his brother naturall, xl lib., &c. In witnes of ye quhilk thing, writtin be the said Johnn Cwnynghame, his brother german, hes subscryvit thir presentis with my hand, at Eschinzairds, the xvii day of Junii 1613 zeiris, befoir thir witness, Hew Campbell of Hullirhirst, Johnn Cwnynghame, my brother german," &c.

It thus appears that Alexander Cuninghame died without issue. Hew Campbell of Hullirhirst was the husband of his sister Jean. He was succeeded by his brother,

III. James Cuninghame of Eissenyards, who married Mareoun Fleming and had issue. He appears to have been alive in 1616, in which year his name occurs in a testamentary document, but to have died soon afterwards, as the name of his successor occurs in a similar document in 1617. His relict died in December 1618. In her testament she constituted John Cuninghame, her lawful son, her only executor. He was succeeded by his eldest son,

IV. James Cuninghame of Eschinzairdis. Whom he married does not appear, but his son,

V. James Cuninghame of Eissenyards was served heir to him 28th July 1627. In 1637 he and his spouse, Jean Campbell, had a charter of the lands of Eissenyards and others. He died in June 1645. His " testament and Inventar " were " ffaythfullie maid and gevin vp be Wm. Conynghame, merchand burges of Edinburgh, in name and behalf of Wm. Conynghame, sone lawfull to the defunct," &c. His successor,

VI. William Cuninghame of Ashinyards, seems thus to have been a minor at the time of his father's death. He was consequently not served heir to his father till 25th January 1671. In 1664 he had a discharge from Hugh Earl of Eglintoun of some incumbrances affecting the properties of Ashinyards and Whitehirst. In 1673 he was appointed tutor to Sir William Cuninghame of Cuninghamehead. In 1712 he disponed his whole lands to his son-in-law, Andrew Martin of Lochridge—the date of the disposition being the 5th of May in that year. This gentleman was one among the many Cuninghame lairds who were obnoxious to Government in the " bad times," and had also his share of sufferings, having been fined in 1684, and imprisoned for nine months for non-conformity to prelacy. He married Margaret Wilkie, of what family is not mentioned, by whom he had two sons and three daughters :—

1. Alan Cuninghame, who, in 1709, is designed younger of Ashinyards in the Archery records of Kilwinning. It would seem that he died soon after this, and before his father.

2. James, who died young.

1. Elizabeth, born in 1677, of whom afterwards.
2. Anna, born in 1678.
3. Jean, who was married, in 1706, to Andrew Martin of Lochridge, in the parish of Beith, preacher of the gospel, who afterwards, by purchase, or probably in part by dowry with his wife, became proprietor of Ashinyards, and various other possessions, as Whitehirst, Nethermains, and others attached to it, consisting of several houses and yards and crofts in Kilwinning, Corsehill, Beith and elsewhere.

I. Andrew Martin of Ashinyards died before the 20th February 1759, and was succeeded by his son,

II. Arthur Martin of Ashinyards, who was served heir of his father on that day. He married Isabel Aitchison, and left a son and two daughters. The son went to the West Indies, where he married, and had two children, who died young. He died there himself at an early period of life. The daughters were :—

1. Margaret, married in 1728, to a Mr Glasgow.
2. Magdalene, married to a Mr Sommerville.

They became co-heiresses of Ashinyards; but both their families being in straitened circumstances, their trustees, by a judicial sale, in 1760 disponed the lands to a near relative of the family, John Bowman, Esq. Lord Provost of Glasgow, who was descended maternally from the family of Ashinyards, thus

V. Elizabeth Cuninghame, eldest daughter of the last Mr Cuninghame of Ashinyards, married in 1695 John Bowman, Esq., an eminent merchant in Glasgow, and who was afterwards chief magistrate of that city in the year 1715. Their son,

VI. John Bowman, who was also at one time Lord Provost of Glasgow, married in 1734 Miss Houghton of Dublin, by whom he had two sons and two daughters :—

1. John, the eldest son, went to North America about the commencement of the contest betwixt Great Britain and her colonies, where he married a lady of fortune, and died there, leaving a family in affluent circumstances.
2. Houghton, the second son, married Miss Vere, a lady from Dominica.

1. Anne, the eldest daughter, of whom afterwards.
2. Elizabeth, the second daughter, married first in 1776 John Weir Vere, of the island of Dominica, uncle of Miss Vere above mentioned; and secondly, Robert Tennent, Esq. of Glasgow; but has no family alive.

John Bowman, Esq. of Ashinyards, (altered, in his time, to Ashgrove), bought also the lands of Mountgreenan, in 1778, and sold them again in 1794 to Robert Glasgow, Esq. He died in 1796, when, by a special destination, he was succeeded in Ashgrove and other property in the parish, by his eldest daughter,

VII. Anne Bowman, who married Miller Hill Hunt, a Captain in the 6th Regiment of Foot, who served under the Duke of Cumberland against the rebels, in the year 1746, at the battle

H

of Culloden, where he received a wound. He died in 1783. His grandfather, Lieut.-Colonel Hunt, was an officer of distinguished abilities and great zeal for the service. He died Lieut.-Colonel of Dormer's Regiment. His own father, Captain Abraham Hunt, was bred also in the army, and saw likewise a good deal of service, in Spain, under Lord Peterborough and General Wade, having been in the severe actions of Almanza, Brihuego, and Sarragossa : as also at the siege of Barcelona, and the taking of Minorca. After serving long as a subaltern, and having seen no fewer than sixteen junior officers promoted over his head, he presented a memorial to the Duke of Devonshire, at that time Lord Lieutenant of Ireland, which had the desired effect, as his Grace introduced him personally to the King (George II). who at once appointed him to a company ; and when the regiment was ordered to embark with the expedition to Carthagena, under Lord Cathcart, his Majesty caused it to be signified to him, that on account of his long services and worn-out constitution, he would excuse him from going to so bad a climate, and provide for him at home. But Captain Hunt declined to accept of this indulgence, as being inconsistent with his ideas of honour and duty, to have received pay so long and then to flinch in the hour of danger ; so he embarked accordingly, and died in that disastrous expedition, from the unhealthiness of the climate, at Carthagena, in 1741.

Anne Bowman, who married as above Capt. Miller Hill Hunt, had three daughters to him :—

1. Maria, who died young.
2. Margaret Anne.
3. Elizabeth Ballantyne, married in 1801 the Hon. Roger Rollo, brother to Lord Rollo, and had issue four sons and two daughters.

She herself died in 1811, when she was succeeded by her eldest remaining daughter,

VIII. Margaret Anne Hunt ; who in consequence of her mother's destination, takes now her grandfather's name of Bowman, as also his arms, and is now proprietrix of Ashgrove, &c.

The *Arms* are, or, a chevron betwixt two bows braced in chief, for Bowman ; and a shakefork in base, sable, for Cuninghame. *Crest*—a quiver of arrows in pale, proper. *Motto*—" Sublimia Cures."

A branch of the Cuninghames of Ashinyards held distinct possession of the property of Whitehirst, part of the estate of Ashinyards. In 1614, Robert Cuninghame was served heir to his mother, Mariotta Fleming, (which lady also appears in the Ashinyards papers about the same period). " Robert Cvnynghame of Quhythirst " is men-

tioned in a testamentary document in 1614. He was alive in 1623, in which year " Rot. Cvnynghame, zounger, of Quhythirst," is a witness to the testament of " Gabriell Cvnynghame," son of " vmquhile James Cvnynghame of Eschinzairdis." Robert Cuninghame, younger, was served heir to his father in 1636. In 1664, Whitehirst was conjoined with the family estate, and still forms part of the property of Ashinyards.

## MOUNTGREENAN.

This estate, about 500 acres of which lie in the parish of Kilwinning, and 400 in that of Stewarton, anciently belonged to the wide-spread family of Ross, who probably acquired it from the De Morvilles. The last of the family who occurs in public records was *John Ross* of Mountgreenan, who appears in almost every public deed in the reign of James III., from 1478 to the unfortunate end of that king's reign in 1488, in which he seems to have been the public prosecutor or king's advocate. Adhering firmly to the interests of that prince, he was afterwards impeached in Parliament by the prevailing party, and on the 14th Oct. 1488, found guilty of treason, and " domed to forfalt to our Sovrane Lord the King his lif, landis, office, gudis, movable et unmovable, and all uther his possessions he haid within the realme of Scotland, evir more to remane with our said Sovrane Lord, his airs," &c. But his talents as a statesman were too well appreciated to allow that he should be disposed of in this manner. The ruling powers soon restored him again to favour ; for, on the 11th Feb. 1489, he appears not only in Parliament, but as a Lord of the Articles, and continued so in every succeeding session down till the 20th Feb. 1491, when he is styled " Sir John the Ross of Mountgrainen." Probably he died soon after, as his name does not again appear on record. Mountgreenan afterwards became the property of the Monastery of Kilwinning.

## CUNINGHAME OF MOUNTGREENAN.

I. ALEXANDER CUNINGHAME, only son of the second marriage of Alexander fifth Earl of Glencairn, and his lady, Janet, daughter of Sir John Cuninghame of Caprington, was appointed Commendator of Kilwinning soon after the Reformation in 1560. He married Jean Blair, of the house of Blair, and had a charter of Mountgreenan, to him and his wife, confirmed on the 2d

March 1582-3.* He was slain in the great feud that arose betwixt the Cuninghames and the Montgomeries, soon after the murder of Hugh fourth Earl of Eglintoun, in 1586. His lady died in 1621:—

"Testament, testamentar, and inventar of the guidis, &c. quhilk perteinit to vmquhile Jeane Blair, Lady Montgrennane, the tyme of hir deceis, quha deceist in the monethe of Januar, the zeir of God 1621 zeiris, ffaythfullie maid and gevin vp be hir awin mouth, &c.

"Inuentar.—Item, the said vmquhile Jeane Blair had, the tyme of hir deceis foirsaid, na vther guidis nor geir except the insyct of the hous in vtincilis and domicills, estimat to xx lib.

"Debtis awand Out.—Item, thair was awand be the said defunct, the tyme foirsaid, &c. viz. to Mr Robert Stewart, hir sone in law, the sowme of ane thowsand merks of tocher guid with hir dochter Jeane Stewart, conforme to hir obligatioune, quhairof scho declairit that he hes in his awin hand, to be allowit in the said sowme, twa zeiris dewtie of hir lyfrent lands, callit the Kirktoune of Cumrae, extending to ii c. l. lib. &c., quhilk twa zeiris dewtie is for the crop 1619 and 1620, &c.

"Legacie.—At the place of Montgrennane, the secund day of Januar 1621 zeirs. The quhilk day the said Jeane Blair, Lady Montegrennane, maid hir testament, quhairin scho nominat Williame Cvnynghame, hir sone, hir executour and full intromittour with hir guidis and geir; and incais of his refusall, to Bryce Blair of that Ilk; and also scho nominats the said Bryce, and Sir Thomas Boyd of Bollinschaw, and Niniane Stewart of Kilcaltane, overscaris to the said William. Item, scho declairis that scho hes disponit, be way of contract and factorie to the said William, hir sone, the haill fermes and dewties addebtit be the tennentis of hir lyferent lands within the Isles of Buit and Inchmarnoche; and that for his releif, and releif of hir oy, the Laird of Montgrennane, of the sowme of nyntein hundrith merks, and vther sowmes conteint in the contract of the date the saxt day of Maij, the zeir of God 1620 zeiris, quhilk dispositioune and factorie be thir presents scho ratifeis and approvis, &c. Item, scho declairis that the haill tocher promeisit be hir with Deame Grissall Cvnynghame, spous to Sir Thomas Boyd of Bollinschaw, is payit; and incaice the said Sir Thomas, or ells the executours of vmquhile Thomas Lord Boyd, or ony alledging ryt thairto, sall cviet ony

sowmes of money alledgit vnpayit of the said tocher; and becaus that vmquhile Johnn Blair of that Ilk was cautiouner for the foirsaid tocher, thairfoir in that caice scho ordanes his guidis and geir to releif the same. . . . And for the testifeying of the commissionour, scho desyrit to subscryve the same, as follows. Befoir thir witnesses, Bryce Blair of that Ilk, Allexander Cochrane of that Ilk, Mr Gavin Blair of Auldmuir, Johnne Sempill of Aikinbar, and Mr William Castellaw, minister at Stewartoune. Sic subr." &c.

The Commendator of Kilwinning was succeeded in Mountgreenan by his son,

II. James Cuninghame of Mountgreenan, who was served heir to his father in the £10 land of Mountgreenan, 31st Aug. 1608. He married *Marcoun Douglas*, but of what family does not appear. He died in 1616. In 1619, "Marcoun Douglas, Lady Montgrenane, zounger," is mentioned in a testamentary document as now the sponse of John Sempill of Aikinbar. He was succeeded by his son,

III. Alexander Cuninghame of Mountgreenan, who was retoured heir to his grandmother in various subjects about Kilwinning, in 1632. His son,

IV. Thomas Cuninghame of Mountgreenan, was retoured heir to his father, Alexander, and his grandfather, James, in 1645; and again, in 1656, to his father, Alexander Cuninghame of Mountgreenan. His son,

V. Thomas Cuninghame of Mountgreenan, was served heir to his father, Thomas, in 1674. He is the last of the family who possessed the property. He lived in the "bad times." He joined the insurrection of the Covenanters in 1679; and on the 8th January 1685, was brought to his trial. "He was indicted for treason and rebellion. His confession that he joined the rebels at Bothwell was the proof. He begged the Lords might intercede for his pardon, and declared that he was willing to take the test. He was brought in guilty, and on the 15th was sentenced to be hanged at the Cross of Edinburgh, on the first Wednesday of April; but it seems he was pardoned. In 1689, in consequence of the Revolution, a general revocation of all these convictions and forfeitures was passed in Parliament, and his name appears in the act. He afterwards lived in the town of Irvine, and died about 1715. He had by his wife two sons, who appear to have died in childhood in 1696—both in the same year. He had also a daughter, his heiress, who married a person of the name of Cuninghame in Irvine.

Though doomed to forfeiture, Thomas Cun-

* Mountgrenane, however, had previously belonged to a family of the name of Cuninghame. "Robert Cunynghame of Montgrenane" occurs in Pitcairn's Criminal Trials in 1551.

inghame seems to have succeeded in disposing of his lands before the act of revocation, though probably, under the circumstances, at a reduced price. The purchaser was Hugh Stevenson, Clerk of the Privy Council. From the records of the Scottish Parliament we find that Mr Stevenson, in 1690, presented a petition, praying that his name might be omitted in the general act, lest it might lead to the forfeiture of his property. He further states that he had purchased Mountgreenan from Thomas Cuninghame, late of Mountgreenan, and his lady and mother, having been induced to enter into a bargain for the lands after Cuninghame's forfeiture. It remained with the Stevensons till 1778, when it was acquired by John Bowman of Ashinyards, who in 1794 sold it to Robert Glasgow, Esq.

### GLASGOW OF MOUNTGREENAN.

I. REV. JOHN GLASGOW, minister of Kilbirnie from 1688 to 1721, when he died. He married, first, 14th January 1690, Jean, daughter of John Cuninghame of Wattieston, Chamberlain to the Laird of Glengarnock, of the family of Robertland; secondly, Margaret, daughter of Robert Scott, merchant in Beith, 19th April 1699.[*] He had fourteen children; but there is no tradition of any of them save his son,

II. Robert Glasgow, who was baptized 17th October 1693.[†] He was Chamberlain to the Viscount of Garnock, and surgeon at Kilbirnie. He was styled of Puddockholm, which was sometimes called the Waters. It lies on the banks of the water of Garnock. Its watery, or marshy situation, gave rise to its picturesque name. He married Margaret Allan of Ladesyde, 15th December 1726. They had nine children, among whom were:—

1. Jean, born in 1727. Married to James White of Woodsyde, parish of Kilwinning, 1st October 1750.
2. Ann, married to Hugh Allan, in Kilwinning, 23d December 1757.
3. Janet, born in 1735; married to William Cochran, younger of Ladyland, 2d September 1756, and left issue.
4. Margaret, born in 1743; married to Andrew Smith of Todholes, in the parish of Dalry, 20th March 1764.
5. Robert, born in 1747. He gained a fortune in St Vincent's; of whom afterwards.
6. James, born in 1756; went to St Vincent's. He died in the parish of Calder, near Edinburgh, unmarried.

III. Robert Glasgow of Mountgreenan. He married Rachael, daughter of Major Dunlop of Dunlop. He died at Mountgreenan House, 19th April 1827, leaving no issue.

[*] Kilbirnie Record.
[†] Ibid.

Robert Glasgow also purchased the lands of Fergushill, being the estate of the Fergushills of that Ilk, which lands form a considerable part of the estate of Mountgreenan. These lands were purchased by Mr Glasgow, about 1800, from a family of the name of M'Vicar. Mr Glasgow left his estate to a daughter of the family, whom he had brought up and educated, and who, during his life was married to Mr Robertson of Prenderguest. The estate was settled on her and her family, who were appointed to use the surname of Glasgow. Mrs Robertson Glasgow, now proprietor, is still alive, but her husband died some years ago. She resides at Pau, in France. Her eldest son and heir, Robert Robertson Glasgow, Esq. is Sheriff Substitute at Paisley. He is married and has a family.

The modern house of Mountgreenan is situated about three miles from Kilwinning. The ancient seat occupied a small knoll, in a pleasant valley, by the side of the Lugton, about half a mile north from the present mansion.

Mountgreenan House is now used as a school, or academy, for boys, under the charge of Mr Wilson, from Glasgow, who can accommodate forty boys within the house, and the academy is in a thriving state, and highly spoken of.

### CUNINGHAMES OF CLONBEITH.

This property belonged to the Monastery of Kilwinning, and was feued out by Alexander the Abbot, 31st March 1534, to nobili viro,

I. JAMES CUNINGHAME of Clonbeith, who is so designed in the charter from the Abbot. The property was to be held of the Abbot of Kilwinning, for the yearly payment of 12 merks, 9 capons, 9 hens, &c., and is described as a six merk land. Nisbet calls the family a cadet of Glencairn, through Aiket.

II. John Cuninghame of Clonbeith appears to have succeeded his father sometime after the 9th July 1572, on which day John Cuninghame, son of John Cuninghame of Clonbeith, is a witness to a charter by John Cuninghame of Glengarnock, to his younger son, John Cuninghame of Caddell. "Johnne Cwnynghame, sone of vmquhile . . . . Cwnynghame of Clonbayth, and John Maxwell, brother to Thomas Maxwell of Southbar," were, in 1576-7, dilatit for the slauchter of James Sandelandis of Calder. He had a son,

III. James Cuninghame of Clonbeith, as appears from a charter by John Cuninghame of Clonbeith to his son, James, dated 28th Nov.

1581. Should this James have succeeded his father, it is probable that he died without issue soon afterwards, for in little more than four years afterwards

IV. John Cuninghame of Clonbeith is implicated in the murder of Hugh fourth Earl of Eglintoun, which occurred on the 19th of April 1586. The next we find in possession is

VI. William Cuninghame of Clonbeith. His wife, Agnes Cuninghame, died in December 1612. From her testament it does not appear that she left any family. William Cuninghame is mentioned in various documents down till 1626. He appears to have been succeeded by

VII. Daniel Cuninghame of Clonbeith, whose name occurs in the testament of Alexander Cuninghame of Cowlyn, in 1626. He sold the property, with consent of his son, William,* to James Scott, Provost of Irvine, in 1633.

This family of Scott also possessed the property of Scots Loch, near Irvine, and different individuals of them appear in the records, as representing the burgh of Irvine in Parliament, at sundry times during the seventeenth century. Their monumental stone is situated close on the right hand of the door next the main entry to the churchyard of Irvine, with the Scott arms upon it, and the initials H. S. and L. S.; for Hugh and Lawrence. They seem to have been cadets of the Millenie branch of the Buccleuch family. In 1694, Clonbeith was sold by Walter Scott to James Park, who, in 1695, sold it to Hew Cuninghame, designed in the disposition, "of Clonbeith," (in all probability a descendant of the original proprietors, who might still have retained the superiority.) On the 3d July 1717, they were sold by George Cuninghame, son and heir of Hew Cuninghame of Clonbeith, W. S., to Alexander ninth Earl of Eglintoun.

*Clonbeith,* the old mansion of the Cuninghames, remains still pretty entire, though roofless. It is situated about three miles eastward of Kilwinning, on a rising bank on the north side of the Lugton water, and is a conspicuous object in the neighbourhood.

### NEVIN OF MONKREDDING.

This property, extending over nearly 700 acres, is situated in the vicinity of Kilwinning, and belonged, in former times, to the Abbey. The first lay proprietor was

* William Cuninghame, fear of Clonbeith, occurs in the testament of Robert Broune of Burrowland, in 1630.

I. THOMAS NEVIN of Monkredding, who had a charter of the lands of East Monkredding to himself and his wife, Elizabeth Craufurd, from Alexander, Abbot of Kilwinning, dated 20th July 1532. This Thomas Nevin seems to have been on terms of intimacy with Hugh second Earl of Eglintoun, who, on a friendly visit to him, was taken suddenly ill, and died in the house of Monkredding, on the 3d of September 1546, his own castle not being more than a mile and a half distant. By his will, which had been previously made, his lordship appointed him one of the tutors in succession to his son, the young Earl. He was succeeded by his son,

II. Andrew Nevin of Monkredding, as appears from an instrument of sasine in 1581. "Andro Nevin de Monkreddin," is witness to a charter of confirmation, by Hugh Earl of Eglintoun, to James Lockhart, son and heir of James Lockhart of Lee, of the lands of Lochwood in Cuninghame, at Edinburgh in 1581. "Andro Neivin of Monkreddin," in 1562, signed the famous *Band* in defence of the Reformed Religion. The next in succession appears to have been

III. Thomas Nevin of Monkredding, whose name occurs, among others, to a discharge granted by John Blair of that Ilk to the burgh of Irvine, for parsonage teinds of some lands in the vicinity of that town, dated the 14th May 1600. "Thomas Neivin of Monkredding," is mentioned in several testamentary documents down till 1621, about which time he probably died. He granted a charter to his son and Margaret Blair, his spouse, in implement of their marriage contract, dated 29th October 1619. He was succeeded by his son,

IV. Thomas Nevin of Monkredding. "Thomas Nevin, *fear* of Monkredding, Niniane Nevin, his father brother, and Mr Hew Nevin, his brother germane," are witnesses to a testamentary deed in 1623. His sister, *Geills,* appears to have been married to Mr Alexr. Wreittoun in Kilwinning, who died in October 1636. In his testament, he "ordanes Geills Neving, his spous, his onlie executrix," and tutrix to his two sons. Failing her he appoints the "Earl of Eglintoun, Thomas Neiving, elder, of Monkridding, and Thomas Neiving, zounger, of Monkridding, ovirscaris." Robertson mentions a resignation of the lands of Monkredding by Thomas Nevin and Margaret Blair, to Thomas Nevin, younger, of Monkredding, their son, dated 5th July 1658. The date should probably be 1650, for "Thomas Neving of Monkredding" died in the month of April 1651. His testament and inventory were given up by James Neving, his second lawful son, as the "cesseoner" of "Hew Baillie and

Anna Buntein, his spous," to whom the defunct was addebted in the sum of three hundred merks. The inventory is interesting in a literary point of view :—

"Item, ane pair of spectacles sett with silver, and ane vther pair with horne, and ane caise thairto, worth xl s. Item, ane greit byble, worth xl s. Item, ane greit psalme buike, worth xxx s. Item, ane lesser psalme buike, pryce xii s. Item, ane greit buike of the Acts of Parliament, worth vi lib. 13s. 4d. Item, vthir thrie buiks of preiching, sett out be Inglischmen, worth xxx s. the peice, &c. Item, in the possessione of Hendrie Kelso, in Kilwinning, and Geilles Neving, his spous, ane hundreth punds money of superplus of the defunct's buirding, payit for him be him to them befoirhand, mair nor he received buirding for fra them.

"Debts awand In.—Item, thair was awand to the defunct the tyme foirsaid, be the Earle of Eglintoun and his factouris, for his *pensione*, j c. lib." &c.

He was succeeded by his son,

V. Thomas Nevin of Monkredding, who appears to have been the father of

VI. Thomas Nevin of Monkredding, who was served heir to his father, Thomas, on the 20th April 1680.

VII. William Nevin of Monkredding was served heir to his brother, Thomas, on the 22d March 1693. In 1698 he alienated the lands of Monkredding to Hugh Cuninghame of Clonbeith, W. S.

## CUNINGHAMES OF MONKREDDING.

I. Hew Cuninghame of Clonbeith was the first of the Cuninghames of Monkredding. He died before 1712. His daughter, *Anne*, was married, on the 4th December 1716, to William Ramsay of Gallery. He was succeeded by his son,

II. George Cuninghame of Monkredding. He married, in 1714, Agnes, daughter of George Dallas of Parklie, representative of an ancient and respectable family in Linlithgowshire, by whom he had a son, *George*, born 28th July 1721,* and three daughters. One of his daughters, *Agnes*, was born 16th August 1716. In the register he is styled of Clonbeith. He died sometime after 1729, and was succeeded by his only son,

III. George Cuninghame of Monkredding. In 1752, he married Janet, second daughter of John

Gemmill of Towerlands, by whom he had a son and four daughters:—

1. Fergusson, born 9th Dec. 1760.
2. Agnes, born 14th Dec. 1752, married to William Miller of Monkcastle, and had issue.
3. Catherine, born 3d April 1758; married 24th Aug. 1785, to the Rev. Thomas Brisbane, minister of Dunlop, and had issue.
4. Anne, born 2d Aug. 1762; married, 28th Aug. 1786, to the Rev. John Monteath, minister of Houstoun, and had issue.

He died in December 1786.

IV. Fergusson Cuninghame, as only son, succeeded to the estate; but, being imbecile, he was cognosed as a lunatic, and Alexander Miller of Monkcastle, his nephew, the son of his eldest sister, was served as tutor of law to him. He died in 1830, and was succeeded by his three sisters, or their descendants, viz. :—

Alexander Miller of Monkcastle, only son of Agnes Cuninghame, the eldest sister; Dr Thomas Brisbane, surgeon in the army, eldest son of Catherine, the second sister; Mrs Anne Cuninghame, spouse of Dr Monteath, the youngest sister.

The estates having since been divided, and the mansion-house allotted to Mr Miller of Monkcastle, as representing the eldest sister, the present proprietors are—

1. William Campbell Miller of Monkcastle, a minor.

2. Dr Thomas Brisbane.

3. James Monteath, writer, Glasgow, eldest son of Mrs Anne Cuninghame, now deceased.

*Monkredding* house is about a mile and a half from Kilwinning. It is situated in a gentle hollow, and is well sheltered with wood.

## BURROWLAND.

This small but valuable property, extending to about 200 acres, belonged to a family of the name of Brown, who were also proprietors of the lands of Nethermains. The first we find of them was

*Robert Broune* of Burrowland, whose name occurs as a witness to the testament of Robert Dickie in Blaksyik, in 1628. He died in October 1630. His testament and inventory were "ffaythfullie maid and gevin vp be *Jonet Couper*, his relict, and be *Jeane* Broune, ane of the defunct's lawfull dochteris, and the said Jeane for hir self, and in name and behalf of *Cristiane* Broune, the vther dochter, and executouris dative," &c. In 1634, his daughter Jeane, appears as a creditor in the testament of Robert Boyd of Portincross for certain sums due to her father. Robert Broune was succeeded by his son,

*James Brown* of Burrowland, who was served heir to his father—5th May 1640—in the lands of Nethermains. At his death he left two daughters, one of whom, *Janet*, married Alexander Blair, second son of Blair of Giffordland. They were succeeded in the lands of Burrowland by their son,

*John Blair*, whose wife, Janet Stewart, daughter of John Stewart of Shawwood, appears to have been infeft in them in virtue of the provisions in her marriage contract in 1671. He was succeeded, in 1736, by his son,

*Alexander Blair*, who died without issue, when the lands of Burrowland descended, in 1742, to his brother,

*James Blair* of Lochwards. He was succeeded by his son,

*James Blair*, who was infeft in the lands of Burrowland, Dec. 1754. On the death of James, who died unmarried, the lands of Burrowland and Lochwards descended to his sister,

*Jean Blair*, who was duly infeft in them in July 1762. She died in October 1804, and was succeeded by her only son,

*James Blair*, as heir to her in the lands of Burrowland and Lochwards. Mr Blair died unmarried upon the 12th of June 1815, having, in the preceding year, executed a settlement, by which he conveyed the lands of Burrowland to

*John Blair Hyndman*, of Springside, one of his relations by his mother.

The family of Hindman for several generations were proprietors of the lands of Lunderston, near Ardgowan, in the parish of Innerkip. John Hindman, uncle of John Blair Hindman, sold Lunderston to the late Sir Michael Shaw Stuart. John Blair Hindman, W. S., had, through his mother's relations, succeeded to Springside, in the parish of West Kilbride, and also to Burrowland. He was succeeded in these lands by his sister, Elizabeth Hindman. At her death the property went to her cousin, Henry Hindman, proprietor both of Burrowland and Springside. He is the grandson of Col. Hindman, who made his fortune in the East India Company's service, and settled at Largs. The eldest son, John Hindman, who was entered advocate, died without issue. The second son, Henry Hindman, was educated for a Writer to the Signet, and practised for some time as a Solicitor in London. He then went to Canada, where he died, leaving several children; and Henry Hindman, his eldest son, is now the proprietor of Springside and Burrowland, having succeeded to them about two years ago, on the death of Elizabeth Hindman.

# PARISH OF KIRKMICHAEL.

ETYMOLOGY, EXTENT, &c.

THE name of this parish is obviously derived from St Michael, to whom the church was dedicated. It was called in former times Kirkmichael of Gemilstoun, from the name, no doubt, of the proprietor, John de Gemilstoun, by whom the church was granted to the Prior and Canons of Whithern. The parish lies north and east, and is in length about twelve miles, and five broad, including an area of upwards of 15,000 imperial acres. It is bounded on the north-east by Dalrymple; on the east by Straiton; on the south by Dailly; and on the west and north-west by Kirkoswald and Maybole.

The topographical appearance of the parish is diversified. The vale of the Girvan, by which it is intersected, is of considerable breadth, and towards the east it undulates in delightful variety of hill and dale. Though not of a mountainous character, the eastern portion of the parish presents much bolder features, rising as it recedes, till it reaches the hill of Glenalla, which is 1612 feet from the level of the sea. From the eminence above the farm-house of Guiltreehill a commanding and delightful view is obtained. Towards the interior are seen the Straiton and Galloway hills, with the well wooded and picturesque windings of the Girvan; and seaward, the beautiful bay of Ayr, indented with thriving towns along the coast, with the bold peaks of Arran, and Benlomond and the Highland hills in the distance. The whole parish, notwithstanding the height to which part of it attains, has a well cultivated and comfortable appearance, almost wholly free from heath and moss. The husbandry of the district is much indebted to the late Henry Ritchie, Esq. of Busbie and Cloncaird, who vastly improved his property by draining

and otherwise. Much has also been done in this respect by the other proprietors. It is long since agricultural ameliorations, however, began to take place in the parish. In the time of Abercrummie, who wrote his *Description of Carrick* before the Revolution, the proprietor of Kirkmichael had drained part of a loch in the vicinity of his orchard, and been rewarded for his labour by good crops of hay. More than a thirteenth part of the parish is wooded, natural and planted—not in one great forest, but in clumps and patches at once ornamental and useful.

The parish is well watered, there being no less than six lochs of considerable extent in it. These are Drumore, containing about nine imperial acres; Kirkmichael, five; Shankston, twelve; Croot, ten; and Spalander, forty-five—in all about 109 acres, less five acres of Loch Spalander, which are in the parish of Straiton. The latter loch is particularly famed for trout, which are plentiful and good. Char are also found in it. The principal streams are the Girvan, Doon and Dyrock burn. The Girvan has its source in the hills of Bar and Straiton, and enters Kirkmichael below Blairquhan, and nearly divides the parish. The Doon, whose "banks and braes" have been immortalized in the strains of Burns, forms the boundary between Kirkmichael and Dalrymple parishes. The Dyrock Burn originates in the lochs of Shankston, Barnshean and Spalander, and flowing past the church of Kirkmichael, joins the Girvan above the farm of Mackailston.

## HISTORY, CIVIL AND ECCLESIASTICAL.

The Church of Kirkmichael, "Ecclesia Sancti Michaelis de Gemilstoun," was granted to the Prior and Canons of Whithern, in Galloway, "by John de Gemilstoun, the son and heir of John de Gemilstoun, knight; and it was confirmed to them by Robert I. in May 1326."* It was also confirmed to them, by James IV., in 1451; and it continued to belong to the Priory till the Reformation. The Prior and Canons enjoyed the greatest part of the revenues, and the remainder was assigned to the vicar. "In Bagimont's Roll," says Chalmers, "as it stood in the reign of James V., the vicarage of Kirkmichael, in the deanery of Carrick, was taxed £3, 6s. 8d.; being a tenth of its estimated value. In 1362, the half of the vicarage was enjoyed by Sir Thomas Montgomery, the vicar of this church, who received from it £15 yearly, and £5 more as the rent of the glebe lands and manse. How the other half of the vicarage was disposed of appeareth not; but the tithes and revenues of Kirkmichael, which belonged to the Priory of Whithorn, were leased to Jonet Mure, for the payment of £100 a-year. The Church of Kirkmichael, with the other property of the Priory, was vested in the King by the General Annexation Act of 1587. The whole was granted by the King, in 1606, to the Bishop of Galloway. In 1641, it was transferred to the University of Glasgow; but it was restored to the same Bishop in 1661; and it was held by the Bishops of that See till the final abolition of Episcopacy in 1689, when the patronage was vested in the King, to whom it now belongs." The old Church of Kirkmichael existed till 1787, when it was replaced by a new building. The site of the church and churchyard, on the banks of the Dyrock, and surrounded by old ash trees, is truly romantic.

The village of Kirkmichael, which extends southwards from the church, is comparatively of modern growth. When Abercrummie wrote, towards the close of the seventeenth century, it had no existence. He says, "the parish of Kirkmichael lyes in length east and west, and is a mensall Kirk of the Bishop of Galloway, who is patron thereof. It stands hard upon the rivulet of Dyrock; *has no clachan by it.*" Kirkmichael village, therefore, has grown up during the last and present centuries. It "struggles picturesquely along both sides of the Girvan, between Cloncaird House and Kirkmichael Castle, three miles and a quarter from Maybole, and ten from Ayr. Around it are finely variegated rising-grounds, and beautiful little expanses of plantation; and interspersed with its houses and trees and little gardens, it has a delightful appearance." Crosshill, another village, of still

more recent growth, in the parish, is about a mile and a half south-west of Kirkmichael, and three miles from Maybole. It is principally formed of a long, regular street of one story houses. It is chiefly occupied by Irish, or the descendants of Irish, who gain a livelihood by the loom.

A good deal of what is called Ayrshire needlework is done in the parish.

The parochial records go as far back as 1638, but have not been regularly kept until the beginning of the present century. The writer in the Statistical Account, (the Rev. John M'Ewen), gives a few extracts, which are curious enough. The first sufficiently accounts for at least one hiatus in the records:—

"In 1692, Mr Gilchrist, after the persecution, having constituted a session of elders that had held office during Mr Cockburn's ministry, he then inquired into the old session book, which had been taken by the late curate, who had been apprehended in a rebellion in the north, imprisoned, and then escaped to France, and taken with him the register, which it is supposed he had destroyed."

The next is characteristic of the stern discipline of Presbyterianism, which was restored by the Revolution:—

"Session, September 24, 1693.—The Session appoints John Forgan to employ a Straitoun tailor to make a coul or covering of sackcloth for the said Jonet Kennedy, like unto that which they have in Straiton; there having been no such thing here for these many years, it's thought none of the tailors of this parish know how to make it."

It appears there had been a bridge over the Girvan at Kirkmichael long prior to 1710, as it had then been in want of repair:—

"Session, June 26, 1710.—Likewise it was concluded by the Session, that there should be a collection gathered for repairing of the bridge of Kirkmichael, which is like to become ruinous, and the next two Sabbath collections that there is sermon here, is to be applyed for that use."

In reference to the building of Dalrymple bridge, we have the following:—

"Session, January 26, 1725.—This day David Armour contracted with the Session to build the bridge over the Doon at Dalrymple for the sum of £76, 1s. sterling."

Besides the Kirk of St Michael, there was at least another in the parish, supposed to have belonged to the Abbey of Crossraguel. It stood on the farm of Lindsaytoun, not far from Casillis Castle, where some ruins point out the site. A well adjacent is still called the Chapel Well.

"In the troublous times of 1685, Gilbert

* Chalmers' Caledonia.

M'Adam was taken prisoner, and carried to Dumfries, on a charge of non-conformity, but was liberated on a heavy caution being given. Soon after, he was again apprehended, and, refusing the oath of allegiance and supremacy, he was banished to the Plantations. In the course of the same year, however, he contrived to return, and, late upon a Saturday night or early on Sabbath morning, in a cottage near the present House of Kirkmichael, when, with some of his friends, at a meeting for prayer, he was surprised by a company of militia, and shot in attempting to escape by a window. In the churchyard, a tombstone was placed over his remains, with an epitaph recording the circumstance of his death by the "Laird of Colzean and Ballochmyl." By some hand these two names were erased. Old Mortality, however, took care to re-insert them, and they now remain as legible as the original lettering. In 1829, a new tombstone was erected, in which the old tablet is preserved."*

*Antiquities.*—" There are," says the *Statistical Account,* "traces of five British or Danish fortlets in this parish, two in the farm of Guiltreehill, one in Keonstan, one in Cassanton, and another in Castle Downans. They are all circular, and are supposed to belong to the early period of the *fourteenth* century." This must be a mistake for the *fourth* century, because, whether British or Danish, their era must be much earlier than the fourteenth century. There is every reason to believe, as the Roman road from Galloway to Ayr traverses the course of the Doon at no great distance, that they are British remains of the Roman period. They are about a hundred yards in diameter, and with a ditch of nearly fifteen feet wide. Where they have been ploughed up, numerous fragments of pitchers, spears, horns, &c. were discovered. From the name of a farm in the immediate vicinity—Dunree, in Gaelic *Dun-righ,* signyfying the King's stronghold—it is inferred that the fort was distinguished by a royal appellative.

*Cassillis Downans.*—The Downans are five beautiful green little hills, about half a mile from Cassillis. They are rendered famous to all time in the " Halloween " of Burns :—

" Upon that night, when fairies light,
   On Cassillis Downans dance:
 Or oure the leys, in splendid maze,
   On sprightly coursers prance."

The highest of the Downans hills, which presents

the form of a cone, has an imposing aspect. The height may be estimated at between four and five hundred feet above the level of the Doon, and as the rise is somewhat abrupt, the difficulty of access is considerable. The summit once gained, however, the visitor is amply rewarded for his toil by the extensive prospect which it commands—the scope of vision ranging from ten to thirty miles. Amongst the woods, in the beautiful haugh beneath, are seen the turrets of Cassillis House, one of the oldest baronial residences in the county. The Doon rolls gently at its base, and the rich green lawns undulate in beautiful perspective amid the magnificent old trees by which it is surrounded. In former times, Cassillis Downans was regarded as a favourite haunt of the fairies of Ayrshire, and a popular tradition still exists illustrative of their peculiar attachment to the locality. The House of Cassillis, it is said, was originally intended to have occupied a site on the top of the hill, but the fairies were so much opposed to this that they invariably demolished at night what had been built during the day—removing the stones and other materials to the spot where the Castle now stands —until the owner, convinced of the folly of contending with his invisible opponents, at length gave up the contest.

*Cassillis House.*—The policies of Cassillis, if enticing, as viewed from the Downans, are still more enchanting when you find yourself on the green lawn under the spreading foliage of many a noble oak and plane, and hear the music of the water

" Among the bonnie winding banks,
   Where Doon rins, wimplin' clear."

The Castle, to which an elegant gothic addition was made in 1830 by the late Lord Kennedy, consisted previously of a massive square tower, with a spiral stair. The lower story is vaulted,* and the walls, as high as the third flat, are upwards of sixteen feet in thickness. At what period the house was built does not appear to be known. Grose, in his *Antiquities of Scotland,* says—" This tower has probably undergone many repairs ; the present appearance (1789) does not bespeak the last to be older than the reign of Queen Mary, or James VI., her son."

Though the Castle is not associated with any

---

* Statistical Account.

* Some years ago, this place was cleared out, with the view of making it a wine cellar. In this process a great many carts of human bones were removed. These, it is to be feared, were the lingering witnesses of deeds and times long gone by, when the devoted guest and the refractory vassal went so frequently amissing, having met a fate which some might suspect, but none durst inquire into."—STAT. ACCT.

remarkable event in history, yet the well-known ballad of the "Gypsie Laddie," and the tradition regarding the Countess to whom the verses refer, have invested the scene of her elopement with a peculiar interest :—

> "The gypsies cam to our lord's yett,
>   An' oh but they sang bonnie;
> They sang sae sweet an' sae complete
>   That doun cam the fair ladye.
>
> An' she cam trippin' doun the stair,
>   Wi' a' her maids before her;
> As soon as they saw her weel-faur'd face,
>   They coost the glamour owre her.
>
> . . . . . . . .
>
> Gae tak' frae me this gay mantil,
>   And bring to me a plaidie:
> For if kith and kin and a' had been sworn,
>   I'll follow the gipsy laddie."

Popular tradition accords with the ballad in attributing the imprudent step adopted by the Countess to the influence of "glamour" or witchery; but Finlay and others attempt to account for the indiscretion, by representing the leader of the gypsies to have been an early lover of the lady—Sir John Faa of Dunbar. The Countess, it is also said, was Lady Jean Hamilton, daughter of the Earl of Haddington, and her husband, John the sixth Earl of Cassillis. Nay, further, the elopement is said to have occured during the Earl's absence at the Assembly of Divines at Westminster in 1643. All these alleged facts have been circumstantially detailed and repeated in Chambers's Picture of Scotland, the New Statistical Account, and the recent Gazetteers of Scotland, as if there were not the slightest dubiety in the statement. Now, there is every reason to believe that the abduction of the Countess of Cassillis, however true it may be, occurred at a much earlier period than the time referred to. The air is older, having been discovered in a book of music written long before the middle of the seventeenth century. But, at all events, that John the sixth Earl and Lady Jean Hamilton were not the parties, seems to be certain. Their marriage took place in 1621, and the lady died in 1642, the year previous to the meeting of the Westminster Assembly. The fact of the Countess' death in 1642 is ascertained from the following correspondence—a letter from the Earl of Cassillis, inviting the Earl of Eglintoun to the funeral of his "deir bedfellow," and the letter of condolence in reply:—

"My noble lord. It hath pleaselt the Almightie to tak my deir bed-fellow frome this valley of tearce to hir home (as hir . . . in hir last wordis called it). There remaines now the last duetie to be done to that 'pairt of hir left with ws, qch I intend to pforme vpoun the ffyft of Januar nixt. This I intreat may be honoured with yor. Lo. presence, heir at Cassillis, yt day, at Ten in the morning, and from this to our buriall place at Mayboille, qch shalbe taken as a mark of yor. Lo. affectioun to

> yor. Lo. humble servant,
>                               CASSILLIS.

Cassillis, the 15th Der. 1642."

[Copy of Lord Eglintoun's reply, scrolled on the same leaf of paper].

"My Lo.
          I am sorrowfull from my soul for yor. Lo. great losse and heavie visitationn, and regraits much that I cannot have ye libertie from my Lord Chancellor to come and doe yat last duty and respect I am byd to. And I will earnestly entreat yor. Lo. not to tak this for an excuse, for I have been veric instant for it. But yor. Lo. appointed day is ye verie day ye meetting of ye Comittee of ye Concert at Air of peace—and further, our partie, ye L. of Glencairne, is so instant yat he will grant no delay in this matter. Yor. Lo. may persuade yourself it is ane very grit grief to me to be absent from you. I will earnestly entreat yor. Lo. to take all this Cristianly, as I am confident yor. Lor. will doe. I pray God to comfort you wt. his wisdom, and resolve to be content with that which comes from his hand, for none sall wish it more than I. You sall still command

> Yor. Lo.
>
>          Most obt. servt."*

From the tenor of these interesting documents it is impossible to conceive that Lady Jane Hamilton could have been the runaway Countess. The funeral, besides, took place from Cassillis House, not from Maybole Castle, which is said to have been the prison-house of the unhappy lady. The second marriage of the Earl of Cassillis did not take place till 1644. It is thus evident that "the most authentic version of this story," to borrow the words of the Statistical Account, is unfounded, in so far as the time and actors are concerned. That tradition is correct, however, in the main incidents, there can be little doubt; but it is equally apparent that they refer to a period anterior to the days of John the sixth Earl, and may possibly, after all, date back to the previous century, when "Johnne Faw, Lord and Erle of Little Egypt," and his followers, first appeared in this country.

The "Gypsies' steps," a few straggling stones across the Doon, at a ford some hundred yards distant from the Castle, are still pointed out as the way by which the Countess and her enchanters escaped from the Castle, and eluded observation by threading their way unseen through the woods. In front of the Castle stands an old and majestic plane tree, on the wide-spreading branches of which Johnnie Faa and his companions are said to have paid the penalty of their temerity with their lives. The tree is called the "Dule Tree," not, as erroneously supposed, from this circumstance—for every baronial residence had its *dule tree*; and the apartment from which

* These letters were found among the Eglintoun papers a few years ago. [See "Ballads and Songs of Ayrshire."]

the lady became an involuntary witness of the revolting spectacle is still pointed out as the *Countess's Room* There are two portraits of her preserved at Cassillis—one before marriage, and the other after her imprisonment The latter represents her in tears. The lady, as tradition affirms, was confined all her lifetime in the Castle of Maybole, where she passed the time in working the story of her misfortune in tapestry. This interesting piece of needle-work is understood to be preserved at Culzean Castle.

*Cloncaird Castle* —Abercrummie describes Cloncaird Castle, in his time, as two miles distant from Blairquhan, and " surrounded with gardens, orchards, and great stores of wood " It was then a vast quadrangular tower, in the style of the sixteenth century It is now modernised into one of the most elegant seats in Ayrshire It has beautiful pleasure-grounds, and occupies a picturesque site

*Kirkmichael House* —" The House of Kirkmichael says Abercrummie, is " a pretty commodious house, within a short space of the church of the same, betwixt which runs the water of Dyrok, above-mentioned which soon swells with rains falling on the higher grounds, and becomes impassible on the sudden The House of Kirkmichael is as desyreable a dwelling as in all the country, having good gardens and orchards,

and was *the first in Carrick planted with apricocks and peaches* This orchard and house is flanked on the south with a loch, part whereof has been drained of late, and rewards the owner's industry with good hay." Kirkmichael House is an excellent and commodious family residence There is still a lake in its vicinity—about five acres in extent—which adds greatly to the picturesque features of the situation Vast improvements have been made on the grounds within these few years There are some splendid trees within the policy, and very thriving plantations throughout the estate.

Abercrummie enumerates *Kilmore* and *Montgomeryston* among the houses in Kirkmichael parish in his time These places are now merely farm houses, although the sites of them still bear evidence of having formerly been places of some consideration.

" There is a local tradition," says the *Statistical Account*, " besides some proofs from ancient documents, that Blairquhan is within the original landmarks of this parish." Abercrummie describes Blairquhan as in the parish of Kirkmichael, so that tradition is quite correct in this instance. As it is now embraced in the parish of Straiton, we shall defer noticing it until we come to that parish.

---

# FAMILIES IN THE PARISH OF KIRKMICHAEL.

## MONTGOMERIES OF CASSILLIS

This branch of the house of Montgomerie seems to have been amongst the earliest of the vassals of the old Earls of Carrick The first of them was

*Alan de Montgomerie* of Stair and Cassillis, second or third son of Sir John Montgomerie, designed of Eastwood, probably before he succeeded his elder brother in the family property of Eagleshame. In the Haddington Collection there is a charter from Robert I , " Carta Alani de Montgomery filii quondam Johannis de Montgomery de terris de Stahare, &c anno regis 22 "

There is reason to believe that he had three sons'

*Sir Neil de Montgomerie,* designed of Cassillis. Taking part in defence of his country against the overwhelming armies of Edward I , he was amongst the gentlemen so treacherously put to death by the English in the Barns of Ayr in 1298. He died without issue, and Cassillis devolved upon his brother John, though he may have been immediately succeeded by

*Alan de Montgomery,* to whom there is a charter by Robert I. of the lands of Stahare, " whilk Allan his father resigned." It appears that he also died without issue, and was succeeded by his brother,

*John de Montgomerie of Stair-Montgomerie and Cassillis.* The elder branch of the family of Montgomerie, Lords of Eaglesbame, appear to have retained some right of property in Cassillis. He died previous to 1361-2, and was succeeded by his only child,

*Marjory de Montgomerie* of Stair-Montgomerie and Cassillis. She joined with Marjory de Montgomerie, daughter of Sir John Montgomerie of Eaglesbame, in a vendition of the lands of "Castlyss" to John Kennedy of Dunure, which vendition was ratified by David II., and is among the charters of the 33d year of that monarch's reign, about 1361-2. In this deed Marjory de Montgomerie, junior, is stated to be daughter of John de Montgomerie, cousin of the other Marjory, who is said to have been married to John Kennedy of Dunure, and to have brought to him the large estates of Cassillis. In the Kennedy papers he is stated to have " acquired from Marjory de Montgomery, senior, *in her pure widowity*, and Marjory, daughter of John de Montgomery, her cousin, the lands of Castlys." In Pitcairn's *Historie of the Kennedys* a tradition is mentioned of John Kennedy of Dunure having obtained these lands from the widow on a promise of marriage, which he did not perform. This, however, may have been a malicious story, put forward during the heat of the feuds which so long prevailed in Carrick. The Kennedy papers, unfortunately, leave the matter in some dubiety. All that is known of the marriage of John Kennedy of Dunure is that his lady's name was *Mary.* He had several children, besides his heir, Sir Gilbert, and it would appear that the barony of Stair had gone to a younger son; for, about 1450, William de Dalrymple acquired the lands of Stair-Montgomery with his wife, Agnes Kennedy, an heiress, whose son, William Dalrymple of Stair, was ancestor of the Earls of Stair, the Baronets of North Berwick, Hailes, &c. The estate of Cassillis has continued, since its acquisition from the Montgomeries, in the possession of the noble family of Kennedy. Cassillis House was long the principal seat of the Earls of Cassillis, until the rebuilding of Culzean Castle, in the parish of Kirkoswald, towards the close of last century, which is now the favourite residence of the Marquis of Ailsa.

### KENNEDIES OF KIRKMICHAEL.

We have already seen that the parish church of Kirkmichael anciently styled " Ecclesia Sancti Michaelis de Gemilstoun," was granted to the Prior and Canons of Whithern by John de Ge-

milstoun, the son and heir of John de Gemilstoun, knight; which grant was confirmed to them by Robert I., in May 1325. Part of the property of Kirkmichael, as appears from ancient charters, was also called Kirkmichael Munterduffy, the name of the clan of whom Roland de Carrick was leader. Gemilstoun is of Saxon derivation, while Munterduffy as clearly indicates the Celtic or aboriginal character of the race by whom it was inhabited. Of the Gemils of Gemilstoun all trace is lost, though the name is not uncommon in Ayrshire. The first of the Kennedies of Kirkmichael was

I. GILBERT KENNEDY of Kirkmichael. He was the son of David Kennedy, sixth son of Sir Gilbert Kennedy of Dunure, one of the progenitors of the noble family of Ailsa. He had a charter of the lands of Kirkmichael, dated 20th August 1429, and in various charters of 1453 and 1455, he is styled " of Kirkmichael."[*] The next on record is

II. Thomas Kennedy of Kirkmichael. In 1503, he and his son, Gilbert Kennedy, are witnesses to a charter by Gilbert Kennedy of Corauchbay,[†] to Gilbert Kennedy, Provost of the Collegiate Church of Maybole.

III. Gilbert Kennedy of Kirkmichael was concerned in the feuds between the Campbells of Loudoun and the Kennedies, having been present at the slaughter of Robert Campbell of Lochfergus, in 1528. In 1529, he was a witness to a charter, by Adam Reid of Starwhite, to John Kennedy of Craigneil, of the lands of Craigfyn and Carslo.

IV. John Kennedy of Kirkmichael is, in 1538, one of the jury on the service of Gilbert third Earl of Cassillis, as heir of his father.

V. John Kennedy of Kirkmichael is one of the jury on the service of Gilbert fourth Earl of Cassillis, as heir to his father, in 1569. In 1585 —Dec. 20—John Kennedy of Kirkmichael, Janet Corrie, his spouse, and Gilbert Kennedy, their son, had a charter of confirmation, from James VI., of the lands of Attiquyn.[‡] He was probably father of

VI. Lamberdo Kennedy of Kirkmichael, who had a charter of confirmation of the barony of Kirkmichael from James VI., 6th May 1576. He is styled in that document " filio Joannis Kennedy de Kirkmichaell." If he was the son of the previous John Kennedy, the barony must

* Culzean charter chest.
† Evidently from the word 'curragh,' a small boat, more peculiar to the Irish. Curragh-bay, the landing place of the curraghs.
‡ Great Seal Reg. In 1594, (19th Dec.) Janet and Susanna Kennedy were served heirs-portioners of their grandfather, John Kennedy of Kirkmichael.

have been resigned to him by his father. In 1595—May 28—he had a charter of the lands of Garfoir and Ballemackessock. The same year—August 16—" Magistro Lamberto Kennedy de Kirkmichael " had a charter " terrarum Ecclesiasticarum vicariæ de Kirkmichael " from James VI   Mr Lambert Kennedy died in 1616 —

" Testament, &c quhilk perteint to vmqnhile Mr Lambert Kennedy of Kirkmichael   . quha deceist in the moneth of Februar 1616 zeiris gevin vp be his awin mouth, in sa far as concernyis the nominatioun of his exceutouris, &c , and puirtlie mind and gevin vp be David Kennedy in Maxwelltoun, his exceutour," &c

" Jonet Kennedy his spous " is mentioned in the legacy , but he appears to have left no children   Allusion is made, however, to a brother's family

He was succeeded probably by his nephew,

VII  David Kennedy of Kirkmichael, who, together with his spouse, " Agnete M'Alexander," had a charter of the lands of Auchinflour, Attiquin &c. from James VI , 23d Dec 1617   He had subsequently a number of charters under the Great Seal, namely, of the lands of Glentig, &c. 21st Dec 1620 , Drumgirnane, 20th July 1632 , Ballochinock, Drumlangford, &c , 23d Jan 1636, Knockdoleone, 29th July 1637 , and Glenmuck, 18th March 1646   He died before July 5. 1653, and was succeeded by his son,

VIII  Thomas Kennedy of Kirkmichael, who was served " heir male of David Kennedie of Kirkmichael, his father," in the " 10 pound land of the bironie of Kirkmichael, of old extent, with the corn and walkmyln," &c , 5th July 1653   Thomas seems to have died early, without issue, for

IX  John Kennedy of Kirkmichael was served heir-male of his grandfather, David Kennedy of Kirkmichael, on the 10th February 1657   He was succeeded by his nephew,

X  " David Kennedie de Kirkmichael, hæres Joannis Kennedie de Kirkmichael," patrui, 17th January 1693   He was succeeded by his son,

XI  David Kennedy of Kirkmichael, born 20th June 1698   He had a charter of resignation, to him and his spouse, of the lands and baronie of Kirkmichael, 29th March 1703 , and another of the lands and house of Grange, Little Brocklock, &c , 26th July 1750.  He had a son, *David*, born 17th March, 1725, who succeeded

XII  David Kennedy of Kirkmichael married Mrs Robina, in the parish of Dailly, 9th December 1765,* by whom he had his successor,

XIII  David Kennedy of Kirkmichael, born

* Parish Records

30th June, 1768.  He married Henrietta Whiteford, daughter of Sir John Whiteford, Bart., of Whiteford, 8th June 1797, and had issue

XIV  David Kennedy of Kirkmichael, born 6th April 1798, died without issue in 1833, and was succeeded by his sister,

XV. Mary Primrose Kennedy, who married James Shaw, second son of Major John Shaw of Dalton, who, assuming the name of Kennedy, is now James Shaw Kennedy of Kirkmichael, C B and Major-General in the army   Issue —

1  John Shaw Kennedy, 36th regiment
2  Henrietta, married to Primrose William Kennedy of Drumellan, Esq

### MURES OF CLONCAIRD

The Mures of Cloncaird were understood to have been an offshoot of the Mures of Auchindrane.  They held the property for a considerable time

I  PATRICK MURE had a charter of the lands of Cloncaird and Barneill, from James IV , dated 19th August 1500   In 1530, Patrick Mure of Cloncaird was concerned in the feuds of the Kennedies and Craufurds

II  Patrick Mure of Cloncaird, " et Mariotæ M'Dowall, ejus conjugi," had a charter of the lands of Brouchjarg and Galdimnoch, in Wigtonshire, from Queen Mary, 30th July 1564

III  Walter Mure of Cloncaird was, in 1600, fined, with a number of others, for abiding from the Raid of Dumfries, under the Earl of Angus  He was also implicated in what has been called " the Auchindrane Tragedy," in 1602   He died before 1687, in which year

IV  Robert Mure of Cloncaird was served heir of Patrick Mure of Cloncaird, his father.  He was thus succeeded, apparently, by a brother, Robert Mure  He died in October 1623   In his testament he constitutes Susanna Kennedy, his wife, his only executrix  He appears to have had no children of his own, and to have disponed his lands to a " Johne Muir," doubtless a relation.  He leaves legacies to his sister, wife of " James Wallace in Dulloris," Margaret Wallace, her daughter, and to " Susanna Peblis, dochter to Mr Rot Peblis, minister at Kirkmichaell "

If John Muir, to whom the lands appear to have been disponed, ever had possession, he did not long enjoy them, for

IV  Jonet Mure, spouse of James Wallace of Dullars, was served heir of her brother, " Roberti Mure de Cloncard, fratres," on the 20th January 1625 ; and again in 1647

Soon after this Cloncaird passed into the hands of the Mures of Auchindraine. John Mure of Auchindraine, heir of Sir John Muir of Auchindraine, was retoured in the lands of Cloncaird and Barneill, amongst others, on the 3d of December 1658. Cloncaird was soon afterwards acquired by Alexander Kennedy, who, together with his spouse, had a charter, under the Great Seal, of the lands of Cloncaird, 17th Nov. 1665.

The estate of Cloncaird now belongs to William Wallace of Busbie and Cloncaird, who succeeded his maternal uncle, the late Henry Ritchie of Busbie and Cloncaird, who died in 1843. (See vol. ii. 219.) The mansion-house of Cloncaird is occupied by the widow of Mr Ritchie, in which she is life-rented.

# PARISH OF KIRKOSWALD.

---

ETYMOLOGY, EXTENT, &c.

This parish derives its name, like many others, from the church, which was dedicated to Saint Oswald, one of the kings of the Heptarchy, who was celebrated for his zealous propagation of Christianity  He was canonized after his death, which occurred in 642, having been slain at Oswastre   From time immemorial a fair has been held at Kirkoswald on the 5th of August, the festival day of the Saint   The church of Kirkoswald stands within the barony of Turnberry, and was anciently called "Ecclesia Sancti Oswaldi de Turnberry

The parish of Kirkoswald is bounded on the north by Maybole, on the east by Kirkmichael and Dailly , on the south by Dailly and Girvan; and on the west by the firth of Clyde   It embraces six miles of sea-coast, and contains nearly 11,000 Scottish acres   It has altogether a picturesque and rich appearance   The surface is hilly, but, with one or two exceptions, not mountainous, and rich in green pasture   The hills of Mochrum and Craigdow, which rise to a considerable altitude, form peculiar and striking objects in the landscape   Mochrum is a flat, broad-based cone, and has been extensively planted with wood   The top is covered with moss   The hill is seen from a great distance, especially at sea   With the exception of a few patches of moss, the whole parish is arable   The shore is less rocky than the generality of the Carrick coast, and is highly favourable for bathing quarters.  A splendid view seaward, and indeed of the interior of the country, is obtained from the hills of Mochrum and Craigdow   There is scarcely any natural wood in the parish , but this defect is amply supplied by the various plantations made by the late Marquis

of Ailsa and Sir Charles Fergusson of Kilkerran, Bart

The parish abounds in excellent springs of water , and although there are no streams of any extent, yet there are numerous rivulets, which afford abundance of pure water   There are, besides, two lochs in the parish , one, covering twenty-four Scots acres, near Mochrum, and another, apparently as large, at Craigdow.

"The parish of Kirkoswald," says Abercrummie, " is pretty populous, because of the coast syde whereof it consists, and is all the pleasure thereof, for the place of the Churche's situation is very obscure and unpleasant, being twixt two hills, at the end of a bogue and marish "  Such was the opinion of the topographer, nearly two hundred years ago.   Modern writers say it " occupies a picturesque site."   Truth to speak, we think the opinion of Abercrummie the most correct for, though the "bogue and the marish" be gone, the church and village are very plainly situated on the west or shore road between Ayr and Girvan, thirteen miles from the former, and eight from the latter town

## HISTORY, CIVIL AND ECCLESIASTICAL

The church of St Oswald, or Kirkoswald of Turnberry, "was granted to the monks of Paisley, by Duncan of Carrick, who afterwards became Earl of Carrick.  It was confirmed, with its lands and tithes, to the monks of Paisley, by Florence, the Bishop elect of Glasgow   It was also confirmed by two Popes, and by Alexander II in 1236   In 1227, it was settled by Walter the Bishop of Glasgow, that the vicar of the church of Turnberry should have yearly 100 shillings in altarage, or in tithes of corn, if the altarage should not be sufficient. Kirkoswald of Turnberry, and some lands appear to have been granted to the monks of Paisley, on the condition that they should establish in Carrick a Monastery of their order: but they did not perform this condition, and Duncan Earl of Carrick, not long before his death, founded the Monastery of Crossraguel. The monks of Paisley complained of this transfer to the Pope, who interfered; but the church continued with the Monastery of Crossraguel. The church of St Oswald of Turnberry was confirmed to the monks of Crossraguel by Robert I.; and it was afterwards confirmed to them by a charter of Robert III., on the 24th of August 1404. Kirkoswald continued to belong to the Monastery of Crossraguel till the Reformation. The monks enjoyed the revenues, which were considerable, and provided a curate to serve the church. Giles Blair, lady of Dow, in Carrick, by her will, which was made on the 31st of August, 1530, bequeathed to the Curate of Kirkoswald one boll of meal, and to Thomas Ferguson, dominical chaplain of Kirkoswald, one boll of meal. She also bequeathed twenty marks, for building an altar in the church of St Oswald. In the rental of Crossraguel Abbey, about the year 1562, which was given in officially by the Earl of Cassillis, it was stated that the tithes of Kirkoswald produced 300 bolls of bear and meal yearly. In 1617, the patronage of Kirkoswald, with all the other property of Crossraguel Abbey, was annexed, by act of Parliament, to the Bishoprick of Dunblane; reserving the same to Peter Hewat, Commendator of Crossraguel, during his life. On the final abolition of Episcopacy, in 1689, the patronage of Kirkoswald was vested in the Crown, to which it now belongs. In 1652, a considerable tract of land, on the north-west side of the river Girvan, and forming about a fourth part of the parish of Kirkoswald, was detached from that parish, and annexed to the parishes of Girvan and Dailly. The old church of Kirkoswald, which had served the parish for ages, and seems to have undergone many alterations, stood in a very low situation, in the midst of a very large burying ground, which is surrounded by a wall. In 1777 a new parish church was built upon a rising ground a little south of the old church."*

Such is Chalmers' ecclesiastical account of the parish. It appears that the "Pennyland of Crossragmol and of Southblan in Carric," were confirmed, along with the three churches in Car-

rick, (Turnberry, Straiton, and Dalmokeran,) to the monks of Paisley, by Alexander II., in 1236. Still earlier mention, however, is made of the gift than this. In a confirmation by Pope Honorius, 1225, of all the lands and churches belonging to the Monastery of Paisley, notice is taken of the donation of the noble man, Duncan Earl of Carrick, of the total lands of Crosragmol and Suthblan, with all their appurtenances, "and one carrucate of land in Ireland, at Dumal's, which is called Tihiror."*

The original charter by "Duncan, the son of Gilbert," is not preserved in the Chartulary of Paisley. The Church of Saint Oswald of Turnberry is mentioned, however, amongst the other churches belonging to the Monastery of Paisley, in the confirmation by Florence, the bishop elect of Glasgow. The document has no date, but is known to have been made between 1202 and 1207. As no other church in Carrick is alluded to, either in this or subsequent confirmations prior to 1236, it is presumable that the church of Turnberry had been originally granted by some of the ancestors of Duncan, and that, in a new donation by that Earl, the churches of Straiton and Dalmakeran had been included.

It seems that Duncan Earl of Carrick contemplated building the Abbey of Crossraguel (Crosragmol) in 1244. In that year the following *Scriptum of Crosragmol*, rendered into English from the original Latin, was issued by the Bishop of Glasgow:—

"William, by the Divine permission, minister of the Church of Glasgow, to all the faithful in Christ, who shall either inspect or hear these present letters, greeting in the Lord, let it be universally known that before us a question being to be moved between the noble lord Duncan Earl of Carric, on the one side, and the Abbot and Convent of Paisley on the other, concerning a religious house of the order of Paisley in Carric, to be founded at Crosragmol, and concerning the property which the said Abbot and monks have possessed in Carric, from the gift of the aforesaid Earl; and at last the parties have submitted, by their own free will, to our decision. We, having God before our eyes, have decided, for promoting religion and good order, with the unanimous consent of the parties, and the assent of the Chapter of Glasgow, in the following manner, namely, that in the aforesaid place, in honour of God and the blessed Virgin Mary,

* The noble family of Ailsa have a burial vault at the Church of Kirkoswald.

* The editor of the Paisley Chartulary says that "Tihiror" may be at Dunamase, in the Queen's county, an early settlement of the De Lacys, who were connected with the Lords of Galloway by marriage.

there may be built a religious house by the monks of the order of Paisley, who may there dwell for ever, and enjoy full liberty, and shall have it in their power freely to appoint, by canonical election, an Abbot, who shall have it in his power to receive those who shall be willing to enter into monastic life, and confirm them in the profession, and to do all which by right belongs to an Abbot; and also that the said House of Crosragmol shall be free in everything from the power and jurisdiction of the Abbot and Convent of Paisley, except only in the recognition of the order, which we declare in the following manner That the monks of Crosragmol shall entirely conform, in order and habit, and the other observances of the Monastery of Paisley, and that the Abbot of Paisley, for the time being, shall visit once a year, with a moderate retinue, and without any heavy expense, the said House of Crosragmol, in which visitation, if he find anything serious or grave to be corrected, that the same thing, (in order that the whole should proceed maturely and with counsel,) shall be corrected by us, along with the same visitor, in canonical form. We have ordered, also, that all the property which for some time the Abbot and Convent of Paisley have possessed in Carric, shall be ceded for ever to the use of the said House of Crosragmol they paying to the House of Paisley ten merks of silver annually at Pentecost, and that, if at any time the said Abbot and monks of Paisley, or the said Earl or his heirs, or the Abbot and monks of Crosragmol, should contravene in any way our ordination, we and our successors shall compel them, by ecclesiastical censure, in the observation of all the aforesaid, plainly, and without any form of law, first giving them an admonition, and also that nothing shall stand valid in the way of infirming the above mentioned, whether as a remedy in canon or civil law, or any privilege of the order of Cluny, either competent, or afterwards to be competent, or any claim whatever in restriction. And in testimony of this transaction, we and the Chapter of Glasgow, and the said Earl of Carrie, have confirmed the present document with our seals. Done in Glasgow, the 15th of August, in the year of Grace, 1244 '

Disputes, arising out of this right of visitation on the part of the Abbey of Paisley, occurred as early as 1265, soon after the completion of the Abbey of Crossraguel In 1370, Rodger the Abbot resigned in consequence of complaints against him by the Abbot of Paisley Similar differences continued to prevail down to the Reformation

The civil history of the parish derives interest from its association with the early and heroic exploits of the restorer of Scottish freedom—Robert the Bruce It was at Turnberry Castle —then held by an English garrison—that he landed with a small band of adherents from the island of Arran, and struck the first successful blow in that series of brilliant achievements which ultimately placed him in security on the Scottish throne.

Under the mild and able ministration of Abbot Kennedy, the Popish religion retained a strong footing in this parish The venerable Abbot frequently preached in the parish church; and here, in 1563, an enthusiastic attempt was made to restore the ancient system A number of influential parties were connected with the reaction *

In future times Kirkoswald will attract no small degree of attention from the circumstance that Burns the Poet spent the summer of 1788 at the school of the village, and that not a few subjects of his muse are identified with the parish Douglas Graham, who occupied the farm of Shanter, is known to have been the hero of the inimitable tale of " Tam o' Shanter." On his tombstone, in the churchyard, he is designed by his fictitious name Burns' mother—from whom he is believed to have inherited his poetical temperament—was a native of Kirkoswald parish, having been the daughter of Gilbert Brown, tenant in Craigenton.

## ANTIQUITIES.

The parish can boast of one of those somewhat rare remains of former times—a vitrified fort It is situated on the shore.

In the *Old Statistical Account* mention is made of two large hillocks, which were situated within thirty yards of the sea-mark, and about ten yards apart. They had existed from time immemorial, and were accidentally discovered to consist of a substance which resembled coal-ashes, and which was found to be good manure for some purposes " Although above 1000 cartloads have been taken," says the writer, " yet there remain in the two hillocks, at a moderate computation, above 3000 loads more. Tradition does not inform us whence these ashes came in such quantities There is no vestige of any building whatsoever nearer than the old farmhouse, and the place is four English miles distant from any coal-work It has been supposed

* See vol. 1, page 73.

they are the effects of barbarous superstition, in times of idolatry in this country."

There are no remains of Pagan worship near to where these ashes existed. In the interior of the parish, however, there are distinct traces of a Druidical circle; and stone-coffins, containing curious ornaments, have been dug up. A very curious spear was discovered some time ago in a moss.

*Turnberry Castle.*—The ruins of this famous Castle—consisting of little more than the foundation—are assuredly the oldest remains in the parish of which any account can be given. They stand upon a small promontory, running into the sea, in the barony of Turnberry. Abercrummie says, " the next (to Culzean) upon the coast, are to be seen the old ruines of the ancient Castle of Turnberry, upon the north-west poynt of that rockie angle that turns about towards Girvan, and is perhaps that place called by Ptoleme, *Perigorium*, of a Greek origination, importing round the corner, and suiting the English designation of Turnberry; and that it cannot be Bargany, as some imagine, the very situation of that castle, and recentness of it, will abundantly show; and to confirme this our conjecture, a tradition amongst the people there will not a little conduce, namely, that near to this very castle there was of old a toune of the same name, of which there is no vestige at present to be seen, but that they perceive some remainders of a causeway; and the reason for this may be, the neighbourhood of the port of greater resort in all that coast, at which the first possessors landed from Ireland, and so might have fixed their habitation near to it, though now the place be but a tract of narrow sands."

There is some probability in the conjecture of Abercrummie. That many of the strongholds of the Romans existed long after their departure is well known, and not a few still exist in various quarters of Britain. This, however, must remain a matter of dubiety. At all events the origin of the Castle of Turnberry cannot now be positively ascertained. It is evident, however, that it was the residence of the M'Dowalls, Earls of Carrick. This may be inferred from the grants of the Church of Turnberry, and from the erection of the Abbey of Crossraguel, by Duncan Earl of Carrick; and it is certain that, in 1271, Martha Countess of Carrick lived at Turnberry, and was in that year married to Robert Bruce, Earl of Annandale.

As the birth-place of King Robert the Bruce, the son of this marriage, Turnberry will be sacred to Scotsmen in all time. It was here, in this Castle, that the first recorded meeting of Scottish nobles, assembled for the purpose of supporting the title of the competitor Bruce to the Crown, was held. This occurred on the 20th September 1286. Here also was it that, in the spring of 1307-8, he struck the first successful blow for freedom. The Castle was then garrisoned by English soldiers. It is generally believed, and so says the *Statistical Account*, that the Castle was destroyed at this time, and that it remained uninhabitable afterwards. The contrary seems to be the fact. In the account of Malcolm, Sheriff of Dumbarton and Baillie of Carrick, between 1326 and 1370, there occur one or two entries in connection with Turnberry :—" And for the expenses of the house of our Lord the King, when he was Earl, £59, 12s. 7¼d.; and seven martis, by the King's letter and precept, showing the same in account; and for the expenses of the King at Turnberry, including the carriage of meal, £21, 17s. 11d. . . . . and to various masons, wrights, and other various operatives, at the works for two years, which he caused to be made about the manor of Turnberry, £85, 18s. 8d. . . . . and seven martis, which are allowed for the works made at the Park of Turnberi." These items refer either to the reign of Robert I. or David II., and they show that, subsequent to the discomfiture of the English garrison at Turnberry, the Castle was not only inhabitable, but had undergone extensive repairs. The demolition of the Castle of Turnberry must therefore have occurred at a later period than is generally supposed.

*Crossraguel Abbey.*—The Abbey of Crossraguel may be regarded as the next oldest building in the parish of Kirkoswald. It was founded, as we have seen, in 1244; but the building was probably not completed for some years afterwards. It has long been in ruins, though great care is now taken to preserve what remains. Abercrummie says, " the fabryck of the Church is entyre, without a roofe. Much of the building is demolished, yet there be two towers still standing entyre in their walls." It is at least 160 years since Abercrummie wrote, and his description of the ruins might serve for the present day. The great injury sustained by the building seems to have been inflicted at the time of the Reformation. The Abbey stands midway between Maybole and Kirkoswald—about two miles distant from each. The public road from Ayr to Portpatrick passes along the north side of the precincts. The situation, as Abercrummie observes, " is noways pleasant "—yet it was well selected in reference to water, a small pelu-

cid stream running along the east of the building  The area of the Abbey grounds measure
about eight acres.  These were enclosed, except
on the south—which was bounded with a marsh—
with a stone wall of considerable strength, having two gates, one to the south, and another to
the south-west.  The former seems to have been
the principal one  The side walls of the church
and choir still remain to the height of fourteen
feet  Towards the east is the niche where the
principal altar stood  " On the right of this is
the vestry, and the Abbot's ecclesiastical court,
all entire, and arched very much in the style of
the Cathedral of Glasgow  There are, besides,
several vaults and cells, all built of fine hewn-
stone "  The tower upon the east, now in ruins,
was the original house of the Abbot; that upon
the west, still very entire, must have been of
more recent construction

According to Keith, the revenues of Crossraguel were £466, 13s. 4d ; bear, 18 c 7 b 3 fi
3 p , meal, 37 c , oats, 4 c 15 b 3 fi 3½ p.

The last Abbot was Quintin Kennedy, brother
to the Earl of Cassillis, well known as the author
of several works, and especially by his disputation with John Knox at Maybole in 1562  Both
the temporalities and spiritualities of Crossraguel were annexed by James VI. to the Bishoprick of Dunblane.  The famous George Buchanan derived a yearly pension from the Abbey.
Allan Stenart, whom the Earl of Cassillis roasted
at a large fire in one of the vaults of Dunure
Castle, for the purpose of compelling him to
subscribe certain documents conveying away the
lands of Crossraguel, was Commendator in 1570
In 1641 the Abbacie was given in tack to Mr
Peter Ewat and his daughter, in consequence
of the losses and hurt he had sustained in the
late troubles as one of the ministers of Edinburgh  He was to have his lifetime of the
Abbacie, and his children, for nineteen years
thereafter, for the yearly sum of five merks
Ewat was at the time advanced in life

The Abbey was afterwards rented from the
Chapel Royal by Sir James Fergusson of Kilkerran, Bart , and the lease still continues in
that family.

*Thomaston Castle.*—The writer in the *Statistical Account* says, " the next old building in the
parish is the house or castle of Thomaston, about
half a mile to the south-east of Culzean.  Tradition tells us that this was built by a nephew of
Robert the Bruce, in the year 1335  It has
been exceedingly strong, and of very considerable extent.  It was inhabited fifty years ago,
and is now the property of the Earl of Cassillis."

It seems to have consisted principally of a strong
tower, and to have had a moat around it  There
are the remains of an extensive orchard in the
vicinity.  Abercrummie notices *Thomaston* as
" once the residence of the Corys, but now of
M'Levain (Mackilveane) of Grimmet ; a very
pretty house, with gardens, orchards, and parks
round it "

*Baltersan.*—Though the statist is silent in
reference to this old building, it nevertheless
claims the attention of the topographer  " Baltersan," says Abercrummie, " is a stately, fyne
house, with gardens, orchards, parks, and woods
about it, lying from Maybole about ane myles
distance "  It is within view of Crossraguel
Abbey  The walls are still pretty entire, but it
has long been roofless, and the orchards, gardens, parks, and woods have given place to corn
and pasture fields  A few solitary trees sym-
pathize with it in its decay.  It bears evidence,
however, of having been at one time a good
house

*Culzean Castle.*—This, the most celebrated of
all the houses of the nobility in Carrick, ought
probably to have had precedence in these notices.
Though the existing mansion is of modern construction, having been built in 1777, it occupies
the site of one of the most ancient residences on
the coast  It was originally called the *Cove*, and
consisted of a strong tower, with minor buildings, in the usual style of the older feudal mansions  " The Cove," says Abercrummie, " is
the mansion-house of Sir Archibald Kennedy of
Colaine, and takes its name hence, that under
the outer area of this house there be three naturall coves, which enter laigh at the water-mark
From the one they enter upwards to a higher, by
ane easie ascent , but the entry to the third is
more difficult, being both low in the entry and
strait ; and in the highest of them there is a
spring of very good water "  Abercrummie elsewhere describes the Cove as " standing upon a
rock above the sea, flanked upon the south with
very pretty gardens and orchards, adorned with
excellent tarases, and the walls loaden with
peaches, apricotes, cherries, and other fruits ; and
these gardens are so well sheltered from the
north and east winds, and ly so open to the south,
that the fruits and herbage are more early than
at any other place in Carrick "  The pre-emin-
ence of Culzean in horticulture and gardening
has thus been of long standing  At the present
day the gardens of Culzean form one of the
chief attractions to visitors, and their produce
bears a high name in local competition

The Coves of Culzean, referred to by Abercrummie, have long been famed in fairy tradition, and are considered curious as objects of nature. The outer cove, which enters at low water mark, is about fifty feet high in the roof, and nearly two hundred feet long, extending inwards. The other two are considerably less, but of the same irregular form. There are other three coves, towards the east, which also communicate with each other. They are nearly of the same height and form as the other. It is popularly believed that these coves extend an unknown distance into the interior; and in corroboration of this, it is said that a piper, who had lost his way amongst them, was heard playing several miles from the sea!

The modern Castle of Culzean is a noble edifice. The projecting rock upon which it stands, immediately above the sea, is about 100 feet in height, and almost perpendicular. The style of the building is singularly elegant. The pleasure grounds are most extensive, comprising nearly 700 acres, studded with numerous plantations. The Castle, from its position, commands a beautiful marine prospect, and is altogether one of the most delightful residences on the west coast of Scotland. Its founder was David tenth Earl of Cassillis.

## FAMILIES IN THE PARISH OF KIRKOSWALD.

### TURNBERRY.

Of the families of Carrick, which originally formed part of Galloway, we have no knowledge prior to the twelfth century, when the rebellion and feuds of Gilbert and Uchtred, the two sons of Fergus, Lord of Galloway, ultimately led to the settlement of Carrick upon Duncan, son of Gilbert, in 1186. That Turnberry Castle was the original seat of the old Earls of Carrick has already been shown. The family can be traced from authentic documents.

I. FERGUS, Lord of Galloway, left two sons, Gilbert and Uchtred, betwixt whom, at his death, 1161, his lands were divided.

II. Gilbert, along with his brother Uchtred, attended William the Lion in his invasion of Northumberland, in 1174, when that monarch was taken prisoner. Upon that event, the men of Galloway broke into rebellion, murdered many of the King's subjects, and threw down his castles. William the Lion is well known to have built various castles throughout his kingdom— amongst others one at Ayr, expressly to repel the inroads of the lawless men of Galloway; and this attempt to throw off the yoke of William may have been induced by the recent erection of certain strongholds for their subjection. The rebellion threw Gilbert and Uchtred into the hands of Henry II. of England, and might have led to the final separation of Galloway from the Crown of Scotland. The cruel assassination of Uchtred, by his brother Gilbert, in 1174, entirely changed the face of affairs, however. On the death of Gilbert, 1185, Roland, the son of Uchtred, took up arms, and, backed by William the Lion, entirely conquered the vassals of his uncle, and slew their commander, Gilpatrick, 4th July 1185. He even showed a determined front against the threatened invasion of the English monarch, who had assembled a large army at Carlisle in 1186. This led to a pacification between the contending parties, and it was settled that Roland should retain all that had been possessed by his father, Uchtred, and that upon

III. Duncan, the son of Gilbert, should be conferred the territory of Carrick. This occurred in 1186. Whether Turnberry Castle had been built by William the Lion, as a means of subjecting Galloway more thoroughly to his sway, or whether it was a still older stronghold, cannot be ascertained; but that it became the residence of Duncan, the first Lord of Carrick, as a distinct possession, can scarcely be doubted. Duncan was created Earl of Carrick soon after this arrangement; and, as we have seen, founded the Abbey of Crossraguel in 1244. He likewise gave various donations to the monks of Paisley and Melrose for the welfare of his soul. He left a son,

IV. Neil second Earl of Carrick, who, like his father, was a munificent patron of the Church. He gave largely to the monasteries of Crossraguel, and Sandale in Kintyre. In 1255, a commission was granted by Henry III., for receiving Neil Earl of Carricke, and other Scotsmen, into his protection. He was one of the Regents of Scotland, and guardians of Alexander III. and his Queen, appointed in the Convention at Roxburgh, 20th September 1255. He died next year. He married Margaret, daughter of Walter, High Steward of Scotland, by whom he had a daughter,

V. Margaret Countess of Carrick, who inherited his title and extensive property. She married, first, Adam de Kilconath, or Kilconquhar, who, in her right, became third Earl of Carrick. Engaging in the crusade, 1268, he went to the Holy Land, under the banners of Louis IX. of France, and died at Acon in Palestine in 1270. The next year, 1271, his widowed Countess happening to meet Robert Bruce, son of Robert Bruce, Lord of Annandale and Cleveland, hunting in her domains, she became enamoured of his personal attractions, and with some violence led him to her castle of Turnberry, where they were married in a few days, without the knowledge of their relations, or the requisite consent of the King. Alexander III. seized her castle and estates, but afterwards accepted of a fine for her feudal delinquency. From this union sprung the hero of Bannockburn—Robert the Bruce.

## BRUCES EARLS OF CARRICK.

The Bruces were of Norman descent. "Robert de Brus," the first of the family, accompanied William the Conqueror from Normandy, and acquired extensive possessions in England. His son, also named "Robert de Brus," visited Scotland, and obtained the lordship of Annandale, and other possessions, from David I. The Annandale property went to the second son of this Robert, who became a subject of the Scottish crown. "Robert de Brus," fifth in descent from the Norman Robert, married Isabel, second daughter of David Earl of Huntingdon, brother of William the Lion, and sister and co-heir of John the Scot, Earl of Chester and Huntingdon. By this marriage his descendants became heirs of the Scottish throne. He died in 1245, his wife surviving him a few years. Their son, "Robert de Brus," took a distinguished part in Scottish affairs. He sat in the Parliament of Brigham, as Lord of Annandale, 18th July 1290; and on the death of Margaret, the same year, entered

his claim to the crown of Scotland, as nearest heir of Alexander III. In 1292, on the crown being adjudged to Baliol by Edward I., Bruce resigned his pretensions to his son, the Earl of Carrick, and died at his castle of Lochmaben in 1295, aged 85.

I. ROBERT DE BRUS, Earl of Carrick, by his marriage with the Countess of Carrick, as already mentioned, was the seventh in descent from the follower of William the Conqueror. He was born about 1245. He accompanied Edward I. to Palestine in 1269, and was in consequence held in much esteem by that prince. In 1281, when Edward lent Bruce £40, he styled him *dilectus bachelarius noster*. He sat in the parliament at Brigham as Earl of Carrick, and swore fealty to Edward I. in 1292. On the death of his wife, the Countess of Carrick, he resigned, in compliance with the law of Scotland, into the hands of Robert de Bruce, his son and heir, the whole earldom of Carrick, with its pertinents, and also all the other lands which he had at any time held in Scotland, or ought to have held, by reason of Margaret, late Countess of Carrick, his spouse, the mother of the said Robert, as the right of inheritance of the said Robert, his son and heir. This resignation was dated 27th October 1292, so that the death of the Countess must have occurred prior to that date. The Earl of Carrick succeeded his father in the Annandale estates in 1295, and was appointed governor of the Castle of Carlisle in his room. He did not sit in the first Parliament of Baliol, but appears, from the summonses, to have sat in those of England. He accompanied Edward I. in his invasion of Scotland against Baliol, and was present at the battle of Dunbar in 1296. According to Fordun, Edward had promised to raise Bruce to the throne in room of Baliol. Bruce now reminded Edward of his promise. "Have I no other business," replied Edward, "but to conquer kingdoms for you?" Bruce silently retired, and passed the remainder of his days in England, in safe and opulent obscurity. He and his son swore fealty to Edward at Berwick, 28th August 1296. They are styled in the record, *Robert de Brus le veil, e Robert de Brus le jeoune comte de Carrick.* Dying in 1304, he was buried at Holmcultram. By Margaret, his Countess, he had issue:

1. Robert Earl of Carrick.
2. Edward, also Earl of Carrick.
3. Thomas, and
4. Alexander, both of whom were taken prisoners in Galloway, 9th Feb. 1306-7, by Duncan Macdowal, when bringing aid from Ireland to their brother Robert. They were grievously wounded in the engagement which occurred on the occasion. Macdowal presented his bleeding prisoners at Carlisle to Edward I., who ordered them to be immediately executed.

5. Neil, a youth of singular comeliness. He was one of those who surrendered at Kildrummie Castle to the Earls of Lancaster and Hereford, in 1306. He was tried by a special commission at Berwick, condemned, hanged and beheaded.

1. Lady Isabel, married, first, to Sir Thomas Randolph of Strathdon, High Chamberlain of Scotland, by whom she had Thomas Earl of Moray, regent of Scotland; secondly, to an Earl of Atholl; thirdly, to Alexander Bruce. The charters of Robert I. to Isabel, Countess of Atholl, and Alexander Bruce, her son, and to Isabel de Atholia, and Alexander Bruce, " filio suo nepoti nostro," do not more particularly describe the parties.

2. Lady Mary, married, first, to Sir Neil Campbell of Lochow; secondly, to Sir Alexander Fraser, High Chamberlain of Scotland.

3. Lady Christian, married, first, to Gratney, Earl of Marr; secondly, to Sir Cristopher Seton of Seton, put to death by the English in 1306; thirdly, to Sir Andrew Moray of Bothwell.

4. Lady Matilda, married to Hugh Earl of Ross. There are two charters of Robert I. to Hugh de Ross, and Mauld, sister to the King, of the lands of Narue (Nairn) with the burgh, and of Crumbachie.

5. Lady Margaret, married to Sir William Carlyle of Torthorwald and Cramington. In the charters of Robert I. there is one to William Karle, the King's sister's son, of the lands of Culyn and Roucan.

6. Lady Elizabeth, married to Sir William Dishington of Ardross, in Fife.

7. Lady ——, married to Sir David de Brechin.

II. Robert the Bruce, Earl of Carrick, the restorer of the Scottish monarchy, was born on the 11th July 1274, and had his mother's earldom of Carrick resigned to him by his father in 1292, when in his eighteenth year. The manner in which he asserted his claim to the Scottish throne, and his ultimate and glorious triumph over the chivalry of England at Bannockburn, in 1314, are all matters of history. He died at Cardross, in Dumbartonshire, on the 7th June 1329, in the 55th year of his age.

King Robert I. married, first, Isabella, daughter of Donald, tenth Earl of Mar, by whom he had a daughter, *Marjory*, who fell into the hands of the English in 1306, and was detained a prisoner in charge of Henry de Percy till 1314, when she was conducted to Scotland by Walter the Steward of Scotland, to whom she was married in 1315, and died in 1315-6, leaving an only child, King Robert II.

Robert I. married, secondly, in 1302, Lady Elizabeth de Burgo, eldest daughter of Richard, second Earl of Ulster. In 1306, she fled to the sanctuary of St Duthac, in Ross-shire; but the Earl of Ross, violating the sanctuary, delivered her up to the English. The directions given for her entertainment are preserved by Rymer. She was to be conveyed to the manor of Brustewick; to have a writing-woman, and a maid-servant advanced in life, sedate, and of good conversation, a butler, two men-servants, and a foot-boy for her chamber, sober and not riotous, to make her bed; three greyhounds when she inclined to hunt; ve-

nison, fish, and the fairest house in the manor. She was removed to another prison in 1308, to Windsor Castle in 1312, when twenty shillings weekly were allowed for her maintenance, and to the Castle of Rochester in 1314. She was the same year, together with the daughter and sister of Bruce, the Bishop of Glasgow, and the Earl of Marr, exchanged for the Earl of Hereford. She died on the 20th October 1327, and was buried in Dunfermline, having had issue :

King David II., born 5th March 1323-4, succeeded his father in 1329, and was crowned at Scone 24th Nov. 1331. His subsequent history shows how strong the Baliol faction still was in Scotland, and how, when relieved of the presence of an overbearing foe, as the country had been by the unparalleled valour and judgment of his father, the feudal heads of the people forgot their patriotism in their personal rancour and love of aggrandisement. He retired to France after the battle of Halidonhill, in 1333, landed at Inverbervie, on his return, in 1341, was taken prisoner at the battle of Durham in 1346, remained in captivity till 1357, and died without issue, in the Castle of Edinburgh, 23d Feb. 1370-1, in the 47th year of his age. He married, first, 12th July 1328, Johanna, daughter of Edward II. of England, who died in 1362; secondly, in 1363, Margaret, daughter or relict of John de Logie, who survived him.

1. Margaret, married, first, to Robert Glen, as appears from a charter of David II. to Robert Glen and Margaret Bruce, the King's sister, of Pittedy, in the shire of Kinghorn, in Fife; secondly, to William fourth Earl of Sutherland. They had a charter of the Earldom of Sutherland, 10th October 1347. She died in 1358, leaving issue by the Earl.

2. Matilda, married to Thomas Isaac, and had two daughters:—Johanna, married to John Lord of Lorn; and Catherine, who died unmarried. Their mother died at Aberdeen, 30th July 1353, and was buried at Dunfermline.

3. Elizabeth, married to Sir Walter Oliphant of Aberdalgy.

III. Sir Edward Bruce, brother of King Robert I., had a grant from that monarch of the earldom of Carrick, with the title and dignity of an Earl—the gift, however, to return to the king in default of heirs. Edward Bruce was also Lord of Galloway. In 1315, the Irish of Ulster, oppressed by the English, implored the aid of the King of Scots, and offered to acknowledge his brother Edward as their sovereign. Edward landed at Carrickfergus, 25th May 1315, was solemnly crowned King of Ireland 2d May 1316, but fell at the battle of Dundalk, 5th October 1318. A dispensation was granted by Pope John XXII., dated at Avignon, 1st June 1317, permitting Edward de Bruss, comes de catrilz, and Ysabella, daughter of William Earl of Ros, to marry, notwithstanding their being within the third and fourth degrees of consanguinity, for the purpose of putting an end to feuds betwixt their parents, relations, and friends. Edward, King of Ireland, had no issue, but left three natural sons :

1. Robert.
2. Alexander.
3. Thomas, successively Earls of Carrick.

IV. Robert, Earl of Carrick, the eldest son, inherited that earldom in virtue of the before recited charter to the heirs-male of the body of Edward Bruce, without restricting the succession to those legitimately procreated. He fell at the battle of Duplin, 12th August 1332, without issue.

V. Alexander, Earl of Carrick, submitted to Baliol after that disastrous action, and was taken in arms at Annan by the Earl of Moray, who saved him from punishment. He atoned for his short defection from his cousin, David II., at the battle of Hallidonhill, 19th July 1333, where he fell valiantly fighting against the English. He married Eleanor, only daughter of Archibald Douglas, sister of William, first Earl of Douglas, and by her had an only daughter, Lady *Eleanor*, married to Sir William de Cunynghame of Kilmaurs.

VI. Thomas, Earl of Carrick, succeeded his brother Alexander, and appears as one of the associates of Robert the Steward, Guardian of Scotland, whom he joined with the flower of the gentry of Kyle, in 1334, but died soon afterwards, without issue.

The earldom of Carrick was now conferred on *Sir William de Cunynghame*, knight, who became ninth Earl of Carrick,* but the title soon reverted to the Crown.

The next, or tenth Earl of Carrick, was *John*, son of Walter the High Steward and Marjory Bruce. The title of Earl of Carrick was conferred upon him by David II., in 1368. He and his wife, Annabella, daughter of Sir John Drummond, had a charter of the earldom from Robert II., his father, to them and their heirs. On the accession of John to the Scottish throne, under the title of Robert III., his eldest son, *David*, became Earl of Carrick, and was created Duke of Rothesay in 1398. When Robert III. instituted the principality of Scotland, in 1404, the title of Earl of Carrick was merged in the princedom.

The barony of Turnberry appears to have continued with the Crown till 1482, when it was acquired by John, second Lord Kennedy.

[The foregoing account of the Earls of Carrick has been abridged chiefly from Wood's Peerage.]

## CULZEAN—KENNEDY MARQUIS OF AILSA AND EARL OF CASSILLIS.

That the noble family of Kennedy is of great antiquity in Ayrshire is unquestionable. Chalmers derives them from the Irish, or rather the Scoto-

* See vol. 1. p. 213.

Irish; but little weight is to be attached to this tradition, as all who spoke the Erse, or Gaelic language, were in later times called Irish. It is at the same time evident that the Kennedies were not of Norman or Saxon origin, but of the unmixed old British stock. Nisbet supposed the etymology of the name to be *Kean-na-ty*, signifying, in Gaelic, the head of a house; but this fancy is set aside by the fact that *Kennedy* was a patronymic in Carrick prior to the gift of chiefship which gave rise to it.* "Marcow Mackennedy," says Chalmers, on the authority of the Melrose Chartulary, "was judge, under the Earl of Carrick, during the reign of Alexander II.," which reign extended from 1214 to 1249. In 1266, according to the Chamberlain Rolls, Fergus Makenedy acted as attorney for the Sheriff of Ayr. One of the earliest notices of the name which has been met, occurs in a charter, by Nicholaus, son of Duncan de Carrick, to the Church of St Cuthbert of Maybole, supposed to be dated in 1250. One of the witnesses is *Murthau Mackenede. Murthauco senescallo*, probably the same person, occurs as a witness in a charter by Duncan Earl of Carrick, some years previously.† The name thus seems to have been originally *Mackennedy*, and was probably derived from a common ancestor of the name of *Kenneth*. In the Chartulary of Glasgow Kennedy is spelled *Kenide, Kenyde*, approaching nearly to the *Mackenede* of the North Berwick Chartulary. Wyntoun, who wrote in the pure vernacular, calls Keneth M'Alpine *Kyned*:—

> " Quhen Alpyne thes Kyng wes dede,
> He left a son was called KYNED."

If Wyntoun is to be regarded as an authority, it would thus appear that *Kennedy, Kenede*, or *Kyned*, were but other modes of spelling or pronouncing the name *Kenneth*. There is a tradition, if we recollect rightly, that one Kenneth, from the Western Isles, was the founder of a family in Carrick. Be this as it may, the name is certainly of long standing in Ayrshire.

The next point in reference to which there seems to be any dubiety, is the more immediate descent of the noble family of Ailsa, who claim to be the head of the clan Kennedy. It has long been held by that family and its numerous branches, that they represent the " old Earls of Carrick"—meaning the first Earls of Carrick, before the marriage of Robert Bruce of Annandale with the Countess of Carrick. A recent search through the charter chest of the Marquis

* The grant of Chiefship by Neil Earl of Carrick to Roland de Carrick, before 1255.
† Chartulary of the Nunnery of North Berwick.

of Ailsa * has failed to establish this point satisfactorily. Duncan, the son of Gilbert, was a mere youth when the district of Carrick was conferred upon him by William the Lion, in 1186. This is apparent from the circumstance that, in the war which ensued after his father's death, between the adherents of his house and his cousin Roland, his forces were headed, not by himself, but by those no doubt entitled to do so during the minority of the chief; but the fact is still more evident from the advanced age to which Duncan attained. He founded, as we have seen, the Abbey of Crossraguel in 1244, and he survived till the 13th day of June 1250.† Supposing him to have been twenty years of age in 1186, he would have been eighty-four at his death. He could thus have had no family on his settlement in Carrick. Marcow Mackennedy, who acted as judge of Carrick, under Earl Duncan, between 1214 and 1249, could not reasonably be supposed to have been of his family, or even of his kin, at all events by the male side, because the patronymic of the Lords of Galloway, of whom Duncan was descended, was Macdowal, and De Carrick was not assumed until after the settlement of 1186—probably a number of years subsequently. The first time we meet with it is in the charter already mentioned, in 1250, by "Nicholaus, son of *Duncan de Carrick*." Thus we see that *Mackennedy* was a surname in Carrick before we find any trace of the *De Carricks*; and that the two names were separate and distinct, and continue so down to our own day, will appear obvious from the comparison of a few dates. The Chamberlain Rolls show that *Roland de Carrick*, who obtained the grant of chiefship, from Neil second Earl of Carrick, was alive in 1265, and that *Fergus Makenedy*, attorney to the Sheriff of Ayr, existed in 1266. Again, *John de Carrick*, chaplain of Glasgow, was living before 1300; *Gilbert de Carrick*, who delivered up Loch Doon Castle to the English, did so in 1306; while *Hugh Kenedy*, knight,‡ and Master *Alex. Kenedy*, canon of Glasgow, were alive between 1272 and 1296.

The way is thus clear, so far. The Kennedies must have been a distinct race from the De Carricks, who obviously sprung from the " old Earls of Carrick." It remains, therefore, to be considered whether the noble family of Ailsa is descended from the De Carricks; and if so, how they abandoned a patronymic already ennobled

for one of as great or greater antiquity probably, but still comparatively of plebeian consideration.

We shall give the editor's statement (Historical Account already referred to) in his own words:

Fergus, Lord of Galloway, died in 1161, leaving two sons, Uchtred and Gilbert. In 1174 Gilbert slew his brother Uchtred, who left a son, Roland. Gilbert died in 1185, and was succeeded by his son Duncan. In the next year William I. interfered between the two cousins, and arranged their feuds, by giving to Duncan that portion of Galloway now called Carrick, while Roland retained the lordship of Galloway. Roland left a son, Alan, who succeeded to the lordship of Galloway, and left three daughters, Elena, Devorgilla, and Christian, among whom his estates were divided.

Duncan, who was created Earl of Carrick by Alexander II. between 1225 and 1230, granted the church of Kirkbride, with its pertinents, to the Cistertian Nunnery at North Berwick. The church of Kirkbride stood upon the sea-coast, on the lands of Dunduff, about half a mile north of the castle of Dunure. The parish of Kirkbride was annexed to that of Maybole before 1597, and now forms the northern part of the united parish of Maybole. It also appears that, in 1193, Earl Duncan granted the lands of Maybottle to the Monks of Melros. Soon after 1216 he granted the church of St Cuthbert at Maybole, with its lands and tithes, to the Cistertian Nunnery of North Berwick, and died about 1249.

This grant was repeated and confirmed by Neil, the second Earl of Carrick. He also granted a charter to Sir Roland de Carrick, previous to 1256, the year of his death, constituting him and his heirs Head of the whole Clan, as " well in calumpniis as in other articles and things pertaining to the Kenkynol,* with the office of bailiary of the said county, and the leading of the men thereof." This charter was confirmed by Alexander II., by a charter dated at Stirling, 20th January, in the 27th year of his reign, 1275-6. It also appears that Earl Duncan had other sons besides Neil, his eldest son and heir. He had a son, John de Carrick, who had the lands of Straiton, and granted the patronage of the church of Straiton to the Monks of Paisley. This grant was confirmed by a charter of Alexander II. in 1244. He is a witness to the charter by Earl Duncan of an annual rent out of the lands of Berbeth. And in other charters, printed in the same collection, granted by Earl Duncan, there are mentioned as witnesses, " Alano Alexandro et Alano filiis comitis." In 1266 there is an entry in the Chamberlain Rolls, in the compotum of Ayrshire, of so much owing " per relivium Rollandi de Carrik," showing that he had succeeded to some property, and possibly as the heir of John de Carrick, son of Earl Duncan.

The first who swore fealty to Edward I. in 1296 of the Ayrshire barons, was " Gilbert fiz Roland," who appears to have been the same as Gilbertus filius Rolandi de Carrick, in the North Berwick Chartulary. In 1342 Gilbert de Carrick received a payment from the Crown; and in 1342 Nigel de Carrick also received a payment.

Sir Gilbert de Carrick, son of Sir Roland de Carrick, submitted, in 1285, a difference between him and the nuns of North Berwick to Robert Bruce, Earl of Carrick, (who married the daughter of Neil, second Earl, and was father of Robert I.), and to Robert, Bishop of Galloway, to which Sir Gilbert de Carrick's seal is appended, having the same coat of arms which the Cassillis family now carries.† If, as is generally supposed, this Sir Gilbert de Carrick is the

---

* Historical Account of the noble Family of Kennedy, Marquess of Ailsa and Earl of Cassillis, &c. Privately printed, 1849.
† Chart. of Glasgow.
‡ Sir Hugh Kennedy swore fealty to Edward I. in 1296.

VOL. II.

* In Gaelic, " Kean" denotes the head, and " Keanel" a tribe or family. It denoted, in Galloway, the right of exacting, under the name of " Canpes," a substantial contribution from the members of the clan, such as a horse, cow, or heifer.
† This charter is in the possession of Lord Panmure, and is printed in the Chartulary of the Nunnery of North Berwick.

J. 2

ancestor of the family of Kennedy of Dunure, and was possessed of that estate, which is situated in the parish of Maybole, and close to the church and lands of Kirkbride. It is very possible that he might have conflicting interests with the Cistertian Nunnery at North Berwick, to whom the church of Cuthbert at Maybole, with its lands and tithes, and the church of Kirkbride, had been granted by Earl Duncan. There is not, in the charter chest of the Marquess of Ailsa, any original grant of the barony of Dunure, whereby it might be seen how that estate came into the family. But that this Sir Gilbert de Carrick was connected, through his father, Sir Roland de Carrick, with the old Earls of Carrick, farther appears from the circumstance, that when Robert Bruce, Earl of Carrick, who married Marjory, heiress of Neil, second Earl, appeared before King John Bahol in 1292, to resign the earldom to his son, afterwards Robert I, Sir Gilbert de Carrick is one of the sureties to the King for obtaining the resignation of the earldom.

A letter of Remission was granted by Robert I to Sir Gilbert de Carrick, which is without date, but must have been granted prior to 16th July 1309, for surrendering the castle of Lochdoon to the English, and restoring him, 'in integrum' to all his lands, tenements, and possessions, and to the office of keeper of the castle of Lochdoon. These lands and castle still belong to the family.

About the year 1290, a charter was granted by Malcolm Earl of Lennox, in favour of Gilbert de Carrick, son and heir of the deceased Sir Gilbert de Carrick, of the lands of Bukmonyn Kennedy, Cromicane, and Blairfode, in the earldom of Lennox.* This Gilbert de Carrick was one of the prisoners taken at the battle of Durham in 1146.

The earliest charter in Lord Ailsa's charter chest is dated 18th January 1357-8, by David II, confirming, in favour of John de Kennedy, all the lands, tenements, and possessions belonging to or acquired by him. This is the first time the name of Kennedy appears in the title deeds. It has been supposed that this John de Kennedy, who, in another charter, about the same period, is called of Dunure, changed the name from Carrick to Kennedy.

There can be little doubt that Sir Roland de Carrick, who was constituted head of the whole of his tribe, (caput totius progenie sui,) bailie of Carrick, and leader of the men, under the Earl, was a near relation, probably the nephew of Nigellus Earl of Carrick, from whom he obtained the charter of Kenkynol. That Earl Duncan had several sons, besides Neil, or Nigellus, is evident from the charters mentioned, and Roland may have been the son of John, as surmised. It is also very clear that Gilbert fiz Roland, and Gilbert de Carrick, son and heir of the deceased Sir Gilbert de Carrick, who had a charter from Malcolm Earl of Lennox, of the lands of Buck-monyn-Kennedy,† in 1290, were his immediate

* On 28th October 1393, Duncan Earl of Lennox, confirms a grant by Sir Gilbert Kennedy of Dunure in favour of John Kennedy, son of Fergus Kennedy, of the lands of Buckmonyn, in the earldom of Lennox. The presumption here is undoubtedly that Sir Gilbert Kennedy of Dunure had succeeded Sir Gilbert de Carrick as heir in these lands when he granted them to John Kennedy, son of Fergus Kennedy.

† There had been a close intimacy between the old Earls of Carrick and the Earls of Lennox. This appears from a dispute, in 1233, between the monks of Paisley and Samuel of Renfrew, concerning the lands of Monach-kennaran. Malcolm Beg, and Rotheric Beg de Carrick, brother of Malcolm, give evidence in the question, and

descendants. But it is by no means so satisfactorily demonstrated that *John de Kennedy*, whose first charter from David II. is dated in 1357-8, was the direct male descendant of these De Carricks. Between the charter by Malcolm Earl of Lennox, in 1290, and 1357-8, a period of nearly seventy years had elapsed, so that more than one generation must have occurred between Gilbert de Carrick and John de Kennedy. The editor of the "Historical Account" must be wrong, we should think, in stating that this "Gilbert de Carrick was one of the prisoners taken at the battle of Durham in 1346." Supposing him to have been only twenty-one years of age in or about 1290, when he succeeded his father, Sir Gilbert, he would have been seventy-seven at the battle of Durham! It seems to be almost certain, therefore, that one or more descendants of the De Carricks had been in possession of the lands belonging to the family before the time of John de Kennedy. In short, there is no evidence that this Kennedy was related to the De Carricks in any way whatever, save that he, or his descendant, is found in possession of certain properties which had formerly belonged to that family, and that Sir Gilbert de Carrick's seal, in 1285, is the same as the coat of arms now carried by the Ailsa family. The former amounts to no proof at all, and the latter, though generally regarded as corroborative evidence, must be held as of little moment in the face of other contradictory circumstances. The arms of Carrick, as worn by Robert the Bruce, and David II, before their accession to the crown, were simply "argent, a chevron, gules," so that the three cross-crosslets of Gilbertus de Carrick, in 1285, must have been additions by that branch of the family altogether independent of the crusades of Adam de Kilconath, or of Robert Bruce, in the Holy Land, the period usually assigned for their adoption; while the addition of John Kennedy of Dunure, in 1371, of two lions sitting on each side as supporters, and a lion erect as the crest, were still later and greater deviations. Indeed, the assumption of the lions suggests a connection with the Stewart family sufficient to explain the position of Kennedy of Dunure. It is certainly singular, if the descent of John de Kennedy from the De Carricks was so immediate as is represented, why no charters of an earlier date than

show that they were intimately acquainted with the locality. Gillekonel Manthac, brother of the Earl of Carrick (Duncan it must have been from the date), was also examined, and agreed in all things with Malcolm and Rotheric Beg. The lands of Buckmonyn-Kennedy, had been so designed before 1290, while the patronymic of De Carrick was still used by the descendants of Roland de Carrick.

1357-8 are to be found in the Ailsa charter-chest. The family, unlike most others of the nobility, is not known to have sustained any disaster destructive of its records; and it is still more singular that this charter supplies no evidence of the family connection. "This is the first time the name of Kennedy appears in the title-deeds," says the editor of the *Historical Account*, in reference to the charter of 1357-8—a fact not at all singular, seeing that, as he previously informs us, it is "the earliest charter in Lord Ailsa's charter-chest." This is an important admission. In the earliest of all the title-deeds of the family the name is *Kennedy*. If this John Kennedy changed the name, as "has been supposed," from Carrick to Kennedy, it is evident that his doing so had no influence on the other members of the De Carrick family, as was usual where the head of a clan adopted a new patronymic. For example, *Gilbert Carrick* had a charter of "ane liferent of the office of coronership betwixt the waters of Air and Doune," from David II., and in 1370, John Kennedy of Dunure obtained from Malcolm, son of *Roland de Carrick*, the two penny land called Treuchan and Kennochen, lying in the parish of Kirkmichael-Munterduffy. The name repeatedly occurs contemporaneously with, and subsequently to, the supposed change of the patronymic of the leader of the clan. Strange enough, there is an incomplete charter by Robert II. to "*Gilberto de Carryk* de omnibus suis terris." It occurs in Book 3, No. 8, of the crown records, and must have been in the early part of that monarch's reign, much about the same time that John Kennedy of Dunure obtained his charter. This Gilbert de Carrick, co-existent with John Kennedy of Dunure, must have been one of the direct representatives of the De Carrick family.

Viewing, as we thus do, the alleged descent of the noble family of Ailsa from the old Earls of Carrick as extremely doubtful, it would be equally difficult, perhaps, to account for the Kennedies being found in all the principal possessions of the De Carricks. It is, nevertheless, perfectly possible to surmise a very plausible solution of the mystery. The editor of the "Historical Account" himself helps us to the suggestion. He says that

In the Cumbernauld charter-chest there is an exemplification of a confirmation in favour of "Joannes Cumyn filius quondam Joannis Cumyn," of a grant made by the deceased William Cumyn, Earl of Buchan, to Cambuskenneth, of a bovate of land in Kirkintulloch—two of the witnesses to which are "Fergusio de Kennedy senescallo nostro, Joanne fratre ejus," &c. It is in a handwriting of the 16th century, and is stated to be taken "de libro registri de Cambuskyaneth." The "curia de Lenzie" is also mentioned in it. This Earl of Buchan died before

1244; and John Cumyn of Badenoch, the son of John Cumyn who grants this confirmation, was one of the competitors for the Crown of Scotland in 1292.

The Cumyns were of Royal descent, and of the highest nobility in the kingdom; and it was not unusual for barons and chieftains to discharge the duties of stewards or judges to such personages or public functionaries, and ultimately come to possess the estates which they originally only managed; and thus the Kennedys may have acquired the barony of Lenzie. Chalmers says in his Caledonia,—' the overpowering influence of the Cumyns during the factious reign of Alexander III., (from 1249 to 1285,) created the new office of Justiciary in Galloway for John Cumyn.' He may at this time have brought Fergus Kennedy and his brother to act judicially under him in his court at Lenzie.

*Marcow Mackennedy*, as we have seen, was judge of Carrick, under Earl Duncan, between 1214 and 1249. Upon the principle that "it was not unusual for barons and chieftains to discharge the duties of stewards or judges to such personages or public functionaries, and ultimately *come to possess the estates which they originally only managed*," what was to prevent the descendants of Marcow Mackennedy from taking the position of the De Carricks? The Kennedies, who are presumed to have thus acquired the barony of Lenzie, were relations of the Kennedies of Dunure, the latter of whom ultimately succeeded to the lands of Kirkintilloch and Lenzie. Marcow Mackennedy may have been the chief of his clan, and the common ancestor of both families. Fergus Kennedy, supposed to have been taken by Cumyn to act under him in the court of Lenzie between 1244 and 1285, may, in point of time, have been the son of Marcow. In a charter by David II., who reigned between 1329 and 1371, "anent the clan of Muntercasduff," *John Mackennedy* is stated to be captain thereof. The presumption is that this clan were Kennedies; and the time precisely corresponds with the era of *John de Kennedy*, the first Kennedy in the genealogical account of the Marquis of Ailsa's family, who had a charter in 1357-8. It is improbable that two John Kennedies, heads of clans, existed at one and the same time; while it is equally probable, from the connection between the Lenzie Kennedies and those of Dunure, that Marcow Mackennedy was the ancestor of both. What farther indicates that there was only one John Kennedy, or Mackennedy, of note at the time referred to (the reign of David II.) is the statement of Fordun and Wyntoun, that in 1346, *John Kennedy*, with Allan Stewart, "sturdily fought" in Carrick against the Gallovidians, though Edward Baliol was there. John Kennedy fights sturdily for his sovereign in 1346, and in 1357-8 John Kennedy obtains a charter confirming him in all the possessions he had acquired. It seems scarcely to be doubted that they were one and the same person; and it is not to be supposed that *Gilbert de Carrick*, who also fought sturdily for the same monarch, and was taken prisoner at the battle of Durham in 1346, could have been the ancestor of the said John Kennedy. There are thus strong reasons for believing that, by whatever mode the Kennedies acquired the property of the De Carricks, they were originally a distinct family. Subject as the earldom of Carrick was to so many changes, in the failure of the main line and otherwise, the acquisition of the lands, by parties who at first only managed them, became all the more easy. It is evident that Sir Roland de Carrick was constituted leader of the men of Carrick, by Earl Nigellus, in the immediate certainty of the title devolving upon a female. He was made leader, *under the Earl*, whoever that Earl might be. Robert the Bruce himself led the men of Carrick at the battle of Bannockburn. The grant of *Kenkynol*, therefore, conferred on Sir Roland, was, perhaps, less a matter of distinction than of profit, as he could only act as captain under a greater than himself, while the "caupes"[*] which it secured were of considerable value. Had the Kenkynolship descended hereditarily, there would have been no necessity for any grants or charters on the subject; but as the earldom was about to pass into the hands probably of the head of some other clan, it became necessary specially to appoint Sir Roland as head of the tribe, to prevent future misunderstandings. No similar necessity, however, could have occurred, had the leadership descended regularly in the family of Sir Roland. And this seems an additional argument against the assumption that John de Kennedy, who obtained a charter in 1357-8, was the genuine male representative of the De Carricks. It was not till 1372, after the accession of the Stewarts to the throne, and that such a connection existed between the monarch and his subject as to be styled " our dearest cousin," that the chieftainship was confirmed to " Joannes Kennedy de Dunnoure."

With these contradictory facts before us we must leave it as an open question for our readers to judge whether the ancestors of the noble house of Ailsa were originally Kennedies or De Carricks. The question is of little consequence—more curious than important. The name of Kennedy is apparently of greater antiquity than De Carrick, and quite as honourable, save that

it happened not to be ennobled at so early a period.

We come now to facts which admit of no dispute. The *Kennedies of Dunure* were the undoubted ancestors of the Ailsa family. The Castle of Dunure, their original seat, now in ruins, is situated on the coast, in the parish of Maybole, and will fall to be described in our account of that portion of the county. The old castle of Culzean is supposed to have been nearly of as great antiquity, and to have formed one of the early residences or retreats of the family. It was subsequently the seat of one of the principal branches of the family, until the title and estates devolved upon the latter.

I. JOHN DE KENNEDY, styled in later charters, of Dunure. He had a charter from David II., dated 18th January 1357-8, confirming him in all the lands, tenements, and possessions belonging to or acquired by him. He was no doubt the same " Johanni Kennedy." whose name occurs in the first roll of David II.,[*] as having had a general charter of confirmation. If so, he must have been considerably advanced in life at the close of the reign of that monarch. "Johanni Kennedy" had also a charter from David II., confirming him in " de terra de Castlys, in vic. de Are, vendita illi per Marjoriam de Mungumry, seniorem, et Marjoriam de Mungumry, filiam Johannis de Mungumry; et de terra de Dalmorton, in comitatu de Carrik, et vic. de Are, illi vendita per Johannem de Turnebery; et de terra de Schauven, illi vendita per Murthacum filium Somerlady." This charter is without date or witnesses; but is supposed to have been granted about 1362. In 1363 John de Kennedy[†] de Scotie had a safe conduct from Edward III., to make a pilgrimage to the shrine of St Thomas at Canterbury. John Kennedy of Dunure was the founder of the chapel near the parish church of Maybole. " Johanni Kennedy, super fundatione, capellæ et trium Capellaricarum Ecclesiæ parochialis de Maybole," was confirmed by Robert II. in a charter dated 4th December 1371, in which he is called " dilectus consanguineus noster Joannes Kennedy de Dunnoure." John Kennedy founded this chapel for a priest and three chaplains to celebrate divine service at the said chapel, for the happy state of himself, *Mary*, his wife, and their children, &c. We thus see that the Christian name of his wife was *Mary*. No surname is given

---

[*] Caupes are described by Skene thus:—" Calpes in Galloway and Carrick signifies ane gift, sic as hors or uther thing quhilk one man in his awin lifetime and liege poustie gives to his minister, or to onie uther man that is greatest in power and authoritie, and specially to the head and chief of the clann, for his maintenance and protection." The caupes were suppressed by James VI. in 1617.

[*] The first roll as given in Robertson's Index.
[†] The same party, apparently, was one of the Commissioners at the Treaty of Newcastle in 1354.

by the editor of the "Historical Account," leaving it to be presumed that it was not to be found in the family records. But this brings us to the secret of the whole mystery. Curious enough, we had written thus far—nay, what we had written was in type—when we accidentally fell in with a small pamphlet, entitled "An Historical Sketch of the very ancient Family and Sirname of Carrick," privately printed at Edinburgh in 1824, by Andrew Carrick, Esq., from the manuscript of Andrew Carrick of Kildees, M.D., Bristol, both of whose families are descended from the Carricks of Moredon, who had properties in the counties of Ayr, Lanark, and Galloway, near Dumfries, a branch of the original De Carricks. Dr Carrick does not give his authorities in detail, but he states that much interesting information was obtained on the subject from George William Johnstone, Esq., M.D., of Lochhouse, a descendant of the family by the mother's side, and Robert Riddel of Glenriddle, Esq., a well-known antiquary. In this pamphlet, it is unhesitatingly stated that Sir John Kennedy married *Mary Carrick,* "daughter, or grand-daughter," of Sir Gilbert Carrick,* who had no surviving male issue. This marriage, it is said, took place about 1350. Here then we have the true source of the very intimate connection between the Kennedies and De Carricks. John de Kennedy married Mary de Carrick, the heiress of Sir Gilbert de Carrick, and assumed the arms and position of the De Carricks. By this marriage, also, from the connection of the De Carricks with the Royal House of Stewart, he was entitled to be called by Robert II. "dilectus consanguineus noster."

John Kennedy, who no doubt obtained Dunure, amongst other properties, along with his wife, had numerous grants of lands. "In particular, he got from Robert II. two charters, dated at Ayr, 1st October 1372, the one confirming the original grant by Neil, Earl of Carrick, to Sir Roland de Carrick, of the chieftainship of the family and bailiary of Carrick, with the leading of the men thereof; and the other again confirming the original grant, and also the charter of confirmation thereof, by Alexander II. He also obtained a charter from Robert II., of the same date, confirming the letter of remission by Robert I. to Sir Gilbert de Carrick, for delivering up Lochdoon Castle, and the regrant thereof," †—all of which was perhaps necessary to secure him in the privileges and position to which he had attained in

virtue of his wife. "In 1370, he acquired from Malcolm, the son of Christynus, the son of Adam de Dalrymple, the half of the barony of Dalrymple; and in 1376, he acquired the other half thereof from Hugh, the son of Roland de Dalrymple. In or soon after 1370, he acquired from Malcolm, son of Roland de Carrick, the twopenny land called Treuchan and Kennochen, lying in the parish of Kirkmichael-Munterduffly. In 1374-5, he acquired, by wadset, the barony of Cumbernauld from Thomas Fleming, grandson and heir of Malcolm Earl of Wigtoun." *

By his wife, Mary de Carrick, he had several children, besides his son and heir. He died about 1385,† and was succeeded by

II. Gilbert Kennedy of Dunure, his eldest son. He is styled "filius primogenitus" in a charter, dated 27th January 1384-5, by Malcolm Fleming of Biggar. He was one of the hostages for David II. in 1358. "In 1364-5, he acquired from his father the lands of Strogilton of Ponton, and two Broughtons of Lethydale; and in 1370, during his father's life, he acquired from Thomas Fleming, grandson of Malcolm Earl of Wigtoun, the town of Kirkintilloch. In 1384, he got a charter from Malcolm Fleming of Biggar, confirming a charter by his father, John Kennedy, of the forty shilling land of Kirkintilloch in favour of Sir Gilbert Kennedy, his eldest son, and of Agnes Maxwell, wife of the said Sir Gilbert, and the longest liver of them, and the heirs male of his (Sir Gilbert's) body, to be lawfully procreated; whom failing, to John Kennedy, brother-german of the said Gilbert, and the heirs-male of his body to be lawfully procreated; whom failing, Roland Kennedy, brother german of the said Gilbert and John, and the heirs-male of his body to be lawfully procreated; whom all failing, the heirs whomsoever of the said John Kennedy of Dunure.

This charter is of importance in a family point of view. These three children, *Gilbert, John* and *Roland,* were not, it will be observed, sons of Sir Gilbert by his wife Agnes Maxwell, but by a previous marriage or otherwise. Nisbet's Heraldry and the Peerages state, but without authority, that Sir Gilbert was first married to Marion, daughter of Sir James Sandilands of Calder, by whom he is said, in Nisbet, to have had two sons, *Gilbert* and *Thomas.* In Wood's

* This Sir Gilbert de Carrick must have been the "Gilberto de Carryk," respecting whom there is, as we have already stated, an incomplete charter in the early part of the reign of David II.

† Historical Account.

* Historical Account.

† There is in the Errol charter-chest, a bond and obligation, dated at Edinburgh, the penult of November 136- (the full date of the year is worn away) by John Kennedy of Dunure, to Lady Margaret, Queen of Scotland, (the second wife of David II.), and to her son, John de Logy, whereby he binds himself to their support against all enemies.

Peerage the marriage is stated, but the children are differently arranged. In the " Historical Account " the editor says " there is no evidence in Lord Ailsa's charter-chest of the first marriage; the only wife of Sir Gilbert Kennedy who is mentioned in any of the titles is Agnes Maxwell, and she is called in various charters, particularly those in 1400 and 1404, the mother of all his children, except Gilbert, John and Roland, and in the charter of 1384, of Kirkintilloch, in which Gilbert is called the eldest son (*primogenitus*), and John and Roland brothers-german of Gilbert, they are only called failing heirs-male of Sir Gilbert's body to be lawfully procreated It would therefore appear that they were not legitimate By our old practice, the word *german* does not necessarily infer legitimacy, but only that the children were born of the same mother "

Agnes Maxwell, the wife of Sir Gilbert Kennedy, was a daughter of Sir John Maxwell of Pollok by his wife, Isabel Lindsay, daughter of Sir James Lindsay of Crawford, by the Princess Egidia, sister of Robert II, not of Sir Robert Maxwell of Calderwood, second son of Sir John, as stated in the Peerages * The eldest son of Sir Gilbert Kennedy and Agnes Maxwell was *James*, who married the Princess Mary, daughter of Robert III In 1392 Sir Gilbert Kennedy gave an obligation, dated 16th September, to James Kennedy his son, obliging himself not to revoke the grant made by him to the said James Kennedy, and the heirs-male of his body,† whom failing, the heirs whatsoever procreate between the said Sir Gilbert Kennedy and Agnes Maxwell, his wife, (mother of the said James Kennedy,) of the Dominical lands of Kirkintilloch, and lands of Sherreve, Bar, Gartchewan, and Badcall, lying in the barony of Lenzie and county of Dumbarton On 2d November 1400 he got a charter from David Earl of Carrick, eldest son of Robert III, of the lands of Dunure, Girvan, and Glenap, in favour of himself and Agnes Maxwell, his wife, in liferent, and after their decease, of James Kennedy, their son, and the

heirs-male of his body, whom failing, Alexander Kennedy, his brother, and the heirs-male of his body, whom failing, Hugh Kennedy, his brother, and the heirs-male of his body, whom failing, John Kennedy, son of the said Gilbert and Agnes, and brother of the said James, and the heirs-male of his body, whom failing, Thomas Kennedy, their brother, and the heirs-male of his body, whom failing, the nearest heirs whatsoever of the said Sir Gilbert Kennedy, their father. He took a charter, in the same terms, in 1404, of the lands of Cassillis and Guletry and two Kilmores, but in this charter each of the younger sons are called brothers of James These charters were all obtained before the marriage of James with the Princess Mary. This event took place in 1405, upon which occasion Sir Gilbert resigned in his favour, and the heirs-male of his body, whom failing his other younger children, in the order above-mentioned, the barony of Dalrymple,* and at the same time he resigned, in favour of his son James, under the reservation of his own liferent, the chieftainship and office of bailie of Carrick. After the death of James, who was killed by his brother Gilbert, Sir Gilbert entered into an indenture with the Duke of Albany, governor of the kingdom, dated 8th November 1408, by which he obliged himself to make a taillie of his estates in favour of himself and Agnes Maxwell, his wife, in liferent, and the heirs-male of his son James *nominatim*, whom failing, to his other sons *nominatim*, and their heirs-male, in the order above-mentioned These sons are in this deed all called brothers of Alexander, who is called son of Agnes Maxwell

In 1386 Sir Gilbert Kennedy granted a bond or obligation to the nunnery of North Berwick as to the church of Maybole It has the remains of his seal attached to it, displaying a chevron between three cross crosslets, with a label of three points on the shield, and a lion for supporter on the left—the rest away

The issue of Sir Gilbert and Agnes Maxwell were —

---

* This is proved by the testament of Sir Robert Maxwell ' yat deid yn France at ye battall off Vernell," in 1421, in which document he orders his body to be buried in the church of the Minor Friars in the county of Anjou, and mentions his wife, his eldest son, " sorror ince d'ne de d'ur," &c.

† The necessity of such a grant is presumptive that the three elder children of Sir Gilbert—Gilbert, John and Roland—were not precisely in the position of illegitimate children Had they been so, it is difficult to understand how it became necessary to exclude them by special grants in this manner There must have been some peculiarity in the case, which does not appear on the face of the transaction. The charters, however, show the precise order of the family

---

1 James, who married the Princess Mary He was slain by his half-brother, as already stated, in 1408 He left issue —

    1 Sir John, who died about 1434 Among the hostages for the redemption of James I was " Joannes Kennedy de Carryk," who is said to be possessed of land to the amount of v c marcas —a large sum at that time, and he had a safe conduct to meet the King at Durham with horses

---

* In the charter of Dalrymple by the King, which is dated 22d January 1405 6, all the sons, except John, are called brothers of James Having two brothers, each named John, the younger one is always distinguished as " son of the said Gilbert and Agnes Maxwell "

and retainers. In 1431 the following notice of him occurs in Fordun:—" For certain causes the King caused Archibald, third of that name, Earl of Douglas, and Sir John Kennedy, his nephew, to be arrested,—the Earl he sent in custody to the castle of Lochleven, and his nephew he kept in the castle of Stirling, where he was kept in prison till the following feast of St Michael: which King then, in a Parliament held at Perth, at the request of the Queen, bishops and prelates, earls and barons, remitted every offence of the Earls of Douglas and Ross, but Kennedy was kept in close custody." A great mystery hangs over this event. Nothing more transpires in his history. But there appears, from the Chamberlain Rolls, under the "Expense" for the year 1434, a payment for the expenses of Sir John Kennedy in the castle of Stirling under the King's Privy Seal, of £14, 18s. 4d., which is the last notice that has been found of him.

2. Gilbert, succeeded his grandfather.

3. James, bishop of Dunkeld in 1438, bishop of St Andrews in 1440, and Chancellor of Scotland the same year. He was one of the regents in the minority of James III, and died 10th May 1466. He founded the college of St Salvator of St Andrews in 1450, reserving to the House of Cassillis the right of presentation to ten prebendaries or bursaries, provided for students in that college. One of the Earls of Cassillis subsequently acquired other four prebendaries from the college. By an act of Parliament, dated 22d July 1644, it was enacted that a Professorship of Humanity should be instituted in St Salvator's College, and that these fourteen prebendaries should be assigned as part of his maintenance. It was also thereby declared that the Earl of Cassillis, his heirs and successors, of the name and arms of Kennedy, should, in all time thereafter, have the right of presentation of the said professor, and of his successors in the said profession, together with the haill rents, profits, and duties of the said fourteen prebendaries. On the 14th and 18th February 1645, a contract was entered into between the Earl and the provost, professors, regents, and remanent members of the college, by which it is provided that the college shall be bound to receive and admit any party presented by the Earl, such party being first tried and found qualified, according to the order of the visitation of the said college. The Earl is bound to present within six months after intimation of a vacancy is made to him by the said college; and failing his doing so, the right may be exercised 'pro lata vice' by the college 'jure devoluto.' By an act passed in the year 1747, the two colleges of St Salvator and St Leonard were united. There being a professorship of Humanity in each college, it was resolved to suppress the one of which the family of Cassillis had the right of presentation, and in its place the patronage of the chair of Civil History was given to the Earl of Cassillis. This right of patronage is still held by the family.

2. Alexander Kennedy of Ardstyncher. He is so styled as a witness to a charter, dated 18th March 1415, by John M'Gillilan to Fergus Kennedy of Bomonyn. He had a son, Gilbert Kennedy, who obtained a charter, dated 31st December 1456, from John M'Dowall of Quarterland, of the twenty-five shilling land of Beoch. In the History of the Kennedies he is said to have been a natural son; and none of his family are called in any of the future entails, although they are frequent witnesses to deeds. In 1464, Gilbert Kennedy acquired the barony of Craigneil, which estate remained with his descendants till the middle of the sixteenth century, when it was sold to Kennedy of Knockdolian, and by him to Kennedy of Carslo, from whom it was acquired by the Earl of Cassillis.

3. Hugh Kennedy, who accompanied the Scottish troops to France under the Earl of Buchan, and distinguished himself at the battle of Baugue, in Anjou, 22d March 1421. He may have accompanied his uncle, Sir Robert Maxwell, first Lord of Calderwood, and fought in his train.

4. John Kennedy, afterwards of Blairquhan.

5. Thomas Kennedy of Bargany. He is called, in a charter by James II., dated 13th February 1450–1, of the lands of Cassillis, &c., Thomas Kennedy of Kirkoswald: and in another charter by James II., dated 23d October 1455, Thomas Kennedy of Bargany. The lands of Kirkoswald were for a long time part of the Bargany estate. In 1597, they were the jointure lands of Lady Agnes Kennedy, widow of Sir Thomas Kennedy of Bargany.

6. David Kennedy. He was one of the retinue who attended Margaret of Scotland on her marriage to the Dauphin Louis, in 1436. He had issue a son, Gilbert Kennedy of Kirkmichael.[*]

With regard to the elder branch of Sir Gilbert's family—*Gilbert, John* and *Roland*—there seems to be some uncertainty in reference to their history. Gilbert is said to have died abroad, whither he fled after the slaughter of his brother James, leaving no issue. This is proved by an infeftment, dated 17th April 1466, in favour of Gilbert, Lord Kennedy, in the forty merk land of Kirkintilloch, on a decree and brieve of recognition, 15th April 1466, against Robert Lord Fleming. John, is believed to have been the ancestor of the first family of Kennedy of Coif, who soon became extinct; and from a curious obligation discovered among Lord Ailsa's titles, it is more than probable that Roland was proprietor of Leffnol. The obligation is dated 28th October 1454, and to the effect that Gilbert Kennedy, son and heir of *Roland Kennedy of Leffnol*, shall not disturb Gilbert Kennedy of Dunure, his master, in his lands and offices specified, under the penalty of £6000 Scots.

Sir Gilbert Kennedy died about 1440, and was succeeded by

III. Gilbert, first Lord Kennedy, eldest surviving son of James Kennedy and the Princess Mary, and grandson of Sir Gilbert Kennedy. He was created Lord Kennedy between 3d August 1456 and 25th March 1457, as he is styled Lord Kennedy, for the first time, in an instrument of resignation of the lands of Glenginnet, of the latter date. In 1466, he was appointed one of the six regents of the kingdom, on the death of

_____

[*] " With regard to the order of seniority of Sir Gilbert Kennedy's children," says the editor of the 'Historical Account,' " the above arrangement is taken from the charters of 1384, 1400, and 1404. Nisbet is clearly erroneous in the order of birth; and his statement, in other respects, of the Blairquhan branch, is quite incorrect. It is clear, from Lord Ailsa's titles, that Thomas was the ancestor of the Bargany branch; and that he was a younger son of James who carried on the main line of the family, is evident from the charter of 1405, in which the sons are all called brothers of James, and from the indenture with the Duke of Albany."

James II. He married Katherine, daughter of Herbert, first Lord Maxwell, of Caerlaverock, by whom he had several children. In 1450, he got several charters from the Crown of the family estates and chieftainship, in which his wife's name is mentioned. He seems to have had the following family:

1. John, afterwards second Lord Kennedy.
2. James Kennedy, afterwards designed of Row. In a charter, dated 14th May 1473, of the half of the barony of Glenstincher, James Kennedy is called 'filio carnali' of Gilbert Lord Kennedy. His wife's name was Egidia Blair. They had no issue.
3. Alexander.
4. Gilbert Kennedy of Crothba, provost of the collegiate church of Maybole. He had no issue. Gilbert, Earl of Cassillis, was served heir of this Gilbert 9th November 1532.
5. Robert.
6. Walter Kennedy of Glentig, and parson of Douglas, acquired Glentig from John Wallace of Glentig, by charter dated 8th December 1504. This was the poet of whom Gawin Douglas, in his "Palice of Honour," written in 1501, says—

> "Of this nation I knew also anone
> Greit Kennedie and Dunbar yet undeid,
> And Quintine with ane huttock on his heid."

And Lyndsay, in a poem written in 1530, exclaims—

> "Or quha can now the warkis countrefait,
> Off Kennedie with termes aureait,
> Or of Dunbar quha language had at large,
> As may be seen intill his Goldin Targe."

It was always supposed that Kennedy was nearly connected with the Cassillis family, but the fact was not demonstrable until the recent search through the Ailsa charter-chest brought the matter to light. In the "Flyting of Dunbar and Kennedy," he makes several allusions to his lineage and position, which are perfectly intelligible, as illustrated by the family documents—

> "I am the kingis blude, his trew speciall clerk," &c.

His claim to the king's blude was well-founded, his grandfather, James, as we have seen, having married the Princess Mary. Dunbar says—

> "In till ane GLEN thow hes owt of repair,
> Ane laithly luge that wes the lippir mennis," &c.

This evidently alludes to his property of Glentig; and Kennedy himself replies—

> "———— I haif landis, stoir, and stakkis;
> Thow wald be fain to gnaw, lad, with thy gammis,
> Under my burde; smooch banis behind doggis bakkis!
> Thow hes ane tome purse, I haif steidis and takkis," &c.

Showing that he was in possession of property, and led a rural life. He was educated at the College of Glasgow, and appears to have been originally intended for the church. He was incorporated with the college in 1475, took his degree as bachelor of arts in 1476, and as a licentiate and master of arts in 1478. In November 1481, he was elected one of the four masters to act as examiner. Of his subsequent history little is known. He continued to reside probably on his estate of Glentig. About 1508, he is alluded to by Dunbar, in his "Lament for the Makars," as at the "pynt of dede;" and in 1530, Lyndsay speaks of him as having been dead some time before. The inference is, that he did not survive the illness alluded to by Dunbar. He married Christian Hynd, and had issue:

1. Walter Kennedy, rector of Douglas. He was incorporated as a member of the College of Glasgow in October 1511. He was chosen rector of the university in 1525, at which time he was provost of the collegiate church of Maybole, and canon of Glasgow.

2. Alexander Kennedy of Glentig, called in the entail of 1540. He had a daughter, Janet Kennedy, who is stated in a contract, dated 3d April 1562, between Gilbert, fourth Earl of Cassillis, and her, to be the heir of Alexander Kennedy of Glentig, Walter Kennedy, parson of Douglas, her granduncle, and James Kennedy in Kirkdominie. She married William Kennedy of Gilespie.

7. Katherine, married to Alexander, second Lord Montgomerie.

8. Marion, who was contracted to marry John, son and heir of William Wallace of Craigie, by indenture dated 12th April 1459; and was also contracted to marry James, eldest son of Robert Lord Boyd, in 1465.

The foregoing sons are all called in succession in a charter by James II., dated 23d October 1455; and failing them and the heirs-male of their bodies, there are called next the said Gilbert Kennedy of Dunure, their father, and the heirs-male of his body; whom failing, Thomas Kennedy of Bargany, and the heirs-male of his body; whom failing, Gilbert Kennedy of Kirkmichael, and the heirs-male of his body; whom failing, the nearest heirs-male of the said Gilbert Kennedy of Dunure.* Lord Kennedy acquired the lands of Balgray, Auchintibbert, &c. from William Earl of Douglas, by charter dated at Stirling, 20th April 1444.† In 1450, he acquired the half of the barony of Glenstincher called Dalquhairn. In 1457 he acquired the barony of Traboyack or Glenginnet. In 1465 he acquired the barony of Thankerton in Lanarkshire. In 1473 he acquired Pinvalley from Kennedy of Bargany. He married, secondly, Isabel, daughter of Sir Alexander Ogilvy of Auchterlonie, and widow of Patrick first Lord Glammis, and was alive 19th October 1478.

Lord Kennedy had bonds of man-rent from Sir John Kennedy of Blairquhan, and John Kennedy, his son and apparent heir, 2d July 1444; Gilbert Kennedy, son of Alexander Kennedy of Ardstincher, 23d April 1447; Gilbert Kennedy, son and heir of Roland Kennedy of Leffnol; and an obligation, dated 20th January 1465, by Robert Lord Boyd, to aid, assist, and defend Lord Kennedy all the days of his life, except his allegiance to the King, and bonds granted to Lord Darnley, Lord Hamilton, Lord Lyle, Lord Montgomery, &c., and to be true and faithful to Lord Kennedy so long as he shall have the keeping of the King's person, and cause solemnize a marriage between James Boyd, his

---

* The elder brothers, Alexander, Hugh, and John, are omitted in this charter, and Gilbert Kennedy of Kirkmichael is called in place of his brother David.

† This disproves the story in the History of the Kennedys, as to the acquisition of these lands by Alexander Kennedy.

eldest son, and Marion, daughter of Lord Kennedy.

He was succeeded by

IV. John, second Lord Kennedy. He was called Lord Kennedy in his father's lifetime in an instrument of Sasine in the barony of Dalrymple, dated 12th April 1475. In 1482 he had a charter of the barony of Turnberry, Traboyack, and Girvanhead. In 1505, he acquired the lands of Coiff, now called Culzean, and other lands, from Gilbert Kennedy of Coiff. He married, first, Elizabeth, second daughter of Alexander, first Lord Montgomerie, by whom he had issue:—

1. Sir David Kennedy of Læswalt, knight, afterwards Earl of Cassillis. He was knighted by James III. on the creation of his second son Alexander Duke of Ross, 29th January 1489.
2. Katherine, mentioned in an indenture, dated 15th September 1465, as contracted to marry Thomas, eldest son of Gilbert Kennedy of Bargany, by whom she had issue.

Before 1471 Lord Kennedy married, secondly, Elizabeth, daughter of George, first Earl of Huntley, and relict of Nicol, second Earl of Errol, and by her had issue:—

1. Alexander, who got a charter of the lands of Girvan Mains from his father, dated 30th July 1481. Hugh Kennedy of Girvan Mains is witness to a precept by the Earl of Cassillis to James Scott of the lands of Ranko, dated 20th May 1536. He married Janet Stewart, Countess of Sutherland, who afterwards married Henry Stewart, Lord Methven. This is the Hugh Kennedy called in the entail of 1540. Gilbert, son of Sir Hugh Kennedy of Girvan Mains, married Margaret, eldest daughter of David Kennedy of Culzean, and is infeft in the lands of Culzean 19th March 1563. They had a son, Hugh Kennedy, afterwards Sir Hugh Kennedy of Girvan Mains. His creditors sold the estate in 1694 to Sir Thomas Kennedy of Kirkhill, Provost of Edinburgh, a descendant of Gilbert, third son of Alexander Kennedy of Bargany. Sir Hugh had a son, Sir Gilbert Kennedy, Bart., who, in 1694, married Jean, daughter of Sir Archibald Kennedy of Culzean, Baronet.
2. John.
3. William.
4. Janet, mistress of James IV., and usually called Lady Bothwell. The King settled upon her the splendid domain of Tarnaway Castle, the principal residence of the Earls of Moray previous to their forfeiture, by a grant in 1501, wherein she is called Jane Kennedy, Lady Bothwell, "als lang as she remanys but husband or uther man, ande dwellande in ye castle of Dernway with ye King's son and nurris, James Stewart." This celebrated beauty, to whom the King was so much attached, and whose jealousy is so forcibly disclosed in the above excerpt, had been contracted to marry Archibald Douglas, Earl of Angus, who was actually imprisoned for attempting to prefer his claim to her hand. On the 7th February 1509 she received a charter from the Crown of the liferent of the barony of Bothwell. On the 21st March 1531 she granted a charter of confirmation and mortification for the sustentation of one prebend in the church of the blessed Virgin Mary in the Field, without the walls of the city of Edinburgh, of certain annual rents and tenements within the city. This was the celebrated Kirk of Field, where the murder of Darnley afterwards took place. She had by James IV. a son, James Stewart, created Earl of Moray

1591, who married Margaret, daughter of Colin, third Earl of Argyle, by whom he had one daughter, Mary, married to John, eldest son of John, third Earl of Buchan. In the Treasurer's Accounts for the period several entries occur in reference to the expenses of the Lady Bothwell.
5. Helen, married to Adam Boyd of Penkill.

John Lord Kennedy is said, in Riddell's Peerage and Consistorial Law, to have married, third, Elizabeth Kennedy, who afterwards married William Power. He died about 1507, and was succeeded by

V. David, first Earl of Cassillis, his eldest son and heir. He was created Earl of Cassillis between 25th July 1509 and 7th January 1510-11, as he is called Lord Kennedy in an assignation of the former date, and Earl of Cassillis in a precept of the latter date. He was a Privy Councillor of James IV., and was at the battle of Flodden Field, where he was killed.* He married, first, Agnes, daughter of William Lord Borthwick, by whom he had issue:—

1. Gilbert, second Earl of Cassillis.
2. William, Abbot of Crossraguel.
3. James of Brunston.†
4. Thomas Kennedy of Coiff, married, according to the "Historical Account," Katherine, daughter of Thomas Corry of Kelwood. Possibly he may have been twice married. We have before us the substance of the testament of "quondam Domine Jonete Stewart, Domine de Culzeane," who died on the 3d December 1551. She appointed as her executors, John Greir of Lag, Patrick Kennedy, her son, and Alexander Stewart of Garmlas. The period of her death seems to indicate a connection with Thomas Kennedy of the Coiff or Culzean. He had issue:—

    1. Thomas, who was infeft in the lands of Coiff and Mackilvairdstain as heir to his father, 1st April 1555.
    2. David, who was infeft in Coiff as heir to his brother Thomas, 7th April 1567. He had issue:

        Alexander of Balvaird, who was infeft in the lands of Coiff and Mackilvairdstain as heir to his father David, 24th August 1586. He married Isobel, daughter of David Kennedy in Maxwelltoun. He had a grandson, David, who was infeft in Mackilvairdstain or Balvaird as heir of his grandfather, 8th September 1675. He had previously sold these lands to the Earl of Cassillis, by disposition dated 18th January 1672.

5. Katherine, married Quintin Mure of Aird, and had issue. She and her husband were infeft by a precept, dated 7th January 1516, in the lands of Kilmore.

* This is proved by a precept, dated 21st May 1534, for infefting Gilbert, third Earl of Cassillis, as heir of his grandfather, Earl David, in the lands of Balgray and others, in which the Earl, though a minor, is declared of lawful age, in virtue of the act of dispensation made by James IV. at Twizelhaugh, dated 24th August 1513, in favour of those who accompanied him to battle.

† He is witness to a contract, dated 29th January 1528, between Gilbert, third Earl, and William, the Abbot. In 1569 there is a William Kennedy of Brunston witness to a letter of reversion by David Kennedy of Coiff to Earl Gilbert; but in a charter by the Abbot of Crossraguel to David Kennedy in Balsarroch, William Kennedy of Brunston is called brother natural of David.

N 2

She married subsequently, before 1533, William Hamilton of Sorn and Sanquhar She had one daughter by Quintin Mure, called Margaret, who was married to John Kennedy of Skeldon

6 Christian, married to John Kennedy of Guiltree, and had issue a son, John She and her husband are mentioned in a discharge, dated 28th May 1526, in favour of the Earl of 200 merks, being her portion

7 Helen, married, first, to Lord Eglinton, secondly, to Graham of Knockdohan

Lord Cassillis married, secondly, Margaret, daughter of Thomas Earl of Arran, and niece of James III, and widow of Alexander, fourth Lord Forbes, but by her had no issue He died 9th September 1513, and was succeeded by

VI Gilbert, second Earl of Cassillis, eldest son and heir In 1516 he was appointed, by the Bishop ot Galloway, bailie of all the lands belonging to the bishopric in Galloway, and captain and keeper ot the manor-place and loch ot Inch He was ambassador to England, 1515-16. He married Isabella, second daughter of Archibald, second Earl of Argyle, and had issue —

1 Gilbert, third Earl of Cassillis

2 Thomas, died before 2d November 1560

3 David of Culzean, according to the "Historical Account,' but there seems to be some mistake He got, it is said, a charter of the lands of Culzean from his brother, Eul Gilbert, dated 30th September 1542, and yet, according to the same authority, David, grandson of the first Earl of Cassillis, was infeft in Coiff, as heir to his brother Thomas, 7th April 1567 We cannot, however, rectify the apparent confusion David married Janet, daughter of Duncan Kennedy of Dalquharugh, and had issue —

  1 Margaret, married Gilbert, son of Sir Hugh Kennedy, of Girvan Mains

  2 Egidia

  3 Katherine, married Richard Kennedy in Largs

4 Quintin, Abbot of Crossraguel, who publicly disputed with John Knox, on the subject of the mass, at Maybole, died in 1564, and was canonized by the Church of Rome

5 Archibald

6 Hugh of Barquhany, married Katherine Bailey, and had issue —

  1 John of Barquhany

  2 Janet, mentioned in a contract of sale of the lands of Mochrumhill

    John, the eldest son, married, and had two daughters, Jean and Helen, his heirs-portioners Helen married Alexander Macdouall of Machermore *

7 James Kennedy of Uchterlure married Agnes Johnston, and had two daughters, his heirs-portioners This appears from a decree by Thomas, Abbot of Glenluce, as to the heritable right to the lands of Uchterlure, dated 1560

8 A daughter, married to Thomas, eldest son of Alexander Kennedy of Bargany, His discharge for £100, part of the lady's portion, is dated 17th July 1527 †

---

* Precept of clare constat in their favour in the lands of Barquhany, dated 9th June 1599

† In the History of the Kennedys Lord Cassillis is said to have had two daughters—Janet, Lady Freugh, and Helen, Lady Kenhilt On 24th November 1571 William Adair of Kenhilt, and Helen Kennedy, his wife, are infeft by Lord Cassillis in the lands of Larg, Steuart, and others, in Wigtonshire, and on the 14th of May 1562 there is an instrument of requisition by Alexander Vans of Barnbar

Lord Cassillis was slain at Prestwick, about Whitsunday 1527, by Hugh Campbell of Loudoun, Sheriff of Ayr, and was succeeded by

VII. Gilbert, third Earl of Cassillis, his eldest son and heir He was born in 1515, and served heir to his father 14th October 1538. He was educated at St Andrews. In Knox's History of the Reformation it is stated that he was compelled to sign the sentence of death of Patrick Hamilton, Abbot of Ferne, who was burned there for heresy On the 30th October 1529 he was discharged of all points of treason from being at the battle beside Linlithgow He was a pupil of the celebrated George Buchanan, who had a high esteem for him, and with whom he travelled abroad for some years, and returned to Scotland in May 1537. On his return he was made one of the Lords of the Secret Council to James V, who admitted him to a very great degree of confidence and favour. He was at the rout of Solway, where he was taken prisoner in November 1542, and was placed under the charge of Archbishop Cranmer, by whom he was converted to the Protestant faith Having procured hostages, he returned home next year, and was engaged in the English interest to promote the marriage of Queen Mary with Prince Edward, for which he got a pension of 300 merks His hostages were his uncle, Thomas Kennedy of the Coiff, and his brothers Thomas and David His ransom was fixed at £1000. His hostages were placed under the care of the Archbishop of York, but were unaccountably neglected by the Earl It was not till they were threatened with immediate execution that the Earl went to London early in 1545, and delivered himself up to King Henry His hostages were immediately released, and he himself was discharged of his ransom, and permitted to return home loaded with presents He afterwards deserted the English party, became a lieutenant-general of horse to Queen Mary, and justiciar of Carrick He was named an extraordinary Lord of Session 31st July 1546 He was appointed Lord High Treasurer in 1554, and was one of the eight members elected by Parliament to attend Queen Mary's marriage with Francis, the Dauphin of France He was appointed a gentleman of the bedchamber to Henry II of France, 28th April 1558. The opposition of the Scottish deputies to give the crown-matrimonial to the Dauphin gave great offence, and three of them died at Dieppe in one night, 18th

roch and Janet Kennedy, Lady Freugh, his wife, to the tenants of certain lands in Galloway to pay their rents These ladies may have been previously married to Thomas M Clelland and Thomas Kennedy

November 1558, among whom was the Earl of Cassillis, and not without suspicion of poison.* His body having been brought home, was buried in the collegiate church of Maybole.

The feud arising out of the slaughter of his father by Campbell of Loudoun, and which continued to disturb the peace of the county for a number of years, was at length made up in 1543 On the 30th August of that year, a bond of manrent was granted by Hugh Campbell of Loudoun to Gilbert, Earl of Cassillis, bearing that the Earl having, at the special request of the Lord Governor and other earls, lords, and barons of the realm, remitted all rancour against the said Hugh Campbell, his servants and dependents, anent the slaughter of his lordship's father, and had taken him into his favour and kindness, and granted to him, and the heir immediately succeeding him, his letter of maintenance, therefore, the said Hugh Campbell obliges him, and the heirs succeeding him in his lands and offices, in manrent and service to his lordship during their respective lifetimes, &c. This bond proceeds upon offers by Hugh Campbell to the Earl for the injuries he had done, and which he humbly beseeches the Earl to accept, in compliance with the request of the King of England and the governor and lords of Scotland, mediators between them, by which he is to give, first, his and his son's bond of manrent to the Earl during all the days of their respective lives, secondly, his son's marriage to be at the Earl's disposal, thirdly, all those engaged on the side of the said Hugh Campbell, who will not bide an assize, to be in the Earl's will; fourth, all suffrages, either public or private, to be referred to the Lords, as the Earl shall think expedient, &c

On the 6th of February 1540 the Earl of Cassillis took a charter of his estates in favour of himself, and the heirs-male of his body, whom failing, to Thomas Kennedy, his brother-german, and the heirs-male of his body, whom failing, to David Kennedy, his brother-german, and the

heirs-male of his body, whom failing, to Quintin Kennedy, his brother-german, and the heirs-male of his body, whom failing, to Archibald Kennedy, also his brother-german, and the heirs-male of his body, whom failing, to Hugh Kennedy, also his brother-german, and the heirs-male of his body, whom failing, to James Kennedy, also his brother-german, and the heirs-male of his body, whom failing, to James Kennedy, uncle of the Earl, and the heirs-male of his body, whom failing, to Thomas Kennedy of Coiff, also uncle of the Earl, and the heirs-male of his body, whom failing, to Hugh Kennedy of Girvan Mains, and the heirs-male of his body, whom failing, to William Kennedy of Glentig, and the heirs-male of his body; whom failing, to Alexander Kennedy of Bargany, and the heirs-male of his body, whom failing, to James Kennedy of Blairquhan, and the heirs-male of his body, whom failing, the nearest heirs-male whatsoever of the Earl, bearing the name and arms of Kennedy, whom all failing, his nearest heirs-female. This charter includes the office of bailiary of Carrick, and all fees pertaining thereto It is valuable in a genealogical point of view, as showing the degree of connection between the different families

On the 10th July 1546 the Earl, for himself, and as taking burden on him for Gilbert, Master of Cassillis, his eldest son and heir, enters into a contract with James Earl of Arran, Governor of Scotland, that the Master of Cassillis, and Dame Jean Hamilton, daughter of the Earl of Arran, shall solemnize marriage as soon as they are of lawful age The Earl of Arran promised to give £2933, 6s 8d of tocher with his daughter. This marriage, however, did not take place The barony of Craigneil was acquired by Lord Cassillis in 1557 He married Margaret, daughter of Alexander Kennedy of Bargany by whom he had issue —

1 Gilbert fourth Earl of Cassillis
2 David, died an infant
3 Sir Thomas Kennedy of Culzean afterwards tutor of Cassillis, from whom descended Thomas, ninth Earl
4 Jean, married Robert, first Earl of Orkney
5 Katherine married, in 1574, to Sir Patrick Vans of Barnbarroch, and had issue

Lord Cassillis died 18th November 1558 Buchanan, who survived his pupil, composed an elegant epitaph upon him, commemorative of his virtues He was succeeded by

VIII. Gilbert, fourth Earl of Cassillis, eldest son and heir, who was served heir of his father 16th October 1562 He had previously, on the 28th and 29th August 1559, entered into two contracts with his mother, the Countess of Cassillis, regarding her provisions By the first contract he provided to her the place of Cassillis,

---

* In an action before the Court of Session 5th May 1565, Gilbert, fourth Earl of Cassillis, produced his father's testaments, to be considered so far as regards his sister Jane, Countess of Orkney He " product ye saidis tua testamentis, ye ane dated Edinburgh 1527," by which he made his wife and Gilbert, his eldest son, his executors, and his brother " ye abbot " Then is this clause —"Item, I leif to Jane, my eldast dochter, to hir meniage scho usand hir honestlie, by ye advise of my wife and my eldest sone, ane thousand pundis " The uyer testament is stated to be maid at Deip, the 14 day of November 1558, by which he ratifies the foresaid testament, and " levis his broder ye abbot of Corshraguel, oversman, and failzing him his broder ye baillie. Item, I leif ye cleyting I send hame—chenyies ringis of gold to my use, &c., and yerafter to be left to Jane, my dochter, which testament is subscribed by Mr Robert Richardson, notar "

with the garden and orchard, for her residence, and assigned to her, yearly, during her life, 110 bolls of meal, 52 bolls of bear, 115 merks money, 89 capons, 35 salmon, and the third part of the meadow of Blairbowie, in full of her terce, to be uplifted and taken out of certain lands. She has also permission to take wood to the place of Cassillis, from the woods of Cassillis and Dalrymple. By the second contract the Earl, for the love and favour he bears to his mother, and for decorating her house, gives her, during her life, the yearly rent of the two and one-half merk land of Craigmulloch, along with 111 milk ewes, 77 yeild ewes, 108 wedders, 40 gimmers, and 40 dinmonts; as also other 80 gimmers and dinmonts, to be received by her at the feast of Belton then next, 1560, together with 11 old goats, and two kids; as also 114 head of nolt, pasturing upon the lands of Kerry Castle, in the forest of Buchan (Kirkcudbright), viz. 16 Nicol cows, and as many calves, 17 farrow and 9 yeild cows, 5 three-year-old cows, 22 old oxen, 2 bulls, 6 three-year-old oxen, and 2 bulls, 5 two-year-old oxen, 3 two-year-old queys, 8 quey stirks, and 9 oxen stirks; which sheep, goats, and cattle, the Countess obliges herself, her heirs and executors, to leave on the ground of the lands respectively above mentioned at her decease, or the like number, and of as great avail, for the use of the Earl and his successors; as also, he gives to the Countess, during her life, a silver bason and a laver, a double gilt cup of silver raised work with a cover, two cases of silver, the one gilt and the other ungilt, a gilt mazer, two silver trenches with two little salt-fatts in their nooks, twelve silver spoons, a silver salt-fatt and cover thereof ungilt, a black velvet bed with the curtains of black damask, and four pieces of tapestry in Edinburgh, and four feather beds and their bolsters; all which silver work, tapestry and bedding, the Countess obliges her and hers aforesaid to leave to the Earl and his successors within the place of Cassillis at her decease, or as much, and of the same avail. The Earl, being under age, obliges himself to choose curators between and Martinmas to ratify the contract. It is accordingly ratified on fifth November 1559 by Quintin, Abbot of Crossraguel, Sir Hugh Kennedy of Girvan Mains, David Kennedy of Culzean, and Mr Thomas Hay, parson of Spynie, the Earl's curators.

On coming of age, the Earl was appointed a councillor to Queen Mary; a gentleman of the Bedchamber to Henry II. of France, 10th February 1558-9; appointed justiciary of Carrick in 1565; was at the battle of Langside with Queen Mary, for which he was forfeited in Par-

liament, but from which he was subsequently reponed. He was afterwards appointed one of the Privy Council to the King.

It was this Earl who was guilty of roasting the Commendator of Crossraguel in "the black vout" of Dunure. On the 1st and 7th of September 1570 he carried Allan Stewart, the Commendator, to the castle of Dunure, where he presented to him for signature various deeds, conveying to the Earl the lands belonging to the abbacy, upon his refusing to sign which the Earl placed him over a large fire in one of the vaults of Dunure to compel him to do so. Kennedy of Bargany, hearing of his position, came to the assistance of the Commendator with a large force, and took the castle of Dunure. The Commendator lodged a complaint with the Privy Council against the Earl, who alleged, in defence, that the complaint was either civil or criminal, and that he ought not to answer thereto to the Privy Council. The Privy Council, however, sent him to Dunbarton Castle until he found security not to molest the Commendator, in £2000, and also in the like sum to Mr George Buchanan, pensioner of Crossraguel, his father's old preceptor.

Illustrative of this affair, there is a curious instrument in Lord Ailsa's charter-chest, dated 9th September 1570, two days after the roasting at Dunure, bearing that the Earl gave possession to Alan, Commendator of Crossraguel, *personally present*, of the place, orchard, wood, and four merk land of Crossraguel, to be enjoyed and possessed by him during the Earl's pleasure, and in token thereof the Earl presented to the said Commendator John Davidson and Patrick M'Cawell, occupiers of the said four merk land, together with the key of the principal tower of the place of Crossraguel; and the Abbot received the said John Davidson and Patrick M'Cawell for his tenants, and that conform to agreement formerly entered into between the Earl and him. Moreover, the Earl obliges himself to pay yearly to the Abbot the sum of £100 money of Scotland; and for the more sure payment of the said sum, the Earl is to find two landed gentlemen as cautioners therefor at the Abbot's pleasure— he being obliged always to give his counsel and service to the Earl. The deed is dated at the Abbacy of Crossraguel, and the witnesses are, David Campbell, son of Charles Campbell of Skeldon, Quintin Mure in Kileckie, Hector Fergusson in Crossraguel, and Mathew Hamilton in Dalrymple.

The conclusion of this affair was as follows:— On the 5th April 1571 there is a memorandum of an arrangement, whereby Lord Cassillis paid 500 merks to Robert Lord Boyd, to be paid to

James Steuart of Cardonald, for which, and the sum of 3000 merks farther, and the discharge of a bond for 300 merks, formerly borrowed from Hugh Kennedy by Lord Boyd, on the one hand, Lord Boyd undertook, on the other hand, to procure from James Steuart all the deeds granted in his favour of the Abbacy of Crossraguel by Alan, Abbot thereof, as also the Abbot's provision to the Abbacy from the Queen, and the instrument of institution by the Pope, and all other deeds relating to the Abbacy *upon his conscience;* as also, to deliver to the Earl, between and the 15th of April next, a feu-charter, signed and sealed by the Abbot in favour of the Earl, or whatsoever other person he shall nominate; as also, to grant an obligation in favour of the Earl for such sums of money as may be necessary to apprise the lands in case the Abbot refuse to accept the resignation thereof; but it is declared that it shall not be lawful for the Earl to apprise any more of James Steuart's lands than the lands of Crossraguel feued to him, as said is, nor yet his moveable goods. All which deeds are accordingly now in Lord Ailsa's charter-chest.

Bargany seems to have had a personal interest to prevent the Abbot falling into the hands of the Earl. On the 28th January 1569 the Abbot obtained letters of relaxation against Bargany from letters of caption which Bargany had taken out against the Abbot, " whom he held in captivity, and would in nowise liberate," although he had found surety to underly the law for being art and part guilty of the slaughter of umquhill James Ballany and two others, at Langside, in May 1568; and therefore charging Bargany to set the Abbot at liberty within three days. And again, on 13th November 1573, Bargany grants a renunciation to the Earl of Cassillis, in implement of a contract between the Abbot on the one part, the Earl on the second part, and Bargany on the third part, whereby he renounces, in favour of the Earl, a great variety of lands, part of the Abbacy of Crossraguel, and renounces and overgives the whole letters of assedation of the said lands and teinds granted to him by the said Abbot, so that the Earl may possess the same, conform to the disposition granted to him by James Steuart of Cardonald, except the proper lands held by Bargany immediately of the King and Laird of Barneil.

The Earl of Cassillis married Margaret, only daughter of John, ninth Lord Glammis. The contract is dated 30th September 1566. The lady's fortune was 10,000 merks Scots; her jointure, 1000 merks. By this lady, who afterwards married John, first Marquis of Hamilton, the Earl had issue:—

1. John, fifth Earl of Cassillis.
2. Hugh of Brunston, Master of Cassillis, died unmarried.
3. Gilbert, Master of Cassillis, from whom descended John, sixth Earl.

This Earl went by the name of " the King of Carrick." He died in December 1576, and was succeeded by

IX. John, fifth Earl of Cassillis, eldest son and heir. He succeeded during his minority, and was placed under his uncle, Sir Thomas Kennedy of Culzean, as tutor. The Earl was served heir to his father 30th August 1588. While his father was alive, and during his minority, a violent feud occurred between Lord Cassillis, his vassals, and the Gordons of Lochinvar, regarding the lands of the abbacy of Glenluce, which had been seized possession of by the Gordons, while Lord Cassillis had been called in by the Abbot to his assistance. On the 28th February 1578, a commission was granted to Mr John Skene and others, advocates, on the narrative that John Earl of Cassillis, Thomas Kennedy of Culzean, his uncle and tutor, and John Kennedy, brother-natural of umquhill Gilbert Earl of Cassillis, had humbly represented to the Lords of Council that they had intended divers actions and causes against John Gordon of Lochinvar, and sundry other persons, inhabitants of the county of Wigtown, stewartry of Kirkcudbright, and earldom of Carrick, within which county, stewartry, and earldom, the Earl's lands and heritages lie; and that by reason of the feud between the Earl's house and friends on the one part, and the inhabitants of the said county, stewartry, and earldom, chiefly of the name of Gordon and Crawford, on the other part, who had lately been guilty of the slaughter of Patrick Macdowall of Logan, the friend and dependent of the Earl, it became necessary to grant commission to the said Mr John Skene and others, constituting them sheriffs of Wigtown, stewards of Kirkcudbright, and bailies of Carrick, with power to them to fence and hold courts within the Council-house of Edinburgh, and to proceed and decide in all actions intruded and depending at the instance of the Earl, Thomas Kennedy of Culzean, and John Kennedy, against the said John Gordon and other inhabitants of the county of Wigtown, stewartry of Kirkcudbright, and bailiary of Carrick. And in 1580, when Lord Cassillis was served heir to his father in his estates in Kirkcudbright, viz., the £10 land of Brachs, called the Forest of Buchan, and fishings thereof, and also the lands called the Free Forest of Buchan, a dispensation was granted for holding the service in Edinburgh, because "it was hazardous that such should proceed before the said steward and his deputies in the burgh of Kirkcudbright, by reason of the feud subsisting between the Earl, his tutor, and their friends, on the one part, and Sir John Gordon of Lochinvar, knight, on the other part—the latter, with his friends and party, having lately committed divers slaughters, mutilations, and other injuries upon the Earl's friends and dependents, as was clearly known to the Lords of Session."

The Earl of Cassillis was High Treasurer of Scotland for a few months in 1599, but was glad to be relieved from the office on payment of 40,000 merks. It was during this Earl's life that most of the events occurred narrated in the History of the Kennedys, and which occasioned the death of young Gilbert Kennedy of Bargany at Brockloch, near Lady Cors, Maybole, on the 11th December 1601, and of Sir Thomas Kennedy of Culzean, by the Mures of Auchendrain, and Bargany's brother, Thomas Kennedy of Drummurchie. It seems to have been in consequence of his uncle's death, and the desire of vengeance upon Auchindrain, that the Earl was led to enter into the following extraordinary contract with his brother Hugh, the Master of Cassillis, for the purpose of taking the Laird of Auchindrain's life :—

We, Johne, Earle of Cassillis, Lord Kennedy, &c., bindis and oblissis ws, that howsovne our broder, Hew Kennedy of Brounstoun, with his complices, taikis the Laird of Auchindraneis lyf, that we shall mak guid and thankful payment to him and thame of the soume of twelf hundreth merkis zeirlie, together with corne to six horsis, ay and quhill (until) we ressaue (receive) thame in houshald with our self: beginning the first payment immediatlie after thair committing of the said deid. Attour howsevne we ressaue them in houshald, we sall pay to the twa serving gentilmen the feis zeirlie as our awin houshald servandis. And heirto we oblise we vpon our honour. Subscryvit with our hand at Maybole the ferd day of September 1602.

                    JOHNE ERLE OF CASSILLIS.

The Earl of Cassillis married Jean, daughter of James, fourth Lord Fleming, widow of John, Lord Maitland of Thirlestane, a lady a great deal older than himself, and against the wish of all his friends. They had no issue. His Lordship died in October 1615,[*] and was succeeded by

---

* In a curious MS. in the British Museum, containing an account of the Scots nobility in the reign of James VI., this is stated :—"The Erle of Cassillis, called Kanethy, being with his friends of the same surname upon the west seas, in the countie of Carrik, a stewardrie and parcel of the shiredome of Ayre. There is of the same name, in that countie, and descended of his house, sundrie lordis and gentlemen, whereof the principall is the Lord Barganye and Blairquhoy, of little less living than the Erle himself. His chief houses he Cassells and Dunnyre, 4 miles from the bridge of Doone. The people are mingled in speeches of Irish and English, not far distant from Carrickfergus in Ireland. [The mode of spelling Kennedy ('Kanethy') seems favourable to the supposition that the name was originally Kenneth.]

X. John, sixth Earl of Cassillis, eldest son of Gilbert, Master of Cassillis, the youngest son of Gilbert, fourth Earl, who married Margaret, daughter of Uchtred Macdowall of Garthland. She afterwards married James Lord Ochiltree. Lord Cassillis was a person of great virtue, and zealously attached to the Presbyterian form of worship. He took an early and prominent part in resistance to the designs of Charles I. in 1638. He was one of the three ruling elders sent to the Westminster Assembly of Divines in 1643. He was served heir to his uncle, John, fifth Earl, on 25th July 1616. He was appointed Lord Justice-General on the 29th June, and admitted an extraordinary Lord of Session 3d July 1649. He is called by Crawfurd, in his *Officers of State*, "the grave and solemn Earl." Being naturally just and upright, he could ill brook to act harshly, much less unjustly, in his legal capacity, even to a decided political opponent, during a turbulent and agitated period. As preses of the court, in 1646, he was obliged to sign the sentence of execution against Sir Robert Spottiswood, President of the Court of Session. His repugnance to act is finely commemorated in the following classical, though rather elaborate, lines of the great lawyer, Sir John Nisbet of Dirleton, who had been counsel for Sir Robert:

Tempore nequicquam Judex Cassilissus Iniquo
Æquior, ei anceps officiumque fuit.
Nam, Judex et Præses erat, sed Judicis albus
Calculus, atrocem Præses utrumque fuit,
Testatus scripsisse manu NON mente—placebat
Quodque aliis, frustra displicuisse sibi.

Lord Hailes remarks, in reference to the last two lines :—"Lord Cassillis dissented from the judgment, although, in virtue of his office, he signed it."

In 1649, the Earl was sent to wait upon Charles II. in Holland with the terms upon which the Estates were willing to acknowledge his cause. These Charles would not agree to, and the Earl returned. He voted against sending commissioners to treat with the king at Breda; but this having been carried, he was himself appointed one of them, and accordingly met the king at Breda. At the Restoration, the Earl was appointed an extraordinary Lord of Session, but did not retain the situation long, having been superseded in July 1662, on account of his refusal to take the oaths of allegiance and supremacy, without an explanation as to the king's ecclesiastical interests. He married, first, Jean, daughter of Thomas, first Earl of Haddington,[*] and had issue:

---

* Contract dated 21st December 1621.

1. James, Lord Kennedy, who died unmarried during his father's life.
2. Margaret, who married Gilbert Burnett, then Professor of Divinity in the University of Glasgow, afterwards Bishop of Salisbury.
3. Catharine, who married William Lord Cochrane, eldest son of William, first Earl of Dundonald, and had issue.
4. Helen, died unmarried.

His Lordship married, secondly, Margaret, only daughter of William, tenth Earl of Errol, and widow of Henry Lord Ker, eldest son of Robert, first Earl of Roxburgh,* and by her had issue :

1. John, seventh Earl of Cassillis.
2. Mary.
3. Elizabeth.

Lord Cassillis died in 1668, and was succeeded by

XI. John, seventh Earl of Cassillis, eldest surviving son and heir, who was served heir to his father 22d September 1668. Of the same religious principles as his father, he was the only member of parliament, in 1670, who voted against the act for punishing conventicles. He was, in consequence, persecuted by the government, and had a large body of Highlanders quartered upon his estates. In 1683, he preferred a petition to Charles II., setting forth the danger in which his estates were placed in consequence of the large sums which had been advanced by his father for the maintenance of the army in Ireland, and the various public debts for which he had become security, and praying that he might have the advantage of the discharge for these debts, under the 6th of his Majesty's current parliament, without taking the test appointed by that act to be administered to all persons in public trust. The petition was favourably received by the king, and referred to the Privy Council of Scotland. The Earl joined in the Revolution, was a Privy Councillor of King William, and one of the Lords of the Treasury. He married, first, Susan, youngest daughter of James, first Duke of Hamilton, and by her had issue :

1. John, Lord Kennedy, died during his father's life, having married Elizabeth, daughter of Charles Hutcheson, Esq. of Owthorpe, in Nottinghamshire,† and had issue :—

John, eighth Earl of Cassillis.

Lord Kennedy died in 1700, and his widow afterwards married John, Earl of Selkirk and Ruglen.

2. Anne, married, in 1694, John, Earl of Selkirk and Ruglen, and had issue.

Lord Cassillis married, secondly, Elizabeth Foix, by whom he had issue :

1. James, who died without issue.
2. Elizabeth.

* Contract dated 20th February 1644, at the Scots League at Heighton in England.
† Contract of marriage dated 5th September 1698. Lady's fortune £4000 : her jointure £500.

In 1695, Lord Cassillis granted a lease to Nicholaus Dupin and Joseph Black, merchants in London, and Alexander Brand, merchant in Edinburgh, for twenty-one years, of the whole mines and minerals of lead, copper, or other metals found within his proper lands in the bailiary of Carrick, at a lordship of an eighth of the metals wrought. The Earl died 23d July 1701, and was succeeded by

XII. John, eighth Earl of Cassillis, his grandson. He was served heir to his father, Lord Kennedy, 22d February 1704. He was born about 1700 ; was governor of Dunbarton Castle. On the abolition of heritable jurisdictions, he was allowed £1800 for the bailiary of Carrick. He executed a strict entail of his estates on 29th March 1759 in favour of himself and the heirs-male of his body ; whom failing, the heirs-female of his body, the eldest always succeeding without division, and the heirs whatever of their bodies, also without division ; whom failing, Sir Thomas Kennedy of Culzean, Baronet, and the heirs-male of his body ; whom failing, to Mr David Kennedy, advocate, brother-german of the said Sir Thomas Kennedy, and the heirs-male of his body ; whom failing, to any person or persons whom he should at any time thereafter nominate or appoint to succeed to his estates, and failing such nomination, to his nearest lawful heirs-male whatsoever ; whom failing, his nearest lawful heirs whatsoever. He married his cousin, Susan,* youngest daughter of John, Earl of Selkirk and Ruglen, by Lady Anne Kennedy, daughter of John, seventh Earl of Cassillis, but by her had no issue. His lordship died in London 7th March 1759, and was buried in Saint James' Church ; but in June 1760 his body was removed to the collegiate church of Mayhole. Lady Cassillis died 8th February 1763, and was buried in the Abbey of Holyrood House.

On the Earl's death the estates went, under the deed of entail, to the heir-male, Sir Thomas Kennedy of Culzean, Bart., descended from Sir Thomas Kennedy, third son of Gilbert, third Earl, and a competition arose for the Peerage between him and William Earl of March and Ruglen, afterwards Duke of Queensberry, as grandson and heir of Lady Anne, Countess of Selkirk and Ruglen, daughter of John, seventh Earl. After a lengthened litigation, it was finally resolved and adjudged by the House of Lords on 27th January 1762, " That the petitioner, Sir Thomas Kennedy, hath a right and title to the honour and dignity of Earl of Cassillis, as heir-male of the body of David, the first Earl of

* Contract dated 25th September and 6th October 1739.

Cassillis, and that he hath also a right and title to the honour and dignity of Lord Kennedy, as heir-male of the body of Gilbert, the first Lord Kennedy."

## Kennedies of Culzean.

*Sir Thomas Kennedy of Culzean* was the third son of Gilbert, third Earl of Cassillis. His immediate elder brother having died in infancy, he was styled Master of Cassillis at the battle of Langside, where he was taken prisoner. He was knighted at the coronation of James VI. He got a charter of the lands of Culzean from his brother Gilbert, the fourth Earl, in which he was infeft 14th September 1569. He married Elizabeth, daughter of David M'Gill of Cranston-Riddell, widow of Robert Logan of Restalrig, and who afterwards, according to the 'Historical Account,' married William Mure of Rowallan. This, however, must be a mistake, for her latter-will bears that " Dame Elizabeth M'Gill, Lady Culzeane," died in January 1622, and that the inventory of her effects, &c. was " ffaythfullie maid and gevin vp be hir self, in the place of the Coiff, the xxvi day of December 1621 zeiris, in sa far, &c. and pairtlie maid and gevin vp be Allexander Kennedy of Craigoche, hir sone," &c. She had issue:—

1. Thomas, died unmarried 1601.
2. James, who succeeded to his father in Culzean. He was served heir to his brother Thomas 18th May 1602. He sold the estate of Culzean to his younger brother, Alexander, by contract dated 30th July 1622, and acquired the estate of Blairquhan. He married Jean Stewart,* and had issue:—
   1. James, who was served heir to his father 12th October 1637. He had a son—
      William, mentioned in a bond, dated 24th June 1662, by him to his cousin, John Kennedy of Culzean.
   2. Jeane, mentioned in her mother's testament.
3. Sir Alexander of Craigoch, of whom afterwards.
4. David, married Margaret, daughter of Hew Kennedy of Garrichorne, whose testament, &c., in 1617, was " ffaythfullie maid and gevin vp be Margaret Kennedy, now spous to David Kennedy, brother-german to James Kennedy of Culzeane," &c.
5. Helen, married to John Mure of Auchindrain, and afterwards John Fergusson of Kilkerran, and had issue.

According to the History of the Kennedys there was another brother, John, and a daughter, Susana, afterwards Lady Larg.

Sir Thomas was murdered on the 12th May 1602

---

* She is called ' Ann ' in the ' Historical Account,' but Jean is the name according to the Commissary records:— ' Testament, &c. and Inventar of the guids, &c. quhilk perteinit to vmquhile Jeane Stewart, Lady Culzeane, within the parochin of Mayboill . . Quha deceist in the moneth of August 1616 zeiris, ffaythfullie maid and gevin vp be James Kennedy, hir spous, in name and behalf of James and Jeane Kennedyis, bairnes lawfull to the defunct, &c.

by Thomas Kennedy of Drummurchie, at the instigation of the Mures of Auchindrain. Sir Thomas was succeeded by his second surviving son, *James,* who sold the estate to his brother,

*Sir Alexander Kennedy of Craigoch,* and ultimately heir. He acquired the estate of Culzean in 1622. He also acquired the barony of Greenan, lands of Baltersan, Mochrumbill, and Glenluie, in 1642, from John Stewart, Earl of Carrick. He married Agnes, daughter of Thomas Kennedy of Ardmillan,* and had issue:

1. John, of whom below.
2. Alexander, called, first, of Craigoch, afterwards of Kilhenzie, from whom descended Archibald, eleventh Earl of Cassillis.
3. Thomas of Baltersan, tutor of Culzean, a major in the army.
4. James, married, first, Anna Campbell, and had a daughter, Anna. She died in April 1650. In her testament, under the head " Inventare," the following occurs:—" Item, the defunct and her said husband being bot newlie maried, and being in house and famille with thesaid Sir Alexander Kennedie, his father, in the plaice of the Cove of Carrick, had no guidis, &c. except allenerlie the ornaments and abuilzements of hir bodie, estimat worth jc lib. money of Scotland." In the list of debtors occurs " John Earle of Lowdoune, heigh Chancellar of Scotland, Jaij lib." James Kennedy married, secondly, Katherine, eldest daughter of Sir John Mure of Auchindrain.
5. Marion, married James Kennedy of Girvan Mains.
6. Margaret, married Alexander Craufurd of Skeldon.
7. Agnes, married Captain James Hamilton of Clintonclare, son of Archibald Hamilton of Halleraig.

Sir Alexander Kennedy died September 1652. By his latter-will, which was dated at the Coiff, 27th September 1652, he appointed John Kennedy, his lawful eldest son and heir, his only executor, and ordained him to pay to the parties aftermentioned, the following sums:—To Agnes Kennedy, his youngest daughter, 7000 merks, as her portion; to James Kennedy, his youngest son, 6000 merks; to Anna Kennedy, " procreat betwixt the said James Kennedy and Umquhile Anna Campbell," 1000 merks; to Gilbert Kennedy of Girvan Mains, and to Marion Kennedy, daughter of the testator, 1000 merks; to Major Thomas Kennedy of Baltersane, 1000 merks; to Alexander Craufurd of Skeldon, and Margaret Kennedy, his spouse, 1000 merks; to Alexander Kennedy of Craigoch, his son, 1000 merks, to be " employit to the vse of Margaret Kennedie, his daughter, gottin of his first mariage, procreat betwixt him and Margaret M'Ilvane;" to Bryce Blair, fifty merks, " with his weiring cloithes, with cloake, net, boots, schanks and bands, and that by and attour his fey." He at the same time ordained Gilbert Kennedy, his son-in-law, to be discharged of two bonds for 300 merks, granted by the late Hew Kennedy of Girvan

---

* She is mentioned in a discharge by James Kennedy of Girvan Mains to John Kennedy of Culzean.

Mains, his father, to him; also, Andro Kennedy, in Lomnoche, and Helen Kennedy, his spouse, his natural daughter, of a bond of 300 merks. His natural daughter, Margaret, he ordained to receive one boll of meal yearly during her lifetime. Sir Alexander was succeeded by

*John Kennedy of Culzean*, his eldest son, who was served heir to his father 8th February 1656; married, first, Ann, daughter of John Blair of Blair, by whom he had no issue; and, secondly, Margaret, daughter of John, first Lord Bargany,* and by her, who afterwards married Sir David Ogilvy of Clova, had issue:

1. John, died without issue.
2. Sir Archibald Kennedy, Baronet, of whom below.
3. Alexander, died without issue.
4. Thomas, who was served heir to his brother Alexander 22d January 1676.
5. Katherine.
6. Jean.

John Kennedy died in 1665, and was succeeded by

*Sir Archibald Kennedy of Culzean, Bart.*, who was served heir to his father 17th April 1672. He was created a Baronet of Nova Scotia to himself, and the heirs-male of his body, 8th December 1682. He married Elizabeth, eldest daughter of David, first Lord Newark, and by her had issue:

1. Sir John, of whom below.
2. David, an advocate at the Scottish bar, died unmarried at Ayr, April 1754.
3. Lewis, collector of the customs at Irvine. He died in 1721, having married Magdalen Cochrane, daughter of the Honourable Alexander Cochrane of Bonshaw, and by her had issue——
   John, lieutenant in the navy, died without issue.
4. Jean, married Sir Gilbert Kennedy of Girvan Mains.
5. Susanna, married Alexander, ninth Earl of Eglintoun, and had issue.
6. Mary.
7. Catherine.

Sir Archibald Kennedy died in 1710, and was succeeded by his son,

*Sir John Kennedy of Culzean, Bart.*, who was served heir to his father 12th March 1711. He married Jean, daughter of Captain Andrew Douglas of Mains, R.N., in Dumbartonshire,† and by her had twenty children—twelve sons and eight daughters—fourteen of whom died young and unmarried. The rest were:

1. Sir John, who succeeded.
2. Sir Thomas, afterwards ninth Earl.
3. David, afterwards tenth Earl.
4. Elizabeth, married, in 1729, Sir John Cathcart of Carleton, Bart., and had issue.
5. Anne, married John Blair, younger of Dunskey, and had issue.
6. Clementina, married George Watson of Bilton Park, and died without issue.

* Contract dated in 1653. Lady's fortune 10,000 merks.
† Contract dated 15th March 1710.

Sir John Kennedy died in 1742, and was succeeded by his son,

*Sir John Kennedy of Culzean, Bart.*, who was served heir to his father 28th January 1743, and died 10th April 1744. He was succeeded by

*Sir Thomas Kennedy of Culzean, Bart.*, who was served heir to his brother, Sir John, 22d July 1747. He became Earl of Cassillis by the decision of the House of Lords already referred to.

XIII. Sir Thomas, ninth Earl of Cassillis. He died without issue in 1775, and was succeeded by his brother,

XIV. David, tenth Earl of Cassillis, who was served heir to his brother, Earl Thomas, 15th April 1776. He executed a supplementary entail of the estates of Cassillis and Culzean, on 2d February 1790, in favour of himself, and the heirs-male of his body; whom failing, to Captain Archibald Kennedy of the navy, late of New York, then residing in London; whom failing, to Archibald Kennedy, eldest son of the said Captain Archibald Kennedy, and the heirs-male of his body; whom failing, to John Kennedy, second son of the said Captain Archibald Kennedy, and the heirs-male of his body; whom failing, to Robert Kennedy, third son of the said Captain Archibald Kennedy, and the heirs-male of his body; whom failing, to any other heirs-male procreated of the body of the said Captain Archibald Kennedy; whom failing, to the other nearest lawful heirs-male whatsoever of John, eighth Earl of Cassillis, maker of the former entail, in their order; whom failing, to such person or persons as he should nominate or appoint to succeed to the said lands and estate; whom failing, to his nearest lawful heirs whatsoever. Earl David was an advocate at the Scottish bar, and died unmarried 18th December 1792, when the Baronetcy became extinct. He was succeeded by

XV. Archibald, eleventh Earl of Cassillis, called in the deed of entail, above-mentioned, Captain Archibald Kennedy of the navy. He was served heir-male of David, the tenth Earl, on 12th March 1793, being descended from

*Alexander Kennedy of Craigoch*, afterwards of *Kilhenzie*, second son of Sir Alexander Kennedy of Culzean. He was infeft in Craigoch 16th May 1644, and afterwards acquired the barony of Kilhenzie. He married, first, Margaret M'Ilvane, daughter of M'Ilvane of Grimmet, by whom he had a daughter, *Margaret*, married to David Kennedy of Drummellan; secondly, Anna, youngest daughter of William Cranfurd of Auchinames, and had issue:—

1. John, of whom afterwards.

N 2

2. Archibald, from whom descended Archibald, eleventh Earl.
3. Alexander.
4. William.
5. Thomas.

He died about 1698, and was succeeded by his eldest son,

*John Kennedy of Kilhenzie*, an advocate at the Scottish bar. He married Helen Monteith, and died about 1748, leaving issue:—

1. Alexander Kennedy of Kilhenzie, who was served heir to his grandfather, Alexander Kennedy, 4th May 1754. He was a captain in the army, and died unmarried 3d May 1766.
2. Helen, who was served heir to her brother 9th November 1773. She married John Shaw of Dalton, and had issue.

*Archibald Kennedy*, the second son of Alexander Kennedy of Kilhenzie, went to New York about 1722, where he was appointed Collector of the Customs. He had a large estate called Pavonia, at Second River. He married, first, Miss Massam, by whom he had issue:—

1. James, who was killed in the expedition against Carthagena.
2. Robert, died unmarried.
3. Archibald, who became eleventh Earl of Cassillis.
4. Thomas, barrister at New Jersey, died in England unmarried.
5. Katherine, married Dr Joseph Mallet, physician to the army.

Archibald Kennedy married, secondly, Miss Waters, a Dutch lady, by whom he had no issue. He died in 1763,* and was succeeded by his son,

*Captain Archibald Kennedy of the navy*, who became eleventh Earl of Cassillis on the death of Earl David. He distinguished himself in many brilliant actions, particularly in one when upon the Lisbon station, in consequence of which he was presented by the merchants of Lisbon with a handsome piece of plate. He succeeded to his father's estate of Pavonia, in the State of New York. His house was burned during the War of Independence, and all his papers destroyed. He married, first, Miss Schuyler, a lady of great fortune in New Jersey, by whom he had no issue; and, secondly, Anne, daughter of John Watts, Esq. of New York, by whom he had issue:—

1. Archibald, twelfth Earl, created Marquis of Ailsa.
2. John, formerly captain of an Independent Company of Foot, married, in 1800, Charlotte, only daughter of Laurence Gill, Esq.
3. Robert, married Jane, sister of General Alexander Macomb, and, dying in 1813, left issue:—
   1. John, secretary to the British Embassy to the United States, married, 5th August 1834, Amelia

* He left a will dated 1733, with two codicils dated 13th March 1745 and 10th December 1749, and recorded in the Probate Office, New York. From this will it appears his two eldest sons were then dead without issue. The death of Thomas appears from the service of Earl Archibald.

Maria, only daughter of Samuel Briggs, Esq., and had issue. He died 14th March 1845.
2. Anne, married Sir Edward Cromwell Disbrowe, G.C.H., and had issue.
3. Jane.
4. Sophia Eliza, married John Levett, Esq. of Wichnor Park, county of Stafford, and has issue.
5. Margaret, unmarried.
6. Frances, married the Baron de Weiller of Heidelberg.
7. Isabella Matilda, twin with Frances, married to Hugh Campbell, Esq. of the Scots Greys.
4. Lady Anne, married to William Henry Digby of Twickenham, Esq. She died in 1820.

Lord Cassillis died 30th December 1794, and was succeeded by his eldest son,

XVI. Archibald, twelfth Earl of Cassillis, and first Marquis of Ailsa, K.T. He was served heir to his father on 29th April 1795. In 1790, he raised an independent company of foot, and was Lieutenant-Colonel of the West Lowland Fencibles. He was created a Baron of the united kingdom in 1806, and a Marquis in 1831, and was a Knight of the most ancient order of the Thistle. He married Margaret, daughter, and eventually heiress, of John Erskine, Esq. of Dun, in Forfarshire, by whom he had issue:

1. Archibald, Earl of Cassillis, died before his father, having married Eleanor, daughter and heiress of Alexander Allardyce of Dunnottar, Esq., by whom he had issue:
   1. Archibald, second Marquis of Ailsa.
   2. Alexander, died unmarried.
   3. John, died unmarried 1846.
   4. David, an officer in the East India Company's service.
   5. Gilbert.
   6. William, an officer in the artillery, married Miss Cecilia de Blois, of Halifax.
   7. Fergus, an officer in the East India Company's service.
   8. Nigel.
   9. Adolphus Archibald, died young.
   10. Lady Hannah Eleanor, married Sir John Andrew Cathcart of Carleton, Bart., and has issue.
2. John Erskine, married Lady Augusta Fitzclarence, daughter of William IV., who afterwards married Lord John Frederick Gordon Hallyburton, and by her had issue:
   1. William Henry Kennedy Erskine of Dun.
   2. Wilhelmina Kennedy Erskine.
   3. Augusta Milicent Anne Mary Kennedy Erskine.
   He took the name of Erskine, as heir to the estate of Dun.
3. Lady Anne, married to Sir David Baird of Newbyth, Bart., and has issue.
4. Lady Mary, married Richard Oswald, Esq., younger of Auchincruive.
5. Lady Margaret, married Thomas, Earl of Newburgh.
6. Lady Alice Jane, married Colonel Jonathan Peel, son of the late Sir Robert Peel, Bart., and has issue.

Lord Ailsa died on 8th September 1846, and was buried at Dun. He was succeeded by

XVII. Archibald, thirteenth Earl of Cassillis, and second Marquis of Ailsa, born 25th August 1816; served heir to his grandfather on the 17th March 1847; married, 10th November 1846, Julia, second daughter of Sir Richard Mounteney

Jephson, Baronet, of Springvale, Dorsetshire, and has issue :

1. Archibald, Earl of Cassillis.

*Creations.*—Lord Kennedy before March 1457, Earl of Cassillis before January 1511, in the Peerage of Scotland ; Baron Ailsa, of the Isle of Ailsa, 1806 ; Marquis of Ailsa, of the Isle of Ailsa, 1831, in the Peerage of the United Kingdom.

*Arms.*—Argent, a chevron, gules, between three cross crosslets, fitchee, sable, all within a double tressure, flowered and counterflowered of the second.

*Crest.*—A dolphin.

*Supporters.*—Two swans, proper.

*Motto.*—Avise la fin.

*Principal Seats.*—Culzean Castle and Cassillis House.

### THOMASTON.

Tradition is probably correct in ascribing the building of this castle to a nephew of King Robert the Bruce. If so, it must have been *Thomas*, third son (illegitimate) of Edward Bruce, who became Earl of Carrick on the death of his brother, Alexander. It could not have been long in his possession, however, as he died soon after 1334, while the date assigned for the erection of the castle is 1335. But tradition is seldom accurate in dates ; and the presumption is, that Thomaston was built prior to that year, before Thomas Bruce's succession to the earldom.

The next we find in possession of Thomaston were the *Corries of Kelwood*, originally a Dumfriesshire family. *Robert Corrie* and Eupham, his spouse, daughter to Thomas Torthorwald, slain at the battle of Durham, had a charter of the lands of Cowlyn and Buchan, in the county of Dumfries, from David II. The first of the name we have found in connection with Ayrshire was

I. THOMAS CORRY DE KELWOOD, who had a charter from James IV., dated 12th January 1507, of the lands of Thomastoun, Craigincalze, Moytoch, Auld Cragachaneane, Dalnacarny, &c. His daughter, *Katherine*, appears to have married Thomas Kennedy of Coiff. He had a charter from James V., in 1517, of the lands of Newby, with the fishings, in Kirkcudbrightshire ; also a charter of the two merk land of Clonlothry, in Ayrshire, from the same monarch, dated 3d February 1528. Thomas Corry of Kelwood, along with David Craufurd of Kerse, was fined in £100 for not entering Bargany for the slaughter of the young laird of Attiquane, in 1512. In 1528, he was concerned, along with Bargany, in the

slaughter of Robert Campbell of Lochfergus. *George*, son and heir of Thomas Corry de Kelwood, had a charter from James V., 1st August 1523, of the lands of Newby, &c., Thomastoun, in the united barony of Kelwood, Dumfries and Ayr. *Thomas*, son and heir apparent of the late Thomas Corry de Newby, had a charter of the lands of Bordland, in Kirkcudbrightshire, from James V., 22d May 1532.

II. Thomas Corry de Kelwood, and Margaret Naper, his spouse, had a charter of the lands of Balmakcawell, in Ayrshire, from James V., 21st July 1536. He had also a charter confirmatory, from the same monarch, 29th December 1537, of the lands of Cragdow and Laggandirre. Again, 29th April 1540, a charter of the lands of Drummurthy, Ayrshire ; and Thomas Corry de Kelwood and Margaret Naper, had a charter of the lands of Drummore, dated 29th February 1542 ; also of Kilhenze, from James V., dated 10th June 1542.

III. George Corry de Kelwood, and Margaret Blair, his spouse, had a charter of the lands of Auld Crag, Thomastoun, Craigincalze, &c., from Mary, 11th May 1546. In 1547 (Oct. 25), he was served heir of his father, Thomas Corry, who died at the battle of Fawside. He is mentioned in the inventory of " quondam Gilberti Kennedy de Balmaclanachan, ab intesto in conflictu de Fawside," which was confirmed 13th January 1547. His name occurs in the list of assize in a criminal trial in 1580.

IV. John Corry de Kelwood appears as a witness in a deed, dated 21st December 1588 ; and on January 16, 1588-9, he was " putt to the horne for non confermeing of the testament of umquhile George Corrie of Kelwood, his fader broder,"[*] &c. He had thus succeeded his uncle. His name occurs in the list of absentees from the Raid of Dumfries in 1600. He was amongst the followers of the Earl of Cassillis at the feud fight at Lady Corse, in 1601, where the laird of Bargany was slain. *Robert Corry, apparent of Kelwood*, had a charter of the lands of Strone, in Kirkcudbrightshire, from James VI., dated 6th July 1597. " John Corre and his brother *David*," are mentioned in the testament of Margaret Hamilton, spouse to Antonie Kennedie of Brigend, as creditors to the amount of 500 merks. She died in 1613 ; but the Laird of Kelwood must have been dead at this time, for

V. George Corrie de Kelwode was served heir to his father, John Corrie of Kelwood, on the 30th March 1610 ; and he and his wife, and *David*, his brother, occur in the testament of

---

* Mason's Notes, MS.

"Williame Broune, merchand burges of Air," who died in 1613. George Corrie de Kelwood, and Margaret Chalmers, his spouse, had a charter of certain lands in Wigtonshire from James VI., 16th July 1612. It was probably the wife of this Laird of Kelwood of whom Wodrow has the following notice:—" 1623. In the moneth of February dyed the Lady Kelwood, at Maybole, my cousin-german, a virtuous and wise gentlewoman, fearing God, and full of good works. She had a large testimony from all good people, and was much regrated by her own and the poor. She bore to her husband twelve children at least, and left eight of them in life." George Corrie of Kelwood appears to have left no male issue, his son and heir having predeceased him. *John Corrie, appeirand heir* of Kelwood, is mentioned in the latter-will of " Capitane James Corrie in Maijboill, quha departed this life at the battell of Afford, in ye moneth of June 1645 zeiris." This testament, part of which is obliterated in the registry, is dated at Maybole, 16th April, and bears that he was " callit out for the public service of the kirk." If his wife should have a son, he left him all his property and money " vpone bandis, except ye band of ane thowsand that is dew to me be James Rosse of Baldneill, quhilk I leive to my dochter, *Margaret*. And I leive the Laird of Grimet, and Alexander Kennedy, sone to the Laird of Collein, and Quintein Kennedy in Maijboill, and Alexr. Crawfurd, lievetennant, my vncle-in-law, overseeris to my wyffe and children," &c. This testament was " pairtlie maid and gevin vp be Florence Crawfurd, his (the Captain's) relict." Captain James Corrie was a brother of George Corrie of Kelwood. This appears from the service of Mariot, daughter of David Corrie, as heir of her uncle, Captain James Corrie, May 13, 1648.

From the Corries, *Thomastoun* seems to have passed to the *M'Ilvanes of Grimmet*, probably through marriage. The first of this family of whom we find any record, was

I. ALANO MAKILVANE, who had a charter of the lands of Grimet and Attiquin from James V., 16th October 1529. He was succeeded by

II. Gilberto M'Ilvene, filio et hæredi Alani M'Ilvene de Grumet, and his spouse, *Jonet Corry*, had a charter of confirmation of the lands of Grumet from Queen Mary, dated 4th May 1546. Gilbert M'Ilvane died at the battle of Fawside, and was succeeded by his son,

III. Patrick M'Ilvane of Grumet, who was served heir to his father, 25th October 1547, in the lands of Nether and Over Grimmet, and Attyqnyne. His name occurs as a witness in a

deed, dated 4th January 1586-7. He and his son, John, were both in the following of the Earl of Cassillis at Lady Corse, in 1601. He died in 1613, and his testament was " maid and gevin vp be Johnn Schaw in Largis of Stratoun, executor." His son, John, seems to have predeceased him. From a charter granted to " Joanni M'Ilvane de Grumet," by James VI., in 1597, his wife's name appears to have been Kennedy.

IV. Johnne M'Kelvane of Grymmet was alive in 1632. His wife was *Anna Corrie*, who died in February of that year. By her latter-will, it appears she left " *Margaret*,[*] *Agnes, Helein*, and *Mareoune M'Ilvanes*, bairnes lawfull to ye defunct." It was probably by this marriage that the M'Ilvanes acquired Thomastoun, as we see by the will of Captain James Corrie, that the heir-apparent of Kelwood died before 1645. If so, this laird of Grimmet must have married again, as Johne M'Alveane of Grimett is mentioned in the testament of *Juliane Schaw*, his spouse, who died in December 1641. She had issue, *Anna* and *Juliane*. Johne M'Ilvane of Grimett occurs in the testament of Sir Alexander Kennedy of Culzeane in 1652.

V. Quintin M'Ilvane of Grimet was served heir to his father, John M'Ilvane of Grimet, in the lands of Thomastoun, 8th October 1669.

The M'Ilvanes possessed Thomastoun towards the close of the seventeenth century; but how much later we are ignorant. The castle was inhabited, however, about the beginning of the present century.

### BALTERSAN.

The first of the Kennedies of Baltersan mentioned in the " Historical Account" of the Ailsa family, is Major Thomas Kennedy, who lived about the middle of the seventeenth century. It had been long previously, however, in possession of a family of the name of Kennedy, no doubt a branch of the main stock. The first occupier, apparently, was

JAMES KENNEDY, second son of Gilbert, first Lord Kennedy, afterwards designed of Row. He is mentioned in a charter dated 14th May 1473. He married Egidia Blair, eldest daughter of John Blair of that Ilk, but died without issue. His death occurred before 1515, which appears from a charter dated 18th April of that year— " Egidia Blair, relictæ quondam Jacobi Kennedy, annui redditus levan, de terris baroniæ de

---

[*] Margaret was no doubt the first wife of Alexander Kennedy of Craigoch, previously mentioned.

Dunure." His lady survived till 1530. Of her latter-will, dated 31st August of that year, and written in Latin, a translation is given in Aiton's Survey of Ayrshire, published in 1811. It was found in the charter chest of Sir John Whyteford in 1796, and translated by Sir Adam Ferguson of Kilkerran. It is interesting as illustrative of the state of society at the time, and may be of service in a genealogical point of view:—

"Seeing nothing is more certain than death, or more uncertain than the hour of death, therefore it is that I, Giles Blair, Lady Row, although weak in body yet sound in mind, blessed be God, make my testament as follows. In the first place, I give and bequeath my soul to God Almighty, and the blessed Virgin Mary, and to all saints, and my body to be buried in the Monastery of Crossraguel, in the blessed Virgin's aisle. I likewise bequeath four pennies, towards the fabric of the church of Saint Mungo. And I appoint and ordain for my executours, David Kennedy of Pennyglen, and Sir John Kennedy, Prebendary of Maybole, and the Reverend Father in Christ, William, by divine permission, Abbot and superior of the Monastery of Crossraguel.

"Inventory of my Goods.

"Imprimis. I confess myself to have sixty-one cows, the price of the piece two merks, summa, eighty-two pounds. Item, twenty-nine oxen, the price of each, thirty shillings, sum, forty-three pounds, ten shillings. Item, fifteen two year olds, the price, per piece, eight shillings, sum three pounds twelve shillings. Item, five hundred and forty-three sheep, the price, per piece, five shillings, sum, one hundred and sixty-two pounds, ten shillings. Item, four score and ten lambs, the price of the piece, sixteen pennics, sum, six pounds. Item, in victual, viz. in bear and meal, one hundred and eighty-two bolls, the price of the boll, twelve shillings, sum, one hundred and twenty-one pounds, four shillings. Item, one hundred and sixty bolls of oats, the price of the boll, six shillings, sum, fifty-four pounds. Item, horses, mares and stags in the muir, the price of them all, thirty pounds. Item, in utensils and domicils, forty pounds. Item, for the rents and profits of Row, twenty pounds.

"Sum of the inventory, five hundred and thirty-four pounds, fourteen shillings.

"There are no debts due to me.

"The debts which are resting by me to others.

"Imprimis. To the Earl of Cassillis, two hundred merks, whom I earnestly beg and entreat to defend my executors, from oppressors, and the violence of oppressors, that they may quietly and freely dispose of my goods, for the health of my soul. Item, to David Kennedy, forty-two

merks, and one-half as the remainder of the tocher. Item, to the Abbot and Convent of Crossraguel, for the farms of Balchristyne and Baltersyne, six pounds. Item, to the Lord Cassillis for the farms of lands, twelve pounds.

"Sum of the debts, eight score and nine pounds, thirteen shillings, four pennies.

"Legacies.

"Imprimis, I leave and bequeath to the Convent of Crossraguel, twenty pounds. Item, to the Minim Friars of Ayr, forty pounds. Item, to the Dominican Friars of Ayr, five merks. Item, to the Friars of Irvine, five merks. Item, to John Whitefurd, forty pounds. Item, to my executors, forty pounds, to be divided equally amongst them. Item, to Alexander Blair, ten merks. Item, to Marion M'Ilquhan, two two year olds and six sheep. Item, to Bessie Davidson, two sheep and two lambs. Item, to John M'Coury, twenty merks. Item, to Fergus M'Mury, twenty pounds. Item, for building an altar in the church of Saint Oswald, twenty merks. Item, to my brother William's daughter, spouse to Richard Lockhart, twenty merks. Item, to Hugh Kennedy, my sister's son, twenty merks. Item, to Bessie Whytefurd, twenty merks. Item, to James Kennedy, baillie of Carrick, twenty merks, conditionally, that he assist and defend my executors, and do not suffer them to be disturbed, or molested by himself, or any other person, otherwise, I do not leave him the said twenty merks. Item, to Sir George Blair, chaplain, twenty merks, six bolls bear and four stones weight of cheese. Item, to Sir John Rays, two bolls of meal, one boll of wheat, and three stone of cheese. Item, to Sir William Cristal, one boll of meal, and one stone of cheese. Item, to Thomas Ferguson, Dominical chaplain of Kirkoswald, one boll of meal. Item, to the curate of Kirkoswald, one boll of meal. Item, to Sir William Johnstoun, one boll of meal. Item, to John M'Mury's wife, a black gown. Item, to Christine Hynd,* a russet gown. Item, to John Steell, a black coat. Item, I leave the web at the weaver's, to Fergus M'Mury, a suit of the said web. Item, to Sir John Kennedy, a gown of the said web. Item, to John Whytefurd, a coat of said web. Also, to Sir John Rays, a gown of said web. Item, to the poor woman the cripple at Maybole, two firlots of meal. Item, I bequeath my uncle, John Whytefurd, for his maintenance, during the space of one year, eight bolls of meal, and four stones of cheese. As also to the said John Whytefurd,

* Wife, probably, of Walter Kennedy of Glentig, the poet, and brother of James Kennedy of Row. She was then, no doubt, in her widowhood.

two silver spoons, and likewise to the said John Whytefurd, other eight bolls of meal, to be received by David Hynd, in his name, for the maintenance of the said John for another year, and that out of the current year's farm, out of the mill of Row, so that the said David Hynd shall have the maintenance of the said John for two years. If the money given out, and bequeathed by me to the said John Whytefurd and David Hynd, be not laid upon land within two years for the use and profit of said John Whytefurd, Item, I bequeath to the said Whytefurd, two pairs of blankets, two coverings, two pairs sheets, and a bed-cover. Item, to David Kennedy of Pennyglen, four ells of linen cloth of russet, and two linen table cloths, and two towels of the same. Item, to Sir John Kennedy, one table cloth, the small board cloth, and one towel of the same. Item, I leave to John Whytefurd, the stone of wool in his mother's possession, for making clothes to him, the said John; and the cloth made, or to be made of the said wool, is to be delivered to David Hynd, in name and for behoof of the said John Whytefurd; and the stone of wool in the hand of John M'Mury's wife, I leave to Fergus M'Mury, her son, to be made into clothes for him. Item, I leave all my goods, wherever they be, to John Whytefurd. Item, I leave to Margaret M'Kellyr, two firlots of meal. Item, to the chaplains and friars, on the day of my burial, twenty merks. Item, to the poor upon the said day, forty shillings in drink, and a chalder of meal, and ten stones of cheese. Item, to the Minim Friars of Ayr, two pair of blankets, three bed-rugs, and one bed-cover of needle-work. Item, to Cristine Adumnell, two pair of sheets, and two coverings or bed-rugs. Item, to Fergus M'Mury, one chest standing in my chamber, and one bolster or pillow. Item, to Navin Dunning, two firlots of meal. Item, to Ambrose Lace, twenty shillings. Item, to Bessie Davidson, one firlot of meal. Item, I bequeath the residue and remainder of all my goods, for building my part of the bridge upon the water of Girvan, formerly built by me; and if anything remain over and above, I bequeath the same to the poor, to be laid out at the discretion of my executors."

This testament bears to have been made at Lady Row's "dwelling-house of Baltersyne," the last day of August 1530, and confirmed by Gaven, Archbishop of Glasgow, 28th September, same year.

It would thus appear that Baltersan belonged at the time to the Abbey of Crossraguel, and that the manor-house or place of Baltersan was not then in existence. The building of this ba-

ronial residence was probably the work of the next possessor.

I. John Kennedy of Beltersane, who also possessed the barony of Greenan—the old tower of which stands upon a rock overhanging the sea, at the Doon foot, near Ayr. He had a dispute with the magistrates of that burgh, in 1591, respecting the salmon fishings at the mouth of the Doon, which then belonged to the town of Ayr.[*] John Kennedy and his wife, Margaret Cathcart, had a charter of the Mains of Grenane, Cuningpark, &c. from James VI., 25th May 1588. Also of the lands of Crokba, Drumbra, Chapeltoun, 26th July 1592.

II. John Kennedy of Beltersane, and Florence M'Dougal, his spouse, had a charter of the lands of Balling and M'Killistoun, and Miltoun of Grenane, " in baroniam de Grenane de novo united," dated 24th May 1597. As the following extract from his testament shows, John Kennedy died in 1609:—

" Testament, &c. of vmquhile Johnne Kennedy of Belterssane . . . quha deceist in the moneth of Februar 1609 . . . and pairtlie maid and gevin vp be Florance M'Dowell, his spouse, quhome he maid and constitute his onlie executrix, &c.

" Debtis awand be ye deid.

" Item, thair was awand, &c. To the King his majestie for the mertimes termes maill of ye lands of greinend of the said crop 1608, &c. . . Item, mair to his majestie for ye few maillis of ye lands of corsraguell ye said crop 1608, &c. Item, to Josias Stewart of bonitoun, for ye teindis of ye rest of ye landis of greinend.

" ffollowis ye Legacie.

. . . And ordanes my bodie to be bureyit in the colledge Kirk of Maybell, in my fatheris grave. And I ordane my wyf to build a rowme about ye grave, quherof scho may be bureyit also. And gif ye erle of Cassillis and the freindis thairof will big ye colledge I ordane hir to pay ane hundrith markis to help to big ye samyn (my dett and legacie being payit).† . . . I ordane na vain in my buriall, nor I forbid to oppin me, bot to burie me without serimonie and honest freinds. . . . Be this my testament, &c. maid and writtin with my awin hand, being seik in bodie and haill of mynd, and subscryvit with my awin hand, at the greinend, the secund day of December, the zeir of God Jai vi c. and aucht zeiris. Sic subscribitur Johnne Kennedy of Beltarssane."

III. Sir John Kennedy of Grenane, miles, was served heir of his father, John Kennedy of Bel-

---

* Ayr records.
† The Collegiate Church of Maybole had not, it appears, been built at this period.

terssane, 22d August 1609. Master John Kennedy, apparent of Baltersane, had " Litera de Abbatia de Saulsaitt," from James VI., dated 25th October 1598. He died before 1616, and was succeeded by his son,

IV. Sir John Kennedy of Barneolin, *miles*, who was served heir of his father, John Kennedy of Belterssane, in the four merk land of Belterssane and Knockrinnellis, &c., 15th February 1616.

The property seems to have passed from the family soon after this. John Kennedy of Culzean was served heir of his father, amongst other lands, in the four merk land of Beltersan and Knokronald, &c., in 1656; and the next we find in possession of it was

*Major Thomas Kennedy of Beltersane*, third son of Sir Alexander Kennedy of Craigoch. He was alive in 1686, in which year he had an obligation from Hugh, son of Thomas Kennedy of Ardmillan, who married his second daughter *Jean*. He had three daughters, but apparently no sons.

[There are few small proprietors in this parish, the greater part of it belonging to the Marquis of Ailsa and the Kilkerran family. The two principal small proprietors are Mr Torrance of Threave, and Sir Seymour Blane, the latter of whom succeeded the late Andrew Blane, Esq. of Blanefield.]

# PARISH OF LARGS.

ETYMOLOGY, EXTENT, &c.

THERE can be little doubt that Chalmers is right in supposing that Largs—there having been more than one place of the same name, occasioned the addition of the final s, the sign of the English plural—is derived from the Gaelic *Learg*, a plain. As a proof of this, it is still called, in ordinary conversation, "the Lairgs." The parish extends along the coast of the Frith of Clyde about nine miles, and embraces a surface of upwards of 24,000 miles. It is bounded on the north by the parishes of Innerkip and Greenock; on the east by Kilmalcolm, Lochwinnoch, and Kilbirnie; on the south, by Dalry and West Kilbride; and on the west by the Clyde. In breadth it does not exceed four miles.

The topographical appearance of the parish is well described in the old *Statistical Account.* "No parish," says the writer, "in the west of Scotland, and few in the Highlands, can afford such a variety of beautiful and romantic scenes. The hills, which begin to rise in the neighbouring parishes of Greenock, Kilmalcolm, Lochwinnoch, Kilbirnie and Dalry, meet in a kind of general summit at the eastern boundary of Largs, from which they gradually descend as they approach the shore, till they terminate at last in a variety of abrupt declivities, some of which are almost perpendicular, as if part of their base had been torn away by force. Notwithstanding the vast height of these hills, they are covered during the greater part of the year with verdure, and afford such excellent pasture for sheep, and some of them for larger cattle, as can hardly be found elsewhere in similar situations. The quantity of heath, even in the highest hills, is comparatively small; and, from indisputable marks, it appears that some of them have once been cultivated." A tract of rich land, averaging about a quarter of a mile in breadth, runs along the coast, from West Kilbride to Kellyburn.

The names of the principal hills are the Stake, which is 1691 feet above the level of the sea; Irishlaw, 1576; and Knockside, 1419. One-half at least, of the parish is hill pasture. Upon the arable portion of it, great improvements have been made of late years.

"The temperature of the town of Largs, which is protected from the east winds by a range of high ground, is considered mild and salubrious; and the situation has become a favourite and fashionable watering-place. The high grounds above Largs afford very delightful prospects. The admirers of nature need not travel out of this district in search of fine scenery, as few scenes can equal in rich variety what the enraptured eye of the beholder can witness from the grounds above Kelburn. There may be enjoyed

> ———— the boundless store
> Of charms which nature to her votary yields,
> The warbling woodland, the resounding shore,
> The pomp of groves, and garniture of fields." *

The view from the range of mountains by which the plain of Largs is enclosed upon the east, is peculiarly beautiful towards the dawn of a summer's day. We recollect visiting Largs many years ago—walking from the interior—just as the hazy evening was gradually enshrouding the more distant surrounding objects. The Clyde Regatta had been engaged in their aquatic competitions during the day. The sea had become as calm as a mill-pond; and many of the gaily decorated yachts, and other boats of pleasure, were slowly beating towards the wished-for port, while hundreds of others lay jauntily at anchor. Here and there a steamer, crowded with passengers, gave animation to the scene, as they cleft their way rapidly amid the gathering and apparently overpowering weight of atmosphere. The scene, so undefined in its outlines, and still with so many bold and impressive objects, leaving so much for

---

* New Statistical Account—Article contributed by James Dobie, Esq. of Crummock, Beith.

fancy to fill up, withal, seemed altogether like enchantment. It was the first time we had seen Largs, and certainly the impression on our then young fancy remains with undiminished effect.

There are only two rivers of any importance in the parish—the Gogo and the Noddle. The former, which rises in the south-east part of the parish, and falls into the Clyde at the town of Largs, has numerous branches and tributaries, being greatly augmented by the waters of the Greeto. The Noddle has its source north-east of the parish, winds through the vale of Brisbane, and loses itself in the Clyde to the north of Gogo. A number of other streamlets either have their source in the parish, or traverse it for a considerable distance. The chief of these are the Rye, Fairly burn, Kepping burn, Routen burn, and Kellyburn—the last of which forms the northern boundary of the parish, and takes its rise in what was of old called "the Forret of Kyith," and which was latterly called the back of the world! "There was formerly a small island opposite the harbour of Fairlie. It is laid down in Bleau's map of Cuninghame; but, owing to the receding of the water, the island is no more visible. At low water, there is a large extent of the channel laid bare between Fairlie and Hunterston, and it has been thought that this land could, by a strong embankment, be entirely gained from the sea; but as this would not be a productive enterprise to the undertaker, it is not likely to be attempted." *

### HISTORY CIVIL AND ECCLESIASTICAL.

"The Lairgs" anciently formed a distinct territory by itself, and was governed by its own bailie. It continued so throughout the thirteenth century; and it seems not to have been until the reign of Robert II., from whom the community of Irvine had their charter, 8th April 1372, settling the privileges of the burgh, that the baronies of Cuninghame and Largs were united under one jurisdiction. In the twelfth century the De Morvilles were superiors of both these districts. In 1196, the lordship passed, by a female heir, the sister of William de Morville, to Roland, Lord of Galloway. On the death of Alan, Lord of Galloway, in 1234, the lordship was inherited by his daughter, Dervogill, who married John de Baliol, the father of John, the competitor; and she held it during her widowhood, in the reign of Alexander III. She granted to Robert, Bishop of Glasgow, and his successors, the lands and pas-

ture of Ryesdale, with the pertinents, and twenty-four acres of land, which were commonly called Belofslands, in her lordship of Largs, and a novate of land, with the pertinents, in her tenement of Largs. This grant was confirmed by Alexander III.* On her death, the lordship of Largs was inherited by her son, John Baliol, who forfeited it upon the accession of Robert Bruce to the throne. It was afterwards conferred by Robert I. upon his son-in-law, Walter, the Steward of Scotland. The barony of Largs became gradually parcelled out among the vassals of the Stewarts.

The most remarkable event in the history of the parish is, of course, the celebrated battle between the Norwegians and the Scots, fought on the 3d October 1263. Various accounts have been given of this national event. In stripping it of the exaggeration and fable of the early historians, our modern writers represent the affair as a mere skirmish. It is impossible, however, considering the reputation of the Norwegians as warriors, and the danger to which Scotland was exposed by the very formidable invasion of Haco, to regard it in this light. Whatever the number of the Norwegians may have been, there were certainly a more numerous force, under Alexander III., at Largs, than what the local chiefs could bring into action. The Chamberlain Rolls show that the invasion of Haco had been expected for some time, and that the Scottish King was not unprepared for the event. Some remarks will be found on the subject in vol. i. of this work.

In the reign of James I., a dispute arose between the Abbot of Paisley and Robert Boyd of Tinwald, who claimed the fruits of the church. The following letter passed under the Privy Seal on this occasion, and proved the means of settling the dispute:—"James, be the grace of God, Kyng of Scottis, till our lovid Robert Boid of Tynwald gretynge: Foralsmekill as we are informit they he adres ybou to be at the Kyrk of Largyss on Friday nextecum, with a multitude of our lieges in feyre of were, in hurtyn and scath of our devote oratours, the Abbot and Convent of Passelay, brekyn of our crya and offens of our maiestie. Our will is, and straitly we charge yhou, gif it sud be, that ye desist tharof, and mak na syk gaderin, undyr all the hiest payne and charge ye may inryne agane our maiestie, and gif ye haif achut aganes our said oratours follond thame as law wills. Gifwyn vndyr our pryve seill at Edinburgh the xxiiii day of Aprile, and of our regne xiiii yhers."

In 1647, the parish suffered severely from the

* Chart. of Glasgow.

plague, which visited the greater part of Scotland. Its appearance was first noticed by the Presbytery of Irvine, on the 29th June 1647. The minister was carried off by the disease, and on the 26th October, the minutes of the Presbytery bear: "The Laird of Bishopton having remonstrate the condition of the paroch of Largs, and the present necessity that the town of Largs was in, and that if it were not tymously removit and helpit, the people wald be forced to break out athort the countrie. The Presbyterie, after hearing, ordains that these brethren of the Presbiterie who, upon the report of their present necessitie, had already gathered something for supply of the same, should presently apply themselves for their relief," &c. Money and victuals were in this way collected in the neighbouring parishes, and the wants of the people supplied. The population, at this period, if we are to judge from the number of communicants (2000), must have been greater than in more recent times.

The parish of Largs was much agitated about the same time by the visit of Montrose to the west country. There appear to have been a considerable number of "malignants" in the parish, the examination and prosecution of whom cost the church courts no small trouble. Some of the cases were frivolous enough, still they show that there was a strong under-current in favour of the royal cause. Robert Boyd, in Closeburn, for example, is taken before the Presbytery for having given utterance to such expressions as the following: "O, thank God, there is ane ill day cum upon the Puritans." He was accused also of having "Cursed all thaim that would not pray for those that went out on the unlawful engagement." But the wrath of the Presbytery was chiefly levelled against Fraser of Knock, who gave the rev. body much trouble, and long evaded their censures.

The first notice of the Church of Largs which we find is in the Paisley Chartulary. On the 30th of January 1318-19, Walter the Stewart, for the safety of his soul, and that of his late spouse, Marjory Bruce, granted to the Monks of Paisley, the Church of Largs, in pure and perpetual alms, with all the tithes pertaining to it.* The Bishop of Glasgow, in 1319, confirmed the church of Largs and the chapel of Cumbray, with all their pertinents, to the Monastery of Paisley. The church of Largs, however, had existed long previously. In the Norwegian account of the Battle of Largs, it is said that a number of the

* The lands of Largs, "sometime John Ballol's, before his forefaulture," were granted to Robert Sympil by King Robert the Bruce.

dead men were buried at the church. The church of Largs continued to belong to the Monastery until the Reformation. At that epoch, the tithes of the church of Largs, with those of the churches of Innerkip and Lochwinnoch, in Renfrewshire, in all produced to the monks of Paisley £460 a year; having been let on lease for payment of that sum. In 1587, Lord Claud Hamilton, the Commendator of Paisley, obtained a grant of the patronage, and tithes of the church of Largs, with the other revenues of the monks of Paisley, the whole of which was then created a temporal lordship, for him and his heirs, with the title of Lord Paisley. He was succeeded, in 1621, in all those estates, revenues and titles, by his grandson, James, Earl of Abercorn. In the reign of Charles I., the patronage and tithes of the church of Largs passed from the Earl of Abercorn to Sir Robert Montgomerie of Skelmorlie. It now belongs to the Eglintoun family. Immediately after the Reformation, in 1567, David Neil was exhorter at Largs, with 40 merks of stipend; and in 1576, Alexander Callender was minister, his stipend being £134, 6s. 8d. Scots. The ancient church of Largs was dedicated to St Columba of Iona, and a fair was annually held at Largs on his birth-day, the 7th of June. It is still held on the second Tuesday in June, and is vulgarly called *Comb's-day*. The old church of Largs stood at the village. In 1812 a new building was erected in a more eligible situation. The manse stood in the immediate vicinity of the old church, near the site of the Brisbane Arms Inn. It was sold by the minister and heritors in 1764, when the present manse and offices were built on part of the glebe. The church and parish were in the Presbytery of Irvine till 1834, when they were transferred to the newly formed Presbytery of Greenock.

Largs town, like other villages, is indebted for its origin to the church. Its growth seems to have been severely checked by the plague—an ignorant dislike to strangers preventing the settlement of families in the village. During last century it began gradually to revive, and its reputation as a watering-place has, within the present century, entirely changed its antiquated and exclusive appearance. It is now one of the gayest and most cheerful of places—vying with its neighbours in all that constitutes a thriving and well frequented watering residence. Largs is thus described by Pont:—" Lairgs. Neir this toune did ye Scotts obtain a memorable victory vnder Alexander ye III. against Acho, King of Norway, quhose armiey they vterly ouerthrew. It is a burghe of barony; it is a fyne plot extended on ye bank of ye grate occeane, laying low. It hath also a small porte for botts on ye mouth of ye river Gogow. Upone the north syde of ye toune ther is a part called by the vulgar ye prison fold, quher ther wer a grate number of Danes enclosed and taken prisoners at ye batell of ye Lairgs. Heir is also a parochiall church of ye same name; heir adjoyning the Lord Boyde hath divers lands called Nodisdaill."

## ANTIQUITIES.

"The principal remains of Antiquity," says the *Statistical Account*, "are those connected with the battle of Largs in 1263. Immediately above Haylie, to the east, there is a small hill on which there are still visible the remains of an encampment. It bears the name of Castlehill. At the back of the mansion house of Haylie there are the remains of a tumulus, which was doubtless erected over the bodies of those who fell in that conflict. It was called Margaret's Law; but this was probably the corruption of some other name. The only other vestige which has withstood the changes of modern times, is the barrow close by the west wall of the burying-ground, which corroborates the Norwegian account of their dead having been interred at the church. Near the spot now enclosed as the gardens of the late Dr Cairnie, there stood a rude stone pillar, which was reputed as commemorative of the place where Haco, the Norwegian Commander fell. The stone was built by Dr Cairnie in the wall of his garden, with an appropriate inscription.

"There is a small piece of land which was originally lying runrig in seven different parts called Breedsorrow. Pont gives the origin of the name thus:—' Breedsorrow is in the possession of the laird of Blare, and being a small hamlet, it is so named, because of grate sorrow it bred amongst neighbours debettaing and contesting for ye heritable right thereof. This place was also called Kempisland.' Thus we find that on 8th May 1610, John Brishane of Bishopton was served heir of his father, Robert Brishane, in the six shilling eight penny land of old extent of Breedsorrow, alias Kempisland; and in 1639, Sir Bryce Blair was served heir-male to his father, Bryce Blair, in the same subject. This change of property proves that Pont's account must have been written between these two dates, as is generally supposed."[*]

Amongst the high grounds, near a place called Padzokrodin, there is one of *those upright stones* called Thor Stones.

[*] Statistical Account.

The old church of Largs, a portion of one of the walls of which only remains, was of unknown antiquity and great strength. It is supposed to have existed before the battle of Largs. The Skelmorlie aisle, built in connection with it, by Sir Robert Montgomerie of Skelmorlie, in 1636, has been left entire. The following account of it is abridged from a description of the aisle by William Dobie, Esq., Grangevale, Beith:—

"The aisle measures, over the walls, 34 feet 10 inches, by 22 feet. It is built both outside and inside, the ceiling excepted, of chiseled freestone, and is covered with a deep roof, the south gable of which is surmounted by a thistle, and the other by a fleur-de-lis. The interior is lighted by a large equilateral arched window in the north gable, divided by a strong mullion into two trefoil-headed lights, with a small circular aperture between the heads; two of the ordinary form in each of the side-walls, and since the removal of the church, by another in the south gable. The entrance-door, the moderate height of which is characteristic of the architecture of the country at the period of its construction, is in the west side of the building. It is ornamented with a moulded architrave, and finished with an ogee arch, ensigned with a fleur-de-lis. Above the door, on a panel enclosed with mouldings, are very neatly sculptured, and but little injured by the weather, the quartered armorials of Montgomerie and Eglintoun, impaled with Douglas and Mar. The shield, in heraldic phrase, is timbered with helmit and mantlings, the former by mistake befitting the degree of an Esquire in place of that of a Baronet. For Crest, an anchor, and on an escroll is the motto: "The . Lord . is . my . svpport;" with the words, "Only . to . God . be . Lavd . and . Gloir," on a compartment, along with the initials and date, S. R. M. 1636. D. M. D. The stone on which this interesting specimen of the "noble science" is insculped, has been skilfully selected for resisting the action of the weather, as all the lettering, though in small raised characters, as well as the equally delicate figures in the shield, have lost little of their original sharpness.

"The aisle within is lofty, being nearly twenty feet in height, and its roof is embowed, or vaulted semi-circularly, with boarding. It is thrown, by painted gothic arches, mouldings and panels, into forty-one compartments of various forms and dimensions, each of which is adorned by the pencil with a religious, moral, emblematical, fanciful, or heraldic subject. . . . The central panel is occupied with the emblazoned coats of Montgomerie and Douglas, quartered and impaled as over the door, and ornamented *secundum artem*, with all the exterior accompaniments of the shield. The family motto, " Gardez bien," is here resumed, and on a compartment is inscribed, in gilt characters, " Sir . Robert . Montgomerie : Dame . Margaret . Douglas." Appended to the achievement is a small cartouch, bearing the date 1638, and the French monosyllable *Ouy*, lettered in the reverse order of the date. . .

" The colouring of the ceiling, though partially faded, has in no part altogether given way, while portions of it appear still to retain much of their original brightness. Considering its long exposure to the influence of so fitful an atmosphere, the free admission of which through broken windows and crannied roof, has been for many years unopposed, it says much for the excellence of the materials employed, that they have so long successfully resisted the most active agents of decay. The embellishments, both in design and execution, it may well be supposed, are not of uniform merit throughout. The ornamented inscriptive tablets, and the various emblazoments, along with the figures of Justice and Fortitude, have been decidedly the most happily conceived, and are the best executed parts of the design. Six landscapes, occupying the upper part of as many large gothic arches, four of which, representing the seasons, and two, apparently allegorical of Agriculture and Commerce, rank lowest in the scale of merit, being alike deficient in composition, perspective, and colouring. Some of these landscapes, it has been said, contain views of Skermorlie House, and of the old church of Largs; but if such were the intention of the artist, he has signally failed in his efforts, both as regards the exterior mien of the buildings, and the natural features of their respective localities. This ceiling, however, with all its defects, has well-grounded claims on the attention of the decorative artist, and the connoisseur in such matters: both of whom, we doubt not, will award it no stinted measure of commendation. A century ago, when in the full lustre of its untarnished brilliancy, and when the stately monument, well worthy of such a canopy, rose unskaithed, either by time or violence, the aisle must have presented a coup d'œil exquisite of its kind, and certainly unequalled for taste and magnificence, at least by any thing reared in Scotland since the era of

> ' That violent commotion, which overthrew,
> In town, and city, and sequestered glen,
> Altar and cross, and church of solemn roof,
> And old religious house.'

" The monument stands across the aisle to the left of the entrance. In length it is eleven feet and a half, in width five feet, and in height eighteen feet. It presents two fronts and profiles responding to each other in every respect, save that the elevation next to the entrance door is three feet ten inches (the depth of the lower stage of the basement) higher than its counterpart. Both elevations may, therefore, be described as a basement, sustaining an arcade between two inter-columniations with appropriate entablatures, surmounted by sculptured compartments, obelisks, and figures: the whole supported by eight Corinthian columns, four in each elevation, and ten pilasters of the same order, distributed between them. The columns stand on pedestals boldly projected, and compose, with the recessed divisions to which the latter are attached, the full basement of the north elevation, and the upper stage of its counterpart. The lower part of the latter has pilasters corresponding with the pedestals over them, but of a slighter relief, and support a congeries of mouldings, in the design of which variety has been studied more than lightness and simplicity. To the right of the monument a stair of seven steps conducts to a small area between the north elevation and the gable of the aisle. From this platform the carved details of the monument may be advantageously examined, though its limited extent precludes the spectator from forming a correct idea of its full outline.

" The monument is, indeed, not less remarkable for the taste, variety, and finish, exhibited in its ornamental details, than for the purity of its architectural profiles and general proportions, considering the period of its construction. . .

" The family vault, as already stated, is situated below the monument. To its low-browed door, which is placed between the central pilasters of the basement, access is obtained by a descent of several steps. The apartment is somewhat stinted in height, and is but obscurely lighted by a narrow aperture in the north wall. A kind of stone bench runs along the side walls, on which, besides two large coffins, and another of smaller dimensions entire, there are placed two broken ones, the contents of which having been embalmed. . . . The two largest coffins are covered with lead, and contain the relics of Sir Robert Montgomery, and those of his Lady. That of the latter bears on the ends her family armorials, and on the cover in raised characters: Dame . Margaret Douglas . Spouse . To . Sir . Robert . Montgomery. The coffin of Sir Robert is ornamented in a similar style, but on the cover, instead of his name, there is the following inscription in latin:—

> ' Ipse mihi præmortuus fui, fato funera
> Praeripui, unicum, idque, Cæsareum,
> Exemplar, Inter tot mortales secutus.'

Signifying, ' I was dead before myself; I anticipated my proper funeral: alone, of all mortals, following the example of Cæsar,' *i. e.* Charles V., who it will be recollected, had his obsequies performed before he died. The explanations usually given of the strange conceits of the inscription, is, that Sir Robert was a very pious man, and used to descend into the vault at night to perform his devotions, there burying himself, as it were, alive."

*Fairlie Castle.*—The square tower called Fairlie Castle is now in ruins. It stands about a quarter of a mile from the sea, on the brink of a deep and romantically wooded ravine, through which runs Fairlie Burn, dividing the parish of West Kilbride from Largs. The situation is altogether so peculiar, that the popular eye had no difficulty in tracing in it the residence of *Hardyknute,* the hero of the well-known beautiful ballad of that name. Whether the story is wholly a fiction seems doubtful. It has long been settled that the ballad itself was an antiquarian hoax ; but it does not follow that it had no foundation in tradition. Pont describes Fairlie Castle as " a stronge toure, and very ancient, beautified with orchardes and gardens. It belongs to Fairlie de eodem, cheiffe of their name."

*Kelburne Castle.*—This baronial residence, to which considerable additions were made by David Earl of Glasgow, was originally a building similar to Fairlie Castle. " Kelburne Castell," says Pont, " a goodly building, veill planted, having wcrey beautiful orchards and gardens, and in one of them a spatious roume, adorned with a christalin fontane, cutte all out of the living rocke. It belongs heritably to John Boll, laird thereof." The Castle is delightfully situated in a valley, amid extensive woods and pleasure grounds, about four hundred yards from the sea. About a furlong from the mansion, on the margin of a romantic dell, stands a monument erected to the memory of John, third Earl of Glasgow, who died in 1775. It " consists of a handsome female figure, placed in a niche, formed in a piece of ashlar work resembling the section of a stunted obelisk. The niche is finished with doric columns, sustaining a pediment, and in a circular panel of white marble, in the upper part of the obelisk, are neatly carved the armorials of the noble family. The statue, which is of the same material, is gracefully proportioned, and exqui

sitely sculptured. It represents, says the writer of the old Statistical Account of the parish, ' Virtue lamenting the loss of one of her favourite sons.' The figure, which is four feet in height, is in a gently reclining position : the right arm leans on an elegant urn, resting on a tripod, in which hand she holds a chaplet of laurel, and in the other, which is slightly elevated, a portion of the flowing tangles of her hair. The expression of the visage, the form and position of the figure, and the style of the drapery, have been all most happily conceived, and as admirably executed. On the basement supporting the columns is engraved the inscription, which is as follows :—

Sacred to the Memory of
JOHN, EARL OF GLASGOW,

Whose exalted piety and liberal sentiments of religion, unfettered by systems, and joined with universal benevolence, were as singular as the candour and modesty which cast a pleasing veil over his distinguished abilities. His loyalty and courage he exerted in the service of his country, in whose cause he repeatedly suffered with fortitude and magnanimity. At the battle of Fontency, early in life, he lost his hand and his health. His manly spirit not to be subdued : at Lafeld he received two wounds in one attack. To perpetuate the remembrance of a character so universally beloved and admired, and to animate his children to the imitation of his estimable qualities, this humble monument is erected by his disconsolate widow.

*Tancrooke Castle.*—The ruins of this old tower stand not far from Greeto Water ; but no memorial seems to be preserved of them.

*Brisbane House,* situated in the vale of that name, is of considerable antiquity, and surrounded with some fine old trees. It was originally called Kelsoland, and is noticed by Pont as " a good house, veill planted."

*Knock Castle.*—The ruins of this ancient residence stand on a steep acclivity between Knock Hill and the sea. Pont says, " Knock is a pretty dwelling, seatted one the mane occeane, and veill planted." Means have recently been taken to preserve the building from farther decay.

*Skelmorlie Castle* is also " seated on the mane ocean." It occupies an eminence commanding a prospect of great beauty and extent. It is thus noticed by Pont: " North Skelmurly is a fair, veill built houss, and pleasantly seatted, decorred with orchards and woodes, the inheritance of Robert Montgomerie, laird thereof, who holds it of ye Earls of Glencairn." It is now one of the seats of the Earl of Eglintoun and Wintoun.

## FAIRLIE OF FAIRLIE.

Of this ancient family, now extinct, comparatively few traces are to be found. According to *Nisbet*, they were a branch of the Rosses of Tarbet, from whom they obtained the lands of Fairlie, and assumed the name of the property as their patronymic. The name was originally spelled *Furnlie* or *Fairulie*.* It is curious that almost no notice of the family occurs in the earlier Crown charters. The first of them of whom there is any record was

*John Fairnlie or Fairlie of Fairlie.* He is one of the executors of Thomas Boid of Lyn, who, according to Robertson, was married to his daughter, *Marion*, which lady afterwards married James Stewart of Bute.† John Fairlie occurs in the Criminal Trials, in 1560. He had also a daughter, or probably a sister, married to Montgomerie, heir apparent of Stane. Montgomerie and his spouse had a charter of certain lands from James V., 3d January 1540.

*David Fairlie of Fairlie*, probably the son of the preceding. He and his two sons, *John* and *William*, were forfeited by the Queen's Parliament in 1571.‡ He married Katherine Craufurd, daughter of Lawrence Craufurd of Kilbirnie, by whom, according to *Douglas' Peerage*, he had two daughters, of whom the youngest, Agnes (not Elizabeth) was married to Robert Boyd of Portincross. In 1585, David Fairlie of that Ilk was appointed to uplift dues from vessels anchoring in Fairlie Roads.‖ He died in 1596, and his lady in 1601. The following is the substance of her settlement:—

"Testament, &c. of vmquhile Katharine Craufurd, Lady Fairnelie, within the parochine of Lairgis, the tyme of her deceis, quha deceist vpone the fyift (or fyrst) day of December, or thairby, anno Jai vic ane zeiris, ffaithfullie maid and gevin vp be hir awin mouthe, at the fortalice of Fairnelie, hir duelling-place, vpone the last day of November, the zeir of God Jai vic ane zeiris, as followis, in particular

"Inuentar.

"Item, the said vmquhile Katharine haid the guidis, geir, insicht plenissing, and vtheris, eftir mentionat, of the availlis and price vnderwrittin, viz., thrie fedder beddis, thrie bowsteris, with thair coddis, price thairof overheid, xviii li; twa nap beddis, with thair bowsteris and coddis, price thairof, vi li; ffyve pair of small scheittis, price thairof overheid, x li; aucht pair of roune scheittis, price vi li; ffyve codwaris, price xl s; ffyve pair of vnwalkit blankettis, price thairof overheid, viii li vis viii d; ane walkit pair of blankettis, price xl s; sevin coveringis, price overheid, viii li; ane arras wark, price iii li vis viii d; ane eadday, price xxx s; twa pair curtingis, with sewit ribbenis, price iiii li; ane pair of plane lyning curtingis, price xxx s; twa pair droggait curtingis, price xl s; thrie small buirdelaithis, price iiii li; four round borelaithis, price liii s iiii d; ten small seruittis, twentie round seruittis, price overheid, l s; twa small towellis, twa round towellis, price xiii s iiii d; twa auld irne pottis, ane auld brasin pot, ane bras pat of ane pynt, twa lytill cruikis, tuelf plattis, sevin trvnscheours, ane brokin chandler, twa pannis, twa speittis, price of all overheid, xiii li vi s viii d; four boynes, four flesche fattis, twa hogheidis, four barrellis but heidis, four aill rub., twa aill boittis, ane gyle fatt, ane mask fatt, twa burnestandis, price thairof overheid, xi li; ane tyne quart, ane tyne pynt stoppis, price xxx s; twa trein stoppis, price x s; nyne , price iiii li; ane auld slaying boitt, price xxiii li; ane mekill auld kist, price iiii li; four litill auld kistis, price v li vis viii d. Item, the defunctis woring claithis, estimat to xxxi li. Item, of reddie money, xl li. Item, in the Fairnelie byre, twa ky, price of ilk peace viii li, summa, xvi li. Item, ane kow in Fairlie waird, price viii li. Item, ane stirk in Fairlie byre, price xxvi s viii d. Item, in buit thrie auld ky, price thairof overheid, xx li. Item, thrie stirkis, price thairof overheid, iiii li. Item, ane twa zeir auld bull, price iii li vi s viii d. Item, threttine auld scheip, sevin hoggis, price of ilk peace overheid, xx s, summa, xx li. Item, in the borne ane mow of vnthressin beir, cassin in be pruif, extending to xvii bolls beir, price of the boll, with the fodder, vi li, summa, ic and twa punds money. Item, in the bairnezaird twa lytill stackis of corne, extending to xlviii bolls aittis, price of the boll, with the fodder, iiii li, summa, iclxiii li money

"Summa of the inventar, vclii li xvi s viii d

"Debtis awand in to the defunct

"Item, awand to the said Katharine be Johne or Edward, or Johne Symsoun, Johne Clark, and thair colligis, tennentis of Fairnelie, ix bs i ft ferme beir, price of ilk boll vi li, summa, lv li xs. Item, be Johne Kyle in Fairlie Mylne, &c

"Debtis awand out to vtheris

"Item, to . Kelso, guidwyfe of Flatt, liii s iiii d Item, to Johne Stewart of Eskok (or Erskok), conform to obligatioun maid to him be vmquhile Dauid Fairlie of that Ilk, spous to the said Katherine, iic li Item, of annuell thairof zeirlie sen ye said vmquhile Dauidis deceis, being aucht zeiris, ilk zeir xx li, summa, iciiixx li Item, and to Robert Lord Sempill and his factouris for teynd in anno Jai saxt hundryt zeiris, saxteen bolls wictuall, price thairof overheid, iiixxxvi li. Item, mawand to thame of teynd, Jai vi ane zeiris, xiii bolls wictuall, price thairof overheid, iiixxx li xiii s iiii d

"ffollowis the said Katherinis legacie and lettir-will

"Item, the said Katherine makis, nominatis, and constitutis John Steward of Erskok his executour and vniuersall intromittour with hir guidis, and leivis to Wa Craufurd, hir brother, twentie li. Item, to Margaret, hir dochtir, vi li xiii s iiii d Item, to Agnes Craufurd, hir ove, vili xiii s iiii d Item, to Katherine Craufurd, hir oye, xx li This was done day, zeir, and place foirsaid, befoir yir witness, Rot Fairlie of that Ilk, Rot Maclane Wa Fairlie in Over (treis?) Allexr Blakburne, Rot Fostir, George Boyde and Johnn Or, induellaris in Fairlie Sic subscribitur ita est Hugo Campbell, notarius publicus," &c.

*Margaret Fairlie,* the eldest daughter, and heiress of Fairlie, married William Craufurd of Drumsoy She was alive in 1618. Her eldest son,

*Sir Robert Craufurd Fairlie of that Ilk,* was served heir of his father, under that designation, in 1596 "Roberto Fairlie, *olim* Craufurd, nepoti Dauidis Fairlie de eodem, ac filio Willielmi Craufurd de Collyland," had a charter of the lands of Fairlie, &c. from James VI , in 1600 He had also a charter from James VI , dated 26th July 1601, of the lands of Fairlie, " in liberum Burgum Baroniæ, cum portis ejusdem," of new united *Douglas* says that Sir John

(a mistake for Robert) married a daughter of Craufurd of Jordanhill, and that he had two daughters, *Agnes* (Anne, according to a charter, 4th February 1612)* and *Janet,* the latter of whom, according to Nisbet, married Cathcart of Carbiston Sir Robert Fairlie was Justice-Depute in 1622.

*Robert Fairlie of that Ilk* was served heir in Fairlie to his father, 27th July 1655 This Robert conveyed the property of Fairlie, 13th December 1656, to David Boyle, afterwards Earl of Glasgow The superiority of Fairlie still continuing in the family, it was taken up by *Adam Fairlie,* the son of Robert, and also disposed of to the same party, 20th June 1661 Both the superiority and property of Fairlie now belong to the Earl of Glasgow

The family of Fairlie, of the old stock, are understood to be extinct, although the name still exists, the offshoots, no doubt, of some of the branches

## KELBURNE—BOYLE, EARL OF GLASGOW

This family is of very considerable antiquity in Ayrshire It has been supposed to have a Norman origin, from the orthography of the name in the *Ragman Roll* " Roberto de Boyvile," and " Richard de Boyvile, vel conte de Air," are both mentioned in that document, and there can be little doubt that they were of the Kelburne family But no great weight is to be attached to the orthography of the Ragman Roll in a matter of this kind, the language of the Court of England being Norman French ; while the fact is the name is written *Boyle* in a document of the reign of Alexander III., many years previous to the usurpation of Edward I It seems as probable that the name is from the Celtic There is an ancient kirk or chapel in Argyleshire, called *Kirkaboill,* and we have *Maybom,* or *Maieboll,* in Ayrshire *Boll* is no doubt the vernacular pronunciation, and may be derived from the locality, the word signifying the heath upon the marsh or meadow And this is pretty accurately descriptive of what is likely to have been the original appearance of the lands now forming the policy of Kelburne House The first of the family hitherto discovered was

I RICHARD DE BOYLE, *Dominus de Caulburn,* whose name occurs in a transaction with Walter Cumin, *Dominus de Rowgallan,* in the reign of

* They had probably another daughter, Christina, married to Stewart in Crevoch-fairlie She is mentioned in a charter in 1607

Alexander III., inter 1249 et 1286. He married Marjory, daughter of Cumin, and had issue.

II. Robert de Boyle of Kelburne, who swore allegiance to Edward I. in 1296. From this Robert descended, though the names of the family cannot be traced at this early period, and several generations must have passed between,

III. Hugo de Boyle, who, in 1399, gave a donation to the Abbey of Paisley, for the good of his soul.

IV. John Boyle de Caleburn, who, on the 24th June 1417, appears as one of a jury on an inquest respecting some lands in dispute betwixt the burgh of Irvine and William Fraunces of Stane. The next in succession is

V. Robert Boyle of Calburn, in all probability son to the preceding. He is witness to a charter by Robert Boyd of Kilmarnock, to John Boyle of Wamphray, of the lands of Ryesholm, Oct. 11, 1446. His son, apparently,

VI. John Boyle of Kelburne, succeeded. He was a strenuous supporter of James III., and lost his life in his cause at the battle of Sauchieburn, in 1488.

VII. William Boyle of Kelburne was served heir to his grandfather, in place of his father, in 1492. This was probably a measure of caution, in consequence of the part his father had taken in the recent struggle. All the lands which had been forfeited by his father were, however, restored to him.* He married Katherine Wallace, and left a son,

VIII. John Boyle of Kelburne, who, in 1495, was infeft in the five pound land of Kelburne, as lawful heir to his father, William, proceeding from a precept of Chancery, holding blanch of the Crown, in a payment of a pair of spurs, dated 28th October of that year. He married Agnes, a daughter of the family of Ross, by whom he had three sons, *David*, *John*, and *Robert* of Ballochmartin; and a daughter, Margaret, married to John Craufurd of Giffordland. David, his eldest son, died in his father's lifetime, leaving a son,

IX. John Boyle of Kelburne, to whom his grandfather assigned the estate in 1549. He married Jean, daughter of John Frazer of Knock, by whom he had a son, John, and a daughter, Margaret, who was married to John Cuninghame, the first of Caddel, son of William Cuninghame of Glengarnock.

X. John Boyle, the only son, succeeded his father in Kelburne, and his great-grandfather in the office of Mayor of Fee, July 16, 1583. He died in 1610. By his lady, Marion, daughter of

Hugh Cranfurd of Kilbirnie, he had a son, *John*, and six daughters:

1. Jean, married to William Barclay of Perceton. She died July 1631.
2. Marion, married, first, to Mathew Ross of Haining; and secondly, to the Archbishop of Glasgow.
3. Margaret, married to Robert Bruce of Auchenbowie.
4. Elizabeth, married to Robert Semple of Millbank.
5. Agnes, married to Robert Boyle of Ballochmartin.
6. Mary, married to William Hamilton of Downshire.

XI. John Boyle of Kelburne succeeded his father. His name occurs, in 1615, in the testament of William Muir of Rowallan, as a debtor, " conforme to his band, 33 lib.; mair to him for releif and non-entres of ye fyve pund land of Polruskane, lx lib. Togidder with the sowme of fiftie pund for ye pryce of fiftie pund of Cumyng (seed) awin of bygonne blanche to ye said sowmes of dewtie, conforme to his band." He married Agnes, the only daughter of Sir John Maxwell of Nether Pollock, by whom he had a daughter, *Grizel*, his only child. He was alive in 1647. His daughter married, apparently in his lifetime, a near relative.

XII. David Boyle of Hawkhill, who is designed *fear* of Kelburne in a testamentary document in 1647. David Boyle was descended of the family thus:

1. John, second son of No. VI., was designed " of Ballahewin" in 1536; married Christian, daughter of Wallace of Cairnhill, by whom he had a son,
2. David of Legdeth in 1578, who married Christian, niece of Lord Boyd, by whom he had,
3. James of Hawkhill, in 1617, who married Margaret, daughter of David Cranfurd of Bedland, by whom he had the above David Boyle of Hawkhill.

David and Grizel Boyle had issue:

1. John, who succeeded.
2. James, of Montgomerieston. He married Janet, daughter and heiress of Mr Robert Barclay, Provost of Irvine, with whom he got the lands of Montgomerieston, and by her had a son, James Boyle of Montgomerieston, a Commissioner of Excise, who died 17th October 1758, and is buried in Irvine Churchyard, where a handsome monument is erected to his memory.
3. Patrick.
4. Grizel, married to William Wallace of Shewalton.

David Boyle died in 1672, and was succeeded by his eldest son,

XIII. John Boyle of Kelburne. He had been a merchant in Edinburgh, and made a fortune in trade.* He married, first, Marion, daughter of Sir Walter Stewart of Allanton, by whom he had two sons:

1. David.
2. William, a Commissioner of Customs, and who, in 1732, purchased the lordship of Stewarton, but afterwards disposed of it to sundries.
3. Margaret, married to Sir Alexander Cuninghame, Bart. of Corsehill.

He married, secondly, Jean, daughter of Sir William Mure of Rowallan, and relict of Gavin

---

* Charter of 1396.

* Scots Magazine, April 1801.

Ralston of that Ilk, without issue. He died in 1685, and was succeeded by his eldest son,

XIV. David Boyle of Kelburne, who was created a Peer by the title of Lord Boyle of Kelburne, &c., 30th January 1699. He took a great share, as one of the Commissioners, in promoting the union with England; and as there was a scarcity of troops in Scotland, offered to maintain 1000 men at his own proper charges. He was created Earl of Glasgow, 12th April 1703. He married, first, Margaret, eldest daughter of Patrick Craufurd of Kilbirnie, by whom he had four sons:

1. John, the second Earl.
2. Hon. Patrick Boyle of Shewalton, who died unmarried in 1761.
3. Hon. Charles Boyle.
4. Hon. William Boyle, who both died unmarried.

He married, secondly, Jean, daughter and heiress of the last Sir William Mure of Rowallan, (and relict of Fairlie of that Ilk, to whom she had issue,) and by whom he had two daughters:

1. Lady Jean, heiress of Rowallan, who married the Hon. Sir James Campbell of Lawers, K.B., third and youngest son of James second Earl of Loudoun, and had issue.
2. Lady Anne, who died unmarried.

XV. John, second Earl of Glasgow, succeeded his father in 1733, and died in 1740. He married Helen, daughter of William Morison of Prestongrange, by whom he had issue:—

1. William, who died young.
2. John, the third Earl.
3. Hon. Patrick Boyle of Shewalton.
4. Lady Helen, who married the late Sir James Douglas, Bart. of Springwood Park, Admiral of the White; but died without issue in 1794;

And other five daughters, who died unmarried.

XVI. John, third Earl of Glasgow, succeeded his father in the 26th year of his age. It is to the memory of this Earl that the monument, described elsewhere, in the policies of Kelburne, was erected. He had been in the army, and saw considerable service abroad. He married, in 1755, Elizabeth, second daughter of George, twelfth Lord Ross, and became ultimately sole heiress of the Ross estates, by the death of her brother, William Lord Ross, in 1754, and of her only sister in 1762. By this lady, who survived him, he had two sons and two daughters:—

1. John, who died young.
2. George, the fourth Earl.
3. Lady Elizabeth, who was married to Sir George Douglas of Springwood Park, and had issue, two daughters, who died before herself, and a son, John-James, who survived her.

XVII. George, the fourth Earl of Glasgow, succeeded his father in 1775. In 1815, he was advanced to the honour of a British peerage, by the title of Lord Ross of Hawkhead; and in 1820, upon the death of the late Hugh Earl of

Eglintoun, his lordship was promoted to the office of Lord-Lieutenant of Ayrshire, from that of Renfrewshire, which he had previously held.

He married, first, in 1788, Lady Augusta Hay, third daughter of James fourteenth Earl of Errol, by whom he had issue:—

1. John, Lord Kelburne, who distinguished himself in the naval service of his country. He died in 1818.
2. James.
3. William, died in 1819.
4. Isabella, died in 1834.
5. Elizabeth, died in 1819.
6. Augusta, married in 1821, to Lord Frederick Fitzclarence.

His lordship married, secondly, November 1824, Julia, daughter of the Right Hon. Sir John Sinclair, Bart., and by her had issue:—

1. George-Frederick, born in 1825.
2. Diana, married, 4th July 1849, to John Hay Slaney Pakington, Esq.

The Earl died in July 1843, and was succeeded by his second son,

XVIII. James-Carr Boyle, fifth Earl of Glasgow, and second Baron of Hawkhead. He assumed, by sign manual, in 1822, the addition of *Carr* to his Christian name. He married, 4th August 1821, Georgina, daughter of the late Edward Hay Mackenzie, Esq. of Newhall and Cromarty, but has no issue.

*Arms.*—Quarterly, first and fourth, or, an eagle displayed, gules, as a coat of augmentation on the creation of the Earldom, being formerly the family crest: second and third, parted, per bend, crenelle, argent and gules, for the surname of Boyle, in England, as a coat of affection: over all, on escutcheon, three harts' horns, gules, two and one, the paternal coat of Boyle of Kelburne.

*Crest.*—An Eagle with two heads displayed, parted, per pale, crenelle, or, and gules.

*Supporters.*—Dexter, a savage, proper; sinister, a lion rampant, parted per bend, crenelle, argent and gules.

*Motto.*—" Dominus providebit."

*Seats.*—Kelburne House, in Ayrshire; Halkhead, Renfrewshire; and Etal, in Northumberland.

## BRISBANE OF BRISBANE.

The vale of Brisbane, where the mansion-house of this family now stands, was formerly called Kelsoland, and belonged to the *Kelsos of Kelsoland*, whose pedigree will fall to be given in another parish. It was acquired by the Brisbane family in 1671, and since then has borne the name of Brisbane. The Brisbanes, or Birsbanes, are an ancient family, originally connected with Renfrewshire. Bishoptoun appears to have been their earliest inheritance, which property they probably held long prior to the date of any charters in their possession.

*William de Brisbane* was Chancellor of Scotland, in 1332;[*] in all probability an ancestor of the family, as the armorial bearings, the three cushions, should seem to be borne in allusion to such civil office.

" *Allanus de Brysbane*, filius Willielmi de Brysbane," obtained " a grant of the lands of Macberach in Stirlingshire, to which Malcolm, Earl of Wigton, (so created in 1334) is witness." This charter is preserved in the archives of the burgh of Dumbarton.

*Thomas* and *Alexander Brisbane*, brothers, are witnesses to a charter dated 9th September 1361; and

*Thomas Brisbane* is witness to a charter dated 22d September 1400.

The first of the family mentioned in the charters of Bishoptoun is

I. JOHN BRISBANE of Bishoptoun, who was succeeded by his son,

II. John Brisbane of Bishoptoun, who, 1st September 1407, obtained a charter from Lord Erskine, the superior, for infefting him as heir of his father in the lands of Bishoptoun. He appears to have been succeeded by his son,

III. John Brisbane of Bishoptoun, and he again by his son,

IV. Thomas Brisbane of Bishoptoun, who, in 1490, was executor to Thomas Sempil of Elliotston, his brother-in-law. He married Mary, daughter of Sir William Sempil of Elliotston, by Agnes, daughter of Alexander, second Lord Montgomerie, by whom he had his successor,

V. Mathew Brisbane of Bishoptoun, who fell at the battle of Flodden, 9th September 1513, when he was succeeded by his brother,

V. John Brisbane of Brisbane, whose service in the lands of Killingeraig and Gogoside in Ayrshire, holding of the crown, relates the circumstance of his brother's death at Flodden; and whose charter, dated 4th July 1514, of the estate of Bishoptoun, is granted by John Lord Erskine, son of Lord Robert, who also fell at Flodden. He was succeeded by his son,

VI. John Brisbane of Bishoptoun, who, as heir of his father, obtained a charter, dated 12th August 1523, from John, third Earl of Lennox, of the lands of Ballencleiroch, in the district of Campsie, Stirlingshire. From a sasine, dated in 1532, it appears that his wife's name was Eliza-

beth Lindsay. He died intestate at the battle of Fawside, 10th September 1547.[*] He was succeeded by his son,

VII. John Brisbane of Bishoptoun, who, in 1530, during the life of his brother, had a crown charter of the eastern quarter of the lands of Henderstoun, in Renfrewshire. He was served heir of his father in the lands of Killingeraig, &c., 20th May 1549. He married, first, ——, by whom he had two sons; secondly, Elizabeth Hamilton, daughter of John Hamilton of Broomhills, by whom he had a son, *William*, who became parson of Erskine, in which office he was succeeded by his son, Mathew, who was father to Dr Mathew Brisbane, physician in Glasgow, a man of great learning. He had also three daughters—Margaret, Janet and Marion. There is a contract of marriage, of rather a singular nature, dated 17th Nov. 1572, entered into betwixt John Frissal (Frazer) of Knok, for himself, and as taking burden on him for John Frissal his grandson, a child, on the one part, and John Brisbane on the other part, as taking burden on himself for his three daughters—by which, in consideration of Brisbane redeeming certain debts on the estate of Knok—Frissal engages that his grandson shall marry, at his lawful age of fourteen years, the said Margaret Brisbane, whom failing by decease, the said Janet, and whom failing, the said Marion. Accordingly, in 1583, there is a charter granted by John Frissal (the grandson), with consent of his curators, for implementing this contract, and infefting her, his future spouse, in certain parts of the estate of Knok. John Brisbane married, thirdly, Elspeth Wallace, relict of Gabriel Maxwell of Stainly, by whom he had a daughter married to Adam Hall of Fulbar. He died in 1591. Many years before his decease he had resigned the fee of his lands to his eldest son of the first marriage,

VIII. Robert Brisbane of Brisbane, who married, in 1562, Janet Stewart, daughter of James Stewart of Ardgowan, the contract being dated 29th August of that year. By this marriage he had issue:—

1. John, his successor.
2. Hannibal, who obtained the lands of Rossland from his father. His son, Hannibal, was served heir to him in 1636, and in 1638, sold Rossland to his cousin, John Brisbane of Bishoptoun.
3. Sarah, married to Robert Hamilton of Dalserf.

He died in 1610. His latter-will was made at " the place of Bischoptoun, the xvi day of Januar." His wife, Janet Stewart, and John, his eldest son, were appointed his executors. Amongst the list of debtors, David Kelso of Kelsoland occurs as owing " ane thowsand thrie hundryith threttie-thrie pund vis viii d." His wife, **Janet Stewart,** survived till November 1614. During their marriage they made large additions to the estate; for besides Nether-Kelsoland, Flat, Kelso, Halie, Hangingbaugh,* and others in the parish of Largs, they acquired lands and annual rents in other counties besides Ayr and Renfrewshire, in Linlithgow, Lanark, Stirling, and Dumbarton; so that at his death a special commission was issued to four persons, as sheriffs, for the service of his son, it being inconvenient and expensive to direct separate brieves to the sheriffs of each of these counties. He was succeeded by his son,

IX. **John Brisbane of Bishoptoun.** He married Anna Blair, daughter of the Laird of Blair, and had a charter, on the resignation of his father, under the Great Seal, of the lands of Killingcraig and Gogosyde, dated 24th December 1595. This charter contained a clause erecting the lands into a free barony of Gogosyde, &c. By this marriage there were:

1. John.
2. John, who died in April 1648. It was not unusual for two sons to be of one name in a family in former times. His latter-will is as follows:—"Testament, &c. John Birsbane, brother to the laird of Bischoptone, within the parochin of Areskyne, the tyme of his deceis, quha deceissit in the moneth of Apryli 1648 zeiris, &c. Inventare.—Item, the defunct had, the tyme foirsaid, perteining to him ane horse and his armes, togethir with his haill abuilzements and cloathes, &c., all estimat worth lxvii ii 13 s 4d., &c. ffollowis the deidis, lattre-will, and legacies.—At Bischoptonne, the xxix day of Marche 1648 zeiris.—The quhilk day, I, John Birsbane, brother to the laird of Bischoptone, being seik in bodie bot haill in mynd, do make my testament and lattre-will as follows: 1 make and constitute John Birsbane, zounger of Bischoptoune, my full, onlie executor, nominatour, and intromittour with my haill guidis and geir, &c. Item, I lieve in legacie to the said John Birsbane, zounger of Bischoptoune, the sowme of ane thowsand merks, &c., adebted to me be the laird of Blakhall, &c. Item, ane thowsand merks money, &c., awing to me be John Birsbane of Bischoptoune, elder, my brother, &c. Item, I lieve to the said John my horse and armes. Item, I lieve to Capitane William Conyngham, my brother, my pairt of that sowme equallie assigned be him to my brother James and me, and discharge him thairof. Item, I lieve to James Wallace of Bardren the whole abuilzement of my body, &c.—Writtan be Mr Mathew Brisbane, minister at Erskine. Confirmed July 18, —48, James Brisbane, brother to the laird of Bischoptoune, elder, cautioner."
3. Robert, who, in 1635, married Elizabeth, daughter of Sir Thomas Lyon of Auldbar. He died in September 1645.
1. Janet, married, in 1611, to Fleming of Boghall, second son of John, first Earl of Wigton.
2. Grissel, married, in 1623, to Walter Denniston of Colgrain.
3. Mary.
4. Elizabeth, married to James Shaw of Balliegellie, in Ireland, of whom afterwards.

* He had a charter of Hanganghauch and Drummies, 18th November 1608.

5. Sarah, married to Sir William Mure of Rowallan.*

John Brisbane married, secondly, April 1612, Jean Sempil, sister of Hugh, fifth Lord Sempil, who is a party to the contract. This lady died in 1626, leaving issue:

1. William.
2. James.
1. Ann, married, in 1628, to James Campbell, son of Sir James Campbell of Ardkinglas.
2. Barbara.

John Brisbane had a grant of the " ward and non-entry of all lands and heritages whilk pertained to James Fleming of Boghall," dated 4th February 1624. He had also a charter to himself, his son and spouse, of the barony of Gogoside, &c., of new united, dated 9th August 1631. He died in August 1635. His testament was " gevin vp be Johne Brisbane, now of Bischoptoune, in name and behalf of *Marie* Brisbane, lanfull dochter to the defunct, and executrix-dative," &c. He was succeeded by his eldest son of the first marriage,

X. **John Brisbane of that Ilk,** who, in 1652, sold the lands of Ballencleiroch, in Stirlingshire, to Sir Mungo Stirling of Glorat. Previous to his father's death, he married Jean Chalmers, daughter of James Chalmers of Gadgirth, by whom he had a son, *John*, and six daughters:

1. Elizabeth, of whom afterwards.
2. Sarah.
3. Anna, married, in 1663, to Robert Hamilton of Barns.
4. Janet, married, in 1662, to Captain William Hamilton of Woodside.
5. Marion.
6. Jean.

In 1644, John Brisbane, younger, during his father's life, married Dame Mary Mure, daughter of Sir William Mure of Rowallan, and relict of Walter, third Lord Blantyre, who was still a minor even at this time (though her first husband died three years before), as her contract required to be entered into with consent of her curators. In this contract, John Brisbane, the father, resigns his estate to his son, and the heirs-male of the marriage, reserving only the liferent to himself and Jean Chalmers, his spouse. His son, however, died before him, in May 1649, leaving issue by this marriage three daughters, in infancy, one of whom, Ann, was afterwards married to William Fullarton of that Ilk.* The two other daughters appear to have died unmarried. On the death of the son, without heirs-male, the estate reverted to the father, John Brisbane, elder, the time of whose death is not mentioned.

* In the testament of Anna Blair, who died on the 18th March 1608, only three daughters are mentioned—Janet, Grissel, and Mary.

† Anna Brisbane, Lady Fullartoun, had a charter confirmatory of the lands of Fullartoun, 3th February 1676.

XI. Elizabeth Brisbane, his eldest daughter, was contracted in marriage, 26th June 1657, to her cousin, James Shaw, eldest son of James Shaw of Balligellic, by Elizabeth, daughter of John Brisbane (No. IX.), her grandfather, by which the estate of Brisbane was to be settled on the heirs-male to be procreated of the marriage, whilst James Shaw himself was to assume the surname and arms of Brisbane. On the other hand, James Shaw, the father, contracted to pay £20,000 Scots, to be applied in paying the provisions to the family of John Brisbane, the younger.

In 1671, James Brisbane (formerly Shaw), acquired the lands of Over Kelsoland, now forming part of the estate of Brisbane. In the charter of these lands, dated 1st March of that year, he is styled "Feodatarii de Bishoptoun." About the same time he disposed of the estate of Bishoptoun to different parties, to be held of himself and heirs, so that the family now possess the superiority only. About thirty years afterwards, the family acquired the estate of Knok; so that their whole property became concentrated in the parish of Largs.

There is a letter of remission to James Brisbane, from James VII., dated 26th Feb. 1686, for fines imposed on him for any irregularities his wife had been guilty of—which irregularities consisted in attending conventicles, or Presbyterian meetings, so obnoxious to the Court at the time.*

Of the above marriage, between Elizabeth and James Brisbane, there were:—

1. John.
2. James, a Writer to the Signet. In 1691, he married Anna, second daughter of John Cranstoun of Glen.
3. William, a Captain in the army, and died unmarried.

The eldest son,

XII. John Brisbane of Brisbane, succeeded to the estate, but in what year is not mentioned. In 1695 (8th Feb.), John Brisbane, junior, of Brisbane, had a charter of the lands of Flatt and Rindaill Muir, so that his father was in existence at that date. He married Margaret, daughter of Sir Archibald Stewart of Blackhall—contract dated 17th and 26th October 1685. Of this marriage there were:—

1. James, who succeeded.
2. Thomas.
1. Prudence, died unmarried.
2. Jean, also died unmarried.
3. Elizabeth, married Alexander Forrester of Carse Cowie.
4. Catherine, married William Fairlie of that Ilk.

XIII. James Brisbane of Brisbane was served

heir to his father on the 2d May 1727, but died unmarried. He was succeeded by his brother,

XIV. Thomas Brisbane of Brisbane, who married, in 1715, Isabel, daughter of Sir Thomas Nicolson of Ladykirk, by whom he had four sons:—

1. Thomas, who succeeded him.
2. John, was an officer in the navy, and distinguished himself in the American war. He rose to the rank of Admiral. He left two sons, Charles and James, both of whom distinguished themselves as naval officers, and four daughters, three of whom were married.

XV. Thomas Brisbane of Brisbane was served heir to his father 15th September 1770. He married Eleanora, daughter of William Bruce of Stenhouse, Bart., by whom he had a son, Thomas, and a daughter, Mary. He died in 1812, and was succeeded by his only son, the present

XVI. Sir Thomas Makdougall Brisbane, G.C.B., G.C.H., LL.D., F.R.S., Lieutenant-General in the army, &c. Sir Thomas early chose the profession of arms, and was actively engaged in many campaigns. He was with the Duke of York in the Netherlands; with Sir Ralph Abercrombie in the West Indies; and with the Duke of Wellington in the Peninsula, where he commanded a brigade in nearly all the battles in Spain, the Pyrenees, and the south of France. In 1814, he commanded a brigade in America, and was with the Duke of Wellington in Paris in 1815. He subsequently had a distinguished command in Ireland, and in 1821, was appointed Governor of New South Wales, where he remained for a number of years. Sir Thomas was created a Baronet in 1836. He married, in 1819, Anna Maria, daughter of Sir Henry Hay Makdougall, Bart. of Makerstoun, in the county of Roxburgh, representative of one of the most ancient families in Scotland, and has issue:—

1. Thomas-Australius, born in 1824, an officer in the army, died 15th November 1849.
2. Isabella-Maria.
3. Eleanora-Australius.

In 1826, Sir Thomas and his lady were authorised, by sign manual, to use the name of Makdougall before that of Brisbane. Sir Thomas is well known in the scientific world.

Arms.—Sable, a chevron, chequy, or and gules, between three cushions, of the second; in the collar point a representation of one of the gold medals conferred on General Sir Thomas Brisbane by the King. Crest.—A stork's head, erased, holding in her beak a serpent, waved, proper. Supporters.—Two talbots, proper. Mottoes.—"Certamine summo." "Fear God and spare not."

* See Law's Memorials, p 271.

### FRASER OF KNOK.

This family, now extinct, was of considerable antiquity. The first of them was

*John Fraser of Knok,* third son of Hugh Fraser of Fairly Hope in Tweeddale, and of Lovat in the north, who settled in Largs parish soon after the year 1400, in the reign of Robert III.

*Alexander Fraser of Knok* was upon the inquest at Irvine, in 1417, respecting a dispute between the burgh of Irvine and William Fraunces of Stane.

*Johanni Fresale* had a charter of the lands of Flatt, from James II., dated 7th July 1450.

*John Fraser of Knok* married, about 1520, Margaret, only child and heiress of Sir John Stewart of Glanderston. John Fresal of Knok and Margaret Stewart, his spouse, had a charter from James V. of the lands of Rowtanbure, 11th November 1537. In 1549 their daughter *Jean,* was married to John Boyle of Kelburne. In 1526, John Frisell of Knok, and his son, John Frisell, were both concerned in the slaughter of Edward Cuninghame of Auchinharvie.

*John Fraser,* grandson of John Fraser of Knok, had a charter of the lands of Knok from James VI., 13th Sept. 1571. In fulfilment of a contract of marriage entered into between his grandfather and John Brisbane of Brisbane, he married, in 1583, *Jeane* (so called in her testament) Brisbane, who died in April 1612. Robert Fraser, her eldest son, was a witness to her latter-will. John Frissel of Knok is mentioned in various testamentary documents down till 1643. James Fraser, apparent of Knok, and his spouse, had a charter of the lands of Grasszairdis and Knok, 27th September 1628. Occasionally afterwards, James Frissel, younger of Knok, occurs in testamentary documents along with his father.

*James Fraser of Knok* alienated the lands of Quarter and Routinburn, in 1630. In the same year the Laird of Knok was a sub-commissioner for valuing the teinds within the Presbytery of Irvine. In 1646 he was summoned before the Presbytery of Irvine for taking " a protection " from Montrose during the sojourn of the royal forces in the west. The Laird of Knok denied having had any concern in the protection, it having been procured by Alexander Beith in his own name. On the 13th March 1649, it was reported to the Presbytery, that " upon the day of tendering the Covenant, the Laird of Knok, becaus it was told him that he wald not be admitted to the Covenant, absented himself from the kirk in the afternoon."

For " his scandalouslie absenting himself fra the kirk the day of swearing the covenant," the Session of Largs were ordered not only to proceed in their process against the Laird, but that this latter offence should be taken into the process. In 1650 the process was still continued against him, though meantime he had fled to Ireland to escape the persecution to which he and others were subjected. Whether this unfortunate Laird of Knok ever returned from Ireland does not appear; but there is no doubt that his affairs were greatly deranged, and his financial embarrassments increased by the unhappy position in which his attachment to the royal cause had placed him. The lash of the church, in these days, was ruinous to all who came under it.

*Alexander Fraser of Knok* had four daughters, but no male heirs. The daughters were served heirs-portioners to the father in 1674, and the following year the lands of Knok were disposed of to Sir Robert Montgomerie of Skelmorlie. In 1696 they were sold by the grandson of Sir Robert to the Kelburne family. In a few years afterwards they were exchanged by David Earl of Glasgow, with the Laird of Brisbane, for the lands of Killingcraig and others, and they still form part of the Brisbane estate.

### MONTGOMERIE OF SKELMORLIE.

The Montgomeries of Skelmorlie were a branch of the Montgomerie family before its conjunction with that of Seton. The first of them was

I. George Montgomerie of Skelmorlie, second son of Alexander, first Lord Montgomerie, by Margaret, daughter of Sir Thomas Boyd of Kilmarnock. From his father he had a charter, dated 6th June 1461, of the lands of Lochliboside, Hartfield, and Colpy, in the barony of Renfrew, and of Skelmorlie in the county of Ayr. This last property had been acquired by Lord Montgomerie in 1453, the first charter of which is dated 25th March of that year. He married Margaret, daughter of Sir John Houstoun of that Ilk, by whom he had issue :

1. John, who succeeded him.
2. Robert, who is designed "frater germanus Johannis Montgomerie de Skelmorlie," in a precept of 'clare constat' by John Lord Ross, for infefting Thomas Ralston of that Ilk in sundry lands, in 1505. It is traditionally believed that certain Montgomeries in the Isle of Cumbray, Arran, and Kintyre, were descended from him.[*]

George Montgomerie died in 1505, and was succeeded by his eldest son,

---

[*] It is more probable that they were from the Braidstone Montgomeries.

II. John Montgomerie of Skelmorlie. He is mentioned in a recognition in 1506. He married the heiress of Lochranza, in the Island of Arran, by whom he became possessed of that property, and by whom he had a son, who succeeded him,

III. Cuthbert Montgomerie of Skelmorlie, born perhaps about 1483. He married Elizabeth, daughter of Sir Patrick Houstoun of Houstoun, by whom he had issue:

1. George, his successor.
2. Alexander of Portray.

Cuthbert was slain at Flodden, in 1513.

IV. George Montgomerie of Skelmorlie was under age when he succeeded his father. His wardship was assigned by the Crown to Lady Catherine Montgomerie, eighth and youngest daughter of Hugh, first Earl of Eglintoun. This lady afterwards became his wife. In 1535, his name occurs as one of the assize on the trial of Patrick and Adam Colquhoun, brother of the Laird of Luss, for being concerned in the slaughter of William Stirling of Glorat. In *Balfour's Annals* it is stated, that, in 1545, the French king sent "5000 soldiers, under the command of George Montgomerey of Largges," which must have been this laird of Skelmorlie, who lived till 1561. By his lady he left two sons:

1. Thomas, his successor.
2. Robert, who succeeded his brother.

V. Thomas Montgomerie of Skelmorlie, who succeeded his father, seems to have been of weak mind, for his brother Robert was appointed tutor to him in 1561. He died without issue, and was succeeded by his brother,

V. Robert Montgomerie of Skelmorlie. In 1572, he entered into a bond of mutual support with Lord Sempill. He was deeply engaged in the feud between the families of Eglintoun and Glencairn. He slew the Commendator of Kilwinning, second son of Lord Glencairn, some time in March 1582-3. The Maxwells of Newark, whose mother was a Cuninghame of the house of Craigens, were also concerned in the quarrel. In a conflict in January 1583-4, Patrick Maxwell of Stainlie was slain by the Montgomeries of Skelmorlie, and others slain and wounded on both sides. In April of the same year, another rencontre took place with the Maxwells, in which the Lairds of Skelmorlie, elder and younger, were both slain. These slaughters occasioned much trouble to the criminal courts, but without any decisive result. The Laird of Skelmorlie married Mary, daughter of Robert Lord Sempill, by whom he had issue:

1. William, slain as already stated.
2. Robert, who succeeded his father.
3. John, died without issue.
4. George, ancestor of the Kirktonholme family.

5. Margaret, married William Cochrane of that ilk, ancestor of the Earls of Dundonald.

VI. Sir Robert Montgomerie of Skelmorlie succeeded his father in 1583-4. He was a man of great courage, and came to the estate at a period when the feud between the Montgomeries and Cuninghames was at the highest. He had not only the wrongs of his chief, but the deaths of both his father and brother to revenge. It appears from a "pleasant story," narrated in Crawfurd's MS. Genealogy,* that he paid a visit to Newark Castle, the residence of the hereditary enemy of his family, with whom, of course, he was at "deidly fead." The Baron of Skelmorlie, the purport of whose visit seems involved in mystery, found himself necessitated to hide in some small closet, or turret of the castle. Newark discovered his hiding-place, but far from resenting this invasion, he called out to him, "Robin, come down to me, who has done you so good a turn as make you young laird and old laird of Skelmorlie in one day." The invitation was accepted, and it appears that Newark and Skelmorlie became reconciled on the occasion. He is, nevertheless, said to have "set no bounds to his feudal wrath, but indulged in it with such eagerness as to occasion very much bloodshed of his enemies. For this he was afterwards seized with remorse, and in expiation performed many acts of charity and mortification in his latter days." He was knighted by James VI., and created a Baronet by Charles I., in 1628. In 1636, he built the Skelmorlie aisle at the old church of Largs, elsewhere described. He married Margaret, daughter of Sir William Douglas, ancestor of the Dukes of Queensherry—a lady whose beauty is the subject of two sonnets by Captain Alexander Montgomerie, author of "The Cherrie and the Slae." It is said they were composed at the request of Skelmorlie. By his lady, who died in 1624, he had issue:

1. Robert, who seems to have been knighted. In the testament of Margaret Cock, relict of umquhile Colein Campbell in Leargs, who died in 1647, occur "Sir Robert Montgomerie of Skelmorlie, knyt, elder, and Sir Robert Montgomerie of Lochrinsay, knyt." He died before his father; but by his wife, Lady Mary Campbell, daughter of the seventh Earl of Argyle, he left two sons:
   1. Robert, who succeeded his grandfather.
   2. Henry, an officer in the army, who died without issue.

Sir Robert Montgomerie of Skelmorlie died in 1651, having enjoyed the estate of Skelmorlie during the long period of sixty-seven years.

VII. Sir Robert Montgomerie of Skelmorlie succeeded his grandfather in 1651. In 1648, the three lairds of Skelmorlie, elder, younger, and

---

* Advocates' Library, Edinburgh.

youngest, were on the Committee of War for Ayr and Bute.* Sir Robert enjoyed a high reputation for honour, virtue, and integrity. He married Antonia, one of the co-heiresses of Sir James Scott of Rossie, in Fife, and by her had issue:

1. Sir James, who succeeded.
2. Sir Hugh, who succeeded his brother.
3. Archibald, stated in the Broomlands Manuscript to have been the second son, and Sir Hugh the third, and to have died without issue.
3. John, who was in the naval service, and died without issue.
5. Christian, married to the Rev. Mr Clark;

and other three daughters, one of whom was named *Antonia*.

Sir Robert was repeatedly subjected to penalties by government, on account of his lady's attendance at conventicles.† He died before 3d February 1685, at which date his son,

VIII. Sir James Montgomerie of Skelmorlie, was served heir to his father. He was chosen to represent the county of Ayr as commissioner at the Convention of Estates, which met at Edinburgh on the 14th of March 1689, and was one of the deputies, along with the Earl of Argyle and Sir John Dalrymple, appointed by the Convention to wait upon King William and Queen Mary with an offer of the crown. He soon after became disgusted with the measures of the new Court, and entered into a treaty with the abdicated King at St Germains to procure his restoration, in which a chief article was to preserve the establishment of Presbytery in Scotland. This plot being discovered, he lay hid for some time in London, and finding that he could not have a pardon, without making a full discovery, he chose rather to go beyond sea. "His art in managing such a design," says Bishop Burnet, "and his firmness in not discovering his accomplices, raised his character as much as it ruined his fortune." He was not even more complying at the Court of St Germains, where on account of his steady adherence to the Protestant religion, he was not so cordially received as he expected; and meeting with little there but disgust, he died, it is supposed of vexation, in September 1694. Sir Walter Scott says that Sir James Montgomerie, "finding himself not promoted by King William to any situation of eminence, thought he could dethrone King William and restore King James (who, it is said, was to raise him to the dignity of Earl of Ayr)." Melville was Montgomerie's successful rival in the appointment of Secretary of State for Scotland. According to the confession of the Earl of Annandale, the Earl of Arran, afterwards fourth Duke of Hamilton, was deeply engaged in the conspiracy. Sir James Montgomerie married Lady Margaret Johnston, second daughter of James Earl of Annandale, by whom he had:

1. Robert.
2. Lieutenant-Colonel William Montgomerie, who was killed in battle in Flanders.*

IX. Sir Robert Montgomerie of Skelmorlie succeeded his father in 1694. He was Lieutenant-Colonel in the army, and governor of a garrison in Ireland, where he died in August 1731. He married Frances, eldest of the two daughters of Colonel Francis Stirling, of the family of Keir, and by her, who died at Skelmorlie, 9th June 1759, he had issue:

1. Lilias, heiress of Skelmorlie, married Alexander Montgomerie of Coilsfield, and had issue.
2. Isabella, died unmarried.
3. Agnes, died unmarried at Edinburgh, 4th September 1752.

Sir Robert was succeeded by his granduncle,

X. Sir Robert Montgomerie of Hartfield, according to the Broomlands MS. He is designed of Busbie in Mr James Blair's mortification to Hutchison's Hospital, Glasgow. Sir Hugh was Provost of that city, of which he was one of the principal merchants, and represented it in Parliament. He was a Commissioner for the Treaty of Union, and took an active part in the discussion of that measure in the last Parliament of Scotland, opposing several of the clauses. It is somewhat remarkable that he attended none of the meetings of the Commissioners in London, and that even his signature is not appended to the copy of the articles of union preserved in the Register House in Edinburgh. The probable reason is that, on finding the objectionable clauses neither omitted nor altered, he declined to sign the document. He was one of the representatives returned to the first united Parliament. He had acquired the estate of Skelmorlie from his nephew before his accession, and made an entail of his extensive landed property in 1728. He married Lilias, daughter of Peter Gemmel, merchant in Glasgow, by whom he had no issue. He died in 1735, and, in terms of his settlement, was succeeded by

XI. Lilias Montgomerie of Skelmorlie.—She obtained an act of Parliament, in 1759, enabling her to sell lands in Renfrewshire, and lay out the proceeds in lands contiguous to her property in Ayrshire. By her husband, Alexander Montgomerie of Coilsfield, she had five sons and three daughters. She died at Coilsfield, 18th November 1783, and her husband survived her only a few weeks. Their eldest son,

* Acts of Parliament. † Wodrow.

* Broomlands MS.

*Hugh*, succeeded his father in Coilsfield, and afterwards became twelfth Earl of Eglintoun.

*Arms.*—Quarterly, first and fourth, azure, three fleur-de-lis, or, for Montgomerie; second and third, gules, three annulets, or, stoned, azure, for Eglintoun. A sword in pale, point in chief, proper for difference.

*Crest.*—A heart and eye over it, proper.

*Motto.*—Tout bien on rein.

### WILSON OF HAYLEE.

This family has been of long standing in the county. From the titles it would seem that the lands of Haylee were originally of much greater extent than at present. About 1516, what is called South Haylee was conveyed by Mr Wilson's ancestors to John Porterfield, brother of Porterfield of that Ilk. It was afterwards acquired by the family of Blair, and is now the property of the Earl of Glasgow. About a century ago, the lands of Ladeside, in the parish of Largs, were also sold to John Beith, whose descendants still possess the property. The family tradition is that the lands were conferred on them for services rendered at the battle of Largs; but little reliance is to be placed on this statement. Their first over-lords were the Sempills of Elliotstone. The superiority afterwards passed to the family of Brisbane, who acquired it under a conveyance from "Dame Anna Lady Sempill, with consent of Francis Lord Glassford her husband," dated 10th April 1488. The first of the Wilsons of Haylee whose name occurs in the charters, was

I. GAWANE WILSON of Haylee. This appears from a gift of marriage by "Thomas Sympile, lard of Elliotstone, sheriff of Renfrew, yat is owr lord to ye lands of ye Weitland and ye Haylee," "to ye forsad Gawane Wilson and Marion Or, he, spous apperant," &c. dated on the 26th December 1483. This deed is curious, as being amongst the earliest instances of the use of the vernacular, in place of Latin, in such documents. He was succeeded by his son,

II. James Wilson of Haylee, who had a charter, by Sir John Sempill, "to James Wilson, son and heir of Gavin," in 1506.

III. James Wilson of Haylee had a charter from William, second Lord Sempill, "to James Wilson, the son and heir of James," in 1516.

IV. John Wilson of Haylee had a charter from the same William Lord Sempill, "to John Wilson, son and heir of James," dated 7th May 1540.

V. James Wilson of Haylee had a charter from Robert, fourth Lord Sempill, "to James Wilson, son and heir of John," dated in 1590.

VI. James Wilson of Haylee had a charter by the same Robert Lord Sempill, "to James Wilson, son and heir of James," dated in 1608.

VII. John Wilson of Haylee had a charter from Robert, sixth Lord Sempill, "to John Wilson, son and heir of James," dated in 1649.

VIII. John Wilson of Haylee had a charter from Robert, seventh Lord Sempill, "to John Wilson, son and heir of John," dated 8th August 1668.

IX. John Wilson of Haylee had a charter from the new superior, John Brisbane of Bishoptoun, in favour "of John Wilson, the elder, (son and heir of the last John), in liferent and John Wilson, junior, his son and heir in fee," dated 20th July 1695. He was succeeded by his son,

X. John Wilson of Haylee as above designed, junior, who, it appears, died without issue.

XI. William Wilson of Haylee had a charter from Thomas Brisbane, tutor at law to James Brisbane of Brisbane, "to William Wilson, nephew and heir at law of James Wilson, junior, of Haylee." This charter is dated in 1744.

XII. William Wilson of Haylee had a charter from Thomas Brisbane of Brisbane, "to William Wilson, son and heir of William Wilson, last of Haylee," dated 18th May 1774. This gentleman died on the 22d March 1821, when he was succeeded by his son,

XIII. James Wilson of Haylee, the present proprietor.

*Arms.*—Argent, a chevron betwixt two mullets in chief, gules, and a crescent in base, azure.

*Crest.*—A demi-lion of the second.

*Motto.*—" Semper vigilans."

*Residence.*—A small but pleasant modern mansion occupies the site of the ancient Haylee, about a quarter of a mile south of the village of Largs. Quarter, part of the family estate, and where they reside, is about a mile and a half north of Largs, and occupies the summit of a high and almost precipitous rocky bank, close by the shore, commanding one of the finest prospects on the Frith of Clyde.

As there is another property called *Haly*, or *Haylie*, in Ayrshire, long possessed by the *Shaws*, it has sometimes been confounded with Haylee in the parish of Largs.

A branch of the Schaws of Greenock held the property of Kelsoland for a few years. They were acquired by Patrick Schaw, second son of John Schaw of Greenock, in 1624, but repurchased from Hugh, the son of Patrick, by the heir-male of the Kelso family. This repurchase is stated, by *Robertson*, to have occurred in 1632, but this must be a mistake, for Patrick Schaw, the father of Hugh, was alive in 1636, and styled " of Kelsoland." *

There are a number of other small proprietors in the parish, but none of them of particular note or standing.

---

* Com. Records.

# PARISH OF LOUDOUN.

### ETYMOLOGY, EXTENT, &c.

THE name of the parish is generally understood to be derived from a very prominent object near its eastern boundary, called Loudoun Hill—a round, conical-shaped mount of remarkable appearance. It springs up abruptly from the surrounding level, and is seen at a great distance. The writer of the old *Statistical Account* derives the name "from the old word *low*, a fire, and *don*, or *dun*, a hill;" and it is scarcely to be doubted that in ancient times an eminence so conspicuous would be used as a beacon. Chalmers, in his *Caledonia*, seeks for its etymology in a conjunction of the Saxon and Celtic *Hlaew*, or *Lau*, and *Dun*; and in proof of this adduces some of the earlier charters, where the name is spelled *Landon*. There is, however, no reason assigned by the learned topographer why the Saxons should have added the prefix *Lau*, since it adds nothing to the meaning conveyed by the Celtic *Dun*. Others have suggested, and not without considerable plausibility, "that the name Loudoun is a corruption of the Gaelic word *Loddan*, which signifies marshy ground; and as the river Irvine, now more confined than formerly to the bed which it has hollowed for its waters, at no distant period flooded the low grounds of the parish, it is not improbable that the valley rather than the hill has had the honour of giving name to Loudoun. The banking of the river and tile-draining have made this name no longer a descriptive one; but the memory of 'the marshy ground' is kept alive in the title of 'Waterhaughs'—a farm skirting the Irvine, on the Galston side of the valley."*

The extent of the parish is about nine miles from east to west. Its greatest breadth, towards Eagleshame, is about seven miles, and its narrowest, at the western extremity, not more than

* New Statistical Account.

three. It is bounded on the west, north-west, and north, by the parishes of Kilmarnock, Fenwick, and Eagleshame; while on the east and south it is bounded by the river Irvine, dividing it from Galston. The western portion of the parish, especially in the vicinity of Loudoun Castle, is well cultivated and beautifully wooded, so much so, that

" Loudoun's bonnie woods and braes"

have become as familiar as the patriotic song of Tannahill in which they are celebrated. For this the district is indebted to John Earl of Loudoun, who succeeded in 1731. He was truly styled the father of agriculture in that part of Cuninghame. In 1733, he caused various roads to be made throughout the parish—had an excellent bridge thrown across the Irvine at Galston, and from thence a highway, the first in the county constructed by statute labour, made to Newmilns. He, no doubt, considered that it was principally owing to the want of good roads that there were so few wheeled carriages in the country. He could recollect when there was not a cart or waggon in the whole parish save what belonged to his father or his father's factor. The Earl is said to have planted upwards of a million of trees, consisting principally of elm, ash, and oak. Loudoun Castle was one of the first places in the west of Scotland where foreign trees were planted. He formed one of the most extensive collections of willows anywhere to be found in this country. During his long military services abroad, he sent home every valuable sort of tree he met with. These were gathered from England, Ireland, Holland, Flanders, Germany, Portugal, and America. The Earl greatly improved his property otherwise as well as by planting, and the result of his care and attention has been a sylvan beauty bequeathed to the locality, which few others can boast of.

The upper, or eastern division of the parish, is of a wilder and less improvable aspect—no small part of it being a deep moss, and covered with heather. The soil, too, is, to a considerable extent of a light, stony nature—although there is much fine loamy land in the valley of the Irvine. Save Loudoun Hill there is only one height of any consequence, the whole surface being of a level or slightly undulating character. Loudoun Hill itself is formed of columnar trap, and is part of an extensive trap dike which is said to "trouble" the whole coal-field of Ayrshire in a north-west and south-east direction.

Besides the river Irvine, which rises in the north-east corner of the parish, there are several small streamlets that intersect and water the parish, the chief of which is Glen Water. There is also a loch in the upper part of the parish, called Lochfield Loch.

## HISTORY, CIVIL AND ECCLESIASTICAL.

As has been frequently stated previously, the De Morvilles were the early over-lords of Cuninghame. Before 1189, Richard de Morville granted the lands of Laudon to James, the son of Lambin, who assumed the name of Laudon, or Loudoun, from the lands. The barony of Loudoun next passed by marriage to a branch of the Cranfurds; again, in the same way, to the Campbells, a branch of the Argyle family; and latterly to the Hastings family.

There are some interesting historical events connected with the parish of Loudoun. The Romans, no doubt, penetrated the district. "Loudoun Hill has been the centre of more than one warlike exploit. The Roman camp, though on the Galston side of the Irvine, is almost beneath the shadow of the hill; the shouts of Bruce's victorious army have been echoed by its gray rocks; and the watchmen who warned the Covenanters of Drumclog (which is in its immediate neighbourhood), of the approach of Claverhouse, were perched upon its summit."* Wallace attacked and defeated a rich English convoy from Carlisle to the garrison at Ayr, near to Loudoun Hill. A small turf redoubt is still pointed out as the spot where he and his small band of warriors lay in ambush. It occupies the summit of a precipitous bank overhanging the old public road. Bruce, in 1307, attacked and defeated the English under the Earl of Pembroke, near the same spot; and in 1679, the memorable battle of Drumclog, between Claverhouse and the Covenanters, was fought, within a short distance of the hill.

Referring to the era of the Persecution, the

* Statistical Account.

writer of the last *Statistical Account* says: "Many tales of more or less interest, connected with that season of trial, are still to be heard from the peasantry. Claverhouse, Dalyell, and Capt. Inglis, have each left behind them records of their ignorant and cruel policy in the graves of some of the headless martyrs of the Covenant, which are to be seen in our churchyards. It may not be out of place to mention one or two current anecdotes regarding some of the leaders of 'the rising' who were connected with Loudoun.

"Captain Nisbet of Hardhill was born upon the present glebe, a few hundred yards from the manse. He commanded the Loudoun troops at Bothwell, and carried his flag (still in good preservation in Darvel), safe out of the ill-fated engagement. On the reported approach of Claverhouse to Drumclog, Nisbet was sent for to Hardhill, and arrived in time to head the successful charge of the Covenanters across the morass. On his way to Drumclog, when passing through Darvel, he induced John Morton, the smith, to accompany him to the field of battle, where his brawny arm would find sufficient occupation. John followed Nisbet in the charge. A royal dragoon, who was on the ground entangled in the trappings of his wounded horse, begged quarter from John, whose arm was uplifted to cut him down. The dragoon's life was spared, and he was led by the smith as his prisoner to the camp of the Covenanters. But the life which was spared on the field of battle, was demanded by those who saw, in the royal party, not merely cruel persecutors, but idolatrous Amalekites, whom they were bound in duty to execute. The smith declared, that, sooner than give up his prisoner's life, he would forfeit his own! The dragoon's life, thus defended by the powerful smith, was spared, but the smith was banished from the army as a disobedient soldier. The dragoon's sword is now in possession of John Morton's representative, Andrew Gebbie in Darvel. Captain Nisbet was afterwards executed at the Grassmarket in Edinburgh, in 1685. His life is in the Scots Worthies.

"The Rev. John Nevay, then minister of Loudoun, and chaplain to David Leslie's army, was the chief instigator of the bloody massacre of Dunaverty in Cantyre, where the whole garrison of 300 were put to death in cold blood, whose bones may even now be seen among the sand banks, on the beach near the fort.—'I hope,' quoth David, after the massacre, 'you have had enough of blood to-day, Maister John.' Nevay, and thousands who acted with him, we believe, had no love for such deeds, but their arguments were first wrong, then their actions.

" James, second Earl of Loudoun, then Lord Mauchline, was flying for his life, having been, with his father, exempted from the general amnesty granted by Cromwell to Scotland. He took refuge in the farm-steading of the Hag-houses, which formerly stood on the rising ground near the lime and coal road, below the wood. He had just changed his dress, and put on the clothes of a labouring man, when some dragoons arrived who had tracked him to the house. His being recognised seemed inevitable, when the tenant, with great presence of mind, struck Lord Mauchline, and said, 'You lazy loon, why do you not go to your work?' and in this way drove him out before the dragoons, who never imagined he would dare so treat his landlord, and he was thus saved. He soon after fled to Holland, and died at Leyden, where he was buried."

" The church of Loudoun," says Chalmers, " belonged of old to the Monastery of Kilwinning, and was probably granted to it by the founder, Hugh de Morville. The monks enjoyed the tithes and revenues of the church, and provided a curate to serve the cure. At the Reformation, and during some years before, the tithes of the church of Loudoun were leased for payment of £100 a-year. The church lands which belonged to the church of Loudoun passed into lay hands after the Reformation. In July 1619, Archbishop Spottiswoode, as Commendator of Kilwinning, resigned to the king the church of Loudoun, with its tithes and revenues, and its glebe and manse, in order that the king might grant the same to Sir John Campbell, the eldest lawful son of Campbell of Lawers, and the heirs procreated between him and Margaret Campbell, the eldest lawful daughter of the late George, Master of Loudoun. The king, accordingly, granted the whole to Sir John Campbell, in March 1620, and confirmed by an act of Parliament of August 1621. The patronage of the church has since continued in the Loudoun family. The present parish church of Loudoun is a modern edifice, and in good repair. It stands at the populous village of Newmilns, which was erected a burgh of barony, 9th January 1490-1, and has a weekly market and five annual fairs."

Besides Newmilns, there is another village called Darvel, of considerable manufacturing importance, in the parish. The lands of this village are said to have belonged to the Knights Templars, and to have been independent of tenure, not even holding from the Crown. There are places in the vicinity called Temple Hill, Temple Darvel, &c.

## ANTIQUITIES.

There are the remains of two Druidical Temples in the parish. One of them occupies the eminence next in elevation to Loudoun Hill. It consists of large broad whinstones. The *Sanctum* is ten feet in diameter, and less injured than the rest. The field adjoining is vulgarly called *Anchor's Field*, but in the old charters its real name is *Acorn's Field*, where probably was a grove of oaks, held in veneration by the Druids. The other druidical remain is within the enclosures near Loudoun Castle. Not far from it, five stone coffins were found some years ago under a large cairn of stones. They "contained what appeared to be the dust of the bodies which they enclosed, and a few cutting instruments made of stone." Similar tumuli are by no means rare in the parish.

The remains of British, or as they are vulgarly called, Danish forts are found at the hamlet of Auldton, and near the village of Darvel—the latter is the most entire. It had been surrounded by a ditch, with a drawbridge, and gate to the castle, as such remains are popularly designated. These round fortifications are invariably to be found in the tract of the Roman invaders, and no doubt belong to that early period. Various Roman implements, dug up from time to time, attest the fact of the "Conquerors of the world" having been within the boundaries of the parish of Loudoun. On the farm of Braidlee, a considerable distance from the course of the Irvine, whose banks the Romans are believed to have traversed, three vessels of Roman Bronze were dug up from the moss. "These vessels were a large and smaller pot, and a kettle, or rather jug, supported by three legs. The two latter vessels were found inside of the large pot. They were very probably a cooking apparatus used by the Roman soldiery. From the remains of large oak trees which are occasionally found imbedded in moss in the upper district of the parish, in which these Roman antiquities were discovered, it is likely that it was at one time an extensive forest."[*]

*Loudoun Castle.*—What is perhaps erroneously called the old Castle of Loudoun was, according to tradition, destroyed by fire, more than three hundred years ago, by the Kennedies of Carrick, headed by the Earl of Cassillis. A deadly feud no doubt existed between the Campbells and Kennedies about that time, Hugh Campbell of

---

[*] New Statistical Account.

Loudoun and his followers having slain the Earl of Cassillis at Prestwick in 1527. The Kennedies afterwards led repeated forays into the Campbell district; but no notice of their having destroyed the castle of their feudal enemy is to be found in the Criminal Records. It may nevertheless have been the case; and it is more probable that the raid was perpetrated by the Kennedies than by " Adam of Gordon and his men." The ballad so called was first published by Lord Hailes, as referring to the burning of Towie Castle, in the north of Scotland, in 1571. The same ballad, or a fragment of it, has been familiar to the peasantry of Ayrshire from time immemorial, as recording the destruction of Loudoun Castle:—

> " O pittie on yon fair castle,
> That's built with stone and lime,
> But far mair pittie on Lady Loudoun,
> And all her children nine."

It is well known, however, that the minstrels of former times were in the habit of altering their ballads to suit the incidents of the locality in which they might be sojourning. The remains of an old tower at Achruglen, a steep eminence on the banks of the Irvine, are still pointed out as the old castle of Loudoun, at all events as the building destroyed by the Kennedies. It may have been one of the strongholds of the family; but the present seems to have been always the principal residence.

The existing mansion is a magnificent one. It stands on a gentle slope, on the north bank of the Irvine, about half a mile from the river. It is embowered among woods, and presents all that is imposing and pleasing in a baronial residence. The structure itself " singularly combines the attractions of massive antiquity with the light gracefulness of modern architecture." One of the square towers, with a battlement, is supposed to have been erected in the twelfth or thirteenth century. This portion of it was partially destroyed when besieged by General Monk. It was defended on the occasion by Lady Loudoun, who capitulated on honourable terms. Another larger and higher tower, built about the fifteenth century, lifts its battlemented head commandingly above the surrounding mass of buildings. A large addition, greatly improving the pile, was made in 1622, by Chancellor Loudoun; but the chief portion of the building, sufficient in itself to constitute one of the most stately mansions in the west of Scotland, was completed so late as 1811. The library, half a century ago, contained about 10,000 volumes. Nearly eighty years ago, ten entire brass swivels, all six-pounders, marked with the Campbell arms, were dug

up in the garden, without tradition or document of any kind to throw light upon their history. They probably had been deposited there during the troubles of the Commonwealth. " The old yew tree of Loudoun, which grows close to the castle wall, is of unknown antiquity. It is said that one of the family charters was signed under it in the time of William the Lion. One of the articles of union, it is also said, was subscribed by Lord Hugh under its deep shade. When Lord James went into voluntary banishment to Holland, he addressed his letters (being afraid of detection) for his lady ' to the gudewife at the Auldton, at the old yew tree of Loudoun, Scotland,' and they always reached their intended destination in safety."* The first " Ayrshire rose" was brought into this country by Lord John from America. The original plant is yet growing fresh and vigorous at the Castle.

*Loudoun Kirk.*—This small church or chapel, the ruins of which stand near the south-west extremity of the parish, was erected by a donation from the lady of Sir John Campbell of Loudoun in 1451. It has been long used as the burial place of the Loudoun family. There was another chapel in the eastern portion of the parish—at least there is a place near Darvel called *Glen-chapel*, although no vestige of any building remains to identify the spot.

*Newmilns Tower.*—This small but very old tower also formed one of the residences of the Loudoun family. It is without history or tradition, save what refers to the era of the Persecution. The writer in the *Statistical Account* says, " This was Captain Inglis's head-quarters when in the district. In one of the expeditions of Inglis's troops in the search of conventicles, eight men, who were discovered praying in the Black-wood, near Kilmarnock, were taken prisoners. One of them, it is said, was immediately executed, and the soldiers in mockery kicked his head for foot-ball along the Newmilns public green! Inglis was about to shoot the others, when it was suggested to him that it would be prudent to get a written order from Edinburgh for the execution. The seven men, in the meantime, were confined in the old tower. But while the troop was absent on one of its bloody raids, with the exception of a small guard, a man name Browning, from Lanfine, with others who had been with him at Airds Moss, got large sledge hammers from the old smithy, (still in existence,) with which they broke open the prison

---

* Statistical Account.

doors, and permitted the Covenanters to escape. John Law, (brother-in-law to Captain Nisbet,) was shot in this exploit, and is buried close to the wall of the tower. The dragoons soon went in pursuit of the prisoners, but they had reached the heather, and there no cavalry could pursue them. The soldiers, however, having ascertained that John Smith of Croonan had given the run-aways food, went to Smith's house, and, meeting him at his own door, shot him dead! Within a short period his grave was to be seen in the garden of the old farm-house."

The indefatigable *Wodrow* relates an anecdote perhaps referring to the same circumstance:— " About the year 1686, or 1687, ther was a party of souldiers quartered in Newmills, and abode in ane old castell of my Lord Loudoun's in Newmills.

If I forgett not, it was one Inglish that commanded them. Some of these souldiers went out to the country about, and gote a man at family worship, and he did not answer ther querys. Upon which they barborously murdered him, and cutt off his head; and ane souldier in particular putt it upon a stick, and brought it to the court of the castell. wher they wer, and plaid [played] at the foot ball with it. Within a day or two, that souldier in the morning was found in the same court with his neck broken, and his brains dashed out. Noe accompt could be given of it, but it was supposed he either throu himself or fell over a high wall of the castle. This my relatour tells me is most certain, and he had it from good hands in the place."

## FAMILIES IN THE PARISH OF LOUDOUN.

### LOUDOUN.

The lands of Loudoun were granted to *James*, the son of *Lambin*, by Richard de Morville, over-lord of the district of Cuninghame, and minister of William the Lion. This must have occurred before 1189, the year in which the granter died. " *Jacobo de Loudon*," who assumed from the lands the surname of *Lawdon*, or *Loudoun*, had a charter from William de Morville, confirming him in his possessions. He had no sons to carry down the name of the family. He had a daughter, *Margaret de Loudoun*, his sole heiress, who married

*Sir Reginald de Craufurd*, one of the leading, and ultimately the main, branches of the very ancient and honourable house of Craufurd. This union is believed to have occurred before 1220. By his lady he had issue:—

1. Hugh, who succeeded.
2. William.
3. John, from whom are descended the Craufurds of Craufurdland.
4. Adam.

Sir Reginald was Sheriff of Ayrshire.

*Hugh de Craufurd de Loudoun*, hereditary Sheriff of Ayr, appears as a witness in a charter by

Alan, the High Steward, of a donation to the Abbey of Paisley, dated in 1226, in which he is styled *Hugo filius Reginaldo*. In the same year he has himself a charter of the lands of Monock, &c. He had two sons:—

1. Hugh, his successor.
2. Reginald, ancestor of Kerse and Drumsoy.

*Hugh de Craufurd de Loudoun*, Sheriff of Ayr. He had a charter of the lands of Stewarton in 1246, and is mentioned as the subject of " a writ, anno 1271, wherein Andrew, Abbot of Kelso, acknowledges 'Dominum Hugonem Craufurd, militem, et aliciam sponsam, ejus, in possessione terræ de Draffen, in vicomitatu de Lanark," which he held of that convent." He had a daughter, *Margaret*, married to Sir Malcolm Wallace of Ellerslie, by whom she was mother of the famous Sir William Wallace, of whom *Wintoun* says—

" His father was a manly knight,
His mother was a lady bright."

*Sir Reginald Craufurd of Loudoun*, also Sheriff of Ayr, succeeded his father Hugh. He appears as a witness of a donation by James, the High Steward, to the Abbey of Paisley, in 1288. In 1292 he was one of the nominees on the part of Bruce in his competition with Baliol. In

1296 he swore fealty to King Edward, and in 1297 he was murdered by the English garrison at Ayr. By Cecilia, his wife, he left two sons:—

1. Reginald.
2. Hugh, who was the first of Auchinames.

*Sir Reginald Craufurd of Loudoun*, his eldest son, succeeded him. " He was," says *Craufurd*, " a strenuous assertor of the honour and independency of his country, in defence of which he lost his life, anno 1303, along with his cousin, the renowned Wallace, leaving only a daughter, Susanne, married to Sir Duncan Campbell," who was the first of the

## CAMPBELLS, EARLS OF LOUDOUN.

I. SIR DUNCAN CAMPBELL, who married Susanna, daughter and heiress of Sir Reginald Craufurd of Loudoun, was the second son of Sir Donald Campbell, second son of Sir Colin More Campbell of Lochow, ancestor of the Argyle family. They had a charter from Robert I., dated 4th January 1318, " to Duncan Cambell and Susanna, sponse sue, of the lands of Loudoun and Steuinstoun, predictos Duncanus et Susannam, sponsam suam, hereditarie contingentes ratione dicte sponse." By this marriage he became Sheriff of Ayr as well as proprietor of the estate of Loudoun. He was succeeded by his son,

II. Sir Andrew Campbell of Loudoun, and Sheriff of Ayr, who is mentioned in a charter dated in 1367. He died in the reign of Robert II., and was succeeded by his son,

III. Sir Hugh Campbell of Loudoun, who is first mentioned in a charter in 1406, and is again mentioned among those barons of Scotland who were nominated to meet James I. at Durham, in 1423. His son,

IV. George Campbell of Loudoun, was one of the hostages for the ransom of James I. in 1424, (his father being then alive,) and was Sheriff of Ayr in 1426. About this time, or sooner, the ancestors of the Campbells of Auchmannoch came off the family, being the oldest known cadet.*

V. Sir John Campbell of Loudoun, supposed to have been the son of the preceding. He accompanied Margaret, daughter of James I., to

France, in 1436, on her marriage with the Dauphin. He died, without issue, before the 16th of May 1450. His widow bequeathed funds to support a chapel on Irvine water, in 1451. He was succeeded by his brother,

V. Sir George Campbell of Loudoun. He had a charter of the Sheriffship of Ayr from James II., dated 16th May 1450. It is supposed the Campbells of Stevenston-Campbell, or Ducathall, were derived from Hew, a younger son of this Sir George, as also those of Barereochill, Cowfauldshaw, Horsecleuch, Boigavroch, and Glasnock, either from him or some previous baron of Loudoun.* He was succeeded by his eldest son,

VI. Sir George Campbell of Loudoun, who appears in a charter (his father then living) in 1465. " Another colony of cadets," says *Robertson*, " appears to have gone off about this time—namely, the Campbells of Shankstoun,† Skeldoun, and Kinganclench."

VII. George Campbell of Loudoun had a charter (his father then living) of the Sheriffship of Ayr, 4th July 1489. He was twice married : first, as is said, to a daughter of Gilbert Lord Kennedy, by whom he had two sons and two daughters :—

1. Hugh, who succeeded.
2. George,‡ of Cesnock. ' George Campbell of Sexnok' had a charter of the lands of Dalmellington, Haly or Hely, &c., 30th August 1511. He was probably also ancestor of the Killoch family, otherwise there must have been two sons in the family of No. VII. of the name of George. This is shown by a charter of confirmation to " Georgio Campbell, filio quondam Georgii Campbell, patrui Hugonis Campbell de Lowdoun, terrarum de Bryntwood," 11th November 1557.
1. Isabel, married to Robert Lord Erskine.
2. Margaret, married to Sir Alan Lockhart of Lee.

He married, secondly, one of the daughters and co-heiresses of Auchinleck of that Ilk, and by her had an only child, *Annabella*, married, first, to Thomas Boswell of Auchinleck, and had issue: secondly, to John Cuninghame of Caprington.§ He was succeeded by his eldest son,

VIII. Sir Hugh Campbell of Loudoun, Sheriff

---

* Robertson. The Campbells of Loudoun Hill were probably an older branch. John Campbell of Loudoun Hill had a charter of the lands of Chalachbreks from the Duke of Albany, Governor of Scotland, dated 15th August 1408. Finlay Campbell, and Margaret Craufurd, his spouse, had a charter of Loudoun Hill, 19th Nov. 1541. This branch has long been extinct. Sir Mathew Campbell of Loudoun had a charter of the lands of Loudoun Hill, 23d August 1570.

* Robertson. There appears to have been, about the same time, also a ' George Campbell of Galstoun,' who had a charter of the lands of Galstoun, with the lordship of Sornyhill, from James II., 12th May 1452.

† George Campbell of Mertinbamie had a charter of one-half the lands of Corehill, Changleichistoune [Shankstoun ?], Schyr, &c. 5th Feb. 1475. George seems to have been a favourite name with the Campbells: George Campbell of Galstoun had a charter of the lands of Galstoun, 26th February 1483.

‡ The name is blank in Robertson, and also in our own account of the Campbells of Cesnock. It now appears, however, from the above charter, that the name was George.

§ She had a charter of a yearly revenue, during her life and that of her son, David Boswell, from the Laird of Overcraikston, 10th February 1513.

of Ayr. "Hugoni Campbell de Lowdoun, militis, et Isobellæ Wallace, ejus, sponsæ," had a charter, dated 1st October 1505, "super terris Dominicalibus de Mertneme," &c. He married Isabel, daughter of Sir Hugh, or Hutcheon, Wallace of Craigie, by whom he had issue:

1. Sir Hugh, his successor.
2. Helen, married to Laurence Craufurd of Kilbirnie.
3. Isabel, married to Mungo Mure of Rowallan.
4. Janet, married to John Campbell of Cesnock.
5. Margaret, married, first, to Thomas Kennedy of Bargany; and, secondly, to Robert Chalmers of Gadgirth.

He died in 1508, and was succeeded by his son,

IX. Sir Hugh Campbell of Loudoun, Sheriff of Ayr. He had a charter of the King's lands of Garvanhoid, Turnberry, &c., 28th March 1526. In 1527, he attacked and killed the Earl of Cassillis at Prestwick, the Earl being then on his way to the court at Edinburgh. There were, of course, a number of followers on both sides. The cause of the feud seems to be unknown; but the death of the Earl was followed by numerous raids and slaughters on both sides, until a reconciliation between the families was effected. He had, in 1544, a remission for all crimes prior to that date. His name occurs in charters and other documents down till 1561. He and his spouse, Margaret Stewart, had a charter of the lands of Newmylns, with the mill and granary, dated 4th October 1533. He had also a charter of the lands of Terrinzeane, 10th August 1546. By his first wife, Lady Elizabeth Stewart, daughter of the Earl of Lennox, he had issue:

1. Mathew, his successor.
2. Marion, married to Sir James Carmichael of Hyndford.

By his second wife, Agnes Drummond,* he had no issue. He was succeeded by his son,

X. Sir Mathew Campbell of Loudoun, Sheriff of Ayr. He had a charter of the lands and lordship of Mauchline, and the church lands of Loudoun, 1st February 1566. He had also a charter of the lands of Loudoun Hill, 22d August 1570. Sir Mathew promoted the Reformation; but such was his sense of loyalty, that he fought on the side of Queen Mary at Langside, where he was taken prisoner. He married Isobel, daughter of Sir John Drummond of Innerpefry, by whom he had issue:

1. Hugh, his successor.
2. Mathew, who signalized himself in the German wars. He settled in Lavonia, and was ancestor of the celebrated Austrian Field-Marshal, Count Lauhdon.

* Sir Hugh Campbell of Loudoun, and his spouse, Agnes Drummond, had a charter of the lands of Spaggok, Renfrewshire, 18th October 1552. On the 5th October 1572, a charter of legitimization passed the Great Seal in favour of Alexander and Margaret, son and daughter natural of Sir Hugh Campbell of Loudoun.

1. Jean, married, first, to Robert Montgomerie of Giffen, and had issue; secondly, to Ludovick, Duke of Lennox, without issue.
2. Margaret, married to Thomas Lord Boyd, and had issue.
3. Marion, married to Sir John Wallace of Craigie.
4. Agnes, married to William Cuningbame of Caprington.
5. Isabel, married to William Craufurd of Leifnorris.
6. Anne, married to Lord Kirkcudbright.
7. Annabella, married, first, to Daniel Ker of Kersland; secondly, to David Dunbar of Enterkine.

Sir Mathew was alive in 1574. The eldest son,

XI. Sir Hugh Campbell of Loudoun, succeeded his father. He was created Lord Campbell of Loudoun 30th June 1601. He was twice married; first, in 1572, to Margaret, daughter of Sir John Gordon of Lochinvar, by whom he had issue:

1. George, Master of Loudoun. He married Lady Jean Fleming, daughter of John Earl of Wigtoun, by whom he had two daughters:
   1. Margaret, of whom after.
   2. Elizabeth, married to Sir Hugh Campbell of Cesnock.

The Master of Loudoun died in March 1612. His latter-will was made at "the Newmylnes, the sevint day of Merche." His lady also died the same month and year. Her latter-will was made also at "Newmylnes, the penult day of Merche." They seem thus to have resided at the tower of Newmilns.

1. Julians, married to Sir Colin Campbell of Glenurchy, without issue.
2. Isabel, married to Sir John Maxwell of Pollok, without issue.
3. Margaret, married to John Kennedy of Blairquhan.

He married, secondly, Lady *Elizabeth* (not *Isabel*) Ruthven,* daughter of the Earl of Gowrie, by whom he had two daughters:

1. Jeane, married to Sir William Cuninghame of Cuninghamehead, without issue.
2. Margaret, married to Sir David Craufurd of Kerse, without issue.

Sir Hugh died in December 1622. His inventory was "ffaythfullie maid and gevin vp be George Campbell, sone to vmquhile Mathew Campbell of Barreochill, tutor-dative to Margaret Campbell, dochter lawfull to the defunct," &c. In 1613, seeing no male issue from his son, who

* This lady died in January 1617. "Legacie.—At the Newmylnes in Lowdonne, ye    day of Januar, ze zeir of God 1617 zeiris, The quhilk day Deame Elizabeth Ruthwane, Ladie Lowdonne, beand seik in bodie, bot haill in spreit, makis hir testament in maner following. In ye first I nominat, mak and constitute my loving spous, Hew Lord of Lowdoune, my onlie executour, &c. with my haill guidis and geir. . . . . Item, I leif my pairt of ye haill frie geir perteining and belanging to my said spous and me, to Jeane and Margaret Campbells, my twa dochteris, procreat betuix the said nobill Lord and me, to be devydit equallie betuix thame. Item, I leif to my saidis dochteris, Jeane and Margaret Campbells, equallie betuix thame, the haill goldsmyth work, jawels, abullzements, and vthers left and disponit to me be vmquhile Deame Margaret Montgomerie, Ladie Boyd, content in ane particular inventar, subscrivit be ye said vmquhile Deame Margaret, of ye date at Sorne ye    day of    the zeir of God 1615 zeiris," &c.

died the year before, he made a deed of entail of his whole property, calling to the succession the following branches of the family, after himself and heirs-male of his body: George Campbell of Cesnock; George Campbell of Killoch; John Campbell of Shenkistoun; Charles Campbell of Skeldoun; Robert Campbell of Kingancleuch; George Campbell of Ducathall, alias Stevenston; Mathew Campbell of Barcreochill; Quintigern Campbell of Cowfauldshaw; Charles Campbell of Horsecleuch; Hugh Campbell of Boigcarroch; and Charles Campbell of Glasnock.

XIII. Margaret Campbell, baroness of Loudoun, succeeded her grandfather in 1622. She married, in 1620, Sir John Campbell of Lawers, of the Breadalbane family. In 1633, he was created Earl of Loudoun, Tarrinzean and Mauchline. He possessed considerable talent and decision of character, and took an active part in the affairs of his eventful time. He was one of the commissioners from the Scottish army who settled the pacification of Berwick with Charles I. in 1639, and sat as a member of the famous General Assembly in 1638. He was made Lord Chancellor in 1642. He had three gifts past to him in 1649: 1st, his haill lands changed from ward to blanch, holding for payment of a red rose. 2d, a gift, *durante vita*, of the sheriffship of Ayr. 3d, a gift to him and his heires, of the bailzirie of Kyle.* Notwithstanding these honours and emoluments, Lord Loudoun suffered severely by the changes to which the period was subjected. He had been a leading promoter of the opposition to the policy of Charles I., and when in that monarch's power, according to *Wodrow*, whose gossip cannot always be looked upon as historical truth, narrowly escaped with his life. " About the 1638, or 1639, John Earl of Loudoun, was sent up to London, at the King's desire, and with the King's safe-conduct then in use. When at London, the business of the letter *au Roy* began to make a noise; and my Lord Loudon's having signed it, was insisted on against him by Laud, Strafford, and the high-flyers, who wer willing to stop the designe of his coming up from the Covenanters. The Earl was put into the Tower; and by Strafford and Laud, ane order was procured from the King to execut my Lord Loudon to-morrow, at such an hour in the morning. The warrand was directed to Sir William Livingston, (if I mind), Deputy-Governor of the Touer. Sir William, when he received this warrand to execut the Earl of Loudon, without

any process or form of law, was extremely concerned, and came and let my Lord Loudon see it. Sir William was a relation, I think, of my Lord Loudon, and he said ther was no help for it, but begged he would shew it to the Marquise (ther being at that time no other Marquisses in Brittain save Hamiltoun, that was his ordinary designation). Sir William went in quest of the Marquise, but he being out of the way, and having left no nottice wher he was, he could not fall on him, till about eleven at night, when they went both streight to the King at Whitehall, and found him abed. Things standing thus, the Marquise said to Sir William, that he knew in lau he, by his office as Lieutenant in the Tower, might demand entrance to the King any time day or night; so the other demanded it and got it. When the Marquise came into the King, he told him he had the above warrand shown him, and it was illegal, and would have many ill consequences, and begged his Majesty might recall it. The King, in a very angry manner, asked him if he believed him such a fool as to grant and signe such a warrand, without considering the consequences?—adding, that he had done it, and he would be obeyed. The Marquis insisted that it would breed ill blood in Scotland: that it was against all lau and equity to cutt off privately a nobleman, that was come up on the publick faith, and that without hearing of him: that this would infallibly make the breach with Scotland irretrievable; and insisted upon other topicks, but in vain. The King continued resolute, and the Marquise took his leave of him, with telling him he would immediately take his horses and go to Scotland; that he could not stay at London to be a witness of the misery his Majesty was bringing upon himself; and that he was of opinion that to-morrow, before this time, the city of London, upon hearing of this unaccountable step, would rise, and for what he knew, tear him to pieces!—or some expression to that purpose, and so he retired. After he was gone doun stairs, a message from the King came to him, ordering him to return. The threatening from the city of London, stuck with the King; and when the Marquise came back, the King said, " Well, Hamilton, I have yielded to you for this once. Take you the warrand and do as you please with it!" My informer adds, that in a feu dayes meeting with Duke William of Hamiltoun, he gave him a hint of what he had heard in conversation; and the Duke answered, ' Mr Frazer, it's all true and fact, and the warrand itself, and a narrative of the whole under the Marquise's hand is among my papers at Hamiltoun.' And that the last Duke, James, confirmed the same

* Balfour's Annals.

to him some years after in conversation." During the Commonwealth Lord Loudoun was excepted out of the Act of Grace, and had his estates forfeited; and two years after the Restoration he was heavily fined by the unscrupulous administration of Charles II. He is mentioned in a testamentary document in 1650. He died in 1652, and was buried in the vault of Loudoun Kirk, where, some years ago, his face might be seen beneath the coffin lid in perfect preservation. He was succeeded by his eldest son,

XIV. James, second Earl of Loudoun. He was obliged to leave the country during the reign of Charles II., and died in Leyden in 1684. He married Lady Margaret Montgomerie, daughter of the Earl of Eglintoun, by whom he had issue :

1. Hugh, his successor.
2. Col. John of Shankstoun.
3. Sir James of Lawers. He was a general officer, and fell at the battle of Fontenoy, at the head of his regiment, the Scots Greys, in 1745, in the seventy-eighth year, it is said, of his age. He married Lady Jean Boyle, eldest daughter of David, first Earl of Glasgow.
1. Lady Margaret, married to the Earl of Balcarras.
2. Lady Jean, married to Sir James Campbell of Aberuchill.
3. Lady Christian, married to George Ross of Galstoun.
4. Lady Eleanor, married, first, to the Viscount Primrose ; secondly, to the Earl of Stair.

XV. Hugh, third Earl of Loudoun, succeeded his father. He was a Privy Councillor in 1697. Argyle, writing to Lord Carstairs, says of him, " Lord Loudoun, though a young man, is an old and noted Presbyterian. His lordship has it in his blood, and he is a mettled young fellow, so that those who patronize him will gain honour by him." He was appointed one of the Commissioners for the Treaty of Union in 1705. He served under Argyle at Sheriffmuir; and was Commissioner of the Assembly from 1722 till 1731, the year in which he died. He married Lady Margaret Dalrymple, only daughter of John, first Earl of Stair, by whom he had issue :

1. John, who succeeded his father.
2. Lady Elizabeth, died unmarried.
3. Lady Margaret, married to Campbell of Shawfield, and died without issue in 1739.

Lady Loudoun lived to the extreme age of 99. She died at Sorn Castle in 1779. Her ladyship possessed rare abilities, and was universally esteemed.

XVI. John, fourth Earl of Loudoun, was distinguished by his military services. In 1745, on the breaking out of the rebellion, he raised a Highland regiment, and served as Adjutant-General under Sir John Cope.[*] He was made Go-

verner of Virginia in 1756; Commander-in-Chief in America in the same year; and was second in command, under Lord Tyrconnel, who commanded the troops sent to Portugal in 1762. It was this Earl who so greatly improved the Loudoun property by plantation and otherwise. He died at Loudoun Castle in 1782, aged seventy-seven. Never having been married, he was succeeded by his cousin,

XVII. James Mure Campbell, son of Sir James Campbell of Lawers, fifth Earl of Loudoun. He married, in 1777, Flora, eldest daughter of John Macleod of Razay, by whom he had an only daughter. He died in 1786.

XVIII. Flora Mure Campbell, Countess of Loudoun. She was married, in 1804, to Francis Rawdon Hastings, Earl of Moira in Ireland, and who, in 1816, was created a British Peer, by the title of Marquis of Hastings,[*] Viscount Loudoun, &c. Her ladyship had issue :

1. George-Augustus-Francis, second Marquis.
2. Flora-Elizabeth, Lady of the Bedchamber to the Duchess of Kent, died unmarried at Buckingham Palace, 5th July 1838. The circumstances attending her death are well known. A posthumous volume of poems, by Lady Flora, were published soon afterwards. Alluding to this publication, the writer in the ' Statistical Account' remarks :—" It will be an enduring monument, not only of the extensive acquirements, refined taste, and lofty poetic genius of its author, but also of the desire, on her part, and on that of her family, to do good to Loudoun, as the proceeds of the volume, in furtherance of a wish she had once expressed, were to be devoted to some object of usefulness in the parish."
3. Sophia-Frederica-Christina, married, 10th April 1845, to the late Marquis of Bute.
4. Selina-Constance, married, 25th June 1838, to Charles John Henry, Esq.
5. Adelaide-Augusta-Lavinia.

The Marquis of Hastings had a high reputation both as a senator and a soldier. He had been Governor of India, and at his death, 28th November 1826, was Governor and Commander-in-Chief of Malta. The Marchioness of Hastings survived the death of her daughter, the Lady Flora, to whom she was much attached, only six months, and was succeeded in the Loudoun estate and titles by her son,

XIX. George-Augustus-Francis, second Marquis of Hastings, &c. He married, in 1831, Barbara, Baroness Grey de Ruthvyn, in her own right, and had issue :

1. Paulyn-Reginald-Serlo, who succeeded.
2. Henry-Weysford-Charles-Plantagent.
3. Edith-Maud.
4. Bertha-Selgarde.
5. Victoria-Maria-Louisa.
6. Frances-Augusta Constance.

His lordship died 13th January 1844. The Mar-

---

* There is a fine portrait of him in his Highland garb in Loudoun Castle.

* The Marquis assumed, by royal permission, his maternal surname of HASTINGS.

chioness married, secondly, 19th April 1845, Captain Hastings-Reginald Henry, R.N.

XX. Paulyn-Reginald-Serlo Rawdon-Hastings, succeeded his father as third Marquis. He was born 2d June 1832, and died at Liverpool a few months ago, from the effects, it is understood, of a fall from his horse while in Ireland. He is succeeded by his brother,

XX. Henry - Weysford - Charles - Plantagent, the present and fourth Marquis.

*Arms of Craufurd and Campbell.*—Gironny of eight, alternate ermine and gules.

*Crest.*—An eagle displayed, with two heads, gules, the sun in splendour betwixt them upwards.

*Supporters.*—Dexter, a chevalier in armour, with feathers, gules, holding a spear in the right hand; sinister, a lady, nobly attired, holding in her hand a letter.

*Motto.*—" I bide my time." *

## NISBET OF GREENHOLME.

*Nisbet*, author of the *Heraldry*, who was himself the representative of the ancient family of Nisbet of that Ilk, in Berwickshire, states that " Nisbet of Greenholm, a family of a good old standing in the shire of Ayr," are " descended of Nisbet of that Ilk." It is not known at what time the Nisbets acquired the property of Greenholme. The first we find recorded was

I. "JOHNNE NESBIT of Greenholme," who grants a discharge, dated 2d November 1576.† He was probably succeeded by a brother,

II. James Nisbet of Greenholme, who died before November 1578.

III. Alexander Nisbet of Greenholme. He was served heir, 25th November 1578, to Margaret Nisbet, eldest sister, and the other heir-portioner of the late James Nisbet of Greinholme, his mother, in the 40s. land of Greinholme, with the mill, granary, and fulling work (*fullonaria*); the 40s. land of Mylnerig; the 20s. land of Sorne; and the 30s. land of Sornehill of old extent, &c.

IV. Alexander Nisbet of Greenholme is the next we meet with, and may have been the son of Alexander. He was one of the cautioners of Hew Campbell in Mauchline, who was charged before the criminal court for being concerned in the

slaughter of John Glencorse of that Ilk, 14th February 1606. His name occurs repeatedly in testamentary documents, from 1603 till 1618. He appears to have married Margaret Lockhart, probably of the neighbouring family of Bar, who died in February 1612. Her testament and inventory were " flaythfullie maid and gevin vp be the said Allexr., in name and behalf of *William** and *Mareoune* Neisbits, lauchtfull bairnes to ye defunct, and executours-dative," &c.

V. Robert Nisbet of Greenholme, who, by his wife, *Barbara*, left issue six sons and four daughters.†

VI. Archibald Nisbet of Greenholme, the eldest son, was born 6th October 1689. He married, in 1727, Elizabeth, daughter of Hogg of Harcarse, by whom he had five sons and seven daughters. His wife died 23d August 1756, aged 46 years. He himself died 25th September 1764, aged 75 years. The monument in Galston church was erected by their fourth son, *David.*

The property of Greenholme had been alienated from the family some years previously.

*Arms.*—Argent, three boar's heads, erased within a bordure, sable.

*Crest.*—A boar's head as the former.

*Motto.*—" His fortibus arma."

Captain Nisbet of Hardhill—a memoir of whom is given in the *Scots Worthies*—though not immediately connected with the Greenholme family, was no doubt an off-shoot from it, as were also the Neisbets of Braidlie, Scheills, &c.

The author of the *Heraldry* mentions Nisbet of Carphin as descended of this family. Also " Mr Alexander Nisbet, chirurgeon in Edinburgh, who carries, argent, three boars' heads erased, sable, within a bordure inverted, gules, for an difference." James Nisbet, sometime in Feoch, and his wife, had a charter of the lands of Ladytoun, Overmuir, &c., in the county of Ayr, dated 2d February 1633. The name still prevails in Ayrshire, though the main branch have long been removed.

The great bulk of the parish of Loudoun belongs to the Loudoun estate; and all the smaller proprietors, of whom Brown of Waterhaughs is the principal, with, we believe, a single exception, hold from the family.

---

* The arms of the Cranfurds of Loudoun, on an old stone inserted in the present Castle of Loudoun, supposed to have been taken from the ruins of the old castle already alluded to, are—gules, on fesse, ermine, supported by two stags.

† Mason's Notes.

---

* There was a William Neisbit minister of Tarbolton in 1626.

† Monument of the Nisbets of Greenholme in Galston church.

# PARISH OF MAUCHLINE.

THERE can be little dubiety as to the derivation of the name of this parish. It is purely Celtic, and signifies " the plain with the pool." Mauchline town and church stand in a plain, " and there runs through the town a rivulet, which has three several falls, or small cascades, that form pools below." " The parish of Mauchline," continues *Chalmers*, " was formerly of very great extent, comprehending the whole of the extensive country, which now forms the three parishes of Mauchline, Sorn, and Muirkirk." The parish, as it now stands, is about eight miles in length, and from two to four in breadth—containing about twenty-four square miles. It is bounded on the north by the parishes of Craigie and Galstoun; on the east by the parish of Sorn; on the south by the parishes of Auchinleck and Ochiltree; and on the west by the parishes of Stair and Tarbolton.

The general appearance of the parish is highly favourable. It has a rich, cultivated aspect. Though generally level, still it is sufficiently undulating to prevent it from being monotonous. Mauchline Hill, which forms part of " the long ridge of Kyle," is the only eminence of any consequence in the parish. It rises a little to the north-east of the town of Mauchline, and running from east to west about a mile in the parish, terminates in Skeoch Hill, in Tarbolton parish. An excellent view is obtained from Mauchline Hill, not only over Ayrshire, but embracing Cairnsmure and other hills in Galloway, and Benlomond, Jura, Arran, Kintyre, and other prominent objects in the western range of the Highlands. From the town of Mauchline, towards the south and south-west, the surface gradually declines till it reaches the channel of the river Ayr, the banks of which are well wooded, and altogether romantic. The Ayr bounds the parish for upwards of a mile. " In its course it passes between steep rocks of red freestone, from forty to fifty feet high. How this passage was formed, whether by some convulsion of nature, or by the water gradually forming a channel for itself, cannot now be ascertained. The scenery is beautiful and romantic. On its banks there are several caves cut out of the solid rock, similar to those at Auchinleck, of which Dr Johnson has taken notice in his ' Tour to the Hebrides.' One of them is known by the name of Peden's Cave, where it is said Alexander Peden, whose name is so familiar to the inhabitants of the west of Scotland, often concealed himself during the unhappy times of the Persecution."[*] The whole parish is arable, with the exception of about three hundred acres under wood, and a few acres of moss. The farms are all well enclosed and subdivided, and the plantations are carefully attended to by the proprietors, so that they have a healthy, thriving appearance. A great improvement has, of late years, been effected in agriculture. There are several other streams, besides the Ayr, which traverse the parish. The Lugar joins the Ayr about a mile above Barskimming, the seat of the late Lord Glenlee, and now of his grandson, Sir William Miller, Bart. Loch-Brown, the *Duveloch* of old charters, was the only lake in the parish, and covered about sixty acres of ground. It used to be the resort of wild-ducks, geese, and occasionally of swans. The whole of the loch, however, has been thorough-drained within the last few years by the spirited proprietor, and goodly crops of grain are now raised upon the land thus reclaimed.

### HISTORY, CIVIL AND ECCLESIASTICAL.

The whole of what is called *Kyle Stewart*, which includes the parish of Mauchline in its

---

* Statistical Account.

original extent, belonged to the family of the High Steward of Scotland. "In 1165," says Chalmers, "Walter, the son of Alan, granted to the monks of Melros the lands of Mauchlin, with the right of pasturage in his wide-spreading forest on the upper branches of the Ayr river, extending to the boundaries of Clydesdale: and the Stewart also gave the same monks a carracute of land to improve in the places most convenient; all which was confirmed to them by King William, at the request of the donor. The monks of Melros planted at Mauchlin a colony of their own order, and this establishment continued a cell of the Monastery of Melros till the Reformation. In the before-mentioned grant of the lands of Mauchlin, or in the confirmations thereof, there is no mention of the church of Mauchlin. It is therefore more than probable that the parish church of Mauchlin was established by the monks of Melros after they had become owners of the territory; and it is quite certain that the church belonged to them. It is apparent that the country, which formed the extensive parish of Mauchlin, was but very little settled when the monks obtained the grant from the first Walter. This fact shows that during the reign of David I., and even during the reigns of his grandsons and successors, Malcolm IV. and William, Renfrew and Ayr were inhabited chiefly by Scoto-Irish, who did not supply a full population of their country. The monks afterwards acquired great additional property in that district, and they contributed greatly to the settlement and cultivation of it. They obtained ample jurisdiction over their extensive estates of Mauchlin, Kylesmure, and Barmure, which were formed into a regality, the courts whereof were held at Mauchlin."

In the Chartulary of Melrose there is a copy of the obligation granted by Hew Campbell of Loudoun in 1521, on being appointed Baillie of this regality. The appointment was doubtless obtained by the shrewd applicant with an eye to the fee-simple of the whole district (at least the superiority of it), on the breaking up of monastic establishments, signs of which were then becoming rife in Scotland. The deed is as follows:—
"Be it kend be thir presents, &c. bundin and oblist, on ye fayth and treuth of my bodie lelely and treulie, and heirs-mail to be gotten of my bodie, myn and their executours, with gudes whatsuever and gear movabbil and immoveabbil, to ane Rev. fader in God, Robert, Abbot of Melrose. That forasmeikle as ye said Rev. fader, in Convent with haill and full assent, has made me and my hears foresaid bailze to all and syndrie ye lands of Kylesmuir and Barmuir, lying within ye Bailzerie of Kyle-Stewart and Sheriffdom of Air, I sall, with freinds and allyes mainteen and defend said Rev. fader and Convent in ye said lands against all whatsoever, ye sovereign alane excepted." Signed, "How Campbell." Witnesses, John Campbell of Little Cesnock; John Hamilton of M'Nairston; John Duncanson, Chancellor of Glasgow; Matho Crawfurd; Hew Craufurd of ye Heateth, &c.

The early charters of the Abbots of Melrose are characterised by singular minuteness of description, and all that simplicity which belonged to the period. The names specified in the boundaries of the district granted are in many instances now unknown; but some of them still remain, such as Derneonner, Auchenbrane, &c.; and the burns (burnæ) Duppol, Nid (or Need), and Garpoll (water). At one point the march is defined by a cross on an oak (quercus ubi crux facta est).

The parish church, or Priory of Mauchline, was no doubt erected by the monks of Melrose, as supposed by Chalmers, after 1165; and the village or Kirktoun of Mauchline gradually sprung up in the vicinity. The church, forming part of the original Priory, it is supposed, and with which the Tower at Mauchline is believed to have been connected, was situated in the middle of the town, having the churchyard around it. The old church was superseded, some years ago, by a handsome new edifice, after the Gothic style, with a tower about ninety feet high. Besides the Priory of Mauchline, there were two chapels in the district—one on the water of Greenock, for the convenience of that part of it now forming the parish of Muirkirk; and the other on the river Ayr, on the lands now constituting the parish of Sorn. The latter was dedicated to St Cuthbert, and stood eastward of the village of Catrine, in a field still called St Cuthbert's Holm.

After the Reformation, the lordship and barony of Kylesmure, with the church of Mauchline, were gifted by the Crown to Hugh Lord Loudoun. The act, erecting the whole into a temporal lordship, was passed in 1606, and is as follows:—
"All and haill the landis, lordschip, and baroneis of Kylismure, and barmure, with castellis, touris, fortalices, maner-places, zairdis, orchardis, houss biggingis, mylnis, multuris, woddis, fischeingis, tennentis, tennandreis, seruice of frie tennentis, fewfermes, annexis, connexis, dependences, pairtis, pendiclis, and pertinentis of the samin quhatsumeuir, lyand within the baillerie of Kyle-stewart and schirefdome of Air, ffra the act of annexatioun maid vpoun the tuentie-nynt day of Julij, the zeir of God Jm. vc. fourscoir sevin

zeiris, annexand the temporalitie of all benefices within this realme to the patrimonie of his Hienes croune; togidder with the paroch kirk of Mach-line, personage and vicarage thairof, with all and sindrie teynd scheves, vtheris teyndis, fruittis, rentis, emolumentis, and duetes perteining and belanging thairto, lyand within the baillerie and schirefdome foirsaidis, firn the Abbacie of Melros and benefice thairof, quhairunto the samin pertenis and pertenit of auld, as ane pairt of the patri-monie thairof: To the effect that his Maiestie may gif, grant, and dispone to the said hew lord of Lowdoun, and his airis-maill, &c. . . . and als to the effect the toune of Mauchline may be erected in ane frie burgh of baronie, to be callit in all tyme cuming the burgh of Mauchlene, with ane ouklie mareat day vpoun Setterday, and tua frie fairis zeirlie . . . . . To be holdin of oure souerane lord and his successouris in frie blenche, frie heretage, frie lordschip, and frie baronie, for evir; payand thairfoir zeirlie, the said hew lord of Lowdoun, and his airis-maill foirsaidis, to oure said souerane lord and his successouris, the ser-uice of ane frie lord and baroun in parliament, with the soume of ane hundreth merkis vsuale money of this realme, at the feist of Witsonday, in name of blenche ferme; and als payand zeirlie to the minister serueing the cure at the said kirk of Machlene fourtie bollis aitmeill and thrie hun-dred merkis money foirsaid, at the termes vseit and wont, and furneschand bread and wyne zeirlie to the celebratioun of the communioun within the samyn kirk, &c.—[The pension granted to Sir William Seyton, brother-german to Alexander of Dunfermaling, Chancellar, furth of the saids lands of Kylismure, and barmure, and teyndis thairof, not to be prejudged by this act.]"

It thus appears that all the then existing castles, towers, fortalices, manor-places, yards, orchards, mills, &c. in the extensive and once barren dis-trict of Kylesmure, were constructed by the monks of Melrose or their substitutes. Unde-niable evidence, in short, of the improved state of the district is borne by the above document, compared with the original grant. In 1510, a charter, erecting Mauchline into a free burgh of barony, was granted by James IV.; and by the act of 1606 it will be observed that Mauch-line was again constituted a free burgh of barony. The charters, however, are said to have been de-stroyed at the burning of the Register Office in Edinburgh, upwards of a hundred years ago, and they have never been renewed. The town of Mauchline has long been considered of im-portance in the district as a market for the sale of cattle. There are no fewer than seven fairs, chiefly for that purpose, in the course of the year.

Mauchline is now somewhat remarkable for its manufacture of wooden snuff-boxes, and numer-ous elegancies for the drawing-room, of the most tasteful design and exquisite execution. There are also two villages in the parish, Haugh and Auchmillan, at the former of which there is a woollen mill, employed chiefly by the carpet fac-tory at Kilmarnock.

The first disjunction of the originally very ex-tensive parish of Mauchline took place in 1631, when the large district now constituting the pa-rish of Muirkirk was separated from it. "In 1636 it was settled that the division now forming Sorn parish should also be taken from it, and a church was built at Dalgain in 1658; but, from the distractions that followed, the establish-ment of this new parish was not fully completed till 1692." The ground for the site of the church and churchyard, with that of the manse, garden and glebe, were the free gift of John Mitchell of Dalgain to the parish in 1656. From the cir-cumstance of the church and manse being erected on the estate of Dalgain, the new parish was known by that name down to the middle of the eighteenth century. "The parish of Mauchlin was thus reduced to less than a fifth of its former magnitude. The patronage of the church has continued in the family of Loudoun since the grant in 1606."[*]

Mauchline parish is not without its share of historical events. An invasion of the Cruithne from Ireland is said to have been repulsed by the old British inhabitants at Mauchline in 681. But it is chiefly with those "troublous times" which followed the Reformation that Mauchline is historically connected. Almost all the lay proprietors in the vicinity were favourable to the new doctrines, which is not surprising, consider-ing that such a large and valuable tract of coun-try fell to be divided upon the Romish priest-hood being denuded of it. In 1544 the celebrated George Wishart was invited to visit Mauchline, and he purposed preaching in the church of the Priory; but entrance was denied him by the Sheriff of Ayr at the head of an armed force. The favourers of the reformer would have at-tempted to take violent possession of the church, but he dissuaded them from it, and retiring to Mauchline Mure, he there preached to a large multitude for about three hours. In 1647 the battle of Mauchline Mure was fought between the King's troops and the Covenanters, when the latter claimed the victory. In 1666, previous to the battle of Pentland Hill, the west country non-conformists are said to have been reviewed

* Chalmers's Caledonia.

on Mauchline Mure. In 1585, during the unhappy reign of James VII. of Scotland, five men belonging to the parish were slaughtered by the emissaries of an obnoxious government. They were buried where they were executed, in the public green at the Townhead. Over their graves was a stone bearing the following inscription :—

" Bloody Dumbarton, Douglas and Dundee,
  Moved by the Devil and the Laird of Lee,
  Dragg'd these five men to death with gun and sword,
  Not suffering them to pray nor read God's word;
  Owning the work of God was all their crime;
  The eighty-five was a saint-killing time."

The hole where the gibbet was fixed is said to be still visible. In 1830 the tombstone was lifted, and a new monument erected in honour of the martyrs, upon which the above lines are carefully engraved.

Under the head of *Antiquities* there is scarcely anything to record—a circumstance owing probably to the district having been so long in the hands of ecclesiastical proprietors, and therefore less liable to change. Now that the church has been removed, the Tower of Mauchline, as it is called, may be said to be the only remain of the ancient Priory. A view of it is given by Grose in his *Antiquities of Scotland;* at which period it was occupied by Mr Gavin Hamilton, the early patron of Burns. It is still in good preservation, and in the possession of Mr Hamilton's family.

Formerly the great feature of attraction to visitors at Mauchline was the " Bridge of Barskimming," built towards the close of last century by Sir Thomas Miller, Baronet, President of the Court of Session, and father of the late Lord Glenlee. It is a noble span, stretching from rock to rock at an immense height above the bed of the river, and connects the parishes of Mauchline and Stair, not far from Barskimming House. The bridge and the scenery on the banks of " the Hermit Ayr " are well worthy of a visit ; though their attractions have been somewhat thrown in the shade by the lately constructed railway bridge across the Ayr near Ballochmyle House. This is a truly magnificent work, and attracts corresponding attention.

The " braes of Ballochmyle," rendered classical by our national poet, have been recently much improved ; and, since the building of the railway bridge, opened to the public. This act of liberality has led to frequent excursion trains from Glasgow, the passengers by which are afforded every facility in viewing the romantic scenery of the place. The spot where Burns saw the " Lass o' Ballochmyle," hallowed in the memory of the old inhabitants, is marked by a rustic cot, within

which, cut out on wood, was set up the song composed in honour of the fair one. It is to be regretted that some ill-disposed excursionist, with as little taste as poetic feeling, pulled down this characteristic memorial of an interesting incident. The railway bridge is in itself a structure of singular dimensions as well as beauty. The height of the arch is 180 feet, and the span about 175. It is placed near the Howford Bridge, a locality long known to tourists as one of the most picturesque in the west of Scotland. Rocks of great height, covered with tall trees, rise up from the crooks or bends of the Ayr, which is seen from the walks on the *braes* stealing along at a great depth below, its murmuring undistinguished on account of the distance.

It would be almost stale to remark how much the town and parish of Mauchline are interwoven with the personal history and poetry of our national Bard. Mossgiel, where the family of Burns resided for many years—the banks of Ayr—Ballochmyle, and Mauchline itself, with its " Belles," its " Jolly Beggars," its " Holy Fair," trysts and masonic meetings, all speak of the youthful, glowing, but yet scarcely developed genius of the never-to-be-forgotten ploughman.

With regard to the records of the parish, the writer in the old *Statistical Account* quaintly remarks that " sometime before the Reformation, the Popish clergy perceived their interest declining, and their downfal approaching in the kingdom. To prepare for the worst, they sold their land in small parcels for ready money, and then departed, carrying with them all their money and effects, and the books and registers belonging to this, and, it is believed, to other parishes in the neighbourhood." It is fully as likely that the records were destroyed by those zealots who were instrumental in pulling down the religious houses. Fanaticism that saw iniquity in stone and lime could scarcely fail to discover it in the written memorials of the discarded priesthood. The existing records of the parish extend no farther back than 1669, a hundred years after the Reformation, and to judge from the evidence they supply of the moral state of the parish then and for a number of years subsequently, it would appear that the real work of the Reformation—the improvement of the moral condition of the people—had been slow in the extreme. In the very centre of the hotbed of the Covenant, Mauchline parish seems to have been, if no worse, at least no better than its neighbours.

From the Presbytery minutes we learn that, on the 15th June 1642, Mr George Young, minister of Mauchline, is ordained to " summon from the pulpit Mungow Campbell, son to Hew

Campbell in Netherplace, to compeir before the Presbiterie, to be halden in Ayr the 20th of July nixtocum, to answer before them for the cruel and unnatural murthering and killing, in the town of Manchline, of John Campbell in Mosgaviel [Mosgiel?] as was gravlie related," &c. On the 12th of April 1643, nearly a year afterwards, a supplication was presented to the Presbytery from Mungo Campbell of Netherplace,* by his brother-in-law, Alexander Pedan [not the famous *Peden*] expressing his willingness to give obedience and satisfaction to the Presbytery, so that his life should not be endangered. In reply to this supplication, Pedan was instructed to say that the Presbytery conceded these terms. The process against Campbell was continued for several years. At length, on the 16th September 1646, " compeired Mungo Campbell of Netherplace, in the habit of sackcloth, and in all humilitie confessed the unnatural murther of and killing of John Campbell, his cousin-german. As also he confessed his frequent falls in fornication sinsyne. The Presbyterie considering hierof, ordane the said Mungo to compeir in the habit of sackcloath in the kirk of Manchline, in the place of public repentance, two lord's days, till the Presbyterie advyse at thair next meiting what further shall be enjoyned to him." The penitent Mungo appeared in the " place of public repentance" accordingly; and on the 18th Nov. 1646 was farther ordained by the Presbyterie to give signs of repentance in the kirks of Ochiltree, Galstonn and Tarbolton. After all this, he again, in December following, appeared in sackloth before the Presbytery, when he was referred to the Session and minister of Mauchline, as having given ample signs of repentance. There is no record of what steps the Session took with the delinquent, but it is to be presumed, from the minute of the Presbytery, that the process would be closed without farther penalty.

The case is altogether a surprising stretch of the power of the Church courts at the time. They no doubt torture the party sufficiently in their own way; but undertake to save, and certainly do so, the murderer from condign punishment. It is true that slaughters, arising out of family feuds, were not uncommon in the previous age; but it does not appear, in this case, that even such a palliation could be adduced in favour of Netherplace. The only plea for the Presbytery, perhaps, is to be found in the unsettled state of the civil government.

The records of the Session, from which we give a few extracts at random, are rather curious as illustrative of the rude state of society at the time, even among a higher grade than the common peasantry :——

" Dec. 26, 1669.—The qlk day, Mr James Veitch, minister of this paroch (the legal restraint under which he had beine from Apryle 1662, being taken off by the Kinge's Counsell), preached publicly againe.*

" May 24, 1670.—Compeirit Johne Campbell in Killbrigend, and acknowledgit Agnes Cock to be his wyffe, and that he was mariet upoun the border, and was ordained to bring testimonialls of his conversatioun thes yeires bygane, and of his mariadge.

" Oct. 15.—The qlk day, compeiring Jean Edward, and partly by her own confession, and partly by witnesses yat were sworn, was conviet of frequent scolding, cursing, swearing, and fighting with her husband, Hew Smyth, and beating of him; qrupon she was ordained to be rebuked publickly, and suspended from the Sacrament of the Lord's Supper.

" Jan. 9, 1672.—The qlk day it was ordained that publick intimatioun be made against disorders and scandalous cariage at likewakes.

" April 22, 1673.—George Campbell, younger in Brigend, and John Duncan, delated for playing on the Saboth.

" May 13.—The elders ordered to try anent the scolding, cursing, and fighting of Isobell Boswell† and her daughter, Marion Reid, and their adversaries John Reid and Jonet Reid, and to cause summond them and witnesses as they shall find sufficient ground.

" There is intimation to be made the next Saboth that people ly not in yairds, nor in the fields, or wander on the Saboths.

" June 15.—Marion Reid compeiring, and being charged with fighting, scolding, and obscene language, abusing Jonet Reid, sister to Adam Reid; she grants she said Jonet Reid drank fyve mutchkins of wine, bot her own mother, Marion M'Caw, was her informer.

" Jonet Reid being charged, and not compeiring, to be cited the second tyme.

" This day Isobell Boswell compeiring, and being charged with scolding and beating John Reid, grants she called him witch-get, bot cannot prove him such.

" John Reid compeiring, and being charged

---

* It would appear from his being designed " of Netherplace," that he had succeeded his father, Hew, during the interval.

* Mr Vetch was minister of Mauchline at the Restoration, and had been ejected in 1662 for nonconformity. He was indulged by Act of Council, 9th December 1669.

† Daughter of James Boswell of Auchinleck, and wife of Mungo Reid of Drumfork.

with drunkenness, and calling the Gudewife of
Drumfork whoore and witch, he grants he called
her a liar like a witch, and a whoore after she
had called him witches get.

"Mathew Baird compeiring, declared, he not
being excepted against by the parties; as also
Jean Campbell, George Bowie, James Wood,
they deponed on oath as follows: Mathew Baird
deponed on oath he heard Marion Reid call Jonet
Reid theif, be the sun that shynes it was true;
and that she brack up the doore upon Jonet Reid,
and that Jonet Reid spak about an apron, bot he
knows not what.

"George Bowie compeiring, deponed that John
Reid danced in his own house, and said he might
make use of it; and that he called Marion Reid
a drunken limmer.

"James Wood deponed on oath, he heard the
Gudewife of Drumfork call John Reid witch-get,
and heard him call her a liar like a witch.

"Jean Campbell deponed she thought both
the Gudewife of Drumfork and John Reid drunk,
and she heard her cry up witches get, and him
cry down that she lied like a witch.

"Jonet Reid to be cited the second time.

"Hew Walker complains that Agnes Wood
called him men-sworne man, and she could not
deny it, qrfor she is to be publicklie rebuked for
saying so in face of the Toune Court.

"June 29.—Jonet Reid being cited the third
tyme, compeired, and being charged with calling
Marion Reid theif, and scolding, grants she said
till Marion that she never did draw any man's
ale, and that she never took a sey apron off the
dyke, after Marion had abused her, and called
her commone theif. The Session orders Isobell
Boswell, Marion Reid, John Reid, and Jonet
Reid, all to be publicklie rebuked on a Saboth
day.

"Adam Reid, younger, being on the street in
a shameful state of drunkenness, was ordered to
appear before the congregation next Lord's day
to be rebukit.

"Robert Mitchell of Braehead is the subject
of a formal complaint to the Session, because that
he "flouted and scorned their officer," when the
latter "delated" him before them.

"Mar. 3, 1674.—George Haldan and Matthew
Hunter are appointed to deliver to Mr Alexander
Craufurd the soume of 60 lib Scots, for relief of
the prisoners with the Turks, and to keep the rest
for the use of the poore.

"April 7.—Adam Reid delate for swearing
and cursing the elders, is appointed to be summoned to the next Session.

"Jan. 12, 1675.—George Campbell and Mungow Gib delate for drinking upon Saturday night

till the Sabbath morning, are appointed to be
summoned to the next Session.

"Jan. 26.—George Campbell and Mungow Gib,
called and not compeiring, are appointed to be
summoned pro 2do. John Millar being also so-
cius criminis with them, is appointed to be summoned to the next Session.

"Feb. 9.—George Campbell, Mungow Gib,
and John Millar, accused of drunkenness and
Sabbath-breaking, denyed the same, wairnt apud
acta, to compeir the next Session.

"Feb. 23.—John Campbell sworne, depont,
that about four houres in the morning, being the
Sabbath, he goeing to the house of Mathew
Campbell, found George Campbell, John Millar,
and Mungow Gib, sitting without their bonets,
in respect they wanted money to pay their reckoning; wherupon he gave them a merk piece to
pay the same; they afterwards going to his house,
his wife would not suffer them to enter in, for
which cause Mungow Gib cast him down at his
own doors, and then the three forenamed persons
went to the house of Netherplace, all being
drunk.

"Jonet Cock depont that she heard George
Campbell, John Millar, and Mungow Gib, at her
door on the Sabbath morning about fyve houres.

"George Campbell in Netherplace depont that
he saw John Millar between six and seven houres
in the Sabbath morning goe to his bed.

"George Campbell, John Millar, and Mungow
Gib, being convict of drunkenness and Sabbath-
breaking, are appointed to be rebuked publiquely
the next Sabbath.

"March 9.—John Millar, George Campbell,
and Mungow Gib, appearing in the publick place,
instead of giving signs of repentance, did strive
all the tyme to break the stoole whereon they
stood, which accordingly they did; for which un-
christian miscariage they were all suspended from
the Sacrament of the Lord's Supper, and other
church privileges.

"Apryle 27.—Given to George Wilson for
mending the stoole of repentance, and knock-
house,  .  .  .  2 lib.

"Given for nailes and bands to the repentance stoole,  .  .  1 lib.

"July 13, 1679.—Given to 2 wounded
men,*  .  .  .  01 00 00

"Aug. 15, 1680.—Scandalous carriage on the
Sabbath-day, such as flocks of children playing
on the street and the churchyard, bearing of
water, and the like, ordained to be reproved and
forbidden after this by the minister.

* The battle of Bothwell Bridge was fought on Sunday, 22d June preceding.

"Jan. 18, 1681.—The Session, considering that one of their members was taken with a caption at the instance of Ludovick Fairfoul, Clerk to the Synod, and forced for his relief to pay tuentic-eight lib. ten shilling for the Synod in Apryl a thousand six hundred and eighty, and eighteen Synods preceding, did allow the same to the person concerned, according to their former custome,*—inde,    .    .    28 10 00

"Item, they allowed the expenses, which was    .    .    04 00 00

"Aug. 8, 1682.—Margret Martine being delated for scandalous carriage with the dragoons at Auchmilling, is appointed to be summoned against the next Session day. George Campbell and his wife are summoned as witnesses.

"Sept. 24.—A contribution appointed to be intymate the next Lord's-day for the supply of John Scot, a brocken sea merchant, being ordained by ane act of the Lords of Councel.

"Aug. 31, 1684.—The which day Mr David Meldrum preached upon 1 Cor. iii. 21, haveing bene admitted minister at Mauchlin upon Friday the 29th preceding by Mr Rob. Simpson, minister at Galston, Mr Jo. Wattson, minister at Achinleck, and Mr William Blair, minister at Sorne.†

---

* Wodrow says—"Upon the 3d of September (1675), the whole of the indulged got a charge of horning to pay the dues ordinary to Ludovick Fairfoul, clerk to the Synod, and Mr David Clunie, bursar. Some hastily went in to the payment of them, and others stood out, and applied for a suspension; In which they found no small difficulty, because the payment of these was one of the things imposed upon them by the act of Council for their indulgence. Those who refused to pay were of different sentiments—some of them reckoning it was lawful to pay these undue impositions when forced and distressed in law, being a part of that passive obedience they reckoned lawful, and what had been generally gone into, as to the stipends of curates, by gentlemen of their persuasion; others of them reckoned it simply unlawful in any case. This matter came not to an issue till some time after this, and I shall have an occasion to give an account of it in the following years." 1.400.

† Mr Vetch was banished by act of Council, 3d January 1684. Wodrow says, "Mr James Veitch at this time went to Holland, where he continued under some trouble from Robert Hamilton and his party, but increasing in learning

---

"Dec. 29, 1686.—Baptized, John, son of a strange gentlewoman, who gave herself out to be ye spouse of John Campbell of Achender, in Argyle.

"Effie Wylie, from Dalgain parish, delated for scandalous conduct with my Lord Cathcart, in being in ane room with him for ane considerable space alone.

"Oct. 30, 1687.—The qlk day Mr James Vetch, minister of this parish of Mauchlein (being returned from Holland, the place of his banishment, legall restraints being taken off) preached publictlie heir againe.

"Aug. 4, 1692.—This day John Wilsone, younger in Brigend, being delate, cited, compeirs, and confessed that he was at the fishing upon the fast day, and likewise that James Wilsone in Brekanhill was fishing, and had a leister in his hand—he is rebuked before the Session, and past.

"Sept. 25, 1695.—The quhilk day, Mr William Metland was ordained minister of Machline.

"Dec. 21, 1734.—John Hamilton of Kype, clerk to the regality of Mauchline, confessed ane irregular marriage with Jacobina Young, daughter of James Young, merchant in Lanark, and had his son, Gavin,* baptized.

"March 8, 1785.—Alexander Sim having committed a scandal by rising from his seat in the church while the congregation was singing the doxology, and with irreverent carriage going forth with his head covered, is to appear next Lord's day to be rebukit in the place of repentance.

"Eo. die.—It was decided that James Miller and Margaret Tailor in Haughead, having entertained several people during service with meat and drink, should be rebukit before ye congregation."

---

and grace, till the toleration, he returned to his charge at Mauchlin." He died at Mauchline in the year 1694.
* This Gavin was Burns's friend.

## CAMPBELLS OF KILLOCH.

This family appears as second in the entail executed by Hugh, first Lord Loudoun, in 1613. Cesnock ranks first in that document; but there seems to be some dubiety in the matter—a doubt which cannot, perhaps, be satisfactorily removed unless by documentary evidence. It has been supposed that Cesnock was a distinct branch of the Loudoun family of a more remote origin than Killoch, and that he was put first in the deed of entail because of his marriage with the second daughter of the Master of Loudoun. This may possibly have been the case, though we find the assumed progenitors of Cesnock and Killoch so closely co-existent as to lead to the conjecture that their fathers were brothers, or that Cesnock was the origin of both. The Campbells of Schankiston, who are placed third in the entail, first occur in public and other documents about the same time—John Campbell of Schankiston appearing in 1488. In short it seems questionable whether the entail alluded to proceeded upon the usual principle of calling the succession in the order of propinquity. Had this been the case, it would have begun with the descendants of *Mathew*, ancestor of the Lauhdons of Germany, great grandson of George Campbell of Loudon, the supposed father of the first Cesnock or Killoch. As Lord Hugh had no prospect of heirs-male of his own body, the calling in the entail may have been, in some measure, the reverse of the usual order of such documents.* Be this as it may, the first of the Killoch family was

I. GEORGE CAMPBELL, whose son,

II. George Campbell, had a charter of confirmation under the Great Seal—" Georgio, filio quondam Georgii Campbell, patrui Hugonis Campbell de Lowdoun, terrarum de Bryntwood," &c. 11th Nov. 1537.

III. James Campbell of Bruntwood, who is known from a renunciation granted by Helen Simson, dated 7th Nov. 1547, of the one-half of the forty shilling land of Killoch, to Hew Campbell, son to James Campbell of Bruntwood.

IV. Hew Campbell of Killoch had a charter of feu from the Commendator of Melrose, dated 20th May 1556, of the four merk land of Lochlee, three merk land of Auchinbrain, and three merk land of Killoch. He was succeeded by his son,

V. Hew Campbell of Killoch, as appears from a procuratory by the said Hew, for resigning these lands in favour of his *son*, *Hew*, in 1567; and, on the 28th October 1577, the said Hew Campbell, designed younger, acquired the lands of Holehouse.

VI. George Campbell of Killoch, who, in 1605, is designed heir of Hew, the younger, his father, in Barnaughthill, and the lands before named. This was the George Campbell of Killoch called in Lord Loudoun's deed of entail in 1613. He is thus mentioned in the list of debts "awand to the deid" in the testament of "vmquhile Williame Campbell of Grenokmaines," who died in December 1607. "Item . . . be the tennentis of Killoch and brwnwoid, perteining to George Campbell of Killoch," &c. He is mentioned in similar documents down to 1616.

* In the absence of positive evidence there seems to be strong reasons for believing that Killoch ought to have preceded Cesnock in the entail:—

1. Lord Loudoun, by that deed, did not set aside his grand-daughters—children of the Master of Loudoun—the eldest of whom became Baroness Loudoun, and the second married Cesnock. In 1620 he executed other two deeds of entail, more in favour of Sir John Campbell of Lawers, husband of his eldest daughter, and afterwards first Earl of Loudoun; but he never meant to exclude from the succession of his title and estates those two grand-daughters. He would, therefore, as a matter of course, put Cesnock as the next after the eldest and her issue, especially as his male next of kin were only distantly related to him.

2. The arms of old Cesnock are those of Argyle quartered with Loudoun, a proof that the origin was directly from Argyle. None of the Loudoun cadets, so far as we are aware, carry the arms of Argyle and Loudoun quartered, except Skerrington, and in this instance the case was somewhat similar to that of Cesnock. Skerrington was originally from Argyle, but a cadet of Loudoun married the heiress of the family.

3. But the strongest proof is in the service of Hugh Campbell of Killoch, "heir-male to Hugh Lord Loudoun, the great-grand-nephew of his (Killoch's) great-grandfather," in the office of Baillie of Kylesmuir, on the 9th January 1634, only twenty-one years after the entail was made. He is here declared heir-male of the very executor of the entail in 1613.

It is thus clear that Killoch, and not Cesnock was the nearest in propinquity to Baron Loudoun, and that both Robertson and ourselves were wrong in ascribing the ancestry of Cesnock to George, second son of George Campbell of Loudoun, (No. VII.) who now appears to have been the origin of the Killoch family.

He had a daughter, *Mary*, married to the Laird of Montgarswood, and a son who succeeded him

VII   Hugh Campbell of Killoch, in 1634, was served heir to Lord Loudoun as Bailie of Kylesmuir.   He was no doubt the same party who, in 1652, disponed the lands to James Dalrymple of Stair, and which conveyance, on the 23d Nov. 1654, was ratified by his sister, Mary Campbell, with consent of her husband, James Campbell of Montgarswood.

*Killoch* is situated near the boundary between the parishes of Mauchline and Galston

### CAMPBELL OF KINGANCLEUCH

This family was one of the most zealous and distinguished in the cause of the Reformation It was a branch of that of Loudoun, and stands fifth in the deed of entail previously alluded to The first we have discovered must, we think, have been a son of Sir George Campbell of Loudoun, and born about the end of the fifteenth century   He is the

I   HEW CAMPBELL of Kingancleuch mentioned by Knox as offended by those who held the kirk of Mauchline against the entrance of Wishart, in 1544, " that they should debar them from entering the kirk, and concluded by force to enter , but the said Mr George (Wishart) withdrew the said Hugh, and said unto him, ' Brother, Christ Jesus is as potent in the fields as in the kirk '*   And so withdrawing the whole people, they came to a dyke on a muir edge, on the south-west of Mauchline.   He was succeeded by

II   Robert Campbell of Kingancleuch, whose name occurs in the list of absentees from the assize on the " Lairds of Lochnorris and Ekles," 14th Nov. 1554,† who were to be tried, but came in the King's will, for intercommuning with Hunter of Ballagane, then a rebel at the horn   He is cautioner, in 1559, for " John Willok, denounced rebel for usurping the right of the Church, and preaching in the burgh of Air, and amerciated for him †   In 1566 he became surety for " William Johnstone, bower, burgess of Edinburgh, for his entry at the next Justice Aire of Edinburgh, to underlie the law for art and part counselling and devising the death of Senzeour Dauid Riccio "†   A number of persons at that period were brought forward on suspicion of being concerned in Rizzio's murder, and especially those who were actively engaged in

promoting the Reformation—even Knox himself did not escape suspicion of being concerned in the " slauchters " of the period *

We have elsewhere† said so much regarding this active reformer that it is unnecessary here to enter farther into detail   The following lines, from the " Memorial " of Kingancleuch and his wife, by Mr John Davidson, may, however, be genealogically interesting .—

> " But to be plainer is nae skaith,
> Of surnames, they were Campbells baith,
> Of ancient blood of the countrie,
> They were baith of genealogie,
> He of the Sheriff's house of Air,
> Long noble, famous, and preclair,
> Sho of a gude and godly stock,
> Come of the old house of Cesnock,
> Quais lord of mony years bygane
> Professed Christ's religion plaine,
> Yea, eighty years sinsyne and mair,
> As I heard aged men declare "

He was an intimate friend of John Knox, and attended him during his last illness, throughout which much friendship and affection was manifested between them   He died in 1574, leaving an only child (by his wife, Elizabeth Campbell), who succeeded him in the estate.   She was

III   Elizabeth Campbell of Kingancleuch, served heir to her father in 1586   *Robertson* could find no notice of whom she married, but concludes that the *Robert Campbell* of Kingancleuch specified in the Loudoun entail was her husband   Her father must have been more than twenty-one, most likely above twenty-five years of age, when he was upon an assize in the year 1654, and supposing his daughter to have been born when he was thirty-one, she would be in 1613 (the date of the deed of entail), at least fifty-three, consequently old enough to have a son upwards of twenty-one.   Therefore it is probable that it was her son, and not her husband, who is called in the Loudoun deed of entail. This is mere conjecture, however, though it is certain that she was married   It is also equally true, if the Commissary records are to be admitted as good evidence, that there was a

IV   John Campbell of Kingancleuch, who appears in various testamentary documents from 1602 down to April 1613 , and again the same name occurs in 1624   In 1627 John Campbell of Kingancleuch was served heir to his mother, Elizabeth, in the lands of Kingancleuch , and in 1636, the same party, apparently, is served heir of his grandfather   In 1634 (19th July) John Campbell of Kingancleuche had a charter, under the Great Seal, of Ballochbrok, Drumlongford, &c   It would therefore appear that *Robert* is a

---

* Knox's History of the Reformation
† Pitcairn's Criminal Trials

* Tytler's History of Scotland.
† See vol L, pages 67 8

misnomer in the entail of 1613. In 1625 the testament of *Charles* Campbell *in* Kingancleuch occurs in the Commissary Records. He is also styled *of* Kinganclench in the same document, and may have been a brother, and in joint possession.*

V. John Campbell of Kinganclench was served heir to the last John, his father, in 1654. He was appointed by Parliament one of the Committee of war for Ayrshire in 1648. He married Agnes, daughter of John Craufurd of Cranfurdland, by whom he had two sons, *Hugh* and *George*, and a daughter. In the testament of Hew Campbell of Netherplace, 1640, "George Campbell, brother to the Guidman of Kinganclench," is mentioned. He was succeeded by his eldest son,

VI. Hugh Campbell of Kinganclench, who married Elizabeth, daughter of Sir Hugh Campbell of Cesnock. He had two sons, *John* and *William*, the former of whom succeeded him.

VII. John Campbell of Kinganclench, who, in September 1681, married Elizabeth, daughter of the Rev. J. Adair,† and had two sons, *John* and *Robert*, who died unmarried. He was a zealous elder of the Kirk, his name appearing in every sederunt of the Session towards the end of the seventeenth century. He died in 1724, and was succeeded by his eldest son,

VIII. John Campbell of Kinganclench, who married Anna, daughter of Kennedy of Daljarroch. He died about 1752, and was succeeded by his only child,

IX. Margaret Campbell of Kinganclench, who married a Mr M'Gill, and died without issue. So far as is known the family is extinct.

On the death of Mrs M'Gill, about the beginning of this century, the property was purchased by Mr Alexander of Ballochmyle, and now constitutes not the least attractive portion of that beautiful estate. Part of the old Tower of Kinganclench still overlooks the romantic scenery around it, and a cottage near was long the residence of Lady Cecilia Brabazon, aunt of the late Mr Alexander, and is now occupied by Mr Buchanan, younger of Catrine Bank.

## CAMPBELL OF NETHERPLACE.

The first of this family we have met with is mentioned as a witness to the summons against

---

* In 1636 George Lockhart, burgess of Ayr, appeared and became cautioner for his relict, Agnes Chalmers, and his dochter, Margaret Campbell, as executors.

† The Rev. William Adair was ordained minister of Ayr in 1639. He was brother to the Laird of Kinhilt. Mr John may have been his son or grandson.

---

John Ross of Montgreenan for high treason, in 1488, under the designation of

I. JAMES CAMPBELL of Brownside, which is known to have been that of the family. Montgreenan had fled from the wrath of James IV., after the battle of Sauchieburn, where he fought on the side of James III., and the Pursuevant, after summoning him at Montgreenan and the "market cross of Irvine," thus discharged his duty at "the merkat corse of Air": "J. Carrich, Pursewant, the xvi day of the moneth of August (1488) past to the merkat corse of Air, and there, be oppen proclammation, sumond and chargeit the said John the Ross to compere before our Sovereign Lorde, at day and place above written. Before thir witnes, Johnne Campbell of Shankstone, Ferguse Fergusson of Kilkerran, Andro Busby, Alderman of Air, James Campbell of ye Brownside, and utheris diverse."

II. Mungo Campbell of Brownside, probably the son or grandson of the preceding, was one of those who kept the church of Mauchline against the martyr, George Wishart, in 1544. He was succeeded by his son,

III. Mungo Campbell of Brownside. *Robertson* says he has "seen a disposition, dated 1569, by Mungo, eldest lawful son of Mungo Campbell of Brownside, to his brother, Hugh, of the lands of Ten-shilling-side, and others, now called Netherplace." He appears to have been succeeded by

IV. Mungo Campbell of Cowfauldshaw, probably his son. He is mentioned in a Crown charter, dated 9th January 1596, to "William Campbell, brother german of Kentigern Campbell of Cowfauldshaws," of the lands of Grenoktoun. He appears to have been the party mentioned in the Loudoun entail, in 1613, and his name occurs repeatedly in testamentary documents in the same year. He was succeeded, apparently, by

V. Mungo Campbell of Cowfauldshaw, who had sasine, in 1620, of the lands of Cowfauldshaw, Netherplace, and others. He married Janet, daughter of John Craufurd of Craufurdland, by Margaret, daughter of Hew Wallace of Cairnhill, and relict of George Campbell of Dueathall. The next in succession is the first who assumed the present designation,

VI. Hew Campbell of Netherplace, the son, we presume, of the last mentioned. His will is recorded in 1640, from which it appears that his first wife's name was Margaret Petheine, probably of the Auchinlongford family; but his second, although alluded to, is not named. The testament is given up by *John*, *Margaret*, and *Mary*, bairns lawful to deceased, in behalf of *George* and *Marion*, likewise bairns lawful, but no doubt young children, as they were the issue of the last wife, who seems to have been also deceased.* He was succeeded by his eldest son,

VII. Mungo Campbell of Netherplace. His name occurs in a testamentary document in 1646. About the year 1650 he married Elizabeth Dalrymple, daughter of Dalrymple of Langlands. The issue of this marriage was a son and two daughters—*Elizabeth*, married to William Mure of Bruntwood, in 1681, and *Margaret*, to William Duncan of Hillar. He was succeeded by his only son,

VIII. Mungo Campbell of Netherplace, Sheriff-Depute of Ayrshire. His name occurs frequently, as an elder, in the Session records from 1672 to 1700. He married, in 1698, Jean, daughter of Sir Alexander Menzies of that Ilk, by whom he had a son and a daughter, Susannah, who died unmarried in 1719. He had another daughter, *Sarah*, baptised 15th Sept. 1699.† He died in 1620, and was succeeded by his son,

IX. Mungo Campbell of Netherplace. He married, in 1720, Magdalene, daughter of William Cuninghame of Craigends, by Christian, daughter of Sir John Colquhoun of Luss, Bart., by whom he had a son and two daughters, *Christian* and *Susannah*. He is frequently mentioned in the Session Records of Mauchline and Sorn as a witness to marriages. His wife died in 1725, and he himself in 1771. His son,

X. William Campbell of Netherplace, is next in succession. He married Lilias, daughter of John Neilson, merchant in Glasgow, by Margaret, daughter of Thomas Wallace of Cairnhill, by whom he had one son and two daughters, *Margaret* and *Lilias*. Mr Campbell of Netherplace died in 1786, and his widow in 1822.

XI. William Campbell of Netherplace succeeded his father. He died a few years ago, and was succeeded by his eldest sister; upon whose death soon afterwards she was succeeded by her sister,

*Lilias Campbell* of Netherplace, who died in April last.

By the settlement of the last laird, her brother, the estate has gone to Col. Hamilton of Cairnhill, who is to be succeeded in it by his second son.

*Arms* as granted in 1694.—Girony of eight, gules and ermine, as descended of Loudoun; the first surcharged with a bezant, or. *Crest*, a right hand erect, holding a hook. *Motto*, "Optime quod opportune."

---

## CAMPBELL OF MONTGARSWOOD.

The first that appears of this family is mentioned by Knox in his "Historie of the Reformatioun" as holding the Kirk of Mauchline, along with others, against the friends of Wishart, in 1544. He was designed

I. GEORGE CAMPBELL of Montgarswood, probably a son of Shankston. Knox farther observes of him that he "yet liveth, anno 1566."

II. John Campbell of Montgarswood is represented, in Shankston's testament, in 1612, as his "oye," or grandson, "and appeirand heir." As he has other sons who are mentioned in the testament, it does not seem probable that Montgarswood was his grandson by a daughter. It would appear, in fact, that this property was an appanage of the eldest, or some other son of Shankston, for soon after the succession of John Campbell of Montgarswood to Shankston, we find a

III. James Campbell of Montgarswood, who, in all likelihood, was either the eldest son or a brother of the preceding. It might be the latter in this instance, for he kept Montgarswood after Shankston had been alienated by the Campbells. He is mentioned in the testament of Hew Crawfurd of Smiddyshaw in 1616. He was cautioner, in 1622, to the executor of Janet Campbell, wife of Arthur Campbell of Auchmannoch; and he is mentioned in the will of Grizzel Crawfurd, relict of umquhile Robert Crawfurd of Nether Possil in 1627. He had a son, who seems to have married a daughter of Campbell of Killoch, about 1654, and who is styled at the time James Campbell, younger, of Montgarswood. The testament of the elder James, who died in 1658, is given in by his son and executor dative 31st Dec. 1661.* This son seems to have succeeded him; but the family does not again appear in any authentic document.

The property has long formed part of the estate of Ballochmyle. It seems to have been early divided into separate possessions. In 1555 James Symyntoun and his wife, Jonet Daw, had a charter of the 4s. land of Montgarswood from James, Commendator of Kelso and Melrose. Symyntoun and his wife were tenants of the land, and the charter sets forth that it was parted with for the purpose of raising money to repair the Monastery.† It is fully as likely, however, that it was alienated because the breaking up of the existing ecclesiastical establishment could not

* Com. Records.
† Session Records.

* Com. Records.
† Chartulary of Melrose.

fail to be seen as close at hand. In 1627 Alexander Paterson, in Burn of Neid, had sasine of the 8s. lands of Montgarswode, called Cultersland, in Kylesmure, on a charter by John Campbell of Schankstoun, dated 2d April 1627, with consent of John, Lord of Loudoun, the superior.*

### REID OF BALLOCHMYLE.

The Reids were at one period a numerous clan in Kyle. Knox speaks of the enemies of the Reformation as endeavouring to create disunion in that quarter, by setting the Reids against the Craufurds," which shows the power the former possessed, the latter being probably the most influential tribe, excepting the Campbells, in that district during the sixteenth century. The first of the name we have met with occurs in the list of " Nobilis Viri," upon an Inquisition held at " Are " on the 10th May 1399,† where " Johannes Reid de Dalrumpill, and Johannes Reid de Barscemyng," are mentioned. From the latter it is probable that most of the numerous families of the surname of Reid in the upper parishes of Ayrshire are descended. Of the Ballochmyle branch we have obtained very scanty notices. The first refers to

I. —— REID of Ballochmyle, whose name occurs in the testament of Robert Harper of Barleith in 1613. He was probably the first lay proprietor of the lands. As there appears from the name, *Ballochmyln*, to have been a mill in connection with the property, it would be amongst the last portions of the lands parted with by the monks.

II. John Reid of Ballochmyle is met with in 1615, in the testament of Alexander Reid, merchant burgess of Glasgow; and again, in 1618, in that of John Reid, burgess of Glasgow.

III. John Reid of Ballochmyle is the next. He had a crown charter of the lands of Ballochmyle, dated 15th March 1634, in which document he is styled " junior of Ballochmyle." His testament was recorded in 1661, " given up by his son, John Reid, now of Ballochmyle, and executour dative."

IV. John Reid of Ballochmyle was admitted a burgess of Ayr, 4th Oct. 1681.‡ His name, along with that of his son, appears frequently in the records of the Kirk Session of Mauchline, after the Revolution, as zealous elders of the kirk. They are invariably designed " Balloch-

myle elder and younger," without any other name or designation. " Kingancleuch," and " Netherplace," are also uniformly to be found along with them in the sederunts. Before that period the Reids were strenuous supporters of the government; and they acquired an odious reputation among the country people as persecutors. The Laird of Colzean and Ballochmyle, according to *Wodrow*, murdered " Gilbert M'Adam, son-in-law of the forementioned James Dun in Benwhat. He had been banished, but had bought his freedom in America, and returned this year. On a Saturday's night, in the house of one Hugh Campbell at Kirkmichael, he was surrounded by Colzean and Ballochmyle, with a company of militia, and when he tried to escape was shot." He was proprietor of Waterhead in Carsphairn, and an ancestor of M'Adam, the road-improver. Ballochmyle had a daughter, *Margaret*, married, in 1681, to John Mitchell of Turnerhill. He died about 1697, and was succeeded by his son,

V. John Reid of Ballochmyle. On 1st February 1688, during his father's lifetime, he had a charter, under the Great Seal, of the lands of Ballochmyle. He married, 22d June 1677, Sarah, daughter of Farquhar of Gilmilnscroft, and by her had four sons, *John*, *Robert*, *Charles* and *James*, and two daughters, *Margaret* and *Sarah*.* It was probably the latter who was married, in 1732, to John Dick of Glasnock. He died early in the eighteenth century, and his son,

VI. John Reid of Ballochmyle succeeded. He appears to have been educated for the Scottish bar, and to have fallen into pecuniary difficulties, for we find " John Reid of Ballochmyle, advocate, prisoner in the Tolbooth " of Ayr, 30th April 1720.† He is mentioned in the parish records of Cumnock as present at the baptism of Sarah, daughter of John Dick of Glasnock, in 1733.‡

Towards the middle of last century the estate was acquired by the Whitefords, who kept it only a few years. *Allan Whiteford* of Ballochmyle appears in a sederunt of heritors at Auchinleck, in 1760. *Sir John Whiteford* of Ballochmyle is mentioned in the parish records in 1776. Sir John was the friend of Burns, and the poet repaid his patronage in kind. Besides lines addressed to Sir John himself, he sung the fare-

---

* Register of Sasines for Ayrshire.
† Chartulary of Melrose.
‡ Ayr Records.

---

* Session Records.
† Ayr Records.
‡ From this circumstance it seems doubtful whether Mrs Dick of Glasnock was his sister or his daughter. If the former, she was born in 1688, consequently rather old to have a child in 1733.

well to Ballochmyle of Maria, his daughter, on leaving the property, which was sold by Sir John in 1786.

## ALEXANDER OF BALLOCHMYLE.

I. ROBERT ALEXANDER of Blackhouse, in the parish of Mearns, resided in Paisley, in the burgh records of which his name occurs frequently early in the seventeenth century. He married Marion Hamilton, by whom he had *James*, his successor, and *Claud* of Newton.

II. Claud Alexander of Newton married, in 1677, Jeane, daughter of William Ralston of that Ilk, and had issue :—

　1. Robert.
　2. Marion, married to Alexander Cochrane of Craigmuir.
　3. Ursula.

III. Robert Alexander of Newton succeeded his father. He married a daughter of his uncle, James Alexander of Blackhouse, and had by her *Claud*, his successor, and a daughter, *Jean*, married to Robert Neilson, merchant in Paisley.

IV. Claud Alexander of Newton married Jean, daughter of Alexander Cuninghame of Craigends, and had issue :—

　1. Robert.
　2. Alexander, who died unmarried.
　3. Claud of Ballochmyle.
　4. Boyd of Southbar, M.P. for Renfrewshire in 1796, and Glasgow in 1802.
　5. John, Major in the 36th regiment. He married his cousin, Jean, daughter of Robert Neilson of Paisley.
　1. Catherine, who died 21st Sept. 1834.
　2. Margaret.
　3. Anna.
　4. Wilhelmina, the lady celebrated by Burns as the "Lass o' Ballochmyle." She died at Glasgow, at an advanced age, in 1843.
　5. Lockart, married to her cousin, Claud Neilson, and had issue.
　6. Lilias.

The eldest brother, Robert, died at Blackhouse in 1795, unmarried. He had previously succeeded to the property.

V. Claud Alexander of Ballochmyle. He went to India in the Civil Service of the Company, and became Auditor-General of army accounts, Paymaster-General, &c. He returned to Scotland in 1786, and took possession of Ballochmyle, which his friends had bought for him in his absence. He married, in 1788, Helenora, eldest daughter of Sir William Maxwell of Springkell, Bart., and by her had

　1. Claud.
　2. William-Maxwell, who succeeded his uncle in Southbar.
　3. Boyd, who married a daughter of Sir John Hobhouse.
　1. Margaret-Maxwell.
　2. Joanna.

　3. Catherine, died in July 1834.
　4. Helena died in childhood.
　5. Mary, married to Jos. Crampton, Yorkshire, and has issue.

He died in 1809, and was succeeded by

VI. Claud Alexander of Ballochmyle, his eldest son, who married Elizabeth, daughter of Colonel Keating, by Lady Martha Brabazon, daughter to the Earl of Meath. They had no issue. She died in 1845, and he the following year, when he was succeeded by his brother,

VII. William M. Alexander of Ballochmyle, who, on obtaining Ballochmyle, relinquished Southbar to his brother, Boyd, now of Southbar.

## REID OF DRUMFORK.

I. MUNGO REID of Drumfork is one of the curators of John Reid of Barskimming in 1577.[*] He was one of the assize on the trial of Jardane of Bernok for the slaughter of Campbell of Over Wellwood in 1609. His son, *Mungo*, died in February 1617, and he was succeeded by his grandson,

II. Mungo Reid of Drumfork, who was served heir of his grandfather (August 16, 1635), in the lands of Drumfork, Brakenhill, and Ballingap, extending to a 3 lib. land of old extent; and in the 17s. 4d. land of Over Logan, in Dalgain parish. It is this laird of Drumfork, we should suppose, whose wife, Isabell Boswell, and her daughter, Marion, appear in the Session records of Mauchline in 1673.

III. Richard Reid of Drumfork had a child baptized in 1757.

These are the only notices we have found of this branch of the Barskimming family. Mungo, the first of Drumfork, seems to have been nearly related to the young laird, probably an uncle or granduncle, he being one of his curators. Part of the property of Drumfork must have been alienated, or perhaps never was possessed by the Reids. A. Dalrymple, minister of Auchinleck, was designated "of Drumfork," previous to 1688.

## REID OF WILLOXHILL.

*James Reid* of Willoxhill was served heir to his father, James Reid of Willoxhill, in the 22s. land of Willoxhill, and the 4s. 8d. land of Rodinghead, in 1604.

*James Reid* of Willoxhill, whose name occurs as a witness to a testamentary deed in 1643, was probably the son of the foregoing.

* Mason's Notes.

This property was afterwards possessed by a family of the name of Millar. *Robert Millar* of Willoxhill was one of the elders of Mauchline for many years previous to the end of the seventeenth century.

## WALLACE OF BRIGHOUSE.

There is a charter from Peter de Curry to the Abbey of Melrose, 1205,* of the lands of Dalhengen (Dalsangan) and Bargour, which lie between the rivulet flowing from the Duveloch (*Anglice*, Black Loch, subsequently Loch Brown) and the Saxnoc (Cesnock), " qui jacent inter rivulem cadentem de Duveloch et Saxnoc." Although it appears rather a loose and indefinite description of boundaries, this simple conveyance was evidently meant to comprehend, under the two names of Dalhengen and Bargour, all the land bounded on the west by the burn running from Loch Brown to the Cesnock, and which the Cesnock itself skirts to the north and east, and as far south-east as to be opposite to Loch Brown in that direction, leaving but a short space between the loch and the river, like the segment of a circle. When their establishment was threatened with destruction by the progress of the Reformation, the monks granted these lands to different parties, among whom the Wallaces of Brighouse, and the Farquhars of Gilmilnscroft, seem to have been the principal. The latter kept their portion, at least the superiority, till 1700, when they were retoured in lands amounting to 50s. of old extent in Over Bargour and Dalsangan. The first of the Wallaces of Brighouse we have met was,

I. WILLIAM WALLACE of Brighouse, who, on the 10th December 1577, " with his awin hand, gaif lifrent stait and sasing of all and haill his lj s. land of Nether Bargour, alias Brighous, with the pertinentis, lyand in the lordschip of Kylesmuir, baillierie of Kylestewart, and shrefdum of Air, to Sibella Stewart, his future spous, personalie present in hir virginitie, in lifrent, for hir lyftyme, be erd and stane, as vs is," &c. Sibella was the daughter of William Stewart of Halrig, and possessed, as her portion, the x s. land of Over Scheelzardis, in Kylestewart. She died in 1627. Her children seem, from her testament, to have been:

1. Robert Wallace, who succeeded.
2. Helen, married to William Wallace of Preistschawis (Prestwickshaws.)
3. Margaret, married to John Cuninghame of Hill.
4. Janet, married to James Hay of Tourlands.

William Wallace of Brighouse was alive in 1614, in which year his name occurs in a testamentary document; but he appears to have died before 1616, his son,

II. Robert Wallace of Brighouse, being then in possession of the property. He is mentioned in the testament of Edward Mure of Park, in 1623.

III. William Wallace of Brighouse.

IV. Hugh Wallace of Brighouse, in 1637, was served heir to his father, William Wallace of Brighouse, in the 40s. land of Brighouse, 5 lib. land of Burnebank and Mossend, 5 merk land of Dollars, 40s. land of Messide, 2 merk land of Whiterig, and 20s. of Riccardton Holms, extending to a 15 lib. land, old extent.

V. John Wallace of Brighouse had a child baptized at Mauchline in July 1676.*

### NETHER BARGOUR.

This property was probably a pendicle of Brighouse. In 1601,

*Hugh Walker* was served heir of his father in the 8s. land of Nether Bargour in Kylesmuir.

*Richard Walker* was served heir of Richard Walker, his grandfather, in the 6s. 8d. land of Nether Bargour, in 1669.

*Hugh Wallace* was served heir, 11th November 1687, to Agnes Walker, relict of —— Wallace in Bargour, his mother, in the 30s. land of Walltoun, and 2d. land of Hawthorn Bank; and on the same day, Hugh Wallace was served heir to his father, —— Wallace in Bargour, in the 8s. 8d. land of Nether Bargour. Hugh Wallace of Bargour is mentioned in the Presbytery records in 1728. He had a child baptized, 26th October 1732.

*Robert Wallace* of Bargour married Elizabeth Blair, of Riccarton parish, in 1779.

The estate of *Rodinghead* is within the boundaries specified in the charter of Peter de Curry, previously referred to, and was doubtless comprehended in Bargour or Dalhangan. It was purchased about the end of last century by *George Douglas*, factor to the Londoun family. At his death he was succeeded by his son, the late *George Douglas* of Rodinghead, who died in March 1850. He married a daughter of Hugh Campbell of Mayfield, by whom he had no issue, and the estate is now the property of Mr Douglas's eldest surviving sister, the wife of Captain Hay, brother to Boyd Hay of Townend.

* Chartulary of Melrose.

* Parish Records,

## MITCHELL OF BRAEHEAD.

I. ANDREW MITCHELL of Braehead.

II. Robert Mitchell of Braehead was served heir, 20th September 1600, to his father, Andrew Mitchell of Braehead, in the 40s. land of Braehead, in Nether Meiklewood; the 8s. land of Mountaineshill; the 4s. land of M'Cleriochstone, in Over Meiklewood; the 8s. 4d. land of Lyik, in Over Meiklewood, called the Hill, "extending to a 9 lib. of old extent;" and in the 8s. land of Haugh, called Damhead; the 40d. land of Dalsaugan; the 8s. land of Grassmilies, and in an annual revenue of £20 from the 40s. land of Kinganeleuch.

III. James Mitchell of Braehead was served heir to his brother-german, Robert Mitchell of Braehead, in the above lands, in 1643. The next we meet with occurs in the session records.

IV. John Mitchell of Braehead, who, March 2, 1673, had a son, *Robert*, baptized.

V. Robert Mitchell of Braehead is "delated," in 1692, before the Kirk-Session for travelling short journeys frequently on the Lord's-day. Subsequently, he is repeatedly called before the Session for "light life and conversation, and breaking the seven command;" but he gives that inquisitorial body great annoyance, by disregarding their summonses, and even, contrary to the spirit of the times, "flouting and scorning" their officer when he cited him. He had his son baptized in 1704, and his name is no more mentioned.

V. Robert Mitchell of Braehead married, in 1739, Margaret Hood, and they had several children baptized before the middle of the century. Their names do not occur in the records after 1750.

Braehead was shortly afterwards acquired by the Auchinleck family, in whose possession it still remains. The other lands possessed by the family belong now either to Sir James Boswell or Mr Alexander of Ballochmyle.

### GIB OF AUCHMILLING.

The Chartulary of Melrose contains a very minute and particular charter, dated 20th Feb., 1555, in favour of the first of the Gibs found in connection with the small property of Auchmilling. After the usual preface, the charter goes on to state that money is required to repair their Place, burnt by our ancient enemies of England, in the time of the last war,[*] and to "give, grant, &c. all and haill the six shilling and eight penny land of old extent of Auchmilling, hitherto subject to the payment, according to rental, of three pennies, in *arreagiis et careagiis*, and in lie bondage silver, to the amount of nine pennies of the usual money of Scotland, with all the houses, places, valleys, moors, lakes, mills, multures and their accompaniments, huntings, fishings, peturies, charcoal, rabbit warrens, dovecots, orchards, brazures, breweries, woods, stones and lime, with mines and carts, *hærezeldo et mercheta mulierum*, and with common pasture, and all the usual liberties named or unnamed, and all privileges and accommodations, paying a feu-duty of 6s. 8d. in *areagiis et careagiis*, and thirty pennies in silver, to our well beloved James Gib in Auchmilling." It is probable that the Gibs possessed the property long before as tenants, without any of those privileges which are here so ostentatiously set forward, as granted and belonging to a small farm. The monks, however, were sagacious enough to append a clause, reserving a right to whatever millstones for the mill, and wood and stones for their place at Mauchline, might be required. The Gibs continued to possess the property until a late period. The next we find is

*Mungo Gib*, who is served heir to his grandfather, James Gib, in the 6s. 8d. land of Auchmilling, in Kylesmure, 30th Aug. 1661. The grandfather, James, was probably the grandson of James who obtained the charter.

*John Gib of Auchmilling* appears, in 1680, in the service of his son,

*John Gib of Auchmilling*, in the 6s. 8d. land of Auchmilling.

*John Gib of Auchmilling* had a child baptized in 1737, and again in 1756. His death is recorded in 1775.

*James Gib of Auchmilling*, had a child baptized in 1778, and died in 1781.

There are several small properties, or farms, of the name of Auchmilling; and there are still descendants of the Gibs in one of them as tenants. So are there also in Mauchline as merchants.

### SPOTTISWODE OF FOWLER.

*William Spottiswode* was denounced, in 1527, as a party concerned in the slaughter of the Earl of Cassillis at Prestwick.[†] He was most likely

---

[*] This must allude to the ruthless spoliation of Evers and Latoun before the battle of Ancrum-mure.
[†] Pitcairn's Trials.

of the Fowler family, as no other of the name appears in the county at that time; and the first that we have found mentioned in connection with the property is in 1581.

*John Spottiswode of Fowler* gives infeftment in that year, as bailie to Mathew Campbell of Loudoun, Knight, of certain tenements in Mauchline, to John Angus; and on the 19th August 1586, at the Temple Court held in Ayr, by "D. Crawfurd, Baillie and Commissar, compeirit personallie Jon. Spottiswode of Fowler, and protestit that ye holding of ye said Court, nor any other court, sould be hurtful to him, ye said Johnne, in his right and title, as he alleges, to the Temple bailliery."[*]

*John Spottiswode of Fowler*, in all likelihood his son, was served heir of Adam Reid of Barskimming, his grandfather, on the mother's side, in the fourth part of the 6 lib. land of Stair Quhyte, called Barskimming. He appears in 1584 as witness to the infeftment, in terms of a marriage contract between Gilbert Kennedy of Dunvene and Margaret, daughter of Hugh Hamilton of Sanquhar, and is there styled "lawful son to John Spottiswode of Fowler."[†]

The testament of *William Spottiswode of Fowlair* is recorded in 1604. His wife's name was Margaret Primrose, by whom he had three sons, *John*, *William*, and *Adam*. His eldest son had been already infeft in all his lands, and he ordains him "to feed, claithe, and sustein the other two whill the time of their perfections, and then to put them to some honest craft, at his awin expences."[‡]

"Fowler Mains" is in the service of *Mariota Richart of Barskimming*, in 1691, and both Fowler and Fowler Mains are now comprehended in the estate of Barskimming.

## VIEWFIELD.

On the south of Mauchline is the residence of the only descendants, in this county, who bear the name of the venerable historian of the Church of Scotland.

*Mr James Wodrow*, long Professor of Divinity in the University of Glasgow, was born, says the Rev. Robert Burns, biographer of the historian, at Eagleshame, on the 2d January 1637. His wife's name was Margaret Hair, daughter of a proprietor in Kilbarchan parish, the name of whose estate is not mentioned, and whose mother was of the family of Stewart of Blackhall. Their second son,

*Robert Wodrow*, was born at Glasgow in 1670, an eventful period in the history of Scotland, the violence of religious and party rancour being then at its height. His mother bore him, according to Dr Burns, in her 51st year. His father, at the time of his birth, was obliged to hide himself from the fury of his persecutors; and when his mother died, which was some years afterwards, it would appear that he was again suspected and watched by them, so that he had to steal into his wife's room, where she was on her death-bed, to obtain a last interview, and with difficulty escaped the clutch of the soldiers. Robert became a student of theology under his father, and was chosen librarian to the College. He soon displayed a talent for historical and biographical inquiry. The study of natural history also attracted his attention in no ordinary degree. On finishing his theological studies, Mr Wodrow left the library of Glasgow, to reside in the family of a distant relation, Sir John Maxwell of Nether Pollock, a Senator of the College of Justice. While there he offered himself for trials to the Presbytery of Paisley, and was licensed to preach in 1703. In the summer following he was ordained minister of Eastwood, in Renfrewshire, in which parish Lord Pollock lived. Although discharging his duties as a minister, both in his parish and in the ecclesiastical courts, in the most exemplary manner, yet he found time to compose his history, which occupied him several years, and was published in two 4to volumes in 1721-2. For a minute and particular account of this work, and the correspondence relating to it, we must refer to the memoir by Dr Burns, who enters fully into the subject. Mr Wodrow married, in 1708, Margaret, daughter of the Rev. Patrick Warner of Ardeer, minister of Irvine. Her mother was a daughter of the celebrated Mr Guthrie of Fenwick. By her he had sixteen children, nine of whom, with their mother, survived their venerable father. Of these—four sons and five daughters—the eldest, *Robert*, was his successor in Eastwood, but he retired from the charge in bad health. He was twice married, and had six or seven children. His eldest son settled in the United States of America; and about thirty years ago, the only surviving daughter went there also with her family. The second daughter of the historian married Mr Biggar, minister of Kirkoswald, and left four daughters, one of whom married the Rev. Mr Inglis, who succeeded her father. Of the other sons, *Alexander* settled in America, along with his elder brother's family, and died during the first years of the revolutionary war. His third son became minister of Stevenston; married Miss Hamilton, daughter of

Mr Gavin Hamilton of Glasgow, and had only one child, a daughter. The second son of the historian was

*Peter Wodrow*, minister of Tarbolton, who married the youngest daughter of Mr Balfour of Pilrig, and had by her

*Robert Wodrow of Viewfield*, father of *William*, the talented and well-known minister of Swallow Street Chapel, London—one who was in every way worthy of his celebrated ancestor. *Robert*, the other son, was a merchant in Glasgow, and was remarkable for his deep research into theological subjects, for his zeal in the cause, and his attention to the duties of religion. They both died some years ago. Of the daughters two survive, *Jane* and *Margaret*, and are now the only representatives of the family bearing the name. *Mary* married the Rev. Mr Thompson, and has issue.

### BEECHGROVE.

To the south of Mauchline is situated this small property, with its mansion-house, the residence of a son of the late Mr Gavin Hamilton, whose name has been destined to go down to posterity in connection with that of Burns as his patron and friend.

"*John Hamilton of Kype*, Clerk to the Regality of Mauchline," (Kylesmure would probably have been more correct, as Mauchline was not a regality,) has the birth of his son, *Gavin*, recorded in the parish register, 27th Dec. 1737. His wife's name was Jacobina Young, daughter of Mr Young, merchant in Lanark.

*Gavin Hamilton*, writer in Mauchline, who is so honourably and so frequently mentioned by the Poet, married, in 1775, Helen, daughter of Kennedy of Daljarrock, and by her had three sons and three daughters:—

1. John, long factor to the families of Loudoun and Portland, who married Miss Paterson of Braehead, by whom he had two sons:
   1. William, married Marjory, daughter of the late William Gordon of Milrig, and had one child, Henrietta. Both Mr and Mrs H. died some years ago.
   2. Gavin, who died in 1840.
   Mr Hamilton married a second time, and now resides chiefly in London.
2. Alexander, married and has issue.

3. Dugald, M.D., married a daughter of John Finlay, of Glasgow, and has two daughters, Mary and Norah. He is proprietor of Beechgrove, in Mauchline; of Catrine Holm, in Sorn; and of Auchtytinch, in Auchinleck parish.

The daughters were, *Wilhelmina*, *Jacobina*, and *Margaret*.

### MOSSGIEL.

This farm, as having once been the residence of the Ayrshire Bard, has acquired a notoriety which perhaps entitles it to be noticed in a work of this kind, though no account can be given of its successive proprietors. The following deed of "backband and service from William Hamilton of Macnairston to ye Abbot and Convent of Melrose," may be interesting:—

"Be it kend, &c. me, William, Hamyltone of Macnairston . . bunden and oblist as above, to ane venerable ffadder, Andro, by permission of God, Abot of Melrose and Caleo [Kelso], &c. fforasmeikle as they have set to me, in feu ferme and heritage all and sundrie the lands of Mossgaviel, with ye pertinents, I am content and consents, by thir presents, fforme, myn heirs and assigns, that I and my friends and our tenants, quhen we happen to be requirit, sall come to ye said venerable fader's, to aid, mak fence, and ride and gang with them, and mak service, and sall tak ye afauld, leel and true pairt in all their gude actions, causes and querels, against all, our Soverane Lord alane exceppit. Signed Wilyem Hamyltone, with my hand. Witnesses, Maister Patrick Ferrers, Thomas Cunday, Thomas Kello." Dated 24th Sept. 1527.

The only other proprietor we have found of Mossgavel, or Mossgiel, in the olden times, is Anabella Wallace, Lady Mossgavil, who is mentioned in the testament of Jonet Dawk, spouse to William Wilson in Lawrieland, "as maistress of ye land," in 1617.

Many anecdotes are related of Burns during his residence at Mossgiel, most of which are already before the public. William Patrick, baron officer at Mauchline, was employed about Mossgiel when Burns was there. He was about ten years of age at the time, and perfectly recollects the Poet, whom he represents as an absent, thoughtful man.

# PARISH OF MAYBOLE.

THE derivation of the name of Maybole is some-what doubtful Chalmers, referring to the char-ter of " Duncan, the son of Gilbert de Galwera,' who, in 1193, gave to God and St Mary of Macl-ros, a certain piece of land in Carrick called *Meybothel*, is of opinion that " the name May-bole is merely an abbreviation of *Maybottle* Botle, in the Anglo-Saxon, signifies a house, or dwelling-place, a farm, a village, and appears in the termination of several names in the south of Scotland The prefix *May*, in Maybottle, may be derived from a man s name or it may be the Anglo-Saxon *Maey*, *May*, signifying a *kinsman*, a *cousin* so *Maybottle* would signify the dwelling of the kinsman or cousin " This is by no means satisfactory, and yet, in support of it, the writer in the new *Statistical Account* says " it may be alleged that several names and usages of this district are undoubtedly Saxon, and to be traced to the period of the Heptarchy, when Galloway and the southern parts of Ayrshire were over-run by the Northumbrians " We should like to know how the writer traces these Saxon names and usages to the Heptarchy! There is, however, so great a similarity between the language and usages of the Celts and Saxons, that they are now considered to have been originally one people But much more likely is it that the names and usages referred to were of later introduction, as in other parts of Scotland, where the Celtic lan-guage has been gradually superseded by the Anglo-Saxon. Carrick was not only originally Celtic, but the Celtic language continued there until comparatively a recent period The ety-mology suggested by Chalmers is not satisfactory —it is not sufficiently characteristic There may have been fifty dwellings of the kinsman in Car-rick—and why should Maybole have been held singular in this respect? Besides, old charters

are not to be regarded as positive authority in matters of derivation. It is more than probable that the charter in question was written by the monks of Melrose themselves, who were foreign-ers, at all events more familiar with the names of localities in the south of Scotland, where the Anglo-Saxon prevailed at an early period, than anywhere else in Scotland The writer of the charter may therefore have spelled Maybole ac-cording to his own idea of its meaning The etymology of places is not to be sought for in a solitary charter, as in this case, but rather in the vernacular pronunciation of the word Now we know that old people used to call May-bole *Minniebole*, and in old writings it is either *Minnyboil* or *Maiboil*, but never *Maybotle*, with the exception of the original charter, where it is *Meybothelbeg* Its derivation is consequently to be sought for in the Celtic, and the writer in the *Statistical Account* himself, attributing it to this source, says, it " will signify the heath ground upon the marsh or meadow, both of which names are so far descriptive of the situation of the town, which stands upon a declivity—no doubt at one time covered with heath, and at the bot-tom of which there is a tract of meadow land which must at one time have also been a marsh " Unfortunately the writer does not give the Gaelic of this very significant and perhaps correct ety-mology A Celtic friend, however, suggests ano-ther meaning *Maigh* (*Mai*, the *gh* in Gaelic being silent), a plain, and *Buile*, a fold for milk cows *Maibuile* would thus signify the fold of the plain *Minniebole*, (properly *Monibuile*), would signify the fold of the hills—*Moni*, in Gaelic, meaning small hills or hillocks Thus *Maibuile-beg* would imply the little fold of the plain The ancient fold consisted of wooden flakes, resembling those now used for turnip-feeding, and the cattle were shifted from place to place, so as to be convenient for manuring the land   Hence the fold would sometimes be on the plain, *Maighbuile*, and sometimes on the table land, or hillocks, *Monibuile*  We do not assert that this is the only correct derivation, but it seems extremely probable, and we are always safest in seeking the etymology of ancient places in the early language of the country.

Maybole originally formed two parishes—*Maybole* and *Kirkbride*  With both combined it comprehends about thirty-four square miles—its greatest length being about nine miles, and its breadth five  It is bounded on the north, and so far on the east, by the river Doon, which divides it from the parishes of Ayr and Dalrymple, on the east and south by Kirkmichael, and the water of Girvan, and on the west by Kirkoswald and the Frith of Clyde

The parish is considerably varied in appearance  Towards the north-east, and stretching along the coast, it is bounded by a ridge of high land, rising about 1000 feet above the level of the sea, called Brown Carrick Hill, forming a kind of natural barrier, besides the Doon, which flows at a short distance, between the coasts of Kyle and Carrick  From this height a magnificent view is obtained both seaward and landward  The rest of the parish is of an undulating character, and has a rich, cultivated aspect  The hill pasture and moorland occur chiefly on the Brown Carrick range of hills, but even these are gradually losing their distinctive character, by the operation of the plough and the spade, and excellent corn and green crops are now raised where recently the heather and whin flourished in all their natural vigour

The only rivers are those of the Doon and the Girvan, which are at the extremes of the parish  There are springs innumerable, however, and several small rivulets, which water the district abundantly  The few small lochs formerly to be found in the parish, have long ago disappeared.

Abercrummie, who wrote immediately prior to the Revolution, describes the parish as " very large and populous, extending from the sea and water of Dun to the water of Girvan, about Dalduffe and westward  Besyde the large church, and Kirkbryde, and other chappells, whereof mention is made above  The Lord Bargany is patron thereof, though he have small or no interest therein. There be a great number of gentry living therein, who have pretty dwellings in commodious places throughout the parish "

HISTORY, CIVIL AND ECCLESIASTICAL

Maybole does not appear in any historical or other document, that we are aware of, prior to the charter of Duncan in 1193  Its history begins with this grant  It is said that of old there was a town in Carrick called *Carrick*, but, unless Turnberry was the site, no other has been condescended upon  Maybole, at all events, does not appear to have existed as a community prior to the grant by Duncan of Carrick  It had not even then a church, and it did not become the capital of Carrick until a much later period  Turnberry, on the contrary, has the first recorded church in Carrick  Even the church of Kirkkryde seems to have existed previously, at all events contemporaneously with that of Maybole, both of which were granted by Earl Duncan to the Cistertian Nunnery of North Berwick—the latter in 1216  This grant was confirmed by Neil, the son of Duncan of Carrick.

" The church of Maybole continued to belong to the nuns of North Berwick till the Reformation  A portion of the revenues of the church was appropriated to the vicarage, which had been established by the Bishop of Glasgow.  In Bagimont's Roll, as it stood in the reign of James V, the vicarage of Maybole, in the Deanery of Carrick, was taxed £5, 6s. 8d, being a tenth of the estimated value  Before the Reformation, the half of the vicarage of Maybole appears to have been annexed to the prebend, called *Saerista Major*, in the Collegiate Church of Glasgow.  In 1562, this part of the vicarage was reported as being only worth ten merks yearly.  At the epoch of the Restoration, the revenues of the parsonage of Maybole, the glebe excepted, were held on lease by Thomas Kennedy of Bargany, for the yearly payment of £22, twenty oxen and twelve cows  In the church of Maybole, a chaplainry, which was dedicated to St Ninian, was founded in 1451, by Sir Gilbert Kennedy of Dunure, who granted to God and to St Ninian, the lands of Largenlen and Brockloch, in Carrick, for the support of a chaplain to perform divine service in the Church of Maybole  On the lands of Auchindrain, which is about three miles north-east of Maybole, there was, before the Reformation, a chapel that was subordinate to the parish church of Maybole " *

The parish of Kirkbride, which was dedicated to St Brigide, also continued in the hands of the Nuns of North-Berwick till the Reformation  It stood on the sea-coast, about half a mile north of the old castle of Dunure  The ruins of the church and churchyard still exist  It does not appear at what time the junction of the two parishes occurred, but it must have been prior to

* Chalmers' Caledonia

1597, in December of which year the church of Maybole was finally separated from the Convent of North Berwick, and established as a rectory, by act of Parliament. Gilbert Kennedy of Bargany obtained a grant of the 40s lands of old extent, which belonged to the church of Maybole, and also of the patronage of the rectory of Maybole, with its tithes. The patronage continued to belong to Lord Bargany till 1696, when it was vested in the Crown.

Alluding to the ecclesiastical state of Carrick, Abercrummie says, " there was also a Collegiat Church at Mayboll, the fabrick whereof is yet extant and entyre; being now used as the burial place of the Earl of Cassillis, and other gentlemen who contributed to the putting a roofe upon it when it was decayed On the north syde of which kirk is the burial place of the Laird of Colaine, within ane enclosure of new square stones, lately built The Colledge consisted of a Rector and three Prebends, whose stalls are all of them yet extant, save the Rector's, which was where these low buildings and the garden are, on the east syde of that which is now the Parson's house. The other three are the Black House, Ja Gray's house, with the orchard, and the Welltrees The patrimony of this church were the Provest (lands) and Priest's-lands, in the parish of Kirkmichael, which fell into the Earl of Cassillis hands, upon the dissolution of the Colledge, at the Reformation, out of which he as yet payes, yearly, to the minister of Mayboll, the sum of 70 merks Scots As for the Church, its present patrimony is out of the tyth of the parish, which, before the Reformation, was all possessed and enjoyed by the Nuns of North Berwick, and on the dissolution of the said Nunnerie became a prize to the Laird of Bargany The present church stands at a little distance from the forsaid Colledge, eastward It does not appear when it was built,[*] but the large Isle, that lyes from the body of the church southward, and makes the figure T, was built by Mr Ja Bonar, minister thereat, in the reign of King Charles the First Within the said parish of Mayboll there have been other chapells of old, as Kirkbryde on the coast syde, whose walls and yard be yet extant, and within the lands of Auchindrain and elsewhere, there have been other chappells, whereof the *rudera* are yet to be seen "

" The schoole," continues Abercrummie, " is upon the east end of the church, separated from it by a partition of timber, wherein doors and windows open not only a prospect into the church, but opportunity of hearing to the greatest distance."

The church which Abercrummie thus describes was superseded by a new building in 1755. It was a large but mean-looking structure, situated near the heart of the town. This again gave way to a more elegant place of worship, which was erected to the eastward of the town, in 1809 It was rather extensively repaired in 1830, and is calculated to hold about 1200 Some years ago a church was opened at Fisherton, not far from the old parish church of Kirkbride, which is a great accommodation to the parishioners in that quarter

Of the rise and progress of the town of Maybole we have no account whatever until the time of Abercrummie, who gives a very interesting description of it as it existed previous to the Revolution " In all this countrey there is not any town corporat, save one, viz Mayboll, which is neither a burgh royal, for it sends no commissioner to Parliament, nor is it merely a burgh of barony, such having only a power to keep mercats, and a magistracy settled amongst them, in dependence on the baron of the place But here it is quyte otherwyes, for they have a charter from the King, erecting them into a burgh, with a toune-councell of sixteen persons, for managing the common concernes of the burgh, with power to them to elect from amongst themselves two baillies, their clerk and treasurer, and to keep courts for maintaining order amongst the inhabitants, and to admit burgesses of their Corporation [*] It is true, indeed, the Erle of Cassillis is the superior of all the land whereupon the town is built, but they deny him to be their superiour, in their constitution as a burgh, and disputed their right with him During the dependence of which action, he, is baron, sett up a baron baillie, to exercise authority over the inhabitants, and to lessen the magistrates' authority, but the people being poor and divided amongst themselves, and the Erle being gott into the government, upon the Revolution, they were forced to submit and yield to his pretensions

" This toune of Mayboll stands upon an ascending ground, from east to west, and lyes open to the south It hath one principall street, with houses upon both sydes, built of free-stone; and it is beautifyed with the situation of two castles,

---

[*] It was built after the Reformation, by the Earl of Cassillis, out of the Kirkmichael lands, aided by private contributions

[*] Maybole was created a burgh of barony 14th November 1516, in a grant to Gilbert Earl of Cassillis, the patron, and to the provost and prebendaries of the Collegiate Church of Maybole, to which belonged the lands whereon the town is situated In October 1639, an act, ordaining that the head courts of Carrick should be held at Mayboll, was passed by the Lords of the Articles

one at each end of this street. That on the east belongs to the Erle of Cassillis; beyond which, eastward, stands a great new building, which be his granaries. On the west end is a castle, which belonged sometime to the Laird of Blairquhan, which is now the tolbuith, and is adorned with a pyremide, and a row of ballesters round it, raised upon the top of the stair-case, into which they have mounted a fyne clock. There be four lanes which passe from the principall street; one is called the Back-Venall, which is steep, declining to the south-east, and leads to a lower street, which is far larger than the high chiefe street, and it runs from the Kirkland to the Welltrees; in which there have been many pretty buildings, belonging to the severall gentry of the countrey, who were wont to resort thither in winter, and divert themselves in converse together at their owne houses. It was once the principall street of the toune; but many of these houses of the gentry have been decayed and ruined, it has lost much of its ancient beautie. Just opposite to this venall, there is another that leads north-west from the chiefe street to the green, which is a pleasant plott of ground, enclosed round with an earthen wall, wherein they were wont to play at foot ball, but now at the gowffe and byasse-bowls. At the east end of the principall street are other two lanes; the one called Foull Venall, carryes northward; the other farder east, upon the chiefe street, passes to the south-east, and is called the Kirk-Venall, and is the great resort of the people from the toune to the church. The houses of this toune, on both sydes the street, have their severall gardens belonging to them; and in the lower street there be some pretty orchards, that yield store of good fruit."

The description thus given by Abercrummie, nearly two hundred years ago, presents a minute picture of Maybole even at the present time. The town has no doubt grown to some extent during so long a period, but not in proportion to many other places in the county, comparatively of modern date. On the east the town is no longer bounded by the castle, and the Earl of Cassillis' granaries. The castle, no doubt, occupies its original site, but an elegant range of buildings, called the New Yards, extend the line of houses very considerably in that quarter. On the west, Whitehall, and a number of recent buildings, have produced a similar extension; while upon the north and south the sides of the town have been swelled by numerous houses, shops, and villas. The introduction of cotton-weaving into Maybole during the last century occasioned a vast increase of the population, by the rapid influx of Irish families; and it may be

said to have wholly lost that aristocratic charac-ter, the decline of which Abercrummie deplores even in his time.

The civil jurisdiction of Carrick was a bail-liary, belonging heritably to the Earl of Cassillis, and, as already mentioned, Maybole was the or-dinary seat of the courts of justice. Capital punishments were repeatedly inflicted at these courts, and the Gallow Hill is still pointed out as the place of execution.

The well-known disputation between John Knox and the Abbot of Crossraguel took place in the house of the Provost of Maybole in 1562.

The parochial records extend no farther back than the beginning of last century. The proba-bility is that they were carelessly kept, and have disappeared.

Among the ministers of Maybole may be men-tioned Dr Macknight, the author of many stan-dard works. He was admitted minister of May-bole in 1753, the duties of which office he faith-fully discharged for sixteen years. He was suc-ceeded by Dr Wright, who was highly esteemed, and who published a volume of sermons.

Mr James Bonnar, of whom *Wodrow* tells the following anecdote, was minister of Maybole about the middle of the seventeenth century: "April 1724. He [Wodrow's informer] tells me that Mr James Bonnar, minister of Maybole, was a poet,* and wrote severall inscriptions on houses; particularly one in the year 1649, which I have forgot. That Mr James Richmond, who was a compresbiter [co-presbyter], I think with Mr Bonnar, told him that a little before Mr Bonnar's death, he came to the Presbytery of Air, and took a very solemn farewell of them, as being never more to meet with them in Presbitery; and he took every one of them by the hand in a most kind manner, save Mr Robert Wallace of Barnweil, whom he refused to take by the hand, telling him that he would be a traitor to the in-terests and kingdom of Christ; and he was the only member of the Presbitery of Air who con-formed to Episcopacy, and was made Bishop of Argyle."

A Mr Fairweather was minister of Maybole in 1717. He came before the Presbytery, on a charge of drunkenness, and his case seems to have occupied that reverend body for a great length of time. The evidence led is curious, as illustrative of the habits of his parishioners at the time. Wine, brandy, and ale, were the favourite beve-rages of the better sort; and it was nothing un-common for the minister and some of the neigh-

* Mr John Bonnar, schoolmaster of Ayr, about 1631, was a poet, and gives a poetical account of a voyage from Bangour, in Ireland, to the port of Ayr.

bouring lairds to spend the greater part of the day " birling at the wine," in one or other of the snug hostelries of Maybole. Alexander Kennedy of Drummellan, aged about forty, was a witness in the case of Mr Fairweather. Was with him in Mr M'Clymont's shop in Maybole, about eight in the morning. Between three persons they had two chopins of ale, and two gills of whisky. David Kennedy of Drummellan, aged about seventeen, another witness, convoyed Mr Fairweather from his father's house on the day libelled. His face was ruddier, and his eye duller, while his tongue faultered. On leaving the gate observed him stagger, but whether from drink or a stone could not say.

### ANTIQUITIES.

There can be no doubt that the Romans traversed the parish. Galloway, of which Carrick formed part, as well as Cuninghame and Kyle, were subjected to their arms. A spear-head of bronze, dug up in the farm of Drumbeg, and a small image, of the same metal, representing Justice, with her equal weights, found in the farm of Drumshang, attest the presence of the Roman legions.

There are various encampments in the parish, and traces of others, enclosed by mounds of earth. Though they may have been British fortlets, of the Roman period, it is probable that they were connected with more recent wars — the invasions of the Irish, or the Danes and Norwegians. On the farm of Trees there is a very distinct encampment, and also on the brow of the eminence near Dunduff Castle.

There are several large standing stones within the bounds of the parish, but no remains of a Druidical circle, so far as we are aware. One is to be seen on the farm of Doonbank, not far from the river Doon, and may have been set up in memory of a battle. Abercrummie says: " There is also upon the descent of *Broun-Carrick-Hill*, near to the mains of Blairstoune, a big whinstone, upon which there is the dull figure of a cross, which is alledged to have been done by some venerable churchman, who did mediat a peace twixt the King of the Picts and the Scots; and to give the more authority to his proposals, did in their sight, by laying a cross upon the stone, imprint that figure thereon." Such was, apparently, the tradition when Abercrummie wrote. It has also been attributed to Wallace as well as Bruce. The stone, which may at one time have been standing, lies apparently in the same position it did in Abercrummie's time.

Tumuli are frequently to be met with in the parish, a good specimen of which exists on the farm of St Murrays.

As previously mentioned, there are several remains of religious houses in the parish. The walls of the Church of Kirkbride, with the surrounding burying-ground, still remain; and an adjoining field bears the name of the Priest's Land. The ruins of the collegiate church of Maybole are still in existence, as well as two of the residences of the priests, the Black House and Well Trees, while the orchards that surround others of the fraternity are well known. " The collegiate church is used as a burying-ground by the family of Cassillis and others, who formerly contributed to its repair. It was, nevertheless, allowed to fall into a most ruinous and filthy condition, from which it was only rescued by the public spirit of Mr Andrews, and the inhabitants of Maybole, who, a few years ago, by subscription, surrounded it with a wall, and tastefully laid out and planted the enclosure." *

" Besides the dwellings of the ecclesiastics and the Earl of Cassillis, commonly designated in these days the King of Carrick, the following houses of the gentry still remain: the present tolbooth, the town residence of the lairds of Blairquhan; the house of Sir Thomas Kennedy of Culzean [possessed by the late Mr Niven of Kirkbride]; the house of Kennedy of Ballemore, in the Kirk Wynd; the garden of Eden, the house of the Abbots of Crossraguel, &c., extending, according to some, to the number of twenty-eight." †

St Helen's Well, to the north of Balloch Mount, was, in Roman Catholic times, famous for the cure of unthriving children, at the change of the quarter, more particularly at May-day. This superstition long outlived the downfal of the Popish religion; and even in the remembrance of persons now alive, the well used to be surrounded by visiters on May-day. The well at Pennyglen Cross also enjoyed a high reputation for the cure of the muir-ill in cattle, and its waters used to be carried to great distances for that purpose.

There are the remains of a number of the ancient seats of the feudal chiefs of the district— more than is to be found in any other parish of the county. These speak of an epoch gone by, and are still a marked and interesting feature of the country. They refer to a period when there were few stone houses in the country, and the land unenclosed. " Within the last forty years," says the writer in the *Statistical Account*, " there was scarcely a hedge, the greater part of the land was in pasture, and the only crops were oats,

---

* Statistical Account. † Ibid.

bear, and a few pease and beans." In such an apparently barren land as this, the stately castles or mansions of the proprietors, with their orchards, gardens, and old trees, planted in the choicest situations, must have had a peculiar effect. But there is probably exaggeration in the averments of most of our statists, in contrasting the low state of agriculture in past times with its present improvement. The writer already quoted elsewhere says: "It is little more than thirty years since wheat began to be partially cultivated; and it has only been raised within the last twenty years." If this is correct, agriculture must have fallen very low during the seventeenth century; for there can be no doubt that Abercrummie's account of Carrick gives a very different idea of its riches and fertility. Indeed, it is quite certain that wheat was cultivated in Carrick during the *sixteenth* century. In the testament of Lady Baltersan, in 1530, elsewhere given, so much *wheat*, as a legacy, is distinctly mentioned; and the various items of the document bespeak a degree of agricultural prosperity not to be expected from such statements as we have quoted. It is probable, at the sametime, that agriculture retrograded after the Reformation, in consequence of the civil wars and disturbances, and the removal of the priesthood, who were the great promoters of husbandry.

*Dunure.*—This, we should think, is one of the oldest family residences in the parish of Maybole. It is thus noticed by Abercrummie :—" This countrey is the ancient seat of the Kennedies, whose principall dwelling was the castle of Dunure, standing on the seasyde, in a rockie shoar, in the parish of Mayboll, and gives a designation to a baronie lying round about it; but this being wholly ruined, their chief mansion is the house of Cassillis," &c. The site of the castle is at once delightful and secure. The shore is studded with rocks, sufficiently large to interrupt the access of enemies seaward, while the beach is beautifully indented with little sandy bays of the most inviting description for sea-bathing. The castle itself occupies the whole of the cliff upon which it is built, the outer wall, towards the sea, appearing as a continuation of the rock itself, while the mass of the building extends landward as far as convenience and safety seem from time to time to have dictated. Assault by land was cut off by a draw-bridge, and the outline of the moat may still be traced; while the anchorage of the boat, used for pleasure or necessity by the inhabitants of the castle, is still to be seen at the foot of the turnpike leading down to the sea. From the style of the building—

having an eye to safety more than ornament—Dunure may be regarded as one of those strongholds supposed to have been built by the Vikingr. Indeed the author of the " Historie of the Kennedyis" attributes the building of the castle to the Danes. He says—

" The Black Book of Scone sets their (the Kennedies) beginning to be in the reign of King Malcolm the Second, who was crowned in the year of God 1010 years, and was the fourscore King of Scotland. There was with the King one M'Kenane of the Isles, who was slain by Danes at the battle of Murink; and of him came the M'Kenane of the Isles, who bruikis the lands of Strowordell to this hour. This M'Kenane of the Isles' succession was at the time of King Donald's reign, when the Danes got possession of the whole Isles, banished by them into Ireland, where he remained to the reign of King Alexander the Third, and then came to King Alexander before the battle of Largs, with threescore of his name and servants; and after that King Acho was defeated, he fled to Ayr, and there took shipping. The principal Man that pursued him was M'Kenane, with his two sons; and after that the King of Danes was received in the Castle of Ayr, M'Kenane followed on a Lord or great Captain of the Danes, to a crag in Carrick, whereon there was a strength built by the Danes, low by the sea side; the which strength M'Kenane and his sons took, and slew the captain and all that was therein. For the which deed, this M'Kenane got the same strength from King Alexander, with certain lands lying thereto; the which he gave to his second son, and there was the first beginning of the name of Kennedy in the mainland. On the strength and crag there is now a fair castle, which the chiefs of the lowland Kennedies took their style of for a long space, and were called Lairds of Dunure, because of the don of the hill above that house.[*] *Of this house the rest of that name are coming.*"

This account of the origin of the Kennedies, and their acquisition of Dunure, is unquestionably fabulous, for it is clear enough that there were Kennedies in Carrick long before the battle of Largs. It is also presumable that the barony of Dunure belonged to Duncan, Earl of Carrick, who granted the church of Kirkbride to the Nuns of Berwick between 1225 and 1230, Kirkbride being situated about half a mile north of Dunure Castle, and that John de Kennedy, who married the heiress of Sir Gilbert de Carrick, acquired the castle and barony of Dunure in a very legal and peaceful manner. Still it is rare that tradition is wholly at variance with fact. The similarity in the ancient armorial bearings is presumptive that the island and mainland Kennedies were of the same stock. In the Highlands there are several small clans of the name of Kennedy—in Gaelic, M'Urick or M'Roriet[†]— and it is rather a striking coincidence that the isolated conical mount on which the flag-staff is erected at Dunure, near the mouth of the harbour, is called *Port-Rorie,* evidently meaning the port of M'Crorie or Kennedy.

There can be no doubt that Dunure Castle was

---

[*] In Gaelic the name signifies the hill or fort of the yew tree.

[†] There are M'Rories in Carrick.

an early residence of the main branch of the Kennedies. The house of Cassillis, after the acquisition of that barony by Sir John Kennedy, became the principal seat, though Dunure, still maintained for its strength, continued to be a place of no small importance during the feudal conflicts in Carrick. Here, in the "Black Vout" (vault), the Abbot of Crossraguel, Allan Stuart, was subjected to a process of compulsion peculiarly illustrative of the insecure state of society at the time. The "roasting of the Abbot," as the circumstance was designated, took place on the first and seventh days of September 1570. The castle was taken by the friends of the Abbot on this occasion, and held for sometime, in defiance of the most desperate attempts of the Master of Cassillis to regain it. The castle has probably been in ruins since the middle of the seventeenth century, as Abercrummie speaks of it as "wholly ruined" in his time. From the calcined appearance of more than one part of the building, it was in all likelihood destroyed by fire. Amid the mass of ruins it would be vain to attempt to identify the "Black Vout" wherein the Abbot was roasted. The whole under buildings seem to have been vaulted, and the adventurous antiquary may possibly push his way into more than one apartment where the "iron chimney" and the fire to which the soles of the Abbot were bound, might have been placed. In former times, we need scarcely remark, the grate in such places stood in the centre of a spacious square or oblong chimney, along three of the sides of which stone seats were arranged, so as to admit of a large number of persons sitting round the fire. The fourth side of the square was left open, so as to communicate light and heat to the rest of the apartment. The castle as well as the barony of Dunure have been in the possession of the Kennedies of Dalquharran since the beginning of last century.

*Greenan Castle.*—This is the only other feudal residence in the parish of Maybole which overhangs the sea. It is situated upon a bold perpendicular cliff, about three miles south-west from the town of Ayr, and within a short distance of the junction of the Doon with the sea. "The Greenand," says Abercrummie, "is a high house upon the top of a rock, hanging over upon the sea, with some lower new work, lately added to it, but never finished. It is too open to the cold and moisture, arysing from the sea, to be a desyreable habitation, and has been designed to be the owner's security against a surprise, rather than a constant residence." The "lower new work" has been wholly removed, and nothing

remains but the ruins of the tower—"a small square building—more resembling a keep than a castle—about fifty feet in height; the lower, or ground story, forming an arched, and totally dark dungeon. . . As seen from the suburbs of Ayr, in the dusk of a summer evening, jutting out upon its craggy eminence, and yet appearing as if indented in the bosom of Carrick Hill, with the ocean flowing to its base, it forms an interesting feature in the 'beautiful romance of nature' which surrounds it:

"It frowns upon the steep,
    Like a monarch, grey and grim;
To its feet the mighty deep
    Bears a never-failing hymn;
And proudly o'er the billow
    Looks the tower, the sunshine through,
When the sailor, on his pillow,
    Dreams of home, and love so true.

"I have heard the rude winds railing
    O'er the bosom of the sea,
And the mariner assailing
    In their mischief-making glee;
But, disdainful, through the haze—
    While the drift flies gloomy past,
And the frightened seaman prays—
    Frowns the ruin on the blast.

*      *      *      *      *

"Old Time, with heedless hand,
    In the city and the wood,
Strews oblivion's darkest sand
    O'er the lonely and the good;
And they moulder on the hill,
    And they fade within the heart;
But the ruin lingers still,
    Though the fair and young depart!"*

The tower is not very old, at least the letters and figures "J. K. 1603," appear over the door-way. John Kennedy was the proprietor at the time, and it is probable that the tower was wholly built by him. At the same time, there is little doubt that some similar stronghold existed on the spot long previously. Mention is made of the castle in the reign of William the Lion, in a grant of the Doon fishings to the Abbey of Melrose. It was then the property of *Roger de Sculebroc*, a vassal of Duncan, Earl of Carrick. In 1510, it is mentioned as "his own mansion-house," in a notarial deed by Thomas Davidson, dated 1st July of that year; and in various other documents it is shown that the barony of Greenan had a tower, or other place of residence, before the date of present fabric. On the day of his slaughter, near the Duppill burn, 12th May 1602, the Laird of Culzean called, in passing, on his kinsman, John Kennedy, at the Greenan, which shows that the proprietor resided there the year before the date over the door of the tower. It is probable that the murder of Culzean, and the disturbed state of

---

* From verses addressed to Greenan Castle, in a small volume of poems published at Ayr in 1845.

the district, arising out of the family feuds of Carrick, induced Kennedy either to build or substantially repair the tower, as a place of safety. That he repaired it only seems probable from the fact that, when Thomas Davidson, in 1576, disponed the barony to Paul Reid, he had " heretabill stait and susing of all and haill the fourtie shilling laud of the Manis of Grenane, with *tour, fortalice, zairdis,*" &c.

The other " pretty dwellings" in the parish of Maybole, enumerated by Abercrummie as existing and inhabited in his time, are—*Dalduffe, Kilhenzie, Auchinwind, Bogend, Smithstoune, Monkwood, Donine* (Dunncane), *Knockdone, Sauchry, Craigshean, Beoch, Garrihorne, Dunduffe,* " a house on the coast never finished," *Glenays, Newark, Bridgend, Blairstoune,* and *Auchindraine.* Of these,

*Dunduffe* still exists in its unfinished state. It had been designed, apparently, to form an oblong square tower of considerable magnitude. The walls are as high as the second story, which seems to have been intended for the dining-room. The windows are large, and the apartment has, even in its unfinished and ruinous state, a light and pleasant appearance. The site of the castle, on the range of hills not far from Dunure, commands a beautiful prospect. The ruins do not seem older than the middle of the seventeenth century. " Near the Castle of Dunduff," says the *Statistical Account,* " a coin of Albert and Elizabeth of Bruges and Brabant, about the size of a crown piece, was lately turned up by the plough. It bears no date, but as they reigned about 1630, its existence in the locality may readily be accounted for in various ways. It was then common for Scotsmen to enlist in the service of the Low Countries, and it may have been part of the earnings of years of hardship, brought back to his native spot by some veteran soldier. Smuggling was also extensively carried on, and it was not uncommon also to pay soldiers serving in the country in foreign money." The writer might have ventured on another suggestion. It was customary to pay workmen, as well as soldiers, in foreign money, and the relic in question may have been part of the pay of some honest craftsman employed in the building of the castle. The age of the unfinished walls, and that of the coin, appear to agree.

*Newark Castle, as it existed previous to the recent additions and improvements.*—The old baronial residence of Newark—now the property of the Marquis of Ailsa—is delightfully situated at the base of the range of hills which distinguish the coast of Carrick from that of Kyle, a short distance south of the Doon. It is still in a habitable condition, though the feudal pomp of former times has long departed from it. Secluded amongst trees, the turrets of the castle are alone observable from the public road. The avenue leading to it—upwards of a quarter of a mile in length—must have been, when in good repair, a very pleasant approach, shaded as it is by tall and beautiful specimens of the ash and pine—the latter exhibiting many fantastic freaks of nature in their growth and form. The castle, originally a single square tower, in the style of those places of strength which began to spring up throughout the country in the eleventh century, is built on a rock, rising gently above the surrounding surface, but at the same time affording ample means of defence, according to the system of warfare which then prevailed. It was surrounded by a moat—only recently filled up—with a drawbridge; and a small streamlet, which now winds past the knoll, supplied the fosse with water. The tower, including the arched keep, consists of four stories, and was ascended, prior to the improvements subsequently made, by an inside spiral stair of very narrow dimensions. The entrance from the drawbridge appears, in olden times, to have been through a portion of the rock. Of the age or history of the building, few particulars, we believe, are extant.

In the " Historie of the Kennedyis," mention is made of the property of Newark as connected with the origin of a deadly fend between the houses of Cassillis and Bargany :—

" There was ane Blak Bessie Kennedy, quha was mareyit first to the Gudmanne of Dinchame; and thanne to the Lord of Colzeane, the Vastor; and to hir third gudmanne, Williame Kennedy of Bronistoune, Baillie of Carrick, quha infeft hir in his sex pund land of Bronistoune. This Bessie Kennedy was fader-sister to the Laird of Bargany, and moder-sister to the Tutour of Cassillis. Scho, being ane widow, held house in this Bronistoune. But befoir hir infeftment, the Baillie of Carrik had infeft the Erll of Cassillis in the samin land; and my Lord had infeft his wyff, Deame Mary Lyone, in the samin lands: And scho, being mareyitt to Johne Lord Hammiltoune, quarrellit this Bessie Kennedyis infeftment, and entirit in proces with hir, befoir the Lordis. The quhilk scho perseaffing, come to her broder-sone, the Laird of Bargany, and gaiff him hir rycht of Bronistoune. For the quhilk, he infeft hir in his sex pund land of New-Wark; he gettand the possessione, in his persone, of Bronistoune, possessit hir in the wther. And eftir ane lang and trubillsume pley, decreitt passis in my Ladyis fauouris, agains the Laird of Bargany ; and remowis him fra the landis of Bronistoune. And he, being remowitt, alledgis that this Blak Bess suld warrand the lands to him, scho being his fader-sister, and haffing dne lewing of her first gudemanne, to interteny hir in the possessione of the New-Wark, and gaiff hir intertenyment in his bons. He wussit na ordour of law agains hir, becaus that scho, being his fader-sister, thocht that nane wald cum betuix him and hir. Scho being content, in ane manner, scho remaynit with him ane lang speace, wnto sik tyme as Sir Thomas Kennedy of Colzeane persuadit hir fra him; and on fair speichis mowit hir to

mak him, quha wes hir sister-sone, assignay to that con-
track. And he, on his assignacioune, maid intimatioune
to the Laird of Bargany, quha was far offenditt with him,
that suld haue melfitt betuix him and hir, quha was hir
awin; and he knew that he had done him, in his distreesis,
(mekil gud seruice?")

From this transaction, which took place probably
about 1580, it would appear that the "sex pund
land of New-Wark" belonged to the Bargany
family. After the death of "Old Bargany," the
Laird of Culzean—the Hon. Thomas Kennedy—
who was tutor to the Earl of Cassillis, "raist
summondes on his auld assignationne, quhilk, as
ye hard, he had gottin fra this Blak Bessy, of the
landis of New-Warke,"—and the young Laird of
Bargany "nocht being acqueintit with the lawis,"
allowed decreet to pass against him for "tuelf
thousand merkis for the byrunnis, quhilk war
awand to hir befoir hir deceise." This, however,
Culzean did not put into execution, but kept it
above young Bargany's head as "ane aw-band,"
which gave the latter great offence, and was the
beginning, according to the author of the "Historie," of those tragical events which Sir Walter Scott has immortalised in the well-known tragedy of "Auchindrane."

The property of Newark, thus acquired by
Culzean, appears to have very soon passed into
other hands. Mure of Auchindraine, as stated
in the "Historie," already quoted, being "har-
dyest persewit off ony of all the friendis" supposed to have been engaged in the murder of Sir
Thomas Kennedy on the 11th May 1602, "left
his awin house and zeid to the Newark, quhilk
was but ane myll different fra Auchindrayne."
Newark was at this period—or at all events
shortly afterwards—possessed by one Duncan
Craufurd, a friend of Mure's. Auchindraine made
a narrow escape on this occasion. The Master
of Cassillis, brother and heir apparent, having
entered into a bond with the Earl, dated 3d September 1602, to "taik the Laird of Auchindrayne's lyf," posted himself, with sixteen horsemen, at the "bak of the Neworkhill," in the
hope of coming upon him as he passed between
the two houses; but the Lady Auchindraine observing them, sent intelligence to her husband of
his danger. Immediately apprising some of his
"friendis in Air" of the circumstance, Auchindraine was soon at the head of a party equal in
number to that of the Master of Cassillis, with
whom he marched against him, and caused him
to "reteir with schame."

A tradition is current that Queen Mary, on
her retreat towards Galloway, after the battle of
Langside, slept the first night of her journey at
Newark. The distance from the field of contest
renders the fact probable; but the apartment

pointed out as Queen Mary's room appears not
to have been then in existence. A tablet above
the main entrance bears the following inscription:
"James Craufurd and Anna Kennedy was married upon the last day of June 1687. They
bought and possessed this house the said yeir.
J. C. A. K." It is presumable, from the tablet,
that the more modern portion of the castle was
erected at the period recorded. It consists of a
large addition to the tower, after the mansion-
house fashion then prevailing, by which the square
of the building became greatly extended, and the
court and court-houses enlarged. A new and
spacious stair, in front of the eastern wall, superseded the former low and obscure entrance; and
portions of the interior flight of steps were altered
and widened, so as to afford access to both the
old and new apartments of the house. But the
improvements effected by the proprietors were
not limited to the castle. Abercrummie says:
"Not far from it (Greenand) lyes the House of
Newark, a good old castle, south-east from the
other; much improved of late by the enclosing
ground for a park, and a well planted orchard."
Prior to this, the castle would appear to have
been a rude unadorned stronghold, with neither
enclosure nor woods, save a few trees, some of
which still exist, and prove by their age the antiquity of the place. The avenue, as well as the
greater part of the wood around the house, was,
in all likelihood, planted about 1687. In the
"Historie of the Kennedyis," it is stated that
when Mure was threatened by the Master of
Cassillis, he went to Newark, because "his hous
of Auchindrayne was inveireyit (environed) with
woidis," thereby implying that such was not the
case at Newark, and that, consequently, he could
not be so easily taken by surprise.

There yet remain many vestiges of the "well
planted orchard" at Newark, and of the taste
displayed by its possessors, "James Craufurd
and Anna Kennedy." Amongst others, there are
one or two walnut trees, which occasionally bear
fruit; but the most remarkable object is a horse-
chesnut, believed to be the finest in Scotland.
That it is very old is unquestionable. It originally branched out into three gigantic arms, but
one of them, it is much to be regretted, was cut
away a number of years ago, by a gentleman who
then occupied the house, because it happened to
spread over his favourite walk in the garden, and
he being very corpulent, could not be troubled
bending as he passed! The trunk of the tree
measures about twenty-two feet in circumference.
There are, besides, two admirable specimens of
the Scots fir, the largest of which may be about
twelve feet in girth. Near the grand stair of

the castle stands the *Dule-tree*, a noble ash, measuring about fifteen feet round. It has five principal branches, and is altogether beautifully proportioned. The popular opinion is, that the *Dule-tree*, common to all baronial residences, derived its name from being the *doom* tree, whereon the condemned of the baron's own retainers, or his enemies, suffered punishment; and Sir Walter Scott gives countenance to the belief in the following anecdote of the last of the Auchindraine family:—

> There was in the front of the old castle a huge ash-tree called the "Dule-tree (mourning-tree) of Auchindraine, probably because it was the place where the Baron executed the criminals who fell under his jurisdiction. It is described as having been the finest tree in the neighbourhood. This last representative of the family of Auchindraine had the misfortune to be arrested for payment of a small debt; and, unable to discharge it, was preparing to accompany the messenger (bailiff) to the jail of Ayr. The servant of the law had compassion for his prisoner, and offered to accept of this remarkable tree as of value adequate to the discharge of the debt. "What!" said the debtor; "Sell the Dule-tree of Auchindraine! I will sooner die in the worst dungeon of your prison!"

With all deference to authority so great as that of the Author of *Waverley*, we are inclined to believe that the *Dule-tree* was set apart for a very different purpose. In Gaelic the *dun deurshuil* (knoll of the tearful eye,) signifies a place where the clan usually assembled to bewail any misfortune that befel the community. The *Dule-tree*—or the tree of sorrow—in the Lowlands is the synonime of the Highland knoll. Under its branches the members of the baron's family congregated, on occasions of particular lamentation, to give expression to their feelings. As illustrative of this, it is known that when David, first Earl of Cassillis, fell at the battle of Flodden in 1513, his fate was deplored for many days by his friends and adherents under the *Dule-tree* in front of Cassillis House. Had there been no more sacred associations connected with the *Dule-tree* at Auchindraine than that it had served the purpose of a gallows, it is scarcely possible that the last representative of the family would have felt so indignant at the proposal to cut it down. Besides, the seat of justice, in the bailliery of Carrick, was at Maybole, where the Gallow Hill still indicates the place of execution.

The Castle of Newark, with the barony—consisting, perhaps, of a thousand acres—came latterly into the hands of the Cassillis family by purchase; and it is averred that the cuttings of the wood of Dalrymple at the time realized more than sufficed to pay for it. The Castle was a favourite resort of David, the tenth Earl, who died unmarried in 1792. It is said he felt so much attached to the locality that he at one time contemplated building an entire new mansion on the spot in preference to Culzean. His intention has been so far carried into effect by the present Marquis, who has recently made extensive additions to the old castle, and otherwise improved and beautified the place.

Newark Hill, forming part of the tract of high land previously described, rises nearly one thousand feet above the level of the sea. The ascent, though occasionally abrupt, is by no means precipitous, and the aspect of the whole is delightfully picturesque. The hand of improvement, however, has done much to pair down the natural ruggedness, and to soften its asperities. Prior to 1825—at which period the Castle and farm of Newark were taken upon lease by Captain Campbell—the hill was clothed in all its native wildness; the greater portion of it being covered with broom, whin and bramble—the haunt of numerous game—while various small lochs of water lay embosomed in the hollows, even to the highest range. A few cattle and sheep alone found scanty pasturage on the hill, and though let, in connection with the arable lands, at a nominal rent of ten shillings an acre, it was not worth much above five. No sooner had Captain Campbell obtained possession than he commenced the work of regeneration in earnest. Between Martinmas 1825 and the following summer he had upwards of fifty acres, densely covered with whin, cleared away, and laid off into fields—intersected with young hedges—while drains were cut in all directions to carry off the water from the spungy portion of the ground. Besides uprooting and burning extensive tracts of bramble and whins, the lessee contributed greatly to the amenity of the locality, as well as added to the number of arable acres, by draining the stagnant lochs, which lay among the hills like so many loadstones to attract the moisture of the clouds. On the north side, in particular, he formed, at great labour and expense, a reservoir, banked towards the declivity by an ingeniously constructed breastwork, to which various cuttings brought the straggling waters of the marshy sides of the hills. Thence leading a deep drain, mostly cut out of the solid rock, across the inclined plain to the farm houses, he conveyed a stream of water ample enough to drive a powerful thrashing machine—thus converting the little pond, secluded among the woods in the rear of the castle, at once into purposes of use and ornament.

Newark Hill is not less interesting to the lover of nature than it is to the agriculturist; whether merely an admirer of external objects, or an explorer of the hidden mysteries of creation. From the summit the view is not surpassed by the celebrated prospects either from Stirling or Edinburgh castles. In any direction the range is not less than twenty or thirty miles, while to the east and north it must be upwards of sixty. From south to east the panoramic circle embraces the Bennan Hill, the valley of Girvan, the hills of Galloway and Dumfriesshire, Lanarkshire, Renfrewshire, Benlomond, Argyleshire, Bute, Arran, Cantyre, &c., while, in the intervening valleys, the beautifully cultivated fields, woods, rivers, and mansions, with the birth-place of Burns, the town of Ayr, and the golden sea glistening in the chastened rays of an autumnal sun, combine in forming one of the most enchanting pictures the human eye ever rested on.

In a geological point of view there is much to engage the attention of the visiter. The limestone quarry at Burnside, near the base of the hill, affords a beautiful illustration of the theory entertained by geologists respecting the formation of the earth. The stratifications of sand and limestone appear to have been torn asunder by some internal convulsion ; and a distinct trap dyke, several feet in thickness, fills up the interstice. The entire hill, indeed, like Salisbury Crags, bears evidence of the volcanic power by which the elevations of the earth have been produced. In the hollows and fissures of the igneous or primitive rock, regular stratas of superincumbent deposits are to be found, together with masses or beds of conglomerate, containing the utmost variety of disintegrated particles. Midway up the eminence innumerable crystallizations present themselves, bursting through the upper stratifications; and many fine specimens of pebble, quartz, rock crystal, &c. have been disembedded with little trouble. At the south-east shoulder of the hill there is a large seam of barytes, which might be wrought to much advantage. But apart from the more minute details of science, a ramble on Newark Hill, amidst so many evidences of a long anterior process of amalgamation, cannot but excite in the mind of the merest tyro in geology a spirit of philosophical inquiry, nowhere so powerful or interesting as when stimulated on the field of contemplation. The numerous ages of growth and decay that must have preceded the present aspect of the earth are demonstrated in a variety of forms. Even on the highest range, a knoll, rising like a little island in the centre of a loch—composed of boulders, sand and disintegrated rock—demonstrates that at some period long gone by the mighty waters must have rolled over its summit.

The antiquities or traditions connected with the hill, so far as we are aware, are not of much importance. The remains of an encampment are still traceable on one of the higher ridges. Prior to the improvements already detailed, it existed in a very entire state. The breast-works ran in parallel lines along the heights, the space between varying from fifty to one hundred yards, according to the form of the eminence. The works were admirably planned for defence, and so extensive that 5000 men might have been accommodated within the trenches. Neither history nor tradition supplies any satisfactory clue to the origin of the encampment. It is probable that it was Norwegian. This is the more likely that Ayr was the debarking place of the Northmen when they invaded Scotland in 1263. According to one of our old historians, " Acho, King of Norroway, landit at Air wt. 160 schipps and twentie thousand men of warre ;" and the presumption is, that in following the course of the Clyde, in their progress towards Largs, where they were defeated, they took possession of the most advantageous eminences. The difference in the form of the encampment on Newark, from those elsewhere met with, cannot be regarded as a distinguishing mark. It appears to have arisen from the peculiar nature of the ground, in the same way that the conic top of the other positions, at Dundonald and elsewhere, gave the breastworks a conical shape. The only other object of traditional interest is a large flat stone, about five feet in length, on one of the eastern projections of the hill. Here, it is said, the inhabitants of Ayr and the surrounding country assembled, in 1588, to watch the approach of the Spanish Armada, and to offer up prayers for its dispersion. All Europe rung with the magnificent preparations of Philip of Spain ; and when it was known that the expedition had at last put to sea a fearful anxiety pervaded the minds of all ranks in Britain. Ignorant on what part of the coast a landing might be attempted, or whether a simultaneous attack would not be made at various points, the inhabitants of all the more assailable estuaries were equally alarmed. The spot chosen for the look-out commands an extensive view of the Firth—and deep and intense must have been the feelings of the beholders, when they saw, in lieu of a formidable array of gallant ships, bristling with armed men, only one or two discomfited, storm-driven wrecks, blown upen their shores.

*Kilhenzie Castle* is perhaps the most entire of all the baronial ruins in the parish. It is delightfully situated on a gentle rising ground, washed by a little rivulet, to the south of Maybole.— Speaking of the " pretty dwellings " of the proprietors, Abercrummie says: " Many of these are sweet, desyreable places; but for the good building, gardens, orchards, and all other accommodations, Kilhenzie is the chiefe, lying about a short myle south from the towne of Mayboll." Though in ruins, and despoiled of its gardens, Kilhenzie still bears evidence of the character given of it by Abercrummie. The knoll upon which it is situated wears a carpet of never-fading green, and the few old trees which surround it maintain a corresponding freshness—the soil in the vicinity being evidently of the best quality. The castle itself consists of a tower and other buildings, of different ages, presenting, as a whole, a picturesque group. It is not a mass of stone and lime, like some of the overgrown feudal residences of former times, yet sufficiently extensive to indicate the medium position of its former owners. Kilhenzie was the residence of the Carrick branch of the Bairds. In the "Historie of the Kennedyis," it is stated that John Baird of Kilhenzie married, for his second wife, a sister of the Laird of Bargany. In his absence, his son took possession of the victual left by his father with his step-mother. She complained to her brother, the Laird of Bargany, who came with an armed force, and "brak the yett" of Kilhenzie, carrying off a quantity of grain equal to that taken by her step-son. Such was the ready-handed mode of obtaining justice peculiar to the times. Old Baird complained to the Earl of Cassillis, on whose side he seems to have acted during the feuds, who professed his willingness to carry fire and sword into the halls of Bargany. The Earl had brought home powder from Italy, when recently there, and he could easily blow up the gate. This was towards the latter end of the sixteenth century, and it would appear that powder was then rather a scarce article in Scotland.

*Auchindraine*, celebrated by the pen of Sir Walter Scott, in his "Auchindrane Tragedy," occupied a well-sheltered situation not far from the banks of the Doon, east a considerable distance of Brown Carrick Hill. Abercrummie describes it as "an high tower, with laigh buildings, surrounded with good orchards and gardens, parks,

and good corn fields. The owner hereof is Moore." The place was environed with wood. Not a vestige of the building now remains. The only memorial left of it is a yew tree, the age of which it is impossible to guess. The *Dule-tree*, respecting which Sir Walter Scott tells a characteristic anecdote of the last Laird of Auchindraine, was cut down and sold to a cabinet-maker in Maybole, who, it is said, made chests of drawers of it. During the feuds in Carrick, the inside plenishing, and much of the outside work of Auchindraine, were destroyed by the friends of Cassillis.

*Blairstone* stands close upon the banks of Doon, in a delightful low-lying bend of the river, nearer Ayr than Auchindraine. It is in good repair, and is the residence of Elias Cathcart, Esq., son of the late Lord Alloway, who took much delight in improving, by plantations and otherwise, a place of great natural amenity and beauty. It has more of the mansion-house style than any of the other residences we have described. Abercrummie speaks of it as "a stone tower-house, with lower buildings about it, surrounded with gardens, orchards, and parks. It lyes low, upon the water syde."

*Bridgend*, "a pretty dwelling," he says, "surrounded also with gardens, orchards, and parks." Of this pretty dwelling scarcely a vestige now remains. It was situated close on the banks of the Doon, and no doubt protected by a moat. From the ruins which remain, it seems to have consisted of a small tower, having a few houses probably attached. The modern mansion is called Doonside. The name originally, we believe, was Nether Auchindraine, and changed to Bridgend after the building of the old bridge of Doon,* near to which it was situated.

Of the other places enumerated by Abercrummie, *Smithstone*, *Sauchrie*, *Craigskean*, *Beoch*, *Garryhorne*, *Glenoyes*, *Brochlock*, and *Dalduff*, are to be traced only by a few ruinous walls.

---

* This bridge is said to have been built by Bishop Kennedy, Chancellor of Scotland, who died in 1466.

## GREENAN.

The first notice we find of this barony and its possessor occurs in a grant of the Doon fishings by *Roger de Scalebroc*, vassal of Duncan, Earl of Carrick, to the Monks of Melrose. This was in the reign of William the Lion. He appears to have had a daughter, *Cristiana*, married to *Raderic Macgillescop*, who bequeathed the lands of Grenane and fishings of Doon to the Monks of Melrose.[*]

The next proprietor of whom we have any notice was

*John Earl of Ross and Lord of the Isles*, who feued the barony of Greenan to

*John Davidson*, his " native esquire," in 1475. Davidson had also a Crown charter of the lands of Grenane, 31st January 1476. In consequence of the forfeiture of the Earl of Ross,

*Thomas Davidson*, the successor of John, and probably his son, was infeft in the barony under a precept from the Crown. The Earl of Douglas, however, had obtained a gift of the escheat of the Earl of Ross, and had infeft his son, William Douglas, in Greenan ; whereupon Thomas Davidson took a notarial instrument, dated 1st July 1510, which states that he compeared at his own mansion-house, and in presence of William Douglas, then taking infeftment of the lands of Greenan, after casting down a certain vessel upon the ground and breaking it, he asserted that such infeftment was broken and dissolved by the breaking in pieces of the said vessel, and protested that such infeftment taken by the said William Douglas should not hurt or prejudge that of the said William Davidson, or his heritage.[†]

This protest seems to have proved effectual, as the property continued in the hands of the Davidsons.

*Gilbert Davidson*, " filio et hæredi quondam Thomæ Davidson de Grenane," had a Crown charter of the lands of Grenane, 8th May 1543.

*Thomas Davidson, apparenti de Grenane*, had a charter of the lands of Blair from Queen Mary, 9th January 1548.

*Thomas Davidsone de Grenane*, hæres Thomæ Davidsone de Grenane, *proavi*, was retoured in the two merk land of Garfour, called Balmokyssog, 23d Jan. 1572. On the 6th September 1576, Thomas Davidson of Grenane, " with his awin hand, gaif heretabill stait and sasing of all and haill the fourtie shilling land of the Manis of Grenane, with tour, fortalice, zairdis, &c. to *Paull Reid*, sone and air of vmquhile *Paull Reid, burgess of Air*," &c.[*]

The property does not appear to have continued long in the hands of the Reids, as we find *John Kennedy of Baltersan* in possession of it in 1591. He held the lands from the Crown. In the list of debts owing by him at his decease in 1609, occurs the following :—" To ye King his Majestie for the Mertimes termes maill of ye lands of Greinand of the said crop 1608." The barony of Greenan was acquired by Sir Alexander Kennedy of Culzean in 1642. Sir Thomas Kennedy of Culzean had sasine, 16th April 1757, of the lands and barony of Greenan, proceeding upon a precept from Chancery, dated 23d February 1757.[†] They seem next to have been acquired by the *Hon. David Kennedy of Newark*, who disponed them to his brother, Thomas Earl of Cassillis. The Earl had sasine, 2d December 1766, of the lands and barony of Greenan, comprehending the 40s. land of old extent of the Mains of Greenan ; the 40s. land of Balbig, alias Balig, and M'Kellyrston ; the one merk land of Miltoun of Greenan ; the 40s. land of M'Crierreston ; the 40s. land of Over and Nether Burntouns, and the two merk land of old extent of Ballyrock and Kylestoun, on a disposition by David Kennedy of Newark, dated 8th April 1765.[‡] Greenan now forms part of the Marquis of Ailsa's estate.

## DAVIDSONS OF PENNYGLEN.

This family was probably descended, and perhaps the direct representative of the Davidsons of Greenan. The property, before they possessed it, belonged to a branch of the Kennedies,[§] whose

---

* Melrose Chartulary.
† The original charter of the lands of Greenan, in 1475, by John, Lord of the Isles, to his native esquire, John Davidson, is in the Ailsa charter chest.

* Mason's Notes.
† Record of Sasines. ‡ Ibid.
§ Die vltimo mens. Februarii 1585-6. The qlk day Morcis M'Murrie in Drummorane, as baillie in that part

names occur frequently in connection with the Carrick feuds.

*John Davidsoun of Pennyglen* was served heir of " Jacobi Davidsoun, nautæ in Air, filli fratris avi," in the ten shilling land, of old extent, of Quhytestaines, in the Burrowfield of Ayr, 6th November 1605. John Davidsoun took part, on Cassillis' side, in the feuds, and his name appears in the Books of Adjournal in 1611. He died in March 1614. Margaret Kennedy, his spouse, and Thomas Davidson, his eldest son, were his executors.

### DUNDUFF.

The earliest notice we find of the lands of Dunduff occurs in a charter of the lands of *Drume-ceisuiene* [Drumasheen], by *Roger de Scalebroc*, to the church or monks of Melrose. It seems to have belonged to *Walter Champenais, de Karrig*, who gave to the Monastery of Melrose " totam terram illam que iacet uicina suæ de Dunduff," &c. These grants were made in the reign of William the Lion.

The next we find in possession of the property is,

*Williame Stewarte of Dundufe*, whose name appears in the list of assize at a criminal trial in 1558. The following year (29th August 1559), " Willielmo Dunduff de eodem et Elizabethæ Corry ejus conjugi," had a Crown charter of the lands of Mekill Sallathane from Queen Mary.

It would thus appear that the family were sometimes called Dunduff and sometimes Stewart —the latter being apparently the real surname. It is probable that Dunduff was an assumed name, in consequence of a marriage with the heiress of Dunduffe.

*Mathew Dunduff* was served heir of his father, " Willichni Dunduffe de Eodem, patris," in the twelve merk land of Dunduff, the ten merk land of Glentig, the five and a-half merk land of Meikill Schallacane, and the four merk land of Litill Schallacane, on the 29th February 1580. In 1581, he had sasine of the lands of Dunduff, as the following extract from *Mason's Notes* attests: " May 8, 1581.—The quhilk day Nicolas Scherar, shref-deput of Air, be vertew of ane precept direct furth of our souerane lordis chancellerie, off the dait the sevint day of Merche last bipast, gaif heretabill stait and sasing of all and haill the xij

merk land of Dunduff, with the milne thereof; the ten merk land of Glentig, with the corne miln of the samin; the fyve merk land and half merk land of Mekill Sallauchane, and the four merk land of Litill Sallauchane, in propertie and tenandrie, with the pertinentis, lyand within the erledome of Carrik, &c., to Dauid Ker, as actornay for Mathew Dunduff (alias Stewart) of that Ilk, eftir the forme and tenour of the said precept, past vpoun ane retour maid befoir the shiref of Air and his deputis to that effect. This wes done first vpoun the saidis landis of Dunduf and miln thereof, at vj houris in the morning, befoir George Stewart, brother-germane to the said Mathew, and William Stewart, his servand," &c.

Thomas Stewart, and his brother, George, appear in another transaction, as stated in the *Notes of Mason*: " Nov. 9, 1586.—The quhilk day Jonet Campbell, relict of vmquhile Dauid Cathcart, burges of Air, as liferenter, and Johne Mure, heretabill fear of the milne and land vnderwrittin, ressauit fra the handis of George Stewart, brother-germane to Mathew Stewart of Dunduff, as cessiouner and assignay, lauchtfull maid and constitut be Johne Erle of Cassillis, sone and air of vmquhile Gilbert Erle of Cassillis, that last deceissit, with aduis and consent of Thomas Kennedy of Culzeane, his tutour, for his entres, in and to the reuersioun following, the sowme of fyve hundreth merkis money of this realme, as for the lauchtfull redemptioun fra thame of all and haill the merkland and milne of Polclewane, lyand within Kingis Kyle, and shrefdome of Air, sauld and annaliit be the said vmquhile erle to the said vmquhile Dauid, and the said Jonet, his spous, vnder reuersion contending the said sowme. The quhitkis landis and milne the said Jonet and Johne grantit to be lauchtfully redemit fra thame be the said George, assignay foirsaid, &c. This wes done within the paroch kirk of Air at vj houris after none, befoir Hew Campbell of Tarringzeane, Ard. Fergushill, Provost of Air, Adame Johnestoun, ane of the baillies thairof, Patrick Mure of Cloncard, Mathew Stewart of Dunduff, Mathew Campbell of Barreochhill," &c. Mathew Stewart of Dunduff occurs in the records of Ayr in 1589. In 1597, " Dinduff of that Ilk *v.* Jameson," appears in the same document, as also " Dunduff of that Ilk," in 1598. In February 1597-8, " Mathew Stewart, *alias* Dunduff of that Ilk," was put to the horn, along with Auchindraine and others, for an attempt on the life of Culzean. Dunduff entered in ward, and was banished from Scotland, England, and Ireland, and all the Isles, and fined 1000 merks. His sentence seems to have been commuted or evaded, for he is in the list of parties " abiding frae the

---

to Johne Kennedy of Pennyglen, be vertew of his precept of sasing insert in ane blanche chartour, maid be him to Johnne Kennedy of Smythistoune and Margaret Cuninghame, his spous, &c. of all and haill his fyve merkland of auld extent of Pennyglen, occupiit be Johne Bard, &c. liand within the Erledome of Carrik, &c.

Earl of Angus' raid at Dumfries" in 1600. He died before 1609,* and was succeeded by his son,

"Willielmus Stewart, alias Dunduff de Eodem, hæres Mathei Stewart alias Dunduff de Eodem, patris," who was retoured in the lands of Dunduff, &c., 24th January 1609.

Passing a generation, we find that the Laird of Dunduff, and William Stewart, his brother, a captain, being malignants, were debarred from renewing the Covenant in 1668.†

The property seems soon afterwards to have passed into the hands of the Whitefords.

James Whyteford of Dunduff is mentioned in certain obligations from James Craufurd of Newark to Alexander Kennedy of Drummellan, in 1700 and 1714.

James Whitefoord of Dunduff had sasine of the merkland of Drumfadd, on a charter under the Great Seal, 12th November 1757.

Mrs Elizabeth Cuninghame, Lady Dunduff, occurs in the town records in 1767.

## NEWARK.

The barony of Newark belonged to the Laird of Bargany in 1576. According to the Historie of the Kennedyis, he exchanged the six pound land of Newark for the lands of Brounstoun with his aunt, by the father's side, "Blak Bessie Kennedy," a widow for the third time, her last husband having been the Laird of Brounstoun. After the death of old Bargany, in 1596, the Laird of Culzean obtained possession of Newark, with a decreet for 12,000 merks, against the young Laird of Bargany, upon an assignation which he had received from "Blak Bessie Kennedy."

In 1601, Quintin Craufurd of Camlarg gave service to his lawful son, Duncan; whom failing, to Quintin Craufurd, his youngest son, and heirs of his body; whom failing, to William Craufurd, the eldest son, and his heirs; whom failing, to the nearest lawful male heir of the name of Craufurd, of " all and haill the three pound land of ye lands of New-wark, occupiet be ——— Wilsone, of auld extent, with ye pertinentis, lyand within ye realme of Carrick, and sheriffdom of Air, haldand of ye said Quintine and his airis, in fee blanche, for payment zerlie thairfoir of twa pennyis at ye feist

of Whytsunday, gif it be requirit," &c. Quintin Craufurd, at the sametime, resigned the lands of Crawisland and Castlehill, within the burgh lands of Ayr, in favour of his son, Duncan.* Duncan Craufurd was in possession of the Castle of Newark in 1602, when Auchindraine sought refuge there from the designs of the Master of Cassillis.

James Craufurd and his spouse, Anna Kennedy, purchased Newark Castle in 1687. They made considerable additions to it, and otherwise improved the place, in commemoration of which, the date, with their initials, are carved above the staircase. His lady was a daughter of Quintin Kennedy of Drummellane, who died in 1691, leaving his son-in-law, James Craufurd of Newark, his sole executor. The latter appears in the burgh records of Ayr, in 1694, as craving permission from the authorities to bury a child in Alloway Kirkyard, which was granted. He is accused of certain derelictions before the Presbytery in 1706, and confesses. Again, in 1717, (31st March) he confesses his guilt with Anna Kennedy, and the Session are ordered to meet in his house because of his infirmity, and there absolve him from the scandal. He was then advanced in years.

Quintin Craufurd of Newark, their eldest son, had one thousand merks left him by his grandfather, Kennedy of Drummellane. "Newark, younger," appears amongst others met at Maybole in 1717, to consider the libel against the Rev. Mr Fairweather for drunkenness. Quintin Craufurd was one of the Justiciary Bailies of the West Seas of Scotland.

Alexander Craufurd of Newark, son of the preceding, had sasine of the merkland of Pennyglen, on a charter of adjudication by Thomas Earl of Cassillis, dated 4th March 1762; and another of the threepenny land of Wester Newark, forty penny land of Easter Newark, twenty penny land of Hillend, the lands of Drummelling, which are part of Hillend, all in Maybole parish, on a charter of adjudication from Chancery, dated 20th February 1762. Alexander Craufurd disponed these lands, with advice and counsel of Mrs Ann Robertson, alias Craufurd, his mother, 6th and 12th April 1763, to the Earl of Cassillis.

Newark, and the lands previously mentioned, were soon afterwards acquired by David Kennedy, advocate, brother-german of the Earl of Cassillis. On succeeding to the earldom, after the decease of his brother, David Earl of Cassillis continued to prefer Newark as a residence.

Though the property of Newark has been long

<hr/>

* His brother, George Stewart, was slain by Roger Gordoun in Glasniche, and John Glendoning of Drumrasche, on the 21st September 1601. The offenders were pursued before the High Court by his nephews, William and John Stewart.
† Presbytery Records.

* Record of Sasines for Ayrshire.

out of their possession, the family of Cranfurd is by no means extinct. Alexander, the last of Newark, who was created a Baronet 8th June 1781, had issue:

1. James, his heir.
2. Charles, G.C.B., a Lieutenant-General in the army. He married, in 1806, Anna-Maria, youngest daughter of William, second Earl of Harrington, and widow of Thomas, third Duke of Newcastle, but died without issue.
3. Robert, a Major-General in the army. He fell while leading his troops to the assault of Ciudad-Rodrigo, 1812; for which service a monument has been erected, at the public expense, to the gallant soldier, in St Paul's Cathedral. He married Bridget, daughter of Henry Holland, Esq., and left issue, Charles, Robert, and Henry.

Sir Alexander died in 1801, and was succeeded by his son,

*Sir James Cranfurd*, born in 1762, who assumed, in 1812, the additional surname of Gregan. He married, in 1792, Maria-Theresa, eldest daughter of the Hon. General Gage, and sister of Henry, third Viscount Gage, by whom he had issue:

1. Thomas, killed at Waterloo.
2. Alexander-Charles, Lieutenant-Colonel in the army. He married, in 1818, Barbara, fourth daughter of George-William, seventh Earl of Coventry, and died in 1848.
3. George-William, who succeeded.
4. Jane, married to the Rev. H. R. Dukinfield, Bart.

*The Rev. Sir George-William Cranfurd* of Kilbirnie, in Stirlingshire. He was born in 1797, and succeeded his father in 1839. He married, first, in 1813, the Hon. Hester King, sister of the Earl of Lovelace, and by her (who died in 1848) has:

1. Charles-William-Frederic.
2. Henry-Thomas-Gage.

He married, secondly, in 1849, Martha, widow of William Cooke, Esq. of Burgh House, Lincoln.

*Arms.*—Gules, a fesse, ermine. *Crest.*—An ermine. *Motto.*—" Sine labe nota."

According to *Burke's Baronetage*, this family believe themselves to be descendants of the Craufurds of Kilbirnie—hence the designation of their property in Stirlingshire. If this was the case, it must have been through his ancestor, James Craufurd, who married Ann Kennedy in 1687; for Duncan Craufurd, who previously possessed Newark, was the son of Quintin Craufurd of Camlarg, and the Camlarg Craufurds were an immediate branch of the Craufurds of Kerse. We have no means of ascertaining whether James Craufurd was the son, or grandson, of Duncan, or whether he was, as supposed by the family, of the Kilbirnie stock.

## KILHENZIE.

The first of the Bairds of Kilhenzie, of whom we have any information, was

*Gilberto Barde*, who had a charter of the lands of Kilhenze, Kilkerane and Makmertinstoun, from James IV., 26th January 1506. He appears to have been the Laird of Kilhenzie who was slain in a feud fight by Schaw of Keirs and others in 1508. He was succeeded by his son,

*John Barde of Kilhenzie*. " Johanni Barde de Kilquhinzie, et Margaretæ Craufurde, ejus sponsæ," had a charter of the lands of Drumbane, &c. from James V., 17th December 1526. Gilbert Barde, who, with his sponse, Cristine Lindsay, obtained a Crown charter of the lands of Glencapok, 14th June 1541, was probably a son of John, at all events the property afterwards appears in the family.

*Robert Barde of Kilhenzie*, whose son,

*John Barde of Kilhenzie* had a charter of the family property during his father's lifetime. "Johanni Barde, filio et hæredi Roberti Barde de Kilquhynzie et Elizabethæ Kennedy suæ sponsæ," had a Crown charter of confirmation of the lands of Glengappok, Kilquhynnze, &c., from Queen Mary, 2d October 1559. He was twice married. His second wife was a sister of the Laird of Bargany, also a Kennedy. A disagreeance between his son, by the previous marriage, and his stepmother, about 1565, was one of the alleged causes of the feud between Cassillis and Bargany. Bargany resented the ill-treatment of his sister, by a foray upon Kilhenzie, and Baird being one of the friends and supporters of Cassillis, the latter was bound to take up his quarrel. He was succeeded by his son,

*Oliver Baird of Kilhenzie*, who had a charter of confirmation of the lands of Glencapok and Kilquhynnze, &c., 21st October 1585. He was served heir of his father in the twenty shilling lands of Dalgervie, of old extent, in the parish of Daily, 29th July 1607. He appears in the Criminal Trials as one of the supporters of the Earl of Cassillis, in the Carrick feuds, in 1611. His brother, John, was concerned, with Hugh Kennedy of Blairquhan, in the slaughter of the Provost of Wigton, in the same year. He was succeeded, apparently, by his son,

*Gilbert Baird of Kilhenzie*, whose name occurs as one of the assize on a criminal trial in 1619. He is mentioned along with his father, in the testament of Jeane Stewart, Lady Culzeane, in 1616, so that his father must have died between that year and 1619.

These are the last notices we find of the Bairds

of Kilhenzie. The name is still prevalent in Maybole and the vicinity—the remains of the Carrick sept of the *Bardes*.

Kilhenzie was acquired by *Alexander Kennedy of Craigoch*, afterwards of *Kilhenzie*, about 1644, and it remained in possession of the family till 1766, when the heiress married *John Shaw of Dalton*.

## AUCHINDRAINE.

Before the Bruce and Baliol wars Auchindraine belonged to Robert Brown, and upon his forfeiture it was granted by Robert the Bruce to Henry Annan,[*] who obtained from that Monarch several grants of land in various districts of Scotland.

The *Mures of Auchindraine* were descendants of the house of Rowallane : " And the house of Auchindraine, the progenie of Andro Mure of Monyhagen, of which Cloneard, held ordinarlie, from one age to another, sonnes of this familie ; however not verie certaine whether or not brethren thairof at one and the same time, do beare the armes of the paternal coat, differenced the one from the other, and both from the cheife bearer, by thair borders of distinction." [†]

I. ANDRO MURE of Monyhagen, in King's Kyle, son or grandson of Sir Gilchrist Mure of Rowallane, who died about 1280.

II. James Mure of Monyhagen, who, by a charter, dated 16th March 1498, granted certain lands, in Wigtonshire, in favour of James Mure, his son, and Margaret Wallace, his spouse. One of the witnesses to this deed is John Mure, " grandson and heir apparent of the said James." We have thus

III. James Mure of Monyhagen, who married Margaret Wallace, and had a son,

IV. John Mure (grandson of James No. II.) whom Pitcairn[‡] supposes to have been the grandfather of John Mure of Auchindraine—one of the principal actors in the *Auchindraine Tragedy.* We should rather think, however, from the great age of the latter—being nearly eighty years old at his death—that he was his father. In 1525 John Mure of Auchindraine was concerned, along with Cassillis, in the slaughter of Martin Kennedy of Lochland. He was also implicated in the slaughter of Robert Campbell in Lochfergus in 1528. John Mure of Auchindraine (still the same party, we presume) was one of the assize at the trial of George Craufurd of Lifnoreis in 1554. At what time the Mures acquired

Auchindraine is uncertain. They had no charters of these lands recorded under the Great Seal before the reign of Charles I., and the family seem to have been originally designed of Monyhagen.

V. John Mure of Auchindraine, who took so active a part in the feuds which divided the Kennedies of Carrick at the close of the sixteenth and beginning of the seventeenth centuries, and led to the slaughter of Sir Thomas Kennedie of Culzean in 1602. In April (11th) 1582, " John Muir of Auchindraine " had sasine of certain lands in the Burrowfield of Ayr, as heir of " his father, umquhile *John Muir of Auchindraine.*" [*] In 1585-6 (21st March) the magistrates of Ayr, proceeding " on a brief furth of the chancel," gave sasine of certain annual rents over tenements in Ayr " to Johne Mure now of Auchindraine, as sone and air of umquhile Johne Mure of Auchindraine, his fader."[†] In 1586-7 Johne Mure gave sasine of the " ane equal half of the xxs. land of Twa-stane-Cors, with syk and medow thairof, &c. liand within the Burrowfield of Air, &c. to Johne Rankene, burges of Air, &c. befoir Mathew Stewart of Dunduf, George Sinclair, brother to the said Jon. Mure," &c. In 1588 he had sasine of the lands of Murrayholme, Lourishoill and Hoill, in the Burrowfield of Ayr, from John Lathis. In 1597-8 he was denounced as a rebel for shooting at the Laird of Culzean in Maybole. He was engaged in the fight at Ladycors, where young Bargany was slain, in 1602 ; and in 1611 he was condemned to death for the murder of William Dalrymple, aggravated by his instigation of the slaughter of Culzean. At the time of his execution he is supposed to have been about eighty years of age. He married Margaret, second daughter of Sir Thomas Kennedy of Bargany (obiit 7th Nov. 1591), by Lady Agnes Montgomerie, sister to Hugh third Earl of Eglintoun. He was for some time Bailie of Carrick. His son, *James*, who was also engaged in the feuds which led to their execution in 1611, married Helen, second daughter of Sir Thomas Kennedy of Culzean, Tutour of Cassillis, by Dame Elizabeth MacGill, daughter of David MacGill of Cranstoun-Riddell, King's Advocate. The lands and effects belonging both to John Mure, elder, and James Mure, younger, of Auchindraine, were forfeited by the doom pronounced against them, but the lands were restored to his successor,

VI. Sir John Mure of Auchindraine, Knight, son of the late James Mure, younger, of Auchdraine.[‡]

* " Carta to Henry Annan, the lands of Aughindraine, qnas Robertus Brown, foresfecit."—ROBERTSON'S INDEX.
† The Historie and Descent of the House of Rowallane.
‡ Criminal Trials.

* Mason's Notes. † Ibid.
‡ Thomas Mure, younger of Auchindraine, had also

He had, under the Great Seal, " Litera Rehabitationis Joanni Muir de Auchindraine," 15th Feb. 1631; and in 1632 (2d April) he had a charter of the lands of Monyhegane, Auchindraine, &c. He was accused of being " friendly to Montrose," in 1645, and severely taken into task by the Presbytery of Ayr in consequence; [*] so was his brother James.[†] Sir John married Bethia Hamilton, daughter of Hamilton of Dalzell, by whom he had, says *Pitcairn*, " at least one son, *James*, who probably predeceased him; for he conveyed Auchindrayne to his brother, *Hugh Mure*, whose son or grandson sold it early in the last century, and the family is now extinct in the male line." This is very inaccurate. Sir John was succeeded by his son,

VII. John Mure of Auchindraine, who was retoured heir of his father, Sir John Mure of Auchindraine, in the eight merk land of Minnihagen and Keyrmoyne, of old extent, within King's Kyle, in 1658.[‡] He had a charter of novodamus of the lands of Leffenhill, dated 29th September 1671, by Chalmers of Gadgirth, in which he is described as heir of John Mure of Monyhagen, *proavi*, (his great-grandfather) who had, in like manner, a charter of the same lands from Campbell of Loudoun, in 1550. It was probably a son of this John who made over his estate to his brother. If so, there would be an intermediate

VIII. John Mure of Auchindraine. At all events, we find

IX. " Hugh Moor of Auchindrane," 2d April 1700, applying to the magistrates of Ayr, who possessed at that time the barony of Alloway, for leave " to bury his late brother, the Laird of Auchindrane," in Alloway kirkyard, which request was granted. Hugh married, and had a son, " William Moor, yr. of Auchindrain," who, on the 20th September 1710, was admitted a burgess of Ayr, along with " Mr Archibald Moor, son to ye deceased Laird of Auchindrain, minister of the gospel at Barro; Robert Moor, son to ye said deceast Auchindraine, apothecary in Air."[§]

X. William Mure of Auchindraine appears to have succeeded his father. He married, but whom we have not ascertained. On 1st April 1735, we find liberty granted by the magistrates of Ayr to " William Muir of Anchindrain to bury his lady in Alloway kirkyard."

another son, Thomas, and a daughter, Mary. The dead body of Dalrymple bled, it is said, on being touched by this girl.
  [*] See Introductory History, p. 103 of this work.
  [†] There was also a Francis Mure, probably another brother, before the Presbytery for the same offence.
  [‡] Printed Retours.            [§] Town Records.

XI. Hugh Mure of Auchindraine, the son, we presume, of the preceding, disponed the property, with the " tower, fortalice, and manor-place," to James Ferguson of Kilkerran, Bart, in 1741.

### BLAIRSTOUN, OR MIDDLE AUCHINDRAINE.

The earliest possessor of this property, of whom we have any record, was William Broune, from whom it was acquired by the Schaws of Sauchy. The Blairs, who succeeded, were a branch, we should suppose, from the intercourse between the two houses, of the Blairs of Adamton. Latterly, they changed the name of Middle Auchindraine to Blairstoun. The first of the Blairs was,

I. JOHN BLARE, who, together with his spouse, Beatrix Mortoun, had a charter of the lands of Mydil Achyndrane from James IV., 10th March 1500. He had " conqueste" the lands from " Jacobo Schaw de Salquhy."[*] He was slain at Flodden. He was succeeded by his son,

II. James Blair of Middle Auchindraine. " I, Allexr. Kennedy of Bargany, and fermerer of the half personage of the Kirk of Maybole, grantis me to haf ressauit be the handis of *James Blar of Mydilauchindrane*, full contentation and payment of xiiij bollis of meile for teindis of Mydilauchindrane, of the zeir of God Javexxxvi zeiris, off the forsaid xiiij bollis for his teindis of the zeir of God forsaid, I haud me weill content, asyth, (?) and payit, for me, to myn airis, and quit clamis, and dischargis the said James and his airis, and of all zeris bigane, for now and euirmair. In witnes of the quhilk thing, I haif subscriuit this present discharge with my hand, at Air, the xx daye of August the zeir of God Javexxxvij zeris, befor yir witnes, Costen. Tayt, Alexr. Kennedy, and Roben Law, with vtheris diuers.

  " Alexander Kenede of Bargany, with my hand."[†]

He had a resignation of the half of the five merk land of Middle Auchindraine from George and John Tait of Knockindale, 11th May 1544. He was killed at the battle of Fawside, or Pinkie, and was succeeded by his brother,

III. John Blare of Myddil Auchindrane, who had sasine of the half of the said lands, 27th June 1548; also of the other half, as heir of his father, killed at Flowden, both on a precept from Chancery, 19th May 1558. He was on the assize at the trial of Barnard Fergusson of Kilkerran, in 1564, for invading the Laird of Camlarg in a fenced court of the schireff of Air.[‡] John

  [*] Instrument of Sasine in Auchindraine charter chest.
  [†] Auchindraine Papers.        [‡] Criminal Trials.

Blair of Middill Auchindraine was one of the "Preloquutouris" for John Blair of that Ilk, when tried, along with a number of others, for "schooting pistolets," &c., in 1576-7 [*] He is repeatedly mentioned in legal documents down to 1580. "James Blair, sone and apperand air to Johnne Blair of Middill Auchindrane," had sasine of the xls. land of Scheilzardis, from William Dunbar of Blantyre, in 1576.[†] In the same year, David Blair of Adamton gave heritable state and sasine to "James Blair, sone and apperand air to Jon. Blair of Middill Auchindrane, of all and haill the xvs. land of Quhitrumrex." In 1579–80, Johne Blair of Middil Auchindraine made over the property to his son, James Blair, reserving a liferent interest. He married Marcoun Kennedy, and had, besides his heir, a son, John, as appears from the following extract: "Sept. 20, 1586.—The qlk day Johnne Blair, lauchfull sone to Johne Blair of Middil Auchindrane, gottin betuix him and vmqle Marcoun Kennedy, his spous, be ressoun of alienatioun, *titulo oneroso*, for sowmes of money for fulfilling of ane contract and appointment maid betuix him on the ane part, and James Blair, his brother-germane, on the other part, of the dait this instant day, and for ane certane sowme of money thairin contenit, resignit and oergaif, purelie and simplie be ane penny, as vsis, all and haill ane annuelrent of li money of this realme zeirlie (&c.) furth of the said Johneis foir tenement of land, vnder and aboue, (&c.) liand within the burch of Air, (&c.)"[†]

IV. James Blair of Middle Auchindraine succeeded his father. In 1579 (13th December), during his father's lifetime, he had a charter, under the Great Seal, of the lands of Myddill Auchindraine. His father and he had a decreet absolviter in the plea John and James Blair v. James Shaw of Sauchy, in 1587. He appears to have died before 1610, in which year,

V. James Blair of Middle Auchindraine was retoured as heir of his father, James Blair of Middle Auchindraine. He died in the month of June 1627. His testament was made at Blairstoun: "Legacie.—At Blairstoun, ye xix day of June 1627 zeiris. The qlk day James Blair of Blairstoun . . maks his testament and lattir-will as followis. In the first, nominats his executoris, viz., James, Jeane, Jonet, and Margaret Blairis, bairnis, onlie executoris and intromettouris. Item, he nominattis Jonet Kennedy,[‡] his spous, tutrix to his eldest sone, Hew Blair, and to ye haill remanent bairnis; and nominattis James Blair,

burges of Air, his fader brother, and William M'Kellar [M'Kerrell] of Hilhous, oursearis to ye said Jonet, his spous . . . David Kennedy of Garriehorne, cautioner." It would thus appear that his wife was of the Garriehorne family. He was succeeded by his son,

VI. James Blair of Blairstoun, who had the following assignation from Jean Blair (his sister) and George Crawfurd of Tempilland, of contract and tack of teinds of Blairstoun, 17th November 1630 :—

"Be it kend till all men be thir present letteris, me, Jeane Blair, eldest lawfull dochter to vmquhile James Blair of Blairstoun, and George Crawfurd of Templand, my spous, for his entres, and the said George for himselff, and takand burdene in and vpoun him for me, and we baith with ane consent and assent, and als with speciall advyse, consent and assent of Jonet Kennedy, reliet of the said vmquhile James Blair of Blairstoun, my mother, for all richt and tytill sche hes had, or ony maner of way may clame to have in tyme cuming, in and to the contract efter specifeit, and sowmes of money and vtheris thairin contenit, that forsamekill as be vertew of ane contract and appointment of the dait the nyntene day of Apryle, the zeir of God Iavic tuentie fyve zeiris, past betuix the said vmquhile James Blair on the ane part, and David Kennedy, sone to Hew Kennedy of Girvenmanis, on the vther part, the said Dauid Kennedy grantit him thairby to haue ressauit fra the said vmquhile James Blair, the sowme of sex hundreth merkis vsualo money of this realme, and band and oblist him, his airis, executouris, assignayis, successouris and intromettouris with his guidis and geir, to have repayit and thankfullie agane delyverit the foirsaid sowme to the said vmquhile James Blair, his airis, executouris and assignayis, vpoun the tent day of Nouember, anno Iavje tuentie sex zeiris, togidder with the sowme of ffourtie pundis money foirsaid of liquidat expensis incais of failzie, and for the said vmquhile James Blair and his foirsaidis forder securitie, the said Dauid Kennedy, as havand richt to the teindis vnderwrittin, sett in tak and assedatioun to the said vmquhile James Blair, his airis and assignayis, all and haill the personage teindis of the flyve merk land of Blairstoun, in satisfactioun of the annuelrent of the said principall sowme during the space and in maner contenit in the said contract, as the samin of the dait abouespecifeit mair amplie proportis, in and to the quhilk contract, sowmes of money, principall, expensis, and teinds foirsaidis contenit thairintill, haill effect and contentis thairof, the said vmquhile James Blair of Blairstoun maid and constitute me, the said Jeane Blair, his doch-

ter, my airis, and assignayis, his vndoutit cessionar
and assignay, procuratour and donatour, in rem
suam, as the assignatioun maid thairanent of the
dait the nyntene day of Junii, the zeir of God
Iavje tuentie sevin zeiris proportis, and now for
the sowme of sex hundreth merkis vsuale money
of this realme instantlie payit and delyverit to ws
at the making heirof be James Blair, lait provest
of the burgh of Air, quhairof we hald ws weill
contentit, satisfeit and payit in nvmerit and tauld
gude gold and siluir, and for ws, our airis, executouris and assignayis, exoneris, quitclamis, and
simpliciter discharges the said James Blair, his
airis, executouris and assignayis of the samin be
thir presentis for euir. Witt ye, thairfoir, ws,
the saidis Jeane Blair and George Crawfurd of
Templand, my spous, for his entres, with ane aduyse and consent, and with speciall aduyse and
consent also of the said Jonet Kennedy, to haue
transferrit, sauld, assignit and disponit, and be
the tennour heirof transferris, sellis, assignis, and
simpliciter disponis fra ws, our airis, executouris
and assignayis, to and in fauouris of the said
James Blair, his airis and assignayis, in vberiori
translationis et dispositionis forma, all and haill
the foirsaid contract and appointment past betuixt
the said James Blair of Blairistoun and the said
David Kennedy, in maner aboue specifeit, with
the foirnamit sowme of sex hundreth merkis,
principall sowme, and flourtie pundis of liquidat
expensis thairin contenit, and with the foirsaid
letter of tak and assedatioun of the personage
teindis of the saidis landis of Blairistoun, specifeit
thairintill, haill heidis, clauses, articles and condi-
tionis thairof, togidder with myne, the said Jeane
Blairis assignatioun thairto abonewrittin, and with
all richt, tytill, entres, clame of richt, actioune,
and instance, quhatsumeuir, quhilkis me or ather
of vs had, hes, or onywyes may clame or pretend
thairto in tyme cuming, surrogatand, and be thir
presentis, with ane consent and assent, substituand
the said James Blair and his foirsaidis in our full
richt, tytill and place of the samin for euir, with
full power to the said James Blair and his abonewrittin to intromet with the sowmes of money,
principall, expensis, annuelrent, teindis, and
vtheris foirsaidis, specifeit in the said contract, to
his awin vse, vtilitie and commoditie, and to gif
discharges vpoun the ressait thairof, quhilkis salbe
als effectuall as gif we had gevin and subscryvit
the samin our selffis, and gif need beis, to call,
follow, and persew thairfoir as accordis of the law,
befoir quhatsumenir juge or juges competent decreitis and sentences thuiruponn, to obtene and
recover, and the samin to caus be put to dew
executioun, compone, transact, and aggrie thairanent at his plessour, as he sall think expedient,

siclyk and als frelie as we micht haue done our
selffis befoir the making of this present transla-
tioun, quhilk we oblige ws, our airis, executouris,
and assignayis, with ane consent and assent, to
warrand gude and sufficient frome all fact and
deid done or to be done be ws, in preiudice thairof: And for the said James forder securitie, we
all thrie, with ane consent, have instantlie delyuerit to him the foirsaid contract and assignatioun
vnregistrat, to be vsit be him and his foirsaidis as
thair awin euidentis at thair plessour. And last,
for the mair securitie, we are content, and con-
sentis that thir presentis be insert and registrat
in the buikis of Counsall and Session, or Shireff'
Court buikis of Air, thairin to remane ad perpetuam rei memoriam, and to haue the strenth of
ane act and decreit of ather the juges thairof, with
letteris and executoriallis of horning vpoun ane
sempill charge of sex dayis, poinding and ward-
ing the ane, but preiudice of the vther, to be direct heirvpon; and for registering heirof, makis
and constitutis our laufull procuratouris, promitten.
de rato, &c. In witness quhairof (thir presentis,
writtin be George M'Calmount, servitour to
George Masoun, toun-clerk of Air), we haue
subscryvit the samin with our awin handis, at
Air, the sevintene day of November, the zeir of
God Iavje and threttie zeiris, befoir thir witnesses, Williame Montgomerie of Bridgend, Hew
Blair of Blairstoun, and Patrik Dauidsone,[*] brother german to Thomas Dauidsone of Pennyglen, inserter of the dait and witness,

GEORGE CRAWFURD of Tempilland.
JEANE BLAIR.
JANET KENNEDY.

W. Montgomerie of Bridgend, witnes.
Hew Blair, witnes.
Patrik Dauidsone, witnes, and insertar of the
    dait and witnesses."

He was succeeded by his son,

VII. Hew Blair of Blairstoun, who was served
heir to his father, James Blair, in 1636, and had
a precept from Chancery for infefting him in the
property, 19th June 1639. Besides the 5 merk
land of Auchindraine, the family at this time
possessed the 5 merk land of Fischertoun. He
was summoned before the Presbytery of Ayr,
in 1646, for having been "friendly to Montrose." He confessed that "he was in Kilmarnock with Alaster [Macdonald]; that he went
to Bothwell Bridge and Loudonn Hill, and was
on the way to Philiphaugh; that he came alongst
with a letter from Montrose, and confessed also
that he said Mr James Bonner[†] suld not preach

---

* This Patrik Davidson married Catherine Cathcart,
sister to Ellas Cathcart, about 1643.
† Minister at Maybole.

such a preaching the nixt day." His brother, James, was also in the list of disaffected laid before the Presbytery. Hew Blair of Blairstoun occurs in the testament of Sir Alexander Kennedy of Culzeane in 1653. He appears to have attained to a long age, having been alive in 1676.

VI. James Blair of Blairstoun had a son, Thomas, born 18th March 1665.* His lady was Isobell Kennedy. They had another son, John, born March 1673. Hugh Blair, grandfather of the child, was a witness at the baptism. A daughter, Agnes, was born 20th June 1674—the grandfather still a witness; Margaret, born 22d March 1676. James Blair was not served heir of his father till 1695. Having, probably, been brought into pecuniary difficulties by the civil war, which ruined many, he, with consent of his son, Thomas, sold the property to Robert Muir, Provost of Ayr, in 1698.† Amongst the witnesses to the disposition were, " Bryce Blair, merchant in Belfast," and James Blair, writer of the document.

## MURES OF MIDDLE AUCHINDRAINE, OR BLAIRSTOUN.

The Mures, or Moores of Blairstoun, were, it is believed, the representatives of the Mures of Park, in the parish of Tarbolton—which Mures were a branch of the house of Rowallane.

I. BERNARD MURE of Park had a Crown charter of the lands of Park, 20th Nov. 1546. He was slain at the battle of Fawsyde, or Pinkie, in 1547. In his testament, his son and heir, John Muir, and his spouse, Agnes Stewart, were appointed his executors, under the direction of Kentigern Muir of Rowallane.

II. John Mure of Park, his son and successor, was served heir of his father in the 40s. lands of Park, with the mill and pertinents, Shelpcoitlois, Parkhill and Barhill, in the barony of Tarbolton, 8th May 1548.

III. " Edward Muir of Park, his Master," is mentioned in the testament of Barnard Greiff in Park, July 1611. *William*, his brother, occurs in the testament of Mareoun Seller, spouse to Robert Brown, merchant, in 1614; also in that of the Laird of Rowallane in 1614. He died in February 1623. In his legacy he nominates " William Muir, his eldest sone, and Marie Muir, his dochter, executours and equall intromittours

with his guids and geir," &c. He " discharges Johnne Muir, sone and air of vmquhile Williame Muir of Lochlichill, of sax hundrith merks, and all sownes of money in wadsett in the Lochliehill, and all vther comptis, with this provisioun, he pay to Edward Muir, his brother, ane hundrith merks;" and he " levis to his sone William " " all the rest of his guidis," &c.

IV. William Muir of Park was served heir of his father, Edward, in the lands of Park, 26th April 1623. His name occurs in the testament of William Muir of Middletoune in 1627. He died in May 1630. His testament, &c. was " ffaythfullie maid and gevin up be Jeane Stewart [of the Halrig family] his relict, in name and behalf of *Williame* and *Alexr.* Muiris, lauchfull barnes procreat betuixt hir and the defunct," &c.

V. John Muir of Park, probably his eldest son, occurs in the testament of Adame Muire of Cocklichill, in 1651. He became, we presume,* a merchant in Ayr, and was for many years Provost of the burgh. He married Janet Dook, or Doak, but of what family does not appear. Amongst the numerous tenements, and other property, he acquired in Ayr, we find him making purchase, in 1666, of the house in the Boat Vennel still known as the Earl of Loudoun's. As the " evidents " connected with this property are locally interesting, we shall copy the following from an old inventory of title-deeds and other documents belonging to Provost John Moore :—

Ane Inventar of the Writs and Evidents of the Houses, Yeard, and Garden Chamber, and Pertinents, which belonged to the Earle of Loudoune, afterwards the Laird of Gadgirth, and was acquired by Provost John Moore.

Imp. Disposition and assignatione by James Dunlop of that Ilk, with consent of John Earle of Loudon, Dam Margaret Campbel, his Countess, and James Lord Mauchline, and them for themselvis, for all right and tittle they had to the tenement efter mentioned, and also with consent of Sir Hugh Campbell of Cesnock, Sir James Stewart of Kirkfield, and Hugh Pennango in Broadlay, in favours of John Chalmers of Gadgirth, of that tenement of land, back and fore, under and above, with the yeard and pertinents thairof, including and comprehending that chamber called the Garden Chamber, lying in the burgh of Ayr, in the Sea Vennel,† upon the south side of it, betwixt the tenement of James Faullusdail, thaireffter John Rankine, on the east, the tenement of Robert Campbell and Hugh Girvan on the south, the wast piece of land of umquil Patherick Broun, and the tenement of umquil Thomas Broun on the west, and of that piece of back

---

* Parochial Records of Ayr.

† Along with the lands of Blairstoun, Provost Mure acquired a right to certain seats in the Kirks of Maybole and Alloway—the clause in reference to which is as follows: " And also my two seats or dasks in the Kirks of Maybole and Alloway."

VOL. II.

* There is no evidence of this beyond the necessary identity of the parties, if Provost John Mure of Ayr was the direct representative of the Mures of Park, which seems probable from the coincidence of name and time. What seems farther confirmatory of the presumption is the fact that the baptism of his two eldest children is not recorded in the Ayr register of births, having probably been born in the parish of Tarbolton. The Wilsons of Barhill, in that parish, were connected with the family, as appears from the family papers.

† Now called the Boat Vennel.

Y 2

land of auld of the said Patherick Brounis, being the yeard of the said tenement, lying contigue thairwith, and on the west part thairof, near the            of old the Gray-friers, for payment of 1000 lib. Scots by Gadgirth to Dunlope; which James Dunlope had right to the foresaid tenement, and to the lands and baronies of Easter and Wester Loudouns from James Livingstone, in the city of London, Esq., with consent of Sir Daniel Carmichael of Hindford, and from the said Sir Daniel, for himself, by disposition dated the         day of      and which James Livingstone had right to the said tenement by a decreet of apprising against the said John Earle of Loudon, dated the 22d of July 1652, by which the said land and baronies of Easter and Wester Loudouns, and the tenement foresaid, with the yeard and pertinents, were apprized for payment to the said James Livingstone, in payment and satisfaction of the accumulate sum of nine thousand six hundred and eighty pounds starline, and sherif fie effeiring thairto, extending to one hundred and eighty-four pounds starline, which decreet was seen and considered be the Commissioners for Administration and Justice to the people of Scotland,* and found orderly proceeded, upon the twenty-eight day of the said moneth of July; conforme whereunto, and be vertue of a chartour, containing precept of seasine granted by the keepers of the liberty of England, daited the 29th day of the said moneth of July 1652, the said James Livingstone was infeft in the subjects foresaid, upon the 12th of August thairafter, which disposition contains also ane assignation to a decreet of declarator of redemption obtained at the said James Livingstone's instance before the said Commissioners, against the said James Lord Mauchline, upon the 15th of July 1653, finding and declaring the lands, baronies, tenements and others foresaid, to be duely and lawfully redeemed fra him by the said James Livingstone; and also to a gift of John Earl of Loudon his escheat, granted to the said James Livingstone; as also containing ane assignation to the foresaid decreet of apprizing and allowance thairof, with the said decreet of declarator and redemption, with the foresaid disposition by the said James Livingstone and Sir Daniel Carmichael to Dunlope, is yet, in so far allenerly as the same concerns, or may be extended to the foresaid tenement, yeard, and pertinents, and piece of back land foresaid, and to the sum of two thousand merks Scots, as a part of the best and readiest of the sums contained in the said decreet of apprizing, and the annual rents thairof from Mertinias 1655, and the proportional part of the sherife fee; as also containing renunciation and overcharge of the reversion by the said Earle of Loudon and James Lord Mauchline, with consent of the said Dam Margaret Campbel to the said Chalmers of Gadgirth; and sicklike containing a clause of absolute warrand; and by the said John Earle of Loudon, the disposition which contains certain other clauses, daited the 5th day of December 1657.

2. Extract disposition by William Gordon of Craichlaw, as having right by apprizing to the tenement above mentioned, &c.

3. Letters of horning at the instance of the said Provost John Moore against the said John Chalmers of Gadgirth, upon the clause of warrandice contained in the foresaid disposition granted by him and the said William Gordon of Craichlaw, daited the 4th and signat the 12th of December 1685.

4. Instrument of seasine in favours of the said Provost John Moore and Jonet Dook, his spanse, of the tenement, &c., daited the 19th day of Feb. 1691.

5. Ratification by the magistrates of Ayr, &c. 13th January 1696.

6. Contract of marriage betwixt the said Provost Robert Moore, with consent of Provost J. Moore, his father, and Agnes Simpson, by which the said John Moore obliged himself to infeft his son and spouse in the tenement foresaid, [date blank].

7. Instrument of seasine following thairon in favours

of the said Provost Robert Moore and his spouse, daited the 2d of Aprile 1684.

There are other five documents enumerated in connection with this property. In one of them "New Mongumry of Bridgend," now Doonside, is mentioned, and in another "James Mar, baillie of Mungnuriston," the citadel of Ayr, which, after the Restoration was gifted to the Earl of Eglintoun, and created a burgh under that designation.

Provost John Mure had issue by his marriage:

1. Robert.
2. Samuel, was designed of Park, which property he probably acquired after the purchase of Blairstoun. "Samuel Muir of Park" appears among the Commissioners of Supply in 1702 and 1704. He married Isobel Chalmer, and had two sons and five daughters.* He was alive in 1731.
3. David, born 22d April 1670.
4. Marion, born 23d August 1671; married to Robert M'Jarrow of Bar, and had issue.
5. Gelis, ⎫ twins, born 23d August 1673.
6. Jane, ⎭

Mr Mure had been in the magistracy as early as 1672, and in 1687 he became highly popular in the burgh by his resistance of the cess proposed to be levied from the inhabitants by Provost William Cuninghame. Mr Mure, together with his son, Robert. Elias Cathcart, Adam Osburne, David Ferguson, and several other burgesses, contributed funds from their own private purses, and successfully opposed the imposition by application to the Privy Council and Session. The Town Council of Ayr, by a special minute, dated 11th January 1689, acknowledged the services of those who took part in this movement, and ordered their respective advances to be refunded from the burgh revenue. In this minute "John Moore" is designed "lait Provost," so that he had been chief magistrate previous to the Revolution, and was probably set aside by the friends of James VII. In 1689, immediately after the Revolution, when the magistrates were chosen by poll election, Mr Mure was made a magistrate, and Robert, his son, a councillor. In the following year he was appointed Provost, and represented the burgh in Parliament, as appears from the following minute of the Town Council:—"Ayr, 2d Septemr. 1690.—Whilk day there was a bill drawn by the Magistrates and Council upon the Thessaurer for paying off ffive hundred merks to the Provost [John Moore, Provost] upon the accompt of his expences and deburscments in the toun's affairs at Edinr., and fees as Commissioner of Parliament for the burgh."† In 1691 he was Provost and Commissioner for the burgh in the General Assembly and Parliament, and was chiefly instrumental in procuring the suppression of the Kirk of Alloway, and the gift of two years' vacant stipends belonging to it, for the

---

* This was during the Commonwealth.

* Parish Records.

† The Commissioners of the Scottish Parliament were paid by their constituents.

repair of the harbour.* His account of expenditure and fees in these matters amounted to £1028, 18s. Scots. The parties appointed to examine and revise the account reported " that they could not impugne or quarrell the said account, referring to the Provost's own discretion if he would quit any part thereof, who, out of kindness to the place, and in consideration of its poverty and great burden the same lies under, of his own goodwill quyt and gave doun the said whole account to the sum of nyne hundreth pounds Scots money, whereupon bill was drawn upon the Thessaurer for payment thereof." In 1692 Provost Mure represented the toun at the Convention of Burghs held at Dundee. In 1696 he again represented the burgh in Parliament, as well as in the General Assembly and Synod of Glasgow. In 1699 he attended the Convention of Burghs; and in 1701, while Commissioner for the burgh in Parliament, procured an act for a new fair to be held annually in Ayr in the month of January. In 1702-3-5, and so late as 1706-7, we find the venerable Provost acting as Commissioner for Ayr in Parliament, the General Assembly and Convention of Royal Burghs. In 1702 he was at the head of the commissioners of burghs on the committee for controverted elections. In 1706 his name occurs as an approver of the first article of the Union, in the terms of the motion at the meeting of 4th Nov. 1706, and afterwards as an approver of the whole act of the Union, on the 12th Nov. following. In 1707 he voted in favour of allowing the proposed sum as the expenses of the Scots commissioners while in London regarding the Union. He voted also in favour of some pecuniary transactions connected with the Indian and African Companies at the sitting 10th March 1707. Provost Mure seems to have been a person of high credit and reputation, not only in the management of his own affairs, but in those of the burgh over which he and his family so long bore sway as chief magistrates. During his lifetime both his sons, Robert and Samuel, were elected to the Provostship, and he evidently took a warm interest in all that concerned the welfare of the town. He was no doubt a staunch Whig, and consequently in favour with the powers that were. In those days

the customs and excise were farmed out; and amongst the papers of the family ample evidence remains of their having been concerned in the collection of these revenues. In 1689 he was collector of the customs at Ayr; and again, in 1696, he farmed one-fortieth of the whole customs of Scotland. Of that amount one-fourteenth was held each by James Hutchison and Elias Cathcart. Provost John Mure died at an advanced age, in the end of 1709 or beginning of 1710, having been engaged in the trade and public business of Ayr during a period of nearly sixty years, remarkable for civil commotions and great events.

VI. Robert Mure, as well as his brother Samuel, continued to carry on business as a merchant in Ayr, and appears to have been very successful. He was, like his father, extensively engaged in the tobacco trade with Virginia, as well as in the wine trade with France. Robert married Agnes Simpson, daughter of Alexander Simpson, merchant in Ayr, prior to which event he had been elected Provost of the burgh. By the contract of marriage his father had become bound to infeft him and his wife in his tenement in the Sea Vennel, the instrument of sasine following upon which is dated 2d April 1684. The issue of this marriage, according to the parish record, was:—

1. Janet, born August 1687.
2. John, who succeeded, born 21st March 1689.*
3. Alexander, born 3d July 1699, merchant in Ayr, died before 1768.
4. Robert, merchant in Ayr, and one of the bailies. He owned lands in Kirkoswald parish, to which his nephew, Robert, succeeded.
5. Samuel, born 30th April, 1698.
6. Agnes, born 6th February 1692; married John M'Jarrow, surgeon in Ayr, and had an only child, Robert. She died before 1737.
7. Thomas, born 19th Dec. 1705.
8. Isobell, married Joseph Wilson of Barmuir, late Provost of Ayr.
9. Giels, born 17th Sept. 1700; married William M'Jarrow of Altonalbany, and died in 1734.
10. Marion, born June 1704, married Bannatyne of Gardrum.

Provost Robert Mure, or Moore, acquired the property of Blairstoun in 1698, and subsequently the lands of Brockloch, also in the parish of Maybole. His name appears in various business transactions down to the year 1730. There is a bond by Samuel Moore (his brother), William Robine, Elias Cathcart, John and David Fergussoun and Stephen Lagail, to Robert Moore, for £740, 8s. 8d. Scots, dated 1st Feb. 1701. " Robert Muir of Blairstone " appears among the Commissioners of Sup-

---

* I, John Alexander of Blackhouse, doe by these presents allow the present magistrates of Aire to make use of my quarrie in Blackhouse for winning stones for repairing their key or harbour, they being always obligded to satisfie the present tenant, George Nisbet, for anie damadge or skaithe he sustaines, and me for the benefite and use of the quarrie, at the sight of William Fullartoun of that Ilk, and John Muire, late Provost of Aire. Given by me att Aire, the second daye of Maye, Jaivic. and ninetie sex yeirs.                                          J. ALEXR.

* The witnesses to the baptism of John were " John Moor, late Provost and grandfather to the child, Mr John Cockburn, Sheriff Clerk, Thomas Millikene, late Bailie, David Fergussone and Samuel Moor, merchants, and uncles to the child."

ply in 1702; and in 1706 " Robert Moor of Blairstone and John Cunninghame of Enterkine " are the only commissioners for Ayrshire in what is called " the Union Parliament of Scotland." Like his father, he and his brother Samuel had taken a deep interest in the affairs of the burgh of Ayr, with which they had been early connected. He represented the burgh at the convention in 1696, and again in 1702. Indeed, it may almost be said, that the welfare of the town of Ayr was wholly in their hands from the Revolution in 1688 till 1722, a period of thirty-three years. The Tory or Jacobite party having then got into power in the burgh, a charge of maladministration was maliciously instituted against the Mures, and a law-suit was the consequence. Some idea of the origin of this law-suit, and the nature of the charge, will be gleaned from the following

MEMORIAL for ROBERT MURE of Blairstoun, late Provost of Air;

In the affair betwixt the Toun of Air and the said Robert Mure.

The minuts being adjusted and laid before your Lordships, the Provost shall not give any further trouble on the point of law, but only must beg leave to informe your Lordships of some matters of fact, that may have some concern in the matter.

In the year 1688, when the magistracy was chosen by a poll election, the defender's father was chosen a magistrat, and himself a councillor, and several others were chosen into the magistracy. After the election, when the magistrats came to consider the toun's circumstances, they found them very low, and that the toun's debt was above 16,000 merks, and that there was no free common good but betwixt 600 or 700 merks yearly for supporting the honour of the burgh, and upholding all the publick works. This made the magistrats despair of being able to keep the magistracy, and would certainly have been obligded to resign, if the Government had not been pleased to give the toun a merk on the boll of malt for ten years within the burgh. This enabled the magistrats to clear a considerable part of the toun's debt, and build the publick entrey to the Toun-house, and a weigh-house under, and repaired the harbour, which cost very considerable sums.

In anno 1722, when the present sett of magistrats came in, the preceding left as many funds as would clear the toun's whole debts, and make them the freest toun in Scotland.

And dureing the former magistracy by their influence in the burrous, procured an ease of the tax roll, by which the toun saved upwards of 1000 merks. Though this was the magistrat's duety, yet this was such a piece of service as ought not to be forgot.

The Provost only mentions these things to show your Lordships how ungratefully he is used by the present sett of magistrats, to pursue him for a lybell of 8000 merks of ommissions, and wherein they cannot condescend upon one shilling of his intromissions with the toun's effects, which, if they could doe, the Provost is willing to pay the double; and if the case be so, your Lordships cannot but see the hardship the Provost is brought under by this process, that he should be obligded out of his private stock to support a plea carried on by humour by the present magistracy, and the expences depursed out of the toun's money, whereas the Provost, who has a numerous ffamily of ten children, must defray the charges out of his private pocket. Its thought there cannot be ane instance of such a process given.

The great noise that is made of the Provost's intromissions is his managdement of the burrow tack, as to which, ls to be observed, that he never received one shilling of that money, and in all that affair did all that was in his power to have procured the toun's payment; but those liable in payment would never come to give such a sourne as the toun would accept of, and a good part of the present magistrats and councill cannot refuse but that some time after the election 1721, when he was speaking in councill about the burrow tack, he told them of the assignation and backbond, and that it was only in security of a debt due to him, conforme to back-bond, which he then judged was either in Baillie David's hands, or in the late clerk's, seeing it was not in the charter chest: and that he could not prevail with the managders to give above five pounds sterling for each penny in the tack roll, which they behooved either to accept of or enter to a plea, and that he advised them rather to accept then enter to a plea, which they declined.

In Jully 1722, when the present magistrats had the plurality, they, without the leist insinuation from the Provost, and to his surprise, sent him the new commission, and he then again dealt with the managders to better the offer quhich he reported at his return, and offered to cleir in these terms, but it was declined, and the not recording of the backbond and assignation was intirely a neglect of the clerk's; and it was wrote by his servant, and he and his servant are witnesses, and is signed by 14 of the Conneillours.

As to the pretence that the debt payed by the Provelst to Ramsay was not the toun's debt, it is a great mistake, for there are two acts of Councell produced whereby the Councell binds and oblidges themselves and their successors to free Baillie Fergusson of any damadge by that process; and one of the toun's lawers just now was of the opinion that what Baillie Fergusson did was legall, and that the toun ought to relieve him of any damadge; and he was accordingly imployed to defend the toun in that affair. And the pretence that the Provelst procured these acts by his power is intirely false, for the Provelst was not in the toun at the tyme of passing these acts, and knew nothing of them."

The Council claimed £2947 10s. 6d., principal and interest, as the sum which ought to have accrued to the burgh from the tack of the custous. It would appear, however, from the above " Memoriall," that Provost Robert Mure was completely exonerated in reference to it. The profits arising from it seem to have gone in liquidation of certain debts due by the town, and that there was an assignation of the tack for that purpose.

Provost Robert Mure married, for his second wife, in 1714, Marion Hamilton, who survived him, and was alive in 1746. He himself died of gout and other ailments in 1734.

VII. John Mure of Blairstoun and Brockloch succeeded his father. He married Jane Fairweather, only daughter of the minister of Maybole, and his wife, Mary Fergusson, and had issue :—

1. Mary, born 10th August 1731, married to David Fergusson, Provost of Ayr, and died in 1782.*
2. Agnes, died in 1746.
3. Robert, born 20th Feb. 1736.

* The witnesses at the baptism of Mary were " Robert Muir of Blairstoune, late Provost, and grandfather to the child, Samuel Muir, late Provost, grand-uncle, and Thomas M'Jarrow of Barr, late bailie, grand-uncle-in-law to the child, Joseph Wilson of Barmuir, late Provost, and uncle-in-law to the child."

4. Marion, born 26th August 1737; married to David Ballantine, Provost of Ayr.

5. James, born 16th March 1740.

He died in 1744. His widow survived him, and was alive in 1747.

VIII. Robert Mure of Blairstoun and Brockloch, the eldest son, succeeded. He became M.D., after studying medicine at Edinburgh, London, and St Omer, and married Mary Michell of London, who died at Richmond in 1784. By her he had issue:

1. John, who graduated as a surgeon at Edinburgh, and died in Jamaica, in 1794, childless.

2. Mary.

3. Eliza, who died young in London.

Robert Mure died at Blairstoun on the 31st December 1801.

IX. Mary Mure of Blairstoun, his only surviving child, was served heir to her father 26th February 1802. She had been married in 1793 to David Cathcart, afterwards Lord Alloway, and died 9th March 1802, leaving a family of four sons and two daughters.

X. Elias Cathcart, younger of Alloway, advocate, her eldest son, was served heir to his mother in the lands of Middle Auchindraine, or Blairstoun, 3d March 1819, and still possesses that property.

### CATHCARTS OF ALLOWAY.

The tradition in this family is, that they are descended from the Cathcarts of Carbieston, or of Bardarroch, ancient branches of the noble house of Cathcart. It is unquestionable that the early merchants of Ayr were almost all offshoots of the landed families in the county—such as the Chalmerses, Wallaces, Campbells, Cuninghames, Craufurds, Blairs, Dunlops, MacJarrows, Rankines, Neils, Mures, Hamiltons, Kennedies, &c. In fact, they were the only parties who possessed means to embark in trading or commercial pursuits. "A business gentleman will be in the eye of a thinking man, as great a character as a gentle ploughman, or a person who has no other thing to improve and instruct his gentry, but the circumstance of his *not* being born in a town."[*]

The Cathcarts can be traced as merchant burgesses in Ayr for several generations. One of them was engaged in the wine trade with Bourdeaux, which began as early as 1466; and they all along took a great interest in the prosperity of the town and harbour. There was an *Adam Cathcart* Provost of Ayr in 1585; a *William*

* M'Ure's History of Glasgow.

*Cathcart*, Provost of Ayr in 1586,[*] and a *David Cathcart*, merchant burgess of Air, whose relict, Janet Campbell, had a sasine of annual rent furth of the "twa merkland of Chippirlagane," in 1586.[†] Who the above parties were, in all probability, will appear from the following extract: "April 14, 1584.—The quhilk day, *Adame* Cathcart of Bardarroch past to his xls. land of Mosblowane of auld extent, liand within the baronie of Auchincruif, baillierie of Kylestewart, and shriefdome of Air, and ther guif heretabill stait and sasing therof with his awin hand, to William Cathcart, his sone and apperand heir, to          Blair, as actornay for Margaret Fullertoun, Lady Fergushill, his spous, to be haldin of the said Adame and his airis in fre blanche for the zeirlie payment of twa d., eftir the forme and tenour of ane chartour to be maid be the said Adame to the said Williame and his said spous," &c. The witnesses to this sasine were William Cathcart, junior, of Carbeston, Gilbert Cathcart, second son of Alan Lord Cathcart, John Cathcart, son natural of the said Lord, David Cathcart, son of David Cathcart, formerly burgess of Air, and John M'Cowll, servant to William Cathcart, junior, of Bardarroch. There can be little doubt that Adam Cathcart of Bardarroch was the Provost alluded to in 1585; and the William Cathcart, junior, of Bardarroch, may have been the Provost mentioned in 1586 ‡ It is as probable, however, that it was *William Cathcart, junior*, of *Carbiestoun*, whose family about this time possessed the "auld tower" at the townhead of Ayr, and which, no doubt, formed their town residence. Whether we may be correct in this supposition or not—for it matters not which of the parties was Provost—it is evident that the whole of the witnesses, with the exception of John M'Cowll, were connected by family ties. Indeed, the nearest relatives were usually, in former times, selected as witnesses to the transfer of family property. The tradition that the Cathcarts of Alloway are descended from the Carbiestoun or Bardarroch families, seems thus to be well founded. "David Cathcart, son of David Cathcart, late burgess of Ayr," may, in all likelihood, have been a cousin of some of the parties mentioned, for the family documents at least prove that David was a favourite name. There can be little doubt, however, that the Cathcarts of Bardarroch and of Alloway branched off before the marriage of the heiress of Carbieston to David Cathcart of Duchray, third

* Town Records.          † Mason's Notes.
‡ Adam Cathcart of Bardarroch had also a brother, William, who is mentioned in the Town Records in 1598.

son of John Lord Cathcart, 1547. We feel warranted, therefore, in the absence of direct evidence on the subject, in tracing the origin of the family to

I. DAVID CATHCART, "late burgess of Ayr," whose relict, Janet Campbell, had an annual rent, as above stated, furth of Chippirlagane in 1586. He had at least a son,

II. David Cathcart, who, in 1584, is styled "son of David Cathcart, late burgess of Air." Whom he married does not appear.[*] He was probably the father of

III. Elias Catcheart, whose second son,

IV. John Cathcart, married Agnes Mertine,[†] relict of Alexander Purveyance, notar and merchant in Ayr—contract of marriage dated 26th December 1643. He had at least two sons:

1. Elias Cathcart, merchant in Ayr, married, first, before 1669, Margaret Hunter, sister of John Hunter, merchant burgess of Ayr,[‡] and niece of Barbara Hunter, wife of Provost John Cuninghame. He had "instrument of seasine of the tenement [mentioned in his father's contract of marriage] in favour of Elias Cathcart, merchant in Ayr, son and heir to the said umquhil John Cathcart, and in favour of Margaret Hunter, his spouse, dated the 9th day of February 1669." He married, secondly, Barbara Maxwell, of the Cardoness family, and infeft her in certain tenements, according to the marriage contract, which is dated 1st August 1695. He had "disposition by John Masson, son to John Masson, town-clerk of Ayr, in favour of Elias Cathcart, merchant, of a seat in the church of Ayr, under the Council loaf, dated 16th of September 1699." He acted along with Provost Muir in resisting the oppressions of the times; particularly in opposing the cess laid on by Provost William Cuninghame in 1687. He was considerably involved in debt prior to, and at the time of his death, as appears from certain family papers.[§] He died childless.

V. David Cathcart, merchant burgess of Ayr, who married Janet Ferguson, and had issue:

1. David, born 7th May 1665.
2. John, born 4th December 1666.
3. Elias, born 19th June 1669.

Elias Cathcart, merchant in Ayr, witnessed the baptism of some of these children;[‖] so also did Robert Doak, merchant in Ayr, a relative, no doubt, of Janet Dook or Doak, wife of Provost Mure.

---

[*] In 1620, Samuel Cathcart was served heir of David Cathcart, the son of the deceased Captain David Cathcart's immediate younger brother. That these Cathcarts were all nearly connected is apparent: but, in the absence of documentary evidence, it is impossible to ascertain their degrees of propinquity.

[†] She had a daughter, Jean Purveyance, married to Archibald Anderson, merchant in Ayr, about 1664.

[‡] Family Papers.

[§] Bailie Thomas Cathcart was probably a younger brother of Elias and David. His name occurs in Elias Cathcart and Margaret Hunter's infeftment. He married Elizabeth Mitchell, and had one son, Elias, and three daughters. He was tacksman of the merk in the boll in Ayr in 1693; and is mentioned also in 1696 and 1699.

[‖] Parochial Records.

---

VI. David Cathcart, "burgess sailor," or "schipper." He married Helen Smith, and had, besides other children,

Elias, born September 4, 1703.

David was afterwards lost at sea, with his ship, on his passage homeward from Bourdeaux.

VII. Elias Cathcart married, first, Helen Mac-Hutchison, daughter of Hew M'Hutchison, or M'Hutcheon, of Changue, in the parish of Bar, Provost of Ayr, by whom he had no issue; secondly, in October 1762, Agnes Fergusson, eldest daughter of James Fergusson of Bank. The children were:

1. David, born December 28, 1763.
2. James, born April 24, 1765, married, and had a numerous family.
3. Jean, born Dec. 24, 1766,
4. Helen, born Nov. 1, 1768,     who all died childless.
5. Margeret, born April 13, 1770,

Elias Cathcart was an extensive merchant, and entered largely into the French wine and Virginia trade. He was a bailie in 1745, and founded the Poor-House of Ayr. He purchased Alloway Nether Crofts and Kirk Crofts from the town of Ayr, when the barony of Alloway was broken up, in 1754. He built a commodious and not inelegant house on the property, which he called Greenfield, and died there in 1776, aged 73. He had been, at various periods, Provost of Ayr. His first wife died in 1756; his second survived him a number of years, and died at Gayfield House, a property belonging to the family, near Edinburgh, on the 26th March 1816, aged 81.

VIII. David Cathcart of Alloway, studied for the Bar, and after practising successfully for some time, was elevated to the Bench, when he assumed the title of Lord Alloway. He was also one of the Lords of the High Court of Justiciary. Greatly respected as a judge, he was not less so as a private gentleman. He married, in 1793, Mary, only surviving child of Robert Mure of Blairstoun, and through her acquired that property. She died at Edinburgh in 1802. He took great pleasure in improving the lands, and usually spent the vacations at Blairstoun House, where he died 27th April 1829, and was buried in Alloway Kirk. He left issue by his wife, Mary Mure, four sons and two daughters, of whom Elias is the eldest.

IX. Elias Cathcart, advocate, succeeded to the paternal estate in 1829. He married, in 1818, Janet, only surviving daughter of the late Robert Dunlop, merchant in Glasgow, and by her has a family of two sons and three daughters. He sold the lands of Brockloch in 1829, and the property of Alloway in 1830. In the latter year, under the old name of Auchindraine, he united his estate of Blairstoun, or Middle Auchindraine, with the adjoining barony of Auchindraine, which he acquired from the Parliamentary Trustees of the late Sir James Fergusson of Kilkerran, Bart. Elias Cathcart's appointment as a Deputy Lieutenant of the county is dated in 1845. He had graduated as L.L.D. in the University of Leyden, in Holland, in 1815.

### MONTGOMERIES OF BRIGEND.

As stated elsewhere, this property was called Nether Auchindraine previous to the building of the "Old Bridge of Doon," so celebrated in the poem of "Tam O'Shanter." Hugh Lord Eglintoun was served heir in the lands, amongst others, of "Auchindraine Nedder," in 1661. The Montgomeries of Brigend were of the Lainshaw branch of this noble family; but some confusion prevails in the various accounts of their origin. *Robertson* states, that *William*, third son of Sir Neil Montgomerie of Lainshaw, married " *Jean Montgomerie*, heiress of Brigend, whose mother was a daughter of Houston of that Ilk;" while the *Broomlands Manuscript* says, that " William Montgomerie, *second* son of Sir Neil Montgomerie of Lainshaw, married          Kennedy, heiress of Brigend," &c. It is extremely probable that Nether Auchindraine belonged in early times to a branch of the Kennedies; and the Broomlands MS. is perhaps right in reference to the fact, though wrong in point of time; for, prior to the date of either of these alleged marriages, we find a

I. JOHN MONTGOMERIE of Brigend, whose name occurs in a legal document dated May 31, 1587. He died in 1612, as appears from the following extract of his latter-will:—

" The testament, &c., of umquhile Johnne Montgomerie, callit of Brigend, quha deceist in ye toun of Irvein in the moneth of March 1612 zeiris," &c.

" Inuentar

" Item, the defunct, the tyme of his deceis foirsaid, being ane aigit blind man of fourscoir zeiris age or thereby, and haveing neyther wyf nor familie, during the haill tyme of his lyftyme, had neyther guidis nor geir except allanerlie ane kist, with certane abuilzements of his bodie being thereintill, standing in the duelling hous of Allexr. Montgomerie, burges of Irwein, quher he depairtit this lyf, thair being in the said kist ane fustiane dowblat cuttit out vpone taffatie, ane pair of reid skarlet breikis, ane coit and ane pair of breikis of broun clayth, ane pair of auld breikis, callit of claith of sylwir, ane cloik of broun Frensch,

ane veluit hat, ane pair of pistolatis, string of sylk, all estimat to the soume of ffourtie pundis. Item, twa hat stringis, estimat to thrie scoir sex pund xiiii s iiii d.

" Debtis awand to the deid.

" Item, Be Thomas Neving of Mounkridding, as principall, and Wm. Cauldwoll of Annandbill, his cautioner, conforme to the band, &c., ane hundrith punds. Item, be Mr Wm. Carstair and Johnne Montgomerie of Cockilbie, &c., ane hundrith punds. Item, be Alexr. Cvnynghame, burges of Irwein, xxvi lib. Item, be Neill Montgomerie of Langsehaw, the tennents of the Kirktoun of Stewartoun, the sowme of thriescoir sex pund xiii s iiii d annualrent out of the saidis landis of the Witsounday and Martimes termes of the crop and yeir of God 1611. Item, be William Cauldwoll of        , xv lib.

" Debtis awand be the deid.

" Item, . . . To Margrat Montgomerie, his naturell dochter, twa hundrith pund. Item, to Hew Gray, prebandar of Mayboill, ane hundrith pundis. Item, to Allexr. Montgomerie, merchant burges of Irwein, for his buirding and intertinement, fiftie pund. Item, to Cudbert Thomesoun, his servitour, for byrun feyis, twenty pund.

" Summa of the debtis out, iiic lxx lib.

" Restis frie geir, debts deducit, xlv lib.

" Na dimisioun.

" At Irwein, the xxvi day of March 1612 zeiris. The quhilk day the said Johnne Montgomerie makand his testament, being seik in bodie, and reddy to depart this mortall lyf, maid and constitute Wm. Montgomerie of Brigend exceutour and onlie intromittour with his guidis and geir. . . . This was done day, zeir, and place foirsaid, befoir thir witness, Thomas Ronnald, baillie deput of Cvnynghame." . . .

It does not appear from this document in what degree of relationship his successor in Brigend stood to the deceased. The latter was no doubt at one time proprietor of Brigend, for his name is mentioned as such in 1587. He seems to have parted with his property to William Montgomerie, his successor, though he was still " callit of Brigend." But as he never was married, William could not be his son-in-law, unless a natural daughter had been constituted heiress, which may have been the case. At all events, his latter-will shows that he had one natural daughter, named Margaret. It is possible, therefore, that William Montgomerie of the Lainshaw family married as stated by *Robertson*, and that it was the father of the deceased John Montgomerie of Brigend, whoever he was, that married the heiress Kennedy.

II. William Montgomerie of Brigend, who is presumed to have married Jean Montgomerie, heiress of Brigend, is repeatedly mentioned in testamentary and other documents down till 1652. In 1636, along with Neil Montgomerie of Lainshaw, he attended the funeral of Hugh, first Viscount Montgomerie of Newton-Ardes, in Ireland. By his marriage he had four sons:

1. John, who predeceased him. He married Agnes Scot, daughter of the Lord Clarkington, by whom he had two sons—Hew and James.
2. James, of Glenays, who married Janet, daughter of Craufurd of Auchenames, but had no issue.
3. William of Belliskeoch. He accompanied his father to the funeral of Viscount Montgomerie, and carried the great banner.* He married Barbara, daughter of John Montgomerie of Cockelbie, but died without male issue.
4. Hugh Montgomerie of Beoch, married Agnes, daughter of M'Ilvain of Grimmet, and had a son. He was alive in 1650.‡

John, the eldest son, who predeceased his father, must have died before 7th December 1647, at which date, "Hugo Montgomerie, haeres Joannis Montgomerie de Brigend, patris," is served heir " in petiis terræ de lie communoune de Crawfuirdstone, alias Terrinzeane, nuncupatis Knokdone in Howanstoune, in parochia de Cumnok." In 1650 we find William Montgomerie of Brigend " takand the burdane in and upon him for Hew Montgomerie, his oy, eldest lawfull sone and air to vmquhile John Montgomerie, zounger, of Brigend," in a contract with Sir William Cuninghame of Caprington, anent "his peice of land of the common of Crawfurdstone, alias Tarrinzeane, callit Knokdone and Howanstoune," &c., possessed by Thomas Richart. He paid 2000 merks Scots for it.

III. James Montgomerie of Brigend, brother of Hew, is said to have succeeded his grandfather, and to have sold the estate to his cousin, John Montgomerie of Beoch.‡ The Broomlands MS. does not mention his having married, and it is certain he left no male issue. He went to America, where he died.

IV. John Montgomerie of Brigend, son of Hugh Montgomerie of Beoch. He married Jean, eldest daughter of George Montgomerie of Broomlands, and had, according to the Broomlands MS., two sons, *George* and *James*, and one daughter. He must, however, have had three:

I. William. He is styled "younger of Brigend" in the parish register of Ayr, where the baptism of two of his children are recorded—the one, "Anna,"

*There is some confusion here. A Hugh Montgomerie of Belliskeoch was also at the funeral in 1636; and Hugh Montgomerie of Belliskeoch has a decreet pronounced against him in the Bailie Court of Cuninghame, 7th Feb. 1694.

† Bailie Court Books of Cuninghame.

‡ It is probable that it was about this time (1661) that Brigend had fallen temporarily into the hands of the Eglintoun family.

in 1691, and "George," in 1693.* His wife's name was Isobell Burnet. He predeceased his father, and his children seem to have died young.
2. George, of whom afterwards.
3. James, merchant, and Provost of Ayr. He married Agnes, daughter of Robert Hunter, merchant there, by whom he had one daughter, Jean, married to James Leggat, merchant in Glasgow, and had issue.
4. Jean, married to William Rankine, merchant in Ayr, and had issue.

John Montgomerie of Brigend died in 1714, when his son, James, merchant in Ayr, obtained leave from the Magistrates and Council to bury his father, the "Laird of Brigend," in Alloway Kirkyard, and have the bell rung.†

VI. George Montgomerie of Brigend was a merchant in Edinburgh. He is so designed in a summons against Robert Muir of Blairstoun, in 1724, before the Lords of Council and Session, for the delivery of a certain discharged bond, granted by him and his father, the deceased "John Montgomerie of Brigend." Though styled "of Brigend" in that document, George Montgomerie had a number of years previously disposed of the property. He married Mary, daughter of Archibald Dickson of Towerlands, by whom he had one son and five daughters:

1. Robert.
2. Janet, married to David Spence, merchant in Edinburgh.
3. Catherine, married to the Rev. Mr Walker, minister of Leuchars, in Fife.
4. Agnes.    5. Jean.    6. Helen.‡

VII. Robert Montgomerie, the only son, was a merchant in Edinburgh, and one of the magistrates of that city. He was one of the Commissioners of H.M. Customs, and Lord Provost of Edinburgh in 1757. He died, unmarried, 7th September 1763. Both he and his father had been successively heirs-male of the house of Eglintoun, and heirs-general of the title of Lord Lisle, which was claimed by Sir Walter Montgomerie Cuninghame after the Brigend Montgomeries had become extinct.

### CRAUFURDS OF DOONSIDE, ALIAS BRIGEND.

The ancestor of the Craufurds of Doonside is understood to have been Duncan Craufurd of Knockshinnoch, brother of Alexander Craufurd of Kerse. He had four sons, the second of whom,

I. JOHN CRAUFURD, Collector of the Customs at Borrowstoness, bought the lands of Brigend from George Montgomerie in 1715. He married and had issue:

1. William, who died young.
2. John, who succeeded.

* George Montgomerie, apothecary, Ayr, and Margaret M'Corn, had a son, George, baptised 28th August 1691. Witness, William Montgomerie of Brigend.—AYR REC.

† Ayr Records.

The name of the property was changed about this time from Brigend to Doonside, and a new mansion-house built in a beautiful holm a short distance farther up the river than the old fortlet.

II. John Craufurd of Doonside succeeded his father in 1746. He married Margaret Hamilton, daughter of Alexander Inglis or Hamilton of Murdiston, but had no issue, and died in 1776. He executed a deed of entail, dated 11th April 1753, in favour of the following series of heirs:—1st, William Craufurd, only son of Captain William Craufurd;* 2d, —— Craufurd, his only sister; 3d, Mary Craufurd, alias Stewart, eldest daughter of the deceased David Craufurd of Allanton, his father's eldest brother; 4th, Katrine Craufurd, the only child of Basil Craufurd, son of the said deceased David Craufurd; 5th, John Craufurd, surveyor of the customs at Borrowstoness.

III. William Craufurd of Doonside, first heir of entail, and second cousin of the entailer, succeeded in 1776. He married Jane Campbell, daughter of Dr Campbell of Wellwood, physician in Ayr, and had issue three sons and three daughters:

1. James Robertson, who succeeded.
2. John, who succeeded his brother.
3. William, the present proprietor.
1. Katharine, married Robert Wallace, Esq., R.N., and has no issue.
2. Margaret, unmarried.
3. Georgina, married William Smith, Esq., deceased without issue.

IV. James Robertson Craufurd succeeded his father in 1807. He died a bachelor, and was succeeded by his brother *John*, in January 1818. John died in October of the same year, and was succeeded by his brother,

*William Craufurd* of Doonside, the present proprietor.

### FERGUSSONS OF DALDUFF.

The Fergussons of Dalduff, "a small stone house, with ane orchard and good corne fields about it," situated about three miles from the mouth of the Girvan, on the south side of that stream, were a direct branch of the Fergussons of Kilkerran, from whom they appear to have originally rented the lands of Dalduff. The first of the family, we presume, was

I. HECTOR FERGUSON in Dalduff, who had a Crown charter of the lands of Riddilliston, 10th February 1557. He was succeeded by his son,

II. Gilbert Ferguson, "filio Hectori Ferguson in Dalduff," had a Crown charter of the lands of Blair and Knokgillo, 20th September 1585. His father was alive at this period. He must have died, however, before 1591, in which year "Gilbert Fergussoun of Dalduff" was appointed, in the testament of "Symone Forgussoun of Kylkerran," one of the tutors to his children. He had not only succeeded his father at this time, but become proprietor of Dalduff. He had a Crown charter of the lands of Dalquhane, Corshill, &c., dated 29th June 1610. He had another charter of the lands of Knokbray and Craigfin, the *penult* of April 1613. Gilbert was alive in 1614, in which year he is mentioned in the testament of "Johnne Dauidsoun" of Pennyglen. He does not appear to have been much mixed up with the feuds which prevailed so violently in Carrick during his time. His name only once occurs in the "Historie of the Kennedyis," where he is described as being in the company of Hew Kennedy of Garriehorne, "quha was ane streker off the Laird of Bargany," when met by the Laird of Auchindraine and his son at the townhead of Ayr, where a short conflict ensued.

III. John Fergusson of Dalduff was served heir of his father, Gilbert Fergusson of Dalduff, October 31, 1615. The property of the family then consisted of the two merk land of Knokbrax; the merk land of Craigfyn; the five merk land of Dalquhonand, Corshill, Dramquhill; five merk land of Crochba, Drumba, Culpanoche, Knockmoill, and Little Auchingarnie; the merk land of Dalduff; and the half merk land of Dalenr. The property seems to have been soon afterwards disposed of to the Cassillis family, as it occurs in the service of John Earl of Cassillis in 1622; and the "stone house" of Dalduff has long been levelled, or nearly so, with the corn fields by which it was wont to be surrounded.

### MONKWOOD.

Monkwood, situated on the banks of the Doon, about a mile farther up than Auchindraine, belonged to the monks of Melrose. Near it a chapel is supposed to have existed prior to the Reformation; and no doubt it took its name from its ecclesiastical owners. After the downfal of the Romish Church in this country, Monkwood seems to have become the property of the Ardmillan family, at least Hugh Kennedy, heir of Thomas Kennedy of Ardmillan, was served heir, March 15, 1644, in the £5 land of Grange, and the £4 land called Monkwood. It thereafter became the property of *John Muir*, probably a

* Eldest son of David, eldest son of Duncan Craufurd of Knockshinnoch. David was secretary to Ann Duchess of Hamilton, and bought the lands of Allanton, Harrischaw, &c. He married Ann Cockburn, and had issue.

branch of the Mures of Auchindraine. The only notice we find of him is in the service of

*Robert Muir of Monkwood,* heir of *John Muir* of Monkwood, his father, January 17, 1693. He was served in the £4 lands of Monkwood, with the new mill, and salmon and other fishings above it in the river Doon; also in the lands of Mossend, and the merk lands of M'Keounstoune, which were part of the £5 land of Nether Culzean, "in regalitate de Mellross et balliatu de Carrick."

We have accidentally fallen in with a curious document among Provost Mure's papers, in reference to Robert Muir of Monkwood. It appears that he was the only son, and a mere youth when his father died. He was placed by his tutors, at board and schooling, with Provost Mure of Ayr, and remained in his house for several years, when an action was brought by the Provost for payment of his boarding, &c. The action was resisted on the ground of overcharge. The following document, entitled "Information for John Muir, Provost of Air, against Robert Muir of Monkwood and his Tutors," dated 18th January 1688, supplies some interesting particulars as to the rate of boarding in the capital of Ayrshire, some two hundred years ago:—

"Muir of Monkwood being deid, his freinds did send Robert Muir, his only sone, to John Muir, Provost of Ayr, that he might intertaine him in his houss, keep him at the scolles, cloath him, and doe everie other thing for him that was requesit. After he had stayed severall yeirs with the Provost, he pursews the said Robert and his curators for payment of his boarding, seholing, and cloathing, quhich is modified by the judge to 20 lb sterling the yeir. Whereupon this decreet being charged, he suspends, vpon this reason, that a person in the toune of Ayr will be boardit for 100 lb in the yeir, and that he is so boardit at present, so that the modificatione is exorbitant, especiallie considering that his estait is lyfrented by his mother, and burdened with debts.

"It was answered for Provist Muir, the charger, that the decreet is opponed where both charger and suspender is compeiring, and the charger deponing upon the tyme of the intertainment and the aliment, modified by the Shireff of Air, who both knew the conditione of the intertainment and the suspender's estait, and that his mother dyed immediately after his going to Provist Muir, and when alyve that she only lyfrented the fift pairt of the estait, and that there are no debts awand out, at least not so much as is awand in; and it is weill known that at the same tyme Sir John Kennedy and Sir Godfray M'Culoch's eldest sons were boardit in the sam house, and that the suspender had the same table and loadging with them, and that they payed ten pund sterling per annum for boarding only, and wer furnished in their cloathes, washing, and scholing, and midicaments, by their parents, so that the other ten pund charged upon the suspender for his loadging, washing, scholing, and others, is verie mean, the suspender being ane active growing youth, and abusing and consuming a great many cloathes.

"Wheras it is pretendit that childring are boardit at Air for 100 lb per annum, and that the suspender is presentlie so, it is replyed that the alledgance is of no import, because boardings differ, conform to the table, ludging, and company; and no person will estime the bnirding in a peitiefull aill-houss, where the suspender getts drinks from severall companies, is the best pairt of his intertainment, to be of equall value with the intertainment in Provest Muir's houss, at a good table, with good company; and, however, he was not only intertained in meat, but in cloathes, scholl wadges, Candilesmes offerings, books bought to him, cloathes washing, made and mendit, periwiges bought and furnished, and whatever els wes necessar to him, even medicine when seik, all which are since furnished to him by his curators, who at pronouncing of the sentence wer satisfied with the modification, though now without cause they reclaim.—In respect whereof, &c."

Robert Mure of Monkwood married Barbara Barclay, of the Pereeton family. They had a son, *Robert,* baptized at Ayr, 30th August 1698. The witnesses at the baptism were, "Sir Robert Barclay of Peirstoune, uncle to the child; Sir John Montgomerie of Auchinhead, uncle-in-law to the child, and Foulis Milliken, merchant in Aire, uncle to and precentor of the child."[*]

This is the last notice we find of the Mures of Monkwood. The property seems to have been soon afterwards acquired by a family of the name of Hutchison, relations probably of the Hutchisons sometime of Underwood, and long merchants in Ayr.[†]

*George Hutchison of Monkwood* appears in the sederunts of the Commissioners of Supply for Ayrshire, from 1711 till 1725. Mr George Hutchison of Monkwood, advocate, no doubt

---

[*] Parish Records.

[†] James Hutchison, "late Provost" of Ayr, was robbed of his saddle bags and pocket-book, on 21st May (1784), betwixt five and six o'clock afternoon, on the high way between Colmonell and Girvan, in the Muir of Aldowers It contained several hundred pounds, in bank notes, bills, accompts, and other valuable papers. A reward of thirty guineas, for the apprehension of the robber or robbers, was offered by the town of Ayr.—AYR RECORDS.

the same person, was admitted a burgess of Ayr, 2d December 1721. He was succeeded apparently by his son,

*John Hutchison of Monkwood*, whose name first occurs among the Commissioners of Supply for the county in 1727. He had probably a sister, Jean, married to James Ferguson of Bank,[*]

*James Ferguson of Bank*,[†] writer, married Miss Hutchison of Monkwood, and by this union became proprietor of that property. They had issue:

1. James, who succeeded; married and had issue.
2. William, M.D. of Windsor; married and had issue.
3. John Hutchison of Trochraigue; married and had issue.
4. Anne, married to Dr Dunlop, and had issue.

The late *James Ferguson of Monkwood*, advocate, sold the estate of Monkwood to his brother, the late John H. Ferguson of Trochraigue, which has since been alienated, and now belongs to *William Paterson* of Monkwood.

### BOGEND.

The old residence of Bogend was situated near to Maybole, "nocht passit ane quarter of ane myll" from the gate of Lord Cassillis' town house.[‡] It belonged to one of the numerous branches of the Kennedies.

"*Antonie Kennedy of Boigend*." We have only gleaned a few particulars regarding him. He was married to Margaret Hamilton, who died in November 1618. The extent of the property belonging to Bogend may be inferred from the testament of the deceased. Dalmorton and Machremore formed part of it:—

"Inventar.—Item, sax drawin oxin.

"Debits awand In.—Item, . . . be the tenants and occupiers of the tuentie pund land of Dalmoirtoun, Carrik, of annuel rent, &c. Item, be the tenants and occupiers of the lands of Boigend and Machriemoir. Item, be the tenants of Bogheid, the said zeir (1613).

"Debtis awand Out.—To David Corre, brother to Wm. Corre of Kilwood, fyve hundrith merks.

"Legacie.—At Altinalbenoche the saxt day of November 1613, the quhilk day I, the said Margaret, being seik, &c., leif my saull to the grit God Almichtie, and my bodie to be bureit in the

Colledg Kirk of Mayboill." Witnesses—Quentin Kennedy of Kilcorane, Hew Kennedy of Pinquhirrie, and John Muir, notar, writer heirof, &c. Mr Hew Blair of Auldmuir, cautioner for Anthonie Kennedy.

Anthony Kennedy of Boigend survived his lady many years. He is mentioned as cautioner in the testament of David Kennedy of Kirkhill, Colmonell, who died in 1630, and to whom he was in all likelihood nearly related, as some of Kirkhill's family appear to have been named after him and his wife.

### CROCHBA.

Another of the numerous clan of Kennedy possessed this property in former times.

*Gilbert Kennedy* of Crochba, third son of Gilbert, first Earl of Cassillis, was Provost of the Collegiate Church of Maybole. He died before 9th November 1532, but left no issue.

*Isabella Kennedy*, heiress of *James Kennedy* of Crochba, her grandfather, was served in the five merk land of Crochba and Drumbu; the forty shilling land of Lettirpyn; the forty penny land of Curfyn, &c., 4th March 1600.

*John Kennedy*, heir male of Isabella Kennedy of Crochba, *nepotis patruis*, was served in the foregoing lands, 20th October 1606. He is mentioned in the testament of Davidson of Pennyglen, who died 1614. They were soon afterwards acquired by Ferguson of Dalduff.

### SMITHSTOUN.

This property also belonged to the Kennedies.

*John Kennedy of Smythstoun* was served heir to his father, *Alexander* Kennedy of Smythstoun, 19th February 1600. He had sasine, in 1655-6, of the lands of Pennyglen, disposed to him by John Kennedy of Pennyglen. The property consisted at this time of the four merk land of Ardmyllane, called Beingrange, and the forty shilling land of Ardmyllane, called Drumfarne. They were probably a branch of the Kennedies of Ardmillan. John Kennedy of Smithstoun appears to have been twice married, first, to Margaret Cuninghame, mentioned in the sasine of Pennyglen; and secondly, to *Agnes Muir*, who survived him, and died in December 1637. Her testament was dated at Ayr. She left two daughters, " *Isobell* and *Mareone* Kennedies," her sole executors.

*John Kennedy of Smithstoun*, the eldest son, succeeded. His name occurs in 1650, as cautioner in the testament of Anna Campbell, spouse to James Kennedy, son of Sir Alexander Kennedy of Culzean, Bart.

---

[*] His brother, William, was an apothecary in London, and acquired a considerable fortune. He had three daughters, married respectively to Fleming of Barrochan, Kelso of Dankeith, and Mr John Hunter, W.S., Edinburgh.

[†] His brother John, of Calcutta, died childless. His sister Agnes, married Elias Cathcart, merchant and Provost of Ayr.

[‡] Historie of the Kennedyis.

## DUNENE, OF DINHAME.

Dunene, or Dinhame, repeatedly occurs in the "Historie of the Kennedyis." It marches with the Brockloch, near Maybole, the scene of the feud fight between Kennedy of Cassillis and Kennedy of Bargany in 1601. The Kennedies of Dunene were of old standing—descendants of "Freir Hew," according to the writer of that history. The first husband of "Blak Bessie Kennedy," "fader-sister to the Laird of Bargany," was "the Gudmanne of Dinehame." He could not have been the first of Dinhame, however, for

*Thomas Kennedy,* and his son *Hew,* of Duneyne, are amongst those against whom criminal proceedings were adopted, for the slaughter of Robert Campbell in Lochfergus and others in 1528. Hew was probably the husband of "Blak Bessie."

On the 26th of May 1582, *Gilbert Kennedy* of Dunene, brother and air of vmquhile, "*George Kennedy* of Dunene," paid "fyve hundreth and threescoir merkis money of this realme," to "Thomas Kennedy of Culzeane, tutor of Cassillis, Elizabeth M'Gill, his spous, James Ross in Mayboill, and Agnes Kennedy, his spous," for the "lauchfull redemption fra thame and ilk ane of thame, of the xl shilling land of the landis of Wester Dunene," &c. He also, at the same time, redeemed the lands of Balkinsay from Thomas Kennedy of Culzeane.

On the same day, also, "Gilbert Kennedy of Dunene past to his four lib. land of Dunene, of auld extent, and thare with his awin handis, for fulfilling of ane part of ane contract of marriage, maid betwix him, Elizabeth Kennedy, his moder, on the ane part, Dame Jane Campbell, relict of vmquhile Sir William Hamiltoun of Sanehair, Knycht, William Hamiltoun of Sanehair, hir sone, and Margaret Hamiltoun, his sister, on the vther part, of the dait at Alloway, the xi day of Merche 1581, gaif liferent susine to the said Margaret for hir lifetyme in her virginitie, being personalie present, of the said four lib. land, with mansionplace, &c.

In 1584, *Jean Kennedy* is served heir of Gilbert Kennedy of Dunene, her father, in the four pund land of Auchnaucht, the four merk land of Balykynna, and the four pund land of Wester Dunene, "in regalitate de Corsreguel." The lands had thus belonged to the monks of Crossraguel, who were the superiors prior to the Reformation.

## KNOCKDON.

Knockdon is about three miles westward of Maybole. The Kennedies of Knockdon were a family of some consideration among the minor landowners of Carrick. They possessed what was called the "Black House" in Maybole, and maintained no small rank among the fashionables in the "good old times," in the capital of Carrick.

*James Kennedy* of Knockdone was engaged in the feud between the Campbells and Kennedies, and was prosecuted as one of the party concerned in the slaughter of Robert Campbell in Lochfergus, in 1528. He was succeeded, apparently, by

*Walter Kennedy* of Knockdon, who was living during the great feud between the Kennedies of Cassillis and Bargany. "June 5, 1576.—The quhilk day Waltir Kennedy of Knokdone grantit him to haue ressauit fra Kennedy in Culnane the somme of thrie hundreth merkis money of this realme, in lauchfull redemptioun of all and haill the twa merkland and half merkland of Culnane, with the pertinentis, liand within the erledome of Currik, &c. This was done within the toun of Mayboill, at twa houris eftir noun, befoir Thomas Kennedy of Barba," &c. He was succeeded by his grandson,

*Walter Kennedy* of Knockdon, who was served heir to his grandfather 30th August 1603. He died in March 1646. His testament, &c., was "faythfullie maid and gevin vp be *John, Jonet, Elizabeth,* and *Annabell* Kennedyes, lauchfull bairnes to the defunct, and executouris-dative," &c. He was succeeded by his son,

*James Kennedy* of Knockdon, who was served heir of James Kennedy, his grandfather by the mother's side, in the four merk land of Monuncheon, &c., 14th May 1639. James Kennedy, younger of Knokdone, was baillie in that part to Archibald Wallace of Strabrakane. He was served heir of his father 18th Nov. 1648. The lands of Knockdon consisted, at this time, of the forty shilling land of Meikill Knokdone, the twenty-four shilling land of Little Knokdone, the five merk land of Tybermorie, alias Lylestoune, within the lordship of Monkland, parish of Maybole.

The Laird of Knockdon was among the Ayrshire gentlemen who were imprisoned for attending conventicles in 1678.

Knockdon continued in the possession of the Kennedies until within a recent date.

*Walter Kennedy* of Knockdon had a precept of *Clare Constat* from the Earl of Cassillis of the two merk land of Doularg, in Girvan parish, dated 15th June 1758.* He had also sasine of the lands of Knockdon, on a precept of Chancery, 18th August 1758.

Part of the property now belongs to *Adam Rankine* of Knockdon.

### BEOCH.

This property, which marches with Knockdon, belonged, in the seventeenth century, to a branch of the Montgomeries of Brigend, and passed, by marriage, into the hands of the *Rankines*, whose progenitors are incidentally mentioned, in connection with the Macquorns of Ballyreagh, in the county of Antrim,† in a foot-note at page 394, vol. i. of this work. The Rankines are a younger branch of the family of Rankine of Orchardhead, in Stirlingshire, the elder branch of which, about the middle of the last century, took the name of Little, on succeeding to the estate of Over Liberton, in Mid-Lothian.

The first of this family who settled in Carrick was

*John Rankine*, who died about 1730, at a very advanced age. He married a daughter of the Rev. David Macquorn, of the family of Ballyreagh (which, about the middle of the eighteenth century, became extinct in every other branch), and had issue:

1. William.

He was, subsequently to the death of his first wife, married three times; and by his third wife, Janet Galloway, had issue:

2. Rachel, who married D'Oyly Broomfield, Ensign in General Whittam's regiment of foot.

*William Rankine* of Knockgray, died 8th November 1728, aged 40 years.‡ He married Jean, daughter of John Montgomerie of Brigend, and had issue:

1. John.
2. Adam, who died December 16, 1745, aged 27, without issue.
3. Margaret, who married James Marshall.
4. Jean, who married Ludovic Houstoun of Johnston.

*John Rankine* of Beoch, &c. His name occurs in the Register of Sasines for Ayrshire in 1753. In 1758, he had sasine of the lands of Beoch and Drumdow, on a precept from Chancery, dated 23d February 1758. His name again occurs in a discharge to the Sheriff-clerk of Renfrewshire, in 1766. He married, 1st, Grizel Cochrane,

daughter of John Cochrane of Watersyde (second son of Sir John Cochrane of Ochiltree) and Hannah de Worth; 2d, Elizabeth Dalrymple of Langlands; 3d, Helen, daughter of —— Shaw of Dawton. He had issue by his first marriage:

1. Macquorn.
2. Hannah, who married George Anderson, merchant in Glasgow;

and by his third marriage, a daughter, who died in infancy. He himself died September 4, 1788, aged 79.*

*Captain Macquorn Rankine* of Beoch, Drumdow, &c., married Jane, daughter of David MacAdam (brother of John MacAdam of Craigengillan) and Sarah Hare, and had issue:

1. Grace, married Captain James Hall, and has issue.
2. Sarah, married James Hunter, and had issue. Died November 10, 1812.
3. Hannah, married Lieut.-Col. James MacIlHaffie of Fulfolk, and has issue.
4. Jane, died unmarried, July 12, 1802, aged 14.
5. John Rankine, advocate, formerly of Drumdow, now of Fort Hill, near Canandaigua, in the State of New York, who married, 1st, Eleanora Ross; 2d, Margaret Reid; and by his second marriage has issue:
    1. Margaret.
    2. Jane.
    3. William Macquorn.
    4. Grace Barbara.
6. David Rankine, Lieut. H.P. Rifle Brigade, married Barbara, daughter of Archibald Grahame, banker in Glasgow, and has issue:
    William John Macquorn.

Captain M. Rankine died 1st November 1819, aged 80 years. His widow survived till 18th January 1838, when she died, aged 82.

This family bears the following arms:—Gules, three boar's heads erased, argent, between a lance issuant out of the dexter base, and a Lochaber axe out of the sinister, both erect in pale of the second. *Crest*—A lance erect, of the second. *Motto*, on an escroll above the crest, " *Fortiter et Recte*."

Beoch now belongs to *John Rankine*, not, however, of the same family.

### BROCKLOCH.

The five merk land of Brockloch, of old extent, formed part of the church lands of Maybole, and belonged to the Convent of Melrose, originally granted to that establishment by Duncan Earl of Carrick. The first lay proprietor since that time was

*John Kennedy of Brockloch*, who had a charter of the lands from " James, Commendator of the Monasterie of Melross and Convent thereof," dated the last day of July and first of August 1579, for " payment of five merks yearly of feu-

---

* Ayr Sasines.
† The Mr Rankine who produced the right to the estate of Drummochrein, as stated in the note referred to, appears to have been of a different family.
‡ Tombstone in Old Churchyard, Ayr.

---

* Tombstone in Old Churchyard, Ayr.

duty, and half a merk of augmentation money." John Kennedy seems to have been the ancestor of the Kennedies of Ochtrelure.

*Hew Kennedy of Ochtrelure*, son and heir to umquhile Hew Kennedy of Ochtrelure, and heritable feuar of the lands of Brockloch, with consent of Uthred M'Dowal of Garthland, his father-in-law, Elizabeth Kennedy, Lady Ochtrelure, his mother, and John Kennedy of Greenand, her spouse, on the one part, and John Kennedy of Baltersan and Florence M'Dowal, his spouse, on the other part, entered into contract, dated 15th January 1598, by which the lands of Brockloch, and certain tenements in Maybole, were disponed to Baltersan for the sum of 8500 merks which he had advanced to Hew Kennedy. In the sasine which followed this contract and disposition, Hew Kennedy is described as "oye and heir to the said John Kennedy of Brockloch," and as under the curatorship of Kennedy of Greenand, his step-father. There is also a "charter of the lands of Brockloch, granted by

*Hew Kennedy of Chapel*, son and heir to umquhile John Kennedy of Brockloch, in favours of the said John Kennedy of Baltersan, and his heirs-male," dated 4th November 1595.

Sir John Kennedy of Baltersan, in 1614, conveyed the lands of Brockloch to his brother, *James Kennedy of Brockloch*, by whom they were disponed, in 1615, to *Lancelot Kennedy* in Glenloy, from whom, again, they were acquired by *George Corrie* of Kelwood, in 1617. Corrie having got into pecuniary difficulties, the lands of Brockloch were acquired by James Chalmers, burgess of Ayr, for himself and the other creditors, upon a deed of apprising, dated 17th April 1628. In 1632, the property, with various others, came to be divided amongst the parties,* James Chalmers retaining for himself, and the bairns of umquhile John Chalmers of Bonnitoun, and William Chalmers and William M'Adam, "the said five merk land of Brockloch, with the mansonrplace, houses,

bigings, yeards, &c., and five tenements of land in Maybole."

Chalmers' affairs having got into confusion, a decreet of apprising was obtained in 1657, at the instance of *Jonet Allison*, spouse of the late John Wishart in Auchin, against *James Chalmers*, son of the late James Chalmers, Bailie of Ayr, upon a bond of 500 merks. There were other creditors (Adam Livingstoun and George Caldwell, merchants in Ayr), interested in the property. *Mr Matthew Baird*, minister at Monktoun, had a disposition of the lands of Brockloch in 1697: and they were acquired by John Moore of Blairstoun in 1738. In 1829, they were sold by Elias Cathcart of Auchindrane to

*James Dunlop of Brockloch*, youngest son of the late Robert Dunlop, merchant, Glasgow.

### GARRIHORNE.

Garrihorne is situated about two miles north-west of Maybole. The superiority of this property belonged, towards the end of the sixteenth century, to a family of the name of Wode, or Wood. James Wode, heir of Lancelot Wode in Semorary, his father, was served in the superiority of the twenty shilling land of Garrihorne on the 16th March 1591.

*Hew Kennedy of Garrihorne* took an active part in the feuds which prevailed in Carrick about that time. He "was ane strekar" of the Laird of Bargany at the skirmish of Ladycors, where Bargany was killed, in December 1601. He was twice married. By the first he had two daughters, *Margaret* and *Jonet*. His second wife was Jonet Kennedy, relict of David Quhytfuird, by whom he appears to have had no issue. He died in January 1617. His testament, &c. "ffaythfullie maid and gevin up be Margaret Kennedy, now spous to David Kennedy, brother-germane to James Kennedy of Culzeane, onlie bairne vnforisfamiliated to the defunct, and executrix-dative," &c. Margaret and Jonet were served heirs-portioners of Hew Kennedy of Garrihorne, their father, 14th August 1617. The family property at this time consisted of the four pound land of Wester Dunnein, twenty shilling land of Garrihorne, twenty-four shilling land of Little Knokdone, &c. Jonet Kennedy, widow of Hew Kennedy of Garrihorne, died in July, the same year. Her testament &c. was made up "be

---

* The contract of division was entered into between "Alexander Kennedy of Culzean, John M'Ilvein of Grimmet, and James Ross, son to Gilbert Ross who were all cautioners for the said George Corrie in several of the bonds upon which the decreet of apprising proceeded, for themselves and in name and behalf of Duncan Craufurd of Drumsoy, and Robert Hunter in Fishertoun, who were also cautioners for the said George Corrie in some other bonds, on the one part, and Mr John Chalmers of Sauchrie, William M'Adam in Auldcreoch, and the said James Chalmers, burgess of Ayr for himself, and in name and behalf of the bairns of umquhile John Chalmers of Bonnitoun wh ch Mr John Chalmers, William M'Adam, and John Chalmers, then deceased, were also cautioners. The lands divided, besides Brockloch and the tenements in Maybole, consisted of Craigdow and Lagandirne, Fishertoun, the Mains of Carswell, with the tower, fortalice, &c (the latter in Wigtonshire.)

* This accords with the "Historie of the Kennedyis," which states, that Sir Thomas Kennedy of Culzean, who married Elizabeth M'Gill, had issue James, Alexander, John, and David.

Adame Quhytfurid, lawfull sone to vmquhile Dauid Quhytfurid, hir first spous," &c.

*David Kennedy of Garrihorne*, who married Margaret Kennedy, as above. He is mentioned in the testament of Lady Culzean, in 1621, as her son, and a legacy is therein left to "Anna Kennedy, dochter to David, my sone, ffourtie punds."

*Hew Kennedy of Garrihorne* was friendly to Montrose in 1645.

The property has long been conjoined with that of the Marquis of Ailsa.

### CRAIGSKEAN.

Craigskean, mentioned by Abercrummie as among the existing residences of families in his time, seems to have been a pendicle of the Mures of Cloncaird. Thomas Mure of Cloncaird, heir of his father Patrick, was served heir to Craigskean, amongst other property, in 1591.

On the 24th May 1577, "Johnne Muir of Craigskeane, with his awn hand gaif heretabile stait and sasing to Archibald Fergushill of Air, . . . of all and haill his xlb land of Craigskeane, liand within the erledum of Carrik, &c., to be haldin of the said Johne and his airis in frie blanche, for payment zeirlie, of ane penny, conforme to ane chartour blanche to be maid tharupon, with clause of warrandice vpoun viij dayis warning; and thareftir the said Archibald grantit renersioun to the said Johnne and his airis, for redemption therof, conteneing the sowme of ane hundreth merkis, &c., to be payit within the paroche kirk of Air, and with ane lb during the nonredemption for payment zeirlie of ten merks," &c. The property was redeemed on the 19th August 1584.

On the 29th October 1590, Johne Mure of Craigskeane received from his mother, Margaret Mure, forty merks as his portion of 'bairns geir' of *William Mure*, his brother—witnesses, Mungo Mure of Alhallowchapell, Johne Mure of Quhytleis, Adame Mure, his brother, and Mr Johne Neshit, writer at Tarbolton.

*John Mure of Craigskean*, probably the same individual, was concerned in the affair at Ladycors in 1601. He was alive in 1611.

### GLENAYES.

This small property, situated on the Carrick coast, and now pertaining to Doonside, was possessed for some time by the Montgomeries of Brigend. It had probably been in the hands of the Kennedies previously. There is a *Lancelot*

*Kennedy of Glenlay* (probably a mistake for *Glenay*) mentioned in the testament of Joseph Ritchard, merchant burgess of Ayr, who died in July 1613.

### SAUCHRIE.

Sauchrie is situated three miles north-west of Maybole. It is mentioned without any comment, in Abercrummie's description of Carrick; but the name is rarely to be found in any of the earlier documents—from which we infer that, though occupying a delightful situation, and now esteemed one of the pleasantest residences in Carrick, it was then of small moment, and comparatively modern. The first of the Sauchrie proprietors we have fallen in with, is

*Mr James Chalmeris of Sauchrie*, an immediate branch of the Chalmerses of Gadgirth. His name occurs in the testament of John Henderson of Woodstoun in 1618.

*Mr John Chameris of Salcharie* was one of the guardians nominated in the latter-will of Hew Kennedy, Provost of Ayr, in 1623. His name occurs repeatedly in similar documents till 1644. In 1636 he is cautioner in the testament of Christian Kennedy, relict of George Craufurd of Auchinway, who died at Sauchrie in that year.

*Robert Chalmeris*, sone lauchfull to Mr John Chalmeris of Sauchrie, is mentioned as head creditor in the testament of Thomas Kennedy of Pinquhirrie in 1644.

Subsequently to the Chalmerses, Sauchrie came into the hands of the *Wallaces*, merchants, we believe, in Ayr, though no doubt, descended immediately or remotely from the Craigie stock. *Mr Wallace of Sauchrie* is mentioned in the Presbytery records in 1729.

In 1834 it belonged to *Archibald Kelso, Esq. of Sauchrie*, and is now the property of Alexander Mitchell, Esq.

### RANKINE OF OTTERDEN.

According to heraldic record, there were only two families of Rankine in Scotland—Rankine of Orchard-Head, in Stirlingshire, and Rankine, merchant in Perth, the former being the more ancient. From this stock it is presumed that all the various branches of Rankine are descended. It is worthy of remark, however, that the Carrick Rankines were called *MacRankine*, *James M'Rankine*, for example, appears in a deed of apprising before us, dated 25th November 1657. The *Mac* has been dropped within the last seventy or eighty years. It does not follow, however, as Robertson supposes, that the Mac-

Rankines were of Celtic origin. It was very natural that, on settling amongst a Celtic people, the descendant of the first Rankine should have been styled *MacRankine*, the son of Rankine. This is a proof that the Carrick Rankines were an early branch of the present stem. The ancestors of

*James Rankine of Otterden*, M.D., which property he inherited from his father, are understood to have been resident in the parish of Maybole for several centuries, as he has himself documents in his possession which carries them back to the year 1600. He is probably the head of the Carrick Rankines, or MacRankines.

In the belief that they are of the Orchard-Head family the arms adopted are precisely similar, the only difference being, that the shield is embraced by two palm branches. Dr Rankine of Otterden is an M.D. of the University of Edinburgh; a Member of the Royal College of Surgeons; and a Fellow of the Linnæan Society of London—a Justice of the Peace, &c. He is married and has a family.

# PARISH OF MONKTOUN.

The names of the parishes of *Monktoun* and *Prestwick*, now united, were originally Prestwic and Prestwic-burgh, signifying, in the Anglo-Saxon, the priests' village or habitation. They existed as separate parishes in the twelfth century, when they were gifted to the monks of Paisley by Walter, High Steward of Scotland. Prestwic, in course of time, assumed the name of Monktoun—*Prestwic Monachorum*—from the monks who resided there, and Prestwic-burgh was known simply as Prestwic, the termination, *burgh*, being no longer required to distinguish it from Monktoun. The parish, as it now stands, "extends to 3½ miles in length by 3½ in breadth, and contains between 9 and 10 square miles. It is bounded by the parishes of Dundonald, Symington, and Craigie on the north and north-east; by Tarbolton and St Quivox on the east; by St Quivox and Newton on the south and south-east; and by the Firth of Clyde on the west." *

The appearance of the parish is flat, with occasional gentle elevations, but rising gradually towards the north-east boundary. The shore is low and sandy, with shoal water, and the beach is studded with sand-hills, some of them of considerable height and magnitude. The soil is various. "Around the village of Monktoun, and towards the eastern and southern bounds of the united parish, it consists of a fine deep loam, varying from a light and very productive sand to a strong, rich clay, all capable of producing every species of crop of the finest quality. To the north and north-east the soil is chiefly a tenacious clay, in some places of excellent quality, and susceptible of great improvement, in others, thin and poor, resting upon a cold bottom, and not so improvable." * Along the coast, including the greater portion of the Prestwick lands, the soil consists of a light sand, so light as to seem scarcely adapted for tillage; yet, of late years, much of it has been enclosed, and so improved as to bear excellent crops. There are two small streams in the parish, the larger of which rises among the high lands in Craigie parish. It is called the Pow-burn, and drives two corn-mills in its course.

## HISTORY, CIVIL AND ECCLESIASTICAL.

Monktoun and Prestwick owe their origin to the religious houses erected at the respective villages. At what time these were planted is unknown. They were in existence at the time Walter, the son of Alan, the first of the High Stewards, founded the Monastery of Paisley, and were granted by him to that Abbey early in the reign of William the Lion. The church at Monktoun was dedicated to St Cuthbert, and that at Prestwick to St Nicholas. They had, in all likelihood, been built and endowed by him. Both the parishes, as well as the patronage of these churches, belonged to him, he being "lord of all the northern half of Kyle, between the rivers Ayr and Lugar, on the south, and the river Irvine on the north." The grant to the monastery was in these terms :—" Ecclesiam de Prestwic, cum tota terra illa quam Dovenaldus filius Yweni eis perambulavit inter terram Simonis Loccardi, et terram de Prestwic usque Pulprestwic, et secundum Pulprestwic usque in mare, et a mari secundum torrentem, inter terram Arnaldi, et terram de Prestwic usque ad divisas Simonis Loceardi; et illam ecclesiam de burgo meo de Prestwie, cum omnibus pertinentiis suis." The grant thus included the whole of the rich flat land now forming the parish of Monktoun, "with the exception of what lies on the east side of the Pow-burn, which probably belonged to the religious house of Ladykirk. The mill of Prestwick, now called Monktoun Mill, was added to this grant in 1368, when the house of Dalmulin, (parish of St Quivox), a house of canons and nuns of the order of Sempringham or Gilbertines, with all its possessions, (of which Monktoun Mill was one), was made over to the Monastery of Paisley."* "In 1227," says Chalmers, "Walter the Bishop of Glasgow made an ordinance respecting all the churches belonging to the monks of Paisley, within his diocese, whereby it was settled that the vicar of the church of St Cuthbert of Prestwic should have, in the name of vicarage, six chalders of meal, yearly, with the altarages; and the monks were allowed to hold the church of St Nicholas of Prestwickburgh solely to their own use, they finding a chaplain to serve the cure. This settlement continued till the Reformation. . . . In Bagimont's Roll, as it stood in the reign of James V., the vicarage of Monktoun was taxed £4, being a tenth of the estimated value." Prestwick was not included, as it was served by a chaplain, and the tithes and profits were drawn by the monks. . . . In 1587 Lord Claud Hamilton, the Commendator of Paisley, obtained a grant of the patronage of the churches of Monktoun and Prestwick, and of their tithes, along with the other property of the monks of Paisley, the whole of which was erected for him into a temporal lordship in fee, with the title of Lord Paisley. In 1621, he was succeeded in these by his grandson, James Earl of Abercorn."

It is not precisely known at what time the parishes of Monktoun and Prestwick were united. "Robert Legat, minister," is mentioned in the records of Prestwick in 1570, showing that the union had not then taken place, while in the same documents mention is made of one clergyman in reference to both parishes. It is probable, therefore, that the junction occurred in the beginning of the seventeenth century. In 1642, James Fullarton of Crosbie (Fullarton of Fullarton) petitioned the Presbytery of Ayr to have the chapelry of Crosbie joined to that of Monktoun. Crosbie belonged to Dundonald parish before the Reformation, after which period the patronage was acquired by Fullarton of Ful-

larton, and the chaplainry converted into a parish church.* In the "New Statistical Account" it is affirmed that "Crosby never was a separate parish." The fact is proved, however, not only by the authority already quoted, but by the Presbytery records, which show that the committee appointed to inquire into the subject, in 1642, reported Crosbie to be a *distinct parish*, and that it should be disjoined from Dundonald, in accordance with the petition of James Fullerton of Crosbie,† and allied with that of Monktoun. It was probably in consequence of this addition that a colleague was appointed to Monktoun. There were, at all events, two ministers of Monktoun in 1645—the Rev. Mr Hamilton,‡ and the Rev. Mr Maxwell. Soon after this period (in 1650) lofts were built in Monktoun church by the Lairds of Crosbie and Adamtoun, by permission of the Presbytery. In 1688, however, Crosbie was again united with Dundonald. "After the union of the two parishes," says Chalmers, "the church of Monktoun was chiefly used as the parish church; but the minister of the united parish preached every third Sunday in the church of Prestwick till 1779.‖ In this year the southern part of the parish of Prestwick, consisting of the lands of Newton-upon-Ayr, was detached from Prestwick, and formed into a separate parish, by the old name of Newton-upon-Ayr." Monktoun church continued to be the principal church of the parish down till 1837, when the present handsome church was built on a pleasant knoll at the Powburn bridge, more intermediately situated for the parishioners. The two old churches were suppressed by decreet of the Court of Teinds, dated 4th June 1834, and are both now rapidly falling into decay.

The burgh of Prestwick is one of the most ancient in the county. In the original grant by Walter the High Steward to the monks of Paisley, as we have already seen, the church is styled " ecclesiam de burgo meo de Prestwic "—the church of *my burgh of Prestwick*. This was in the beginning of the reign of William the Lion, about 1165. According to the renewed charter granted by James VI., as administrator for his son, " Henry, Duke of Rothsay, Earl of Kyle, Carrick and Cunningham, Lord of the Isles," &c. dated 19th June 1600, the burgh had existed as a free burgh of barony for 617 years before the period of renewal. This would carry the erec-

---

* Inquisit. Special.
† It would appear from this, that although erected into a distinct parish at the Reformation, it had been practically included in that of Dundonald.
‡ Respecting this gentleman some curious notices are given at pages 118, 119, 120, vol. i. of this work.
‖ The church was used at a much later period.

tion of the burgh back to the year 983, " far beyond the epoch of record," as Chalmers observes, " and still farther from the truth !" It is well known that James VI., as well as most of the writers of his time, were inclined to the fabulous, in reference to matters of antiquity ; and there can be little doubt that it was indulged in to some extent in the renewal of the Prestwick charter. The burgh was in all likelihood erected by Walter the High Steward ; and consequently his styling it " my burgh of Prestwick," was in every sense highly proper. He was lord of the northern portion of Kyle (Kyle-Stewart), and Prestwick was the head baronial burgh of the district—where the head courts of the bailliery were held. By their charter the freemen of Prestwick were entitled to choose a provost, two baillies, and councillors, with power to grant franchises to several trades, to hold weekly markets, and a fair upon the 6th of December, the feast of St Nicholas, the patron of the burgh. The lands belonging to the burgh extend to about " 1000 Scots acres, and are divided among thirty-six freemen, or *barons*,* as they are called, each of whom possesses a lot of arable land, and a right of pasturing a certain number of sheep and cattle on the common. None of them can sell their freeholds but to the community, who have a right to sell them again to whom they please.† The magistrates have power to regulate the police of the burgh, and a jurisdiction over the freemen, for enforcing the recovery of small debts. Though they have the power of committing a freeman to prison, they cannot lock the doors upon him ; but if he come out of the prison, without proper liberation by the magistrates, he loses his freedom or baronship in the

burgh."* The authority of the burgh is limited to its own proper lands, which extend in all to about 700 acres, of which nearly 200 have been feued out, leaving 500 divisible among the freemen.

The records of the burgh of Prestwick are preserved as far back as 1470.† They contain little of general interest—referring as they do chiefly to local matters—debts, disputes about land, and occasionally assaults. At Prestwick there was and still is a jail, which has recently been rebuilt, with a school-house attached.‡ and a cross, the almost only one remaining in the county, where the process of the law was usually executed. Prestwick had also a gallows, as appears from the records. In a state of the " Rodis and landis " belonging to the burgh, made up in 1470, the locality of this necessary adjunct to a barony, is thus indicated :—" In the first, on the west sid of the toun, fra the venall, passand doun to the gallous." Monktoun had also its instrument of capital punishment. This is attested in an enumeration of the " labourit lande " of the burgh, under the date 24th April 1490— " Item, the medoxe liand besid *the Monktoun gallouse*." The right of " pit and gallows " was thus possessed equally by both places. It does not appear from the records that any one ever suffered the punishment of death. Scourging seems to have been the severest penalty inflicted : " Feb. 1, 1574-5—and sick lyk, the inquest hes ordainit the first resetting ony stollen geir be Meg Black, scho to be benneist and scurgit af the toune gif euir scho resset ony in tyme cuming ; and ordainit this act to be maid first vrang. And gif scho beis found in the nixt scho salbe puneist to the rigour." Prestwick and Monktoun have always been mere villages, but the greater fertility of the soil in the vicinity of Monktoun, and its being the seat of the vicarage, seem to have given it a degree of superiority over Prestwick, notwithstanding the chartered and ancient rights of the latter. Prestwick, however, was early in possession of two important adjuncts to the prosperity of a locality— a coal-work and salt-pans. In 1575-6 " the coil-heuch, besyd the pannis," was set by the community to " Michael Wallace of Wasfurd, his airis and assignayes," for nineteen years, for which he was to pay " xij d. at twa termes in the zeir, Witsonday and Mertimes." There is no tradition or record of any residence in Monktoun belong-

---

* In ancient times the barons of Prestwick bore arms according to the most approved fashion. By one of their statutes (Oct. 1561) it was ordained that " ylk freman of this burght at has hors, at thai haf ryden geyr, wyth ane sadyl, brydyll, gak, steyl basnet and ane slot staf, or ane pow ax, suerd and bucklar."

† This law seems to have been first enacted in 1580-1. At a meeting of " the Burrow Court" held on the 3d Feb. of that year, John Wallace of Craigie Provost, it was " statut and ordainit, that everie freman within the said burch sall haif be equal diuisione, heretable infeftment of thair landis quhilk ar teiltable, and the wtinland to be sowmit be geraing, and everie freman to be infeft in samony sowmes gers as efferis to his infeftment of the teil land withe thair pertineatis, and thair merchis to be according to thair decreit. And that na man sall sell, dispone, nor away put his portion of land. The quhilk infeftment sall be gevin in this maner to the freman and his airis, prowyding that gif the air leif the toun, or be nocht ane fre man him self, nor bruick nocht, and duellis within the town, according to the custume of the toune, that thane his portioun of land sall fall into the tounes handis, and salbe disponit to thame be ane condigne inquelst. Sua that yt sall nocht be tesum to na ane to bruik tounes "

---

* Chalmers's Caledonia.

† These records were privately printed by Mr Smith of Swindrigemuir, and presented to the Maitland Club, in 1834.

‡ The former jail was rebuilt in 1780.

ing to the early monks, or rector of the parish. All remains of it had been swept away at the Reformation.

The parochial registers do not extend farther back than the beginning of last century, and are therefore too modern to throw much light on the moral state of the community. From the Prestwick records, and those of the Presbytery of Ayr, sufficient evidence is afforded to show that the parish of Monktoun was no exception to the rule throughout the county. Deep-drinking and bastardy seem to have prevailed even to a greater extent than in other districts. Nor is this to be wondered at, perhaps, considering the loose behaviour of at least some of their clerical instructors,* and the extent to which smuggling was carried on along the coast, in which the inhabitants of Monktoun largely participated. A curious example of this occurs in the Presbytery books. On the 31st Dec. 1728, evidence is led before the reverend court in reference to certain charges against "Mr Foultoun, presentee to Monktoun." Marion Blair, daughter of the deceased David Blair of Adamtoun, stated, in the course of her evidence, that he was "a deep drinker," and could "fill three companies drunk while he himself kept pretty sober." He used to drink with the tide-waiter, keeping him from his duty, while anchors of brandy were being landed. This must have been a strong recommendation to Mr Foultoun in the eyes of no small number of the parishioners, however much it might militate against him in the eyes of the Presbytery. The reverend gentleman, at the same time was not altogether invulnerable, though unquestionably a strong champion of Bacchus. The same witness, Marion Blair, saw him so drunk one night at a kirn feast at Midtoun, that on sitting down he fell fast asleep, and had to be awakened twice to say grace, in the middle of which he fell asleep again, and slept during the supper.

### ANTIQUITIES.

There are no remains of antiquity in the parish older probably than the two dilapidated churches themselves. That of Prestwick is a good specimen of the small churches existing before the Reformation—the ruins of which are so frequently to be met with in remote districts. Monktoun Church is of greater extent, built in the form of a cross. Both are supposed to be the original structures, though the latter may have had additions made to it at a subsequent period. It has a

Saxon arch over what was once the main entrance, and otherwise bears an air of great antiquity. The bell bears the popish inscription of *Sancte Cuthberti ora pro nobis*—"St Cuthbert pray for us." "Tradition says that it is the same fabric in which Sir William Wallace attended divine service on the occasion of his having the remarkable dream mentioned in the seventh book of Blind Harry's Poem."* The records of Prestwick notice the fact of a *Justice Aire* having been held in the burgh church in 1440. It is said that a number of Knights Templar lie buried in the grave-yard of Prestwick Church. There are no doubt several flat stones without any inscription upon them, save the form of a sword, or, in the estimation of some, a cross—but these may be the graves of the Pope's Knights, as a certain class of the priesthood were called. Repeated mention, however, is made in the burgh records of the Templars' lands, from which yearly sums were paid to St John of Irvine—as for example —"anent Johne Syncleir, Sr. William Walas, chaplane, in stat of twa rodis of *temple* [land], qnhilk acht zerli at the ascencioun dai xviijd. to Sanct Johne of Irvine."

Besides the churches of Monktoun and Prestwick, there was a chapel, in the barony of Adamton, of considerable note, popularly styled "our Lady Kirk of Kyle." Chalmers gives the following account of it:—"It stood on the common pasture lands of the manor, or barony of Adamtoun. The building formed a square; having turrets upon each corner; and there was a chapel in the middle of the square. The chapel was dedicated to the Virgin Mary, from which it obtained the popular name of 'our Lady Kirk.' In a charter of James IV., in 1490, it is called 'Capella de le Grace.' In a grant of the same king, in 1505, which is entered in the Privy Seal Register, in the Scottish language, it is called 'the Preceptory of our Lady Kirk of Kyle.' There appears to have been connected with this establishment a *Pardoner*, who was popularly called 'our Lady of Kyles' Pardoner;' and he seems, like other Pardoners, to have travelled the country for the sale of his pardons. On the 8th of December 1511, the king, then being at Edinburgh, gave a gratuity of 3 shillings 'to our Lady of Kyles' Pardoner.' On the same day he gave a gratuity of 5 shillings 'to a Pardoner with St Dutho's coup.'† On the 24th of the same month the king gave 14 shillings to a Pardoner in Leith The Pardoner is one of the characters brought forward and held up to ridicule by Sir David Lyndesay, in his satyre of *The Three Estates*.

---

* Vide vol. i. p. 18—the Rev. Mr Hamilton.

* New Stat. Account.          † A Cup.

Our Lady Kirk of Kyle appears to have been a place of some note before the Reformation. James IV. never passed through that part of the country without making an offering at 'our Lady's Kirk of Kyle;' generally giving 14 shillings at a time. The patronage of Our Lady's Kirk of Kyle belonged to the family of Blair of Adamtoun, who were proprietors of the barony in which it was situated. They acquired this estate of Adamtoun in the reign of David II.; but whether Lady Kirk was in existence then does not appear. They certainly held the patronage of our Lady Kirk during the reigns of James III. and James IV., and as low down as the Reformation. Long after the reform of such establishments the same family maintained their right to the patronage of this establishment; and they had it inserted, as usual, in their several charters. The ruins of Lady Kirk are still extant, though much dilapidated. One of the old turrets, and a part of the chapel, still remain. They are included in the garden, near to a mansion named *Lady Kirk*, the seat of the proprietor of the lands of Lady Kirk, which were formerly a part of the barony of Adamtoun. There appears to have been a cemetery at Lady Kirk; as many human bones have been found when digging near the ruins." So far Chalmers' interesting account of this establishment, which is not noticed by Spottiswoode in his catalogue of religious houses. Chalmers is doubtful whether Our Lady Kirk of Kyle was in existence in the reign of David II., when the Blairs of Adamtoun acquired that estate. In "The Historie and Descent of the House of Rowallane," it is stated that Robert II. (when High Steward of Scotland) was married to Elizabeth Mure "by Roger M'Adame, Priest of our Ladie Marie's Chapell," who also drew out "ane testimonie, written in Latine," to that effect. This must have occurred as early as 1347,* so that the chapel was in existence in the reign of David II., and probably had been for some considerable time previously. Lady Kirk now belongs to the proprietor of Auchincruive.

A part of the ruined walls of *Kilcais* or *Kincase*,† an ancient hospital for indigent persons affected with leprosy, are still to be seen on a gentle elevation within fifty or sixty yards seaward of the high road between Prestwick and Prestwick Toll. Tradition, as recorded by Chalmers, assigns the origin of this charity to Robert the Bruce, who had been cured of an eruptive disease of the nature of leprosy—brought on by

his arduous struggles and fatigue—by drinking of the water of Kilcase Well. It is probable, however, that the house existed previously, as Wallace and his uncle, "Schyr Ronald," are described by Blind Harry as *coming to Kingcase* on their way to Ayr, on the morning of the "Blac Parliament."* This hospital was dedicated to St Ninian. "It was endowed," says Chalmers, "with the lands of *Robert-lone*, which is now called *Loans*, in Dundonald parish; with the lands of Sheles and Spital Sheles in Kyle Stewart, and with other lands which cannot now be specified. As the foundation charter of this hospital does not exist, it cannot be ascertained what number of persons were originally maintained in it. It appears, however, to have been governed by a guardian, or prior, and it had a chaplain. In the reign of James II. Wallace of Newton acquired the lands of Spital Sheles, which belonged to this hospital, as the name implies, and the hereditary office of keeper, or governor, of the hospital, and of the lands belonging to it. In January 1515-16, all these were resigned by Hugh Wallace of Newton in favour of his brother Adam. After the whole property of this hospital was thus granted away, the only revenue that remained to it was the feu-duties payable from the lands, in this manner granted in feu-firm, and these, amounting to 64 bolls of meal, and 8 merks Scots of money, with sixteen threaves of straw, for thatching the hospital, are still paid. For more than two centuries past, this diminished revenue has been shared among eight objects of charity, in equal shares of eight bolls of meal, and one merk Scots to each. The leprosy having long disappeared, the persons who are now admitted to the benefit of this charity, are such as labour under diseases which are considered as incurable, or such as are in indigent circumstances. The right of appointing these belonged to the family of Wallace of Craigie for a long time, and was purchased about 1790, by the burgh of Ayr, which still holds this patronage. The old hospital, which existed in the better days of this charity, has been long in ruins. In the description of Kyle, by Robert Gordon, in the reign of Charles I., he mentions the chapel of this establishment, and says "that the persons admitted to the charity were then lodged in huts, or cottages, in the vicinity." Kincase repeatedly occurs in the Prestwick records. Various acts were passed by the "burrow Court," prohibiting all intercourse with the hospital, for fear of infection, and not a few individuals were punished for contravening the

---

* Sir William Pethede was Rector of our Lady Kirk in 1485.—PREST. REC.

† It is Kincase in the Prestwick Records.

* See some remarks in reference to this institution at page 26, vol. i.

law. In the records of the Presbytery of Ayr a commission is intimated from the Lord Chancellor to visit the Hospitals of Kingkesse, Air, and Mayboile—all having interest in these hospitals to compeir.

---

## FAMILIES IN THE PARISH OF MONKTOUN.

### ADAMTOUN.

The property of Adamtoun, which is of considerable extent, is situated about four miles northward of Ayr. The *Blairs of Adamtoun* were an ancient cadet of the family of Blair of that Ilk, and acquired the lands of Adamtoun in the reign of David II.

I. Sir JOHN BLAIR of Adamtoun was the second son of Blair of that Ilk. That he had the honour of knighthood appears from a writ in the chartulary of Paisley, dated in 1390—"*Licentia per Johannem Blair militem, dominum de Adamton, cum consensu Johannis Blair, filii sui, &c., trahendi aquam per Alamton*," &c. In a donation to the Monastery of Paisley, by Sir Adam Fullarton of that Ilk, John Blair, *miles*, dominus de Adamtoun, in Kyle, is a witness in 1392. Again, Sir John, with consent of John, his son and apparent heir, made a donation himself to the Monastery of Paisley, out of his lands of Adamtoun, of 40s. yearly, dated in 1397. It is not known whom he married, and he is supposed to have died early in the reign of James I.

II. John Blair of Adamtoun, who got a charter of the lands of Adamtoun, under the Great Seal, dated 16th June 1430. He married Agnes, daughter of Sir William Douglas of Peirstoun, near Irvine, which property Sir William had acquired by the marriage of an heiress of the Stewarts of Dreghorn.* John Blair died in the reign of James II., and was succeeded by his son,

III. David Blair of Adamtoun. He is witness to a confirmation charter of James II. to the Monastery of Paisley in 1451; and again in a writ of agreement betwixt Robert Bishop of Glasgow and the Abbot and Convent of Paisley, dated in 1485. In this document he is designed "David Blair de Adamton, *armigeri*." His name occurs

repeatedly in the Records of Prestwick, of which community he was "oversman" for a number of years. He appears as such in 1484-5. He died in or about 1487, in which year "Johne Blair, sone of David Blair of Adamton" was elected "oversman" in his stead.

IV. John Blair of Adamtoun, his son and successor, married Elizabeth, daughter of John Colquhoun of Camstrodden, and got a charter under the Great Seal, "Johanni Blair de Adamtoun, et Elizabethæ Colquhoun, ejus sponsæ, terrarum baroniæ de Adamton," &c., dated 22d April 1490. Like his father, he presided many years over the affairs of the burgh of Prestwick. He is mentioned as "oversman" in 1492; and in 1499 his name occurs as "balie to my Lord of Paslay." He died before 1515, in which year his son,

V. David Blair of Adamtoun, was allowed to "enter the fredome of the burght [of Prestwick], sic lik as ys gutsour wes of before, Johne Blayr of Adamton." David Blair was chosen "oversman" of the burgh, in the room of Adam Wallace of Newton, the same year. He had a charter, under the Great Seal, from James V. of the lands of Holmstoun in Renfrewshire, dated 29th May 1527. He had a son,

VI. David Blair of Adamtoun, who married in his father's lifetime, Margaret Hamilton, but of what family is not stated. On his father's resignation, he got a charter, under the Great Seal, "Davidii Blair, apparentii de Adamtoun, et Margaretæ Hamilton, ejus sponsæ, terrarum de Adamton," &c.—dated 13th March 1542. He was for many years "overman" of the burgh of Prestwick, which office he resigned in 1571, when John Wallace of Craigie was elected. He and his spouse had a charter of the lands of Reddenhall, 22d November 1586. He probably married, a second time, a daughter of Mure of Rowallane, "Elizabeth Muir, Ladie Adametone," occurs in the testament of Alexander Cuninghame, merchant burgess of Irvine in 1611. She after-

---

* Sir William left three daughters, co-heiresses:—one married as above; the second to Craufard of Thirdpart; the third to Robert Barclay, the progenitor of the Barclays of Peirstoun.

married Creichton of Liberry, and died in 1632. He was succeeded by his son,

VII. David Blair of Adamtoun,* who married Grisel Blair, daughter of John Blair of that Ilk. He and his spouse had a charter of the lands of Adamtoun, Barstoun, &c., 21st July 1598; and another of the £3 lands of Hillhouse, 6th May 1607. In 1576-7, while *younger* of Adamtoun, he was surety for William Blair, brother of the Laird of Blair, in a prosecution arising out of the feuds of the time; and in 1600 he was amongst those fined for abiding from the Raid of Dumfries in 1600. David Blair of Adamtoun was alive in 1647, when his son, David Blair, junior of Adamtoun, had a charter, on his resignation, of the lands and barony of Adamtoun. He died, however, before 1650, in which year, "umquhill David Blair of Adametone, and Grissell Blair," and "David Blair, *now* of Adametone" are mentioned in the testament of "Johne Blair, tailzeour, merchant burgess of Air." He had at least four sons :—

1. David, who succeeded.
2. James, of Over Mains of Monktoun. Borrowing from "Douglas's Baronage," Robertson makes James the successor of his father. In the charter to which he refers, of the Over Mains of Monktoun, dated 19th January 1643, he is styled James Blair, son of David Blair of Monktoun, whereas David, the eldest son, is repeatedly mentioned in testamentary and other documents.
3. William, sailler burgess of Air, sone lauchfull to David Blair of Adamtoun."

VIII. David Blair of Adamtoun had a charter under the Great Seal of the lands of Adamtoun in 1647, during his father's lifetime; and another, dated 28th March 1654; and a third, dated 2d July 1669. He was one of the Committee of War for Ayrshire in 1648, and appointed one of the Justices of the County in 1663. In 1689 he and his son were amongst the commissioners appointed by Parliament for ordering out the militia. He married Margaret, daughter of David Boswell of Auchinleck, by whom he had :—

* He had a brother, Adam Blair, merchant in Ayr, who died in June 1622. He married Elizabeth Caldwell. His latter-will says—"Item, I leif the said Bessie Caldwall, my spous, tutrix, testutor to the said Agnes Blair, my dochter, during hir minoritie, and ineais of the deceis of my said spous I nominat David Blair of Adametoune, my brother, hir tutour," &c. He had probably a sister also, married to Malcolme Cranford of Pathelott, Kilwinning, who died in 1630. In his testament he "levis his part of all fre geir, gif ony be, to Wm., Joseph, and Bryce Craufuirdis, lauchfull sones, and to Jeane, Agnes, and Annas Craufuirdis, his lauchfull dochteris; as also quhat he can be befall frome his lauchfeiria of the wod of Eglintoun. He levis the aquavite pott, pold kettill, with the brewing vesehell, to his wyf, Bessie Blair, quhame he nominats his executouris, to do all to pay his debt, &c., and that be the specialle advys and consent of David Blair, younger of Adametoune.

1. John, who succeeded.
2. Margaret, married to William Blair of Giffordland and had issue.
3. Marjory, died unmarried.

IX. John Blair of Adamtoun. He married Janet Blair, eldest daughter of John Blair of Dunsky, in the county of Wigton, by whom he had two sons :—

1. David.
2. John.
3. Margaret, married to John Cameron of Barlay, and had issue.

X. David Blair of Adamtoun, the eldest son, succeeded his father. He was twice married : first, to a daughter of Campbell of Glendaruel, in Argyleshire, without issue : secondly, to Anne, eldest daughter of William Blair (Scot) of Blair, by whom he had one daughter,

XI. Catherine Blair of Adamtoun. She married, in 1776, her cousin, Sir William Maxwell of Monreith, Bart., by whom she had three sons and six daughters. She sold Adamtoun, in Nov. 1783, to the late Robert Reid, Esq., and died 2d April 1798. The representation of the family now devolved on the issue of her father's brother,

XII. John Blair, merchant in Glasgow. He married, in June 1732, Agnes Alexander, eldest daughter of Robert Alexander, merchant, and one of the bailies of Glasgow, by whom he had issue, one son, John, and two daughters. Janet died unmarried, and Margaret, was married to the Rev. James Thorburn, minister of Kingarth, in Bute.

XIII. John Blair, the only son, was a merchant in Glasgow, and afterwards in Ayr. He married Mary, the only daughter of William Davidson of Garshake, in Dumbartonshire, merchant in London, by whom he had seven sons and three daughters :—

1. John, of whom afterwards.
2. William, who died young.
3. William Davidson, Deputy-Colleetor of Cess for the city of Glasgow. He married Jane Bruce, niece of Dr Gilbert Stuart, the historian, descended of the Stuarts of Lochridge, and daughter of the late Alexander Bruce, surgeon in Musselburgh. He had four sons and four daughters.

XIV. John Blair, Esq., W.S., Edinburgh. He married, in December 1813, his cousin, Margaret Cannan, third daughter of Horatius Cannan of Barlay, and had one son, John, who died in 1823, and two daughters, Catherine and Mary.

*Arms.*—Argent, on a saltier engrailed, sable, five mascles of the first : being those of Adamtoun. *Crest*, a falcon's neck and head erect, proper. *Motto*, "Post Astra Lucem."

*Robert Reid, Esq. of Adamtoun* was, we believe, the architect of his own fortune. He married Barbara, daughter of William Macredie of Perceton, who still survives, and is life-rented in the property. Having no issue, the heirs of entail are the descendants of Col. John Reid, brother of Adamtoun.

## LADYKIRK, OR LADYLAND.

This appanage of the Blairs of Adamtoun—the lands of "Our Lady Kirk of Kyle"—was possessed as a separate property, after the Reformation, by an immediate off-shoot of the family, the first of whom we have fallen in with was

*James Blair of Ladykirk,* whose name occurs as a witness to a proclamation at Ayr in 1597.* It also occurs as a debtor in the testament of William Brown, merchant burgess of Ayr, who died in 1615. He died in September 1616. He left his wife (name blank) and *James Blair,* his eldest son, executors, under the superintendence of David Blair of Adamtoun.

*James Blair of Ladykirk* is mentioned in several testamentary documents. In 1630 his name occurs in that of Michael Wallace of Inchgotterick. In the testament of Walter Kennedy of Knokdone "David Blair, sone to vmqle. James Blair of Ladyland," is a witness.

The lands of Ladykirk seem to have continued in the hands of the Blairs till about the middle of last century, when they were acquired by William Gairdner, writer in Ayr. He was appointed "clerk, and doer for the town and community" of Prestwick, in the room of James M'Dermeit, deceased, 20th November 1755. William Gairdner of Ladykirk died in 1780. He was succeeded by his son, the late

*Alexander Gairdner of Ladykirk,*† who died a bachelor.

The property was afterwards acquired by the late A. R. Oswald, Esq. of Auchincruive, and is now incorporated with that estate.

## MONKTOUN.

The ecclesiastical lands and superiority of Monktoun, which, as we have seen, belonged to the Monastery of Paisley, were included in the temporalities forming the lordship of Paisley

conferred on Lord Claude Hamilton in 1587. These descended to his grandson, James Earl of Abercorn, who, in 1650, disponed them to John, first Lord Barganie. The lands and barony of Monktoun were acquired by John Cuninghame of Enterkine from John second Lord Barganie, in 1674. In the disposition, however, the feu-charters and infeftments granted by Lord Barganie were exempted from the warrandice. In 1688, they were disponed by John Cuninghame of Enterkine, "with consent of Mrs Mary Cuninghame, his spouse," to Hugh Cuninghame, writer in Edinburgh, by whom they were sold to "William Baillie, merchant in Edinburgh, nephew to Major Hugh Bunten of Kilbride." The

## BAILLIES OF MONKTOUN

claim to be descended from the Baillies of Lamington. Be this as it may, the first of the family seems to have been

I. "HEW BAILLIE in Kilwinning," whose wife was *Anna Buntein,* sister of Major Buntine of Kilbride.* Their son,

II. William Baillie, who acquired the property of Monktoun, was a merchant in Edinburgh. He married Margaret Cuninghame, daughter of the Laird of Enterkine. William Baillie occurs in the list as one of the "restorers of the ancient practice of archery at Kilwinning, in 1688. He is there designed merchant in Edinburgh, and resided at the time in "that large house built by his uncle, Major Buntine of Kilbride, on the south side of the Green of Kilwinning." By his marriage he had issue:

1. Hugh.
2. John, born in 1694. He was a merchant in Glasgow, and marrying, had two daughters, Anne and Robina.
3. Anne, born in 1695. She was married, in 1719, to Hugh M'Bride of Baidland, to whom she brought a marriage portion of £5000 Scots, and had a numerous family.
4. Robert, who commanded an India ship. He married a lady in India, by whom he had two daughters.
5. Francis, a Captain of Dragoons. He was a very handsome man, and esteemed the greatest beau of his time. He married an Irish lady, by whom he had a daughter, who married a gentleman of the name of More, possessed of a large estate in Ireland.

William Baillie of Monktoun was a Commissioner of Supply for the county of Ayr in 1695, the year after his purchase of the estate of Monktoun. In 1714, he had a great addition to his fortune, by receiving from his uncle, Major Buntine, a disposition to the valuable barony of Kilbride. He died in the year 1740, at the age of 84, as appears from a monument erected to his memory

---

* Masoun's Notes.

† Alexander Gardener, son to William Gardener, late baillie, and Elizabeth Glasgow, born at Ladykirk, 25th April 1762—SESSION RECORDS.

* He and his spouse are mentioned in the testament of Thomas Neving of Monkridding, who died in April 1631.

in Kilwinning Churchyard, on which, also, is engraved his coat of arms. He was succeeded by his eldest son,

II. Hugh Baillie of Monktoun, LL.D. He had, eighteen years previously, been invested in the barony of Kilbride.[*] He married Grizel, daughter of George Kirkton, surgeon-apothecary in Edinburgh. In the marriage contract, dated 16th and 22d February, and 6th May 1720, the parties are thus described:—"Hugh Baillie, younger of Monktoun, advocate, eldest son of said William Baillie, and Mrs Grizel Kirkton, only daughter of George Kirkton, surgeon-apothecary at Edinburgh, with consent of Mrs Jean Gray, her mother, and Mr George Baillie of Jerviswood,[†] whereby the said William Baillie disponed the said lands and barony to the said Hugh Baillie and the heirs male, whom failing, to the heirs female of the marriage." By this lady he had eleven children, of whom

3. William, in the E.I.C.'s service. He was amongst those who unfortunately perished in the Black Hole of Calcutta, in 1756. He was twenty-eight years of age, and had acquired a considerable fortune, which was remitted to his father.

5. Jean, married to Mr Kennan, second son of Mr Kennan of Dirletoun, near Dublin, after whose death she came to Scotland, and died at Newfield, in the parish of Dundonald.

6. Margaret, married to Counsellor Harding in Dublin, and left one daughter, Frances, married to William Ryves of Ryves Castle, near Limerick.

7. Leslie was bred to the sea, and died a Commodore in the Company's service.

8. Robert, commanded a ship in the E.I.C.'s service. After acquiring a moderate fortune, he returned home, at the early age of 28. He married May, eldest daughter of Mr Reid Cuninghame of Auchenharvie, by Anna, the eldest co-heiress of Auchenharvie. By this lady he had two sons and five daughters—one of whom, John, was with Colonel Baillie at the desperate battle of Conjeveram, fought on the 10th September 1780, when the small body of British were defeated by an overwhelming force led on by Hyder Ally and Tippoo Saib in person. John Baillie was taken prisoner, and kept in durance for some time. He died in India. Robert Baillie, soon after his marriage, bought a small part of the lands of Seabank, where he built a pleasant villa near Stevenston. He died at Southwick, the seat of General Dunlop, in 1807, at the age of 77.

11. Hugh was also bred to the sea, and at an early period of life went to India, where he got an appointment in Calcutta. After acquiring a handsome fortune, he married Anna, daughter of Mr Pearce, Chief Judge of Calcutta. He and his family latterly resided at Newfield, in Dundonald parish, where he died 27th September 1813, in the 81st year of his age. His eldest daughter married, whilst in India, Mr Davies, Judge-Advocate of Calcutta. Hugh, his only son, went to India, and died there in 1806. Julia was married to Lieutenant-General James Dunlop of Dunlop, and had three sons and two daughters.

* Crown Charter, dated 22d June 1722.
† George Baillie of Jerviswood and Mr Kirkton, the father of the bride, were cousins. The Rev. James Kirkton, minister first at Merton, and secondly at Edinburgh, married Grizel Baillie of Jerviswood, and had, amongst other children, Mr Kirkton, surgeon.

Dr Bailie had the misfortune to get into embarrassed circumstances, by having large shares in the South Sea Company. He sold the barony of Kilbride, in consequence, to his brother, but retained Monktoun, upon which he built a large house, now called Orangefield. In the end, however, he was obliged to sell Monktoun also, as well as all his property about Kilwinning. He afterwards had a farm left him, near Mid-Calder, called Selms, which was also sold. On a particular occasion he accompanied George II. to Hanover, when his Majesty presented him with his picture, which is still in the family. He was soon afterwards appointed to be Chief Judge of the Admiralty in Dublin. During his stay in Ireland, he was left an estate called Balleymeen, in the county of Wicklow, which he also sold. After his wife's death, he returned with his two unmarried daughters, and lived in Ayrshire. His son, the Commodore, died about this time in India, and left him the life-rent of his property. He then went to London, where his society was much courted, on account of his intelligence, and conversational talent. He married after the age of 80, Miss Spence, by whom his latter days were rendered comfortable.

*Arms.*—The arms of the Baillies, as engraved on the monument in Kilwinning churchyard, were, *argent*, nine stars, *or*, 3, 3, 2, 1. *Crest*—a boar's head couped. *Motto*—"Quid clarius astris"—being precisely the arms of the Baillies of Lamington.

### M'CRAE, OR M'QUYRE, AND DALRYMPLE OF ORANGEFIELD.

In consequence of Dr Baillie's embarrassments, the estate of Monktoun, or Orangefield, was put into the hands of trustees, by a deed dated 9th and 11th November 1734. The parties were, "Hugh Rodger, late Provost of Glasgow, Hugh M'Bride of Baidland, John Gemmel of Tourland, chirurgeon-apothecary in Irvine, and D. Logan, writer in Kilwinning." From these trustees the estate was purchased, in 1736, by

"JAMES M'CRAE OF BLACKHEATH, in the county of Kent, Esq., late Governor of Fort St George, in the East Indies." Such is the purchaser's designation in the title-deeds.[*] The history of this individual is curious. It is said he was an orphan, and in early boyhood endeavoured to gain a livelihood by running messages. A person of the name of Hew M'Quyre, "violer," or musician, in Ayr, is said to have been kind to

* The Disposition is dated 27 July 1736.

the boy. He put him to the schools for several years. Macrae went to sea—fortune favoured him, and he rose from one step to another, until he obtained the Governorship of Madras. After amassing a large fortune in India, he came home, and purchased several estates in the west of Scotland. This must have occurred before 1733, in which year, August 1, he was admitted a burgess of Ayr. He is styled in the record, "James Macrae, late Governor of Madras." In 1734, he presented the city of Glasgow with a metallic statue of King William III., which stands at the cross;* and in 1745, 17th December, he lent the burgh £1500 sterling, at 4½ per cent., to make up the sum levied by Prince Charles Edward. But for the kindness of M'Quyre, the violer, who gave the orphan boy education, Macrae never could have attained to such distinction and wealth, and it is creditable to his memory that he remembered this with gratitude. On his return to Scotland, he sought out the family of his benefactor, and showered his riches upon them. Whether old M'Quyre was dead we know not; but the probability is that he had previously "paid the debt of nature." In 1742,† "James Macrae of Orangefield" executed a disposition and deed of tailzie of the lands and barony of Orangefield, in favour of "Miss Macrae Maguire, daughter of Hugh Maguire, wright in Ayr, and Isabella Gairdner, cousin of the said James Macrae, and the heirs-male of her body, whom failing the heirs-female of her body," &c. This Hugh Maguire, or M'Quyre, must have been a son of the violer, not the violer himself, who could scarcely be expected to have so long survived. In 1749, 20th December, we find "Hugh M'Queir of Drumdow" admitted a burgess of Ayr; and in 1753, "Charles Dalrymple of Orangefield, son-in-law to Hugh M'Queir of Drumdow," also admitted a burgess. Drumdow was a small property, now a farm, in the parish of Stair, which, no doubt, had been acquired through the munificence of Governor Macrae, who, himself a bachelor, bequeathed the greater part of his property and money to the descendants of the old violer. Hugh M'Quyre of Drumdow had, besides a son,‡

* M'Ure's History of Glasgow.

† Date of Disposition 12th August 1742.

‡ James, son of Hugh M'Quyre of Drumdow was left the great estate of the Barony of Houston, comprehending a whole parish, by Governor Macrae, on condition that he assumed the name of Macrae. This property belonged to Sir John Houston, who had no male heirs. His daughter carried it in marriage to Sir John Schaw of Greenock, about 1730 or 1740. Schaw sold the barony to Sir James Campbell, whose heirs sold it again to Governor Macrae. The said James M'Quire, afterwards James Macrae, was succeeded by his eldest son, James Macrae, who demolished the manor, or castle of Houston, in 1780-81, except one

three daughters who were esteemed handsome. They were well educated by Macrae, and all of

square, and applied the stones thereof to the building of a new town which he had lately feued off. In April 1782, he alienated the barony of Houston to Alexander Speirs of Ellerslie, Esq. Fowler, in his "Sketches of the Towns of Renfrewshire," says—"This James Macrae was a Goth, and committed a most barbarous deed, to demolish the great and splendid castle in 1780, and apply the stones to the building of a new village for lappet weavers."

James Macrae, afterwards styled of Holemains, was better known in the fashionable world as Captain Macrae. In "Chambers' Traditions of Edinburgh," we have the following notice of him:—

"The Misses Ramsay had their shop at the east side of the old Lyon Close, north side of the High Street, opposite the upper end of the City Guard-House. They made a fortune in business, and built, towards the end of their lives, Marion Ville, a splendid villa near Restalrig. People called it Lappet Ha', in contempt of their profession. Here, about thirty-seven years ago, lived Captain Macrae, celebrated for having killed Sir George Ramsay in a duel fought upon Musselburgh Links, which took place in consequence of an insult which Captain Macrae thought he had received from Sir George's servant at the door of the theatre. Captain Macrae was very fond of theatricals, and had a private theatre fitted up in his own house. After the duel he escaped abroad."

In "Kay's Edinburgh Portraits," the Captain is represented as practising, with a pistol, at a barber's block, and, in the accompanying letter-press, some additional particulars are given of the parties engaged in the unfortunate affair:—

"James Macrae of Holemains, Esq., had the misfortune to obtain a celebrity, by no means enviable, as a duellist. He was a capital shot, and, it was said, attained his excellency by firing at a barber's block provided by him for that purpose. In April 1790, the event occurred which had the effect of exiling him from his native land. On Wednesday, 7th April, Captain Macrae, thinking himself insulted by a footman of Lady Ramsay at the theatre, beat him severely. Macrae, the next day, met Sir George Ramsay in the street, when he told him he was sorry to have been obliged to correct a servant of his last night at the play-house. Sir George answered, that the servant had been a short time with him, was Lady Ramsay's footman, and that he did not consider himself to have any concern in the matter. Macrae then said he would go and make an apology to Lady Ramsay, which he did. On Monday, 12th, the footman commenced an action against him. Macrae wrote to Sir George, requesting him to turn off his servant, which he refused to do. A great many notes passed between them. At last Captain Macrae challenged Sir George. The duel took place at Musselburgh. Sir George was killed. There can be little doubt that Macrae, in this unfortunate affair, was highly blameable. He fled to France. He was cited upon criminal letters, dated 26th May 1790, to take his trial for murder on the 26th July following. Sentence of outlawry was pronounced against him. Previous to his outlawry, he took the precaution to convey his estate to trustees, who subsequently executed an entail of it. The servant had given a good deal of abusive language to Captain Macrae, yet their lordships were of opinion that no abusive language whatever could justify the act of beating a man to the effusion of blood. Sir George Ramsay, although married, left no issue, and was succeeded by his brother William. The indictment runs in the name of Dame Eleanor Fraser, relict of the deceased Sir George Ramsay of Banff, Bart., and Sir William Ramsay of Banff, Bart., his brother-german. Before his exile, Macrae married Miss Maria Cecilia le Maistre, by whom he had a son and a daughter. He died abroad on the 10th January 1820."

Captain Macrae was a strange character. To those of his own class he was a tyrant and a bully; whilst his conduct to those below him was kind and obliging.

them had ample doweries—the gift of the Indian Governor. The hand of the eldest, *Elizabeth*, was sought by no less a personage than William, thirteenth Earl of Glencairn. The second daughter, *Margaret*, married James Erskine of Barjarg, who was one of the Barons of Exchequer in 1754, and elevated to the bench, as one of the Lords of Session, in 1761. He changed his title from Lord Barjarg to Lord Alva. The third daughter, *Macrae*, married Charles Dalrymple, sheriff-clerk of Ayr. Governor Macrae died in or before 1748, and was buried in the churchyard of Monktoun. In the *Memorandum Book of John Dickie, farmer in Loans*, from 1715 to 1750, it is stated that "the monument was built at the Whiteside, above the Monktoun, for the deceased Governor Macrae, in 1748, by John Swan, and fell, being near compleat, on 13th August 1749. Rebuilt again by John Swan, 1750." This monument still exists, and being situated on a rising ground, is a prominent object in the vicinity. The lands on which it is built were formerly part of the Orangefield estate, anciently called Prestwick or Monktoun.

*Charles Dalrymple*, Sheriff Clerk of Ayr. His father, James Dalrymple, was Sheriff Clerk of the county. He was admitted a burgess of Prestwick in 1726. He obtained the lands and barony of Orangefield, alias Monktoun, through his marriage with Miss Macrae M'Quyre. "Mrs Macrae Maguire, spouse of Charles Dalrymple, Sheriff Clerk of Ayrshire, and the others, heirs of tailzie," had a charter of resignation of these lands, 12th February 1747. The marriage, however, had taken place previous to the obtaining of this charter, for, on being admitted an honorary burgess of Prestwick, in 1746, Charles Dalrymple is styled "of Orangefield."

*James Dalrymple of Orangefield*, the son of this marriage, was served heir of his mother, in the lands and barony of Orangefield, 20th April 1785. He was one of the early patrons of the Poet Burns, and continued throughout a warm friend to him. He subscribed for ten copies of his poems, and introduced him to his consin, James, fourteenth Earl of Glencairn, upon whose death, in 1791, Burns wrote the well-known "Lament." In a letter to Gavin Hamilton, Esq., dated "Edinburgh, December 7th, 1786," he says,—"I have met, in Mr Dalrymple, of Orangefield, what Solomon emphatically calls 'a friend that sticketh closer than a brother.' The warmth with which he interests himself in my affairs is of the same enthusiastic kind which you, Mr Aiken, and the few patrons that took notice of my earlier poetic days shewed for the poor unlucky devil of a poet." Amongst the published letters of Burns there is

one addressed to "James Dalrymple, Esq., Orangefield," from Edinburgh in 1787, in reply to a packet from Mr Dalrymple, enclosing some rhymes, and making kind inquiry as to the success of the Bard. In this epistle Burns speaks favourably of the *extempore* effusions of Mr Dalrymple, from which it is to be surmised that he had at least a poetic taste. The Laird of Orangefield was, it is said, extremely fond of hunting, and lived somewhat freely, so that his affairs became embarrassed. In 1791, 3d February, he executed a disposition in trust of the lands and barony of Orangefield, in favour of the Rev. William Dalrymple, one of the ministers of Ayr, John Ballantine, banker there, William Paterson, writer in Kilmarnock, and John Murdoch and Robert Aiken, writers in Ayr. The estate of Orangefield, though entailed, was ultimately disposed of, and after passing through several hands, is now in the possession JAMES F. MURDOCH, Esq., writer, Ayr. James Dalrymple of Orangefield married and had a family. His eldest son, Captain Dalrymple, of the 71st Regiment, died at Gill's Cottage, Coleraine, Ireland, some years ago, in the 73d year of his age.

## PRESTWICKSHAWS.

The ten pound land of Prestwickshaws formed part of the barony of Newton. They are first mentioned in the Prestwick records in 1497, but not as a separate possession. There was a mill at Prestwickshaws, and Sandy Fyndlay was miller in 1562. The first proprietor, apart from the lairds of Newton,[†] appears to have been

*Thomas Somervell of Prestwikschawis*, whose name occurs in the Prestwick records in 1514.

*James Somervell*, heir of John Somervell of Cambusnethane, his grandfather, was served in the "10 libratis terrarum de Prestwikschawis," 3d July 1599. The property, however, must have been sold previously, for

"*Adam Stewart*, burgess of Air, and his tenentis and occupiaris of his landis of Prestwik-

---

* Thomas Wilson, Esq. of Orangefield, died 27th Sept, 1829, in the 78th year of his age.—(Tombstone erected in Monktoun Churchyard by his nephew, Robert Pettigrew Wilson.)

A person of the name of Turner also possessed Orangefield prior to its acquisition by the late Mr Murdoch.

† The lairds of Newton appear to have retained the lordship. In 1563-4, Dame Katrene Kennedy, lady of Newton, appeared in the burgh court of Prestwick, by her prolocutors, against Adame Myller, "for hyr fyrme mallis and dewite for hyr landis of Prestwikschawis," &c.

schawis," are mentioned in the Prestwick records in 1597. Adam Stewart was succeeded by his son,

*John Stewart*, who was served heir to his father, in several small properties, beside Prestwickshaws, 16th November 1616. Prior to this, however, the property appears to have been acquired by

*William Wallace of Prestwickshaws*, whose name occurs in the testament of William Browne, merchant burgess of Ayr, 1613.* He is repeatedly mentioned in similar documents down till 1640, when it appears for the last time in the testament of John Neill, one of the barons of Prestwick. He seems, from the testament of Jeallis Stewart, relict of William Wallace of Brighouse, to have been married to her daughter, Helen Wallace.

*James Wallace of Prestwickshaws*, and Anna Kennedy his spouse, had a son, *James*, baptized 7th Oct. 1677. The witnesses were—" Robert Wallace of Holmstone, Mr Robert Stewart, advocate, Hugh Wallace, W.S., and James Kennedy of Gardenrose, goodseer to the child."† Also a daughter, *Elizabeth*, born June 30, 1679.

*Robert Wallace of Prestwickshaws*, whose sister *Elizabeth Wallace* seems to have been the last of the family. In 1720 she disposed of some property in the Sandgate of Ayr, to

*William Adair of Prestwickshaws*,‡ who acquired the property on the death of her brother. " William Adair of Prestwickshaws and Elizabeth Crawford, had a son, *William*, born 11th December 1730." It was presented for baptism " by John Vans, merchant, in regard the parents are lying under the scandal of uncleanness, before their supposed marriage."∥

### CAMPBELL OF FAIRFIELD.

This family, originally styled of *Whitehaugh*, Muirkirk parish, were merchants in Ayr for several generations, as the burgh records distinctly show. The first of them we meet with is

I. WILLIAM CAMPBELL of Whytehaugh, who on the 11th October 1583, " actually ressavit fra the hands of John Cochrane, burgess of Are, twa hundred and fifty merks, in redemption fra the said William of the back tenement of land, with yards and pertinents, of Thomas Kennedy of Ardmillan."§ He appears, also, in 1585, in

a transaction regarding a portion of the burrowfield. The next we find is

II. Hugh Campbell of Whytehaugh, who is left fifty merks by Charles Campbell of Glaisnock in 1629.*

III. John Campbell of Whitehaugh (probably the son of the preceding), married Helen Stevenson, and dying before the year 1660, his widow married, in 1661, John Mitchell of Turnerhill.† He was succeeded by his son,

IV. John Campbell of Whytehaugh, who married Jean Paterson, daughter of Alexander Paterson in Blairkip. This is instructed by a registered bond, over the lands of Burnhead, granted to Alexander Paterson, father of the above mentioned Alexander, which bond was inherited by his grand-daughter, the wife of Whytehaugh, and discharged by her about the year 1680. He had a son who succeeded him, and a daughter, *Janet*, married to Hugh Mitchell of Dalgain.

V. John Campbell of Whytehaugh, some time Provost of Ayr, married Catherine Fergusson of Auchenblain, and had a son who took the designation of

VI. William Campbell of Fairfield, which property he had recently acquired. He married, in 1747, Betty Metcalf, of Virginia. He entailed his property conditionally, that his heirs should always bear the name and arms of Campbell, with the designation of Fairfield. His son was

VII. William Campbell of Fairfield, advocate,‡ who sold the lands of Whytehaugh. He was twice married: first, to Sarah Cuninghame, of Cambridge, New England, by whom he had six children. *Martha Kilby*, the eldest, married Charles M'Vicar of Tobago; and the second, *Elizabeth*, was married to Lord John D. Campbell, only remaining brother to the Duke of Argyle. The other children died young. He married, secondly, Catherine Gunning, niece of Sir Robert Gunning of Eltham, Kent, by whom he had twelve children :

1. William Gunning.  2. George.
3. Charles, Major in the E.I.C.'s service. He married Jane Wemyss, daughter of the Hon. Leveson Granville Murray, second son of the Earl of Drummore, and has left three sons and three daughters.
4. Alexander, married and has two sons.
5. Napier, married, and has a son and daughter.
6. James.  7. Andrew.  10. Argyle.
1. Charlotte.  2. Isabella.  3. Marion.  12. Catherine.

* It belonged to the Laird of Craigie in 1605—from which it may be inferred that William Wallace was an immediate off-shoot of that family.
† Ayr Session Records.
‡ Ayr Records.
∥ Session Records.
§ Mason's Notes.

* Commissary Records.
† Contract of marriage between Turnerhill and H. Stevenson.
‡ William Campbell of Fairfield, advocate, was chosen commissioner for the burgh of Ayr to the General Assembly in 1773. He had previously been elected by the Presbytery as their representative.—BURGH RECORDS.

He was Provost of Ayr in 1784. His eldest son is the present

VIII. William Gunning Campbell of Fairfield. He married, in 1811, Diana, daughter of Sir John Ingilby, Bart., of Ripley-Park, Yorkshire, by whom he had one son, *William Ingilby*, Lieut. in the 6th Dragoon Guards, who was un-fortunately drowned by falling overboard a steamer between Leith and London in 1835. Mr Campbell married, secondly, in 1845, Maria M'Naughten, only daughter of J. H. M. Menzies, second son of John Menzies of Culdares.

The *Arms* are those of a cadet of Cesnock.

# PARISH OF MUIRKIRK.

ETYMOLOGY, EXTENT, &c.

THE parish of Muirkirk anciently formed part of the extensive parish of Mauchline, and belonged to the Monks of Melrose. It was erected into a separate parish in 1631, and the church built at that period was styled "the Kirk of the Muir," or "the Muir Kirk of Kyle." Latterly it came to be simply styled *Muirkirk*. "The parish is about eight miles in length, from east to west, and seven miles broad, from north to south. Its area must therefore contain 56 square miles, or above 30,000 acres. It is bounded on the east and south-east by the parishes of Douglas and Crawfordjohn; on the north and north-east by the parishes of Avondale and Lesmahago; on the south and south-west by Auchinleck; and on the west and north-west by Sorn and Galston."

The topographical appearance of the district is bleak and wild, the greater portion of the high ground being covered with dark heath. In ancient times, as appears from the charters of the monks of Melrose, it was a dense forest. The surface is extremely unequal, rising here into abrupt eminences, and there into hills which may well be called mountains. Cairntable, the highest of these, is also the highest in the county —being 1650 feet above the level of the sea. The medium height of the other hills is estimated at about 1000. Hence *Muirkirk* may be regarded as a somewhat mountainous district. With a soil composed in a great measure of moss, humidity must be the prevailing characteristic of the locality. Rain predominates to a considerable extent; yet, though disagreeable, it has not been found injurious to health, there being certain corrective substances in the soil which neutralise the bad effects of too much moisture. There are, of course, innumerable springs and streamlets in the parish, and some of them possess the peculiar power of petrifaction. There are no natural lakes in the parish; but, in 1802, a vast reservoir, covering about twenty-one acres, was formed at Glenbuck, by the proprietors of the cotton works at Catrine, for the purpose of driving their machinery. The water of Ayr, the second largest in the county, and one of the classic streams of the "Land of Burns," takes its rise from this reservoir, a body of water having previously existed there, and, before leaving the parish, is augmented by several smaller streams, such as the Garpel, Greenok, and Whitehaugh. But a small portion of the land has been cultivated—the greater part lying unenclosed, and devoted to sheep farming. Still great improvements have been made in particular instances, and the time is probably not far distant when skill and capital will effect an ameliorating change on the features of the district. The parish, however, is rich in minerals, such as iron, coal, lead, and even manganese has been found in it.

## HISTORY, CIVIL AND ECCLESIASTICAL.

Muirkirk may be said to have no history previous to its disjunction from Mauchline in 1631. In the twelfth century, when Mauchline was granted to the monks of Melrose, Muirkirk, as well as Sorn, was thickly covered with wood. The process of clearing, however, has been carried too far—as the want of shelter is now severely felt. Various attempts have been made by the proprietors to remedy the evil, by planting belts of wood.* The Lairds of Loudoun were hereditary baillies for the Abbots of Melrose before the Reformation, at which period they obtained a grant of the lordship and superiority of the lands. Most of the land, after it had been reclaimed, was in possession of the Campbells. After they lost their properties, the different small estates were acquired by the Stuart M'Kenzies of Seaforth and Glasserton, and were collectively known as the Muirkirk estate. More than twenty years ago, the Duke of Portland bought it, and it has since been an appanage for one of his younger sons. The late Lord George Bentick was proprietor of Muirkirk, and he was succeeded in it by his brother Lord Henry.

When the "Kirk of the Muir" was built in 1631 there does not appear to have been a single house in the vicinity. Now a considerable village has sprung up, and what between the manufacture of iron, and the working of coal, Muirkirk has long been in a thriving and comfortable condition. The Muirkirk iron company was established in 1787, and has since gone on successfully.† Lord Dundonald had previously commenced making coal tar in the neighbourhood of the village, and some of the buildings still remain. The adoption of copper for sheathing the vessels of the navy ruined the speculation, and the Earl suffered great pecuniary loss in consequence.

The parish of Muirkirk has some claim to the notice of the historian in connection with the civil and religious struggle which preceded the Revolution of 1688. Aird's Moss, where Mr Richard Cameron, and several others were killed in a skirmish with the royal troops in 1680, is situated within a short distance of Muirkirk.‡ So is Priesthill, where John Brown was shot by a party of soldiers under Graham of Claverhouse, while in the act of kneeling in prayer. New monuments, both at Aird's Moss and Priesthill, have been erected in commemoration of these tragic events. Another martyr's stone, unnoticed

by topographists, exists near Wellwood. It is truly a greystone, covered with moss, and occupying a romantic spot at the bend of a gurgling rivulet, which murmurs past the lonely grave with Arcadian sweetness. The stone bears the following inscription :—" Here lyes William Adam, who was shot in this place by Captain Dalzeal and his party, for his adherence to the word of God and Scotland's covenanted work of Reformation, March 1685." It is stated as a tradition, that Adam, in attempting to escape, had cleared the rivulet, and was shot as he was about to take the cover beyond.

The parish register is not older than 1772, so that it is uninteresting as a record of the past. Certain glimpses from the Presbytery Books afford some idea of the social state of the community—which could not boast any degree of superiority over the rest of the county. On the 13th September 1643, Alexander Laurie, Muirkirk, compeired before the Presbytery, (having previously been taken in task by the Session,) and admitted having accused the Gudeman of Gilmilnscroft of theft; but that he had got his corn back again. Gilmilnscroft explained that his servants, while inning corn, had negligently taken some of Laurie's, the field being runrig, in the dark; but that as soon as he learned the circumstance, he caused the corn to be given back again. Laurie was ordained to stand two sabbath days in the kirks of Mauchline and Muirkirk, by way of repentance for the slander.

It ought not to be forgotten that *John Lapraik*, the poet and friend of Burns, was born in the parish, and that his mortal remains rest in the churchyard of Muirkirk.

## ANTIQUITIES.

On the top of Cairntable there are two cairns or tumuli—but so far as we are aware they have never been opened. There are numerous single standing stones in the parish, put up, no doubt, to commemorate events long ago forgotten.* The largest of these, about eight feet high, is on the farm of Laighshaw. There are no ancient houses in the parish, the oldest being that of Wellwood, which bears the date 1600, and the initials T. C. M. C. on one of the gables of the building, which has the appearance of a commodious and comfortable farm-house.

---

* The charters defining the boundaries of the ancient forest of "Ayre" are curious. It comprehended what was afterwards styled Kyle's-muir, and probably the name, "Aird's Moss," should properly be, from this circumstance, "Ayr's Moss," as the Moss is just where a principal portion of the forest stood. In one spot the boundary line is said to be marked by a cross on an oak, "Quercus ubi crux foeta est."

† The iron works belonged for many years to James Ewing & Co. of Glasgow, by whom they were sold, some time ago, to Messrs Wilson & Dunlop, and they are now the property of Mr Wilson's son. The discovery of blackband ironstone, a few years since, in Wellwood, in addition to the clayband previously worked, enhanced the value of the factory, and increased the production of the iron, and they have now three furnaces in blast.

‡ The scene of the skirmish, however, is within the bounds of the parish of Auchinleck.

* The district was much harassed in olden times by the Annandale thieves, and several of these stones, it is said, were erected to commemorate the defeat of these marauders.

# FAMILIES IN THE PARISH OF MUIRKIRK.

## WELLWOOD

In the seventeenth century, three families of the name of Campbell, all descended from Glaisnock, possessed the three Wellwoods. We cannot trace their affinity to its source, or ascertain the period when either of them branched off from the parent stock, but it would seem that Under Wellwood was the more immediate connection, Middle Wellwood the next, and Over Wellwood the more distant. They might have been originally three younger brothers of William Campbell of Glaisnock and Under Wellwood, the eldest of the three, which would account for the succession of his son (Charles) to his uncle of Glaisnock in 1629 and also for the bequest of that estate by the son of the latter to Middle Wellwood. We may infer that he was sprung from the second of the three younger brothers.

## OVER WELLWOOD

I WILLIAM CAMPBELL of Over Wellwood was killed at the kirk of Douglas, in 1597, by Jardine of Birnock, a crime for which, among many others of even a blacker die, that ferocious freebooter was beheaded in 1609 * His son

II William Campbell of Over Wellwood appears as one of the prosecutors of his father's murderers at the above period †

III William Campbell of Over Wellwood, son of the preceding, suffered much from the troubles of the times, and his two sons, youths of eighteen and twenty, were seized by a party of Ross's dragoons, on Wellwood Hill, and carried to the Canongate Jail, where they endured many grievous hardships, but whence they effected their escape ‡ The eldest, however, died not long afterwards in consequence of his sufferings The old gentleman survived till the year 1715 When, as Wodrow says, "he went to heaven in a full gale of joy" He was succeeded by his second son,

IV John Campbell of Over Wellwood—Captain of Dragoons, he having been offered a troop

after the Revolution He is the last of whom we have any account He was alive at the time Wodrow wrote his history (about 1715,) and he seems to have alienated the property some time afterwards *

## MIDDLE WELLWOOD.

I. THOMAS CAMPBELL of Middle Wellwood is witness to the testament of Hugh Campbell of Garallan, in 1602

II. William Campbell of Middle Wellwood, occurs as a legatee in the testament of Charles Campbell of Glaisnock, in 1629. The next was probably his son,

III William Campbell of Middle Wellwood, who, as Wodrow says, was taken along with his brother by Claverhouse (about 1684,) and sent to Dunnottar Castle† after much harsh treatment. It would appear that he was heir-male of the Glaisnock family, and was accordingly constituted successor by testament; but, in consequence of his opposition to the government of the country, and the risk of forfeiture which he had incurred, the deed was cancelled and a new one executed, leaving Glaisnock to Robert Farquhar of Gilmillscroft, but burthened with a sum (equal to its value,) of 40,000 merks to Middle Wellwood This transaction gave rise to much litigation, but, we presume the money was paid, as this family did not succeed to Glaisnock He married Jane Thompson, (of a Lanarkshire family,) who survived him, and was married to Thomas Logan of Knockskinnoch They had a son,

IV John Campbell of Middle Wellwood, who was in possession of his paternal estate soon after the Revolution Whom he married does not appear. He had issue one son, who succeeded him, and three daughters—

1 Anne, married John Ranken of Adamhill, (Burns' friend,) and had issue
2. Jean, married Mr Sutherland, a merchant, and had issue
3 Mary, married Dr Wilson of Cumnock

V John Campbell, M D of Wellwood, married

---

* Pitcairn's Criminal Trials      † Ibid
‡ Wodrow's History of the Church of Scotland

---

* Wodrow's History of the Church of Scotland
† History of the Sufferings of the Church

Jean, daughter of John Reid of Mid Hillar, and had three daughters—

1 Jean married John Craufurd of Doonside, and had issue
2 Joan, married Lieut.-Col George M'Kenzie (son of Sir James M'Kenzie of Seadwell,) and had issue—
  1 John, who married a French lady and had several children
  2 Lewis, who married Jane Logan, daughter of William Logan of Camlarg, and had issue, Margaret, who married the Rev Starr M'Quhae of St Evox
  3 Jane, married Dr Bow
3 Mary, married —— Maxwell of Williamwood, without issue

Dr Campbell was one of the shareholders of the Douglas and Heron Bank, which stripped him, like many other Ayrshire lairds, of nearly all he possessed, and led to the sale of his estate

We have no gleanings respecting the Campbells of Under Wellwood which are not stated above That property, soon after the accession of its owner to Glaisnock, is found in the retour of one of the Browns of Waterhead, and "Brown of Wellwood" is in Middleton's list of recusants in 1662

## CAMPBELL OF AULDHOUSEBURN

The lands of Auldhouseburn and Crossflat seem to have been united in former times In the year 1608, James Chalmers of Gadgirth was retoured in the "4 merk land of Corseflat and Auldhouseburn" The first of the Campbells was, in all likelihood, a branch of one of the numerous families in the neighbourhood

I JOHN CAMPBELL of Allersburn is mentioned in the testament of John Beg in Weltries, parish of Auchinleck, in 1617

II John Campbell of Auldhouseburn is retoured heir to his father in the merk land of Freshaw, 11th June 1644 He is probably the same John Campbell, who, on 13th April 1646 is retoured, under the designation of "Crossflat," heir to his brother William Campbell of Holehouse, in "Holehouse, Brochledyke, and Sund," in that part of Mauchline parish now constituting the parish of Sorn. His son,

III John Campbell of Auldhouseburn is mentioned by Wodrow* as suffering from the measures of Government directed against the Covenanters,

* Wodrow's History

in 1685 He was entrusted with the flag of the Muirkirk division of malcontents, which venerable relic is still preserved by his descendants He married Margaret, daughter of Alexander Muir of Bruntwood, and by her had his successor,

IV William Campbell of Auldhouseburn, who married, in 1716, his cousin, Marion Muir, daughter of William Muir of Bruntwood —Witnesses to contract, Thomas Brown of Waterhead, Robert Aird of Crossflat, William Campbell of Waterhaugh, and William Muir, yr of Bruntwood By her he had two sons—

1 John
2 William, who married Agnes Aird daughter and coheiress with her sister of William Aird of Holt and had issue

The eldest succeeded his father, and was

V John Campbell of Auldhouseburn, who married, in 1756, Sybella, daughter of James Hutchison of Nether Mains —Witnesses to contract, Andrew Brown of Waterhead, John Campbell of Wellwood, Alexander Muir, yr of Brunt wood He had by her two daughters—

1 Mary, married to John Lamb and had issue, Sybella, married to John Gemmel in Garpel, by whom she has a large family
2 Marion, married to John White of Craigheadpen Jamaica, and had issue, the present Thom is White of Sawerston and a daughter

John Campbell of Auldhouseburn died in 1761 The property was sold some years ago by Mr Gemmel, and now belongs to Mr Swan

ESHAWBURN was the property of another family of Campbells in this parish, but we have few, or rather no notes respecting it

## WATERHEAD

The Browns of Waterhead possessed that property for upwards of three hundred years, and by the female side, it still remains in the family The Browns of Waterhaugh are of the same stock. The heiress of Waterhead, Innabella Brown who was married to the late Mr Anderson, father of Thomas Anderson, the present proprietor, and the late Nicol Brown of Waterhaugh, were cousins, and her mother was Helen M'Jarrow, of the M'Jarrows of Altan-Albany, Auchinsoul, &c —in the parish of Bar The Waterhead family, by the mother's side, Mr Anderson being from Perthshire, are widely connected in Ayrshire

# PARISH OF OCHILTREE.

THERE can be little question that Chalmers is correct in deriving the name of this parish from the British, which was just a dialect of the Gaelic—*Uchel-tree*, signifying the high town or dwelling place. The name is precisely descriptive of the locality, as the village and church stand on the slope of the hill, on the south side of it. In corroboration of this, the orthography of old, and even down to a late period, was *Uchiltre*. It matters not that the village is modern—the church is of ancient institution; and it is from the sites of such buildings that the names of parishes have generally originated. The parish was formerly of much greater extent, as it included the parish of Stair. It is about eight miles in length, by five in breadth, and contains upwards of 15,000 imperial acres. It is bounded on the south by the parishes of New Cumnock and Dalmellington; on the east by Old Cumnock and Auchinleck; on the north by the parish of Stair; and on the west by Stair and Coylton.

The surface is uneven, being from 400 to 1000 feet above the level of the sea. The hills, or ridges, which diversify it, generally run from east to west, the flats or valleys between being mostly composed of moss. With a northern exposure, and a variable climate, it may be conceived that Ochiltree is not the most favoured parish in reference to agriculture. The crops are often late, and of course inferior. Besides numerous springs of excellent water, there are two lochs, one of which is about twenty-seven acres in extent. The Lugar divides the parishes of Ochiltree and Auchinleck; and the Kyle separates Ochiltree from Coylton. The Burnock, and other small streams, are tributaries of the Lugar and Kyle, which empty themselves into the sea.

## HISTORY, CIVIL AND ECCLESIASTICAL.

" In the twelfth and thirteenth centuries, Ochiltree was a rectory, the patronage whereof belonged to the proprietors of the manor or barony of Ochiltree. In 1296, Symon de Spalding, the parson of the church of Ochiltree, swore fealty to Edward I. at Berwick. During the reign of Robert I., and before 1321, Eustace de Colvil, the relict of Sir Reginald le Chene, and the daughter and heiress of Sir William Colville of Ochiltree, granted to the monks of Melrose the church of Ochiltree, with all its pertinents. It was confirmed by a charter of Robert de Colvil of Oxnam and of Ochiltree, in 1324. The church of Ochiltree belonged to the monks of Melrose till the Reformation. Those monks enjoyed the tithes and revenues, while the cure was served by a vicar, who had a settled stipend from them. In 1527, James Colville of *Uchiltre* granted an annualrent of £10 for the support of a chaplain, to officiate at St Mary's altar, in the church of *Uchiltre*; and this grant was confirmed by the King in March 1527-8. In 1530, Sir James Colville transferred the barony of *Uchiltre* to Sir James Hamilton of Finnart, in exchange for the barony of East Wemyss, in Fife. In 1534, Sir James Hamilton transferred the barony of Ochiltree to Andrew Stewart, Lord Avondale, in exchange for the barony of Avondale, in Lanarkshire; and in consequence of this exchange, Stewart was afterwards created Lord Stewart of *Ochiltre*, in place of Lord Stewart of Avondale, in March 1542-3. Andrew, Lord Ochiltree, the son of the preceding Lord, was a zealous reformer; and he reformed the church of Ochiltree, by appropriating to himself the whole of the lands which belonged to that church. He obtained from David Creichton, vicar of the church of *Uchiltre*, with consent of the Commendator of Melrose, the patron of that church, a charter of fee-farm of all the church lands of *Uchiltre*, except the vicar's manse and garden; and of this charter he obtained a confirmation, under the Great Seal, on the 10th of May 1567. His grandson, Andrew Lord Ochiltree, obtained, in March 1601, a grant of the Kirklands of *Uchiltre*, called the Vicar's Holms, and also the advowson, donation, and patronage of the parsonage and vicarage of *Uchiltre*; and this charter was ratified in the Parliament of 1606. In 1653, the western part of the parish of Ochiltree was detached from it, and formed into a separate parish, called *Stair*. The patronage of the church of Ochiltree, which was granted to Andrew Lord Ochiltree, in 1601, afterwards passed through several hands. In 1792, it belonged to the Countess-Dowager of Glencairn, who was then proprietor of about three-fifths of the parish, and who died in 1801. The patronage of Ochiltree now belongs to Boswell of Auchinleck. A new church was built in 1789 at the village of Ochiltree." * The want of accommodation had been complained of long previously. In May 1642, at a Presbyterial visitation of the parish of *Uchiltrie*, it was recommended to apply to the Lords of the Committee. There were then 1200 communicants connected with the parish.†

Ochiltree parish shared to no small extent in the feuds to which the greater part of Scotland was subjected in those early times, when the power of the law was less strong than it is now. There is record of a hostile encounter between the Lairds of Ochiltree and Auchinleck as early as 1449;‡ and in 1498, such was the state of matters between Sir William Colvill of Ochiltree and Hugh Campbell of Loudoun, Sheriff of Ayr, that the King granted the former and his tenants exemption from the jurisdiction of the latter, "because it was notoriously known that there is a deadly feud betwixt them." After the battle of Flodden, Ochiltree house was violently taken possession of, the owner having been slain on that fatal occasion.

Ochiltree was repeatedly visited by Knox, who was married to a daughter of Lord Ochiltree, in the course of his missions to Kyle; and in the times of Prelacy Ochiltree had its own share in the vicissitudes of the eventful period. In 1683, John Cochrane of Waterside, son of Sir John Cochrane of Ochiltree, was accused of participating in the rising at Bothwell. He was said to have met the Galloway men, at the head of a party of his own and his father's tenantry, at Cumnock, and to have proceeded with them to Bothwell. Though not guilty, according to Wodrow, yet he deemed it prudent to withdraw from the country for a time. Sir John Cochrane of Ochiltree, his father, having been concerned in Argyle's insurrection in 1685, both he and Waterside were apprehended, and carried to Edinburgh, where, after examination, they were "put aboard the King's Yacht, and transported to London." They both narrowly escaped execution, their pardon having been purchased by the Earl of Dundonald, and Sir John was restored in 1689 —the year after the Revolution—an event in which he, as may well be supposed, heartily rejoiced. Following the example of other districts of the country, he raised a body of volunteers, with the view of defending the Revolution settlement against all attempts of the exiled monarch. The banner displayed on this occasion by the Ochiltree Volunteers, is still preserved. In 1844 it produced a sort of paper war, and a correspondent gave the following account of it in a local paper—the *Ayr Observer:*—

#### " OCHILTREE ' COVENANTING BANNER.'

" As much ignorance and misunderstanding prevail here in reference to the origin and history of an ancient flag, which the inhabitants regard as the palladium of the village, a few remarks on the subject, so far as can be ascertained by history and local tradition, may not be unacceptable to those curious in such matters, and tend to throw some light on the disputed point—who is the legal owner of the relic? A notion generally prevails in this neighbourhood that it was taken at the battle of Ayrs-Moss, and brought to Ochiltree House by the lord of the manor, Sir John Cochrane of Ochiltree. This, however, is a popular error, and may have arisen from the circumstance of Sir John having sent Bruce of Earshall with a band of troopers to attack Cameron and his followers, who were holding a conventicle in the Moss, the tragical issue of which is well known; but although this cannot be denied, it does not follow that the flag in question was taken on that occasion. On the contrary, it can be distinctly proved, from its date, that it was not in existence till nine years after the battle of Ayrs-Moss, that it never was in the hands of the Covenanters, or was made for Covenanting purposes, and that it never was unfurled in any engagement.

* Chalmers' Caledonia. † Presbytery Records.
‡ See vol. i. p. 236.

The battle of Ayrs-Moss was fought on the 22d of July, 1680, during the reign of Charles II., whilst the date upon the flag, 1689, is nine years subsequent to that event, and in the second year of the reign of William, whose name it bears, and during whose Government no such thing as persecution took place for religious opinions, and when all cause of Covenanting had ceased to exist.

"For some time after the accession of the Prince of Orange to the crown of Great Britain, his predecessor, James, made several attempts to regain the throne of his ancestors, and for this purpose kept up a large force in Ireland; and as a descent by him was anticipated on the west of Scotland, the noblemen and gentlemen in this part of the country, favourable to the Revolution, raised volunteer corps in aid of the government of William; and amongst others who showed their loyalty on this occasion was the former noted persecutor of the Covenanters, Sir John Cochrane,* who, accommodating himself to the times, raised a company of volunteers among his servants and dependents, and caused this notable flag to be made in honour of William's accession to the throne, and used it as a banner to his newly-made soldiers. That this is the true history of the flag can be shown by something better to be depended upon than tradition. As William, Prince of Orange, ascended the throne in 1688, and the date of the flag being 1689, a few months only after his accession, every reasonable person must infer that it was made in honour of that great event, and by order of Sir John Cochrane; for as neither village nor villagers then existed, it could not be made or purchased by them. This is farther corroborated from the motto which it bears, and which is as follows:—

' Deus est
S E M.        P E R.
I D.           E M.
Ochiltree.
W. R.
For God, the Covenanted Presbyterian Reformation, Crown, and Country.
1689.'

A little attention by any person acquainted with the Latin language will perceive that the capital letters that follow 'Deus est' are 'semper idem,' and signify that 'God is unchangeable.' This motto was very appropriate for the times and the purpose for which the flag was got up, viz., to be borne against King James, who was well known

to be a despot and a bigoted Papist; and, no doubt, it was also intended as a compliment to King William, who ascended the throne on Protestant principles, and confirmed the Presbyterian form of church government, as we enjoy it. The decisive battle of the Boyne, which soon after followed, having extinguished all hopes of James' ever regaining the Crown, the Ochiltree Volunteers, amongst others, were disbanded by their feudal superior; and their flag deposited in Ochiltree House, where it remained in possession of the descendants of its original owner, Sir John Cochrane, till a person of the name of Millar, who held the situation of cook in the family, surreptitiously carried it from the house. Sometime after, it was about to be consigned to oblivion, by being wrapt as a winding-sheet about the body of a pauper, when a patriot of the village had the good sense to rescue it from this disgraceful end, by furnishing the article wanted, of less-famed material, and taking the relic into his possession. It subsequently passed through several hands, when Mr Simson, schoolmaster, became custodier, by receiving it from an old woman, who was about to remove from the village to the town of Ayr; and in whose hands it remained till the year 1818, when the late Sir Alexander Boswell obtained possession of it, as superior of the village, and deposited it in the old baronial house of Ochiltree, whence, it has been shown, it originally came; and thus became the last legal possessor of the flag. It remained there till 1832, when a deputation of the villagers, smitten with the reform mania, repaired to the house, and requested of the lady who then resided there to let them have it, for the purpose of parading through the village in honour of reform. This request was granted, with a full understanding that it was to be brought back to its original destination; but this was, as a matter of course, forgotten; and assuming a right to that to which they never had the slightest claim or title, a self-called meeting elected a committee into whose hands the flag was committed, one of their number being made custodier. This person, for some cause or other, gave up his charge a few years ago, and the 'sacred relic' was delivered over to another of the committee who now holds it. The box in which it was kept having three locks, it could not be opened without the consent of the other two members of committee, who each held a key. As this arrangement scarcely suited the peculiar views of the custodier, who, pretending a great veneration for the 'precious relic,' and anxiety for its preservation, represented to the other two members of committee, that the flag would soon be destroyed, unless it was regularly aired, and

* The writer, otherwise well informed, must be mistaken in reference to the character of Sir John Cochrane: as already shown, both he and his son suffered in the liberal cause.

by this means got possession of the other two keys, which, of course, he forgot to return; and thus has become, in the meantime, sole dictator of that which he has not the shadow of a legal title to retain.

"As the said flag was not originally purchased by the people of Ochiltree, nor ever in their lawful possession, they had no right to *meet*, or *elect* a committee, or *deliver* it to any one. The flag, such as it is, undoubtedly belongs to the proprietor of the mansion-house of Ochiltree, whence it originally came, and may be claimed at pleasure; and be it remarked—the several individuals who have held it from time to time never claimed it as their own, all admitting that it was taken out of the old house, and by illegal means. In 1689, the date of the flag, the village of Ochiltree did not exist, and, of course, could have neither villagers nor banner. The baronial house of Sir John Cochrane, and a few huts to accommodate his immediate dependents, then constituted Ochiltree; which remained nearly in that state till within the memory of people still alive."

### ANTIQUITIES.

Tradition states that the village of Ochiltree is built on what was formerly a camp. but of its history nothing is known. At the Moat, on the road to Ayr, an urn containing calcined bones, was found some years ago; and subsequently a crown piece of James I. of England, in good preservation.

The foundation of the old *Castle of Ochiltree*, which stood on the banks of the Lugar, is all that remains of the building. The present Castle of Ochiltree, the residence of the Dowager Lady Boswell, is not a modern building—being probably two or three hundred years old. "There are," says the writer in the *Statistical Account*, "the ruins of an old castle at Auchincloich, but by whom, or for what purpose it was built in that hilly district, is not known. There is, detached from the rock on the banks of the Lugar, a large stone, about 60 feet high, by 40 feet in length, and 20 feet in breadth, partially covered on the top with shrubs, heather, and grass. It is regarded as a great curiosity, and called, from its peculiar form, Kemp's Castle." The name of this rock, or stone, can hardly be derived from its "peculiar form," though possibly from the Scottish word *kemp*, to contend, or compete. Other places in Scotland, as Kemp's Castle near Forfar, bear a similar name. At the same time, there is a tradition of a famous robber, called Kemp, having at one time existed in Scotland, whose name may have been given to such retreats for the lawless as Kemp's Castle at Ochiltree.

## FAMILIES IN THE PARISH OF OCHILTREE.

### BARONY OF OCHILTREE.

The original possessors of this barony, as far as record goes, were the *Colvilles*—a family, according to Dugdale and others, of Norman descent. The first of them who came to Scotland was *Philip de Colville*, one of the hostages for the release of William the Lion in 1174. His earliest possessions were Heton and Oxnam, in Roxburghshire. There can be no doubt that he was the ancestor of the *Colvilles of Ochiltree*, the two properties being afterwards found in the possession of the representative of both branches of the family. He had a son, *Thomas*, who again had a son, *William*. Sir *John Colvill* was proprietor of Oxnam and Ochiltree in the reign of Alexander III., about 1250. The first styled of Ochiltree, and who seems to have been the main stem, was

Sir *William Colvill of Ochiltree*. He left no male issue, and his heiress, *Eustace*, married Sir Reginald Chene, who died, at an advanced age, in 1291. She survived her husband, and swore fealty to Edward I. in 1296. From the extent of her possessions in the shires of Aberdeen, Ayr, Banff, Forfar, Inverness, and Kincardine, it is evident that this lady was the heiress of the principal house of Colville.

*Robert de Colvill*, dominus de Oxnam, was designed *of Ochiltree* in 1324, and is witness to a donation to the Monastery of Kelso in 1354. He had a charter of the barony of Ochiltree from David II. The Oxnam branch having succeeded to the bulk of the property after the death of the heiress, they seem to have retained the designation of Oxnam for some generations.

*Robert Colvill of Oxnam and Ochiltrie*, occurs in 1390. So does

*Thomas Colvill of Oxnam and Ochiltree*, about 1384; and it is probable that he was the person who formed one of the numerous train of Scottish barons who attended Margaret of Scotland on her marriage with Louis the Dauphin of France in 1436.

*Robert de Colvill of Oxenham and Ochiltree* had a charter of the lands of Barnwell and Symontoun, on his own resignation, 26th May 1441. Sir Robert de Colvill had a charter of the barony of Uchiltre of the same date, on his father's resignation. He married Margaret Colvill, who had a charter from her son, Robert, of the lands of Crabelgyn, in the barony of Uchiltre, 10th September 1441.* He appears to have been twice married; for, on the 16th February 1450-1, he had a charter of the barony of Ochiltree to himself and Cristina de Crichton, daughter of Sir Robert Crichton of Sanquhar, Knight. According to Nisbet, he had two sons, *Richard*, his eldest, slain by the Earl of Douglas for killing John Auchinleck of that Ilk, in 1449; and his successor,

*Sir Robert Colvill of Oxnam and Ochiltree.* He had a charter of several lands lying in the barony of Ochiltree, dated 9th March 1477. He had two sons, *Sir William*, his heir, and *Robert* of Hilton, in the barony of Tillicoultry, and shire of Clackmannan. He and his spouse, Margaret Logan, had a charter of the lands of Hilton, dated 16th October 1483.

*Sir William Colville of Ochiltree and Oxnam* died in 1502, leaving two daughters, co-heiresses:

1. Elizabeth, married to Robert Colvill of Ravenscraig, a cadet of the family.
2. Margaret, married to Patrick Colquhoun of Drumskeith.

*Sir Robert Colvill of Ochiltree*, son of Robert of Hilton, carried on the representation of the family He was steward to Queen Margaret, and being a person of distinguished merit, was highly esteemed by James IV., who appointed him master of his household, and director of the chancery. He seems to have acquired nearly all the lands belonging to the Colvill family. In the charter, under the Great Seal, of the barony of Ochiltree, he is styled *Roberto Colvill de Ochiltrie*. He attended his royal master to the fatal field of Flodden, in 1513, where he was slain. By his wife, Elizabeth Arnot, daughter and co-heiress of Walter Arnot of Balberton, he left two sons:

1. Sir James, his he'r.
2. Robert, who married Margaret Scougal, and got a Crown charter of the lands of Easter Wemyss in 1599.

* This lady had been of some of the branches of the Colville family in Ochiltree. The Colvills of Lesnesok, for example, continued down till a late period.

*Sir James Colvill of Ochiltree* was made director of the chancery by James V., and one of the Senators of the College of Justice, when that judicature was first instituted. He had four charters of different lands and baronies between 1520 and 1228. In 1527, be granted an annual-rent of £40 out of the barony of Ochiltre for the support of a chaplain to serve at St Mary's altar in the church of Ochiltree. In 1530, he exchanged his lands of Ochiltree with Sir James Hamilton of Finnart, for the lands of Easter Wemyss, which afterwards became the chief title of the family. He married Alison Bruce, of the family of Clackmannan, by whom he had a son:

1. Sir James, his heir.
2. Margaret, married to James Lindsay of Dowhill.

He had also a natural son, *Robert*, to whom he gave the barony of Cleish, and who was ancestor of Lord Colville of Ochiltree.

[For the continuation of this family, see *Woods' Douglas' Peerage*.]

*Arms*—Quarterly, 1st and 4th, *argent*, a cross moline, *sable:* 2d and 3d, *gules*, a fess cheque, *argent* and *azure*.

*Crest*—On a wreath, a hind's head, proper.

*Supporters*—On the dexter side, a rhinoceros; on the sinister, a savage covered with a lion's skin, holding on his exterior shoulder a baton.

*Motto*—" Oublier ne puis."

Sir James Hamilton of Finnart did not long retain the barony of Ochiltree, having disposed of it to Lord Evandale for the barony of Evandale, in 1534.

### STEWART, LORD OCHILTREE.

*Andrew, third Lord Evandale*, lineally descended from Robert Duke of Albany, was the first of the Stewarts Lords of Ochiltree. He was Governor of Dumbarton Castle, and Groom of the Stole to James IV. Having exchanged his lordship of Evandale, as we have seen, for that of Ochiltree, he had charters under the Great Seal of the barony of Ochiltree, and several others, in 1536 and 1540. He also obtained a change of his title from Evandale to Ochiltree, which was confirmed by act of Parliament in 1543. He is thus mentioned in the testament of Alexander Hamiltone, tutor of Silvertonhill, who died in 1547: " Debita sibi Deben.—Imprimis, Andreas Stewart, dominus de Uchiltrie, lxiii lib. computate betuix him and me at his departing of Scotland," &c. He himself died in 1548. He left by his lady, Margaret, daughter of Sir John Ken-

nedy of Blairquhan, three sons and three daughters.

1. Andrew, his heir
2 Henry Lord Methven
3 Sir James Stewart, ancestor of the Earl of Murray
1 Agnes, married to John Boswell of Auchinleck
2 Anne, married to Bartholomew Cranfurd of Kerse
3 Barbara, married, first, to James Sinclair of Sanday,
   secondly to Roderick Macleod of Lewes

*Andrew, second Lord Ochiltree*, died soon after
his father. He married Margaret Hamilton,
daughter of James, Earl of Arran, by whom he
had a son and successor,

*Andrew, third Lord Ochiltree*, usually styled
the "Good Lord." He was a zealous promoter
of the Reformation. He had four charters under
the Great Seal, of several lands and baronies,
including the church lands of Ochiltree, between
1570 and 1592. He married Agnes, daughter of
John Cuninghame of Caprington, by whom he
had five sons and two daughters —

1 Andrew, Master of Ochiltree, who predeceased his
   father. He had charters of the lands and barony of
   Ochiltree, and the five merk land of Portcarrick besides others, between 1578 and 1584. He married
   Stewart, daughter of Henry Lord Methven, by whom
   he had two sons and six daughters —
   1 Andrew, afterwards Lord Ochiltree
   2 Josias Stewart of Bonnyton, died without issue
   1 Anne, married to Sir Andrew Kerr of Fernyhirst,
      afterwards Lord Jedburgh
   2 Margaret, married to John Stewart of Traquair,
      and was mother of the Great Earl
   3 Marjory, married to Sir Roger Ashton, of Eng-
      land, Gentleman of the Bed-chamber to James VI
   4 Martha, married to Nicol Rutherford of Hundely
   5 Mary, married to Sir George Craufurd of Lif-
      norris
   6 Isabel, married to Gilbert Kennedy of Bargany
2 Sir James Stewart of Bothwelmuir afterwards Earl
   of Arran, but better known as Captain Stewart *
3 Sir William Stewart of Monktoun, who was killed by
   the Earl of Bothwel without issue †
4 Sir Henry Stewart, knight
5 Robert Stewart of Wester-Braes
1 Isabel, married to Thomas Kennedy of Bargany
2 Margaret, married first, to John Knox, secondly, to
   Sir Andrew Ker of Faudonside

*Andrew, fourth Lord of Ochiltree*, succeeded his
grandfather. He had a charter of the ecclesiastical lands of Ochiltree in 1601. He was one of
the Gentlemen of the Bed-chamber to James VI,
General of the Ordnance, and Governor of the
Castle of Edinburgh. He is mentioned in the
testament of "Jeane Houstoun, spous to Williame
Cranfurd, elder of Lefnoreis," who died in 1608
—"Andro Stewart, Lord Uchiltrie, and Margaret
Stewart, his dochter." He married Margaret,
daughter of Sir John Kennedy of Blairquhan, by
whom he had issue —

1 Andrew afterwards Lord Castle-Stewart

* For some account of Captain Stewart, see vol 1 p 83,
&c
† He is mentioned in the testament of Michael Dalrumpill, merchand burges of Ayr, who died in 1613

2 William. He is not mentioned by Douglas, but his
existence is proved by the following extract from
Masoun's Notarial Book —"Apud burgum de Air,
December 5, 1612—The quhilk day (&c) compeirt
personalie Hew Dowok, wrycht, burges of Air, and
Margaret Dowok, his spous, quha of thair awin fre
motive (&c) for ane certane soume of money now instantlie at the date hierof returalie payit and deliverit
to thame, be Williame Stewart, brother-germane to
Andro Lord Stewart of Uchiltree, and Marioun M'Alexander, his spous, to the extent of thir presentis, quhairof thai held thame weill content, satisfeit and payit
and dischargeit the saidis Williame and Marioun thairof for evir, witt ane consent and assent ratifeit and
apprevit, as be the tenour hierof thai ratifie (&c) the
alienatioun maid be thame to the saidis Williame
Stewart and Marioun M'Alexander, thair
airis and assignayis, of all and haill thair fourt tenement of land heigh and laigh, with the pertinentis
lyand within the burch of An, in the Sandgait thairof, upoun the eist syd of the Kingis Streit, betuix
the tenement sumtyme of David Wallace and umquhile John Porterfield minister of Air on the south
and ane part, and the tenement of umquhile John
Lower on the north and uther part, (&c.) This wes
done within the dwelling hous of me John Masoun,
noter, common clerk of Air, within the burch thairof,
(&c.) befoir Alexander Schaw of Clauchfyn James
Hunter lait thessaurer and burges of Air, Robert
Hunter, in Dachertoun, his brother (&c.)
3 Margaret, married to Sir George Craufurd of Lifnorris

Lord Ochiltree, with consent of his son, the
Master, sold the lordship of Ochiltree to his
cousin, Sir James Stewart of Killeth, son of his
uncle, the Earl of Arran, who upon the resignation of Andrew, Master of Ochiltree, became
Lord Ochiltree, and the Master, in lieu thereof,
was created Lord Castle-Stewart of the kingdom of Ireland, by patent in 1615.

The male line failing on the death of Andrew,
second Lord Castle-Stewart, the representation
of the Ochiltree family devolved upon the purchaser of the barony.

*Sir James Stewart of Killeth*, who, as already
stated, became Lord Ochiltree. He had charters,
under the Great Seal, of the lands and superiority
of Polquharn, and others, in 1616. His name
occurs as "James, Lord Uchiltrie," in the testament of "George M'Calmount, merchant burges
of Air," in 1615. Having accused the Marquis
of Hamiltoun, as having a design upon the Crown,
and failing in his proof, he was ordered to be
confined in Blackness prison for life, but he was
liberated by Cromwell, after the decisive battle
of Worcester, in 1562. He died in 1569. By his
wife, Margaret, daughter of Uchtred M'Dougal
of Garthland, he had a son, who predeceased
him, but who left a son,

*William, Lord Ochiltree*, who died at the age
of sixteen, while attending the University of
Edinburgh, in 1675, upon which the honours became extinct.

## COCHRANES OF OCHILTREE.

The barony of Ochiltree having been acquired by William, first Earl of Dundonald, it was bestowed upon his second son,

*Sir John Cochrane of Ochiltree,* who obtained a charter of it from the Crown, 6th March 1667. By his forfeiture, in 1685, the property fell to the Crown, but was restored to his son in 1686. He married Margaret, daughter of Sir Thomas Strickland of Bmytonn, in Yorkshire, by whom he had two sons and one daughter:—

1. William, his heir.
2. John Cochrane of Waterside.
3. Grisel, married to John Ker of Morriston, Berwickshire.

Sir John was alive in 1687, in which year his name occurs in the Presbytery Books of Ayr. He was succeeded by his son,

*William Cochrane of Ochiltree,* who married Lady Mary Bruce, eldest daughter of Alexander, Earl of Kincardine, by whom he had nine sons and four daughters:—

1. William, who died before his father, without issue, in 1797.
2. Charles, his heir.
3. John, a Lieutenant in the fleet, perished at sea with Sir Cloudsley Shovel.
4. Alexander, a Captain in the army, cast away on his return from Holland, without issue.
5. George, a Captain in the army, killed in Spain, in 1709, without issue.
6. James, a Lieutenant-General in the British service.
7. Thomas, afterwards Earl of Dundonald.
8. Robert, died unmarried in 1721.
9. Basil, a Captain in the army, and Deputy Governor of the Isle of Man under the Duke of Athol, and afterwards one of the Commissioners of Excise for Scotland. He figures in "Kay's Edinburgh Portraits." He died at Dalry, near Edinburgh, 2d October 1788.
1. Eupheme, married to Colonel John Erskine, brother to Sir Charles Erskine of Alva.
2. Mary, died unmarried.
3. Anne, married to Sir George Preston of Valleyfield.

"Mr Cochrane of Ochiltree" is mentioned as "Manager to Lord Dundonald" in some of the local records, from which it would appear that he had acted as his chamberlain or adviser. He died in 1728, and was succeeded by his son,

*Charles Cochrane of Ochiltree.* He is said, by *Douglas,* to have been "a man of great honour and hospitality." The family papers show numerous discharges of bonds and other debts which had been incurred by his father. Amongst them is a bill by "Cornet Thomas Cochrane"* to George Chalmers, writer in Edinburgh, for £20, drawn upon "Mr Charles Cochrane." He died in 1752, and was succeeded by his next surviving brother,

*Lieutenant-General James Cochrane,* who mar-

* Afterwards Earl of Dundonald.

ried Miss Margaret Hawkison, by whom he had two daughters:—

1. Mary-Anne, married to Robert Sibthorp, Esq. of Dimany, counsellor at law in Ireland.
2. Elizabeth, married, first, to Cary Hamilton, Esq.; secondly, to —— Gould, Esq., in the same kingdom.

Lieutenant-General Cochrane died in 1758, and was succeeded by his brother, *Thomas,* who, upon the death of William, seventh Earl of Dundonald, in 1758, succeeded as heir-male to the estate and honours, and became the eighth Earl of Dundonald.

## BARONY OF TRABOCH.

This, the only other barony in the parish, is the property of Sir James Boswell, Bart. Little is known of its history. *Robert Boyd,* ancestor of the Lords Boyd of Kilmarnock, had a charter " of the 5l. land of Trabeache, in Kyle regis" from Robert the Bruce. How long it remained in the Kilmarnock family we know not. At the beginning of the seventeenth century Chalmers of Gadgirth possessed part of the barony, and so did Reid of Barskimming. The writer in the *Statistical Account* says,—" on this estate there is a farm called Hoodstone, which the ancestors of the present tenant have rented from about the middle of the thirteenth century. About that time, three brothers of the name of Hood came from England, and settled, one of them, in Hoodstone, and the others in the neighbourhood. According to the tradition in the family, the death of their renowned progenitor, Robin Hood, was the immediate cause of their emigration."

## COCHRANE OF WATERSIDE.

*John Cochrane of Waterside,* was the second son of Sir John Cochrane of Ochiltree. He was forfeited, when only sixteen years of age, for being in arms at Bothwelbrig, in 1679. He went abroad, and was with Charles II. in Holland. He accompanied his father in the invasion of Scotland, under the Duke of Argyle, when both were taken prisoners. He was pardoned, along with his father. He married Hannah de Worth, of London, by whom he had eight sons and seven daughters. He was admitted a burgess of Ayr in 1686.* He was succeeded by his son,

*John Cochrane of Waterside,* who was bred as a lawyer, and admitted advocate in 1724. He was alive in 1733, in which year his name occurs in the Presbytery Records. He held the office of

* Ayr Records.

Judge-advocate for Scotland, which situation he resigned in favour of his son.

*William Cochrane of Waterside*, Judge-advocate for Scotland in 1764.

### COLVILL OF LESNESOK.

The *Colvills of Lesnesok* were no doubt a branch of the Colvills of Ochiltree. We have no information respecting the family save what is to be found in the following extract from the testament of

*Robert Colvill of Lesnosok*, who died in June 1643, " gevin up be    lauchfull creditor to the defunct, &c., as the said umquhile Robert Colvill was justlie addebtit and awand to

" *Williame Colvill*, now of Lesnossok, the sowme of flyve hundrithe merkis money, principall sowme, conforme to the contract of mariage past betuixt the defunct Jeane Stewart, his spous, and the said Williame Colvill, and Kathrein Kennedy, relict of umquhile Robert Stewart of Robertoun, and Jeane Stewart, his lauchfull dochter, on the ane and uther pairtis, of the daite the 22d day of Julij 1631."

### BONNYTOUN.

*Josias Stewart of Bonnytoun* was the second son of the Master of Ochiltree. His sister, *Isabel*, was married to Gilbert Kennedy of Barganie, who unfortunately lost his life in the feud fight with the Earl of Cassillis at Ladyeors in 1602. His brother, Andrew, fourth Lord Ochiltree, having obtained the escheat of Barganie from the Crown, he was appointed, in opposition to those who had better claims, tutour to the infant Laird of Barganie. From his position as tutor, and other influences, he seems to have acquired considerable property. He is styled " Josias Stewart of *Blairquhan*," in a testamentary document in 1621. His name occurs for the last time in a similar document, wherein " Williame Stewart, brother german to Josias Stewart of Bonytoune," is mentioned, in 1625. He died without issue.

### BARQUHARRIE.

This property belonged to the Craufurds.

*Hew Craufuird of Barquharrie*, mentioned in a testamentary document in 1603, seems to have been proprietor of Corsflatt, in Muirkirk parish. Mareon Craufuird, his spouse, died in 1616. From her testament it appears she left issue—*Hew, Margaret* and *Agnes*.

" Hew Craufuird of Barquharie, and *Andro* Craufuird, son to Barqubarie," appear in the testament of " Johne Adame, merchant in Kilmarnok," in 1617.

The property soon afterwards passed into the hands of the *Campbells*, latterly of Sornbeg.

In 1725 the heritors of Ochiltree were—" Mr Charles Cochrane, Hugh Campbell of Barquharie, and John Chalmers of Bonnytoun."

### POLQUHAIRN.

*James Cuninghame of Polquhairn* paid to Hew Campbell in Pottirstoun, burgess of Ayr, " the sowme of fourtie pundis money of this realme, in lauchfull redemptioun fra thame of all and haill the merkland of the Manis, of auld extent, with the pertinentis, lyand within Kingis Kyle, and sherefdome of Air." on the 4th June 1576.* " Oct. 38, 1578. The quhilk day Williame Cuninghame of Polquharne, zounger, fear of the lands underwrittin, and James Cuninghame of Polquharne, his fader, liferenter therof, with there awin handis, guif heretabill stait and sasing of all and haill there vjs. viijd. worth of land of Burntoun, of auld extent, &c., lyand within there landis of Eister Polquharne, Kingis Kyle, &c., to Johne Cuninghame,† mariner, burges of Air, sone lauchfull to the said James. personalie present, conforme to ane chartour," &c.

*Williame Cuninghame of Polquhairn* succeeded his father. His name occurs as a witness to a sasine, 21st April 1585. He had a brother, *Robert*, " above the toue, burges of the burgh of Air," who disponed the " Nolt Fauld " to David Fergushill, Provost of Ayr, in 1600.

*James Cuninghame of Polquharne* witnesses a document in 1597. " Henrie Cunynghame, brother to the Laird of Polquharne," occurs in the testament of umquhile " Michaell Dalrumpill, merchand burges of Air," in 1613.

*Williame Cuninghame of Polquhairn.* " Agnes Muir, relict of umquhile Adame Muir of Brounehill, and William Cunynghame, elder, of Polquharne, hir spous." The Laird of Polquhairn had thus, it seems probable, been twice married. " William Cunynghame, younger, of Polquhairne, appears in the testament of William Wilsoun, Uchiltrie, in 1618. The property seems to have been parted with shortly after this period, for we no longer meet with the Cuninghames of Polquhairn in any document.

---

* Masoun's Notarial Book.

† John Cuninghame acquired the four merk land, of auld extent, of Barturk, within the barony of Ochiltree, from Andro, Lord Stewart of Uchiltre, in 1582.

"*Joseas Stewart of Westir Polquharne*, his minister," occurs in the testament of Agnes Hunter, in 1613. He was tutor of Burganie. Wester Polquhairn and Bonnytoun seem to have been synonymous.

*David Chalmer*, heir of John Chalmer in Ballochneil, his father, was served in the four merk land of Wester Polquhairne, called Bonnytoun-Polquhairne, namely, the two merk land of Bonnytoun, &c., Aug. 25, 1627.[*] In March, 1642, *John Chalmer*, heir of James Chalmer, junior, of Polquhairne, his brother, was served in the eight merk land of Easter Polquhairne, with the mill and granary. And in the same month and year,

*James Chalmers*, heir of James Chalmers, notary public, burgess of Ayr, his father, had service of the lands of Waterside, Greenside, Richartoun, and certain parts of the lands of Wester Polquhairn. These were the same Chalmerses formerly mentioned in reference to the properties of Sauchrie and Brockloch, in the parish of Maybole.

Polquhairn afterwards occurs (1646) in the service of John Chalmers of Gadgirth, and in that of the Earl of Stair (1696).

*Adam Crawfurd of Dalleagles* had sasine, on the 31st March 1756, of the eight merk land of Polquhairn, and the 33s. 4d. land, old extent, of Knockguldron, in Ochiltree parish, on a precept from Chancery, dated 23d Feb. 1756. It is now the property of

*James Pettigrew Wilson of Polquhairn.*

### FERGUSHILL OF BURNOCKSTONE.

The Fergushills of Burnockstone were no doubt a branch of the Fergushills of that ilk, in the parish of Kilwinning. The first of them, however, so far as we can trace, was

I. ARCHIBALD FERGUSHILL, burgess of Ayr. He had a precept of sasine of the xls. land of Gallisholmes, in the baillierie of Kyle-Stewart, dated 22d May 1577.[†] June 19, 1579, "Archibald Fergushill, burgess of Air . . . gaif stait and sasing of all and haill his landis of Sanctleonardis, &c. lyand besyd the Corrachanburne, within the territorie of the burgh of Air, to Johne Cuninghame," &c.[‡] Again, August 19, 1584, "Archibald Fergushill, burges of Air, grantit him to haif actuallie ressavit fra the handis of John Muir of Craigskean, the sowme of je merkis,

money of this realme, in lawful redemptioun fra the said Archibald, of his xls. land, of auld extent, of Craigskeane, with the pertinentis, liand within the erledome of Carrik, &c., annaliit to the said John, under reversioun, contening the sowme foirsaid," &c.[*] On the 27th July 1586, "Archibald Fergushill, burges of Air," paid two hundred merks to Sibella Stewart and William Wallace of Brighouse, her spouse, for the redemption of an annualrent o twenty-two merks "that thai had zeirlie to be upliftit furth of the said Archibald's tenement in the meilmercat of Air," &c.[†] In 1587 Archibald Fergushill was Provost of Ayr.[‡] He had a son,

II. David Fergushill, merchant burgess of Ayr, and Provost of the burgh in 1600. He had a charter of confirmation, under the Great Seal, "Davidi Fergushill, filio et hæridi quondam Archibald Fergushill, Praepositi de Air, terrarum de Cunning-park," 27th September 1596. "March 10, 1600. The quhilk day, &c., compeirt personally Robert Cuninghame, above the Tour,[‖] burgess of the burgh of Air, and brother germane to umquhile William Cuninghame of Polquharne, quha of his awin frie motive, &c., gaif reall and actual possession to David Fergushill, Provest of Air, and Jonet Kennedy, his spous, being personalie present, of all and haile the said Davidis croft land, callit the Nolt Fauld, with housses, &c., occupyit of befoir be the said Robert," &c. Wodrow *gives some account of John Fergushill, minister at Ochiltree, and subsequently at Ayr, son of the Provost, and preserves a letter written by the elder Fergushill to Boyd of Trochrig, his relative, then in France, in reference to the education of his son. It was written during one of the visitations of the plague, and is interesting as showing its effects :— "*Laus Deo*. From the town of Air, the 10 of September 1604. Right honourable, and loving Emc—my humble commendations remembered. Seeing the eminent danger of God's heavy wrath against the maist part of the inhabitants of this land, especially the partis eastward, plagued with that fearfull plague of contageous Pestilence, whereupon already great mortality has ensued, that the best towns there are almost left desolat. Yet this west part, from Glasgow westward, in the Lord's great mercy, is hitherto protected, preserved, and hitherto delivered free of all danger, praised be his name! Now, seeing that schools, discipline, and vertue are dissipat and dispersed diversly, that there is no place left in this land,

[*] The published Retours.
[†] Masoun's Notarial Book. [‡] Ibid.

[*] Masoun's Notarial Book. [†] Ibid.
[‡] Ayr Records. [‖] Wallace's Tower.

where learning safely may be recovered, I therefore on this respect, having my only son, bearer hereof, who I have these three years past entertained at the Colledge of Edinburgh, and this present year should have passed his course, I have determined to make his recourse towards Montauban, where I am informed your residence is, as a place most fitt and frequent for him, in respect of your presence there. I am therefore humbly to request you, that, as he has the honour to be your kinsman, ye would take a care over him, assist him with your counsell, favour and countenance, in preferring and advancing him forward in virtue, learning, and chiefly in the fear of God. In which doing, besides all duty that I am by blood bound unto you I will ever think me yours more obligat, and shall require it with what service in me lies for recompence. I hope you shall find him plausible enough to receive instruction; for of his awin naturall he is inclined to good. Gif ye think good that he pass his course there, I am to initate your opinion thereuntill. Not that I mean to give him the title of a master, but just as the effect shall be. As to the defraying of him of such things as should be requisite to his advancement, I have taken orders thereanent, appointing an honest man in Bourdeaux to furnish him, as he shall have to do; so that ye shall be exeemed from all other trouble, save counsell and countenance. This I am bold to importune you, reposing assuredly on your goodwill thereanent. I end, committing you to the protection of the Most High, what mot augment your graces, and make you an instrument of his glorie.

Your loveing Eme and servant,
DAVID FERGUSHILL, Provost of Air."

Provost Fergushill married Janet Kennedy, a sister or near relative of Hugh Kennedy, Provost of Ayr. He died in April 1613. From his testament it appears that beside his only son, he had a daughter, *Janet*, married to John Cuninghame, and a brother, James Fergushill, burgess of Ayr. Amongst the "Debtis award to the deid," there were the following:—" Item, there was award be the said umquhile David, the tyme foirsaid, to James Herreot, in Edinburgh, twa thousand punds. Item, to Mr Johne Welsche, sax hundrith, thrieseoir sax pund xiiis. iiijd. Item, to Mr James Inglis, ane thousand pundis. . . . Item, to Johnne Lockhart of Bar, sax hundrith thrieseoir sax pund xiiis. and viijd. Item, to Johnne Cwynghame of Mylne Quarter, ane thousand pundis, &c.

"Legacie.—Item, the said David ordanes his executouris to gif up inventar of all uther debtis and sownes of money awing to him. In witnes heirof the said David gave command to Mr George Dumbar, minister at Air, to subscryve for him, becaus he was nocht abill himself. And this he did befoir thir witness, Johnne Lockhart of Bar, writter of thir presents, and James Fergushill, burges of Air, his brother."

III. Mr John Fergushill of Burnockstone, the only son of Provost Fergushill of Cuningpark, studied for the ministry under his distinguished relative, Robert Boyd of Trochrig. His name appears twice in the register of matriculations of the University of Glasgow, first in March 1600 and secondly in 1614. He was ordained minister of Ochiltree, and in 1620, " was cited before the Court of High Commission, at Glasgow, for nonconformity to the Perth Articles. He declined the jurisdiction of the court, and was suspended and sentenced to confinement within the town of Perth, but, by the good offices of Trochrig and Mr John Chalmers the last part of his sentence was modified, and he was allowed to return to his parish of Ochiltree, under certain restrictions."* While minister of Ochiltree he acquired the property of Burnockstone, which is in the vicinity. He was appointed minister of Ayr in August 1639, and continued there till his death, which occurred on the 11th June 1644. The year before (1643) he administered the solemn League and Covenant to his people with great solemnity.

IV. Robert Fergushill of Burnockstone, son of the preceding, we presume, is mentioned in the Presbytery Records, 2d May 1695. He was alive in 1746.

V. Mr John Fergushill of Burnockstone, minister, son of Robert Fergushill of Burnockstone, gave a bond of relief to Mr Charles Cochrane of Ochiltree, from certain cautionary obligations entered into by his father, dated in 1730. Bailie David Fergushill, merchant in Ayr, is mentioned in the document. There was also a George Fergushill, merchant in Ayr, in 1649,† from which it would seem that Provost Archibald, the first apparently of the family in Ayr, had more sons than his successor, David Fergushill of Cuningpark. *Jean M'Dermeit*, relict of Mr John Fergushill, had sasine of the lands of Burnockstone, 25th June 1754.

VI. James M'Dermeit Fergushill of Burnockstone had sasine of the lands of South High Cortoun, High Broomberry-Yards, High Carcluie, and Aikers, from the magistrates of Ayr, 15th Feb. 1755.

---

* Statistical Account.
† He was married to a daughter of Mr William Birnie, minister at Ayr, who died in January 1619.

VII. John M'Dermitt Fergushill of Burnock-stone, had sasine of the four merk land of old extent of Burnockstone, with houses, biggings, yards, &c. 24th May 1763, on a charter by the Right Hon. Elizabeth, Countess of Glencairne, dated 19th and 21st March 1763. He was the father, we presume, of the present

VIII. Robert M'Dermitt Fergushill of Bur-nockstone.

# PARISH OF RICCARTON.

WE can see no reason to doubt that the name of this parish was anciently derived from the name of a person. In ancient documents it is spelled two ways—*Ricardstoun*, and *Richards-toun*—both evidently meaning the same thing—*Richard's Town*. There are several other places in Scotland, the names of which are obviously of the same Anglo-Saxon origin. The parish is about eight miles in length, from east to west, and its greatest breadth is three miles. It is bounded on the north by the river Irvine, which separates it from Kilmarnock; on the south by Craigie, Manchline, and Galston; and on the west by Symington and Dundonald.

Though boasting of no scenery of peculiar beauty or picturesque effect, the aspect of the whole is diversified and pleasing. The surface rises gently towards the south and east " till it terminates in a ridge of hills of no great elevation, not being above 500 feet in height. The exposure is northern, which lays it open to the severe and chilly blasts from that direction. As the ground towards the south is considerably elevated above that on the north, or Cuninghame side of the river, the view towards that quarter is very imposing, commanding a vast extent of beautiful country, but especially of the vale of the Irvine. The soil is rather of a stiff clayey nature, but when drained is capable of raising excellent crops. The holm lands immediately adjoining the river are, in general, of superior quality.* Great improvements have been made for a series of years, by thorough draining

* Statistical Account.

and otherwise, so that the parish has a well cultivated appearance. It is not deficient in belts of planting, and though with a northern exposure, is not altogether unprotected. There are only two streams of any size in the parish, the Irvine, which bounds it on the north; and the Cessnock, which enters the Irvine about three miles above the village of Riccarton. The banks of the Irvine are somewhat flat and tame, so far as it bounds the parish; but those of the Cessnock have rather a picturesque effect. There are numerous perennial springs in the parish, but many of them are of a mineral quality, and unfit for domestic use.

## HISTORY, CIVIL AND ECCLESIASTICAL.

The parish is supposed to have derived its name from *Richard Waleys* of Riccarton, ancestor of the renowned Sir William Wallace. This may or may not be the case, although it is well known that Richard Waleys held considerable estates in various parts of Kyle in the reign of Alexander II. There can be no doubt that the family of *Waleys*, or *Wallace*, was one of the most powerful vassals of the Stewarts, Lords of Kyle, under whom they held their lands. It is rather curious, however, if the barony derived its name from the *Waleys* family, that it was not called *Waleystoun*. If it is argued that patronymics were not in existence when the first of the family is supposed to have settled in Scotland, it follows that *Waleys* was a local name; and hence it may be inferred that *Ricardstoun*, or *Richardstoun*, existed prior to the possession of that property by the Wallaces. Had they been the first of Riccarton, they would, in all probability, have adopted, as other proprietors generally did, the patronymic of their lands—*Riccarton*. The family name of *Symington*, which is also the name of a parish, for example, is derived from *Symon's Town*. It is supposed that the Wallaces were Normans or Saxons, followers of the High Steward; but it is equally as probable that they were of the aboriginal race, who were called *Walenses*, and adopted the name of *Walens*, or *Waleys*. The stern patriotism of Sir William Wallace, and his popularity with the great body of the people, at a time when most of the nobility — foreigners by descent—had sworn fealty to Edward I., seems to favour the idea that the patriot had sprung from the native stock. Be this as it may, the Wallace family were in possession of the barony of Riccarton, and other properties in Kyle, in the reign of Alexander II. Riccarton was made a burgh of barony in 1638; but the civil powers conferred upon it do not seem to have ever been exercised. Though of considerable antiquity, it is not more than a century since the village came to be of any size. The greater part of it was then feued from the Earl of Marchmont, to whom the adjoining lands belonged.

The church of Riccarton was anciently a chapelry, subordinate to the church of Dundonald, and both were granted, by the second Walter the Steward, to the Convent which he founded at Dalmulin, in 1229. When this institution was broken up, in 1238, Riccarton, along with the other property belonging to it, was transferred to the Monastery of Paisley. "The chapel of Ricardtoun," says Chalmers, "was afterwards established as a parish church, which belonged to the monks of Paisley; and it remained as such till the Reformation. The monks, meantime, received the tithes and revenues, while the church was served by a chaplain, who was appointed by them. In a rental of Paisley Abbey, which was given up to government in 1562, it was stated that the monks derived from the church of Ricardtoun, 17 chalders, 6 bolls, and a firlot of meal, yearly. In 1587, the patronage of the church of Ricardtoun, and the tithes belonging to it, which then appertained for life to Lord Claud Hamiltoun, as *Commendator of Paisley*, were granted to him and his heirs, with the other property of the monks of Paisley, which was erected into a temporal lordship to him in fee. In 1621 he was succeeded in the whole by his grandson, James Earl of Abercorn. The patronage of the church of Ricardtoun was afterwards transferred to Cuninghame of Capringtoun, who held it at the end of the reign of Charles II.:

and it still belongs to that family. After the Reformation, the parish of Ricardtoun was united to the parish of Craigie, and both were placed under the charge of one minister. But they were again disunited in 1648; and have since remained distinct parishes."

Chalmers states that the church of Riccarton was almost wholly rebuilt in 1772. From the Presbytery Records it would appear to have been rebuilt in 1725. The present church, built on what had formerly been the *Moat*, or justice-seat of the barony, was erected in 1823. The old church, the ruins of which still remain, stood in the centre of the burying-ground. In 1742 £1000 Scots was contributed by the heritors, according to their respective valuations, " for repairing of the old, or building of a new manse."[*] According to the Statistical Account, the present manse was built about half a century ago. If so it may be inferred that the old manse was only repaired in 1742.

## ANTIQUITIES.

Under this head there is little to note. Though the Romans are known to have traversed the banks of the Irvine, nearly from its source to its junction with the sea, we are not aware that any remains of that people have been found in the parish of Riccarton. Nor does any cairn, or other memorial of the native inhabitants exist, so far as we are aware. Of the old Castle of Riccarton, the ancient residence of the Wallaces, not a vestige remains. Its site, however, is understood to have been where the farm house of Yardside now stands. Some of the trees by which it was surrounded still maintain their position; and a venerable pear-tree, said to have been planted by the hand of Sir William Wallace himself, still flourishes in what no doubt formed the orchard connected with the Castle. Craigie Castle having become the chief residence of the family so long ago as the close of the fourteenth century, that of Riccarton appears to have been allowed to fall into decay; and its entire removal must have occurred some years since. It is not noticed in Pont's topography of the county, drawn up about 1608. It is said "that the stone now set over the fire-place of the manse kitchen is the identical mantel-piece of the dining-room of that once venerable mansion."[†] The *Castle of Caprington*, now modernised by additional buildings, is of considerable antiquity. It belonged of old to a branch of the Wallace

[*] Presbytery Records.  [†] Statistical Account.

family, and is mentioned in one of their charters, dated in 1385. It is built upon a basalt rock which juts out of the vale below, and is within a few yards of the water of Irvine. As it now exists, the castle is a massive, noble building, exceeding anything of the kind in the parish. *Treesbank*, about a mile south of Caprington, was a plain old-fashioned house originally, but a recent and extensive addition to it has rendered it in every respect a desirable residence. Of the house of *Knockmarloch* only a portion of one of the gables remains. It seems to have been a small building. In 1738 the only residences of heritors in the parish were *Knockmarloch, Auchinskeith, Caprington, and Treesbank.** 

## EMINENT PERSONS CONNECTED WITH THE PARISH.

Under this head the name of *Sir William Wallace* must have precedence. Though born of the Ellerslie branch of the Wallace family, he is understood to have passed many of his younger days at the castle of his relative at Riccarton. This is known to every reader of Blind Harry, a poet whose veracity was unduly criticised by Lord Hailes. Though incorrect in various particulars, the general accuracy of the poem of "Wallace" has been established beyond question by the author of the "Wallace Papers," published by the Bannatyne Club. It is not necessary here to enter into any detail of the glorious, yet unfortunate career of Wallace. His story is an undying one. As Burns says—

> " At Wallace' name what Scottish blood
> But boils up in a spring-tide flood?"

The " bickering bush," a thorn tree, which grew near the farm-house of Maxholm, until removed by some Gothic hand within these last twenty years, marked the spot where Wallace is said to have been set upon by five English soldiers, while fishing in the Irvine, whom he defeated.

*Sir John Cuninghame of Caprington*, created a baronet by Charles II., was a distinguished lawyer, and esteemed one of the most learned and best men of his time. His second son, John, was the first who read lectures on the Roman law in Scotland, and which he continued till his death in 1710.

The late *Sir James Shaw, Bart.,* Lord Mayor of London, and latterly Chamberlain of the metropolis, was born at Mosshead, a farm on the property of Treesbank, in this parish. As we will not elsewhere in this work have an oppor-

* Presbytery Records.

tunity of paying the respect to the memory of this gentleman so well merited, we consider no apology necessary for inserting the following " Memoir of Sir James Shaw," from an excellent little work, the "History of Kilmarnock," by Archibald M'Kay:—

" This distinguished baronet was the son of a highly respectable farmer, and was born at Mosshead, in the parish of Riccarton, in the year 1764. On the death of his father, which occurred about five years afterwards, his mother and family removed to Kilmarnock, where he was educated at the grammar school, then taught by the accomplished, but unfortunate, John Graham, A.M.

" At the age of seventeen the subject of our sketch went to America at the request of his brother David, who held an appointment in the *commissariat*, and by his interest was placed in the commercial house of Messrs George and Samuel Douglass of New York. After being with them on the most amicable terms for about three years, he returned to this country, and in a short time became a junior partner of the same company in London. From the great respectability of the firm he soon became widely known among the more wealthy and influential circles, and gradually attained that estimable character, as a gentleman and a citizen, which led to his future success and elevation in society.

" In 1805, he was elected Lord Mayor of London; and while holding that dignified and important office, he took a warm interest in everything connected with the welfare and honour of the city. The spirited manner in which he obtained the warrant of precedence, soon after his election, is here worthy of particular notice. This is a privilege which, in virtue of his office, the mayor enjoys in taking the lead at all public processions in the city. However exalted in birth or station, none save the Sovereign have a right to precede him on these occasions. Whether his predecessors in office had ever availed themselves of this prerogative, or whether it had, in earlier times, been acted upon by them and fallen into disuse, is a point we are not qualified to decide. The latter, we think, is most probable, —at all events, Sir James (then Mr) Shaw, resolved to establish his claim, and make use of the privilege at the funeral of Lord Nelson, in January 1806. He therefore waited on Lord Liverpool, then prime minister, to whom he introduced the subject. His lordship, however, appeared unwilling to move in the matter, probably from being aware that the Prince of Wales and his six brothers were to attend the funeral, (which was to take place on the following day,) and would be at the head of the procession. Mr Shaw, with the honour of the city at heart, said, ' Well, my lord, if you do not grant my request, I shall put another pair of horses to my carriage, which is at the door, and go forthwith to his Majesty at *Windsor*, from whom I have received much kindness, and *he*, I have no doubt, will not hesitate to favour my wishes.' His lordship, who was taken by surprise at the firmness displayed by the mayor, replied, ' Give me a little time and I will see what can be done.' ' There is not a moment to lose,' rejoined the mayor; 'there is to be a meeting of council early to-morrow morning, and I trust I shall then be able to state my success.' ' Then give me *till to-morrow morning*, and I will see about it,' returned his lordship. Here the conversation ended, and the mayor left. His object, however, was gained. The deed was forwarded in due time to the city on the following morning, to the great satisfaction of the corporation. At the funeral procession, Mr Shaw took precedence of the Prince of Wales and his brothers, but courteously gave way to his royal highness on entering the Cathedral of St Paul's.

' By integrity and diligence in the discharge of the important duties of mayor, Mr Shaw continued to rise in respectability and eminence. In 1809, his Majesty, George III., conferred on him the rank of baronet. During his mayoralty, he was also elected one of the members for the city of London, and occupied that honourable position in three successive Parliaments.

' Sir James retired from Parliament in 1818; but continued to discharge the duties of alderman with great honour till 1831. At that period, upon the decease of Richard Clerk, Esq., he was elected to the honourable and lucrative office of chamberlain of the city of London, which situation he continued to hold till May, 1843, when he resigned it. His death, which was deeply lamented, took place on the 22nd of October of the same year, after a long illness, which he bore with the utmost resignation.

' In person Sir James was tall and commanding, with none of the obesity usually imputed to a London alderman. He possessed great energy and muscular power; as an instance of which we may state, that, in 1815, when the mob surrounded and broke open the gates of the Royal Exchange, he seized one of the leading rioters, and retained him till he was perfectly secured.

" Few men have left behind them a more undying name for integrity, in public and private life. He was indefatigable in his exertions to serve, not only his youthful relatives but many others who had little claim on his benevolence, as the numerous cadetships, as well as civil appointments, which he procured for them in India will testify. Literary and artistic merit, especially that of individuals belonging to his native place, he always encouraged with his patronage. After the death of Burns he showed his deep appreciation of the genius and talents of the poet, by taking a leading part in London to raise the sum which was then collected for behoof of his widow, and by afterwards procuring respectable situations for his sons. Kilmarnock, too, has frequently experienced his liberality. In times of commercial or other public distress, his princely donations have often been the means of lessening the wants of many of the inhabitants, and, we may venture to say, of restoring, in many instances, the blessings of health to the humble invalid, who, without his bounty, might have pined in protracted debility, or drooped into an untimely grave, the victim of cheerless penury.

" These philanthropic actions, we are proud to say, have not been forgotten in this locality, but, on the contrary, are still remembered with a grateful feeling. In 1845, in consideration of the many public and private deeds of benevolence conferred by Sir James on the town of Kilmarnock, the magistrates and council took the lead in opening a subscription for the purpose of erecting the monument to his memory, and, in the most handsome manner, subscribed £50 for that object. The scheme was highly appreciated by the numerous friends and admirers of the baronet; and subscriptions, amounting to nearly £1000, were soon added to the sum subscribed by the council.

" Sir James Shaw is succeeded in his title and fortune by his estimable nephew, John, now Sir John Shaw, son of John Macfee, Esq. of Greenholm, Kilmarnock, by the sister of the late baronet. He assumed the name of Shaw in 1813, in lieu of his patronymic Macfee.

" Sir John, from his generous public acts, appears to have inherited the philanthropic virtues for which his distinguished relative was so widely and justly esteemed."

## WALLACE OF RICCARTON.

The barony of Riccarton, so far as record goes, was first possessed by the progenitor of this truly national family. It has been attempted to trace the origin of them to *Eimerus Galleius*, who witnesses a charter to the Abbey of Kelso, founded by David I., about the year 1128. There seems little affinity, however, between the names, and it is unworthy of attention. The first to be met with, connected with the barony of *Ricardtoun*, is

I. RICHARD WALENSE, who is witness to a charter of Walter the first Steward, before 1174.* The name *Walense* signified the native inhabitants —so that it is anciently to be found in England and Wales, as well as in Scotland; and no doubt that *Vallence* is just another mode of spelling the same patronymic. It is not, however, presumable that the family of Wallace came from England or Wales—because the aboriginal inhabitants of Strathcluyd were designated *Walenses* as well as the natives of Wales.

II. Richard Walense succeeded. He granted to the monks of Melrose the lands of Barmore and Godeneth, with their pertinents; and this grant was confirmed to them by the second Walter, the Steward.

*Henry Walense*, supposed to have been a brother of Richard, held lands in Renfrewshire under the Steward, in the early part of the thirteenth century. He is believed to have been the ancestor of Malcolm Waleys of Ellerslie, who married a daughter of Sir Reginald Craufurd, Sheriff of Ayr, and by her had issue:—

1. Sir Andrew Wallace, Knight, killed by the English.
2. Sir William Wallace, styled "Wallace Wight." He first appears in May 1297, and was executed 23d August 1305, s.p.
3. John Wallace, taken prisoner, and executed in 1307.

The estate of Ellerslie went to the Wallaces of Riccarton, as the nearest male heirs.

III. Richard Walense, or Waleys, (for it is spelled both ways in the chartularies) lived contemporaneously with the second Walter the Steward. According to *Dalrymple* he held the estate of Auchencruive, as well as the original barony of Riccarton. This, however, admits of doubt; although it is unquestionable that Richard Wallace of *Hackencrow* is mentioned in a charter to the canons and nuns of Dalmulin-upon-Ayr, in 1208. He may have been the same Richard who is elsewhere styled of Riccarton. Be that as it may, *Auchencruive* immediately afterwards became the patrimony of a branch of the family. Richard Wallace of Riccarton appears to have been succeeded by

IV. Adam Wallace of Riccarton, who is said to have been alive in 1258. His successor bore the same name.

V. Adam Wallace of Riccarton, who is called *Adam le Waleys*, in the Ragman Roll, in 1296. He was succeeded by

VI. John Wallace of Riccarton, who in the early part of the reign of David II. had a charter of the lands of Moorlecere, in Forfarshire. In that document he is styled " John Wallayis of Richartoun."* He married the heiress of Lindsay of Craigie, about the year 1371, and from that period Craigie became the chief residence of the family.

## CUNINGHAME OF CAPRINGTON.

I. THOMAS, third son of Sir William Cuninghame of Kilmaurs, who lived in the reign of David II., was the first of the Cuninghames of Caprington. He obtained the lands of Baidbnd in patrimony from his father, and had the gift confirmed by charter from his brother, Sir William, dated 9th August 1385. He died in the beginning of the reign of James I., leaving a son,

II. Adam Cuninghame of Capringtoun. He married, according to *Douglas*, one of the daughters and co-heiresses of Sir Duncan Wallace of Sundrum, with whom he got the lands and barony of Caprington.‡ In consequence of this

---

* Paisley Chartulary.

---

* Duncan Wallayis had a charter of Sundrum, &c., at the same time.
† See page 336, vol. i.
‡ It is more probable, however, as elsewhere explained, that she was a sister, and not a daughter of Sir Duncan.

marriage, the family was long in the habit of quartering the arms of Wallace with their own Adam Cuninghame of Caprington was one of the hostages for James I in 1431 He died towards the end of the reign of James II, leaving by his lady a son,

III Sir Adam Cuninghame of Caprington, who succeeded He had a charter, under the Great Seal, to himself and Isobel Craufurd, his spouse, of the lands and baronies of Budland, Greenside, &c. dated 19th December 1488. He was knighted by James IV, and had a charter of the lands of Dunlophill, &c, 18th November 1505 and another of the lands and barony of Tarbolton, 9th March 1506 By his lady, a daughter of Malcolm Cranfurd, progenitor of Viscount Garnock, he had a son and successor He had also a daughter, Margret, married to John Farfie of that Ilk, who was alive in 1513

IV John Cuninghame of Caprington, married first Annabella, daughter of Sir Mathew Campbell of Loudoun, Sheriff of Ayr, by whom he had a son, William his heir He married, secondly, Lady Elizabeth Cuninghame, daughter of William fourth Earl of Glencairn, by whom he had no surviving issue This Laird of Caprington greatly improved the family estate and had various charters of lands between 1525 and 1564 He died soon after the latter year, and was succeeded by his son,

V William Cuninghame of Caprington He had a charter, under the Great Seal, of the lands and baronies of Brounhill, Spittleside, Byrehill, Bourtreemuling, &c dated in 1573 In 1577 (October 19) he had sasine from William Hamilton of Sanquhar of his "merk land of Chapelland and of milns of Dalmelling miln, lands, mailures and sakin of the samin, with three pertinentis, lyand with the heathene of Kyle-Stewart,' &c In 1579 he had sasine of certain lands fishings &c, from William Hamilton of Sanquhar In 1580 he had a charter of confirmation of the lands of Curley, Montgarswood, &c, and another of the lands and barony of Glenure, in 1582 In 1583 (May 24) he "resignit and our gif, be ane penny, as us is, all and haill, ane annuelrent of xxv merkis money, to be zeirlie uphiftit, &c, furth of all and haill his tenement of land, bak and ton, &c, in the burgh of Air, in the handis of Adame Johnstoun, baillie, in favouris of Johne Porterfield, minister of Air, and Margaret Smollat, his spous, and of the langer levar of thame," &c In 1585 he is styled, in a legal document, "Williame Cuninghame, sone and heir of umquhile Johne Cuninghame of

Caprington " He married a daughter of Sir William Hamilton of Sanquhar, and left issue —

1. William, his heir
2. Adam, who occurs as a witness, along with his father, in the contract of marriage between James Craufurd of Auchinames and Elizabeth Cuninghame, daughter of the Earl of Glencairn, dated 2d September 1579
3. John, of Brounhill,* who carried on the line of the family
4. Hugh, of Previck, predecessor of the Enterkin family

He died about the year 1596 or 1597, and was succeeded by his eldest son, =

VI William Cuninghame of Caprington, who had a charter, under the Great Seal, of the ten pound land of Cambuskeith, &c, in Ayrshire, dated the 9th December 1598 He had also a charter to him and William his son and heir, of the whole lands and barony of Caprington, de novo unit, dated 19th June 1601, and another to him and Agnes Campbell, his spouse, of the lands and barony of Cumnock, 26th July 1602. Agnes Campbell was the daughter of Sir Hugh Campbell of Loudoun, Sheriff of Ayr. In 1596 he was concerned in the great feud between the Montgomerie and Cuninghame families. His name occurs in a proclamation at Ayr, 29th June 1602, at the instance of Mr Andro Boyd, minister of Inglishame, as assignee to the estate of Lord Kilmarnock wherein he is represented as owing the said cedant the sum of "twa hundreth and thre scor merkis' His name occurs in the testament of Jonet Clerk, in Caprington, in 1603 In 1608 the "Lands of Cuninghame, elder and younger," are mentioned in a similar document In 1612-13, he claimed the lands of Genoch, as heir of his father, and was served accordingly † In 1611 'Dame Agnes Campbell, Ladie Capringtoun,' is mentioned in the testament of Malcolm Seller, spouse to Robert Browne, merchand in Kilmarnock William Cuninghame of Caprington died before 1616 He was succeeded by his son,

VII Sir William Cuninghame of Caprington, whose name occurs in the testament of George Craufurd of Auchincross, in 1616 He had a charter, on his father's resignation, of the ten pound land of Cambuskeith, 4th July 1599 He was Knighted by James VI, who granted him a charter of the lands of Auldton, Schaw-miln, Bushet, Dykehead, Knockallan, Meadowfullwood, Redheads, &c, dated the penult day of July 1618 Between the years 1619 and 1637, he had no less than six charters, under the Great Seal, of lands and baronies, so that his estate must have been immense In 1637 he had infeftment of part of the lands of Knockdone, called the

---

* Masoun's Notarial Book

* Erroneously "Proonhill" in Douglas Baronetage
† Ayr Records

Common of Terrinzean, from George Craufuird of Liffnoreis; and in 1644 he leased the lands of Knockdone from John Montgomerie of Bridgend. He was at first engaged on the Parliament side, in the reign of Charles I., and appointed one of the committee for stating the debts of the nation in 1641, as also for the plantation of kirks the same year. He was a sincere loyalist at heart, however, and joined Montrose in 1645, for which he was imprisoned in Edinburgh Castle in 1646, and had a fine of £15000 imposed upon him by Parliament. This sum he could not pay, nor yet find security for the amount, and was liberated on giving a bond to appear before the committee when called upon. Though possessed of large estates, it appears, that, partly by heavy outlays in building, expensive living, and the unfortunate part he latterly took in politics, he became so thoroughly embarrassed, that he was finally evicted from his estate by his creditors. He married Lady Margaret Hamilton, second daughter of James first Earl of Abercorn, and died without issue. The representation of the family now devolved upon

*John Cuninghame of Brounhill*, second son of Sir William Cuninghame of Caprington, No. V. He obtained the lands of Brounhill from his father. He married Eleanor, daughter of Andrew Macadam of Waterhead, by whom he had a son, his successor,

*William Cuninghame of Brounhill*, whose name, "Mr Williame Cunynghame of Brounehill," occurs in the testament of William Muir of Middleton, in 1626. He got a charter, under the Great Seal, *Magistro Willielmo Cunningham de Brounchill*, of the lands of Polgaris, Kilfossets, &c., in Stirlingshire, dated 1st April 1629. He was engaged on the Parliament side in the reign of Charles I., and was one of the Commissioners from the Covenanters to the King in 1639. He married, first, Janet, fourth daughter of Patrick first Lord Lindores, by whom he had three daughters, all of whom were married—secondly, Elizabeth, daughter of William Sinclair of Rattar, by whom he had three sons and four daughters:—

1. Sir John, his heir.
2. James Cuninghame of Geise.
3. Adam, a Captain in the army.
1. Janet, married to Murray of Clerdon.
2. Isabel, to Sinclair of Telstence.
3. Anne, to Bruce of Itam.
4. Mary, to Stewart of Ascog.

He was succeeded by his eldest son,

VIII. Sir John Cuninghame of Caprington, who was one of the most distinguished lawyers of his time. He, along with Sir George Lockhart,

was employed to appear before Charles II. against Lord Lauderdale, the issue of which was the downfal of Lauderdale not long afterwards. Sir John was created a knight-baronet, 19th September 1669. He possessed the lands of Lambruchton before he repurchased the barony of Caprington from the Chancellor Glencairn, who had bought it from the creditors of Sir William, and bestowed it on his son, Lord Kilmaurs. He sold it with the burthen of the jointure of Lady Betty Hamilton, Lady Kilmaurs, a daughter of William, Duke of Hamilton, who lived in the Castle of Caprington fifty years a widow, so that Sir John is supposed to have paid in this manner about three times the value of this estate. He married Margaret, daughter of William Murray of Polmais and Touchadam in Stirlingshire, by whom he had two sons and one daughter:—

1. Sir William, his heir.
2. John, an eminent lawyer, who, about the beginning of last century, was the first that undertook to read lectures on the Roman law in Scotland, as well as on the Scots law. These lectures he continued to read till 1710, when he died. He kept up a constant correspondence with the celebrated Dutch lawyer Voet; and by this method he perfected his colleges on the Roman law, and saved many families from the expense of a foreign education.
3. Janet, his only daughter, was married to George Primrose of Dunipace. Her son, Archibald Primrose of Dunipace, suffered at Carlisle in 1746.

Sir John died in 1684, and was succeeded by his eldest son,

IX. Sir William Cuninghame of Caprington, Bart. He married Janet, only child and heiress of Sir James Dick of Prestonfield, Bart., by whom he had six sons and four daughters:—

1. Sir John, his heir.
2. James, who died without issue.
3. William,  } both succeeded to the estate of Prestonfield; their mother's property.
4. Alexander, }
5. Adam,  } both died unmarried.
6. Archibald, }
1. Anne, married to Sir Robert Dalrymple of North-Berwick.
2. Margaret, married to Robert Keith of Craig, at one time Ambassador to the Courts of Vienna and Petersburgh.
3. Janet, married to Sir Alexander Ferguson of Caitloch.
4. Christian, married to Sir John Douglas of Kellhead.

Sir William died in 1740, and was succeeded by his eldest son,

X. Sir John Cuninghame of Caprington. In 1711 "John Cuninghame of Caprington" was made a burgess of Ayr.* His name occurs in various documents connected with the county from that year downwards.† He married Lady Elizabeth Montgomerie, eldest daughter of Alexander, ninth Earl of Eglintoun, by Susanna, daughter of Sir Archibald Kennedy of Culzean, Bart., by whom he had issue:—

---

* Ayr Records. † Ibid.

1 William, his heir
2 Alexander Montgomerie Cuninghame

He died in 1777, and was succeeded by his eldest son,

XI Sir William Cuninghame, Bart, who married Mrs Græme, but had no issue. Sir William died at an advanced age in 1829, when the Baronetcy devolved upon his cousin-german, Sir Robert Keith Dick of Prestonfield, who assumed the name of Cuninghame.

Caprington is now the property of *John Smith-Cuninghame, Esq*, *W S*, who married *Anne*, second daughter of Sir William Dick of Prestonfield, one of the co-heiresses of Caprington

*Arms* — Argent, a shake-fork sable, within a border, ermine
*Crest* — A dexter hand holding a plumb-rule proper
*Motto* — " Ad amussim "

### KNOCKMARLOCH

Knockmarloch formed part of the ancient barony of Riccarton It was in the hands of the Mures towards the close of the sixteenth century " *Robert Mure of Knockmarloch* " is witness to a document dated July 26 1586 William Mure of Park was served, among other properties, in the five pound land of Knockmarloch, 26th April 1623

Soon after this it seems to have been acquired by

*Richard Brown of Knockmarloch*, whose son, *Mr Robert Brown*, minister at Cotheburn, was served heir to his father in the five pound land of Knockmarloch, 14th July 1657 He was succeeded apparently, by his son, *Andrew Brown of Knockmarloch*, who had a son *George*, and a daughter, *Elizabeth* * He must have died before 1739, in which year, *George Brown of Knockmarloch* is mentioned in the Presbytery Books In 1710 he was admitted a burgess of Ayr He was then styled " younger of Knockmarloch " He married Elizabeth Shedden, only daughter of Robert Shedden of Roughwood, and had issue

The property of Knockmarloch having come into the market, it was purchased by *Robert Shedden*, grandson of Robert Shedden of Roughwood, and nephew of Mrs Brown of Knockmarloch, with whom he had passed the greater part of his younger years He died in London, in 1826, and left Knockmarloch to his eldest son,

* Her name repeatedly occurs in the Presbytery Books

*George Shedden* of Paulerspury Park, Northampton, and Knockmarloch, in this county He married his cousin, Mary, eldest daughter and co-heiress of William Goodrich of Spring Hill, in the Isle of Wight, and had by her four sons and eight daughters *William-George* is his eldest son and heir

### TREESBANK

This property was also comprehended in the barony of Riccarton According to Robertson, the first of its proprietors, as a separate possession, was

I JAMES CAMPBELL of Treesbank, second son of Sir Hugh Campbell of Cessnock, from whom he obtained the lands, and by whom the old mansion was built He married Jean, daughter of Sir William Mure of Rowallan. The contract of marriage is dated 16th December 1672. The issue of this marriage was

1 George, his heir
2 Anne, married to —— Cuninghame, and had a son, George Augustus Cuninghame, a surgeon in the army
3 Mary, died at an advanced age, unmarried, in 1752

He lived to an advanced age. He was alive in 1730, being then upwards of 90. He must have died, however, before 1742, in which year his son is designed as proprietor of Treesbank.

II George Campbell of Treesbank had the greater part of the estate resigned to him during his father's lifetime He married, in 1708, Ann, youngest daughter of David Boswell of Auchinleck, by whom he had issue —

1 James, his heir
2 John, minister of Riccarton, and died unmarried
1. Anna, died unmarried
2 Jean married in 1746, to the Rev George Reid of Barwharrie, minister of Ochiltree.

III James Campbell of Treesbank, married, first, in 1764, Helen, second daughter of Andrew M'Credie of Perceton, by whom he had an only child, *Jean*, who, in 1787, married Robert Reid of Adamton, and died in August 1789, leaving a daughter, *Helen*, who died in April 1790 He married, secondly, in 1768, Mary, second daughter of David Montgomerie of Lainshaw, by whom he had two sons.—

1 George-James, his heir
2 David, who entered the army in early life, and became Lieutenant-Colonel, and Major of the 9th Foot

He died in 1776, and was succeeded by his eldest son,

IV George-James Campbell of Treesbank, then in infancy He married, in 1797, his cousin, Elizabeth Montgomerie Beaumont, only daughter of Mrs Elizabeth Montgomerie, in her own right, of Lainshaw. He died at Edinburgh in 1815, and left issue:—

1. George-James, his heir.
2. John.  3. David.
1. Jane-Maxwell; 2. Elizabeth-Montgomerie; 3. Mary; 4. Anne.

He was succeeded by his oldest son,

V. George-James Campbell, now of Treesbank. He married in December 1822, Elizabeth M'Kerrel, only child of Colonel John Reid, of the E.I.C.S., by whom (who died in 1826) he has two surviving daughters. He married, secondly, Miss C. J. Jones, second daughter of the late Major Jones, of the 25th Light Dragoons, and has a son, George-James, and a daughter. Mr Campbell is a Justice of the Peace, and a Deputy-Lieutenant in Ayrshire.

Both in Robertson's *Ayrshire Families*, and in Burke's *Landed Gentry*, he is set down as the chief of the Campbells of Cessnock and of Loudoun; but, from what we have observed elsewhere, this appears extremely doubtful, in so far as the Loudoun Campbells are concerned. Although George Campbell of Cessnock is first called in the deed of entail executed by Lord Loudoun in 1613, his preference may be attributed to his marriage with Elizabeth, co-heiress of the Master of Loudoun. Campbell of Killough seems to have been the undoubted male representative of the Loudoun family.

*Arms* precisely similar with ancient Cessnock.

## CUNINGHAMES OF AUCHINSKEITH.

The Cuninghames of Auchinskeith are frequently to be met with in connection with the parish of Riccarton, and in the records of the county, of a modern date, but we can give no proper account of the family. *Auchinskeith* occurs as one of the proprietors of Riccarton in 1738. The first we meet with is

*William Cuninghame of Auchinskeith*, mentioned in the Records of Ayr. He died in 1727, and his representatives, on the 6th June of that year, gave six pounds Scots for ringing the town bell at his funeral. He was succeeded by

*William Cuninghame of Auchinskeith*, who was admitted a burgess of Ayr in 1738. On the 12th October 1764, William Cuninghame of Auchinskeith, and *William Cuninghame*, his son, had sasine of the 20s. land of Inchbean; the 10s. land of Commonend; the 40s. land of Whatriggs; the 2 merk land of Wester Mosside; the one merk land of Easter Mosside; the 2½ merk land of Hole of Commonhead and Clayslope; the 40d. land of Commonhead, &c., on a charter of resignation and confirmation, by James Pringle of Bowland, one of the Clerks of Session Commissioners of Hugh, Earl of Marchmont, dated 23d August 1764.

*William Cuninghame of Auchinskeith* is mentioned in a sasine of the lands of Langlands to Dr Park, 28th November 1767. *Alexander Cuninghame*, second son of William Cuninghame of Auchinskeith, was admitted a burgess of Ayr in 1775.

There were several small families in the parish of Riccarton, such as the *Hasties* of Kaimshill, of whom we can give no account. *James Hastie of Kaimshill* is mentioned among the heritors of Riccarton in 1743.[*] Mr Brown, merchant, Liverpool, and Mr Malcolm, printer, Glasgow, are descendants of the family by the female side.

* Presbytery Records.

# PARISH OF ST QUIVOX.

ETYMOLOGY, EXTENT, &c

THE name of this parish anciently was Sanchar, or Senechar, from the Gaelic Sean-Chaer, the old fort. Other places in Scotland called Sanchar have a similar derivation. St Quivox may have been a fortification in the days of the Romans. It is quite such a position as that people were likely to choose—and from certain remains recently dug up in the parish it is evident that they were in the vicinity.* In charters of the thirteenth and fourteenth centuries the name was written Senechar, or Sinchar. In subsequent times it was changed to Sanquhar, the quh being substituted for the "ch." Latterly the church came to be called after its patron Saint—Saint Kevoc—supposed to be derived from "Santa Kennocha Virgo in Coila," who lived in the reign of Malcolm II., and was distinguished for her zeal in promoting monastic institutions.* Both the church and the parish were so named before the Reformation. After passing through various modes of spelling, the name has now settled into Saint Quivox. The name of the ancient territory, or manor, is still called Sanquhar. The parish is bounded on the south by the river Ayr, and on the east, north, and west, by the parishes of Tarbolton, Monkton, and Newton. It is about five miles in length, and three in breadth, and contains about 5000 acres.

Except towards the east, where the surface becomes somewhat elevated and uneven, the surface of the parish may be described as a perfect level. The scenery is consequently of a monotonous character, save, perhaps, along the wooded banks of the Ayr, which are at all times delightful. The soil, towards the sea, is of a light sandy nature, with occasional patches of moss and clay. The higher lands consist chiefly of a stiff clay. Notwithstanding these apparent drawbacks in point of soil, which are increased by a naturally humid climate, the parish has attained a first class position in reference to agriculture. So great have been the improvements effected within these few years that it may be described as a garden—so well is it enclosed, wooded, and cultivated.

## HISTORY, CIVIL AND ECCLESIASTICAL.

The church of Sanquhar was a rectory, and existed prior to 1208.* When the second Walter the Steward founded, in 1229, a convent at Dalmulin for canons and nuns, of the order of Sempringham, which was dedicated to the Virgin Mary, the church of Sanquhar was amongst the numerous gifts bestowed upon the institution. Dalmulin, signifying the mill-field, where a mill had existed from the earliest times, and does still exist, is situated on the north bank of the Ayr, and is altogether a delightful spot. The canons and nuns were brought from Sixile, in Yorkshire, and were called Gilbertines, from Gilbert, the founder of the order. All the grants of Walter, which comprised many lands and fisheries, with the churches of Dundonald and Sanquhar, and the chapels of Crosbie and Riccartoun, were confirmed to the Gilbertines by Alexander II., at the town of Ayr, in May 1230. The church of Auchinleck was also granted to them subsequently to the convent. "The Gilbertines did not remain long at Dalmulin. Pretending the want of health, they resigned their establishment here, and returned to Yorkshire in 1238. The monks of Paisley contrived to obtain from Walter the Steward a grant of Dalmulin, with its property and pertinents, on condition of paying 40 merks yearly to the Gilbertines of Simpingham.* The monks of Paisley, as soon as they had secured Dalmulin, with its rights, possessed it by a detachment of monks, who held it as a cell of Paisley till the Reformation. The ruins of the house of Dalmulin were extant at the beginning of the eighteenth century."† The resignation of the property was in name of the "Master of the House of Simpringham of Dalmulin," whose seal was attached to the document.

Although the church of Sanquhar was thus gifted first to the Convent of Dalmulin, and secondly to the Monks of Paisley, the territory, or barony of Sanquhar, continued in the hands of a lay proprietor. This we learn from the Paisley Chartulary, wherein we find a document of which the following is a free translation:—

"Charter of the Boundaries of the lands of the House of Paisley and William of Sanchar.

"To all the faithful in Christ, who may see or hear this present writing, William of Sanchar, son and heir of the deceased Hugh the Porter (or Door-keeper) greeting eternally in the Lord.

"Let you all know that a controversy has often arisen between the Abbot and Convent of Paisley, on the one part, and we on the other, concerning the boundaries and divisions between my lands of Sanchar, and their lands, as well of their church of Sanchar as of Dalmulin. In order to extinguish for ever the said contention, and to have an everlasting peace and remembrance of these boundaries, by faithful men, and by the consent of parties attested and sworn on the Holy Gospel of God, have been recognised and declared divisions between the foresaid lands, the following, namely, from the boundaries of Auchincro, by a certain ditch, made between my land and the land of the foresaid church, and ascending by ditches somewhere made, and crosses erected, as far as the ford, which is called Crossford, and so on from that ford, descending by a certain hollow in the marsh, as far as a certain ditch made in the same marsh, and so on by other ditches made, descending into the rivulet, which is called Muclath Burn; besides, between my land of

Sanchar and the land of Dalmulin, from the boundaries of Auchincro, by a certain hollow descending to the boundaries of Auchincro, and by the same hollow ascending the ditches made, and crosses here and there erected, as far as a certain cross which is called the cross of *Walter the son of Roger*, and so on descending as far as the Great Moss. Moreover it has been agreed, as well for me and my heirs as for the aforesaid Abbot and Convent and their successors, that from Martinmas no field shall be enclosed between my domain and my other lands, from the aforesaid rivulet westward, and the land of the aforesaid church, until the festival of the Purification of the Blessed Virgin; but that the animals of said Monks and Convent, or their servants, should freely pasture in my land, and *vice versa*, my animals, of my heirs, and of our dependents, in the land of the aforesaid church; however, so that no damage shall be done to my granges, ditches, or sown land, at any time to me or my heirs. However, on the other side of the aforesaid rivulet, for a fortnight after the corn has been carried from the lands, and also everywhere throughout my whole land on the same side of the rivulet, the animals of the persons inhabiting the land of the aforesaid church shall freely graze; nor shall they be impeded by me, or my heirs or assignees; neither shall they be prevented from pasturing in any part beyond my land which we had in common at the time of the making of this document. And in order to keep by the aforesaid limits, thus known and declared, and also in all other and each thing faithfully in time to come, for me and my heirs and successors, I have given my bodily oath into the hands of the official of the Court of Glasgow. And the aforesaid Abbot and Convent have considered all this agreeable and accepted, and promised to keep by the same faith fully. Moreover, by the said Abbot and Convent there has been granted to me and to my heirs, that we shall have at all times a footpath for ourselves and our family, from our house to the church aforesaid, through the lands of said church. Witnesses—Master Alexander Kennedy, Walter Kemblock, John the son of Allan, John Calvo, William of Knox, Walter Diknoe, Richard the son of Osanne, and many others. Done at Sanchar, on the first Friday after the feast of St Martin, A.D. 1280."

This document, which is of considerable local interest, is followed by another, dated "at Paisley, the first day of March after the feast of Saint Katherine, 1280," wherein "William of Sanchar, the son of Hugh the Porter, or Door-keeper, binds himself, under a penalty of ten pounds to be paid for the fabric of the church of Paisley,

* The Gilbertines transferred their right to the 40 merks to Sir William More of Abercorn, in 1668.
† Chalmers' Caledonia.

that he or his heirs shall put no impediment in the way of making ditches and erecting crosses, as land-marks between his lands and the lands of Sanchar and Dalmulin, belonging to the Monks of Paisley; the said crosses and ditches to be made by men mutually chosen; one-half of ditches to be taken from the lands of both parties, and the ditches to be six feet wide." Part of what is called "the Great Moss," mentioned in the first of the foregoing documents, still exists, and evidence is afforded, by the numerous roots of trees which have been dug up in the vicinity, that the soil had been thickly studded with timber at some period or other. In a charter of Walter the Steward to the Monks of Paisley, about 1208, liberty is granted to them to take wood for burning out of his forest of *Seanceathre* (Sanquhar?) in Kyle, at the sight of his forester.

After the Reformation, the church lands and patronage of this parish, "came first to Lord Claud Hamilton, and settled at last on the Earl of Abercorn. The patronage of Saint Quivox Church has belonged to Oswald of Auchincruive for many years.     When the church was repaired in 1767, a new aisle was built by Oswald of Auchincruive, the patron, for the accommodation of his family."* The church itself is old, having been built before the Reformation; but it was recently repaired and enlarged. The manse was built in 1823.

## ANTIQUITIES

There is little to remark under this head—all remains of antiquity, including the Convent of Dalmulin, having long ago been swept away by the hand of improvement. Several small urns, however, supposed to be Roman, were discovered some years ago, in levelling a sand-bank at Content, in the vicinity of Newton-upon-Ayr.

---

## FAMILIES IN THE PARISH OF ST QUIVOX

### AUCHINCRUIVE

The earliest possessor of this property, of whom there is any record, was *Richard Wallace of Hackencrou*, mentioned in a charter by Walter the Steward to the canons and nuns of Dalmulin, supposed to have been dated in 1208, although that convent is generally held to have been founded in 1229. According to Lord Hailes, this Richard also possessed the estate of Ricardtoun, the original patrimony of the family. This, however, seems doubtful. We seldom or ever had the chief of a family designed by any other than the original title. It is more probable that the Auchincruive Wallaces were a branch of the Riccarton family. But the compilers of the genealogies of the Wallaces are so inaccurate that it is difficult to arrive at any thing like a satisfactory conclusion in reference to certain particulars. It is evident, however, that *Sir Duncan Wallace*, the next we find of Auchincruive, and who got charters of Sundrum, and various other lands, could not have been the son of John Wallace of Craigie—as set down by *Robertson*—though he might have been his brother, if the Wallaces of Riccarton and Auchincruive were one and the same family. "*Johanni*

"*Walays de Ricardtoun*," and "*Duncano Walays, militi*," had both charters of the same date from David II in 1371. What makes it more probable that Sir Duncan Wallace was the representative of the Auchincruive branch, is the fact of his marriage with Eleanora de Bruys, Countess de Carrick.† A younger son of Wallace of Riccarton could scarcely be supposed equal to the hand of a Countess in her own right. Be this as it may, there can be no doubt of the identity of

*Sir Duncan Wallace of Auchincruive and Sundrum.* The latter property was acquired, not inherited by Sir Duncan. "Hew Loocky, had a charter of the 4d land of Sundroun, with many other lands within the sheriffdom of Air," from Robert I.‡ A *Robert Wallyis* had a charter of the lands of Ballmckeran, in Carrick, from Robert I., and *Robert Walleyis* had a charter of "the lands of Drumferne, in King's Kyll," from David II. Also, "*Robert Wallayis* and his heirs-male only," had a blanch charter of "the lands of

---

* Caledonia

† Robertson makes this lady Eleanora Douglas, Countess of Alexander Bruce Earl of Carrick, but she is plainly styled in the charters "Eleanorae de Bruys, Comitisse de Carryk."

‡ Robertson's Index

Somdrome and Quyltoun, in baronia de Kyll." What relationship this Robert Wallace bore to Sir Duncan it is impossible to say; but about the same time we find the latter obtaining a charter from the same monarch of "the lands of Somdrome, and Drounferne, and Swild," in Ayrshire; of the lands of Achterbannak, in Stirlingshire, and "of ane annuell furth of the lands of Barres," in Kincardineshire. Sir Duncan does not appear to have married the Countess of Carrick at this time; but, on the 11th August, 1370, "Duncano Wallayis, militi," resigns the lands of Sundrome, Drumferne, and Sywyld, and obtains a new charter of the same, in favour of himself and "Elianore de Bruys, sponse ejus," dated at Perth, 22d October 1371. He and his spouse had various other charters of lands and baronies. "Duncano Walays, militi, et Elianoræ de Bruys, Comitisse de Carryk, sponsæ sue," had a charter "baroniarum de Dalyell, de Modirvale, de Oxinhame, et de Hetton, de terra de Maxtoun de Erthbyset," &c., from Robert II., 22d October 1374. It seems doubtful whether Sir Duncan had any children. Nisbet states that one of his daughters, a co-heir, married Cuninghame of Baidland, and by her got the barony of Caprington. But it is probable that this lady was a sister of Sir Duncan. Another of his sisters was married to Alan de Cathkert, ancestor of Lord Cathcart, and we know that the baronies of Dalmellington and Sundrum were devised by Sir Duncan to Alan de Cathkert, his nephew. Sir Duncan died, apparently without issue, before 1384, in which year we find Alan de Cathkert entering into an indenture with Roger Craufurd of Daleglis, at Sundrum, the Thursday after Christmas, 1384, by which part of the lands of Dalmellington were ceded to Roger for £46, 3s. 4d. The Cathcarts also obtained the barony of Auchincruive through the death of Sir Duncan, which seems further confirmatory of the belief that he died without issue; because, if he had left two or three daughters, as is usually said, his property would have been more equally divided. It also seems that these inheritances, Auchincruive, Dalmellington, and Sundrum, were Sir Duncan's own property, prior to his marriage with the Countess of Carrick. Most of the other lands were entailed to James de Sandylands, son of the Countess by a previous marriage.

The lands of Auchincruive, Sundrum and Dalmellington, continued long in the hands of the Cathcarts. The lands of Auchincruive, however, were possessed for some time by the Drongane family. John Craufurd of Drongane had a charter of the house and lands of Auchincruive, 10th May 1532. Also of the mains of Auchincruive,

5th August 1535. In 1733 the heritors of St Quivox parish were Charles Lord Cathcart; William M'Taggart, late Provost of Irvine; Sir Thomas Wallace of Craigie, and Robert Wallace of Holmstoun.

The lands of Auchincruive were acquired by the ancestor of the present possessors, the

## OSWALDS OF AUCHINCRUIVE,

about 1760. According to Sir John Sinclair's account of Thurso, the progenitor of the Oswalds was one of the bailies of that burgh. He had a son,

I. THE REV. JAMES OSWALD, minister of Dunnett, in Caithness, who had two sons:

1. Rev. Dr James.
2. Richard, merchant in London, and minister plenipotentiary to sign the articles of peace with the United States in 1782.

II. The Rev. Dr James Oswald is said, in *Burke's Commoners*, to have acquired the estate of Auchincruive, by purchase, about the time already mentioned. It seems rather to have been purchased by his brother, Richard, who is styled *Richard Oswald, Esq. of Auchincruive*, in the deed of sale of the Greenhead manufactory of Kilmarnock, in 1773. Dr Oswald married Miss Murray of Pennyland, Caithness-shire, and had two sons:

1. George, of Scotstoun, his heir.
2. Alexander, of Shieldhall, merchant in Glasgow. He married Mary-Anne, daughter of John Dnudes of Mona, Perthshire, and had issue:
  1. James, who succeeded to Auchincruive.
  2. John, died unmarried in 1806.
  3. Richard-Alexander, married Elizabeth, daughter of John Anderson, Esq. of London, and died in 1822, leaving two sons and two daughters:
    1. Alexander, M.P. He was born in 1811, and married in 1844, Lady Louisa Johnstone, widow of Sir George-Frederick Johnstone, Bart., and daughter of William, first Earl of Craven.
    2. George, born in 1823.
    1. Margaret.   2. Mary.
  1. Agnes.  2. Elizabeth.
  3. Lillias, married to Andrew Mitchell, Esq., Glasgow.
  4. Margaret, married to Alex. M'Fadzean, M.D.
Mr Oswald of Shieldhall died in 1813.

Dr Oswald died in 1819.

III. George Oswald of Scotstoun and Auchincruive, married Margaret, daughter of David Smyth of Methven, Perthshire, and had issue:

1. Richard-Alexander, who succeeded.
2. David, Major of the 38th Foot. Died in 1798.
3. James, Capt. R.N., died in 1822.
4. Alexander, advocate, married, in 1819, Anne, daughter of the late Sir Hew Hamilton, Bart., and died without issue in 1821. His Lady died in 1820.

1. Elizabeth of Scotstoun.
2. Catherine, married to Robert Haldane, Esq.
3. Margaret, married to General J. Wilson.
4. Christian, married to Alexander Anderson, Esq.
5. Mary, married to James Dennistoun, Esq.

IV. Richard-Alexander Oswald of Auchincruive, M.P. for Ayrshire. He was born in 1771, and married, first, in 1793, Louisa, daughter of Wynne Johnston, Esq. of Hilton, in the Merse. It was in honour of this " accomplished and lovely woman," that Burns wrote—

> " O, wat ye wha's in yon town,
>   Ye see the e'enin' sun upon?
> The fairest dame's in yon town,
>   That e'enin' sun is shinin' on."

Mrs Oswald died at Lisbon, in 1797, leaving issue:

1. Richard, who married, in 1823, Lady Mary Kennedy, daughter of the Marquis of Ailsa, but died in January following.
2. Mary-Hester, married in 1819 to Thomas-Spencer Lindsay, Esq. of Hollymount, Ireland.

Mr Oswald married, secondly, in 1817, Lady Lillias Montgomerie, widow of Robert-Dundas Macqueen, Esq. of Braxfield, and daughter of Hugh, twelfth Earl of Eglintoun, but by her had no issue. He died in 1841. Mr Oswald was greatly respected by all who knew him, and especially by his tenantry, who, previous to his death, subscribed for a marble bust of him, and were at the expense of sending Mr Fillans, sculptor, to his residence abroad, to take a model. His Lady survived him a few years. Leaving no male issue, Mr Oswald was succeeded by his cousin,

V. James-Oswald Oswald of Auchincruive. He was a merchant in Glasgow, and first elected M.P. for that city in 1832.

Auchincruive, the family seat, is delightfully situated on the banks of the Ayr, a few miles from the county town.

# PARISH OF SORN.

ETYMOLOGY, EXTENT, &c.

THE original name of this parish was Dalgain, from the property so called on which the church was built. It signifies, in the Celtic language, the field of sand or gravel, which is characteristic of the place. It was occasionally called the Church of Sorn, from Sorn Castle, which stands at a short distance, and ultimately the designation of Sorn altogether supplanted that of Dalgain. Sorn is also Celtic, and means a projection, or rough visage, which may have been applicable to the site of the castle. The parish is nearly a square, about six and a half miles. It is bounded on the east by the parish of Muirkirk; on the west by the parish of Mauchline; on the north by the parish of Galston; and on the south by the parish of Auchinleck.

The parish is intersected by the river Ayr, which enters it from the east, and runs in a westerly direction. The Ayr is augmented by several tributary streams, the principal of which is the Cleugh, which flows close by Sorn Castle. The topographical appearance of the parish is highly diversified, and in some respects picturesque. The highest eminence is Blackside-end, on the north-east boundary, supposed to be about 1600 feet above the level of the sea. From this height a beautiful and commanding view of the surrounding country is obtained. The level holms and romantic hollows along the banks of the " hermit Ayr" are exceedingly beautiful, while the scenery of the deep glen through which the Cleugh finds its way, is said to equal, on a small scale, the far-famed scenery of the Falls of Clyde. There is a great deal of moor and moss land in the parish, though what is arable is generally well cultivated, and numerous plantations and belts of wood give a sheltered aspect to a considerable portion of the district. Blackcock, and other game birds, abound in the parish.

In 1845 blackband ironstone was discovered on the lands of Glenlogan, and a considerable body of miners were employed in extracting it until recently. Since the end of March, (1852), owing to the existing depression in the iron trade, the operations at the pits have been discontinued.

## HISTORY, CIVIL AND ECCLESIASTICAL.

Sorn did not exist as a separate parish till 1658, when it was disjoined from the overgrown parish of Mauchline. It consequently formed part of the original grant to the monks of Melrose, and was then in a state of nature. In 1652 a settlement was made for detaching the parish from Mauchline; but owing to the distraction of the times the separation was not finally effected till 1692. From a stone in one of the walls of the church it appears to have been built in 1658. When the settlement took place in 1692, the patronage of the church was conceded to the Earl of Loudoun; and in 1782, it was disposed of, along with the Castle of Sorn, to William Tennent, Esq. of Poole, by whom both were sold to Graham of Limekilns, and Stevenson of Dalgain, who again parted with them to Somervell of Hamilton Farm, and they are now held by Mrs A. Somervell of Sorn Castle and Dalgain.

" From Wodrow's History it appears that a Mr John Campbell was ejected from Dalgain in 1662 for noncompliance with Episcopacy; and

according to Cruickshanks, Mr Andrew Dalrymple, minister at Auchinleck, was 'indulged'
to Sorn in 1669. Nor is it improbable that, previous to the Revolution in 1688, there was an
Episcopalian incumbent settled in the parish, as
a tradition prevails that he was obliged to flee
at that period; and a small pass at the side of
the river Ayr, near Sorn Castle, over which he
is said to have passed during his flight, is still
called the Curate's Steps. It is not unlikely that
he was one of those to whom Bishop Burnet alludes as being so obnoxious to the people, that
they tore their gowns, and carried them in mock
procession through their parishes previous to ex-
pelling them. In 1826, the church was thoroughly
repaired, and the seating so arranged as to accommodate about fifty persons more than formerly. It is conveniently enough situated for
the parish—has 611 sittings, of which 64 are set
apart for the poor, and those not otherwise entitled to church accommodation. There is, besides, a chapel of ease in the village of Catrine,
which was built by Claud Alexander, Esq. of
Ballochmyle, in 1792, and cost £1000. In 1829,
this chapel was purchased from the late Claud
Alexander, Esq. of Ballochmyle, by the feuars of
Catrine, who, by their feu-rights, are bound to
maintain a chapel in connection with the Establishment, as well as a churchyard." *

The manse has been rebuilt since the last Statistical Account was published, and in a style of
elegance which is rarely seen in a rural parsonage.

In the year 1849, a set of school-houses were
erected, which, in beauty of design and in ampli-
tude of accommodation, surpass any to be found
in the district.

Catrine, now a considerable village, has long
been famed for its extensive cotton mills. These
works were commenced in 1786 by Claud Alexander, Esq. of Ballochmyle, and David Dale,
Esq., merchant in Glasgow. At that time only
two families lived at Catrine—those of the miller
and blacksmith. The population now amounts
to nearly 3000.

The population of the parish, at last census,
was about 5000.

### Extracts from the Session Records.

"Dec. 18, 1692.—Whilk day, after calling on
the name of the Lord, the minister, Mr Mungo
Lyndesay, inquired whether or no there was any
parish register belonging to the session or congregation; and it being answered and declared
that there was none since the disjoining of the

paroch from the paroch of Mauchline, the late
prelacy being not long thereafter introduced
into the national church, and during it the said
paroch not being planted with any ordained minister, but men of a prelatick stamp intruded
thereupon, and in such tymes of confusion there
was no register kept.

"The minister farther inquired if any other
elders used to sit as members of the session than
those present; and it was declared that Robert
Farquhar of Catarin, Andrew Wylie, portioner
of Logan, John Peden of Blindburn, and Alexander M'Kerrow in Blackside, were yet living in
the paroch, that had been established elders;
that Robert Farquhar, though in late times,
through the power of temptation, and through the
persecution, did swear that abominable oath called
the test, yet, to the knowledge of many, he grievously repented that sin; of the others, two were
also guilty of the same desertion." They were
all finally re-elected.

This is the first entry in the Session Records,
and it shows forcibly the zeal with which the first
minister after the Revolution entered on his duties. Throughout, indeed, he manifests the same
anxiety for the interests of his parish, and in matters temporal as well as spiritual. The entries
during his incumbency are written in a remarkably neat and distinct hand, and the style is clear
and forcible. In 1698, we find him urging the
heritors to fix a salary for a schoolmaster to the
parish, and on 24th February of that year, a
meeting was held for the purpose; but although
a considerable number attended, they, "not being the major part of the heritors of this paroch,
found and declared themselves not to be in a capacity to stent the paroch in a salary for schoolmaster." It was some considerable time afterwards when this object was effected.

"Nov. 23, 1698.—Whilk day Jean M'Latchie
was dilated by authority of two magistrates, James
Farqhar of Gilmillscroft, and Adam Aird of Ka-
tarin, and was by them put in the jougges, from
the ringing of the first to the ringing of the third
bell, and then appeared to be rebuked before the
congregation, for profanation of the Sabbath.

"May 11, 1700.—Hugh Mitchell of Dalgain
was this day, according to the 31st Act of the
present Session of Parliament, entitled 'Ane Act
against Profaneness,' named and chosen magistrate unanimously for this parish to carry said
act into effect, Sir Geo. Campbell of Cessnock,
Sher. Princ., having given him full powers.

"July 10, 1700.—Christian Beg in Corsebogue
confesses voluntarily that she inned some stuff on
Saturday near the Sabbath, and on Sabbath night
she caved some corn from the Shaw, and gave it

* Statistical Account.

to the calfs. She was dismissed with a sessional rebuke, as she had not waited for a judicial summons, but told voluntarily; but the congregation is to be told that she was rebuked, and the magistrate has decerned her in a personal fine, which she is to pay.

"At Dalgane Kirk, this 30th Oct. 1702.—The Earl of Loudon and many other heritors present, met for the purpose of appropriating his room to every heritor for a seat, the aisle for the Earl was determined on, and for Dalgayne three pews south of the pulpit," &c. So on the minute runs, till the whole is apportioned, and it is resolved farther to erect "lofts" or galleries. This minute is signed by all the heritors of whose families an account is here given, and then existing in the parish, and also by the following: Patrick Boyle of Smiddyshaw; J. Beg of Heateth; Beg of Over Clewis; J. Smith, portioner of Logan; Wylie, portioner of Logan; J. Brown of Hill of Auchmannoch; Gibson of North Limmerhaugh; Peden of Blindburn.

### EMINENT PERSONS CONNECTED WITH THE PARISH.

The two Professor Stewarts, both connected with the University of Edinburgh, resided chiefly during the summer season at their villa of Catrine. Burns, who experienced great kindness at their hands, and frequently dined at Catrine, thus compliments them in the *Vision:*

> " With deep-struck reverential awe
> The learned sire and son I saw,
> To nature's God, and nature's law,
> They gave their lore;
> This, all its source and end to draw,
> That, to adore."

The reputation of the father, for his original genius, and high attainments as a geometrician, and of the son, Dugald Stewart, as a metaphysician, is too well known to require any eulogium here.

The Countess-Dowager of Loudoun, after having lived for a considerable time at the Courts of Queen Anne and George I., took up her abode at Sorn Castle in 1727, and for a long series of years carried on those improvements in hedging and planting which so much adorn the surrounding landscape.

Though not properly ranking under the title of eminent men, it must not be forgotten that the famous Alexander Peden, of prophetic memory, was a native of Sorn parish. He was born in 1626, as asserted by some, at the farm-house of Auchencloigh, and died at his brother's house, near the place of his nativity, in 1686.

### ANTIQUITIES.

"There is nothing," says the writer in the *Statistical Account,* "particularly worthy of being noticed under this head except Sorn Castle. This castle, which stands upon a rock overhanging the river Ayr, and within a short distance of the church and manse, is supposed to have been erected at a very early period, but by whom is unknown. There is, however, a tradition that the labourers who were engaged in building it had their option either of a peck of meal or 1½d. per day." The earliest possessors of Sorn were the Keiths of Galston. Janet de Keith, heiress of Galston, was married, first, to Sir David de Hamilton, ancestor of the ducal house of Hamilton; and secondly, to Sir Alexander Stewart of Darneley. Amongst other lands, she granted Sorn to her son, Andrew de Hamyltoun, which charter was confirmed, under the Great Seal, on the 11th December 1406. In the reign of Charles II. Sorn Castle was garrisoned by a troop of dragoons, for the purpose of overawing the Presbyterians in that quarter. The following relic of these eventful times is preserved amongst the family papers at Auchmannoch:—

"God save the King.

"I, Lewis Lauder, Governor of Sorn Castle, dow heirby certifie and declare, viz. —— Kirkwood, servitour to Arthur Campbell of Auchmannoch, in the parish of Sorne, did compeir before me, on solemn oath before Almightie God, did abjure and renounce the late traitourous apollogeticall declaration, in so far as it declares war against his Majestie, and asserts that it is lawful to kill all such as serve his Majestie in church, state, armie, or countrie, conform to his Majestie's late proclamation of the 30th daye of December last.

"Given at Sorne, the aught day of February 1688 zeirs.
                              "LEWIS LAUDER."

There is a tradition that James V. visited Sorn Castle on the occasion of the marriage of the daughter of his Chancellor, Sir William Hamilton, to Lord Seaton. It is also averred, that it was while on this visit that his Majesty alighted at a well, half-way between Glasgow and Sorn, to refresh himself; hence the name of "King's Well," which the place still bears; and that he was so much annoyed by the bad roads as to declare, that if he wished to do the devil an ill turn he would send him to Sorn on the occasion of a marriage.

## BARONY OF SORN.

The estate of Sorn, as we have seen, belonged of old to the Keiths of Galston, and was granted by the heiress of her family to her son, Andrew de Hamyltoun, son of Sir David Hamyltoun, ancestor of the ducal house of Hamilton, in 1406 The writer in the old *Statistical Account* may be so far correct in stating that ' this Andrew Hamilton married Agnes, a daughter of Sir Hugh Campbell, Sheriff of Ayr, and by him had a son, Sir Robert Hamilton of Sorn and Sanquhar," and that Sir Robert married a daughter of Sir William Craufurd of Loch Norris. But, as we have elsewhere shown, Sir William Hamilton of Sorn and Sanquhar, Lord High Treasurer to James V could hardly be a son of this marriage, because he is designed of MacNairston, in the parish of Ayr, prior, apparently, to his acquiring the properties either of Sorn or Sanquhar He seems to have been of the Cumbuskeith family, and may have succeeded to Sorn by inheritance or purchase

## SOMERVILL OF SORN

The estate of Sorn, with its castle and romantic domain was purchased in 1795 by Mr Somervell of Hamilton Farm, who was a partner in the house of Somervell, Gordon, and Company, of Glasgow, long known as one of the most eminent mercantile establishments connected with our colonies Mr Somervell died soon after he acquired the estate, and his widow, with her son and two daughters, came to reside in Sorn Castle These were

1 William Somervell of Sorn who died in 1815, and was succeeded by his sister
2 Christina Somervell or Brown of Sorn who, before that period, had married Nicol Brown of Lanfine She died some years afterwards, and was succeeded by the youngest sister
3 Agnes Somervell of Sorn, the present proprietrix

## MITCHELL OF DALGAIN.

This family would seem, from the cadets which it gave off, and the lands with which it endowed them, to have been possessed of considerable property long before we meet with them in authentic records

I JOHN MITCHELL of Dalgain is the first we have met with. He is a party to the marriage contract of his second son, Andrew, with Marion, daughter of Alexander Nisbet of Greenholme, in 1600, [*] and becomes bound to infeft the couple in the lands of Turnerhill in Mauchline parish, and Nether Hylar in what is now Sorn. George Dunbar of Knockshinnoch is also a party to the contract. He married, first, a daughter of John Dunbar of Knockshinnoch, by whom he had

1 John      2 Andrew
3 Janet, married to James Campbell of Clewis

He married, secondly, Janet Wilson, without issue He was succeeded by his son,[†]

II John Mitchell of Dalgain, who married Mary Campbell, apparently of the Wellwood family, for Middle Wellwood is witness to several documents soon afterwards relating to the family. He died in 1643, and was succeeded by his son,

III John Mitchell of Dalgain, whose name occurs in a special charge to enter heir upon an apprising to his relative, John Mitchell of Burnhead, of date 1654 The lands of Burnhead had been given to a son early in the sixteenth century by Dalgain He granted a site for a church and a churchyard, and also a glebe for the minister, in 1656, when the parish—which, from its situation on the estate of Dalgain, was called, first, Dalgain, and afterwards Sorn—was separated from Mauchline It retained the former name till the middle of last century. His wife's name does not appear, but he left two sons, *John* and *George*—the first succeeded his father, he was also

IV John Mitchell of Dalgain He had a Crown charter in 1670, "Joanni Mitchell, junior, de Dalgaine " He died unmarried, and was succeeded by his brother,

V George Mitchell of Dalgain, who married Isabel Hamilton, and by her had three sons and two daughters —

1 Hugh      2 Gavin      3 James

---

[*] Contract of Marriage, of date May 1600
[†] Commissary Records

1. Jean, who married William Hutchison in Dalgig.
2. Sarah, who married Thomas Gemmel of Braehead.*

VI. Hugh Mitchell of Dalgain succeeded his father. He married Janet, daughter of John Campbell of Whitehaugh, and had many children, several of whom died in infancy. Those who attained to maturity were

1. Jean, born 1697, married 1719, John Campbell of Auchmannoch.
2. Margaret, born 1702, married 1725, Rev. M. Younger of Muirkirk.
3. Agnes, born 1713, married 1731, Hugh Logan, yr. of Logan.
4. Hugh, born 1719.†
5. Andrew, D.D., born 1725, minister of Monkton for many years. He died early in the present century, leaving his property of Avisyard, in Cumnock, to the Auchmannoch family.

Hugh Mitchell of Dalgain was appointed magistrate for Dalgain parish, under an act of the Scottish Parliament, anent the profanation of the Sabbath. He died about 1730, and was succeeded by his son,

VII. Hugh Mitchell of Dalgain, who was bred to the law, and resided in Edinburgh. The estate was sold by his father's trustees during his minority, to Mr Stevenson, whose grandson, the late John Stevenson of Dalgain, dying in embarrassed circumstances, was succeeded by his brother, the late Lieutenant-General Sir James Stevenson Barnes, who sold Dalgain by public roup in 1827, when it was purchased by Colonel Burnet of Gadgirth, who sold it in 1831, to the present proprietrix, Mrs A. Somervell of Sorn.

### MITCHELL OF BURNHEAD.

I. ROBERT MITCHELL of Burnhead is the first we find of this family, though from the deed of apprising mentioned in the preceding article, it must have been his father or grandfather who was a son of Dalgain. He is mentioned in a Crown charter to his only daughter, Agnes, " of the lands of Dalsangane," of date 1602, (21st August.) The words are, to " Agnes, only daughter of the late Robert Mitchell of Burnhead." The next is

II. Patrick Mitchell of Burnhead, who is only known by the retour of his son,

III. John Mitchell of Burnhead, dated 1626, as heir to his father, Patrick Mitchell of Burnhead. He had a charter of confirmation from Lord Loudoun, superior of the lands, of the same date. This deed was witnessed by " Dalgaine" and " David Dunbar of Enterkine." He left a son,

IV. John Mitchell of Burnhead, who being burthened with debt, parted with his land in 1654, to John Mitchell of Dalgain, and all claims against him were discharged by a deed, witnessed by John Reid of Ballochmyle, George Logan of that Ilk, Allan Logan his brother, and William Logan " ye writer hereof." This discharge is dated 1680, and is signed by Alexander Paterson, Jean Campbell, (Whitehaugh's wife,) &c.

According to tradition the Dalgain family had their residence in a tower on this property, which was partly in existence about the middle of last century. Besides the branches here mentioned, there are others—such as Braehead in Mauchline, and some in Galston parish—which sprang from it. Burnhead was sold soon after the year 1700, to Logan of Logan, in which family it continued till the death of the last of the name— Hugh Logan of that Ilk, in 1802, who left it (subject to the payment to the heir of a nominal price) to George Ranken of Whitehill, his relative. But the heir (H. G. Campbell of Auchline,) disputed the will, and after long litigation it was set aside, on account of an informality, by the House of Lords. Mr Ranken bought it some time afterwards, at the judicial sale of Logan's property, along with Nether Hillar, and he changed the name to Glenlogan, in grateful remembrance of Logan's friendly intentions.

### MITCHELL OF TURNERHILL AND NETHER HILLAR.

I. ANDREW MITCHELL of Turnerhill,* second son of John Mitchell of Dalgain, married in 1600, Marion, daughter of Alexander Nisbet of Greenholm,† and by her had his successor, and another son, (William,) who obtained part of Clewis from the Campbells. He died in 1643, and was succeeded by his eldest son,

II. John Mitchell of Turnerhill, who married Helen Stevenson,‡ relict of John Campbell of Whitehaugh, and by her had an only son,

III. John Mitchell of Turnerhill, who married in 1683, Margaret, daughter of John Reid of Ballochmyle. He acquired, before 1700, the estate of Daldilling, and, in 1710, he disposed of Nether Hylar to George Logan of that Ilk. The disposition is witnessed by John Boswell, son of David Boswell of Auchinleck, and Captain H. Campbell, son of Sir Hugh Campbell of Cessnock. Hylar remained, along with Burnhead,

* Turnerhill had previously been possessed by his elder brother, John, as appears by a charter of date 1596.
† Contract of Marriage.
‡ Contract of Marriage.

* Sorn Register of Births and Marriages.
† Sorn Session Records.

in possession of the Logans and their heirs until 1819, when they were purchased by the present proprietors Some years afterwards, Daldilling and Turnerhill were both alienated, and the family is no longer noticed in the local annals Daldilling now forms part of Mrs Somervell's estate.

### RANKEN OF WHITEHILL AND GLENLOGAN

The lands of Burnhead and Nethar Hillar being now one property, under the name of Glenlogan, we have to give some account of the family of the present proprietor The family of Sheill in Ochiltree, from which it descends, seem to have been in possession of their estate long before we first meet with them, for they are then found entering deeply into the feuds of the district, in which inhabitants recently settled would scarcely be involved

I PETER RANKEN of Sheill, in 1508, is found "banded" with Craufurd of Kerse and several others, chiefly Craufurds and Cathcarts His son, William, is also in the number Kerse was fined five pounds, and the rest forty shillings each, " for convocation of the lieges, and coming to the court of the bailliery of Carrick, on occasion whereof the baillie (Hew, Earl of Eglintoun,) was obliged to resume the brief of the Laird of Kilhenzie, and thus impeding the said baillie from holding his court ' * His son,

II William Ranken of Sheill was father of

III " Lawrence Ranken, Laird of Sheill," as he is styled by Knox, who represents him as much affected by the preaching of Wishart at Mauchline in 1544 † His son,

IV William Ranken of Sheill, being of improvident habits, and his eldest son also, a great many debts were contracted, which led to the sale of the bulk of their property In 1577, he gave "stait and sasine" to James Campbell " apperand of Shankston,' of the 10s land of "Mains of Sheill, with the manorplace, house, yards, orchards, and pertinents "‡ and before his death the 8 merk land of Sheill had also been alienated, together with Sheilhill, (at present called Sheill, the eight merk land being only known now by the names of its different farms respectively), for they are both found annexed to the barony of Drongan, of which they constitute half, in 1621 They afterwards passed through various hands and Sheill Mains, soon

after this period, became the property of Patrick Davidson, burgess of Ayr. He is mentioned in several testaments of the period; in that of " Jeanne Houston, Lady Lochnorris,"* and in that of John Reid, burgess of Glasgow, and as a witness to an infeftment in 1585.† He married Agnes Craufurd, of the family of Lochnorris, and had by her three sons and a daughter —

    1  John, who died before his father, unmarried
    2  William
    3  James, (ancestor of this family)
    4  Agnes

Robertson, who seems to have been ignorant of the existence of both these Williams, father and son, represents John and James as the sons of Lawrence, No III., and the former as continuing the line of the family; but they are more likely to be the sons of William, as the dates will show That the last William and James were brothers, is evidenced by a correspondence, preserved among the family papers, between their grandchildren, in which casual but distinct allusion is made by the latter to their " two grandfathers at Sheill " This being the case, they could scarcely be brothers to William, the son of Lawrence, though brothers of the same Christian name are met with sometimes. William Ranken of Sheill died in 1623 his testament dative is recorded in May of that year, by which it appears that he still possessed some property in land His only daughter, Agnes, is sole executrix, and " William Ranken, now of Sheill, of his awn free will, cautioner "‡

V William Ranken of Sheill, son of the preceding, married Helen, daughter of John Craufurd of Craufurdland, and by her had one son and one daughter, named William and Agnes He is mentioned in the testament of George Craufurd of Auchincorse, as " apperand of Sheill," in 1617,‖ in that of Alexander M'Ghie in Shielmilne, in 1626,§ as a creditor " for the ferme of ye land," which shows that he was still proprietor of that farm He was succeeded by his only son,

VI William Ranken of Bankhead, he having discontinued the designation of Sheill He married Abigail, daughter and heiress of Robert Cathcart of Drumjoan, (a branch of Lord Cathcart's family,) and by her had one child only, Abigail Ranken, who married John Campbell of Horseclough or Skerrington She succeeded to the property of her father and mother, and the arms of the two families she represented are still borne quarterly by her descendants.

---

    * Pitcairn's Criminal Trials.
    † History of the Reformation
    ‡ Masoun's Notes

    * Commissary Records
    † Masoun's Notes
    ‡ Commissary Records
    ‖ Ibid                    § Ibid.

VII. James Ranken, third son of William No. IV., obtained in lease Fardenreoch and Carniven, part of the barony of Torringan in Cumnock parish, where he settled prior to 1619, when he first appears in a receipt of multures of that date. He married a daughter of George Douglas of Pennyland, (then at Glenshamrock,) and had two sons, *George* and *James*. The eldest was designed

VIII. George Rankon "of Ardgrene," he having married Elizabeth, only child and heiress of John Blackwood of Ardgrene, and succeeded to that property. By her he had two sons:—

1. George.
2. William, grandfather of the late John Ranken of Adamhill, commemorated by Burns.

The eldest,

IX. George Rankon of Ardgrene, married Agnes Farquhar, daughter of William Farquhar of Lochingerroch, (formerly of Castle Cavil,) and had one son and two daughters:—

1. James.
2. Jean, married George Cranfurd of Rig.
3. Ann, married James M'Rierick of Cairn.

He sold his maternal property, and his son, some years after his death, bought the estate of Whitehill. He died in 1740.

X. James Ranken of Whitehill, married, 1750, Jean, daughter of William Hutchison in Dalgig, by Jean, daughter of George Mitchell of Dalgain, and by her had one son and one daughter:—

1. George,
2. Agnes, married James Paterson, next brother to John Paterson of Carmacoup, Lanarkshire, and had issue, two sons and three daughters:—
   1. James, now of Carmacoup.
   2. John, Captain, E.I.C.S., died 1850.
   3. Jean.
   4. Mary.
   5. Grace.

James Ranken of Whitehill died 1779, and was succeeded by his only son,

XI. George Ranken of Whitehill, who married Janet, youngest daughter of James Logan of Knockshinnoch, by Margaret, daughter of John Beg of Dornal, and his wife Sarah Chalmers, daughter of Ronald Chalmers of Polquhairn, a son of Gadgirth, and by her had fourteen children, four of whom died in infancy. Those who grew up were

1. James.
2. Thomas, writer and collector of cess in Ayr, married Jane, daughter of John Logan of Knockshinnoch, and had issue, three sons and two daughters:—George, John, Thomas, Wilhelmina, and Agnes. He died in 1831.
3. George, in Australia, married Janet, daughter of William Hutchison of Kiltoside, Dumfriesshire; surviving issue, four sons:—William, James, Thomas, and Andrew.
4. William, M.D., formerly of Demerara, now in this country, married Marianne, daughter of John Campbell, M.D. of Edinburgh, son of Sir James Campbell of Aberuchil, Bart. She died in 1846, (July 12.) Surviving issue, one son and two daughters:—William, Regina, and Janet.
5. Hugh Logan, M.D., Ayr. He died in 1831, of a fever caught in the discharge of his duty at the Dispensary.
6. Andrew, M.D., late of Demerara, now in this country, married Agnes, daughter of John Koert of that colony. She died a few months afterwards.
7. John, Lieutenant, H.E.I.C.'s service, volunteered to serve in the Burmese war with 40 of his company, and was killed in storming a stockade near Prome, on 25th November 1825, in his 22d year.
8. Arthur, in Australia, married Annabella, daughter of John Campbell of Lochend, (Argyleshire,) issue, six sons and one daughter:—George, John, James, Andrew, Arthur, William, and Annabella.
1. Jane.
2. Agnes, died on 19th February 1825.

George Ranken of Whitehill died on 2d December 1844, and was succeeded by his son,

XII. James Ranken of Whitehill and Glenlogan, who was more than thirty years in the H.E.I.C.'s service, and for a large portion of that time Postmaster-General of the North-Western Provinces—an office, for the efficient discharge of which he received, more than once, the marked approbation of the Governor-General. He died unmarried, 30th May 1848. The next in succession is his nephew, the eldest son of his brother Thomas,

XIII. George Ranken.

The *Arms*, as quartered with those of Skerrington, Loudoun, and Drumjoan, on the occurrence of the marriage above-mentioned, about the end of the 17th century, are the same as those of Rankine of Orchardhead in Stirlingshire, with a difference in the tincture of the field, viz.:— Azure, three boars' heads erased, argent, between a Lochaber axe issuing out of the sinister base, and a lance issuing out of the dexter.

*Crest.*—A hand and forearm in armour, grasping a battle-axe.

*Motto.*—Fortiter et Recte.

## FARQUHAR OF OVER CATRINE.

The first we have observed of this family, which was probably a branch of Gilmillseroft, is,

I. Bernard Farquhar of Over Catrine, mentioned in a Crown charter of confirmation to his son,

II. George Farquhar of Over Catrine, in which he is styled Bernard Farquhar of Over Catrine. It is dated 22d July 1597. The next met with is,

III. George Farquhar of Over Catrine, who has a Crown charter of date 15th March 1634, and was probably the son of the preceding. The next we find may be his son,

IV. George Farquhar of Over Catrine, who is mentioned in the retour, 1681,[*] of his son,

V. Robert Farquhar of Over Catrine. He was deeply involved in the religious discussions of the age, but, at last took the test and submitted to Government. He was an elder of Dalgain in 1693, having been re-elected on the accession to the ministry of the parish of Mr Mungo Lyndsay, although "he had taken the abominable oath called the Test," "because he had grievously repented thereof."[†] His wife's name was Margaret Campbell, and by her he had one son and three daughters:—

1. Agnes, married, 1701, to John Aird, son of Adam Aird of Wester Catrine.[‡]
2. Mary, married, 1714, to William Beg, second son of James Beg of Dornal.—Witnesses, John Beg of Dornal, and William Beg of Dernlaw.[§]
3. Margaret, married to the Rev. Mr Connal, minister of Sorn,[¶] after Mr Lyndsay.

It would seem that he had been twice married, as the son and Mrs Connal must have been born many years after the first two daughters. He was succeeded by

VI. Robert Farquhar of Over Catrine, his son, who married, first, Annice, daughter of James Beg of Dornal; and secondly, Anna, daughter and co-heiress of John Chalmers of Gadgirth. He had no issue by either of his wives, the last of whom long survived him, she having died about 1790. The property was then sold to a Mr Allan, who possessed it some years, when it was purchased by the present proprietors, the Buchanans of Catrine Bank. It was sometimes called Townhead, probably to distinguish it from the other Catrine.

### AIRD OF NETHER CATRINE AND STEWART OF CATRINE.

I. WILLIAM AIRD of Nether Catrine had a Crown charter, dated 26th October 1593, of these lands, and his son,

II. Adam Aird of Nether Catrine had a Crown charter to him and his son, of the lands of Catrine, dated 15th March 1634. This son, whose name is not given, was probably father to

III. Adam Aird of Nether Catrine, who is witness to the marriage of John Mitchell, yr. of Turnerhill, with Margaret Reid, in 1683.[**] His wife's name does not appear, but he had a daughter named Agnes, married, 8th June 1693, to the Rev. Mr William Fleming, minister of the gospel at Innerkip.[*] He was succeeded by his son, who is several times mentioned, during his father's lifetime, as witness in the parish records,

IV. Adam Aird of Nether Catrine, whose wife's name was Jean Dunbar, and they had two daughters, Christian and Helen, baptized, respectively, in 1697 and 1700. We find no other issue of this marriage, and it is known by tradition that one of his daughters married the Rev. Mr Stewart of Rothsay,[†] (minister there,) and that Professor Mathew Stewart, of Edinburgh University, was the offspring of that marriage. The Professor succeeded to the estate of Nether Catrine, but whether by purchase or in right of his wife, does not appear. He married Marjory, daughter of Archibald Stuart, Writer to the Signet,[‡] and by her had Dugald Stewart, Professor of Moral Philosophy in the same University, afterwards so famous for his works. The lives of both these eminent men will be found detailed, at greater length than our limits will permit, in the Biographical Dictionary of Eminent Scotsmen. Dugald Stewart married, first, Helen, daughter of Neil Ballantine, merchant in Glasgow, and by her had one son, Mathew, and one daughter, Margaret, married to the Rev. Dr Miller of Cumnock, and had issue; secondly, Helen D'Arcy, daughter of the Honourable George Cranstoun, without issue. He died in 1828, and was succeeded in Catrine by his son, Lieutenant-Colonel Mathew Stewart, who served long in India, and was the author of an able pamphlet on Indian affairs. Colonel Stewart was an accomplished scholar, and deeply versed in the learning of the east. He died in 1851, and in 1852, his estate was purchased by Arthur Campbell, W.S., son of the late Arthur Campbell of Auchmannoch.

### BUCHANAN OF CATRINE BANK.

Archibald Buchanan of Catrine Bank was the second son of James Buchanan of Carston in Stirlingshire. He married, first, Miss Robertson, daughter of the Rev. Mr Robertson, and by her had two sons, James and John; secondly, Hannah, daughter of Robert Struthers, merchant in Glasgow, and by her had four daughters and one son:—

1. Hannah, married to the Rev. Dr Keith, minister of Hamilton, and has issue.
2. Margaret, married George Bogle of Rosemount, and had issue. She died in 1839.
3. Janet.
4. Agnes, died in 1837.

* Old Retours.
† Sorn Session Record.
‡ Ibid.  † Ibid.  § Ibid.  ¶ Ibid.
** Mauchline Session Register.

* Sorn Session Register.
† He was perhaps twice married. See "Robertson," v. 15.
‡ Biographical Dictionary of Eminent Scotsmen.

1. Archibald, Partner in, and Manager of the Catrine Cotton Company.

Mr Buchanan purchased the lands of Daldorch about forty years ago, and subsequently those of Townhead or Over Catrine and others, and built an elegant mansion on them, to which he gave the name of Catrine Bank. He will long be remembered in the district for the admirable manner in which he conducted the cotton works of Catrine, of which he was manager, and (of the company,) a principal partner for many years. Mr Buchanan died about 1841. His eldest son, James, is a merchant in Glasgow, and his second, John, resides in England. The youngest, Archibald, as stated above, occupies his father's position in the Catrine Cotton Company. He married, 1847, Miss Foster of Northumberland, and by her has one daughter.

## CRAUFURD OF SMIDDYSHAW.

This was one of the oldest families in the parish. The first we meet with among our very scanty notices is,

I. HUGH CRAUFURD of Smiddyshaw, who is one of those who was cited on suspicion of being concerned in the murder of the Earl of Cassills, in 1527.*

The next is,

II. Robert Craufurd of Smiddyshaw, who is mentioned in the testament of Robert Farquhar of Lightsbaw, in 1612 ;‡ also in the testament of his son, Hew Craufurd, yr. of Smiddyshaw, 1616,‡ who appoints his father and George Campbell of Killoch, and Arthur Campbell of Auchmannoch, "overseers," and his wife, Margaret Campbell, and his daughter, Sarah Craufurd, executrices. Robert Craufurd of Smiddyshaw occurs in the testament of Janet Fleming in Manchline, 1629.‖ In all probability he was son of the other Robert, but he may be the same person. The next, of a different name, is,

III. William Craufurd of Smiddyshaw. He is mentioned in the testament of Hew Campbell of Netherplace, in 1641.§

IV. ——— Craufurd of Smiddyshaw is in Middleton's list of those who were fined in 1662. He seems to have been the last of them, for soon afterwards, Daldorch, which, with Smiddyshaw, constituted their estate, is found in the retour of Cessnock; and in 1702, Patrick Boyle of Smiddyshaw appears in the list of heritors of Sorn. It now forms part of Mrs Somervell's estate.

## PEDEN OF AUCHINLONGFORD.

The first notice we have of this family is in the old retours, under date 16th March 1648, when

I. ALEXANDER PETHEIN is served heir to his grandfather, Alexander Pethein of Auchinlongford ;* but from the number of families of the same name that existed in the parish during the seventeenth century, we may infer that they had been settled there long previously.

II. James Peden of Auchinlongford had a child baptized on 5th March 1693.§ His wife's name was Agnes Miller. They had several other children baptized. His son succeeded in 1728, and was also styled

III. James Peden of Auchinlongford. He married Isabell Rob, and had several children baptized before the year 1733.§ He was succeeded by his son,

IV. James Peden of Auchinlongford, who sold his property before the year 1780 to Mr Innes of Stowe, in whose family it continues. It consisted of the farms of Burntshields and West Auchinlongford.

There were six families of farmers named Peden in the parish towards the end of the seventeenth century, doubtless all derived, either directly or indirectly, from Auchinlongford, and from one of them sprang the revered Covenanter, Mr Alexander Peden; but it is doubtful (although it is allowed by every one that he was a native of Sorn), to which of them he belonged. The Pedens in Auchmannoch have the name of Alexander more frequently mentioned in the session records than any other, which is an indication, at least, of nearer affinity. The first entry in the register is the baptism of a son of Alexander Peden in Auchmannoch.

## RICHMOND OF AUCHINCLOIGH.

Andrew Richmond is retoured, 7th October 1663,‖ heir to

I. JOHN RICHMOND of Auchincloigh, his brother, in the 40s. land of Carlieth. The next we find any notice of is (at a long interval),

II. James Richmond of Auchincloigh, who

---

* Pitcairn's Criminal Trials.
‡ Commissary Records of Glasgow.    ‡ Ibid.
‡ Ibid.    § Ibid.

* Old Retours.
§ Session Records of Sorn.    ‡ Ibid.
‖ Old Retours.

married, 27th August 1724,[*] Isobell Paterson, portioner of Carlieth, and had subsequently several children baptized.

III. John Richmond of Auchincloigh was married, 8th November 1774, to Janet Harvie. It was probably their son who alienated the property, about the beginning of the present century, to Mr Falconer, who sold it to the Duke of Portland ten or twelve years ago. A family of the name of Harvie were joint proprietors with the Richmonds of Auchincloigh, as the parish register shews, from 1696 to 1729, and most likely before and after these dates. Both portioners sign the minute of heritors meeting in 1702, at which the church pews were apportioned. The Richmonds acquired the whole estate at some subsequent period.

### RICHMOND OF CARLIETH.

This, as we have seen in the preceding article, was a branch of the Auchincloigh family.

*James Richmond of Carlieth*, apparently the son of Andrew, mentioned above, married, 1700, April 7, Janet Richmond.

*John Richmond of Carlieth* had a child baptized June 1704. He was probably the brother of James.

*John Richmond of Carlieth* had a child baptized in 1746; and his son, John Richmond, younger, had an illegitimate child baptized in 1767. This is the last entry of them in the session records.

### PATON OF SAWERSTON.

*John Paton of Sawerston* is one of the heritors who signed the distribution of church seats in 1702. He had a child baptized 1727.

*Robert Paton of Sawerston* had a child baptized 1759, and several other children before 1770.[*] His son,

*Robert Paton of Sawerston*, sold the property about the beginning of the present century to Mr White, who is now the proprietor.

*Auchincloigh, Carlieth*, and *Sawerston*, are all on the north and west sides of the parish, near the boundaries of Galston and Mauchline with Sorn.

### CAMPBELL OF CLEWIS.

1. JAMES CAMPBELL of Clewis is denounced as a rebel, and put to the horn, along with Shank-

ston and many other Campbells, for the slaughter of Patrick Dunbar of Corsinton in 1512.[*] Subsequently, Cessnock appears as his cautioner, from which it may be inferred that Clewis was of his family. The next we find is, after a long interval,

II. James Campbell of Clewis, whose testament is recorded 1621, by which it appears that he was married to Janet, daughter of John Mitchell of Dalgain.[†]

III. John Campbell of Clewis is retoured heir to his father in Clewis and Moss-side in 1643.

IV. Robert Campbell of Clewis is mentioned in the marriage-contract of John Mitchell of Turnerhill, 1683, as having disponed part of Clewis, called Over Clewis, to William Mitchell. This was done, apparently, about 1648.

V. John Campbell of Clewis is mentioned, 1681, in the retour of his son,

VI. John Campbell of Clewis, who then enters heir to his father.

VII. James Campbell of Clewis had a son baptized in 1747.[‡] This is the last notice we find of the family.

*Clewis* now forms part of the Auchinleck estate.

### CAMPBELL OF AUCHMANNOCH.

Robertson assumes the traditional account preserved in this family, that they were directly descended from Loudoun, to be correct. We incline to think that all the primary branches of that family were comprehended in the entail of the first Lord Loudoun, and therein set down in their respective degrees of propinquity, and that many families of that period subsequently sprang from them. In corroboration of this is the fact, that in the sixteenth century there were no fewer than twenty-two families of the name in the parishes of Mauchline and Cumnock alone (both being then undivided), all of whom, from their being engaged in the same quarrels, and being mentioned in each other's documents, were evidently of one blood; while, in the entail just mentioned, only eleven are called to the succession, and these are scattered over many parishes of the county. It will be seen by the following account, that the Killoch family was in intimate connection with this one; and the near proximity of the places, taken in connection with this circumstance, may appear to indicate the source of the latter, and to support the tradition in so far as that Killoch

---

[*] Pitcairn's Criminal Trials.
[†] Commissary Records, Glasgow.
[‡] Session Register.

was latterly the unquestionable chief of the Loudoun Campbells.

I. ARTHUR CAMPBELL of Auchmannoch has a renewed charter from the Commendator of Melrose, of date 8th August 1565, to him and his spouse, Margaret Cuninghame (of the Caprington family). He was succeeded by his son,

II. George Campbell of Auchmannoch. He had a charter from James VI., dated 20th September 1590. He was succeeded by his son,

III. Arthur Campbell of Auchmannoch, who married, 10th November 1606, Janet, daughter of John Campbell of Eshawburn. His retour is dated 1601. He is mentioned in the testament of Robert Craufurd, younger of Smiddyshaw, in 1616,[*] whose wife's name was Margaret Campbell. George Campbell of Killoch, and Arthur Campbell of Auchmannoch, are overseers under the deed. The testament of his wife is recorded 1622, "given up by the said Arthur in behalf of Arthur, Hew, Agnes, and Janet Campbell, lawfull bairns to defunct." Smiddyshaw and Montgarswood are cautioners. Auchmannoch appears also in the testament of John Campbell, Baillie of Mauchline, 1622.

IV. George Campbell of Auchmannoch succeeded his father, the preceding, in 1637. He took an active part in support of the Presbyterian Church, during the reign of Charles I., having taken the field with General Leslie in 1638, as appears from a will executed by him in 1639, wherein he appointed John Campbell of Eshawburn, John Campbell of Killoch, and his father, trustees in his absence. From this it appears, also, that his father had conveyed the lands to him during his own lifetime. He married Jean Mure, daughter of John Mure of Stacklawhill, descended of Rowallan, and by her had two sons, *Arthur* and *John*, designed of Netherton.

V. Arthur Campbell of Auchmannoch was retoured heir to his father in 1668. He, like his father, was engaged in the cause of the Covenant. He is accordingly among those who were fined by Middleton in 1662, "as Campbell, younger of Auchmannoch." He was afterwards imprisoned at Strathaven. His name is to be found, among those of many other gentlemen of Ayrshire, appended to an address regarding grievances, in 1701. He married, 1671, Margaret, daughter of John Schaw of Kiers, in Carrick (afterwards of Dalton), by whom he had three sons, *John*, *William*, and *Allan*. The last two died unmarried. Arthur Campbell of Auchmannoch died 1703, and was succeeded by his eldest son,

VI. John Campbell of Auchmannoch, who

married Jean, daughter of Hugh Mitchell of Dalgain, by Janet Campbell, daughter of John Campbell of Whitehaugh, by whom he had two sons, *John* and *Arthur*. He died in 1740, and was succeeded by his son,

VII. John Campbell of Auchmannoch, who was for many years a merchant in Bristol. He died unmarried, in February 1794, and was succeeded by his brother,

VII. Arthur Campbell of Auchmannoch, who married Burella, daughter of Robert Hunter of Pisgah, Professor of Greek in the University of Edinburgh, and by her had four sons and one daughter:

1. John, who died at Calcutta, in the service of the Hon. East India Company, unmarried.
2. Robert.
3. Andrew, Lieut.-Colonel in the service of the East India Company, succeeded the late Rev. Dr Mitchell in the lands of Avisyard, in Cumnock parish. Col. Campbell married Nicola Anna, daughter of Colonel Maxwell of Birdstown, county Donegal, and has one son.
4. Arthur, W.S., of Catrine, who married Miss Barstow, and has one son and four daughters. He bought the estate of Nether Catrine in 1852 from the heirs of the late Colonel Stewart.
1. Elizabeth, married to James Cuthbert of Dalleagles, and had issue.

Arthur Campbell of Auchmannoch died in 1828, and was succeeded by his son,

VIII. Robert Campbell of Auchmannoch, the present proprietor.

*Arms*—Girony of eight, gules and ermine, for Loudoun, surcharged, with the arms of Mure of Rowallan in a canton; a silver cup in chief for Schaw of Hailly; and a bugle horn on base for Hunter of Pisgah.

*Crest*—A double-headed eagle issuing from flames, and looking to the sun.

*Motto*—" I byde my tyme."

*Auchmannoch* is in the northern quarter of the parish, near the march with Galston. A family of the name of Brown possessed part of it until the beginning of last century. In 1691, William Brown is retoured heir to James Brown of Auchmannoch in the 10s. land of Auchmannoch; and in 1649, Margaret and Janet, daughters of William Brown of Auchmannoch, are retoured heirs to him. John Brown of Auchmannoch signs at the kirk distribution meeting in 1702. The hill of Auchmannoch was their part of it.

## CAMPBELL OF BROCKLERDYKE.

In 1646, John Campbell of Crossflat (and Auldhouseburn) is retoured heir to his brother in Brochlerdyke, Holehouse, and Sands, (now Holehouse Mill.) From this it would appear that these two families were intimately connected, but which was the oldest, and consequently the parent stock, cannot be ascertained. The first who is found after the above date is

*George Campbell of Brochlerdyke,* who, in 1695, had a child baptized. His wife's name was Elizabeth Logan. They had subsequently several children baptized. His son,

*William Campbell of Brochlerdyke,* was a writer in Mauchline. He appears in the Session-books as witness to a marriage in 1719; and the last notice of him is in 1740, when he appears as an elder of Mauchline. He died some years afterwards. His tombstone is still extant in Sorn kirkyard, with the arms of Loudoun on it.

### CAMPBELL OF LITTLE MOUNTGARSWOOD.

This was a family distinct from that of the Larger Mountgarswood in Mauchline parish, but probably a branch of it.

*William Campbell of Mountgarswood* was an elder of Dalgain in 1695. He had a daughter,

*Mary Campbell of Mountgarswood,* who married, in 1700, John Marshall; witnesses to marriage, Arthur Campbell of Auchmannoch, and Andrew Paterson in Blairkip. They had several children baptized previously to 1724; but after these entries, nothing farther appears regarding them.

This small property was bought some time afterwards by the father or grandfather of the present proprietor, Henry Richmond of Mountgarswood.

### FARQUHAR OF GILMILLSCROFT.

Robertson says that the first of this family was

I. Robert Farquhar of Gilmillscroft, whose wife was Agnes Wallace, "Gudewife of Gilmillscroft," as she is styled in an infeftment granted by her to her son,

II. Alexander Farquhar of Gilmillscroft, dated in the year 1407.

III. Thomas Farquhar of Gilmillscroft is the next mentioned by Robertson, who states that he had a charter from King James I. (not among the recorded Crown charters.) He was succeeded by his son,

IV. John Farquhar of Gilmillscroft, who had a charter from the Commendator of Melrose of the lands of Castle Cavil, in 1445. He married

Margaret, daughter of the Laird of Barwharrie. Robertson says that a chasm occurs here in the genealogy which he cannot fill up. It is doubtful whether they were not, up to this period, tenants of Gilmillscroft, although they may have had other lands, and that Robertson has been misled by the illegible state of the documents he quotes; for the next in succession, and the first we find in public records, is

V. Alexander Farquhar of Gilmillscroft, who obtained a charter of Camys and Glenshamrock from the Abbot of Melrose, in 1535; and in the chartulary of that abbey his obligation in consequence will be found. It is as follows: "Be it kend til all men, me, Alexander Farker, to be bonden and oblisset to ane reverent fadder in God, ye Abbot of Melrose and Convent, notwithstanding they have laitten to me in feu heritage, and myn airs, the lands of Ower and Nether Camys and Glenshamrock, I neertheless bin and obliss me and myn airs to the said reverend fadder and convent, that I sall never molest nor trubul, nor mak requisition to, the persouns which are at this present tyne namit and wrytten in the rental of the said abbey, under payn of forfaultin my feu (Signed) Alex. Farchar, with my hand."[*] He is simply styled "Alexander Farker," without the designation "of Gilmillscroft;" and a Crown charter is granted to him, 7th June 1541, of the lands of Gilmillscroft, in which he is styled *in*, not *of* Gilmillscroft. This charter is to him and his wife, Janet Campbell.

VI. Andrew Farquhar of Gilmillscroft is the next mentioned by Robertson, as son of the preceding, and father of

VII. Alexander Farquhar of Gilmillscroft, who married, in 1586, a daughter of Charles Campbell of Glaisnock (of the Loudoun family.) He had a Crown charter, under date 11th May 1583, " of the Mill of Dalsangan." He died in 1625, and was succeeded by his son,

VIII. Robert Farquhar of Gilmillscroft, who had a ratification from Parliament of the lordship of Kylesmure to him and George Reid of Daldilling. He had a Crown charter, dated 15th March 1634, of the "holdings of Gilmillscroft united," to him and his son.[†]

IX. Robert Farquhar of Gilmillscroft, who succeeded him in 1646. His retour is of that date, and the property is considerable, but not above half the extent stated by Robertson (viz., £37, 10s. old extent.) He has evidently mistaken the new for the old valuation. He married, 22d September 1651, Elizabeth, daughter of James Ross of Balneill, in Wigtonshire; her tocher 8000 merks.

---

* Chartulary of Melrose.          † Ayrshire Families.

Witnesses to marriage, James Dalrymple of Stair, John M'Dowall, brother of Sir James of Garthland, and Alexander Baillie. There was no issue of this marriage, and he was succeeded by his cousin,

X. Robert Farquhar of Gilmillscroft, formerly of Lightshaw, grandson of Alexander Farquhar (No. VII.) and —— Campbell, his spouse. He was engaged in the broils of the period, but contrived to get better out of them, by prudent management, than others. He married Julian, daughter of Nisbet of Greenholm, by whom he had three sons and three daughters:

1. James.  2. Hugh, a Colonel in the army.
3. George.
1. Sarah, married to John Reid of Ballochmyle.
2. Margaret, married to Robert Craufurd of "ye parochine of Cumnock."
3. Barbara, married to Rev. Mr Steel of Lochmaben: witnesses, James Farquhar of Gilmillscroft, and Pat. Nisbet of Greenholm.*

His eldest son,

XI. James Farquhar of Gilmillscroft, succeeded in 1698. His retour is dated 2d May 1700. He married, in 1700, Jean, daughter of William Porterfield of Duchal and of that Ilk, by Anabell, daughter of Stuart of Blackhall, by whom he had three sons and five daughters:

1. Robert, who predeceased him.
2. Alexander.  3. William.
1. Annabell, married to Andrew Brown of Waterhead.
2. Jean, married to John White of Neuk.
3. Anna, married to John Wylie in Burnhead.
4. Margaret, married to Duncan Campbell of Barbieston.
5. Mary, married to Charles Campbell, brother of Barbieston.

He was succeeded by his eldest son,

XII. Alexander Farquhar of Gilmillscroft, who married, first, Agnes, daughter of John Campbell of Whitehaugh, without issue; secondly, Elizabeth, daughter of Joseph Wilson of Barmuir, Provost of Ayr, by whom he had a daughter, Jane, of whom afterwards. He married, thirdly, Jean, daughter of Alexander Cuninghame of Polquhairn, without issue. He was succeeded by his only child,

XIII. Jane Farquhar of Gilmillscroft, who married, in 1777, John Gray, son of the Rev. James Gray of Strathblane. He had previously succeeded his uncle, the Rev. Andrew Gray of New Kilpatrick, in the property of Kilmardinny, near Glasgow. They had by this marriage six sons and one daughter:

1. James.  2. Alexander.
3. John, Lieutenant 40th Regiment, killed at the battle of Salamanca.
4. William, a merchant in Glasgow, died 1823.
5. Andrew, Comptroller of Customs, Glasgow, married

Margaret, daughter of the late Benjamin Barton, Commissary Clerk of Glasgow, and has issue one son.
6. Robert, died in 1807.
1. Eliza, married John Ashburner, M.D., of London: no issue.

Mrs Gray Farquhar died in 1809, and was succeeded by her eldest son,

XIV. James Gray Farquhar, Lieut.-Colonel of the Ayrshire Militia, who married Margaret, daughter of Major J. Baillie, by Margaret, daughter of Lord Anchorville, a Senator of the College of Justice, by whom he had one son and two daughters, John, Margaret, and Jane. Colonel Farquhar died in 1828, and was succeeded by his son,

XV. John Gray Farquhar of Gilmillscroft, who died in 1835, and was succeeded by his sister,

XVI. Margaret Gray Farquhar of Gilmillscroft, the present representative.

Arms—Argent, a lion rampant, sable, armed and langued, or, between three sinister hands, two and one, paleways, gules.
Crest—A dexter hand, couped.
Supporters—Two greyhounds, proper.
Motto—"Sto, cado, fide et armis."

### REID OF DALDILLING.

This was an ancient family and probably one of the oldest cadets of the Barskimming Reids. They seem to have been, from an early period of the Reformation, staunch supporters of the Government and the form of worship it desired to maintain. The first we have found, is

I. GEORGE REID of Daldilling. He is one of those accused of being concerned in the murder of the Earl of Cassills in 1527.* And he is probably the same, who, in 1544, held the Kirk of Mauchline against Wishart, who desired to preach in it. The four who did this are stated by Knox to have been, George Reid of Daldilling, the Campbells of Brownside and Mountgarswood, and the Laird of Templand.§

II. George Reid of Daldilling is the next. He had a charter of the lands of Douray, 1596. His son, John, got a charter of Weltown, dated 20th March 1598. His testament was recorded in 1615. He might be the son, but more probably was the grandson of the preceding. All that his inventory contained, was "ane black naig nine years auld." He was succeeded by

III. George Reid of Daldilling. This appears by the retour of his son in 1651, wherein the

* Session Register of Sorn.

* Pitcairn's Criminal Trials.
§ History of the Reformation.

latter is styled heir of George Reid of Daldilling, his father.

IV. John Reid of Daldilling succeeded his father, as stated, in 1651. His retour contains the £4, 5s. land of Daldilling, 11s. 4d. land of Holehouse, 22s. land of Newton, 29s. land of Dernhunch, 6s. land of Craighead, and 4s. 2d.* land of Over Meiklewood. Some of these were merely superiorities, for it appears that his father and Robert Farquhar of Gilmillscroft "got a ratification from Parliament of the lordship of Kylesmuir to themselves and remanent vassals;"† and it would seem that part of the superiority of this extensive lordship thus obtained from Government, which probably had taken it from some friend of the Covenant, (and very likely Lord Loudoun,) remains in the possession of the Gilmillscroft family to this day. He was a noted persecutor, as were most of his name at that time, and he seems to have been in the employment of Government, for he was placed with some troopers, in Kinginclouch-house for a considerable period. Yet, before this, both he and his kinsman of Ballochmyle had been considerably taxed by the insatiable Middleton, as they are in his list of 1662. It is difficult to account for this. The next we find, is in the retour of his successor,

V. "William Reid of Daldilling," as he is styled, "minister of the gospel in Ireland." He was probably the younger brother of the last mentioned Laird. He was succeeded by

VI. William Reid of Daldilling, whose retour is dated 1691, and it comprehends a great many properties. A few years after this, and before 1700, Daldilling was sold to John Mitchell of Turnerhill, whose family only kept it for about forty years, when it was alienated to Mr Stevenson of Glasgow, who, about the sametime, purchased Dalgain.

### REID OF MERKLAND.

I. JOHN REID of Merkland possessed the property early in the seventeenth century. It is probable that he (or his ancestor,) branched off from Daldilling, which is only separated from Merkland by the farm of Nether Burntshields, (or Benthead.) His son,

II. Mungo Reid of Merkland succeeded. His retour is dated 1654, and is to "the 14s. 6d. land of Burntshields, called Merkland, and Green of Burntshields."‡

III. Margaret Reid of Merkland is retoured, 1674, heir to her father and her brother, Mungo Reid of Merkland, in the lands of Merkland and East Auchinlongford.*

IV. John Reid of Merkland is the next we find. He appears in the parish register as having his daughter, Agnes, married to "Charles Campbell of the parish of Auchinleck," in 1702;‖ and in 1716, when he is described as "deceast," another of his daughters was married to Adam Davidson, eldest son of Patrick Davidson of Holehouse;‖ and in 1719, another daughter, named Elizabeth, was married to Thomas Hamilton of Inchgotrie—Witnesses, George Campbell of Treesbank and Patrick Davidson of Holehouse.‖ Merkland and East Auchinlongford, came into the possession of Gilbert M'Adam, son of James M'Adam of Waterhead, about the middle of last century, and by him they were sold about 1780, to the present proprietors, the Campbells of Fairfield.

### DUNCAN OF HILLAR.

The lands of Over Hillar, about the year 1600, were possessed by a family of the name of Durie,¶ who seem also to have been proprietors of the neighbouring farm of Garpel, and to have taken occasionally the designation of both. Durie, of Hylar** appears as one of an assize about the period mentioned, and Durie of Garpell married a daughter of Campbell of Shankston in 1608.†† The first of the Duncans we notice,

William Duncan of Hillar, who married, 1682, Margaret, daughter of Mungo Campbell of Netherplace. Their son,

Mungo Duncan of Hillar, married Jean Cochrane, and they had a child,‡‡ John, baptised, February 1717; and in 1722, another son named Alexander, was baptised.

John Duncan of Hillar succeeded his father. His wife's name was Marion Hamilton, and by her he had Mungo, born in 1762; Lily, 1764; William, 1765; Jean, 1766; Agnes, 1775; and John, 1776.‖‖

Mungo Duncan of Hillar succeeded. He seems to have died unmarried, and to have been succeeded by his brother, William, a writer in Hamilton, who alienated the property, in the beginning of the present century, to the Fairfield family. William died many years ago, and his

---

* Old Retours.
† Robertson's Ayrshire Families.
‡ Old Retours.

* Old Retours.
‖ Sorn Session Register.   ‖ Ibid.   ‖ Ibid.
¶ Commissary Records.
** Pitcairn's Criminal Trials.
†† Contract quoted, vol. 1. Art. Shankston.
‡‡ Session Records of Sorn.   ‖‖ Ibid.

children emigrated to North America. *John*, the younger brother, a captain in the army, was killed at the battle of the Pyrenees, in 1814. One at least of the sisters married, and left issue.

### AIRD OF HOLL.

*William Aird of Holl* is mentioned in a deed of apprising, of date 1654, in which it is set forth that his son, afterwards

*William Aird of Holl*, is his heir. His son's retour is among those published (dated 1687.) He was also

*William Aird of Holl*. He married Agnes Reid, and had a son named *James*, baptized July 1693. He had several other children baptized before the year 1712. The next is his son,

*James Aird of Holl*. His wife's name does not appear, but he left two daughters, one of whom (Sarah) married William Campbell, son of John Campbell of Auldhouseburn, and had issue. The other sister disponed her half of Holl to James Peden of Auchinlongford. Both portions became again united; and the place, after being in possession of the late Robert Steele of Holl and his family for nearly half a century, was sold about 1833 to Mrs Somervell of Sorn.

### REID OF MID HILLAR.

This family would seem to have been tenants of the Abbots of Melrose, previous to the Reformation, and to have acquired a feu-right to the lands, (when the monks clearly foresaw the overthrow of their establishment), like other families of the district. " James Reid in Helar," son of Wm. Reid in Clare, was convicted of the murder of John Reid of Cronberry, in 1539, on the Moss of Darn Dougall.[*] Clare seems to have been the name of Nether Hillar in ancient times; and the Reids appear to have possessed both farms, for Mid Hillar marches with Cronberry, and the Moss of Darn-Dougall is just at that march, near the place where both properties abut on Templand Shaw,[†] the Lanehead of the Shaw in Reid's "dittcy," being the end of the lane that is the march between the latter and Cronberry. Little more is known of these Reids, excepting that one of them had a daughter married in 1715 to James Mac-Adam of Waterhead, and another had also a daughter, who, about 1740, married John Campbell of Wellwood. The farm now belongs to Mr Campbell of Fairfield.

[*] Pitcairn's Criminal Trials.
[†] See vol. i. p. 56.

# PARISH OF STAIR.

ETYMOLOGY, EXTENT, &c.

THE parish of Stair derives its name from the ancient residence of the Earls of Stair. In old charters, the name is written *Stahare, Stayhar,* &c. The parish lies between the waters of Ayr and Kyle, and is about six miles in length by two in breadth. It is bounded on the north by Tarbolton; on the east by Mauchline; on the south by Ochiltree; and on the west by Coylton. The river Ayr separates it from Tarbolton and Mauchline, and Kyle from Coylton. The parish is diversified by hill and dale, and the scenery on the banks of the Ayr and Kyle, particularly at Barskimming, is highly picturesque. There are extensive plantations on the estates of Barskimming, Drongan, and Stair. There is only one loch in the parish, but springs are numerous. The soil is chiefly of a stiff clay, with a retentive bottom. Minerals abound in the parish, and on the estate of Dalmore, on the banks of the Ayr, there is a quarry for whetstone, long known by the name of the Water-of-Ayr stone.

## HISTORY, CIVIL AND ECCLESIASTICAL.

Stair was formerly a part of Ochiltree parish, from which it was disjoined, according to *Chalmers,* in 1653, and according to the *Statistical Account,* in 1673. The new parish and church of Stair were first established by a decree of the Commissioners for the plantation of Churches, and confirmed by Act of Parliament, 22d July 1690. It does not appear, however, that the settlement of the new parish was fully carried into effect till about 1706, in which year the church of Stair was built. The erection of the new parish was ostensibly for the accommodation of the Stair family, whose seat was about five miles from the church of Ochiltree. The Earl of Stair, in consequence, agreed to pay one-half of the stipend of six chalders of victual settled on the minister of Stair, the other half to be drawn from the stipend of the old parish of Barnweil, which was then suppressed, and annexed to the parishes of Tarbolton and Craigie. Though suppressed by Act of Parliament, a minister still continued to preach at Barnweil. On the 27th Nov. 1706, we find the Presbytery intimating to the parish of Barnweil that they must proceed with the settlement of Stair, which no doubt was then done. In 1709, when a new arrangement was made as to the stipend, some lands were disjoined from the parish of Stair, and others annexed to it. The patronage was also settled on the Stair family, with whom it still continues.

## ANTIQUITIES.

There are the remains of a tower on the property of *Tribboch Mains,* no doubt the residence of the proprietors of that barony, most of which is situated in the parish of Ochiltree. The structure bears the evidence of considerable antiquity. The walls are of immense thickness, and arrow slits are the only openings. On removing a cairn on an adjoining knoll, a grave was discovered, cut out of the solid rock, and covered with a large flag-stone. It contained blackish dust, and some beads.

On the farm of *Drongan Mains* there are the remains of another tower, of larger dimensions.

The walls, until lately, were almost entire. It was the residence of a branch of the Cranfurds.

The old house of *Barskimming* was superseded by an elegant modern mansion, built by Sir Thomas Miller, Bart., Lord President of the Court of Session, who died in 1789. About 1817, two wings and other considerable additions were made to it, and great improvements effected in the interior. The library, forming the east wing, is a splendid apartment, and contains upwards of 18,000 volumes. The house stands close on the banks of the river Ayr, which are naturally picturesque; but the hand of art has done much to improve the general effect. The lawn is extensive and truly delightful, with numerous trees remarkable for height and thickness; while the bridge across the river, and by which the house is approached from the north, has long been the admiration of every visitor. The small holm, a little farther up the river, where Burns is said to have composed his "Man was Made to Mourn," is surrounded with a row of beeches of great size and beauty.

*Stair House* stands in a delightful holm, about three miles farther down the river. The older portion of it is much decayed, but the modern part is occupied by the tenant who farms the lands. Close by the house there is a willow tree, which, about six feet from the ground, measures 22 feet 10 inches in girth; and on the same holm there is a Lombardy poplar, nearly ninety feet in height. Two beeches, on the banks of the river, measure from 13 feet to 13

feet 6 inches each, about two feet from the ground. These are the remains of a fine plantation, which has only recently been cut down. Field-Marshal Stair planted a good many clumps, arranged, it is said, precisely after the manner in which the British troops were drawn up at the battle of Dettingen. A solitary tree, called the General, stands on an adjoining eminence. "It is well known," says the writer in the *Statistical Account*, "that Field-Marshal Stair had the misfortune, when a boy, to kill his elder brother, by the accidental discharge of a pistol; and that his parents found it necessary, for their own comfort, to banish him from their sight, as his presence awakened the most painful associations. The tradition in the neighbourhood is, that this melancholy event took place in a room on the ground floor, (which, it is said, was long after kept locked by the succeeding proprietors) and was the reason for the property being disposed of. After passing through several hands, it was purchased by the present [late] Earl, about fifteen years ago, and is understood to be now entailed." General Stewart was proprietor of Stair for some time, and during the residence of his family there, the Poet Burns made repeated visits, and was kindly encouraged by Mrs Stewart, a lady of high accomplishments and poetic taste. She was heiress of Afton Lodge, where she afterwards resided. The song of "Afton Water" was composed in honour of his lady patroness.

*Drongan House*, though not a very old building, is in a dilapidated state.

---

## FAMILIES IN THE PARISH OF STAIR.

### STAIR.

"Ade Quhyt" had a charter of the lands of *Stayhar*, from Robert I.; so also had Alan Montgomery of the lands of *Stahar*. Hew de Eglintoun, Knight, had a charter of certain annuals within the sheriffdom of Air, which Robert de Bruys resigned, viz.:—50s. out of Drumdow, 8s. 4d. out of *Stayre*, 33s. 4d. out of Cars, [Kerse], and 40s. out of Monyhagen. The lands of Stair and Cassillis were carried, in marriage, it is understood, by the heiress, to Sir John Kennedy of Dunure, in the reign of David II. Stair is believed to have gone to a second son of this

marriage, as William de Dalrymple, about 1450, acquired the lands of Stair-Montgomerie with his wife, Agnes Kennedy, an heiress, whose son, William Dalrymple of Stair, was ancestor of the Earls of Stair, the Baronets of North Berwick, Hailes, &c.

### DALRYMPLES EARLS OF STAIR.

The name is undoubtedly local, assumed from the barony of Dalrymple, which the ancestors of the Stair family at one time possessed. The charter of the 30th May 1371,* embraces three

* See vol. i. p. 437.

generations, *Adam de Dalrumpil*, *Gilcrist*, his
son, and *Malcolm*, son of Gilcrist, the latter existing at the date of the charter, in 1371. *William de Dalrymple*, who obtained the lands of
Stair-Montgomerie, in 1450, may therefore have
been the son of Malcolm. We shall assume as
the first—

I. ADAM DE DALRYMPIL of Dalrymple.

II. Gilbert de Dalrympil of Dalrymple.

III. Malcolm de Dalrympil of Dalrymple, the
last of the barons of Dalrymple. His lands were
acquired, in 1371, by John Kennedy of Dunure.

IV. William de Dalrymple, who married Agnes
Kennedy, heiress of Stair-Montgomerie, and who
acquired these lands in 1450. His son and heir,

V. William Dalrymple of Stair, married
Marion, daughter of Sir John Chalmers of Gadgirth. She was one of the Lollards of Kyle,
summoned, in 1494, as heretics before the Council,
when the accused were dismissed by James IV.,
and the charges against them treated by him
with contempt. *William*, their son and heir,
died during their lifetime.

VI. William Dalrymple of Stair, their grandson, succeeded. He married Margaret, daughter
of Wallace of Cairnhill, and was alive in 1531.
His son,

VII. John Dalrymple of Stair succeeded. He
married Isabel, daughter of George Cranfurd of
Lechnorris, and was alive in 1555. He was a
great advocate of the Reformation. His son,

VIII. James Dalrymple of Stair, married Isa-
bel, daughter of James Kennedy of Bargany.
He opposed the marriage of Lord Darnley and
Queen Mary, and joined the association of King
James, in 1567. He died in 1586. His son,

IX. John Dalrymple of Stair, was alive in
1612. He died, however, before 1613, in which
year "James Dalrumpill, brother to umquhill
Johne Dalrumpill of Stair," occurs in the testament of Robert Muir, merchant burgess of Ayr.

X. James Dalrymple of Stair, his son, married Janet, daughter of Fergus Kennedy of
Knockdaw. He died in 1625: "Testament, &c.
of James Dalrumple of Stair, Uchiltrie, Quha
decist in the monethe of Januar 1625, ffaythfullie maid and gevin up be Fergus Kennedy of
Knockdaw, guidsire [grandfather] to James Dalrumple, lawfull sone to the defunct, procreat betuixt him and Jonet Kennedy, his relict: in name
and behalf of the said James, executour dative,
decernit to the said defunct's guids and gear, be
decreit of the Commissary of Glasgow, the viii
day of July 1626."

XI. James, first Viscount Stair, grandson of
Knockdaw, was born in 1619. He studied at
the University of Glasgow, where he took the
degree of A.M., but entered into the Earl of
Glencairn's regiment of foot, 1638. Shortly
afterwards he became a successful candidate, in
"his military uniform," for the philosophical
chair of his Alma Mater, and continued for some
time to combine the discharge of his military
with his academical duties. In 1648 he was admitted a member of the Faculty of Advocates, and
in 1657, upon the recommendation of Monk to
Cromwell, was constituted a Lord of Session.
On the approach of the Restoration, he had a
private conference with General Monk, on the
day previous to his march into England, and was
re-constituted a Lord of Session, 1661, and
created a Baronet, 1664. Subsequently he was
made, 1671, President of the Court of Session,
but having, by his propositions, embarrassed the
projects of the Duke of York, in favour of the
Catholics, he found it convenient, upon a hint of
imprisonment, in 1682, to retire to Holland. He
married, in 1643, Margaret, daughter of James
Ross, of Balneil, county Wigton, and by her,
who died in 1692, had issue:—

1. John, created Earl of Stair.
2. Sir James, first Baronet of Borthwick, so created in
    1698, author of "Observations on Scottish History."
    He married thrice, and by his first wife, Katherine,
    daughter of Sir James Dundas of Arniston, had issue.
3. Sir Hugh, first Baronet of North Berwick, so created
    in 1698, President of the Court of Session. By his
    wife, Marion Hamilton, he had issue. He died in
    1737.
4. Sir David, first Baronet of Hailes, Haddingtonshire.
    Created in 1700, and died in 1721. He married
    Janet, daughter of Sir James Rochead of Inverleith,
    and had issue.

James, Viscount Stair, returning with the Prince
of Orange, in 1688, was reinstated as President of the Court of Session, and created
Baron Glenluce and Stranraer, and Viscount
Stair, in 1689. He was the author of some legal
and polemical works, and of a MS. "Apology
for his own conduct," in the Advocates' Library.
He died, aged 74, 25th November 1695.

XII. John, first Earl of Stair, born about
1648, was a member of the Faculty of Advocates,
and counsel for the Earl of Argyle, in 1781. He,
however, although on some pretence he suffered
three months' imprisonment himself, so far made
his peace with the Government as to become
King's Advocate of Scotland, in 1687; and in
that office obeyed his royal master's commands
absolutely and without reserve. Nevertheless,
in 1688, he was signally instrumental in promoting the Revolution, and was one of the three
commissioners deputed by the Convention to
offer the Crown to the Prince and Princess of
Orange, in 1689. He was reinstated as King's
Advocate, in 1690, and being constituted one of
the Secretaries of State the following year, held

the Seals of Office till 1695, when he was compelled to resign on account of his concern in issuing the orders for the massacre of Glencoe. Though he succeeded to the title, by the death of his father, the same year, he so far submitted to the guidance of his friends, or was awed by public opinion, as to forbear taking his seat among his peers till 1701. He was, however, called to the Council Board on the accession of Queen Anne, and was created, in 1703, Baron Newliston and Earl of Stair, with remainder to the issue male of his father. He married Elizabeth, daughter and heir of Sir John Dundas of Newliston, and by her, who died about 1731, had issue:—

1. John, second Earl.
2. William of Glenmure, a Colonel in the Army, died 1744. He married, in 1698, Penelope Crichton, Countess of Dumfries, fourth in that Earldom, and by her, who died in 1742, had issue:—
   1. William, fifth Earl of Dumfries, and fourth Earl of Stair.
   2. John, a Captain of Dragoons, and the favourite nephew of John, Earl of Stair, the General. He died unmarried in 1742.
   3. James, third Earl of Stair.
3. George, of Dalmahoy, a Baron of the Exchequer, died in 1745. He married, in 1720, Eupheme, daughter of Sir Andrew Myrton, Bart. of Gogar, Edinburghshire, and had issue:—
   1. John, fifth Earl of Stair.
   2. William, a General in the Army, died in 1807. He married, in 1783, Marianne Dorothy, daughter of Sir Robert Harland, Bart. of Sproughton Hall, Suffolk, and had issue:—
      John-William-Henry, seventh Earl.

The Earl, who interested himself deeply in the Union, in 1707, died suddenly after a day of exhaustion from his earnest advocacy of that measure. "He was," says Lockhart of Carnwath, "so great a master of eloquence, and expressed himself so copiously and pointedly, and with so much life and rhetorick, that there were none in the Parliament capable of taking up the cudgels with him. He died on the 8th January 1707.

XIII. John, second Earl of Stair, K. T., son and heir, born 1673, served as a volunteer in Flanders under King William, and just before his death was nominated to a lieutenant-colonel's commission in the Scottish foot guards. On the accession of Queen Anne, he attended the Duke of Marlborough in his first campaign, 1702, and was at Ramilies, Oudenarde, and Malplaquet, 1706, 1708, 1709, in the former battle as Brigadier, and in the latter as Major-General, and took rank as Lieutenant-General, 1710. On the accession of King George I., 1714, he was called to the Council Board, and in 1715 undertook the appointment of ambassador to the court of France, in order to combat the intrigues of the Jacobite party, when the house of Hanover could

not be said to be firmly established on the throne. This important station he sustained for five years with extraordinary hospitality and magnificence, and, as it proved in the sequel, at his private expense; the British ministry resolving, in 1720, to sacrifice his lordship to their terror of Law, the French financier, "who," says Lord Stair, "was very much displeased with him because he did not flatter his vanity by putting into the Mississipi; but he did not think it became the King's ambassador to give countenance to such a thing, although it had been wrong to himself to the value of thirty or forty thousand pounds, which he could easily have gained if, as others did, he had put himself into Mr Law's hands." The bubble burst, as is known to all the world, and the Earl retired to agricultural pursuits at Newliston, to improve his estate, as well by planting, in which the predominance of his military ideas is visible in the design, as by retrenchment to retrieve the expenses of his embassy, and was the first person also who introduced to his countrymen the cultivation of turnips and cabbages in the open fields.

The Earl was appointed Vice-Admiral of Scotland in 1729, but was deprived of that command on joining the opposition to Sir Robert Walpole. On the dissolution of the Walpole administration, in 1742, he was made a Field-Marshal of the forces, and the same year went ambassador to Holland, and was constituted Commander-in-Chief of the allied army in Flanders till the arrival of George II., in 1743. Under his majesty he served at the battle of Dettingen; but being disgusted at the preference shown by the King to the Hanoverian generals, he presented a memorial, and resigning his command, retired to the Hague. The public mind being much inflamed against the King's partiality to his native troops, opposition took up the matter warmly in the Commons, and in the lords it was said that "the man so long celebrated for his courage, his wisdom, and his integrity; the man who had so frequently signalised his zeal for the royal family, was reduced to a statue with a truncheon in his hand, and was permitted only to share the dangers of the campaign, of which the electoral divan regulated the operations."

He married Eleanor, daughter of James Campbell, second Earl of Loudoun, widow of James, first Viscount Primrose, but having no issue, he obtained a charter, in 1707, extending the entail to a nomination of his own, such person being descended from the first Viscount; and failing such nomination, to his elder brothers and younger sons in succession, failing which, to the eldest son. This power of nomination he executed by deed, in 1747, but in favour of his younger brother's son. It was unimpeached as to the estates; but it was set aside as to the title, as giving the power of creation to the Peerage, of which the Crown could not be divested. The Earldom, of course, devolved to the next heir of entail, although the three cousins all eventually inherited it.

The Earl, who was restored to his command in 1744, died at the age of seventy-three, 9th May 1747.

XIV. James, third Earl of Stair, nephew and heir of entail, succeeded in terms of the resolution of the House of Lords, 1748. He died unmarried, 13th Nov. 1760.

XV. William, fourth Earl of Stair, styled *Earl of Dumfries and Stair*, having succeeded his mother as fifth Earl of Dumfries, 1742, elder brother of the third Earl of Stair, and heir of entail, married, but died without surviving issue, when the Earldoms separated, that of Dumfries to his sister's son, and that of Stair to his cousin, 27th July 1768.

XVI. John, fifth Earl of Stair, cousin and heir, as also heir of his uncle by nomination. He voted as Earl of Stair at the election in 1747, but was dispossessed of the Earldom by the decision of the Lords, in 1748, to which, twenty years after he succeeded. He married, in 1789, the daughter of George Middleton, Esq., banker, London. He alienated Newliston, and died 13th October 1789.

XVII. John, sixth Earl of Stair, son and heir, born in 1749, was ambassador to Warsaw in 1782, and to Berlin in 1785. He died without issue, 1st June 1821, and was succeeded by his cousin,

XVIII. John-William-Henry, seventh Earl of Stair. He was born in 1784, and married, in 1808, Laura, youngest daughter of John Manners, Esq. of Grantham Grange, which marriage was dissolved in 1809, in consequence of a prior contract, in 1804, with Johanna, daughter of Charles Gordon, Esq. of Cluny, deemed a valid marriage by the laws of Scotland when it took place. The latter marriage was annulled, however, in June 1820. The Earl died in Paris, 22d March 1840, without issue; and was succeeded by his kinsman,

XIX. Sir John Hamilton Dalrymple, Bart., eighth and present Earl. He is a General in the army, and Colonel of the 26th Regiment. Married, first, in 1795, Harriet, eldest daughter of the Rev. Robert-Augustus Johnson of Kennilworth, who died in 1823, without issue; secondly, in 1825, Adamina, daughter of Adam, Viscount Duncan. His lordship was created a

Baron of the United Kingdom, 11th August 1841, with remainder to his brother.

*Arms*—Or, on a saltier, azure, nine lozenges, of the field.

*Crest*—A rock proper.

*Supporters*—Two lions proper.

*Motto*—Firm.

*Seats.*—Stair House; Culhorn, Wigtonshire; and Oxenford Castle, Edinburghshire.

As already stated, the property of Stair was alienated for some time. On the 20th January 1756, we find *Thomas Gordon, younger, of Earleston*, seised in the lands of Stairfarm, Shaw Holm, &c., on a disposition by John Dalrymple of Stair, (subsequently Earl of Stair,) dated 17th and 29th Aug. 1755; and on the 18th Oct. 1764, " Thomas Miller of Barskimming, his Majesty's advocate for Scotland," has sasine of " these parts of the lands and estates of Stair, viz. lands of Easter and Wester Davistons; lands of Mackieston, lands of Meadowhead and Kemphouse; of Stair; Stairbill, and Pant, on a disposition and assignation by Thomas Gordon of Earleston, in favour of Thomas Miller, of said lands, by William Dick of Crombie, to said Thomas Gordon, dated 28th February 1757." Dick of Crombie thus seems to have been the original and principal purchaser of the Stair property. About the close of last century, Stair was in the possession of *General Stewart*, whose lady was one of the early patrons of Burns. The property now belongs to the Earl of Stair.

*Major-General Stewart of Stair* is understood to have been a grandson of the Earl of Galloway. He married Catherine, daughter of Gordon of Afton, and grand-daughter of Sir William Gordon of Earlston and Afton. Mrs Stewart succeeded her father in the estate of Afton, in New Cumnock parish. They had three daughters:—

1. Grace.   2. Ann.
3. Catherine, married William Cuninghame of Enterkine, and had issue, William Cuninghame now of Logan and Afton. Mrs Cuninghame died many years ago, and her two sisters, Grace and Ann, in 1835 and 1842.

Mrs Stewart of Afton resided long at Stair, and subsequently at Afton Lodge, which she built. She is beautifully complimented by Burns as representing benevolence—" a female form from the towers of Stair."

## BARSKIMMING.

The first possessor of this property, which was also called *Starquhyte*, was, so far as charters show,

*Willielmo Rede*, who had a charter of the lands of Barskemyn, from Robert II., dated 12th Oct. 1377. That he was the ancestor of the Reids of Barskimming, and of the once numerous branches of the name in Ayrshire, there can be little doubt. We have no means, however, of tracing the family in genealogical order. The next who turns up in our notes is

*Adam Rede de Sterquhite*, (alias Barskimming). He had a charter of the fortalice of Ardcardane, and the ten shilling land adjacent to it, dated 15th Sept. 1498. He had also a charter of the lands of Arkerden, Glencarden, Auchinsaull, Rannydoch, Auchinbrek, Keironasche, &c. 27th August 1499.

*Adam Reid*, son and heir of Bernard Reid of Stairquhit, and Jonet Campbell, sponsæ suæ, had a charter of the lands of Stairquhyt, alias Barskimming, 13th July 1551.

*John Reid of Barskemming*, on the 21st Sept. 1577, " with his awin hand, with advis and consent of Mungo Reid of Drumfork, William Reid of Makistoun, and David Reid in Thridpart, his curatouris, for thare interes, gaif heretabill state and sasing of all and haill that ane four merk land of his mainis of Barskemming of auld extent, occupiit, &c., lyand in Kingis Kyle, &c., to David Cruther, burges of Air, &c., conforme to ane blanch chartour maid therupon," &c.* The last of the Reids we find mentioned was

*John Reid*, " fear of Barskimming," who occurs as a debtor in the testament of George Reid of Daldilling in 1615. The property seems to have been acquired some time previously by

*Sir Henry Stewart, Knight*, brother to the well-known James Stewart, Earl of Arran. He was the fourth son of Andrew, third Lord Ochiltree. He seems to have been alive in 1614, at least " Henrie Stewart of Barskimming " is mentioned in a testamentary document of that year. " Henrie Stewart of Barskymming, Uchiltree, deceised in the month of December 1622." His testament is dated " at the dwelling-hous of Barskymming," Nov. 1621. He " nominat and names, *Jonet Reid*, his spous, only executrix, &c.

and levis his pairt of the frie gier to Jonet Reid, his executrix......Item, he ordanis the thowsand merks awand to Adame Stewart, his sone, to be payit of the first end of thrie thowsand merks that is awand be Lefnoreis and his cautioners." " Jonet Stewart, his dochter," is also mentioned.

*Adam Stewart of Barskimming*, mentioned in the testament of John Campbell, bailie of Mauchline, died before his father, in January 1622. His testament was " faythfullie maid and gevin up be *Marie Ros*, his relict, in name and behalf of *James, Jonet, Marie*, and *Elizabeth* Stewarts, bairns lauchfull to the defunct, and executouris datives, decernit to the guids and geir," &c.

*Henry Stewart* was served heir of " Henrici Stewart de Barskimming, avi, in six libratis terrarum antiqui extentis de Stairquhyt, alias Barskimming," &c., June 23, 1632. He died, apparently without issue, in Sept. 1646. His testament was " gevin up be David Hamilton in Monivey, executour dative, &c........Inventar— Item, the defunct had adebtit and awand to him the tyme of his deceis foirsaid, be umquhile Robert Craufurd of Munkland [in Kilmarnock] his airs, executouris, the sowme of fyve hundreth merks, Scots money, promittit and obleist to have been payit by the said umquhile Robert to the defunct efter the deceis of umquhile Christian Wallace, mother to the said umquhile Robert."

The property of Barskimming appears to have been immediately afterwards acquired by

*Gilbert Richart*, who is styled of Barskimming in the testament of James Thomsone, merchant, Irvine, in December 1646. He was probably a son of Robert Ritchart of Clonnayis, or Clonnochis, in Maybole parish, by Jonet Chalmer, formerly married to John M'Lurge of Kilmoir. She died in 1621, and, from her testament, it appears that she had a son to her husband, Robert Richart, called *Gilbert*, who survived her. The next was

*James Richart of Barskimming*, whose son,

*James Richart of Barskimming*, was served heir to his father in the six pound land of Stairquhyt, alias Barskimming, &c., 20th December 1687. He died without issue, before 1691, on the 6th October, of which year,

*Mariota Richard*, wife of Ninian Ross, in Mauchline, was served heir of entail and provision of James Richard, her father's brother.

Barskimming soon afterwards was acquired by the ancestor of the present possessor.

* Adam Reid seems to have died without heirs-male; for, on the 23d May 1601, John Spottiswode of Fowlair, was served heir-portioner, on the part of his mother, to Adam Reid of Barskimming, his uncle, in the fourth part of the six pound land of Stairquhyte, alias Barskimming.

## MILLER OF GLENLEE AND BARSKIMMING.

I. Thomas Miller, Esq. of Glenlee, in the Stewartry of Kirkcudbright, married Agnes, daughter of the Rev. William Guthrie, minister of Fenwick, and was succeeded by his eldest son,

II. John Miller, Esq. of Glenlee, who married Grizel, daughter of Sir Hugh Cathcart, Bart.; but dying without issue was succeeded by his brother,

III. William Miller, Esq. of Glenlee. This gentleman married Janet, eldest daughter of Thomas Hamilton, Esq., and had issue:—

1. John.        2. Thomas.
3. Patrick, married and had issue,
1. Grizel, married to George Chalmers, Esq.
2. Martha, married to John Davison, Esq.

John, the eldest son, died unmarried; and his second brother succeeded.

IV. Thomas Miller, Esq. of Glenlee. He studied for the bar, and eventually became Lord President of the Court of Session, and was created a Baronet 19th February 1788. He married, 1st, Margaret, eldest daughter of John Murdoch, Esq. of Rose Bank, Provost of Glasgow, by whom he had issue:—

1. William, his heir, Lord Glenlee.
2. Jessie, married to John Dunlop, Esq.

Sir Thomas married, 2dly, Anne, daughter of John Lockhart, Esq. of Castle Hill, but had no issue by this lady. He died in 1789, and was succeeded by his son,

V. Sir William Miller of Glenlee, Bart.; a Lord of Session, by the title of Lord Glenlee. He married, 5th November 1778, his cousin, Grizel, daughter of George Chalmers, Esq., Fifeshire, and had issue:—

1. Thomas, married Edwina, daughter of Sir Alexander-Penrose-Gordon-Cumming, Bart., and died in 1827, leaving five sons:
    1. William, present Baronet.
    2. Alexander, late Captain 92d Regiment; married Julia-Monica, daughter of the late S. Shiel, Esq. of Ballyshannon.
    3. George, an officer in the 54th Regiment.
    4. Thomas, R.N.        5. Mathew.
2. William, Lieut.-Colonel 1st Foot Guards, mortally wounded at Quatre Bras, 16th June 1815; died next day at Brussels.
3. John, married and has issue.
4. George.
5. Mathew, Captain 31st Regiment, deceased.
6. James, advocate; died in 1849.
1. Grizel, married, in 1808, to William MacDonald, jun., Esq. of St Martin's, advocate, who died in 1841.
2. Margaret-Lockhart, married in 1827.
3. Martha, married to Captain Houston Stewart, R.N.

Sir William resigned his office as a Lord of Session in 1840, and died 9th May 1846. He was succeeded by his grandson,

VI. Sir William Miller of Glenlee, Bart. He was born 12th September 1815, and married, 27th April 1839, Emily, second daughter of Lieut.-General Sir Thomas MacMahon, Bart. K.C.B., and has issue:—

1. Thomas-Macdonald, born 1st January 1846.
2. Edwina-Constance; and another daughter.

Sir William was an officer in the 12th Lancers.

*Arms*—Argent, a cross-moline, azure; in chief, a lozenge, between two mullets, of the last; in base a bar, wavy, vert.

*Crest*—A hand, couped at the wrist, the third and fourth fingers folded in the palm, argent.

*Seats*—Barskimming; and Glenlee, Kirkcudbright.

## DRONGAN.

The property of Drongan is situated about six miles from Ayr. A family of the name of Craufurd possessed it as early as the fourteenth century—but of what stock, does not appear. The first of them on record[*] was

I. John Craufurd of Drongan, who granted a charter—8th November 1406—to John Shaw of Haly, of certain lands in the barony of Dalmellington.

[A long interval elapses between this John and the next who is found mentioned.]

II. John Craufurde of Drongane was concerned, along with Alan Cathcart of Clowlynan, in "the treasonable taking of the Castle of Lochdone," in 1511. He was also engaged, together with his sons, John and William, in the slaughter of the Earl of Cassillis, in 1527; and took part in most of the feuds, until his death, which ensued between the Craufurds and Kennedies.[†] He married the eldest daughter of John, second Lord Cathcart. He had a charter of the Mains of Auchincreaf, on an apprising against John, Lord Cathcart, dated 16th May 1532.[‡] Also of the lands of Brockelhill, &c., 6th November 1532; and the Mains of Auchincruive, 5th August 1535. He was succeeded by his son,

III. John Craufurd of Drongan, who in 1537-8, "came in the King's will for art and part of the sedition and insurrection made between the neighbours and the inhabitants of the burgh of Ayr: and for art and part of the common oppression of his neighbours. In 1528 he had a remission for

----

* Robertson's Ayrshire Families.
† Pitcairn's Criminal Trials.
‡ Lord Auchinleck's Notes.

his share in the slaughter of the Earl of Cassillis in 1527. He married Margaret, eldest daughter of Duncan Cranfurd of Camlarg. In 1539 (4th March), he had a charter to himself and his spouse, of the four merk land of Camlarg and Pennyvenzies-wester, and Mill of Dalmellington, on his own resignation."* From this it would seem that Lady Drongan was the heiress of Camlarg. Her second son, *David*, succeeded her in that property.

IV. John Cranfurd, the eldest son, succeeded his father in Drongan. He was married to a lady of the name of Kennedy, but of what family does not appear. In 1552, he granted a charter of the Mains of Drongan, and of the four merk land of Smithstoun, and lands of Skeoch-hill, on a life-rent right, in favour of his spouse, Margaret Kennedy.† In 1554 he had to find security for intercommuning with the Laird of Ballagane, then at the horn. He appears to have died without issue, and to have been succeeded by

V. Alexander Cranfurd of Balgregan,‡ the nearest heir. That he did succeed to the Drongan property is evident from the *retour* of his son,

VI. John Cranfurd of Balgregan, who, on the 31st July 1584, was served heir to his father, Alexander Cranfurd of Balgregan, in the ten shilling land of Knockgowr, and the four merk land of Over and Nether Drongan; and the twenty shilling lands of Hannayston, in Carrick.

Robertson, in his "Ayrshire Families," says "I have met no more accounts of this family of Cranfurd of Drongan, nor of the place itself, till in the year 1621, when it was in the possession of the Craufurds of Leifnorris"—and he quotes, from *Lord Auchinleck's Notes*, a charter to Sir George Cranfurd of Leifnorris, of the "eight merk land of Drongan, called Sheil-Ranken," &c., in corroboration of the statement. It had previously been in possession of Sir George's father. From Sir George it was acquired by his brother Mathew, who had "carta magistro Mathæ Craufurd, nunc de Drongane, et suæ sponsæ, baroniæ de Drongane," &c., 20th December 1622. He had also the escheat of Sir John Wallace of Cairnhill, Knight, 22d June 1624.

*William Cuninghame* had a charter of the barony of Drongane, 8th July 1624.

* Lord Auchinleck's Notes.            † Ibid.
‡ Of the House of Kerse.

The "Laird of Drongan," but whether he was a Cuninghame or not does not appear, is mentioned in the list of disaffected persons laid before the Presbytery in the time of Montrose in 1645.

*John Smith of Drongane* is mentioned amongst the Commissioners of Supply for the county of Ayr in 1757. The last Laird of Drongane, who died in India several years ago, is understood to have contemplated great improvements on the estate of Drongan, by building a new mansion-house and otherwise.

## DRUMDOW.

In 1604, Lady Margaret Montgomerie, heir of Robert, Master of Eglintoun, was served in the 50s. lands of Drumdow. It thereafter came into the hands of William Huntar, burgess of Ayr, whose son, William Huntar, was served in the four merk land of Drumdow, 23d April 1642. The superiority, however, seems to have continued in the Eglintoun family. Janet and Esther Huntar, heirs-portioners of their father, William Huntar, had service of the four merk land of Drumdow, 14th April 1682; and Esther, as heir of her sister, Janet, was served in the said lands, 21st Nov. 1682. "Hugh Craufuird of Drumdow, land-waiter in Leith," occurs in the town records of Ayr, 16th May 1749.

Drumdow was afterwards purchased by Governor M'Crae, and gifted to James M'Quire, son of William M'Quire, violer, Ayr, his former benefactor. As formerly stated, James M'Quire was styled "wright," in certain documents connected with the property. An outline of the history of Governor M'Crae, and the M'Quires, has already been given in the account of the parish of Monktoun.

## DALMORE,

Another small property, formed part of the barony of Gaitgirth. In 1615, it belonged to a family of the name of Scherar, burgesses of Ayr; and in 1696 it is amongst the numerous properties mentioned in the service of the Earl of Stair. Latterly it belonged to the late *James Heron* of Dalmore.

# PARISH OF STEVENSTON.

## ETYMOLOGY, EXTENT, &c.

THE name of the parish is believed to have been derived from Stephen, or Steven, son of Richard Loccard, who acquired a grant of the lands from Richard Morville, Lord of Cuninghame, about 1170. The greatest length of the parish is about five miles, and its extreme breadth about three. It is bounded on the north by Ardrossan and Kilwinning; on the south by the Frith of Clyde; on the west by Ardrossan; on the east by Kilwinning and the river Garnock, which separates it, for about three miles, from the parish of Irvine; and on the south-east by the confluence of the Garnock and Irvine.

The highest land in the parish is not more than 398 feet above the level of the sea, yet the surface is varied, and not altogether defective in rural beauty. "The aspect of the parish," says the writer in the Statistical Account, "indeed, from various points of view, is remarkably pleasing. One of the best views of it is, as you approach Stevenston from Kilwinning. In the foreground you have the church and part of the village. The noble back-ground is formed by the wooded heights above Sea Bank, surmounted by the magnificent peaks of Arran in the distance. The view from the south, though of quite a different character, is scarcely inferior to this. From the shore, all the principal residences in the parish are seen on the gentle acclivity before you. Ardeer, with its green wood and terraced gardens, is conspicuous on the right. More inland, you have Hullerhirst on a very commanding site, and Hayocks still prominent over a thriving young plantation. Worthy of the centre of the scene, you behold the mansion-house of Grange, and the ivy-mantled turrets of ancient Kerila, embowered in woods, stretching onward to the distant glen. In the foreground you have the stately church and modest manse above the subjacent village, on a situation not surpassed by any one on the coast. Lovely Mayville salutes you on the left, breathing odours from a thousand shrubs and flowers. Sheltered, and sweet, and cheerful, Sea Bank presents itself on the west, with its green fields, and woody braes, and martello tower, and mounted battery. And the town and spire of Saltcoats form a good termination on the left; for though it has few surrounding trees to give softness to chimney tops and architectural angles, it compensates at times by its forest of masts, a most interesting feature in a sea-coast scenery."

The upper part of the parish is a stiff clay, part of the centre of a flat tract of loamy ground, and towards the sea there are about 1200 acres of sand-hills. This large piece of barren ground had at one time been encompassed by the sea, and it has settled into its present form after various mutations. The shifting of the sands, in consequence of the high winds, is understood to have entirely changed the course both of the Garnock and Stevenston burn. In Pont's Cuninghame, in place of the Lugton joining the Garnock, and the Garnock and Irvine uniting near Irvine Bar, the three streams are delineated as running separately into the sea at considerable distances. The changes effected by the sand-drift are still further manifested by the fact that in quarrying and sinking for coal, a rich alluvial soil has been reached, bearing evident marks of having been at one time under the plough. Instances of this occurred at Ardeer and at Misk. At the latter place, not long ago, the workmen, after digging through many feet of sand, came upon ridges evidently formed by the plough, and found several fragments of earthen vessels, and an entire tobacco pipe. If the use of tobacco was unknown before 1560, when it is understood to have been introduced by Sir Walter Raleigh, the sand-drift must have made rapid progress. On this now desolate tract it is evident, from remains that have been dug up, that the bison and deer roamed through its glades at some period or other.

The Irvine and the Garnock are the only streams of note which water the parish. The windings of the Garnock have been compared, on a small scale, to the links of the Forth of Stirling. Its banks, especially at Grange, display considerable beauty, and at the Glen there is a small cascade.

### HISTORY, CIVIL AND ECCLESIASTICAL.

The lands of Stevenston, as we have already seen, were granted by Morville, Lord of Cuninghame, to Stephen Loccard, from whom the parish obtained its name. They subsequently came into the possession of the Loudoun family, from whom the name of Saltcoats-Campbell is given to a portion of the parish, and some of the best lands in it still hold of the Loudoun family. "Duncan Campbell and Susanna, sponse sue," had a charter of the lands of "Loudoun and Steuinstoun," from Robert I. From the Campbells it seems to have been acquired by the Glencairn family, who possessed it both before and after the Reformation.* Kerila Castle, the ancient residence connected with the property, was one of their strongholds. The leases granted by Glencairn, to nine fishermen of Saltcoats, were dated at Kerila 1545. These fishermen were bound to carry the Earl's furniture, in their two boats, from the Creek of Saltcoats to Finlayston, every spring, and bring it back again in the fall, when the family returned to their residence at Kerila. Also to furnish him yearly with half a barrel of herrings.

The barony of Stevenston became the property of Sir Thomas Boyd of Bonshall in 1609; and in 1627 he disponed it, with consent of Dame Grizzel Cuninghame, his spouse, to Sir William Cuninghame of Cuninghame-head. In 1656 it was purchased by Sir Robert Cuninghame, Physician for Scotland to Charles II. In 1685, the

mansion-house of Kerila, and the adjoining lands, were sold to John Hamilton, formerly of Cambuskeith, and afterwards of Grange. They continued to reside at Kerila until about sixty years ago, when they built the present mansion of Grange, on a fine situation, at a short distance from the old castle of Kerila. About 1707, other portions of the parish were sold—Ardeer, to the Rev. Patrick Warner; Townhead of Saltcoats, to the Earl of Eglintoun; and Hullerhirst to a family of the name of Kelso.

"The town of Stevenston is of considerable antiquity, being mentioned in a charter of the Loudoun family as far back as 1240. There was a small village of some antiquity, called Piper-Heugh, of which there are still some remains in the wood at Ardeer. The inhabitants were chiefly trump-makers; and there were some, it would appear, in Stevenston of the same profession, for in the Commissariat of Glasgow, we find the record of the death, in 1627, of 'Agnes Glasgow, spous to Johnne Logane, trump-maker in Stevenstoune.' The trump which they manufactured at Piper-Heugh was the Jews' Harp; and from the name of their residence, it would appear that this little colony possessed the united accomplishments of Jubal and Tubal, being not only 'artificers in brass and iron,' but 'handlers of the harp,' and it is probable of the pipe."*

The coal mines of the parish of Stevenston have long constituted one of the chief branches of trade connected with the district. In the account of Ardrossan parish we had occasion to speak of the rise and progress of Saltcoats, and the great exertions made by Robert Cuninghame of Auchinharvie to improve the coal trade. "He began his operations at what is called the *deep shank*, in the little holm to the east of Stevenston kirk and burn; and erected a water-wheel to draw the water out of that pit. He also, with great spirit, and judgment, and perseverance, put down several shafts or pits in the coal-field, at considerable distances from each other, to ascertain the thickness, quality, and declivity of the various strata, as well as the position of the chief *troubles*; and the papers which he left to his successors showed the surprising exactness of the knowledge he had thus obtained, and proved of great service to them in their operations. On the west side, too, of the parish, he drove a level mine, for a mile and a half, through his own coal-field and part of Lord Eglintoun's, which laid the upper part of several of the seams dry; and the coal which was wrought at the townhead of Saltcoats and some other places, was carried

---

* "Willielmo Cuninghame, militi, filio et hæridi Cuthberti, Comitis de Glencarne, had a Crown charter of Western Lowdoun and Stevenston, 22d January 1527.

* Statistical Account.

up by stairs, on the backs of the wives and daughters of the colliers."[*]

The construction of a harbour at Saltcoats, and other expenses into which the public spirit and comprehensive views of Mr Cuninghame led him, so encroached upon his means that he was compelled to part with several valuable portions of his property, and he died in 1715.

"At the time of his death, the public works were in a low state, and a manager was appointed, who carried them on for two years. Afterwards, the coal and saltworks were let to the shipmasters of Saltcoats, for the yearly rent of £250. Having heard that steam-engines had begun to be employed for pumping water, these spirited shipmasters employed Provost M'Taggart of Irvine, who had joined them in the lease, to go to London to purchase a steam-engine, and to engage an experienced person to set up the engine, and to superintend its operation. This was in 1719, only five years after the steam-engine had begun to be employed at Newcastle; and this was the second that had been set up in Scotland. The cylinder, however, of Newcomen's engine, which was purchased, was only eighteen inches in diameter, and the engineer, after carrying on for some time an unsuccessful contest, decamped in the night. Another engineer from Newcastle was engaged, but still the water could not be kept under. Seeing, however, a good field of coal, he took, as one of the partners of an English company, the lease, which the shipmasters willingly gave up, agreeing to pay, as they had done, £250 a-year, for thirty-one years. This new company carried on the works till 1728, when they failed. The coal and salt-works came then into the hands of a company in Falmouth, who carried them on till 1731, when they also failed. A law-suit having taken place, the Lords of Session, in 1732, appointed Mr John Cuninghame of Windyhall, as factor and manager, to carry on the works. About this time, James Cuninghame of Auchinharvie died, and was succeeded by his son, Robert, a minor. Mr Cuninghame of Windyhall seems to have proceeded with great spirit, and set up an engine of thirty-eight inches cylinder at the deep shank at Stevenston. In 1733, Robert Cuninghame of Auchinharvie died, and his sisters succeeded as heirs-portioners. In 1737, the eldest of them was married to Mr John Reid, second son of the Rev. Mr Reid, minister of Stevenston; and soon after this Mr Cuninghame of Windyhall ceased to be manager of the public works—Mr John

Reid of Sea Bank, we believe, taking the charge of them.

"From this time, for more than a quarter of a century, they were carried on under the direction of the heirs-portioners, but with little success, it would appear, as in 1763, they were let for nineteen years to Mr A. Crawford, with two breaks in the lease. He died in 1765, and his friends availed themselves of the first of these breaks, and gave up the lease about 1767.

"Brighter days, however, were now about to arise. In 1770, Robert, the eldest son of John Reid of Sea Bank, succeeded his father, and, in consequence of a special agreement with the heirs-portioners, became possessed of the estate of Auchinharvie, and added the name of Cuninghame to his own. The right for fifty-seven years, which had been retained when Ardeer was sold, having now expired, he entered into a co-partnery with Mr Warner of Ardeer, to work the coal on their respective properties, Mr Reid Cuninghame of Auchinharvie being the sole manager. One of the first operations of this enterprising and successful manager, was to improve the harbour of Saltcoats, and to form a canal from the coal field to the harbour, a distance of more than two miles. In these days this was no small undertaking, but it was accomplished—the canal navigated in 1772, being the first on which business was done in Scotland. It would lead us greatly to overpass our limits to trace his proceedings; but the best proof of the judgment and spirit with which he acted is, that, for some years previous to his death in 1814, the profits shared by the partners were from £2000 to £6000 a-year."[*]

The coal mines of Stevenston are still carried on successfully.

"The church of Stevenston belonged of old to the monks of Kilwinning, who were patronised by the opulent Morvilles. The monks enjoyed the parsonage tithes and revenues, and a vicarage was established for the service of the church. In Bagimont's Roll, as it stood in the reign of James V., the vicarage of Stevenstoun, in the Deanery of Cuningham, was taxed £2, 13s. 4d., being a tenth of the estimated value. At the epoch of the Reformation, the vicarage of Stevenstoun was held by James Walker, who also held the parsonage of Inchcailloch, in Dumbartonshire. In January 1561-2, he made an official return; stating that the vicarage of Stevenstoun was worth 80 merks yearly, or thereby, a part of which was paid to his under reader,

---

who was placed in the church of Stevenstoun by the Reformers. In 1603, the patronage of the church of Stevenstoun, with the tithes and church lands, were granted to Hugh Earl of Eglintoun. Not many years after, the church, and the pertinents belonging to the same, passed to William Cuninghame of Rathillet, and were inherited by his son, Richard, in 1627. In the reign of Charles II., the same property belonged to Cuninghame of Auchinharvie ;"* and the presentation continued to be exercised alternately by his family and that of Hamilton of Grange.

The old church of Stevenston was dedicated to St Monach, or Monk. This is shown by the will of Archibald Weyr, dated 7th October 1547. It stipulates that " corpusque meum sepeliendum Ecclesia Sancti Monachi de Steynstoune... Testis Dominus Stephanus Wilkynsoune, Curatus de Steynstoune." † The church then in existence was superseded by a new church about the year 1670, to which the people of Saltcoats added an aile about 1744. Part of the old fabric was supposed to have been retained. This picturesque building, however, has been entirely removed within these few years, and a comfortable new building, of much greater extent, erected in its place.

None of the parish records are older than 1700.

*Antiquities.*—Wodrow, the church historian, relates, in a letter to Sir Robert Sibbald, dated 23d November 1710, that, in consequence of the blowing of the sand, the ruins of what appeared to have been a building were laid bare, about a mile to the south-east of Saltcoats, a little from the shore, and that a coin of Faustina, and a spear of a mixed metal, were discovered—thus proving, beyond all doubt, that the Romans had been at one period in the vicinity.

In 1332 a pavement, about six yards long, and two feet broad, was discovered, in a sandy field at Dubbs, about five feet under the surface. " There was laid across one end of it a stone of about a ton weight. At the other end of it there was a stone coffin three feet in length and two in breadth, containing two urns, the one of gray and the other of black pottery. There was nothing in the urns but earth. Within the stone coffin they found five buttons formed of jet, and as finely polished as if they had been newly deposited. The buttons were of different sizes ; the largest more than an inch in diameter. They were concave on one side, and convex on the other, with knobs for attaching them. The urns were broken."

*Kerila Castle* may be considered the oldest building in the parish. Previous to 1488 it was partially destroyed by fire by the Montgomeries, who were at feud with the Cuninghames. According to tradition Kerila was for some time the residence of the Abbot of Kilwinning. This may have arisen from the fact of the office of Commendator having been conferred, after the Reformation, on Alexander Cuninghame, third son of Alexander, Earl of Glencairn. Kerila may have been the residence of the Commendator. It is further stated, and consequently not at all improbable, that the ancient hall of Kerila was ornamented with the coats of arms of the Scottish nobility, taken from the Abbey of Kilwinning, when it was destroyed at the Reformation.

At *Castle Hill*, on the estate of Grange, it is supposed that a castle, or fort, had existed at some early period.

" Strangers, in proceeding from Stevenston to Saltcoats, observe an old castle near the shore. We blush not to tell, that it is the remains of the engine-house, in which was erected, in 1719, the second steam-engine that had ever been employed in Scotland!"*

*Eminent Men.*—Under this head the name of *Robert Cuninghame*, nephew of Sir Robert Cuninghame of Auchinharvie, certainly deserves to be mentioned. He decidedly led the way in the science of mining in Ayrshire, and it is to his enterprise and skill that the coal trade of the district is chiefly indebted.

*General Alexander Hamilton*, of the family of Grange, was highly distinguished in America as a soldier, an orator, and a statesman. He is said to have been " the mentor of Washington, the framer of the present Constitution of America. and, moreover, a man of strict honour and integrity; equally esteemed in public and in private life." The following paragraph recently went the round of the newspapers :—" Great interest has been excited in New York by the discovery that Alexander Hamilton was the author of ' Washington's Farewell Address.' This composition, which has become known throughout the civilised world, and reflected upon the first American President so much honour, has always been regarded as one of the best written state papers in the English language."

The *Rev. Patrick Warner*, minister of Irvine, and the purchaser of the estate of Ardeer, in this parish, was an eminent divine, and one of the sufferers during the era of persecution.

---

* Chalmers's Caledonia. † Commissary Records.

* Statistical Account.

# FAMILIES IN THE PARISH OF STEVENSTON.

## CUNINGHAMES OF AUCHINHARVIE.

The origin of this family is probably as *Robertson* conjectures.

I. Edward Cuninghame, fourth son of Alexander, first Earl of Glencairn.

II. Robert Cuninghame of Auchinharvie was in possession of that property before 1523.[*] He married Christian, eldest daughter, and one of the co-heiresses of William Park of that Ilk, by whom he acquired the lands of Park. Her eldest daughter, Janet Park, became heiress of Park, and married George Houstoun, afterwards Houstoun of Park.[†] He had a son,

III. Edward Cuninghame of Anchinharvie. The Earl of Eglintoun and others were pursued for the slaughter of Edward Cuninghame of Auchinharvie, 26th June 1526.[‡] In the Eglintoun MS. he is called son and heir of Robert Cuninghame of Auchinharvie. He appears to have left no male issue.

IV. "Margaret, Janet, Elizabeth, and Helen, heirs - portioners of Edward Cuninghame of Auchinharvie," were served in the lands of Auchinharvie, &c. 27th July 1545. One of the daughters, probably the eldest, seems to have married *Adam Cuninghame, who is styled of Auchinharvie.* He is presumed to have been of the Craigends family.

V. Robert Cuninghame of Auchinharvie is one of the Ayrshire barons who subscribed the famous *band* in 1562. He had a Crown charter of the lands of Chapeltoun, 27th March 1566.

VI. Robert Cuninghame of Auchinharvie was served heir of his grandfather, Adam Cuninghame of Auchinharvie, 27th March 1606. He seems to have been twice married, first, to Catherine, daughter of Mr Robert Cuninghame, minister of Barnweil, by Jean, a daughter of the Laird of Hunterston; secondly, before 1613. to "Kathrein Huntar, relict of vmquhile Hew Garven, Baillie Clerk of Cvnynghame."[§] He had a charter of the lands of Auchinharvie 11th February 1615,[‖] and is mentioned in a testa-

* MS. history of the Montgomerie family.
† Craufurd's History of Renfrewshire.
‡ Criminal Trials.
§ Commissary Records.
‖ Index of Crown charters.

mentary document, November 1615; but he appears to have died soon afterwards, for

VII. "Johnne Cwnynghame of Auchinharvie," is mentioned in the testament of Mareoun Hamiltoun in Hunterstoun, as a debtor to the amount of "ane thowsand merks." He seems to have died prematurely, for

VIII. Robert Cuninghame of Auchinharvie occurs in the testament of "Johnne Steinstoun in Irwein," in 1617. He had a Crown charter of the lands of Auchinharvie, 23d April 1623. He had a son, Adam, styled younger of Auchinharvie on an inquest serving Robert Fergushill of that Ilk heir to his father, dated in 1625. He no doubt predeceased his father, for the next successor was

IX. Sir David Cuninghame of Auchinharvie, probably his nephew. He had a Crown charter, " Davidi Cuninghame, filio quondam Patricii Cuninghame de Kirkland, terrarum de Auchinhervie," &c. 19th February 1631. He was created a Baronet in 1633. " Domino Davidi Cuninghame de Auchinharvie" had a charter of confirmation of the lands of Bolinshaw, &c., 26th July 1634; and another of the lands of Drummylling, 13th February 1636. He appears to have left no children, and was succeeded by

X. Robert Cuninghame, second son of John Cuninghame of Baidland, probably his nephew. Having been brought up to the study of medicine, Robert Cuninghame was appointed physician to Charles II. for Scotland. He was much employed at Court, and having much practice otherwise, he acquired considerable property. In 1656 he purchased the barony of Stevenston, which then comprehended the whole parish, besides other lands in the parishes of Stewarton and Kilbride. He attended Charles II. in the expedition conducted by the Duke of Hamilton, in 1651, and was present at the battle of Worcester. He was taken prisoner and carried to the Tower of London, but was not long detained a prisoner. On the Restoration, in 1660, he was reinstated in his office as Physician to the King; and in 1673 was raised to the hereditary dignity of a Baronet of Nova Scotia. He married, first, Miss Elizabeth Dundas, by whom he had a son; secondly, Elizabeth Henderson, of the family of Fordel, in Fife, who had issue a daughter. He died before 1674, and was succeeded by his only son,

XI. Sir Robert Cunioghame of Auchinharvie, who enjoyed the honours and estate for only a short period. He was succeeded by his only sister,

XII. Anne Cuninghame of Auchinharvie, who had a Crown charter of the baronies of Stevenston and Auchinharvie, 1st March 1676. She did not long survive her brother. At her death, by a special deed of entail, the estate fell to the nephew of her father,

XIII. Robert Cuninghame, surgeon, Edinburgh. As already stated in our account of the parish of Stevenston, he made great improvements on the estate, and devoted no small portion of his time and means to the improvement of the coal mines and harbour; in consequence of which he was latterly compelled to dispose of the greater part of the barony of Stevenston.* He married, in 1669, Miss Anne Purves, by whom he had seventeen children, of whom only six came to maturity. He died on the 10th of July 1715, and was succeeded by his son,

XIV. James Cuninghame of Auchinharvie, who married, about four years previously, Marion Fullarton, daughter of Fullarton of that Ilk, by whom he had a son and three daughters. He died in December 1728, and was succeeded by his son,

XV. Robert Cuninghame of Auchinharvie, who died of a brain fever in 1733, in the sixteenth year of his age. He was succeeded by his sisters—*Anna, Elizabeth*, and *Barbara*, heirs portioners. Elizabeth died unmarried, and Barbara married Mr William Cuninghame in Kilwinning.

XVI. Anna, the eldest, carried on the line of the family. In July 1737, she married John Reid, second son of the Rev. William Reid, minister of Stevenston.† The children of this marriage were—

1. May, married to Robert Baillie, Esq. of Mayville, and had two daughters:—
   1. Leslie, married to Mr Cumming of Logie.
   2. Grace.
2. Robert, of whom afterwards.
3. Elizabeth, married to Mr Andrew Donald, merchant, Greenock, and had issue:
   1. Anne.
   2. Christian, married to Mr Learmont, merchant in India, and had issue.
4. Anne died unmarried.
5. Sarah, married Alexander Cuninghame, Esq., Collector of Customs, Irvine, brother of the late William Cuninghame of Fairlie, and had issue:

* William Cuninghame of Cuninghamehead had a charter of the barony of Stevenston in 1673.
† The eldest son, Thomas, was father of the late Robert Reid of Adamton.

1. Anne, married to Mr Anthony Dunlop, son of John Dunlop of that Ilk, and had issue.
2. Jane, married to William Smith of Jordanhill.
3. William, E.I.C.S.
6. John, married Miss Boilean, in India, died there, and left a numerous issue.

XVII. Robert, the eldest son, in consequence of a special agreement with the heirs portioners in 1770, became possessor of the property of Auchinharvie, and assumed the name of Cuninghame, in addition to his own. As already stated, he was a person of great judgment and enterprize, and carried on the coal-works at Stevenston with much spirit and success. He also vastly improved and embellished the estate of Sea Bank. He was twice married, first, to Elizabeth Hamilton, sister of Colonel Alexander Hamilton of Grange, by whom he had one daughter,

1. Elizabeth, married to Major George Vanbury Brown of Knockmarloch. She died at Tours, in France, and left a son, John, and three daughters, Elizabeth, Hamilla, and Mary.

He married, secondly, Annabella, daughter of Mr Thomas Reid, merchant in Saltcoats, and by her had issue:—

2. John, who died unmarried in India.
3. Anne, married to Col. Alexander Robertson of Hallcraig, in Lanarkshire, and had issue.
4. Robert, of whom afterwards.
5. Thomas, R.N., who died at Chatham in 1818.
6. Marion.

Mr Reid Cuninghame died in November 1818, and was succeeded by his only surviving son,

XVII. Robert Cuninghame, now of Sea Bank.

*Arms*—Argent, a shake-fork betwixt two lozenges in fesse, sable, with the badge of Nova Scotia.

*Crest*—A dexter hand, proper, presenting a lozenge, or.

*Motto*—" Cura et Candore."

*Residence*—Sea Bank, in the vicinity of Stevenston. Auchinharvie Castle, now in ruins, from which the family take their designation, is situated in the parish of Stewarton, about four miles north from Irvine. Pont thus refers to it in his description of Cuninghame:—" Auchinheruy, the etimologie of ye vord signifing a fold, or manured croft of corne, vpon a zellow knoppe. It is ane ancient, old touer, vell planted, and does belong to a gentleman of the name of Cuninghame, who is Bailzie of the Lordschipe of Killmaures, called ye Laird of Auchinheruy."

### HULLERHIRST.

This property formed part of the barony of

Stevenston, and was acquired by Dr Robert Cuninghame, along with it, in 1656. It had previously belonged to a family of the name of *Campbell*. The first of them we find mentioned is

*Hew Campbell* in *Hullerhirst*. His name occurs in the testament of Margaret Cowan, spouse to James Wilson in Little Dubs. Hew Campbell *of* Hullerhirst is mentioned as one of the curators in the testament of Ashinyards in 1613. His name appears in a similar document in 1620. In the testament of Stein Hog, merchant burgess of Irvine, he is thus set down—" Item, be Hew Campbell of Hullerhirst, for work to ye lle of ye Kirk, fyve marks." He married Jean Cuninghame, but of what family we know not. She died in the month of August 1621. Her testament and inventar were " faithfullie maid and gevin vp be the said Hew [Campbell of Hullerhirst] in name and behalf of *James, George, Jonet, Jeane, Margaret,* and *Marie Campbells,* lauchfull bairnes to ye defunct, and executouris datives," &c. Hew Campbell of Hullerhirst frequently appears in testamentary and other documents down to 1630. He was one of the Sub-Commissioners for valuing the teinds within the Presbytery of Irvine, and died prior to November in the above year.

### KELSO OF HULLERHIRST.

This property was purchased from Cuninghame of Auchinharvie about 1707 by

I. WILLIAM KELSO, at that time one of the Baillies of Campbeltown, in Kintyre. He had previously resided at Carwinin-Hill, in the parish of Dalry, and is supposed to have been an offshoot of the Kelsos of Kelsoland. He married Mary Montgomerie, daughter of Hugh Montgomerie of Broomlands, near Irvine, and died in 1742, at the advanced age of eighty. By this lady, who died in 1739, aged 75, he had his successor,

II. William Kelso of Hullerhirst. He married, on the 19th December 1741, Dorothea Hunter, fourth daughter of Patrick Hunter of Hunterstoun. He died on the 12th September 1750, aged 55. By this lady, who afterwards married Mr Weir of Kirkhill, he had issue two sons, *William* and *Patrick,* and a daughter, *Mary.* He was succeeded by his eldest son,

III. William Kelso of Hullerhirst, who died unmarried on the 6th January 1778, in the 33d year of his age. He was succeeded by his brother,

IV. Patrick Kelso of Hullerhirst, who died

on the 28th December 1791, in the 42d year of his age. He married, 8th April 1777, Mary Hamilton, third daughter of Robert Hamilton of Saltcoats, by whom he had :—

1. William.
2. Robert, who died in Jamaica, 22d December 1802.
3. Alexander Hamilton, of whom afterwards.
1. Anne-Barclay, married to John Howe of Irvine, and had issue.
2. Mary, died 4th July 1804.
3. Dorothea, died in infancy.

IV. William Kelso, the eldest son, succeeded his father in Hullerhirst, but died unmarried on the 27th January 1805, in the 27th year of his age, when he was succeeded by his only remaining brother,

V. Alexander Hamilton Hamilton of Hullerhirst, and of the Retreat, in the county of Devon. This gentleman was about ten years—from 1800 till 1811—in the E.I.C.S., on the Madras establishment ; during which period he filled important offices in the revenue and judicial departments, and latterly in that of Civil or Diplomatic Commissioner, in charge of the Danish settlement of Tranquebar, during a part of the war. In 1809, on the death of his maternal uncle, Sir Alexander Hamilton, of the Retreat, in the parish of Topsham, and county of Devon, he assumed the name, and quartered his arms with those of his own family, having succeeded him in that property, which has since been the principal residence of the family. In 1809 Mr Hamilton (then Mr Kelso) married Maria Rosalie, daughter of Edward James Colbiornsen, of an ancient family, and who had been Chief Justice, and a member of the Danish Government of Tranquebar. Issue :—

1. Alexander Kelso, died 25th May 1818.
2. Maria Frances Anne.
3. Emma, died 14th February 1818.
4. Harriet.
5. Edward Kelso.

*Arms*—Quarterly, first and fourth for Hamilton ; and second and third for Kelso ; with two crests.

*Hullerhirst,* the seat of the family in Scotland, is a handsome, modern, small mansion, occupying a pleasant and commanding situation, about a mile north-east of Stevenston.

### ARDEER.

This property also formed part of the barony of Stevenston, and was purchased by the present family in 1708.

I. JOHN WARNER, in 1656, purchased a tenement in the burgh of Irvine, together with the Braid Meadow adjacent, from John Mure. He had two sons, both of whom were eminent ministers of the Church of Scotland, and both were sufferers for their principles in the persecuting times of Charles II. The eldest son, Thomas, was minister of Balmaclelan in Galloway, whence he was ejected in 1679, for attending Conventicles, but seems to have been restored again at the Revolution. He died on the 10th September 1716. He was generally called *Vernor* in his own parish, and it is under that name he appears in the history of the times. There is a beautiful story of him recorded in the " Lights and Shadows of Scottish Life." The second son was the

II. Rev. Patrick Warner, who was educated at St Andrews, and licensed about the year 1667. He was minister of Fort St George, on the coast of Coromandel, in the East Indies, but returned to Scotland in 1677. Having been engaged, along with the celebrated John Welsh, in various field preachings in Galloway, he found it necessary to retire to Holland after the battle of Bothwell Bridge. He returned to Scotland before 1681, and still taking part in conventicle meetings, was forced once more, after a long imprisonment and various persecutions, to proceed to Holland. In 1687, he took advantage of King James' Indulgence, and returning to Scotland, was ordained minister of Irvine in 1688, where he officiated for about twenty years. Having resigned in 1709, he retired to his own house of Ardeer, where he lived till after the year 1722, being then the oldest minister of the Church of Scotland.

In 1691, he purchased from Walter Scott of Clonbeith the lands of Scots-Loch and the Trindle-Moss, in the vicinity of Irvine, which he improved so effectually, by a large drain, still called *the Minister's Cast*, that, from being a swampy field of little value, it has become among the most valuable land in the parish. In 1692 he bought the lands of Hallbarns, in the parish of Kilmaurs, from Sir Robert Barclay of Peirceton, and in 1708 he acquired the lands of Ardeer and Dovecothall, from Robert Cuninghame of Auchinharvie.

He married, in 1691, Mary, one of the daughters of the Rev. William Guthrie of Fenwick (eldest son of the laird of Pitforthy, in Angus), by whom he had three sons and three daughters, all of whom died young except *William*, his heir, and *Margaret*, married, first, to the Rev. Ebenezer Veitch, Lecturer in the Tron Kirk of Edinburgh, afterwards, in 1703, minister of Ayr, who

died in 1706;[*] and secondly, to the Rev. Robert Wodrow, the church historian. By her second marriage she had a large family.

III. William Warner of Ardeer. He married, first, Janet, daughter of Alexander Hamilton of Grange, by whom he had issue:—

1. Patrick, born 18th June 1712.
2. John, born 28th August 1713. He was minister of Kilbarchan, and died in 1786.
3. William, born 19th February 1717, drowned in India.

Also two daughters, who both died unmarried. He married, secondly, Mary Mowat, widow of James Rae of Walstone, in the parish of Kilmarnock, with whom he acquired that property, but without issue. He died before the year 1764, and was succeeded by his son,

IV. Patrick Warner of Ardeer. He married Helen, daughter of Mr Russell, shipmaster in Saltcoats, by whom he had:—

1. William John, died in infancy in 1781.
2. Patrick, his heir.
3. John, surgeon E.I.C.S. Bombay, died in 1826.
1. Janet, died unmarried in 1800.
2. William-John, married to the late A. Miller of Monkcastle, died in 1844.
3. Agnes.
4. Helen, married to the late R. Hunter, Esq., Ardrossan, died in 1839.

Mr Warner died in 1793, aged 81, and his widow in 1810.

V. Patrick Warner of Ardeer, (Lieut. R.N.), married, on the 21st October 1816, Catherine, daughter of Quintin Johnston of Trolorg, and had issue:—

1. Patrick, his heir, born 4th Oct. 1818.
3. Catherine, born 1820, died in infancy in 1823.

Mr Warner died 27th Sept. 1824, and Mrs Warner, 10th Dec. 1828.

VI. Patrick Warner of Ardeer, married, 28th June 1838, Lucy-Campbell, eldest daughter of the late Captain Joseph Pearce, R.N., and Forbes, his wife, eleventh daughter of Colonel George Mackay of Brighouse, Sutherlandshire, and has issue:—

1. Patrick, born 19th Dec. 1840.
2. Joseph-Pearce, born 22d April 1845.
3. William-Frederick, born 20th June 1846.
1. Lucy-Josephine.
2. Forbes-Anna-Georgina.
3. Katherin-Elenor-Mary.
4. Anne-Forbes.

In 1838, Mr Warner purchased a portion of the neighbouring estate of Grange from the trustees of the late Col. Alexander Hamilton.

*Arms*—Azure, a fesse, argent, betwixt three

---

* He was the third son of the famed Rev. William Veitch of Dumfries.

boars' heads crazed—two in chief, and one in base.

*Crest*—An open Bible.

*Motto*—" Manet in æternum."

*Ardeer House*, the family residence, is in the immediate vicinity of Stevenston. It has been greatly improved of late years.

### FULLARTON OF KERILA.

The manor of Kerila, with its extensive lawns, lies contiguous to the quiet little village of Stevenston, and remains intact, untainted, and undisturbed by intrusive railways, dusky ironworks, or bustling cotton factories.

The avenue leading to the modern mansion-house is shaded by old patrician trees, preparing the visitor for a view of the ancient Castle of Kerila, which looms in the distance in all the ruined pride of feudalism and hoar antiquity. The arrow slits, and twisted cable, denote a date anterior to the fourteenth century.

The shrubbery around the spacious mansion-house exhibits specimens of the gigantic flowering *Mimosa*, and the *Ribes*, with its scarlet petals, which can safely challenge rivalry in wide Scotland.

The estate of Kerila was acquired by the present proprietor, GAVIN FULLARTON, Esq. a West India merchant, by purchase, from the trustees of the late Col. Alexander Hamilton of Grange.* The property has been greatly improved, under the auspices of the proprietor. The immediate ancestor of Mr G. Fullarton was the Rev. John Fullarton, minister of the parish of Dalry, who married Miss J. Donald of the Broome, in Stevenston parish. John Fullarton was preceded by his father of the same name, who was also an incumbent of the parish of Dalry. He married Miss Catherine Ralston, sister of Gavin Ralston of that Ilk. John Fullarton was a cadet of the very ancient family of the Fullartons of Kilmichael, in Arran, who hold their charter from the days of "guid King Robert the Bruce," and are hereditary Crowners in the island of Arran. The armorial bearings are, the Fullarton arms, quartered with the Ralston in the left compartment of the shield. The motto is " Lux in tenebris."

---

* An account of the Hamiltons of Grange is given in the Parish of Kilmarnock.

# PARISH OF STEWARTON.

ETYMOLOGY, EXTENT, &c.

THE name is no doubt from the surname *Stewart*, but as *Stewartoun* existed prior to the end of the twelfth century, before the patronymic of Stewart was adopted, it becomes a question how it originated. Speaking of " Stewarte-toun Castell," Pont describes it as "a strong old donjoun, the ancient inheritance of the predecessors of our Scotts Kings, now possessed by Neil Montgomery of Langeshaw." This is the popular belief as to the derivation of the name. It is true that the family of the High Stewards were not called *Stewards*, or *Stewarts*, till the time of Walter the Second, in 1204; and Chalmers, in his *Caledonia*, supposes that the name may have been derived from some settler who held the office of steward to the De Morvilles, Lords of Cuninghame. But the High Steward of Scotland was surely as likely to give the name to a place as the steward of the De Morvilles; hence the popular belief, as expressed by Pont, may be correct. The parish of Stewarton is bounded by the parishes of Neilston and Mearns, in Renfrewshire, on the north-east; Fenwick, on the east and south-east; Dreghorn on the south; Irvine and Kilwinning on the west, and Dunlop on the north-west and west. The parish contains about twenty square miles, and is about ten miles long, and from three to four broad.

The district has a rich, diversified appearance, abounding in fine sloping grounds and gentle eminences, and withal well wooded—especially in the lower part of the parish—by thriving plantations. The surface rises gradually towards the boundary line of Renfrewshire, where the heights are of considerable altitude, commanding a beautiful view of the far-stretching Clyde, and not a few of the surrounding counties. The parish is refreshingly watered by numerous springs, and not a few streams of considerable size, amongst which the chief are the Annock, the Swinsey, and the Glazart, Corshill and East burns. The Annock flows from the White Loch, in the Mearns parish, six miles east of Stewarton, and is joined by the Glazart at Water-meetings, four miles below Stewarton. There is also a mineral spring, called the Bloak Well. It was first discovered, about forty years ago, by the resort of pigeons to it from neighbouring parishes. A handsome house was built over it, in 1833, by the late Mr Cuninghame of Lainshaw, when he appointed a keeper to take care of it. The soil is admirably adapted for green-cropping, and the district is an excellent dairy one. Considerable improvements in agriculture have been effected within these few years. The humidity of the climate, however, is against the culture of wheat.

## HISTORY, CIVIL AND ECCLESIASTICAL.

Stewarton formed part of the extensive district over which the De Morville family held sway at the commencement of the recorded annals of Scotland. The Ross family, now represented by the Earl of Glasgow, had at one time extensive possessions in the parish of Stewarton. Godfridus de Ross, *miles*, son and heir of Sir Godfrede de Ross, Knight, confirms the lands in Stewarton, which the Abbacy of Paisley got from Sir James Ross in 1281. Patrick Murray had a grant of the half of the lands of Stewarton from Robert the Bruce. In 1283, the lands of Stewarton were erected into a separate lordship, and became the inheritance of James, High Steward, in whose family it remained after their accession to the throne, and were repeatedly bestowed upon the favourites or relatives of the Crown. In the reign of Robert III., John Stewart, Earl of Buchan, the Regent's son, and Elizabeth de Douglas, his spouse, daughter of Archibald Earl of Douglas, had a charter of the lands of Stewarton, Armshengh, and Dunlop, on the resignation of the Earl of Douglas. In 1564-5, Queen Mary granted a charter of the lands and lordship of Stewarton, amongst others, to John Sempill, son of Lord Sempill, and Mary Livingstone, sister to William Lord Livingstone, his spouse.

The church of Stewarton belonged to the Monastery of Kilwinning, having probably been granted to it by Hugh de Morville, the founder of the Abbey. " The monks enjoyed the rectorial revenues of the church, and a vicarage was established for serving the cure. In Bagimont's Roll, as it stood in the reign of James V., the vicarage of Stewarton, in the deanery of Cuninghame, was taxed £4, being a tenth of the estimated value. At the Reformation, the tithes, and other revenues of the church, yielded yearly to the monks of Kilwinning, 133 bolls of meal, 1 boll of bear, 254 bolls of oats; and £34, 6s. 8d. for part of the tithes, which was leased. The lands which belonged to the church of Stewarton passed into lay hands after the Reformation. On the lands of Langshaw, which is now called Lainshaw, in the parish of Stewarton, there was, in former times, a chapel, which was dedicated to the Virgin Mary, and which had an appropriate endowment. After the Reformation, the endowment was appropriated by the patron, and the chapel was allowed to fall into ruins. In 1661, the patronage of this chapel belonged to the Earl of Eglintoun. The place where the chapel stood was denominated, in the seventeenth century, Chapeltoun; and it is now called Chapel."* The patronage of the church of Stewarton latterly belonged to Cuninghame of Lainshaw.

The town of Stewarton has long been a place of considerable manufacturing importance. Bonnet-making has been a staple branch of trade for many centuries. " Almost the whole regimental and naval bonnets and caps are made here, as well as those worn by the people in the country at large. Upwards of fifty families, besides a great number of boys and girls, are thus employed. Their deacon was styled *Princeps Pileorum Artifex Scotiæ*. Steel clockwork is peculiar to this place,* and is in great demand, not only in Britain, but in America. There is a large manufacture of spindles for cotton and woollen mills."† There are also mills for carding and spinning wool and tow, and for fulling bonnets, besides several carpet works. The weaving of silk and cotton for the Glasgow and Paisley manufacturers gives employment to a considerable number of inhabitants. Altogether, Stewarton is a thriving community.

### ANTIQUITIES.

About forty years ago, " while Mr Deans of Peacock Bank was rooting out some trees in a small plantation, in Carnduff Brae, on his property, he discovered three urns containing human bones. The urns were covered with a great quantity of stones, forming, it is conjectured, one of those cairns in which the ancient inhabitants of this country buried their dead."‡

Recently a tumuli, or ancient place of sepulture, was discovered about a mile north-east of Kennox House. One of the graves, which was opened by direction of the proprietor, C. S. M'Alester, Esq., contained two rudely formed urns, made of dark brown clay, a number of oddly fashioned beads, of the substance known as *Druid's glass*, and several arrow heads of flint. The grave itself, formed of rough flags, was small in size, being only about three feet square.

Some years ago the ruins of a chapel were discovered near the farm-house of Low Chapelton, about a mile below Stewarton.

There are the ruins of three castles in the parish—Robertland Castle, the stronghold of the Cuninghames of Robertland; and the Castles of Corshill and Auchinharvie. The former " has been lately celebrated by Gabriel Alexander, Esq., advocate, the author of ' My Grandfather's Farm,' who is a native of this parish, and now resides in London. The critics of the day were pleased to ascribe this work to Miss Mitford."§

Lainshaw Castle, spoken of by Pont as the residence of the High Stewards of Scotland, still exists, though surrounded by buildings of a modern description. It consists of a large square tower, with a lesser one of a different style, and a number of buildings of more modern date, connecting them together, and a large and elegant modern addition.

*Eminent Characters.*—Stewarton parish can boast of having given birth to not a few distin-

---

* Caledonia.

* The neighbouring burgh of Kilmaurs used to be famed in this respect.
† Statistical Account.      ‡ Ibid.      § Ibid.

guished individuals. Amongst these are the well-known David Dale, father-in-law of Mr Owen, the founder of Socialism. He was the son of a grocer, and born in 1739. By his own industry, he rose to be one of the first manufacturers and merchants in Scotland, and at his death, it is said, left upwards of £100,000. Dr Robert Watt, compiler of the "Bibliotheca Britannica," was born on the farm of Bonnyton, on the 1st May 1774. "The Rev. John Brown of Clerkhill, preacher, author of Sermons and Prayers, posthumous works in two volumes, not printed for publication, besides numerous manuscripts on theological subjects, died in 1833, aged thirty-nine

years. John Gilmour, son of James Gilmour of Clerkland, who died in 1828, at the age of eighteen, was the author of a volume of "Poetical Remains," printed after his death."[*] James Gillies, M.D., was long a successful practitioner in Bath, and one of his Majesty's Physicians for Scotland. James Miller, tenant in Woodhead, was the inventor of an improved reaping machine. David Craig of Craigton made several improvements on the thrashing machine, and Alexander Reid of Bollingshaw received several premiums for the invention of various agricultural implements.

# FAMILIES IN THE PARISH OF STEWARTON.

## MONTGOMERIE OF LAINSHAW.

The first of this family was

I. NIGEL or NEIL MONTGOMERIE of Langshaw, second son of Hugh, first Earl of Eglintoun, by Lady Helen Campbell, daughter of Colin, first Earl of Argyle. He had a Crown charter of the lands of Uretoun, 4th October 1545. He married Margaret, daughter and sole heiress of Quintin Mure of Skeldon, by whom he got the lands of Skeldon, Hollow-Chapel, Laganafie, Charlewraek, &c. By this lady, according to *Robertson*, he had

1. John.
2. Neil.
1. Christian, Lady Luss.
2. Elizabeth, married to Hume of Fastcastle.
3. Helen, married to Maxwell of Newark.[*]

He was slain in a rencontre at Irvine, from old feud, by Lord Boyd, Mowat of Busbie, and others, in December 1547. He was succeeded by his eldest son,

II. John Montgomerie of Lainshaw, who married Margaret, daughter of the third Lord Boyd, but died without issue.

III. Sir Neil Montgomerie of Lainshaw succeeded his brother. He married Jean, only daughter of John, fourth and last Lord Lyle, whose only son, James, Master of Lyle, died un-

married about the year 1556, on which the estate of Lyle came, by a special deed of entail, to Sir Neil, who quartered the arms of Lyle with his own. By this lady he had three sons, besides daughters. The two younger sons went to Ireland. By a charter in 1558, it appears that Sir Neil possessed very considerable property, chiefly holding from the Earl of Eglintoun. He was succeeded by his eldest son,

IV. Sir Neil Montgomerie of Lainshaw, who was served heir to his mother, Jean Lyle, in 1575, in the lands of Gallowberry. By a contract dated 1559, he resigned all claim to the estate of Duchal, or of Lyle, and others, for a certain sum of money paid him by Porterfield of that Ilk, according to a decreet arbitral, but he still assumed the arms of Lyle, as heir of line of that noble family. He had a precept of *Clare Constat*, by Alexander, Earl of Eglintoun, dated 18th March 1616, of the lands of Lainshaw, with the patronage of the chapel of Lainshaw, Peacock-Bank, &c. He married Elizabeth, eldest daughter of Cuninghame of Aiket, and had four sons and two daughters:—

1. Neil, who is mentioned as the "zong Laird of Langschaw" in the testament of Issobell Wylie in Gabrochhill.
2. James, minister of Dunlop, who died at Lainshaw in May 1613. There was owing to him at his death "be ye Laird of Langshaw, his brother, fyve hundrith fiftie marks." His testament is dated "at ye toun of Langshaw, the xi of May 1613 zeiris." He left his

---

[*] According to the Commissary Records his testament and inventory were made and given up in behalf of Bisseta, Cristina, and Helen Montgomerie, his daughters.

[*] Statistical Account.

sons, Robert and James, his only executors, and his wife, Elizabeth Montgomerie, his only tutorix and intromittcrix with his guids and gear. William Montgomerie of Bridgend, and John Montgomerie of Cockilbie, were to be overseers.

3. William, of Bridgend.
4. John, of Cockilbie. He married Jean, daughter of Captain Daniel Forrester of Carden, envoy of James VI. to Spain, by whom he had:—
 1. David, who became Laird of Lainshaw.
 2. John, of Crevoch, who had a son a merchant in Glasgow, and three daughters, Mary, Jean, and Agnes.
 1. Jean, married to William Caldwell of that Ilk.
 2. Barbara, to William Montgomerie of Mackbiehall.
 3. Agnes, to Kennedy of Kirkmichael.
 4. Catherine, to M'Cubin of Knockdolian.
 5. Margaretta, to the Rev. Andrew Miller, minister of Dalry, and afterwards of Neilstoun.
 1. ——, married to Graham of Grugar.
 2. Mariot, married to Johnston of Wamphray.

He was succeeded by his eldest son,

V. Neil Montgomerie of Lainshaw. The precept of sasine of his lands, as successor to his father, is dated 28th April 1629; but his father must have died in or before 1621, for in that year "Johnne Montgomerie, brother to Neile Montgomerie, sone of Langschaw," appears in the legacy of Lady Culzean. He married Marcoun,[*] daughter of Sir William Mure of Rowallan, by whom he had a son, Neil, and four daughters, who were married respectively to Buntin of Ardoch, Montgomerie of Auchinhood, Campbell of Skeldon, and Houstoun of Park. He died in or before 1635, and was succeeded by his only son,

VI. Neil Montgomerie of Lainshaw. The first sasine in his favour is dated 23d August 1646; but he must have succeeded many years previously, for in the testament of Patrick Houstoun of Park, in 1635, we find the following:— "Item, their was awand, &c., be Marioun Muir, Ladie Langschaw, as principall, and Neill Montgomerie of Langschaw, hir sone, as cautioner for hir, the sowme of twa thousand pundis money obleist be thame to the defunct, in name of tocher, with Agnes Montgomerie, dochter to the said Marcoun Muir, for the marriage solemnizat betuix hir and George Houstoune." He married Margaretta Lockhart, daughter of the Laird of Barr, by whom he had:—

 1. John, his heir.
 2. Neil, who married Elizabeth Kirkwood, by whom he had two daughters, who both died unmarried,

and four daughters, who were married respectively to Mr Thomas Orr; Mr Watson, Provost of Dumbarton; Mr Ramsay, in Ireland; and Hugh Montgomerie in Lumford. He was succeeded by his eldest son,

VII. John Montgomerie of Lainshaw, who married Helen, daughter of Sir Ludovick Houstoun of that Ilk, but died without issue. His father and he seem to have died or resigned much about the same time, for in 1654 a disposition was granted by his father, with his consent, in which he is designed of Lainshaw, of the estate to

VIII. David Montgomerie of Cockilbie, son of John Montgomerie of Cockilbie (see No. IV.) who married Marcoun Dunlop, eldest daughter of James Dunlop of that Ilk, by whom he had two sons, *James* and *David*; and one daughter, *Jean*, married to the Rev. Alexander Laing, Rector of Donaghadee, of whom afterwards. Having been concerned in the insurrection of *Bothwell Brig*, in 1679, he suffered severely in consequence.[*] By an act of attainder in 1685, his whole property was vested in the Crown; and by a precept from James VII., dated 26th August 1686, the lands of Lainshaw and others were gifted to Lieutenant-General William Drummond of Cromlex, (afterwards Lord Strathallan), and Lord Montgomerie commanded to enter and infeft him therein. Lord Strathallan afterwards resigned his rights to these lands; and a charter proceeding on that resignation, and on a disposition from David, was granted by Alexander Lord Montgomerie and Kilwinning, to James, son and heir of David, dated 6th October 1688. In 1690 the forfeiture was rescinded in Parliament, and David restored to all his civil rights. There is a sasine in favour of James, by his father David, dated 28th October 1692. How long he lived afterwards does not appear; but

IX. James Montgomerie of Lainshaw appears in full possession of the estates, by charters, in which his father's name is not mentioned, in 1696, 1698, and 1701. He appears in the list of Commissioners of Supply for the country in 1696; and about the same time was appointed Clerk of Justiciary for life. He assumed the title of Lord Lyle, and bore it till his death, as representative of that noble family. He married Barbara, daughter of John Kennedy of Craig, or Barclanachan, in Carrick, but had no issue. He died about the year 1726, and was succeeded by his nephew,

X. David Laing, afterwards Montgomerie of Lainshaw, son of his sister, Jean Montgomerie, and Alexander Laing, her husband, Rector of Donaghadee. This appears from various legal documents from 1726 down till 1738. He married *Veronica*, daughter of James Boswell of Auchinleck, by whom he had issue:—

---

* She is called Mariota in a Crown charter, dated 2d August 1601: "Carta Nigello Montgomerie, juniori, de Langschaw, et Mariotæ Muir, ejus sponsæ, terrarum de Falwood, Balgray, &c., in Baroniam de Peacock-Bank."

* Law's Memorials.

1. James, his heir.
2. Elizabeth, of whom afterwards.
3. Mary, married to James Campbell of Treesbank.
4. Margaret, married to James Boswell of Auchinleck.

He died before the 3d September 1752, of which date his only son,

XI. James Montgomerie of Lainshaw, had a precept of *Clare Constat* from Alexander, Earl of Eglintoun, as heir to his father, David Montgomerie, in all his lands. "Jacobi Montgomery, de Lainshaw, armigeri," gave a charter of resignation of the lands of Mackbichill, 23d February 1759. He married Jean, daughter of Sir John Maxwell of Nether-Pollock. He died in 1767, without issue.* He was succeeded by his eldest sister,

XII. Elizabeth Montgomerie-Cuninghame of Lainshaw, who had been previously married to Alexander Montgomerie-Cuninghame of Kirktonholme, son of Sir David Cuninghame of Corshill. After the death of her husband, in 1770, she married, secondly, J. Beaumont, Esq., to whom she had a daughter, *Elizabeth*, who was married to George-James Campbell of Treesbank, and had issue.

*Arms*—Those of Eglintoun, Montgomerie, Mure, Lyle and Marr; and latterly, in addition, those of Cuninghame; all arranged in due heraldic order.

*Crest*—A cock rising.

*Supporters*—Two leopards proper.

*Motto*, being that of Lyle—"*An I may.*"

The mansion-house of Lainshaw is in the immediate vicinity of Stewarton.

#### CUNINGHAME OF LAINSHAW.

*Adam Cuninghame*, in Caprington Close, Kilmarnock, a cadet of the family of Caprington, was the first of this family. He purchased the lands of Kirkland Holm from William Wallace of Burnbank, in 1663; and the lands of Bridgehouse from Hugh Wallace of Bridgehouse, in 1673. He had a son,

*George Cuninghame*, who succeeded him, and who, again, was succeeded by his son,

*Alexander Cuninghame of Bridgehouse.* He was a merchant in Kilmarnock, and married Barbara, daughter of Robert Hodgert,† surgeon in Kilmar-

nock, and widow of William Findlay. On his death, in 1751, he was succeeded by his eldest son,

*John Cuninghame of Bridgehouse*, minister of the parish of Monkton, who died without issue in 1777, when the estate passed to

*William Cuninghame of Bridgehouse*, who purchased the estate of Lainshaw in 1779, and that of Kirkwood in 1781. He was thrice married. By his first marriage he had surviving issue a son; and by his second, with Elizabeth Campbell, second daughter of James Campbell, merchant in Glasgow, a son of Campbell of Glendaruel, in Argyleshire, he had also a son, his only surviving issue. By his third wife, Margaret Nicolson Cranston, daughter of the Hon. —— Cranston by a daughter of Brisbane of Brisbane, he had also issue. On his death, in April 1799, the estates of Lainshaw and Kirkwood, by a deed of entail, passed to his only son by his second marriage, and his estates in Galloway and Peeblesbire, by another deed of entail, to John Cuninghame of Duchrae, his youngest son by his third marriage.

The late *William Cuninghame of Lainshaw* was, at the time of his succession to Lainshaw, in the Bengal Civil Service of the E.I.C. He returned in 1804, and from that period down till his death in November 1849, in the 74th year of his age, he constantly resided on his estate, with the exception of a short annual visit to England. As a country gentleman Mr Cuninghame acted a useful and exemplary part; and during the war he commanded a body of volunteers with characteristic energy. He became a skilful agriculturist, and exhibited in his home farm the results

---

* His lady afterwards purchased the lands of Auldhouse from Robert Wardrop of Auldhouse.

† Robert Hodgert, a minister in Galloway, who fled to India during the Persecution, and died there, married Annabella Boyd, daughter of Robert Boyd of Piteon, (grandson of Lord Boyd,) and of Anne Blair, daughter of Bryce Blair of that Ilk, whose mother was Grizell, daughter of the third Lord Sempill, and whose younger brother, Alexander, married Margaret, heiress of William Cochrane of that Ilk, through which marriage the noble line of Blair has merged in the Earldom of Dundonald.

The above Robert Hodgert (or Hodzart) was succeeded by his son, Robert Hodzart, (already mentioned) who married Janet Brown, daughter of Robert Brown, minister of Quothquhan and Laird of Knockmarloch, by —— Hay, daughter of Andrew Hay of Craignethan, whose brother, John Hay of Hayston, was principal Clerk of Session in the reign of Charles the Second.

This Andrew Hay was one of four deputies appointed to present the Remonstrance to Charles for his breach of pledge of adherence to the Solemn League and Covenant after the Restoration, and Wodrow states in his history that he was the only one of the four who escaped a violent death; but that his wife, Lady Craignethan, was turned out of Craignethan in the depth of winter by the soldiers sent to search for her husband, and perished in the snow.

Of the above marriage there was no male issue, but four daughters, of whom Annabella was married to Robert Paterson, and Barbara, in 1715, to William Findlay, who died in early life, leaving his widow and an infant son, Robert, afterwards Dr Findlay, Professor of Theology in the University of Glasgow, the grandfather of Robert Findlay, Esq., now of Easter Hill.

of the more improved modes of cultivation. He surprised his neighbours by showing that wheat could be successfully cultivated in the district.

"Though he never gave up his farm, and within a few weeks of his death explained an experiment he was making, and personally pointed out his young wheat to one who accompanied him over his farm, yet his mind, for thirty years back, had been engrossingly occupied with pursuits of another kind, and in the preparation of the numerous works which rapidly proceeded from the press, and by which his name became widely known as an expositor of prophecy and a critic on Scriptural chronology. The infirmity of deafness, which gradually increased, caused him to withdraw, in a great measure, from ordinary society and public business, and devote all his time to prophetical and chronological studies.

" Mr Cuninghame was early impressed with strong religious convictions. They were felt by him when a boy at school at Kensington, where he received most part of his education. He was a thoughtful boy, with a weakly constitution, and a most delicate organization. Before going to India, he was for a short time at the University of Utrecht, where he had as his companions General Sir Thomas M. Brisbane, G.C.B., and George Ross, Esq., of Edinburgh, with both of whom he continued to live in habits of intimacy, and had returned from a visit at Brisbane House only ten days before his death. While in India his religious convictions deepened, and his spiritual progress was greatly aided, as he himself acknowledged, by the opportunities he enjoyed of meeting the celebrated Dr Carey of Serampore, and other Baptist missionaries. His spontaneous generosity to some of those missionaries, on hearing accidentally of their difficulties, is acknowledged in the ' Memoirs of Dr Carey.' While in India, he wrote some letters on the Evidences of Christianity, addressed to his countrymen. These letters, under the signature of ' An Inquirer,' were afterwards collected and published for the benefit of the Serampore Mission, and subsequently republished in England.

" With the cause of missions to the heathen, but more particularly to the Jews, the feelings of Mr Cuninghame were warmly embarked. He was a liberal supporter of the leading religious societies in London ; but to the London Society for promoting Christianity among the Jews, his time, his purse, and his talents were given in its seasons of difficulty with the greatest zeal and self-devotion. No cause lay so near to his heart as the promised Restoration of Israel. In the year 1810, Mr Cuninghame appeared a second time before the public as an author, by an answer to David Levi's ' Dissertations on the Prophecies relative to the Messiah,' which Mr Cuninghame had written for the prize proposed for the best answer to that learned Jew's work ; and, having obtained the prize, the late celebrated Thomas Scott, being one of the competitors, the work appeared under the signature of ' Talib.'

" In 1813, Mr Cuninghame's work on the Apocalypse was first published. It immediately attracted attention, and was most favourably noticed in many of the religious critical journals. The fourth and last edition, greatly enlarged, was published in the year 1843.

" The subsequent publications of Mr Cuninghame succeeded each other rapidly, and are too numerous to be specially noticed. Some of them were directed to an exposure of the idolatrous character of Popery, and its identification with prophetic announcement—some to the support of the doctrine of the pre-millennial advent and reign of our Lord—and his latest to a vindication of the superiority of the Septuagint, or Greek chronology of the Scriptures, to that of the Hebrew or vulgar chronology.

" Mr Cuninghame, on his return to this country, joined the communion of the Established Church, to which his family had belonged, but he declined becoming an elder, though pressed to do so, as he could not assent to the doctrines of the Confession of Faith, especially on the subject of the limitation of the Atonement. In 1822 he ceased to be a member of the Establishment, for reasons which he assigned in a pamphlet published at the time, entitled ' Narration of the Formation of a Congregational Church at Stewarton.' He became the pastor of the church, and continued to perform the pastoral duties every Lord's day when at home, with occasional assistance, till the year 1843, when the Rev. Robert Smith, of the Congregational Church of Irvine, became assistant minister. This church has always had a respectable body of adherents, and will form a permanent congregation in the town of Stewarton. Mr Cuninghame has not only left it in possession of a commodious place of worship, and of a comfortable manse for the minister, but also bestowed a suitable endowment to maintain the church."[*]

Mr Cuninghame was never married, and is succeeded by his younger brother, Mr John Cuninghame of Hensol, in the Stewartry of Kirkcudbright.

* Notice of Mr Cuninghame's death in the " Ayr Observer."

ARNOT OF LOCHRIG.

The first of this old family, of whom there is any record, was

I. JOHN DE ARNOT of Lochrig, whose name occurs as one of the jury in a cause between the burgh of Irvine and William Fraunces of Stane, in 1417. From his position at that time it may be inferred that the property had been for some time previously in the possession of the family. The Arnots of Lochrig were probably a cadet of the Arnots of that Ilk, in Fifeshire. This is countenanced by the fact that " Andro Arnot, elder, of that Ilk," was cautioner for Andro Arnot of Lochrig, in reference to the *testament of David,* his son, in 1604. The next, in all likelihood, was

II. Edward Arnot of Lochrig, who had a gift of the two Fenwicks from Sir Gilbert Mure of Rowallan, for the " yearlie payment of ane pair of gloves at S. Lawrence Chapell, and of ane paire of spures, at S. Michaell's Chappell, embleames of reddie service."* He was succeeded by

III. Andrew Arnot of Lochrig. He was designed of Fenwick during the life of his father: " Andreus Arnot de Watt'fenik, filius et heres apparen. Eduardi Arnot de Lochrig," granted a charter of confirmation to Robert Mure, of the two merk land of Wattfenike, in the barony of Rowallan, dated at Irvine, 7th Sept. 1497. He was probably succeeded by

IV. Henry Arnot of Lochrig, of whom nothing is known save that his name occurs in the precept of sasine of his son,

V. Andrew Arnot of Lochrig, who had a precept of sasine from the Crown, as heir of his father, Henry Arnot, 11th May 1505.

VI. Robert Arnot of Lochrig. His name occurs in the testament of William Wallace of Ellirsly in 1549. " In 1556," says Robertson, " he obtained a charter of the lands of Lochrig from Mary Queen of Scots. There are other deeds in which the names of 'Robert Arnot elder and younger of Lochrig are associated. Another son, Andrew, is also mentioned. Robert appears to have died before his father, who was succeeded by his second son,"

VII. Andrew Arnot of Lochrig. He had a Crown charter of confirmation—" Andrew, filio et hæredi Roberti Arnot de Lochrig, terrarum de Lochrig"—22d November 1555, his father being then apparently alive. In 1573 (1st Feb.) the Laird of Lochrigis gave a bond of man-rent to

Robert Lord Boyd—" Andro Arnot, zoungare," binding himself and heirs at all times to " ryde and gang" with the said Lord Boyd. In 1574, he had a charter of the five merk land of Rosfynnich and Wattosfynnich, with a share of the common muir of Rowallan. He married Elizabeth Craufurd, of the Cranfurdland family, who died 28th December 1610. He had two sons:

1. Andrew, his successor.
2. David, who died in 1604.—" Testament, &c., of vmquhile David Arnot, secund lawfull sone to Andro Arnot, elder of Lochrig, faithfullie maid and gevin vp be his awin mouth, the penult day of November 1604 zeiris, and deceist the first day of December nixt thaireftir following. Quha nominat, &c., the said Andro Arnot of Lochrig, his father, to be his onlie executour, &c. Inuentar.—The said vmquhile David declairit that he was super-expendit in chargie of chyrurgeanes, in hoip of cuiring of his diseis, quhilk availlit not, and whatsumeuir guidis eftir-mentionat that he had was wairit vpone his chargis in furneising him sic necessaris as he neidit, and wytting vpone him in lang lying the space of twa zeiris. Item, the said David hade perteining to him ten hoggettis ticht and sufficient neis, price of the peice o'thed, xx s., summa x li., quhilk neis he delyuerit in custodie to his wae to Andro Muir, sone to vmquhile Adam Muir, sometyme of Kittiemuir; summa patet, x li. Debtis awand in. —Item, awand to the said vmquhile David, the tyme of his deceis foirsaid, be Andro Arnot, zonger of Lochrig, xxli money, lent syluer. Item, be Johne Steinson in Pacokbank, the sowme of ix li xiiis iiiid lent siluer, qlk said haue beine payit at ane certane terme ellis bypast, togidder with iiiili money as annuell thairefir, permittit be the said Johne to the said vmquhile David, for the qlk Patrick Wallace becums cautioner, baith for principale and annuell above specifit, . . . This testament was maid at the Lochrig, . . . writtin be Johne Neven of Kirkwode, nottarpublick, befoir thir witness, Adam Muir of Carsedossie, &c.—Confirmed, Oct. 15, 1609, Andro Arnot, elder, of that Ilk, cautioner."

VIII. Andrew Arnot of Lochrig. He had a Crown charter—" Androw, filio et hæredi Andreæ Arnot de Lochrig et Margaretæ Cuninghame, suæ sponsæ, terrarum de Lochrig"—17th July 1602. In 1616, he had a tack of the teinds of Lochrig, for the space of his own life, the lives of his two next heirs, and for five nineteen years thereafter, from William, Archbishop of St Andrews, Commendator of Kilwinning. His lady, Margaret Cuninghame, of the Corshill family, died in April 1616. Amongst the debts " awand in," in her testament, " thair was awand to ye defunct and hir spouse, be ye Laird of Carnell and his cautioner, conforme to yair obligatioune and contract of marriage maid with Andro Arnot, ane thowsand merks." This Andrew Arnot was no doubt their son.* It appears also, from her legacies, that they had a daughter, Janet Arnot, married to John Montgomerie. She directed that the " frie geir," after the debts were paid, was to be distributed " amangis hir bairnes," but

---

* The Historie and Descent of the House of Rowallane.

* " Andro Arnot, fear of Lochrig," occurs in the testament of Lady Culzeane in 1621.

they are not mentioned by name. "Allexander Cvnynghame of Corshill, elder, and Allexander Cvnynghame of Corshill, zounger," were witnesses. Andro Arnot was succeeded by his son,

IX. Alexander Arnot of Lochrig, who had a charter, on a precept from Chancery, as heir of his father, dated 29th May 1623. He married Jonet Ros, but of what family does not appear. He died in November of the same year, leaving issue *Alexander*, *John*, and *Elizabeth*.

"Testament, &c. of Allexander Arnot of Lochrig, Kilmarnok, quha deceist in the monethe of November 1623, &c. Legacie.—At Fynnick, ye xxi day of November 1623 zeiris.—The qlk day Allexander Arnot of Lochrig maid his testament as followis: In ye first, he commits his saull in ye handis of ye Lord, &c. Nixt, he levis and nominats Jonet Ros, his spous, and failzeing hir, Allexander Cvnynghame of Corshill, Allexander Cvnynghame, his sone, Thomas Craufurd in Walstoun, tutours-testamentars to Allexander, Andro, Johnne, and Elizabeth Arnot, his sones and dochter, to be guydit and governit be the said tutours, &c. Item, he levis and nominats Jonet Ros, Andro, Johnne, and Elizabeth Arnot, his executouris, &c. Thir presents ar writtin be me, Allexander Cvnynghame of Corshill, at the directioun of the said Allexander Arnot, in his awin hous of Fynnick, &c. Compared, October 26, 1624, Mr David Fullertoun, cautioner. *N.B.*—In this testament, as creditors, occur 'his fatheris childrein gottin on Jeane Cvnynghame,' which makes it probable that Jean was his father's second wife."

X. Alexander Arnot of Lochrig, the eldest son, succeeded. He seems to have been a minor when his father died, for he was not served heir to him till 10th August 1637. He married Jean Sempill, daughter of William Sempill of Fulwood (by Jean, daughter of Sir Patrick Houstoun) one of the oldest cadets of the Sempill family. Their contract of marriage is dated February 1639. Alexander Arnot built the present house of Lochrig. He died in July 1649. His testament is dated at "ye place of Dunlope," where he seems to have died. He appointed Andro Arnot, his brother (probably by the second marriage, formerly alluded to), his only executor, and tutor to *Alexander* Arnot, his son and heir.

XI. Alexander Arnot of Lochrig, whose long minority is attested by many papers relating to the transactions of his curators. He was served heir to his father 16th June 1657. He married Janet Arnot, daughter to Arnot of that Ilk, in Fife, and had by her two sons and two daughters. His uncle and tutor, Andro Arnot, was present

at the battle of Pentland Hills, in 1666, and having been taken prisoner, was executed at the Watergate of Edinburgh. In 1689, his name is included in a numerous list of those sufferers whose sentence of forfeiture, in the preceding reigns, was revoked, and their families restored to their rights. In 1696, Alexander Arnot of Lochrig, with consent of his wife, Janet Arnot, and of Alexander, his eldest son, disposed of the lands of Rosefinnick and others to Robert Barns of Kirkhill; and at the same time the farms of Mosside and Mosshead, in the parish of Fenwick, to Wilson, afterwards of Haghouse. He died in 1714. His eldest son, Alexander, dying on the Continent about the same time, the property devolved upon the second son,

XII. James Arnot of Lochrig, an officer in the Foot Guards, who died unmarried in 1728, and was succeeded by his sister,

XIII. Anna Arnot of Lochrig. She died unmarried in 1745, as did also her second sister, Catherine. Isabella, the youngest, married Mr John Galt, in 1723, and had an only child,

XIV. Jean Galt Arnot, who, in 1741, was married to Mathew Stewart of Newton, a descendant of the Stewarts of Blackhall. Of this marriage there were three sons, *Alexander*, *Mathew*, and *Archibald*, and four daughters, who survived their parents. *Ann*, the eldest daughter, married the Rev. Dr Taylor, Principal of the University of Glasgow, and was the only one who left descendants. Mathew Stewart of Newton died in 1764, and was succeeded by his son,

XV. Alexander Arnot Stewart of Lochrig, a Lieutenant in the Scots Greys, who sold his paternal property of Newton, and died in 1769. He was succeeded by his brother,

XVI. Mathew Arnot Stewart of Lochrig, a Lieutenant in the 56th Foot. He married Mary, only child of John Brown of Gabrochhill, by whom he had issue a son, *Mathew*, and a daughter, *Eliza*. He died 8th January 1796, and was succeeded by his posthumous son,

XVII. Mathew Arnot Stewart, an officer in the Queen's Bays. He was a Stipendiary Magistrate in the West Indies, and died some years ago, unmarried. His sister, Eliza, married Mr Brown of Auchintorley, in Renfrewshire. She is still alive, but has no issue. Mrs Stewart sold Lochrig to her son-in-law, by whom it was disponed, in 1830, to *David Provan*, Esq., surgeon in the E.I.Co.'s service, who also purchased Peacock Bank. He married Miss Reid, daughter of the late Mr Reid, bookseller, Glasgow, by whom he had *David*, now of Lochrig, (a minor); *James*, of Peacock Bank, and three daughters. Mr Provan died in 1851.

The house of *Lochrig* is a goodly old mansion, still in excellent repair, and possesses considerable accommodation. It has the initials of the founder, Alexander Arnot, and the date, 1636, in the front. It is well sheltered with plantations, and stands on a rising ground about a mile south of the village of Stewarton.

*Arms*—On a large polished stone in the front wall of the house there are two shields engraved. On the one side is a chevron betwixt three stars, apparently for Arnot; on the other a chevron cheque, with a bugle in base; and for a crest, two doves cooing, probably for Sempill of Fulwood. The stone being much weather-worn, the tinctures cannot be discerned.

*Crest* is now, a lion's head erased.

*Motto*—" Spero meliora."

### CUNINGHAME OF CORSHILL.

I. ANDREW, second son of William, fourth Earl of Glencairn, was the first of the House of Corshill. His father, while Master of Kilmaurs, had a royal charter of the lands of Doura, Robertland, &c., 18th January 1531: also, of the same date, of the lands of Blacklaw, Hairschaw, Littill Corshill, Meikill Corshill, and Armsheuch. " Andreæ, filio Willielmi Cuninghame, militis, Magistri de Glencarne," had a royal charter " terrarum de Cuttiswray, Clarklands, et Hillhouse," 4th May 1538. The original grant to him by his father, of the lands of Doura, Potterton, Little Robertland, with the two Corshills, is shown by the family papers to have occurred in 1532. Like his elder brother, Alexander, fifth Earl of Glencairn, Andrew was actively engaged in support of the Reformation, and being convicted of heresy before the Lords Spiritual in 1538, his estate was forfeited. However, he was afterwards pardoned, and had his property restored; in confirmation of which he obtained another charter from the King—" Carta Andreæ Cunynghame, filio Willielmi, Comitis de Glencarne, et Margaretæ Cuninghame, sponsæ dict. Andræ, terrarum de Cuttiswray," &c., 5th Aug. 1541. His wife, Margaret Cuninghame, was of the Polmais family. He died in 1545,[*] and was succeeded by his eldest son,

II. Cuthbert Cuninghame of Corshill. This appears from an instrument of sasine in his favour of the above year. After his marriage with

Mauld Cuninghame, daughter of Cuninghame of Aiket, Cuthbert resigned his estate in the hands of the sovereign, for new infeftment, and thereupon obtained a charter from Henry and Mary to himself and his spouse, and their heirs. He left two sons, *Patrick* and *Alexander*, who were for some time under the guardianship of their grand-uncle, Hugh Cuninghame of Watterston, and two daughters, *Jean* and *Margaret*.

The long-continued feud between the Cuninghames and Montgomeries appears to have been at its height about this time. Patrick Cuninghame of Corshill was implicated in the slaughter of the Earl of Eglintoun, when on a visit at Lainshaw in 1586. Patrick was himself slain afterwards by the Montgomeries, as appears by a commission by the King in reference to the feud between the families of Cuninghame and Montgomerie, dated in 1588.

III. Alexander Cuninghame of Corshill, the second son, carried on the representation. He married Marion Porterfield, daughter of Porterfield of Duchal, by whom, according to the family papers, he had two sons:—

1. Alexander, his heir.
2. David, of Dalbeith, who married Margaret Cuninghame, and had issue—
   1. Jean, married to Cuninghame of Aiket.
   2. Elanour, married to John Craufurd of Craufurdland.
   3. Janet, married to Blair of Adamton.

He had also a daughter, as appears from the Commissary Records :—

3. " Jonet Cwnynghame, dochter lauchfull to Allexr. Cwnynghame of Corshill."[*]

IV. Alexander Cuninghame of Corshill, the eldest son succeeded in May 1546. He had several royal charters—one of the lands of Lambruchtoun, Thirdpart, &c. penult day of July 1618; two of the lands of Cuttiswray, &c. 11th Dec. 1622. By his wife, Mary Houstoun, (of the family of Houstoun of that Ilk,) he had issue :—

1. Alexander.
2. Cuthbert.[†]
1. Elizabeth, married to James Dunlop of Dunlop.
2. Margaret, married to James Stewart of Torrance.

Alexander, the eldest son, died before his father, leaving by his wife, Anne Craufurd,[‡] of the

---

[*] " Androwe Coninghame, sonne to the Earl of Glencarne, was concerned in the murder of Rizzio." Orig. Letters, edited by H. Ellis, vol. ii. p. 221.

[*] Testament of William Porterfield of that Ilk, who died in October 1616.

[†] " Mr Cuthbert Cunynghame, son lauchfull to Alexander Conynghame of Corshill, occurs in the testament of William Hume, chamberlain to the Earl of Eglintoun, 12th Feb. 1659.

[‡] " Anna Crawfurd, Lady Corshill, youngare," died in August 1649. The inventory of her effects is as follows: " Inventare,—Item, the said umquhile Anna Crawfurd had, the tyme foirsaid, &c. viz. ane rid cloath bed, with ane rid and zallow silk lace vpone it, with fyve peices of curteins thairto; ane inner pand, ane vttir pand, ane large rid covering conforme to it; ane heid peice, with the cover

Craufurdland family, an only son, on whom, and his affianced wife, his grandfather settled the estate, 13th April, 1663, by disposition and charter, reserving to himself the liferent. Alexander Cuninghame, senior, died about 1667, and his grandson,

V. Sir Alexander Cuninghame of Corshill, who, on the 20th January 1672, obtained a charter from the Crown, in favour of himself and spouse, and their heirs, in confirmation of the disposition made by his grandfather; and on the 26th Feb. 1672, the dignity of a Baronet, by diploma, was conferred on him and his heirs-male. By his wife, Mary Stewart, daughter of John Stewart, younger of Blackhall, he had issue:—

1. Alexander.
2. Mary, married to Cranfurd of Dalleagles.
3. Elizabeth.

VI. Sir Alexander Cuninghame of Corshill, the second Baronet, succeeded in March 1685, and married, the following year, Margaret Boyle, sister of David, first Earl of Glasgow, by whom he had an only son, *David*, and a daughter, *Jean*, married to William Newall of Barskeoch.

VII. Sir David Cuninghame of Corshill, Bart. married Penelope Montgomerie, neice and heiress of Sir Walter Montgomerie of Skelmorlie, by whom he had three sons :—

1. Alexander.
2. David, who died in Jamaica, and left issue.
3. Walter.
4. Margaret, married to —— Craig, Esq.

Alexander, the eldest son, was in the army, and served in the wars in Flanders. On succeeding to the estate of Kirktonholm, he adopted the name and arms of Montgomerie, in consequence of a clause to that effect in the deed of entail.

of the stoupps, ane cover of the beid conforme to the same, with ane table cloath, price liii lib. 6s. 8d. Item, ane imbroideret taffetie matt, pryce thairof xl s., &c. Item, three carpet cushenis and fyve sewit cuscheines, pryce of all viii lib. Item, three peices of hingings to windoes, pryce xxs. Item, ane zallow canople, pryce thairof xxxs. &c. Item, three leathered chyres, pryce thairof ix lib. Item, three red leathered stooles, &c. Item, three chyres coverit with arrare worke, pryce xii lib., &c. Item, two lint quheillis, pryce thairof iii lib. 6s. 8d. Item, an mekle quheill, in the Hacket, pryce xxxvi s. Item, ane dissane of silver spunes, and ane silver porringer, and a cruik, pryce of all i c. xiii lib. 4s., &c. Item, twa puncis (?) pryce xxxiv s., &c. Item, ane silver watch, pryce xxvi lib. 13s. 4d., &c. Item, ane womanis sadle, with a covering, pryce xxiii lib. Item, ane old Byble, pryce xxx a.; ane old velvet gowne, pryce xxx lib; ane peice of gold, iii lib. &c. Item, ane flourit waskot, and ane blake taill of damase, pryce v lib. 6s. 8d. Item, the defunctis ryding clothes; ane qubyt petticot, with a blake lace, pryce iii lib. &c. [Lady Corshill nominated the Laird of Craufurdland her executor, from which it may be inferred that she was of that family.]

He married Elizabeth, eldest daughter, and thereafter heiress, of Sir Neil Montgomerie of Lainshaw, a representative of the family of Lyle, Lord Lyle. He predeceased his father, Sir David, by a few months, in 1770. His children, by his wife, were :—

1. Walter.                     2. David.
3. Eglintoun, died young.
4. Alexander, who served with the army in the American war, died unmarried.
5. James.
6. Henry-Drumlanrig, R.N. He was a lieutenant on board the Alfred, in Rodney's great engagement, 12th April 1782. He died unmarried.
1. Anna; 2. Elizabeth; both died young.

VIII. Sir Walter-Montgomerie Cuninghame, Bart. of Corshill succeeded his grandfather in 1770, and died unmarried in March 1814.

IX. Sir David Cuninghame, Bart. of Corshill, second son, and fifth Baronet, had been in the R.N.B. Dragoons. He died unmarried in November following, when his next surviving brother succeeded.

X. Sir James Cuninghame, Bart. of Corshill, married Jessie, second daughter of Thomas Cuming, Esq., banker in Edinburgh, representative of the ancient family of Cuming of Earnside, Nairnshire, by whom he had :—

1. Alexander.                  2. Thomas.
3. James, who died in 1835.
4. George.                     5. Henry.
1. Jessie-Jane, married to Sir James Boswell, Bart. of Auchinleck.
2. Grace-Matilda, died 11th October 1842.

Sir James died in March 1837, and was succeeded by his eldest son,

XI. Sir Alexander-David-Montgomerie Cuninghame, Bart. of Corshill, who died, unmarried, 8th June 1846. He was succeeded by his brother,

XII. Sir Thomas-Montgomerie Cuninghame, Bart. of Corshill, present and eighth Baronet. He married, in 1832, Charlotte, only child of the late Hugh Hutcheson of Southfield, Renfrewshire, and has issue, three sons and three daughters. As the representative of Andrew, second son of William, fourth Earl of Glencairn, Sir Thomas is claimant, and apparently rightful heir of the honours of Glencairn.

*Arms*—Argent, a shakefork; in chief a crescent, azure.

*Crest*—An unicorn's head erazed, proper.
*Supporters*—Two conies, proper.
*Motto*—" Over fork over."

*Seats*—Corshill, and Kirktonholm in Lanarkshire.

## CUNINGHAME OF ROBERTLAND.

Robertson states, that *David Cuninghame of Bartonholme* was the ancestor of this family, and that he was the only son of the second marriage of the first William Cuninghame of Craigends with Dame Marion Auchinleck, to whom he was married in 1499. This seems probable enough; at least that there was a family relationship, appears from the intercourse between the houses in subsequent times. In 1599, for instance, "Craiganis and Danid Cwnynghame of Robertland," were joint tacksmen of the teinds of Kilmaurs, as well as at a later period.

I. DAVID CUNINGHAME of Robertland was an active assistant in the feud between Cuninghame of Glengarnock and the Sempills, in 1530-33. He had a charter from the Crown of the seventh part of the lands of Watterland and Hacket, 26th February 1535; while *David* Cuninghame of Bartonholm had a charter of the lands of Corssynkell and Myddilpart, 25th May 1536. These two could not be one and the same party, though they might have been related. On the 4th August 1537, David Cuninghame of Robertland had a charter of the lands of Corserag, *Corsinkill*, &c., which probably he had acquired by the death of his relative; also, 5th March 1539, of the lands of Bartaneholm, Snodgers, &c. He and his spouse, Dame Margaret Cuninghame, had a charter of the lands of Baidland and Spittall, 8th July 1541. He was alive in 1555.

II. David Cuninghame of Robertland had "Carta Davidi Cunninghame, filio et hæredi quond. Davidis Cunninghame de Robertland, terrarum de Hoilhouse," 30th April 1566. He and his spouse, Margaret Cuninghame, had a Crown charter of the lands of Brydeland and Spittal, 18th April 1593. It must have been this David Cuninghame of Robertland who was concerned in the slaughter of the Earl of Eglintoun, in 1586.

III. David Cuninghame of Robertland, and Jean Cuninghame, his spouse, had a charter of the seventh part of the lands of Watterland, Aiket, and Hesilbank, 14th February 1597. It was no doubt this Laird of Robertland who was "takisman of the teindis of Kilmaris" along with the Laird of Craigends, in 1599, and again in 1602. He probably died without issue, as his successor,

IV. David Cuninghame of Robertland, was served heir to his grandfather, *Sir* David Cuninghame of Robertland,[*] 24th October 1607. He

had a Crown charter to him and his spouse,"[†] of the barony of Glengarnock, 18th January 1614, He died in April 1619, when the inventory of his effects was faithfully made and given up "be *Margaret Flemyng*, his relict,[*] in name and behalf of *Allexander, Johnn, James, Williame,* and *Ewphame* Cwnynghames, bairnes lauchfullie procreat betuix thame." They had, besides, *David,* the eldest son, and *Jeane,* "dochter to ye Laird of Robertland," mentioned in the testament of Lockhart of Bar, in 1614. He was succeeded by his eldest son,

V. Sir David Cuninghame of Robertland, who was served heir to his father in 1628. Lady Robertland occurs in the testament of "Johnn Niniane, in Smith Dickvoy, Largs," who died in 1624, as a creditor for "sax thowsand salt herring, pryce of ye thowsand, vi lb, inde xxxvi lb. to be payit zeirlie, betuixt Zuill and Candilmes."[†] And "Sir Dauid Cwnynghame of Robertland, Knicht," who was created a Baronet of Nova Scotia in 1630, occurs in similar documents in 1642 and 1647. He was alive in 1652, in which year "Alexander Conynghame, brother to the Laird of Robertland, appears in a testamentary document. It is probable, however, that he died soon afterwards, and was succeeded by his son, also

VI. Sir David Cuninghame of Robertland, who was a Commissioner of Supply in 1661. He apparently died without issue, for

VII. Sir Alexander Cuninghame of Robertland was served heir to Sir David, *filii fratris,* in 1672. He married the heiress of John Cuninghame of Kilmaronock, son of James, seventh Earl of Glencairn, by whom he had issue:

1. David.
2. Alexander.
3. Jean, married to Sir Alexander Forrester.

He was succeeded by his eldest son,

VIII. Sir David Cuninghame of Robertland, who appears as a Commissioner of Supply in 1685. He had a son, *David,* who, in a charter of an annuity from the barony of Caprington, dated 26th Februry 1686, is styled "junioris de Robertland." He predeceased his father, however, who left an only daughter, and sole heiress,

IX. Diana Cuninghame of Robertland, who was married to Thomas Cochrane of Polkelly, but died without issue.

[Much of the estate is supposed to have been alienated about this time. "Magistri Cuninghame de Milnecraig, advocate," had

---

[*] Christierne Cvnynghame, sone lauchfull to vmquhile Sir David Cvnynghame of Robertland, Knyt, was the

writer of the testament of James Cuninghame, son of the Laird of Ashinyards, who died in 1623.
[*] She was alive in 1652.
[†] Evidently a payment of rent for the land he possessed.

a charter of adjudication of the lands and barony of Robertland so early as 10th Jan 1632.]

X Sir Alexander Cnninghame of Robertland, uncle of Mrs Cochrane, succeeded to the titles, and what remained of the estate. He was served heir of his brother, Sir David, in 1692, but must have died soon after He was succeeded by his son,

XI Sir David Cuninghame of Robertland, who, in 1696, had a protection in his favour from Parliament He died before 1778, in which year,

XII Sir William Cuninghame of Auchinskeith was served heir to him, and assumed the title He was descended from Christian, second son of Sir David Cuninghame of Robertland, who was killed at the siege of Namur His grandfather, John Cuninghame of Wattiestoun, was the second son of Christian, and his father, William Cuninghame, who married Miss M'Ilvain of Grimet, was designed of Auchinskeith Sir William married Margaret, sister of Alexander Fairlie of Fairlie, and by her acquired that property *

Robertland was purchased about forty years ago by *Alexander Kerr*, Esq, a native of Stewarton, who had spent a number of years in America He also acquired the property of Haysmuir, which previously belonged to a family of the name of Dunlop Mr Kerr died about five years since, and was succeeded by his son, *John James Kerr*, the present proprietor

### SOMERVILLES OF KENNOX.

The Somervilles of Kennox were originally from Lanarkshire The first of the family was *James Somerville of Kennox*, in the parish of Douglas, a younger son of Sir William Somerville of Cambusnethan. He married a daughter of Inglis of Ingliston, and died in 1764, as recorded on his tombstone in Douglas churchyard He was succeeded by his son,

*William Somerville of Kennox*, who was twice married, first, to a daughter of Sir —— Vere of Blackwood, without issue, secondly, to a daughter of Sir Archibald Fleming of Ferme, (a cadet of the Earls of Wigton) by a daughter of Archibald Stewart of Scotston, who was the second son of Sir Archibald Stewart of Blackhall, by Margaret, daughter of Bryce Blair of that Ilk. Mrs Somerville's grandmother, Lady Fleming, was daughter of Colquhoun of Luss,

and her grandmother daughter to [Stirling of Kerr His son,

*James Somerville of Kennox*, disposed of the estate of Kennox, in Lanarkshire, about the beginning of last century, and purchased the barony of Bollingshaw in this parish, also Little Peirceton, now Annick Lodge, in the parish of Dreghorn, where he at first resided This, and also part of his other property in Stewarton, he afterwards disposed of, and . built a mansion at Montgomerie Crevoch, which he called Kennox, after his paternal inheritance, and which has from that time been the seat of the family He married Janet, eldest daughter and heiress of Alexander Montgomerie of Assloss, by the only daughter of Alexander Montgomerie of Kirktonholm, grandson to Robert Montgomerie of Skelmorlie, by Dorothy, daughter to Robert, third Lord Semple. Mrs Somerville's mother's mother was daughter to Corbett of Tollcross; her father's mother daughter to William Wallace of Shewalton

Alexander Montgomerie of Assloss was third son to George Montgomerie of Broomlands, the direct representative of the Hon. William Montgomerie, fourth son of Hugh, first Earl of Eglintoun He had four daughters —1. Janet (Mrs Somerville), above mentioned, who succeeded him in Assloss, which she afterwards disposed of, 2 Margaret, married to Forbes of Waterton, in Aberdeenshire, 3 Penelope, married to Sir David Cuninghame of Corshill, Bart ; 4 Anne, married to Moir of Leckie, and was left the estate of Kirktonholm by the will of her uncle, Sir Walter Montgomerie, Knt , and dying without issue, bequeathed it to Captain Alexander Cuninghame, younger, of Corshill, her youngest sister's son , and it is now possessed by his grandson, Sir Thomas Montgomerie Cuninghame of Corshill and Kirktonholm, Baronet.

By this marriage with the heiress of Assloss, James Somerville had a very large family, most of whom died without issue The descendants of John, who settled in America, enjoy large possessions in Virginia and Maryland The eldest son,

*William Somerville of Kennox*, succeeded his father in 1743. He married Lilias, youngest daughter of Gabriel Porterfield of Hapland, (a cadet of Porterfield of that Ilk), by Elizabeth, daughter of William Cuninghame of Craigends (a cadet of the Earl of Glencairn), and Christian, daughter of Sir James Colquhoun of Luss, Bart

The last Porterfield of Hapland was killed by a fall from his horse in the year 1765, when his estate was divided among his three sisters as co-

* See p 24 of this volume

heiresses. The eldest, Johanna, was married to Thomas Trotter of Mortonball; the second, Margaret, married John Hamilton of Barr; the third, Lilias, Mrs Somerville.*

By his marriage, as stated, William Somerville of Kennox had two sons, *James* and *William*, both of whom died unmarried. The eldest daughter, *Elizabeth*, having displeased her parents by her marriage, they entailed the estate of Kennox, and a portion of Hapland, on their second daughter, *Janet*, the present proprietrix, who had previously married, in 1792, Charles M'Alester, only son of M'Alester of Loup, chief of the clan. This gentleman, who was a Deputy Lieutenant of Ayrshire, and Commandant of the first regiment of Ayrshire Local Militia, died in 1847. She has issue two sons and two daughters:

1. Charles, married, in 1828, Mary Brabazon, only child of Edward Lyon, Lieut. R.N., by Anna Catherine, eldest daughter and co-heiress of George Frederick Winstanley of Philipsburgh, county Dublin. Issue:—
    1. Charles, Lieut. 46th Regiment.
    2. Edward.
    1. Anna-Catherine.
    2. Mary.
2. James, of Chapeltoun, a part of the barony of Bollingshaw alienated, as above stated, by James Somerville, and re-acquired and bequeathed to him by his father.

---

* These marriages are incorrectly stated at page 52 of this volume, as there were only three daughters, married as above.

1. Williamina.
2. Jane.

The mansion-house of *Kennox*, built by James Somerville, about 1720, still exists, but has been extensively added to by his successors, at different periods. It is set down amidst fine old woods in a curve of the water of Glazart, about two miles west from Stewarton. Close to the house is a yew tree, of remarkable size and beauty. From its dimensions it is computed to be upwards of nine hundred years old, and is still vigorous. As the yew tree, in this country, was usually planted in the immediate vicinity of family residences, this would infer great antiquity for the site of Kennox, formerly Crevoch.

### GIRGENTI.

This property was acquired by the late *John Cheape*, Esq., from Stirlingshire. It was formerly called Muirhead. He built a magnificent house on the property, which, at his death, a few years ago, he bequeathed, together with the whole of his fortune, to the five principal Infirmaries in Scotland. He had an only sister, married to the late Earl of Strathmore, who, according to his will, would have been life-rented in his property and fortune; but she died a short time before him, so that the whole passed at once to the institutions for which it was designed.

# PARISH OF STRAITON.

In early charters the name of this place is spelled variously—Strattan, Stratton, Strattoun, Strattin, &c. It is no doubt of Celtic derivation, though not perhaps formed, as Chalmers supposes, by a union of the Gaelic *Strath* (*th* being silent), and Saxon *toun*, but rather by the addition of *don*, deep—so that *Stradon* would signify the deep valley—which is precisely descriptive of the site occupied by the church and village of Straiton, which stand between two hills on the upper part of the Girvan water. Abercrummie, in his description of Carrick, says "The parish of Stratoune lyes east and south, toward the Stewirtrie of Galloway. The church stands upon a ground declining to the westward." The parish is one of the largest in Ayrshire. "Its extreme length, from Carnochan on the river Doon, to the farm of Star, at the head of Loch Doon, is more than twenty miles. Its extreme breadth from the Doon, near Dalmellington, to the farm of Knockgarner, is upwards of eight miles. The number of square miles may be about eighty-two. It is bounded on the north by Kirkmichael and Dalrymple parishes; on the east by Dalmellington, on the south by Carsphairn, Kells, Minigaff, and Barr, and on the west by Dailly and Kirkmichael."[*] Straiton village is about fourteen and a half miles from Ayr.

The topographical appearance of the parish is extremely varied. The hills, which are numerous, rise to a considerable height. Craigengower, or the hill of the goats, in the immediate vicinity of the village, rises to the height of 1300 feet, and

Benan-hill (*Beinan*, the little mountain) whereon a small obelisk was built more than half a century ago, is about 1150 feet high. In such a district the scenery must be both pastoral and picturesque. The valleys are generally rich, alluvial lands, and are either in crop or meadow; but towards the south-east boundaries of the parish, the aspect of the country is altogether wild and rocky.

If the hills are numerous, the number of lochs in the parish is scarcely less so. The principal of these is Loch Doon, long celebrated for its castle —one of the ancient strongholds of the Scottish crown—built on an island near the head of the lake. The loch itself is about seven miles long, and one broad. The high lands by which it is encircled are extremely barren, and its margin is almost wholly destitute of wooding—still there is a something pleasing in its very wildness. Much of its rocky or gravelly bottom was laid bare a number of years ago, by the sluices made to regulate the supply of water for the river Doon, of which classic stream it is the source. Much of the picturesque beauty of the water-fall, into Berbeth Glen, through which the river flows, was destroyed by this utilitarian improvement. Berbeth Glen, or the Crags of Ness, are justly considered one of the most interesting of natural objects in the wide range of the county. The glen is about a mile in length, and the rocks rise on each side to the height of 230 feet. The cliffs are thickly covered with trees of the richest foliage, through which is seen the pent up river below, confined within a bed of a few yards wide, leaping and boiling over the rocky channel, with almost fearful impetuosity. "From the glen the Doon flows in great beauty through the grounds

---

[*] Statistical Account,

of Berbeth, and then expands into a loch much frequented by water-fowl. From this loch to Patna it runs sluggishly for five miles through meadows, without the ornament of a single tree."

The principal other lochs are called, Braden, Dercleugh, and Finlas, in the whole of which numerous and excellent trout are to be found; and they are usually much frequented by anglers. The water of Girvan takes its rise above Loch Braden, about twelve miles distant from the village of Straiton, towards which it flows through a well-cultivated valley. "From Straiton it winds for three miles through the richly wooded grounds of Blairquhan, and then enters Kirk-michael parish. The river Stinchar bounds this parish for a mile or two, near its source among the lochs in Barr parish."

"There are two waterfalls in the parish. Dal-kairney Linn, which is formed by a small stream near Berbeth, is a perpendicular jet of forty feet, and is noticed in old books for tourists. Tarelaw Linn is upon the Girvan, above Straiton. The stream rushes down several successive falls, forming together a descent of more than sixty feet, and then opens into a deep and wooded dell."*

### HISTORY, CIVIL AND ECCLESIASTICAL.

"The church of Straiton was dedicated to St Cuthbert, to whom other churches in Ayrshire were dedicated. In the reign of Alexander II., Duncan, Earl of Carrick, granted to the monks of Paisley the church of Stratoun, with its tithes and lands; and this grant was confirmed, 1236, by a charter of Alexander II. At this time the lands of Stratoun were held by John de Carrick, a son of Duncan, Earl of Carrick. He appears to have engaged in the rebellion of the Galloway-men, in 1235, and committed injuries to several churches in the diocese of Glasgow. In consideration of his getting from William, the Bishop of Glasgow, a pardon for this offence, John de Carrick granted to the Bishop " Una denariata terræ in feodo de Strattun, que vocatur Achin-clebyn, cum jure patronatus ecclesiæ de Strattun, in perpetuum, quam quidem denariatum terre idem Johannes assignavit dicto episcopo pro qua-tor marcatis terre.' And if John's right to the patronage of the said church should not be good against the Abbot of Paisley or others, then he granted to the Bishop, and his successors, 100 shillings land, in some competent part of his property in Carrick. This grant of John de Carrick was confirmed by his father, Duncan Earl of Car-

rick, and also by a charter of Alexander II., in 1244. John failed in making good his right to the patronage of the church of Stratoun, as the Abbot of Paisley had obtained a grant of the church from Duncan, Earl of Carrick, the father of John. The church of Stratoun was transferred from the monastery of Paisley to the monastery of Crossragwell, which was founded by Duncan Earl of Carrick, and planted with Cluniac monks from Paisley. This church was afterwards confirmed to the monks of Crossragwell by Robert I.; and it was specially confirmed to them by Robert III. in his charter of August 1404, in which it was called ' Ecclesia Sancti Cuthberti de Stratoun.' The church of Stratoun continued to belong to the monastery of Crossrag-well till the Reformation. The monks received a considerable part of the revenues, and the vicar received the remainder. In Bagimont's Roll, as it stood in the reign of James V., the vicarage of Stratoun, in the deanery of Carrick, was taxed £4, being a tenth of the estimated value. In 1562, William Bothwell, the vicar of Stratoun, made a return of the income of his vicarage; stating that the revenues were let to the Earl of Cassillis, for the yearly payment of £46, and the vicar's glebe, extending to a half merkland of old extent, was worth 20 marks yearly; and from this revenue he was obliged to pay 20 marks annually to a minister who was placed in the church by the Reformers. About the same time, that part of the revenues of the church of Stratoun which belonged to the monks of Crossragwell, was reported as yielding £60 yearly. In 1617, the patronage and tithes of the church of Stratoun, with all the other property of Crossragwell Abbey, were annexed by Act of Parliament to the Bishopric of Dumblane; reserving the revenues to Mr Peter Hewat, the Commendator of Crossragwell, during his life. On the final abolition of Episcopacy, in 1689, the patronage of the church of Stratoun was vested in the King, to whom it now belongs."

So far *Chalmers*,* whose general accuracy can be relied on. It appears, however, that the patronage of the church of Straiton had belonged to the Crown before the Revolution. Aber-crumnie, who wrote before that period, says: "The King is in possession of the patronage thereof, having slipt from the Abbot of Cross-raguel, to whom it seems to appertaine, because the tyth hold of that Abbacy." A pair of communion cups, with an inscription—" for the Kirk of Straiton"—are still preserved. The tradition is, that they were presented to the parish in the

---

* Statistical Account.

* Caledonia.

reign of Charles II., possibly by the monarch himself. It was probably because the King was patron, that the minister of Straton (Mr John M'Corne) was so friendly to the royal cause in 1645, and opposed to the covenant with England. The "edict," as it was called, of the Marquis of Montrose, was publicly read from his pulpit, while he (the minister) was present in the church. Sundry charges, and this amongst others, was afterwards brought against him, and he was ultimately deposed. The parish generally appears to have been rather friendly than otherwise to the cause of monarchy.

The church of Straiton was probably built immediately subsequent to the Reformation. It is a plain, oblong building, and does not contain above 500 sittings. There is, however, an aisle attached to it, of Gothic architecture, now the private gallery of Sir David Hunter Blair, which is believed to have formed part of the old structure before the Reformation.* The church underwent alterations and repairs in 1787, and again in 1813.

The churchyard, which is a large one, contains a few memorials of some interest. The oldest stone in the burying-ground bears the following inscription in raised letters:—"Heir rests the bodie of J.o.n. Macquoren, younger, in the hop of the joyful. He died in peace, 1 May 1628, aged 23. Anchora spei. vivi. vivo melius. optime vivam. Al Fleshe is Gras." This John Macquorn, younger, was in all likelihood a son of Mr John M'Quorn, minister of the parish in 1645, who is then spoken of in the Presbytery Records as "aged and paralitick." The churchyard contains, also, one of those venerated relics—a martyr's grave-stone. Beside the old stone a new one has recently been erected, and both have an inscription in memory of the martyr.

Besides Straiton, there is another thriving village called Patna, from the name of a place in India, where its founder, the late Mr Fullerton of Skeldon, was born.

### ANTIQUITIES.

On the summit of Benan-hill, more than half a century ago, two carved urns, filled with ashes, were dug up. There are no Roman remains in the immediate vicinity, so that they were probably relics of the British aboriginals.

"The most remarkable object of antiquity in the parish," justly remarks the writer in the *Statistical Account*, "is the ruinous Castle of Loch

Doon." The building occupies nearly the whole extent of an island situated at the head of Loch Doon. It has eleven irregular sides, and measures about 230 feet without the walls. The tower is square. The style of the building is a mixture of Saxon and Gothic, and is of superior execution; while every expedient, by battlements, embrasures, and portcullis, has been had recourse to, to render it secure, and which, from its situation—being surrounded by the lake—must, prior to the invention of gunpowder, have been almost impregnable. It seems to have been capable of holding a considerable number of retainers. The main entrance, which is arched in the Gothic style, with its portcullis aperture, is still entire; as are also the sallyport and the greater portion of the tower. The well-prepared ashler stones, of which the outward facing of the building is composed, are entirely different from the rocky strata in the vicinity. Hence it has been a subject of conjecture where they were obtained, and how conveyed to so remote and inaccessible a spot. About sixty years ago, a person well skilled in geology, and who felt an antiquarian enthusiasm in the question, discovered a quarry about two miles from Dalmellington, the stone of which corresponds exactly with the quality of those of the castle. He farther traced a route by which they might have been conveyed on sledges to the bottom of the loch. His supposition, therefore, was, that the stones, having been prepared at the quarry, were floated to the castle on rafts. This opinion was partly confirmed some time ago by the discovery of several oak beams or joists, in a squared state, which had probably dropped by accident from the rafts employed in floating materials to the building. If this conjecture is correct, the stones must have been carried a distance, between land and water, of not less than eight or ten miles. In 1823, after the waters had been reduced to a lower level, by the construction of sluices at the lower extremity of the loch, as already stated, three canoes were discovered at the bottom, near the entrance of the castle. They had each been cut out of a solid trunk of oak. One of them was sent to the Museum of the Glasgow University. In 1831, other three were discovered, of a similar description. The largest measures 23 feet long, 2 feet 6 inches in depth, and 3 feet 9 inches in breadth at the stem. In one of them were found an oaken war-club, a battle-axe, a number of large animal teeth, and a quantity of hazel-nuts. The canoes are supposed to have been used at the building of the castle; but from the remains found in them, we should suppose them to belong to a much earlier period—as the castle is not likely to be older than

---

* Straiton was no doubt one of the many churches despoiled by the zealots of the Reformation.

the reign of William the Lion, who built a number of castles, at Ayr and elsewhere, to overawe the wild men of Galloway.* The canoes, with the exception of the one sent to Glasgow, are preserved in a pond near Berbeth. As the district is now wholly destitute of wooding, except some modern plantations, the wonder is where the huge trees came from out of which they were scooped. There can be no doubt, however, that the country was thickly covered with wood at one time. One of the titles of the De Carrick family, and subsequently of the Earls of Cassillis, was Ranger of the forest of Buchan.

Loch Doon Castle was anciently a royal fortress, and is associated with more than one of our national events. One of the principal of these is the betrayal of Sir Christopher de Seton.

Sir Christopher—of the noble family afterwards distinguished as the Earls of Winton—is known to have been an early and warm supporter of the Bruce in his claim to the Scottish throne. We have no precise account of his participation in those plans which led to the assertion of Bruce's rights; but from his intimate family connection —being married to Lady Christian, sister of the future King—there can be little doubt that he was privy to all the secret proceedings by which the eventful crisis was brought about. He was present when Bruce struck down the Red Comyn in the Convent of the Minorite Friars in Dumfries, and he was among the few who afterwards rallied round the standard of the King, when he was crowned at Scone, on the 27th of March 1306. In the disastrous battle of Methven which followed, Sir Christopher bore a conspicuous part. The Scots, relying, in the chivalrous spirit of the times, on the statement of the Earl of Pembroke, that the day being too far spent he would not be ready to join battle until the morrow, neglected to plant proper outposts round their camp; so that they were set upon during the night, and nearly cut to pieces, before they could offer any effectual resistance. Bruce and the few leaders who were with him had scarcely time to arm, and though they performed prodigies of valour, it was impossible, taken at such disadvantage, to resist an overwhelming force. The King was three times unhorsed; and, according to Barbour, Sir Philip de Mowbray had so nearly taken him prisoner, that the knight cried aloud—"I have the new-made King!" The ready hand of Sir Christopher Seton, however, at that moment dealt Sir Philip a well-aimed blow, which felled him to the

earth, and rescued Bruce from his perilous situation. The result of the battle of Methven proved disastrous to the hopes of Bruce for a time. He and all his party who escaped the fray were compelled to seek safety in the fastnesses of the country. While the King and a few of his adherents directed their course towards the Highlands, Sir Christopher Seton sought refuge in the Castle of Loch Doon.

The castle was justly deemed a place of importance in the war of independence, not only because of its strength, but from its being one of the strongholds on the paternal property of Bruce. When Sir Christopher Seton took shelter within its walls in 1306, it was under the hereditary governorship of Sir Gilbert de Carrick, a maternal ancestor of the Kennedies, Earls of Carrick. As is well known, Edward I. vowed the deepest revenge against Bruce, and all his supporters, for the slaughter of Comyn, and their subsequent appearance in arms against his authority. Sir Christopher was, in consequence, hotly pursued, and the castle invested by a strong body of English troops. The governor made a very impotent defence, and the castle, along with the gallant knight, fell into the hands of the enemy. Tytler, in his history of Scotland, states, on the authority of documents which he quotes, that the castle is "said to have been pusillanimously given up;" and it further appears from the evidence, under a commission of the Great Seal, appointed to inquire into the circumstance, that "the delivery of Sir Christopher de Seton to the English was imputed to Sir Gilbert de Carrick." The historian, however, is not altogether satisfied on the subject, as the charge cannot be established; and he seems to be even in doubt whether Sir Christopher had taken refuge in the Castle of Loch Doon or in that of Loch Urr, as conjectured in the Statistical Account. The remission to Sir Gilbert de Carrick, granted by Robert I., which is without date, but must have been obtained before 16th July 1309, for surrendering Loch Doon to the English, and restoring him to his former possessions and office, he at the same time admits, fully proves the delivery of the castle into the hands of the English, at the period alluded to, by Sir Gilbert de Carrick—which is an important fact, strongly corroborative of the capture of Sir Christopher de Seton at Loch Doon— if not of the imputation against its keeper. The circumstance is not without suspicion. Barbour, indeed, in his Life of Bruce, boldly affirms, what the historian appears to have overlooked, that Sir Christoper was actually betrayed; and that by a person of the name of MacNab. After describing the disasters which befel the monarch

* Loch Doon was anciently called Loch Balloch. How its name came to be changed is unknown. As "dun," in Celtic, signifies a fort, it may have been called Loch-Dun, or the Loch of the Fort, after the erection of the castle.

in his flight from Methven, and detailing the cruelties exercised by Edward upon such of his coadjutors as fell into his power, he says:

> " And worthy Crystall of Seyton
> In to London betresyt was,
> Throw a discipill of Judas,
> Macnab, a fals tratour, that ay
> Wes off his duelling nycht and day."

This account of the betrayal of Sir Christopher de Seton is confirmed by a tradition preserved in the neighbourhood of Loch Doon. A portion of the farm at the lower end of the Loch, called the Beoch, is yet known by the name of *Macnabston*, which is said to have been given to the "fals tratour," as the price of his treachery. The ruins of Macnabston house, we believe, are still visible. Macnab is represented by Barbour as one of the domestics of Sir Christopher. He

> " Wes off his duelling nycht and day."

Hence, in the opinion of the Poet, the blacker die of the "tratoury." Though Barbour is thus supported by tradition, it may be argued that the character of the hereditary keeper is in no respect affected by it. Perhaps not; but his pusill nim ous defence of the fort, coupled with the imputation or belief that he had delivered up Sir Christopher, are rather convincing proofs that he was not sakeless in the matter. Macnab may have been the mere tool of Sir Gilbert de Carrick, who, thinking the cause of Bruce hopeless, might be anxious to propitiate Edward; and, aware of the price set on the brave Seton's head, he could not have hit on a more effectual mode of doing so. But, be this as it may, the tradition gives the highest countenance to the fact that Sir Christopher de Seton took refuge at Loch Doon, and not in the Castle of Urr. In whatever manner the betrayal was accomplished, it is clear that Macnab could only have held the lands awarded to him through the medium of the hereditary keeper, as any direct grant from the English would have been cancelled on their expulsion from the country. In the appendix to the "History of Galloway," another version of the tradition about Macnabston is given. It runs thus:—

"When the English, in 1319, besieged the Castle of Loch Doon, being unable to take it by storm, they raised an embankment of earth and stone, lined with raw hides, to prevent the water from oozing through the rampart, across the place where the lake discharges itself; hoping thereby to inundate the castle. The work was finished; and the water rising rapidly, one of the soldiers, named M'Nab, volunteered to destroy the caul; and being a good swimmer, he took the water at midnight, with a large 'bonnet sword' folded in his cap, with which he succeeded in cutting several large holes in the hides, through which the water rushed with such force, sweeping away everything in its course, that he was carried down in the current, and consequently lost his life in saving his companions; but in gratitude for the service he had rendered his country, a grant of land was conferred on his son, which bears the name of Macnabston to this day."

This improbable story is countenanced by tradition only in so far that it is said the Castle was upon one occasion—though assuredly not by the English in 1319, for they were not then in the country—attempted to be taken by damming back the lake; but the project failed, some of the *lanes* or feeders being lower than the level of the castle. The fiction, however, challenges itself. If the embankment had been composed of such solid material as "earth and stone," faced with raw hides, how could a few thrusts of a *bonnet sword* produce such an avalanche as to carry all before it, more especially as the swimmer by whom it was handled must have previously swam, or partially walked, picking his way amongst enemies, at least six miles—the castle being that distance from the foot of the loch! As described by Barbour, Sir Christopher Seton was cruelly put to death by his captors, not in London, but at Dumfries. The charge against him was not only rebellion, according to the definition of Edward, but of murder and desecration, having been present in the convent of Minorite Friars when Comyn was struck down by Bruce. He is alleged, by an English historian, to have slain a brother of Comyn; but this charge is not corroborated by any other writer. The character and prowess of Sir Christopher was so much esteemed by Bruce, that "he afterwards erected, on the spot where he was executed, a little chapel, where mass was said for his soul."

Loch Doon Castle was one of the five strongholds held during the minority of David I., when the friends of Baliol had so far succeeded, backed by the English, as to have all but subjected the kingdom wholly to their power. Its gallant defender was John Thomson, who, according to Tytler, is believed to have been the same person who led back the remains of the Scottish army from Ireland, after the death of Edward Bruce.

The castle is supposed to have been destroyed by fire in the reign of James V.,—about the same period that Kenmore, and other strongholds of the nobility in Galloway, were reduced—the policy of the monarch being to increase his own power by crippling that of the feudal barons. A portion of the roof, which seems to have been thrown over into the loch, is visible in clear calm weather. So is the iron portcullis. In attempting to carry the latter away during frost, the ice broke down under the immense weight, and it sank to the bottom, to the no small disappointment of the parties, who had calculated on a valuable prize.

The only other remain of feudal greatness in

the parish, is *Keirs Castle*, the residence at one time of the Shaws. It stands prominently on the brow of a ravine, about half way up the rising ground from the valley of the Doon. It is wholly in ruins—but enough remains to show that it had been a house of considerable size and strength. In Abercrummie's time, the only resident gentry in the parish were "*Shaw of Keirs*, and *Shaw of Grimmet*, toward the water of Dun." At the castle there still flourishes a noble yew, which must have been planted many hundred years ago. The arms of the Shaws of Keirs, cut out in stone, and which had formerly graced the entrance of the castle, are preserved in the wall of the farmsteading which has been recently built in the immediate vicinity of the castle, partly, with the materials of the ruins.

The old *Castle of Blairquhan* has been superseded by the splendid mansion built by Sir David Hunter Blair, Bart. in 1824. Some of the windows and mouldings only are preserved in the kitchen court. The writer in the Statistical Account states that a considerable portion of it had been built in 1570, but that M'Whirter's Tower, concerning which a curious legend is given in Chambers' "Picture of Scotland," was some centuries older. According to Abercrummie, it must have been a magnificent building. "Next to it (Straiton)," he says, "is the great Castle of Blairquhan, the fyne building and huge bulk whereof, is a plain demonstration of the some time greatness of that family; which, besyde their possessions in Carrick, had large territories in Galloway. It is well provyded with wood, covered with planting of barren timber, and surrounded with large orchards." During the persecution a garrison was stationed at Blairquhan, consisting of one hundred foot soldiers and twenty horsemen. Four persons were shot at this period in the parish, one of whom, Thomas M'Haffie, has a tombstone erected to his memory in the churchyard.

Blairquhan was formerly in the parish of Kirkmichael, hence the statement of Abercrummie that "no gentry live heire (in Straiton parish) save Shaw of Keirs, and Shaw of Grimmet."

# FAMILIES IN THE PARISH OF STRAITON.

## SCHAWS OF KEIRS.

The Schaws of Keirs seem to have been originally designed of Halie, a property in Kyle-Stewart, the original stock from whence appear to have sprung the various families of Schaw in Ayrshire. The first of them is supposed to have been

*William Shaw*, who is a witness to a charter by "*Jacobus Seneschallus Scotiæ*" to the Monastery of Paisley, in 1291. The same party, it may be presumed, is styled *Willielmus de Schaw* in the Ragman Roll. "*Willielmo dicto del Schaw*, pro homagio et servitio," had a charter from James the Steward of Scotland, of the lands of which Hayley, Wardlaw, and Drumchaber, in this county, the date of which must have been before 1309, when the granter died.

*John Shaw of Hayley* entered into an indenture with Sir Allan Cathcart anent the wadset of certain lands, in 1407.

*John Schaw of Hale* had a royal charter of confirmation of the lands of "Marselmerk et de Knapbyrney, Mulenath et de Lethanys," 31st May 1446. *Andrew Schaw*, son of Haylie, was infeft, under the Great Seal, in the lands of Sornbeg, Polkemmet, Whitburn, &c., 21st May 1447;[*] and *William Schaw of Polkemmet*, and his spouse, Margaret Campbell, had a charter of the lands of Snowdane, Hirst and Dalloy, from James IV., dated 1st November 1491; and another of Sornbeg, 15th June 1490.

*John Schaw of Haylie*, in 1469, was conjoined in an embassy to Denmark, along with several parties of distinction, to treat of a marriage between James III. and a daughter of Christiern

---

[*] See parish of Galston, where some account of the Sornbeg Schaws is given.

of Denmark. This Laird of Halie must have been succeeded by another,

*John Schaw of Halie*, probably his son. April 11, 1576:—"Johne Schaw of Halie," gives "heretabile stait and sasing to Gilbert Schaw, his sone, personalie present, of all and haill his xxxiii s. iiij d. worth of land of Cruikis, of auld extent, occupiit be Johne Vaus, &c., liand within the baillerie of Kyle Stewart, &c., to be holden of the said Johne Schaw, his airis and successouris, in fre blanche, for payment zeirlie of ane penny," &c. The witnesses to this deed were "Johne Schaw, younger, of Haly, David Schaw, brother to the said Johne Schaw, elder, and John Schaw, his servand."[*]

The first time the name occurs in connection with the property of Keirs, occurs in the same year. When "George M'Ilmorrow in Kerris, as Baillie of Carrik in that part," gave sasine of certain property, "David Schaw, sone to Johne Schaw of Haly," was one of the witnesses.[†]

John Schaw, younger of Halie, seems to have predeceased his father,

*David Schaw*, son of John Schaw of Halie, had a royal charter of the landis of Kerris, Dalvyne, Halie, &c., 26th March 1584. His elder brother, however, was alive in May 1582, when "Davidi Schaw, frater-germane Joannis Schaw de Haly," is witness to a sasine.[‡] Keirs was succeeded by his son,

*John Schaw of Keiris*, who was served heir of his father, David Schaw of Keiris, in the £10 land of Halie and Hielies, together with the mill; also the £5 land of Scalilour, 11th May 1608. He had previously been served heir in the £5 land of Dawyne, and £10 land of Keiris.

*John Schaw of Keirs* was served heir of John Schaw of Keiris, his great-grandfather, in the lands of Camlarg, &c., 1st February 1623. He and his spouse had a royal charter of the lands of Keiris, &c., 23d April 1623. He appears to have been alive in 1651. His sons, if he had any, seem to have predeceased him, for

*William Schaw of Keiris* was served heir to his uncle, John Schaw of Keirs, 15th August 1671. He appears to have been alive in 1729, when Anthony Schaw, brother-german to the Laird of Keirs, is mentioned in the resignation of the lands of Clongall by Hew Schaw of Clongall, eldest son of the deceased Anthony.[§] Hew Schaw's mother was the only daughter of Hew Kennedy, Provost of Ayr, and he was the nephew and nearest of kin to the deceased Alexander Kennedy of Clongall, in which property he had been infeft in December 1691.[*]

Part of the property of Keirs had been some time previously alienated, as we find the £10 land of Keirs in the service of John Binning of Dalvenan, March 19, 1672. It has since passed through various hands, and at present is held in nearly equal proportions by the Marquis of Ailsa, the Hon. Col. M'Adam Cathcart, Sir David Hunter Blair, Bart., &c. The Castle of Keirs has long been in ruins.

## SCHAWS OF GRIMMET.

This family was a cadet of the Schaws of Halie and Keirs. Part of the lands of Grimmet belonged to the M'Ilvanes. The first of the Schaws we find mentioned in connection with the property was

*Quintin Schaw of Grimmet*, who had a royal charter of the lands of Carsilloch and Calloptis, 24th May 1558. He appears to have been succeeded by

*Quintin Schaw*, who, in a Crown charter of Over-Grymmet, 19th August 1618, is styled "*nunc de Grymmet*." He was served heir to Quintin Schaw of Grymmet, his great-grandfather, 17th August 1622. In another charter, to him and his son, John Schaw, of the lands of Dalwyne, &c., 23d April 1623, he is designed "Quintino Schaw, mercatori, apud Straitoun," from which it would appear that he had carried on merchandise at Straiton. His son,

*John Schaw of Dalwyne*, was served heir to his father, 1st February 1625. He had a Crown charter of the six merk lands of Grimet, 3d December 1628. He was served heir to his father in the lands of Nether Grumet, 28th Aug. 1630. He was succeeded by

*Quintin Schaw of Grimmet*, who, togetherwith the heirs of his late brother, *David*, is mentioned in the will of "Mr Gavine Stewart, lait minister at Dalmellingtone," who died in November 1646. He was succeeded by

*John Schaw of Grimmet*, whose name occurs as a witness to the latterwill of Mr Robert Spreule, minister at Dalrymple in 1660.

Among the other branches of the Halie family were the *Schaws of Keirhill*. Alexander Schaw of Keirhill died in September 1625. His latterwill and inventary were "faithfullie maid and gevin vp be Margaret Stewart, his spous, in name and behalf of Elizabeth and Eister Schawis,

---

* Masoun's Notarial Book.
† Ibid.                          ‡ Ibid.
§ Ayr Records.

* Ayr Records.

bairnes lauchfull to the defunct, and executouris datives, dewlie decernit be decreit," &c.

There were also the *Schawis of Dunassine*. *John Schaw of Dunassine* had sasine of the muir of Laights, with coal and other mines, on a feu charter and disposition from William Logan of Camlarg, 28th April 1752

### KENNEDIES OF BLAIRQUHAN.

The first of the Kennedies of Blairquhan was

I. JOHN KENNEDY, fourth son of Sir Gilbert Kennedy of Dunure. On the 2d July 1444, Sir John Kennedy of Blairquhan, and John Kennedy, his son, grant a bond of maanrent to Sir Gilbert Kennedy, his nephew. He had another son, Thomas Kennedy of Carslo, Coroner of Carrick,[*] which office he disponed to his son, Thomas Kennedy of Craigfyn, in 1513.

II. Sir John Kennedy, son and apparent heir of John Kennedy of Blairquhan, infefts Margaret Campbell, his second wife, in lands in Galloway, 27th June 1500.

III. Gavin Kennedy of Blairquhan infefts John, his brother, (consanguinian) in the lands of Skeith, &c., 26th September 1505.

IV. James Kennedy of Blairquhan enters into a contract with the Earl of Cassillis relative to certain lands, dated 28th May 1528. This is the James Kennedy of Blairquhan called in the Cassillis entail of 1540. He was succeeded by his son,

V. John Kennedy of Blairquhan.

VI. John Kennedy of Blairquhan was served heir to his father, John Kennedy, 3d May 1608. His name occurs in the testament of Davidson of Pennyglen, in 1614.

VII. John Kennedy of Blairquhan was served heir to his father and grandfather, 7th September 1620. He sold the estate of Blairquhan, about 1622, to James Kennedy of Culzean, eldest son of Sir Thomas Kennedy of Culzean.

The estate of Blairquhan, however, was apprised from James Kennedy, in 1623, by John Gilmour, W.S., who disponed it to William MacAdam of Waterhead, and Humphry Dowie, who afterwards disponed it to Adam Whitefoord in Trochrigg, and he to John Whiteford, who got John Kennedy, a descendant of the old family of Blairquhan, to make up a title and convey the estate to him.

The old family of Blairquhan, however, not

only continued to be designed of Blairquhan, but held the property, in defiance of the various legal transfers of it. In 1645, *John* and *Hew Kennedy*, sons to the *Laird of Blairquhan*, were favourable to Montrose, and are cited in the Presbytery books to underly the censures of the church.

In 1648, the town of Ayr agreed to pay "*John Kennedy*, son of *umquhile Laird of Blairquhan*, 2000 merks, in satisfaction to him and others for their richt to the teinds of the parish of Air."[*] This would probably be the John Kennedy who made up the title and conveyed the estate of Blairquhan to John Whiteford.

The attempt to eject the Kennedies of Blairquhan led to a feud between them and the Whitefoords; and it is supposed that the old house of Drummellan was destroyed by fire by the adherents of Blairquhan, the Kennedies of Drummellan having taken part with the Whitefoords, the two families being connected by marriage.

James Kennedy of Blairquhan, of the Culzean family, was served heir of his father, James Kennedy of Blairquhan, 12th October 1637.

"Anna Steuart, Lady Blaehquhan," died in 1661. Her testament, &c., was "ffaithfullie maid and gevin vp be *Katherin Kennedy*, dochter lauchfull to the defunct, and executrix-dative," &c. "Inventar.—Item, the defunct being ane old woman the tyme of hir deceis foirsaid, had no other goods, &c., except allenarly the soume of sextein hundreth merks Scots money, addetit to hir be Johne Whitefoord of Balloch, conform to his band, &c., dait xxv day of May 1661 zeiris. Confirmed 28th October 1661. Mr Alexr. Kennedy, brother-german to the said Katherin Kennedy, cautioner to her."

This "Anna Steuart, Lady Blachquhan," was not of the old race of Blairquhan, but the wife of James Kennedy, eldest son of Sir Thomas Kennedy of Culzean, who sold Culzean to his brother, as already stated, and acquired the estate of Blairquhan.

### WHITEFOORDS OF BLAIRQUHAN.

The Whitefoords were an ancient Renfrewshire family.

*Walter de Whytfoord* is witness to a charter by Alexander II. He was probably the same Walter who obtained the lands of Whitefoord from the Stewart of Scotland for his services at the battle of Largs, in 1263.

*John Whitefoord of that Ilk*, who died in the reign of King James I. His son,

---

* This appears from a charter amongst the Ailsa papers, dated in 1398.

* Ayr Records.

*Patrick Whitefoord of that Ilk* obtained from the King a confirmation of the lands, upon the resignation of John Whitefoord of that Ilk, his father, in 1431. His son,

*John Whitefoord of that Ilk*, was father of

*Quintine Whitefoord of that Ilk*, who had sasine of the lands of Whitefoord in 1507. He was father of

*Adam Whitefoord of that Ilk*, served heir to his father in 1519. His son,

*John Whiteofoord of that Ilk*, lived in the reign of Queen Mary. He married Margaret, daughter of Robert Lord Semple. His son,

*John Whitefoord of that Ilk and Miltoun*, who lived in the reign of James VI. He had been twice married, first to Elizabeth Lindsay;* and secondly, to Elizabeth Houston,† daughter of Houston of that Ilk, but died without issue in 1606. He and John Sempill of Beltrees were put to the torture by the Regent Morton in 1577, in reference to an alleged conspiracy on the part of the Duke of Hamilton's party. His estate devolved upon

*Adam Whiteefoord of Milntoun*, his brother.‡ " Adami, filio Joannis Whytfurd de Eodem," had a charter of the lands of Whytfurd, 24th June 1579. Adam married a daughter of Sir James Somerville of Cambusnethan, by whom he had two sons:

1. James, his successor.
2. Dr Walter Whiteoford, sometime Dean of Glasgow, Parson of Moffat in 1635, and afterwards elevated to the Episcopal see of Brechin, where he continued till 1638, when he was deprived of his benefice by the Assembly of Glasgow. He was forced to retire to England, where he died in 1643. He appears, from the Commissary Records, to have married a daughter of Hew Ritchie in Knockindaill, parish of Symington. Nisbet says he married a daughter of Sir John Carmichael of that Ilk, and had a son, Colonel Walter Whiteofoord, who had to fly to Holland on account of his loyalty. While there he killed Dorislaus, the Dutch lawyer, who drew up the indictment against Charles I.

*James Whiteofoord of Whiteofoord and Milntoun*, who succeeded, appears to have been the father of

*Sir John Whiteofoord of Whiteofoord and Miltoun*, who, according to Nisbet, died without issue in 1689, and with whom ended the principal stem of the family. He, however, had a daughter, who may have predeceased him. From the Criminal Records, January 1674, it appears that

---

* John Quhytefuird of that Ilk and Elizabeth Lindsay, his lady, resigned the half of Danielston, 2d March 1591.
† "Bessie Houstoun, Lady Quhytfuird," was alive in 1617, in which year she occurs, with "Wm. Ros, her spous," as creditors "of ferme for ye crop 1616," in the testament of Kathrain King in Quhytfuird."
‡ Nisbet says he was succeeded by his brother John, but this is evidently a mistake.

Sir John Whytefoord presented a petition against Robert Forrest, Margaret Scot, and Janet Young, his servants, prisoners in the tolbooth of Lanark, who, while he and his lady were from home, carried away *Agnes Quhytfoord*, their daughter, under cloud of night, and detained her by violence for several days, until she was recovered by warrant of the Sheriff Depute. As farther stated in the petition, they broke up a cabinet, and took away four or five thousand merks. Forrest had also counterfeited Sir John's hand, and given discharges to his tenantry and other debtors.*

The lands of Whiteofoord, as well as those of Miltoun, ultimately passed from the family—the former to the Earl of Dundonald, and the latter to Sir John Hamilton of Hallcraig, one of the Senators of the College of Justice.

"The eldest branch of the family," says Nisbet, " is Whiteofoord of Blairquhan, in Ayrshire, descended of a younger son of Whiteofoord of that Ilk and Miltoun, who took up his residence in Ayrshire with his brother, who was Abbot of Crossraguel in the reign of James IV."

At the beginning of last century there were several families of the name of Whiteofoord in Carrick. *Adam Whiteofoord* in Trochrigg, about 1622; *John Whiteofoord*, in Maybole, who had a Crown charter of the lands of Kirkland, 24th March 1632, and of the lands of Balmaclanachan, 27th July of the same year. There was also *John Whiteofoord* in *Balloch*, who had a Crown charter of the lands of Girvan, 27th March 1621. The latter seems to have been the purchaser of Blairquhan. The oldest we have met with, however, is

*David Whytefurd*, who married, in 1852, a daughter of Gilbert Kennedy of Drummellan, and who was probably the common ancestor of the Carrick Whiteofoords.

*David Whytefurde in Balloch* succeeded his father, *David, in Balloch*, and was served heir to him in the 20s. lands of Devochty, and the 20s. lands of Garleffin, 30th April 1605. He appears to have died without issue, and was succeeded by his brother,

*John Whytefurde in Balloch*, who was served, as his heir, in the three and a half merk lands of Dallamfuird, 29th July 1620. He acquired the lands of Girvan in 1621. He was evidently the same party who bought the lands of Kirkland, and is designed as living in Maybole in 1632; for, although John Whiteofoord bought the lands of Blairquhan, about 1622, we have seen that he did not get possession of that property until a much later period, and may, con-

---

* MS. Books of Adjournal, Register Office.

sequently, have taken up his abode in Maybole during the tedious process of ejecting the Kennedies from Blairquhan. He is mentioned in the Presbytery Books, in connection with the church of Straiton in 1643.

*John Whytefurde of Balloch* was served heir of John Whytefurde of Balloch, his uncle, in the lands and barony of Blairquhan, 4th February 1664. John Whytefoord of Blairquhan, the same individual, we presume, had a charter of the lands of Dalhowan, 25th March 1686; also of the lands of Machrimore, 16th March 1688. His son,

*Adam Whytfoord of Blairquhan* had a Baronetcy conferred upon him by Diploma, 30th December 1701. Nisbet states that Sir Adam disponed to his brother, *Bryce Whiteffoord*, the lands of Dunduff and Cloncaird. Dunduff, however, had previously belonged to a branch of the family, for we find *George Whiteffoord of Dunduff*, giving a charter of resignation of the lands and barony of Whytfoord, 10th April 1702, from which it might be inferred that George Dunduff was the representative of the family. This may have been the case, though devolving soon afterwards upon the Blairquhan branch. Sir Adam of Blairquhan is mentioned in the Presbytery Records as soliciting a seat in Straiton kirk for his family. He married Margaret, only daughter of Allan Lord Cathcart. Captain John Whiteford, younger, of Blairquhan, was admitted a burgess of Ayr in 1723. Sir Adam died in 1728, on the 2d February of which year the Town Council of Ayr ordain " the representatives of Sir Adam Whiteford of Blairquhan to pay two dollars, or what more they may think fit to give, for the privilege of having the bells rung at the transportation of the corps of the said Sir Adam Whiteford, from his lodgings to the New Church of Ayr." Sir Adam was succeeded by his son.[*]

*Sir John Whiteford*, who assumed the family designation, *of that Ilk*. In 1732 (26th July) Sir John, with consent of his lady, gave a charter of resignation of the lands of Bishopland. Sir John, Major-General in the army, gave a charter of resignation of one-half of the barony of Whiteford, commonly called Blairquhan, 23d Feb. 1758. " Margaret and Alice Whiteffoords, daughters to Sir John Whiteford of that Ilk, and Dame Allice Muir, baptized 3d May 1730. Witnesses Capt. John Dalrymple, son to Sir Hugh Dalrymple, Lord President of the

Session, Thomas Garven of Cambuscescan," &c.[*] He was succeeded by his son,

*Sir John Whiteford of that Ilk*,[†] better known probably, as Sir John Whiteford of Ballochmyle, which property had been acquired from the Reids of Ballochmyle by his uncle, *Allan Whiteffoord of Ballochmyle*, about the middle of last century. This Allan was of the Ballochtoull, or Girvan branch of the family. " Mri. Alani Whyteffoord de Ballochtoull, armigeri, Receptoris Generalis Regis Subsidii terracie in Scotiæ, terrarum et tenandrie de Ballochtoull et Air, 29th Nov. 1739." This was, we should suppose, the Allan Whiteffoord who was taken prisoner by the Highlanders at Prestonpans, and whose story has been so well interwoven in *Waverley*. Sir John Whiteford of Ballochmyle was the friend and patron of Burns; and his eldest daughter, Mrs Cranston, was the subject of the Poet's " Farewell the Braes o' Ballochmyle," which property was disposed of in 1786, Sir John having been ruined by his connection with the Douglas and Heron Bank. Blairquhan, about the same time also, was alienated to the curators of the present proprietor, Sir David Hunter Blair, Baronet.

*Arms*—Argent, a bend betwixt two cottises, sable, with a garb in chief of the last.

*Crest*—A pigeon, proper, on the top of a garb.

*Motto*—" D'en haut."

## HUNTER BLAIRS OF BLAIRQUHAN.

This family is descended paternally from the ancient house of Hunter of Hunterstoun, and maternally from the noble houses of Glencairn and Cassillis. Cadets of the principal families of the county were to be found located as burgesses of Ayr, and from their superior means, were usually the most enterprising amongst the traders of the burgh. The Hunters of Milnholm, afterwards of Brounehill, ancestors of Sir David Hunter Blair, were of the Abbothill branch of the Hunters of Hunterston; but the first of them must have been earlier than *John Hunter of Milnholm*, who was born 11th August 1702, as stated in Robertson, and at page 204, vol. i. of this work,

---

[*] He had also another son, David, born 1st January 1708.—AYR PAR. REC.

[*] Ayr Session Records.

[†] On the 2d June 1758, " John Whiteffoord, junior, of that Ilk, Coronet in the horse regiment commanded by Lieut.-General Colmondly," had sasine of the lands of Glenstincher, comprehending South Balloch, &c., on a precept from Chancery, 23d February 1758. He disponed of them to his father, Sir John, who had sasine of them, 2d June 1758.

for we find that *William Hunter of Milnholm*, and *Elizabeth Coltron*, his wife, had a daughter, *Agnes*, baptized 17th February 1714.* This William, we should think, must have been descended thus:

I. ADAM HUNTER, in Abbotshill, was twice married; first, to Marion Blair, and secondly, to Janet Wallace, daughter of Wallace of Mainholm and Woodhead. By his second marriage he had several children, as well as by his first.

II. William Hunter of Milnholm and Milnquarter (now Craigie House) may have been a son of this marriage, and obtained the lands of Milnholm from the Wallaces, through his mother. Mr Robert Wallace, son to Wallace of Holmstoun, witnesses the baptism of one of their family. William Hunter of Milnholm, and his wife, Elizabeth Coltron, had several children. Amongst others, we find the following baptisms recorded in the session books of Ayr:

1. Agnes, baptized 17th February 1714.
2. Thomas, son to William Hunter in Mainholm, merchant, and Elizabeth Coltron, baptized 23d May 1716.

III. John Hunter of Milnholm and Milnquarter, who married *Anne*, daughter, and one of the co-heiresses of "the deceased Mr William Cuninghame of Brounehill, advocate." Their marriage was celebrated on the 20th October 1798.

The first of this branch of the Cuninghames of Brounehill was

*William Cuninghame*, Provost of Ayr in 1664. He is so designed as witnessing the baptism of James Cuninghame, son to John Cuninghame, Dean of Guild, and Barbara Hunter, his spouse, on the 26th March of that year. He obtained the lands of Brounehill from Mr John Cuninghame of Lambruchton, afterwards of Caprington, 26th June 1667. The old Cuninghames of Brounehill were a branch of the Lagland family, cadets of the house of Glencairn. Though, as Nisbet asserts, Provost Cuninghame was descended from the Earls of Glencairn, the precise link is awanting. He was a merchant in Ayr, where there were several others of the same name. For example—"Agnes Cunynghame, daughter of William Cuninghame, merchant burgess of Ayr, and Jonet Ritchie, his spouse, was baptized 23th February 1666.—Witnesses, William Cuninghame, Provost, and Maister James Cunynghame, Sheriff-depute of Ayr." Who the Provost married does not appear. He, however, had a son,

*William Cuninghame*, younger of Brounehill, who was twice married; first to Giels Hamilton. Their eldest son and successor, William, was born in 1669. His baptism is thus recorded—"William Coningam, sone lauchfull to William Con-

ingam, younger of Brounehill, and Giels Hamilton, his spouse, born on Friday the 28th of May 1669, and baptized on Friday the 15th day of June.—Witnesses, the Earl of Eglintoun, William Earl of Dumfries, William Lord Cochrane, William Blair of Blair, and William Cuningam, grandfather to the said child." Their next son,

2. James, was baptized on the 3d September 1670.
3. John, baptized 19th January 1673.
4. Isobell, baptized 22d February 1674 (died young.)
5. Isobell, baptized 1st April 1675.

William Cuninghame of Brounehill married, secondly, in 1695, Dame Margaret Ramsay, relict of Sir John Lauder of Fountainhall. He was Provost of Ayr in 1670-1, and again in 1686-7. He was succeeded by his eldest son,

*William Cuninghame* of Brounehill, advocate, who married Elizabeth Hamilton, second daughter and co-heiress of Sir Archibald Hamilton of Rosehall, Bart., M.P. for the county of Lanark. By this marriage he had four daughters, *Anne*, *Frances*, *Elizabeth*, and *Margaret*, co-heiresses, the eldest of whom, as already stated, married John Hunter of Milnholm and Milnquarter. Mr Hunter died in 1755,* leaving two sons, *William* and *James*.

V. William Hunter of Brounehill, born in 1739. He entered the army in 1757, attained the rank of Lieutenant-Colonel, and died unmarried in 1792, bequeathing the estate of Brounehill to his nephew, *David*, and was succeeded by his brother,

VI. James Hunter of Robertland, born in 1740. He married, in 1770, Jane, eldest daughter and heir of John Blair of Dunskey, Esq., by Anne, sister and co-heiress of line (with her only sister, Lady Cathcart) of David, tenth Earl of Cassillis, upon which occasion he assumed the name of Blair in addition to his own. Mr Hunter Blair was some time Lord Provost of Edinburgh, and represented the city in Parliament. As one of the partners of the eminent banking establishment of Sir William Forbes and Company, he was well known and highly esteemed. He was created a Baronet 27th June 1786. By his marriage Sir James Hunter Blair had fourteen children:

1. John, his successor.
2. David, present Baronet.
3. James, who inherited the estates of Dunskey and Robertland. He was Lieutenant-Colonel of the Ayrshire Militia, and thrice M.P. for the county of Wigtoun. He died unmarried in 1822.
4. Robert, a Captain in the army, died unmarried in 1799.
5. Forbes, succeeded to the estates of his brother James; died unmarried in 1832.
6. Thomas, Major-General in the army, C.B., inheritor of the estates of his brother James. He was wounded and made prisoner at the battle of Talavera, and de-

* Ayr Records.

* His widow afterwards married Robert Hamilton of Bourtreehill.

tained in France until the peace of 1814. He was again wounded at Waterloo, in 1815; and subsequently promoted to the rank of Lieutenant-Colonel. He afterwards served as Brigadier-General in the Burmese war, in India. He married, in 1820, Eliza, daughter of J. Norris, Esq., and died 3d August 1849.

7. Archibald, died at sea, in the E.I. Co.'s service, 1798.
8. Henry Dundas, died in 1799.

1. Anne, married, in 1791, to William Muir of Caldwell, Esq., and has issue.
2. Clementina, married, in 1808, to Gen. Birch, Royal Engineers, and died 19th June 1844, leaving issue.
3. Jane, died unmarried in 1831.
4. Jemima.

Sir James was succeeded by his eldest son,

VI. Sir John Hunter Blair, Bart., who died unmarried in 1800. The title then devolved upon his next brother,

VII. Sir David Hunter Blair, Bart., of Blairquhan, who served as Colonel of the Ayrshire Militia during the war, and is now Convener and Vice-Lieutenant of the county. He married, first, 2d July 1813, Dorothea, second daughter of the late Edward Hay Mackenzie, Esq. of Newhall and Cromartie (brother of George, seventh Marquis of Tweeddale), by the Hon. Maria Murray M'Kenzie, eldest daughter of George, sixth Lord Elibank, by whom (who died 22d May 1820) he had issue:

1. James, born 22d March 1817, Captain and Lieut.-Colonel in the Fusileer Guards.
2. Edward, born 24th March 1818; 93d Highlanders.
3. Maria-Dorothea, married, in 1839, to Walter Elliot, Esq., younger of Wolflee.

Secondly, 15th January 1825, Elizabeth, second daughter of Sir John Hay, Bart. of Hayston, Peeblesshire, by Mary-Elizabeth, second daughter of James, sixteenth Lord Forbes, by whom he has issue:

1. John, born 18th October 1825.
2. David, born 22d January 1827.
3. William, born 18th January 1828.
4. Charles-Forbes, born 15th May 1829.
5. Archibald-Thomas, born 5th January 1832.
6. Henry-Arthur, born 18th June 1843.
1. Mary-Elizabeth.
2. Jane-Anne-Elizabeth.

*Arms*—Quarterly: 1st, argent, on a chevron, gules, between three bugles, vert, garnished, of the second, an annulet, or, for Hunter; 2d, argent, on a chevron, gules, between three crosscrosslets, fitchee, sable, three fleurs-di-lis, all within a double tressure, flory, counterflory, or, for Kennedy of Culzean; 3d, argent, on a saltier, sable, nine mascles of the field, and in chief, a star of eight points, gules, for Blair; 4th, argent, a shake-fork, sable, and in chief, a rose, gules, for Cuninghame of Brounehill.

*Supporters*—Dexter, a dog of chase, saliant, argent; sinister, an antelope, springing, proper, gorged with an open crown, and a chain hanging thereat.

*Crest*—A stag's head, caboshed, proper.
*Motto*—" Vigilantia, robur, voluptas."

*Seat*—Blairquhan Castle. This splendid mansion was finished in 1824. It is built in the architectural style of Henry the Seventh's time, and is altogether a magnificent building. The saloon, communicating with the principal apartments, is sixty feet in height. The porch is in the Tudor style. The castle is about a mile from Straiton village, and stands on the banks of the Girvan, occupying nearly the site of the old castle. The approach winds through the wooded and rocky banks of the river for nearly two miles and a-half, and enters by a handsome bridge and lodge. The situation is altogether delightful—the river gliding in front of the castle, and the hills of Craigengower and Benan forming a background, which, in their dark outlines, form a truly picturesque contrast to the variegated woods, the winding avenues, the green lawns, and rich gardens of Blairquhan.

### M'ADAMS OF CRAIGENGILLAN.

The M'Adams of Craigengillan were probably a branch of the Macadams of Waterhead, in the same parish. The first of them we have noticed was

*Williame M'Adame of Craigullane* (Craigengillan) who remained, by license, from the Raid of the Isles, under Lord Ochiltree, in 1611.

The family seems to have remained for some time in comparative obscurity. They are not noticed in any of the general or local records, nor yet by Abercrummie in his account of Carrick. " Quintin M'Adam, scribae, Edinburghi," had a Crown charter of the lands of Nether Grimmet, 23d February 1677. He was probably a descendant of John M'Adame, merchant in Edinburgh; and his spouse, Mariot Geichane, who had a Crown charter of the lands of Previck, 23d June 1607. The M'Adams of Grimmet were, at all events, related to the M'Adams of Craigengillan.

*James M'Adam of Craigengillan* is mentioned among the proprietors of Straiton parish in the Ayr Presbytery books, 27th October 1725.

*John M'Adam of Craigengillan*, to whom Burns addressed the verses quoted in the first volume (page 398), added extensively to the originally small property of Craigengillan. He acquired the two merk land of Upper Berbeth in 1757. It had previously belonged to a family of the name of Stevenson.* He acquired the lands of

* William Stevenson of Bairbeth had a child, Janet, baptized 8th October 1704.—SESSION RECORDS. He is

Over and Nether Leicht in 1758; and of Loch-
maharle, New Cumnock parish, in 1764, besides
various other properties at a later period. He
not only added to, but greatly improved the
estate. Mr M'Adam was succeeded by his son,
the "young Dunaskin's Laird" of Burns,

*Colonel M'Adam of Craigengillan,* whose only
surviving child, *Jane,* was married to the

*Hon. Col. Frederick M'Adam Cathcart,* now of
Craigengillan. Colonel F. M. Cathcart is the
second son of the late William Schaw, Earl Cathcart, a name and title assumed from the barony
of Kerkert, or Cathcart, in Renfrewshire. The
family can be traced from *Rainaldus de Kethcart,*
who witnesses a charter, in reference to the church
of Kethcart, in 1178. *Sir Alan Cathcart* was a
stout supporter of Robert the Bruce at the battle of Loudoun Hill. Barbour thus describes
him :

> " A Knight that then was in his rout,
> Worthy and wight, stalward and stout,
> Courteous and fair, and of good fame,
> Sir Alan Cathcart was his name."

The son of this Sir Alan inherited the baronies
of Dalmellington, Auchincruive, and Sundrum,
from his maternal uncle, Wallace of Auchincruive
and Sundrum, which properties continued in the
family until the latter half of last century. *Alan,
fifth Baron Cathcart,* died at Auchincruive in
August 1628. " Legacie.—At Auchincrue, the

mentioned as one of the proprietors of Straiton parish in
1772.

penult of Julij anno Jajvi₆ and twentie-aucht
zeiris.—The qlk day Allane Lord Cathcart maid
his testament as followis : Forsamekill as thair is
nothing moir certane nor daithe, I, Allane Lord
Cathcart, ffirst recommend my imortall sawll to
God, to be saved in the immaculat Lamb of
J. C. Nixt, I direct this my mortall bodie to
be bureit in the sepulchir of my progenitours.
Thridlie, in respect of ye assurance I have that
my loveing spous, Dame Jeane Colquhoun, will
have singular cair, as a loving mother, to ye educatioune of our zoung sone, the appeirand air
and hope of my hous, I leive her onlie tutrix and
administratrix unto him. And last of all, I leif
hir onlie executrix and intromissatrix with my
guids and geir, to be used at hir pleasour. This
my testament and latter-will, writtin be Andro,
Bischop of Argyll, at Auchincrue, the penult day
of July Jaivie and twentie-aucht zeiris." The
" hope of the house," who was born the same
year that his father died, became sixth Baron
Cathcart, and died at the age of eighty. *Charles,*
eighth Baron Cathcart, was distinguished as a
military officer, as most of his descendants have
also been. The present Earl, elder brother of
Colonel F. M. Cathcart of Craigengillan, has
recently been appointed Governor of the Cape of
Good Hope.

[We have thought it unnecessary to give a
genealogical detail of the Cathcart family, as it
is to be found at length in the Peerages.]

# PARISH OF SYMINGTON.

SYMON LOCCARD is known to have held the lands of Symington as early as the reign of William the Lion, and from him they are understood to have derived the name of *Symonstoun*, now called Symington. In the same way the parish of Stevenston derived its name from *Stephen* Loccard, a branch, no doubt, of the same family. The parish is about four miles in length, and one-and-a-fourth broad. It is bounded on the north by Dundonald parish; on the east by Riccarton; on the south by Craigie; and on the west by Monkton.

The topographical appearance of the parish is varied, and from several eminences commands excellent views of the Clyde. The soil is generally clayey, on a hard subsoil, and there is no natural wooding to give warmth and shelter to the land. Several belts and clumps of trees, however, have been planted by the proprietors, especially in the vicinity of Dankeith and Rosemount, the lands of which were greatly improved by their respective owners many years ago. As early as 1740 young plantations were springing up around Dankeith, the then proprietor of which was the first to use compost in dressing his fields, as well as to introduce ryegrass in the district. Thirty years afterwards, the example was followed on the estate of Rosemount. Dr Fullertoun, who returned about 1770 from India, set about improving the property, by building a new mansion, planting timber, and cultivating the lands in a style greatly beyond his compeers, and which still distinguishes the lands. There is plenty of good spring water in the parish, but no streams or lochs of any extent, save an artificial sheet of water at Cowdam house.

## HISTORY, CIVIL AND ECCLESIASTICAL.

Symington village, or the *town of Symon*, has an antiquated and somewhat romantic appearance. The site, too, was well chosen in reference to the quality of the soil, which rests upon rotten-rock, and is of a light, dry nature. The church is old—the period of its erection being unknown; and a few large, venerable trees, surrounding the churchyard and village, convey rather a favourable impression of the site of *Symonstoun*.

There are few historical memorials connected with the parish. At the earliest dawn of our mutilated national records Symontoun was held under Walter the first Stewart, by Symon Loccard, in 1165. The same Symon also held a manor in Lanarkshire, which obtained the same name—*Symonstoun*. He was ancestor of the Lockharts of Lee. His son, Malcolm Loccard, who succeeded him in both his Lanarkshire and Ayrshire properties, granted to the monks of Paisley, in pure alms, for the salvation of the soul of Walter, the son of Alan, six acres of land, ' in villa Symonis de Kyil.' " The church of Symonstoun was granted to the convent, which was founded at Feil, or Faile, in Kyle, during the year 1252; and it continued to belong to that convent till the Reformation. The cure was served by a vicar pensioner, who had a settled income and a glebe; and the minister and brothers of Fail enjoyed the remainder of the tithes and revenues. In Bagimont's Roll, as it stood in the reign of James

V., the vicarage of Symonstoun, in the deanery of Kyle, was taxed £2, 13s. 4d., being a tenth of its estimated value. After the Reformation the patronage of the church of Symontoun passed through several hands, and was at length acquired by the Earl of Eglintoun,"* in whose family it still remains.

The church underwent a thorough repair about the middle of last century, and again in 1797, when an addition was made to it. The manse was built about 1786.

We know not when the lands of Symonstoun passed from the Loccards; but they seem to have been at an early period in the hands of the Wallaces. On the 21st Feb. 1581-2, "Johnne Lindsay in Symontoun, as baillie in that part to Hew Wallace of Carnell and Robert Wallace, his sone and apperand air," gave "stait and sasing of lifrent to Thomas Masoun, actornay for Jonet Campbell, Lady Barskemming," of the five lib. land of Fowtoun, and four lib. land of Symontoun, liand within the baillerie of Kyle Stewart," &c. Again, "Feb. 18, 1583-84.— The quhilk day, Johne Wallace of Cragy past to the landis vndirwrittin, viz. the lands of Goldring (Rosemount), Instelsyd and Cruiksyd, extending to iij lib. land; the x lib. land of Prestuikshawis, with milne thereof; the v lib. land of Symontoun, and v lib. land of Helentoun, liand within the baillierie of Kylestewart, &c., and thare, with his awin hand, gaif heretabill stait and sasing of the saidis landis to Johne Wallace in Burnbank, as actornay for Johne Wallace, sone and apperand air to the said John Wallace of Cragy, haldand of the said John and his airis in fre blanche," &c.

There was, it seems, a property called the Trinity lands of Symontoun, no doubt belonging originally to the church. "March 9, 1584-85.— Hew Wallace in Dundonnald grantit him to haif ressauit fra Adam Wallace in Hilhous, the sowme of lxx merkis money of this realme, in lauchfull redemptioun of the said Adamis landis, callit the Trinitie landis of Symontoun, liand," &c.*

*Antiquities.*—" This parish," says the *Statistical Account*, "can scarcely boast of any antiquities. Formerly there was a round mound called the Law-hill, at the foot of the village, partly natural and partly artificial, when the proprietor, Mr Boyd, in improving his land, caused the Law-hill to be levelled with the adjacent field. Those employed in doing so, found at no great depth from the surface, several arrow-heads, made of iron, most of them barbed, and very rudely constructed. They also found combs made of horn, in a pretty good state of preservation. . . . . . There is also an eminence near Helenton, called the Mote-hill, upon which a ruin stands; but of which tradition takes no notice." The Law-hill here mentioned was no doubt the seat of judgment for the barony of Symontoun; and the Mote-hill that of Helenton.

The heritors of the parish of Symington in 1734 were—William Kelso of Dankeith; Adam Baird of Cowdam; Alexander Cunningham, Bailie in Kilmarnock, for Mr Findlay of Waxfoord; George Boyd of Townend of Symington; and James Boyd of Kerrix.

## FAMILIES IN THE PARISH OF SYMINGTON.

### CUNINGHAMES OF DANKEITH.

This property was of old frequently spelled *Dalkeyth*. The Cuninghames were a branch of the Caprington family. The first of them was *Daniel Cuninghame*, son of William Cuning-

hame of Caprington. He appears repeatedly in the local records, though unnoticed in the genealogies of the Caprington family. His relationship is distinctly stated in the following extract from the *Notarial Book* of John Masoun, Town Clerk of Ayr:—" Mercij (April) 28,

* Chalmers's Caledonia.                    * Masoun's Notarial Book.

1595.—The quhilk day, &c. Johnne M'Cra, ane of the servandis and officeris of the shirrefdome of Air, past, at the desire of William Mure, fear of Middiltoun, in name and behalf [of Daniel] Cuninghame of Dalkeyth, sone lauchfull [to vmquhile] Williame Cuninghame of Capringtoun, assignay vnder mentionat, past to the mercat croce of the burgh of Air, and thair, be opin proclamacioun, maid dew and lauchfull intimatioun to all and sundrie our souerane lordis liegis, that Annabell Cuninghame, dochtir to the said vmquhile Williame Cuninghame of Caprintoun, had lauchfullie maid and constitute the said Daniel Cuninghame, hir brother, his airis and assignais, hir veray lauchfull, vndoutit and irreuocable cessionaris and assignayis, in and to the sowme of auchtene hundreth merkis money of this realme, contenit in thrie seueral reuersionis maid and grantit be hir to Williame Cuninghame, now of Caprintoun, hir broder, for redemption of the xl s. land of Dolquhoyis, xl s. land of the Mainis of Cumnok, with the corne milne thairof, thirle, multure and sukin of the sammin, lyand within Kingis Kyle, &c. And in and to all and sundrie vther guidis, geir and sowmes of money pertening, or that may appertene to hir ony maner of way, during hir lyftyme. As als that the said Annabell had oblist hir and hir airis to renunce and owergif the said Daniellis xl s. land of the Kirkland of Symontoun, quharin scho wes infeft be him vnder reuersioun, contening the sowme of tuelf hundreth merkis, with the byrun proffeitis thairof, how sone sebe or hir airis wer requirit thairto, vpoun thrie dayis warning, as in the letter of assignation maid be hir to the said Daniell thairvpoun, of the dait, at Colisfeild, the ferd day of Februar, the zeir of God Imvc. foirscoir tuelf zeris [1592], contening speciall reseruacioun and prouisioun, that incais of the said Annabellis marriage with ane husband, hir said assignatioun to be null and without reseruatioun, siclik to hir of the malis and dewiteis," &c.

The same Daniel Cuninghame of Dalkeyth occurs again in Masoun's notes, as having, " in the queir of the Kirk of Air," 1st June 1598, presented to the Moderator of the Presbytery " our souerane lordis presentacioun " of Mr Johne Cuninghame to the vicarage of Symontoun. William Wallace, minister of Failfurd, also presented the King's letters in favour of Mr William Wallace to the same vicarage. Both parties took instruments, &c.

" Danieli Cuninghame de Dankeyth, et Mariotæ Wallace, ejus conjugi," had a Crown charter of the lands of Clasens, 25th January 1606. Daniel Cuninghame of Dankeith was alive in 1612, in which year his son, Daniel, is mentioned

as a witness to the testament of Jonet Boyde, spouse to David Hardie, Symontoun. He must have died soon afterwards, however, for

Daniel Cuninghame of Dankeith, and his son, William, occur in a testamentary document in 1613.

William Cuninghame of Dankeith is mentioned in another testamentary document in 1619, and again in 1623.

Johnne Conynghame of Dalkeyth occurs in the testament of Jonet Baird, in Staflour, in 1628. The next and last we meet with is

David Cuninghame of Dalkeith, mentioned in the Presbytery Records in 1642.

The lands of Dankeith appear in the service of Sir William Cuninghame of Caprington, 25th March 1685, and were acquired by the ancestor of the present proprietor in 1693.

## KELSOS OF DANKEITH.

The original designation of this family was Kelso of Kelsoland, in the parish of Largs, which property they finally alienated in 1671. The first of them, according to the continuator of Nisbet, was

I. HUGO DE KELSO, whose name occurs in the Ragman Roll, 1296, ancestor, as is supposed, of

II. Andrew de Kelcho, or Kelso, Prior of the Abbey of Paisley in 1328, who appears in a deed of submission to which he was a party.

III. John de Kelcho, dominus de Kelsoland, who, with consent of

IV. John de Kelso, his eldest son, and Elizabeth Livingstoun, his spouse, apparently of the house of Callendar, gave in donation the lands of Langley-Bank, lying betwixt Kelsoland and Largs, to the church of St Mary at Paisley, by a deed of mortification, dated 5th January 1403.

V. Thomas Kelso of Kelsoland succeeded his grandfather. In a charter of the lands of Kelsoland from James II., dated 4th September 1444, he is styled oye and heir of the late John Kelso of Kelsoland. He married a daughter of Boyle of Kelburne. He was succeeded by his son,

VI. John Kelso of Kelsoland, who married a daughter of William Stewart of Fynock, second son of William Stewart of Bute, and by her had

VII. Thomas Kelso of Kelsoland, designed, in a charter from James V., in 1521, " filius et hæres Joannis de Kelso de Kelsoland." His son and successor,

VIII. Thomas Kelso of Kelsoland, had sasine of the lands in 1536. He married a daughter of Frazer of Knock, and left a daughter, Giles, married to Hugh Cranfurd of Cloverhill, and a son,

IX Archibald Kelso of Kelsoland, who was served heir to his father, 10th November 1576 He married Margaret, daughter of James Stewart of Ardgowan and Blackball, by Janet, his wife, daughter of George Maxwell of Newark, and had issue:

1 David, his heir
2 William, whose son,
   Robert, repurchased Kelsoland in 1632, and continued the line of the family
3 Giles, married to John Stewart of Ascog, in Bute, and had a son, Ninian Stewart of Ascog, who married Janet, daughter of Sir Bryce Blair of that Ilk, and a daughter, the wife of Fullarton of Greenhall

The elder son,

X David Kelso of Kelsoland, was served heir to his father 2d November 1601 He married his cousin, Elizabeth, daughter of James Stewart, tutor of Blackhall, second son of James Stewart of Ardgowan His name repeatedly occurs in testamentary documents from 1603 downwards He is said by Robertson and Burke to have been succeeded by his son, Archibald, who died without issue, but this was not the case, for the son predeceased him "Archibald Kelso, zounger, of Kelsoland,' died in April 1613 He left a daughter, Elspeth Kelso, by his wife, Sara Brisbane, who subsequently married Sir William Mure of Rowallan Archibald Kelso is said by Robertson and Burke to have been succeeded by his brother,

XI Robert Kelso of Kelsoland, in 1613, and that he also had no issue. This, however, does not appear to have been the case, for "Henrie Kelso, sone to ye Laird of Kelso," is mentioned in a testamentary document in 1614 He may at the same time have died young Robert Kelso is said to have sold Kelsoland in 1624 to Patrick Schaw (second son of John Schaw of Greenock) and that it was repurchased in 1632 by Robert Kelso of Halrig This statement, however, is to a certain extent inaccurate, for we find

XII David Kelso of Kelsoland mentioned in the testament of John Kyle, in Kelsoland-milns, as his maister, in 1619 David Kelso, sometime of Kelsoland, occurs in the testament of Kathrein Wode, Largs, in 1630 It is therefore evident that it was David, and not Robert, who sold the lands in 1624

XIII. Robert Kelso of Halrig, who repurchased Kelsoland, was the grandson of Archibald Kelso of Kelsoland. He married, in 1639, Jean, daughter of John Osborne, Provost of Ayr, and commissioner for the burgh to Parliament in 1644 By this marriage he had two sons, John and William

XIV. John Kelso of Kelsoland succeeded his father. He sold the old family estates, in 1671, to James Brisbane of Bishopton, who altered the name to Brisbane. Mr Kelso, who enjoyed, until his demise, the office of collector and sole surveyor of the Customs of Port-Glasgow, married Mary, daughter of the Rev Archibald Hamilton, minister of Wigton, brother of James, first Viscount Claneboye, and son of the Rev Hans Hamilton, vicar of Dunlop, and had,

1 Robert, who was Captain of an Indiaman in the merchant service. He married Jane Oakley, widow of Captain Norris, R N, and dying in 1752, left a daughter, Mary, and a son, John, of whom hereafter as inheritor of Dankeith
2 William

The second son,

XV William Kelso, WS, acquired, in 1693, the lands of Dankeith. He married Mary, daughter of John Dunlop of that Ilk, and had one son and two daughters —

1 William, his heir
2 Mary, who married Dr Macgill, an eminent physician in Edinburgh, and had a daughter married to Walter Stewart, Esq, who died without issue
3 Jean, who died unmarried

William Kelso was succeeded by his only son,

XVI. William Kelso of Dankeith He is frequently mentioned in the burgh records of Ayr, in connection with the property of Friar Dankeith On the 29th May 1725, "William Kelso of Dalkeith produced in Council a decreet of sale of the two merkland of Frier Dalkeith, alias Gilhead, lying within the parochin of Symington, Bailliery of Kyle Stewart, and Shirrefdom of Air, holding from the magistrates, obtained before the Lords of Council and Session, at the instance of the deceased William Kelso of Dalkeith, his father, against Hew-Archibald, eldest lawful son and appearand heir to the deceased Hew-Archibald of Dalkeith, and his tutors and curators, &c, dated in 1698, to which the said William had a right as heir of his father, and desired he might be entered and received vassal," &c. William Kelso died, unmarried, in 1763, and was succeeded by his sister, Mrs Macgill, at whose decease, in consequence of an entail, Dankeith passed to his cousin,

XVII. John Kelso, Captain in the 32d regiment of foot, son of Captain Robert Kelso, eldest son of John Kelso of Kelsolands. He married, 13th June 1758, Margaret, daughter of William Mowate, Provost of Aberdeen in 1754, and had issue

1 William, his heir
2 Robert, Major-General in the army, who married Miss Burtsell of Suffolk, and had a son, John Edward, of Horkesley Park, near Colchester, and two daughters, Margaret-Augusta and Louisa General Kelso

died at his residence at Bungay, in Suffolk, 13th October 1823.

3. John, an Ensign in the 51st regiment, deceased.

4. Millar, R.N., drowned in the river Ganges, near Calcutta.

5. Alexander Stuart, } both died in the West Indies.
6. Berrie.

7. Archibald, born 18th March 1771, who purchased the estate of Sauchrie. He married, in February 1806, Miss Macharg, daughter of Macharg of Keirs, and had issue:

    1. Archibald.

    2. Andrew-John.

    3. John.

    4. Cecilia-Margaret.

    5. Margaret-Georgiana, ⎫
    6. Jane,          ⎬ deceased.
    7. Elizabeth,    ⎭

8. George, Captain of an Indiaman, who married Miss Plumb, but died s. p.

9. Andrew, died unmarried.

    1. Jane.

    2. Frances, died unmarried

    3. Mary, married to the late Patrick Ballantyne, Esq. of Castlehill.

    4. Margaret, died unmarried.

    5. Charlotte-Christina.

Captain Kelso died in 1781, and was succeeded by his eldest son,

XVIII. William Kelso of Dankeith, Major of the 23d Light Dragoons, subsequently Colonel of the Ayrshire Militia, a Justice of the Peace, and Deputy-Lieutenant of the county. He married, 30th August 1784, Susanna, daughter of William Fergusson, Esq. of Doonholm, and had issue :

    1. John, who died unmarried

    2. William, his successor

    3. Fleming, Lieut. 16th Light Dragoons, died unmarried.

    1. Elizabeth, married to John H. Martin, Esq. of Glenorce, Wigtonshire, son of Samuel Martin, Esq. of Antigua, and has issue.

    2. Margaret.

    3. Mary-Susanna, married to the Rev. Alfred G. Utterson (son of John Utterson, Esq. of Mile-End House, Sussex, and Marwell Hall, Hants), Rector of Layer Marney, Essex.

    4. Eleanora.

Colonel Kelso died 22d April 1836. He was succeeded by his son,

XIX. William Kelso of Dankeith, Lieut.-Col. E.I.C.S. He died unmarried, 18th April 1844, and was succeeded in the property of Dankeith by his youngest sister,

XX. Eleanora Kelso of Dankeith, the present proprietrix.

*Arms*—Sable, a fesse, engrailed, between three garbs, or.

*Crest*—A garb, or.

*Motto*—" Otium cum dignitate."

*Dankeith*, the family seat, is about five miles south-east of Kilmarnock.

## ROSEMOUNT (FORMERLY GOLDRING.)

This property, forming part of the lands of Symontoun, belonged at one time to the *Schaws of Sornbeg*, a branch of the *Schaws of Halie*.

*Andrew Schaw* of Sornbeg, heir of William Schaw of Sornbeg, his grandfather, was served amongst other lands, in the 5 lib. land of the Mains of Helentoun, with the mill; the 5 lib. land of Knokindail; the 50s. land of Goldring, &c., 10th December 1549.

*Robert Schaw of Goldring* (no doubt a younger son of Schaw of Sornbeg), gave sasine to George Jamesoun, burgess of Ayr, " of all and haill his fiftie shilling land of Goldring," &c., 9th November 1578.* The same Robert Schaw of Goldring, apparently, (by his baile) " be vertew of his precept of sasing insert in ane charter of alienatioun maid be him, with advis of Katherine Hamiltoun, his spous, to George Jamesoun, burges of Air, and his aires, of all and haill his merkland of auld extent of Woodheid, &c., lyand within the landis of Maynholm, in Kylestewart." &c., 15th February 1580-81. He also, with consent of his spous, " gaif heretabill stait and sasing of the Mains of Maynholme, extending to ane xl s land or thairby, with mansioun place, &c., to George Jamesoun, burges of Air," &c., 7th December 1581. " Johne Schaw, as sone and air to vmquhile Johne Schaw of Polkemmet," had sasine of " all and haill the v lib. land of Helentoun, with toure, mains, and milne of the samine, and with those parts of the landis of Helentoun muir, being ane pendicle thereof; of all and haill the v lib. land of Knokindaill, and 1 s. land of *Goldring*, in propertie and tenandrie," &c.†

Goldring seems to have reverted to the Sornbeg family, for Patrick Schaw of Sornbeg, heir of his father, was served in the 50s. lands of Goldring, amongst others, 25th August 1631. It soon, however, passed to the M'Kerrells of Hillhouse, Goldring being in the service of Mr. William MacKerrell of Hillhouse, 24th November 1636. From the M'Kerrells the property was next acquired by the Cuninghames of Previck, as it appears in the service of William Cuninghame, heir of Mr. Adam Cuninghame of Previck, 17th October 1647. Goldring subsequently passed to the Dundonald family, and is mentioned in the service of the Earl of Dundonald, 28th October, 1690. It was next acquired by

*Patrick Fullartoun*, second son of Patrick Fullartoun, younger of that Ilk. He married Margaret Harper, by whom he had issue :

* Masscun's Notarial Book.      † Ibid.

1. William, a surgeon in India.
2. John, a Major in the E.I.C.S., married and had issue:
   1. Robert, who died in 1774, aged 5 years.
   2. William, of Skeldon, Provost of Ayr, who married Susan, daughter of the late Dr. Whiteside, and had issue. He died 10th January 1855.
3. Patricia, died 23d February 1830, aged 89.

Patrick Fullartoun of Rosemount died 3d June 1743, aged 35. His lady survived him till 30th April 1785. He was succeeded by his eldest son,

*Dr. William Fullartoun of Rosemount*, who, on his return from India in 1770, added greatly to the paternal estate, and so improved it that it became one of the finest and best cultivated domains in the county. Dr. Fullarton married Annabella, third daughter of Ronald Craufurd of Restalrig, W.S. He died October 22, 1805, aged 68, leaving no issue. His lady survived till 11th November 1826.

*Rosemount* was, for a considerable period, the property of Lord James Stuart, brother of the late Marquis of Bute, by whom it was sold, a few years ago, to George Bogle, Esq.

The only other properties of any extent were *Knokindaill*, *Helentoun*, and *Cowdam*. They, of course, formed originally part of the lands of Symontoun, and latterly were united in the barony of Sanquhar-Hamiltoun, so called from the sometime flourishing house of Hamiltoun of Sanquhar. They were appropriated, for a brief space, by the notorious James Stewart, Earl of Arran; and on his fall, came chiefly into the hands of Wallace of Craigie, whose family and its branches appear to have been amongst the earliest proprietors of these lands. William Wallace of Ellerslie had sasine of "the xxx s. land or thereby of the Mains of Helentoun and Bogend, with the tour, fortalice, and manour-place thereof, with the half of the milne of Helentoun," &c., 3d March 1583-4.

*Knokindaill* was possessed, in 1600, by a family of the name of *Tait of Adamhill*; and by the *Stewarts of Halrig* in 1609.

### FAIRLIE OF COWDAM, OR COODHAM.

This small property was purchased by the late' Mrs. William Fairlie, widow of William Fairlie of London, and formerly of Calcutta, about 1826, who built a splendid mansion upon it, at a cost, *together with the improvements in the vicinity*, of little short of £20,000. *William Fairlie* was the son of John Fairlie, by Agnes, daughter of Mungo Mure of Brentwood. He made a large fortune as a merchant and banker in Calcutta. His son,

*James Ogilvie Fairlie*, the present proprietor, married, first, in 1840, Anne-Eliza, daughter of Macleod of Macleod, and had issue: and secondly, in 1845, Elizabeth Constantia, only surviving daughter of William Howieson Craufurd of Craufurdland and Braehead, and has issue.

There are one or two other resident proprietors.

# PARISH OF TORBOLTON.

WE quite agree with the author of the well-written article—"Parish of Torbolton"—in the *New Statistical Account*, as to the derivation of the name—"*Tor*, or *Thor-Bol-ton*, or toun, is the town at Baal's hill, *i.e.* the toun at the hill where Baal was worshipped." The hill referred to is a mound, partly natural and partly artificial, in the immediate vicinity of the village; and was no doubt the court-hill of the Barony. Of its ancient use, as the site of the worship of *Bal*, or *Bol*, a popular custom still remains as evidence, and is thus recorded by the reverend statistician, "On the evening preceding the Torbolton June fair, a piece of fuel is demanded at each house, and is invariably given even by the poorest inhabitant. The fuel so collected is carried to a particular part of the hill, where there is an altar or circular fire-place of turf, about three feet in height, and is placed upon the altar. A huge bon-fire is kindled, and many of the inhabitants, old and young, men and women, assemble on the hill and remain for hours, apparently chiefly occupied with observing a feat performed by the youths, who are to be seen leaping with indefatigable zeal upon the altar, or turf wall, enclosing the ashes of former fires, and supporting the present one." The parish, which is of irregular shape, is bounded on the north by the parish of Craigie; on the east by Mauchline; on the south by Stair; and on the west by St. Quivox and Monkton.

The highest elevation is not more than 400 feet above the level of the sea, yet the topographical appearance of the parish is extremely varied and undulatory, and some of the eminences command extensive views — embracing, amongst others, "the great valley of Ayrshire, which stretches from the Doon to Ardrossan, a distance of nearly twenty miles." The banks of the richly wooded Ayr, which forms the southern boundary of the parish, present numerous picturesque scenes. As in most other parishes, great improvements have recently been made in agriculture.

Besides the river Ayr, so well known to the admirers of Burns, the parish is watered by several other streams, the largest of which is "the Fail." It originally had its source in Lochlee Loch, and flowing through the pleasure grounds of Coilsfield House, joins the Ayr at a place called Failford. There are numerous springs in the parish; and formerly there were three lochs, or rather flooded plains, called Lochlee, Fail, and Torbolton Lochs. The former was drained some years ago. The proprietor, the Duke of Portland, having relieved his tenantry from the thirlage to Milburn-mill, the collected waters of the loch were no longer necessary for the mill.

## HISTORY, CIVIL AND ECCLESIASTICAL.

*Tor-bol*, or "the hill," may be regarded as the nucleus of the village of Torbolton. As its name implies, it was used as a place of Pagan worship, long before the era of Christianity. One of those instruments used by the Druids, termed *celts*, was dug up some years ago in a field to the north-west of the hill. It would seem, from the remains of trenches, that the hill had been used as an encampment, probably by the ancient Britons, or during the Scoto-Irish wars. It is well known that the Culdees, the first introducers of Christianity, usually planted their *cels* on or near the sites of the Druidical temples, and their example was generally followed by their successors. Hence, as in the case of Torbolton, most of our old parochial churches are to be found in close proximity to the ancient altars of Druidism. The church of Torbolton was in existence in 1335, and probably at a much earlier period.

The first proprietor of the lands of Torbolton, under the Stewarts, who were Lords of Kyle, of whom we have any record, was John de Graham. In 1335, he granted the patronage of the church of Torbolton, with the lands of Unzaak (Unthack) on which the church is built, to Robert de Graham of Wolston, his cousin. This charter is dated at the convent of Falle (Fail), 21st September of the above year, having, no doubt, been written by some of the friars. Divested of its sacred character, the hill of Torbolton was used, in the feudal system, as the court hill of the barony; and Chalmers says, "the hall formerly [...] on this moot, was the chief messuage of the barony, where seisin was given of the same."

"The church of Torbolton was a rectory, the patronage of which belonged to the proprietors of Torbolton. In January 1387-8, John de Graham of Torbolton granted to the convent of [...] the patronage of the church of Torbolton, and this grant was confirmed by John, Earl of Kyle, and Earl of Carrick, in August [...]. In July 1413, John de Graham of Torbolton granted to the monks of Melrose the patronage of the church of Torbolton, and this grant was witnessed by Robert the Steward. It does not appear that either the convent of [...] or the monks of Melrose enjoyed the church of Torbolton, in consequence of the above grant. Torbolton continued a free rectory, and the patronage appears to have gone with the barony of Torbolton to the Stewarts of Dernley, in 1561-2. In 1429, John Cameron, the Bishop of Glasgow, erected the church of Torbolton into a prebend, or canonry, of the Cathedral Church of Glasgow. This was done with the consent of John Stewart of Dernley, the patron of the church, thus converted into a prebend; and the patronage of the prebend was settled to belong to him and his heirs. It was established, at the same time, that a vicar pensioner should have the cure of souls at the parish Church, with a stipend of twenty merks yearly, and a manse and glebe. The canon who held this prebend had the whole revenues of the church of Torbolton, with the dedication of the twenty merks to the vicar; and he was, moreover, taxed £3 a-year for the bene-

fit of the Cathedral Church of Glasgow. The rectory of Torbolton continued a prebend of the Church of Glasgow till the Reformation; and the patronage continued equally with the Stewarts of Dernly, who became Lords of Dernly and Earls of Lennox. In Bagimont's Roll, as it stood in the reign of James V, the rectory of Torbolton, a Prebend of Glasgow, was taxed £16, being a tenth of its estimated value. At the period of the Reformation, the rectory and prebend of Torbolton was held by James Cheisholm, who let the tithes and revenues thereof to Cuninghame of Capringtoun, for the yearly payment of £160; out of which Chisholm paid £20 yearly to the chaplain who served in his stall within the quire of Glasgow. There were several lands which belonged to the church of Torbolton, which were granted in fee-firm to Cuninghame of Capringtoun at the period of the Reformation. One of the titles which were given to Esme Lord D'Aubigny, when he was created Duke of Lennox, was Lord of Torbolton, on the 5th of August 1581. The lands of Torbolton, with the patronage of the church, appear to have continued with that family in 1655. The lands and patronage of the church seem to have passed to the Earl of Eglintoun before 1661. The patronage of the church of Torbolton now belongs to the Earl of Eglintoun. The village of Torbolton wherein the church stands, was erected a burgh of barony in 1671."*

The history of the church of Torbolton forms only a minor part of the ecclesiastical history of the parish of Torbolton as it now exists. The Monastery of Fail, though originally in the parish of Barnweill, is now within the extended bounds of Torbolton. The parish of Barnweill has been at least ecclesiastically suppressed since 1714, although it still stands in the Cess Books of the county as a distinct parish. Fail Monastery was founded in 1252, but by whom is unknown. It belonged to the Red Friars, who were called Matharines, from the house dedicated to St. Matharin in Paris. They were also styled "Fathers of Redemption "—(*Patres de Redemptionis Captivorum*), it being part of their duty to redeem captives from slavery. When this monastery was founded, the *serf* system, or locally slavery, prevailed. The peasantry were actually bought and sold along with the soil. We have innumerable instances of this in the feudal transfers of property, even down to a comparatively recent date. In a charter of vendition in reference to certain lands in Girvan parish, so late as the 29th November 1739, before feudal jurisdic-

---

* Chalmers' Caledonia.

tions were done away with, we find the old style of conveyance still retained, though *serfage* had long previously ceased to exist—"terrarum et *tenandrie* de Ballochtoull and Air." Such, no doubt were the slaves originally designed to be redeemed by the Monastery of Fail; but long after their local vocation may be supposed to have disappeared, there remained ample scope for their exertions abroad. Our early merchant-men suffered greatly from foreign piracies, and many of our ships' crews were made captives, and remained in captivity until redeemed by large sums given for their liberty. The Friars of Fail therefore, had a wide field for their benevolent exertions. Unquestionable evidence remains in the Presbytery Books to show that the benevolent objects of the Monastery of Fail were carried out long after the era of the Reformation. For example the following minute:—

"*Ayr, 3d August* 1642.

"This day William Hunter, ruling elder, presented two letters from sundrie captives of Ayr, now in Salio, taken by the Turkes, for their redemption, qubilk being read and considered, the Presbytery appointed the brethren to intimate the samyn to their people, and desire them to prepare themselves with their charitable contributions to the effect foresaid."

It was therefore a noble mission consigned to the Friars of Fail—to strike off the manacles of their fellow-creatures. Unluckily we have no record of their services in the way of redemption; but they have left an imperishable memento of their character as the merriest of the friars of old:—

"The Friars of Fail drank berry-brown ale,
    The best that ever was tasted,
The Monks of Melrose made gude kale,
    On Fridays, when they fasted."*

There is another version of this ditty, more characteristic of the jolly fathers of redemption:—

"The Friars of Fail
Gat never ours hard eggs, or ours thin kale;
For they made their eggs thin wi' butter,
And their kale thick wi' bread;
And the Friars of Fail they made gude kale
On Fridays when they fassed,
And they never wanted gear enough,
As long as their neighbours' lasted."†

The principal of the convent was styled "Minister," and, as head of the order, had a seat in Parliament. The Monastery of Melrose is associated with that of Fail in the first of the rhymes we have quoted, and very properly so, for no small portion of the lands of Torbolton were gifted at an early period to the Monks of Mel-

rose. From the chartulary of that establishment the talented author of the account of Torbolton parish, in the *Statistical Account*, has furnished some interesting notices in reference to the acquisition of property by the ghostly monks and friars of Melrose and Fail. "The earliest of the 'Friars of Faill,'" he says, "in regard to whom anything has been ascertained, is 'Brother John,' who was the chief or Minister of Failford in the year 1348. There are some documents extant relating to this 'Brother John' and a 'White Horse,' which seem deserving of notice, as bringing to light some of the methods taken by monks and friars for obtaining land and patronage, and displaying the ignorance and credulity of landowners in Scotland in the fourteenth century. In a notarial instrument, dated 20th November 1343, Johannes de Graham, nuper dominus de Torbolton, confesses that, after his grant to his cousin, Robert de Graham, which grant had been confirmed by the Seneschal of Scotland, and approved by the Chapter of Glasgow, 'Brother John,' Minister of the House of the Holy Trinity at Fiele, in the diocese of Glasgow, had given him a White horse for the right of patronage to the Church of Torbolton, which horse the said 'minister John' had afterwards forcibly taken away (*nanc parte abstulit*) from the said John de Graham. . . . This confession was made at Torbolton, in the church of that parish, before Thomas de Gethrath, monk of the Cistertian order, and others."

"Another document, entitled 'Revocatio Johannis de Graham fil,' sets forth, 'that things which are done through impetuosity of temper and facility of disposition, are revocable; that, being ignorant of law, 'Brother John,' of the House of the Holy Trinity of Fiele, in the diocese of Glasgow, had, by his flattering and most pernicious present (*non sine aerate prostino*), persuaded him to annul his former grant to his dear cousin, Robert Graham of Wolston, of the right of Patronage to the church of Torbolton, and land called Unthank . . . . that he recalls this error, and will subject himself, as is fitting, to the correction due to his offence.—Datum apud Torbolton, 21st February, for the salvation of his soul, and that of Emma, his wife.'

"A Charter by Robert de Graham of Wolston, granting to the Monks of Melrose the patronage of the Church of Torbolton, and seven acres of the lands of Unthank, and three acres of Carnegolayn, the nearest to the church—and another charter by the same Robert de Graham, conveying to the monks of Melrose, for the salvation of his soul, and that of Emma, his wife, the following lands situate in the territory

* Ramsay's Evergreen.
† Statistical Account.

and Lordship of Torbolton, viz., ' Dernehunche, Qayltisfield, and Auldtounburne,'—give us to understand why John de Graham was compelled to make and to put on record such humiliating confessions ; and show that the affair of the white horse was a struggle betwixt the monks of Melrose and the Friars of Fail, for the increase of their patronage and the extension of their lands —John de Graham being the dupe of the one party, and Robert de Graham the prey of the other.

" The monks of Melrose, by a promise to Robert of what they could not give—' salvation for his soul and that of his wife '—had obtained from him not only the advowson to Torbolton Church and glebe, but also a grant of the estate of Coilsfield, and other valuable lands.

" The superior of Fail, by his flatteries, and by the gift of the horse, had prevailed with John de Graham to convey to the house of Fail what was no longer his to bestow.

" Neither John de Graham, nor Robert de Graham, appears to have been able to write his own name. Each charter bears that the person granting it had affixed his seal before witnesses."

In the reign of Robert II., " the patronage of the Kirk of Faill " was granted, by royal charter, to James de Lindsay of Crawforde.* In 1470, " John Quhit of Fale " is mentioned in the burgh records of Prestwick.

The rental of the Ministry of Faill, as given in by Robert Cunninghame, who was Minister in 1562, amounted to £174, 6s. 8d. in money ; 3 chalders of bear ; 15 chalders 4 bolls of meal ; 30 stones of cheese ; 10 hogs (young sheep) ; 3 stirks (young cows) ; 2 dozen grilse or salmon. There belonged to the monastery five parish churches, viz., the churches of Barnweil, Symington, and Galston, in Kyle ; of Torthorwald, in Dumfriesshire ; and the church of Inverchoalan, in Argyleshire.

The lands of Fail now belong to Edward H. Blair of Dunskey and Brounehill, second son of Sir D. H. Blair, Bart., of Blairquhan.

In common with most of the other districts in Ayrshire, Torbolton suffered considerably during the Persecution. In the churchyard there is a martyr's stone, bearing the following inscription : " Here lys William Shillilaw, who was shot at Woodhead by Lieut. Lauder for his adherence to the word of God and Scotland's covenanted work of Reformation, 1685."

In virtue of the charter of *novodamus* granted by Charles II to John Cuninghame, Esq. of Enterkine, in 1671, constituting Torbolton a free burgh of barony, the community is governed by two bailies and twelve councillors who are annually elected on Christmas-eve. A Town-house and lock-up were erected by subscription in 1836. The inhabitants are chiefly occupied in weaving, obtained from Glasgow. Hand-sewing is also carried on to a considerable extent by the female portion of the community. At Failford, about two and a-half miles from Torbolton, there was, till recently a manufactory for hones, made of the Water-of-Ayr stones, and razor strops. The cases were finished in a very tasteful manner. Two fairs are held annually in Torbolton.

## ANTIQUITIES.

The remains of a Roman camp are still to be seen at Park-moor. Near to this, and also on the farm of Law, several sepulchral urns have been found under cairns of stones. Near to Fail Monastery similar remains were discovered some years ago in pits or graves, covered by flat stones. In these ancient depositories of the dead, ample evidence was furnished, from the geometrical position of the pits, in reference to each other, that they belonged to the Druidical era in Scotland.

On one of the farms of Failford, named Adamcroft, there were formerly several ancient sepulchres, of which, however, one only now remains entire. These sepulchres consisted of green mounds, of an oval form, regulary built in the interior with large rough stones, and containing urns of baked clay, ornamented with diagonal lines, and full of the remains of burned bones. Some of the sepulchres were opened by the late Alexander Cooper, Esq., who presented one of the most perfect of the urns to the Antiquarian Society of Edinburgh, but it is believed that it soon fell to pieces. A portion of the burned bones was long preserved at Smithstone House. One of the mounds appears to have been thirty-six feet long by eighteen wide ; but the one remaining unopened is smaller, being about twenty-four feet by eighteen.

The mound, popularly understood to contain the remains of Old King Coil, was opened in

* Robertson's Index of Royal Charters. "There is a curious document extant (Liber de Melrose) in the shape of a letter, in the old Norman frank of the time, addressed to John de Grahame, Séjneur de Torbolton, to all who shall see or hear this letter, complaining that Sir John de tymlessly had maliciously, falsely, and wickedly, intromitted with the church of Turbolton, and with the support and maintenance of William of Douglas, had presented to said church. He then states the grant of the advowson of the church and lands pertaining thereto, to his cousin Robert Graham, confirmed by the Seneschal, and ratified by the See of Glasgow ; and that the said Sir John, and whoever should maintain him, should be held as intromitters against the law of the church and the civil law." BY s L. ACCOUNT.

May 1837, when it was satisfactorily ascertained to have been a place of sepulture of no ordinary description.*

The only other remain of antiquity of any note in the parish is the gable and part of a side-wall of the manor-house of the chief, or minister, of the Monastery of Fail. There is a tradition that the last laird, or minister, of Fail, who inhabited the old building was a warlock; and it is said that the house was blown down by the storm which prevailed at his funeral.†

*Notable Persons connected with the Parish.*— *Alexander Peden*, popularly regarded as a prophet, held the office of schoolmaster in Torbolton previous to his being admitted to the ministry. "He frequently preached at a secluded spot in the Coilhome Wood, called Peden's Cove. The pulpit is a jutting out mass of red sandstone overlooking a level piece of ground bounded by the Ayr, and hid from view by precipitous cliffs and lofty banks covered with copsewood. It is remembered that many of his admiring hearers used to assemble before the pulpit with their loaded firelocks in their hands."* *Burns*, the poet, passed not a few of the happiest of his days at Lochlee, a farm in the upper part of the parish —and many of the surrounding scenes are alluded to in his poems. *Thom*, the self-taught sculptor, whose figures of "Tam o' Shanter and Souter Johnnie," have obtained a world-wide notoriety, was born in a thatched cottage about a mile from Lochlee. The late *Rev. Dr. Ritchie*, one of the ministers of the High Church, and Professor of Divinity in the University of Edinburgh, was for some time minister of Torbolton.

# FAMILIES IN THE PARISH OF TORBOLTON.

We have seen that the earliest possessor of the lands or barony of Torbolton, under the Stewarts, was *John de Graham*, Lord (or Laird) of Torbolton. He lived in 1335, and *Robert de Graham of Welston* was his cousin. Who these Grahams were does not appear. Both the barony and patronage of the church of Torbolton passed to the *Stewarts of Darnley* in 1361-2, with whom they remained till the Reformation—one of the oldest families connected with the parish, apart from the great house of Darnley, was the

### DUNBARS OF ENTERKINE,

a branch of the Dunbars of Cumnock and Blantyre. On the 22d May 1576, William Dunbar of Blantyre gave sasine of his 40s. land of Schielzardis to James Blair, son and heir of John Blair of Middle Auchindraine.‡ The first of the Dunbars of Enterkine we meet with was

*William Dunbar of Enterkine*, whose son, Mr. Johne Dunbar, on the 19th August 1600, "past to the personal presens of Dauid Dunbar of Daldork, and laufullie warnit him &c. to pay and deliuer to the said Mr. Johone, within the paroche kirk of Terboltoun, upoun the tent day of Nonember. now nixt to cume, the sowme of nyne hundreth merkis, &c. as for the lawfull redemptioun, &c. fra the said Mr. Johone and his airis, of all and haill the said Dauidis merkland of auld extent of Daldork, with the pertinentis, lyand within the parochin of Terboltoun, &c. This was done &c. befoir the said William Dunbar of Interkine, *Gavin Dunbar his sone*, and Eduard Wallace of Sewaltoun, witnesses," &c. The next we find is,

*Dauid Dunbar of Interkine*, who is mentioned in the testament of James Hutchesoun in Mauchline, in 1613. "Davidi Dunbar de Enterkin" had a Crown charter of the lands of Beandris, Leifnoreis, &c. 10th June 1623. His name occurs in various local records down till 1643, when he died. He had a son, named Hew Dunbar, as appears from the inventory of his effects, which was "faythfullie maid and gevin vp be Hew Ker of Kerisland, lauchfull creditor to the defunct, &c., in sua far as the said vmquhile Dauid Dum-

* For some particulars regarding Coilus, and the opening of his tomb, see vol. i. pp. 2, 3.

† See Part II. of the "Ballads and Songs of Ayrshire."

‡ Masoun's Notarial Book.

* Statistical Account.

bar of Enterkin, as one of the cautiouneris, conjunctlie and scuerallie with Hew Dunbar, his sone, as cautiouneris and soverties for William Catheart of Wattersyd, was justlie addetit and awand to Mr. Thomas Garvane, sumtyme scholemaister at Irwein, and now minister at Collingtoun, the sowme of ane thowsand pundis money," &c.

This is the last notice we find of the Dunbars of Enterkine.* The property afterwards passed into the hands of a branch of the Cuninghames of Capringtoun.

### CUNINGHAMES OF ENTERKINE.

Adam Cuninghame of Prieet was the fourth son of John Cuninghame of Rudelands. He died in March 1656. From his testament it appears that he married Ester Fullartone, probably a relative of Mr. William Fullartone, minister of St. Quivox, who is mentioned as a debter to the deceased. Amongst his debts he was owing "Margaret Conynghame, for ye bairding and enterduing of William, John, and James Cuninghame, the defunctis bairnes, preceiding Witsonday 1st, 1656 zeiris, xl. lib." These children were probably of a former marriage. His son,

Robert Cuninghame, was served heir to his father, "Mr. Adam Cuninghame of Prestick," in the lands of Gabbrug (now Rosemount), Enterkine, &c. 7th Oct. 1657.

Mr. Cuninghame of Enterkine acquired the superioritie and baronie of Monktoun from Lord Bargeny in 1674. In 1678 he disponed these lands, with consent of Mrs. Mary Cuninghame, his spouse, to Hugh Cuninghame, writer in Edinburgh, who again sold them to William Baillie, merchant in Edinburgh, son-in-law to Enterkine, Baillie having married his daughter Margaret. He had another daughter, Esther, who married, first, William Fletcher of New Cranstoun, advocate; and secondly, Sir James Dalrymple of Killoch, Bart., and had issue by both. John Cuninghame of Enterkine, who had been brought up as a lawyer, was for several years "furnisher of the News-Letter" to the burgh of Ayr. He was appointed to the Office in 1775, in the room of Robert Craufurd of Craufurdstone, who had acted as "furnisher" for eighteen months, and was succeeded by Mr. Craufurd, who was re-appointed on the 16th Feb. 1788.

John Cuninghame of Enterkine was admitted a burgess of Ayr, 12th April 1723, and appointed elder to the General Assembly for the burgh,

20th March 1738. He was succeeded by his grandson.

William Cuninghame of Enterkine, who had a precept of Clare Constat, for infefting him in certain burgh property, dated 4th February 1760. He married Catherine, daughter of Major-General Stewart of Stair, by whom he had a son,

William Allason Cuninghame Logan, of Logan and Afton. He married Miss Allason, heiress of Logan, and assumed the name of Allason.

Enterkine is now the property of John Bell, Esq.

### COILSFIELD.

This property, no doubt, derived its name from the grave of King Coel, or Coil, which is situated in the immediate vicinity of the Mansion-House of Coilsfield. It is called Quyltisfield in the charter of John de Graham, conveying it and other lands to the monks of Melrose in 1342. It formed part of the original lordship of Torbolton, but continued in the hands of the monks of Melrose till the Reformation. It was then acquired, with other church property, by Cuninghume of Caprington, from whom it was purchased, with the patronage of the Church, by the Hon. Colonel James Montgomerie, fourth son of Alexander, sixth Earl of Eglintoun, before 1661. The lands of Coilsfield remained with the Eglintoun family until a few years back, when they were sold by the present Earl to William Orr, Esq., who changed his name to Paterson, in compliance with the will of a relative, which name only he now bears. By the same will, he was bound to call the estate which he was to purchase with Mr. Paterson's funds Montgomerie, which is accordingly now the name of Coilsfield. Montgomerie House is an elegant modern building, situated on the southern bank of the Fail rivulet, and embosomed among woods. The situation is delightful. Burns, in his song of "Highland Mary," alludes to it as "the Castle o' Montgomery"—

"There summer first unfolds her robes,
And there they langest tarry."

### FAILFOORD OR SMEITHSTON, AND TEMPLEBOGWOOD.

The regality of Failfoord, or, Smeithston, and lands of Templebogwood, the property of William Cooper, Esq., lie in the eastern part of this parish, stretching continuously from the river Ayr, the boundary of the parish of Stair, northwards to the march with Craigie parish. The scenery on that part of this property adjoining the river Ayr is highly picturesque.

At the little village of Failford, in a beautiful situation, near the junctions of the rivers Fail and Ayr, a very handsome range of alms-houses was erected, about twenty years since, with funds left by the late Alexander Cooper, Esq. for the accommodation of eight aged poor persons, four to be chosen from the parish of Torbolton, and four from the parish of Mauchline, who receive a weekly aliment. It was at one time feared that this institution might have the effect of increasing the number of paupers in these parishes, but this result has not followed, as the trust deed requires of the inmates a previous residence in the parishes of five years, without begging.

The lands comprehended in this regality were originally parts of the barony of Torbolton and regality of Darnley. Part of them, at least, are contained in a charter, in favour of John Wallace of Craigie, dated 18th November 1557. William Wallace of Failfuirde, is retoured as heir to his father, William Wallace of Failfuirde, on 23d December 1630, "in terris de Smythistoun, Ladyzairde, Adamecroft, et Litell Auchinwet, extendentibus ad 10 mercatas terrarum antiqui extentus cum salmonum piscariis in aqua seu rivolo de Air, infra balliatum de Kyle Stewart. A. E. 10 M. N. E. 50 M." These lands, together with " the four merk land of Middleton, Younderstoun, Redcraig, Outlands, Newlands and Largieside," were erected into a regality by charter in favour of Sir Thomas Wallace of Craigie, dated 12th August 1706, with all the privileges of the regality of Darnley within the bounds, and with a grant of a "free chapel and chancery," which is believed to be of unusual occurrence.

It is uncertain at what particular period the name of " Failfoord " was first applied to these lands. In the older titles they appear to have no generic appellation, but are described by the names of the various farms. The Wallaces of Failfuirde being proprietors of the manor place and precincts of Fail, or Failfuirde, the old residence of the Friars of Fail, in the adjoining Parish of Barnweill,* as well as of the lands of this regality, it is supposed that they designated their whole property by the name of Failfuirde. When their lands in Barnweill parish fell into other hands, their lands in Torbolton still retained

the name. From the earliest date to which the county valuation rolls in the hands of the Clerk of Supply go back, viz.—19th May 1759, the whole lands of the Wallaces in the parish of Torbolton, with their entire valuation, amounting to £542, 6s. 4d. Scots, (all now in the hands of Mr. Cooper,) appear in these Rolls under no other name than that of " Failfoord." This designation is continued down to the present time, and the name of " Smeithston " is in no case applied to these lands in the Valuation Rolls now extant. The Rolls for the parish of Barnweill also contain an article " Failfoord," with a valuation of nine pounds, twelve shillings, Scots, being the old Manor Place and Precinct of Fail. So that it appears in this instance, as in others in the county, there are, in different parishes, two properties of the same name.

In 1776 Sir Thomas Wallace Dunlop sold this regality to John Coghlan of Crutchedfriars, London, who soon afterwards disposed of it to Messrs Brown and Collinson, of that city, by whose creditors it was sold, in 1786, to William Cooper, Esq., with right to the rents from Martinmas 1785. William Cooper built the mansion-house, and laid out the grounds. During his lifetime the lands were popularly designated " Smeithston," but his son, soon after his succession, revived the old and more correct name of " Failfoord." The mansion-house, however, is still commonly called Smithstone House.

The adjoining lands of Templebogwood, on the eastern march of the parish, have, obviously from the name, been at one time the property of the Knights Templars. They afterwards, with the other Temple lands of Kyle, fell into the hands of the Cuninghames of Caprington, who appear to have disposed of them to the Farquhars of Gilmilnscroft, but at what date is uncertain. Alexander Farquhar of Gilmilnscroft disponed these lands to William Gibb, son of James Gibb in Templebogwood, by feu disposition, dated 15th October 1750. William Gibb, son of the said William Gibb, was infeft, as heir of his father, in 1783 ; and in 1796, the trustee for his creditors, sold the lands to Alexander Cooper, Esq., who executed an entail thereof in 1817, in virtue of which he was succeeded, at his death in 1829, by his nephew, William Cooper, now of Failford.

### COOPER OF FAILFORD.

The surname of this family was formerly written " Couper," and sometimes " Cowper." Playfair, in his Baronetage,* states that it is taken

---

* It is erroneously stated in the Statistical Account of Scotland, parish of Torbolton, vol. v. p. 761, that the parish of Barnweill was suppressed. That parish still occupies its place in the county valuation rolls, though attached QUOAD SACRA to the parishes of Craigie and Torbolton.

* Appendix, p. 128.

from the town or lands of Couper, and that it is nearly as old as the time of Malcolm Canmore; but Sir George Mackenzie, in his "Science of Heraldry," first published in 1680, says that "the Cowpers do for more security carry the flower de luces and ermines in one shield, to signify their descent from France, and from Bretaigne in that kingdom."[*] The name frequently occurs in the records, at an early period, among the landed proprietors, in various counties, particularly in the county of Fife; but the principal families were Couper of Gogar in Midlothian, raised to the Baronetage about 1638, and Couper of Fentounbarns, county of Haddington, descended from William Couper, Bishop of Galloway, and they appear to have been nearly related.

SIMON COUPER, whom Playfair states[†] to have been the first ancestor on record of the Coupers of Gogar, swore fealty to Edward I., anno 1296, and he is accordingly mentioned in the Ragman Rolls.[‡] Playfair's statement is corroborated by the Lyon Register of Arms,[§] where it is said that the Coupers of Gogar are descended in a direct male line from the above mentioned Simon, "one of the Barons of Scotland who was compelled to swear fealty to Edward I. in 1296." Of this family was

I. JAMES COUPER, who, by marriage with Elizabeth Young, daughter and co-heiress of John Young, burgess of Edinburgh, and neice and co-heiress of Roland Young, acquired considerable properties in that city, of which he and his wife had various sasines in the years 1556 and 1558. He was alive in 1592, as appears from a sasine, dated 7th August of that year, in favour of his son Adam, reserving his father's liferent. He had issue :—

1. John, who sold his right of succession to his brother Adam, who consequently succeeded his father and mother.
2. Adam, of Gogar.

II. ADAM COUPER of Gogar. Various sasines appear in the records in his favour in 1586, 1592, and subsequent years. He was one of the principal Clerks of Session. He married Margaret Danielstoun, of the family of Colgrain, and died 3d December 1608, leaving issue :—

1. John, his heir.
2. Elizabeth, baptized 21st January 1596.
3. James, b. 30th October 1597.
4. Alexander, of Foulfoord, in Midlothian, W.S., b. 15th November 1598. He married, first, Catherine Cochrane, of the family of Barbachlay, and, secondly,

* Edition of 1722, vol. ii. p. 589.
† Playfair ut supra.
‡ The "Ragman Rolls," printed for the Bannatyne Club, p. 151.
§ Lyon Register vol. i. p. 510 and 511.

Isobel Rae, and had issue by both. On 10th September 1641, he was served tutor to the children of his eldest brother.[*]
5. George, b. 26th August 1600.
6. Thomas, b. 4th October 1601.
7. Robert, b. 23d January 1603; he was minister at Temple, and died 1668.
8. Margaret, b. 15th February 1604.
9. Andrew, b. 24th February 1605.
10. Adam, b. 23d March 1606; he died in 1653.

III. JOHN COUPER of Gogar succeeded his father. He is said to have been created a Baronet in 1638, but does not appear to have assumed the title. It is, however, alleged that the Baronetcy was not created till 1646, in the person of his son. He married Helen Skeine, of the family of Halyards, who survived him. He was killed, 30th August 1640, in the blowing up of Dunglass Castle. His issue were :—

1. Sir John Couper, of Gogar, born 18th March 1621. He married Margaret Inglis, and had issue several daughters. In 1685, he executed an entail of his estate in favour of his daughter, Mary, and her husband, but his creditors reduced the entail in 1697. After his decease, which took place previous to 1690, the Baronetcy lay dormant till the service of Sir Grey Couper, 1st August 1775.
2. James, whose birth is not recorded, but who is mentioned in his father's testament. He is said to have been minister of Humbie and Holy Island. From him Sir Grey Couper, who, in 1775, revived the Baronetcy, claimed descent.
3. Margaret, baptized 12th August 1623.
4. Alisone, b. 28th June 1624.
5. Helen, b. 24th June 1625.
6. William, b. 22d May 1629, from whom the family now settled in Ayrshire claim descent.
7. Alexander, b. 11th February 1634, died young.
8. Robert, b. 17th April 1635. He was alive 28th December 1685, when he acted as baillie in the sasine of Gogar, under his brother's entail.
9. Alexander, b. 18th July 1637.
10. Rebecca, b. 22d March 1639.
11. Jeane, b. 7th April 1640.

IV. WILLIAM COUPER, the ancestor of the Ayrshire branch, served as an officer of dragoons in the time of the Commonwealth. He married Christian Scot, and settled in the county of Dumbarton. Robert Couper is witness to the baptism of two of his children. He had issue :—

1. John, of whom afterwards.
2. Mariah, b. 16th August 1657, died young.
3. Daniel, b. 17th April 1659. He married Janet Wallace, in 1698. He is mentioned in his brother John's testament in 1687.
4. Maria, b. 22d June 1661.
5. Janet, whose name occurs in her brother John's testament 1687.

V. JOHN COUPER, the elder son, resided at the Tower of Banheath, in the county of Dumbarton. He married, in January 1676, Christian Gray, by whom he acquired property, and who survived him. He died March 1687, having had issue :—

* Inquisitiones de Tutela, Nos. 1346, 1347, 1348, and 1349.

1. William, born 1676, died young.
2. John, of whom afterwards.
3. William, baptised 20th January 1684.

VI. John Couper, the eldest surviving son, born 25th August 1677. He also resided at the tower of Banheath. In November, 1708, he married Margaret Thom, a relative of the Rev. William Thom of Kirkdales, minister of Govan, celebrated for his wit and eccentricity, and by her had issue :—

1. John.
2. William, of whom afterwards.
3. Robert, b. 28th May 1713.
4. Christian, b. 8th December 1714.
5. James, b. 28th April 1717, died young.
6. Margaret, b. 4th March 1721.
7. Alexander, born 1720, was a merchant in Glasgow, and died unmarried 30th June 1785, leaving considerable property to his brothers.
8. and 9. Katherine and Mary, the dates of whose births are not recorded.

VII. The Rev. John Couper, the eldest son, b. 12th November 1709, was settled as a clergyman in the county of Lincoln, where he resided long. He considered himself entitled to the baronetcy of Gogar, and was proceeding to claim it, but desisted therefrom on the appearance of Sir Grey Cooper, claiming descent from an elder branch, in imitation of whom he changed his name to the English name of Cooper, and died at Glasgow, unmarried, 21st September 1789, leaving the greater part of his property, which was considerable, to the children of his brother William.

VIII. William Couper, the second son, afterwards of Smeithstone and Failford, b. 5th August 1711, was a merchant in Glasgow. He was taken prisoner by the rebels at the battle of Falkirk, and carried to the North, but effected his escape. He purchased the regality of Failfoord, or Smeithston, from the disponees of Sir Thomas Wallace Dunlop. He married, in 1753, Mary* eldest daughter of Hugh Stewart, Esq., merchant in Glasgow, and by her, who died in January 1768, had issue :—

1. Mary, born 11th August 1754, died in infancy.
2. Mary, born 17th February, 1756, died unmarried 9th May 1783.
3. Cecilia, born 1st September 1757, married, 16th June 1800, Lieut. Colonel, afterwards Lieutenant General David Shank, an officer who highly distinguished himself in the American War. She died, without issue, 9th December 1842.
4. Helen, born 8th August 1759, died young.
5. William, born 22d July 1761, died in May 1768.
6. Alexander, }
7. Samuel, } of whom afterwards.

* In a note, page 221 of this volume, it is incorrectly stated that two of the daughters of Hugh Stewart of Castlesalt, merchant in Glasgow, married respectively William Cooper of Smithstone, and William Parker of Barleith. Mary Stewart, Mrs. Cooper, and Mary Stuart, Mrs. Parker, were not sisters, though, it is believed, they were relations.

William Couper, like his elder brother, latterly changed his name to "Cooper," which name he entailed on his successors, along with his lands. This change took place subsequently to 1754, as in his postnuptial contract of marriage, dated 9th July of that year, he subscribes his name "Couper." He died 16th May 1793, and was succeeded by his eldest surviving son,

IX. Alexander Cooper of Failford, born 12th May 1765, who revived the former name of his lands, and added to them the adjacent lands of Templebogwood, by purchase, in 1796. He held a commission in the 61st regiment of foot, and served abroad. He was afterwards appointed Captain Commandant of the Mauchline Volunteers, Lieutenant-Colonel of the 2d regiment of Ayrshire Local Militia, and a Deputy-Lieutenant of the County. He died, unmarried, 19th September 1829, and was succeeded by his brother,

X. Samuel Cooper of Failford and Ballindalloch, born January 1768. He married, 18th August 1795, his cousin, Janet, daughter and heiress of Henry Ritchie, Esq. by Esther, daughter and eventually representative of William Crawford of Balshagray and Scotstoun, the head of one of the most recent branches of the family of Crawfurdland. Janet Ritchie died in May 1818, leaving a numerous family. In 1799, Samuel Cooper purchased the barony of Ballindalloch, in the county of Stirling, where he chiefly resided. He was Lieut.-Colonel of the Western Battalion of Stirlingshire Local Militia, and a Deputy Lieutenant of that county. He died 14th July 1842. His issue were :—

1. Janet Crawford, married, in January 1821, her cousin, William Wallace,* formerly of Rhynd, now of Busbie, and has issue.
2. Mary.
3. Cecilia, born 7th August 1799, married, in July 1835, Robert Strachers, Esq. She died at Adelaide, South Australia, on 7th February 1841, leaving issue a son.
4. William, born 29th May 1801, died the same year.
5. Henrietta, born 1st August 1802, married, in April 1823, John Crooks, Esq. of Levan, county of Renfrew. She died 20th March 1827, leaving issue a daughter.
6. Frances, born 27th October 1803, married, in February 1830, Herbert Buchanan, Esq., son of Herbert Buchanan of Arden, county Dumbarton. She died 9th October 1843, leaving issue three sons and three daughters.
7. Ann, married, in June 1829, George Ross Wilsone, Esq., late of Benmore, county of Argyle, and has issue one son and one daughter.
8. William, of whom afterwards.
9. Ellinor, married, in April, 1844, Thomas Gray Scott, Esq., W.S., Edinburgh, and has issue a son and three daughters.
10. Esther Ritchie, born 30th December, 1814, married in July 1843, Alexander Dunlop, Esq., younger of Gairbraid, county Dumbarton. She died at Montego

* See page 220 of this volume.

Bay, Jamaica, on 16th May 1844, leaving issue one son, who died 28th September, 1844.

11. Henry Ritchie, of Ballindalloch, married, in October 1846, Mary Jane, only surviving child of the deceased Gerald Butler, Esq., representative of a family who long held lands in the county of Wexford, by Catherine Byrne, of the family of Cronakeera, county Wicklow, and has had issue—

   1. Esther Mary Catherine, born 7th September 1847, died 29th March 1851.
   2. Mary.
   3. Geraldine.
   4. Henry.

Samuel Cooper was succeeded by his eldest surviving son.

XI. William Cooper of Failford, and of Solsgirth, county Dunbarton, who married, first, on 30th July 1835, Isabella, daughter of Robert Clarke, Esq., of Comrie Castle,* county of Perth, but she died without issue 4th May 1841; and, secondly, on 17th October, 1845, Margaret, eldest daughter of the Rev. Dr. Hill, Professor of Divinity in the College of Glasgow, by Margaret, only daughter of Major Crawford of Newfield,† county of Ayr. Mr. Cooper is representative of the Craufurds of Balshagray, county of Lanark, and of one of the co-heiresses of the Fletchers of New Cranstoun, county of Edinburgh. He has issue:—

   1. William Samuel.
   2. Margaret Craufurd.
   3. Janet Ritchie.
   4. Alexander Hill.

Arms.—The arms of Couper of Gogar, recorded in the Lyon Register, and quoted by Nesbit, are, "argent, a chevron, gules, charged with another ermine, between three laurel slips, vert. Crest, a dexter hand holding a garland of laurel, both proper." Motto, "Virtute." From Sir George Mackenzie's work on heraldry, already quoted, it appears that the laurel slips had been originally fleurs de lis, in evidence of the French origin of the family.

In consequence of the change of name, arms were granted to Cooper of Failford analogous to those of various English Families of the name of Cooper, and with these they quarter the arms of Ritchie, Craufurd, and Couper or Cowper, all by authority of the Lord Lyon, in whose register they are thus blazoned, viz. Quarterly. First argent, on a bend engrailed between two lions rampant gules, three crescents of the field, within a border cheque, argent and azure, for Cooper. Second and third, quartered first and fourth, argent on a chief, gules, three lions' heads erazed of the first, all within a border ermine, for Ritchie; second and third, gules, a

fesse, ermine, and in chief a mollet of the last, for Craufurd. Fourth, argent, a chevron gules, surmounted of another ermine, between three laurel slips vert, all* within a border cheque as the former, for Couper or Cowper.

Crests.—On the dexter side, issuant out of a wreath argent and gules, a dexter hand holding a garland of laurel, both proper. Motto—"Virtute." On the sinister side, upon a wreath argent and azure, an oak tree with a branch borne down by a weight. Motto—"Resurgo."

### BROOMHILL, OR BROUNEHILL.

This property was acquired by *Adam Cuninghame,* second son of William Cuninghame of Laglane, a branch of the Cuninghames of Caprington (see Appendix to this volume), soon after the Reformation. He was designed "in Potterhill," and "Tutor of Laglane," in 1553. He is said to have had a son, *John Cuninghame of Rudelands,* father of *William Cuninghame of Broomhills,** who died without issue, when the property devolved upon his next surviving brother, *John.* Adam Cuninghame died before 1598, as appears from the following extract from Masoun's *Notarial Book:*—"Apud Air, Sept. 15, 1598.—The quhilk day, &c. comperit personalie ane honorable man, Dauid Craufurd of Kerss, with Alane Cathcart, the spous of Eistir Fullertoun, relict of vnquhile Adam Cuninghame of Brounhill, quha presented to Alexander Lockhert, ane of the baillies of the burgh of Air, &c., ane commissioun, direct be the Lordis of Counsale to the Prouest, &c. for ressauing of the said Dauid Craufurde's aith of veritie vpoun the treuth and veritie of ane decreit arbitrall producit befoir the saidis Lordis, be Daniel Cuninghame of Dalkeyth, in the mattir movit be him aganis the said *Eistir Fullertoun* and her said spous, and *Williame Cuninghame,* hir sone, &c. of the daitt the xxvij day of July last bipast," &c.

Adam Cuninghame had thus a son, *William,* as well as John of Rudelands. William Cuninghame, *Laird of Brounehill,* appears in various testamentary documents from 1613 downwards till 1636, in which year he is mentioned as "his maister" in the testament of "Johnne Livingstone in Faill."

Brounehill was disponed by Sir John Cuninghame of Lambruchton and Caprington to Provest William Cuninghame of Ayr, in 1667, and is now possessed by his descendant, E. H. Blair

---

* See Burke's History of the Commoners.
† See page 40 of this volume.

* See Appendix.

of Dunskey and Brounehill, to whom also belongs the lands of

### FAIL, OR FAILFORD.

Failfurde, after the Reformation, was held by a branch of the Wallaces of Craigie, under the title of Ministers of Fail. *William Wallace*, son of *William Wallace, Minister of Fail*, was served heir to his father in the manor and Monastery of Fail, 22d April 1617. "Agnes Boyd, spous to William Wallace of Faill," occurs in the testament of John M'Kildune, merchant burgess of Glasgow, in 1630.

### MURES OF PARK.

Some account of this branch of the Mures of Rowallan is given in the account of the parish of Maybole. They are supposed to have been the ancestors of Provost Mure of Ayr, afterwards of Middle Auchindraine.

### DRUMLEY.

This property belonged to the Coilsfield estate, and was purchased by *Captain Robert Davidson*, of the E.I.C.'s navy, from Hugh Montgomerie, Esq. of Skelmorlie and Coilsfield, in 1791. The Davidsons were merchants in Ayr. The first of them mentioned in the parochial registers was *Patrick Davidson*, who married *Catherine Cathcart*. They had a numerous family. Robert Davidson, who purchased Drumley, never married, and left the property, in liferent, to his brothers—1. William (father of the present proprietor), a physician in the E.I.C.'s service; 2. Thomas, a merchant in India; 3. James, a major in the army of the E.I.C., who died before Thomas, from the effects of a kick received from his horse—and subsequently to his nephew, *Thomas Davidson*, the present proprietor, in fee. Mr. Davidson married Janet, daughter of Robert Montgomerie of Craighouse, and has four sons and two daughters, the eldest of whom is named *William-Robert*.

### SMITHFIELD.

This small but fine property was, previous to the end of last century, a part of Enterkine estate. In 1798, Robert Paterson, Esq., purchased the lands of Gedshall, Sandgate, and part of Gallowhill, from William Cunningham, Esq. of Enterkin, and soon after built the present mansion-house, and named the property Smithfield. Mr. Paterson was a blacksmith to trade, went to the island of Tobago, W.I., where he acquired a considerable fortune; hence the name of *Smithfield*. He died soon after the house was built, in 1843. His heirs sold the property to William Forrest, Esq., formerly a merchant in Glasgow; who very much improved it by draining and planting for ornament and shelter. The property now belongs to James M'Naughton, Esq., who purchased it from Mr. Forrest.

### TOWNHEAD OF DRUMLEY.

This fine property includes the lands of Rosemailing, Roughlay, Alley of Drumley, Galriggs, Temple-house, &c., &c. It is about two miles south-west of the village of Torbolton, and five from Ayr, and is intersected by the road from Mauchline to the county town. It was purchased in 1852 from the heirs of the late Colonel Neil of Barnweil, by George Clarke, Esq. of Kilmarnock, lately merchant in Rio-de-Janeiro, S. A. These lands were in the possession of the Neil family from 1788, having then been acquired by James Neil, Esq., writer in Ayr. There had, it is probable, from the names and the old dipping wells about it, been a village or clachan on this property, and, in all likelihood, a place of worship at or near Temple-house; which, no doubt, was in former times a place of some note, having until of late a fine orchard connected with it. The fine old fruit trees were recently removed in making improvements on the estate. In 1591, Temple-house was the residence of a Marion Sawers. In her testament, of date that year, she left part, or all her property, to the family of Wallace of Cairnhill.

APPENDIX

# APPENDIX.

The following additional account of the

has been drawn up chiefly from the family papers :—

William, Lord of Kilmaurs, with consent of William, his son and heir apparent, by a charter, of date 9th May 1385, granted the lands of Bedlan to " Thomæ Cuningham, filio suo juniori," the Caprington ancestor*—and both Bedlan and Caprington were duly inherited and transmitted by the subsequent line of Caprington, with the important feudal hereditary office of " Crownar," or Coroner of King's Kyle, Kyle Stewart, and Cuninghame.

The next in order to the preceding Thomas, is William Cuningham, who obtained a charter from Robert III.,† (who reigned from 1390 to 1406), of the superiorities of Perston, Warwickhill, Drummore, and Caprinstane, in the barony of Cuninghame.

" Adam de Cuningham, dominus de Capringtoun," figures as the Caprington heir and representative on the first of December 1462, of which date he grants by charter,‡ the lands of " brokalmuir, in dominio de Dunlop, in ballia de Cuningham, Karissimo fratri meo Thomæ de Cuningham," while the latter Thomas, on the 3d of December 1462, under the explicit designation of " Laglane," (thus identifying him, as younger brother of Adam of Caprington), resigns the same lands of Brokalmuir, into his hands, for an heritable regrant—Adam being designed " nobilis vir " in the instrument.

This Thomas was the ancestor of the Cuninghams of *Laglane*, of repute and distinction in Ayrshire, and, from them, the late and present line of Cuningham of Caprington are descended through a younger branch, which came eventually to be the possessors and representatives of Caprington on failure of the former line.

On the 7th of November 1497,§ Adam Cuningham was infeft as heir of the preceding Adam Cuningham of Caprington, his father, in the twenty pound land of old extent of Caprington, in Kyle Stewart, Ayrshire ; in the three merk land of old extent of *Badlane* (Bedlan), and *brodokle*, with pertinents, in the bailiery of Cunyngham, " et de officio Coronatoris de Kileregis, Kilestewart et Cunyngham," all held of the Stewart of Scotland (James IV.) upon a special retour and precept, dated 28th October 1497—the instrument bearing that seisin was given " apud *turrim* de Caprington, hora xi. vel eo circa ante meridiem, presentibus ibidem honorabilibus ac providis viris Willielmo Cunyngham de Laglane," the then Laglane representative, and others, &c.

---

* Proved by writs in the Caprington charter chest.
† Index of charters extant and missing, by the kings of Scotland, published in 1798, by William Robertson, Esq., Deputy-Keeper of the Scotch Records, p. 140, No. 34.
‡ Caprington charter chest.        § Ibid.

On the 6th of March 1564, John Cuningham of Caprington, the direct Caprington representative, had a charter from Queen Mary,* creating and incorporating his estates "in unam integram et liberam baroniam, baroniam de Caprington, omni tempore nuncupandam," and ordaining "Castrum de Caprington fore principale messuagium dictæ baroniæ." Thus the family held by a baronial tenure directly of the Crown.

John was succeeded by William Cuningham of Caprington, his son and heir,† and this elder Caprington line (who were occasionally knighted), continued to figure in the seventeenth century, after the middle of which they lost their estates, and shortly thereafter the branch failed—when the male representation of Caprington devolved upon the Cuninghams of Rudeland and Broomhill, a branch of the Cuninghams of Laglane, who are proved to have sprung from Thomas, younger brother of Adam Cuningham of Caprington, in 1462, and to whom the remaining portion of this pedigree or family deduction necessarily is confined.‡

I. The above Thomas Cuningham of Laglane had issue,

II. Alexander Cuningham of Laglane, who was succeeded by his son,

III. William Cuningham of Laglane, (figuring *ante* in 1497), who had issue :—

1. Alexander Cuningham of Laglane whose descendants continued to hold that estate till 1663, when it was sold by Andrew Cuningham of Laglane to Mr. John Cuningham of Broomhill, advocate, afterwards of Lambruchton and Caprington, and created baronet in 1669.
2. Adam, who immediately follows.

IV. Adam Cuningham (the said younger son) figured in 1553, and is designed in writs as "in Potterhill" and "tutor of *Laglane*," and hence the next Laglane heir, or heir male, at the time. He was the father of

V. John Cuningham of Rudelands, who married Janet Macadam, and had issue :—

1. Mr. William Cuningham of Rudelands, (in 1613) of Broomhills, which last property he acquired,§ and of Privet Ac, but died without issue,
2. Hew.                                   3. John.
4. Mark of Privet, ancestor of the Cuninghames of Enterkine.

VI. John Cuningham of Broomhill, and of other lands, and of Geise in Caithness, where he was Admiral-Depute in 1630. He married, first, Jean Leslie, and had three daughters; secondly, Elizabeth, daughter of Sinclair of Ratter, (a cadet of the Earl of Caithness), by whom he had five sons and four daughters :—

1. Sir John of Lambruchton.          2. James of Geise.          3. George, a writer.
4. Adam, merchant in Edinburgh.      5. Alexander.
6. Jane, marr'd to David Murray of Clerdon.
8. Anne, married to Walter Brune of Stair.                7. Isabel, married to Alexander Sinclair of Telletone.
                                                          9. Mary, married to John Stewart of Ascog.

VII. Sir John Cuningham of Broomhill, Lambruchton, and Caprington, who was one of the most distinguished lawyers of the time. By patent, 21st December 1669, he was created a baronet to him and the heirs-male of his body. He possessed the lands of Lambruchton before he acquired, in 1683, the barony of Caprington from John, Earl of Glencairn. He married Margaret, eldest daughter of John Murray of Polmaise and Touchadam, Stirlingshire, by whom he had four sons and two daughters :—

1. Sir William, his heir.
2. John, an eminent lawyer. He kept up a constant correspondence with the celebrated Dutch lawyer, Voet, and was the first who read lectures on the Roman law, in Scotland, as well as on the Scotch law. He died in 1710.
3. James.                                4. Adam.
5. Janet, married to George Primrose of Dunipace.
                                         6. Elizabeth.

Sir John died in 1684, and was succeeded by

II. Sir William Cuningham, second Baronet of Caprington  He married Janet, only child and heiress of Sir James Dick of Prestonfield, Baronet, whose patent of Baronetcy, in 1707, limits it to those of the Cuninghames of Caprington, who were his heirs of entail. By her, Sir William had six sons and four daughters :—

1. Sir John, his heir.
2. James,        }
3. Sir William,  } who died without issue.
4. Sir Alexander,

The two last succeeded to the baronetcy and estate of Prestonfield.

---

* Caprington charter chest.        † Proved by writs in the Caprington charter chest        ‡ Ibid.
§ The property must have been acquired by Adam Cuninghame, Tutor of Laglane, who appears to have had a son William, as well as John of Rudelands.

5. Adam, } died unmarried.
6. Archibald }
7. Anne, married to Sir Robert Dalrymple, Bart. of North Berwick.
8. Margaret, married to Robert Keith of Craig, Esq. for some time Ambassador to the Courts of Vienna and St. Petersburgh.
9. Janet, married to Alexander Fergusson of Caltloch, Esq.
10. Christian, married to Sir John Douglas, Bart. of Kelhead, ancestor of the Marquis of Queensberry.

Sir William died in 1740, and was succeeded by his eldest son,

III. Sir John Cuningham, third Baronet of Caprington. He married Lady Elizabeth Montgomerie, eldest daughter of Alexander, ninth Earl of Eglintoun, by Susanna, daughter of Sir Archibald Kennedy, Baronet of Culzean, and by whom he had two sons :—

1. Sir William, his heir.                    2. Alexander Montgomerie Cuninghame, who died unmarried.

Sir John died in 1779, and was succeeded by his eldest son,

IV. Sir William Cuninghame, fourth Baronet of Caprington. He married Mary Swindell, relict of Captain John Græme, and died in 1829, without issue.

The Baronetcy devolved upon his cousin german, Sir Robert Keith Dick, Baronet of Prestonfield, who, by an Act of Parliament 8 and 9 Victoria, cap. 23, was enabled to take the surname of Cuninghame along with Dick, which otherwise he could not have done, through the entail of Prestonfield, by which alone he held that estate.

The direct senior representation of the family of Cuninghame of Lambruchton and Caprington, as well as of Dick of Prestonfield, with the estate of Caprington, then descended to the heirs of line of Alexander Cuninghame, younger son of Sir William Cuninghame, second Baronet of Caprington, by his wife, Dame Janet Dick, only child and heiress of Sir James Dick, first Baronet of Prestonfield. This Alexander Cuninghame, afterwards Sir Alexander Dick, third Baronet of Prestonfield, and holder of that title and estate in virtue of the Prestonfield patent and entail, left issue, three sons and five daughters :—

1. Sir William, his heir.
2. Sir John, who succeeded his nephew, Sir Alexander Dick, as sixth Baronet of Prestonfield, and died without issue.
3. Sir Robert Dick Keith, already mentioned, who succeeded the said Sir John, his brother, as seventh Baronet of Prestonfield.
4. Janet Dick, } who died unmarried.
5. Anne Dick, }
6. Elizabeth, married to the honourable Robert Lindsay of Balcarres.
7. Mary, married to Alexander Pringle of Whytbank, Esq.
8. Margaret-Alexander, married to James Stark of Kingsdale, Esq.

Sir William Dick, fourth Baronet of Prestonfield, married Dame Joanna Douglas of Garvaldfoot, and left issue, one son and four daughters :—

1. Sir Alexander, his heir.
2. Mary, married to the Rev. David Wauchope, whom she predeceased, leaving only one child, John-Mary Wauchope, who died on 5th January 1820, without issue.
3. Anne, to be immediately mentioned.
4. Agnes-Joanna, married to Alexander Pringle of Whytbank, Esq., her cousin-german.
5. Elizabeth-Douglas-Trotter Dick, married to Major-General Sir Duncan M'Gregor.

Sir Alexander Dick, fifth Baronet of Prestonfield, (the only son), died unmarried in 1808. His sisters, above-mentioned, became the heirs of line, while the Prestonfield baronetcy and estate devolved to the next heir-male, Sir John Dick, sixth Baronet of Prestonfield.

Sir William Cunninghame, fourth Baronet of Caprington, died without issue, upon 16th January 1829, and, by the failure of nearer heirs, the senior representation of the family of Caprington, together with the castle and principal portion of the estate, and in like manner the senior representation of the family of Dick of Prestonfield, were vested, by special service of 10th December 1829, in the before-mentioned Anne Dick or Cuninghame, second, but then the eldest surviving daughter of Sir William Dick, fourth Baronet of Prestonfield. This Lady married John Smith, Esq., who obtained a licence from King William IV. to use the surname of Cuninghame. She died on 1st March 1830, and left issue by her said husband two sons and two daughters :—

1. Thomas Smith Cuninghame, her heir.
2. William Cathcart Smith Cuninghame, in the Civil Service of the East India Company, married Maria, daughter of James Anstruther, Esq.
3. Joanna Trotter Smith Cuninghame, married to the Rev. William Henry Cooper.
4. Mary Anne Keith Smith Cuninghame, died unmarried on 9th October 1842.

*Armorial Bearings*—Quarterly, first and fourth, argent a sheaf-fork sable, within a bordure, ermine ; second and third, ermine, a fess azure betwixt two mullets in chief and a hart's head erased in base, attired with ten tynes gules. Above the shield is placed a helmet with a mantling gules doubled argent, and surmounting the achievement are placed two crests, viz:—on the dexter side upon a wreath argent and sable, a dexter hand holding a plumb-rule proper, and in an escroll over the same, this motto, " Ad Amussim." And on the sinister upon a wreath argent and azure, a ship in distress proper, and in an escroll over the same, this motto, " At spes infracta; " and on a compartment below the shield, which is entwined with an escroll, whereon is inscribed the words " Via tuta virtutis," are placed for supporters, two horses at liberty, argent, maned and hoofed, or.

*Seat*—Caprington Castle, Ayrshire.

### CRAUFURD OF BALSHAGRAY AND SCOTSTOUN.

Although the estates of Balshagray and Scotstoun lie in the counties of Lanark and Renfrew, and, consequently, do not fall to be noticed in the body of this work, yet as this family of Craufurds is one of the most recent cadets of Craufurdland, and as a notice of them is given by Robertson, which is, however, neither very full nor very accurate, we here, in the Appendix, insert an account of the family taken from authentic documents. In a note on page 200 of vol. ii. of this work, where the family are mentioned, some inaccuracies have also occurred, which we shall here correct.

I. John Craufurd of Craufurdland,* who succeeded his grandfather in 1612, married, in 1630, Janet, daughter of William Cuninghame of Craigends, and by her had issue seven sons and five daughters. The third son was

II. William Craufurd, merchant and burgess of Glasgow, b. 1642, died 21st June 1703, aged 61, and was interred in the High Church yard at Glasgow on the 25th of the same month. He mortified £100 for the poor members of the merchants' rank, also £100 for the poor under the charge of the Kirk Session of Glasgow.† He married Martha, daughter of John Miller, of the Barskimming family, and by her had issue :‡—

1. Anthony, stated by Robertson to have been the eldest son, and who, if he ever existed, must have died in his youth. We have seen no old document in which he is mentioned.
2. Matthew, of Balshagray and Scotstoun, of whom afterwards.
3. John, b. 5th March 1685.
4. Agnes, b. 1687. She was interred in the High Church yard at Glasgow, 2d June 1758, aged 70. She married John Cross, merchant in Glasgow, and had issue. Her marriage contract is dated 16th October 1708, and among the parties subscribing it is Alexander Craufurd of Fergushill, her father's brother.
5. Alexander, b. 28th February 1684.
6. James, b. 28th August 1689, interred in the High Church yard at Glasgow, 25th May 1756.
7. Martha, b. 11th November 1696. She must have died previous to 10th March 1696, when another daughter was baptized, of the same name.
8. Janet, b. 16th October 1692, interred in the High Church yard at Glasgow, 3d August 1703.
9. Margaret, b. 15th January 1695, was interred in the High Church yard at Glasgow, 15th December 1699.
10. Martha, b. 10th March 1696. She married James Dalrymple of Harvieston, § whom she survived, being mentioned as his relict in the testament of William Craufurd of Balshagray, 1756. She had issue.
11. Robert, b. 26th October 1698, was buried in the High Church yard at Glasgow, 5th February 1699.

III. Matthew Craufurd, of Balshagray and Scotstoun, succeeded his father. He married, first, in 1705, Agnes, daughter of Alexander Stewart of Torrance, (the marriage contract is dated 28th April 1705,) and by her had issue an only child,

Agnes, born 16th July 1706. She married, about 1726, Mr. William Dalrymple, younger of Cousland, afterwards Sir William Dalrymple of Cranstoun, Baronet—her post-nuptial contract of marriage is dated 31st August 1741. She died 13th September 1755, leaving issue,—now represented by the Earl of Stair, her grandson.

Matthew Craufurd, married, secondly, in 1712,|| Esther,¶ youngest daughter and co-heiress, (with her sister, Elizabeth, wife of Sir John Dalrymple, Baronet,) of William Fletcher of New Crans-

---

* No. XVIII. of that pedigree. Vol. ii. p. 198.
† M'Ure's History of Glasgow.
‡ In the note on page 200 of vol. ii. of this work, William Craufurd is said to have had four sons and one daughter. The same mistake also occurs in the text at p. 198. His family was much more numerous.
§ Son of Sir James Dalrymple of Killoch, Baronet, by Esther Cunningham of Enterkine, mentioned below.
¶ The marriage contract is dated 17th September 1712. Among the relations, at whose instance execution is to pass and subscribing witnesses, are Sir James Dalrymple of Killoch, Baronet, and his sons, Andrew Fletcher of Saltoun, and his brother Mr. Henry Fletcher, George Home of Kaimes, John Cunningham of Enterkine, George Munro of Culrain, William Baillie of Monktoun, John Miller of Glenlee, Daniel Campbell of Shawfield, and others.
¶ General Retours.

toun,* (by Esther,† third daughter of John Cunningham of Enterkine,) and by her, who was interred in the High Church yard of Glasgow, 6th June 1751, he had a numerous family.

In 1714, Matthew Craufurd had sasine of tenements in Glasgow. In 1719, he acquired the estates of Balshagray, Balgray, and Hyndland, in the county of Lanark, of which he had sasine in 1720, and obtained a Crown charter thereof 15th February 1721. He also held the adjacent estate of Scotstoun, in the county of Renfrew, in satisfaction of a large heritable debt, apparently at first redeemably, but afterwards irredeemably. He died in March 1744, and was buried in the High Church yard at Glasgow on the 26th of that month. On the 23d and 27th October 1741, he granted bonds of provision in favour of his younger children. His issue by Esther Fletcher were :‡

1. William, of Balshagray and Scotstoun, of whom afterwards.
2. Esther, b. 25th July 1714.
3. John, b. 1715, or 1716 and who died at Glasgow in July 1763. He was a surgeon, but was also engaged in various mercantile speculations along with his brothers. On 10th April 1754 he was infeft in part of Stobcross under a bond. He married Janet, daughter of John Orr of Barrowfield and Orugar, and had issue—
   1. Matthew, who died unmarried at Edinburgh in 1815.
   2. John, of the island of Jamaica, who married Miss Mary Johnstone of New York, and had issue.
   3. Esther, who married James Whyte of New Mains, and had, with other issue, Janet Esther, who married, in 1808, William Howieson Craufurd of Craufurdland,§ and has issue.
   Also four daughters, Ellen, Agnes, William, and Janet Craufurds, who all died unmarried.
4. Mathew, b. 17th September 1717.
5. Martha,‖ who married, on 13th September 1743, William Orr, younger of Barrowfield. She died, at Kailzie 14th April 1780, leaving issue.
6. Thomas b. 3d July 1722; he was educated at Oxford.
7. Alexander, b. 2d July 1723, and died in May 1754. His testament dative, given up by his brother John Craufurd, surgeon in Glasgow, is in the Commissary Record, 22d June 1758.
8. Elizabeth, b. 31st January 1725.

IV. William Craufurd, of Balshagray and Scotstoun, the eldest son, b. 14th August 1713, was a merchant in Glasgow. He married Mary, daughter of Peter Murdoch, Lord Provost of Glasgow, by Anne, daughter of John Alexander of Blackhouse and Janet Cunningham of Craigends. Mary Murdoch, who died in November 1755, was aunt to Margaret Murdoch, wife of Sir Thomas Miller of Glenlee, Baronet.

On 11th November 1741, during the lifetime of his father, William Craufurd was infeft in the lands of Balshagray, Balgray, and Hyndland and others, and on 13th December 1742 he had another sasine of these lands. In 1749, 1750, and 1755, he had various sasines of other lands in the same district, and in 1751, he was infeft in the lands of Easter and Wester Scotstouns. His estates were valuable and extensive.

William Craufurd was the intimate friend of the poet Hamilton of Bangour—a fact of which we were not aware when editing a new edition of his works in 1850. His character is highly praised in the dedication of the posthumous edition of Hamilton's works, which we quote below.¶ We also give some verses, hitherto unpublished, addressed to Mr. Craufurd by the poet.**

* William Fletcher of New Cranstoun, advocate, was son of David Fletcher, Bishop of Argyle, and nephew of Sir John Fletcher of New Cranstoun, who was appointed Lord Advocate, 5th February 1661, and who appears to have been a brother of Sir Andrew Fletcher of Innerpeffer, one of the Senators of the College of Justice. The estate of Over or New Cranstoun, (also called Cranstoun Daw,) in the county of Mid Lothian, [now belongs to John Earl of Stair, the representative of Elizabeth, the eldest daughter of William Fletcher. The arms of the family were borne by Sir William Dalrymple, in right of his mother, and are, "Sable, a cross flory, cantoned with four escallops, argent."

† Esther Cuningham married, secondly, Sir James Dalrymple of Killoch. Baronet, being his second wife

‡ At page 198, vol. ii. of this work, as also in the note on page 200, it is stated that Matthew Craufurd had seven sons and one daughter,—his family according to the evidence of the registers, consisted of five sons and three daughters. In the same note it is also erroneously stated that Matthew was the eldest son of Matthew Craufurd and Esther Fletcher. The same mistake is made by Robertson, but it is corrected in manuscript, by his own hand, in the copy of his work in the Library of the Faculty of Advocates at Edinburgh, [now belongs to John Earl of "Matthew" being erased and "William" substituted. The hand-writing in which this is done is the same as that of the very numerous corrections all through this copy, and that it is the author's own is evident from the note at the foot of p. 182, vol. ii. (Robertson.) This correction is printed in a small pamphlet of corrections published afterwards, a copy of which is deposited in the Lord Lyon's Office.

§ See vol. ii. pages 199 and 200.

‖ In the note before referred to Martha is said to have been the only daughter. This is a mistake.

¶ "To the memory of Mr. William Craufurd, merchant in Glasgow, the friend of Mr. Hamilton—who to that exact frugality, that downright probity and plainness of manners so suitable to his profession, joined a love of learning and of all the ingenious arts, an openness of hand and a generosity of heart that was free both from vanity and from weakness, and a magnanimity that could support, under the prospect of approaching and unavoidable death, the most torturing pains of body with an unalterable cheerfulness of temper, and without once interrupting, even to his last hour, the most manly and the most vigorous activity in a vast variety of business:

"This edition of the works of a gentleman for whom he, who was candid and penetrating, circumspect and sincere always expressed the highest and the most affectionate esteem, is inscribed by the editors, as the only monument which it is in their power to raise of their veneration and of their regret."

** "Lines addressed to Mr. William Craufurd upon his having gone to live in the country, by Mr. Hamilton:

William Craufurd died in 1755, and was interred in the High Church yard of Glasgow on the 11th November of that year—nine days before his wife. He made a general disposition, *omnium bonorum*, in favour of his only surviving son Peter, by whom, and by Mr., afterwards Sir John, Dalrymple, his nephew, Provost John Murdoch of Rosebank, and Provost Cochrane of Cochranelodge and Bridgehouse, his brothers-in-law, and others, tutors to the said Peter Craufurd, who was a pupil, his testament dative is given up, 6th May 1756. His issue were :—

1. Anna, b. 22d September 1742, died unmarried, as is shown by her testament dative confirmed at Glasgow 5th February 1782.
2. Esther, of whom afterwards.
3. Matthew, b. 2d January 1748, died before his father, as is shown by the testament dative of William Craufurd, given up by Peter Craufurd, ONLY SON of William, in which the decree dative is dated 6th May 1756, and by general disposition, 'omnium bonorum,' granted by William Craufurd in favour of Peter Craufurd, dated 23d October, 1755, and registered in the books of the Commissary Court of Glasgow.
4. Peter, of whom more below.

V. Peter Craufurd of Balshagray, b. 24th August 1753. In 1757, he was infeft in various lands lying in the regality of Glasgow and shire of Lanark, but the estates appear to have been disposed of during his minority. In 1776 he is designed merchant in Virginia, but he afterwards went to Calcutta, and, having fitted out an armed ship, engaged in the China trade. In 1782 he had a severe action with a French privateer, which he beat off, with considerable loss to both ships, but principally to the French vessel. Peter Craufurd died at Calcutta on the 26th of April 1783. By his will, dated 17th December 1782, he bequeaths legacies to his cousins, John Craufurd, of the Island of Jamaica, and Helen, Agnes, William, and Janet Craufurds, children of his uncle John, as also to the daughters of his aunt Mrs. Orr. The residue of his estate, which was considerable, he left to his cousin, John Orr of Barrowfield, and his only surviving sister, Esther. He appoints as his executors his cousins, Sir John Dalrymple of Cousland, Baronet, and John Orr of Barrowfield, and his brother-in-law, Henry Ritchie. His only surviving sister,

VI. Esther Craufurd, b. 28th April 1745, became, on the death of Peter Craufurd, representative of this family. She married Henry Ritchie, merchant in Glasgow, son of John Ritchie of Craigton,*—the marriage contract is dated 31st October 1767. Her husband died 14th June 1792, and she died 19th November 1812, and was interred in the north-west burying-ground at Glasgow on the 25th of that month. She had issue :—

1. Mary.
2. Helen, b. 5th February 1770,   }   Those two daughters both died previous to 18th July 1776, as is shown by a settlement of Henry Ritchie's of that date (afterwards cancelled) wherein his daughter Janet is designed " his only child now in life."
3. Janet, of whom afterwards.

VII. Janet Ritchie, b. 1772, or 1773, was interred in the north-west burying-place of Glasgow 15th May 1818, aged 45. She was served heiress to her father, as his only child, by ward of Court at Glasgow on 6th July 1792, and, on 21st July 1813, had sasine of the lands of Cranstonhill, proceeding on a charter of confirmation and precept of *Clare Constat* in her favour as heiress of her mother. She married, 18th August, 1795, her second cousin, Samuel Cooper of Ballindalloch, afterwards of Failford,† bringing to him a considerable fortune. She is now represented by her eldest surviving son, William Cooper of Failford, who is heir of line of the Craufurds of Balshagray.

The arms of Craufurd of Balshagray, viz. " Gules, a fess ermine, and, in chief, a mollet of the last," were borne by Samuel Cooper in right of his wife, and by authority of the Lord Lyon. He also claimed right to quarter " sable, a cross flory, cantoned with four escallops argent," in right of Esther Fletcher, co-heiress of New Cranstoun.

> " When Balshagry's rural seat
> Received you in its calm retreat,
> Trees you planted round you growing,
> Flowers you set around you blowing,
> Every wish resigned or granted,
> All enjoying, nothing wanted,
> Fond to be pleased, and fond to please,
> Seeking but for health and ease,
> This pleasing character review
> Which Horace praised and Virgil drew."

* See vol. ii. p. 219.                    † See p. 492.

## COCHRANE OF BRIDGEHOUSE.

In the first volume of this work* we have given a short account of Andrew Cochrane of Bridgehouse, a person of considerable celebrity in his day, and who seems worthy of a more lengthened notice.

This gentleman, who was Provost of Glasgow in 1745, 1746, as also on two subsequent occasions, was much distinguished on account of his prudent management of the affairs of that city during the rebellion, and for his unwearied exertions in subsequently obtaining compensation for the losses sustained through the neglect of all precautions on the part of the authorities in Scotland. He was a person of great learning, and considerable literary abilities. In 1836 the "Cochrane Correspondence," regarding the affairs of Glasgow, was published by James Smith, Esq of Jordanhill, with a prefatory notice by James Dennistoun, Esq. of Dennistoun, and presented to the Maitland Club. This correspondence consists principally of letters from Provost Cochrane to the parties at the head of affairs in Scotland, at the time of the rebellion, and of their replies, and is extremely interesting as matter of authentic local history.

Andrew Cochrane of Bridgehouse was infeft, on 1st May 1760, in parts of the lands of Stobcross, called Cochrane Lodge. He married the eldest daughter of Peter Murdoch, Provost of Glasgow. He was, for more than forty years, Preceptor of Hutcheson's Hospital, and his portrait had been taken for that institution, from which it has now disappeared; there is, however, a curious miniature of him, on copper, still in existence.† His library was bequeathed to James Browne, junior, merchant in Glasgow, who, again left it to John Ballantyne, "late merchant in Glasgow, now in Ayr," with a request that the said books should not be sold. There are in the hands of William Cooper, Esq. of Failford, several letters addressed by Provost Cochrane to his wife's sister, Mary Murdoch, wife of William Craufurd of Balshagray, which are written in an elegant and amusing style. From reference in these letters to the state of health of Lord Dundonald, it may possibly be inferred that Provost Cochrane was a relative of the Dundonald family.

Andrew Cochrane died on 9th July 1777, in the 85th year of his age, and the Magistrates of Glasgow erected, in the High Church of that city, a handsome monument, with a Latin inscription, to his memory, which is still in existence. Among the papers in Mr. Cooper's possession there is the following epitaph, which would appear to have been inscribed on a monument, but where this monument was erected is not known :—

" Sacred to the memory
Of Andrew Cochrane, Citizen of Glasgow;
A gentleman descended from a reputable family,
Who, after receiving a liberal education,
Prosecuted mercantile business in this town with success;
And having several times
Discharged offices of Magistracy in the City
Exhibited an instance of upright and prudent behaviour,
While supporting the character of Lord Provost,
During the rage of the late rebellion:
Who, by conducting the business of the Community
Before the British House of Commons,
With his usual sagacity and wisdom,
Obtained for his fellow citizens
The restitution of a sum of money
Carried away from them
By the enemies of this country and of liberty;
Who, eminently skilled in the laws and history
Of his native country,
And improved by a long course of experience
Was respected by his friends for his eloquence and learning;
And at convivial meetings, even in his old age,
Was an agreeable and cheerful companion;
And who, at last, finished a long and illustrious life,
Upon the 9th day of July 1777,
In the 85th year of his age.

His heir erected this Monument."

---

* Volume i. p. 202 and 221.          † In the possession of Henry Ritchie Cooper, Esq. of Ballindalloch.

## FERGUSHILL OF FERGUSHILL.

*(Omitted in its proper place—the Parish of Kilwinning.)*

The property of Fergushill is situated on the north banks of the Lugton, about four miles eastward of Kilwinning. The Fergushills of that Ilk were, no doubt, an ancient family.

*Robert de Fergushill de Eodem* appears as one of the jury in a trial respecting property between the burgh of Irvine and William Fraunces of Stane in 1417. At that time the estate is known to have been much more extensive than it was latterly.

No regular account of the family can be given either before or subsequent to this period. In 1590 (1st March) they had a charter of legitimation:—" Legitimatio Roberti et Johannæ Fergushills, filij et filiæ naturalium Alexandri Fergushill, tutoris de Fergushill." Of the same date, *Alexander Fergushill*, tutor of Fergushill, and Robert, his son, had a charter of confirmation of the lands of Nethermains.

*Robert Fergushill of that Ilk* was served heir to his father, *John Fergushill of that Ilk*, in 1596. The same Robert, apparently, had a Crown charter of the lands of Annanhill Hunter, 22d May 1616. He is supposed to have married Elizabeth, daughter of John Craufurd of Craufurdland. He and his spouse had a Crown charter of the lands of Busbie Fergushill, &c., 22d November 1621. Robert Ferguson of that Ilk is mentioned in various testamentary documents; amongst others, in that of Margaret Cvmyng, in Busbie Fergushill, Kilmaurs,' in 1618. He must have died previous to 1625, in which year

*Robert Fergushill* was served heir to his father, " Robert Fergushill de Eodem." He married in 1622, Marion, daughter of Alexander Porterfield, younger of that Ilk. He had a Crown charter of the lands Middle Auchintibber, 2d March 1633. This was the last of the old Lairds of Fergushill. He appears to have died without male issue.

In 1658, " Jeane Fergushill, dochter of ye lait Laird of Fergushill, left, at her death, " a hundred merks to Jean Porterfield, relict of umquhille Robert Hamiltoun of Torrence.

## CRAUFURD OF FERGUSHILL.

The estate of Fergushill appears to have been acquired by the Craufurdland family—probably as the nearest heirs on the female side—immediately after the death of the heiress, *Jeane Fergushill*, who died, as above, in 1658.

*Alexander Craufurd of Fergushill* was the second son of John Craufurd of Craufurdlands and Janet Cuninghame, daughter of the Laird of Craigends. He appears in the list of Commissioners for ordering out the Militia of Ayrshire in 1689. He was twice married: first, to Elizabeth, daughter of Maxwell of Southbar; and, secondly to Isabel Henderson, relict of Bryce Boyd of Pitcon, by both of whom he had issue. John Craufurd, his eldest son by the first marriage, married Anna, the younger sister of Major Daniel Ker of Kersland, (killed, in 1692, at the battle of Steinkirk,) and by an arrangement with her elder sister, Jean, became proprietor of Kersland, and assumed the name of Ker. He wrote the well-known *Memoirs*, and was politically notorious during the reign of King William. He had also a son.

*James Craufurd*, surgeon, who predeceased his father. By his wife, Agnes Kincaid, he had a son.

*Thomas Kincaid*, also of the medical profession, who, together with his mother, alienated the lands of Fergushill to Neil Macvicar and Elizabeth Montgomerie, his spouse, by a disposition, dated 17th March 1728.

The lands of Fergushill remained with the Macvicar family till 1802, when they were acquired by Robert Glasgow of Mountgreenan.

## CUNYNGHAME OF MILNCRAIG.

*(Omitted in its proper place—the Parish of Coylton.)*

This family claims to be descended from the Earls of Glencairn, through the Craigends branch of the Cuninghame stock. They were originally of *Polquhairn*, in the Parish of Ochiltree (see page 401 of this volume.) *James Cuninghame of Polquhairn*, living in 1578, was probably the first of the family. They are said to have acquired " the estate of Milncraig by intermarrying with one of the daughters and co-heirs of William Cathcart of Carbiestoun,"* but this must be a mistake, as none of the Carbiestoun family left co-heiresses save William, who died in 1547, and one of them dying, the other became the sole heiress. The statement may be right, however, in the main fact, that the property was acquired by marriage with the Carbiestoun family. The first of the Cuninghames of Milncraig (or Milnquarter, as it was sometimes called) appears to have been

*Johnne Cunynghame of Milnquarter*, whose name occurs in the testament of David Fergushill of Conyng Park, as a creditor for " ane thousand pundis," in 1613. The next, apparently, was

*David Cuninghame of Milncraig*, who died in December 1659. According to his latter-will, he left a son, *David*, his heir, and two daughters, *Agnes* and *Catherin*, to whom he gave portions of two thousand merks each. His wife's name was *Margaret Maisson*, sister of John Maisson, writer in Ayr, and daughter of John Masoun, Town Clerk of the burgh, whose *Notarial Book* we have so often quoted from. He was succeeded by his son,

*David Cunyngham of Milncraig*. He was a distinguished lawyer, an able debater in the Scottish Parliament, and the friend and coadjutor of Fletcher of Saltoun. He acquired the property of Livingstone, in Linlithgowshire, and was created a *Baronet of Nova Scotia*, 3d February 1702. He married, first, Isabella, youngest daughter of James, first Viscount Stair : and, secondly, Elizabeth, daughter of Sir Robert Baird, Bart. of Soughton Hall. Sir David died before 1733, and was succeeded by his eldest son,

*Sir James Cunynghame of Milncraig and Livingstone*, who purchased Roodlands, and other properties in Ayr parish, 27th November 1733. He died, married, in 1747, and was succeeded by his brother,

*Sir David Cunynghame of Milncraig and Livingstone*. He was a Lieutenant-General in the army, and Colonel of the 57th Regiment of Infantry (1751.) He married Lady Mary Montgomerie,† only daughter of Alexander, ninth Earl of Eglinton, by whom he had, with other children, *William Augustus‡* and *Margaret*, married to the Hon. James Stuart Wortley Mackenzie. Sir David died suddenly, 10th October 1767, and was succeeded by his son,

*Sir William Augustus Cunynghame of Milncraig and Livingstone*. He married, first in 1768, Frances, daughter and heir of Sir Robert Myrton, Bart. of Gogar, county of Mid-Lothian, by whom he had :—

1. David, present Baronet.
2. Robert. Married, 8th April 1813, Maria, daughter of Dundas of Dundas, and left issue :—
    1. Caroline Stirling. Married 9th December 1830, Sempster-John-Henry Bulkeley, Esq., Captain of the 40th Regiment, son of the late Colonel Bulkely, by Katherine Feilding, his wife, sister of the first Lady Ribbesdale.
    2. Frances Jane-Myrton. Married, 19th July 1844, to Adolphe le Croix, Esq., Her Britannic Majesty's Consul at Nice.
    3. Mary Montgomerie. Married, in July 1846, to Alexander Woodford, Esq., third son of Lieutenant-General Sir Alexander Woodford.
    4. Francis. Married Miss Jane Whiteford.

Sir William married, secondly, in 1785, Mary, only daughter and heir of Robert Udney, Esq. of Udney, and had issue :—

1. William-Augustus, born in 1788; died in 1827.
2. George-Augustus-Frederick, born in 1790.
3. Frederick-Alexander
4. James Stuart Wortley (deceased).
5. Mary.

He died 17th January 1828, and was succeeded by his eldest son,

*Sir David Cunynghame of Milncraig and Livingstone*, the present Baronet, a Colonel in the army. He married, first, in 1801, Maria, daughter of Edward Thurlow, Lord Chancellor of England, by whom (who died 21st February 1816) he has had issue :—

1. Edward Thurlow, born 23d September 1802; died in 1825.
2. David Thurlow, born September 1804, married in 1833, Anne, third daughter of the Hon. General Robert Meade.
3. Robert S. Thurlow, born 27th March 1807 ; died in 1828.
4. Francis Thurlow, born 11th August 1808.
5. Arthur Thurlow, born 3d August 1812.
1. Mary Frances Thurlow, married to the Hon. Augustus Ellis, second son of Lord Seaford.
2. Caroline Anne Thurlow, died in 1830.

Sir David married, secondly, in 1817, Gertrude-Henrietta, daughter of William Kimpton, Esq. of Ampthill, in Bedfordshire, and has surviving issue by that lady :—

---

* Burke's Peerage and Baronetage.      † The subject of one of Hamilton of Bangour's Poems.
‡ He and his father, Sir David, were admitted burgesses of Ayr in 1754.

1. Henry-Sydney-Myrton, born 6th August 1817.
2. William-Augustus-Charles-Myrton, born 6th January 1824.
3. Augustus-Myrton, born 8th January 1829.
4. Julia-Myrton. Married, 4th January 1844, to Frederick-William, second son of R. C. Kirby, Esq. of Blandford London.

*Arms*—Argent, a shake-fork between three fleurs-de-lis, sable.
*Crest*—An unicorn's head, armed and crined, or.
*Supporters*—Dexter, a knight in armour, holding in his exterior hand a spear; sinister, a countryman, in his exterior hand a hay-fork.
*Motto*—Over fork over.
*Seats*—Livingstone and Milncraig.

---

## CORRECTED VERSION OF THE HAPLAND PORTERFIELDS.

### (*From the Duchall MS., drawn up in* 1708).

*Magister John Porterfield of that Ilk* (No. IX. in the Porterfield pedigree) married, first, Beatrix Cunyngham, daughter of the Laird of Craigends, in 1540; and secondly, Jean Knox, daughter of the Laird of Ranforlie, in 1545. He had by Beatrix Cunynghame :—

1. William, his successor, of whom afterwards.
2. Gabriel, infeft in the 40s. land of Aikenbar; Blairlin, Bellcroft, and St. Mungo's Bell, in the lordship of Provan, near Glasgow, and the vicar-land of Ardrossan, called the Stanlie, in 1568, left by his uncle, Sir William Porterfield, Vicar of Ardrossan. He died unmarried, or without issue, about 1577. His brother, William, succeeded him in the said land.
3. Marion, Lady Culbertswood.

Mr. Porterfield had issue by his second wife :—

4. John, of Greenend.
5. Elizabeth, married to Archibald Campbell of Oailan, Dumbartonshire.

---

*William Porterfield of that Ilk, and of Duchall*, married Isobel, daughter of John Cunyngham of Glengarnock, in 1560. He died in 1616. They had issue :—

1. Alexander, his successor.
2. Jean. Married, first, Alexander Cunyngham, younger of Waterstonn, in 1580; and, secondly, William Muir, younger (his second wife), of Rowallan, 1605.
3. Married to the Laird of Corshill, in 1594.
4. Marion, married to Patrick Maxwell of Dargavill, in 1595.

---

*Alexander Porterfield*, younger, born about 1561. He died in 1609. He married Agnes, daughter of Patrick Houston of that Ilk, in 1587, and had issue :—

1. Jean, married to Robert Hamilton of Torrance.
2. Alexander, of that Ilk, married Ann, daughter of John Blair of that Ilk, in 1613.
3. GABRIEL PORTERFIELD OF HAPLAND. He got the four lib. land of Hapland in 1616.
4. George, Provost of Glasgow, married Janet Patonn, a merchant's daughter.
5. Agnes, married, first, to William Cathcart of Waterheid; and, secondly, to William Wallace of Johnston.
6. Marion, married to Robert Fergushill of that Ilk, in 1622.*
7. Mary, married to Robert Hamilton, younger of Aikenbead, in 1625.

---

*Gabriel Porterfield*, the second son, obtained the four lib. land of Hapland, with the 6s. 8d. land, called the Temple Land thereof, in the parish of Dunlop, from his grandfather, William Porterfield of that Ilk. This he had in virtue of a contract betwixt William, his grandfather, and Alexander, his brother, heir to the said William. The discharge, under Gabriel's hand, is dated at Duchall, 25th May 1616. He married, first, in 1618, Margaret Craufurd of Lochnorris, by which union he acquired the house and yards, and some part of the lands of Lochnorris, which he afterwards sold to Lord Crichton. By this marriage he had :—

1. William, who died young.

---

* The writer of the Duchall M.S. remarks that "Johnstoun and Fergushill ran themselves headlong into poverty."

2. Anna, married to Mr. Hugh Peebles of Mainshill.
3. Jean, married to James Anderson of Stobcross.

Gabriel Porterfield married, secondly, Jean Maxwell, sister to John Maxwell of Dargavill, and got 2400 merks of tocher, as per contract, dated at Glasgow, 22d July 1624. He had issue by this marriage :—

| 4. John, of whom afterwards. | 5. Alexander. | 6. Gabriel. |
| 7. George. | 8. Marion. | 9. Elizabeth. |

Gabriel Porterfield of Hapland married, thirdly, Jean, daughter of Douglas of Muirstown, who was a senator of the College of Justice. She was the widow of Edmiston of Umit. (After Hapland's decease, she married Cuninghame of Dankeith.) By this marriage there were :—

10. William, a soldier, who went abroad and never returned.
11. Mary, married to a Mr. Fullarton, merchant in Irvine.
12. Isobel, who died unmarried.

Gabriel Porterfield died in 1648, and was succeeded by his son,
*John Porterfield of that Ilk.* He was a youth of great promise. He was a Captain in the Scotch army when Cromwell was in Scotland, for which his estate was sequestrated. He was a person of good courage and magnanimity, and of a good presence. He was to have been married to a daughter of the Laird of Corshill, and to have got 10,000 merks of tocher, but he fell sick when the marriage was to have been solemnized, and died much lamented. He was succeeded by his brother, *Alexander,* in 1653, who held the lands only for a short time, and died unmarried at the house of Duchall. He was succeeded by his next brother,
*Gabriel Porterfield of Hapland,* who occurs in 1675. He married Jane, daughter of Robert Hamilton of Barns, and got with her 8000 merks of tocher. Of this marriage there were, besides others, who died young :—

| 1. Gabriel, his successor. | 2. Margaret. | 3. Mary. |
| 4. Ann. | 5. Jean. | |

Gabriel Porterfield died in 1687. He was, in the words of the Duchall MS., "a very discreet and virtuous person."
*Gabriel Porterfield of Hapland* succeeded his father. He married, as stated in the former account, Elizabeth Cuninghame, daughter of the Laird of Craigends, and had issue :—

1. Alexander, killed by a fall from his horse.
2. Johanna, married to Thomas Trotter of Mortonhall.
3. Margaret, married to John Hamilton of Barr.
4. Lillias, married to William Somerville of Kennox.

## COCHRANES OF THAT ILK.

*William Cochran of that Ilk.* He lived at the Place, or Castle of Cochran on the borders of Paisley and Lochwinnoch parishes. He married Margaret, daughter of Sir Robert Montgomerie of Skelmorlie, and by her had an only daughter, Elizabeth, in whose favour he made a settlement in 1593.
*Elizabeth Cochrane* was married to Alexander, third son of John Blair of that Ilk, by Grissel Sempill, daughter of the great Lord Sempill. She occurs 7th February 1601-2. This gentleman assumed the name of Cochrane, in compliance with the settlement made by her father. Alexander Cochrane of that Ilk, and Elizabeth Cochrane, his spouse, superiors, feued out ane seven shilling land of Halshill, or Auchincreuch, in the barony of Cochran, 12th March 1640, to Richard and William Robesoun, father and son. To this document, dated at the place of Cochran, Alexander Cochrane of that Ilk appends his name. Witnesses—Hew Craufurd, servitor to Magister William Cochrane of Cowdoun, John Hamiltoun, Maister of the Music School at Pasley, and John Quhyt, notar. Witnesses to the subscription of Elizabeth Cochrane at Glasgow—Ochter Cochrane, Gavine Cochrane, her sons, and Andro Trimbill, servitour to Mr. William Cochrane of Cowdoun. Elizabeth Cochrane could not write herself, and James Gray, notar, signed for her.
Alexander Cochrane of that Ilk seems to have died before 1646. He had issue :—

1. Sir John, Colonel in the army. He married one Butler, of the Ormond family. He had no issue, and died before the Restoration.
2. Mr. William Cochrane of Cowdoun, or Cowdounhall, afterwards Earl of Dundonald.*

Cowdoun is in the parish of Neilston, and now one of the baronies of Col. Mure of Caldwell. It was the ancient site of the original castle, or *domus vitus*, of the High Stewards, or royal family of Scotland, before the Castle of Renfrew was built in the twelfth century.† A part of the Scots army at the Battle of the Standard, 1138, in all likelihood commanded by Walter, the Dapifer, were called *Lavernani*, from the water of Lavern, which runs past Coudounhall. The county of Renfrew had previously been called Strathgryffe, from the neighbouring water of Gryffe. Walter, the third Steward (from 1204 to 1206), had a daughter, Elizabeth, married to Maldwin, Earl of Lennox. He probably gave Cowdoun, or Cowdounhall (useless as the family residence) to her in tocher ; at all events it was afterwards granted by the Earl of Lennox to his factor or chamberlain, Walter Spreull. The Spreulls were, for many ages afterwards, in high estimation. James Spreull of Cowdoun sold his estate to Alexander Cochrane of that Ilk in 1622, whose son, always styled *Mr.* Cochrane of Cowdoun, from his College degree, until his elevation to the peerage in 1647, bought the lordship of Paisley and the barony of Glen from the Earl of Angus, in 1653, for £160,000 Scots. Lord Angus bought the same from the Earl of Abercorn in 1652. His Lordship was banished from the kingdom by the inquisition of the Scots Kirk in 1649.

3. Alexander, of Auchincruoch, a Colonel in the army. He married Agnes Richieson, who died before 30th May 1668. The Colonel died between 1671 and 1674. They had issue :—
  1. William, served heir of his mother, 30th May 1668.
  2. James, made a burgess of Glasgow 23d April 1674. He was a writer in Edinburgh in 1677 and 1681. He married, first, Marion, daughter of Mr. Hugh Peebles of Mainshill (parish of Beith), and Minister of Lochwinnoch, by whom he had no surviving issue. He married, secondly, Ursula, daughter of William Hamiltoun of Brinmore (parish of Beith), ancestor of Lord Belhaven, before 1691. He had an only daughter, Elizabeth Cochrane, married to Robert Sempill of Beltrees, 20th June 1722. He was chamberlain to his uncle, the Earl of Dundonald, from 1697 to 1707, when he is supposed to have died.
4. Colonel Hugh Cochrane of Ferguslie, near Paisley. He served under Gustavus Adolphus, King of Sweden ; and also during the civil war in Ireland. Col. Hugh Cochrane married a daughter of Hugh Savage, county Down, Ireland, and had issue :—
  1. John, of Ferguslie, married Barbara, daughter of James Hamilton, merchant in Glasgow, and nephew of Woodhall. He died without issue before 1697.
  2. William, who succeeded to Ferguslie, and was served heir of his brother, 18th November 1697. He married Bethia, daughter of Mr. William Blair of Auchinvale, and had issue.
  3. Grizel, married to Mr. Robert Millar, minister of Ochiltree, who was "outed" in 1662, and died in 1685, leaving issue.
  4. Margaret married to John Hamiltoun of Barr, parish of Lochwinnoch, about 1670. Issue :—
    1. Alexander Hamiltoun of Barr, married Margaret, daughter of John Hamiltoun of Udstoun, in 1700. The Udstoun Hamiltouns were forefathers of Lord Belhaven.
    2. Agnes Hamiltoun, baptized in 1674, was married to Dr. Thomas Foster, physician in Port-Glasgow, and had issue.
    3. Jean Hamiltoun, born in 1677, and married to John Crawford of Birkhead, parish of Dalry in 1698.
  5. Eupham, married to Archibald Stewart of Newtoun, in 1688. They had two sons.
5. Sir Bryce, born at Cochran Place, or Castle, about 1620, a Colonel in the Royal Army. He lost his life in the King's service in 1650.
6. Arthur, or Ochter, Captain in the Royal Army. Crawfurd called him Orighter, or Captain Ochter.
7. Captain Gavin, of Craigmuir, in Lochwinnoch parish. He occurs in 1640. He died in 1701. He married a sister of Captain Clelland of Faskin, parish of Monkland. Captain Clelland fell in the battle of the Muirdykes, in 1685. Captain Gavin's wife, out of revenge, discovered Sir John Cochran and his son to the Royalists. They were brought to Edinburgh as prisoners 3d July 1685. "July 1, 1685.—We had the news that Sir John Cochran and his son, Waterside, and one Dunbar, a surgeon, were apprehended at Gavin Cochran, his uncle's house (of Craigmuir) near Killmalcolm, in Renfrewshire, being discovered by Gavin's wife, out of revenge, because she was sister to Captain Clelland, who in the rebels retiring was slain by them, he being on the King's party. Sir John, his son, &c., were brought into the Tolbooth of Edinburgh on the 3d of July."‡ Issue :—
  1. Alexander of Craigmuir. He was baron bailie to the Earl of Dundonald in 1719, over the baronies of Calderbaugh and Glen. He married a daughter of Claud Alexander of Newtoun, in Paisley. Issue :—
    1. Agnes was married to John Cathcart of Genoch, in the parish of Maybole, in 1719.
    2. Gavin of Craigmuir, a Colonel in the 54th regiment in 1782.
    3. Robina was married to Mr. Henry Millar, minister at Neilstoun, to whom she had :—
      1. Alexander, married E. Edmonstoun of Walkinshaw.
      2. Marion, who was married to William Fulton of Park.
      3. Elizabeth, married to Alexander Napor of Blackstoun.
  2. William, born in 1662.          3. Gavin, baptized 18th June 1676.
8. Elizabeth, married to John Lennox of Woodhead, in the county of Stirling.
9. Grizell, born about 1615, at the auld tower, or Place of Cochran. She was married to Thomas Dunlop of Household.

---

* See parish of Dundonald.      † For this discovery we are indebted to the research of Dr. A. Crawford, Lochwinnoch.
                                ‡ Fountainhall's Decisions, vol. i. p. 366.

## Additional Particulars regarding the Family of WODROW, the Historian.

*Mr. Patrick Wodrow* was vicar of Eggleshame, and a notar-publick. He was a convert from the Church of Rome.

*John Wodrow*, his eldest son, had the Hill, the Picket, and other maillings, in the parish of Eagleshame and Mearns. He killed a man called Hamiltoun, on a Sabbath-day, in Eagleshame Kirkyard. His son,

*Robert Wodrow*, in the Hill, was chamberlain to the Earl of Eglintoun, over his Lordship's estate of Eagleshame, from about 1640 to 1660. He was in the Battle of Pentland, in 1666, on the side of the rebels. He was taken prisoner, and confined for some time. His son,

*Maister James*, born in 1637, was tutor to the young Lord Blantyre. He was licensed to preach in 1673, and became one of the ministers of Glasgow * He was subsequently, in 1692, appointed Professor of Divinity. He died in 1707. He married Margaret Hair, from Kilbarchan parish, and among others had

*Mr. Robert Wodrow*, the Historian, born at Glasgow in 1679. He published his *Sufferings*, &c., in 1720, on account of which he was presented with a hundred guineas by the King. He married, in 1708, Margaret, daughter of Mr. Patrick Warner of Ardeer, minister of Irvine, and by her had **sixteen** children :—

1. Robert, who succeeded his father as minister of Eastwood. He fell into dissipated habits, and resigned his charge.
2. Peter, minister at Torbolton.
   3. James, minister at Stevenstoun or Saltcoats. He married a daughter of Gavin Hamilton, bookseller in Edinburgh, and left one daughter, who was alive in Saltcoats in 1829.
4. Alexander, settled in America.
   5. Mary, unmarried.
6. Margaret, married to the Rev. Mr. Biggar, minister of Kirkoswald.
   7. Marion, unmarried.
8. Janet, unmarried.
   9. Martha, unmarried.
   10. John, died in infancy.
11. William, died young.
   12. Kitty, died young.
   13. A daughter, died in infancy, &c.

Mr. Wodrow died in 1734, but his wife survived till 1759.

The surviving representative of the family in this country is Mr. Wodrow of Mauchline, whose son, William, is minister of the Scots Kirk, Swallow Street, London.

---

### ALEXANDERS OF BLACKHOUSE.

*Robert Alexander of Blackhouse*, in the parish of Mearns, a small estate of about fifty acres. He was born in 1604, and apprenticed to John Quhyt, writer in Paisley. He had a long and prosperous career: writer and Town-clerk about 1636, and Bailie of Paisley in 1648, and again at various times in subsequent years. He acquired the lands of Blackhouse, near Ayr, in 1648. The feu-charter, by James second Earl of Abercorn, is dated 17th June of that year, in favour of Robert Alexander, Esq., of all, &c., the two merk land of Blackhouse, with houses, &c., glebes, fishings, used and wont, in the water of Ayr, parts and pertinents ; and all and whole the lands of Chappel-lands, comprehending therein the lands of Dykes and Smiddybill, and the mill of Dalmilling, lying in the barony of Monkton and Dalmilling, regality of Paisley, bailliary of Kyle-Stewart, and shire of Ayr. Mr. Alexander acquired various other properties in the vicinity, all of which were incorporated under the designation of Blackhouse. On the 25th May 1668, he had a disposition in favour of himself in liferent, and of his son, James Alexander, in fee, of the 42s. land of Woodquarter, called Thornyflat, from Allan Hunter, who had a feu-charter of the same from John, second Lord Barganie, 31st May 1665. He had also a disposition and assignation, in the same terms, of the lands of Boghall, from John Cuninghame, Esq. of Baidland, and Robert Gordon of Boghall, and John Gordon, his eldest son, dated 22d June 1665. These lands were formerly held by the Lockharts of Boghall, a branch of the Lockharts of Bar, who appear to have obtained them from the Earl of Abercorn, successor to the Abbots of Paisley. John Lockhart of Bar was served heir to his grandfather, Alexander Lockhart of Boghall, in all and whole the 16s. 8d. land of Taitsquarter, with the pertinents. &c. ; the 3 merk land of Dalmilling of old extent, also called Taitsquarter ; the 16s. 8d. land of Dalmilling, of the same extent, called Jasperscumstead, with the pendicles, &c. ;

---

* His kirk was called Merkdaillie Meeting-House. In Chapman's "Picture of Glasgow," published in 1818, it is said ; "Before Charlotte Street was formed, near seventy years ago, its site was occupied as a kitchen-garden, at the annual rent of £365—hence the name of Merk-daily-Street, which it still occasionally gets." If this be true, the spirit of the Professor may look down from its mansions of bliss, grieved at the change which has taken place. The Kirk is erased, and the Nunnery of the Sisters of Moray is now erected in its place.

as also the merkland now called Chappelland, &c., 24th June 1630. These lands were alienated by John Lockhart of Bar to Robert Gordon, Provost of the burgh of Ayr, and John Gordon, merchant burgess there, his eldest son, dated 25th June 1647. They had thereafter become the property of John Montgomerie, whose son, Patrick Montgomerie of Blackhouse, disposed of them to John Cuninghame of Baidland, 11th June 1663. On the 28th of April 1664, a decreet of apprising of the lands of Boghall was obtained by Mr. Cuninghame of Baidland, for payment of the money he had some time before advanced upon them; hence the sale of the lands by the parties concerned to the Alexanders in 1665. Robert Alexander, of Blackhouse and Boghall, married Marion Hamiltoun, and had issue :—

1. Maister James, his successor.                          2. Claud, of Newton (ancestor of Alexander of Ballochmyle.)
3. Mr. Robert, writer in Paisley, from 1677 to 1699.
4. John. He and Robert are mentioned as the "breither-german" to Claud, in a document in 1678.
1. Jonet, married to Robert Love, maltman in Paisley. Her "breither" Claud, Mr. Robert and John, were bound to give the somme of 2000 merks in 1676, if Marion, as under should die before her marriage. Robert Love died before 1678.
2. Marion, married John Maxwell of Braidieland, parish of Paisley, in 1678. Braidieland consisted of 20s. old extent, and and another mailing of 40s. She brought a tocher of 3600 merks, and her jointure was 400 merks.

*Mr. Alexander of Blackhouse and Boghall*, Minister of Kilmalcolm, to which charge he was ordained in 1656. He married Mary, daughter of the Laird of Southbar, and aunt of Mr. James Stirling, minister of the Barony of Glasgow. This marriage took place in 1657. A contract was entered into upon the occasion, "between the said Robert Alexander and James Alexander, commissar at Kilmalcolm, his eldest son, on the marriage of the latter with Mary Maxwell, daughter of John Maxwell of Southbar, whereby the former became bound to convey to the latter his lands of Blackhouse, Chappelland, mill of Dalmilling, £3, 11s. land of Dalmilling, called Gairdner Hunter and Lauchland's mailings, and the one half merkland of Dalmilling, called Greystack, under the reservation of his own liferent of one half thereof," dated 9th June 1657. Mr. Alexander was among the "outed" ministers in 1662. He is said to have died of fever in 1669; but this could not have been the case, for, on the 30th October 1685, he grants a disposition in favour of *Robert* Alexander, his eldest lawful son, of the lands and estate of Blackhouse. He had issue :—

1. Robert, of Blackhouse.
2. John, born about 1660, was a merchant in Glasgow, and at his death, in 1712, he mortified £100 for the use of the poor members of the merchant rank in Glasgow, and also to the poor of the Kirk Session, £66, 13s. 4d. Scots. He married, about 1690, Janet Cuninghame a daughter of the Laird of Craigends, and had issue :—
   1. Robert, Physician.                          2. William, Provost of Edinburgh.
   3. Anna, married to Peter Murdoch, merchant, and Provost of Edinburgh (his second wife.) They had a daughter, Mary.
3. Jean, married to William Greenlies of Auchlamont (Paisley parish) writer in Ayr. Contract dated 24th August 1682. He died before 1698.

*Robert Alexander of Blackhouse* had a charter of that property, under the Great Seal, 5th March 1686. With consent of his father, James, he disposed of part of the lands of Chappelland to Sir Thomas Wallace of Craigie, Bart. He was one of the Principal Clerks of the Court of Session. He married Sophia, daughter of John Blair of Innerwick. He was an able, virtuous, benevolent, and friendly man. On his death, in 1723, Allan Ramsay wrote a laudatory poem in honour of his memory. He left an only daughter, Jean, married to Lockhart of Lee. Amongst the title-deeds are—" Retour of the special service of Mrs. Jean Alexander of Blackhouse, as only child and heir to the said Robert Alexander, and spouse to John Lockhart, Esq. of Lee, in the said lands of Boghall and Dalmilling," dated 26th June 1733. Also, "Precept of *Clare Constat*, by Hugh Baillie, Esq. of Monktoun, in favour of the said Mrs. Jean Alexander, or Lockhart, for infefting her as heir foresaid." &c., 26th March 1734. Mrs. Alexander excambied, for certain parts of the lands of Dalmilling, with Sir Thomas Wallace of Craigie, the upper holm of Blackhouse, with four rigs of land, with the bog and brae above the holm, all parts of the lands of Blackhouse.

*Robert Alexander*, fifth of Blackhouse, was served heir to the said Mrs. Jean Alexander, or Lockhart, his cousin, in the lands of Blackhouse, 1769.

*William Alexander*, sixth of Blackhouse, next succeeded as heir apparent.

On the 29th November 1786, a decreet of sale was obtained before the Lords of Council and Session, at the instance of George Home of Branxton, Esq., one of the Principal Clerks of Session, against the Messrs. Alexander, merchants in Edinburgh, of the lands and estate of Blackhouse. In 1787 the property came into the hands of the Ayr Coal Company, represented by David Balfour, Esq., W.S., from whom it was acquired by John Taylor, Esq., W.S., for himself, and as trustee for the other partners, 14th August 1789. In 1829, it became the property of the Messrs. Hunter and Co., bankers, Ayr, who disposed of it a few years ago to *John Taylor Gordon*, Esq. of Newton Lodge.

---

\* Mr. Campbell of Craigie bought Dalmilling, or Milton Mill, from Mr. Home in 1790.

## BOYDS OF KILMARNOCK.

### From "Ayrshire Notes and Queries" of the Ayr Observer.

Although much has been written in regard to the origin of this family, we doubt exceedingly if any one of the theories can be considered as quite satisfactory. It was the opinion of the author of " Caledonia " that the Boyds could not show " very distinctly, either the *origin* of their *name* or their *family* ; " and greatly various have been the accounts of different writers. It has, however, become popular, as well as general, to connect them with the earliest of the High Stewards ; but it is only necessary cursorily to examine the different views that have been promulgated to be entirely satisfied, that the only safe conclusion was that adopted by the author of " Caledonia."

1. For, looking at the " Genealogical Deduction," which was found in the family charter chest, and written, as it is supposed, in the beginning of the eighteenth century, it will be found that the writer mentions having seen a very ancient genealogy of the family, whereby it appeared that the *first* of the family was Robert, a younger son of the Stewarts, who lived as far back as the reign of Alexander I., who reigned from 1106 to 1124, and was the predecessor of the Sainted David, who came to the throne in the latter year.

2. Nisbet's theory is, that the first who took the surname of Boyd was " Robert, the son of Simon, third son of Allan, second Lord High Steward of Scotland, who died 1153, which Robert is designed, in the charters of Paisley, " *nephew to Walter, the son of Allan Dapifer Great Steward of Scotland.*" The inaccuracy, as well as gross inconsistency, of this view, is tangible. For it will be seen at a glance, that if Robert was the son of Simon, the third son of Allan, the second High Steward, the Paisley Register, instead of saying he was the *nephew* of Walter, the first High Steward, ought to have called him his *great-grandson*. Nisbet refers to Crawfurd's History, and to Sir James Dalrymple's collections ; but they afford no proof satisfactory to the inquirer of the origin of the family. In 1205 *Robert Boyl* of Gavan and Risk is a witness to the execution of a contract between Ralf de Eglintoun and the burgh of Irvine ; and Dalrymple mentions that, in the charter of the lands of Halkhill, dated 1262, he found a person who is called " *Robert dictus de Boyl.*" But although these instances prove that the family had by that time adopted a surname, they go no way to show what was its origin.

3. Again, Mr. Paterson, in his recent History of Ayrshire (who adopts very nearly the theory of Douglas and Wood), goes minutely into the genealogy of the family. It is he who adduces the family deduction already referred to, and, although he does so, he by no means abides by it. On the contrary, he holds it manifestly inaccurate in some particulars. His deduction is from Simon, *not the son* of Allan, the second High Stewart, but the *brother* of Walter, the first High Steward—mentioning that Simon is to be found as a witness to the foundation charter of the Monastery of Paisley, which was dated about 1160 ; and true it is that a Simon there occurs, who is designed the brother of Walter. The next step downwards is *Robert*, who is said to be the son of this Simon, and designed as the *nephew* of Walter, the first Stewart, this Robert being, as the author adds, called " *Boyt or Boidh*," from his having had a *fair complexion*, the term in the Gaelic being of this signification. But this is the chasm. Although there is a Robert, who is called the *nephew*, or it may be as well the *grandson* (the word *nepos* having both meanings), of the first High Steward, there is no *Robert Boyt, Boidh*, or *Boyd*, who is so called or characterised ; and it is only by the exercise of considerable ingenuity that Robert the nephew or grandson, is identified with *that* Robert Boid, who, in 1205, witnesses the contract before referred to. There is no grounds, as we conceive, for doing so, except that of bare conjecture. It is said, however, that the Boyds bear in part the same arms as the Stewarts ; and this, it is asserted, is proof of a connection or relationship. According to Nisbet, the families of Boyd and Monteith carried " *their figures cheque, to shew their descent.*" The carrying of this *cheque*, however, proves too much for the argument that is attempted to be raised on the fact ; for Nisbet himself has this statement—" There are many other families, of *different surnames*, who, in *imitation* of the Stewarts, or as *vassals* to them, have chequered their armorial bearings, as the Semples, Rosses, Houstons, Spreuls, Brisbanes, Fleming of Barochan, and Schaw of Bargaron." And, accordingly, may it not be inquired, if these families did so, where there was no relationship, might not the Boyds do so equally well ? They were not in different circumstances from these families ;—all of them were in, and connected with, Renfrewshire, the ancient inheritance and patrimony of the Stewarts : all were their immediate vassals, not excepting the *Boyds ;* and, we presume, it must have been some misunderstanding of the early residence and possessions of this family which led to their being looked upon in a light different from the Semples and other families, who have *chequered* their armorial bearings.

It seems not to have been known, or, at least, understood, that the *earliest* possession of the Boyds was *Gavan* and *Risk*, in the parish of Lochwinnoch, and barony of Renfrew,—a barony which, it is well known, was the *first* and *chief* possession of the Stewarts. Consequently, the Boyds were the immediate vassals of this family, and hence arose the cause for chequering their armorial bearings. Gavan and Risk was the designation of *dominus Robertus de Boyd*, who witnessed the contract in

1205; but the author of "Caledonia" supposed that these places were "*near Irvine*," and writes them "*Giruan and Rysk*," which is an evident mistake, inasmuch as there are no such places near Irvine, and the barony of Gavan and Risk, in Lochwinnoch, is one that is universally known. On this point a charter, granted by Robert III., as tutor to his dearest son, James, the Steward of Scotland, may be opportunely referred to. This charter is dated on the 15th of June, 1405, about two hundred years after Sir Robert Boyd witnesses the contract, and by it the King gives, grants, and confirms in "*nomine suo, et tutorio nomine*." "*Willielmo Boyd, filio et hæredi* Willielmo Boyd de Baddynkath, totas et integras terras de *Garan* et *Rick*, cum pertinen., jacen. in *Baronia* de Renfrew, et intra vicecomitatum nostrum de Lanerk, quæ fuerunt dict. Gulielmi Boyd de Baddynkath.' A copy of this curious deed will be found in Carm. Tracts (p. 104), who took it from the collections of Mr. John Cors, regarding the principality, that gentleman having had a perusal of the original charter, which was preserved in the Boyd charter chest, from the Earl of Kilmarnock's doer. This William Boyd of Baddyngath, the father, is known to have been the second son of Sir Thomas Boyd, who accompanied David II. to the battle of Durham, and was there taken prisoner, as well as his sovereign, and he is supposed to have been the *first* of the Boyds of Badenheath, in Stirlingshire.

We, therefore, do not see proper reasons for coming to the conclusion that Robert, the *nephew* (or grandson) of the first Stewart, was Sir Robert Boyd of Gavan and Risk; and, with reference to the orthography of the surname, we are forced to remark, that we have never found it written in the Gaelic form of "*Boyt*," or "*Boidh*," in any very ancient deed. Boyd is now, and has been for a considerable time, the form of the surname, which is certainly similar to the Gaelic term "Boyt," but in ancient times it stood differently. For instance, in the Chronicles of Lanercost, written during the 14th century, the term is spelled "Boide." In a Bond of Friendship, dated in February 1573, it is also written "Boid" several times; and in the Glasgow Register it is "Boid, Boyd, and Boyde." Such an appellation, however, existed some time prior to the era of the Stewarts, as we will immediately show; and there is no reason for supposing that the Kilmarnock Boyds sprung from a person of the name of Robert, who lived about the latter end of the 12th century, rather than from a party who was named "Bœd," in the reign of Alexander I. Such a name, however, is to be found in the well-known Inquisition of David, made about the year 1116, when he was Prince of Cumberland, and in regard to the possessions of the Kirk of Glasgow, in order that, after being ascertained and defined, they might be restored, all for the love and glory of God, and the support of that Kirk. Accordingly, the Prince, as the Inquisition bears, appointed five persons out of the whole of Cumbria, who were of mature age, and possessed of wisdom, to inquire into these possessions, and determine of what they consisted; and one of these was called "*Gill filius Bœd*;" the others being "*Uchtred filius Waldef, Leysing et Oggo Cambrenses judices*, and *Halden filius Eadulf*." Gill is evidently a contraction of *Gillise*, a name which occurs several times in some of the oldest writings extant, during the reigns of Edgar, Alexander, and David I. Mr. Innes, in editing the Register of Glasgow, paid great attention, as he himself says, to insure the accuracy of his copy of this Inquisition; and he prints the name "Gill" with a line across the two final letters as a mark of contraction. At the time of this Inquisition, there is no evidence of the Stewarts or Fitz-Allans having come into Scotland from Oswestrie in Shropshire; and at least, in this writ, there is no notice of them, although the witnesses are both distinguished and numerous. We will not say that this *Bœd* was certainly the remote ancestor of the Boyds of Kilmarnock; but it is as likely, indeed more likely, that he was, than that they sprung from Robert the son of Simon.

Here is a *Bœd*, a person in existence, of wisdom and distinction, in the first quarter of the 12th century, and acting in a most momentous matter on the commission of Prince David; while Sir Robert Boyd is, in 1205, less than a century later than the date of the Inquisition, found mingling with the *magnates* of the times. There is, therefore, no impropriety in supposing that the family of Boyd was of considerable importance nearly a century earlier; and in adopting this *Bœd* as the progenitor of Sir Robert, it will be perceived that the necessity will be avoided of originating a surname, solely, as it would appear, for the sake of escaping a difficulty, and finding a remoter ancestor who was highly connected.

It may be inquired, however, who was "*Gill, the son of Bœd*," and we must be candid enough to confess that it will be difficult to make any very satisfactory answer to the question. Sir James Dalrymple (Coll. p. 344) would have the whole of the persons, who reported upon oath as to the Kirk's possessions, to be *Judges of Cumbria*; but it is doubtful if the clause of the Inquisition warrants such a view. His statement is this: "The declaration in favour of the Church of Glasgow bears to be *rogatu et imperio supradicti Principis*, and before four witnesses called *Cumbrenses Judices*, who, it is like, were the chief magistrates in Cumberland under that Prince;" and what he adds is, that "*Halden* and *Eadulf* are known names in that country, the first from the time of Haldanus the Dane, and perhaps has given occasion to the surname of Halden in Scotland." The clause stands exactly thus: "Uchtrede filius Waldef, Gill. filius Bœd, Leyssing, et Ogga Cumbrenses Judices, Halden filius Eadulf," &c.; and on the best consideration which we can give, it would rather appear that the term "*Cumbrenses Judices*" applied exclusively to *Leyssing et Ogga*, names which immediately precede the term. If the term, however, had stood at the *end* of the clause, and after the names of all the Inquisitors, it might reasonably have been said to apply to *all*; but unfortunately, as we think, for Sir James Dalrymple's view, it is followed by another name to which it certainly cannot apply, namely, *Halden filius Eadulf*. Sir James does not pretend to give any information as to this *Gill, filius Bœd*; indeed, knowing probably nothing about his extraction, he passes him over in silence, although others of the Inquisitors and witnesses are commented on by him at some length. We are not sure, however, if this author was wrong when he said that the witnesses were all magistrates of Cumbria, or at least were connected with that district. For it will be found, on referring to the foundation charter of Holyrood by David I. granted about the year 1128, that *Ogga and Leyssing* occur as witnesses as well as *Gill, filius Bœd*, although in this instance, the latter is not described with the *addition of "filius Bœd."* He, however, as in the Inquisition, stands in juxtaposition with Ogga and Leyssing; and the name, in the contracted form of *Gill*, is lengthened into *Gillise*. The following is the concluding part of the testing clause, as it is called: " Petro de Bruys, Normanno Vicecomite, Oggil, Leisying, *Gillise*, Williel de Grame, Turstano de Crectune," &c. Here, then, the three parties, Ogga, Leisyng, and *Gillise*, not only stand together, but all of them are without designations, and between the names of the other witnesses, who are designed—Petro de Bruys, we presume, has either the designation of being a Norman Sheriff, or *Normanno* is the name of a witness with the designation of Sheriff, as " *Norman the Sheriff.*" Sir James Dalrymple remarks upon the witnesses to the charter of Holyrood, that " Robertus Burnvilla Lieffin, Gilles, and others, are witnesses who are to be found in the charters of Edgar, Alexander, and David, before, and in the beginning of David's reign," (p. 391). And accordingly, on referring to the charter of King Edgar to the Priory of Coldingham, of the lands of Swyntoun, which is one of the oldest Scottish documents extant, we find Leisyng and Ogga as witnesses, although Gillise cannot be distinguished.

In these circumstances, then, it must appear pretty evident that *Gillise*, in the charter of Holyrood, is no other person than *Gill, filius Bœd* in the Inquisition of David; and that Gillise, as well as Leisyng and Ogg, was, if not a Judge of Cumbria, at least connected with the district, and in close contact, generally, with Leysing and Ogga. It is clear that they were all persons of repute, and of great sway and authority. The next point is, has it been discovered that there was any person in Cumbria, in the end of the 11th or the beginning of the 12th century, of distinction, who was called *Gillise* or *Bœd*? We are inclined to answer in the affirmative, after making a search into the ancient history of Cumberland. In doing so, it was discovered that a large barony, lying on the east side of the river Eden, is called *Gillisland*, which, as the learned Camden thinks, had its name from one *Gil, the son of Bueth*, the ancient lord of it; and as to a place, *Irthington*, which is said to be the capital of this barony, it is stated that there the lord had a mansion called Castlesteed, of which great ruins were to be seen. It is added that at this place *Gil de Bueth* dwelt, and after him Hubert or Robert de Vallibus, who, suffering the castle to go into disrepair, built the Castle of Naworth from the materials. Bueth Castle, too, or, as it was afterwards called, *Bew* Castle, is said to have been built about the time of the Conqueror, by one *Bueth*, a man of Cumbria, and one who was so potent that he had the government of the whole of that country in his own hands. It appears also that one Ranulph or Ralph was the first Earl of Cumberland by grant of the Conqueror, and that he was succeeded by his son of the same name, who, on obtaining the more important Earldom of Chester, resigned, as it is said, the Earldom of Cumberland into the hands of Henry I., who immediately, or soon afterwards, conferred it on Malcolm King of the Scots, on the condition of that King protecting the north parts of England from its enemies, both by land and sea. In consequence, the eldest sons of the Scots king came to be appointed to the charge, and to be called Princes of Cumberland. It is related, however, that Ranulph did not resign Cumberland quite unconditionally, as, according to the accounts of the writers of those times, he either gave or attempted to give, *Copeland* barony to his brother, William de Meschines, and *Gillisland* to Hubert de Vallibus. This latter grant appears to have been attended with the displacing of *Gilles de Bueth*, *against the desire of the Scots;* for it is reported that De Vallibus was dispossessed by *Gilles de Bueth*, who held the barony for some time by force of arms, and with the assistance which he required from the Scots. It is added, however, that Gilles was slain some time afterwards by Robert de Vallibus, the son of Hubert, at a meeting which took place for the purpose of arranging differences, and reconciling the parties. This Robert was espoused to Ada, the daughter and heiress of William Engaine, and widow of a Simon de Morville. In consequence of the death of Gillise, the De Villibus prevailed, and succeeded in wresting Gillisland from this family; but the murder was so uncalled for and barbarous, that Robert, as it is said, lamented it so grievously, that as an atonement, he not only built the Abbey of Lannercost, but endowed it with a great portion of the land which had occasioned the quarrel. From the De Vallibus the barony came to the De Multons, thence to the Dacres, and latterly to the Howards, who are now believed to be the representatives of the ancient Lords of Gillisland. Sir Richard de Morville was constable from 1162 to 1189, and we find that in a charter granted by him in favour of Henry de St. Clair of Edmund, and Gillemichel, as bondsmen, and their offspring, one of the witnesses is, " *Howen de Buth.*" Of this person, however, we have met with no other notice, and whether he was a Cumbrian or not, we cannot pretend to say.

We feel constrained, then, in these circumstances, to submit that there is strong evidence of "*Gill filius Bæd*" being connected with, if not the same person, as *Gilles de Bueth*, the ancient Lord of Gilhsland. We see the latter standing up against the family of De Vallibus, with the assistance of the Scots, after they received Cumberland, and we also see that, with all the assistance received, he was dispossessed by the De Vallibus family, and forced to leave his patrimonial inheritance. On this, where, it may be asked, is it probable that he went? Is it not likely that he put himself under the powerful protection of his abettors, the Scots, their King and Prince? We think that it is so; and that there is the strongest probability of the Scottish King taking the family of De Bueth within his own kingdom, for, as the De Vallibuses were in Cumberland in strength and force, it cannot be supposed that they would be inclined to remain there, where the strongest feelings of both families would be engendered, and were likely to be vented in revengeful deeds. This view is confirmed, as we think, by Sir James Dalrymple's statement, that in the charter of Halkhill in 1262, before referred to, Robert Boyd is called "*Robertus dictus de Boyd*" (pref. p 80), that is, "*Robert, called of Boyd*," the term Boyd being evidently *here* meant to express some particular *locality* or *district*, while, if it had been descriptive of a *person* with a fair complexion, the word "*de*" would not probably have been used, and in the latter case the expression would, we think, have been simply, having regard to the sense, *Robertus dictus Boyd or Boyt;* that is, *Robert called the Fair.* For, if the preposition "*de*" had been used, the English interpretation of the clause would be, *Robert called of the Fair*, which we conceive is far from having any feasible or palpable significancy. We would remark also, in conclusion, that there appears no very material difference between the appelations "*Gill or Gilhse filius Bæd*" and "*Gilhse de Bueth*," the former only being characterised as the son of the latter, or at least a son of one of the family of De Bueth, and this will the more evidently appear, on considering that the one term is in a Latin, and the other in an English dress.

We now leave the matter for the consideration of those who take an interest in such inquiries, and having attempted to afford the public such information as we possess upon an antiquated and greatly mysterious point in history, we hope that some one will be induced to come forward ere long, and afford such information as they may have happened to collect.

*July* 1852                                                                                                          VIDIMUS

Our attention has been drawn to the foregoing article. With the writer we are unacquainted, but it falls appropriately enough within the scope of our Appendix, and we hold the origin of distinguished families—such as that of the Boyds—to be an interesting and important subject of inquiry. *Vidimus* has made a plausible conjecture, still we do not see that it rests on any solid foundation. There are not many points in the question at issue, yet as they are somewhat mystified by the manner in which they are treated, it will be as well to take them up in detail.

1. It is admitted that *Simon*, who lived in 1160, was the brother of Walter the first High Steward. It is true that the word *nepos* may signify grandson as well as nephew, but of the two meanings we must adopt the one most in keeping with probability. *Robert* is more likely, in point of time, to have been the son of Simon than the grandson of his brother Walter, both of whom were living in 1160. Besides, in one of the foundation charters of Paisley Monastery, dated 1177, *William, son of Walter*, is distinctly mentioned as a witness, so that, with these dates, we could not well have *Robert Boyd* of Gavan and Risk, the grandson of Walter, witnessing the Irvine charter in 1205. It is perhaps possible, but not at all probable, therefore it is right to infer that Robert, mentioned in the Paisley charters, was the *nephew* of Walter, and consequently the son of Simon. It is true, there is no positive proof of the fact, but, as already stated, the genealogist, in such a case, must assume what appears to be most consistent with truth. It seems to be a tradition in the family—countenanced by the manuscript deduction of 1709—that the surname of Boyd originated, as described, from the fair complexion of Robert, and we have generally found that tradition rests upon some foundation. There is nothing extraordinary in the circumstance, for surnames were invariably adopted either from the names of places, or from some personal feature—such as *Roy*, red, or *Dhu*, black.

2. It seems to be rather in favour of our deduction than against it, that Gavan and Risk were amongst the first possessions of the Stewarts in Scotland, although not the seat of the family. By reference to page 508 of this volume, it will be seen that there is reason to believe that Cowdoun was the site of their original stronghold. It is reasonable to suppose that the lands nearest to the head of the family would be given to the immediate branches of it rather than to a stranger or new comer. Nor does it at all militate against the fact, that the same lands are granted to the Badinheath branch of the Boyds by Robert III. in 1405. The property may have originally formed part of the patrimony given by Sir Thomas Boyd to his second son, William, who was the first of the Boyds of Badinheath, and been granted of new by the Crown upon a formal resignation. As to the orthography of the name, which is of no great moment, *Vidimus* might have found it written *Boyt* in the Ragman Roll, in 1297. There is also a *Walter de Boht*, witness to one of the Paisley charters in 1272.

3. It is rather unfortunate for *Vidimus* that *Bæd*, whether the person so called was a judge of Cumberland or not is of little consequence, is not a patronymic, and therefore could not have been

the original surname of the Boyds of Gavan and Risk. *Gill* or *Gillise*, was merely son of *Bœd*, (as Alan, son of Walter the first High Steward),—and according to the showing of *Vidimus* himself, if he really was the same person whose name occurs in the charter of Holyrood (1128), he is designed simply as Gill, or Gillise, and never afterwards appears in any Scottish or even English record, as "Gill, filius Bœd," or Gillise de Bœd, or in any form that could point him out as the remote or immediate ancestor of the Boyd family. There is no evidence whatever, nor even good conjecture, for identifying him as *Gilles de Bueth*, the ancient lord of Gillisland ; and even if there were, it would still remain to be shown that *Bueth* and *Bœd*, or *Boyt*, were synonymous. We need hardly remind *Vidimus* that *Gillies* is quite a common surname in Scotland.

4. Even allowing that the discomfited De Bueth was brought to Scotland by the King, it must have been so contemporaneously with the introduction of the Stewarts as to render it highly improbable that two distinct families could have possessed the same property, for *Vidimus* himself coincides in the fact that Gavan and Risk were amongst the earliest possessions of the Stewarts. If they were located anywhere in Renfrewshire, it is rather surprising that neither *Gill*, nor *Gillise*, nor *Bœd* or *Bueth* once occurs amongst the witnesses, or otherwise in the Paisley charters. And it is still more surprising that, if "Gill, filius Bœd" was the ancestor of the Boyds, "Gillise" should not have been handed down in the family, while we see that *Robert* was a prevailing name amongst them. The distinction sought to be established by the use, or non-use, of the preposition *de*, is of little consequence, as it is often found misapplied, or in a sense differing from what we conceive to have been the common acceptation. In the very charter of Holyrood, quoted by *Vidimus*, "Petro *de* Bruys" is the first witness. He could not be Peter *of* Bruys, because there was no such locality. The restorer of Scottish independence—the great King Robert—was called Robert *de* Bruce, or *the* Bruce. So, in the Halkhill charter of 1262, we no doubt ought to understand the terms "Robertus dictus de Boyd," as signifying Robert, called *the Boyd*. And here, we think, a most conclusive argument, against his proposition, starts up under the very nose of *Vidimus ;* for, if Boyd was a new patronymic assumed, as is supposed, by Robert, the son of Simon, or his grandson, who fought at the battle of Largs, nothing could be more proper than to designate him Robert *the* Boyd.

We might have said more, but we think we have fully exhausted the arguments of *Vidimus*, and shown that his theory rests on a mere shadow. Until we see a more satisfactory origin propounded for the Boyds we must adhere to the old. It is pleasing, however, to find the readers of a newspaper taking an interest in such topics ; and although, as we opine, unsuccessful in this instance, we would by no means discourage *Vidimus* in his researches.

---

EXPLANATION of the terms "Laird," "Ladie," "Gudeman," and "Gudewife."

These terms frequently occur in the body of this work ; and as many of our readers may not be familiar with their meaning, we beg to offer a brief explanation, drawn up chiefly from notes kindly handed to us by Dr. A. Crawfurd, Lochwinnoch.

A *Laird* was anciently a thane, a baron, a crown vassal, with the privilege to hold a baron court, and the right of "pit and gallows." He was equal in rank to the lord of the manor in England. For example, in a charter of Montgrennan, granted by James VI. of Scotland, in 1615, this passage occurs : "Administrator, tutor, et gubernator nostri filio Caroli, Duci de Rothesay, Comite de Carrik, Kyll et Cunynghame, Domino Insularum, *Baroni Baronie de Renfrew*, et Senneseallo de Scotie ;" and in another, under the signet of the Commissar of Glasgow, 28th Nov. 1607, in reference to the twelve pund land of Auchinames, the Prince and his titles are similarly stated : Henrie, Duik of Rosaye, Erle of Carrik, Lord of ye Ylles, *Barroune of ye Barronie* of Renfrew, and Prince and Stewart of Scotland." In these charters, the difference between *Lord* and *Laird* is obvious. *Laird*, or baron, in the Scots sense, does not mean *Lord*. Dominus Sympill, for example, would mean Lord Sympill ; but Dominus *de* Ranfurlie signifies the *laird*, or baron of Ranfurlie. The preposition *de*, in this case, makes the distinction * Sir George Mackenzie, in his "Science of Heraldry," printed in 1680, describes the meaning of *Laird* as one who held his office from the Crown, King, or Prince. All *Lairds* had a right to sit in Parliament till 1587, when an Act passed, dispensing with their attendance, but requiring the lesser barons to send commissioners to Parliament to represent them. The Lairds were, in short, the same as the ancient squires in England.

*Ladie*, in like manner, either held her lands directly from the Crown, or was the wife of a *Laird*, or vassal of the Crown. Marie Livingstoun, or *Domina* Beltreis, in 1582, for example, held certain lands granted to her by Queen Mary.

*Gudeman* and *Gudewife* signified parties who were feuars or vassals of a subject-superior. In this

---

* Lord Kames' Antiquities.

case there was no barony or baron court.   James V, as we are informed by Captain Mackay, who wrote in 1723, used to make *incognito* excursions among his subjects, under the title of the *Gudeman of Ballangeich*, and the Captain explains, at the same time, that "Goodman," in Scotland, is the same as "Yeoman" in England—yeoman being a feuar   The popular rhyme, in reference to the titles of the Duke of Hamilton, supplies an accurate illustration of the respective ranks of *Laird* and *Gudeman* :—

> " Duik Hamiltoun and Brandoun,
> Erl Chatelrow and Arran,
> The *Laird* of Kinneill,
> The *Gudeman* of Draffen "

Wishaw says, that " the Lord Hamilton was long since vassall to the Abbot of Kelsoe in the lands of Draffan, and many others lyand in the paroch of Lesmahagow, till the Reformation, about 1560 "   Innumerable examples could be given of the legal as well as popular application of the distinctive titles   In a removing, in 1632, pursued by James Hamilton against Mathew Wallace, the latter is styled *gudman* of Dundonald   Sir Walter Stewart was styled *gudman* of Allantoun under the superiority of the Earl of Tweeddale   The Earl feued out the lands of Auchtermuir to several heritors, the most considerable of whom was William Stewart of Allantoun, " who hath a good and substantious house lyand upon the water of Calder, well planted with barren timber, long possessed by his predecessors "   Hamiltoun of Wishaw was styled *gudeman*.   He held his lands under the superiority of the Duke of Hamiltoun   Sir James Hamiltoun of Broomhill, under the superiority of the Duke, was similarly designated   Caldwell of that Ilk thought fit to sell the superiority of his five merk land of Wester Caldwell to Lord Cochran, between 1662 and 1666, and thereafter he was styled *gudeman*   Gabriell Conynghame, a descendant of the Lairds of Craigends, was called in 1620, " Gudeman of Carncurran," which lands he held of Lord Lyle   The " Guidwyfe of Glanderstoun," in 1649, held the lands of Glanderstoun from Lord Cochran   Margaret Hamiltoun heiress of the lands of Fergushie, adjacent to the town of Paisley, held these lands from the Earl of Abercorn, and was styled " Gudewyfe of Fergushie "   Her husband, John Wallace, chamberlain to the Earl, was a Roman Catholic, and he and his lady were in consequence subjected to great annoyance by the Presbytery, in the records of which she is invariably designated the " Gudewyfe of Fergushie "   Agnes Sympill, " Gudewyfe of Clotherick," appears in the session books of Kilbarchan in 1651   Lord Sempill was her overlord   In later times we have the " Gudewife of Wauchope House" corresponding with the poet Burns.

  The term *Laird* is still in common use, though frequently misapplied   but *Ladie*, *Gudeman*, and *Gudewife*, have altogether become familiar expressions, entirely irrespective of their meaning. Even the late worthy Mr George Robertson was ignorant of the proper signification of the terms, and it is amusing to read the following passage in his *Ayrshire Families*   He says—" In the account of the family of Rowallan, it appears that John Mure of Rowallan, who came to the estate in 1547, had a daughter who was married first to the Laird of Collellan, and, secondly, to the *Gudeman* of Dundonald      As to the appellation of gudeman, it was not usual in those times to bestow it on gentlemen of considerable property, being rather a familiar expression of personal esteem than at all inferring a diminution of dignity   I have found it applied to landed proprietors, otherwise of great respectability, as besides this gudeman of Dundonald (an estate of £1100 valued rent), there was Hamilton of Broomhill, Stewart of Allantoun, Caldwell of that Ilk, &c   All, at times, even the most wealthy of them, *gudemen* of their several places, down even to the commencement of the eighteenth century "

  Thanks to our worthy friend, Dr. A Crawfurd of Lochwinnoch, whose notes we have thus thrown together, our readers can no longer plead ignorance of the once distinctive and important designations of LAIRD, LADIE, GUDEMAN, and GUDEWIFE

---

## FOULTONS OF GRANGEVALE AND FOULTON

  The marine boundary line of Ayrshire is serrated and indented with numerous harbours, bays, and estuaries   which afforded many inducements and facilities to the bold contrabandist of the last century for running and landing his various commodities, upon which Custom-House duties were leviable, but which exactions our less scrupulous forefathers deemed as items in a tariff, oppressive in principle, and vexatious in practice   Beith, from its adjacency to the coast of Largs, which formed one of the formidable smuggling resorts, was an entrepot for choice Hollands, brandies. tobacco and teas, from whence these articles of merchandise were distributed inland, by organised bands of well armed receivers. Indeed, so bold were these Dirk Hatteraicks down to the very commencement of the present century, that a regiment of soldiers was stationed in 1800 at Beith to repress this dauntless band of revenue defaulters. During the troublous times between the two rebellions of 1715 and '45, the contraband trade was carried to a great extent in Ayrshire, and families of note and good repute did not scruple to enter themselves in the list of bluff freeholders of the sea. In sooth many of the spruce present generation of "bonnet lairds" owe either their origin or aggrandisement to the smuggling propensities of their forebears.

It is a matter of local history that John Fulton of Auchinbathie, a cadet from the old Grangehill family, who was married to Jean, daughter of William Fulton of Broomknowes, about 1723, being a staunch Jacobite, and a favourer of Prince Charles Stuart in 1745, therefore a thorough despiser of Hanoverian enactments, was deeply engaged, and acquired much wealth in the contraband trade, which, like the border raids of a former era, were not thought disparaging nor dishonourable, although not free from danger to those implicated. But a dash of peril heightens the zest of excitement. The goods were transported inland on horseback, owing to the bad state of the roads ; and for ease and the quickness of transit, a man rode upon each pad horse, leading another in hand, back-laden.

> Your armour gude ye maunna shaw,
> Nor ance appear like men o' weir,
> As country lads be a' arrayed
> Wi' brauks and ankers on ilk mare.

Fulton of Auchinbathie came to an untimely end. He was shot by one Malloch, a gauger, from behind a hedge, in 1748, at the Shauswood, on his journey to Edinburgh, with a great retinue of horses, carrying "a cargo of smuggled guids, brandie, tea, tobacco, and silks." His remains rest in the churchyard of Lochwinnoch with the bones of his forefathers.

---

## MONTGOMERIES OF BRIGEND.

The last sheet of this work was on the eve of being sent to press when a gentleman called from America. He said he had seen the account of the "Montgomeries of Brigend" in the fourth part of Vol. II., and that it was, in a main fact, incorrect—the family being still in existence, and not extinct, as represented. In asserting that the Brigend Montgomeries were extinct, we followed Robertson, and had been misled by the Broomland MS. From the facts now in our possession, the real descent of the family appears to stand thus :—

I. *William Montgomerie* of Brigend, of the Lainshaw branch of Montgomeries, "who is presumed to have married Jean Montgomerie, heiress of Brigend."* He had issue, four sons, as mentioned in the History of the County. John, the eldest, married, not Agnes Scot, but *Elizabeth Baxter*. According-to the marriage contract—which is much destroyed by damp, or otherwise—it appeared that the marriage took place in 1626. In that document he is styled eldest "son of William Montgomerie of Brigend," and his spouse, "Elizabeth Baxter, dochter laufull of umqle. Thomas Baxter." . . . Amongst others, "Adame Montgomerie of Magbe, and William Weddro, writer in Glasgow," gave their consent to the union.† John died before his father, leaving issue by his wife, Elizabeth Baxter, the eldest of whom, Hew, succeeded his grandfather.

II. *Hew Montgomerie* of Brigend married, in 1653, Catherine Scot, daughter of William Scot of Clerkington, and had issue :—

1. William, styled "younger of Brigend."
2. James, who married in Glasgow, and had issue, a daughter, married to Robert Maxwell of Arkland, and a son who died in Brazil.
3. Two daughters.

III. *William Montgomerie*, "younger of Brigend," married, in 1684, Isabel Burnet, daughter of Robert Burnet, laird of Lethentie.‡ The birth of two of their children—*Anna*, born in 1691, and *William*, born in 1693—are recorded in the parish books of Ayr. In 1701, William and his family emigrated to America, and settled at Doctor's Creek, in East Jersey. He seems to have had another son, *Robert*, the eldest of the family—whose birth may possibly be recorded in the parish books of Maybole, and two younger sons, *James* and *Alexander*.

---

* Page 367, Vol. II. of the *History of Ayrshire*.
† The Earl of Eglintoun gave a life-rent charter of "half of the five merk land of Brigend, with the anueties made and ranted, in favour of Elizabeth Baxter."—*Contract of Marriage.*
‡ The marriage contract is dated at Edinburgh, 8th day of January 1684. It was written by Charles Johnston, servitor to William Stirling, writer to the signet, and witnessed by Robert Scott, minister of the Abbey of Holyrood House.

The following is a copy of a letter addressed by James, the second son, to his brother William —

"Glasgow, February 2d, 1709

"BROTHER,—I write this at venture, not knowing of your being in life  for I have written to you several times, but have had none from you these three years past   So my friend, Mr Andrew Gibson, being coming to Virginia, I send you this by him, in expectation in his travels he may chance to meet you   This only informs you that your father and both sisters are alive, and in health at present, as also my wife and familie.  No alteration is here, so that I would desire to know how you are, and in what condition you and your familie are in , and for that business, I believe there will not a great be recovered, for he will not so much as aliment your father, so you know by this time how I am left *  I shall not insist on               All I desire to know is, what was done with William M'Grean s (?) agreement, when your father cautioned for him, and what became of that discharge ?  Also, if David Montgomerie's bond and diligence was reduced by said David Cunninghame of Milncraig., being now dead , and if there be any trade with you, and how to be addressed, and how it fares  with you and familie, and friends are all well in general —Being all from your affect brother,                                   JAMES MONTGOMERIE

" P S.—My service to Lathentie, your wife and children—farewell."

It would thus appear that Hugh Montgomerie of Brigend was alive in 1709
There are several other letters which serve to render the identity of the family still more indisputable  James Montgomerie of Lainshaw writes to " Robert Montgomerie, Monmouth County, New Jersey,' as follows —

"Edinburgh, March 1, 1720

' SIR—I received your letter  by which you give me an account that you are the son of William Mongomerie of Brigend, who was son of Hew Montgomerie of Brigend, and that Francis Montgomerie your cousin-german, was with you   I rejoice to hear of your welfare, and entreat you may let me know by the first occasion whether your father be alive, and how many of his children are living, and how many children they have.—I am, Sir, your affectionate cousin and humble servant,
"JAS MONTGOMERIE "

In another letter, dated 29th January 1723, the same party says —

As to Brigend, your father sold it to his cousin, John Montgomerie of Bcoch, and his son has sold it to one Mr  Cranfurd' cousin to you both   I doubt no, but the Earl of Eglinton and I may prevail with him to part with it at a reasonable rate '

From this it would appear that Robert, or his father, had entertained the idea of repurchasing their paternal property
We have no data as to the death of William Montgomerie, " younger of Brigend "  His grandson Robert married, about 1715, Sarah Stacey  in New Jersey, and had issue one son, James, who married Esther Wood, and had a son, Robert, who died without issue
IV  William Montgomerie, born in Ayr in 1693, carried on the representation of the family.     He was married three times to ladies of the respective names of Wood, Ellis, and Paschale  He, however, had only one son by the latter, named William  He seems to have been anxious to record his descent, as the following extract from the minutes of the High Court of Chancery, New Jersey, shows —

By His Excellency, William Franklin, Esquire  Captain General, Governor and Commander-in-Chief in and over the province of New Jersey and territories therein, &c  &c
To all whom these presents shall come greeting

These are to certify that Charles Pettit, Esquire, before whom the depositions, or affirmations of William Montgomerie and Esther Wood + were taken  is one of the masters of the High Court of Chancery of the province of New Jersey, and Deputy Secretary  and duly and fully authorised to take such depositions, or affirmations, and that full faith and credit is due to his attestations   In testimony whereof, I have caused the great seal of the said province to be hereunto affixed, at the city of Burlington, this seventh day of May, in the year of His Majesty s reign, anno domini, 1770
(Signed)                          " CHARLES PETTIT, D  Secretary '

' New Jersey —Be it remembered that  on the fifth day of May in the year of our Lord, one thousand seven hundred and seventy, personally appeared before me, Charles Pettit, one of  the Masters of the High Court of Chancery of the Province of New Jersey, &c
William Montgomerie, Esq , of the county of Monmouth, a person well known and worthy of credit, who, being one of the people called Quakers, and duly affirmed according to law, did thereupon declare, testify, and say, that he is now about seventy-six years of age,‡ and that he was born in the city of Aire  in Scotland, in the Island of Great Britain, where his father usually resided in the winter season  that his father, William Montgomerie, was commonly called and known by the name of William Montgomerie of Brigend  or Bridgend, and was the owner and possessor of the estate of Brigend, about a mile from the said city of Aire, and frequently resided on the said estate in the summer season , that the said William Montgomerie, father of this affirmant, was married to Isabella, the daughter of Robert Burnet, Laird of Laithentonn, or Laithentie, by whom he had issue four sons—Robert, his eldest son , William this affirmant, James and Alexander, that in, or about the year of our Lord, one thousand seven hundred and one, or two, the said William Montgomerie of Brigend moved with his family to New Jersey  in America
(Signed),             " WILLIAM MONTGOMERIE "

V  William Montgomerie, the only son of the " affirmant," married Mary, daughter of Rober Rhea, and had four sons, William, Robert, John, &c

---

* This possibly refers to the sale of Brigend                † His wife, no doubt
‡ This agrees with the date of his birth, 1693

VI. William Montgomerie, the eldest son, born in New Jersey in 1778, married a French lady from the island of St. Domingo, daughter of one of the King's (Louis XVI.) Commissioners, by whom he has four sons and two daughters.

1. *Henry*, unmarried.
2. *Richard*, married to Elizabeth, daughter of the Hon. Horace Binney, Member of Congress.
3. *Augustus*, married to Margaret, daughter of William Kernochan, Esq.
4. *Alfred*.

*Alfred Montgomerie*, one of the four sons, the gentleman who called upon us, is at present in Paris.

From this account of the Brigend Montgomeries, which may be relied upon as genuine, it follows that the statements regarding III. and IV. in the genealogy as given in the History of Ayrshire, vol. ii., p. 368, is incorrect. It also follows that the representative of the family, William Montgomerie of New Jersey, is entitled, so far as we are aware, to take precedency of all the Montgomeries, being descended, in a direct line, through the Lainshaw branch, from the old stock, previous to the amalgamation of the Eglintoun and Seton families.

[In the year 1830 there was published "The Montgomery Manuscripts 1698-1704, containing Notices of the Viscounts Montgomery, &c." Since then there has appeared a new and enlarged edition entitled "The Montgomery Manuscripts, (1603-1706): compiled from Family Papers by William Montgomery of Rosemount, Esquire; and edited, with notes by the Rev. George Hill, Queen's College, Belfast. Sm. 4to.]

---

## FAIRLIE OF COODHAM (*Additional Account*).

This is a junior branch of Fairlie of Holmes, Galston, in the account of which parish some links of the ancient and once opulent family of Fairlie are but imperfectly given. Robertson, in his *History of Ayrshire Families*, endeavoured to furnish an unbroken line of the Fairlies of that Ilk; but his researches terminated at the transfer of the widely extensive lands of Fairlie and its castle, now a noble ruin on the banks of Clyde, in the possession of the Earl of Glasgow. These lands were alienated to Boyle of Kelburne in 1650. About that period—

1. Thomas Fairlie settled in Irvine, and married Jane, daughter of Francis of Stone Castle, and had one son.
2. James, who was twice married, and had by his first wife three sons and one daughter, John, Thomas, James, and Margaret.
3. John, the oldest, born 1717; married Agnes, daughter of Mungo Muro of Brantwood, and had issue:—
    1. James. See Fairlie of Holmes, Galston.
    2. Mungo.
    3. William.
    Jean married John Mure of Nethcraith.
    Margaret married P. Clark, Esq.
    The third son, William (who died in 1825), married January 1798, Margaret, daughter of John Ogilvy of Murtle, and had issue:—
    1. William, born in 1798; died in 1822.
    2. John, born 1799; married, and has issue.
    3. James Ogilvy, born 1800.
    Agnes Maria m. James Fairlie of Holmes.
    Margaret Eliza m. John Stuart Hay, Esq., and has issue.
    James Ogilvy, the third son, formerly an officer in the 2d Life Guards (born October 10th 1800) succeeded his mother in the property of Coodham: married, first, in 1840, Anne Eliza, daughter of MacLeod of MacLeod (who died 1843), by whom he has
    Henry James, born in 1841.
    Isabella Catherine, born in 1842.
    He married, secondly, in 1845, Elizabeth Constance, daughter of William Houison Craufurd of Craufurdland, and has
    William Frederic, b. 1847.
    James Ogilvy Reginald, b. 1848.
    Reginald Norman, b. 1850.
    Esther Constance, b. 1851.
    Margaret Anne Alice, b. 1853.
    Francis Archibald, b. 1854.

---

## KENNEDY OF KIRKMICHAEL (*Omitted in its proper place*).

Issue of General and Mrs. Shaw Kennedy :—

Henrietta, married, 1840, to Primrose William Kennedy, Esq. of Drumellan, died 1841.
Wilhelmina, died young.
John, married, January 1848, to Eleanor, daughter of Joseph Green Wilkinson, Esq., and has issue:—
    James Frederick, born January 7, 1849.
    Henry John, born October 13, 1850.
    Mary Eleanor Whiteford, born July 2, 1852.

## DALRYMPLES OF CUNINGPARK

BARGANY, *November* 16, 1853

SIR,—I have accidentally observed in the *History of the County of Ayr*, by Mr. James Paterson, under the head of "Dalrymples of Cuningpark," that the compiler mentions, "that he had not been able to discover who the Captain Dalrymple was that purchased that estate"

Captain John Dalrymple was the third son of Sir Hew Dalrymple of North Berwick (President of the Court of Session), who was third son of James, first Viscount of Stair

He had been captain in the Inniskilling dragoons, of which his cousin-german, field-marshal the Earl of Stair, was then colonel He married Mary, sister of Major Ross of Balkail, Glenluce, his son, Hew Whiteford Dalrymple was born at Ayr, *November* 22, 1850, O S. (*December* 3) In 1772 (when, it appears, he sold the property), he was captain in the royal regiment of foot, and died in the year 1830, having for some years attained the rank of general, and having been created a baronet in 1815, (of High Mark, county Wigton) See, for account of the family, Lodge's and Burke's *Peerages*

I am his eldest and only surviving son, and should be obliged, if any other edition should be published of the *History of the County of Ayr*, that you would make the alterations that I have pointed out

I am obliged to your history for the knowledge of where the estate was situated that my father once possessed in Ayrshire I return the farm of High Mark, on the border of Wigton and Ayrshire, which is valuable to me as an inheritance from my grandfather —I am, Sir, your obedient servant,

ADOLPHUS JOHN DALRYMPLE.

The Editor of the *History of the County of Ayr*

---

## LATTERWILL OF ROBERT BOYD OF BADINHEATH

The testament, testamentar, latterwill and inventar of ye guidis and geir perteining to vmquhile Robert Boyde of Badinaith, within the parochin of      , quha deceisit in the moneth of      the yeir of God Jai vic and ellevin zeiris, pairtlie maid and gevin vp be his awin mouth, in swa far as concernis the nominatioun of his executouris and legacies vnderwrittin, and pairtlie maid and gevin vp be his executouris eftir specifeit, in sa far as concernis the vpgeving of the inventar of his guidis and geir awand in and out as heir eftir followis

### Inuentar

Item ane littel quhyt naig, by the airschip horse, pryce xvi lib      Item, in vtincillis and domicilis, with the abulzement of ye defunctis bodie (by ye airschip) estimat to twa hundrith pundis

### Debtis awand to ye deid

Item, yair was awand to ye defunct the tyme of his deceis, &c, viz be Hew, Erle of Eglintoun, and be

his cautioneris, for the dewtie of Little Cumray, of the termis of Witsonnday and Mertimes, of ye croppis and zeiris 1608, 1609, 1610, and Witsonnday 1611 zeiris, being zeirlie one hundrith thrie scoir sex pund xiijs iiijd, inde      hundrith fourscoir thrie pund vi s viijd mony.      Item, be the tennents and occupieris of the landis of Lochwoid, ten bollis twa firlotis meill, for ye equal half of ve fermes de anno 1611

### Debtis awand be ye deid

Item, the defunct the tyme of his deceis forisaid was awand, &c      To my Lord Abircorne for ye tak maill of ye landis of Gawand de anno 1610 zeiris, sevintein pund xvs      Item, to my Lord of Blantyre, for ye tak maill of ye landis of Medrois, Myvettis, and vtheris, seven pund xs. .      Item, to James Cleland of Mounkland, for ve defunctis blanch dewtie of ye defunctis landis of Mounkland, for ye Mertimes termes 1610, and Witsonnay terme 1611 zeiris, fourtein pund vi s viijd      Item, to my Lord Archiebischope of Glasgow, for ye few dewtie of ye defunctis landis of Lochwoide.. fyve pundis v s. Item, to ye principall and regentis of ye Colledge of Glasgow, for annuell of ve mans of Lus, of Witsonnday terme 1611 zeiris, fourtie shillings      Item, to Mr. Allexr Andro, for ane zeiris maill of his hous, fourtie sex lib viijs iiijd      (The following are stated among the creditors as his servants James Cvnynghame, John Vrie, Jonn Miller, Jobnee Ker, Jonn Brache.)

### Followis the Deidis Latterwill and Legacie

At Badinyath, the xiii day of Julij, 1611 zeiris      The qubilk day the said Rot Boyd of Badinath, makand his testament and latterwill Vnderstanding thair is nathing mair certane nor daith, nor mair uncertane nor ye hour and tyme thairof, thairfoir, he being diseasit in bodie, zit haill in sprit and myne, makis this my testament and latterwill as followis, leveand my saull to God to be savit be his mercie throw the bluid and daith of Jesus Chryst, my saviour, and ordanes my bodie to be bureyd in my predicessouris Isle, at ye kirk of Leinzie, and creatis, constutis and ordanes Adame Boyde of Tempiltoun, my brother sone, Mr Rot. Boyde of Kippis, Johne Cleland of Fostan, my onlie executouris and intremittouris, with my guidis and geir, dischairgeand all former testamentis and legacies maid be me preceiding the daite of yir presentis, and all benefeit that ony personcs quhatsumevir can sute or cleame thairby. I desyre, requistis and ordanes my verie guid Lord James, Erle of Abircorne, and Mr. Patrik Scharp, principall of ye colledge of Glasgow, to be oversearis of this my will, be fulfillit, my puir tennentis and servitouris vntrublit, my legacie geivin, and to keip my tennentis and servandis frae oppressioun, to keip thame in thair richt, and get thame it that pertenis to thame. This humlie requestis thame to do, as I have evir bein and salbe during my lyfetime, willing to serve thame in thair awin . In ye first, as to my proper guidis and geir, gould, sylvir, joellia, sylwir work, domicillis, inspreth of my hous, debtis awand to me and be me, and all vther thingis perteining to me, I refer ye samyne to ane inuentar, wryttin be my servand, James Cvnyngame, of ye dait ye xviij day of August, ye zeir of God Jai vic and four zeiris, daitit and suberyvit with my awin hand, and farder to be gevin vp be my domestick servandis and offiœris of my landis, as they will answer to God. Item, in ye first of my reddiest guidis and geir, I ordane that I be honestlie careyit to my buriall, and friendis that cumes to my convoy honestlie tret as becumes ; and that sax stand of duill gownes be maid to sex of my speciall servandis, at ye discretioun of my saidis exeentouris ; and tuelf puir follouris with duill gownes, hois, and schone, and fourtie pund to be delt to ye puir incuming. Item, I ordane my saidis execntouris, as they will answer to God, of my rediest guidis and geir, to lay fyve hundrith merkis vpone land to ye kirk of Leinze, for ten merkis ye hundrith, and ye proffeit of ye samyne to be laid on agane in ane vther place, for ye same proffeit, and to ye sumes, and sua to remane for evir. Of ye quhilk proffeit of fyve hundrith merkis, extending to fiftie merkis mony, I ordan that xxs. be gevin zeirlie to the beddell of the kirk for dichting and keiping cleane of my said Ile, and xlvi s. viijd. money to be applyit zeirlie to vphauld of ye said Ile, in glas, sclait, poynting, and vther necessaris requesit thairto. And als I ordane that ilk Soneday in the zeir, for ewer, that ten s. money of ye said annuell be delt and deliverit to ye puir folk of ye parochin of Leneze in thair awin hand, at ye said kirk dur. And speciallie, git ony puir of my awin land happinis to be thair, that they be considederit befoir vtheris ; begynnand the first distributioun of ye samyn vpon the first Soneday aftir my deceis, and sa furth ouklie everie Soneday for ewir. As to ye rest of ye said fiftie merkis money, extending to four pundis money, I ordane ye samyne to be delt and distribut zeirlie to ye puir folk of ye said kirk of Leneze vpone ye day of ye moneth that I sal happin to deceis vpone, begynnand ye first distributioun thairof vpone ye day tuelf moneth that I sal happin to deceis vpone, and sua furth zeirlie for ewir ; and that the puir people be warnit be ye minister furth of ye pulpet vpone Soneday befoir ye day of my deceis, to cum and ressave ye samyn. And that ye said annuell be collectit and distribut according to this my will be the honestest elder zeirlie that beis chosin within my fyve pund land of Badinhaith, and failzeand him be ye honestest men and of best lyf and conscience duelland thairvpon, with ye advys of ye minister and elderis of ye said kirk. And that quhat beis left zeirlie of ye said sowme of fourtie saxs. viijd. vnapplyit of ye vphauld of ye said Ile, in manner foirsaid, I ordane the same to be delt zeirlie with ye said sowme of four lib. money, vpon the day of my deceis as said is. And quhill the said sowme of fyve hundrith merkis be gettin land on land to ye vse foirsaid, I have mortifiit, resignit, and ouergevin, and be ye tennour heirof mortifeis, resignis and ourgevis to ye vse of the saidis puir and Ile foirsaid in maner foirsaid, ye zeirlie proffeit of my four akeris of landis in Kirkintulloch, callit ye Lairdis land, lyand within the territorie thairof, quhilk payis me zeirlie fyve bollis twa peckis beir. And that the samyne be applyit to ye vse of ye said puir and Ile in tyme cumiug, I ay and quhill my airis and executouris lay on and bestow the foirsaid sowme of fyve hundrith merkis money in maner and to ye use foirsaid. Item, I leif to the Laird of Lus, my sister sone, my ryding sword. And farder, I dischairge and levis the said Laird of Lus, all debtis or sowmes of money that I or my saidis executouris can ask or crave of him, eithir for himself or his vmquhile brother, for ony caus quhatsumevir preceiding the daite heirof ; provyding alwayis that the said Laird of Lus exonor and dischuirge me, my airis and executouris and assessouris of all sowmes of money that he can crave of me, vtherwayes nocht. Item, I leif to the Laird of Hessilheid, my sister sone, in ane remembrance, my signet of gold, of ane vnce weicht, and my best stand of silk claithis to his sone my god sone. Item, I leif to James Hamiltoun of Ardoch, my cousing, my auld servand, my best hors, my ganging sword, and fyve hundrith merkis money, to be distribut be him amang his bairnes at his awin discretioun. minister at the kirk of Leinze, ane hundrith pundis money. Item, I leif to Johne Cleland of Fostan, my nixt best hors, and ane hundrith pundis money. Item, I leif to James Cleland, elder, his brother pundis. Item, I leif to Robert Cleland, his brother, the sowme of ffourtie pundis money, quhilk he is awand to me be his obligatioun, and siclyk dischairges him of all hous maillis that he is awand to me for my hous in Glasgow at the kirk styll, quilk he duelt into. Item, I leif to James Cvnynghame, my servand, ane hundrith pundis money, with all ye money that he restit awand to me at ye of his compt maid ye ferd day of March last by past [except] the sowme of twa hundrith merkis money thairof, to be gevin to my saidis executouris. Item, I leif to James Craufurd in Dyk, fourtie pundis money. Item, I leif the sowme of ane hundrith merkis money to be bestowit amang the remanent of my servandis for ye tyme, at ye discretioun of ye saidis executouris. Item, I leif my ryding stand of claithis . . . with my hors, geir, saidill, brydill and bittis, to my [ryding] boyis . . . of my hors for ye tyme, and all the rest of my new claithes I leif thame to Thomas Hill, James Cvnynghame and James Craufurd, equallie amanges thame. Item, I dischairge and . . . to my haill tennentis, all restis of entres sylwer that they or thair cautiouneris is bund to pay to me for ony set, tack, or rentall maid be me to thame, without prejudice to thair . Item, I leif to Hugh Erle of Eglintoun, my sister sone, my gould signet, innamulit with ane quhyt gravin stane thairin. Item, I leit to Margrat Boyde, Ladie Cvnynghame, my sister, the sowme of twa hundrith merkis money, . . . forsameikle as wrongfullie, quhilk my conscience is burdenit with, I gat fra vmquhile Thomas Pettigrew of Coittis, twa hundrith merkis; I leif and ordanes my saidis executouris, quhat evir vthir thing they do, to pay the samyne tua hundrith merkis to ye neirest of ye said unquhile Thomas Pettigrew, quha ather is his air, or ony vther quham it wald have pertenit, or to quhome he wald have best leit it. . . . Item, I leif to the neirest of vmquhile William Fairlie of Bog, in maner forsaid, xl lib. money quhilk . . . him for wrang that I thocht I did to him. Item, I leif to ye said Mr. Patrik Sharp all my buikis, to tak his will of, telland him the kyndes of thame. Item, as to the tak of the teyndis of my landis of Mounkland, set to me be Walter Lord of Blantyre, I mak ane trust . . . my teindis payeris of ye saidis teyndis, ilk ane of thame for thair awin partis, sa far as they are addebted zeirlie . . . I leif ye samyne to ye said Adame Boyde of Tempiltoun, my cousing, Mr. Robert Boyde of Kippis, and Johnne Cleland of Forstane, equallie amangis thame, exceptand my legacie, will, and ordinance abovewritten. . . . In witness quhairof I have subscryvit this my testament and latterwill with my hand, quhilk is vryttin be James Cvnynghame, my servand, at my duelling hous of Badinhaith, the ffourtein day of Julij, the zeir of God Jaɪ vic and elleven zeiris; befoir thir witnesses, Mr. Wm. Strutheris, minister at ye kirk at Leinze, James Hamiltoun of Ardoch, Robert Craufurd in Wodmylne, James Craufurd in Deirdyk, Johnne Craufurd, his brother, and ye said James Cvnynghame, writer heirof. [They all subscribe.] Confirmed at Glasgow, the fferd day of Maij 1612.

---

### PLENISHING OF THE EARLE OF DUNDONALD'S HOUSE AT PASLAY, 1691.

At Pasley the second of Octr. ninetie ane yearis, Lady Housbill, Mrs. Cochrane and Mrs. Dunlope, did divid the plenishing of the Earle of Dundonald's house as æqualie as they could, the one half to the Countesse, and the other half to the Earle.

| *The Countesses Half.* | lib. sh. d. | *The Earles Half.* | lib. sh. d. |
|---|---|---|---|
| Imp. In the great room of dinning room, 4 pieces of arras, hangings, valued to ... | 144 00 00 | Imp. 4 pieces of arras hangings in the dinning room valued to | 144 00 00 |
| ib. 2 armed kain chairs at 8 shillings sterling per piece, and 4 litle kaine chairs at 5 shillings sterling per piece, in the room of the dining room, is | 021 00 00 | ib. 18 carpett chairs in the dining room, valued to ... | 036 00 00 |
| | | ib. 2 carpetts in the dining room, valued to 9 lib. ... | 009 00 00 |
| ib. Ane oval table, and tuo course by tables, valued to 10 lib. | 010 00 00 | ib. The chimni shovell and tongs in the dining room, valued to | 003 00 00 |
| ib. In the great room ane chimnie, shovell and tongs, valued to | 012 00 00 | ib. In the dining room ane knok, valued to 12 lib. ... | 012 00 00 |
| ib. In the great room ane japan cabinet and glass ... | | ib. In the Countesses studdie ane black ibonie cabinett, and ane other cabinet, with whit mother of pearl and strong box | |
| ib. Mrs. Stuart's chamber, a feather bed, bolster, ane pillow. two pair of blanquets, and a coverlet, tuo chairs, table, chimni and tongs, and tuo window curtains, valued | 012 00 00 | ib. In the painted room ane old laigh bed, with ane old chimny and tuo pair of old blanquets, valued to ... | 012 00 00 |
| ib. The red damasse bed that was in the wardrop, now in the great room, ane fether bed, bolster, 3 pair of blanquetts, tuo pillous, valued to ... | 096 00 00 | ib. In the middle room in the high gallerie ane gray cloath bed that was in the wairdrop; ane shewed gray cloathed bed, limon tabie lining, and quilted cover, 3 pair of blanquets, 2 pillous, bolster, valued to | 114 00 00 |
| ib. 3 scringes in the painted room, valued to ... | 036 00 00 | ib. The gilded leather hangings in the dining roome, of the | |

| | lib. sh. d. |
|---|---|
| 18 carpett chairs, in the little dining room, valued to | 036 00 00 |
| ib. In the litle dining room ane chimni, shovell and tonge, valued to ... | 012 00 00 |
| ib. The 4 pieces of arras hangings in the wardrop. valued to | 148 00 00 |
| ib. In the room above the green room, ane red and whit droged bed, fether bed, bolster, 2 pillous, 4 piece of arras hanging, a table, carpett, and old fashioned glasse, 6 chairs, with old moyhaw covers, chimny shovell, tongs, and 2 stands, valued to | 120 00 00 |
| ib. In the room next the green room, ane dark cloak bed, with cesnut lining, and tuilt fether bed, bolster, 2 pillous, and sute of old coloured hangings, with gilded strips, 4 chairs, table and carpet, ane old glasse, 2 pair blanquets, chimny and tongs, valued ... | 036 00 00 |
| ib. In the stair foot room, ane purple bed, fether bed, bolster and 2 pillous, 3 pair of blanquets and ane cover, 6 old carpett chairs, ane chamber box and pan, chimny shovell and tongs, and ane resting chair, valued to ... | 024 00 00 |
| ib. In the wairdrop, ane table carpett that lay on the old dining roome, valued to ... | 240 00 00 |
| ib. In the wairdrop, ane table and tuo stands, valued to ... | 009 00 00 |
| ib. Ane hundreth eightie ane pound penther, valued to 10 shilling per pound, is ... | 090 10 00 |

| | lib. sh. d. |
|---|---|
| end of the great hall, valued ... | 036 00 00 |
| ib. Ane oval table in the litle dining room, valued to ... | 006 00 00 |
| ib. In the nurserie, wher the children are, ane chimni shovell and tongs, valued to | 012 00 00 |
| ib. Tuo pieces in the middle room in the high gallerie, and one piece in the wardrob, valued | 108 00 00 |
| ib. In the middle room in the high gallerie, ane table and 2 stands, valued to ... | 012 00 00 |
| ib. Ane chimny shovell and tongs in the middle room in the high gallerie, valued to ... | 006 00 00 |
| ib. In the green room, ane sarge bed, with silk slips, lined with red and whit sesnett, fether bed, bolster, 2 pillous, 2 pair of blanquets, and ane half, 6 chairs, 2 piece of hangings of green and whit stuff, chimny, shovell, tongs, glasse, table and stands, and windou curtains, valued to ... | 133 06 08 |
| ib. In the room next the room above the green room, a fether bed, with yellou curtains, and ane box bed, three pair blanquets, valued ... | 012 00 00 |
| ib. In Mr. Cochrane's chamber, fether bed, bolster, 2 pair of blanquets and covering, chimny, shovels and tongs, valued | 012 00 00 |
| ib. In the blue room in the laigh gallerie, ane blue bed, fether bed, bolster, 2 pillous, 3 pair of blanquets and ane cover, ane table, 2 stands, ane table cloath, 6 chairs, and ane resting chair, 3 piece of bleu hangings, chamber pott, box, chimny, shovell and tongs, valued to ... | 048 00 00 |
| ib. In the middle room in the laigh gallerie, ane green bed, fether bed, bolster, 2 pillous, 3 pair of blanquets, some old strip hangings, 4 old chairs, chamber box and pan, chimny, shovell and tongs, chamber pott, valued to .. | 012 00 00 |
| ib. Ane hundreth and eightie one pound peuther, valued to 10 shillings each pound, vnde | 090 10 00 |

The kitchen graith and linnings, and velvett bed, not divided, and brewing veshell and candlesticks.

[The foregoing we copy from the original. We know not the occasion of the division of furniture between the Earl and Countess, but we doubt not the list will be interesting to some of our readers, and it is worthy of preservation.]

## TESTAMENTUM THOME KENNEDY DE KNOKDAW.

He appoints "corpusq. meum sepelie pulueribus Colmoneli," and "constituo meos executores Dauid Kennedy, filium meum senior, et Jota. Kennedy, meam sponsam."

Legacie.—Item, xxiii Messas celebra. Item lego tres petras cere. Item, I leif, &c., Jonet Kennedie, my spous, my wery lauchfull cessioner, &c., (and he leaves her lands which he held in tak of William Edzare of Kynhilt.) Item, lego Thome Kennedy, filio meo, xl s., &c. (Issobell and Cristyn, his daughters, are mentioned, and have provisions) . . . Testamentum p. me, Thoma Kennedy de Knokdaw, apud mansionem eiusd. xxvi. die mens. Aprilis, Anno Deu Jajvcxlix.

Confirmed—x. Januarii 1549.

## TESTAMENTUM QUOND. JO'TE SPREULL, D'NE DE CATHCART.

Que obiit apud villam eiusd. xxii die mens. Octobris, Anno Jajvlmo, coram hiis testibus Will·mo Pollok de eod. D·no de Coldame, Valtero Spreull, Niniano Merschiall and Johanne Spreull cum diueris aliis.

In Dei nom., amen.—Ego, Jo·ta Spreull, infirma corpe. tamen mente condo testamentum meum in hine modum sequeter. Imprinis, do et lego animam meam Deo omnipotenti, beati Marie Virgini, omnibus felicis corpusq. meum seplend. in choro S·cti Osualdi in Cathcart, ac. iiii d. face. S·cti Kentigerni. Et hos constituo meos executores, viz., Robertum Sympile, meum filium, et Maldelmum Sympile, meum filium juniores; et constitus et ordinis Willielmum Sympile, meum filium seniores, et Gabrielle Sympile, meum filium juniore, viz., lie o·rmen et vt dictum executoris et superiores disponat, de bonis meis vt volunt rndre. prosalute.

Legacia.— . . . Item, Jo·te Pollok, mea filie seniori, iiii bs et vnum togam de lie Scottis blak, et meam quotidianam lie kirtill. Item, Bessete Sympile, mea filie, iiii bs., et meam optimam togam et vnum lie kirtill de worsett, et vnum lie pair of Franche blak clokis. Item, Jon. Pollok xx s. Item, Jon. Pollok, de eod. xx meas. morte, &c. &c.

Itu est Joes. Coluill, curtus de Cathcart, manu ppa.

Confirmat—Penultis Octobris, Anno (Jajvc et) lmo.

*The Wallace Family.*—In a note on page 220 of this volume, it is said, that failing Robert Wallace of Kelly, the representation of the family of Wallace will devolve upon the descendants of Hugh Wallace of Biscany. This is incorrect as Mr. Wallace of Kelly has a brother, Major-General Sir James Wallace; but in the event of his decease without male issue, the representation would fall to the Biscany branch, as stated in the note referred to.

*Cuninghame of Polquhairn.*—We were in error in supposing (p. 505, Appendix) that *James Cuninghame of Polquhairn*, living in 1578, was the first of that family. In the Acts of Council we find "Marion Craufurd, the spous of the vmquhile *Robert Cunyngham of Polquhairn*," pursuer in an action against "William Coluile of Ochiltre, Knyt," 21st June 1493, so that the family is much older than we imagined. It does not appear, however, from what branch of the Cuninghame stock they are descended.

# PAROCHIAL REGISTERS OF AYRSHIRE.

[EXTRACTED from that very interesting publication entitled "Memoranda of the state of the Parochial Registers of Scotland, whereby is clearly shown the imperative necessity for a National System of regular Registrations, by WILLIAM B. TURNBULL, Esq., Advocate. Edinburgh; T. G. STEVENSON. 1849." 8vo.]

## AYRSHIRE.

[This county, which is about sixty miles in length and twenty-six in breadth, comprises the districts of Carric, Kyle, and Cunningham.]

ARDROSSAN.—" From a memorandum in one of the volumes, of date 1755, it appears that

Registers of baptisms, from May 28, 1682, till May 23, 1725, had been regularly kept, but which have been lost. From 1742 till 1787, lists of baptisms and marriages have been regularly kept, and with a little interruption at this period till 1802, from which last date till 1816 they are very imperfect; but they have since been kept with great accuracy."

AUCHINLECK.—" Previous to the appointment of the present schoolmaster, these were not very regularly kept; and they go no further back than to about the beginning of last century."

AYR.—No return.—The session-clerk informs me that :—" The register of births and baptisms in this parish commence January 1664, and continues down to 26th January 1720. Commences again on 26th June 1721, and continues down to the present date. The register of marriages in the parish of Ayr commences 18th November 1687, and continues down to 13th February 1708. One marriage recorded on 31st October 1708. One marriage recorded on 12th October 1711. The record again commences August 1714, and continues down to the present date. The register of deaths in the parish of Ayr commences 13th March 1766, and continues down to November 1786. Three deaths recorded in 1787. The register commences again 31st January 1789, and continues down to 10th September 1806. Two deaths are recorded in the year 1816. The record then commences on 7th January 1817, and continues down to present date. Many births in this parish are not recorded. In particular the Roman Catholics do not record the births of any of their children."

BALLANTRAE.—" The parochial registers do not reach farther back than 1744, and contain only marriages and baptisms. They are not in a good state of preservation till near the end of the century: since then they have been kept with greater accuracy and care, though still there is no register of the deaths."

BARR.—No return,—but the clergyman informs me,—" that there have been no records kept in this parish, except of births and proclamations. These commence on the 22d March 1689. They are all engrossed in one volume, which has been kept by the session-clerk, and there appear to be no blanks."—" The registers are not very exact and faithful, many parents neglecting their duty in the registration of their children; and of deaths there is no register."

BEITH.—" The earliest volume of the Beith register commences in 1659, and ends in 1758. It is imperfect, and for some years no entries are made; sometimes births, baptisms, and marriages are entered promiscuously. Of late years, the register has been kept with greater accuracy and care, but there are comparatively few births registered."

COLMONELL.—" The register of births commences in 1759, and there are no sessional records of older date than 1786."

COYLTON.—" The session records extant commenced on 6th February 1723. Baptisms and marriages have been registered for upwards of a century. The earliest registration of births is dated 15th February 1723; and of marriages, 29th May 1725. Since that time, these registers have, with few exceptions, been regularly kept. The present session-clerk has kept, with great accuracy, a register of deaths for the last fourteen years."

CRAIGIE.—" The parochial records are, 1st, A Register of births and baptisms. The first baptism recorded is in 1679, and for many years this register appears to have been irregularly kept. The births commence to be recorded along with the baptisms in 1807, and from that time the record is kept pretty regularly. 2d, A register of proclamations of marriage, commencing in the year 1679,—not regularly kept till 1776. 3d, A minute-book of the transactions of the kirk-session from the year 1775, kept regularly. 4th, Cash accounts of the poor's funds from 1788, regularly kept since 1804. Minutes of meetings of the heritors, commencing in the year 1787."

CUMNOCK (Old).—" The register of baptisms begins in 1704. There are blanks in it from 1706 to 1724, from 1739 to 1740, from 1746 to 1751, and from 1752 to 1753. The baptisms only are recorded up to the year 1768. After this period, the births also are, for the most part, entered along with them. A few only of the dissenters register their children. The register of proclamations for marriage begins in 1758; but up to the year 1782, no notice is taken of the marriages. Subsequent to this period, the date of the marriage is also entered. No register of deaths is kept."

CUMNOCK (New).—" The earliest entry in the parish registers is dated 1709; but the register has not been regularly kept, till within these few years."

DAILLY.—" The parochial registers, and the records of the kirk-session, have been uniformly kept together. They occupy seven volumes. The first volume includes the period from April 1691 to the year 1711, and is perfectly legible, but in some places much decayed. There is reason to believe that, during the early parts of the last century, the registers were not accurately kept. From the year 1751, every attention has been paid to them."

DALMELLINGTON.—" The most ancient account of parish transactions is to be found in the session-records. The first date of them is 7th March 1641. For twenty-one years they were exceedingly well kept, and very voluminous, and again, for the same period, at the beginning of the last century.— The register of births and marriages begins at the same date, and, except during ' the time of the curate,' as the last period of the Episcopacy is usually designated, all the records of which are a few scarce readable entries of baptisms, it has been, with little interruption, well kept to the present day."

DALRY.—" The earliest existing registers are of births and marriages, and commence in 1683, but have not been regularly kept till 1724 ; from which period they are complete till the present time. The records of the transactions of the kirk-session commence in 1693, and, excepting a blank from 1701 to 1717, have been most accurately kept to 1765. From that time till 1821, it appears that the minutes of session were written on detached slips of paper, and, as might be expected from such a slovenly practice, they have all been lost."

DALRYMPLE.—" The parochial registers of births and marriages and the minutes of the kirk-session, commence in 1699. The register of deaths commences in 1739, and ends in 1793. A new volume, however, was begun in 1816.—The whole have been kept pretty regularly."

DREGHORN.—No return.

DUNDONALD.—" The registers of this, as in most other parishes in Scotland, from the accidents of time, but more especially from the slovenly way in which they have been originally kept, are in a very imperfect state. The oldest volume, containing the records of session, and bearing date 1602, is tolerably entire ; indeed, much more so than any of the succeeding ones. It extends over a period of forty years, comprising a silent interval of sixteen years, and contains a great deal of parochial information that is curious and interesting.—The minutes of session, after the conclusion of this volume, till within the last few years, have been very carelessly and imperfectly kept. The next entry after 1643, is in 1702, the commencement of another volume. And for more than half a century after this date, there are scarcely ten consecutive years of their transactions recorded. The register of baptisms, extending to four volumes, begins in 1673 ; that of deaths, in one volume, in 1763 ; and that of marriages, also in one volume, in 1823. The first of these is, in comparison, tolerably correct. But the other two are very incorrect, *and hopelessly so, until some stringent measures are taken to compel the people generally to attend to such matters.*"

DUNLOP.—" The register of proclamations commences in 1700, and that of baptisms in 1701. With the exception of two or three short intervals, they have been kept with extreme inaccuracy till the year 1780. Since that time they have been kept with great regularity."

FENWICK.—No return.—The clergyman writes,—" That the registration of births, marriages, and deaths, commenced in the year 1691. I have not discovered any blanks, and the records seem to have been kept in an orderly and correct manner. All the dissenters do not register."—" During many years there has been no register of deaths preserved, and only a partial one of births."

GALSTON.—" The parish records are very imperfect and mutilated previous to the date of 1692, from which date there is a regular series of baptisms and minutes of session. The earliest entry is dated 1578."

GIRVAN.—" The parochial registers commence in 1733, since which period a pretty regular account of births has been kept ; but of marriages and deaths the account was very imperfectly kept, down to the year 1825, when a correct record of marriages commenced ; but a record of deaths is still wanting."

IRVINE.—No return.

KILBIRNIE.—" The register of baptisms and marriages commences in the year 1688. A blank occurs between the 9th July 1724, and 5th December 1725, ' in consequence,' as is stated on the record, ' of their being no schoolmaster during that period ; ' and another, from the same cause, between the 10th January 1731 and the 16th March 1732. Again, the register of marriages, from 3d July 1729, to 15th June 1738, has been lost, but from this date to the present time, there are apparently no omissions. The registry of deaths begins in 1753, and is preserved entire. Minutes of the kirk-session also commence in 1688, but there is an unregretted gap in these impure records, excepting some illegible scraps, extending from 1725 to 1791."

KILBRIDE (WEST).—" The registers of this parish commence pretty early, are very complete, and in good preservation ; certainly much more so than is usually the case with such documents. The register of births begins November 6, 1691, and is regularly continued to the present time. It is to be noted however of this record, that at no time has the law been uniformly complied with, many births never having been entered at all ; *which of course very much lessens its value to the community.* The registry of marriages is continued from 1693, and is preserved entire. Minutes of the kirk-session commence February 15, 1716, and now occupy nearly two thick quarto volumes."

KILMARNOCK.—" The earliest entry in the register of baptisms is dated 6th February 1644 ; but little seems to have been entered till January 1663. From that period almost nothing is entered, till January 1665 ; but there are many omissions till August 4, 1687, from which time it appears to have been regularly kept."

KILMAURS.—" The register of births and marriages commenced in 1688, but was not regularly kept till 1783."

KILWINNING.—" The earliest minute of session is dated 12th March 1656, since which time, with the exception of a few intervals, they appear to have been regularly recorded. The record of baptisms begins 27th April 1669, and that of proclamations, 14th July 1676, and both are continued, with few interruptions, to the present day. In recent times the *register of births* is far from being complete, and there is none of deaths or burials."

KIRKMICHAEL.—" The sessional records were kept somewhat irregularly till about the year 1711. The date of the earliest entry is 8th July 1638."

KIRKOSWALD.—" There are registers of births, baptisms, marriages, and deaths, all regularly kept."

LARGS.—" There is no regular record of births and baptisms prior to the Revolution, and long after that epoch the record was very imperfect. It has of late been better kept."

LOUDOUN.—" There are two parish registers. 1. Marriages. The earliest date of this register is 3d December 1673, and it has been kept regularly since November 1759. 2. Baptisms. Earliest date 16th October 1763 ; kept regularly since November 1759. Few Dissenters register their children in this register."

MAUCHLINE.—" The ancient parochial records are now lost. The date of the earliest entry in the parochial register is 17th January 1670. The whole records of the parish are contained in ten volumes. Till about eighty years ago, they were most irregularly kept, being written mostly on detached leaves, so that they are almost useless."

MAYBOLE.—" The earliest entry of a birth is in January 1772 ; and the register of births is continued regularly from that date to the present day. The register of proclamations of banns and marriages is of a much more recent date, and does not seem to have been accurately kept. The earliest date of minutes of session is December 1777. A very accurate register of deaths, and the ages and diseases of the deceased, has been kept for the last few years ; and the mode of furnishing a document so important is at the same time so simple, that its general adoption is much to be desired. A small fee leads the church-officer to make the requisite enquiries at every funeral. The result is given into the kirk-session every Sabbath after sermon, and is then entered into a book. If there is any defect in the information, the elder best acquainted with the relatives of the deceased makes farther inquiry, and reports to the succeeding meeting."

MONKTON AND PRESTWICK.—" The parochial registers are the records of the kirk-session, and the register of births and baptisms. The earliest entry in the latter is in 1702. The former does not extend so far back, the earlier volumes having been lost. Both are now kept with considerable regularity."

MUIRKIRK.—" Before the year 1772 the parish registers are very imperfect and irregular; but since that period they have been regularly kept. The first entry is dated in the year 1739."

NEW CUMNOCK.—*Vide* Cumnock (New.)

NEWTON-UPON-AYR.—" The registers have been regularly kept since the erection of Newton into a separate parish, which took place in 1779.

OCHILTREE.—" The registers of baptisms and marriages go back to the year 1647, but there was no register of deaths till about forty years ago. The registers begun in 1647 were regularly kept for a considerable time, but were afterwards, for a long period, very much neglected. For the last fifty years they have been kept in a most regular manner."

OLD CUMNOCK.—*Vide* Cumnock (Old).

PRESTWICK AND MONKTON.—*Vide* Monkton.

RICCARTON.—" The only registers existing, or which seem ever to have been kept, are the session records, commencing with the year 1695, the registers of births and marriages and the minutes of heritors' meetings. Except the registers of births and marriages, none seem to have been regularly kept ; and it is only within these last ten years that the minutes of the heritors have been at all accurately kept."

SAINT QUIVOX.—" The parochial registers do not extend farther back than the year 1780, but since that time they have been kept with great regularity."

SORN.—" The parish registers commence in 1692, and have since been regularly kept. The registers of baptisms is not by any means complete, as parents belonging to different dissenting bodies frequently neglect the registration of their children. Care, however, is taken to enforce this duty on parents belonging to the establishment. There is no record of deaths, although the minister, in the course of his visitations, is in the habit of taking an exact account of them."

STAIR.—" The earliest parochial register is of date 1736 ; the early part not very correctly kept. A register of births and marriages has been kept since 1805, and one of the deaths since 1815."

STEVENSTON.—" None of the parish registers go farther back than 1700, and many portions of them have been lost. The register of marriages has been regularly kept from April 1701 till May 1717 ; and from May 1737 till January 1746, and from January 1747 till the present time, February 1837. The register of baptisms has been regularly kept from July 1700 till November 1718 ; irregularly kept from 1718 till 1737 ; and regularly from 1737 till near the end of the century ; but from that time to the present, it cannot be considered as regularly kept, as the dissenters do not record the names of their children. A register of deaths has been kept from 1747 till the present time ; but for a considerable time, those only whose friends have paid for the mortcloth have been recorded."

STEWARTON.—" The registers of baptisms and marriages have been preserved since 1693, though the first were not regularly kept till 1747, nor the second till 1794. The burials have been regularly recorded since May 1745. There is no distinction of the sexes of children under twelve years. The minutes of session from 1757 to 1776, and from 1810 to the present time, are in good preservation. The minutes of heritors have been regularly kept since February 1774. Very few of the dissenters register; and *great are the inconveniences often felt from this omission.*"

STRAITON.—" The registers of the parish commence in the year 1644. They are regular in the registration of births and marriages, excepting during the reign of James, till 1770. From that period till 1825, they are very imperfect. During the last twelve years they have been kept with great care, embracing almost all that have been born or that have died within the parish, not, as is sometimes the case, only those that were baptised or buried in the parish. The session records begin in 1734, and, with the exception of a few years, about fifty years ago, are complete from that period."

SYMINGTON.—" The registers have been kept so far back as the year 1642, but very irregularly till about 1780."

TORBOLTON.—" The date of the earliest entry in the register of baptisms is 1730. The earliest minute of session is of date 1774. The register of baptisms is defective, owing to the carelessness of some parents in not having their children registered."

WEST KILBRIDE. –*Vide* Kilbride (West.)

THE END.

EDINBURGH:
PRINTED BY J. & W. PATERSON, 90 SOUTH BRIDGE.